Lecture Notes in Networks and Systems

Volume 219

The series "Lecture Notes in Networks and Systems" publishes the latest developments in Networks and Systems—quickly, informally and with high quality. Original research reported in proceedings and post-proceedings represents the core of LNNS.

Volumes published in LNNS embrace all aspects and subfields of, as well as new challenges in, Networks and Systems.

The series contains proceedings and edited volumes in systems and networks, spanning the areas of Cyber-Physical Systems, Autonomous Systems, Sensor Networks, Control Systems, Energy Systems, Automotive Systems, Biological Systems, Vehicular Networking and Connected Vehicles, Aerospace Systems, Automation, Manufacturing, Smart Grids, Nonlinear Systems, Power Systems, Robotics, Social Systems, Economic Systems and other. Of particular value to both the contributors and the readership are the short publication timeframe and the world-wide distribution and exposure which enable both a wide and rapid dissemination of research output.

The series covers the theory, applications, and perspectives on the state of the art and future developments relevant to systems and networks, decision making, control, complex processes and related areas, as embedded in the fields of interdisciplinary and applied sciences, engineering, computer science, physics, economics, social, and life sciences, as well as the paradigms and methodologies behind them.

Indexed by SCOPUS, INSPEC, WTI Frankfurt eG, zbMATH, SCImago.

All books published in the series are submitted for consideration in Web of Science.

More information about this series at http://www.springer.com/series/15179

Nancy L. Black · W. Patrick Neumann ·
Ian Noy
Editors

Proceedings of the 21st Congress of the International Ergonomics Association (IEA 2021)

Volume I: Systems and Macroergonomics

 Springer

Editors
Nancy L. Black
Département de génie mécanique
Université de Moncton
Moncton, NB, Canada

W. Patrick Neumann
Department of Mechanical and Industrial
Engineering
Ryerson University
Toronto, ON, Canada

Ian Noy
Toronto, ON, Canada

ISSN 2367-3370   ISSN 2367-3389 (electronic)
Lecture Notes in Networks and Systems
ISBN 978-3-030-74601-8   ISBN 978-3-030-74602-5 (eBook)
https://doi.org/10.1007/978-3-030-74602-5

This Springer imprint is published by the registered company Springer Nature Switzerland AG
The registered company address is: Gewerbestrasse 11, 6330 Cham, Switzerland

Preface

The International Ergonomics Association (IEA) is the organization that unites Human Factors and Ergonomics (HF/E) associations around the world. The mission of the IEA is "to elaborate and advance ergonomics science and practice, and to expand its scope of application and contribution to society to improve the quality of life, working closely with its constituent societies and related international organizations" (IEA, 2021). The IEA hosts a world congress every three years creating the single most important opportunity to exchange knowledge and ideas in the discipline with practitioners and researchers from across the planet. Like other IEA congresses, IEA2021 included an exciting range of research and professional practice cases in the broadest range of Human Factors and Ergonomics (HF/E) applications imaginable. While the conference was not able to host an in-person meeting in Vancouver, Canada, as planned by the host Association of Canadian Ergonomists/*Association canadienne d'ergonomie*, it still featured over 875 presentations and special events with the latest research and most innovative thinkers. For this congress, authors could prepare a chapter for publication, and 60% chose to do so. The breadth and quality of the work available at IEA2021 are second to none—and the research of all authors who prepared their publication for this congress is made available through the five volumes of these proceedings.

The International Ergonomics Association defines Human Factors and Ergonomics (HF/E) synonymously as being:

the scientific discipline concerned with the understanding of interactions among humans and other elements of a system, and the profession that applies theory, principles, data and methods to design in order to optimize human well-being and overall system performance.

Practitioners of ergonomics and ergonomists contribute to the design and evaluation of tasks, jobs, products, environments and systems in order to make them compatible with the needs, abilities and limitations of people.

Ergonomics helps harmonize things that interact with people in terms of people's needs, abilities and limitations. (https://iea.cc/definition-and-domains-of-ergonomics/)

The breadth of issues and disciplines suggested by this definition gives one pause for thought: what aspect in our lives is not in some way affected by the design and application of HF/E? For designers and managers around the world, a similar realization is growing: every decision made in the design and application of technology has implications for the humans that will interact with that system across its lifecycle. While this can be daunting, the researchers and professionals who participated in IEA2021 understand that, by working together across our disciplines and roles, we can achieve these lofty ambitions. This is especially relevant as we continue our collective journey into an increasingly "interconnected world"—the theme for the 21st IEA Congress. With the rise of a myriad of technologies as promulgated by Industry 4.0 proponents, we need now, more than ever, the skills and knowledge of HF/E researchers and practitioners to ensure that these tools are applied in a human-centric way towards resilient and sustainable systems that provide an enduring and sustainable road to prosperity—as advocated in the new Industry 5.0 Paradigm (Breque et al. 2021). Where the trend of Industry 4.0 aims primarily at encouraging technology purchasing and application, Industry 5.0 includes goals of resiliency and sustainability for both humans and our planet. These proceedings provide examples of research and development projects that illustrate how this brighter, human-centred future can be pursued through "*Ergonomie 4.0*", as stated in the French theme of the Congress.

While the theme of the Congress concerns human interactions within a rapidly evolving cyber-physical world, the devastating impact of the COVID-19 pandemic has given an added dimension to the Congress theme and its delivery model. As the pandemic began to engulf the world, the traditional in-person Congress became increasingly less viable and gave way to the creation of a hybrid model as a means to enhance international participation. In early 2021, it became clear that holding an in-person event would not be possible; hence, the Congress was converted to a fully virtual event. The uncertainty, mounting challenges and turbulent progression actually created new possibilities to engage the global HF/E community in ways that were never previously explored by the IEA. Indeed, one of the scientific tracks of the congress focuses explicitly on HF/E contributions to cope with COVID-19, and readers will find some submissions to other tracks similarly focus on what HF/E practitioners and researchers bring to the world during this pandemic period. This journey epitomizes broader transformative patterns now underway in society at large and accentuates the urgency for resilience, sustainability, and healthy workplaces. No doubt, the notion of globalization will be redefined in the wake of the pandemic and will have far-reaching implications for the connected world and for future society, and with new paradigms emerge a host of new human factors challenges. The breadth of topics and issues addressed in the proceedings suggests that the HF/E community is already mobilizing and rising to these emerging challenges in this, our connected world.

IEA2021 proceedings includes papers from 31 scientific tracks and includes participants from 74 countries across 5 continents. The proceedings of the 21st triennial congress of the IEA—IEA2021—exemplify the diversity of HF/E, and of the association, in terms of geography, disciplines represented, application domains, and aspects of human life cycle and capability being considered. Our diversity mirrors the diversity of humans generally and is a strength as we learn to weave our knowledge, methods, and ideas together to create a more resilient and stronger approach to design than is achievable individually. This is the strength of the IEA congresses, in the past, in the current pandemic-affected 21st occasion, and in the future. There is no other meeting like it.

A substantial number of works were submitted for publication across the Scientific Tracks at IEA2021. This gave us the happy opportunity to group contents by common threads. Each volume presents contents in sections with papers within the track's section presented in alphabetical order by the first author's last name. These proceedings are divided into five volumes as follows:

VOLUME 1: SYSTEMS AND MACROERGONOMICS (ISBN 978-3-030-74601-8)

Activity Theories for Work Analysis and Design (ATWAD)
Systems HF/E
Ergonomic Work Analysis and Training (EWAT)
HF/E Education and Professional Certification Development
Organisation Design and Management (ODAM)

VOLUME 2: INCLUSIVE AND SUSTAINABLE DESIGN (ISBN 978-3-030-74604-9)

Ageing and Work
Ergonomics for children and Educational Environments
Ergonomics in Design for All
Gender and Work
Human Factors and Sustainable Development
Slips Trips and Falls
Visual Ergonomics

VOLUME 3: SECTOR BASED ERGONOMICS (ISBN 978-3-030-74607-0)

Practitioner Case Studies
Aerospace Ergonomics
Agricultural Ergonomics
Building and Construction Ergonomics
Ergonomics in Manufacturing
HF/E in Supply Chain Design and Management
Transport Ergonomics and Human Factors

VOLUME 4: HEALTHCARE AND HEALTHY WORK (ISBN 978-3-030-74610-0)

Health and Safety
Healthcare Ergonomics

HF/E Contribution to Cope with Covid-19
Musculoskeletal Disorders

VOLUME 5: METHODS & APPROACHES (ISBN 978-3-030-74613-1)

Advanced Imaging
Affective Design
Anthropometry
Biomechanics
Human Factors in Robotics
Human Modelling and Simulation
Neuroergonomics
Working with Computer Systems

These volumes are the result of many hours of work, for authors, Scientific Track Managers and their reviewer teams, student volunteers, and editors. We are grateful to Springer for making it available to you in book form and are confident you will find these works informative and useful in your own efforts to create a better, more human-centred future.

References

Breque, M., De Nul, L., Petridis, A., 2021. Industry 5.0: Towards More Sustainable, Resilient and Human-Centric Industry, in: Innovation, E.D.-G.f.R.a. (Ed.), Policy Brief. European Commission, Luxembourg, p. 48. https://ec. europa.eu/info/news/industry-50-towards-more-sustainable-resilient-and-human-centric-industry-2021-jan-07_en
International Ergonomics Association (2021) Definitions and Domains of Ergonomics. https://iea.cc/definition-and-domains-of-ergonomics/; accessed March, 2021

Nancy L. Black
W. Patrick Neumann
IEA2021 Scientific Co-chairs

Ian Noy
IEA2021 Conference Chair

IEA2021 Acknowledgements

The IEA Congress organizing committee acknowledges many individuals whose contributions to the event have been invaluable to its success.

First and foremost, we acknowledge with deep appreciation the tremendous work of Steve Marlin, CEO of Prestige Accommodations, International Inc. His firm, hired to assist with organizing and executing the Congress, delivered unparalleled service throughout the planning process. Tragically, Steve passed away in early 2021. He provided outstanding support and wise counsel, always with a smile. He is sorely missed. We remain indebted to the Prestige staff, whose expertise and outstanding professionalism guided us through the planning process. In particular, we are grateful to Laurie Ybarra, Sr. Meetings Manager, who oversaw the many diverse aspects of our ever-changing plans and Christine Reinhard, Director of Operations, who skilfully managed the budget, website and registration system. Laurie and Christine's friendly approach, and their unique combination of technical and interpersonal skills, made it a pleasure to work with them. Marie-Hélène Bisaillon, Executive Director of the Association of Canadian Ergonomists/ *Association canadienne d'ergonomie*, supported their work.

The Organizing Committee is also indebted to those contributors who were instrumental in developing and promoting IEA2021. Joanne Bangs, our freelance Communications Specialist, provided engaging news blogs and other promotional collateral to help get the word out about the Congress. Sadeem Qureshi (Ryerson University), Elizabeth Georgiou, Elaine Fung, and Michelle Lam (Simon Fraser University) helped to create widespread awareness of the Congress as well as the HF/E field and profession through creative use of digital and social media. We are also grateful to those who worked diligently to ensure that the Congress provided meaningful opportunities for students and early career researchers, including Daniel P. Armstrong and Christopher A.B. Moore (University of Waterloo), Owen McCulloch (Simon Fraser University), Dora Hsiao (Galvion, Inc.), Chelsea DeGuzman and Joelle Girgis (University of Toronto), and Larissa Fedorowich (Associate Ergonomist, self-employed). The ePoster presentation option, new to IEA triennial congresses in 2021, was defined with care by Anne-Kristina Arnold (Simon Fraser University). Colleen Dewis (Dalhousie University) was key to interpreting our technical submission software and adapting its capacities to our needs. Hemanshu Bhargav (Ryerson University), Rachel Faust (Université de Québec à Montréal), Myriam Bérubé (Université de Montréal), Charlotte Bate, Vanessa DeVries, Caleb Leary, and Marcelo Zaharur (Fanshawe College), Tobi Durowoju (EWI Works), Issa Kaba Diakite, Mariam Keita, Mouhamadou Pléa Ndour, Shelby Nowlan, Faouzi Mahamane Ouedraogo, Jenna Smith, and Israël Muaka Wembi (Université de Moncton), and the aforementioned Larissa Fedorowich assisted with technical submission database verification and clean-up. We are particularly grateful that so many came to us through the Association of Canadian Ergonomists/Association canadienne d'ergonomie, witnessing to the active and motivated ergonomics and human factors community in IEA2021's host country.

The organizers are especially grateful to our sponsors, whose generous contributions made the Congress possible and readily accessible to the global HF/E community. Their recognition of the Congress as a valuable opportunity to advance the field of HF/E, as well as their steadfast support throughout a very trying planning period, was critical to the success of the Congress. The IEA 2021 sponsors include:

Benefactor Level:
> Amazon.com, Inc.

Platinum Level:
> Anonymous

Diamond Level:
> Healthcare Insurance Reciprocal of Canada

Gold Level:
> Huawei Technologies Canada
> Institute for Work and Health (Ontario)
> WorkSafe BC

Silver Level:
> Fanshawe College
> Simon Fraser University
> Aptima, Inc.

Organization

IEA2021 Organizing Committee

IEA2021 Congress Chair

Ian Noy — HFE Consultant and Forensic Expert, Toronto, Ontario

Technical Program Committee Co-chairs

Nancy L. Black — Department of Mechanical Engineering, Faculté d'ingénierie, Université de Moncton

W. Patrick Neumann — Human Factors Engineering Lab, Department of Mechanical and Industrial Engineering, Ryerson University

Media Outreach

Hayley Crosby — Options Incorporated

Developing Countries

Manobhiram (Manu) Nellutla — Actsafe Safety Association

ePosters Coordinator

Anne-Kristina Arnold — Ergonomics, Simon Fraser University

Exhibits Coordinator

Abigail Overduin — Workplace Health Services, The University of British Columbia

Early Career Researcher Program Coordinator

Sadeem Qureshi
Human Factors Engineering Lab, Department of Mechanical and Industrial Engineering, Ryerson University

Media Relations

Heather Kahle
Human Factors Specialist/Ergonomist, WorkSafeBC

Jenny Colman
Human Factor Specialist, Risk Analysis Unit, WorkSafeBC

Events/Social

Gina Vahlas
Human Factors Specialist/Ergonomist, Risk Analysis Unit, WorkSafeBC

Era Poddar
Specialist Safety Advisor-Ergonomics, Manufacturing Safety Alliance of BC, Canada

Alison Heller-Ono
CEO, Worksite International

French Language Coordinator

François Taillefer
Faculté des sciences, Université de Québec à Montréal

Communications Coordinator

Joanne Bangs
Free-lance consultant

EasyChair Platform Technical Liaison

Colleen Dewis
Department of Industrial Engineering, Dalhousie University

Scientific Committee of IEA2021

Nancy L. Black (Co-chair)
Université de Moncton, Canada

W. Patrick Neumann (Co-chair)
Ryerson University, Canada

Wayne Albert
University of New Brunswick, Canada

Sara Albolino
Coordinator of the system reliability area for the Center for Patient Safety—Tuscany Region, Italy

Thomas Alexander
Federal Institute for Occupational Safety and Health (BAUA), Germany

Anne-Kristina Arnold
Simon Fraser University, Canada

Rafael E. Gonzalez	Bolivarian University, Petróleos de Venezuela, S.A. (PDVSA), Venezuela
Ewa Górska	University of Ecology and Management in Warsaw, Poland
Maggie Graf	International Ergonomics Association - Professional Standards and Education, Certification Sub-committee, Switzerland
Alma Maria Jennifer Gutierrez	De La Salle University—Manila, Philippines
Jukka Häkkinen	University of Helsinki, Finland
Gregor Harih	University of Maribor, Slovenia
Veerle Hermans	Vrije Universiteit Brussel, Belgium
Dora Hsiao	Revision Military, Canada
Laerte Idal Sznelwar	Universidade de São Paulo, Brazil
Rauf Iqbal	National Institute of Industrial Engineering (NITIE), India
Nicole Jochems	University of Luebeck, Germany
Marie Laberge	Université de Montréal, Centre de recherche du CHU Ste-Justine, Canada
Fion C. H. Lee	UOW College Hong Kong, Hong Kong
Yue (Sophia) Li	KITE, Toronto Rehabilitation Institute— University Health Network, Canada
Peter Lundqvist	SLU - Swedish University of Agricultural Sciences, Sweden
Neil Mansfield	Nottingham Trent University, UK
Márcio Alves Marçal	Universidade Federal dos Vales do Jequitinhonha e do Mucuri, Brazil
Blake McGowan	VelocityEHS, USA
Ranjana Mehta	Texas A&M University, USA
Marijke Melles	Delft University of Technology, Netherlands
Marino Menozzi	Swiss Federal Institute of Technology, ETH Zurich, Switzerland
Francisco Octavio Lopez Millan	TECNM/Instituto Tecnológico de Hermosillo, Mexico
Karen Lange Morales	Universidad Nacional de Colombia, Colombia
Ruud N. Pikaar	ErgoS Human Factors Engineering, Netherlands
Dimitris Nathanael	National Technical University of Athens, Greece
Yee Guan Ng	Universiti Putra Malaysia, Malaysia
Jodi Oakman	La Trobe University, Australia
Udoka Arinze Chris Okafor	University of Lagos, Nigeria
Paulo Antonio Barros Oliveira	Federal University of Rio Grande do Sul, Brazil
Vassilis Papakostopoulos	University of the Aegean, Greece
Maria Pascale	Uruguayan Association of Ergonomics (AUDErgo), Uruguay

Gunther Paul	James Cook University, Australia
Chui Yoon Ping	Singapore University of Social Sciences, Singapore
Jim Potvin	McMaster University, Canada
Valérie Pueyo	Université Lumière Lyon 2, France
Sadeem Qureshi	Ryerson University, Canada
Sudhakar Rajulu	NASA - Johnson Space Center, USA
Gemma Read	University of the Sunshine Coast, Australia
David Rempel	University of California Berkeley; University of California San Francisco, USA
Raziel Riemer	Ben-Gurion University of the Negev, Israel
Michelle M. Robertson	Office Ergonomics Research Committee, Northeastern University, University of Connecticut, University of California, Berkeley, USA
Martin Antonio Rodriguez	Universidad Tecnológica Nacional Buenos Aires FRBA, Argentina
Gustavo Rosal	UNE (Spanish Association for Standardisation), Spain
Patricia H. Rosen	Federal Institute for Occupational Safety and Health (BAUA), Germany
Ken Sagawa	AIST, Japan
Paul M. Salmon	University of the Sunshine Coast, Australia
Marta Santos	Universidade do Porto, Portugal
Sofia Scataglini	University of Antwerp, Belgium
Lawrence J. H. Schulze	University of Houston, USA
Rosemary Ruiz Seva	De La Salle University, Philippines
Fabio Sgarbossa	Norwegian University of Science and Technology, Norway
Jonas Shultz	Health Quality Council of Alberta, University of Calgary, Canada
Anabela Simões	University Lusófona, Portugal
Sarbjit Singh	National Institute of Technology Jalandhar, India
John Smallwood	Nelson Mandela University, South Africa
Lukáš Šoltys	Czech Ergonomics Association, Czech Republic
Isabella Tiziana Steffan	STUDIO STEFFAN—Progettazione & Ricerca (Design & Research), Italy
Daryl Stephenson	Occupational Health Clinics for Ontario Workers, Canada
Gyula Szabó	Hungarian Ergonomics Society, Hungary
Shamsul Bahri Mohd Tamrin	Universiti Putra Malaysia, Malaysia
Andrew Thatcher	University of the Witwatersrand, South Africa
Giulio Toccafondi	Center for Clinical Risk Management and Patient Safety GRC, WHO Collaborating Center, Florence, Italy

Andrew Todd	Rhodes University, South Africa
Judy Village	University of British Columbia, Canada
Christian Voirol	University of Applied Sciences Western Switzerland, University of Montreal, Switzerland
Michael Wichtl	AUVA-Hauptstelle, Austrian Ergonomics Society, Austria
Amanda Widdowson	Chartered Institute of Ergonomics and Human Factors (CIEHF), Thales, UK
Sascha Wischniewski	Federal Institute for Occupational Safety & Health (BAuA), Germany

Contents

Contents

Part III: Ergonomic Work Analysis and Training (EWAT)
(Edited by Catherine Delgoulet and Marta Santos)

Part I: Activity Theories for Work Analysis and Design (ATWAD) (Edited by Pascal Béguin and Francisco José de Castro Moura Duarte)

Classes and Dimensions of Task Microprojects: A Case Study on Cargo Handling

Mateus Pereira Abraçado[1,2(✉)], Francisco José de Castro Moura Duarte[1], and Pascal Béguin[2]

[1] Coppe, Federal University of Rio de Janeiro, Rio de Janeiro, RJ, Brazil
[2] Institut d'Etude du Travail, Université Lumière Lyon 2,
UMR 5600 – LABex IMU, Lyon, France

Abstract. This communication aimed at identifying the different classes of microproject, a specific type of situated design performed by users facing an unpredictable situation of great uncertainty. Our hypothesis is that microprojects work differently, depending on the heterogenous actors and the intermediary objects involved. The research presented three case studies carried out on oil extraction platforms in Brazil, focusing on cargo-handling work. Each case presented unique characteristics, which were analyzed and compared in order to understand the situated design process comprehensively. It was observed that the situated design process has different characteristics depending on the level of interdependence of actors involved in solving the problem. The greater the distance between the realms of the actors involved in the design, the greater the need for formal decision procedures and the use of intermediary objects in situated design. Therefore, design must provide material (equipment, zones, routes) and immaterial (competences, intermediary objects) resources for action and for the situated design.

Keywords: Microproject · Situated design · Design ergonomics · Design in use

1 Introduction

Design does not end when an artifact "leaves" the project office. On the contrary, situated design is observed during the operation [1]. Usually, it is considered that design continues in use due to a lack of understanding of the work process by the designers. While working, users define how to fill the gaps left by designers for the needs of their activities [2–4].

Situated design, however, cannot be seen as one thing. The characteristics, methods, and motivations of situated design can lead to different interpretations of the nature and relevance of the design and work processes.

This communication is centered on "Microprojects," defined by Gotteland-Agostini et al. [5] as a specific type of situated design in which users face an unpredictable situation of great uncertainty. In these situations, the prescribed tasks are usually far from the actual work since the action to be taken depends on the context. The authors understand the design of such tasks as occurring in the form of microprojects, whose central characteristics are a short duration of time and an execution that is guaranteed by the

N. L. Black et al. (Eds.): IEA 2021, LNNS 219, pp. 3–11, 2021.
https://doi.org/10.1007/978-3-030-74602-5_1

person in charge of the task, designing the users' tasks according to local circumstances. Microprojects, in this sense, incorporate the main dimensions of the traditional design process, but the tasks are designed by the users in the operational context.

Abraçado [6] argues that microprojects have three main characteristics: (a) the design emerges from the situation, (b) it has an intentional and original character, and (c) it is ephemeral. It does not deal with the incorporation of new technology by the system. On the contrary, this design category is part of a problem that emerges from the field and requires the mobilization of the constructive dimension of activity to develop a solution [1].

The microproject is also essentially original and intentional. When faced with a problem, users design a new task through their skills and experience. Because of the high uncertainty, microprojects take on original forms. Many tasks of this nature are not anticipated by the designers, and others are carried out in ways completely different from those designed.

Finally, microprojects are ephemeral and contingent by nature. They are developed to solve a specific problem, with unique applications in time and space. If the same problem occurs again, the experience gained while developing the previous microproject might be reused, but all stages of implementation should be reconsidered, because local conditions affect use.

Under these circumstances, a work project should provide resources for action that can be used openly in different situations. In addition, one can think of resources for microprojects, such as drawings, schemes, sketches, plans, and reports [7].

This means that constructive activity may require mediation to be understood and validated, especially when dealing with microprojects involving heterogeneous actors. These resources can facilitate dialog with the situation [8], thus supporting reflection on the problem and development of a solution. Alternatively, the resources act as inter-mediary objects, facilitating the dialog of heterogeneous actors on the representation of situations and translation of knowledge [9, 10], especially with actors from different professional worlds [13].

Our study aimed at better identifying the different classes of microproject, under-standing the dynamic of these situated design processes, and identifying the resources that users need. Our hypothesis is that microprojects work differently, depending on the diversity of actors involved in the process and their shared knowledge.

2   Method

The research was carried out on oil extraction platforms in Brazil, focusing on cargo-handling work. The method implemented follows the six steps explained by Yin [11] (i.e., plan, design, preparation, evidence collection, evidence analysis, and reporting), described in the subsections below.

With regard to the first step, the case study method is appropriate for identifying the different characteristics of microprojects developed on-site and to understand how they differ from each other. Since task design dynamics are based on interactions of workers in the field, the combination of observation and other evidence becomes a central feature of this research when the case studies provide an opportunity to pose "how" questions about a contemporary phenomenon outside experimental control [11].

The design step embraces the combination of a microproject background and identification of theoretical references related to situated design and intermediary objects, as described in the Introduction section.

The preparation step defined the procedures for the direct observations, followed by open interviews with users [12]. The purpose was to analyze typical work situations and identify the classes and characteristics of the microprojects undertaken in order to solve a situational problem. Interviews were guided by decisions made by operators in the field. Important actions undertaken by a supervisor or assistant had its motivations questioned in order to understand non-observable activity aspects [14].

The evidence collection considered 18 real situations at an oil production company to understand the nature of cargo-handling work conducted on an offshore platform. From these, the current research presents two typical work situations to illustrate the characteristics of microprojects in cargo-handling activities. In addition, one situation observed on a visit to an oil platform in a shipyard was used.

The cargo-handling team responds to a marine coordinator and is led by a logistics technician, who is responsible for inspecting the cargo-handling work and for tracking and controlling cargo arriving and leaving the oil platform. The logistics technician also participates in the design of risky and critical tasks. The crane operator is the only one responsible for crane usage, which is the main cargo-handling resource in the field. He participates in all cargo entry and exit and in internal maneuvers using this device. Assistants, led by a supervisor, are responsible for the entry and exit of cargo and for any internal handling that weighs over 25 kg. They perform services for all platform teams but the main demands arise from the maintenance team because capital-intensive production warrants automated processes (see Fig. 1).

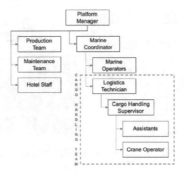

Fig. 1. Formal organization

The evidence analysis adopted a simultaneous deductive and inductive method as discussion elements were based on pattern matching. For Yin [11], this is a technique based on the comparison of an empirically based pattern and a predicted pattern generated before the data collection. The technique involves the development of different theoretical propositions articulated in operational terms, and the identification of independent variables. In this study, two main variables were identified in the literature: (1) number of heterogenous actors and (2) intermediary objects used. These variables were analyzed within a context of microproject development. This comparison resulted in the classification of microprojects according to these variables.

The reporting is observed within this paper.

3   Results

3.1   Moving a Flange to a Process plant's First Floor

The team received a flow meter about 4 m long and moved the equipment to the installation site. Initially the maneuver was performed with a trolley, but to reach the final destination it was necessary to overcome a floor elevation, a maneuver for which no resources were available.

The supervisor and assistants examined the environment, seeking resources for action, and verbally discussed possible solutions. They used (1) a beam that passed over the installation site to tie two straps with mobile hoists, one for each side of the flow meter, and (2) two pilasters to roll cables, one for each hoist (Fig. 2). The idea was to develop a system in which, while the load was lifted by the hoists, the operators would loosen the cables, thus avoiding the pendular movement of the load. The maneuver was carried out in this manner, with intense mobilization of the operators, making manual adjustments during the operation, eventually managing to place the load in its place of installation.

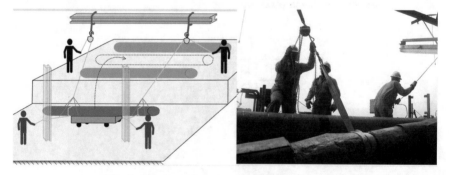

Fig. 2. Moving a flowmeter to its installation point

3.2   Moving a Trolley to a Process plant's First Floor

This case deals with the movement of a trolley (2000 kg) on rails, used for the removal of the beam from heat exchangers during a maintenance campaign. After performing an inspection in a heat exchanger on the top floor of a process plant module, it was necessary to descend with the trolley. The trolley tracks gave access to a hatch, which was accessed from a high-capacity fixed hoist. The certification of the hoist, however, had expired, so it could not be used.

Because of this restriction and the high risk of the operation, a new task was designed. A broad dialog was established, involving team leaders, maintenance, safety, the platform manager, and some engineers who were on board for the campaign. The actors used resources, such as plans and technical specifications, to discuss technical issues related to the structural capacity of the beams, the safety of the maneuver, and the operational risks. The result of this discussion was the design of a more elaborate plan, with the drawing of an outline, involving risk analysis and a safety plan.

The plan could be divided into three main parts: (1) a pulley installed in a beam in the central area of the hatch to lower the equipment using a manual lever hoist, (2) a second pulley with a crane used as safety system in case of breakage of the main cable, and (3) an auxiliary hoist used to give stability to the load, avoiding strong pendular movements (see Fig. 3).

Fig. 3. Representation of the system composed of a lever hoist and pulleys

The system was assembled by industrial climbers, and the task was developed by the cargo-handling team itself. Six workers were allocated to manipulate the lever hoist, taking turns in groups of three, to allow for rest periods. The activity was adjusted over time. The use of guide cables to avoid shocks to structures, for example, helped the equipment pass through different locations.

3.3   Removing a Diesel Engine from the Generator Room

This work situation also occurred at the shipyard during the integration stage of platform P-R1. The emergency generator room consisted of three main pieces of equipment: a generator, a diesel engine, and a radiator. During the construction period at the shipyard, the emergency generator engine had to be replaced.

The shipyard team of engineers developed a plan for the removal from the stern through the air outlet duct, taking advantage of the existing resources. The aim was to perform the removal through the following steps:

1) Removal of the air outlet duct from the generator room: The cover had to be cut and removed to allow the equipment to pass through.

8   M. P. Abraçado et al.

2) Removal of the radiator: The generator engine could only be removed after the radiator had been removed. The radiator was a large piece of equipment and had sensitive parts, which made it difficult to perform the maneuvers.
3) Removal of the engine: After removal of the radiator, the engine could be removed through the air outlet.

Access through the outlet duct was restricted. The duct was located immediately below the helipad, making direct access with a crane impossible. Thus, the entire process was developed using two cranes from the shipyard, which worked in tandem. The main crane was responsible for carrying a scale (see Fig. 4), which was used to allow access to the air outlet, even though the crane cable was located beyond the reach of the helipad structure. The plan made it possible to balance the weight of the removed equipment with a counterweight, ensuring the balance of loads during the process. However, for this process to work, a second crane was required to ensure the stability of the scale on the counterweight side. Because the weight was never the same, the second crane generated a force in the same or in the opposite direction of the load, ensuring system stability. Moreover, the auxiliary crane ensured that the scale remained stable, even without a load on the opposite side of the counterweight.

This system allowed the generation room equipment to be removed with a secondary cable on a different axis from the one holding the scale, thus avoiding any kind of contact with the helipad. All distances were measured first and put on paper for conference and discussion between the different disciplines to avoid any kind of failure in the process. The fall of the engine (8.8 t) could have meant major damage to the structure of the platform and cranes, ultimately resulting in accidents involving operators.

The equipment was removed from the generation room with hoists installed in eye-bolts, lever hoists, and skateboards to bring the equipment to the base of the air outlet so that it could then be removed with the crane. The new equipment was placed in reverse order.

Fig. 4. Moving the generator room cargo using a scale with a counterweight

3.4   Analysis of Cases

The cases presented show task microprojects developed to respond to uncertain work situations. Working in this context requires a high level of inventiveness, competence, and autonomy on the part of the operators, who design solutions for each demand that arises. The performance depends on the continuous development of expertise among workers, who learn new combinations of resources for solving problems.

In the first case, task definition was the responsibility of the cargo-handling team. The operators analyzed the local conditions, identified resources and possible solutions, and developed an original task based on their previous experiences.

In the second case, the task design involved members of other teams because of the risks involved. The expansion of the number of actors from different knowledge domains required the formulation of a plan and the use of intermediate objects for discussion during task design. The actors mainly used a sketch of the maneuver to be performed, which was continuously transformed during the discussion.

In the third case, the discussion involved a maneuver based on an engineering project. The maneuver was of such difficulty that the risks involved required precise calculations and the participation of different project disciplines. In this case, different intermediate objects were used for discussion, such as design plans, specifications, and maneuver sketches. The plan was formalized as a technical specification and was approved and agreed upon by the leaders involved.

These cases show tasks that required different microproject processes depending on the level of interdependence between the teams required to solve the problem. The more the task requires the participation of heterogeneous actors, the more the decisions are procedurals, and the number of intermediate objects grows. In the tasks that the cargo-handling team designed alone, all decisions were made verbally.

Some cases go through a design process in loco, with no formal procedures, whereas others, which involve greater difficulty, require resources and expertise that are beyond the capabilities of the workers in the field and therefore require the integrated participation of other teams. As a consequence, the use of intermediary objects and formal decision procedures are needed.

On the basis of these observations, three classes of microprojects can be identified, according to the degree of interdependence of heterogeneous actors.

- **Low**: Tasks that a professional design without the need for intermediary objects. These require the use of different load-handling equipment (e.g., installation and operation of hoists) and coordination between operators. They may require the intermittent support of other operating teams (e.g., scaffolding construction).
- **Medium**: Tasks that require prior planning by the operation team and that can integrate other teams of the platform during task design. These require a careful study of the working environment, the restrictions on the execution of the maneuver, and a formal plan, validated internally. Execution generally requires extensive coordination between the operators involved.
- **High**: Tasks that require a detailed engineering project. In addition to having a high degree of difficulty and risk or demanding high precision in maneuvers, their execution may require special services, such as the cut of structures and the use of specific

handling equipment. These tasks require the participation of teams from outside the operation or even the hiring of specialized companies.

The intermediate objects used for the design and the degree of decision procedural-ization of the project depend directly on the actors involved. As distance between the professional worlds [13] becomes greater, the need for resources and the risks involved in action grows.

4 Conclusion

All the presented cases show that situated design in highly uncertain situations, repre-sented by the development of microprojects, preserves the three central characteristics presented by Abraçado et al. [6]: (a) emergence from the situation, (b) an intentional and original character, and (c) ephemerality.

However, microprojects can also assume different forms depending on the degree of interdependence between heterogeneous actors. This study has demonstrated that the greater the distance between the actors' realms, the greater the need for formal decision procedures and the use of intermediary objects, demonstrating the main characteristics of different microproject classes.

Designing for microproject activity thus demands more than static prescriptions. Design must provide material (equipment, zones, routes) and immaterial (competences, intermediary objects) resources for action and design. As tasks from different classes have different requirements, experience must be constructed from the early stages of the design process so that the design can meet operational needs.

References

1. Rabardel, P., Béguin, P.: Instrument mediated activity: from subject development to anthropocentric design. Theoret. Issues in Ergon. Sci. **6**(5), 429–461 (2005)
2. Béguin, P.: Argumentos para uma abordagem dialógica da inovação, pp. 72–82. Laboreal, IV (2008)
3. Wisner, A.: A inteligência do trabalho: Textos selecionados de ergonomia. Fundacentro, São Paulo (1994)
4. Béguin, P.: The design of instruments as a dialogical process of mutual learning. In: Falzon, P. (ed.) Constructive Ergonomics. Taylor & Francis Group, Boca Raton (2015)
5. Gotteland-Agostini, C., Pueyo, V., Béguin, P.: Concevoir des cadres pour faire et faire faire: l'activité d'encadrement dans une entreprise horticole. Activités **12**(1), 24–45 (2015)
6. Abraçado, M., Duarte, F., Béguin, P., Fontainha, T.: Micro-projets pour des tâches imprévis-ibles. Actes du 12e Congrès 01. Design. Saint Ferréol (2021, Forthcoming)
7. Agre, P., Chapman, D.: What are plans for? Robot. Auton. Syst. **6**, 17–34 (1990)
8. Schön, D.A.: The Reflective Practitioner. Basic Books, New York (1983)
9. Vinck, D., Jeantet, A., Laureillard, P.: Objects and other intermediaries in the sociotechnical process of product design: an explanatory approach. In: Perrin, J., Vinck, D. (eds.) The Role of Design in the Shaping of Technology, pp. 297–320. European Commission Directorate-General Science, Brussels (1996)
10. Boujut, J., Blanco, E.: Intermediary objects as a means to foster co-operation in engineering design. Comput Support Coop. Work **12**, 205–219 (2003)

11. Yin, R.: Case Study Research: Design and Methods. Sage, London (1989)
12. Guérin, F., Laville, A., Daniellou, F., Duraffoug, J., Kerguelen, A.: Compreender o trabalho para transformá-lo: a prática da ergonomia. Editora Blucher, São Paulo (2001)
13. Béguin, P.: Conduite de projet et fabrication collective du travail: une approche développementale. Habilitation a diriger des recherches. Ecole Doctorale: Sciences Sociales. Université Victor Segalen Bordeaux 2. Bordeaux (2010)
14. Mollo, V., Falzon, P.: Auto- and allo-confrontation as tools for reflective activities. Appl. Ergon. **35**(6), 531–540 (2004)
15. Bittencourt, J., Duarte, F., Béguin, P.: From the past to the future: integrating work experience into the design process. Work **57**, 379–387 (2017)

Analysis of Well Intervention Team Meetings: Understanding the Actual Work of Integrated Operations

Carolina Maria do Carmo Alonso[1]([✉]) [iD], Luciano do Valle Garotti[2] [iD],
Janaína Silva Rodrigues da Costa[3] [iD], Eliel Prueza de Oliveira[1] [iD],
William Silva Santana de Almeida[3] [iD], and Francisco José de Castro Moura Duarte[3] [iD]

[1] Department of Occupational Therapy, Medical School, Federal University of Rio de Janeiro,
Rio de Janeiro, Brazil
carolina.alonso@medicina.ufrj.br
[2] Petrobras, Rio de Janeiro, Brazil
[3] Production Engineering Program, COPPE, Federal University
of Rio de Janeiro, Rio de Janeiro, Brazil

Abstract. Given the specificity and complexity of activities related to the Integrated Operations (IO) in well interventions, many studies focused on the development and use of information and communication technologies, with fewer investigations addressing the human and organizational factors related to the actual work of its different actors. To overcome this gap this manuscript present and analyze data that demonstrates the main characteristics of well intervention team meetings and aspects that facilitate or hinder IO work. The strength of this study refers to the generate knowledge about actual work situations related to discussion spaces that bring together different specialists around well intervention projects. The lack of another published research focusing on the sharing of information and the exchange of experience in IO at drilling operations reinforces the relevance of the results of this paper for Ergonomics.

Keywords: Ergonomics · Well construction · Drilling · Integrated Operations · Team meetings

1 Background

Operational Integration (IO) refers to a type of work organization characterized by the sharing of data in real-time and communication between professionals from different specialties located in different geographical areas and organizational environments. In most companies, IO is operationalized through the implementation of shared workspaces, where onshore and offshore personnel cooperate through the integration of work processes, and technology [1].

Concerning drilling wells the development of technology for real-time data transfer has enabled remote monitoring and support for interventions in offshore wells, providing faster access to onshore information, reducing personnel on board, and costs of this type of operation [1]. Given this, we observed an increase in studies that focused on the development and use of information technologies that favor IO [2, 4]. However, because of the specificity and complexity of activities related to drilling, construction, and maintenance of wells, remote monitoring and operational support encounter challenges related to human and organizational factors that still need to be more investigated [1, 2].

Hence, since 2019, a team of researchers has been working on the study entitled. The operational support onshore in wells interventions: integrating performance and safety, which aims to increase the knowledge about the human factors linked to the work in this context.

In this realm, this article highlights the daily well intervention team meetings which are a pillar for collective work that supports IO. The objective is then to present and analyze data that demonstrates the main characteristics of these meetings and aspects that facilitate or hinder IO work.

2   Methods

This study was a qualitative investigation, and its procedures for collecting and analyzing data were guided by the theoretical framework of Activity Ergonomics (AE), which includes the following research stages: 1. demand analysis; 2. organizational, technical, economic, and social environment analysis; 3. Activity analysis and 4. A review of the results, a validation of the study, and formulation of recommendations to improve the work [5].

As mentioned in the previous section, this article presents some results of the project entitled *The operational support onshore in wells interventions: integrating performance and safety*. This research was carried out during the period from May 2019 until January 2021 and the first stages of ergonomic analysis (demand analysis, analysis of the technical and social environment and analysis of tasks, validation of the partial report) occurred between the months of May to December 2019.

Data and analysis specifically related to well intervention team meetings come from the time period between july and december of 2020. The data collection strategies were concentrated on non-participant observation of the Daily Meetings and on interviews held with professionals from different hierarchical levels who work in support of offshore well drilling operations.

Thus, 55 meetings were systematically monitored remotely, using the Teams® application, during the months of August to November 2020, comprising 68 h of observation. To validate the information collected by the researchers a remote meeting with the team leader and the Directional Engineer took place in december of 2020.

3   Results and Discussion

The results of this paper are presented from two perspectives: the first describes the well intervention team meetings context and organization and the second presents data from the observations of meetings that demonstrate, through actual work situations, aspects which facilitate or hinder IO work.

3.1 Well Intervention Team Meetings: Context and Organization

The well intervention team meetings are held daily and have an average duration of 1 h 30 min. The participants of these meetings are located in different onshore spaces and on the rigs as shown in Fig. 1.

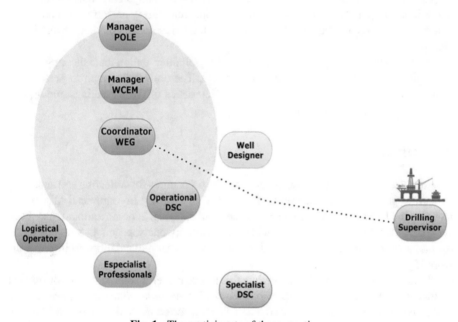

Fig. 1. The participants of these meetings.

In addition to the supervisors, who are located in the rigs, and the onshore operational support team, professionals who design the well interventions projects and specialists in different disciplines related to the field (i.e. cementation, fluids, logistics, safety, etc.) also participate in those meetings.

A member of the Decision Support Center (DSC) assumes the role of meeting coordinator. In general, there are three distinct moments in each meeting. The first takes about five minutes and consists of a presentation related to Health and Safety Management issues aiming to disseminate the safety culture.

The second moment of the meeting is the longest, as it focuses on the operational situation of all the rigs operating in a given field. In this stage, the whole team is presented with what has happened in each rig in the following sequence a) expose a summary of what happened in the operation from the last meeting to the present moment; b) address issues related to logistics, which may include the activity of support vessels, the need for material or equipment, among others; and c) if applicable, address the schedule regarding the embarkation and disembarkation of supervisors in the rig.

The final moment is reserved for general announcements, announcements about courses, disclosure of the day's meeting agenda, and other administrative reports.

3.2   Aspects Which Facilitate or Hinder the IO Which Were Observed Through Well Intervention Team Meetings

Regarding the role of this meeting for the IO work, the researchers identified that participation in these meetings favor a panoramic view of what happens in each rig. Since, outside business hours, only DSC members continue to monitor field operations. Therefore, the daily meeting allows the entire support team to become aware of what each rig faced the previous day (challenges faced, solutions found), what is happening at the moment, and the next steps of the operation.

This dimension of the meeting can be demonstrated by the discussion of a problem with a coring operation, that went unheard for an hour during the night. At the risk of compromising the sample or leaving equipment at the bottom of the well, the professionals opted to interrupt the operation and restart the maneuver.

The presentation of this situation at the well intervention team meetings allowed all members of the onshore support team to become aware of the challenges faced during the night, as well as of the decisions that were made. Also, it was possible to think about the consequences of the delay in the operation and to plan future actions to support the progression of operations concerning this rig.

The work analysis of the professionals involved in onshore support for well drilling operations, carried out in the first stages of the research, showed that the experience of these workers is fundamental to guarantee the safety and performance of interventions in wells.

In this scenario, the well intervention team meetings became a privileged stage for exchanging experiences, as professionals from different specialties and experiences, in different scenarios, come together to identify problems and build solutions for situations that cannot be fully anticipated.

To illustrate this dimension, we take the case of a rig that had problems in one of the stages of completion. During the presentation of this situation at the meeting, the support team initiated a debate to find hypotheses that would justify the reported difficulties, as well as the identification of possible risks and alternatives to face the problems. Previous events with similar characteristics were discussed and difficulties, that could increase the cost of that operation, were also listed.

The operational support work in well interventions deals with situations of high risks, high costs, and considerable uncertainty. Given this, it is often necessary to create discussion groups to deal with more complex situations. It was observed that during the well intervention team meetings, these complex situations are identified, as well as the planning of specific workgroups to address them is carried out.

Aspects observed in this research that can restrict the IO work in well intervention team meetings are related to the time restriction of the meeting and the volume or complexity of the cases discussed.

About the time restriction, it was found that the structure of the meetings does not allow in-depth discussions about the cases under analysis. This limit is imposed by the structure of the meeting, which establishes an average duration.

Although this barrier is mitigated by the possibility of creating new discussion groups, it should be noted that this resource reduces the group, restricting integration to a small fraction of the team, in addition to being subject to the availability of the actors for meetings at other times of the workday.

Another barrier to IO work identified in the well intervention team meeting analysis occurs as the number of rigs to be presented at the meeting begins to increase. Since the greater the volume of rigs the shorter the time allocated for the presentation and discussion of each case. It is worth showing out the number of complex cases to be addressed at the meeting, which may aggravate this limiting factor, further reducing the sharing time of the other rigs.

4   Conclusions

This research aimed to present and analyze data that demonstrates the main character-istics of well intervention team meetings and aspects that facilitate or hinder IO work in these encounters. The strength of this study refers to the generate knowledge about actual work situations related to discussion spaces that bring together different special-ists around well intervention projects. The lack of another published research focusing on the sharing of information and the exchange of experience in IO at drilling operations reinforces the relevance of the results of this paper for Ergonomics.

References

1. Bento, F.: Complexity in the oil and gas industry: a study into exploration and exploitation in integrated operations. J. Open Innov. Technol. Market Complex. **4**(1), 11 (2018)
2. Lauche, K., Sawaryn, S.J., Thorogood, J.L.: Capability development with remote drilling oper-ations. In: Intelligent Energy Conference and Exhibition. Society of Petroleum Engineers, Amsterdam, p. 289 (2006)
3. Cao, D., Loesel, C., Paranji, S.: Rapid development of real-time drilling analytics system. In: IADC/SPE Drilling Conference and Exhibition. Society of Petroleum Engineers, Texas, pp. 1171–1193 (2018)
4. Gooneratne, C.P., Li, B., Deffenbaugh, M., Moellendick, T.: Instruments Measurement Princi-ples and Communication Technologies for Downhole Drilling Environments. Springer, Cham (2019)
5. Guérin, F., Laville, A., Daniellou, F., Duraffourg, J., Kerguelen, A.: Compreender o trabalho para transformá-lo: A prática da ergonomia, 1st edn. Edgar Blücher, São Paulo (2001)

The Survival of Life. For an Ecology of Human Work

Michelle Aslanides[(⊠)]

Universidad Favaloro, Buenos Aires, Argentina

Abstract. The notions of human ecology and ergonomics were linked by Pierre Cazamian, one of our discipline founders [4]. The concept of sustainable development leads us to consider nature as part of the environment that conditions human work, but also as one of the dimensions of environment affected by human work. The aim of this communication is to discuss the ways future work will guarantee the survival of life within work systems and between layers of the overall ecosystem [6]. We start from our experiences of two types of interventions: reactive and requirement based classical ergonomic approaches, pulled by industrial and market needs, and prospective ergonomics based on people's needs approaches [10], inspired by the evolution of human activities in ecovillages and in socio-environmental projects. We find some trends in both contexts related to design, management and field activities and the need to guarantee life in all the ecosystem layers.

Keywords: Human ecology · Prospective ergonomics · Work · Life

1 Introduction

According to different Ergonomics Systemic frameworks that we have described some years ago [1] life could be described as the effect of work but also as a property of work itself. Indeed, life means health, safety, wellbeing and absence of stress, fatigue, harassment, etc. These are all the consequences of having "a good job", as we say. As the System's ergonomics view states that a working situation includes five main elements: external conditions, worker or internal conditions, activity, effects of activity and results of activity [8]. Amongst worker's activity and its effects on worker's health we find other ways to describe life in the whole system. Wellbeing and Performance (reliability) are therefore the two main aspects on which we should intervene to improve the chances of preserving life in our working sociotechnical systems. This presentation explains a little bit how we have proceeded until now and how we could proceed in futur interventions.

2 Life, Present in Different Ways in the Analyzed and Designed System

2.1 Life as the Consequence of Reliability

Life could be present in activity results, when the work process affects potentially the environment, other people and nature. In this case, we talk about human or organizational

N. L. Black et al. (Eds.): IEA 2021, LNNS 219, pp. 17–20, 2021.
https://doi.org/10.1007/978-3-030-74602-5_3

reliability impacting sustainability of the safety critical system. A larger description of the whole ecosystem in terms of sustainable development leads us to identify layers and stakeholders that need to cooperate to maintain life at each layer level [6].

2.2   Life in Interventions "Pulled" by Industry: Safety Critical Systems

Our experience of ergonomic interventions happened in systems that potentially lead to death, where design, management and operational teams think about preserving life in a special way: preventing accidents and only sometimes improving comfort in work-stations. We experienced Safety critical systems like aviation, nuclear, railway, con-certs/shows and medical industry. In all of them the design is supposed to be human centered and ergonomists should intervene, but in the real world the situation is very different. Life is not taken into account as we would expect.

In all these systems life is little evoked in design stages, and each layer of the whole ecosystem reasons independently one from another. The overall emergent life is not imagined. It is only after starting manufacturing stages than life emerges as an issue, as an incident, an accident, a complaint, a disease, etc. The workers daily working life is not understood nor included in the scenarios of the simulations done by the project leaders. Future work is not well anticipated nor protected. Life is a little bit preserved in some extreme scenarios like the worse ones, for which some of the solutions are planned and take into account operators needs (accessibility, workload, etc. in case of emergencies for instance). In all other scenarios of daily life very basic errors are being done by designers, simply because the design is not centered in workers needs at that stage.

2.3   Life in Prospective Ergonomists Driven Interventions

Our experience of ergonomics interventions in these new contexts are few but enough to extract some learnings from them. Indeed, we have shared in Argentina, France and Spain different projects where the main goal was protecting life in a wide way: 1) environment-friendly projects as ecovillages developments, 2) NGO's networks prevent-ing governments and companies from poisoning our lands and oceans and 3) assemblies of self-organized citizens acting at their neighborhood level to defend different causes linked to pollution of waters, rivers modifications and wetlands alterations. These experi-ences showed us that life is present in all the activities as a main goal, since the collective motivation is focusing the environmental challenges as a society.

For the moment Ergonomics is not present in all these changing and challenging worlds. Our colleague's findings [2] in these contexts arrive to a similar conclusion: *"hu-man work has tended to be overshadowed by the environmental and economic dimen-sions, and one could argue that work is the great forgotten dimension of sustainable development"*.

We believe at least through Permaculture concept we can be sure very soon sustain-able development will be focusing on the need to improve the quality of life in a global sense as stated by Cazamian [4], in 24 h a day activity. This is our goal, to little by little enter these worlds and bring our knowledge about designing workplaces to be able to design future working situations the best way possible. Besides country-side activities, in transportation system, other colleagues point out the need to be proactive [7]: *"There is a fundamental need for HFE professionals to be more vocal and active in infrastructure upgrade projects in IDCs".*

Even if the population that leads these interesting and life-prone projects don't know us ergonomists nor usually contact ergonomists or other experts to enhance their working conditions, it is worth it to pull these communities and convince them to work together.

2.4 Ergonomics at the Crossroad of Health and Performance

We have certainly encountered the "generation unity" mentioned by Pueyo [10] quoting Mannheim: *"when socio-cultural upheavals impose a pace that accelerates the change of attitudes to the point that the latent and continuous change of traditional forms of lived experience, of thought and of shaping is no longer possible, then new points of rupture crystallize somewhere forming a new impulse and a new structuring unity".* In these contexts, sometimes "solidarity and cooperation economy" model is present, sometimes not. The stake is ergonomists can help hold together life and economic stakes at once, in an ecological and sustainable human work approach. Ergonomics also turns out to be full of hopes and expectations for correcting work situations to design products and uses, and also to define needs and innovations that do not yet exist. We used to say "Ergonomists rarely initiate projects" [3] but this is changing. We have worked in Argentina recently in the design of a tool enabling to transport seedlings easier, with a team of Industrial Designers. It is possible, now it has to become the rule. The new sustainable development goals (ONU's ODS) are a good context, as described by our colleagues [6]: *"In an economy convinced of the challenge of Sustainable Development and of the opportunity that it opens in developing Service based dynamic, the strategic question concerns the desindexation of volume/value and the promotion of the "performance of use" concept: coping with this challenge require the recognition of the centrality of work in economic innovation and the centrality of the subjectivity in the activity".*

3   Conditions for Prospective Ergonomics Interventions

In our experience, the economic aspect of the intervention is the main issue, with the absence of knowledge about our existence as design professionals. Sometimes we can intervene but not get paid fairly for our service, and sometimes we are totally absent in projects because people don't know our potential work. This has to change in sustainable projects.

As remarqued by Hutchings [7], sustainable transportation's design principles need to integrate ergonomics in industrially developing countries: *"HFE professionals, through their knowledge and understanding of design principles and system optimization, should play a more active role in designing safer and accessible transportation systems. In the railway industry, this could be for both passengers and train drivers, and may include secure station design, ergonomics of the train driver's cabin, and the implementation of communication systems both auditory and visual that can ease commuter frustration and improve train services."*

Moore [9] observations can also lead us to some reflective thoughts in terms of required evolution of our intervention skills: *"HFE practitioners to a degree, and HFE researchers almost inevitably, can be prone to hiding behind the iterative process and standing back while others make the first design decisions, after which we happily step in and critique. HFE advertises itself as being part of the design community, and yet too often in practice, we are reactive in the way medical doctors wait for patients – and our tools and methods currently reflect that. We need to be involved at the beginning because some critical strategic decisions in sustainable development projects are made then".*

4 Conclusions

The stake has been making ourselves as ergonomists identified by other designers and remaining available during projects lifecycles as one of the professionals who can generate a positive change in people's life. We did this in the "regular industry" where the challenges are safety and operational reliability. We didn't succeed much. Life is still far away from the priorities in the effective design work. The design process is too taylorized and parcelized. Therefore, coping with the needs of future workers becomes almost impossible. Ergonomists are not present in the desing process at the necessary levels, therefore "life" is always at risk. The new scenario of sustainable projects is hopefully a good one, pulled by people who want to respect life. Guimarães [5] went even further detecting the sustainability needs of a town in Brazil to reduce its ecological footprint. The stake is to be able to design working conditions to enable life in those contexts. We need to go on working on this direction.

References

1. Aslanides, M.: «Modelo», Laboreal **11** N°2 (2015). https://doi.org/10.4000/laboreal.3832. https://journals.openedition.org/laboreal/3832
2. Béguin, P., Duarte, F.: Work and sustainable development. Work **57**(3), 311–313 (2017)
3. Brangier, E. (2013). https://www.canalu.tv/video/universite_de_lorraine/histoire_s_de_l_erg onomie_7_7_prospective_perspectives_sur_le_futur_de_l_ergonomie.11586
4. Cazamian, P.: Entretien avec Antoine Laville (2000). https://ergonomie-self.org/wp-content/uploads/2016/06/Pierre-Cazamian.pdf
5. Guimarães, L.B.M.: Sustainability and cities: a proposal for implementation of a sustainable town. Work **41**, 2160–2168 (2012)
6. Hubault, F., De Gasparo, S., Du Tertre, Ch.: Sustainable development arguments for an immaterial ergonomics. In: Bagnara, S., et al. (eds.) IEA 2018, AISC, vol. 825, pp. 702–706 (2019)
7. Hutchings, J.: Transport system in industrially developing countries (IDCs) – the role of human factors and ergonomics (HFE). In: Fischer, K., Thatcher, A., Zink, K. (eds.) Human Factors for Sustainability: Theoretical Perspectives and Global Applications (2021)
8. Leplat, J.: L'analyse psychologique de l'activité en ergonomie. Aperçu sur son évolution, ses modèles et ses méthodes. Octarès Editions, Toulouse (2000)
9. Moore, D., Tedestedt George, C., Qadir, J.: HFE practice within complex teams. what we bring. In: Fischer, K., Thatcher, A., Zink, K. (eds.) Human Factors for Sustainability: Theoretical Perspectives and Global Applications (2021)
10. Pueyo, V.: Pour une Prospective du Travail. Les mutations et transitions du travail à hauteur (2020)

Emancipation and Work: An Outmoded Ambition?

Pascal Béguin[(⊠)]

Institut d'Etude du Travail de Lyon, UMR 5600 EVS, Labex IMU, Lyon, France
pascal.beguin@univ-lyon2.fr

Abstract. The notion of emancipation belongs to a long social tradition, but it is curiously absent from the HF/E community as if it is an outdated ambition. Starting from the idea that emancipation is a heuristic notion for discussing the purposes and mobiles of HF/E, the aim of this communication is to discuss the relationships between emancipation and work. Two main focuses are well identified: emancipation from and within work. But a third focus, still to happen, could be named emancipation by work.

Keywords: Work · Labor · Activity · Emancipation

1 Problem Statement

The notion of emancipation is part of a long social tradition, and has been central for the development of the workers' movements that emerged in the first half of the 19th century [1]. Indeed, this notion was at the center of the first international workers' organization (the "International Workingmen's Association", often called "the First International") founded on September 28, 1864 in London, whose objective was to unite proletarians of all countries "*in the struggle they waged for their social emancipation, beyond the artificial divisions created by the borders of nation-states*". But to my knowledge, the notion of emancipation is far to be a reference for the HF/E community. Probably the reason comes from it appears as an outdated ambition (although other reasons may explain this absence: assumed divergence, too strong political anchorage for a scientific discipline, etc.). But anyway, the analysis of this "omission" would be difficult, as that idea of emancipation seems to be a blind spot of our discipline.

However, this notion has never disappeared, and emancipation stays an active idea concerning work. It is still used by the International Labor Organization, concerning social rights at work for oppressed peoples (home workers, rural workers, etc.), and in relation to contemporary issues (gender, decolonization). Moreover that notion makes a still timid, but assumed occurrence in recent publications in the ergonomics of activity. Guérin and Coll. [2] for example, argued that the aim of the discipline should be to "*contribute to the making of the work we want, by pursuing a goal of emancipation of human activities*". But it should be noted that, in a curious reversal, the idea of emancipation at work is also claimed as an aim by the financial world, by confusing work and employment in a context of increased deregulation of the Labor market [3].

N. L. Black et al. (Eds.): IEA 2021, LNNS 219, pp. 21–28, 2021.
https://doi.org/10.1007/978-3-030-74602-5_4

The notion of emancipation remains contemporary, and disputed. And there is the need to clearer the purpose.

Starting with the idea that emancipation may be a heuristic topic for discussing the purposes and mobiles of ergonomics, the aim of this communication is to initiate a debate within the HF/E community on the relationships between emancipation and work. It is by no means a question of saying the last word, but rather of proposing some ideas on that issue in the renewed context of the beginning of the 21st century. It will be argued that three different outcomes need to be identified: emancipation *from* work, emancipation *within* work and emancipation *by* work. Emancipation *from* work is an historic, but still actual focus of the social movement. Emancipation *within* work can be understood as a central topic for activity-centered ergonomics approach. However the third focus, so call emancipation *by* work, is still to better define. But in order to facilitate my point, I will begin in introducing a difference between "*labor*" on the one hand, and "*activity*" on the other hand.

2   Work as Labor and as Activity

As the IEA website asserts, the word ergonomics means "science of work" (and it is assuming that HF and Ergonomics are used interchangeably). However, the daily notion of work is not without ambiguities. Between the men and women who go to work for having money, and the baker who works the dough for human consumption, it is not at all the same thing. On the one hand, work as a historically constructed productive regime (namely "labor"), and on the other hand, work as a finalized human action names an "activity" [4].

Contemporary forms of Labor result of a socio-historical construction, which began in pre-modern times but which spread nowadays over a large part of the planet due to the hegemony of the capitalist system. It is not the purpose of this text to make the history of Labor. We will only point out that from the 17th century, labor has been understood as a factor of production that needs to be rationalized. In this context, John Locke will consider work as the main principle for creating value, and he considers it is thanks to the existence of money we can measure this value. So, workers exchange their "labor power" for money, which becomes a commodity. And Adam Smith will defend the virtues of the division of labor, reducing in the same movement the social to a contract and to its commercial corollaries (a point questioning issues related to the fair distribution of the wealth). It is in that context that questions about subordination will emerge. And as a result of capital and division of labor, the dominant form of "labor relations" is established: wage earning and employment (and its corollaries: the employment contract, working time, etc.), as well as hierarchical links and constraints (wage-earning being the provision of one's labor force by the employee during a given period of time). From the 19th century onwards, these "labor relations" will gave the birth to a whole set of regulations (and particularly work laws), deemed necessary to deal with the very unbalanced relations of subordination between the holders of capital and the workers, who held their labor force alone. This evocation is too brief (see [5] for a extended debate). But it makes possible to draw structuring dimensions of current production situations that cannot be avoided by ergonomists, such as "division of labor", "wastefulness" (central to lean production), or "prescription" for giving only few examples.

Quite different is speaking of work understood as an Activity. According to this acceptance, human activity is characterized by the relationship that human beings have with an environment in order to satisfy their needs of life: food, health care, clothing, etc. This is the main sense of activity in the cultural-historical activity theory approaches [6, 7]. During activity, humans are acting "through" instruments (i.e. material and immaterial historico-cultural resources) in order to give form to an object (the dough that the baker kneads, the plant that the peasant cultivates) in order to satisfy needs and to serve collective purposes.

Understood in that sense, an activity is before all an anthropological question, and for the people at work a human experience in the sense that something essential to life in society is performed. But each activity at work is situated in an historical and social context of labor. The current forms of labor are then obviously questioned, given that they either may support or, on the contrary, undermine and finally *alienate* the workers and the human life in all its anthropological dimensions.

3 Emancipation *from* Work

It is to the extent that labor is alienating for proletarians that emancipation has historically appeared as a goal to be achieved in workers' and trade unions movements. This conceptual couple emancipation/alienation being a key point of Marx's works [8], it is usefull to come back on Marx's meaning of alienation in order to define this first issue: emancipation *from* work.

To grasp Marx's understanding of alienation, it is necessary to start from the place he gives to activity, since it is in the socio-historical metamorphoses of labor that capitalism imposes alienation on activity. As with the cultural-historical approaches to the activity discussed above, Marx starts from the idea that an activity is aimed at satisfying needs that are useful to life. To work is to implement means to satisfy other needs. Activity here refers to the production of an (material or immaterial) object with use value in relation to life. Marx names that process an *objectification*.

But the capitalist form of labor doubly dispossesses the workers of their activities. On the one hand, the workers are dispossessed of the result of their activity (Marx speak of an "objective alienation"). But it is above all a "subjective alienation" that Marx insisted on in 1844. The workers are dispossessed of their activity because the concrete activities carried out by the workers are goods that belong to others. It is then a loss of oneself, which is akin to alienation in act, insofar as it is no longer what is done that counts, but the productive act itself that is counted and measured. Workers then maintain a relation of externality to their own activity. And accordingly to Marx, this "subjective alienation" must be understood as a loss of humanity. A human being whose whole life is spent to carry out a small number of simple operations, whose effects are always the same, has no need to develop his intelligence none to exercise his imagination. Labor causes a withdrawal from what constitutes the specificity of human life, and ultimately intended the human to fulfill "animal functions". It is finally in the context of this analysis that the notion of emancipation must be understood. Emancipation consists in an act of re-appropriation of the human world, which the organization through labor faces to the worker as an autonomous power, which turns against him.

It is on that bases that *emancipation* will be widely included in workers' and trade unions movements. In France, the charter of Amiens (1906) defined its program as improving working conditions on the one hand, and preparing a "full emancipation" of the workers on the other hand. The main idea (which joins that made by Marx-Engels in Volume III of The Capital [9]) is that activity, whatever efforts will be made, is within the "*domain of the necessity*". And as such, working conditions must be improved. But it is mainly outside of work settings, i.e. within "*the domain of liberty*" that humans being flourish. In other words, emancipation resides in an appropriation of the production tool, which will ultimately be intended to allow the reduction of working time. A fair redistribution of the wealth produced will make it possible to reduce working time, and will offer free time for the service of all, and for everyone's fulfillment.

The focus is clearly emancipation *from* work. Work activity is understood as a necessity (inevitably defined by its constraints). And emancipation means fair redistribution of wealth, offering the possibility for the workers to access free time which is leisure, and also "higher" human activity.

4   Emancipation *Within* Work

The reduction of weekly working hours is a central struggle in the history of labor and trade unionism. And the point here is not to question its relevance. However, defining the challenge of emancipation outside of work setting avoids important questions about work understood as an activity. Such an understanding reduces work activity to elementary operations realized under constraints.

However, activity at work question anthropological dimension. Having an activity is to make an experience in which something essential to human life is played out regardless of its social and historical forms. This position is known as the idea of *a human centrality of activity at work*. And in order to present it, one can situate the difference made below between *labor* and *activity* within a work setting.

In a given work setting, what has been called above « the labor» will be implemented in the form of a "*prescribed task*". The task is an actualization in a given setting of a certain "regime" of work, a labor (for speaking quickly, the regime of the globalized industrial dynamics under the domination of market finance, particularly in the case of industry 4.0). But the gap between the task and "real" work (i.e. activity), so important for activity-centered ergonomics approach, testifies that, in their activity, the worker(s) question, redefine and renormalize prescribed work based on their own understanding, perception and norms of life [10]. In so doing, the workers implement something from themselves in making a labor. And the analysis shows that such an implementation refers to three dimensions.

First of all, work is a specific place of socialization where human beings are engaged in shared activities that produce specific intellectual, moral and emotional effects. A positive work experience is an irreplaceable developmental factor. Conversely, when labor does not offer this potential, it becomes a disruptive factor, causes psychological dysfunctions and leads to the formation of pathological complexes in the cognitive, social and affective life. Secondly, activity is finalized. It is an action within the human world. The usefulness, the meaning and value of what is done are always questionning. Third, to work understood as a finalized activity inevitably questions the contribution made to the community, and the place occupied among others.

Labor, especially in its capitalist form, exploits the human activity; it dispossesses the protagonists of their activity and sometimes abuses them. But under no circumstances does the contemporary form of labor eradicate human life. The gap between prescribed work and real work bears witness to this expression of humanity at work. It testifies that, in their activity, the worker(s) question, redefine and renormalize prescribed work based on their own living experiences. From that point of view, work settings and labor are arenas in which debates on living norms are conducted.

Emancipation *within* work designates such a process of appropriation and renormalization. The aim of ergonomics intervention, as it has been developed in activity-centered ergonomics approach, may be understood as the process which support this emancipation [2], knowing that the space left for these renormalizations within labor is often too narrow to be fully deployed. The appropriation of the task in the activity is obviously not free, it comes up against relations of subordination (because of the wage relationship, or even more pernicious forms where the wage relationship is replaced by a market form) according to which: "*your activity does not belong to you!*". Intervening in this context means tooling, supporting and promoting the possibilities of a renormalization process of labor by the workers.

5 Emancipation *by* Work

The previous idea of an emancipation *within* work may nevertheless seems insufficient. To argue that humans renormalize labor in their activity, does not eliminate an anxious concern about the socio-historical evolutions of Labor. Never any company has abandoned the principles of line work on the basis of such an observation. This concern reaches a paroxysm in the face of technical prospective, which promises us a future without human work, where everything would be carried out by automata called "artificial intelligence". Everyone feel that such a "progress" is in fact very far from bringing about any improvements, due to the centrality of the work mentioned above. Faced with this dystopian future, the sole possibility is to assume the historical necessity in which we stand to contribute to the writing and definition of Labor. The ILO centenary initiative "the future of work we want: a global dialogue" is a manifestation of such an ambition, which is far from being limited to the countries of the South. But it raises considerable questions, and the idea of emancipation *by* work can help us to better define the stake at hand.

To introduce this third orientation, one can come back to the definition of work as an "objectification process" and to the idea of "objective alienation" pointed out by Marx. As previously seen, Marx's notion of alienation mainly focused on the dispossession of their own activity by the workers (what he named the "subjective alienation"). But he also pointed an "objective alienation": the workers are dispossessed of the results and values of their own activity. The central idea is that work is characterized by the relationship that man has with nature to satisfy the needs for life.

In fact, the place given by Marx to this "*objective alienation*" will evolved in his work. He argued in 1844 that work is "the first need of life" and that the "objectification of work" is positive for the human being. But in volume III of the Capital, the process of objectification is finally apprehended as a necessity quite distinct from "the realm of freedom", which is situated outside the sphere of work. In doing so, Marx falls in line with a dualism whose the origin goes back to Greek philosophy [11], where work tends to be reduced to a servile activity and a chore, which socially valued activities must get rid of.

However, work, understood as a "finalized instrumental" activity, can convey aesthetic and moral values, as well as dimensions of intelligent experimentation, freedom and self-expression [12]. It is in fact the socio-historical conditions of work (i.e. the labor) that alter this possibility. The division of labor in fact decomposes any finalized activity into elemental operations without meaning [13], and makes opaque the finalities pursued insofar as it becomes impossible for the protagonists to perceive the ends and mobiles of their activity. Activity then appears as a means at the service of ends over which those who work have no influence, and do not even have the perception. This loss of the finalized instrumental dimension of activity was already very present in taylorism. And it increases in post-Taylorian organizations, where mediation chains are more and more longer (especially due to information and communication technologies). The perception of the goals pursued is made even more opaque. The workers are then alienated, in the sense that they are dispossessed of the instrumental purposes of their activities, its meaning and value. But as the UNDP points out, "Human development … is about creating an environment in which people can develop their full potential and lead productive, creative lives in accord with their needs and interests." (www.und p.org).

To speak of emancipation by work then consists to understand work activity in that it constitutes a "useful contribution to the world" in the words of Valérie Pueyo [14]. Emancipation *by* work may then be understood as the process of re-appropriation not only of the working process, but also of work as a resource for creating environments and utilities that contribute to a useful and sustainable life. Such a focus needs to a change of our paradigm. The question is less to adapt labor in order to make it viable, than to redefine our current development trajectory of labor (deeply marked by globalized industrial forms under the domination of market finance) in order to contribute to the definition of another work "regime", capable of responding to societal and environmental challenges we are facing.

6   Discussion

The aim of that paper is by no means a question of saying the last word, but to initiate a debate on the relationships between emancipation and work, starting from the idea that emancipation may be a heuristic topic for discussing contemporaries' purposes and mobiles of HF/E. On that basis, three positions have been identified.

The first one, emancipation *from* work, questions the dialectic of working time and free time. The second one, emancipation *within* work, designates a process of labor renormalization by the workers and through their activity, which need to be supported during intervention. The third one, emancipation *by* work, concerns activity as a resource for creating environments and utilities that contribute to a useful and sustainable life.

However, this third orientation is still to happen. The categories from which we can develop such a program are barely defined, and the task is huge. From my point of view, three fields are questioned. The first, which I have already mentioned above, consists in redefining philosophical categories about work that we have inherited from the ancient Greeks, but which continue to be active in our ways of thinking. The second field consists in resuming the analysis of the economic infrastructure from which labor developed, starting from a reflection on the notion of *value*. Our entire economic edifice is centrally based on exchange value. But what counts for life, i.e. the usage value, is far more important and far more extensive than what could be counted in monetary terms [15]. Approaches centered on the servicing dimensions of work activity have already opened this second field [16]. The third one concerns the links between work and environmental sustainability. Human beings interact with a natural environment, and societies are based on the metabolism of human and nature, whose the operator is work. We are linked, and dependent on a nature that is being destroyed by labor understood as a contemporary forms of work: deforestation and urbanization, destruction of animal environments, production of poison, toxics and pollutants, spread on a large scale in the natural environment. Everyone still confusedly perceives that what we do on and with the world is inseparable from what we do to ourselves. Damage to our natural environment is in fact a new form of alienation.

The scientific integration of these dimensions is a hard job. But ergonomics is a discipline at the crossroads [17]. We need to carrefully meet the challenges of integrating economic and environmental dimensions.

References

1. Léonard, M.: L'émancipation des travailleurs, Une histoire de la Première Internationale. Paris, La Fabrique (2011)
2. Guérin, F., Pueyo, V., Béguin, P., Garrigou, A., Hubault, F., Maline, J., Morlet, T.: Concevoir le travail, le défi de l'ergonomie. Toulouse, Octarès (2021, in press)
3. Penicaud, M.: L'émancipation par le travail est notre projet de société. La croix 04/06/2018 à 11:48 (2018). https://www.la-croix.com/Economie/France/Muriel-Penicaud-Lemancipation-travail-notre-projet-societe-2018-06-04-1200944173
4. Béguin, P., Robert, J., Ruiz, C.: Travail et Travailler. In: Brangier, E., Valey, G. (eds). Dictionnaire encyclopédique de l'Ergonomie. 150 notions clés. Dunod, Paris (2021, in Press)
5. Lavialle, C. –coord.-: Le travail en question, XVIIIe-XXe siècle. PUF, Coll. Perspectives historiques, Paris (2017)
6. Rabardel, P., Béguin, P.: Instrument mediated activity: from subject development to anthropocentric design. Theor Issues Ergon. Sci. **6**(5), 429–461 (2005)
7. Nicolini, D.: Practice Theory, Work, and Organization. An Introduction. University Press, Oxford (2012)
8. Marx, K.: Les manuscrits économico-philosophiques de 1844, trad. Vrin, Franck Fischbach, Paris (2007)
9. Marx, K., Engels, F., Le capital, Livre III. (1894) Trad. Louis Évrard & Coll. Editions La Pleiade, Paris (1968)
10. Schwartz, Y.: Expérience et connaissance du travail. Editions Sociales, Paris (1988)

11. Arendt, H.: Condition de l'Homme moderne. Paris : Calmann-Levy, Coll. Agora (1961/1983)
12. Renault, E.: Dewey et la centralité du travail. Travailler, 2012/2 n° 28 (2012)
13. Friedman, G.: Le Travail en miettes : Spécialisation et loisirs. Gallimard, Paris (1956)
14. Pueyo, V.: Pour une prospective du travail. Les mutations et transitions du travail à hauteur d'Hommes (2020). https://hal.archives-ouvertes.fr/tel-02480599
15. Rist, G.: Le développement. Histoire d'une croyance occidentale. Presses de Sciences po, Paris (2007)
16. du Tertre, C.: Economie servicielle et travail : Contribution théorique au développement d'une économie de la coopération. Travailler **2013**(29), 29–64 (2013)
17. Teiger, C.: L'approche ergonomique : du travail humain à l'activité des hommes et des femmes au travail. Education permanente **116**, 71–97 (1993)

Industry of the Future, Future of Work: The Case of Collaborative Robotics

Tahar-Hakim Benchekroun[1]($\boxtimes$), Mouad Bounouar[2], Richard Bearee[3], and Ali Siadat[2]

[1] Conservatoire National des Arts et Métiers, CRTD, 41 Rue Gay-Lussac, 75005 Paris, France
Tahar-hakim.benchekroun@lecnam.net
[2] Arts et Métiers Institute of Technology, LCFC, 4 Rue Augustin Fresnel, Metz, France
[3] Arts et Métiers Institute of Technology, LISPEN, 8 Bd Louis XIV, Lille, France

Abstract. This communication discusses the resulting changes in the field of design project management generated by the industry of the future and its promises, with a special focus on collaborative robotics. Among the guiding issues of this work, we will focus on the importance of including such an intention to cobotize some or all of the tasks initially assigned to human operators, during the strategic stakes of the design process and to instruct and support it by the potential contributions of a bottum up approach centered on the real activities, mobilized and deployed during the realization of the tasks which are objects of cobotization. This discussion is based on an industrial case study, aimed at assisting a finishing workstation (the last stage of a production process) for fragile mechanical parts used in the manufacture of metal parts for the aeronautics sector.

Keywords: Industry of the future · Collaborative robotics · Design project management

1 Introduction and Methodology

1.1 Introduction

The emergence of new technologies presents a major challenge to the transformation of the work and activity of human operators. These technologies once again raise questions about the place of humans in the new work organizations, and about their potential impact on the work and activity of operators [1, 2].

The appearance of robots that can share the same workspace with human operators (cobot(s)) [3] generates multidisciplinary discussions related to the multi-stakeholder aspect of these new technological devices [4], including the nature of the new forms of human - cobot(s) interactions, called collaborative interactions, and the health and safety of users [5], the transformation of their work [6], its organization, the relationship to work and the collective, the new skills to be acquired and developed as well as the profitability of these investments (impact on the quality and productivity of the existing system) [7, 8].

In this sense and in order to contribute to the new classes of problems and debates raised by these emerging technologies, we present in this paper a brief feedback of a

N. L. Black et al. (Eds.): IEA 2021, LNNS 219, pp. 29–35, 2021.
https://doi.org/10.1007/978-3-030-74602-5_5

research-intervention study conducted in a French SME, interested in these new techno-logical devices (cobots), with the aim of assisting manual finishing stations for fragile mechanical parts intended for the manufacture of technical devices in the aeronautical and other sectors.

This research and development involve a multidisciplinary team of engineers and ergonomists with the main objective of carrying out a feasibility study to answer the following questions: how could the use of industrial cobotics provide a relevant, realistic and feasible response to the strategic issues of improving production performance, health (MSD risks) and working conditions? In which way does a mobilization and involvement approach of the operators concerned by the cobotization project, in particular through the analysis of their actual activities, represent an essential condition to succeed the design project?

1.2 Methodology

To address the issues and objectives outlined above, we have conducted an action-research project with a French SME. This project aimed to integrate a collaborative robotics solution for the refining workstations used to manufacture mechanical parts for the aeronautics sector with high quality, reliability and safety standards.

During this project, we sought to:

- Understand and analyze the strategic issues of the different stakeholders of the design project in order to contextualize the choice of this technology as an answer and solution to the issues of customer retention, the perspectives of modernization of the manu-facturing equipments, a more efficient performance by reducing rejects, prevention of MSD risks and global work conditions improvement, etc.;
- To mobilize and involve the concerned operators, in particular by the precise analysis of the gestural refining activities, to model the operations of manipulation and refining of the cores; to investigate the possibilities of cobotisation of the refining operations to support the gestural activity and to reduce the hardship of these workstations.

All these steps are part of a mobilization process of the involved design project participants, including the refining operators, and required the setting up of a strategic monitoring group of the project.

2 Analysis and Modeling of the Refining Activity

2.1 Analysis of the Refining Activity

Initially, the team focused on understanding the issues related to the finishing activity targeted by the cobotization project. The exploratory interviews conducted with members of management, local managers and finishing agents highlighted the following strategic dimensions:

– The strategic stakes of winning new shares of the product market, higher reliability of the produced products answering more and more strict specifications, etc.;

- The strategic stakes of increasing product market share, greater reliability of the produced products in response to the more and more demanding specifications, etc.;
- Quality and reliability requirements: A high product rejection rate is observed in the manufacturing process. This is due to customers' strict standards for aviation safety reasons.
- Dimensions related to the employment, training and hiring of finishing operators, their overall cost and the insecurity of retaining them;

2.2 Modeling of the Refining Activity

After the strategic analysis phase, the team focused on the analysis of finishing activities. Observation campaigns equipped with audio and video tools were organized following a schedule consisting in observing the finishing activity of parts of different complexity (parts qualified by the workshop manager from complex to simple) by operators with different levels of experience (4 months, 5 years, 10 years and 17 years of experience).

These observation campaigns were followed by exchanges and explanatory interviews with the observed operators, with the aim of understanding and analyzing their finishing activity. This phase made it possible to propose and validate (by the finishing operators) a characterization of the finishing gestural activity according to a view of the professional gestures not only from a biomechanical and physical point of view but extended to a greater complexity mobilizing the cognitive, collective and psychic dimensions. Such a conception of the professional gesture will make it possible to enrich the reflection and the choice of the technological solutions in the perspective of an allocation of the functions between the human and the cobot. An allocation of functions that takes into account the usefulness of the cobot and its integration in the course of the actions of the operators concerned, its participation in reducing the risks of Musculoskeletal disorders (MSD) related to the manipulation of parts and to preserve, or even develop new forms of efficient activities that produce meaning and recognition for the final users.

In order to go more deeply into this characterization, and inspired by the work of Chassaing [9] and Benchekroun et al. [10, 11], gestural activity would be located, invested, constructed and developing:

- Situated as long as the gesture is permanently inscribed in changing and evolving contexts on the organizational, technological, spatio-temporal, historical, social and cultural levels;
- The invested character of the gestural activity refers to its subjective dimension of the moment that it is singular and that everyone attaches values and meaning to it. The invested character of the gestural activity refers to its subjective dimension of the moment that it is singular and that each person attaches values and meaning to it. The gesture is not reduced to what is realized, it is also this activity that cannot be done and that risks being prevented;
- The constructed and developmental character of gestural activity refers to the processes of training and learning on both the individual and collective levels. In these processes of construction and development, Weill-Fassina [12] gives an important place to reflexive activities which, according to her, can be spontaneously made by

the subject, develop in the work group or be provoked by various forms of questioning or interviews.

On the basis of this characterization of the gestural activities of the finishing operators, we come to represent them according to the following model (Fig. 1):

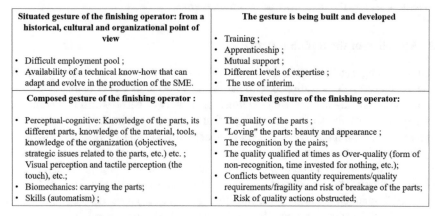

Situated gesture of the finishing operator: from a historical, cultural and organizational point of view	The gesture is being built and developed
• Difficult employment pool ; • Availability of a technical know-how that can adapt and evolve in the production of the SME.	• Training ; • Apprenticeship ; • Mutual support ; • Different levels of expertise ; • The use of interim.
Composed gesture of the finishing operator :	**Invested gesture of the finishing operator:**
• Perceptual-cognitive: Knowledge of the parts, its different parts, knowledge of the material, tools, knowledge of the organization (objectives, strategic issues related to the parts, etc.) etc. ; Visual perception and tactile perception (the touch), etc.; • Biomechanics: carrying the parts; • Skills (automatism) ;	• The quality of the parts ; • "Loving" the parts: beauty and appearance ; • The recognition by the pairs; • The quality qualified at times as Over-quality (form of non-recognition, time invested for nothing, etc.); • Conflicts between quantity requirements/quality requirements/fragility and risk of breakage of the parts; • Risk of quality actions obstructed;

Fig. 1. The 4 squares scheme for the analyzed activity

This type of analysis made it possible to broaden the discussions and to develop the project on dimensions that had not been questioned until then, with a projection of the finishing operators on the part of their activity to be assisted possibly by a cobotic solution. If the right hand fulfils the essential role of finishing the part by filing, sanding, filling, using different finishing tools, operations considered to be the key role of the finishing operator, which valorize them and give a recognized brand image of the SME; the role of the left hand remains essential as long as it carries the piece, manipulates it to prepare and anticipate the actions of the right hand, but capitalizes on the complaints of all finishing operators in terms of pain, discomfort and potential risk of Musculo-skeletal disorders (MSD). They unanimously believe that if their work is to be helped and relieved, it must be through a solution to reduce the discomfort felt in the left hand and left shoulder (see Fig. 2 which details the distribution of operations between the right and left hands).

This diagram shows the following dimensions:

– Finishing work mobilizes knowledge about products, their destination, their complexity, their sensitivity, the different kind of methods and used tools, gestural finishing skills mobilizing precision, accuracy, detection of imperfections, caution not to break the products; the different uses made of the light source to support and anticipate the lighting and its quality on the different treatment areas, etc.;
– The left hand has an essential role in preparing the operations of the right hand and protecting the pieces -which are very fragile- from breakage by continuously adapting their position according to the operations to be carried out by the right hand, the orientation in relation to the light source, the effort exerted by the right hand, etc.

Perceptive and Cognitive Mobilization	
- Initial inspection of the workpiece;	
- Continuous control of the progress of the finishing operations on the different areas of the part;	
- Choice of the appropriate tool according to the step and the finishing zone (sandpaper, file, blower, binocular).	
- Coordinate operations of both hands;	
- Maintain product quality requirements ;	
- Meet the assigned time;	
- Protect the part;	

Left Hand	Right Hand
- Carry the workpiece;	- Remove the burrs ;
- Preparing right hand operations ;	- Polishing the worked surface;
- Present the workpiece;	- Blow to clear the material (blower/mouth);
- Anticipate right hand operations;	- Turn the workpiece;
- Protect the workpiece against damage;	- Caution not to break or damage the worked part;

Fig. 2. Schematization of the finishing gesture activity targeted by the cobotization project

– Dimensions related to the health and hardship of the work: observation of significant solicitations of the upper limbs, in particular the hands, fingers and wrists. These solicitations are described as painful by the operators, particularly those of the left hand, which seems, to an outside observer, "not to be strongly solicited", etc.

Par un travail systématique d'observation, de traitement et d'analyse, nous avons identifié différents « patterns » de port et de manipulation des pièces par la main gauche. Ces patterns présentent les pièces à la lumière selon des plans longitudinaux et sagittaux rendant possible les opérations précisent, rapides et délicates de la main droite.

3 Discussion and Perspectives

The analysis of the finishing activity in this case study has made it possible to direct the reflection of the finishing station' assistance (the objective of this case study) towards a more precise objective which is the assistance of the left hand (the hand that carries the parts during the finishing activity).

In fact, the analyses and modeling carried out have shown, on the one hand, that it is this part of the gestural activity that causes the most pain to the finishing operators, especially if the parts are heavy or too small. On the other hand, the perceptive-cognitive activity mobilized and the skills developed by the finishing operators constitute the central part of the finishing activity, and any intervention on this part will transform the central part of the finishing activity. With regard to the gestural activity of the right hand that performs the intervention on the parts to be finished (burr removal, polishing, drilling, turning the parts to be finished, etc.), the great variability of the operations performed makes it difficult to think about technological assistance paths. This assistance track was subsequently discussed with the finishing operators who expressed their curiosity and interest in seeing what a solution of this kind could look like, and that they were in favour of testing a prototype of this technological solution.

Based on the analyses carried out, the design team pointed out that a few constraints must be considered in this potential future system in order to ensure its goal of providing assistance without compromising too much on the quality and scrap rate of the manu-factured parts, the productivity of the finishing department and the sense of this activity. These constraints are formalized below (see Table 1).

Table 1. Table of necessary constraints the future system must consider

Constraint reference	Example
Constraint 1	Ensuring parts carrying
Constraint 2	Allow to carry a variety of parts
Constraint 3	Allowing parts to be rotated and inclined smoothly
Constraint 4	Allow to feel the forces applied on the parts (force feedback)
Constraint 5	Do not damage or break the carried parts
Constraint 6	Allows parts to be assembled and disassembled quickly and easily
Constraint 7	Ensuring user safety & CE conformity (Machinery Directive)

Currently a feasibility study is underway to propose technological directions that would be able to meet all the constraints related to the activity to be assisted. As the strate-gic analysis and activity analysis stages, this phase is conducted by a multidisciplinary team of robotics engineers and ergonomists. Potential technological approaches will be discussed with the finishing operators and the piloting committee to decide whether to go further in this assistance track or iterate to specify or modify the constraints to be fulfilled by the assistance system.

4 Conclusion

The development of collaborative robotics and the emergence of new technologies more generally will continue to transform production systems and the activities of human operators. These new technologies, although they present significant potential for the future, must be thought out and implemented with great caution. In fact, what is supposed to improve performance or improve working conditions represents at the same time a risk of disturbing the existing system, degrading productivity [9] or even placing additional constraints on human operators [10].

To avoid undertaking unnecessary investments, it is necessary to verify the need in terms of these technologies and the presence of a real potential added value for the existing system (increased productivity, improved quality, reduced effort and hardship). A preliminary analysis of the strategic challenges and the real activity targeted is essen-tial before starting the technical feasibility study of any new technology, especially technologies with high interactivity with humans, such as collaborative robotics.

Even after the emergence of potential technical solutions, they must be tested and evaluated to ensure their adequacy with the requirements of the activity being trans-formed. This transformation must not downgrade the activity of human operators; the dimensions related to the perception of this transformation, its acceptability and the meaning of the work of human operators must be at the heart of the design, evaluation and deployment processes of potential technological solutions.

References

1. Benchekroun, T.H.: Intervenir en ergonomie: analyser le travail pour le comprendre et transformer le travail pour le concevoir. In: Proceeding of the 51th Congress of the SELF, Marseille (2016)
2. Garrigou, A., Thibault, J.-F., Jackson, M., Mascia, F.: Contributions et démarche de l'ergonomie dans les processus de conception. Pistes **3**(2), 1–20 (2001). https://journals.ope nedition.org/pistes/3725
3. Bounouar, M., Bearee, R., Benchekroun, T-H., Siadat, A.: Etat des lieux de la cobotique industrielle et de la conduite de projet associée In 16ème édition S-mart colloque (AIP-Primeca), Les Karellis-France (2019). https://smart2019.event.univlorraine.fr/243184
4. Bounouar, M., Bearee, R., Siadat, A., Benchekroun, T-H.: L'ergonomie, la robotique collaborative et le génie industriel: Vers une conception pluridisciplinaire des systèmes Humains-Robots. Proceeding of the 55th Congress of the SELF, L'activité et ses frontières. Penser et agir sur les transformations de nos sociétés.. Paris (2020)
5. Safeea, M., Neto, N., Bearee, R.: Efficient calculation of minimum distance between capsules and its use in robotics in IEEE. Access **7**, 5368–5373 (2019). https://doi.org/10.1109/ACC ESS.2018.2889311
6. Thibault, J.F., De La Fontaine, F., Martin, C.: L'ergonomie dans la conception de systèmes cobotiques. In: Proceeding of the 55th Congress of the SELF, L'activité et ses frontières. Penser et agir sur les transformations de nos sociétés. Paris (2020)
7. Quenehen, A., Pocachard, J., Klement, N.: Process optimisation using collaborative robots - comparative case study. IFAC-PapersOnLine, vol. 52, Issue 13, pp. 60–65, ISSN 2405-8963 (2019). https://doi.org/10.1016/j.ifacol.2019.11.131
8. Bounouar, M., Bearee, R., Siadat, A., Klement, N., Benchekroun, T-H.: User centered design of a collaborative robotic system for an industrial recycling operation. In: 1st International Conference on Innovative Research in Applied Science, Engineering and Technology (IRASET), Meknes, Morocco, (2020). https://doi.org/10.1109/iraset48871.2020.9092178
9. Chassaing, K.: Elaboration, structuration et réalisation des gestuelles de travail: les gestes dans l'assemblage automobile, et dans le coffrage des ponts d'autoroute. Thèse de doctorat en ergonomie, Cnam, Paris (2006)
10. Benchekroun, T.H., Arnoud, J., Arama, R.: Vitalité des activités et rationalité du Lean: deux études de cas. Pistes, **15**(3) (2013). http://journals.openedition.org/pistes/3589
11. Benchekroun, T.H.: Caractérisation pluridisciplinaire de l'activité en ergonomie. In: Proceeding of the 53th Congress of the SELF (2018)
12. Clot, Y.: La fonction psychologique du travail. PUF, Paris (1999)
13. Cherubini, A., Passama, R., Crosnier, A., Lasnier, A., Fraisse, P.: Collaborative manufacturing with physical human–robot interaction. Robot Comput. Integr. Manuf. **40**, 1–13 (2016)
14. Theurel, J., Atain-Kouadio, J-J., Desbrosses, K., Kerangueven, L., Duva, C.: 10 idées reçues sur les exosquelettes, INRS, (2018)
15. Weill-Fassina, A.: Activité. Psychologie du travail et des organsaitions, 100 notions clés. Dunod, Paris, pp. 25–31 (2016)

The Invisible Risk in the Work of Live Line Electricians

Flavia Traldi de Lima[1] , Gustavo Tank Bergström[1] ,
Sandra F. Bezerra Gemma[1(✉)] , José Roberto Montes Heloani[1] ,
José Luis Pereira Brittes[1], Milton Shoiti Mitsuta[1] , Amanda Lopes Fernandes[2],
and Eliezer Silva Franco[2]

[1] University of Campinas (UNICAMP), Campinas, Brazil
{gemma,heloani,jbrittes,msmisuta}@unicamp.br
[2] CPFL Energy Group, Campinas, Brazil
{amandaf,esilvafranco}@cpfl.com.br

Abstract. The article's purpose is to analyze the psychosocial risks involved in the Live Line Electricians (LLE) work and the collective risk management strategies. The research was carried out with workers who perform electrical structures maintenance in an advanced power station belonging to a private sector electric company, located in the countryside of São Paulo/Brazil. For this, it was used as a methodological resource the first stages application of Ergonomic Analysis of Work (AET). Psychosocial risks, also called invisible risk, which generates fear and anxiety, are associated with a job when a large tasks volume are involved, an intensified and dangerous routine, thermal constraints, repetitive movements, great cognitive load for the planning and replanning execution, action synchronicity between the team(s) and assertive and safe decision-making for the preservation of life.

Keywords: Work · Risk · Electricians · Ergonomics

1 Problem

The work performed by electricians is considered dangerous to the worker's life and physical integrity, especially due to the subject's exposure to risks of different orders.

According to the National Electric Energy Agency (ANEEL), in Brazil (2020), there were 28 deaths in the electric sector due to work accidents, adding own and outsourced employees.

Unlike other electrician's categories linked to electric power companies, Live Line Electricians (LLE) have characteristics that confer even more risks to the worker's safety, health and life. This is because the LLEs operate through the contact method in energized medium voltage networks (13.8 kV or more), using trucks with aerial baskets.

In addition to the shocks, fires, explosions risks, directly related to electrical hazard, the electricians work is also associated with thermal risks, which added to own clothing and other Personal Protective Equipment (PPE) can cause dehydration (Scopinho 2002).

Other risks must also be considered, such as falling from a height and falling materials on workers (Hembecker 2010), physical risks due to repetitive stress such as Work-Related Musculoskeletal Disorders (WMSDs) and Repetitive Stress Injuries (RSI) (Moriguchi et al. 2008), risk of poison animals in vegetation pruning activities, exposure to noise from urban workplaces and vibrations related to the truck that attaches the aerial basket, and also vibrations derived from tools (Gonçalves 2019).

In addition to the risks described above, the electricians work includes psychosocial risks (Nogueira 1999; Martinez and Latorre, 2009, Souza et al. 2010). The psychosocial risks related to work derive from the interactions between the individual, the environment and work, where factors related to the work's content, organizational conditions and capacities, worker's needs and other individual and family characteristics (ILO, 1986).

According to the European Agency for Safety and Health at Work, psychosocial risks are subjective perceptions that the worker has about the work organization. Contained in the psychosocial risks' idea, are the emotional, interpersonal stressors and those linked to the work organization (Heloani; Barreto, 2018).

In accordance to Nogueira (1999), the psychosocial risks associated with working in the electricity sector are related to pressure for deadlines and responsibilities, workload, problem solving and decision making, need to adapt to new technologies, pressure from managers, customers and others. Due to the dangerous context and the stressors present at work, the research by Souza et al. (2011) found that the prevalence of common mental disorders in electricians was similar to that found in civil police.

Because it is a worker constituent subjectivity element, the psychosocial risks seen in the electrical sector are named by Salvagni and Veronesi (2017) as invisible risks, responsible for psychological suffering at work.

Therefore, the objective is to analyze the psychosocial risks involved in the Live Line Electricians work and the collective risk management in a private sector electric power company, located in the countryside of São Paulo/Brazil.

2 Methodology

This research presents partial data from the Research and Development Project (R&D) "Ergonomics, biomechanics and cybernetics - Technologies for the future electrician: Continuous increase of productivity with Health, Safety and Quality of Life improvement", carried out from the partnership established between the School of Applied Sciences (University of Campinas), the CPFL Energy Group and Restart Brazil, a company focused on the development and production of tools and equipment for the electrical sector.

The research was conducted on an advanced power station located in the countryside of São Paulo/Brazil.

In order to know the real work and the risks related to the tasks performed by twelve LLE energy's distribution maintenance, company's own employees, the methodology used was Ergonomic Analysis of Work in your first stages application (Guérin et al. 2001).

As a result of the demand, terms and objectives defined in the R&D, the Ergonomic Analysis of Work first stages were applied. For this, global and open observations, individual and collective interviews were performed with the 12 LLEs.

Individual interviews were also carried out with professionals related to safety, health, engineering and human resources, besides interviews with local company managers.

The electrician's activity was also studied through visits to the workplace, both at the electric company and at the addresses for carrying out LLE tasks (streets and avenues), where conversations and data validation were possible.

The survey data were recorded using field notebooks, tape recorders, camcorders and cameras. It is noted that it was a demand oriented but built together with the company's interlocutors.

3   Results and Discussions

LLE work is performed in different locations in the municipalities covered by the electric company, with different activities being carried out, depending on the electrical structures that need maintenance.

To guide tasks, the company has a Task Manual, called Standard Operational Step, used by Live Line Electricians, which also supports the operations management for different sectors and for compliance analysis (included incidents and accidents), training and reviews.

Live Line category corresponds to the top electrician's career in an electricity distribution company. The activity performed is extremely specialized, requiring a large number of training hours and professional experience. Due to the risk degree conferred by LLE activity, work is prevented from being carried out at night or under rain, wind or humidity conditions.

The electrician's team is constituted in pairs, so that the functions are previously established. The electrician (executor) who climbs into the aerial basket attached to the truck is concerned with developing the structures maintenance. The electrician who stays on the ground, called in this company "lifeguard", is responsible for observing the activity and ensuring the partner's safety in the work's execution, communicating with the executor whenever necessary. However, depending on the complexity required by the task, it may be necessary to add another truck and another pair of electricians.

Organizational dynamics are guided by workload and productivity. Most tasks are marked as priorities, given that the electrical structures malfunction directly influences the company's performance. Depending on the complexity, the execution each task time can vary from 1 to 8 h.

The LLEs, under the conditions studied, have certain decision's autonomy on the time they have to carry out the activities. Despite this, new technologies implemented by the company through tablets and Smartphone's have been used, providing different assessing ways and controlling work.

As mentioned in the literature, risks related to constant and intense exposure to the sun were observed, aggravated considering especially the use of flameproof uniforms and other PPE (Personal protective equipment) such as boots, gloves, sleeves and balaclavas.

Aspects related to the activities repetition and movements were also pointed out, situations that cause pain and inflammation, especially in the upper limbs. The insect bites occurrence such as bees and wasps has also been reported by workers when carrying out the pruning vegetation task.

Regarding the risks related to shocks, fires, explosions from contact with an electrical network, they were related to tension feelings due to fear of accidental electric shock. In addition to the body, there is an air basket contact concern with the wires. This is because the work situation is extremely close to the energized network intersection. This tension comes not only from the body contact with the wire network, but also from a possible operational failure that can provide an electrical arc discharge or explosions.

The tasks complexity performed by the LLEs brings a significant cognitive demand, given the need to observe the structures, perceive risk and make decisions regarding the operations sequence to be carried out based on the activity's specifications, competence and technical experience, as well as on the security questions.

This means that the task execution depends on prior planning and constant replanning given that the work situation seen below the post may not be the same as that found in the actual execution situation in the structures. Thus, they also include overloads derived from responsibilities and constant decision making in the work face situations that need to be constantly assertive.

As a result, communication between electricians and teams in this work type becomes essential, since the lifeguard role is to guide and care for the executing electrician. However, on this aspect, it is observed that workplaces with an intense cars and pedestrians flow, for example, impair communication between the electricians.

In work situations in which failures can be fatal, the noises interference in the communication established by the "lifeguard" with the executor is a risk factor, since possible guidelines in relation to safety may not be fully understood by the electrician in the air basket.

From this, it is clear that the dynamics and work situations, that is, the psychosocial aspects that involve working in the electrical sector, can make the individual live daily with an insecurity feeling, which can generate anxiety and fear.

However, despite this, workers develop strategies to manage the risks inherent to work, which involve organizational, individual and collective factors. The intersubjective analysis relations, facilitated by the Ergonomic Work Analysis, allowed to identify the strategies used by the LLEs to manage the work risk focuses on considering the inter and intra-individual task variability and the electricians themselves.

In practice, the pairs perform relay roles as lifeguard and executor in different activities throughout the day. LLEs prefer that pairs be fixed, alternating only when one of the electricians is absent due to vacation or other complications.

The team's permanence allows a trust relationship, a fundamental element for this work type, because when exercising the guardian role, the electrician ensures not only that the work goes well, but especially for the worker safety and life.

This means that cooperation in this work type is indispensable to manage the different risk types present in the electricity activities sector.

In the total impossibility standardization and anticipation of the various factors involved in work situations such as those presented, trust and cooperation allow individuals to create strategies that enable work oriented in the same direction and for the same objective, in a more secure manner.

4   Conclusions

The analyzes showed that the psychosocial risk evidenced in the Live Line Electricians activities is associated with the factors present in a highly dangerous work environment, in which different risks are involved, a large tasks volume, intensified and dangerous daily routines, associated thermal constraints the great physical demand that involves the force application and repetitive movements.

In addition, there is a great cognitive load for the action execution plans and replanning and assertive and secure decision-making.

The fact that LLEs operate in energized networks is aggravated, that is, without the electric interruption. This generates the shocks, fires and explosions possibilities give the worker a high degree of pressure and tension, demanding precise actions, responsibility, care, evaluation and work supervision situations to prevent accidents and preserve life.

The psychosocial risks present at work, directly imply how individuals perceive and interpret work organization and interpersonal relationships. It is estimated that the content and work characteristics, associated, can often give LLE a feeling of insecurity, which generates fear and anxiety and, therefore, suffering. Despite this, LLEs use collective strategies against such emotional states in order to manage risks and perform tasks satisfactorily.

It is perceived that for the risks management, there is a certain autonomy granted by the company for the tasks completion, which is identified as positive because it allows greater flexibility, organization, planning and caution in the activities execution in which variability and risk.

As for the collective risk management performed by workers in their daily work practice, it is possible to identify the preference for pairs or fixed teams, coexistence and involvement among operators that give them tacit knowledge to identify the inter and intra-individual variability, from the task, to the physical and mental conditions of colleagues for the division between workers. This makes elements such as trust and cooperation essential for synchronous operations, carried out with technical quality and safety.

5   Acknowledgements

The authors would like to thank the CPFL Energy Group for technical and financial support, through the Research and Development project PD-00063-3036/2018 with resources from ANEEL's R&D program.

References

ANEEL Homepage. http://www2.aneel.gov.br/aplicacoes/IndicadoresSegurancaTrabalho/pesqui saGeral.cfm. Accessed 17 June 2020

ILO - International Labour Organisation. http://www.ilo.org/public/libdoc/ilo/1986/86B09_301_ engl.pdf. Accessed 20 June 2017

Guérin, F., Laville, A., Daniellou, F., Durraffourg, J., Kerguelen, A.: Compreender o trabalho para transformá-lo: a prática da ergonomia. Edgar Blücher, São Paulo (2001)

Guardia, M.La., Lima, F. Cooperação e relações de Confiança: a construção da segurança e da saúde no trabalho de alto risco. Laboreal, Porto, v. 15, n. 1 (2019)

Gonçalves, M.S.R.: Poda de vegetação em linha viva: complexidade e risco na atividade dos eletricistas. Dissertação de Mestrado, Mestrado Interdisciplinar em Ciências Humanas e Sociais Aplicadas, Faculdade de Ciências Aplicadas, Universidade Estadual de Campinas (UNICAMP), Limeira-SP (2019)

Heloani, R., Barreto, M.: Assédio Moral: Gestão por humilhação. Curitiba, Editora JURUA (2018)

Hembecker, P.K.: Conjunto de segurança para trabalhos em altura: uma análise comparativa de cintos tipo paraquedista no setor de distribuição de energia elétrica. Dissertação submetida ao Programa de Pós-Graduação em Engenharia de Produção da Universidade Federal de Santa Catarina (2010)

Martinez, M.C., Latorre, M.R.D.O.: Saúde e capacidade para o trabalho de eletricitários do Estado de SP. Clín. Saúde Coletiva, Rio de Janeiro, v. 13, no. 3, June (2008)

Morigochi, C.S., Alencar, J., Miranda-Junior, L.C. e Coury, H.J.C.G.: Sintomas musculoesqueléticos em eletricistas de rede de distribuição de energia. Rev. bras. fisioter. [Online]. vol.13, no.2 (2009)

Nogueira, V.A.: Reestruturação do setor elétrico: um estudo qualitativo das condições de trabalho e saúde dos eletricitários frente à privatização da CERJ. Dissertação de Mestrado, Programa de Pós-graduação em Saúde Pública, Fundação Oswaldo Cruz, Escola Nacional de Saúde Pública, Rio de Janeiro (1999)

Salvagni, J., Veronese, M.V.: Risco invisível: trabalho e subjetividade no setor elétrico, p. 29. Soc., Belo Horizonte, v, Psicol (2017)

Scopinho, R.A.: Privatização, reestruturação e mudanças nas condições de trabalho: o caso do setor de energia elétrica. Cadernos De Psicologia Social Do Trabalho 5, 19–36 (2002)

Souza, S.F., Carvalho, F.M., Araújo, T.M., Porto, L.A.: Fatores psicossociais do trabalho e transtornos mentais comuns em eletricitários. Rev. Saúde Públ. 44(4), 710–7 (2010)

The Work of Live Electricians: Postural Analysis in Vegetation Pruning Task

Flavia Traldi de Lima[1] , Gustavo Tank Bergström[1] ,
Sandra Francisca Bezerra Gemma[1(✉)] , José Roberto Montes Heloani[1] ,
José Luis Pereira Brittes[1] , Milton Shoiti Mitsuta[1] , Amanda Lopes Fernandes[2],
and Eliezer Silva Franco[2]

[1] University of Campinas (UNICAMP), Campinas, Brazil
{gemma,heloani,jbrittes,msmisuta}@unicamp.br
[2] CPFL Energy Group, Campinas, Brazil
{amandaf,esilvafranco}@cpfl.com.br

Abstract. The paper aims to present an analysis about pruning vegetation with hydraulic pole pruner, a task considered critical, performed by Live Line Electricians (LLE). The research was carried out at an advanced power station, located in the countryside of São Paulo/Brazil through the application in Ergonomics, Biomechanics and Cybernetics methods. It was possible to identify the critical determinants of the activity under study through the Activity Ergonomics, as well as to explain the physical issues through the movements simulation (biomechanics) in terms of medium and high pruning that confer bigger postural problems, especially of the trunk and upper limbs, validated by cybernetic analysis (3D), which allowed quantifying such elements in order to create demands for the tools design to alleviate this condition. It is suggested that the articulation between qualitative and quantitative analyses, explained here through the methods triangulation, although anchored in different epistemological keys, provide more complex and broad understandings about the working reality and the possibilities of transformation.

Keywords: Electric sector · Ergonomics · Biomechanics · Cybernetics

1 Introduction

It is known that the work performed by electricians presents physical demands associated to Work-Related Musculoskeletal Disorders (WMSDs) and Repetitive Stress Injuries (RSI), derived from repetitive movements (Mendonça 2004; Moriguchi et al. 2009).

In 2010, a research conducted with maintenance, live line and commercial electricians by Oliveira, Martins and Costa, showed that 72% of them presented some physical painful manifestation.

Official government data extracted from the *Observatório de Segurança e Saúde no Trabalho* - SmartLab (2018) indicate that in Brazil the fourth most frequent injuries in the electrical power distribution area were related to contusions or superficial

N. L. Black et al. (Eds.): IEA 2021, LNNS 219, pp. 42–47, 2021.
https://doi.org/10.1007/978-3-030-74602-5_7

crushing, resulting in 200 cases, while fracture, distortion or torsion and superficial abrasion/abrasion, presented more than 150 cases in the same year.

In addition to physical risks, the electrician's activity presents mechanical, biological, chemical and psychosocial risks, which can lead to illnesses and fatal accidents. The category of Live Line Electricians (LLE), research focus, confers even more risks to safety, health and live, since these workers act in contact to energized medium voltage networks (13.8 kV or more), using trucks with overhead baskets.

From this context, the article's objective is to present an analysis on plant pruning with hydraulic pole pruner, a task considered critical, performed by LLE. The research was carried out in an advanced power station, in a private electric company, located in the countryside of São Paulo/Brazil through the application of methods in Ergonomics, Biomechanics and Cybernetics.

2   Methodologies

This research presents partial data from the Research and Development Project (R&D) "Ergonomics, biomechanics and cybernetics - Technologies for the future electrician: Continuous increase of productivity with Health, Safety and Quality of Life improvement", carried out from the partnership established between the School of Applied Sciences (University of Campinas), the CPFL Energy Group and Restart Brazil, a company focused on the development and production of tools and equipment for the electrical sector.

The study included the triangulation of methods in Activity Ergonomics, Biomechanics and Cybernetics. The triangulation aimed at employing and combining different techniques of data collection and analysis, aiming to broaden the understanding about the object of study (Minayo, Assis, Souza 2010).

2.1   Population

12 (twelve) Live Line Electricians (LLE), own employees, who worked with electrical structures maintenance in the CPFL Energy Group, in a specific advanced power station.

2.2   Procedures

2.2.1   Activity Ergonomics

First stages application from the Ergonomic Work Analysis (Guérin et al. 2001) aiming explore the LLE real work, that allowed to elect the task of vegetation pruning as critical and identify the physical demands, cognitive and organizational aspects from work.

Individual and group interviews were conducted with 12 LLE, professionals from engineering, safety and health areas, local and outside managers, besides image and audio records. The global and open activity's observations were made through visits to the advanced electric company station and the addresses for carrying out the LLE field tasks, with interviews and posterior data validations with the operators.

2.2.2 Biomechanics

Vegetation pruning movement simulation by Motion Capture *Optitrack* system with 11 cameras. The use of such technology aimed to integrate the images obtained with higher resolution quality and closer analysis with the movement simulation.

The volunteer handling the hydraulic pole pruner in his hands performed upper limbs movements, drawing the letter "W" trajectory in the air (Bento da Silva et al. 2019), which presented variations similar to the real action of pruning vegetation. Five W movements were performed from right to left and five movements from left to right.

The movement was carried out in three different situations: a) Medium pruning: placing the tool in front of the volunteer; b) High pruning: positioning the hydraulic pole pruner above the shoulder line; and c) Low pruning: placing the hydraulic pole pruner below the waistline.

The activities were outlined in the DELMIA tool present in the ergonomic 3D simulation module, experience software from *Dassault Systèmes®*, where the LLE's Personal Protective Equipment (PPE), clothing and the hydraulic pole pruner weights were considered, totaling 9.5 kg (see Fig. 1).

Fig. 1. Volunteer with a hydraulic pole pruner - image captured by an *Optitrack* system with eleven cameras.

2.2.3 Cybernetics

Reconstruction of the vegetation pruning motion simulation images obtained by the Motion Capture and DELMIA *Optitrack* system by 3D Experience software from *Dassault Systèmes®*.

Afterwards, the Rapid Upper Limb Assessment (RULA) protocol was applied (Mcatamney and Corlett 1993). The use of such tools aimed to perform quantitative postural analysis, focused on the upper limbs (see Fig. 2).

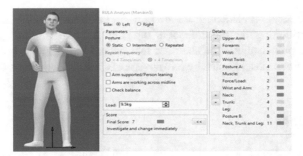

Fig. 2. Simulation in DELMIA with RULA analysis.

Through the Ergonomic Work Analysis application, qualitative data was collected and analyzed in terms of the real work, the content and characteristics surveys of the work performed by LLE in the vegetation pruning task.

The procedure performed by Biomechanics, through the low, medium and high simulation pruning movements and the technologies used, became preparatory for Cybernetics analysis, by favoring greater image fidelity to body postures. Using the RULA tool, related to this last field, it was possible to raise postural components of the upper limbs, in a quantitative way.

The articulations between qualitative and quantitative analyzes, explained here through the methods triangulation, although anchored in different epistemological keys, provide more complex and broader understandings about the work reality and the possibilities for transformation.

3   Results and Discussions

The analyzes derived from the Ergonomic Work Analysis application for vegetation pruning demonstrated that the activity comprises a series of variations, which involve the local traffic conditions and flow of cars and pedestrians and determine the truck's position, the weather sunny and thermal constraints associated with Personal Protective Equipment (PPE), the winds direction that interferes with the trees scenery and shrubs and the proximity and risk to the power grid, which generate anxiety and fear.

It was observed that keeping the arms permanently stretched or elevated above the shoulders is a posture performed frequently and repetitively. This also occurs with neck and torso movements. The justifications are related to the conditions imposed by the activity itself, considering the trees diversity composition, branches and trunks in different sizes and thicknesses, task execution time and frequency performed 3 to 5 times a week, during the two journey periods of work. In addition to these factors, wear and tear related to vibrations resulting from both the operations truck and hydraulic pole pruner.

The high, medium and low pruning simulation movements derived from the procedures performed by the Biomechanics field were classified in order of critical conditions by RULA score. The sum of the Upper Limb and Lower Limb points, for the right and left sides, reflects how much the respective cinematic chains are requested throughout the activity as a whole, indicating a potential for cumulative wear.

The most critical movement, from the RULA's perspective, is the medium pruning movement, positioning the tool in front of the body and high pruning, positioning the hydraulic pole pruner above the shoulder line, which have similar criticality scores. Likewise, the limbs most affected by the movements performed include the trunk, neck, wrist and arms.

4 Conclusions

The research aimed to present results on Vegetation Pruning with hydraulic pole pruner, a task considered critical, performed by Live Line Electricians, through the application of methods in Ergonomics, Biomechanics and Cybernetics.

It was possible to identify the critical determinants of the activity under study, as well as postural measurement and analysis for upper limbs related to its execution.

The qualitative analysis provided by Ergonomics demonstrated the physical, cognitive, emotional and organizational work wear, especially those related to the content and characteristics of the vegetation pruning task. From the movement's simulation, high, medium and low pruning postures, in high resolution, through Biomechanics, the images were applied by the Rapid Upper Limb Assessment (RULA) protocol for upper limbs quantitative postural analysis, using a specific software. It was identified that the upper limbs and torso, neck, wrists and arms movements are the most critical in terms of wear, with emphasis on the medium and high pruning movements.

Such findings, associated with the pruning activity frequency execution performed by the company and the exposure's intensity for long periods over the sun, the truck's operation and the hydraulic pole pruner vibration, the emotional stress for knowing the risks and cognitive stress for planning the operation and safe decision-making, can corroborate even greater criticisms in terms of physical wear and tear. Through the knowledge generated, there are demands for tools design mitigate this condition, leading to the belief that analyzes may be useful for the health and safety sectors of electric power companies, in order to improve working conditions.

Finally, it is suggested that the qualitative and quantitative articulation analyzes, explained here through the triangulation of methods, although anchored in different epistemological keys, provide more complex and broader understandings about the reality of work and the possibilities for transformation.

Acknowledgements. The authors would like to thank the CPFL Energy Group for technical and financial support, through the Research and Development project PD-00063-3036/2018 with resources from ANEEL's R&D program.

References

ANEEL Homepage. http://www2.aneel.gov.br/aplicacoes/IndicadoresSegurancaTrabalho/pesqui saGeral.cfm. Accessed 17 June 2020
Bento da Silva, S., Gemma, S., Brittes, J.L.P., Lacusta Junior, E., Misuta, M.S.: Variabilidade do CM em Simulação com Motopoda para Eletricista de Linha Viva: Estudo Preliminar. In: Anais do XVIII Congresso Brasileiro de Biomecânica (2019)

Guérin, F., Laville, A., Daniellou, F., Durraffourg, J., Kerguelen, A.: Compreender o trabalho para transformá-lo: a prática da ergonomia. Edgar Blücher, São Paulo (2001)

Mcatamney, L., Corlett, E.: A survey method for the investigation of work-related upper limb disorders. Appl. Ergon. **24**(2), 91–99 (1993)

Mendonça, M.S.: Análise Ergonômica do Trabalho de Manutenção de Linhas de Transmissão. 2004. Dissertação (Mestrado). Programa de Pós-Graduação em Engenharia de Produção, Universidade Federal de Pernambuco, Recife (2004)

Minayo, M.C.S., Assis, S.G., Souza, E.R.: Avaliação por triangulação de métodos: Abordagem de Programas Sociais. Rio de Janeiro: Fiocruz **2010**, 19–51 (2010)

Moriguchi, C.S., Alencar, J.F., Miranda-Junior, L.C.: Sintomas musculoesqueléticos em eletricistas de rede de distribuição de energia. Rev. bras. fisioter. vol.13, no. 2 (2009)

Oliveira, K.P., Martins, M.P., Costa, J.A.: Prevenção de dores osteomusculares em eletricistas: uma análise ergonômica. vol. 6, no. 2. Revista científica da FAMINAS (2010)

The Role of Participatory Ergonomics Meetings on the Development of an Electronic Health Record for Support Collaborative Care of Children and Youth

João Marcos Bittencourt[1]([⊠]) ⓘ, Eliel Prueza de Oliveira[2] ⓘ,
Vitória de Araujo Melo[1] ⓘ, Melissa Ribeiro Teixeira[2] ⓘ,
and Carolina Maria do Carmo Alonso[1] ⓘ

[1] Technical Drawing Department, Engineering School, Federal Fluminense University,
Rio de Janeiro, Brazil
joaobittencourt@id.uff.br
[2] Department of Occupational Therapy, Medical School, Federal University of Rio de Janeiro,
Rio de Janeiro, Brazil

Abstract. Usability studies are focused on heuristics of efficiency, effectiveness, and completeness. However, they generally ignore the content of the work performed. Seeking to overcome this gap this paper aims to present and discuss the role of participatory ergonomics meetings on the development of an EHR for collaborative care of children and youth. As we will present, the construction of a common world will help integrate users to understand different work situations based on this understanding, they could propose solutions to support different phases of care and embracing different professional worlds. This process was developed based on the knowledge about work situations and the dynamics during the collaborative meeting, but also with the support of Intermediary Objects developed by the ergonomist for this purpose.

Keywords: Work simulation · Activity · Intermediary object · Usability · Electronic Health Records

1 Background

Electronic Health Records (EHR) encompasses a variety of information systems ranging from the compilation of data from individual departments to longitudinal collections of patient information that can be used by different health system services [1]. These systems have been used as a resource of monitoring of individual treatment plans as well as in providing epidemiological analyzes of populations, subsidizing health organizations and management [2, 3]. Patient's health data may be imputed from different levels of the health system, different health agents and can be provided in various formats such as text, images, vital signs, prescriptions, stories originated from clinical meetings, multidisciplinary care or hospitalizations [4].

Usability practices improve the overall functioning of digital applications, and interfaces like EHR. In general, usability heuristics focus on criteria of efficiency, effectiveness, and completeness of the tasks performed. However, this type of contribution has limits because it disregards the content of the work and context of use [5, 6].

The poor consideration of the actual conditions of use in the EHR project, according to several researchers, may limit the potential of these tools and have deleterious impacts on the work process of health professionals [5–9]. A literature review that addressed this topic suggests a strategy to overcome the limits of the "heuristic decontextualization" using the framework of Activity Ergonomics since this approach can subsidize the development of knowledge regarding the content of the actual work situations [6]. Hence, a deeper understanding of the activities encompassing the use of EHR may allow the enhancement of EHR design in areas where traditional studies based on general heuristics have already reached their frontiers.

Thus, this paper presents aspects of the designing process of an Electronic Health Record (EHR) which was developed by an ergonomist team for a group of professionals that works collaboratively in the care of children and youth that lives in low-income neighborhoods in Rio de Janeiro. In the first phase of this project, the ergonomist team has explored the actual work of the professionals who would become the future users of this EHR [10].

In the second phase of this project, ergonomists promoted meetings to put the user's perspective of the system in evidence seeking to develop tailor-made solutions to their specific needs. During those meetings, ergonomists used two intermediary objects (IO) [12], and also the dynamics during the meeting were conceived to stimulate and help users to present their logics of their professional worlds [11, 13].

The objective of this article is to present and discuss the role of participatory ergonomics meetings on the development of an EHR for collaborative care of children and youth. As we will present, the construction of a common world will help integrate users to understand different work situations based on this understanding, they could propose solutions to support different phases of care and embracing different professional worlds. This process was developed based on the knowledge about work situations and the dynamics during the collaborative meeting, but also with the support of Intermediary Objects developed by the ergonomist for this purpose.

1.1 Theoretical Framework: The Concepts of Professional Worlds and Common Worlds

According to Béguin [13], the need to integrate different points of view in a project, as well as in a given health care situation, creates additional complexity to the work process. Whatever the project is to be conceived, it cannot be conceptualized by overlapping different technical systems. Therefore, it will always be necessary to integrate the different views concerning a work objective in a coherent and coordinated manner [11, 13].

To analyze this integration of knowledge in a multi-professional teamwork situation, Béguin [13] introduced the concepts of the professional world and the common world. The term professional world is defined by Béguin as a set of implicit, conceptual, and practical values that forms a system with the object of the action. Consequently, the professional world concept features the background that guides the interpretation of the tangible dimension of action that permits the worker to build unique strategies to achieve a certain goal [11, 13].

The objective of a professional world is organizing systems, solving problems using abilities, skills, and strategies, to avoid staying on the sidelines of the event. To be a specialist is to have a particular skillset, but also to build a more integrated professional world. Thus, the creation of a common world enables the possibility of mutual learning and coordination among different professional worlds [11, 13].

2   Methods

We carried out a case study on the design process of EHR conducting, firstly, an Ergonomic Work Analysis [14] on the activity of different potential users of this system which was occurred from July of 2017 until December of 2018, and the preliminary results of this research can be consulted in a paper published by Alonso and colleagues [10].

Therefore, this manuscript outlines three collaborative design meetings, that took place during 2019, in which the ergonomist team brought together the potential users of the EHR. The participants of these meetings were from different fields like education, health, and social assistance, that has been working on the project of collaborative care of children and youth, from two different low-income neighborhoods of Rio de Janeiro.

The first two meetings lasted about 3 h with the support of 3 ergonomists and 2 software developers. The last meeting, which also lasted 3 h, was intended to simulate the use of a beta version of the system to validate the proposed solutions and included participants who were present in the first two meetings.

Besides the participation in the meetings, we collect data from recordings from the meetings made with both workgroups. As the ergonomists were involved in the project acting as facilitators during the meeting, the authors used the video for further analysis of discussions on research questions. During video analysis, we selected excerpts when the different heath agents referred to characteristics of their professional worlds.

3   Results and Discussion

Ergonomists created two Intermediary Objects (IO) to support the collaborative meetings to discuss design solutions and highlight different work logics. The first IO consisted of a model for building the application's resource hierarchy which is illustrated in Fig. 1. All resources were identified with post-it notes, to permit users to change their position. The base of the hierarchy was made of paper and pens of different colors were made available so that relations between the tools could be established.

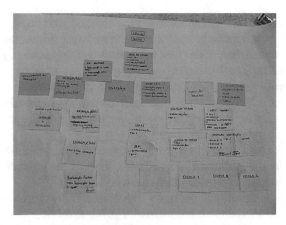

Fig. 1. System hierarchy representation

The second IO represented a continuous scrolling screen with the records of fictional cases developed to improve the thoughts of each participant about what they expect from the new ERH. With an impression made to refer to a cell phone, a continuous column was made so that health workers could put the information and order of presentation that they considered important. Each agent worked individually on setting up a patient registration screen, following their work logic. Afterward, everyone discussed their results to put together a unified proposal as shown in Fig. 2.

Fig. 2. System hierarchy representation

The design process can be characterized as a social process, where dynamics among people are determinant for the project results, we also need a method to study a phenomenon outside experimental control. In these sense the participatory meetings supported by IO used in this research was adequate since the ergonomist wanted to investigate discussions and dynamics for a factual project [12, 13, 15].

The unit of analysis [16] was the reveal process of professional world and the development of a common world based on the support and the dynamics created for the collaborative meeting [11, 13]. By observing the different work logics, criteria and prioritized processes, we could realize how workers uses the ER system and the health agent could better understand their colleagues point of view. Design solutions were selected which enabled relating how these professional worlds operate.

The results presented show the importance of studying work activity to design tools and the importance of workers' collaboration. Based on work analysis and discussions with health agents it was possible to evidence work logics, priorities and strategies. This study also points to other practical evidence.

First, user participation was essential for improving the organization of the application. Even with the study of activities conducted, the professionals' direct contribution is essential to adapt the digital resource to the work's reality.

Second, although usability studies show improvements in information systems, these studies generally do not address the work's content. Based on the knowledge constructed collaboratively it was possible to develop solutions aimed at work context and their own constraints. The solutions presented on this approach pointed to solutions that would hardly be discussed based on usability heuristics. Still, this does not substitute the mentioned heuristics, but help to go further on design solutions.

Third, the proposed intermediary objects focused on the organization of information and not on the system itself. These characteristics made it possible to focus the discussion on work situations and not on application characteristics. The content of these discussions allowed improvements in the systems' proposition, taking into account the work activities and not the "optimization of the system".

Forth, through the construction of a common world, it was possible to develop an application tool with resources to aid different categories of health agents. The different health agents externalize their logics, practices and criteria; and based on that they could confront different ideas and negotiate priorities. This made possible for the group to understand and visualize with information and resources were important to evidence to attend the whole chain of healthcare process instead of valorize one logic over others.

4   Conclusion

Usability studies are focused on heuristics of efficiency, effectiveness, and completeness. However, they generally ignore the content of the work performed, as if the efficiency of use does not depend on the context. When we have an application used in different contexts and with different users, the efficiency and effectiveness will differ. Therefore, designers should not center their studies on usability based on a single logic of use alone. Integrate different logics will help to ensure a better result for extensive use. In this sense, the user's participation can improve the design of devices aimed at collaboration. One way to build this collective integration is to create a common world. In this paper, ergonomists made an effort to bring together professionals who collaborate throughout the process -although hardly directly to each other. From building the common world, these different agents understood better the role, limitations, and criteria of different areas. Based on this collective learning, they proposed solutions that contemplated a larger group of professionals in the process.

References

1. Häyrinen, K., Saranto, K., Nykänen, P.: Definition, structure, content, use and impacts of electronic health records: a review of the research literature. Int. J. Med. Inform. **77**(5), 291–304 (2008)
2. Detmer, D., Bloomrosen, B., Tang, P.: Integrated personal health records: transformative tools for consumer-centric care. BMC Medicak Inform. Decision Making **8**(1), 45 (2008)
3. Hillestad, R., Bigelow, J., Bower, A., Girosi, F., Scoville, R., Taylor, R.: Can electronic medical record systems transform health care? Potential health benefits, savings, and costs. Health Aff. **24**(5), 1103–1117 (2005)
4. Marin, H., Massad, E., Azevedo Neto, R. S.: Prontuário eletrônico do paciente: definições e conceitos. In: Massad, E., Marin, H., Azevedo Neto, R. S. (eds.) O prontuário eletrônico do paciente na assistência, informação e conhecimento médico. São Paulo (2003)
5. Ellsworth, M., Dziadzko, M., O'Horo, J., Farrell, A., Zhang, J., Herasevich, V.: An appraisal of published usability evaluations of electronic health records via systematic review. J. Am. Med. Inform. Assoc. **21**(1), 2018–226 (2016)
6. Alonso, C.M.C., Oggioni, B.P., Bittencourt, J.M.V.Q., Duarte, F.J.C.M.: Usability of electronic health records: what does the literature reveal about the work dimension?. In: Proceedings of the 50th Nordic Ergonomics and Human Factors Society Conference. Copenhagen, Denmark (2019)
7. Almeida, S.R., Dal Sasso, G.T., Barra, D.C.: Computerized nursing process in the Intensive Care Unit: ergonomics and usability. Revista da Escola Enfermagem da USP **50**(6), 996–1002 (2016)
8. Sidebottom, A., Collins, B., Winden, T., Knutson, A., Britt, H.: Reactions of nurses to the use of electronic health record alert features in an inpatient setting. Comput. Inform. Nurs. **30**(4), 218–226 (2012)
9. Sitting, D.F., Wright, A., Ash, J., Singh, H.: New unintended adverse consequences of electronic health records. Yearbook Med. Inform. **1**, 7 (2016)
10. Alonso, C.M.C., Lima, N., Teixeira, R., Oliveira, E., Silva, E., Couto, M., Duarte, F.: Contributions of Activity Ergonomics to Design a Virtual Tool for Sharing Mental Health Care: Advances in Intelligent Systems and Computing. Springer, pp. 683–690 (2019)
11. Alonso C.M.C.O: Trabalho do Agente Comunitário de Saúde na concepção dos projetos terapêuticos singulares na perspectiva dos conceitos mundos profissionais e mundo comum. Rio de Janeiro, 2017. (Doutorado em Engenharia de Produção). Universidade Federal do Rio de Janeiro (2017)
12. Vinck, D., Jeantet, A.: Mediating and commissioning objects in the sociotechnical process of product design: a conceptual approach. In: MacLean, D., Saviotti, P., Vinck, D. (eds.) Management and New Technology: Design. Networks and Strategy. COST Social Science Series, Bruxelles (1994)
13. Béguin, P.: O ergonomista, ator da concepção. In: Falzon, P. (ed.) Ergonomia, vol. 1, pp. 317–330. Editora Blucher, São Paulo (2007)
14. Guérin, F., Laville, A., Daniellou, F., Duraffourg, J., Kerguelen, A.: Understanding and transforming work: the practice of ergonomics, 1st edn. ANACT, England (2007)
15. Bucciarelli, L.L.: Reflective practice. engineering design. Design Stud. **5**(3), 185–190 (1984)
16. Yin, R.K.: Case Study Research. Design and Methods. Sage, London (1989)

Forensic Police's Work Simulation to Support Product Development in Times of Pandemic

João Marcos Bittencourt(✉) ⓘ, Manela D'avila de Moraes Rosaⓘ,
and Sarah da Silva Diasⓘ

Technical Drawing Department, Engineering School, Federal Fluminense University,
Rio de Janeiro, Brazil
joaobittencourt@id.uff.br

Abstract. Work simulation is a strategy to integrate work knowledge into the design process. Although it a recurrent approach among ergonomists, few paper present information on simulation preparation and the material used. This paper presents a work simulation planning to support forensic ballistics packaging for evidence collected in the crime scene. The study was conducted with the forensic police department of a statue Brazilian Civil police. Because of the COVID-19 pandemic restrictions, the ergonomist had to restrict their interaction with workers to remote meetings. Based on the initial field study interrupted by the pandemic and remote discussions on work constraints, the ergonomist team develop a design for ballistic evidence packaging and prepared a simulation to test it. The simulation plan presented englobes different materials, intermediary objects designed, workgroup composition. Also is shown the general dynamics, including rules, points of interest, and typical action situations selected for work simulation.

Keywords: Work simulation · Activity · Intermediary object · Participatory ergonomics

1 Introduction

Ergonomists have been using various participatory methods to integrate users into the design process of workspaces, equipment and other elements of the work system. These simulations technics generate benefits such as focusing on user needs, thus improving solutions and increasing project acceptability [1]. Several authors use work simulation methods to integrate knowledge from work activity [2–5]. These simulation methods involve users' participation, but the ergonomist must plan these meetings and select the intermediary objects [6] to organize participatory dynamics. Despite of some author proposes frameworks for simulations and presents details on the material used (see for example [7, 8]; usually, these subjects are not well described in articles.

This text report part of a project related on developing packaging for forensic police department in Brazil. Police officers use these packaging to protect, manipulate and control the evidence collected in crime scenes during all custody chains. When these forensic packagings are poorly designed, they can interfere in these police officers' work

© The Author(s), under exclusive license to Springer Nature Switzerland AG 2021
N. L. Black et al. (Eds.): IEA 2021, LNNS 219, pp. 54–60, 2021.
https://doi.org/10.1007/978-3-030-74602-5_9

activity. This paper will present and discuss the simulation planning for testing forensic ballistics packaging developed based on the discussion on these police officers' work conditions.

The activity analysis stage is essential for the Ergonomic Work Analysis [9]. However, the project reported here had analysis restrictions due to work-related safety issues and limitations imposed by the pandemic. To overcome these limitations, three ergonomists' design team worked with a forensic group to develop forensic evidence packaging. The group reported difficulties related to work situations, discussed usage particularities and design propositions to support various evidence packaging development. The design team organized work simulations with forensic police officers who manipulate this material during the chain of custody in more advanced stages. The simulation was planned to test the design proposals and allow the design team to analyze better these work situations that were previously only discussed.

2 Method

We conducted a case study with a police forensic department, where a team of three ergonomists organized a participatory approach in the project of new forensic evidence packaging. The team worked on the project for one year, analyzing work procedures, legal and technical requirements, and forensic police officers' work situation to collect and precede analysis on evidence collected on crime scenes and/or on civilians involved in the investigation. The project's purpose was to develop forensic packaging for different departments related to computer crimes, ballistics, forensic medicine, among others. The purpose of the study presented in this paper is to analyze the planning on simulations held to test one of the packing developed for ballistics. This ballistic packing is used to collect ammunition and projectiles on crime scenes.

Authors conduct this study as a case study [10], a methodological approach suitable to investigate phenomenal in their environment. Work simulation is a methodological tool used in the design process, where people's dynamics interfere in the design results. Besides, case studies are applied in a situation outside experimental control, such as the social interactions, reactions, and discussions during the design process.

The project was developed based on the Ergonomic Work Analysis [9]. The ergonomist team started the project by visiting all laboratories that analyze evidence collected in crime scenes, discussing with officers difficulties related to manipulating evidence. Access to crime scenes to follow the evidence collecting was not possible due to legal and security restrictions. Subsequently, due to the Covid-19 pandemic, the design team need to stop the work analysis on police laboratories. The strategy for gathering information on the work situations was changed, centered on meetings with a forensic police officer and forensic technician. They also consulted other colleagues specialized in other departments. Although this approach limited the study, it was the possible strategy to keep the study without exposing the design team and the police officers in forensic laboratories.

Based on these remote interactions with forensic officers and laboratory technicians, the design team proposed several design solutions for forensic packing and laboratory material to manipulate and preserve evidence. To test the design propositions, the ergonomists prepared prototypes very close to the proposed materials and respecting their real scale. The objective was to conducted simulations focused on the work activity based on selected typical action situations [2, 3, 11]. This way, the ergonomist could observe how forensic officers would use the proposed material. This was a strategy to compensate the limited access to work activity. Because of restriction related to the COVID-19 pandemic, this paper will focus on simulation planning since it was not yet possible to conduct these tests on the police premises.

This study's data was collected from planning prepared by the ergonomist and its summary presented to the directress of the forensic police unit. This plan was prepared in two stages, an executive summary presentation to the directress and an extensive plan submitted to the remote support team composed of forensic officers who work with the ergonomist team.

3 Results

The simulation was planned to allow observing a simulated work activity, trying to maintain the temporal continuity of collecting ammunition on the floor in some scenarios prepared by the ergonomist team. To better organize the results, the planning will be present in three different items.

3.1 Simulation Structure

The first element is the team composition. Because we have the interest to observe a simulated work activity, it's necessary to include who actually collect and manipulate this kind of evidence. The proposition was to include three forensic offices and one police officer. Because both professionals can collect evidence, it is essential to have both points of view. The meeting would also involve the three ergonomists in the project and forensic offices who worked remotely with the design team. This composition would totalize nine people with different backgrounds and points of view on the manipulation process.

A second element of the planning is the simulation place. The proposition is to hold a simulation on the ballistic laboratory. The selection has two motivations: first, hold the simulation meeting in a place where users know well and feel comfortable. Secondly, inside the ballistic laboratory, extra material can be used in the tests if the ergonomist team's initial material is not enough. This includes ammunition material that cannot be moved from places to be used on the tests.

3.2 Simulation Material and Intermediary Objects

To conduct the simulation as planned, a series of materials is necessary. First, to test collecting ammunition, it necessary to have the disposal of ammunition. For safety reasons, all ammunition used for the test are inert, which means they have inside material removed to not work on weapons anymore. All the shells prepared for the test is provided and inerted by the police. For the test it was select a variety of calibers so packing could be tested with the more common ammunition for pistol, revolvers and rifles.

The primary material for this simulation is the ballistic packaging. They are the intermediary objects that represent the design developed. Although it was not possible to prepare a packaging with the same material specified, dimension and resources are functions on the prototype. The packaging comprises three parts (Fig. 1): a plastic piece to put the ammunition individually, a paper casing to protect the ammunition on the plastic piece, and an adhesive seal to block the packing and to allow officers to write information regarding the collection. The two last elements have material very close to real on the prototype. The plastic piece, on the other side, is made with 3D printing.

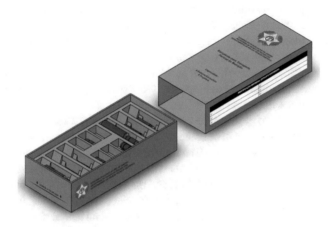

Fig. 1. Different elements from the ballistic packing

The packing was designed in two different sizes for different ammunition quantities. Because there is no pattern to how many ammunition police officers can found in a crime scene, the two sizes were conceived to give more flexibility to organize the collected material. Also, as the selection of size packing is an item of interest for the simulation, it was necessary to plan equivalent quantities for both sizes.

A second intermediary object is a variation for the adhesive seal. On the seal, the collector officer will describe information relative to the evidence, such as the officer responsible for the collection, date and summary description. The information selection related to the custody chain and its organization on the label was discussed with the remote workgroup. However, during the simulation, it is possible to have a new discussion on the material, conducting to new propositions. The variant adhesive seal intermediary object is simply the label dimensioned without written information (except for organizational identification). Rather grid lines so they could rewrite a new proposition with reference to the label size to avoid inputing too much information.

A third object is a piece of chalk. Because we will be presented some "simulated crime scenes," to help the officer doing the task proposed, it will be drawn on the floor three "bodies" to use as references for the ammunition collection. The mark on the floor will remain the same during all "simulated crime scenes"; their role is only to mark situational with multiple shooters and multiple points of ammunition collection.

Lastly, the equipment for simulation recording. For these simulations, ergonomists planned to use three cameras: one for continuous video recording, one for photographs, and one in case of need. The discussion will also be audio recorded to guarantee the discussion continuity and easier editing for further analysis.

3.3 Simulation Dynamics

The ergonomist team programmed the simulation meeting to occur in three hours and it is structured in four phases. The first phase consist on dynamics introduction. Explain that participants will perform some collections using the packing. Also, they will be asked to explicit their thinking process during the use so other participants can understand how he is using the material and explain that the packing is developed to support his fieldwork and process control during the custody chain. Therefore, it is important to explicit his difficulties related to his real problems and strategies. It will also be presented the recording material and explicated that all videos will be used for the study propose and their anonymity will be preserved.

The second phase is to perform the typical action situations selected with the remote support team. The third phase will be centered on discussing their opinions on the material developed and possible propositions. The fourth phase will be to thank everyone for their availability and inform that all participants will receive a summary presentation on the most important results from the simulation and the modification of the material.

To perform the simulated work activity, it was selected some typical work situations, all of them with prior interest of analysis. Four of the typical action situations are related to the "crime scene" organization:

(1) collection of small amount of low caliber ammunition around one body mark and one shooter;
(2) collection of small amount of hight caliber ammunition with around two body marks and two shooter;
(3) collection of large amount of different caliber ammunition around three body mark and multiple shooter;
(4) collection of large amount of different caliber ammunition with one body and new shooting risk imminent.

Each of the selected situations will create an opportunity to observe characteristics of possible work activity. For example, some point of interest is related to how officer moves around the crime scene, how simple is to handle the packing during collection, how the collector officer uses the spaces inside de plastic piece to organize ammunition collected, among other elements. The last situation with a shooting risk imminent is to evaluate the possibilities of a sad situation that police officers often meet: do the collection under pressure due to risk involved on the local.

After each collection, the officer will be asked to perform a new situation: seal the packing and fill in the information regarding the crime scene. They will then simulate to deliver the evidence material to the forensic ballistic laboratory to finally reach the forensic who will open the analysis's packing. Simulate the "processing of the process" to register in the packaging's label all department the evidence passed before getting to analysis. Each responsible will fill the label. This way, it will be possible to evaluate if the label helps the control during the process.

4   Discussion

This work highlights some aspects: first, the importance of collaboration with professionals in the field. Without constant meetings with the work team, developing the evidence packaging proposal for the situation's specificities would not be possible.

Second, ergonomists designed the simulation dynamics aiming also to simulate work temporality. Not every simulation and not every simulation support allows this type of use. The ergonomist aim was to test the product in a simulated work situation to test the product in real-time. Also, to observe a work activity (even if simulated) that could not be observed in real conditional for safety and biosafety reasons.

Third, the dynamics is not centered in validating a design proposal, but to discuss design solution with the workgroup and edit the project during the meeting. Although the simulated task's performance is sent to be central, during the next moment, that participant will have the opportunity to present new ideas and new work strategies that could lead to further modification of the design. In this sense, modifying the design after the meeting will not be a sign of design failure but a sign of the dynamic's success.

This work presents the limitation on access to work activity analyses due to the restrictions caused by the COVID-19 pandemic restrictions. The strategy to discuss work situations and design solutions remotely is not optimal but rather a resource for this particular situation. Also, the simulation was not yet realized. Even with the planning, the simulation is subjected to work variability not anticipated and new aspects that can emerge during the discussion.

5   Conclusion

Work simulation is a methodological resource to ergonomist integrate knowledge on work activity. A well-defined plan, procedure, intermediary objects, and selection of material can play a role in the dynamic's success. This paper presents elements from this planning, helping other ergonomists prepare similar simulations during other projects. An important factor is to prepare situations to induce discussions on work activity, their variabilities, and strategies to overcome these situations. Based on this reference, an ergonomist will have better conditional to reevaluate the design proposal and address new design solutions to support better work strategies.

References

1. Wilson, J.R.: Solution ownership in participative work redesign: the case of a crane control room. Int. J. Ind. Ergon. **15**(5), 329–344 (1995)
2. Garrigou, A., Daniellou, F., Carballeda, G., Ruaud, S.: Activity analysis in participatory design and analysis of participatory design activity. Int. J. Ind. Ergon. **15**(5), 311–327 (1995)
3. Daniellou, F.: L'ergonomie dans la conduite de projets de conception de systèmes de travail. In: Falzon, P. (ed.) Ergonomie, PUF, Paris (2005)

4. Maline, J.: Simuler le travail. Une aide à la conduite de projet. 1st edn. ANACT, Montrouge (1994)
5. Beguin, P., Weill-Fassina, A.: La simulation en Ergonomie. Connaître, agir, interagir. 1st edn. Octarès, Toulouse (1997)
6. Vinck, D., Jeantet, A.: Mediating and commissioning objects in the sociotechnical process of product design: a conceptual approach. In: MacLean, D., Saviotti, P., Vinck, D. (eds.) Management and New Technology: Design, Networks and Strategy. COST Social Science Series, Bruxelles (1994)
7. Broberg, O., Duarte, F., Andersen, S., Bittencourt, J.M., Conceicao, C.S., Edwards, K., Garotti, L., Lima, F.: A framework for using simulation methodology in ergonomics interventions in design projects. In: Proceedings of the XI International Symposium on Human Factors in Organizational Design and Management, Copenhagem (2014)
8. Bittencourt, J.M., Duarte, F., Béguin, P.: From the past to the future: integrating work experience into the design process. Work **57**(3), 379–387 (2017)
9. Guérin, F., Laville, A., Daniellou, F., Duraffourg, J., Kerguelen, A.: Understanding and Transforming Work: The Practice of Ergonomics, 1st edn. ANACT, England (2007)
10. Yin, R.K.: Case Study Research. Design and Methods, Sage, London (1989)
11. Béguin, P.: O ergonomista, ator da concepção. In: Falzon, P. (ed.) Ergonomia, 1st edn., pp. 317–330. Editora Blucher, São Paulo (2007)

The Territorial Dimensions of Solid Waste Management Systems: A Global-Local Dialectic for Sustainable Work Systems

Leïla Boudra[1]([⊠]), Marcelo Souza[2], Pascal Béguin[3], and Francisco Lima[2]

[1] Conservatoire National des Arts et Métiers, CRTD (EA 4132), Paris, France
[2] Federal University of Minas Gerais (UFMG), Belo Horizonte, Brazil
`fpalima@ufmg.br`
[3] Université Lumière Lyon 2 – Institut d'Étude du Travail de Lyon – UMR 5600, Lyon, France
`pascal.beguin@univ-lyon2.fr`

Abstract. Waste management systems are heavily dependent on the territorial dimensions of waste production from residents and collection and sorting dynamics. Such local anchorage is supposed to be integrated in ergonomic research to improve work conditions and design sustainable work systems. Based on studies led in France and in Brazil, this communication analyzed the effects of the territorial dimensions over the work of the sorters, that raise work systems sustainability challenges for waste sorting facilities in both countries.

Keywords: Territory · Work · Work systems sustainability · Organization · Design

1 Introduction

Waste management systems are heavily dependent on the territorial dimensions of waste production from residents and collection to sorting dynamics. Through studies in France and in Brazil exploring the links between work activity and territory in material recovery facilities (MRFs), this paper analyzes the territorial relations that raise work systems sustainability challenges for waste sorting facilities in both countries.

It is useful to point out that the history of the industrial development of recycling is quite different in France and Brazil. In France, recycling has been developed since the 1990s based on an industrial mass production model with mechanized and automated equipment following the principles of work organization on a production line and most frequently hiring people from the popular classes. In Brazil, recycling begins with informal picking by unemployed and marginalized people, some of them (10%) organized in cooperatives since the 1990s. The work process remains essentially manual, using only a few machines, like conveyor belts and balers. And the industrialization with mechanized and automated equipment is more recent.

In spite of these differences, the two models have in common a commitment to sustainable development as proposed by the UN commission in the late 1980s. Waste management and recycling offer new opportunities to limit the volumes of waste landfilled

N. L. Black et al. (Eds.): IEA 2021, LNNS 219, pp. 61–69, 2021.
https://doi.org/10.1007/978-3-030-74602-5_10

or incinerated and the use of raw materials consumed. By creating new industrial fields, it also contributes to employment at the territorial level for people from the working and popular classes.

It should also be noted that the French and Brazilian political organizations are significantly different (unitary state vs federal state). But for both countries, waste management policies are territorialized following a rationale of decentralization of public policies [1, 2].

Consequently, urban solid waste depends on their territory, as observed in France [3]. Firstly, the production of waste is territorially anchored related to the consumption patterns of residents and the economic flows on a geographical space. Secondly, public policies are territorially specified, local authorities decide the technical and social dimensions for waste collection and sorting. Thus, waste management systems are territorialized. And groups of actors - external to the sorting firm, involved in the territory - influence the sorting work in MRFs, even if they are far from the work situation. One main analytical issue dealt with the coherence between waste management into the territory and working conditions into the MRFs, and the possibility to maintain such coherence over time [4].

And concerning Brazil, it has also an aggravating element, since it was a result of a technology transfer made from a technocentered perspective [5]. São Paulo's local authorities had decided to import Europeans MRFs to increase the city's sorting and recycling capacity, but the designers have given little importance to the economic, geographic, social and cultural aspects, neither to the territorial dimensions involved. As a result, in France as in Brazil, efficiency, quality and work conditions concerns emerged.

In this paper, we will discuss the implications of taking into account the territorial dimension in ergonomics studies in waste sorting management. We will first present the two case studies from France and Brazil, starting with a presentation of the context of the research, method and material. Then, we will focus on the technical and organizational functioning of the MRFs, their relations with the territory and the effects of territorialized collection systems on sorting work. In the last part, we will discuss these findings regarding the notion of territory and its relations with the sorting work systems.

2   Presentation of the French Case

2.1   Context, Material and Method

The research, funded by the French *Institut National de Recherche et de Sécurité* (INRS) and carried out in partnership with the University of Lyon, aimed to contribute to the design of sustainable work systems and to develop work-related risks prevention for sorting workers. It concerned five MRFs in France, all belonging to local authorities and whose facilities had been commissioned to the private sector (4/5) or directly operated by the local authority (1/5).

The methodology is based on an activity-oriented and participatory ergonomic approach [6]. We proposed a systemic and multiscale analysis in order to understand the organizational systems and the interactions between the different actors involved in the waste management systems at national level (macro), territorial level (meso) and firms' level (micro) [7]. For 42 months, we conducted 22 in situ analysis campaigns involving

102 waste sorting operators from the 5 MRFs. Firstly, an analysis of the work activity was elaborated with the workers, articulating observations, semi-directive interviews and reflexive interviews with visual supports (photos, videos, etc.). Secondly, an objectification of the work was produced with the findings of the work analysis and used as an instrument for developing a mutual process learning [8], during meetings with workers and managers, and during meetings with managers, executives and heads of local authorities to support changes in practices.

2.2 MRFs Work Systems and Working Conditions in France

In France, MRFs are industrial facilities whose purpose is to separate waste from selective household collections by material (paper, cardboard, steel, aluminum and different types of plastic). This includes only packaging and papers (for instance, glass or organic waste is collected separately). Sorted waste is then sold to recovery companies for recycling. Non-recyclable waste (called refusals), mistakenly included or having been degraded during transport, is stored separately and transferred for landfilling or incineration. They are owned by private national or international companies or by local authorities. And in the second case, the production and staff management can be carried out by the community or by a private company. MRFs are equipped with different technical systems and have different annual processing capacities, depending on the strategic industrial choices made by the owner at the design stage. Among the five MRFs concerned by our research, the gap was from 4 500 tons per year for the least mechanized MRF to 32 000 for the most mechanized and automated MRF.

Work in MRFs is done on production lines. Workers, placed around an automated sorting belt, have to perform a predefined task that consists in removing three types of waste on average (recyclable or not) by taking waste in hands. Such work activity is affected by considerable biomechanical load and repetitive efforts in upper limbs, often maintaining awkward postures (for example, due to the depth of the belt which forces to be positioned over the belt to catch the waste) and fixed and quasi-static standing posture, this work also requires continuous cognitive and visual attention. All of these conditions can be the cause of musculoskeletal and psychosocial disorders. Rhythms and cadences are imposed by machines, on which the workers have few margins of actions. Moreover, workers are asked to realize operations that do not take into account the variety of wastes and the variability and production hazards they have to face.

2.3 Effects of Territorialized Collection Systems on Sorting Work

Flows of waste are directly linked to territorial dimensions that influence collection processes, quality and types of waste. The conditions of the waste, its density and size, for example, cannot be known precisely before the sorting operation. More particularly, these material dimensions appear to be territorialized: economic, social, political, geographical or meteorological factors impact the incoming waste and thus affect the work of sorting workers.

Consequently, waste is a territorialized object. Its characteristics fit territorially defined dimensions and territory needs to be regarded as a determinant of work. Such dimensions are:

– the sorting instructions given to residents (e.g., instructions could be collection of packaging and paper called mix-materials or packaging only).
– the method of collection (e.g., collection at a voluntary delivery point, in bags or in individual and collective containers placed on sidewalks).
– the modes of transport (e.g., transport to the MRF organized directly after the collection or organized weekly with an intermediate storage in a center for the most geographically distant zones).

Such territorial anchorage of waste corresponds in fact to the choices of local authorities for waste management and collection. It is important to specify that in France, regarding the regulatory obligations affecting local authorities, various municipalities joined together into intercommunal structure, one of their missions being to organize the collect and treat waste, including recycling dealing with local issues. And as a consequence, according to our observations, there is no uniformity of these dimensions in a given territory. Indeed, each of the choices taken corresponds to specific local issues. One example: organizing intermediate storage in a transfer center is a preferable choice from an environmental point of view (e.g., limited CO_2 emissions linked to transport) and from the point of view of the working conditions of the collection workers (e.g., limiting working time, travel time and distances, etc.). However, there are consequences on the work of sorting workers: the time between waste production and sorting is therefore longer for these landlocked areas and quality can be degraded with potential consequences on the health of workers (e.g., proliferation of bacteria and respiratory risks [9]. Another example: implementing voluntary drop-off points appears preferable to limit road congestion with individual or collective containers and to facilitate waste collection and management for example in a city district in a metropolitan area of 75,000 residents with a population density of approximately 2,600 people per square kilometer. But from the perception of the workers, there seems to be more non-recyclable waste to be taken out of the waste flow. It appears that this channel contains a larger amount of non-recyclable waste than the other collection channels. According to the data provided by the firm management, an average of one third of the waste coming from this channel was recyclable (compared with an average of 75% for the other channels). For the local authority, the problem is related to the size of the trap openings designed for the voluntary delivery of selective waste, which did not allow for a clear differentiation from the non-recyclable household waste located nearby. As a consequence, workers need to implement adaptive strategies to preserve the economic variable on which the industrial and market criteria are based.

In conclusion, sorting work activity is not limited to the action of separating waste by material types, activity gives an industrial and market value to the waste in a process of transformation into a product that is territorialized. It thus appears that the way choices are made in the territorialized sorting chain influences the working conditions and the work activity of sorting workers. Consequently, the transformation of work systems cannot be limited to the boundaries of the firm and must examine the dialectical relations between the MRF and its territory.

3 Presentation of the Brazilian Case

3.1 Context, Material and Method

It was 2014. The city of São Paulo had carried out a participatory process to review its Integrated Solid Waste Management Plan. In this review, guidelines from the National Solid Waste Policy [10] were emphasized, mainly with regard to the technological hierarchy in waste management. Priority was given to non-generation, reuse and recycling strategies. In order to increase recycling, the main bet was anchored in the implementation of four Material Recovery Facilities (MRFs), which should be able to respond to a 500% increase in the processing capacity of the municipality's official recycling system [11]. This system was based so far on the work of waste pickers' cooperatives included in the municipality's public policies, all of which operating sorting sheds with essentially - if not entirely - manual work. With this, it was expected to go from approximately 200 tons of recyclables processed per day (5% of the recyclable waste generated in the city) to 1 thousand tons per day (23% of the recyclable waste generated in the city). They would be the first semi-automated plants for sorting recyclable waste implanted in the city, in the country and in Latin America. The first two plants were implemented in 2014 and were purchased from two European suppliers.

Besides the Brazilian plants, we also studied a MRF in San Francisco (USA). To study them, we developed a methodological framework based on the ergonomic and anthropotechnological analysis [6, 12]. The methodological strategies were to compare a given technology implemented in different countries to highlight the technological adaptation process [5]. We also analyzed activities situated upstream (selective collection, environmental education and mobilization activities…) and downstream (sales processes, market prospective…). Finally, we investigated the work in the waste pickers' cooperatives that became responsible for the sorting operation in the MRF. In total, it took 125 h of field research, for 20 months, to carry out this case study. We then analyzed three major problems, related to the system efficiency, the product quality and the work conditions. Here we will focus our attention on one of São Paulo's plants, which were imported from a French supplier (MRF01).

3.2 MRFs Work Systems and Working Conditions in Brazil

MRF01 is a clean MRF, with single stream and centralized manual sorting. It means that this plant processes with source separated waste, collected in a single stream (all recyclables mixed), and has one single section where all the manual work is done (manual sorting cabin), at the end of the production line. Some waste pickers from one cooperative included in the official municipality recycling system operate in this cabin, and also work in the feeding process. Other workers from one of the private companies responsible for the municipal scavenger services also work on the plant, mainly in maintenance processes and in the control room.

In the manual sorting cabin, the prescribed work was limited to "quality control", i.e., the waste pickers must only act in the machine's sorting failures, "cleaning" the flow. The ergonomic work analysis could demonstrate features of the real activity developed by the waste pickers, who regulate their work in face of situated constraints, some of them territorially anchored. We will explore in the next section three cases that illustrate these findings, highlighting the interrelations between the work process and the territory.

3.3   Effects of Territorialized Collection Systems on Sorting Work

The first case is related to a specific material: glass. It is known that in France, the country that sold the technology used in MRF01, collection systems with glass segregation at the source are very common, with 93% of the population served with this type of collection [13]. But in São Paulo, as in most Brazilian cities, the collection systems are designed to collect all recyclable materials together, leaving both the first and the finest separation in charge of the waste pickers. The MRF01 was, however, designed without considering processes for glass recovery; the justification presented by the supplier for such a decision focused on the financial unfeasibility of a possible recovery process. This design decision, disregarding other possible impacts of the operational contradictions between the territorial collection system and the work at the plant, would lead to serious consequences for the sorting work and for the production efficiency [14].

Along the production line, there are several transitions of the material in unevenness, from belt to belt or from belt to equipment, which leads to the breaking of this material. This broken glass runs along the entire line and is one of the causes of work accidents, tears in the conveyor belts (leading to production stoppages), wear of belts and other equipment, increased refuse rate in the plant – since it was not recovered, glass accounted for 40% of the refuse. It is still a problem for some buyers, since broken glass, a prohibitive material in some industrial recycling processes (plastic for example), sometimes falls into separated material silos, and impacts the quality of the bales of sorted waste.

The second case relates to the consumption and packaging patterns found in the local market. Two materials are exemplary in this regard. Polypropylene (PP) is an abundant material, representing 10% of the plastics present in Brazilian waste [15]. However, in MRF01 there was not a process to recover this type of material. More importantly, it is identified in one of the optical separators and sent to the conveyor that receives the high-density polyethylene (HDPE), generating additional work for the waste pickers who work there. As HDPE is a material with high quality requirements, sending the PP to a conveyor with an already densified flow ends up intensifying the work even more.

At the other extreme is the case of colored polyethylene terephthalate (or colored PET), which is PET packaging in colors other than transparent or green. This type of material is very little present in Brazilian waste, and it is even difficult to sell it. However, an entire line was designed at MRF01 to work with this material, with an optical separator and a dedicated conveyor belt in the manual sorting cabin. This line was underutilized – its silo took 15 days to fill, that is, less than 1 ton of material every 15 days in a plant that processed 100 tons daily. It was so idle that it was redesigned by the waste pickers and other plant workers, to work with mixed fiber, abundant (50% of MRF01 production) and problematic material in the production process [5].

Finally, we can mention materials with serious quality problems, such as the mixed fiber itself, whose commercialization presented serious difficulties. This material is worked in the manual sorting cabin on a belt that receives the product of the negative sorting of all lines of flat materials. Due to the great diversity of materials present in the Brazilian waste, mainly flexible plastics – material that is prohibitive in industrial fiber recycling – this conveyor received a very abundant and assorted flow. The pickers then had to "clean up" the flow, that is, remove everything that was not fiber, which was impossible to do at the speed the plant operates, even when working at an intensified pace. Besides the incidence of the same work health problems seem in the French case, these conditions also led to highly contaminated material. It could not be absorbed by the local industrial fabric and needed to be sold for a low price – 10 times less than those obtained by waste pickers' cooperatives – to intermediaries who exported the waste to China. With the recent increase in restrictions on waste imports by Asian countries [16, 17] and even the complete ban on these imports by China in January 2021 [18], the situation tends to worsen, not only for MRF01, but for several MRFs around the world, mainly in central countries, whose recycling depended on these more permissive global markets.

4 Discussion and Conclusion

This article analyzed how territorialized anchorage for waste influences the work in MRFs. The results of these studies conducted in France and Brazil show that territory is a determinant of work and that decisions made on the territory will have an impact on working conditions. Moreover, the results also show a certain disconnection between the MRF and its territory, which makes sorting activity more complex, intensifies work and has a negative impact on the quality of recycled waste. Such disconnection negatively influences MRFs' performance, both internally (low quality, maintenance problems, work risks, etc.) and externally (buyer network, logistics, integration of waste pickers into the system, etc.). The sustainability of work systems - i.e., economic, environmental and social performance- is then hindered.

To the large-scale production of waste, it is attempted to respond with technologies that operate large-scale logistics and sorting systems, with the adoption of automated technologies. These technical options necessarily lead to increasing deterritorialization and a logic of standardization of collection systems and waste management and recycling organizations. But as we observed in France and in Brazil, there are historic-local dimensions that defy any attempt at standardization.

In fact, our results provide arguments for the creation of places for direct relationships between collection teams and residents, and between MRFs' workers and collectors, who may even be from different companies. The treatment option in MRFs thus creates counterproductive effects that cannot be solved under the terms in which these systems operate and produce a high refuse rate and the low quality of the sorted waste intended for commercialization and recycling (i.e., transformation in new products) as we observed in France and in Brazil. Furthermore, our results may also open relationships with recyclers and open new reflections on a global-local dialectic. As we see for Brazil, the low quality of materials has become a more critical problem in recent years with the tightening of international trade standards in some countries that historically received low quality waste. But this should not fail to question the impossible standardization of the mechanized and automated forms of the MRF's that must be in fact territorially anchored.

As a consequence, the territory appears as a blind spot in the design of work systems, even though it is a determinant of waste production and work. Such results do not neglect to question the integration of the work activity in the design of technical systems. Human activity must be interwoven with the technical system, from the initial processes, as collection and pre-sorting, eliminating materials that damage machines and optical sensors, to the final ones, in machine supervision and in quality control by making the final sorting. In the case of MRFs, the challenge is to create interfaces that integrate better human activity and waste territorialized anchorage.

The discussion we are presenting here appears increasingly important in the context of technology transfer as seen for the Brazilian case. The transferred technology also exports the design problems already identified in France. The transfer of a technology developed and operated in Europe to a peripheral country functioned as a "quasi-experiment" that made it possible to show, as if they were magnifying glasses, the causes of the problems of efficiency and quality of MRFs, which persist even in central countries. The problems evidenced in France and Brazil can be observed in the light of the concept of "anthropotechnology" by Alain Wisner [12], by the designers involved in these transfers to generate projects more adherent to the realities of the situations found in the destination countries. And, as a boomerang effect, even the MRFs of central countries can adopt this perspective to rethink the relationships between collection and sorting systems in a given territory, including relations with the local, national and international market.

References

1. Chaves, G.L.D., Jr. Santos, J.L., Rocha, S.M.S.: The challenges for solid waste management in accordance with agenda 21: a Brazilian case review. Waste Manag. Res.: J. Sustain. Circ. Econ. **32**(9), 19–31 (2014)
2. Defeuilley, C., Lupton, S.: The future place of recycling in household waste policy: the case of France. Resour. Conserv. Recycl. **24**, 217–233 (1998)
3. Boudra, L., Pueyo, V., Béguin, P.: The territorial anchorage of waste sorting activities and its organization for prevention. In: Bagnara, S., Tartaglia, R., Albolino, S., Alexander, T., Fujita, Y. (eds.) Proceedings of the 20th Congress of the International Ergonomics Association (IEA 2018), vol. 825, pp. 923–931. Springer (2018)
4. Boudra, L.: Durabilité du travail et prévention en adhérence. le cas de la dimension territoriale des déchets dans l'activité de tri des emballages ménagers (doctoral thesis). Lyon, Université de Lyon (2016)
5. de Souza, M.A.: Catador e a Máquina: transferência de tecnologia e reprojeto em Centrais Mecanizadas de Triagem. UFMG, Belo Horizonte (2016)
6. Guerin, F., Laville, A., Daniellou, F., Duraffourg, J., Kerguelen, A.: Understanding and Transforming Work - The Practice of Ergonomics. ANACT Network Editions, Lyon (2007)
7. Boudra, L.: Activité humaine, espace et territoire. Éléments de réflexion à partir d'une analyse systémique et multiscalaire. Ergologia **22**, 69–90 (2019)
8. Béguin, P.: Acting within the boundaries of work systems development. Hum. Factors Ergon. Manuf. Serv. Ind. **21**(6), 543–554 (2011)
9. Schlosser, O., Déportes, I.Z., Facon, B., Fromont, E.: Extension of the sorting instructions for household plastic packaging and changes in exposure to bioaerosols at materials recovery facilities. Waste Manag. **45**, 47–55 (2015)
10. Brasil: Lei n° 12.305, de 2 de Agosto de 2010. Política Nacional de Resíduos Sólidos. Brasília, DF: Presidência da República (2010). https://www.planalto.gov.br/ccivil_03/_ato2007-2010/2010/lei/l12305.htm. Accessed 25 Jan 2021

11. São Paulo: Plano de Gestão Integrada de Resíduos Sólidos da cidade de São Paulo. São Paulo, SP: Prefeitura Municipal (2014). https://www.prefeitura.sp.gov.br/cidade/secretarias/upload/servicos/arquivos/PGIRS-2014.pdf. Accessed 25 Jan 2021
12. Wisner, A.: Quand voyagent les usines: essai d'anthropotechnologie. Syros, Paris (1985)
13. Djemaci, B.: Public waste management services in France: National analysis and case studies of Paris, Rouen, and Besançon (Working Paper, CIRIEC No. 2009/02). CIRIEC, Belgian (2009)
14. de Souza, M.A., Lima, F.P.A., Varella, C.V.S.: A conformação social do lixo e das tecnologias de triagem: o caso da transferência de Centrais Mecanizadas de Triagem em São Paulo. Urbe. Revista Brasileira de Gestão Urbana **13**, e20200073. (on press)
15. Varella, C.V.S., Campos, L.S.: Reciclar - Catálogo de padronização dos materiais recicláveis. Centro Mineiro de Referência em Resíduos – CMRR, Belo Horizonte (2012)
16. Brooks, A.L., Wang, S., Jambeck, J.R.: The Chinese import ban and its impact on global plastic waste trade. Sci. Adv. **4**(6), 1–8 (2018)
17. Ip, K., Testa, M., Raymond, A., Graves, S.C., Gutowski, T.: Performance evaluation of material separation in a material recovery facility using a network flow model. Resour. Conserv. Recycl. **131**, 192–205 (2018)
18. Bureau of International Recycling (BIR) Homepage. https://resource-recycling.com/recycling/2020/12/01/china-confirms-expanded-import-ban-starting-jan-1/. Accessed 25 Jan 2021

Distribution of Visual Attention in High-Risk and Dynamic Environment: An Eye-Tracking Study with Submarine Team Leaders

Léonore Bourgeon[(⊠)], Vincent Tardan, Baptiste Dozias, and Françoise Darses

French Armed Forces Biomedical Institute, Brétigny-sur-Orge, France
`leonore.bourgeon@def.gouv.fr`

Abstract. Distribution of visual attention in high-risk and dynamic environment is an important issue for safety since missed or delayed information detection is a significant factor of accidents. In complex socio-technical systems operators need to draw their attention on numerous visual displays, yet auditory information from verbal exchanges plays also a major role in the development of their situation awareness. Team leaders may then develop strategies to gather information both from visual and auditory sources. The aim of our study was to identify how team leader's attention is distributed among visual displays and interactions with team members as a function of their level of performance during a highly demanding situation. Ten leaders from the Diving-Safety Team in French nuclear submarine were equipped with a mobile eye-tracker in a full scale simulator during training sessions. Areas Of Interest were grouped into four categories: technical displays, navigation displays, team members and written documentation. Two critical AOIs related to two failures were analyzed. Our results showed that most part of leaders' attention was directed toward interface displays (78% of all dwells). Significant differences showed that high-performance leaders performed more frequent visual scanning and were also able to monitor longer and more frequently critical AOI. The allocation of attention showed that high-performance leaders directed more frequently their attention on commandment team members suggesting a higher level of hindsight on the situation. Further research is needed to identify more accurately the distribution of attention between visual and auditory channel in relation with situation awareness.

Keywords: Visual attention · Situation awareness · Eye-tracking · Team leader · Submarine

1 Introduction

Safety in high-risk and dynamic environment highly depends on the quality of operators' visual information gathering. Early detection of critical data is indeed crucial to develop and maintain accurate situation awareness which can be defined as the ability to perceive information that emerge from the evolving situation, to understand the current situation and to project how the situation will evolve [1]. Studies dealing with visual attention

© The Author(s), under exclusive license to Springer Nature Switzerland AG 2021
N. L. Black et al. (Eds.): IEA 2021, LNNS 219, pp. 70–74, 2021.
https://doi.org/10.1007/978-3-030-74602-5_11

distribution showed that the more frequently operators look at critical information in the environment, the higher is their level of situation awareness [2–4].

Yet, in complex socio-technical systems, operators' attention is not only drawn by visual channel but also by auditory channel since team members must exchange verbal information. The way information is communicated and distributed among team members impacts their performance [5]. Hence, team leaders who are in charge with making decisions must distribute their attention among visual and auditory information in order to ensure that all critical information is detected. This is especially true for complex socio-technical systems, such as submarines, which require to monitor numerous displays and which involve frequent interactions within- and between-teams. Such environments are highly demanding in cognitive and attentional resources and leaders face several cognitive challenges, such as projecting current data into the future or quickly getting and integrating environmental information to make a decision under time pressure and high stress [6]. For instance, the Diving-Safety Team (DST) in French nuclear submarines comprises a leader interacting with three team members, tightly coupled with the commandment team, in order to ensure the submarine safety and navigation. The leaders plays a crucial role as he must gather and share information from interfaces and operators in different teams so as to build a mental representation of the situation, share his situation awareness with the commandment team and make appropriate decisions dealing with operational and safety goals. Team leaders may then develop strategies to gather information both from visual and auditory sources. Although both visual and auditory attention is crucial for safety, especially through development of accurate situation awareness, few studies have dealt with the distribution of attention between these two sources of information.

The aim of our study was to identify how team leader's attention is distributed among visual displays and interactions with other team members during a highly demanding situation. We compared high- and low-performance leaders in order to bring out effective strategies and to suggest some areas in which future research is needed to prevent loss of situation awareness and accidents.

2   Methodology

The study took place in a French military nuclear submarine DST full-scale simulator during training sessions. Five operators from two teams participate in these training sessions. DST team members included a helmsman, a technical operator and a team leader. From the commandment team, an officer of the watch was present to provide operational goals and a commanding officer located outside but close to the simulator could also interact with team members. Participation was voluntary, and all participants signed an Informed Consent Form prior to participation.

A realistic scenario was conceived in order to meet both research and training needs. Data was collected during a specific phase of the mission where teams had to maintain periscope depth in shallow area, with a failure impeding immersion management. Meanwhile team members faced an overpressure on board which should lead them to regularly monitor the air pressure gauge. Performance assessment was based on depth immersion reflecting maintenance/loss of periscope depth.

Team leaders' eye movement data were recorded using a mobile eye tracker (*Mobil'Eye*, ASL). Twenty-four Areas Of Interest (AOI) were defined in collabora-tion with a submarine instructor. They belonged to four categories: technical displays, navigation displays, team members and written documentation. Among AOIs, two of them were considered critical given the scenario: The AOI providing information about submarine attitude (depth, velocity, and pitch angle) which is necessary to manage depth immersion, and the AOI related to air pressure gauge necessary to monitor the overpres-sure on board. The number and duration of dwells on AOIs were identified through a frame-by-frame analysis of the video-recordings.

The study was approved by the Ethics Committee for research of Paris-Saclay University (CER-Paris-Saclay-2018-029R).

3 Results

Ten team leaders were included in the study (all males). Their experience ranged from 8 to 14 missions in submarines. Four teams were associated to low-performance level and six to high-performance level. Level of experience did not differ as a function of performance level.

Results showed that visual scanning was more frequent among high-performance leaders than low-performance leaders, with respectively 88 AOIs and 80 AOIs dwelled per minute $[t(8) = -2.87; p < .05]$. Mean dwell time did not differ significantly as a function of level of performance.

Distribution of visual attention among the four categories of AOIs was significantly different $[\chi^2(3) = 119.8; p < .0001]$, with high-performance leaders looking more frequently at technical displays (45% of all dwells) and less frequently at the helms-man displays (34%) than low-performance leaders (respectively, 33% and 44%). No significant difference was found for team members nor written documentation. Addi-tionally, results showed that high-performance leaders dwelled significantly longer on AOIs than low-performance leaders $(p(F) < .05)$. No effect of interaction between level of performance and category of AOI was observed.

Distribution of visual attention among the four team members differed significantly $[\chi^2(3) = 116.9; p < .0001]$. High-performance leaders dwelled more frequently on the officer of the watch (34% of dwells on operators) and the commanding officer (26% of dwells on operators) than low-performance leaders (respectively, 19% and 10%). On the opposite, low-performance leaders dwelled more frequently on the helmsman (47% of dwells on operators) and on the technical operator (24% of dwells on operators). An interaction effect showed that high-performance leaders dwelled significantly longer on the officer of the watch and on the commanding officer than low-performance leaders $[p(F) < .05]$.

The critical AOI related on submarine attitude was more frequently dwelled by low-performance leaders (27% of all dwells) than by high-performance leaders (23% of all dwells) $[\chi^2(1) = 16.5; p < .0001]$. By contrast, the critical AOI related to air pressure gauge was more frequently dwelled by high-performance leaders (6% of all dwells) than by low-performance leaders (3% of all dwells) $[\chi^2(1) = 38.83; p < .0001]$. No significant correlation was found between dwell time on the AOI related to submarine attitude and depth of immersion. Yet, a negative significant correlation was found between dwell time on the AOI related to air pressure gauge and depth of immersion ($r = -.65$; $p <$ .05), meaning high-performance leaders dwelled longer on that critical AOI.

4 Discussion

Our results show that leaders' attention is mostly directed to interface devices, which represented 78% of all dwells. The orientation of their attention toward team members represented only 15% of all dwells, regardless of their performance level. This result comforts the importance of visual search on interface devices within the activity of team leaders and also comforts the importance of visual information in the development of situation awareness. Yet, the allocation of attention on team members might be underestimated since it is possible that team leaders listen to conversations between other team members while their gaze is directed to interface displays.

The analysis of how their attention is distributed among team members showed a significant difference with high-performance leaders looking more frequently and longer on the two officers from the commandment team whereas low-performance leaders looked more frequently on DST team-members. This result suggests that high-performance leaders would collect information from the evolving situation through interface devices and interact with team members rather at a higher level of situation awareness to discuss the adequacy of their assessment of the situation with operational goals. This strategy of allocation of attention shows a higher level of hinsight in high-performance leaders. On the opposite, low-performance leaders seem to allocate their attention mainly within DST intra-team. This result may be interpreted as a lack of hindsight on the situation but it may also be interpreted as a strategy to concentrate their resources in DST-team in order to overcome their difficulty to maintain periscope depth. In the same way, it is low-performance leaders who look more frequently and longer on the critical AOI related to the submarine attitude, which is inconsistent with the findings of most research showing that high situation awareness is related to higher frequency of fixations and longer dwell time on hazardous AOIs [2, 3]. This result can also be interpreted as the leader's strategy to concentrate his attention on the part of activity where he encounters difficulties and hence monitor more closely this hazard.

Additionally, our study shows that successful team leaders perform more frequent visual scanning which highlights a more regular monitoring of the evolving situation. Their visual attention is also more frequently and in a longer duration oriented toward the critical information related to air pressure gauge meaning they choose to allocate their attention to specifically monitor and be aware of the evolution of this failure.

These results may reveal a profile of high-performance leaders who have high ability to distribute their attention on all interfaces and who are also able to monitor more closely specific hazards. They also choose to allocate their attention on interactions mainly with commandment team members suggesting a higher level of situation awareness.

5 Conclusion

The outcomes of this study are both theoretical and practical about distribution of visual attention of successful team leaders in high-risk and dynamic environment. Efficient visual attention seem to be related to more frequent visual scanning, higher ability to detect and monitor critical information and allocation of resources on interactions with officers to develop more hindsight about the evolving situation. Further research is needed to identify more accurately the distribution of attention between visual and auditory channel in relation with situation awareness, with use of self-confrontation interviews for example.

References

1. Endsley, M.R.: Toward a theory of situation awareness in dynamic systems. Hum. Fact. **37**(1), 32–64 (1995)
2. Hasanzadeh, S., Esmaeili, B., Dodd, M.D.: Examining the relationship between construction workers' visual attention and situation awareness under fall and tripping hazard conditions: using mobile eye tracking. J. Const. Eng. Manage. **144**(7), 04018060 (2018)
3. Moore, K., Gugerty, L.: Development of a novel measure of situation awareness: the case for eye movement analysis. In: Proceedings of the Human Factors and Ergonomics Society 54th Annual Meeting, pp. 1650–1654 (2010)
4. Behrend, J., Dehais, F.: How role assignment impacts decision-making in high-risk environments: evidence from eye-tracking in aviation. Saf. Sci. **127**, 104738 (2020)
5. Artman, H.: Team situation awareness and information distribution. Ergonomics **43**(8), 1111–1128 (2000)
6. Dominguez, C., Long, W.G., Miller, T.E., Wiggins, S.L.: Design directions for support of submarine commanding officer decision making. In: Proceedings of 2006 Undersea HSI Symposium: Research, Acquisition and the Warrior, pp. 6–8 (2006)
7. Bourgeon, L., Tardan, V., Dozias, B., Darses, F.: Understanding Situation Awareness development processes through self-confrontation interviews based on eye-tracking videos. In: Proceedings of the 20th congress of the International Ergonomics Association, vol. VI, pp. 369–378. Springer, Cham (2018)

Extending System Performance Past the Boundaries of Technical Maturity: Human-Agent Teamwork Perspective for Industrial Inspection

Garrick Cabour[1]([✉]), Élise Ledoux[2], and Samuel Bassetto[1]

[1] Department of Mathematics and Industrial Engineering, Polytechnique Montreal, Station Centre-ville, P.O. Box 6079, Montreal, QC 3C 37, Canada
garrick.cabour@polymtl.ca

[2] Physical Activity Department, Université du Québec À Montréal, Montréal, QC 3C 3P8, Canada

Abstract. Cyber-Physical-Social Systems (CPSS) performance for industry 4.0 is highly context-dependent, where three design areas arise: the artifact itself, the human-agent collaboration, and the organizational settings. Current HF&E tools are limited to conceptualize and anticipate future human-agent work situations with a fine-grained perspective. This paper explores how rich insights from work analysis can be translated into formative design patterns that provide finer guidance in conceptualizing the human-agent collaboration and the organizational settings. The current manual work content elicited is disaggregated into functional requirements. Each function is then scrutinized by a multidisciplinary design team that decides its feasibility and nature (autonomy function, human function, or hybrid function). By doing so, we uncover the technical capabilities of the CPSS in comparison with subject-matter experts' work activity. We called this concept technological coverage. The framework thereof allows close collaboration with design stakeholders to define detailed HAT configurations. We then imagined joint activity scenarios based on end-users work activity, the technological capabilities, and the interaction requirements to perform the work. We use a study on technological innovation in the aircraft maintenance domain to illustrate the framework's early phases.

Keywords: Cyber-physical-social system · Human-autonomy teaming · Activity analysis · Work system design

1 Introduction

The technical maturity during the system design cycle is generally measured on the technological development of its features, which does not consider the social-organizational-operational environment in which the technology is implemented [1]. Automation is switching towards autonomy, requiring a more holistic/socio-technical approach to appraise the joint Human-Agent performance in process-tasks completion: "*as the system cannot be neatly divorced from the evaluation of the performance of the user, or the performance of the Human-Machine System [or Cyber-Physical-Social System (CPSS)] as a whole*" (p.22) [2]. An intelligent system can perform well in experimental circumstances in terms of accuracy and output sensitivity (technical maturity). However, this validity does not embrace the operators who will use it in an industrial context or joint Human-Agent performance [3, 4]. The joint performance should be anticipated, evaluated, and iterated during the system design cycle as it will influence the overall CPSS performance, acceptance, and integration [2].

Before implementing a technological solution in complex domains, previous research emphasized the need to understand better how work is currently performed to capture the embedded context ecologically [5]. HF&E methods are well suited to elicit the relevant contextual factors that shape the work domain and taskwork settings. Ergonomic Work Analysis (EWA) is a robust analytical framework that elicits relevant content regarding work domain features and end-users' work activity [6]. However, the challenge is how to use the rich data elicited to formalize efficient Human-Agent Teaming (HAT) configurations? The transition between descriptive fieldwork data obtained with EWA and design remains unclear [7]. Bridging this gap requires formative design models that guide artifact design, human-agent collaboration (HA), and the organizational settings in the envisioned world. [8]. Indeed, current HAT taxonomies offer general design guidelines that encompass function allocation, interaction design, etc. However, two main issues emanate from them. First, the analytical layer is "coarse-grained." It does provide requirements and abstracted design patterns for specific system features (communication modes, type of interaction) [9, 10]. Yet, it limits the guidance provided to designers to conceptualize how human and artificial agents will engage together in a joint activity [4]. Second, the traditional methods of assigning human-machine functions do not systematically impregnate the socio-technical context and the work to be done [5]. These generic taxonomies do not provide a clear integration plan of work analysis, whereas the performance of CPSSs is highly context-dependent [4]. A fine-grained design perspective should adequately conceptualize the HA joint activity to deliver optimal HAT configurations that enhance the overall performance.

2   Methods

This research is part of a partnership research project aiming to develop an automated cell to inspect aircraft parts in the aeronautics sector. We present the basis of a framework to show how to provide useful guidance and actionable design patterns from fieldwork inquiries to design a CPSS (that encompasses a HAT perspective).

2.1   Research Design

This study is grounded within the *Ergonomic Work Analysis* (EWA) and *Knowledge Engineering* (KE). We conducted qualitative fieldwork to obtain rich insights into the industrial inspectors' work activity: information intake mechanisms, meaning-making and decision processes (steps, variables, assessment of decision outcomes), the knowledge required, rules and strategies applied.

2.2   Data Collection and Interpretation

We realized 11 on-site observations with concurrent verbalization, 26 mixed-methods interviews (semi-directed, retrospection with work activity content, self-confrontation), and six operational experiments (*microworld*) for a total of 43 h spent with 12 inspectors. We deployed several units of analysis with different layers of granularity to elicit conceptual and tacit knowledge from the head of subject-matter experts. A "scaffolding" construction of the expert's mental models related to their work context is realized by triangulating data collection methods (fieldwork inquiries and documentation analysis) during nominal/off-nominal working conditions. A detailed description of the fieldwork methodology deployed, from activity analysis to empirical modeling, can be found in [11].

We interpreted the results with a combination of EWA and KE. EWA enables a systemic perspective of end-users work activity, linking the "*what are they doing?*" with "*why are they doing it in such a way?*", i.e., identifying and understanding how the contextual factors shape the work of inspectors. Several iterative steps were carried out with experts to validate the accuracy and reliability of the data collected in the field. We then used KE to identify and capitalize the knowledge captured through *in situ* analyses. The descriptive knowledge models developed can be found in [11].

2.3   Early Phases of Cyber-Physical-Social System Design

From Induction to Deduction. We deduced functional requirements that the HAT should execute from the work activity content elicited (e.g., meaning-making and decision-making tasks). For example, in the task "*the inspector detects a nick on the upper area of the part*," at least three functional specifications emerged:

1. The system must detect the defects
2. The system must classify defects type (nick)
3. The system must map and recognize the different area of the part

Determination of Technological Coverage. Then, we introduced the concept of *technological coverage*. Technological coverage represents the functional capabilities of the technical system being design. Instead of focusing on the system components' technical maturity (e.g., hardware equipment's: cameras, sensors), the emphasis is placed on the different tasks to be accomplished for the targeted work activity to endorse a bottom-up approach. Based on the functional description of the current work system, we determined with the design engineers (4 *focus groups* of one hour via videoconference applications) what functions can we automate. For each function, we identified the possible configurations that could be endorsed:

1. Fully automated (autonomy function)
2. Partially automated(hybrid function)
    a. Requiring manual data entry
    b. Not requiring manual data entry

3. Not automated (human function)

Fine-grained HAT Hypotheses. The next step was to define each function's configuration, the content of each entity's work and the requirements for human-agent interaction. We took a slight switch from traditional function allocation methods ("who does what"). Instead of solely segmenting the human work content and the artificial agent work content, we identified the *inter-functional dependencies* [12] or *interdependencies* [4] that allocation decisions would generate on the other party. In other words, if the agent is in charge of Function A, what does it means for the operators? Based on technological capabilities, in which function/situation does the agent need human intervention (e.g., manual input or performance monitoring) during real-time process tasks execution? Is the output sensible and must be validated by human operators? What information does the operator/agent need to know to continue the sequence of operations?

The work analysis performed in the earliest phases was essential to identify the constraints (or work determinants) that restrict which functions each party can assume or not [5]. As aeronautics is a domain where safety is paramount, the design team decided that the operators would make the final decision on each part inspected.

3 Activity Analysis of Industrial Inspection in Aeronautics

Industrial inspection for aircraft maintenance is a highly regulated and safety-critical domain, where human inspectors process multiple sources of knowledge distributed in their environment to diagnose a component's condition. This diagnosis compares the component's state with existing standards that specify the acceptance/refusal criteria and rules to be applied. Inspectors are the central pillar of a decision-making ecosystem that involved other workers (operators, engineers, and technical representatives) with whom they interact to diagnose and repair service-run components correctly. Their work can be broken down as follows (adapted from [13]):

1. Work preparation: inspector sets up the workstation, collect inspection equipment, tasks aids, and aircraft parts to inspect
2. Multi-sensorial search: he examines the part using visual, tactile and perceptual-motor senses until he detects an anomaly
3. Diagnosis: he classifies the type of anomaly encountered and measures/estimates its physical characteristics (depth, length, width). Then, he interprets the measures, process the decision-making variables (Table 1) and the rules to apply to decide whether a defect is acceptable as is, needs to be repaired or is unacceptable
4. Execution: he takes the necessary actions following the previous diagnosis. He decides about the overall part's condition and prescribes the set of repair operations required to restore it and conduct computerized tasks (e.g., record part's information in the database). He repeats operations 2 to 5 until no other anomaly is detected.
5. Work completion: he dispatches the item to the corresponding department

Operations 3 and 4 intertwine the most critical aspects of inspectors' work. During these meaning-making and decision-making steps, inspectors collect, process, and apply relevant knowledge/criteria from their cognitive environment (paperwork, computerized procedures, inspection aids, vibro-engraved information on aircraft part, communication

Table 1. Decision-making variables shaping inspectors' diagnosis*

	Decision-making variables (DMV)	Explanation	Importance
1	Depth, width, length, circumference of a defect (physical characteristics)	Tolerance thresholds (TT) are based on dimensional measures	Very high
2	Physical characteristics borderline with the tolerance threshold	Human judgment under uncertainty. Will be removed with automatic measurement	Very high
3	Family of defect (defect identification)	TT differ according to the types of defects	High
4	Blending/dressing restrictions	Some repairs operation can only be applied once or twice; some areas cannot be blended etc	Very high
5	Area of defect's occurrence		Very high
5.1	Defect occurrence on critical area (attachment zone)	Material removal on critical areas can engender harmful stress and constraints for adjacent parts	Very high
5.2	Defect occurrence on unregistered area ("gray area")	If a defect appears in an ill-defined zone, it must be rejected	Very high
5.3	Defect occurrence on repaired area (e.g., material thickness with defect removal)	Repairing a defect removes parent material. The thickness of a part must not fall below a certain threshold	Very high
…	…	…	…

* These decision-variables were first compiled by the analyst from the raw and processed data collected. He then asked three inspectors to range them by order of importance. We present here only five variables out of 18.

with colleagues, and experiential knowledge) to inspect and decide about each defect's state. We have grouped under the heading of "decision-making variables" all the criteria and factors that modulate inspectors' diagnosis process (Table 1). The next section shows how we translated work activity content into formative insights for the CPSS design.

4   Formative Patterns for HAT Configurations

This paper presents how we use descriptive analysis in the on-going research project to configure efficient HAT that takes both entities' advantages. For interested readers, we present how the activity analyses were formalized into design patterns to support software development in [11].

The previous section was inductive, where we gathered relevant knowledge on inspectors' work activity. Here, we switched to a deductive perspective to use the field-work analysis in the process design. We first have extracted from each task (either physical, cognitive, or perceptual) decision variables and domain constraints, functional requirements that the technical system must execute in a fully autonomous scenario

(Table 2, 1st column). By doing so, we disaggregated each function into sub-function to detail the overall work content and subsequently verified the *technological coverage* for each of them (only the "parent" functions are shown in Table 2). We started to examine whether some functions would disappear, be added, or be modified in the envisioned HAT situations during this stage. Based on technological coverage, the work determinants, and the taskwork requirements, we defined the types of function (autonomy, human, or hybrid) with the HAT teamwork hypotheses' associated work content (Table 2, 4th column).

Table 2. Formative table of HAT configurations with technological coverage and work content

Function	Technological coverage	Function type	Human-agent teamwork hypotheses
I. Work preparation			
1. Collect and process relevant data and information on equipment	Yes (limited extend)	Hybrid function with manual input	System: know the areas of the part inspected and the tolerance threshold associated (TT) Inspectors: manual input of the Serial Number and Part Number, as the system is not able to recognize vibro-engraved characters on the aircraft components
2. Assess the quantity of repairs operation allowed by areas (DMV #4 -blending/polishing restrictions)	Yes	Autonomy function	System: calibrated to understand how much repair is allowed for each registered part of the aircraft component. Whenever a repair operation is required, the system display on-screen the remaining number of repairs authorized, inspectors then validate it
3. Check correspondence between the information on paperwork, the physical part and computer procedures	No	Human function	Inspectors: continue to double-check the exactness of information before inserting the parts in the automated cell
II. Multi-sensorial search			

(continued)

Table 2. (*continued*)

Function	Technological coverage	Function type	Human-agent teamwork hypotheses
4. Detect eliminatory defects (cracks, burnt zone)	Yes (limited extend)	Hybrid function without manual input	The system can detect major defects; however, it can struggle to classify the defect as significant and eliminatory. The system warns the human operator of a significant defect with the associated zone, and he continues the rest of the operation
5. Detect minor defects	Yes (limited extend)	Hybrid function without manual input	The system can detect almost all types of defects (mick, dent, scratch, pit, corrosion) but can have difficulty with complex combinations (erosion on the part's edges). Inspectors can check these known areas of difficulties, as they are easily perceptible to them
III. Diagnosis			
6. Classify defect (DMV #3 – Types of defect)	Yes (limited extend)	Hybrid function with manual input	The system is not able to classify all defects. It will have to display an alert for "unknown" defects if necessary. The inspector will then decide if classification is required (some types of defects have the same tolerances threshold and others do not)
7. Defect measurement (DMV #1 – Physical characteristics)	Yes	Autonomy function	System: can measure the physical characteristics of a defect and display the results on the screen if required by the inspector
...	...	...	...

5   Discussion and Conclusion

The literature review and practitioners' feedback showed that existing HF&E tools lack fine-grained formative design models to support the engineering of highly innovative and interactive technologies. In this paper, we have presented the preliminary results of some of the key aspects that our design team prospect in designing a Cyber-Physical-Social System. We show how to construe work content elicited from activity analysis into formative patterns that guide HAT configurations in the envisioned situations. By translating descriptive fieldwork data into functional specifications, we can compare system capabilities with inspectors' expertise in cross-functional collaboration with automation engineers. We called this step *technological coverage*. Having in mind the strength and weakness of both entities – plus a detailed vision of the socio-technical context of inspection – the design team can define and choose among the best HAT configurations possible that enhance the overall CPSS performance. We believe that this type of fine-grained framework allows early anticipation of the changing work system: people role, work organization (work added, reassigned, and removed for affected stakeholders), and *inter-functional* needs/requirements for the coordination of the joint activity (Table 2).

However, the nature of these scenarios is prescriptive by nature. They uncover software requirements, HAT requirements, and design decisions. Design assumptions should be validated by eliciting the future joint activity through participatory workshops with relevant stakeholders [14]. To proceed with the design process, we plan to animate work simulations with different materials (interactive workflow diagram and hi-fi prototypes in this project) to elicit and evaluate the Human-Agent joint activity: the orchestration of the activity, the fluid coordination of shared human-agent functions, the difficulties encountered (types and causes) and alternatives solutions or "prevented actions" and the other potential work configurations.

Acknowledgments. This research is supported by the *Consortium for Research and Innovation in Aerospace in Québec,* funded by Mitacs accelerate program (contract IT11797).

References

1. Boy, G.A.: Human systems integration: a mix of human-centered design. In: Systems Engineering, Ergonomics, HCI and Artificial Intelligence (2019)
2. Hoffman, R.R., Mueller, S.T., Klein, G., Litman, J.: Metrics for explainable AI: challenges and prospects. ArXiv Prepr. ArXiv181204608 (2018)
3. Markman, A.B.: Combining the strengths of naturalistic and laboratory decision-making research to create integrative theories of choice. Nat. Decis. Mak. 10 (2018)
4. Johnson, M., Bradshaw, J.M., Feltovich, P.J.: Tomorrow's human-machine design tools: from levels of automation to interdependencies. J. Cogn. Eng. Decis. Mak. (2017). https://doi.org/10.1177/1555343417736462
5. Roth, E.M., Sushereba, C., Militello, L.G., Diiulio, J., Ernst, K.: Function allocation considerations in the era of human autonomy teaming. J. Cogn. Eng. Decis. Mak. **13**(4), 199–220 (2019). https://doi.org/10.1177/1555343419878038
6. St-Vincent, V., Bellemare, D., Ledoux, and Imbeau: Ergonomic Intervention. Institut de recherche Robert-Sauvé en santé et en sécurité du travail (2014)
7. McDermott, P.L., Walker, K.E., Dominguez, D.C.O., Nelson, A., Kasdaglis, D.N.: Quenching the thirst for human-machine teaming guidance: helping military systems acquisition leverage cognitive engineering research, May 2018. Accessed 19 Nov 2020. https://www.mitre.org/publications/technical-papers/quenching-the-thirst-for-human-machine-teaming-guidance-helping

8. Seeber, I., et al.: Machines as teammates: a research agenda on AI in team collaboration. Inf. Manage. **57**(2), 103174 (2020). https://doi.org/10.1016/j.im.2019.103174

9. Dubey, A., Abhinav, K., Jain, S., Arora, V., Puttaveerana, A.: HACO: a framework for developing human-AI teaming. In: Proceedings of the 13th Innovations in Software Engineering Conference on Formerly known as India Software Engineering Conference, New York, NY, USA, February 2020, pp. 1–9 (2020). https://doi.org/10.1145/3385032.3385044

10. van Diggelen, J., Barnhoorn, J.S., Peeters, M.M.M., van Staal, W., Stolk, M.L.: Pluggable social artificial intelligence for enabling human-agent teaming (2019)

11. Cabour, G., Ledoux, É., Bassetto, S.: A work-centered approach for cyber-physical-social system design: applications in aerospace industrial inspection, ArXiv210105385 Cs, January 2021. Accessed 15 Jan 2021. https://arxiv.org/abs/2101.05385

12. Dekker, S., Hollnagel, E.: Coping with Computers in the Cockpit. Routledge (2018)

13. See, J.E., Drury, C.G., Speed, A., Williams, A., Khalandi, N.: The role of visual inspection in the 21th century. Proc. Hum. Factors Ergon. Soc. Annu. Meet. **61**(1), 262–266 (2017). https://doi.org/10.1177/1541931213601548

14. Van Belleghem, L.: La simulation de l'activité en conception ergonomique : acquis et perspectives. @ctivités, **15**(1) (2018). https://doi.org/10.4000/activites.3129

Autonomy and Singularity - Work, Ubiquity and Operational Fluidity

Juan A. Castillo-M[1]([⊠]) [iD], Carlos Alberto Cifuentes Pinzón[2],
and Jose Luis Gil Gomez[2]

[1] GiSCYT Research Group, Universidad del Rosario, Bogotá, Colombia
`juan.castillom@urosario.edu.co`
[2] Occupational Health Department - Ecopetrol, Bogotá, Colombia

Abstract. The differential value of an ergonomic intervention is to bring an innovative approach in the models and practices of treatment of risks at work, in the assessment procedures and in the models used for data processing. These procedures are based on an approach to occupational health that must be elaborated by the worker and must also be understood as a construction directly linked to the work context. The ubiquitous approach of the ergonomic intervention presented here was developed and designed as a process of specialized knowledge production in the field of occupational health, specifically in the operational field of the activities of an oil company. The objective of this ergonomic intervention was to transfer the practices, models and strategies developed in the laboratory or from the theory to the practices developed by the workers and the company. A flexible structure was developed according to the new models of workers involved in the field of occupational health.

Keywords: Ergonomics · Knowledge · Operational autonomy · Situational autonomy

1 Introduction

The dynamics of the transformations of work in its conventional expression presents multiple questions that begin to outline the singularity of work for the various productive models that societies have adopted, referring to the creative capacity Attridge indicates that "the singular is what is, at a given moment, outside the cultural horizon of thinking, understanding, imagining, feeling, perceiving of certain agents" [1], i.e. transferred to work, it is about the new ways of establishing a productive link mediated by a type of remuneration that is beginning to be strongly modified. In countries with strong industrialization, the irruption of artificial intelligence and robotics have resulted for example in the suppression of certain types of jobs, causing in parallel an increase in productivity and deterioration of the economic possibilities of workers who have been replaced, these workers, the specificity of their work has been transferred to another medium and these workers have been exposed by the limited field of skills and the repertoire of options available to them.

N. L. Black et al. (Eds.): IEA 2021, LNNS 219, pp. 84–90, 2021.
https://doi.org/10.1007/978-3-030-74602-5_13

In ergonomics and sociology of work, the problem of autonomy has been widely and extensively studied, [2, 3] in the act of working, autonomy is associated with the capacity for self-determination, self-awareness and self-regulation has been key to understanding and, in some cases, explaining the contributions of individuals to productive systems, it has also been understood as a sort of balancing agent, sometimes as the source of restoration, control and continuity.

However, it has also been a problematic source given the rationality of productive processes, where ideas derived from security have entered to fight, on many occasions, for and against these individual capabilities. Some currents of human resources even seek strategies to promote autonomy in certain fields of human activity, as well as resources to understand some of the psychological and social aspects at work [4], in fact many studies consider autonomy as a lever of power to achieve better productivity standards.

Autonomy has given place to discussions about the participation and possibility of control of work by workers, this has undoubtedly been a valuable way to focus the role and role of the worker in achieving the goals of organizations, however, the transformations of work that have progressively eliminated the boxing of activities taking them from rigid places to scenarios in which ubiquity and immateriality gain strength. The accelerated developments since the beginning of the 21st century in terms of communication, connectivity, new forms of manufacturing and decentralization of services and jobs have given a new dimension and value to these concepts, especially when thinking about the operational fluidity of the new modes of production in which it seems that the value is in the data and not in the acts, in fact, the data can contribute to predict or modify the acts of individuals. [5] The new technologies and the new modes of production have given a new dimension and value to these concepts.

In this order of ideas, a tremendously unbalanced world of work appears on the horizon, where inequality surfaces, not only in economic terms where deregulation opens the space for fierce competition for access to jobs, but also in terms of competencies that establish distances between individuals that can sometimes seem insurmountable, even if the continuity of learning is promoted, it finds its limits in the cognitive resources available.

1.1 New Patterns of Work and Types of Workers

The changes brought about by public health conditions, simultaneously accompanied by the introduction of new technological possibilities inscribed in the fourth industrial revolution, have led to the appearance of different ways of being productive and working and achieving a stable labor position. These could be classified into the following categories:

a. Traditional workers, those are workers who in the conventional model of linkage perform activities in fixed physical spaces, with externally defined goals and objectives and that require physical permanence. This is a group that is progressively shrinking.
b. Home workers, some professional fields have been making use of this strategy, which has been accelerated by global public health conditions, it is considered that at least 60% of the activities may in a short period of time move to this modality.

c. Co-Workers is the development of forms of collaboration measured by communication technology and self-employment generation, they are mobile workers who collaborate in physical spaces for limited times and within the framework of precise and concrete objectives.

d. Cloud Workers. They are workers who have specific skills that allow them to work providing solutions to the needs of companies without physical presence, sometimes they are responsible for small parts of a project or solve specific aspects of a problem, for this they use their own means and resources, they can be located anywhere geographically.

e. Digital Nomads' is an option of continuous mobility, in which the worker establishes a contractual link with an organization and solves the tasks fulfilling objectives without having a specific place for them, they only depend on their own competences, resolutive and creative capacity in addition to their own resources.

f. Autonomous workers. They are the logical development of the deregulation of work, they are workers who make their resources available to the objectives of an organization, they have a formal link with the organization, but their income depends on their own management, it has been a model widely used in marketing and sales.

g. Zero Hours workers is a new ethically controversial modality, but in full development thanks to mobile applications, workers do not have any kind of link, they are a sort of gear between service demanders and service providers, they are exposed to variations in requests and do not have a defined labor link framework (Fig. 1).

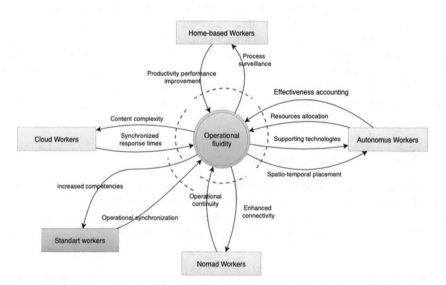

Fig. 1. The fluidity operating in a hyper-flexible work structure, raises the need to develop innovations in the domain of communication, support and synchronization of the actions of the different workers operating in this model.

The new working modalities and the new worker profiles invite to reflect on the role of ergonomics and human factors, the singularity of work scenarios and of work as a productive act, profoundly modify the practices of specialists in the new spheres of work. The barriers between working life and family or social life are progressively diluted, and the resources that are used are still to be understood.

The structure of work and workers that is in the process of consolidation presents a challenge for operational fluidity, this can be understood as synchronization of structures to ensure the continuity and stability of the processes of each organization; when it is decided to operate in a structure where new workers will be present, the problem of synchronization becomes critical, therefore the concern for time becomes critical for both the organization and the workers, the "just in time" becomes central in these synchronization processes that determine the operational fluidity of an organization.

Operational fluidity poses challenges to the management model focused on the stability of the system, in practice organizations have had to learn to accept the instability resulting from innovations and the innovation process itself; classically in the face of any change the organization tried to integrate it quickly to return to a stable structure sometimes rigid, the transformation of work and workers implies the need to develop agile models that are integrating the operational fluidity, this includes the new techniques of organizational learning adopted in artificial intelligence that helps in these complex processes of stabilization and productivity.

The point of view presented here has been developed to anticipate the future practices of ergonomics and human factors, today in fact any intervention to be developed in an organization that adopts these types of workers implies having tools and means adapted and flexible to these realities, In fact, the central notion of workplace is diluted in some cases, in others the idea of work situation and scenario is reaffirmed, and the idea of ubiquity transforms many of the concepts commonly accepted in ergonomics. This also increases the complexity of the approach of ergonomics to these operational spheres where the work will be developed in the near future.

2   Practical Application in Ergonomics Intervention

The objective of this experience was to transfer practices, models and strategies developed in ergonomic studies of the ErgoMotion-lab laboratory of the Universidad del Rosario, Colombia, whose differential value lies in providing an innovative approach by introducing models and practices of ergonomic intervention, in the evaluation procedures and in the models used for data processing and treatment. These were based on an approach centered on the idea of health being elaborated by the worker and understood as a construction directly linked to the work context.

A ubiquitous model of fluid intervention was designed for which there was a control node, a management node (with two pilot units) and operational nodes; the localized interventions were established in sequences according to the epidemiological analyses. Each operational node intervened using a flexible structure of procedures, monitoring and control of the intervention is autonomous and successful and unsuccessful actions were reported, recording is done by activity, according to the specific objectives established by the specialized nodes. The control node collected the data obtained from the localized interventions and, according to the requirements of knowledge transfer, designates the contents of the material intervention and the design of the training, based on the micro-training methodology.

The intervention was developed as a process of specialized knowledge production in the domain of occupational health in the operational sphere of the activities of an oil refinery. The service was deployed in activities that covered three dimensions according to the requirements of the organization:

1. Operational dimension: it was in the hands of interprofessional binomials made up of 26 professionals operating independently in well-delimited geographical areas, where a flexible structure of intervention procedures adapted to each operational situation, data capture and systematization was agreed upon.
2. Conceptual dimension: where contents and recommendations were elaborated based on the analysis of the data processed in each operational unit and validated by the pilot units, which were made up of an operational technical team and another one in charge of the conceptual technical aspects.
3. Prospective dimension: where the prospective prevention axis was built with statistical analyses that determined the behavior of variables that focused actions based on hypotheses derived from the data.

A total of 3675 interventions were carried out over a period of 14 months, for which a team of professionals with situational autonomy was formed with permanent access via a communications network with an internet and voice platform, in order to achieve quality technical results, which was reflected at the end of the process in an evaluation that exceeded 90% compliance in terms of the technical quality of the products generated.

To achieve these results, the process included continuous conceptual, methodological and operational support to each professional and to the different groups of autonomous operational professionals with technical contributions in terms of report elaboration, data collection techniques and data processing, as well as special emphasis on generating added value to all products and service actions executed through well-adapted recommendations.

The progress of the intervention was monitored in systematic weekly meetings, and the progress report of the operational node was reviewed at each meeting, together with the progress schedule of the interventions located at the different levels. A nonconformity follow-up model was developed, designed and used in the development of the activities (field incident log). In addition, a support network of 12 professionals was formed to assist and generate specific solutions required by the organization at different times.

Figure 2 shows the conformation of the operational network of intervention, as can be seen, the different nodes were interconnected throughout the process, and elements of flexibility were introduced to allow the rapid formation of response teams. According to the design of the intervention, professionals participated as co-workers, cloud workers and autonomous workers.

All of them were linked through a common interaction platform where the communication axis was the technical contents, the resolution of conflicts or methodological problems was solved collaboratively, and the interventions were well contextualized in order to find specific and not generic solutions. The control node was made up of traditional workers.

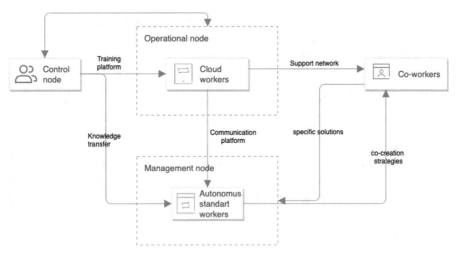

Fig. 2. Structure of the intervention adopting a functional model centered on autonomous but interconnected nodes to facilitate management, technical and operational processes, each node was formed with professionals in specific operational units.

3   Discussion

It is a reality that the digital revolution has increased the availability of data, the degree of connectivity and the speed with which decisions are made, however, this requires the design of intervention models adapted to these new realities. Companies need dynamic and flexible ergonomic and health risk management to navigate an unpredictable future where change comes quickly. In the near future, companies will need hyper-dynamic risk identification and prioritization to keep pace with the changing environment. They will need to anticipate, assess and observe threats based on disparate internal and external data.

The experience presented here is a way to address these challenges, defining, structuring and organizing a flexible, operational and technically performing network is the means to respond, this implies a high degree of mobility and the availability of means that facilitate focusing on local problems and specific to each risk control need, the model presented here was tested and obtained excellent technical results, however it also revealed difficulties and challenges related to logistics.

This was specifically due to the clash in the negotiation between a highly flexible and adaptive management structure and a structure with difficulties to adapt to change with highly formalized administrative procedures, where the main challenges to respond to the hyperdynamic of production situations are located, where paradoxically the phenomenon of different categories of workers operating in parallel on common units is also being installed.

In order to improve and optimize working conditions and manage risks at work, companies need to find a systematic way of deciding which risks to take and which to avoid. This implies having operational field risk research networks that provide an objective and external view of operationality and efficiency.

Today, many productive organizations think of risk in purely static and financial terms, which can lead to inflexible and imprudent organizational perspectives. Given the changing ways of monitoring and managing risks to workers' health, it is found that companies that do not take sufficient risk to innovate may lose control over their own processes, including the loss of intangible but essential operational knowledge essential to process stability, it is important to keep in mind that companies that focus on purely financial metrics of the effects of occupational risk may run unintended operational risks.

For most ergonomic, technical and health risks, the lines are not clear where worker structures have changed, so each company will need a nuanced perspective built on a solid, objective factual base. Companies will need to develop more flexible intervention networks by adopting views on these issues and continually updating them as ways of working evolve with consequent changes in operating environments and their corresponding databases.

References

1. Attridge, D.: The Singularity of Literature. Routledge, London (2004)
2. Terssac, G.D., Friedberg, E., (sous la Dir. de): Coopération et conception, Toulouse, Octarès (1996)
3. Naville, P.: L'automation et le travail humain, p. 741. Edition du CNRS, Paris (1961)
4. Karasek, R.A.: Job demands, job decision latitude, and mental strain: implications for job design. Adm. Sci. Q. **24**(2), 285–308 (1979). https://doi.org/10.2307/2392498
5. Shoshana, Z.: The Age of Surveillance Capitalism: The Fight for Human Future at the New Frontier of Power. Profile Books, London (2019). 692 pp., ISBN 978–1–7881–6316–3

The Work System: A Scale to Capture the Systemic Design Activity of Farmers in Agroecological Transition

Marie Chizallet[1]([⊠]), Lorène Prost[2], and Flore Barcellini[3]

[1] Université de Paris and Univ Gustave Eiffel, LaPEA, 92100 Boulogne-Billancourt, France
marie.chizallet@u-paris.fr
[2] Université Paris-Saclay, INRAE, AgroParisTech, UMR SAD-APT, 75005 Paris, France
[3] Ergonomics Team, CNAM, CRTD, 41 rue Gay-Lussac, 75005 Paris, France

Abstract. This paper aims to provide some support for the widespread claim that agroecological transition entails a wide variety of changes for the farmers. It focuses on farmers' work systems (combining several subsystems: biological and technical, socio-economic, family, and related to the farmers' characteristics) and shows how agroecological transition deals with every part of these work systems. One case study is used to illustrate how farmers' concerns, which are drivers of change, are constructed at the interface of these subsystems. The paper focuses on the Chronicle of Change method (Chizallet et al. 2020) to dissect the work subsystems to which the farmer refers in relation to this concern and to analyze how farmers make their work system evolve in the course of their agroecological transition. The perspective of this research paper is to offer tools and methods to support the agroecological transition of farmers in a systemic approach. It is thus shedding light on the transition from a work point of view and not only from a technical point of view.

Keywords: Work system · Agroecological transition · Farmer's work · Ergonomics · Systemic approach

1 Problem Statement

Agriculture today is widely challenged as to its sustainability. Many actors, whether institutional or political, associations or citizens, including actors from the agricultural world, are calling for a transition of agriculture. We speak of agroecological transition (AET). AET is claimed to imply a very deep transformation of farmers' work, in many different directions. A review of the literature (Chizallet 2019) shows that most studies have underlined the technical dimensions of AET. However, few have focused on social and economic dimensions, or on the role of family in the management of the farm, and almost none of them have combined all these dimensions.

We mobilize the notion of system and work system by combining two series of approaches which have explored the systemic nature of work: ergonomic ones on the one hand, from activity-oriented approaches to ergonomics (e.g. Leplat 2000; Falzon

N. L. Black et al. (Eds.): IEA 2021, LNNS 219, pp. 91–95, 2021.
https://doi.org/10.1007/978-3-030-74602-5_14

2013) and Human Factors (e.g. Carayon and Smith 2000; Carayon et al. 2006; Thatcher and Yeow 2016), and agronomic ones on the other hand (e.g. Osty 1978; Flichman and Jacquet 2000; Laurent et al. 2003; Gafsi, 2006). The crossing of these approaches allows us to propose an understanding of the work system in which the farmer is at the core as follow in Fig. 1.

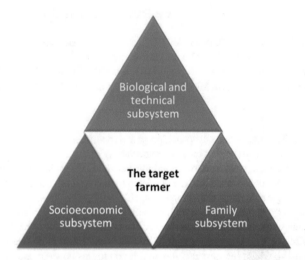

Fig. 1. Proposition for the representation of farmer work system

2   Objective

Based on Chizallet (2019, 2020), this paper assumes that farmers engaged in an AET are developing a design activity of a new work system. Indeed, this transition involves many transformations in the work that farmers have to manage, and more than that, it is a new work system that farmers have to design in order to progress towards more agroecological practices.

The scale of the work system seems an interesting one for people who support such a process of change for three reasons:

1) It reveals the scope of the elements that impact farmers' work and that should be taken into account in the design process.
2) It leads to the identification of work subsystems, their internal functioning and inter-actions. This provides a better understanding of farmers' design activity on these subsystems in order to progress in their AET.
3) Thus, this representation could guide discussions with farmers on all the dimensions of AET to support their design activity.

To sum up, our objective is to challenge this representation of farmer work system by testing it at various stages of an ergonomic intervention carried out with farmers in AET and see if it provides a useful characterization of the challenges faced by the above-mentioned farmers.

3   Methodology

We designed and implemented the Chronicle of Change method (CC) (Chizallet et al. 2017, 2020) to reveal the process of farmers' design of their work systems. The CC is based on an artefact, Fig. 2, which allows the explanation of farmers' difficulties, goals and resources, throughout the design process, i.e. during their AET.

Fig. 2.   The artefact of the Chronicle of Change method

The use of this artefact generates discussions between the animator(s) (here an ergonomist and an agronomist) and the famer(s), which are traced on a paperboard via post-it© notes. The ergonomist questions the farmer about his/her difficulties, objectives and resources, thus promoting the exploration of the work situations experienced and narrated by the farmer. It gives farmers the opportunity to explore (i) all dimensions of their work; (ii) their past, present and potential future work situations as they are built through the design process.

We base this paper on the analysis of the work system of a cattle breeder in transition to a low-input, self-sustaining grassland system. This analysis is based on two meetings with the cattle breeder mobilizing the Chronicle of Change method. The meetings have been recorded and the verbatim are analyzed according to 1) their belonging to the farmer work subsystems and 2) according to their temporality (past, present, future).

4   Results

Three main results emerge. First, the farmer takes a systemic vision of his work system by using the CC. For example, when the farmer talks about his economic difficulties, he links them to his complicated relationship with his bank and the support of an initiative center to increase the value agriculture and the rural environment (socioeconomic subsystem), the support of his wife (family subsystem), his project to obtain certification in organic agriculture and to build a pedagogical farm (biological and technical subsystem), and the desire to "*find a balance between [his] social life, [his] work and [his] profitability*" (farmer's own characteristics). Our analysis shows that the farmer refers to all the work subsystems when he describes a work situation and he creates links between his work subsystems. Secondly, the CC method reveals the design object through the mobilization of past, present and future work situations. For example, the farmer's objective of finding "*a balance between [his] social life, [his] work and [his] profitability*" was built over time, during his transition, on an accumulation of situations that were within the scope of:

– economic difficulties related to the choice of farming practices made by the farmer's family several years earlier;
– meetings with new agricultural players who have gradually built up their new professional network;
– exchanges with members of his family who have been involved in certain decisions for the farm.

Moreover, in the projection of the farmer in his new work system, he projects his situations in different temporalities. For example, when he mentions the certification to organic farming and the pedagogical farm, the situations projected are exclusively of an organic and technical subsystem to respond to economic difficulties and require a long period of time. This long-term projection is possible because he has already put in place shorter term responses in other subsystems such as changing banks or contracting a bank loan.

It shows a coherence between the elements of the work system reported in the discussions of actual work situations and those projected in future work situations. Finally, we show that this object is designed by the farmer through the experience he makes of his work subsystems and the articulations he creates between these subsystems.

5   Discussion

This research proposes a representation of a farmer's work system. The representation of the farmer's work system proposed in this paper is a way to help farmers and those who accompany them to have a global view of the agroecological transition and not focus on only one dimension of the transition. Indeed, the AET seems to mobilize or even transform all the dimensions of the farmer's work. It goes beyond simple technical issues and encompasses everything that makes the activity of farmers.

Such a representation could be discussed with farmers, agricultural actors, or people who directly support farmers in AET. With this representation, we propose an understanding of how this work system is designed: (1) the farmer's experience of his work subsystems and of the articulations of these subsystems seems to be the key to the progress of his design process; (2) the farmer develops a systemic approach when designing his work system. This understanding, already tested with several farmers, could be tested in other farms with different productions.

6   Conclusion

When engaging in AET, the farmers are designing and experimenting their work system. The experience they make of their work subsystems but also of the articulations of these work subsystems seem to be key in the progression of their agroecological transition. Furthermore, this work supports the postulate that AET involves a set of systemic transformations for the farmers in their work and farms. Finally, this work makes a methodological proposal by the Chronicle of Change that could be more widely remobilized to support transitions beyond the agricultural world.

References

Carayon, P., Smith, M.J.: Work organization and ergonomics. Appl. Ergon. **31**(6), 649–662 (2000). https://doi.org/10.1016/S0003-6870(00)00040-5

Carayon, P., Hundt, A.S., Karsh, B.T., Gurses, A.P., Alvarado, C.J., Smith, M., Brennan, P.F.: Work system design for patient safety: The SEIPS model. BMJ Qual. Saf. **15**(suppl 1), 50–58 (2006)

Chizallet, M.: Comprendre le processus de conception d'un système de travail dans l'indivisibilité du temps. Le cas d'agriculteurs en transition agroécologique. Thesis, Conservatoire National des Arts et Métiers, Paris (2019)

Chizallet, M., Barcellini, F., Prost, L.: Supporting agroecological transition on farms: Co-designing a change management support approach. In: Proceedings of the 48th Annual Conference of the Association of Canadian Ergonomists & 12th International Symposium on Human Factors in Organizational Design and Management, Banff, pp. 308–313 (2017)

Chizallet, M., Prost, L., Barcellini, F.: Supporting the design activity of farmers in transition to agroecology: Towards an understanding. Le travail humain **83**(1), 33–59 (2020)

Falzon, P.: Ergonomie constructive. PUF, Paris (2013)

Flichman, G., Jacquet, F.: Le couplage des modèles agronomiques (bio-techniques) et économiques. Acquis et perspectives. Séminaire en économie de la production, p. 17 (2000)

Gafsi, M.: Exploitation agricole et agriculture durable. Cahiers Agric. **15**(6), 491–497 (2006). https://doi.org/10.1684/agr.2006.0035

Hill, S.B., MacRae, R.J.: Conceptual framework for the transition from conventional to sustainable agriculture. J. Sustain. Agric. **7**(1), 81–87 (1996)

Laurent, C., Maxime, F., Mazé, A., Tichit, M.: Multifonctionnalité de l'agriculture et modèles de l'exploitation agricole. Economie rurale **273**(1), 134–152 (2003)

Leplat, J.: L'environnement de l'action en situation de travail. Dans Centre de recherche formation Conservatoire national des arts et métiers (eds.) L'analyse de la singularité de l'action, pp. 107–132. PUF, Paris (2000). https://doi.org/10.3917/puf.derec.2000.01.0107

Nicourt, C., Souron, O.: Incidences de quelques innovations sur les conditions de travail des agriculteurs. Économie Rurale **192**(1), 110–114 (1989)

Osty, P.-L.: L'exploitation agricole vue comme un système. Diffusion de l'innovation et contribution au développement. Bulletin technique d'information, **326**, 43–49 (1978).

Thatcher, A., Yeow, P.H.: A sustainable system of systems approach : A new HFE paradigm. Ergonomics **59**(2), 167–178 (2016). 10(1080/00140139), pp.1066876 2015

The Workplace Role in Integrated Operations: Contributions and Limits of a Collaborative Environment

Cláudia Vieira Carestiato Cordeiro[(✉)] [iD], Nora de Castro Maia[iD], and Francisco José de Castro Moura Duarte[iD]

PEP/COPPE - Universidade Federal do Rio de Janeiro, Avenida Horácio Macedo 2.030, COPPE, Bloco G, sala G209, Cidade Universitária, Rio de Janeiro/RJ 21.941-914, Brazil
{claudiac,noramaia}@pep.ufrj.br, fjcmduarte@coppe.ufrj.br

Abstract. The creation of collaborative environments is one of the first practices adopted by companies that intend to implement an integrated operation (IO). The participation of ergonomists in a collaborative environment project for the subsea installations sector of a Brazilian oil and gas company and the subsequent space evaluation during operations, prompts reflections on the contributions and limits of this initiative.

The research shows that this workplace design, based on a participatory approach, can contribute to greater integrated operations. However, the workplace is only a means, and, in this context, what is at stake is the design of a new work system.

Keywords: Collaborative environment · Integrated operations · Oil and gas industry

1 Introduction

The questions presented in this article were based on a case study and are the result of a reflective approach, carried out following an ergonomic intervention in the design of a collaborative environment. The objective of this new workplace was the operational integration of teams from the subsea services sector of a Brazilian oil company. The ergonomics team took part in two stages of this project. In the first, preliminary layout studies and recommendations for the new workplace were developed. In the second, the collaborative environment performance assessment was carried out at the integrated operation startup and recommendations made for adjustments.

From 2005, the Brazilian oil industry started its own integrated operations (IO) program, following the international oil and gas sector trends [6, 14].

The studied company's main objectives were to facilitate the continued exploration of old fields and start production of fields located in ultra-deep waters - the pre-salt[1].

---

[1] The term pre-salt refers to a layer of rocks below a layer of salt, formed, in general, by carbonate rocks, where the deposit of organic matter accumulated over millions of years potentiated the generation and accumulation of oil. In Brazil, the pre-salt fields can reach up to 8.000 m above the sea surface, requiring high technological investments.

N. L. Black et al. (Eds.): IEA 2021, LNNS 219, pp. 96–103, 2021.
https://doi.org/10.1007/978-3-030-74602-5_15

The exploration of these new fields demanded the development of new technologies. The company's goals aimed to reduce the high operational, logistical (cargo and people transport) and maintenance costs, through onshore-offshore integration.

Generally, IO initiatives are based on high investments in Information and Communication Technology (ICT) that allow data exchange and remote communication in real time. For the most part, they envisage the creation of workplaces equipped with these technologies, where the operational support teams are located [9, 10, 14]. These locations are referred as "collaborative environments" in the IO's literature for the oil sector [8]. Its role is to promote greater collaboration between these teams.

Over time, the creation of these spaces has been one of the first practices adopted in the implementation of IO projects. According to Moltu [15], operational support rooms, in their most varied formats, have become an IO icon. Nevertheless, in the Brazilian context, there is an unstated expectation the integration of different teams on land will occur, based on the occupation of the same workplace.

According to Arnoud and Falzon [11], cooperation in the development of work activity can be enhanced by sharing the same workplace in activities in which discussions and arguments are important. For Carballeda [2], in addition to sharing the same physical space, it is necessary to think about the organization, so that the individual's work is incorporated in the collective work.

Moltu [15] seeks to demystify the need for a common physical space, stating that the rooms that support the IO processes do not need to be restricted to four walls. They may be a network that connects different physical locations, with several ICT solutions and different organizational and managerial models, however, all focused on supporting operations.

Maia et al. [12], based on this same article's case study, demonstrate that these workplace designs require the understanding and reflection of how future teams can work, cooperate and coordinate their actions, because what is at stake is the design of a new work system.

Collaborating with this discussion, this article examines the question to what extent the simple action of allocating all teams in the same workplace, with collaborative environment characteristics, can ensure an integrated operation and guarantee improvement goals desired by companies.

2   Context

In the studied company, IO initiatives, prior to this project, did not produce the expected results, despite high technological investments and the creation of collaborative environments with advanced resources.

The subsea services sector, studied in this research, sought to reduce operating costs and increase productivity. For this, they aimed at better planning of vessel use and a faster response, in relation to the unforeseen operational problems, based on the integrated operations of different teams.

The high operational cost was borne by its main resources - contracted vessels - that served the various types of services, all along the Brazilian coast. The vessels, each with specific technical characteristics, were managed by five operational sectors, according to the operations served. The five operational sector teams worked in different locations, planning and controlling resources (vessels, people, and materials) to carry out subsea operations.

One of the main initiatives of this IO project was to design a space, to which the teams were to be transferred, to work in an integrated manner. The company itself had started studies of possible layouts to place 90 workstations in a single location. There was a 900 m^2 area on the roof of a building nearing completion for this. The layouts to be analyzed and approved by the IO project managers.

Faced with the difficulty to analyze such studies, management demanded an external team, for an ergonomic study of the future collaborative environment. The first stage of which was carried out between November 2013 and April 2014. This resulted in preliminary layout studies and recommendations to develop the architectural project. This also included requirements for furniture, equipment, lighting and acoustics, as described in Cordeiro et al. [3], Duarte et al. [5], Maia [11] and Maia et al. [12].

In parallel, another external team was hired to develop a single data entry and consultation system, so that everyone could see, in real time, the progress of each team's resource planning and the variability to which their routine activities were subjected.

In 2014, following the ergonomic intervention first stage completion, the collaborative environment project was developed by the company's team of designers, who were also responsible for the construction supervision.

The transfer of teams to the new workplace started in mid-2015. During this period, the ergonomics team began the case study's second stage: to monitor the collaborative environment start-up, based on its performance analysis. The objective was to identify workplace needs for adjustments and transformations, which generated recommendations involving: layout, furniture, ambiences, information presentation devices, software and other resources provided to support the work activity.

3   Methodology

In this project's initial phase, the various teams' work characteristics to be integrated were identified, to incorporate their individual needs to the new workplace design process. The adopted methodology had as its theoretical references: the Ergonomic Work Analysis - EWA [7] and the future activity simulations [13].

Initially, individual and collective interviews were conducted with the various teams, followed by work activity observations and a self-confrontation process. These facilitated a more detailed understanding of the problems faced and the resources needed to achieve the intended transformations.

Presenting Power Point slide floor plans, several meetings were simulated depicting future work situations involving the multi-sector operational representatives. Several proposals were made to the initially proposed layouts.

The research's second stage objective was to conduct a performance analysis of the collaborative environment. The methodology adopted was a double approach combining EWA with questionnaires, measurements and interviews based on the principles of Post-Occupancy Evaluation - POE [16, 17]. This stage lasted only 30 days and was aimed to assess the need for project adjustments.

4 Results

4.1 First Stage of Ergonomic Intervention

This study's first phase results were described in detail by Cordeiro et al. [3], Duarte et al. [5], Maia [11] and Maia et al. [12].

As these articles reported, a discussion regarding the future organization of work was raised from the participatory approach and the layout simulation dynamic studies, performed in the ergonomic design project. This discussion strongly impacted the workplace design project, imposing important changes in the number of workstations forecast and the resources needed to develop the activity (furniture and equipment), which consequently led to several rearrangements.

During the project, the teams started to be treated as nuclei or work cells. To give an idea of the organizational changes discussed, there was more than a 60% increase of initially foreseen employees for one of the teams and all foresaw workstation expansions. Important changes were established in the number of information screens necessary for the workstation activities and to share information in and between cells.

One interesting, highlighted aspect regarding layout, was the separation of cells in individual rooms, but integrated with others, through passages and mobile partitions. Opened doors and partitions facilitate quick communication between cells. When closed, they maintain the privacy required to develop each group's tasks. Between the work rooms, small rooms were foreseen, where it would be possible to hold quick meetings involving members of the same nucleus, from different nuclei or external people.

The integrated operations center was provided with support environments such as: pantries, bathrooms, cafeteria, meeting rooms and training rooms. To deal with incidents and accidents, a set of rooms was created, called the contingency complex, where multidisciplinary teams could meet and deal with problems 24 h a day, without interfering or suffering interference from other operations.

The layout solution, discussed and built with collective participation, broke the company's initial paradigm projecting all workstations in the same open plan space, to achieve integration.

4.2 Second Stage of Ergonomic Intervention

During the collaborative environment performance analysis, several factors were evaluated: questions related to the characteristics of the working population; aspects of physical arrangement and environmental comfort in work rooms and support environments; and aspects of operational and communications integration. In general, the collaborative environment performance for these aspects was considered good by users. However, some evaluation results allow us to reflect on the workplace role in the integrated operations process desired by the company.

The workforce population was mainly composed of people with technical or higher education. Approximately 34% of workers had less than 5 years in the company and 63% of operators had worked for less than 6 years in their current activity. This result demonstrates that the transformations of the teams' work had already been occurring in recent years. At the time of the research, the work in the performed function was recent, even for those who had been in the company for a longer time.

As for the physical arrangement, changes were identified in the use of some spaces and in the foreseen position for the workstation occupation (position/function ratio); besides the need for space for unforeseen functions.

The relative operator positions at the various benches has changed for several reasons, such as: allow better integration considering not yet occupied workstations; admit that functions requiring more concentration were distant from others, that intensely communicated; enable the videowall proximity for functions that constantly used it; increased expected operator numbers for certain cells; among others.

Complaints were raised about the circulation within rooms, showing frequent different routes from those projected and complaints related to light and air condition control devices.

Some complaints were linked to the existing building's imposed limits, and by changes made to meet demands throughout the project's development. The solutions adopted in this period did not always follow the logic of the ergonomic intervention first stage choices, which privileged the work activity logic and now implemented a participatory dynamic to the project. Nevertheless, some issues were related to a still immature organizational design when the collaborative environment project started, making it difficult to find adequate design solutions for the various work requirements.

According to Duarte et al. [5], the layout simulations of this study's first stage demonstrated the need to discuss and reflect on the organizational changes to be implemented in the new workplace and created a space to launch this discussion based on the activity's characteristics. However, this late start did not allow several aspects to be thought and so planned. For example, a planned circulation routes change intensified people circulating within the work rooms and increased the routes to reach certain support environments. This result was due to a set of factors such as: (i) apply an access control system on doors that would allow a shorter and external circulation to the work rooms; (ii) use a support room as a shift coordinator room - a function that did not previously exist and was frequently accessed by operators through a work room; (iii) to concentrate personal use lockers in a single area, when the previous forecast was to distribute them close to users; (iv) the little used mezzanine floor cafeteria moved to the work room floor, leading to greater use of a pantry, now accessed through the work rooms; among others (Fig. 1).

The integration and communication devices and the integration software system made available were considered satisfactory for the activity development and as integration facilitation factors. However, there were demands for larger or more monitors, that provided better data visualization in the workstation - and for system user training - which was still under development at the operation startup.

The larger screens, distributed along the operation benches to share information, could not be used as such, due to their command being linked only to certain computers. The lack of advance definitions of what should be possible to view at each workstation, via integration software, also made it difficult to adequately forecast information sharing resources, leaving installed resources unused.

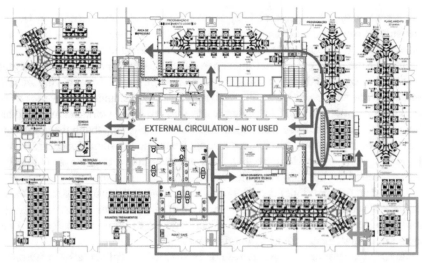

Fig. 1. Doors with access control (blue); changing the position of the lockers (red); creation of the shift coordinator's room (green) and use of pantry for meals (pink).

These examples reveal a mismatch between what the layout discussions foresaw, which involved thinking about a certain form of operation, and the design of computer resources.

5 Discussion and Conclusions

During the ergonomic study first stage, participatory dynamics stood out, where the layout proposals simulation became an organizational discussion instrument about the future new way of working. Each team had the opportunity to explain its operating methods, its actions, its limits and its needs given the identified operational situations. This exchange between teams brought a greater understanding of the impact of a cell's work on the others, as well as the various interfaces necessary to carry out operations in an integrated manner.

Discussions on organizational issues, based on the layout proposals, covered topics such as: (i) the need for operators in the same nucleus to interact and/or between nuclei; (ii) the creation of unforeseen functions; (iii) the addition of people in expected functions; (iv) the needs for future expansions; (v) the needs for furniture, equipment and technologies for communication and data visualization; (vi) future work processes, among others.

These debates and the construction of commitments between the desirable and the possible to meet the demands of each group were, in summary, the beginning of integration between the teams. However, the evaluation carried out at the integrated operation startup, revealed that the participatory dynamics implemented in the project's first stage was reduced, creating difficulties in exchanges between the operating teams, managements and designers throughout the project development. Changes and complaints identified in this period were linked to unforeseen or unaddressed organizational issues, which impacted the space projects, integration software and operator training. The analysis results also showed that there were major changes in the work context and even the most experienced professionals had their roles reconfigured.

Although there was managerial concern to identify processes to design the integrated operations, the organizational planning did not go into the level to identify characteristics specific to each team's work activity, to design a new work system. This new system was based on collective work involving teams that previously worked independently, although their processes were interdependent. One element supporting the construction of this new work group was the collaborative environment. However, for collective work to happen, it is not enough to just put all teams together in the same space. This will not bring the desired collaboration and integration.

It is evident that proximity between people can bring benefits to certain work activities. However, it can also bring some problems, such as: (i) difficulty in concentrating on complex tasks; (ii) compromising the confidentiality of certain information; (iii) more frequent interruptions in activities, among others.

Integrated operations programs cannot be limited to collaborative environment design. The space and physical definitions and technical resources alone are not sufficient to transform output developed in a fragmented way, into an integrated and collaborative work. It is a new work system conception, where it is necessary to design, in addition to a workplace, other work requirements and, in particular, the organization and training necessary to enable each worker to efficiently play their role in this new system.

The collaborative environment must be seen as a means for the organization to function effectively. For this to happen, the work needs to be understood; spaces for the participatory construction of solutions have to be created; and the future work organization must to be designed, in order to portray it in the solutions to be adopted. In addition, the work tools designs should provide adjustment possibilities, resulting from the constant evolution of new work systems, which arises from the integration of the teams.

Although the collaborative environment studied has been positively evaluated, at the operational and managerial level, and has collaborated with the integration of the teams, aspects identified in this ergonomic study show the lack of formalized organizational planning and a worker training program, to support the teams' integration and the company's pursued goals.

References

1. Arnoud, J., Falzon, P.: Favoriser l'emergence d'un collectif transverse par la co-analyse constructive des pratiques. Le travail humain **77**, 127–153 (2014)
2. Carballeda, G.: La contribuition des ergonomes à l'analyse et à la transformation de l' organisation du travail: l'exemple d'une intervention relative à la maintenance dans une industrie de processus continu. Thèse de Doctorat d'Ergonomie, Conservatoire National des Arts et Métiers (CNAM), Paris (1997)
3. Cordeiro, C., Castro, I., Maia, N., Duarte, F.: As simulações em projeto de integração operacional: do espaço à concepção organizacional. In: Proceedings of the 11th International Symposium on Human Factors in Organizational Design and Management (ODAM), and 46th Annual Nordic Ergonomics Society Conference (NES): Selected and peer reviewed papers, pp. 873–878. International Ergonomics Association, Copenhagen (2014)

4. Daniellou, F.: Métodos em ergonomia de concepção: A análise de situações de referência e a simulação do trabalho. In: Duarte, F. (ed.) Ergonomia e projeto na indústria de processo contínuo, pp. 29–33. COPPE/RJ, Lucerna, Rio de Janeiro (2002)
5. Duarte, F., Maia, N., Cordeiro, C.: Contribuições das simulações organizacionais para projetos de ambientes colaborativos na indústria de óleo e gás. Ação Ergonômica 12(2), 62–69 (2017)
6. Edwards, T., Mydland, Ø., Henriquez, A.: The art of intelligent energy (iE) – insights and lessons learned from the application of iE., SPE Intelligent Energy Conference and Exhibition, SPE 128669, Netherlands (2010)
7. Guérin, F., Laville, A., Daniellou, F., Duraffourg, J., Kerguelen, A.: Comprendre le travail pour le transformer. ANACT, Paris (2001)
8. Guldemond, E.: Collaborative work environments in smart oil fields: The organization matters! In: Rosendahl, T., Hepsø, V. (eds.) Integrated operations in oil and gas industry: Sustainability and capability development, chapter 4, pp. 59–75. Business Science, USA (2013)
9. Lilleng, T., Sagatun, S. I.: IO methodology and value proposition. In: SPE Intelligent Energy Conference and Exhibition, SPE 128576, Netherlands (2010)
10. Liyanage, J.P.: Integrated e-operations-e-maintenance: applications in North Sea offshore assets. In: Kobbacy, K.A.H., Prabhakar Murthy, D.N. (eds.) Complex System Maintenance Handbook, pp. 585–609. Springer, London (2008)
11. Maia, N.: O projeto de ambientes colaborativos: a dimensão coletiva do trabalho na integração operacional na indústria do petróleo. Tese de Doutorado, PEP, COPPE, UFRJ, Rio de Janeiro, RJ, Brasil, março (2015)
12. Maia, N., Duarte, F., Cordeiro, C., Castro, I., Oggioni, B.: Lições aprendidas de um projeto de ambientes colaborativos: o caso do Centro Integrado de Operações Submarinas. In: Rio Oil & Gas Expo and Conference, IBP 1960_16, Rio de Janeiro (2016)
13. Maline, J.: Simuler le travail. Editions de l'ANACT, Paris (1994)
14. McCann, A., Omdal, S., Nyberg, R.K.: Statoil's first onshore support center: the result of new work processes and technology developed to exploit real-time data. In: SPE Intelligent Energy Conference and Exhibition, SPE 90367, Houston (2004)
15. Moltu, B.: Good IO-Design is more than IO-Rooms. In: Rosendahl, T., Hepsø, V. (eds.) Integrated operations in oil and gas industry: sustainability and capability development, Chapter 9, pp. 141–153. Business Science Reference, USA (2013)
16. Ono, R., Ornstein, S.W., Villa, S.B., França, A.J.G.L.: Avaliação pós-ocupação: Na arquitetura, no urbanismo e no design: Da teoria à prática. Oficina de Textos, São Paulo (2018)
17. Preiser, W.F.E., Rabinowitz, H., White, E.: Post-Occupancy Evaluation (Routledge Revivals). Routledge, London (2015)
18. Resende, A.E.: Salas de controle: do artefato ao instrumento. Tese de Doutorado, FAU, USP, São Paulo, SP, Brasil (2011)

Health Crisis, Work Crisis: What Place for Ergonomics in Society Now?

Fabien Coutarel[1]([✉]), Valérie Pueyo[2], Marianne Lacomblez[3], Catherine Delgoulet[4], and Béatrice Barthe[5]

[1] ACTé Lab., Clermont Auvergne University, Labex IMobS3 I SITE CAP 20-25,
63530 Clermont-Ferrand, France
fabien.coutarel@uca.fr
[2] Environnement Ville Et Société Lab., Institut Für Kontinuumsmechanik, Leibniz Universität
Hannover Lyon 2 University, UMR 5600, Labex Intelligence Des Mondes Urbains, Hanover,
Germany
[3] Porto University, Porto, Portugal
[4] CRTD Lab., Conservatoire National Des Arts Et Métiers, Gis-CREAPT, Paris, France
[5] Toulouse Jean Jaurès University, Toulouse, France

Abstract. The present context of health crisis and unprecedented lockdown is an opportunity for thinking, position-taking, indignation and controversy. As a social activity, work redefines itself every day, according to circumstances. Work is a central object of ergonomics and ergonomists can learn from crisis: behind the health crisis, we highlight the work crisis. Ergonomics must take part in the social debates that accompany this crisis, and make its contribution to better reconciling the human challenges of work and organizational issues in the future. To do this, we need criteria: the crisis highlights the need to experience the recognized contribution, individually and collectively, of one's own work to meaningful social issues, and therefore to renovate our approach to occupational health.

Keywords: Work · Health · Occupational risks · Subjectivity

Occupational health is widely understood in terms of the risks involved. The integrity of employees must be protected. The health crisis reveals that workers are taking risks in contracting Covid-19 to preserve the meaning of their work, which is also essential to their health. Ergonomics can contribute to thinking and action around this apparent contradiction: exposing oneself to risks in order to build one's health.

1 Dead Ends and Blind Spots of Pre-crisis Work

Major characteristics of contemporary work organizations have contributed to this crisis. These same characteristics are at the origin of major and well known difficulties in work itself as well:

- globalization of value chains and the hyper-specialization of each of the actors in the chain. Hyper-specialization leads to the devaluation of know-how, the individualization of tasks, fragmentation of the activity [1], loss of meaning, and impeded quality

N. L. Black et al. (Eds.): IEA 2021, LNNS 219, pp. 104–107, 2021.
https://doi.org/10.1007/978-3-030-74602-5_16

[2]. The impoverishment of work is not the only consequence: more transport, more pollution, more mobility of workers at the interface of production entities, less local and autonomous production capacity for many necessary products (masks, respirators, medicines, etc.).

- The absence of stocks upstream of, during and downstream of means of production, reduces the risks of unsold products. But this also makes human work dependent on the market, a dependency that can be integrated through the increasing flexibility of work contracts and working hours: staggered hours, part-time work, short-term contracts, etc. Job insecurity and non-standard working hours are major risk factors for employee health [3]. Lack of stocks also makes a region more dependent on supplies. The slightest break in these supplies immediately puts a system under stress and very quickly leads to the absence of essential products.

- To a large extent the digital revolution in our society reinforces the growing trivialization of atypical working hours and social or even family precariousness, as the balance between family life and professional life is sometimes upset. From this standpoint, compulsory remote working, combined with childcare (these same parents having to ensure educational continuity for their children) offers a vast shared experience of the difficulties associated with the deregulation of the system of activities [4]. All these principles lead to intensification of work, that is the ever-increasing. The meaning of work for those who carry it out is often abused.

2   The Experience of the Recognized Contribution of One's Own Work to Meaningful Social Issues During Crisis

In experiencing the crisis, many workers also experience new work situations, alone or in existing or (re)composed groups, often revealing other ways of doing things and of thinking about Work and Society: united, proud to be useful, authentic, inspired by moral values and alternative conceptions of "living together". Very small companies in the textile field are modifying their production methods in order to make masks; one of a multinational cosmetics company's sites has begun to manufacture hydroalcoholic gel; nurses are transforming painter's suits into smocks; car manufacturers are making respirators; bakeries are recruiting personnel to deliver to people isolated in their homes, and so on. This reconfiguration of ways of doing things is changing the daily life of hospitals, nursing homes, the market gardening sector, the building and public works sector and many others. In the health crisis and its urgency, the standard rules and norms of everyday life no longer apply, allowing each individual to reinvent in situations where they were previously shut away.

Many workers have taken the risk of contamination and exhaustion to make themselves useful. How can ergonomics take care of this? We believe that work experience must once again become an essential issue in the ergonomic approach to working conditions: how can work be a health operator? We can see that preserving the integrity of worker is not enough to understand work. Exposures say nothing about the subjective experience of social utility that work allows (or not). "The broadening of the scope of action is a typical and fundamental feature of human development. The competency of workers is very much linked to their ability to change register according to circumstance", said Wisner [5]. The "cumbersome subjectivities" [6] of the past have become the salutary subjectivities of today, to the extent that the usefulness of local and solidarity-based economies embedded in their regions and living environments reveals the true conditions of subsistence for each individual and his/her loved ones.

During a crisis, life is re-invented and health is built with, and in the face of, risks. This is how Canguilhem, [7]: "I am well to the extent that I feel able to take responsibility for my actions, to bring things into existence and to create between them relations that would not come without me and that would not be what they are without them".

3   Meaning of Work and Ergonomics

The historical moment we are currently experiencing is an extremely powerful indicator: this pandemic is what anthropologist Mauss [8] calls a "total social fact", a phenomenon which "sets in motion the whole of society and its institutions", which involves society in its entirety, with all its members. His understanding supposes that the phenomenon is not broken down or dissected according to its various dimensions (biological, historical, political, legal, geographical, demographic, psychological, economic, etc.), because "it is by considering the everything as a whole that we [can] perceive the essential". The pandemic imposes on us all the global and systemic vision claimed by ergonomics as we understand it. In this way, a major challenge lies in the appropriate delineation of the system's boundaries: it is both necessary to identify the major determinants of situations, while preserving realistic transformation horizons. In any case, the range of dimensions to be taken into account is much wider than that of the workstations and their displays. This is what Carayon and Perry [9], for example, propose for the health care system. For these authors, the level of action is the system governance, to allow to: defer to local expertise; support adaptive "real time" behaviours, enhance system interactions; repurpose processes; and support dynamic continuous learning. These perspectives on managing and transforming organizations are aimed at restoring a central status to work experience. The pragmatist approach to organizations [10] and organizational interventions approaches [11] are essential supports in this direction, where each individual activity, these effects on health and performances, are oriented by its intimate meaning for the person who carries it out [12]. This theoretical framework gives to ergonomics possibility to join individual sensemaking of work with organizational and systemic perspectives.

So, ergonomics must be re-examined: do our approaches to work often concern the fundamental questions that this social activity raises? Can we imagine contributing to the evolution of our societies without addressing these aspects?

Similar orientation where built in Ergonomics. Professor Alain Wisner's anthro-potechnology [13] already marked this questioning, taken up in its own way and in other words by macro-ergonomics [14]. Resilience of systems requires taking into account of culture and societal aspects [15].

Constructive ergonomics [16] requires us to return to the fundamental questions of work: is work an opportunity for self-construction? This question is largely absent when health is approached in terms of physical or psychosocial exposure, displays design, etc. The health crisis is forcing ergonomics to return to the essentials: working is living, and living implies conditions.

References

1. Friedmann, G.: Le travail en miettes. Gallimard (1956)
2. Clot, Y.: Le travail à Coeur. La Découverte (2010)
3. Seifert, A.M., Messing, K., Riel, J., Chatigny, C.: Precarious employment conditions affect work content in education and social work: results of work analyses. Int. J. Law Psychiatry **30**(4–5), 299–310 (2007)
4. Curie, J., Hajjar, V., Baubion-Broye, A.: Psychopathologie du travail ou dérégulation du système des activités. Perspect. Psychiatriques **22**, 85–91 (1990)
5. Wisner, A.: Aspects psychologiques de l'anthropotechnologie. Le Travail Humain **60**(3), 229–254 (1997)
6. Le Blanc, G.: Les maladies de l'homme normal. Vrin, Paris (2004)
7. Canguilhem, G.: Ecrits sur la médecine. Seuil, Paris (2002)
8. Mauss, M.: Essai sur le don: forme et raison de l'échange dans les sociétés archaïques. In: Sociologie et Anthropologie, PUF, pp. 274–275 (1973)
9. Carayon, P., Perry, S.: Human factors and ergonomics systems approach to the COVID-19 healthcare crisis. Int. J. Quality Health Care **33**(1), 1–3 (2021)
10. Lorino, P.: Pragmastism and Organization Studies. Oxford University Press (2018)
11. Nielsen, K., Noblet, A.: Organizational interventions for health and well-being. Routledge (2018)
12. Récopé, M., Fache, H., Beaujouan, J., Coutarel, F., Rix-Lièvre, G.: A study of the individual activité of professional volleyball players: Situation assessment and sensemaking under time pressure. Appl. Ergon. **80**, 226–237 (2019)
13. Wisner, A.: Ergonmics and anthropotechnoloy, a limited or wider approach to working condition in technology transfer. In: Ergonomics in developing countries, Lulea University Press, Sweden (1984)
14. Hendrick, H.W., Brian M.K.: Macroergonomics. Theory, Methods and Applications. LEA (2002)
15. Falzon, P.: Constructive Ergonomics. CRC Press (2013)
16. Amalberti, R.: Optimum system safety and optimum system resilience: agonistic or antagonistic concepts? In: Resilience Engineering, Concepts and Precepts, pp. 253–271, ASHGATE, England (2006)

Organisations Without Employers, Reflection on Future Work in Workplaces

Gabriela Cuenca[✉]

Universidad Tecnológica Nacional, Regional Buenos Aires, UTN/FRBA, Buenos Aires, Argentina
gcuenca@frba.utn.edu.ar

Abstract. During the 1980s and 1990s Argentine economy was unstable until finally in early 2000s the economic model collapsed. People demonstrated in the streets. Many factories closed down or went broke. In 2001, the President resigned. Under urgency and uncertainty a new social movement emerged. Workers could face unemployment developing the so-called recovered factories.

In 2020, the pandemic reveals an unpredictable world, where it is no longer possible to rely on structures based on certainties. I resumed my research on recovered factories conducted during 2008/2011, looking for clues, traces and creative practices undertaken by workers in the face of sudden and unexpected events, I chose the terms urgency, uncertainty, inhabiting, trace, prospection and emancipation as useful elements in times of crisis.

Thinking about the future of work in the context of a pandemic or crisis led me to analyze the practices carried out in the recovered factories and then address our own practices as ergonomists. I seek through a new theoretical approach to enrich the transition to future work in general and ours in particular.

Keywords: Crisis · Urgency · Uncertainty · Ergonomics · Self-management

1 Recovered Factories (RF)

In the early 1990s, the first evident symptoms of deindustrialisation process and loss of jobs appeared. In this context, the productive system ceased to be the driving force of national economy, resulting in the collapse of several productive activities. When companies started to close down or go bankrupt, workers started taking over those companies. This mechanism of appropriation became the only alternative to structural unemployment and a way of recovering and maintaining work sources. The first experiences of factory takeovers took place in large industries with more than 300 workers. There were many recovery circumstances: those collecting and/or repairing what former owners had left behind; those returning to old production practices because their owners had sold the new machinery; those taking up production as usual and those closing down due to lack of raw materials and supplies. At the same time, small significant initiatives were arising among the sectors already excluded from the labor market. All these experiences turned into a new struggling tool for this new "social movements" and new social actors promoting a different behavior and implementing the concept of "social economy".

© The Author(s), under exclusive license to Springer Nature Switzerland AG 2021
N. L. Black et al. (Eds.): IEA 2021, LNNS 219, pp. 108–114, 2021.
https://doi.org/10.1007/978-3-030-74602-5_17

Recovered factories attracted the interest of local and international researchers who wanted to know and understand the phenomenon. A link was established between the recovered factories and national and provincial universities and institutions that made possible the transfer of technological and scientific knowledge to the productive environment through research and programs created to these workers' needs. During 2008–2011 our research-action generated a link between the University-Recovered Factories that allowed us to work with and for the workers. The result -product of a collective construction- allowed the workers to become the owners of what was produced. (Cuenca, Zotta 2012).

2   Approach

Based on my own research on recovered factories, I intend to create a new network relating some theorical viewpoint.

To build the future of work, I developed two concepts: inhabiting and thinking time.

I choose Heidegger's notion of "inhabit", I continue with "inhabiting the world" (Béguin 2007), I develop the term uncertainty, I focus on "inhabiting uncertainty" (Cuenca 2020) and "inhabiting time" (Chesnaux 1996) as well. I continue with the binomial emancipation/alienation concepts by Marx. I recover the past by investigating the "unrealised potentialities", as they represent "what is still at a project stage" (Harshaw 1997). I am interested in Marc Bloch's approach (2001), who rescues the past through traces taken from a historical consciousness that can explain the causes, motives and reasons why someone did something. I understand the present as "an opportunity to rethink work from a prospective viewpoint" and the need to present real alternatives beyond the existing ones (Valérie Pueyo 2020). I decide to take up Heidegger's notion on the future and I take Pueyo's "prospective" concept as well.

3   Theoretical Issues

3.1   Building the Future of Work

I choose Heidegger's notion of "inhabiting". In his 1951 lecture "Building, Inhabiting, Thinking", the author explains that man is, insofar as he inhabits. The essence of man, his way of being, is to inhabit. In inhabiting, we find the matrix of all others. Each man's only option for being is to be in the world. One of Heidegger's structures that describes inhabiting is "being-in-the-world" (*In-der-Welt-sein*). Being-in-the-world implies being with others and sustaining a common world.

Inhabiting the World: I take the structure "being-in-the-world" to introduce Pascal Béguin's (2007) concept "Inhabiting the world", in which there are heterogeneous professional worlds related through a process where a group of actors use their skills, their competences, their strategies to organise these worlds and therefore, build a common world. "*Actors do not negotiate their worlds but reaffirm their identities*". Hence, the need for a common world where professional worlds are coordinated and can inhabit it from their conceptual frameworks but constructing a common operational framework. "*The concept of world postulates a situated creativity*".

In these recovered factories, there is the world of the workers, which initially replicates the previous system, and the world of the former owners, which endures through their practices. The ways of inhabiting each world differ in knowledge, experience, seniority and interests. Through a process of appropriation that integrates both worlds, a common world emerges.

Inhabiting Uncertainty

After the pandemic or any other types of crisis, it seems necessary to think about the future of work in this kind of contingency. I therefore introduce a few words such as "urgency" and "uncertainty" to express two variables that will be present in our future work. Urgency corresponds to unthinkable or unexpected events. Reinforcing this idea Dewey (1952) says that in an immutable order, the object of knowledge, other than finding certainty, is to pursue certainty so as to direct change in line with genuinely human goals and interests. However in a changing world, where absolute certainty disappears, intelligence constitutes the main function to direct change and adapt it to our purposes. In novel and complex situations that cannot be solved with existing knowledge, we ignore what is at stake or what we are risking with every decision taken, that's when uncertainty appears.

In 1927, Heisenberg formulated the "uncertainty principle", which revealed to physics that the mere fact of observing a phenomenon in order to measure it causes its conditions to change; i.e., reality is modified when we try to observe it. In other words, the observer intervenes and modifies the object conditions each time he wants to study it. Following Jonas (1996) about responsible action, I propose the concept "Inhabiting uncertainty". We are as responsible for actions taken in the past as in the present since with both of them we are building the future.

Inhabiting uncertainty, we must be responsible for what we observe and what we fail to observe; for what we reject and what we aspire to. We should appeal to creativity and inventiveness in order to build this desired future collectively.

In our research on recovered factories carried out in 2008, our responsible action was when trimming was focused on jobs analysis. For this presentation, I recover socioeconomic data obtained at that time and I intend to point out their value. In 2001, fearing losing their jobs, workers at recovered factories were – unawarely – inhabiting uncertainty and giving rise to a new way of producing goods, know-how, a new group indentity, all this was achieved through their creativity, and which is more relevant, collectively.

Inhabiting Today: in his doctoral thesis, Ramón Vanaquen Navarro (2018) states that in globalisation times and in contemporary inhabiting a new habit emerges: virtualisation. Globally connected, virtual reality enables to experience multiple habits of inhabiting, such as playing, learning, teaching, communicating, organising and producing.

Inhabiting Time: Chesnaux's (1996) tells us that man *"inhabits his time"* when he lives his present, looking at his past and at his future as well. He argues for a democratic temporality involving "a present as an opening to the future through resourcing in the past", a true dialectic between "field of experience" and "horizon of expectation". Pierre Bourdieu says, "the presence of the past in the present makes possible the presence of the present in the future".

Thinking the Past. Paul Ricoeur (1985) says that one way of restoring the past and not forgetting it is to work with the notion of collective memory. He also proposes the need to write the past so that the burden of the past falls on the future.

Another view belongs to Marc Bloch (2001) who proposes rescuing the past through footprints obtained from a historical consciousness that can explain the causes, motives and reasons why someone did something. And Finally, according to Harshaw (1997), to think these traces towards the future, - and from a literary point of view - is to consider "unrealised potentialities" in the past, as they represent "what still remains as a project".

In recovered factories, workers inhabited their "past" by reproducing previous organisation and practices, their "present" by learning to manage and their "future" by constructing innovative ways of inhabiting it. The re-reading of our work has allowed us to update the forgotten and to collectively reconstruct the workers' experiences and our own ones. Finally, I consider unrealized potentialities in the past when I take this research and extract only socio-economical and self-management processes to give them deeper analysis.

Thinking the present from the prospective of the present, I choose Valéry Pueyo (2020) who tells us that *"Prospective does not try to promise a better world but to build, experiment and support alternatives starting from the experiences of the "present" and in the present". "The purpose of the prospective of the present is to experiment, to face the challenges of daily life, to identify the tensions that, in the mismatches, appear between the macro and micro levels".* Prospective seeks to innovate by describing future needs.

My proposition regarding prospective and the present is to inhabit uncertainty. By living the present as it presents itself without looking away from the past and the future, we can inhabit time in "full length" through experience and through hope in the realization of projects that give meaning to uncertainty.

Thinking the Future: For Heidegger, the main phenomenon of time is the future. The human being is not confined to the present, but always projects himself into the future. OECD defines prospective as a set of systematic attempts to take a long-term view of the future of science, technology, economy and society in order to identify emerging technologies that are likely to produce the greatest economic and/or social benefits. I agree with Valerie Pueyo (2020), who, based on Berger, says that *in times of crisis, prospective helps us to think about and create desirable futures.* By observing the action deployed in recovered factories, it is possible to project a proposal for the future, because the self-managed economy is not only a way out that the working class has developed to face crisis, but it must be seen as a perspective of a future economy as an alternative to neoliberal capitalism.

Emancipation/Alienation

I choose to explain Marx's emancipation/alienation binomial because in recovered factories workers managed to emancipate themselves. To the author, alienation resides in the strangeness of the work performed by a worker and emancipation in the use of his free and creative time. Work is external to the worker and only satisfies his essential needs. Alienation then has to do with the relation of the worker to the object of his work and to his own activity, which in both cases are alien to him and do not belong to him. The process of these recovered factories went from alienation to emancipation when their workers became owners of their actions and of their decisions. Both, the object of work and the process become meaningful through their appropriation. The ability to negotiate constitutes a form of emancipation of work from the domination of capital and are at the heart of the political debate on the future of work.

But above all it appears the essential of emancipation which is the creativity and inventiveness put in value to solve a complex and adverse situation.

Why is Self-Management the Key in the Recovered Factories?
The self-management experience allows the appropriation of material resources and transforms the old capitalist management into a management technique at the service of workers. Production-units self-management processes contributed to the development of a new management model that linked the factories with other actors and social movements. A new proposal for cooperativism appeared and modified the inherited work processes. Workers' control over the production process strengthens a new management technology that encompasses all aspects. Through their actions, these organisations recovered terms such as "common wellbeing" and "citizenship".

Palomino (2020) says that currently, much of business literature on personal management, under the title of "new form of management" reflects this relationship between capital and labor proposed in the recovered factories. Expert advise delegating and empowering. The authority and control of workers should be exercised with a view to ensuring their loyalty and the organisations of work should be a responsibility and commitment of each one.

4   Result

Recovered factories are part of a collective experience in the midst of a violent economic, productive and social crisis. Those recovered factories are a reflection of the impossibility of postponing. The actions taken were necessary in order to keep their jobs, clients, colleagues, knowledge, skills, raw materials, among others. The urgency appears in the face of the crisis through unthinkable or non-existent events, which led them to change the paradigm since the system was put in check.

As for the initial question of what the transition will be like after crisis' times, one possible answer is what happened in the recovered factories as they moved from a pyramidal and hierarchical organisational culture to cooperative and solidarity-based forms. To stop obeying and to make their own decisions. By building a collective identity from their labor practices. By transforming alienation into labor emancipation by negotiating their working conditions. By making their own decisions about work processes. By directing change and adapting it to their purposes through inventiveness and creativity.

The most common words used by them are self-management and autonomy, masters of their destiny, but also cooperation, learning and inventiveness. All these actions contribute to think and build our future work.

5   Discussion

With the Pandemic, processes that were in developing stage or embryonic state had to be implemented urgently. Making the parallelism with the approach to recovered factories, a possibility of analysis appears here to take into account in future labor situations. If we think of the Argentine case as a test laboratory on an event that transformed the reference situation and that was replicated in our continent and in Europe, it may help us to inhabit other crises.

But, as ergonomists, what have we learned while going through this experience under urgency?

Some ideas -that must continue to evolve-, have shown us that the possibility of projecting ourselves towards a new horizon should not be based on prescription but on proscription. We must use prospective to think the future because prospective ergonomics is concerned with future needs. As ergonomists our work is built with each client. The impossibility of going to the field leads us to create new and hybrid ways of approach. We were also able to see which professional sectors, with protocolized urgency, had to resort to the non-protocolized knowledge of experience so that the system would not collapse. In urgency, action is reactive, so, the novelty in urgency will be our inventive capacity. To inhabit uncertainty, ergonomists should be able to rethink our own work collectively.

6   Conclusion

In the face of the crisis, it seems necessary to build a "culture of exception", based on cooperation, solidarity, self-management, assembly and care for others.

A democratic use of scientific knowledge appears as central in the linkage of researchers and workers, but more important is the product of this linkage, since the idea of action-research allows the appropriation of knowledge. One way of thinking about current and future work is to analyze the actions implemented by workers facing urgency and uncertainty produced by the paradigm shift and the globalized conflict. The object of knowledge is to pursue certainty so as to direct change according to genuinely human goals and interests.

Although crises change in scale, urgency and uncertainty will be repeated, it will then be necessary for us to integrate them as a constant in life and work. Future work will be variable, contextually mutable, articulated with other knowledge, circumstantial and labile. Workers will be more creative and will absorb change more quickly. Apparently, change will be the constant.

References

Béguin P.: Innovation et cadre sociocognitif des Interactions concepteurs/opérateurs. Le travail humain. **70**, 369–390 (2007). ISBN 9782130561361

Bloch, M.: Apología para la historia o el oficio del historiador, trad. M. Jiménez y D. Zaslavsky. 2a ed. rev. Fondo de Cultura Económica (2001)

Bourdieu, P.: Méditations pascaliennes. Seuil, Paris (1997)

Chesneaux, J.: Habiter le temps, p. 339. Coll, Société, Éds Bayard (1996)

Cuenca, G., Zotta, G.: Ergonomic Analysis Jobs in Recovered Factories. IOS Press. pp. 549–551 (2012)

Dewey J.: La búsqueda de la certeza. México D.F., F. C. E., p. 175 (1952)

Harshaw, B.: Ficcionalidad y campos de referencia. En Teorías de la ficción literaria. Arco Libros, Madrid (1997)

Heidegger, M.: 1964. L'Être et le temps, Paris, Gallimard (1927)

Heidegger, M.: Conferencias y artículos. Ediciones del Serbal, Barcelona (1994)

Jonas, H.: The phenomenon of life: toward a philosophical biology. Harper and Row, New York (1966)

Marx, K.: "Sobre la cuestión judía", *Escritos de Juventud*, pp. 461–490. FCE, México (1987)

Palomino (2020), El marco social y político de los interrogantes sobre el futuro del trabajo. Revista del Plan Fénix año 10 número 80.

Pueyo V. (2020). Pour une Prospective du Travail. Les mutations et transitions du travail à hauteur d'Hommes. Anthropologie sociale et ethnologie. Université Lumière Lyon 2.

Ricœur, P.: Temps et récit 3. Le temps raconté, Paris, Seuil (1985)

Ricœur, P.: Soi-même comme un autre. Seuil, Paris (1990)

Vanaquen Navarro Ramón: El concepto de habitar. Tesis doctoral bajo el Programa Nacional de Becas CONACYT, Méjico (2018)

Territory as a Construct of Work Activity and an Operative Dispositive For and Through Action

Liliana Cunha[1,2](✉) ⓘ and Marianne Lacomblez[1,2] ⓘ

[1] Faculty of Psychology and Educational Sciences of the University of Porto, Porto, Portugal
[2] Centre for Psychology at University of Porto (CPUP), Porto, Portugal
{lcunha,lacomb}@fpce.up.pt

Abstract. The relationships between territory and work are still insufficiently explored from the point of view of the work activity [1]. In what way does the territory cease to be only the "ground" where the history of work activities and its protagonists are daily constructed to become a category of analysis?

The territory is asymmetric, and it often assumes the status of constraint, as evidenced in the case study in the road passenger transport sector we present here. However, the territory is also acted upon, it is enriched through the actors' work activity. How does the activity compensate territorial inequalities? How to methodologically apprehend these territorialization processes?

The concept of place emerges full of pertinence from this analysis as mediator and the visible side of these processes. Given their heuristic nature, we identify these places as "markers", material or symbolic, of how the work activity contributes to the reconfiguration of the territory.

Keywords: Territory · Work activity · Territorialization processes

1 Introduction

The territory must be interpreted, and not only taken into account, as a variable describing the differences in economic or employment distribution. Territory is more than just a physical set of material landscapes together with their biophysical system, it is the product of its protagonists, their interactions, powers, capacities, and initiatives [2, 3]. The territory is, then, socially built, and it can congregate simultaneously coexistence, conflict, and contingence [4].

Hence, we abandon the notion of territory as an object, *per se*, and instead we consider it a process, though it is frequently envisioned as heterodetermined (as a political institution), and less as revealing about the work activities, which is our goal here.

Such a territorial perspective, which encompasses the point of view of the work activity, goes beyond translating the methodological option "for a scale of analysis that stays closer to reality, a kind of descriptive thoroughness (…). Understanding the territory <u>demands</u> [our own emphasis], such an understanding since the beginning" [5,

© The Author(s), under exclusive license to Springer Nature Switzerland AG 2021
N. L. Black et al. (Eds.): IEA 2021, LNNS 219, pp. 115–122, 2021.
https://doi.org/10.1007/978-3-030-74602-5_18

pp. 62−63], and reveals there is an analysis category missing, the one that distinguishes macro and micro perspectives [6], once the territory is, in itself, its synthesis.

In order to demonstrate the pertinence of this theoretical assumption, that the work activity intervenes in the territorialization processes – that is, in the processes inherent to the territory production and development −, we will revisit a study developed in the transport sector. The "territory sensitivity" [5] when planning a public transport service is particularly noticeable in the case of road passenger transport. The bus routes suffer changes according to the densities some places produce and to their mobility generating poles.

In redesigning the layout of the mobility networks, some territories tend to be left out of the discussions inscribed on the "mobile society" paradigm [7]. The case study we hereby present takes place in a territory with such characteristics − it has a vast area and a low population density.

Despite the widespread awareness that the territory characteristics play a role in the production of differentiated mobilities (e.g., territory geomorphology, access structures, population density and type of economic activities), sometimes reproducing social inequalities in the access to the public transport service, the added value of an analysis of the drivers activity in a context with these characteristics consists in also highlighting alternatives to compensate such inequalities [8].

This study also raised other questions: how to methodologically apprehend such territory appropriation and transformation through the work activity?

2 Objective/Question

As far as the mobility projects are concerned, the designers of the transport networks play the starring role in the definition of the bus lines, their perimeter and boundaries, and of the bus stops. Which conceptions of territory do their practices reveal?

How do the workers that use this transport network in their activity on a daily basis take part in the debate about the evolution of the mobility path? May their knowledge about life in this territory grant them the status of legitimate actors in the redesign of the mobility network? Which mediators can be used to methodologically apprehend the territorialization processes through the work activity?

3 Methodology

The research was part of a project to redesign the public transport network by bus in a municipality in the center region of Portugal, characterized as a "predominantly rural" territory.

The improvement of the public transport services in rural areas and low on population density is considered as a matter of priority to foster territorial cohesion and social equity. Well, the mobility conditions by public transport in this territory have the following traces: (i) scarce offer – limited to two journeys per day, in each bus line, at the beginning and at the end of the day, to meet roughly the school schedules, and also limited to working days and to the school year; (ii) lack of interface between the different lines (radial configuration of the transport network); (iii) there is no offer of journeys adapted to the work schedules in force at the local companies (e.g., wood industry;

metalworking industry; pharmaceutical industry); (iv) reinforcement of the transport offer circumscribed to the day of the weekly fair.

As a result, the drivers work schedules are, in this case, "cut" and defined by the pendular movements. Additionally, some of the journeys are "empty", because the passengers ride is only in one direction in each journey (from the outskirts to the center in the morning; on the other way round at the end of the day), as stated by the drivers, as if their activity demanded a permanent confrontation with alterity - an "empty" circulation, instead of driving passengers, is itself a constraint.

3.1 Participants

The team of designers who took part in the redesign of this transport network was composed by three engineers, two geographers and one mathematician.

All the drivers (N = 6) from this network joined the sample, whose characterization is presented in the following table (see Table 1).

Table 1. Drivers' characterization'

Drivers	Gender	Age	Seniority in the company (years)
M1	Female	36	1
M2	Male	37	6
M3	Male	54	8
M4	Male	35	2
M5	Male	58	19
M6	Male	54	9

3.2 Data Collection and Analysis

Observation of the drivers' activity (around 160 h), as well as interviews with each of them (average duration of 1 h) and with different territory stakeholders (representatives from local authorities and company) (average duration of 1 h 40 m), and members of the design team responsible for redesigning the layout of the mobility network (average duration of 1 h).

These analyses gave a strong contribution for a better understanding and interpretation of the territory's cartography, developed by the designers' team. In return, as the work activity contribution was not inscribed in this cartography, we highlighted later on traces, both physical and symbolic, capable of illustrating such legacy, to avoid that one territory might "hide" the other and exploring the "sense of place" for the work activity.

4   Results and Discussion

4.1   The Territory as a Set of Space-Related Indicators

The designers and the drivers reveal a different appropriation of the territory. The first look at the territory, invoking Latour [9], as a *matter-of-fact*. An example thereto is the collection of indicators (e.g., populational density; mobility generator poles; origin-destination matrices of movements), and the creation of maps – using cartography and Geographic Information Systems as resources –, considered the main tools to know and represent the territory (see Fig. 1 and Fig. 2).

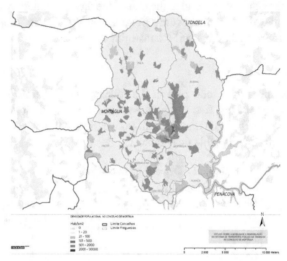

Fig. 1. The designers' perspective: representation of the territory according to the variation in populational density – "why are the dynamics or deficits produced here and not somewhere else?"

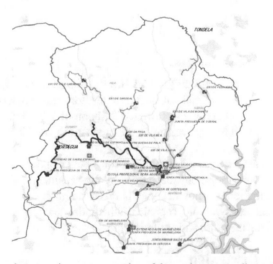

Fig. 2. The designers' perspective: representation of the territory according to the density generator poles and, consequently, mobility poles (e.g., schools, health center providers, public services) – "how do the uses of public transport change in these locations?"

In order to illustrate the contrast between this perspective of territory and the one translated by the work activity we will hereafter refer to a specific bus line — "Meligioso - Mortágua" – identified with the bolder line in Fig. 2.

4.2 When a Territory "Hides" Another Territory: Which Territorializations Are Produced by the Work Activity?

These drivers live in the municipality where they work and are legitimate actors in that territory. Unlike an urban context, here the drivers know their clients, their names, where they live, and their distance to the nearest bus stop.

The observations and the interviews reveal strategies that are followed in the work activity so to shorten the distance for some territory inhabitants to the transport network and to expand the limits of the line layout. The introduction of unplanned detours in specific points to transport those who are further from the route or making more stops than defined (see Fig. 3), are strategies the drivers develop to compensate the inequalities the transport system ends up reproducing.

The analysis to these territorialization processes enables a heuristic opening to the concept of territory, as it moves from the territory as a result (as the activity "ground") to its production.

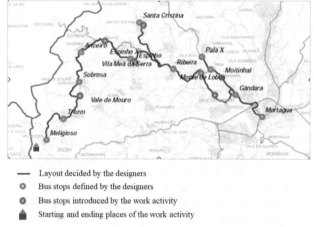

— Layout decided by the designers
○ Bus stops defined by the designers
● Bus stops introduced by the work activity
▉ Starting and ending places of the work activity

Fig. 3. Representation of a line in the transport network conceived by the mobility designers (base layer) and of the signs of the deviations made along this line, and solidified in the territory, due to and in the drivers' activity (layer with the signs of the activity)

The knowledge of the drivers as citizens-workers from this territory is brought to the activity to answer the population actual needs: is it necessary or not to make a detour to the line layout to "catch" someone that stays far away? Is it necessary to stop elsewhere, even though it is not expected nor properly signed? The mobility potential that may benefit those who use public transport comes partly from the drivers' activity in this context, and from the alternatives that activity has been consolidating. As such, we share the reflection that space needs time thickness, silent repetitions, slow maturations, to become territory [10].

Following this reasoning it is important to clarify the "equivocation of the heritages" [11, p. 5, free translation] of designers and drivers. In fact, we cannot ignore that they "(…) belong to two different worlds and if they are different it is, before anything else, because the solutions (…) they advocate for the problems result from the different spot occupied by ones and the others (…)" [12, p. 200, free translation].

Let's say that rather than a *matter-of-fact*, the territory constitutes a *matter-of-concern* [9] of debate and of dialectic between different scales of analysis [5]. For example, debate about the notion of public service that crosses the drivers' activity, reinforcing that the guarantee of their delivery cannot leave hidden the inherent conditions to access such service.

This study also led us to additional questions from a methodological point of view: which mediators can be used to apprehend the territorialization processes through the work activity?

We have dared to try and represent the territory in a map that does not considers exclusively the indicators used by the designers but shows an overlapping layer (see Fig. 3), with reference to bifurcations, interactions or forms of sociability that set up the territorialisations processes. These processes unravel daily, with more or less repetition, in specific locations. Still, there is always something unprecedented about it.

We have explored the sense of "place" assumed by the drivers as spots along the way where there are bifurcations, and there are alternatives that the activity proposes to face the asymmetries of resources reserved to those places (e.g., distance greater than 3 km/1.86 miles between stops; stops with no shelter). And we have identified these places as "markers", physical or symbolic, of the territory. They are pivotal-points [13] in the interactions and the uses of the territory by the citizens.

As an example, we have identified as physical markers places where a stop is improvised (see Fig. 3), for example, an outdoor, a post box on the road, but also the doorstep of a café because the effective stop offers no shelter for the passengers. Other examples are related to the place where the journey begins and ends (see Fig. 3) — in this case, it is actually the driver's house, bearing in mind that the drivers in this network were assigned the line closer to their houses; the bus is taken home, avoiding additional costs for the company if the bus had to drive "empty" around 35 km/27.75 miles until the collection site, located in a different municipality. In turn, examples of symbolic markers are: the inexistence of separation between the passengers entry and exit out of the bus (there are no barriers to entry, the passengers do not show the commutation ticket – they are everyday passengers!); the existence of "regular" seats in the bus (e.g., one of the drivers has established an order, based on age criterium, reserving the front seats for smaller children and the adults in the back of the bus); or the definition of a place inside the bus to place the schoolbags (thus avoiding carrying the schoolbags while standing).

Unlike a territory approach based on indicators – for example, count the number of passengers per stop properly signed along the path, as the designers do it – the identification of these markers, from the work activity perspective, reveals other places that shape the territory. They are places of debate and normative activity, by the work activity, they consolidate interactions and mark collective identities [14].

Hence, to address the territory as an operative device implies showing its permanent update, its daily maturation, as something acknowledged and shared as a collective resource.

5 Conclusions

This study allowed us to reinforce the idea that the territory is not merely a form to index the phenomena under analysis; it is not simply a geographic invariant of the work activity; nor is it limited to the observation slots the researchers cut out and define as their spaces for context appropriation. Here is the challenge: if the territory is not only a space described by the researcher, if it is acted upon and its existence is permanently kept or renewed by the work activity, how to depict the territory from "the inside"? How to reveal the territorialization processes, built from discreet daily actions? And how can they be given back to all the territory legitimate actors? These are the questions that make us pursue the debate on territory as a collective resource.

The territory-place relationship, considering the place not as a strict location, but as a pivotal-point, a material or symbolic marker of the territorialization processes, makes it possible to explore how the work activity contributes to produce territory. The concept of place is the visible side of the territory and it is the synthesis of the debates about the norms and values of the protagonists, workers, and citizens.

These findings, and their discussion with the designers, were determinant for the redesign of the local transport network and the extension of its territorial coverage.

Nevertheless, the territorialization processes keep evolving, following the changes in the places where their main users start the journey, and their needs: some places will disappear, while other will reify.

Despite the petitions the population does every now and then, asking for a deviation or asking for an addition stop, the request is not always attended nor is the time to answer compatible with the evolution of the population's needs. The challenge then persists: how to guarantee the sustainability of the territorialization processes while at the same time settling their recognition as a territory asset?

References

1. Boudra, L., Béguin, P., Delecroix, B., Pueyo, V.: Taking into account the territory in occupational risks prevention. The case of work activity in waste sorting centers. Le Travail Humain **82**, 99–128 (2019)
2. Reis, J.: Ensaios de economia impura. Almedina, Coimbra (2007)
3. Vanier, M.: Territoires, territorialité, territorialisation: controverses et perspectives. Presses Universitaires de Rennes, Rennes (2009)
4. Lefebvre, H.: La production de l'espace. L'Homme et la Société. Anthropos, Paris (1974)
5. Reis, J.: Uma epistemologia do território. Estudos Sociedade e Agricultura **13**(1), 51–74 (2005)
6. Berdoulay, V., Entrikin, J.: Lieu et sujet: Perspectives théoriques. L'Espace géographique **2**, 111–120 (1998)

7. Cunha, L., Lacomblez, M., Schwartz, Y.: Traces de l'activité et tracés de son analyse dans deux pays du(des) «Sud(s)»: Les débats qui dépassent le rapport entre empirie et théorie. In: Prévot-Carpentier, M., Paltrinieri, L., Nicoli, M. (eds.) Le philosophe et l'enquête de terrain: Le cas du travail contemporain, pp. 149–166. Octarès Éditions, Toulouse (2020)
8. Cunha, L., Lacomblez, M.: From the "terrain" to "territory": Which contributions from mobility and bus drivers' activity towards local development? Work 41, 6156–6161 (2012)
9. Latour, B.: Reassembling the Social - an introduction to Actor-Network-Theory. Oxford University Press, New York (2005)
10. Marié, M.: Un territoire sans nom. Pour une approche des sociètés locales. Librairie des Méridiens, Paris (1982)
11. Schwartz, Y.: Travail et Philosophie: Convocations mutuelles. Octarès Éditions, Toulouse (1992)
12. Oddone, I., Re, A., Briante, G.: Redécouvrir l'expérience ouvrière. Editions sociales, Paris (1981)
13. De La Garza, C.: Aportes del método de los "puntos pivote" a un estudio prospectivo de seguridad en el campo de la interoperabilidad ferroviaria. Laboreal 1(1) (2005).
14. Banos, V.: Réflexion autour de la dimension spatiale des processus normatifs. Géographie et cultures 72, 80–98 (2009)

Reward, Social Support and General Health in Colombian Teleworkers. A Mixed Study

Jonathan Duque Porras$^{(\boxtimes)}$ and Luz Amparo Pérez Fonseca$^{(\boxtimes)}$

Universidad Nacional de Colombia, 110111 Bogotá, Colombia
{jduquep,laperezf}@unal.edu.co

Abstract. The expansion of teleworking, driven by the COVID-19 pandemic, places at the center of the research agenda, the possible implications for the teleworker´s health. This research aims to explore the lived experience in reward, social relationships and mental health in Colombian teleworkers, reported in phenomenological interviews, and to compare in which extent such experience matches with the scores obtained in sub-scales of recompense, social support, and the Goldberg general health scale, in a sample of Colombian teleworkers. A convergent mixed method QUAN + QUAL = corroboration, was used. The participants were adults, living in Colombia, with a teleworking contract for more than six months. Recruitment was done through social networks (Facebook and Twitter); a typical case sampling method was used. A comparison of the quantitative and quantitative results was made according to the common concepts identified in the two data sets. We identified in which way the data converge, diverge, or expand the understanding of the results. The quantitative and qualitative results confirmed each other in all cases. The main protective factors for the Colombian teleworker health identified were being able to avoid the use of public transport, saving time, and the comfort and tranquility of work from home. The main risk factors identified were reduction in social activity, reduction in physical activity and overwork.

Keywords: Telework · Reward · Social support · Mental health · COVID-19

1 Telework

Telework refers to the work modality in which the worker carries out his work through information and communication technologies (TIC), without requiring his or her presence in a specific place. At the present day, this modality of work has been positioned as a first option for workers and employers. The consulting firm in solutions for telework *MySammy* [1], reports that, by 2019, 20% of the world's workforce teleworks. In Colombia, the implementation of the teleworking modality has experienced a constant growth in the last decade. According to the Ministry of Telecommunications [2], between 2012 and 2018, the number of Teleworkers in the country went from more than 31,000 in 2012, to almost 123,000 in 2018.

We highlight the contingent character that has taken the modality of teleworking during the social isolation produced by covid-19. A survey carried out in Spain with

N. L. Black et al. (Eds.): IEA 2021, LNNS 219, pp. 123–130, 2021.
https://doi.org/10.1007/978-3-030-74602-5_19

280 people [3], found that 40% of them continued working during the crisis in the telework modality. In Colombia, the Ministry of Labor issued guidelines indicating to employers that they must authorize teleworking for all those workers for whom it is possible (Resolution 385, March 12, 2020).

Telework Risks and Benefits for the Teleworker. The main topics investigated are job satisfaction and quality of life. The studies mostly report an improvement in quality of life and an increase in job satisfaction [4]. Nevertheless, some studies have reported overwork [5], perception of workaholic [6], and conflicts between work and personal life responsibilities [7].

Regarding mental health, the main protective factors of teleworking identified in the studies were the increase in autonomy [6], work flexibility [8], reduction in travel times and being able to avoid the use of the public transport [9]. With respect to the risk factors for mental health that have been identified, the main risks are associated with a decrease in social interaction accompanied by a feeling of isolation, perception of loneliness and loss of contact with peers [6]. Regarding to overwork, this causes recovery times to get shorter and shorter [8, 10, 11]. All these mediating factors can lead to a higher level of fatigue and to an increase risk of exhaustion [10].

The research about teleworking experience in Colombian context remains scarce. The analysis of the teleworkers experience, their working conditions, and the implications for their health, can provide important information for the development of strategies that seek to eliminate or mitigate the negative effects related to teleworking and enhance its positive effects.

2   Objective

The objective of this research was, to explore the lived experience in reward, social relationships, and mental health in Colombian teleworkers, reported in phenomenological interviews, and to compare in which extent such experience matches with the scores obtained in sub-scales of reward, social support, and the Goldberg general health scale, in a sample of Colombian teleworkers.

3   Theoretical Framework

Reward. The self-regulation of the individual depends on the successful exchange through social roles in adult life [12]. Based on this theory, Siegrist [13], develops the work stress model: effort-reward imbalance. His model suggests that the perception of the worker of an imbalance between the effort he invests in carrying out his work and the rewards he receives, promotes a state of emotional distress and sustained tension that affects his health [12].

Social Support. Some studies have shown that receiving adequate social support can have a moderating effect on work stress. The demand-control-social support model [14] propose that the higher risk of negative effects on psychological well-being and illness occurs in workers with high demands at work, low autonomy, and low social support [15].

Mental Health. Mental health has been defined as: A state that can be indicated by moods and positive or negative affects. As a process that is indicated by the behaviors that are carried out; for example, an effort behavior or a resignation behavior. And also as the outcome of a process, such as suffering a loss or a significant event. Mental health has been associated with personal characteristics such as coping styles, personality traits and competitiveness [16].

3.1 Methodology

A convergent mixed method QUAN + QUAL = corroboration was used. The participants were adults, living in Colombia, with a teleworking contract for more than six months Recruitment was done through social networks (Facebook and Twitter); a typical case sampling method was used.

We did a parallel collection of qualitative and quantitative data. For qualitative data, a scripted semi-structured individual interview was used. It included 10 questions about the teleworker experience at his work. The sessions were held in a video-call with the google meets platform in the free version. The quantitative data were collected with three questionnaires answered on the web platforms surveymonkey.com and survey-planet.com. The quantitative variables were: 1) Sociodemographic data; 2) Score in the subscale of Reward (Effort-Reward Imbalance) Spanish version [17]; 3) Score on the social support subscale of the Questionnaire JCQ (Job Content Questionnaire) version in Spanish [18]; and 4) Score in the Goldberg General Health Scale (GHQ-12), 12-item version [19].

Data Analysis. Qualitative data were analyzed following the phenomenological method descriptive proposed by Moustakas [20]. Quantitative data were analyzed with univariate descriptive statistics of the results on each scale. The sample was divided by marital status, sex, and age range into groups. A bivariate analysis was performed with the Mann-Whitney nonparametric U test for independent samples. The SPSS software was used. Secondly, for the data integration, a comparison of the quantitative and quantitative results was made according to the common concepts identified in the two data sets. We identified in which way the data converge, diverge, or expand the understanding of the results.

4   Outcomes

The participants were six (N = 6) Colombian teleworkers - three women and three men. Average age was 32 years (S.D: 6.52) – minimum 24 years old, maximum 42 years old. Two participants married, four singles. Three of them have children. The average length of time teleworking was 22 months (S.D: 14.59) – minimum 8 months and maximum 48 months. Educational level of all participants was technical level. All participants had an indefinite term contract. The participants were: two sellers of products and services, a quality analyst, a changes coordinator, a person in charge of training processes and a web manager. In three cases the company requires that they have a suitable workplace at home with some minimum characteristics and provides a computer with specific characteristics and with the necessary software for the job. In the other cases, the worker can access the information necessary for their work and carry out their work from any device and anywhere.

Qualitative Outcomes. The description of the shared phenomenon telework was organized into the following core themes:

Teleworking Working Conditions

- Not having to commute and not having to use the public transport allows to start the working day on time and avoid crowds and insecurity. This reduces stress, provides peace of mind, and promotes increased quantity and quality of sleep.
- Have delayed work or significant increases in workloads cause concern. Sleep and rest hours are reduced, they work longer hours and even on non-working days.

Reward

- Receive an enough payment on time, to cover all expenses, and the comfort of working at home doing what you love, makes them feel calm, comfort, satisfaction, and economic security.
- Having indefinite term contracts leads them to feel that their job stability depends only on their good performance and compliance. They do not feel their position threatened.
- Meeting colleagues and bosses with long careers in the company, as well as receiving congratulations and recognitions, reinforces the perception of job stability and promotion possibilities.

Social Support

- The group receives timely and almost immediate support from their bosses in case of doubts and incidents of the work. This makes them feel supported and secure.
- There is no constant pressure from bosses, in this way stress at work is reduced. They work more calmly, make fewer mistakes, and have a higher performance.
- Not sharing the same workspace with colleagues is seen as an advantage. In this way there are no interruptions, noise and rivalries between peers.
- The group identifies a reduction in their social activity, represented in the little "face-to-face" contact with other people. This can cause negative mood effects portrays in boredom and demotivation at work.

Mental Health

- It is difficult for the group to disconnect from work. Especially when they leave pending tasks. This situation affects the quantity and quality of sleep.
- Telework promotes good health due to the peace of mind and convenience of working at home without pressure from bosses or colleagues and not having to use a public transport system with many problems.

Affectations related to mandatory isolation (COVID-19)

- The group has had increases in the workload and has seen the need to find more activities to do without leaving home.
- The sense of social isolation has been heightened during the pandemic.

Quantitative Outcomes. The group of teleworkers, on average, receives a high reward (23.67/28) and high social support (28.83/32) in their work. On Goldberg's health scale (GHQ-12), the average scores were 18.33/48. Higher scores indicate further deterioration in health. From these results it can be stated that do not exist affectations in their psychological well-being. No statistically significant differences were found between the groups by sex, age or marital status (Table 1).

Mixed Outcomes

Table 1. Mixed outcomes

Main Concept	Average Score	Qualitative Findings	Mixed Method Meta-Inferences
Reward	**23,6/28**	*"(…) more than the money is doing what I like, that's the best. So I'm happy and peaceful" (ET1) -- "It is very good, to share more with your family, you are a little more rested on the subject of sleeping more and that you do not have to go out" (ET5) "I do not see my work threatened because I have done my work very well" (ET5) -- "My stability depends only on that, on being good at what I do. Of my performance"(ET4) --- "I cannot change the stability I currently have with this company" (ET7)*	**Confirm quantitative outcomes:** The group perceives that they receive a reward that compensates for their effort at work, this perception is congruent with the scores on the reward scale

(*continued*)

Table 1. (*continued*)

Main Concept	Average Score	Qualitative Findings	Mixed Method Meta-Inferences
Social Support	28,8 / 32	*"And so it is with my boss, support is immediate, you know you can count on him at any time" (ET1) ---- "(…)Well, I don't have pressure from my bosses, so I work my way and I'm doing well…" (ET7) "Yes of course, I feel recognized by my bosses. They like how I do my job and they have told me" (ET7) -- "That support makes me feel very happy, I think that motivates to be more loyal and more comfortable with the work" (ET4) "And the thing is that in the office environment one becomes saturated a lot, with noise, having the boss by the side, information and problems and talks with others, that saturates" (ET1) -- "Working at home is better, you work alone and have no problems with your coworkers". (ET3)*	**Confirm and expand understanding of quantitative outcomes:** The group perceives that they receive high social support at work, mainly from its immediate bosses. This perception is congruent with the scores on the Social Support scale. Peace of mind and performance benefits that allow not sharing the same workspace with colleagues and bosses are highlighted
Main Concept	Average Score	Qualitative Findings	Mixed Method Meta-Inferences
General health	18,33 / 48	*"My current mental health, excellent, I'm happy with my job, I don't handle stress, I sleep well" (ET1) "My health is good, I feel that I live less stressed, I am calm. This has been the best thing that has happened in my life, teleworking" (ET3) "(…) I think work promotes it. I think it promotes it in a positive way, because if I'm good at my job then I'm calm. That helps a lot to not have stress" (ET4)*	**Confirm quantitative outcomes:** The group perceives that their current state of health is "very good", this perception is congruent with the scores on the General Health scale. It stands out as a promoter of good health not having to use means of transport and autonomy

5 Discussion

The results of this research are consistent with the research around the world. This study contributes to the identification of distinctive features of telework: the importance of having effective communication channels for the teleworker; appreciation for avoiding the need to use the public transport (mainly in cities with mobility problems and insecurity); and the importance of family support in the teleworker activity. Note that the group of interviewees, in general, do not depend on other co-workers for the realization of their tasks. The productivity benefits of working without boss pressure and without interruptions from colleagues have been identified in several investigations [6].

Some findings in the experience of the teleworker group, such as overwork, short recovery times, reduced physical activity and the perception of low social activity, have been classified as important psychosocial risk factors that can increase stress in the worker [5]. In this study, the feeling of isolation was not investigated in any way, the issue of reducing social activity emerged during the interviews.

The limitations in this research were the small sample size and the low control over the data collection conditions. For future research it is recommended to consider gender differences in relation to the integration and organization of work and the non-work roles. In addition, to inquire in the context and individual conditions the cases where isolation and low social interaction problems are excessive.

6 Conclusions

The main findings in relation to reward and social support allow us to affirm that the subscales of reward and social support remain valid in the evaluation of teleworkers. Some additional aspects should be investigated such as the social interaction of the teleworker, communication channels and control of time and work schedule.

The mixed approach allowed us to identify specific conditions that constitute protection factors and risk factors in the group of teleworkers. The main protective health factors for the group of study participants were avoid insecurity and traffic jams, time savings, comfort of working at home, flexibility in schedules, and autonomy in the development of work. The main risk factors for the group of participants in this study were reduced social activity, overwork, inability to mentally disconnect from work, and reduced physical activity.

The main effects caused by the mandatory isolation by the covid-19 emergency, occurred in those workers linked to small companies that suffered losses. This situation increased job instability.

References

1. MySammy: Telecommuter Infographic - Statics and Stats on Telecommuting Workers (2019). https://www.mysammy.com/infographics-telecommuter
2. MINTIC. Cuarto estudio de penetración del teletrabajo en empresas colombianas (2018). https://www.teletrabajo.gov.co/622/articles-75985_archivo_pdf_estudio_teletrabajo.pdf

3. Fernández Rosa. Valoración de la experiencia con el teletrabajo durante la cuarentena en España en abril 2020. España (2020). https://es.statista.com/estadisticas/1116451/covid-19-valoracion-del-teletrabajo-durante-el-confinamiento-en-espana

4. Varas, C.I.: Apoyo organizacional percibido y satisfacción laboral en Teletrabajadores. Universidad de Barcelona (2019). https://diposit.ub.edu/dspace/bitstream/2445/145639/1/TFM_Ignacio_Varas.pdf

5. Madden, M., Jones, S.: 'Networked workers'. Pew Research Center's Internet & American Life Project. Pew Research Center, Washington, DC (2009)

6. Gallardo, E., A.: Teletrabajo: La percepción que tiene el teletrabajador sobre su salud laboral, en la ciudad de Quito. Facultad de ciencias psicológicas. Universidad central del Ecuador (2019). https://www.dspace.uce.edu.ec/bitstream/25000/19073/1/T-UCE-0007-CPS-147.pdf. Accessed 02 Jan 2021

7. Allen, T.D., Johnson, R.C., Kiburz, K.M., Shockley, K.M.: 'Work–family conflict and flexible work arrangements: deconstructing flexibility. Personnel Psychol. 66(2), 345–376 (2013)

8. Kandolin I., Tuomivaara, S.: Work, creating flexibility at work. In: Työ, terveys ja työssä atkamisajatukset. Institute of Occupational Health, Work and Human Research. vol. 41, pp. 27–41. Helsinki (2012)

9. Mello, A., Dal-Colleto, A.: Telework and its effects in Brazil. In: Telework in the 21st Century. An evolutionary perspective. International Labour Organization, Suiza (2019)

10. Messenger J.C.: Introduction. In: Telework in the 21st Century. An Evolutionary Perspective. Editorial International Labour Organization. Suiza (2019)

11. Ojala, S., Pyöriä, P.: Working at home, the prevalence and consequences: a European comparison Finland. Työpoliittinen Aikakauskirja, 56(1), 52–64 (2013)

12. Siegrist, J.: Place, social exchange and health: Proposed sociological framework. Soc. Sci. Med. 51(9), 1283–1293 (2000)

13. Siegrist, J.: Adverse health effects of high-effort/low-reward conditions. J. Occupat. Health Psychol. 1(1), 27–41 (1996)

14. Johnson, J.V., Hall, E.M.: Job strain, work place social support, and cardiovascular disease: A cross-sectional study. Am. J. Public Health 78(10), 1336–1342 (1988)

15. Kristensen, T., S.: The demand-control-support model: methodological challenges for future research. Stress Med. 11(1), 17–26 (1995)

16. Hurrel, J., Murphy, L., Sauter, S., Levi, L.: Salud Mental. In: Enciclopedia de la salud y seguridad en el trabajo. Capítulo 5, pp. 5.1–5.23 España (2012)

17. Fernández-López, J.A., Fernández-Fidalgo, M., Martín-Payo, R., Rödel, A.: Confirmatory factor analysis of the Spanish version of the effort-reward imbalance questionnaire. Atención Primaria, vol. 38, pp.465–466 (2006)

18. Gómez, V.: Assessment of psychosocial stressor at work: Psychometric properties of the Spanish version of the JCQ (Job Content Questionnaire) in Colombian workers. Revista Latinoamericana de Psicología. 43(2), 125–138 (2011)

19. Goldberg, D.P., Williams, P.: An user's guide to the General Health Questionnaire. UK: NFER-NELSON (1988)

20. Moustakas, C.: Phenomenological Research Methods. Sage Publications, USA (1994)

Integrated Operations in Times of Pandemic: Communication at Distance and Knowledge Sharing

Raquel M. Faraco$^{(\boxtimes)}$ (ID), Claudia V. Carestiato Cordeiro (ID),
and Francisco José de Castro Moura Duarte (ID)

PEP/COPPE - Universidade Federal do Rio de Janeiro, Avenida Horácio Macedo 2030, COPPE,
Bloco G, Sala G209, Cidade Universitária, Rio de Janeiro, RJ 21941-914, Brazil
{rmfaraco,claudiac}@pep.ufrj.br, fjcmduarte@coppe.ufrj.br

Abstract. The social distance imposed by the pandemic required new strategies from experts who support the decision-making for drilling rig operations, guaranteeing the flow of information. However, they have not been shown to ensure the agility provided by physical proximity. This article investigates the limits of remote work and its impact on knowledge transfer during pandemics. Based on the ergonomic work analysis methodology, the research identified that, without face-to-face interaction, the team had to develop new collective and individual strategies to ensure the construction of situational awareness and knowledge transfer. The pandemic situation made it impossible for the ergonomists to monitor the team in person, limiting observation possibilities. The continuity of the research will allow focusing on observing selected events remotely to be validated with the team members involved.

Keywords: Remote work · Knowledge sharing · Ergonomic work analysis · Integrated operations · Collective work

1 Introduction

The social distance imposed by the pandemic required new strategies from experts who support the decision-making for drilling rig operations.

This Operation Support (OPS) team brings together experts from different specialties involved in drilling, maintenance, and demobilization operations of subsea wells in oil and gas exploration fields. The OPR service functions uninterruptedly, with five groups of 13 experts rotating in 12-h shifts.

The OPS team had always worked collocated, interacting in person, sharing the same workspace. During the research, the first cases of COVID-19 appeared in Brazil, leading to changes in the means of work and the insertion of new tools, with significant and definitive transformations for the work activity. The team members were dispersed in different locations, a few in the original room and the others in remote work from different parts of the country. The monitoring of activities in person initiated by the ergonomists

N. L. Black et al. (Eds.): IEA 2021, LNNS 219, pp. 131–138, 2021.
https://doi.org/10.1007/978-3-030-74602-5_20

in September 2019 was suspended in April 2020. The social isolation required the ergonomists to find new ways of observing the OPS team.

The team's internal face-to-face communication changed to the remote communication platform, adopted by the company by the end of 2019. External communication, with offshore and other onshore teams, has mostly migrated from the telephone to the remote communication platform due to the easiness to share images and the quality of the connection. However, in the absence of face-to-face interaction, there were reports of losses in the communication agility inside the team, which could affect the anticipation of problems, delaying their solution. The researchers identified individual and collective strategies developed by the team to face remote communication limitations.

This article is part of a research that intends to integrate performance improvement and operations safety for operational support and inspection teams of offshore rigs. The study presented here has the general objective of building guidelines for the design of new OPS Centers.

In this context, this article intends to investigate the limits of remote work activity and its impact on the construction of situational awareness and knowledge transfer.

2 Methodology

The methodology adopted throughout the research followed the Activity-oriented Ergonomics and Ergonomic Work Analysis (EWA), according to Guerin [1], to identify the work characteristics and the demands for improvement under the point of view of the activity.

In the face-to-face observation stage, before the pandemic, the ergonomists interviewed around 83% of the work population. They monitored the activity of at least one representative of each team's experts. EWA tools were used to understand the work activity and Post-Occupancy Evaluation (POE) tools were used to assess the original work environment.

Systematic observations have started but were soon interrupted by the pandemic. The imposition of social distance made it impossible for ergonomists to access the workplace in person. Contact with the OPS team was made possible through the remote communication platform. Two moments of individual and semi-structured interviews were held: (a) between May and June of 2020 (b) and between August and September of 2020.

As there was already a previous face-to-face contact between ergonomists and workers, and a social construction established at the managerial and operational levels, this approach's result proved to be positive. The interviewees reported the changes they were subjected to, the facilities implemented, the difficulties faced, and the expectations regarding the ongoing transformations, which, in part, should last after the pandemic.

Although the researcher kept his camera open in all interviews, the interviewee was free to open his camera or not. As a result, eventually, it was possible to glance at the new workplaces. The repetition of themes and situations experienced, reported by workers, allowed ergonomists to gather a set of aspects common to the group, validated later with some team members. The prior knowledge of the activity that ergonomists acquired in the first phase of the research (before the pandemic) helped to understand the activity transformations from the workers' point of view.

With the ergonomists' visits suspended and the OPS team geographically dispersed, it was necessary to adapt the research objectives. The ergonomists started to monitor the changes resulting from remote work that impacted both space and work organization. Since some of these transformations may last after the pandemic, their understanding allows a necessary update to design new Operation Support (OPS) Centers.

The collected data also included at least monthly conversations with the OPS leaders, and, after September 2020, a researcher attended at least ten team meetings. These meetings occur daily at the remote communication platform, in the beginning of shifts, with an approximate duration of 40 min each. The platform allows team members to share documents and screens of the systems used.

The method adopted by the research during the pandemic did not pretend an adaptation of the tools recommended by the EWA to carry out remote observations. Observing the work activities remotely was not feasible because of the workers' geographical dispersion. Although limited if compared to the face-to-face observations, the method applied remained faithful in the intention to understand the strategies adopted by the specialists to carry out their tasks through a different and unexpected context. The results obtained were validated with the workers.

Shortly, it is planned to continue the remote observation of team meetings. This monitoring will deepen the understanding of the interaction between the OPS team and the drilling rigs in operation, with subsequent validation with the experts involved, expanding the knowledge of the work activity in the limits imposed by the pandemic on the research team.

3 Original Context, Before the Pandemic

Before the pandemic, the OPS team used to interact collocated, sharing the same work environment. The members of the OPS team collaborated internally in person. The OPS team interacted remotely with external interlocutors, teams on board of the rigs, or other onshore teams, using Information Technology and Communication (ICT) systems. Their work environment included individual work consoles with computers and two or three monitors, telephone with audio conference facilities, video wall for sharing monitoring screens, and TVs to share images from the closed-circuit television (CCTV) system of the drilling rigs. They also had two meeting rooms with video conference facilities.

Each member of the OPS team has a distinct specialty related to the stage of the drilling, maintenance, or well abandonment process, and is under the leadership of a specific manager. Therefore, it is a multidisciplinary team whose leader is not their direct manager. Another six employees worked in the same room in related activities.

The layout of the room consisted of consoles facing the video wall. The experts are distributed in the workstations by interdependence in the operation's processes. This arrangement contributes to easy communication and allows the rapid formation of workgroups, whether to participate in an audio conference, discuss a monitoring parameter on the video wall, watch a video generated by the drilling rigs CCTV system or discuss a common subject (Fig. 1).

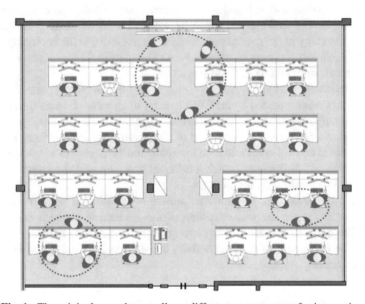

Fig. 1. The original room layout allows different arrangements for interaction.

4   Changes Due to the Pandemic

With the start of the pandemic, the company needed to adopt emergency measures, among them: (1) the geographical dispersion of the OPS team, to assure social isolation; (2) the changing of the shift regime, to reduce weekly trips; and (3) the implementation of ICT improvements, to make remote work feasible.

The OPS team members started to interact remotely, working from different locations. The criterion adopted by the company established that employees from the risk group would work in the home office and the rest would stay working in the original office or start working remotely in offices of the company close to their residences. The objective was to avoid trips and reduce commuting, as several team members came from different Brazilian states. In December 2020, the working population's monthly average working from home was 42% (Fig. 2).

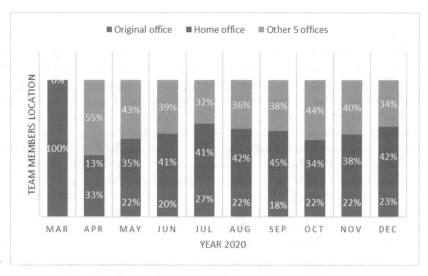

Fig. 2. Team members location during the pandemic.

5   Comparison and Results

The interviews revealed that the team's geographical dispersion had a direct impact on work activity. Although it did not impede carrying out the tasks, it required new team strategies. In distance work, the exchange of information and experiences between team members has changed substantially. The work activity took a different form, without the intense interaction of the face-to-face work.

The original collocated work had allowed the team members to interact more: (1) One could listen to the speech of another at their side while talking on the telephone with others involved in the process, intervening to participate and contribute with their expertise to the analysis and solution of an issue; (2) one could quickly call the attention of another to a monitoring detail on the video wall; (3) one could ask a question to another without interrupting him at an inappropriate time. In all these situations, because there was oral and visual communication, the discussion could expand and quickly involve other experts present in the room, building a collective representation of the problem and discussing possible risks and solutions. As a result, the developments ended up involving the team more broadly. Even those who did not contribute directly to a particular analysis could closely follow the solution.

In the new reality of remote work, the research identified significant differences. Remote discussions, most of the time via chat (text message with the possibility of attaching documents and images), usually involved only those called to discuss a problem. Chat groups are numerous and often set up for a specific discussion. If someone were not included in the chat, it would be difficult to find out about the meeting, impacting problems anticipation and solutions agility. The following speech of a team member exemplifies the issue: *"It turns out that the impact is great because there is a delay of the information that would have arrived faster if everyone were in the same room.*

Something happens and may take a long time to be informed. A loss on a well started yesterday. I only knew because the drilling rig chemist called me."

The research identified, through conversations with OPS team leaders, new strategies applied collectively using the company's communication platform. At the beginning of the shift, a daily meeting was included, sharing information about wells operations, generally without video for better audio. A chat group was also created for the OPS team, where each member could formalize information about their specialty during the shift, using text messages with the possibility of sharing documents and images.

The research also identified individual strategies adopted by team members. Interviews indicated the need for more attention to monitoring parameters when working remotely, though most of these team members had reduced screens' availability. OPS team members also reported looking for more accurate information about events in the chat message history, although the number of chat groups is enormous. The speech presented next, from a team member following chats with events in two different wells, exemplifies the issue: *"When you arrive, you have to read* [the chat history] *to keep up with what's going on. Yesterday I had an operational situation that I thought was dangerous unless they had done an oil cleaning".* The specialist contacted another offshore team who first said the equipment was clean and shortly afterwards said it was not clean. The rig team claimed it was clean but with no details because the shift had changed just before. "[Searching the chat history], *I found a record that it had already been cleaned. It was not the best cleaning... but it was clean."* The equipment in question remains in the well for up to 20 years. *"There is a great risk of having oil and gas trapped underneath. When removed, you need to be careful. The proximity* [of the OPS team members] *gives agility* [to communication]. *In the distance, you need to be more attentive, looking carefully for problems."*

Since the company adopted the remote work in an emergency, there was no time to implement ICT and physical resources in the workers' homes. The company quickly provided external access to the systems, but not all residences had a high-speed internet connection with the necessary quality. Sometimes it was required a cell phone as a backup, other times the audio of a remote meeting could oscillate. Regarding physical resources, as corporate notebooks were initially intended for occasional use, not all specialists had one in conditions for continuous use. The notebook is not the most suitable equipment for OPS team members to carry out their activities. Due to the typical characteristics of Integrated Operations (IO), the original work environment had dedicated workstations with two or three monitors, videowall, and TV. Most team members do not have a dedicated physical space and equipment at home that can mirror the original workstation, including desk, chair, lighting, air conditioning, and noise control. In addition, experts working from home continued to work on a shift basis (night shift from 7 pm to 7 am; day shift from 7 am to 7 pm) though, during the pandemic, family members were all at home. In addition to spouses working remotely, classes at schools and universities throughout 2020 remained almost exclusively remote in Brazil.

6 Discussion

The results indicate that the OPS team's internal interaction impacts two processes in particular: (1) The construction of collective situational awareness and cognitive synchronization: Chat interactions are frequent but segmented into events and specialties. Remotely, each team member is very focused on the activities of their specialty. The circulation of information between specialties is dependent on the OPS team leader's effort to encourage the sharing of information and on the individual response of each member of the team. (2) The knowledge transfer between team members: The lack of face-to-face interactions weakens the trust between team members, critical for knowledge transfer. Besides, tacit knowledge originated from work experience is difficult to transmit orally or in writing. There is a lack of interdisciplinary spaces for sharing work experiences. The adoption of remote work immediately at the beginning of the pandemic was possible because of the company's efforts to provide the necessary ICT improvements and the OPS team's cohesive relationship, based on the daily face-to-face work. It is expected that trust will be partially lost with the pandemic extending and the team's constant renewal. Segmented and less spontaneous communications can also result in difficulties in the knowledge gaps identification that would be easily recognized and corrected in collocated work.

According to Shon [2], "our knowledge is in our action". In the face-to-face interaction, this knowing-in-action is present in a more concrete way, facilitating its sharing and the construction of collective decisions. Filstad, Hepso and Skarholt [3] use the same word "knowing" to describe IO knowledge sharing across boundaries. They define "knowing" as "being able to frame the situation and find ways of collaborative working" [3]. The collective strategies adopted by the OPS team, though it involves an additional effort, facilitates knowledge sharing internally and externally, outside the OPS team boundaries.

According to Dixon [4], the generation of collective knowledge involves reflecting on actions and their results before moving on. This dynamic is observed today in the team meetings at the beginning of the shift. Experts from different specialties discuss the progress of operations on each drilling rig, highlighting the most significant events and building common knowledge around these experiences that may be used a few days or months later. Through this dynamic, experience is transformed into knowledge [4].

Explaining the need for physically open working arenas, Moltu [5] states that "the work process between onshore and offshore operations are what constitutes the need for powerful workstations, more permanent and based in a physical room rather than laptop-based." Although the pandemic justifies each member of the team's personal effort to carry out their activities remotely with the available resources, it is important to highlight that the face-to-face interaction of the team in an environment equipped with ICT technologies seems essential for performance improvement.

Filstad, Hepso and Skarholt [3] state that knowledge sharing in virtual teams requires trust among team members, ICT infrastructure and "a sufficiently shared situational awareness". The confidence and integration of the OPS team had allowed the rapid adoption of remote work without significant losses in meeting the operations' demands. However, it is impossible to reproduce the ICT infrastructure and physical resources from the original environment in all team members locations. Additionally, remote work revealed difficulties in building a collective situational awareness. These aspects end up interfering in the team's knowledge sharing.

Moltu [5] considers that collaborative work in operation support (OPS) rooms requires a large degree of self-synchronization. Differently from the traditional synchronization of more hierarchical teams, Filstad, Hepso and Skarholt [3] explain that, in self-synchronization, tasks are commonly distributed between peers and require "all members having a peripheral awareness of priority tasks and resources".

7   Conclusions

The new dynamic of remote interaction of the OPS team has been improving every day, introducing new individual and collective strategies. Although it is quite effective in fulfilling tasks, there are signs of impact on the agility of responses and the transmission of knowledge due to the reduced interaction of the remote work.

The multidisciplinary OPS team interaction is characterized by exchanging information and transferring specific knowledge from different specialties to build a collective solution. Some of the drilling rig operations may simultaneously involve more than three experts. The construction of new strategies proved to be fundamental. It had been possible because there was already trust among team members, rooted in the face-to-face work activity before the pandemic.

However, interview results suggest that remote communication between OPS team members requires an additional team effort and may compromise performance in the medium and long term. The ICT infrastructure of the original work environment makes it easier to distribute information in real-time and simultaneously to the entire team. The collocated work facilitates interaction allowing face-to-face communication.

The limitations resulting from social isolation prevented the ergonomists from observing the activities in person as required by the EWA methodology. This research's continuity will allow to deepen and validate the results obtained so far.

Acknowledgments. This work has been carried out with the support of the Conselho Nacional de Desenvolvimento Científico e Tecnológico – Brasil (CNPq) and from the Coordenação de Aperfeiçoamento de Pessoal de Nível Superior – Brasil (CAPES) - Financing Code 001.

References

1. Guérin, F., Laville, A., Daniellou, F., Duraffourg, J., Kerguelen, A.: Comprendre le travail pour le transformer. Anact, Lyon (1996)
2. Shon, D.A.: The Reflective Practioner: How Professionals Think in Action. Basic Books (1983)
3. Filstad, C., Hepso, V., Skarholt, K.: Connecting worlds through self-synchronization and boundary spanning. In: Rosendahl, T., Hepso, V. (eds.) Integrated Operations in Oil and Gas Industry: Sustainability and Capability Development, pp. 76–90. Business Science Reference (2013)
4. Dixon, N.: Common Knowledge: How Companies Thrive by Sharing What They Know. Harvard Business School Press, Boston (2000)
5. Moltu, B.: Good IO-design is more that IO-rooms. In: Rosendahl, T., Hepso, V. (eds.) Integrated Operations in Oil and Gas Industry: Sustainability and Capability Development, 141–152. Business Science Reference (2013)

Supporting Digital Transition within SME through Multilevel Cooperation, A Work Use Lab Experimentation

Viviane Folcher[✉]

ComUE Paris Lumière, Paragraph Lab, University Paris 8, Vincennes-Saint Denis, France
viviane.folcher@univ-paris8.fr

Abstract. Supporting an organization in its future means betting on its development by building a work use lab experimentation at different levels of its organization. A mission conducted in a company in charge of supporting digital transition of SME is an opportunity to present the multi-scale cooperation device that we implement during twelve months. The productions of the actors involved at each scale highlight the protagonists' learnings and the development path that open for the organization as whole. In discussion we are exploring the ways and means of an organizational development through a work use lab that setup an ephemeral and transitional learning device whose vocation is to become sustainable.

Keywords: Work use lab · Learning process · Design project · Capability and power to act

1 A Work Use Lab Experimentation as a Developmental Learning Process

A work uses lab is meaning a developmental learning process proposed through a multi-level cooperative system that unfolds at different scales, crossing borders within an organization as well as connecting various organizations. Within this multilevel device, we're building transitional spaces [1] for human activities that are valuable for organization's cooperation and transformation [2].

In order to allow mutual learning process we are connecting various stakeholders considered as "designers-for-use" and "designers-in-use" [3]. Designers-in-use are equipped to collect their work situations, to share those with the designers-for-use. Protagonists are both tooled to co-design the future work forms, its organization, the new products and offered clients services.

1.1 The Mission Conducted

The mission was conducted in a company in charge of supporting digital transition within SME. Four SME were involved, in legal and health fields (judicial officers and pharmacies). Digital challenges coped by those SME, were mainly related to their relationships

N. L. Black et al. (Eds.): IEA 2021, LNNS 219, pp. 139–143, 2021.
https://doi.org/10.1007/978-3-030-74602-5_21

quality with various professionals and their missions scope enlargement, including client as actor.

To drive the mission, we're articulating three action scales as illustrated in Fig. 1.

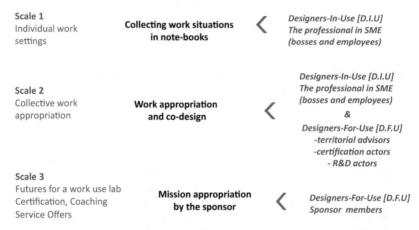

Fig. 1. A work use lab experimentation as a multi-level cooperation device

As to the first scale, the designers-in-use collect their daily work situations in a note-book that reports frequency, period concerned, tools and resources mobilized, difficulties and tips found, desired futures and visual associated.

As to the second scale, the designers-for-use and the designers-in-use were invited to identify keys work activities that are the core of actual work and significant for future.

At the third scale, the sponsors deliver their appropriation about the conducted mission, and explore the possible device usages.

1.2   The Involved Stakeholders and Their Productions

On scale 1, eighteen (18) designers-in-use harvested their work situations during 1,5 months. After a short training session, 18 notebooks were produced over a period of 45 days.

119 situations were collected revealing an abundant and exhaustive harvest: the situations collected are mainly frequents (70 situations/119), and mobilize a range of numeric resources (114 situations/119). For a large part, the harvesters imagine paths for the future (99 situations/119). They frequently illustrate their work-lived with visuals (92 situations/119).

On scale 2, the eighteen (18) designers-in-use meet eight (8) designers-for-use during work appropriation. They identify six (6) keys work activities, three (3) in judicial officers and three (3) in pharmacies. During co-design stage, the same stakeholders has projected the digital evolutions and the competences and know how required at short, medium and long term.

On scale 3 our sponsors are producing various documents - argumentation sheet-that prospect futures uses based on this experimentation.

26 actors were involved in the mission.

2   Results: The Stakeholders Capabilities to Produce Desirable Futures for Work

The main results are highlighting protagonist's capabilities to produce desirable futures in the real work footsteps. These productions are witnessing their new capabilities to act emerging during this learning process:

- As they're collecting their own work, the designers-in-use are precisely reporting their difficulties, revealing their tips and reporting tangible explorations of future work forms as illustrated in Fig. 2:

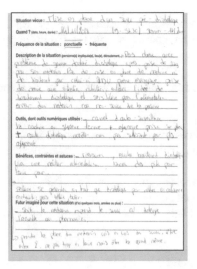 

Fig. 2. Note book extract: "setup of a pre-diabetic follow-up"

What does it tell about the professional situation:

- Resources diversity: self-monitoring diary, blood glucose device
- Method: "Reassure, avoid diabetic treatment through a better diet, frighten, spike".
- Tips: "Introduce yourself as a diabetic to build confidence".
- The professional dilemmas he's coping with: "Taking doctor's place in terms of follow-up, being in between, not overdoing it but being there".
- The articulation issues with other professions: "Either the doctor takes over the follow-up or he delegates to the pharmacist".

Collecting work situations reveals a both retrospective and prospective portrait. Retrospective, it takes note of the work's current resources, the main difficulties and tips. Prospective, this portrait projects desirable for future work and its sustainability requirements that are already being experienced as illustrated in the notebook extract.

- As the "designers-for and in-use" are engaged in work appropriation and co-design for future, they will evolve from individuals work settings towards the genericity of their professions in a present-future continuum. For example, "**come along with the patient through a range of diversified services**" means new medical knowledge of chronic diseases, digital skills for cross-data analysis, patient file chaining and finally, assistance in the usage of dematerialized services.

At this point, designers-for and-in use are identifying the need to support this digital transition: work organization, customer relationships, network of professionals involved in services delivery.

The first need deals with the control of the digital data chain in the network of professionals involved:

- Debtors, creditors, partners, lawyers, regalian institutions for the Bailiffs of Justice;
- Patients, guardians, family, caregivers, doctors, hospital staff, nurses, physiotherapists for the Pharmacies.

The second need deals with the role that users may play in a co-construction the professionals are engaged in order to:

- Co-elaborate an evolving care process based on a shared medication review allowing for long-term follow-up of patients (chronic diseases, poly-medicalized patients) in the case of pharmacy dispensaries;
- Co-elaborate with the debtor the decision in a perspective of accountability that takes into account the respect of the law and integrates a debtor actor who can be accompanied in his negotiation steps, with banks for example, and potentially loyal as a future customer.

- Involved during the mission our sponsor evolved from a focus on digital technology impact on work, towards an ambition to build a "work uses lab" that could serve a set of targets as illustrated in Fig. 3.

As a tool for monitoring skills evolution in real work setting, this "work use lab" would serve a set of targets to come along with the SME, enriching the missions of our sponsor. It deals with collecting learning work situations to reinvest into AFEST[1], identifying what's emerging from digital changes in work and translates into support needs at the upper level (professional certifications).

3   From Learning to Development

Our working hypothesis is that the proposed learning process to those actors, allows the development of new professional capacities. The proposed device is settled at several

[1] The French law for the freedom to choose one's professional future of September 5th, 2018 recognizes the possibility of training in a work situation. The AFEST is part of an "educational path to achieve a professional goal".

Collect learning work situations to reinvest in AFESTs

Identify the needs for cross-sectoral support to the professional branches

A work use lab as tool for monitoring skills evolution in real work settings

Identify professional activities impacted by digital and/or emerging technologies

Enrich and update professional certifications

Fig. 3. A work use lab: tool for monitoring skills evolution in real work settings

scales of one organization: it temporarily redraws its boundaries and offers a space enabling contact within the work experience for diverse professionals in the exercise of new action capability.

By doing this, a reflexive and prospective capacity is developed individually and collectively. Its enables SME workers to collect their daily work situations and project the future working forms with protagonists coming from others professional worlds [4]. It enables the territorial advisors to renew their mission content, based on the working realities discovered with the harvesters. Our results enables our sponsor's to draw and enrich the future of his company.

The learning device we install into organizations is transitory and ephemeral, its lifespan is variable, between 12 and 18 months. It could be crystallized within an organization through an instance such as a work use lab whose vocation is to be perennial. As it creates potentials for the future of work, this laboratory needs to be invested at the strategic level, then architecturally designed and orchestrated in its implementation.

References

1. Bationo-Tillon, A., Folcher, V., Poret, C., Couillaud, S.: Understanding the development of organizations at the cross road of the course of action and the instrumental approach: the transitional perspective. Activités **17**, 2 (2020)
2. Folcher, V., Batono-Tillon, A., Poret, C., Couillaud, S.: Des genèses instrumentales aux genèses organisationnelles, voies et moyens d'un défi développemental. In: Arnoud, J., Barcellini, F., Cerf, M., Perez Toralla, M. (eds.) Développement et Intervention, Octarès, Collection Travail et Activité Humaine (2020, to appear)
3. Folcher, V.: Innovation at work, lessons learned from a design-for-use design-in-use approach. In: Proceedings of the 20th Triennal Congress of International Ergonomics Association, Florence, Italy, 26–29 August 2018 (2019)
4. Beguin, P.: Conduite de projet et fabrication collective du travail, une approche développementale. Document de synthèse en vue de l'obtention de l'Habilitation à Diriger des Recherches, Université de Bordeaux 2, 19 November (2010)

Contribution to the Industry 4.0 Design Project Based on Exposure Situations

Louis Galey[1,2]([⊠]), Nathalie Judon[3], and Alain Garrigou[4]

[1] University Paris Nanterre, Department of Psychology, LAPPS (EA 4386), Team TE2O, 200 avenue de la République, 92001 Nanterre Cedex, France
louis.galey@parisnanterre.fr
[2] Ergonomics Team, CNAM, CRTD, 41 rue Gay Lussac, 75005 Paris, France
[3] Institut National de Recherche et de Sécurité (INRS), Rue du Morvan, CS 60027, 54500 Vandoeuvre Les Nancy, France
[4] University of Bordeaux, Inserm, Bordeaux Population Health Research Center, Team EPICENE, UMR 1219, 146 rue Léo Saignat, 33000 Bordeaux, France

Abstract. Industry 4.0 generates risks renewing stakes for design project integrating work activities, as it can be done in activity centered ergonomics and participatory ergonomics. From a case study supporting a design project for a plant of the future assembling metal additive manufacturing processes in aeronautics, this article aims to show the contribution of using typical situations to define requirements for industrial design projects 4.0.

The method is based on a construction of the approach, the identification of typical exposure situations (through video and measurement), collective confrontation interviews (using typical situations) similar to reflexive and constructive simulations, and the setting of requirements.

Results highlights specific exposure situations during the work, which the interviews made it possible to understand, enabling to collectively debate organisational, technical or social determinants, in order to transform them from the point of view of the work, within the framework of the design project.

Keywords: Participatory ergonomics · Design project · Industry 4.0 · Typical exposure situation · Metal additive manufacturing

1 Introduction

The industry of the future induces the automation and digitalization of the means of production, leading inexorably to radical transformations of human work. In this context, workers are going to be exposed to emerging hazards. It is necessary to act on them as early as possible in the design projects mobilizing these new technologies. The challenge is to promote safe working conditions by taking action at the stages of design projects, which will lead to decisions that integrate health issues. The results presented in this paper are based on an industry of the future design project in aeronautics. The aim is to use metal additive manufacturing production equipment to print aircraft engine parts in

3D. Worker interventions on these processes lead to potential exposures to micro and nanoparticles with known health effects such as cancer.

Today, some *safe by design* and prevention approaches seek to make innovations (such as those related to nanotechnologies) safer by focusing mostly on the technical dimensions or without taking into account the actual work and associated potential exposures. Yet, activity-centered ergonomics approaches contribute to a better consideration of work activities in design projects. This article is based on a theoretical framework founded on the work carried out over the last 30 years in design ergonomics, to take into account real work situations (typical action/exposure situations and settings of usage) in order to define requirements for design projects (Garrigou et al. 1995; Duarte and Lima 2012; Barcellini et al. 2014; Galey et al. 2020a, b; Souza da Conceição et al. 2020; Kadir and Broberg 2021). These technological and societal innovations therefore bring new challenges to which ergonomics can provide answers.

The objective of this paper is to present preliminary results of a case study to accompany the design project of a metallic additive manufacturing industry 4.0 based on the identification of typical exposure situations in order to set up requirements for 4.0 design projects.

2 Method

The research was carried out in an aeronautics company as part of a project to design a $10,000 \text{ m}^2$ site comprising 50 SLM type metal additive manufacturing machines. The company's objective is to gather and mutualize the group's production means spread over 5 sites in France (15 machines in operation).

The company's request initially focused on the understanding of exposure situations on a metal additive manufacturing pilot workstation to develop prevention strategy. In the course of the intervention research, it appeared that the results could make it possible to define preventive actions for similar workstations in other factories of the group as well as within the framework of a project for the design of a 4.0 plant integrating means of production for metal additive manufacturing.

After a construction of the approach (Judon et al. 2019) with the company's stakeholders, reference situations were analysed at one of the group's sites. The analysis of two reference situations resulted in the production of videos of the work activity and real time aerosol exposure measurement (CEN 2018; Galey et al. 2020a, b) during the stages of human work on the additive manufacturing machine.

The synchronization of real-time aerosol measurements with videos of the work activity (Rosén et al. 2005) allowed the identification of several typical exposure situations. Variations in exposure could be associated with the workers' actions.

Then, collective confrontation interviews were conducted with the management, the health and safety committee, and the workers. These interviews consisted in presenting extracts describing typical exposure situations based on videos of the work activity and measurements to company stakeholders, similar to "*reflexive and constructive*" simulations (Bobillier Chaumon et al. 2018).

The aim of these simulations was also to collectively build design requirements for the choice of future machines and the organization of future work situations.

3 Results

Typical exposure situations have been identified within these reference situations.

Confrontation interviews based on these typical exposure situations helped to understand several determinants of these exposure situations. These determinants are notably associated with the choice of machines and their techno-centric design, the organization of work, and the perceptions and representations of risks by operators leading to exposing work activities.

At this stage of the design project, several requirements for the future plant have been co-constructed, as illustrated by these verbatim statements by the initial site preventionist.

> *"Then it's the* [serial additive manufacturing machine] *that will change, with more capacity, I think. From memory, from memory, we were told that there would be an automatic sifting... But from memory we will have more, when we reload, we won't have to compact the powder as we used to do."*

These requirements concern the choice of additive manufacturing machines to automate stages of the work activity leading to exposure; the installation of sensors in the future plant to monitor in real time variations in particle concentrations; the separation of production areas; or the involvement of operators in the design of the plant and in training courses for this new profession for example.

4 Discussion

The project in progress does not yet allow to observe the final outcome on the work of the integration of the design requirements into the overall plant construction project. However, we observe that the exposure situations made visible by approaches of ergonomics and the development of requirements have been transferred from the reference situations to the management team of the new plant design project. In order to reinforce consideration of real work, new work observations in diversified reference situations, as well as simulations with the design project stakeholders, should be carried out. More generally, we note that the industry of the future will lead to the disappearance of certain machining trades (turners, millers) and the appearance of new trades (additive manufacturing technician).

The theoretical and methodological lessons of this research intervention for design ergonomics can be summarised in several points. First, it is necessary to start from existing work situations in order to define typical situations. By making these situations and their determinants visible through exchanges with operators, it becomes possible to specify these typical situations. Then, on the basis of reflexive practices (simulations, confrontation interviews, debate spaces, etc.). These practices notably enable the understanding of exposure situations, the comparison of situations, the projection of the work activity, and design choices. The temporal dimensions are mobilised by these approaches (Chizallet et al. 2020). The discussion of current situations reveals past work situations, perceived exposures, and their determinants, influencing current situations and future projections according to the subjects. Prospects for re-constituting past situations appear.

Following this, a projection into future work activity is promoted, based on the characteristics of the project and the nature of current work activities. The future activity is mainly based on the discussions on the transformation of current determinants and associated design choices. Finally, it will be necessary to accompany the work of the designers, the implementation by the project management, the start and the design in the use of these work situations whose determinants may still be brought to evolve.

The transformations brought about by the industry 4.0 have consequences on both the work of operators and the nature of the work of ergonomists. In addition to exploring the *how* and the *why* (Béguin et al. 2015), it seems as if industry 4.0 is an opportunity to question the *where* and the *when* of work activities.

5   Conclusion

The study carried out shows the challenge of pursuing a better integration of real work in the industry of the future design projects. Indeed, risk situations that did not exist before the advent of the industry of the future may be generated, requiring discussion and mobilization of specific stakeholders in design projects. However, the automation and real-time monitoring of work environment characteristics opens new perspectives for the development of favorable working conditions. A better consideration of real work can therefore be achieved using new exposure characterization techniques, without forgetting to systematically involve stakeholders with knowledge of real work in the project.

References

Barcellini, F., Van Belleghem, L., Daniellou, F.: Design projects as opportunities for the development of activities. In: Falzon, P. (ed.) Constructive Ergonomics, pp. 187–204. CRC Press, Boca Raton (2014). https://doi.org/10.1201/b17456-16

Béguin, P., Duarte, F., Sznelwar, L.I.: Introduction to the special section on activity theory for work analysis and design. Production **25**(2), 255–256 (2015). https://doi.org/10.1590/0103-6513.ED2502

Bobillier Chaumon, M.-É., Rouat, S., Laneyrie, E., Cuvillier, B.: De l'activité DE simulation à l'activité EN simulation: Simuler pour stimuler. Activités **15**(1) (2018). https://doi.org/10.4000/activites.3136

CEN: Pr EN 17058—Workplace exposure—Assessment of inhalation exposure to nano-objects and their agglomerates and aggregates. CEN (2018)

Chizallet, M., Prost, L., Barcellini, F.: Supporting the design activity of farmers in transition to agroecology: towards an understanding. Le travail humain **83**(1), 33–59 (2020)

Duarte, F., Lima, F.: Anticiper l'activité par les configurations d'usage: proposition méthodologique pour conduite de projet. Activités **09**(2) (2012). https://doi.org/10.4000/activites.314

Galey, L., Audignon-Durand, S., Brochard, P., Debia, M., Lacourt, A., Lambert, P., Bihan, O., Martinon, L., Pasquereau, P., Witschger, O., Garrigou, A.: Towards an operational exposure assessment strategy to airborne nanoparticles by integrating work activity analysis and exposure measurement. Archives des Maladies Professionnelles et de l'Environnement **81**(3) (2020). https://doi.org/10.1016/j.admp.2020.03.831

Galey, L., Audignon, S., Witschger, O., Bau, S., Judon, N., Lacourt, A., Garrigou, A.: What does ergonomics have to do with nanotechnologies? A case study. Appl. Ergon. **87**(103116) (2020). https://doi.org/10.1016/j.apergo.2020.103116

Garrigou, A., Daniellou, F., Carballeda, G., Ruaud, S.: Activity analysis in participatory design and analysis of participatory design activity. Int. J. Ind. Ergon. **15**(5), 311–327 (1995). https://doi.org/10.1016/0169-8141(94)00079-I

Judon, N., Galey, L., Saint Dizier de Almeida, V., Garrigou, A.: Contributions of participatory ergonomics to the involvement of workers in chemical risk prevention projects. Work **64**(3), 651–660 (2019). https://doi.org/10.3233/WOR-193001

Kadir, B.A., Broberg, O.: Human-centered design of work systems in the transition to industry 4.0. Appl. Ergon. **92**(103334) (2021). https://doi.org/10.1016/j.apergo.2020.103334

Rosén, G., Andersson, I.-M., Walsh, P.T., Clark, R.D.R., Säämänen, A., Heinonen, K., Riipinen, H., Pääkkönen, R.: A review of video exposure monitoring as an occupational hygiene tool. Ann. Occup. Hyg. **49**(3), 201–217 (2005). https://doi.org/10.1093/annhyg/meh110

Souza da Conceição, C.S., Broberg, O., Duarte, F.: A six-step model to transform an ergonomic work analysis into design guidelines for engineering projects. Work **66**(3), 699–710 (2020). https://doi.org/10.3233/WOR-203212

The Work of the Logisticians and the Collective Dimension of Integrated Operations of Logistics in the Oil & Gas Industry

Luciano do V. Garotti[1]([✉]) [iD] and Fausto Leopoldo Mascia[2] [iD]

[1] Petrobras Research and Development Center, Rio de Janeiro, Brazil
luciano.garotti@petrobras.com.br
[2] Production Department, University of São Paulo, São Paulo, Brazil
fmascia@usp.br

Abstract. In this paper, we analyze the work's collective dimension of the logisticians dedicated to supporting the offshore drilling oil and gas industry, in the context of Integrated Operations (IO). We approach the work of the logistics team focusing on the articulation and activation of collective dimensions within a Logistic Integration Center.

Keywords: Integrated Operations · Logistics · Ergonomics · Collective work

1 Introduction

Mainly due to the exhaustion of the closest fields, the oil industry has increasingly explored more remote areas [1]. Such expansion has presented challenges the oil & gas industry tries to solve through Integrated Operations (IO) initiatives. IO's practices consist in the implementation of special offices in the onshore installations, with facilities such as videoconference equipment and other Information and Communication Technology (ICT) tools. Ensuring the supply of remote offshore areas has become essential. Simultaneously, the offshore operation supportive logistic chain followed such expansion and adopted IO practices. Thereby, the IO practices in logistics represent an attempt to overcome such related challenges. These practices seek greater efficiency and continuity of the offshore operation logistical support in increasingly more remote areas.

The implementation of IO concepts in the oil industry aims to increase the integration among different operational disciplines, geographically dispersed, and collaborating companies [2]. In this context, the workers have been working in dynamic environments, inserted in a collective activity [3]. Tasks are interdependent [4] and this type of organization demands complex social processes with the joint intervention of several actors [5].

In this context, the work effectively done is still poorly mentioned in the literature. It is known that workers face several challenges: collaborating with workers in other departments; overcome organizational segregation barriers and integrated companies' different areas and their particularities in terms of routines, tasks, and goals.

N. L. Black et al. (Eds.): IEA 2021, LNNS 219, pp. 149–155, 2021.
https://doi.org/10.1007/978-3-030-74602-5_23

Thus, this study focuses on the collective dimensions. We emphasis on the work of logisticians and their interactions with company's areas, that demand logistic services. The logisticians are the main workers involved in the articulation and activation of collective dimensions in the studied situation. We highlight a plan adjustment situation through an example in which logisticians intervene to recover from unforeseen variability that occurred in scheduled operations.

2 Theoretical Bases

The worker's activity is always collective, to a greater or lesser extent, according to the working situation [3]. From this point of view, it becomes impossible to understand an operator's individual activity without considering the collective dimensions of the work in which the analyzed situation is inserted [6].

Collective work involves sharing goals [7] and presupposes the construction of a collective representation of the situation in which the workers are engaged [8]. The mobilization of several workers in a situation of collective activity results in a constitution of a transversal collective of work, in which several workers engage in different, but coordinated actions, belonging to the same process [9].

In order to carry out the collective work, it is necessary for the workers to build a current status representation of the collective situation in which they are engaged, based on facts regarding the situation status and the contributions of the other workers also engaged in the task [8]. It is essential to define what the workers engaged in the collective work need to share. This definition is important to understand the difficulties and possibilities for the satisfactory operation of distributed work groups and of remote collaboration [10].

The common referential is a functional representation shared among the actors of a collective work, which guides and regulates the collective activity in which they are engaged. This referential is a guide to action, constituted by a set of knowledge, principles and values [11], and serves as a guide for the construction of mental representations regarding goals, strategies, procedures, knowledge of the domain, limitations and criteria.

The construction and evolution of this "Common Operational Referential" along the collective activity occurs dynamically among the operators. In situations of common knowledge about the problem domain, the operators resort to recovery dialogues in order to equalize the general knowledge. Thus, verbal or nonverbal communication makes it possible to ensure that each engaged worker is aware of the facts regarding the status of the situation, and that the same general knowledge about the domain is shared [12].

The understanding of his own role and of the role of the others by each engaged worker is possible through a process established by the "Common Operative Referential". In order to it happens is necessary the workers' engagement in activities of clarifications and explanations, which allow the building of mutual intelligibility [13].

3 Method

This paper is the result from a study carried out at the Logistics Integration Center (LIC), composed of 6 workers from the Logistics IO and 7 workers from operational areas: ground transportation (GT) and maritime transportation (MT). These workers were divided in two teams, working in day and night shifts. During the study, the LIC supported 33 drilling rigs (divided in 5 drilling areas) and 16 maritime unities (platforms, production ships and special ships). The work was done with the support of five information systems, electronic spreadsheets, and simultaneous message systems.

The research method was based on the work ergonomic analysis [14, 15] and was developed in phases: (1) research and analysis of processes documents related to the process of drilling and logistics adopted by the company; (2) research and analyses of documents relating to the logistics process and installations and resources capacity; logisticians work – procedures, processes mapping, etc.; (3) interview with the logistic manager in order to have the access to the LIC; (4) observations of logisticians work in different moments to know the diversity of work concerning different participants in the LIC; (5) analysis of data collect during logistics works observations; (6) Work observation and interviews of rig onboard workers; (7) validation interviews with study involved actors; (8) presentation of study results to workers and logistic management.

4   Results

The central point of this study refer to the work of the logistic operators, considered here as the central actors and activators of the collective dimension present in logistics operations. Into this paper, the term logistic operators comprehends the different workers that take part in logistic planning, negotiation and decision, such as logistic integrator, drilling offshore supervisors, drilling onshore coordinator, maritime transport coordinator, storekeeper and cargo deck supervisor. Thus, this article presents an analysis of the logistical service planning work followed by the situations of planning adjustments, resulting from the variability and unforeseen factors inherent to drilling operations. We consider that through these two main actions that the Logistic Integrator activates the different collective dimensions in the studied situation.

The logistic integrators of the LIC prepare the logistic plan based on the request issued in the ERP system and in accordance with the supply ships' schedule. These issuers generate transportation requisitions of materials with different origins, destinations and responsibility for the transport up to the respective port. Besides the company's warehouses, other origins are workshops, internal or external to the installations of the studied company, and warehouses of outsourced companies. The materials destined to the rigs must forcefully go through one of the ports used by the company. Then they update the status of the requisitions and complete the plans.

This information serves as basis for work in the different logistic operational areas. For instance, the logistic technicians analyze the information consistency together with the drilling engineers residing in the offices of the pertinent rigs. The view per maritime transport (MT) service cluster allows for specific works, both by the ground transport (GT) and the MT. The GT representative at the LIC can calculate the necessary transport cubage per truck and estimate the necessary fleet for the transport, as well as request priority or other types of adjustments in case of need. The MT representative at the LIC can calculate the necessary deck area on the supply vessel to be designated to the transport.

Once the logistic plan have been completed, the worksheet's updated version can be accessed and checked by the logistic technicians allocated in the different drilling poles served by the local port. If there is the need to update the registered transportation requisitions, such as postponing the delivery date, alterations may be requested by the Advanced Post technician. These requests are made via email, phone call or instant messaging system to the Logistic Integrator, located at the LIC.

The principal reasons for changing logistic plan are:

- Maritime transport – difficulties to level fleet capacity and demand in face of demand's quantity and variation, supply boats out of functioning due to maintenance needs, deadline for crew changing and meteorological conditions.
- Port operations – variation in the duration of transferring cargo between port and ships, specific functioning rules due to local infrastructure; weather conditions and also cargo characteristics
- Drilling rig type – semi-submersible rigs are less stable and with less capacity to receive cargo comparing to ship rigs, demanding more agility of the logistic chain.
- Drilling rig equipment – rigs with double rotating table are faster than regular rigs while connecting drilling rigs and drilling the well.
- Incompatibility between rig equipment and drilling materials as well as service providers' tools and materials. Adjusting it can demand time, space on board and or agility of the logistic chain.

4.1 A Drilling Rig

The situation here described occurred in a drilling rig, semi-submersible, located around 250 km from the coast. A rig normally accommodates nearly 200 workers between rig equipment operators, drilling equipment operators, drilling service, equipment providers, hospitality, maintenance, health and safety technicians, drilling rig management and client company representatives (drilling engineers as offshore supervisors, geologists, and health and safety technicians). The logistic chain supports the rig delivering food, potable water, diesel, drilling equipment, tools and tubes, chemicals and others. Due to restricted space on board, since its high coast in terms of steel and construction, the rig needs to store as less material as possible, paying attention to not disturb its operation because the absence of some necessary material or equipment. Because the high costs of its daily functioning, stopping rig operations to wait for some material input is undesirable and, consequently, it demands a lot of attention of the drilling offshore supervisors and rig managers.

Three main teams take part in planning and operational decisions. The rig team knows about rig capacities and tries to keep it as much available as possible. The service providers go onboard with specific equipment, materials and drilling or special tubes to be used together the drilling floor rig team. The contractor representatives team (mainly the drilling offshore supervisors) knows about the client company needs, the well construction plan and specificities, decides each step of the operations to be performed, including preparation, and intermediates service providers, rig team, and the logistic operations.

4.2   A Demand for Logistic Adjustment

Rig A, Day 1: onboard rig A, on day 1, there was identified a necessity of adjustment. The drilling tubes to be used the next drilling phase were different from the usual. These tubes were shorter than regular ones and incompatible with handling equipment that supports their connection. Until this moment, the involved actors were **drilling team and drilling offshore supervisors**.

As **Alternative 1,** they consider to prepare and connect the tubes on the cargo deck. It requires space on cargo deck for positioning the tubes with enough free area around so the workers can assembly it in safety conditions according to companies safety norms. However, there is a **restriction**: the cargo deck was full loaded with materials whose backload was planned for day 6. Wait until day 6 would impede the assembly of the tubes in time. It was necessary to anticipate this backload.

The **opportunity** was to transfer this backload to the supply boat SR that was delivering other cargos to the rig A on day 1. The boat SR cargo deck would be empty after transferring the cargo to rig A. Still on day 1, the **involved actors (drilling offshore supervisors, drilling onshore coordinator, cargo deck coordinator, and drilling team)** decided to anticipate the backload of these materials on boat SR.

In order to make this anticipation feasible, it was necessary to change the transport requisition of these materials to emergency status. The storekeeper should do this change and the emergency costs would be afforded by contractor. According to the supervisor, these costs would be compensated by the possibility in anticipating the preparation of the drilling tubes and to not stopping drilling operations.

After this decision, the **negotiation** of this logistic alternative was done between **the drilling offshore supervisor and the logistic integrator**. The solicitation for using the boat SR was initially accepted by the logistic integrator. During the night of day 1, the client supervisor informs the other actors. It was necessary the **storekeeper and the cargo deck coordinator** get the cargos prepared in time for the transferring them to boat SR just after the ongoing transferring operation finished. The cargo deck coordinator should also arrange the deck in order to guarantee the demanded space on it to start drilling tubes preparation.

Day 2: On the morning of day 2, the **Logistic Integrator** informs the drilling supervisor about the **impossibility of the backload anticipation** through boat SR. **The supervisor calls the logistic integrator and the Maritime Transport Coordinator,** both located onshore, **and arguments about the importance of transferring this cargo to boat SR**. As an option (**Alternative 2**), the MT Coordinator proposes to do the backload through supply **boat 2**, already near the rig A area. According to the MT Coordinator, this boat could approximate the rig A area still in day 2.

In the MT Coordinator point of view, the boat SR would receive scheduled backloads from other rigs before returning to the port. Receiving the anticipated backload from rig A would limit boat SR capacity to receive the planned backloads of other rigs (differently from port, offshore operations difficult accommodating cargo until boats full capacity). These other backloads were tubes and rig A needed to backload other materials that could damage if hit by some tube. In addition, the boat would demand more time on port to transfer rig A backload and it would postpone port operations.

However, according to the drilling supervisor, the **Alternative 2 would lead to an efficiency loss** due to the time of boat 2 approximation of the rig (it demands safety equipment tests and slow maneuvering before operating). The goal was to anticipate as much as possible the rearrangement of the cargo deck to allow beginning the preparation of the drilling tubes needed in the next phase.

After the argumentation, **the MT Coordinator agrees to do the backload through boat SR** despite the related consequences.

5   Discussion

In this example, what seems to be a possible solution for those directly impacted is seen as not feasible due to the technical conditions of the moment. Therefore, the anticipation of the backload to guarantee space to allow the fixing of the equipment onboard is considered impossible. Several workers, from distinct company areas – representatives of maritime transportation and port operations, drilling supervisor, onboard logistician – participate in the building of a solution to the problem.

The negotiation before related highlights a conflict between different logics. From the Drilling rig A logics, the space on cargo deck is necessary to avoid postponing its operations. From the MT logics, the boat SR needs to leave rig A empty in order to achieve enough conditions to attend backload of tubes from its next scheduled rigs according to planning and, consequently, to avoid disturbing their programed operations. Finally, from the Port point of view, the main necessity is to allow fast operation with the cargos in order to avoid disturbing its internal operations.

Thus, the search for solutions goes through other interlocutors. In this context, workers in different sectors of the supply chain have a fundamental role to mobilize different representations and build a collective representation that allows them to elaborate a compromise alternative.

6   Conclusion

This situation illustrates the aspects related to the activation of collective dimensions among involved actors. The case shows a strong interdependency between departments. The search for a solution involves negotiating each proposed alternative, while handling the problem. Initially, the construction of a common representation is difficult to achieve. The possibility of sharing different representations between involved actors turns out to be an essential condition to achieve a solution. As negotiations take place, collective representation evolves and becomes a common reference. New alternatives will be analyzed until the group reaches a solution considered satisfactory for the involved interlocutors.

Finally, this situation shows the double dynamism that affects logistic planning. Drilling variabilities alter needs and deadlines and impose new conditions to the logistic chain, which also has its own inherent variabilities. In face of it, the consequent ephemeral character of the logistic planning demands the logistic operators to activate collective dimensions to achieve an enough common reference that allows negotiation and decision.

References

1. Barreto, R.: A produção de petróleo e o desenvolvimento nacional. Revista de divulgação do Projeto Universidade Petrobras e IF Fluminense **2**(1), 101–107 (2012)
2. Ramstad, L., Holte, E.: Integrated Planning in Oil & Gas Industry Designing and Cultivating IPL Practices (2013). www.iocenter.no
3. Caroly, S.: L'activité collective et la réélaboration des règles: des enjeux pour la santé au travail, These HDR, Université Victor Segalen Bordeaux 2 (2010)
4. Owen, C.A.: Analyser le travail conjoint entre différents systèmes d' activité. Activités **5**(2) (2008)
5. Lorino, P., Neussif, J.: Tertiarisation des filières et reconstruction du sens à travers des récits collectifs. Revue Française de Gestion **1**(170), 75–92 (2007)
6. De La Garza, C., Weill-Fassina, A.: Régulations horizontales et verticales du risque. In: Benchekroun, H., Weill-Fassina, A. (eds.) Le travail collectif en ergonomie: perspectives actuelles en ergonomie, pp. 217–236. Octares, Toulouse (2000)
7. Nascimento, A.: Produire la santé, produire la sécurité: développer une culture collective de sécurité en radiothérapie. Sciences de l'Homme et Société. Conservatoire National des Arts et Métiers (2009)
8. Caroly, S., Barcellini, F.: Le développement de l'activité collective. In: Falzon, P. (ed.) Ergonomie Constructive, pp. 33–46. PUF, Paris (2013)
9. Lorino, P.: L'activité collective, processus organisant. Un processus discursif fondé sur le langage pragmatiste des habitudes. Activités **10**(1), 221–242 (2013)
10. Carroll, J.M., Rosson, M.B., Convertino, G., Ganoe, G.H.: Awareness and teamwork in computer-supported collaborations. Interact. Comput. **18**, 21–46 (2006)
11. Raspaud, A.: De la compréhension collective de l'activité réelle à la conception participative de l'organisation: plaidoyer pour une intervention ergonomique capacitante. Sociologie. Conservatoire national des arts et metiers – CNAM (2014)
12. Darses, F., Falzon, P.: La conception collective: une approche de l'ergonomie cognitive. In: Terssac, G., Friedberg, E. (eds.) Coopération et conception, pp. 123–136. Octares, Toulouse (1996)
13. Salembier, P., Zouinar, M.: Intelligibilité mutuelle et contexte partagé. Activités **1**(2), 64–85 (2004)
14. Guérin, F., Laville, A., Daniellou, F., Duraffourg, J., Kerguelen, A.: Compreender o trabalho para trasnformá-lo: a prática da ergonomia. Edgard Blücher, São Paulo (2001)
15. Daniellou, F.: The French-speaking ergonomists'approach to work activity: cross-influences of field intervention and conceptual models. Theor. Issues Ergon. Sci. **6**(5), 409–427 (2005)

Co-creation Workshops for Innovation in Places: The Role of Boundary Objects

Thiago Gomes de Lima[1](✉), Ole Broberg[2], and Francisco de Assis Esteves[3]

[1] Federal University of Rio de Janeiro, Macaé, Brazil
[2] Technical University of Denmark, Kongens Lyngby, Denmark
[3] Federal University of Rio de Janeiro, Macaé, Brazil

Abstract. The innovation of places is a field of knowledge focused on the design and development of destinations such as regions, tourism, national parks, among others. For that, co-creation workshops involving stakeholders were considered. This article aims to provide a greater understanding of the role of boundary objects used in co-creation workshops, where the knowledge of the participants is integrated into the local innovation processes. This is an exploratory case study, applied to a single Brazilian National Park. It was realized that boundary objects are of great relevance since it facilitates the process in which individuals can, together, transform their knowledge. Among the findings is the possibility of generating intangible knowledge about places, strengthening the engagement of different participants during facilitation, generating insights aligned with the objectives of the workshops, and applying individual knowledge throughout the process of collaboration regardless of previous experience in co-creation.

Keywords: Co-creation · Boundary objects · Place innovation · Prototyping · Self-confrontation

1 Introduction

The research directed towards place innovation has been the focus of different researchers and research fields (Lindberg et al. 2020). The term 'place' refers to a destination, city, municipality, or region, that is, any type of geographically delimited area (Lindberg et al. 2015). Social, environmental and economic changes in places provide opportunities as well as threats, given this fact, there is a need to plan, take advantage of opportunities, and anticipate changes, aiming at the resilience and sustainability of places (Kenny 2017).

Place innovation, is a new concept, has its origins in social innovation and seeks to involve stakeholders in the co-creation process, at the defined location. In practice, it aims to design interesting environments for organizations, communities, and people who are inserted in these spaces (Ericson et al. 2016).

To strengthen the attractiveness of these places, during the innovation process, cultural, social, economic, and technical aspects are developed together, in order to increase the attractiveness of the place among visitors (existing and potential), residents, and investors (Lindberg et al. 2015). Involving the various stakeholders in the innovation processes of places is a paradigm shift that has contributed to the development of society (Lindberg et al. 2015).

In order to involve stakeholders in co-creation processes, researchers and designers develop workshops. Co-creation workshops have been adopted by researchers in different contexts and aim to generate solutions to different problems together with stakeholders (Egusquiza et al. 2021; Akasaka et al. 2021). Co-creative practices are considered practices in which one or more communities participate in creating new desired futures. During the workshops, different tools, methods, technical or objects will be important for co-creation activities (Holmlid et al. 2015).

The aim of this study is to provide a greater understanding of the role of boundary objects used in co-creation workshops, where the participants' knowledge is integrated into the place innovation processes. This is an exploratory case study (Thomas 2015) applied to a Place Innovation case. The location of this study is a Brazilian National Park, which sought to understand the role that boundary objects play during co-creation workshops, aiming at the design of products and services. According to Broberg et al. (2011), the characteristics of boundary objects are very relevant to allow the participation and collaboration of stakeholders in design activities.

The article is organized as follows: First, co-creation workshops will be contextualized. Secondly, boundary objects will be conceptualized. In the third part, the boundary objects applied to the analyzed case study will be presented. In the fourth part, the research design is defined. Finally, based on the theoretical approach, is presented the case in a national park and the results will be discussed in relation to the role of boundary objects in the co-creation workshops for local innovation.

2   Contextualization of Co-creation Workshops

It is important to note that there are different ways of conducting co-creative practices and a diversity of tools, methods, objects, and techniques that can be used. Mattelmäki and Sleeswijk Wisser (2011) suggested four types of co-design. In the first mode, users receive the voice and their reports are used in the design process. In the second mode, the contribution of users is facilitated with tools (co-creative) made available by designers or researchers. In the third mode, the design is not only a facilitator but also plays an important role in collective creation. In the fourth mode, designers and researchers conduct the collaborative process of several stakeholders, not just a user.

Although different co-creation processes are found in the literature. Holmlid et al. (2015), suggested the lens model. This model describes perspectives that direct the process towards innovations in four lenses, being: (1) generation of insights, aims to identify needs, desires, and potentials, (2) exploration of concepts, which can meet these needs and desires, (3) convergence to specifications, participants converge on a shared understanding of the service, as well as their responsibility in the development and delivery process and (4) implementation, aims to make products and services viable. It is not a linear model, and a co-creative practice can benefit more than one step.

Therefore, co-creation workshops are common mechanisms to involve users and various stakeholders and to explore insights together with researchers or designers (Holmlid et al. 2015). In this sense, the design objects are manipulated during the workshops, generating a new potential design for the desired future through the collaboration process (Broberg 2010).

3   Concept of Boundary Objects

For Wenger (2000) boundary objects can be intentional forms developments, they are instruments to help facilitate the learning process. According to Carlile (2002), boundary objects have three characteristics. First, they establish a language that individuals can represent their knowledge. Second, they provide a concrete means that people can use to specify and learn about the particularities and dependencies of a given boundary. Third, it facilitates the process in which the subjects are able to transform their knowledge together.

Wenger (2002), divided the boundary objects into three, being: 1) Artifacts, 2) speeches, and 3) processes. Artifacts can be physical and conceptual as words, tools, concepts, methods, stories, documents, links to resources, and other ways of reification that show our shared experience and around which we organize our participation. The speeches refer to a common language that collaborates for people to communicate and negotiate meanings across boundary. The processes are related to the explicit routines and procedures existing in organizations.

Broberg (2010) classified boundary objects in the categories of Carlile (2002) and Wenger (2000), and structured them into four types: (1) standardized forms and methods, (2) objects, models, and maps, (3) discourses and (4) processes. Thus, two objects to be discussed in this work were organized as follows: prototyping, in the typology of processes, and self-confrontation, in the typology of discourses.

Prototyping is related to the process of mutual learning that occurs in a collaborative configuration of co-creation. During the process, a prototype can be built and manipulated (Brodersen et al. 2008). For the author, developing participatory prototyping is a challenge that aims to create a common area within which participants can be involved in co-creating possible futures.

On the other hand, self-confrontation interviews offer the opportunity to make certain aspects of the participant's experience updated and explicit, still implicit in the situation. This interview aims to confront an individual about his behavior in a given situation through the use of video or photography exposure. In this context, the subject must observe this physical record of his actions and describe the course of his actions to the researcher, making the moment, as lived, more intelligible (Theureau 2003). In this way, the next topic intends to present the role of the respective boundary objects used in co-creation workshops, where the participants' knowledge is integrated into the local innovation processes.

4   Research Design

This study aims to provide a greater understanding of the role of boundary objects used in co-creation workshops for Place Innovation. Therefore, it is a unique case study, carried out in a Brazilian National Park.

According to Flyvbjerg (2006), a case study provides the researcher with proximity to real-life situations, therefore facilitating the understanding of a social phenomenon. For Yin (2005) the case study can be considered a research strategy that has in essence to clarify a decision or a set of decisions, as well as the reason why they were taken, how they were implemented, and with what results obtained within a specific situation.

Thus, the present study has an exploratory descriptive character, that traces a sequence of events over a given period of time, describing a particular phenomenon, within a singular reality. The data collected comes are from four co-creation workshops, realized according to the fourth mode of Mattelmäki and Sleeswijk Wisser (2011) in which designers and researchers lead the collaborative process with several stakeholders, not just a user. Data were collected by one of the authors through observations participating in the workshops.

For the present study, the fourth workshop will be contextualized, in which two boundary objects were applied, being self-confrontation and prototyping. Thus, according to Broberg (2010) prototyping is in the typology of processes, and self-confrontation is in the typology of discourses. Therefore, the case will be analyzed based on the four-lens model of Holmlid et al. (2015) with an emphasis on the lens (1) insights generations, although the process can reveal important contents of other lenses.

5 The Case Project: Co-design of Products and Services in a National Park

5.1 Case Settings

The Restinga de Jurubatiba National Park (RJNP) is an environmental conservation unit (UC) linked to the Chico Mendes Institute for Biodiversity Conservation (ICMbio). The Park is located in the north of the state of Rio de Janeiro, has 44 km of beaches, and in this stretch, there are 18 coastal lagoons of rare beauty and of great ecological interest. This conservation unit has an advisory board, with 33 representatives of the government, business, organized civil society, and surrounding communities (ICMBio 2008).

In March 2018, the RJNP received approval from the ICMbio Public Use Plan, however, between the strategies to make this plan viable, it was decided to develop the Environmental Interpretation. Caetano et al. (2018) define Environmental Interpretation, as a set of communication strategies designed to reveal the meanings of environmental, historical, and cultural resources, with the aim of provoking personal connections between the public and the protected heritage.

The means of carrying out the interpretation can be divided into personal and non-personal. Personal interpretation is performed through a guide or interpreter that accompanies the visitor throughout the UC experience and non-personal interpretation is developed through physical tools that promote interpretation, that is, interpretive products and services. Therefore, ICMbio recommends that the process of designing products and services be developed through participatory methodologies. Given this context, were opted for co-creation processes involving the various stakeholders that are part of the board of the RJNP, therefore, a researcher became responsible for planning and facilitating co-creation workshops.

5.2   Co-creation Workshops for Service and Product Design

Four co-creation workshops were held with the involvement of stakeholders between the period of March and August 2019. Therefore, the first workshop aimed to contextualize the importance of the project to be developed. The second workshop presented the methodology for the design of interpretive products and services and the alignment of the priority areas for design activities. The third workshop presented the case of a Brazilian national park that developed interpretive products and services. In the fourth workshop, the stages of product and service development were presented and the generation of insights began, using the prototyping and self-confrontation boundary objects. The co-creation activities of the fourth workshop will be detailed in topic Sect. 5.2.1.

5.2.1   Boundary Objects in Co-creation Workshops

The activities of generating insights are about identifying needs, desires, and potentials and, therefore, it is about opening space to encourage participants to reflect on what they are experiencing and what they can experience in the desired future situation. Insights can be considered as starting points for the product and service design process. (Holmlid et al. 2015). In this sense, this step was carried out using self-comfort and prototyping boundary objects.

After deciding on the priority area to start the product and service design processes by the participants, the researcher accompanied two professionals developing activities in this place, being an environmental analyst at the conservation unit and an external researcher, as shown in Fig. 1. The audience for these activities were high school and university students. Along the way, the researcher photographed six spots where professionals stopped to talk to visitors.

Fig. 1. Immersion at the visitation activities

In this way, it was possible to map the visitor's journey throughout this experience. The visitor's journey aims to identify the main elements of a service, understand the links between all the different, elements over time, identify problem areas in a service or areas, where new things can be added, and finally create empathy with different types of participants (Design Council 2020).

From the photographic records, were adopted the self-confrontation with professionals, which was applied separately. With the researcher, it was carried out in his working office at the university and recorded, and with the Environmental Analyst, the technique was applied during the fourth workshop. Through the ordered pictures, the professionals were asked, what they were doing at that moment, what they were seeing, feeling, and hearing, as well as, what resources they were using and how the visitors interact with the experience.

The photos were included on the map that represented the journey made in the priority area (From the visitors' center to Lagoon of Jurubatiba). Therefore, throughout this process, stakeholders were able to understand how professionals perceived the visitors' experience, which tangible and intangible aspects were present in the context, and therefore, how we could improve and innovate in that place. An example of one of the professionals' speech when verbalizing about the characteristics of the sandbank. An important step for visitors, who, when they arrive at the Conservation Unit, are contextualized about what a "Resting" is in the visitation room. Restinga are coastal ecosystems endemic to the Atlantic Forest biome (Scarano 2002).

Researcher: How do you see the Resting? "[…] I see the Restinga as a multivariate environment, it is not homogeneous, typical beach vegetation, then the Restinga vegetation formed by thickets, we have the lagoons, lagoons of black water, lagoons of clear water, the lagoon of brackish water, freshwater lagoons…. You need to go with a very open eye, not pre-conceived, for you to see different forms of life […]".

Researcher: What about the smell of this place? "[…] The smell near the sea has the full of sea… At the end of the afternoon the smell of the sea is stronger, as you go towards the continent, this smell will diminish and you will be no smell […]".

Researcher: What about the color of the Restinga? "[…] the color is a very strong green due to the vegetation, mixed, contrasting, with white, white sand, it is a strong and dark green, with white sand, and it is very beautiful, like a typical picture of paintings, landscape painters, very beautiful.

Researcher: What about the light? "[…] The Renting, unlike an Amazonian forest, is an environment with a lot of light, light and with the possibility of seeing everything, there is almost no shading in the bushes, little shade, shade only within the bushes […]".

Researcher: What about the texture? "[…] The texture reminds me of the sand, thick sand, typical of this Restinga, during the day it can be very hot, that nobody can set foot, in the months of January February and March, you can hardly not walk rest in Restinga, the temperature is very high […]".

Researcher: Is there sound in the Restinga? "[…] Above everything close to the sea, you have the sound of the waves, the sound of the sea birds […] As you enter the Restinga, it is a calm, peaceful environment, that you will hear the noise of birds, or in the late afternoon or early in the morning, the rest and a very pleasant silence […] "[…] Silence is very important in the Restinga because the species that have evolved in the Restinga have suffered adaptations with an environment without noise […]".

Researcher: What about the atmosphere in this space? "It is a clear atmosphere, except on foggy days, and this fog is stronger near the sea, otherwise it is a clean, transparent atmosphere, and especially when the sky is very blue, it makes up the atmosphere with the green of the Restinga one of the most beautiful sceneries that I consider […].

In the verbalization of this professional, important aspects about the place are identified, it is an important content for the process of designing products and services that can contribute to maximizing the experience in the place. According to Holmlid et al. (2015), many organizations carry out the prototyping of experience design as a way to get out of the box and co-create "the feeling of things".

In another scenario, it would be common to hear scientific concepts about what a sandbank is, generating few values and intangible content about the place. Considering that the map of the priority area was attached to the flipchart, with the respective photos of the journey (Fig. 2), and the participants already with information obtained from the self-confrontation about the journey, the prototyping process began.

Fig. 2. Prototyping on the map around the priority area.

For this, the participants signaled their insights for each of the stages of the journey, the ideas were recorded in a post-it and attached to the map. This prototyping process is very important for the second lens by Holmlid et al. (2015), referring to the co-creative practice in concept exploration and development, in which, during practice, possible futures collaboratively materialize, explore and develop.

Twenty new product and service insights were raised, and a matrix of products and services was subsequently developed, classifying them according to the type of service, target audience, location, and which were informative and interpretive.

6   Discussion of Results

The two boundary objects used in the present case study, self-confrontation and proto-typing, were of great relevance for co-creation activities. They contributed to facilitating the constructive dialogue between stakeholders and to make insights generation more tangible. As presented, the interpretive products and services, consider tangible and intangible aspects, in this sense, the verbalization of professionals during self-confrontation showed essential intangible values that will guide the co-design process, like feelings, values, sounds, and perceptions of the place. The verbalizations also allowed the transformation of scientific knowledge about the place, in a language more accessible to the participants, thus serving an important objective of environmental interpretation.

The self-confrontation interviews explained the tacit dimensions of the knowledge and behavior of the professionals who interact with the present case study. Self-confrontation also allowed access to knowledge formed by competent action, errors, and decisions, located in the body, in an incorporated and tacit way. This knowledge was accessed whenever the subjects were invited to describe their activity through verbalizations and gestures. For Lima (1998, p. 19), real behavior is always richer and more complex than the representation that the subject himself consciously elaborates. However, it is not possible to explain the meaning of the "outside" action, therefore it is necessary to explain the reasons and reasons of the individuals, which cannot be done without resorting to the speech of the actors themselves, ultimately, those who can validate the proposed interpretations.

According to Carlile (2002), an effective boundary object is able to establish "a shared syntax or language" and in different fields of knowledge (Carlile 2002, pp. 451–452), on the present study the boundaries objects helped the researcher to conduct the workshops aligned with the proposed objectives, among participants with different profiles, educational levels, professions and knowledge level of co-creation.

The prototyping developed using a map of the national park, in which stakeholders designed the future based on current reality. The twenty Insights for improvement in the visitor's journey were raised, which will make possible should contribute to the place innovation. Certainly, without the use of boundary objects, the number of insights for the development of products and services would be less than the number raised and probably not aligned to the context of innovation. Working with boundary objects is not just representing and transform knowledge, but also facilitate collaboration design through work practices (Suchman 1995; Button and Harper 1996). According to Holmlid et al. (2015) prototyping can take the form of several ways and can be adopted for different purposes. They can assist in the identification and construction a general understanding of the design challenge, as well as eliciting expressions and practices of stakeholders.

7 Conclusion

This study aimed to broaden the understanding of the role of boundary objects used in co-creation workshops, where the participants' knowledge is integrated into the local innovation processes. The paper showed that boundary objects can play an important and often unrecognized role in co-creation workshops for innovation in places. Prototyping activities contributed to add value to the dialogue between stakeholders and to put individual knowledge into action in the co-creation process. The self-confrontation interview proved to be an assertive method to access work activity and a differential in relation to other methodologies for analyzing the visitor's journey. Self-confrontation also brought intangible values essential to the product and service design process, which we would hardly have access to if it were not for verbalization. The facts strengthen the important role of boundary objects in the facilitation process among stakeholders, especially in a universe of participants with different profiles and little familiarity with co-creation activities. Finally, the selection of boundary objects in co-creation workshops for places is of great importance, since different objects allow the participation of interested parties and collaborative design in different ways.

References

Akasaka, F., Nakatani, M.: Citizen involvement in service co-creation in urban living labs. In: Proceedings of the 54th Hawaii International Conference on System Sciences, p. 4374, January 2021

Broberg, O.: Workspace design: a case study applying participatory design principles of healthy workplaces in an industrial setting. Int. J. Technol. Manag. **51**(1), 39–56 (2010)

Broberg, O., Andersen, V., Seim, R.: Participatory ergonomics in design processes: the role of boundary objects. Appl. Ergon. **42**(3), 464–472 (2011)

Brodersen, C., Dindler, C., Iversen, O.S.: Staging imaginative places for participatory prototyping. CoDesign **4**, 19e30 (2008)

Button, G., Harper, R.: The relevance of 'work practice' for design. Comput. Support. Coop. Work **4**, 263e280 (1996)

Caetano, A.C., et al.: Interpretação ambiental nas unidades de conservação federais. In: ICMBio 2018, 73 p (2018)

Carlile, P.R.: A pragmatic view of knowledge and boundaries: boundary objects in new product development. Organ. Sci. **13**(4), 442–455 (2002)

Design Council (2020). https://www.designcouncil.org.uk/. Accessed 02 Dec 2020

Egusquiza, A., Ginestet, S., Espada, J.C., Flores-Abascal, I., Garcia-Gafaro, C., Giraldo-Soto, C., Claude, S., Escadeillas, G.: Co-creation of local eco-rehabilitation strategies for energy improvement of historic urban areas. Renewable Sustainable Energy Rev. **135**, 110332 (2021)

Ericson, Å., Holmqvist, J., Wenngren, J.: Place innovation: using design thinking in live cases. In: 12th Biennial Norddesign 2016 Conference "Highlighting the Nordic Approach", Trondheim, Norway, 10–12 August 2016, vol. 2, pp. 398–317 (2016)

Holmlid, S., Mattelmäki, T., Visser, F.S., Vaajakallio, K.: Co-creative practices in service innovation. In: The Handbook of Service Innovation, pp. 545–574. Springer, London (2015)

Kenny, M.J.: Urban planning in the arctic: historic uses and the potential for a resilient urban future. In: Arctic Yearbook 2018, pp. 133–146 (2017)

Lima, F.P.A.: Fundamentos Teóricos de Metodologia e prática de análise ergonômica do trabalho. Curso de introdução à análise ergonômica do trabalho. Belo Horizonte. Departamento de Engenharia de Produção (mimeo) (1998)

Lindberg, M., Ericson, Å., Gelter, J., Karlberg, H.: Social change through place innovation. Design Res. J. (1), 9–13 (2015)

Lindberg, M., Nilsson, Å.W., Segerstedt, E., Hidman, E., Nilsson, K.L., Karlberg, H., Balogh, J.: Co-creative place-innovation in an arctic town. J. Place Manag. Dev. (2020)

Mattelmäki, T., Sleeswijk Wisser, F.: Lost in Co-X—interpretations of Co-design and co-creation. In: Proceedings of IASDR Conference, Delft (2011)

Scarano, F.R.: Estrutura, função e relações florísticas de comunidades vegetais em habitats estressantes marginais à Mata Atlântica brasileira. Ann Bot. **90**, 517–524 (2002)

Suchman, L.: Making work visible. Commun. ACM **38**, 56e64 (1995)

Theureau, J.: Course-of-action analysis and course-of-action centered design. In: Handbook of Cognitive Task Design, pp. 55–81 (2003)

Thomas, G.: How to Do Your Case Study. Sage, Thousand Oaks (2015)

Yin, R.K.: Estudo de caso: planejamento e métodos, 3rd edn. Bookman, Porto Alegre (2005)

Work Activity, A Link Between Networks and "Living" Territories: The Case of Express Package Distribution

Nadia Heddad[1]([✉]) and Sylvain Biquand[2]

[1] Département ergonomie et Écologie humaine, Université Paris 1, Panthéon Sorbonne,
21 rue Broca, 75005 Paris, France
nadia.heddad@univ-paris1.fr
[2] Abilis Ergonomie, 10 rue Oberkampf, 75011 Paris, France
sbiquand@ergonome.com

Abstract. This article aims to study the link between the network organization of an express parcel service and work activity in parcel distribution centers. The increase in parcel flows leads to rationalize production on a national and global scale. The organization on this scale is based on the industrial vision of the network as the processing of flows transiting between sites. However, the final sorting for delivery to the recipient obeys a local territorial rationality. In the delivery agencies, space use and circulation, work organization, work intensity and the physical involvement of workers, all adapt to distribute the parcels over a singular territory, despite the variability of volume or type of parcels. The activity of the workers has a normalizing role that allows adaptation to territorial singularities.

Keywords: Industrialization · Territory · Work · Sustainable development

1 Introduction

Express parcel services require to link a national (or international) territory to different local territories and conversely. The network is designed to process flows in an industrial approach through standard automated equipment and work organization over the country.

The work activity in parcel sorting center is directly impacted by the way parcels are received and dispatched to the final delivery vehicles. This level is generally considered as a simple sorting operation and is not taken into account in the design of national level flows. As a result, the workers in local sites face time pressure and service requirement.

The capacity of the express parcel service (as a work system) to offer next day delivery lays in suppressing the distance constraint between the origin of the goods and the delivery point by transferring parcels during the night between local sites. For the customer, getting a parcel within a day by ordering online is today a standard service offered by most express compagnies. Buying online does not consider the provenance of goods and leads to sustainable development concerns. Concomitantly, the second-hand market between private individuals is growing, fueled by customers' concern for

N. L. Black et al. (Eds.): IEA 2021, LNNS 219, pp. 165–168, 2021.
https://doi.org/10.1007/978-3-030-74602-5_25

sustainable development and avoiding waste. The pandemic context and confinement boosted this tendency. Packed at home, parcels with non-standard wrapping are more and more frequent and specific, in opposition to the industrial standardization of flows. Here again, workers performing the final sorting for delivery face a tension between the industrial system designed for bulk and the need to locally identify and dispatch individual parcels to their destination.

2   Methodology

The collected data comes from a case study in separate parcel sorting sites in different parts of France. We proceeded by observations and interviews with the workers in Paris, Bordeaux, Tours and Montpellier sorting centers. We observed work activity in real-work situations carried out at several delivery sites. In Bordeaux site, work groups were conducted with local workers to discuss work activity, technical setup, and organizational issues for a safe and efficient parcel processing. The results of the analysis were presented and discussed in a steering committee including designers and managers at the national and local level.

The objective was to understand complaints about health effects and contribute to set up new criteria for site design considering observed work needs and constraints.

3   Connecting the National Territory to the Local Territories

The express parcel company designs its network over the national territory. The routing layout and automatic industrial sorting nodes are set to process flows (Blanc 2020). This organization is a macro system (Gras 1997) consisting of an industrial complex of parcel processing sites linked by a routing scheme to take charge of parcel transport and delivery. Large automatized sorting center (called Hubs) are installed close to big cities. They are linked by motorways or airlines.

This industrial approach leads to standard equipment and work organization over the country. This organization is efficient by concentrating the flows of parcels transported between hubs within the national network. Sorting in Hubs takes place during daytime or evening and is generally highly automatized, using automatic scanners in an industrial approach. The industrialization of flows and sorting means that local specificities of parcel handling and delivery are eliminated.

However, the parcel flows need to reconnect to a local territory to be delivered. The identification and sorting in the local sites receiving parcels for final delivery is not automatic, the workers need to touch each parcel for scan reading and push it on the conveyor leading the parcel to the right zone for loading to delivery vans by address.

As the last link before final delivery, workers in each sorting center face time pressure as a result of the connection between the national territory and the local territory. The national network links 90 points on the territory every night, but thousands of local addresses are served each morning from these network nodes.

For example, parcels arrive at Bordeaux sorting center by trucks late in the night, usually between 2 et 3 am, and must leave the center to their final destination in delivery vans between 5 and 7 am early in the morning. Considering the daily quantity of 10 to

15 thousand parcels, and a team of less than 10 people, workers facing fatigue in night shifts must cope physically with the workload. Individual regulation, through slowing or taking a pause, is limited, as operators are linked by the conveyor system is a processing chain where each position must be manned. All employees work intensively for the 2 to 3 peak hours, and the high cardiac cost for this intense activity has been established.

Each local site has to adjust the standard bulk flow to local singularity. The activity of sorting workers is continuously adjusting to fit the peculiarities of a situated territory. The industrial system can absorb increasing flows through automatic processing and larger hauling trucks; however, it does not manage sorting tasks at destination. The workers must find the necessary flexibility to perform sorting within the short time allocated between trucks arrival and the departure of delivery vans. Their work is compressed under a double time pressure. The adjustment variable, in case of delayed route or airlines, remains the workers flexibility to face harder time pressure in sorting parcels.

The activity of workers has a normalizing role that allows the handling of territorial singularities (Heddad 2017). This activity relies on fundamentally human skills. It would be too expensive or complex for automatization. It requires the individual and collective activity and experience at local sites to adjust to the specific set of geographic, institutional and delivery coordination singularities, and their variability.

4   Increased Local Variability

In addition to the time pressure, workers in local sorting center must consider different customer requests and process the parcels accordingly. For example, time and delivery location can be changed by the customer, deciding to receive a parcel later or asking for delivery to a shop near home (relay point). This feature is put forward by the national network and promoted through advertising.

This flexibility has a cost for the workers sorting the parcels. For each redirection, they have to identify the parcel, read the request and process it specifically to it to the right driver at the right time. This redirection task is to manage by the workers late at night.

5   Sustainable Development Concerns Increasing Local Variability

On the other hand, recent sustainable development concerns change the nature of the flows. Local trade has become a trend specially during this pandemic period. People got interested in second-hand goods purchase, local small shops or buying direct from the producer.

These new connections do not go through warehouses where standard and efficient packaging is a need, and the goods are sent in a variety of shapes, wrapping and labelling, far from the standard cardboard box.

The shape and wrapping of these new types of parcels are often not truly adapted for transport and delivery, even for short distance. Workers must adapt to take care of a very large morphology spectrum, constantly adjusting their hand grip, manipulating the parcel to find the routing label, avoiding breakage. Owing to their varied shapes, these parcels do not fit in stacks, and are not adapted to roller conveyors.

The typology of parcels is changing and becomes less adapted to industrial type automatic process, and imposes an increased workload for their handling.

6 Conclusion

Parcel delivery face two contradictory movements. On one hand, the necessary national network should be designed with an industrial approach to process the increasing flow. On the other, the growing variability due to customer requirements and new purchase habits imposes an additional load on the workers.

The objective of our study was to understand complaints from workers about health effects, reduce physical workload through proper workplace design, and overall contribute to build new design criteria considering work needs in addition to the flow capacity criteria currently in use. Even if designers and managers at the national and local level are today aware of the workers work situation, changing design criteria for the macro-system, the industrial complex of parcel processing sites, is not realized yet. Time pressure is still a characteristic in work situations.

References

Blanc, Y.: La chaîne de valeur de l'entreprise. Séminaire du pôle ergonomie. Université Paris 1. Panthéon Sorbonne (2020)

Gras, A.: Les macro-systèmes techniques. Que sais-je? PUF, Paris (1997)

Heddad, N.: L'espace de l'activité: Une construction conjointe de l'activité et de l'espace. Le travail humain 2017/2, vol. 90, pp. 207–233 (2017). https://doi.org/10.3917/th.802.0208

From Integrated Operations to Remote Operations: Socio-technical Challenge for the Oil and Gas Business

Vidar Hepsø[(⊠)] and Eric Monteiro

NTNU Norwegian University of Science and Technology, Trondheim, Norway
{Vidar.Hepso,eric.monteiro}@ntnu.no

Abstract. Remote operations started with integrated operations (IO) some years ago where designated tasks and roles were shifted from off- to onshore. Remote operations, however, is more than remote control as the operational model or concept is key: it defines the scope for the tasks to be conducted remotely. With this increased ambition and scope, sociotechnical concerns play an increasingly important role. With increased autonomy and automation in the oil and gas business, the reliance upon digital representations of the process conditions that the center/control room follow up becomes more complex, technically but not the least organizationally and institutionally. Operational, organizational and information infrastructure issues are key considerations for remote operation including employer-employee relationships and collaboration with vendors. How will these new centers differ from traditional control rooms and the previous generation of collaboration centers that came with integrated operations 10–15 years ago? What are the key capabilities around which you build scalability and replicability in the design of such control centers? We discuss and empirically illustrate different configurations of remote operations.

Keywords: Control room · Remote operations · Integrated operations · Information infrastructures · Autonomy · Operational model · Center of calculation

1 Introduction

Technologies for collaboration within the oil and gas industry Integrated Operations (IO), allowed real-time data sharing between remote locations that challenged traditional geographical, disciplinary, and organizational boundaries [1]. According to the Norwegian oil industry association (OLF) [2] the first generation (G1) processes would integrate processes and people onshore and offshore using ICT solutions and facilities that improve onshore's ability to support offshore operationally. The second generation (G2) processes would help operators utilize vendors' core competencies and service more efficiently. Utilizing digital services and vendor products, operators would be able to update reservoir models, drilling targets and well trajectories as wells are drilled, manage well completions remotely, optimize production from reservoir to export.

© The Author(s), under exclusive license to Springer Nature Switzerland AG 2021
N. L. Black et al. (Eds.): IEA 2021, LNNS 219, pp. 169–176, 2021.
https://doi.org/10.1007/978-3-030-74602-5_26

In this paper we address this development of opening of boundaries into ecosystems, from integrated operations to remote operations. This process took many years and we analyze it as an *infrastructuring* process [3, 4]. Infrastructuring highlights the ongoing, provisional and contingent work that goes into working infrastructures of IO or remote operations. Working infrastructures share similar properties to ecosystems as they evolve along with their spread. Our analysis of integrated operations and remote operations specifically targets the evolution of emergent infrastructures over time. The key here is to focus on the increasing degree of entanglement of the infrastructure with internal and external stakeholders and agendas [5] in an everchanging ecosystem.

Crucially, an infrastructural perspective on IO emphasizes how collaborative practices are achieved through collections of – rather than singular – artefacts. One of the key components related to IO was the establishment of onshore support centers which enabled companies to move work tasks from offshore platforms to land. To enable such control centers several artefacts and practices were bundled: fiber-optic networks to shore, proper standards for communication and sharing of data, collaboration tools and new work practices and competence. This was a socio-technical bundling that made it possible for local and bounded distinct readings/data to be transferred to any place in a larger ecosystem [6]. Bruno Latour's [7] concept of *centers of calculation* underscores an important precondition to understand the unboundedness that comes with the development of IO and remote operations [8]. Collaboration centers and collaboration rooms were centers of calculation. Our research question is: *How do infrastructuring process transforming IO to remote operations change the content of the centers of calculation?* IO collaboration centers opened bounded offshore sites a process that has expanded with remote operations where boundaries are more obscure and where all control functions ultimately can be operated from anywhere given the proper barriers and cyber security mitigation.

IO grew out of Human Factors work methods and the research and consultants that worked with control room and control center development around the legacy of ISO11064 'Ergonomic design of control centers'. Even though the ISO standard had ways to deal with communication outside the control room, this method was still bounded in space. It was also criticized for not dealing with the change management and the multifaceted stakeholders and challenges that came with IO. It focused to a large extent around the development and construction of a control room, a bounded centre of calculation. Much of the new demand in IO came from understanding collaboration/work and IT support outside the control room, in the interaction between onshore and offshore staff during maintenance and operations and collaboration inside and across company borders more in general. Finally, how the existing situation could be changed through change management. The traditional HF methods could not address the ecosystem perspective and the existing methods were not able to address the dynamic features of the larger ecosystems [9]. New MTO/HF methods and conferences were developed as joint industry/research developments (see example center for integrated operations (https://www.iocenter.no/ and CRIOP (www.criop.sintef.no) to deal with this challenge where HF methods and around risk and change management were incorporated into new frameworks to address the increasing boundaryless features of IO.

However, IO lost remote operation along the way. When Rosendahl and Hepsø [1] co-edited the book on Integrated operations, 2012–2013, remote control had not proven to be as important as heralded, largely due to the socio-technical complexity of operational and technical aspects of remote operations. There were two main lessons that were incorporated according to Edwards [10].

The first was a move from the understanding that the operational model of the installation was a consequence of design, where the operational model was recognized as a precondition for the design rather than the other way around. Linked to the first lessons was a focus on maintenance hours. As Edwards et al. argue [10], they are normally a function of how much equipment you have on the installation that will require maintenance. Maintenance hours is a key parameter for how many people you will need to maintain the proper technical condition of the installation. When one was able to combine these two lessons into a profitable business case, the path to remote operations was possible. Edwards [11] describe the road to low manning, remote operation as a configuration of complexity of the installation systems, instrumentation needed to remotely control and a low number of maintenance hours. All these together form a path to an operational model based on remote control.

As a consequence of these two lessons the focus changed from the technical concept of remote control, that includes the technical capabilities that needs to be in place to make remote control possible, to remote operations that is a socio-technical configuration. This is where the operational model/concept is the key and where the technical, organizational and competence capabilities are included in the concept.

2   The Current Centers of Calculation

In what follows we describe the main configurations of centers of calculation as they appear with remote operations. We use the IOGP recommended practice as the basis for these types of configurations [11].

2.1   Remote Onshore Control Room

This is the first centre of calculation configuration. It can exist in various socio-technical realizations based on instrumentation level, manning and operational principles, installation reliability and maintenance load. It can also operate several installations from the same location regardless of geography. The main control room is located outside the production site boundary and in a safe zone. This location can be far away from the actual production site but is within the premises managed by the company. The primary purpose is to remotely control and operate the production site(s), but it may also include dedicated remote engineering or maintenance rooms. As these connections allow interaction with the production process or equipment, physical access controls are typically strictly enforced. Remote control refers to remote actions such as control commands (including: adjusting plant or equipment operational parameters, set point changes, alarm acknowledgement, manual start/stop commands), set point changes and operations monitoring on detailed graphical displays (e.g., process conditions, equipment status, alarms, errors).

Safety functions can also be performed from the remote-control room (such as executing manual shutdowns, operating critical action panels, etc.). Remote control requires read and write access to the system to enable operator interaction with the process and equipment on the production site. There are different preventive controls and recovery preparedness principles/measures in manned or unmanned situations and if there are people on site, or not. This is sought presented in the four-field table below (Fig. 1). This table describes four ideal situations, normal operations vs. emergency and if the installation is manned vs. unmanned installation.

	Normal operations	**Emergency**
Manned installation	• Lean crew close to emergency preparedness requirements • Onshore control room always in control • Can use operators to verify situation in the field	• Traditional onsite emergency organization and roles • Offshore has most functions • Offshore crew can verify situation in the plant, if safe
Unmanned installation	• Normal situation is unmanned • Onshore control room always in control • Campaign based maintenance and ad-hoc visits when necessary • When unmanned must use instrumentation/ actuators, camera, mobile fixed sensors to verify a situation in the field, ad-hoc shuttling last resort • Crawling, swimming or flying drones for check and report	• During campaigns normal emergency preparedness on site • Unmanned, the standard, roles filled by onshore or by nearby installation • Automatic or camera, fixed/mobile sensor identification during emergency

Fig. 1. Four ideal situations of remote operations

A remotely operated but manned installation can have a local offshore control room, but during normal operations the command and control of the installation are conducted from an onshore control room. Examples of this on the Norwegian continental shelf are the Martin Linge (Equinor) and Ivar Aasen (AkerBP) installations. Such an installation typically has a lean organization close to the emergency preparedness role requirements and the crew are always on the installation in shift rotation. During an emergency the local control room can be manned, and the offshore organization performs emergency preparedness roles. The offshore organization has a fully manned emergency preparedness organization. Compared to traditional oil and gas platforms the biggest difference is that the onshore control room is always in control. We exclude subsea installations here since they are always unmanned and remotely operated. Subsea fields like Ormen Lange and Snøhvit that are controlled from an onshore control room, but most subsea assets and tie-ins are usually controlled from the installation into which they deliver their production.

An unmanned installation can have a local control room, but command and control are always undertaken from an onshore control room. There can also be no offshore control room or just simplified control and shut-down functions on the installation. The remote sensor capabilities (CCTV coverage, remote actuation capabilities of equipment and sensor systems) are more advanced since the installation is operated most of the time without any crew. The visit intervals are dependent upon the maintenance load and instrumentation level of the installation, often scheduled in maintenance campaigns. Ad-hoc visits by helicopter can happen as last resorts. Maintenance campaigns typically range from manned for two out of six weeks, to as little as one or two scheduled short campaigns in a year. Examples of such installations are Valemon (Equinor) that are unmanned four out of six weeks, or well-head platforms like Oseberg H (Equinor) that have two scheduled campaigns every year. When unmanned the emergency function is handled onshore or by a nearby installation. In a period with campaign manning a simplified emergency organization exists locally (rescue teams) on the installation while emergency management functions can be divided between a nearby field or by the onshore organization. The normal operations model-unmanned in Fig. 1 above is the emerging model on the Norwegian Continental Shelf but this is already the standard in highly automated domains like wind-farms and power production/utilities more in general.

We do not have the possibility to address the larger ecosystem around remote operation in this short paper, but we mention these other types of centers of calculation since they bear witness of the movement from local control to centralized global or unbounded control more in general. Neither do we address the cybersecurity aspects and risks around control functions executed through these types. These ideal types also build on the IOGP recommended practice for control systems [11].

The first is the remote collaborative centre which is the collaboration center we recognise as a center of calculation from IO. Remote collaborative centre refers to an open office-based environment where personnel from multiple disciplines collaborate to manage the performance of one or more sites or specialised system across sites, like monitoring of rotating equipment. Such centres typically host collaboration, monitoring, visualisation, and analytical functions. They are similar to remote control rooms in terms of geographic location but may sometimes be distributed over several locations (i.e., multiple interconnected collaborative centres). Collaborative centres sometimes have less access controls than a control room however this depends on operational or security risks. Remote collaborative centers typically perform remote monitoring, or monitoring and diagnostics of production, operations and equipment conditions remotely using data generated and exported from the production site outside the control room. It also includes remote security monitoring using systems and network logs. It requires appropriate data needs to be available at the remote location. Access is usually made available inside the company firewall with either a vertical or horizontal integration, see next section. Remote at vendor premises also came with IO and refers to a centre of calculation at a remote location belonging to a vendor (or subcontractor). This location is usually located in private premises managed by the vendor or contractor. Contracts may define physical access and security restrictions at the vendor premises. Connection to these premises usually involves communications links via public networks. The external user at the vendor location accesses a fire wall (DMZ) with a strong user authentication process. This center normally does monitoring but can also conduct remote operation of equipment given the right access and cyber physical safety. Both these two centres and their access solution existed in the IO period, but they now can execute more control functions than earlier. The newest center of calculation is remote access from anywhere. Here control can in principle be done from any external location, in a private or public area (e.g., a home, hotel, or airport) where people can sit distributed outside company/vendor premises and can access/execute control functions given the proper access rights and functions. This option is increasingly seen as an opportunity with the coming of Internet of Things and becomes possible via control of devices via cloud services and new standards developed like OPC UA coming with Industry 4.0.

3   Basics of Industrial Automation and Control Systems (IACS) and Enterprise Systems OT and IT

IACS refers to collection of personnel, hardware, and software that can affect or influence the safe, secure, and reliable operation of an industrial process [11]. This area is called the operational technology (OT) domain. Most IACS can be remotely operated. Most new facilities include connections to enterprise networks to enable data export for plant monitoring, and other types of administrative systems whether these are collaboration systems, portals that are more open to the external world. The latter is the administrative domain defined as IT. Typically, the separation between OT/IT are implemented using firewalls that create a zone and conduit model to achieve appropriate network segmentation and restrict any direct connections between the OT/IT systems. An intermediate network or de-militarized zone (DMZ) network between OT/IT networks is typically used to prevent direct connections between enterprise network and control system networks. This makes it possible for office network-based systems and users to view data from control systems in a secure manner. The DMZ acts as a protection gateway between the safe zone and the enterprise network. Remote connectivity to control systems can be provisioned in two key ways, referred to here as 'horizontal' or 'vertical' connectivity [12]. First as 'horizontal' connectivity, an extension of control system 'zones' whereby the local control network is extended to a remote location. This provides identical level 2 control system network access and functionality at the remote location to that at the local site or operational site. The remote location retains the same security requirements as the IACS on the main site as they are fundamentally on the same zone. A 'horizontal' connectivity essentially maintains the remote functions within the IACS zone, thus relatively reducing the potential for external access as compared to vertical connectivity. But it increases the access points on the network, making them more distributed and may create new vulnerabilities or common mode of failure especially when the extension is not using dedicated network infrastructure.

'Vertical' connectivity – happens via implementation of connectivity from a remote, higher level (typically office/IT based) network to the local control network through a segregated and controlled 'zone' and 'conduit' architecture. Access to control system networks is managed through strong authentication and network traffic controls (typically a firewall or IDPS). 'Vertical' connectivity however connects control systems to enterprise network or external networks. This is sometimes achieved using third party networks. As all enterprise networks will have external, internet connectivity and often run a managed service to allow inbound connections, 'vertical' connectivity typically introduces the threat of external access to control system networks. In most facilities, some form of 'vertical' connectivity between control systems and enterprise networks as well as 'horizontal' connectivity are used.

Both the vertical and horizontal approach has its pros and cons. The recommended practice [12] describes the trade-offs and considerations that should be undertaken in the design process of the onshore control room. Thus, in the provision of remote operating centers, it is common that hybrid architectures will be present. The architecture is based on the IEC 62443 architecture reference model [11]. For details in the architecture and use-cases we refer to the IOGP Remote Control, monitoring and engineering architectures and security Recommended practice [12].

4   Quo Vadis - Remote Operation Industrial Control Systems

Each remotely operated facility has their own IACS (also referred to as safety and automation system – SAS) with functionalities for control and safety distributed between the facility itself (local) and the control center (remote). The dominant model for enterprise reference architecture in IACS is the Purdue Enterprise Reference Architecture (commonly known as the Purdue Model) for control systems and network segregation. Once the Purdue model became the industry standard, many companies started using these network models for safety systems. Purdue provides a model for enterprise control, which end users, integrators and vendors can share in integrating applications at key layers in the enterprise. Over time the industry has moved from a stable order informed by the Purdue model to a situation below where the network architecture is opening up, providing new possibilities and configurations coming with cloud infrastructures and IoT, but also new risks. In other words, Purdue has over time shifted towards an infrastructural system facilitating an evolving ecosystem.

Acknowledgement. This research is a part of BRU21 – NTNU Research and Innovation Program on Digital and Automation Solutions for the Oil and Gas Industry (www.ntnu.edu/bru21).

References

1. Rosendahl, T., Hepsø, V.: Integrated Operations in the Oil and Gas Industry: Sustainability and Capability Development. IGI Global Publishing, Hershey (2013)
2. OLF (Norwegian Oil Industry Association). Integrated Work Processes: Future Work Processes on the Norwegian Continental Shelf (2005). https://www.olf.no/getfile.php/zKo nvertert/www.olf.no/Rapporter/Dokumenter/051101%20Integrerte%20arbeidsprosesser,% 20rapport.pdf. Accessed 21 Sept 2009
3. Karasti, H., Baker, K.S., Millerand, F.: Infrastructure time: long-term matters in collaborative development. Comput. Support. Coop. Work (CSCW) J. **19**(3–4), 377–415 (2010)
4. Monteiro, E., Pollock, N., Hanseth, O., Williams, R.: From artefacts to infrastructures. Comput. Support. Coop. Work J. **22**(4–6), 575–607 (2013)
5. Bossen, C., Markussen, R.: Infrastructuring and ordering devices in health care: medication plans and practices on a hospital ward. Comput. Support. Coop. Work (CSCW) J. **19**(6), 615–637 (2010)

6. Østerlie, T., Almklov, P.G., Hepsø, V.: Dual materiality and knowing in petroleum production. Inf. Organ. **22**(2), 85–105 (2012)
7. Latour, B.: Science in Action: How to Follow Scientists and Engineers Through Society. Harvard University Press, Cambridge (1987)
8. Rolland, K.R., Hepsø, V., Monteiro, E.: Conceptualizing common information spaces across heterogeneous contexts: mutable mobiles and side-effects of integration. In: Proceedings of the 2006 20th Anniversary Conference on Computer Supported Collaborative Work Conference, pp. 493–500 (2006)
9. Hepsø, V.: When are we going to address organizational robustness and collaboration as something other than a residual factor? In: SPE Intelligent Energy Conference and Exhibition, Amsterdam, The Netherlands, 11–13 April 2006 (2006)
10. Edwards, A.R., Gordon, B.: Using unmanned principles and Integrated Operations to enable operational efficiency and reduce Capex and OPEX costs. SPE-Number-MS176813 (2015)
11. IEC/TS 62443: Industrial communication networks – Network and system security (2009). https://en.wikipedia.org/wiki/IEC_62443
12. IOGP (International association of oil and gas producers): Selection of system and security architectures for remote control, engineering, maintenance, and monitoring. Report 626, October 2018

Monitoring Return to Work Processes at a University Hospital: Ergonomics Contributions

Selma Lancman[1(✉)] ⓘ, Thaynah Pereira Oliveira[2] ⓘ,
Rafaela da Silva Roberto Dutra[1] ⓘ, Danielly Ferreira[1] ⓘ,
and Talita Naiara Rossi da Silva[1] ⓘ

[1] Universidade de São Paulo Medical School, São Paulo, Brazil
lancman@usp.br
[2] Clinical Hospital of Universidade de São Paulo Medical School, São Paulo, Brazil

Abstract. This study aims to reflect on the necessary adjustments in the program's conduct for monitoring removal and return to work (PAART), considering its principles, the reality, and challenges imposed by the pandemic. This is a report on the PAART experience in a medium- and high-complexity hospital during the pandemic. The program was restructured, given the need to understand work situations from workers' and managers' reports and previous knowledge about hospital dynamics. These reports were retrieved by information and communication technologies. A total of 571 workers were included in the PAART, and 277 could be contacted. Work organization relocation and changes in the period resulted in disrupted services, modified work routines and teams, and directly affected the implementation of the PAART. This raised concerns about the contributions of activity ergonomics and work ergonomic analysis in unpredictable work context situations. Also, we asked about the possible outcomes of the PAART if observations and analyses of real work situations were maintained. Despite questionings, we understand that the PAART experience in the pandemic is an opportunity for theoretical and methodological reflections.

Keywords: Health workers · COVID-19 · Activity ergonomics · Return to work

1   Introduction

Return to work is the reintegration process into work activities after a period of disability that results in the absence and removal of workers [1, 2]. This process is dynamic and associated with several factors, for example, length of removal, company type and policy, worker's health conditions, environmental, organizational, and relational work conditions, and involvement of various stakeholders underlying the work situation [3–11].

Work conditions and organization must be considered and adapted to facilitate this process and support job retention during workers' return. Therefore, work evaluation aspects become essential. Franco-Belgian ergonomics principles are fundamental as

N. L. Black et al. (Eds.): IEA 2021, LNNS 219, pp. 177–182, 2021.
https://doi.org/10.1007/978-3-030-74602-5_27

they provide that understanding work is fundamental to transform it and that it must be adapted to the worker's characteristics [11, 12].

Understanding work by observation and from the workers' expertise, including the peers of the one who is returning, allows reorganizing activities and support and cooperative processes among the workers involved in the work situation [13, 14].

The reality that emerged from the outset of the COVID-19 pandemic in 2020, especially in hospitals, implied the disruption of services and changes in teamwork routines and several developed programs. Several workers at the largest Hospital Complex in Latin America were at a higher risk for contracting COVID-19 due to the inherent exposure in their work plus age and comorbidities.

In 2020, the Central Institute of this Complex (CI) allocated its 900 beds during the most critical period of the pandemic, exclusively to assist patients with COVID-19, 300 of which were adapted for intensive treatment. The severe and unprecedented disease's characteristics brought about the need to recruit new staff, redirect teams, rearrange and train staff in the procedures for infection prevention and specific care to COVID-19 patients. Functions, work dynamics, and service flows were redefined. The respective treatment protocols were built and tested simultaneously with the most significant knowledge about the disease.

In this context, work removals, workers' difficult return, and team restructuring and reallocation were observed. Circulating within the Complex was also restricted due to the high disease infection level. This constraint included worker's health and safety teams, such as, for example, the Occupational Therapy team that develops the Removal and Return to Work Monitoring Program (PAART). This program is linked to the Hospital Complex's Specialized Service in Engineering, Medicine, and Occupational Safety.

Supporting the return to work and job retention, the PAART follows the principles of ergonomics. It aims to assess the worker, meet with immediate managers, and validate work situations and recommendations with workers, managers, and the health teams. The actions to assess the work situation and monitor the agreed changes' implementation had to be suspended during the period studied.

This study aimed to reflect on the necessary adaptations in conducting PAART considering its principles, the reality, and challenges imposed by the COVID-19 pandemic.

2   Method

This is a report on a PAART experience in a medium- and high-complexity hospital during the pandemic. The program was restructured following interruption of visits to work situations and face-to-face contact with workers and their managers. Understanding of work situations was based on the workers and managers reports and previous PAART team experience on hospital dynamics. These reports were obtained remotely through information and communication technologies. CI workers with removals equal to or greater than seven consecutive days or totaling seven days and over in any given month were included in the PAART. The Human Resources Department facilitated information on removals. Workers' personal and professional data were selected and organized according to the proposed objective.

A protocol with standardized questions to identify the reason for removal, the worker's health condition, work before removal, the return activity, and possible constraints among workers was elaborated. This information produced orientations regarding COVID-19, contacts with managers for arrangements and agreements required for the return to work, and continuous monitoring under PAART and other care programs to worker.

3 Results

In the Hospital Complex, 6,981 workers were removed due to suspected, confirmed, or risk for COVID-19, other physical and mental illnesses or work accidents, and maternity leave from March 16 to August 27, 2020.

Of the 2,420 workers removed in the CI, the three professional categories with the highest number of leaves were Nursing Technicians/Assistants/Attendants (28%), Medical Residents (14%), elementary and high school level health professionals (FMS) (13%). Another 12 categories made up the remaining 46% of removals.

A total of 571 workers met the PAART criteria, of which the program monitored 277: 71.75% were female, and 28.25% were male. The age of the workers ranged from 20 to 79 years, with a mean of 37.5 years.

This monitoring evidenced in the reports the difficulties of relocating and reconfiguring the teams and reorganizing work. Twenty-two percent of the monitored workers were unaware of whether they would return to the same function or sector after removal, and 6.8% would not return to the same place.

A nurse monitored by the PAART reported that she felt unsafe, first, because she was no longer in her work sector, as she had been transferred to another unfamiliar location. This professional coordinated a ward with a small team and did not know whether she would return to work in the same team. The team had been working together for a long time, and she feared the team's definitive breakdown. The nurse said, *"the feeling was that people were thrown into other sectors, unprotected, unsupported"*.

Regarding return to work, the workers shared doubts and concerns primarily regarding COVID-19, and the main ones were disease immunity after being infected, risks of transmitting the disease to their peers and families, peer prejudice, fears vis-à-vis the end of isolation and social distancing, and testing opportunities.

During the pandemic, follow-up by PAART also revealed the invisibility of workers not working directly in caring for COVID-19 patients but who are also essential for hospital functioning.

The hospital will no longer conduct tests for this type of employee. If we are unimportant, we could have been dismissed. Everyone has to work, but they only look at those who come close to the patient. (Administrative professional monitored by the PAART)

The workers also stressed the importance of the follow-up initiated even during removal from work.

If I were to summarize the monitoring carried out by PAART, I would say that it is "welcoming". You put yourself on this side to try to understand what's on the other side of the phone. I liked the program, a global work that can hear us in every way. (Nursing assistant monitored by the PAART)

4 Discussion

Hospitals are complex sociotechnical organizations in which work is necessarily carried out through multidisciplinary teams that seek to ensure the necessary care for patients. Providing care to the population is exhausting and a product of physical, psychological, and emotional illness for those working in these services [15, 16].

Due to the pandemic, hospital work organization has become even more intricate. It was necessary to restructure the services for a temporary and undefined period to respond to the demands for care to the population with barely known needs, a high infection level, and, in parallel, provide care to patients with other diseases.

These changes, the infection risks, and the necessary procedures for protecting workers also disrupted worker's health and safety programs and, consequently, rephrased PAART actions.

According to the principles of ergonomics, PAART recommends workers' involvement in the actions and the analysis of real work situations. However, some adaptations were made to ensure the program's remote development. This enabled the continuous monitoring of both sick workers at work due to COVID-19 and the rest. Performing remote actions during sick workers' removal did not allow assessing real work situations.

Following the health protocols, teams should circulate exclusively in their respective work areas, including worker's health and safety professionals, such as the PAART team. Thus, observing work situations and interacting with workers at their workplaces were not allowed.

The workers recognized the importance of the work performed and felt welcomed at a time of uncertainty and fears produced by the pandemic and the proximity of returning to work in this context. Also, there was a concern, mainly, with the infection of peers and possible fear and prejudice upon return. Social and peer support is crucial for the success of this process and staying at work [11, 12].

To assess the need for adjustments at work and facilitate the return, the discussion with the workers considered the previous knowledge of the PAART team about the hospital dynamics and the reports of each worker concerning their tasks and work activities. However, some workers were unaware of their returning place, given the hospital's organizational changes. Moreover, the distance from work during the period of removal, and, above all, the uncertainties, doubts, and fears brought about by the pandemic, became the central theme of the workers' reports, leaving other aspects of work conditions and organization in the background.

This new hospital work context generated doubts about the limited contributions of activity ergonomics and the ergonomic work analysis (EWA) in situations with such unpredictable context and when in loco real work analysis is not feasible [17]. In the situation presented, the real work was approached to monitor employees reflecting on their concerns regarding their activities upon actual return to work.

This space for reflective conversation allowed workers to learn from experience, build an understanding of their work and peers, and develop professional competences and prepare for the next activities. Reflection on productive activity transcends the temporal logic of the course of action and can potentially transform workers. These, in turn, transform their actions and relationships at work. It is the articulation of action learning with action analysis learning [18].

We also inquired the possible outcomes of PAART if observations and analyses of real work situations were maintained. Workers showed the need to talk about their health conditions and concerns about COVID-19 throughout the follow-ups, which limited the development of strategies to improve other work situations that could be negotiated with the managers.

Despite the questions, we understand the experience of the PAART in the pandemic as an opportunity for theoretical and methodological reflections, closer partnerships with other hospital sectors, and expansion of the program's actions to include the work removal period.

5   Final Considerations

The principles of activity ergonomics and EWA contributed to constructing reasoning and protocols for performing the return to work in the COVID-19 pandemic. The structuring of work-centered PAART allowed identifying situations of greater risk of removal and development of approaches that could facilitate the new introduction and permanence of the worker in the activity. Given the distancing from the work situation, whether due to the removal of sick workers or the team's restricted access to the sectors due to infection risks, remote contact with workers and reflecting on work allowed the continuous monitoring of employees' return to work, preserving the consideration of the real activity in the actions.

References

1. Silva Júnior, E.J.: Contexto de trabalho e estresse ocupacional entre os profissionais de Enfermagem de um hospital universitário. 112f. Dissertação - Centro de Ciências Humanas, Letras e Artes, Universidade Federal do Rio Grande do Norte, Natal (2018)
2. Lima, M.A.G.: Retorno ao trabalho. In: Mendes, R. (ed.) Dicionário de Saúde e Segurança do Trabalhador: conceitos, definições, história, cultura, pp. 998–999. Proteção, Novo Hamburgo (2018)
3. Young, A.E., Roessler, R.T., Wasiak, R., Mcpherson, K.M., Van Poppel, M.N.M., Anema, J.R.: A developmental conceptualization of return to work. J. Occup. Rehabil. 15(4), 557–68 (2005)
4. Young, A.E., Viikari-Juntura, E., Boot, C.R.L., Chan, C., Porras, D.G.R., Linton, S.J.: Workplace outcomes in work-disability prevention research: a review with recommendations for future research. J. Occup. Rehabil. 26, 434–447 (2016)
5. Silva, T.N.R., Alves, G.B.O., Assis, M.G.: Return to work in the perspective of occupational therapists': facilitators and barriers. Revista de Terapia Ocupacional da Universidade de São Paulo 27(2), 116–122 (2016)

6. Cumming, K., O'Brien, L., Harris, J.: Predictors of employment participation following lung transplant. Aust. Occup. Ther. J. **63**(5), 347–351 (2016)
7. Dunstan, D.A., MacEachen, E.: Bearing the brunt: co-workers' experiences of work reintegration processes. J. Occup. Rehabil. **23**(1), 44–54 (2013)
8. Morrison, T., Thomas, R.: Survivors' experiences of return to work following cancer: a photovoice study. Can. J. Occup. Ther. **81**, 163–172 (2014)
9. Young, A.E., Choi, Y.: Work-related factors considered by sickness-absent employees when estimating timeframes for returning to work. PLoS ONE **11**(10), e0163674 (2016). https://doi.org/10.1371/journal.pone.0163674
10. Lancman, S., Barros, J.O., Jardim, T.A.: Theories and practices of return and permanence at work: elements for the performance of occupational therapists. Rev. Ter. Ocup. Univ. São Paulo **27**(2), 101–108 (2016)
11. Nilsson, A.O., Eriksson, G., Asaba, E., Johansson, U., Helman, T.: Being a co-worker or a manager of a colleague returning to work after stroke: a challenge facilitated by cooperation and flexibility. Scand. J. Occup. Ther. **27**(3), 213–222 (2020)
12. Edgelow, M., Harrison, L., Miceli, M., Cramm, H.: Occupational therapy return to work interventions for persons with trauma and stress-related mental health conditions: a scoping review. Work **65**(4), 821–836 (2020)
13. Guérin, A., Kerguelen, A., Laville A., Daniellou, F., Duraffourg, J.: Understanding and transforming work: the practice of ergonomics. ANACT Network Editions, Lyon (2007)
14. Falzon, P.: Ergonomia, 1st edn. Blucher, São Paulo (2007)
15. Carayon, P.: Human factors of complex sociotechnical systems. Appl. Ergon. **37**(4), 525–35 (2006)
16. Carayon, P., Cassel, C., Dzau, V.J.: Improving the system to support clinician well-being and provide better patient care. JAMA **322**(22), 2165–2166 (2019)
17. Daniellou, F., Béguin, P.: Metodologia da ação ergonômica: abordagens do trabalho real. In: Falzon, P. (ed.) Ergonomia, 1st edn, pp. 281–301. Blucher, São Paulo (2007)
18. Mollo, V., Nascimento, A.: Práticas reflexivas e desenvolvimento dos indivíduos, dos coletivos e das organizações. In: Falzon, P. (ed.) Ergonomia Construtiva, 1st edn, pp. 283–303. Blucher, São Paulo (2016). Author, F.: Article title. Journal 2(5), 99–110 (2016)

Inter-organizational Design for Sustainable Transition in Agri-Food Systems: The Case of the Paris-Saclay Territory

Chloé Le Bail[1]([✉]) and Marianne Cerf[2]

[1] Université Paris-Saclay, CNRS, LISN, UMR 9015, 91400 Orsay, France
chloe.le-bail@universite-paris-saclay.fr
[2] Université Paris-Saclay, INRAE, AgroParisTech, UMR SAD-APT, 75005 Paris, France

Abstract. To reach their desirable vision of what actors mean by sustainable agri-food systems, transition processes take place in which the work activities evolve. The present paper investigates such an evolution through the conceptual framework of organizational design in ergonomics. It aims to understand how evolves the work of actors involved in the transition towards more "localized" production, distribution and consumption of food. We propose to consider the sustainability transition of agri-food systems as an inter-organizational design process, a process by which people redesign rules that guide coordination between organizations. We approach local food systems at the territorial scale to grasp the news forms of coordination in their cultural, spatial, economic, technical, political and ecological context. We consider the inter-organizational design process as the meso-level of actions, which articulates with the micro-level (work activities) as well as the macro-level (public policies, norms in food consumption). The paper presents the case of the association C, which manages catering for a public organization on the Paris-Saclay Plateau. We investigate the ecosystem of actors of the association C, as well as the way by which the catering manager develops and redesigns coordination at the various levels of actions.

Keywords: Food systems · Sustainability transition · Organizational design · Work activities · Multi-level of actions

1 Introduction

For several years, health and economic crises have highlighted the vulnerability of globalized agricultural value chains. It is now well recognized that agri-food systems need significant transformation of the existing standardized food regime to become more sustainable [1]. One approach on the definition of sustainable agri-food system is: a set of practices, from the production to the consumption of food products, economically viable, socially sustainable and ecologically responsible [2]. In this definition, sustainable food is not only about organic food. It concerns the quality of the food, the number of intermediaries and the geographic proximity as well [3]. The main objectives are to guarantee self-sufficiency and food security, to support the local economy, and to reduce GES emissions [4].

Sustainable agri-food systems require sustainability transition, namely a process of change from one sociotechnical system to another [5]. Over the last two decades, the field of *Sustainability Transitions Studies* has explored processes of innovation in agri-food systems towards more sustainability [2]. Many scholars analyze bottom-up initiatives, namely innovations developed by some actors for their own benefit. They identify local food systems as social innovations, which encourage fair prices, solidarity, democracy and participatory processes between different actors, especially farmers and consumers [6]. Here, Social Innovation refers to a set of innovative activities and services that are motivated by the goal of meeting a social need [7]. It generates new forms of collaboration between people and promotes community values such as equity and mutual aid.

However, in local food systems, work activities might be quite different from what they ought to be in globalized agricultural value chains. The aim of this paper is to understand how evolves the work of actors involved in the transition towards more "localized" production, distribution and consumption of food. We propose to consider the sustainability transition of agri-food systems as an inter-organizational design process, namely a process by which people redesign rules and tools that guide coordination between organizations. We approach local food systems at the territorial scale to grasp the news forms of coordination in their cultural, spatial, economic, technical, political and ecological context. The objective is to understand local food systems as anchored in particular territories, which implies the existence of social networks at this scale (local authorities, distribution platforms), institutional regulations (for example, Territorial Food Program) and specific forms of sharing knowledge, know-how and traditions [8].

Therefore, we grasp the concept of territory as the result of the combination of geographical, economic, cultural and socio-political factors and try to capture its dynamics through the lens of a transition process to address a societal function (here, food). We see the territory as a complex and situated system, which takes shape according to human interactions, interactions between individuals and organizations, and interactions between humans and the natural environment [9]. It implies to consider different scales of actions, and to understand how work activities evolve within and throughout these various scales. We consider the inter-organizational design process as the meso-level of actions, which articulates with the micro-level (work activities) as well as the macro-level (public policies, norms and conventions in food consumption). We question how, in such a design process, the various actors deal with their interdependencies and debate about their way to define what local and more generally sustainable food means. How evolves inter-organizational coordination to produce and consume sustainable food and to build a territorialized agri-food system? How does it change the work of the actors involved?

2 Method

2.1 Context

We have conducted a case study in the Paris-Saclay Plateau located in the south of Paris. It is a peri-urban area, which is favorable to the emergence of local food systems. Paris-Saclay Plateau is close to a dense urban area where prosperous agricultural activities remain, despite huge construction sites for the installation of both private companies and public infrastructures (universities and research centers). Local stakeholders try to preserve agricultural and natural spaces to develop the well-being of people and an area is identified as a protected agricultural land reserve (ZPNAF). The past few years, local initiatives (i.e., short food-supply chains) have emerged to help the connection between local consumption and local production [10].

More precisely, we have focused on the delivery of local products in the canteens of companies and universities based on the Paris-Saclay Plateau. In France, the Egalim law was passed in 2018, with the objective to promote a healthy, safe, sustainable diet for all by introduction in school and university canteens of 50% quality-labeled or organic products starting on January 1st 2022. Canteens are encouraged to source products obtained via Territorial Food Program even though these products are not counted in the 50% of sustainable products. In this context, we have explored how actors that have key roles in inter-organizational coordination (local producers, canteen managers, NGOs that aim at developing sustainable food practices in the area) articulate their actions to develop the local food system.

2.2 Data Collection

Data collection was carried out between October 2019 and May 2020 by researchers in Ergonomics and Management Science. Twelve interviews were conducted with:

- Experts, to understand the functioning of company canteens in France, and the changes related to the introduction of sustainable products, including local products (three interviews);
- Managers in charge of sustainable development issues in companies, in the case where companies do not have canteens (two interviews);
- Catering managers, for companies which have canteens (three interviews);
- Producers and processors of local products included in the menus of the canteens where we interviewed the managers (three interviews);
- The most important local NGO, which works with public authorities on the definition of the Territorial Food Program in Paris-Saclay Plateau (one interview).

Furthermore, we collected some documents that help actors to coordinate their work (e.g., contracts, invoices).

2.3 Data Analysis

Data analysis was based on the framework of organizational design in ergonomics, where organizational change is seen as a collective design process distributed in time and space.

In such a perspective, the operator is considered as the "designer" of his own work, and as the designer of its own work organization [11, 12]. Collective work refers to the way in which operators cooperate in a more or less effective manner to achieve a common goal. It implies processes of task allocation, coordination of activities and "re-design" of rules to articulate individual objectives, as well as to guarantee a "good" job that satisfies all stakeholders [13].

Firstly, we have identified the ecosystem of actors of the managers and the producers interviewed, and who are involved in the development of local food consumption in the canteens. Secondly, we have focused on how these managers and producers articulate three types of coordination to develop local food consumption: 1) a coordination within organizations at the micro-level of actions (work activities); 2) a coordination between organizations at the meso-level of actions (inter-organizational coordination); and 3) a coordination which aims at changing some norms and conventions in food consumption at the macro-level of actions. The multi-level perspective refers to the complexity of actors within the ecosystem in terms of governance (i.e., how entities are directed and controlled, how and by whom rules are decided). Therefore, such a perspective refers to how actors can change the structure and the rules of coordination that guide the interactions between them. We have considered that an upper level is more complex and more stable than a lower one.

3   Results

We present the ecosystem of actors of the association C, which manages catering for a public organization in the Paris-Saclay Plateau. The association C manages three restaurants. Each one has its own kitchen and employs between 16 and 20 employees distributed as follows: a chef, cooks, a storekeeper, catering staff. The three restaurants are open only for lunch, Monday to Friday, and approximately 230 days per year. Each year, the catering manager creates a provisional financial plan that must be approved by the direction. The plan includes food needs, equipment needs, cleaning needs and labor needs. The manager is also in charge of the respect of hygiene norms, nutrition and provision of meals. He chooses suppliers according to the possibilities which the financial plan offers to him. For example, sustainable products are generally more expensive than other products, so the manager adapts the number and the type of sustainable products he orders to cope with the financial conditions.

The Fig. 1 illustrates the ecosystem of actors of the association C and the three types of coordination: 1) coordination of activities within restaurants (micro-level); 2) inter-organizational coordination, which concerns restaurants and local producers (meso-level); and 3) coordination which takes place on a more macroscopic level and which concerns institutions, public policies and catering national societies.

3.1   Variability of Coordination with Producers

Relationships between the association C and local producers-processors are diverse. Such a diversity shows that the catering manager wishes to adapt the functioning of the association C to the characteristics and the needs of the various farms. The result highlight three categories of relationship (see Fig. 1):

- Regular order: the producer delivers always the same quantity in a regular and on-going manner (e.g., every day). It is the case of the producer 1 who delivers systematically its chickens every month, and the producer 2 who delivers regularly its yoghurts. These two producers are located in the Paris-Saclay Plateau.
- Irregular order: the producer does not deliver the same quantity each time and/or the delivery days are not the same over time. It is the case of the producer 3 who delivers various quantity of bread according to the period of the year. Indeed, the catering manager has accepted to buy more bread each week before schools holiday to support the producer in the loss of income during holidays. The producer 3 is located in the Paris-Saclay Plateau.
- Exceptional order: the catering manager helps a producer-processor who needs to find urgently a market for its products. It is the case of the producer 2 who sometimes has a surplus of vegetables and the catering manager buys the surplus to avoid waste. It is also the case for producers who are not usually in the ecosystem of the association C, such as the producer 4 who is located in Brittany. Once, the manager accepted to help the producer who had 500 chickens to sell urgently. He wanted to help the producer to rebuild up its cash flow.

The three categories of relationship highlight that the catering manager wants to support local food consumption, in the Paris-Saclay Plateau, as well as in the "best possible proximity". The manager wants to support French agriculture as a whole. But the expansion of the criterion of "locality" is also due to the absence of some products in the Paris-Saclay Plateau. In other words, the area does not offer enough food resources to meet the requirements of the restaurants.

3.2 Influence at Micro-level

The actions that the catering manager develops at meso-level of actions (coordination with producers-processors) affect the micro-level of actions (work within the canteen). For example, the purchase of a surplus of vegetables "in the last minute" requires to change the menus and to adapt other orders. Normally, the process by which the menus are elaborated and then ordered is as follow (see Fig. 1):

1) Menus are created during a committee which involves the catering manager, the administrative staff, the direction, a dietician, cooks, consumer representatives. The committee approves the menus for a period of twenty days, which corresponds to the national recommendations for respecting a dietary balance.
2) The restaurants order the food they need at least one week before. This time of one week is necessary for the buyer of the association to prepare the orders. The buyer centralizes the requests and places orders with suppliers.
3) The products are delivered directly to the restaurants according to a delivery schedule established with the supplier.

To help a producer or to support local production, the catering manager does not hesitate to change the rules (of elaboration of menus) that he has himself designed.

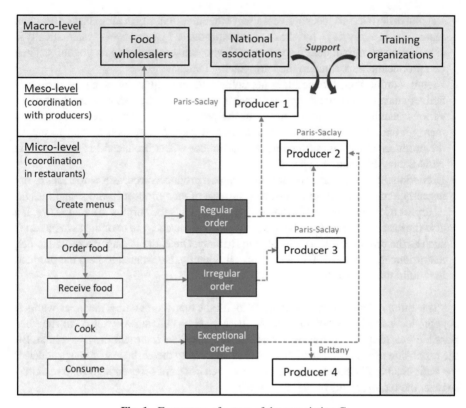

Fig. 1. Ecosystem of actors of the association C.

3.3 Relation with Macro-level

At the macro-level of actions, the catering manager coordinates its actions with dominating food wholesalers that help him to find products less expensive, as close as possible to the restaurants. As well, he coordinates its actions with catering national societies to obtain a certain degree of latitude. For example, the association C is very engaged in a national association for catering professionals. During the elaboration of the Egalim law, the catering manager of the association C has contributed to increase the limitation from which suppliers are put into competition on the basis of a call for tenders. The limitation has been increased from 25,000 euros to 40,000 euros per year, excluding taxes. Such an augmentation is favorable for "little" suppliers such as local producers for which competition is hard to manage.

In the same idea, the association C works with private national training organizations to develop the skills of employees. Indeed, collective catering involves specific skills and know-how to re-introduce fresh and local products in cooking practices.

4 Discussion

The transition of agri-food systems to provide more sustainable food to employees-consumers in the Paris-Saclay area implies an organizational work at both micro and meso-levels of actions. Furthermore, it implies that the organizational work articulates with the macro-level of actions.

To produce and consume sustainable, local food, and to build a territorialized agri-food system, actors must redesign "during the use" the inter-organizational coordination between restaurants and producers. Such a redesign is constrained by the macro-level of actions (the public policies, the norms and convention), by the geographical and cultural dimensions of the territory (e.g., what resources are existing, how people consider these resources), and by the possibilities of transformation and evolution of work situations (i.e., do the transformations respect health and safety?).

Implications for ergonomics intervention are twofold. Firstly, it implies to identify at least two processes of coordination and their reconfigurations, one inside the organizations, the other between the organizations. Secondly, it implies to identify which criteria are in stake in the reconfigurations (e.g., sustainability, locality, territoriality), and their signification from the point of view of the actors involved in inter-organizational design process.

References

1. Meynard, J.M., Jeuffroy, M.H., Le Bail, M., Lefèvre, A., Magrini, M.B., Michon, C.: Designing coupled innovations for the sustainability transition of agrifood systems. Agric. Syst. **157**, 330–339 (2017)
2. Gaitán-Cremaschi, D., Klerkx, L., Duncan, J., Trienekens, J.H., Huenchuleo, C., Dogliotti, S., Contesse, M.E., Rossing, W.A.: Characterizing diversity of food systems in view of sustainability transitions. A review. Agron. Sustain. Dev. **39**(1), 1–22 (2019)
3. Renting, H., Marsden, T.K., Banks, J.: Understanding alternative food networks: exploring the role of short food supply chains in rural development. Environ. Plan. A **35**(3), 393–411 (2003)
4. FAO. Sustainable healthy diets – Guiding principles. Rome (2019)
5. Rip, A., Kemp, R.: Technological change. Hum. Choice Clim. Change **2**(2), 327–399 (1998)
6. Chiffoleau, Y., Loconto, A.M.: Social innovation in agriculture and food. Int. J. Sociol. Agric. Food **24**(3), 306–317 (2018)
7. Mulgan, G.: Social Innovation: How Societies Find the Power to Change. Bristol University Press, Bristol (2019)
8. Lamine, C., Garçon, L., Brunori, G.: Territorial agrifood systems: a Franco-Italian contribution to the debates over alternative food networks in rural areas. J. Rural Stud. **68**, 159–170 (2019)
9. Moine, A.: Le territoire comme un système complexe : un concept opératoire pour l'aménagement et la géographie. L'Espace géographique **35**(2), 115–132 (2006)
10. Tedesco, C., Petit, C., Billen, G., Garnier, J., Personne, E.: Potential for recoupling production and consumption in peri-urban territories: the case-study of the Saclay plateau near Paris France. Food Policy **69**, 35–45 (2017)
11. Coutarel, F., Petit, J.: Le réseau social dans l'intervention ergonomique : Enjeux pour la conception organisationnelle. Manag. Avenir **7**(27), 135–151 (2009)

12. Arnoud, J., Falzon, P.: Changement organisationnel et reconception de l'organisation: des ressources aux capabilités. Activités **10**(2) (2013)
13. Caroly, S., Barcellini, F.: The development of collective activity. Constructive ergonomics. In: Falzon, P. (eds.) Constructive Ergonomics, pp. 19–32. CRC Press, Boca Raton (2014)

Experimenting Sustainable Orchards: How to Cope with Different Territorial Levels?

Agathe Legendre[1]($\boxtimes$), Nadia Heddad[1], Marianne Cerf[2], and Servane Penvern[3]

[1] Université Paris 1 Panthéon Sorbonne, Département Ergonomie et Écologie Humaine, 21 rue Broca, 75005 Paris, France
[2] Université Paris-Saclay, INRAE, AgroParisTech, UMR SadApt, 75005 Paris, France
[3] INRAE, UR Ecodeveloppement, Domaine Saint Paul, 84914 Avignon Cedex 09, France

Abstract. Research institutes seek solutions to reduce the use of pesticides in fruit production. They redesign new orchards, pesticides free (or nearly). It implies new forms of interactions with the local stakeholders as well as a change in the experimental paradigm and the content of work, with a key role of observations on the agroecosystem. This leads us to distinguish two territorial levels: the "ecological one" and the "sector one". The first is related to the territory as a production environment (e.g. climate, type of soils, plants, animals, growers) whereas the second is related to the territory as a geographical space where different players of a production sector are located. We analyze how these two territorial levels are handled by the experimental stations. We discuss how the change in experimental paradigm brings questions to the experimental stations' workers, regarding territories issues and suggest that giving more centrality to work activity might create new relations between the stations and their territories.

Keywords: Experimental work · Sustainability · Territory · Observation

1 Introduction

Agricultural systems are always situated in a territory; agricultural production in one territory couldn't be the same in another. Thus, work in agriculture also depends on the territory in which it is performed. We distinguish the "ecological territory" to give account of the territory as a production environment with abiotic and biotic processes mostly impacted by the activities of neighborhood actors, and the sectorial territory, as a geographical space where different players of a sector are located (processing industry, suppliers, growers). In this paper we will focus on two experimental stations, working on fruit production in the South-East of France. They are located in two different fruit production areas with regard to both territorial dimensions (environmental and sectorial). Their longstanding implementation in these areas gave them the opportunity to develop knowledge on their ecological environment as well as relations with the different players involved in fruit production. Such relations enable their workers, if desired, to involve these players in the research process or to share the results obtained in the experimental orchards.

N. L. Black et al. (Eds.): IEA 2021, LNNS 219, pp. 191–195, 2021.
https://doi.org/10.1007/978-3-030-74602-5_29

Nowadays, reducing the use of pesticides in agriculture is an important research issue. However, it has been proven difficult to reduce pesticides levels below a certain level in classical orchards (Simon et al. 2011, Navarrete et al. 2012). To overcome this difficulty, the managers of these two experimental stations decided to redesign disruptive multi-species and multifunctional orchards, pesticides free (or nearly), based on ecosystem services. It changes the experimental design and purposes. Indeed, most experimental stations are dedicated to test production factors and their effects on crop performances in factorial trials or started more systemic trials aiming at comparing combinations of cultural operations but without calling into question the classic orchard schemes, in particular the online organization of species and varieties, and the main objective: production. Within such stations, work is organized in a quite hierarchical fashion: engineers or researchers define protocols, technicians are dedicated to scoring data on the field, while others have in charge the crop management. As stations are always embedded in a local production area, local farmers visit them mainly to seek information on technical references and performances obtained in the station fields. On the contrary, maximizing ecological processes to avoid pesticide use implies to reconsider the organization of the orchard, its objectives and the trial scale (from blocks to the whole agroecosystem). Such disruption changes the content and the scale of the design, management and evaluation work. It also seems to enhance the role of observation activities, within the stations' staff activity.

 A first work was conducted within these two stations and revealed the centrality of observation activity within the stations' workers activity. It also led to several questions about work in experimental orchards in connection to the territory. In this paper, we will illustrate such questions.

2 Methodology

We focused on two experimental stations (G and B) run within two different institutions and located in the South-East of France. We collected data during the design phase (co-design workshops), as well as documents on decision processes and protocols developed during the implementation phase. We conducted interviews with the workers of the station to identify the changes which occurred in the work organization in relation to the new orchards, and observed the course of various tasks (pruning, harvest, data collecting, etc.). The observations we performed in the orchards were focused on the observation activity.

3 Reconnecting with the Territory in Both Design and Implementation Phases

3.1 Designing Orchards with the Local Stakeholders

Being aware that pesticide free orchard will be more context dependent and will rely on local ecological processes, people in charge of the experimental stations organized co-design workshops involving stakeholders of their local territory with various backgrounds (Penvern et al. 2018). The idea was to value local knowledge hold by them on local species and ecological processes and to favor exchanges with an extended knowledge base (e.g. empiric and scientific knowledge from various disciplines) to design disruptive orchard prototypes. This process inaugurates changes in the work done to produce and mobilize knowledge within the station and with the local stakeholders. It also developed a new understanding of the ecological territory by reconnecting to the stakeholders' knowledge on the local ecosystems.

The prototypes were then discussed and modified by experimental stations workers. In G., these ones built from scratch a circular and multispecies orchard completely pesticides free; in B., they chose a multispecies orchard in which biocontrol products can still be used as a last resort. They diversified existing specialized rows with new species and varieties.

The experimental stations also opened their door to the local stakeholders for visits, and organized events where growers and scientists could exchange on their experience of a particular topic (Cardona et al. 2018).

With this type of process, experimental stations embrace the "sectorial territory", and become more and more an actor of this territory as they try to take into consideration the commercial outlets and production circuits.

3.2 Observation Activities: A Pivotal Role Which Specifications Requires In-depth Reconnection to the Ecological Territory

Observation activities are central in the ecosystem services-based orchards. It is performed by all the workers. It is a constant and highly embedded activity. Observations serves different functions: to answer to the task requirements, gather information on orchards' health, build landmarks and skills. This activity is pivotal for understanding and managing any orchard, as well as for defining the experimental protocols. Without observation, no work activity is possible in the orchards. This is true regardless the "ecological territory" in which the experimental station is situated and regardless of the design of the orchard, or the work organization. However, what can change depending on the location are the components of the "ecological territory" on which to focus, the signals that workers are looking for. Indeed, depending on the location, pests and diseases can be different, and fruit trees can be more or less sensitive to them. For instance, in our study, the workers of one station considered peach trees as more resistant than apricot trees, whereas it was the other way round in the other station.

The new spatial organization of the orchards also requires to build new landmarks to identify the spots on which relevant observations have to be carried on for both management and experimental tasks. The workers also grasp many signals to build a living picture of the agroecosystem, e.g. a picture in which they are aware of the various habitats for both fruit trees, fruit bushes and their pests and auxiliaries. Observations are key to enable the workers of the experimental stations to rebuild a new environmental territory and make it tangible for other local producers.

4 Questions Regarding Territorial Issues

4.1 How to Generalize Knowledge When Produced in a Local Situation?

Those new orchards, based on ecosystem services, are more dependent on their environment than conventional ones. Indeed, the new orchard's biodiversity means that new interactions between its components occur, while the short range of solutions when a pest or a disease occurs brings new constraints. As pointed above, this leads to a pivotal role of observation activity, to prevent any outbreaks and better understand/assess the agroecosystem. The stations' workers are then closer and closer to their environment, they are, as they say, "connected" to the orchards. But, while this connection to this territory is growing, it become more and more difficult for the stations' workers to generalize their results, to define how they will valorize their experimentation. Indeed, if the results obtained in the experimental orchards are highly dependent of the *hic and nunc* context and not reproducible elsewhere, then which knowledge and results can be produced and shared with growers and other actors? Should they share their questions and the changes in their work? Should they share their way to connect to the orchard rather than the performance obtained?

4.2 Which Potential Impacts of Pesticide Free Experimentation on Local Commercial Orchards?

Some workers pay attention to the potential impacts their pesticide free management can have on surrounding orchards. If such orchards may host and increase biodiversity, including auxiliaires useful for pest regulation, it can also host pests. For instance, a worker acknowledges the dissemination risk of drosophila suzukii which could damage the quality of commercial harvests. This concern not only points an awareness of the quality requirements for most of the commercial orchards but also show that workers feel somehow uneasy with the pesticide free experimentation: what if their experimentations, instead of helping growers, might have negative impacts for them?

4.3 Which Room for Work Requirements in the Step-by-Step Design of Pesticide Free Experimental Orchards?

Although the spatial and landscape design were defined during a first stage, the way to manage the pesticide free orchard and to collect data, to document its dynamics and performance is designed "step-by-step". Our observations enable us to point out that the decisions were mainly driven to promote biodiversity, production, resilience of the trees, reducing pests and disease, but no goals regarding work were clearly identified. As well, the feasibility of the tasks within the new orchards was not often discussed. Yet, maximizing biodiversity, for instance, can lead to constraints for the work activity. For example, during raspberries' harvest, the workers had to dig in the raspberries, sometimes intertwined with other shrubs. These constraints are perceived differently among the workers. The important point here, is not so much the constraints that maximizing biodiversity bring to the stations' workers, but the fact that those constraints are not discussed, that, as one of the workers said *"it's true that we take work for granted"*.

However, balancing biodiversity issues with work ones might be required for commercial growers to accept the experimentation results. Indeed, if growers assume that developing such orchards will cost too much, in terms of work thus of money, there is a risk that they will never be developed. Our last question will then be: Why is work feasibility not considered as a goal and workload not assess apart from time allocated to tasks within the step-by-step design process if one of the aims of the experimentation is to favor the adaptation and design of pesticide free orchards by growers?

5 Conclusion

Orchards based on ecosystem services are more than ever situated in their territory, which leads the experimental stations to exchange with the local stakeholders and the workers to "connect" themselves to their ecological environment. This "connection" is possible thanks to the observation activities, which are central in their work. However, as the connection between the experimental stations (and their workers) and their local territory increase, the difficulty to generalize results of the experimentation also increase. Other issues have also been revealed as the potential impact of the pesticide free experimentation on the surrounding orchards through pest dissemination, or the lack of requirements regarding working activities in the step-by-step design of the experimentation. In fact, recognizing the centrality of work in the experimental orchards could open the experimental stations to new connections to their territories. To which extent could/should workers share their questions and changes in their work with the local growers, in order to help them to design and manage their own production system? It would be interesting to investigate such an avenue in the future.

References

Cardona, A., Lefèvre, A., Simon, S.: Les stations expérimentales comme lieux de production des savoirs agronomiques semi-confinés. Revue d'anthropologie des connaissances **12**(2), 139–170 (2018)

Penvern, S., Chieze, B., Simon, S.: Trade-offs between dreams and reality: Agroecological orchard co-design. IFSA (2018)

Navarrete, M., Bellon, S., et al.: L'écologisation des pratiques en arboriculture et maraîchage. Enjeux et perspectives de recherches. Le courrier de l'environnement de l'Inra, no. 62, pp. 57–70 (2012)

Simon, S., Brun, L., et al.: Pesticide use in current and innovative apple orchard systems. Agron. Sustain. Dev. **31**(3), 541–555 (2011)

Constructing the Place of Ergonomics as a Design Discipline: The Case of the Basic Design of Oil Platforms

Camila P. Marins[1][(✉)] , Priscila B. C. Leite[1] , Marina P. Mercado[1] ,
Luciano do V. Garotti[2] , and Francisco J. C. M. Duarte[1]

[1] Department of Production Engineering, Federal University of Rio de Janeiro, Rio de Janeiro,
RJ, Brazil
{camila.marins,marinapmercado,duarte}@pep.ufrj.br,
priscila.blasquez@coppe.ufrj.br
[2] Petrobras Research and Development Center, Rio de Janeiro, Brazil
luciano.garotti@petrobras.com.br

Abstract. Ergonomics is currently in the process of building its space as a discipline in energy sector design, as well as in the continuous process industry. This issue emerges from the expectation organizations have in regard to participation and products developed by the discipline in projects. The purpose of this study is to report the participation of a team of ergonomists in an oil platform basic design, discussing ergonomics structuring. To that effect, this study used participant observation as a methodology, as well as data collected along 14 months for this case study. The results show the challenges faced and strategies adopted to integrate remote work to the design dynamics. Even though ergonomics' scope of action has not yet been clearly understood, it was possible to observe how the practice of the discipline has evolved during this project. This work highlights how ergonomics can potentially help integrate the different rationales which make up the design.

Keywords: Ergonomics · Design process · Offshore

1 Introduction

Design processes, such as the ones involving oil platforms, have specific organization, which is often guided by technology-centered criteria [1]. In Brazil, ergonomics has increasingly stood out in the energy industry, and one of the reasons for that is the increased rigor of governmental inspections.

Design dynamics itself goes through transformations, as new technological resources become available. In addition to that, ergonomics must build its own space in the design, making it possible for knowledge on real work to be used to establish design requirements from the early stages [2].

This paper discusses the participation of an ergonomics team in an oil platform basic design. The premises of this participation accommodated a double ambition: the

N. L. Black et al. (Eds.): IEA 2021, LNNS 219, pp. 196–200, 2021.
https://doi.org/10.1007/978-3-030-74602-5_30

design was conceived with the purpose of being a benchmark project for platforms in the future, and, as for ergonomics itself, the project would be a benchmark for the discipline, with the purpose of generating documents which would serve as the grounds for future projects.

The purpose of this study is to discuss the structuring of ergonomics actions, as well as the challenges faced in this project.

2 Methodology

This is a qualitative research based on a single case study and grounded in activity ergonomics references proposed by Guérin et al. [3]. The study was developed based on the monitoring of an oil platform basic design, which took place between October 2018 and June 2020.

Three researchers collected the data during the 14 first months of the project. Participant observation was the methodology adopted by the researchers, who monitored and participated in the activities as members of the project's ergonomics team [4, 5].

As proposed by Daniellou [6], 12 visits were made in 4 units identified as reference situations to understand the real work. These units were chosen for having characteristics similar to the ones proposed for the project. The information collected in these visits fostered the discussions on the project.

During the five first months, the research team took part in specific meetings, upon invitation made by the project coordination team. During that time, researchers' participation was limited to the referred meetings and to the preparation of draft technical reports and technical specifications addressing Ergonomics. Even though those were not final versions of the documents, they were developed to serve as the basis to discuss the actual work, based on observations made in reference situations. They were also used to support the development and validation of final recommendations [7].

These documents are structured according to a structure which had been predefined for the project. Table 1 presents Ergonomics-related activities planned by the company.

Table 1. Ergonomics team activities foreseen in the project schedule.

Task	Discipline	Start	End
Ergonomics Requirements for Hull	Ergonomics	07/16/18	12/21/18
Ergonomics Report for Hull	Ergonomics	12/18/18	03/21/19
Descriptive Memorandum - Ergonomics	Ergonomics	07/11/19	09/30/19
Comments on documents from other disciplines	Ergonomics	07/16/18	02/10/20
Ergonomics Requirements for Hull	Ergonomics	07/16/18	10/01/18
Ergonomics Report for Topsides	Ergonomics	10/30/18	05/08/19

After that time period, research team's access to the location where the project was being developed increased, allowing the three researchers to monitor the project on site. Six hundred and five hours of monitoring took place during the project, including the following actions: observation, meetings, and assistance with demands from other disciplines, project documentation development, events, and interviews.

As of the fifth month, interviews were made with some specific stakeholders, from which we highlight: members of the arrangement, automation, architecture, and ergonomics teams. Interviews were short and semi-structured, lasting approximately 10 to 15 min. The purpose of these interviews was to gather information on new work practices in design in a context which involves changes.

The information gathered was organized into two categories for analysis: primary and secondary sources. Primary sources included the field notebook, meeting minutes, records of events and interviews made by the researchers.

The field notebook contained records of observations related to how the project worked, as well as records of dialogues between designers and actions developed. In addition to the records in the logbook, independent documents were also developed to record specific events such as meetings, constructability events and design review sessions. All records were made in digital format and files were shared from the cloud among all members of the research team.

Secondary sources consisted of documents provided by the company such as, for instance, technical specifications from other disciplines, plan views and 3D models.

3   Results

The design in question differed from previous designs developed by the company for having relied on 3D-model-oriented organization. This type of organization encouraged a new work dynamics, with more integration around the resource in question.

As for the participation of ergonomics, practice transformation was related to how independently the discipline acted in a platform basic design. In previous designs, ergonomics studies were scattered across documents related to other disciplines, mainly architecture. Moreover, ergonomics used to be called upon to contribute in more advanced phases, such as the detailed design phase.

Considering the aforementioned context, ergonomics practice had to be structured during the course of its actions in the project. To that effect, the meetings held in the early months of the project helped understand design objectives and dynamics, as well as the demands related to ergonomics as a discipline.

Design organization was defined in a way that teams from every discipline were allocated on the same floor. The purpose of doing so was to use this proximity to encourage and facilitate exchanges and interactions throughout the project. From the moment researchers had access to this location, it was possible for them to monitor and effectively participate in ergonomics-related topics within the dynamics.

Thus, in addition to the meetings which included the participation of the ergonomics teams, they were also able to engage in spontaneous discussions related to the design. This closeness also made it possible for interviews to take place, which, in turn, helped researchers grasp the perception designers had of the new design dynamics and the role of ergonomics.

This participation made it possible for other teams to better understand the discipline's scope of action, going beyond the six actions initially attributed to Ergonomics, shown in Table 1.

4 Discussion

The participation of the team prior to the detailing phase was a unique opportunity to potentially make it possible to make changes to the design at a time guidelines, specifications and basic concepts were still being defined [8]. However, especially when it comes to engineering designs, the role of ergonomists does not yet seem to be well defined.

The scope of action of ergonomics does not seem to be clearly understood at this point, which means to say that some teams still have questions as to how, or even to which extent, ergonomics can contribute to other disciplines.

Creating deliverables for the discipline requires its own specific development process, which involves, among other actions, understanding the actual work by analyzing reference situations. Reference situations in the project in question consisted of visits of the ergonomics team in some of the company's oil platforms already in operation.

Ergonomic practice in projects involves hard-to-quantify actions, which is made evident, for instance, when the number of design actions attributed to the discipline is considered. Among over three thousand actions in the general schedule for the basic design phase, ergonomics was effectively responsible for six items. Even though this number might seem small when compared to the whole, these attributions represent a step forward when we consider the participation of ergonomics in this type of project.

It is worth mentioning that, in addition to the fact that recognition of the ergonomics team's work is related to deliverables, social construction was a resource which brought visibility to ergonomic actions [9]. Space given for discussions intended to develop technical specifications ensured the alignment and validation of information and solutions.

One of the main limitations of the research is related to the fact ergonomists were both observers and observed in the study. Nonetheless, this bias was mitigated because the team was made up of three ergonomists-researchers who mutually validated design records [10].

A suggestion for future studies is to delve into the theme as to how to better translate ergonomics' participation in engineering design evidence. Another possibility would be to monitor corresponding studies in another design stage, such as the conceptual and detailed design phases.

5 Conclusion

Contrary to the situation identified during a diagnostic context, in a project situation, ergonomists do not have autonomy to take action and must find their place in other design disciplines.

Ergonomists' participation in this project leads to the hypothesis that this discipline can potentially play a key role in integrating different specialties in the design, as its object of study - the work itself – relates to the scope of other disciplines. On the other hand, ergonomics still "seeks" more than it "is sought", that is, it is more likely for ergonomics teams to reach out to other disciplines to align content and, somehow, offer their contribution.

This study allowed for considerations to be made on the way the participation of ergonomics is set up, considering the corporate standpoint in corresponding projects.

References

1. Duarte, F.: Complementaridade entre ergonomia e engenharia em projetos industriais. In: Duarte, F. (ed.) Ergonomia e Projeto na Indústria de Processo Contínuo. Lucerna, Rio de Janeiro (2002)
2. Cordeiro, C., Oggioni, B., Duarte, F., Lima, F.: From the ergonomic guidelines to the configuration of use in the offshore platforms design context. Production 25(2), 298–309 (2015)
3. Guérin, F., et al.: Compreender o trabalho para transformá-lo: A prática da ergonomia. Edgard Blücher, São Paulo (2002)
4. Minayo, M.: Trabalho de campo: contexto de observação, interação e descoberta. In: Minayo, M. (org.) Pesquisa social: teoria, método e criatividade. 34a ed. Vozes, Petrópolis (2015)
5. Patton, M.Q.: Qualitative Research and Evaluation Methods, 3rd edn. Sage Publications, Thousand Oaks (2002)
6. Daniellou, F.: L'ergonomie dans la conduite de projets de conception de systèmes de travail. In: Falzon, P. (ed.) Ergonomie. Presses Universitaires de France, Paris (2004)
7. Conceição, C., Silva, G., Broberg, O., Duarte, F.: Intermediary objects in the workspace design process: means of experience transfer in the offshore sector. Work 41, 127–135 (2012)
8. Oggioni, B., Duarte, F., Cordeiro, C.: Ergonomics in projects of oil platforms in a change context. Work 41(1), 107–113 (2012)
9. Daniellou, F.: The French-speaking ergonomists' approach to work activity: cross-influences of field intervention and conceptual models. Theor. Issues Ergon. Sci. 6(5), 409–427 (2005)
10. Jackson, J.: Entre situations de gestion et situations de délibération. L'action de l'ergonome dans les projets industriels. Thèse de Doctorat en ergonomie. Collection Thèses et Mémoires Laboratoire d'Ergonomie des systèmes complexes Université Victor Segalen Bordeaux 2-ISPED éditions (1998)

Work Dimensions of the Inclusion of Autistic People: An Integrative Literature Review

Vitória Araujo Melo[1](✉) ⓘ, Carolina Maria do Carmo Alonso[1] ⓘ,
and Pauline Dibben[2] ⓘ

[1] Department of Occupational Therapy, Medical School, Federal University of Rio de Janeiro,
Rio de Janeiro, Brazil
[2] Management School, Sheffield University, Sheffield, UK

Abstract. This paper analyzes evidence on how the literature approaches the work dimension in the process of inclusion of autistic people. A bibliographic search was made at different healthcare databases and following the exclusion of the duplicates and applying the inclusion/exclusion criteria 47 papers were reviewed by the authors. This literature review showed that autistic people can be more disadvantaged in the workplace than (other) disabled people which shows that attitudinal barriers can be more limiting than infrastructural ones. Moreover, there is a lot of focus on the autistic worker needing to adapt to work. Studies focusing on workplace changes point to the use of sensory accommodations without describing them. In this aspect, studies based on Activity Ergonomics might strategically fill this gap, since they develop solutions based on actual work situations, including the point of view of autistic workers on the challenges they face in their daily work, as well as on the appropriateness of the accommodations to be developed for them. Given this scenario, and knowing that the inclusion of disabled people is a right, it is a duty of researchers who study and discuss work processes, like ergonomists, to further research how inclusion can be ensured, so that appropriate techniques can be adapted not only for a 'disability' but also for individuals. The development of studies that deepen our knowledge of workplace inclusion for disabled people and promote equity is absolutely necessary for the full inclusion of autistic people at work.

Keywords: Autism · Equity · Social inclusion · Activity ergonomics

1 Background

Autism is a term used to describe a group of symptoms which usually manifests itself in childhood, characterized essentially by different forms of social communication and the use of repetitive sensory-motor behaviors [1, 2] as well as heightened sensitivity to stimuli. Regarding the impacts of autism on social inclusion, studies have focused mainly on infancy rather than other life stages. However, in the last decade, we have seen an increase in publications that address the needs of this population in youth and adulthood, encompassing issues related to sexuality and independent living [3–5].

© The Author(s), under exclusive license to Springer Nature Switzerland AG 2021
N. L. Black et al. (Eds.): IEA 2021, LNNS 219, pp. 201–210, 2021.
https://doi.org/10.1007/978-3-030-74602-5_31

Given the role of work in youth and adult life, authors have also begun to address facilitators and barriers faced by autistic people in the workplace [6–8]. However, a substantial number of these studies are centered on the individual's behavior with little regard to how work might be changed or adapted.

Thus, for a better understanding of this theme, this work aimed to collect and analyze evidence on how the literature approaches the work dimension in the processes of inclusion of autistic people.

2 Methodology

This article presents an integrative review using the following databases: PubMed and Virtual Health Library (VHL). An integrative review allows the generation of new insights based on the results presented by previous research [9]. The inclusion criteria used were: peer-reviewed empirical papers published in the last five years written in Portuguese or English that discuss the inclusion of autistic people in the workplace which encompassed any form of human resource practice (such as recruitment, training or accommodations) as well as ergonomics. Conference proceedings, review articles, case studies, conceptual papers, theses and dissertations were excluded.

The search strategy performed on the databases mentioned above used the following terms: (Autistic Disorder[mesh] OR Autism[tiab] OR Autism Spectrum Disorder[mesh]

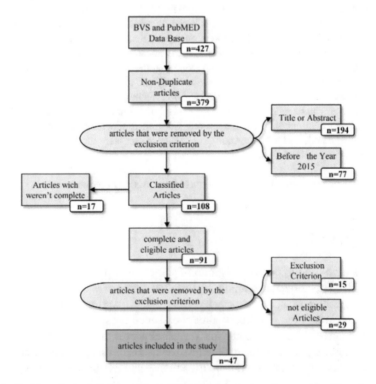

Fig. 1. Flowchart of study search, inclusion and exclusion. Prepared by the authors.

OR Autism Spectrum Disorder[tiab] OR Asperger Syndrome[mesh] OR Asperger Disorder[tiab]) and (workplace[mesh] OR Workplace[tiab] OR Job Site[tiab] OR Employment[mesh] OR Employment[tiab]). 427 articles were found after the exclusion of duplicates. The articles were selected in two stages: analysis of the title and abstracts, and analysis of full texts. Thus, we removed 290 articles after analyzing the title and abstract, and we fully analyzed 91 of them. In this last phase, we also removed 14 articles since they were not directly relevant. Figure 1 shows the flow diagram of study search and selection. For data extraction one researcher used the data collection form that encompassed:

- title,
- author,
- year,
- country,
- journal,
- purpose,
- method,
- how the study addressed work dimensions of the inclusion of autistic people.

The other researchers reviewed the extracted data, and consensus was achieved between the three researchers.

3 Results and Discussion

Data on the 47 studies included in this systematic review are presented in the Table 1.

Among those papers, more than half were written in the United States of America (26), followed by Australia (7), Sweden (8), Canada (4), Germany (3), and the United Kingdom (1). Ireland and Turkey had 1 article each. Israel, Denmark, South Africa, India, and Japan contributed 1 article each.

Most of the studies included in this review were carried out in developed countries and none of them were based in Latin America, even with the incorporation of a database focused on this region. This result is in line with other studies that point out that the inclusion of disabled people at work needs more investment in low and middle income countries [10, 11].

Figure 2 shows that the studies included in this research were published predominantly in journals in the area of developmental disabilities or in journals with a specific focus on autism, followed by publications in the area of psychology and health, and with fewer publications related to the human factors/ergonomics field.

Autistic people sometimes face challenges in social forms of communication within the workplace which can affect whether they are recruited, and can affect their work performance unless employers make appropriate accommodations [12, 13]. However, often employers lack knowledge of autism and therefore do not adjust the workplace, job role or expectations of autistic workers in order that they can perform effectively. As a result, autistic workers can end up being underemployed, in jobs that do not match their capabilities.

The review also showed that autistic people can be more disadvantaged in the workplace than (other) disabled people which shows that attitudinal barriers can be more

Table 1. List of studies included in this literature review

Author(s) (year of publication)	Studies objectives
Frank et al. (2018)	To examine employment status, type of occupation and inadequate employment in a sample of clinically mostly late-diagnosed and most likely not intellectually disabled adults with ASD in Germany
Baric et al. (2017)	To describe the occupational transition process to upper secondary school, further education and/or work, from the perspectives of young adults with Asperger syndrome or attention deficit/hyperactivity disorder
Ohl et al. (2017)	To examine the employment characteristics and histories of both employed and unemployed adults with ASD, and the factors that contributed to their employment status
Snell-Rood, et al. (2020)	To understand the interdependent impacts of policy, organizational, provider, and individual factors that shape the transition planning process in schools, and the subsequent process through which transition plans are implemented as youth access services and gain employment
Lee et al. (2020)	Explores the components and associated outcomes of a strengths-based program designed to support autistic children and adolescents to develop interests and skills in Science, Technology, Engineering, Arts, and Mathematics
Halladay et al. (2015)	Summarizing evidence gaps and identifying emerging areas of priority regarding sex and gender differences in autism spectrum disorder including unique challenges to females with ASD as they transition into adulthood?
Chen et al. (2019)	To explore how parents express their future visions (i.e. hopes and expectations) for their autistic transition-age youth
Nicholas et al. (2019)	Assessment of the outcomes of the program CommunityWorks Canada®
Knüppel et al. (2019)	To compare groups of young adults diagnosed with ASD in childhood and currently engaged in different types of daytime activity using a large and nationwide sample from the AutCome survey
Friedman et al. (2019)	Longitudinal study examined conversational language and its impact on vocational independence and friendship status measured 5 years later in a sample of 84 adults with ASD
Sung et al. (2019)	Details the iterative development, feasibility, and preliminary efficacy of an 8-week work-related social skills intervention, Assistive Soft Skills and Employment Training, for young adults with high-functioning autism spectrum disorder

(*continued*)

Table 1. (*continued*)

Author(s) (year of publication)	Studies objectives
O'Connor (2019)	To clarify whether diagnostic disclosure affects social marginalisation in workplace contexts
Yamamoto et al. (2019)	To examine the efficacy of a brief intervention of textual prompts with performance feedback for increasing social niceties of adolescents and young adults with autism spectrum disorder in a simulated workplace
Lee et al. (2019)	To explore the key factors contributing to successful work placement experience and the perceived benefits of these placements from the perspective of adolescents with ASD (n = 5), their parents (n = 6) and employers (n = 6)
Black and al (2019)	To identify the factors perceived to determine gaining and maintaining employment for autistic individuals
Dreaver et al. (2020)	To explore organisational and individual factors facilitating successful employment for adults with ASD across Australia and Sweden, including the supports and strategies underpinning employment success from an employers' perspective
Griffiths et al. (2019)	Measure the frequency of negative life experiences in autistic adults and explore how these are associated with current anxiety and depression symptoms and life satisfaction
Rast et al. (2020)	To use Vocational Rehabilitation administrative data to describe rates of Postsecondary education training services among versus Transition-age youth with autism with other intellectual or developmental disabilities
Finke et al. (2019)	To begin to fill the gap in the current literature regarding the hopes of parents of children with ASD
Taylor et al. (2017)	To examinate vocational/educational disruption in the 2–3 years after high school for 36 youth with ASD
Zwickera et al. (2017)	To describe the unmet employment, education and daily needs of adults with DD, with a sub analysis of persons with ASD and CP in Canada, to inform efficient and equitable policy development
Eismann et al. (2017)	To identify the characteristics of people with disabilities who received occupational therapy services during their transition to adulthood and determine factors associated with their successful postsecondary transition
Lerman et al. (2017)	To evaluated an assessment of job-related social skills for individuals with ASD by arranging conditions that simulated on-the-job experiences in a clinic setting

(*continued*)

Table 1. (*continued*)

Author(s) (year of publication)	Studies objectives
Wehman et al. (2017)	To develop and investigate an employer-based 9-month intervention for high school youth with ASD to learn job skills and acquire employment
Scott et al. (2017)	To examined the benefits and costs of employing adults with ASD, from the perspective of employers
Bush et al. (2017)	To examine the current state of employment for three groups of adults with ID, individuals with ASD, individuals with DS, and individuals with idiopathic ID. Choice-making and its relation to improved employment outcomes was explored
Meiring et al. (2016)	To gain an understanding of the factors parents and professionals regard as important in preparing for transition of adolescents with ASD to adulthood, vocational, and residential arrangements
Cheak-Zamora et al. (2016)	To understand youth's desires for and perspectives on becoming adults
Wehman et al. (2016)	To provides a retrospective review of 64 individuals with ASD who came to our program from 2009 to 2014 for supported employment services as referred by the state vocational rehabilitation services agency
Baldwin et al. (2016)	To provide an overview of the health, education, work, social and community activities of a large sample (n = 82) of adult females with high-functioning ASD.A secondary aim of the study was to identify any note-worthy ways in which the experiences of females with high-functioning ASD differed from those of a comparable sample of males
Gilson et al. (2016)	To study was to extend previous work on CAC by examining the effect of a job coaching package comprised of audio cuing, social-focused coaching, and reduced job coach proximity
Lorenz et al. (2016)	To discover how individuals with autism succeed in entering the job market
Johnson et al. (2016)	To unpack the phenomenon of stigma associated with developmental disabilities such as an autism diagnosis at work
Smith et al. (2016)	To evaluate the vocational outcomes of the participants at 6-month follow-up with a focus on whether or not they attained a competitive position

(*continued*)

Table 1. (*continued*)

Author(s) (year of publication)	Studies objectives
Hayakaw et al. (2015)	To examine the effect of ASD tendencies and psychosocial job characteristics on health-related quality of life (HRQOL) among factory workers
Katza et al. (2015)	To measure the trajectory of the work performance and Quality of life on jobs in the open market of the people with ASD
Lounds et al. (2015)	To examined correlates of participation in postsecondary education and employment over 12 years for 73 adults with autism spectrum disorders and average-range IQ whose families were parto fa larger, longitudinal study
Roy et al. (2015)	To determine which psychiatric comorbidities occur in adults (age range, 20–62 years) with AS. We also made note of accompanying psychiatric circumstances, such as past and current psychotherapy and drug therapy
Sung et al. (2015)	To determine whether there are gender-specific VR service predictors of employment status in transition aged individuals with ASD after controlling for the covariates of demographics and work disincentives
Scott et al. (2015)	To explore the key factors for successful employment from both the viewpoints of adults with ASD and employers. A secondary aim was to contrast the viewpoints of adults with ASD and employers to explore whether their views on factors for successful employment were similar or different and how these viewpoints impact the process of employment
Chen et al. (2015)	To investigated: What are the employment outcomes of individuals with ASD in different age groups? How do demographic covariates and cash or medical benefits associate with employment outcomes among individuals with ASD in different age groups? What rehabilitation services are related to the successful employment outcomes of individuals with ASD in different age groups, and who receive services from the VR
Tint et al. (2018)	To address the following broad research questions: How do women with ASD perceive their service and support experiences? What, if any, are the unmet service needs of women with ASD? What, if any, barriers to care do women with ASD identify?

(*continued*)

Table 1. (*continued*)

Author(s) (year of publication)	Studies objectives
Nicholas et al. (2018)	To offer a conceptual model for determining and nurturing the employment ecosystem for individuals with ASD
Kaya et al (2018)	To offer a conceptual model for determining and nurturing the employment ecosystem for individuals with ASD
Chan et al. (2018)	To investigate the proportions of adults with ASD with co-occurring ID who were successful in sustaining community employment over an 18-month period of time. And to examine how individual characteristics, family factors, and contextual influences contributed to sustained employment for this subgroup
Miller et al. (2018)	To report on the service needs and experiences of adults with ASD in two separate Medicaid-funded programs in Pennsylvania as reported in focus groups
Thompson et al. (2018)	To explore the experience of parents during the transition to adulthood for young adults with ASD. Specific research objectives included identifying factors that supported the transition process and unmet needs during this period in Australia

limiting than infrastructural ones [14]. Prejudice, bullying, lack of clear instructions, inflexibility in the hours worked, lack of help with motivation and incentives, and lack of clear instructions at times of crisis are all examples of barriers that autistic people can face in the labor market [15].

Most studies included in this review discuss vocational rehabilitation programs which do not sufficiently address the needs and inclusion of autistic workers. The most helpful work adaptations include: careful explanation of requirements, constant feedback in clear language, and flexible hours and routines.

In particular, autistic workers are not included in decision-making. Moreover, there is a lot of focus on the autistic worker needing to adapt to work. Studies focusing on workplace changes point to the use of sensory accommodations without describing them. In this aspect, studies based on Activity Ergonomics might strategically fill this gap, since they develop solutions based on actual work situations, including the point of view of autistic workers on the challenges they face in their daily work, as well as on the appropriateness of the accommodations to be developed for them.

Changes are important since in the future there might be more autistic people entering the workplace who have a diagnosis and are entitled to support. Work is one of the most important areas of human life and it is to be hoped that autistic adults who seek to enter the workplace will gain successful careers. It is the responsibility of researchers and professionals to find effective strategies to enable the transition of autistic people into work, improving the quality of life for autistic people and improving the world of work.

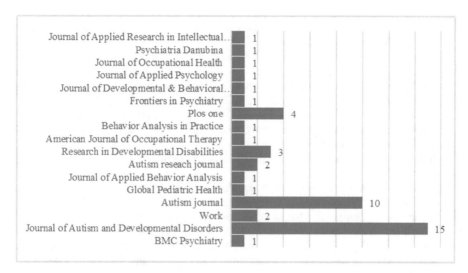

Fig. 2. Numbers of publications included in this review regarding the journals.

4   Conclusion

This research aimed collected and analyzed evidence on how the literature approaches the work dimension in the processes of inclusion of autistic people. Among the limitations of this review, we can mention the non-inclusion of all existing databases. The strengths of its results refer to the selection and evaluation of peer-reviewed articles, clear inclusion and exclusion criteria on paper selection and on data extraction. The lack of another published review focusing on work dimension in the processes of inclusion autistic people in the labor market reinforces the relevance of the results for public health.

Also, although, many journals of ergonomics and human factors are indexed in databases used in this study, we do not find many studies that addressed the inclusion of autistic people in those journals. Given this scenario, and knowing that the inclusion of disabled people is a right, it is a duty of researchers who study and discuss work processes, like ergonomists, to further research how inclusion can be ensured, so that appropriate techniques can be adapted not only for a 'disability' but also for individuals. The development of studies that deepen our knowledge of workplace inclusion for disabled people and promote equity is absolutely necessary for the full inclusion of autistic people at work.

References

1. Klin, A.: Autism and Asperger syndrome: an overview. Braz. J. Psychiatry **28**, s3–s11 (2006)
2. Lord, C., Elsabbagh, M., Baird, G., Veenstra-Vanderweele, J.: Autism spectrum disorder. Lancet **392**(10146), 508–520 (2018)
3. Howlin, P., Magiati, I.: Autism spectrum disorder: outcomes in adulthood. Curr. Opin. Psychiatry **30**(2), 69–76 (2017)
4. Parchomiuk, M.: Sexuality of persons with autistic spectrum disorders (ASD). Sex. Disabil. **37**(2), 259–274 (2019)

5. Vortman-Shoham, I., Kenny, S.: Emerging adulthood and ASD. In: Autism in Adulthood, pp. 1–19. Springer, Cham (2019)
6. Brownlow, C., Werth, S., Keefe, K.: Autism spectrum disorder: emotion work in the workplace. In: Work and Identity, pp. 23–37. Springer, Cham (2018)
7. Khalifa, G., Sharif, Z., Sultan, M., Di Rezze, B.: Workplace accommodations for adults with autism spectrum disorder: a scoping review. Disabil. Rehabil. **42**(9), 1316–1331 (2020)
8. Lindsay, S., Osten, V., Rezai, M., Bui, S.: Disclosure and workplace accommodations for people with autism: a systematic review. Disabil. Rehabil. **43**(5), 597–610 (2021). https://doi.org/10.1080/09638288.2019.1635658
9. Whittemore, R., Knafl, K.: The integrative review: updated methodology. J. Adv. Nurs. **52**(5), 546–553 (2005)
10. Fritz, M.: Towards inclusive workplaces. Requirements for the inclusion of people with disabilities in small and medium sized organizations in the Global South (2019)
11. Hiranandani, V., Kumar, A., Sonpal, D.: Making community inclusion work for persons with disabilities: drawing lessons from the field. Community Dev. **45**(2), 150–164 (2014)
12. Roy, M., Prox-Vagedes, V., D Ohlmeier, M., Dillo, W.: Beyond childhood: psychiatric comorbidities and social background of adults with Asperger syndrome. Psychiatr. Danub. **27**(1), 50–59 (2015)
13. Lerman, D.C., White, B., Grob, C., Laudont, C.: A clinic-based assessment for evaluating job-related social skills in adolescents and adults with autism. Behav. Anal. Pract. **10**(4), 323–336 (2017)
14. Taylor, J.L., Henninger, N.A., Mailick, M.R.: Longitudinal patterns of employment and post-secondary education for adults with autism and average-range IQ. Autism **19**(7), 785–793 (2015)
15. Baldwin, S., Costley, D.: The experiences and needs of female adults with high-functioning autism spectrum disorder. Autism **20**(4), 483–495 (2016)

Responsibility of Action and Situated Cognition in Artefact—User Relationship

Juan Carlos Mendoza-Collazos[1,2(✉)]

[1] Universidad Nacional de Colombia, Bogotá, Colombia
`juan.mendoza@semiotik.lu.se`
[2] Lund University, Lund, Sweden

Abstract. I discuss the dilution of responsibility of action and the idea of a symmetrical relationship between artefacts and humans. In doing so, I argue that meaning making is an activity unilaterally performed by agents, leading to an asymmetrical relationship between agents and artefacts. Therefore, the study of the one who is responsible for the action, the meaning-maker (with the capability to act) is crucial for a theory of action responsibility. The latter should not be transferred to derived agents, an abstract brand or impersonal technologies. The study of the origin of actions is crucial for a better understanding of situated cognition in relation to responsibility. Therefore, the role of artefacts in human actions has to be reconsidered, since artefacts acquire functions by means of designing and they do not act for themselves. These issues have consequences for our understanding of situated cognition and for the current debate on responsibility of AI technologies, as well as for work analysis and design.

Keywords: Agency · Cognitive semiotics · Situated cognition · Artefact—user relationship

In the quest for taking cognition back to the ground, scientific and philosophical research have built a thick corpus challenging the idea of the body as a puppet controlled by an ethereal mind. There is a growing – almost unchallenged – consensus on the situated character of cognition, and a myriad of derivative outcomes of this approach are part of the state-of-the-art, for a detailed review see [1].

However, a discussion on the implications of this paradigm is important when the notion of agency is extended to artificial entities or inert matter, and especially when the concept of responsibility is at stake. The following lines emerged as a digression from a cognitive-semiotics research on the role of artefacts in relation to agency [2–7]. These papers defend the thesis of an asymmetrical relation between artefacts and agents, arguing that "agency and intentionality are exclusive properties of living beings, and not properties of things" [4].

I present arguments for understanding of situated cognition into a cognitive semiotics and phenomenological frame, restating the volitional role of true agents and their responsibilities, regardless if such are blurred by new automatized technologies. Section 1 briefly summarizes the notion of situated cognition and its relation to agency. Section 2 explains the artefact—user relationship as symmetrical, and why it should be better

© The Author(s), under exclusive license to Springer Nature Switzerland AG 2021
N. L. Black et al. (Eds.): IEA 2021, LNNS 219, pp. 211–216, 2021.
https://doi.org/10.1007/978-3-030-74602-5_32

understood as asymmetrical. A boundless interpretation of situated cognition could lead us to fade responsibility of action away, which has implications for work analysis and design, as explained in the closing Sect. 3.

1 Situated Cognition and Agency

A comprehensive review of the history of situated cognition was compiled and edited by Robbins & Aydede [1]. In this handbook, situated cognition is mainly assumed in the broad philosophical frame beyond its common delimitation to learning studies and cognitive science. Thus, situated cognition is the genus of derivative approaches such as "embodied, enactive, embedded, and distributed cognition" [1]. The origin of the concept is located in the twenty century, although its roots are extended to Aristotle's concept of practical wisdom and some few philosophers before last century such as Nietzsche [8].

Situated cognition refers to contextual dimensions of meaning-making when meaningful actions "are inseparable from the setting of action, or from a form of life" [8]. This can be understood as the online, ongoing process of meaning-making taking into account all resources involved in such a process. For Cognitive Semiotics, meaning is inherent to life, and life is a required condition for agency. My approach to the polysemy-laden concept of agency [9] is taken from agentive semiotics [3, 10]. It is a sort of intentional agency – in opposition to "causal agency", according to the distinction offered by Johnson & Verdicchio [9] – but agentive semiotics proposes a more comprehensive definition of agency framed in the cutting edge of cognitive semiotics research. Thus, for the understanding of agency "the principle of ontological continuum [11–16] is the main epistemological orientation" and "The irreducible conditions for agency are animation [15, 16], situatedness [17, 18] and attention [19]" [3].

The cognitive semiotics approach clarifies the relation of situated cognition and agency proposing that "an agent acts only if it is situated. Its action must be embedded and embodied, and have a kineto-perceptual basis and a specific place and time. An agent's action is always affective; it tends to interact with other agents and it is under several degrees of control (from unconscious to highly concentrated actions)" [3]. Agency requires cognitive capabilities only present in living organisms such as perception, memory, volition, autopoiesis and an intrinsic value system [3, 20, 21]. With these concepts of situated cognition and agency in mind, following sections elaborate on possible implications for – understood as such – moral agents.

2 The User-Artefact Relationship

In the text "On Interobjectivity" [22] Latour tries to introduce the importance of artefacts for sociological studies. He claims sociology needs to be "materialized", studying the role of artefacts as symmetrical to the role of true agents, taking seriously the "social life of things" [23].

Interestingly, Latour does not assume the notion of agency as an intrinsic characteristic of artefacts, unlike what has been replicated by other authors (see [24–27]). In contrast, Latour proposes the concept of *dislocation*, understood as a delegation of human tasks to artefacts, similar to the notion of derived agency [2, 10]. However, he diminishes the importance of who originates the actions and thus, of the person responsible for the action [28].

Latour argues that the notion of "social actor" has to be redefined to include non-human animals and even inert objects. The concept of interaction between living beings is important only at the level of non-human primates for direct social relationship. In contrast, human interactions are mediated by artefacts. Thus, human interactions become more complex with this mediation.

The human capacity to dislocate actions into artefacts – regardless of spatio-temporal sequentiality – is a semiotic resource that works through the reification of symbolic representations. This delegation is materialized in concrete artefacts [22]. However, it is important to notice that the way in which artefacts "do something" is completely different from the way that agents do it, establishing, unlike Latour, a completely asymmetric relationship. Artefacts deploy functions assigned by agents, which is not equivalent to the way of acting of the latter. In Latour's approach, the dynamics of the process and interactions between elements is the only relevant issue while the person responsible for the action is secondary, since such action is distributed in a socio-technical network within a balanced (symmetrical) relationship [28].

The argument for dissolving the importance of the originator of actions is based on this idea of network: each action connects with the previous and the next in a permanent flow that has a completely diffuse origin. The responsible agent is therefore ungraspable. The argument avoids discussions on agents with intentionality and purpose. In contrast, as stated in Mendoza-Collazos [4], understanding of situated cognition implies a central consideration of the nature of agents, understood as living organisms with different degrees of complexity: biological and cognitive. Artefacts are mediators of interactions between *living organisms*.

I emphasize the importance of both agents and things "while, at the same time, positing an asymmetrical relationship between artefacts and human beings" [5]. The elements in a socio-technical network establish – although ecological – clearly asymmetrical relationships, since agents endow artefacts with meaning and functions by means of design. This derived agency allows artefacts "to mediate interactions between true agents, to enhance the agent capabilities for action, and to achieve the purposes of the agent" [5]. The mediational role of artefacts has considerable implications for responsibility of actions, as elaborated in the next section.

3   Responsibility of the Action in Situated Cognition

The Gibson's notion of *affordance* [29] is crucial for situated cognition. Actually, Gibson can be regarded as a pioneer of situated cognition studies, although he did not coin the coupled term [1]. The notion of affordance is useful to discuss the approach I offered so far to situated cognition, and its implications for responsibility of actions. Contrary to a common understanding of affordances as inherent features of artefacts representing the agency of things [27]; I argue that the only intrinsic characteristics of things are materials, shapes and colors, although they are often confused with possibilities for action, also called affordances. Only a situated agent can *discover* new possibilities of action and they are not present in artefacts by default. These possibilities of action are ongoing built exclusively by agents acting in the world. It is in this sense that we consider artefact—user relationship as a profoundly asymmetrical.

This has practical consequences, for instance, in the way that public policy is assumed or how work environments are designed. If artefacts are taken as equal partners (symmetrical relationship), the analysis of work and its design could lead us to put the emphasis only on interactions between the elements of a system, disregarding who is the originator of actions, who defines the purpose of actions, and who is responsible for such actions. This explains the recurrent approach to analysis of work activities as if they were part of "immanent" systems that omit the deep understanding of situated experience, opting for explanation instead of comprehension, as De Sousa Santos [30] points out.

On the contrary, I propose to assume the complexity of situated experience within multiple factors, where unexpected courses of action are possible. This experience cannot be reduced to the analysis of activity in causal terms, but rather requires a more systemic integration between the entire set of the socio-technical network, highlighting the asymmetric emphasis put by true agents.

Moreover, the study of the role of artefacts in situated cognition – with phenomenological accuracy, as proposed here – is crucial for optimal work design. Let's see the case of an abandoned factory where, for some reason, robots are still working automatically on the production line: their actions are useless. Actions only make sense when a true agent enters the scene. On the other hand, robots wouldn't be there if someone hadn't designed them in the first place. This has been omitted by radical versions of situated cognition and those who defend the concept of material agency [27, 31–39].

For some of these scholars, the speed bumps in the streets – using a famous example – are not just reminders to reduce speed, they are even moral agents [27]. The original intention of the designer is overlooked and the existence of things *ex nihilo* is taken for granted. I insist, the speed reducer is not a moral actor, it is a *mediator* of the interaction between two moral agents: the designer and the driver. Urban designer decides on the location and type of bump with the remote intention [40] of warning the driver. The activity of design highlights the teleology of human actions.

As explained elsewhere [7], in public presentations of a project of design and manufacturing of an autonomous vehicle [41], questions arose about who was responsible in the event of a pedestrian run over on the road. The responsibility must always rely on true agents – designers and manufacturers – as the vehicle embodies the remote intentions of its creators. Parthemore & Withby, elaborating from Zlatev [20], claim "A moral agent must be embedded in a cultural and specifically moral context, and embodied in a suitable physical form. It must be, in some substantive sense, alive" [21]. Therefore, responsibility of actions cannot be diluted in artificial intelligence or similar technologies, and situated approaches to work analysis and design should to include these moral dimensions. The analysis and design of sociotechnical networks should not consider their elements as playing symmetrical (neutral) roles.

References

1. Robbins, P., Aydede, M. (eds.): The Cambridge Handbook of Situated Cognition. Cambridge University Press, Cambridge (2008)

2. Mendoza-Collazos, J.C.: Semiótica del diseño con enfoque agentivo: Condiciones de significancia en artefactos de uso. Utadeo, Bogotá (2015)
3. Mendoza-Collazos, J.C.: Design semiotics with an agentive approach: an alternative to current semiotic analysis of artefacts. In: Zlatev, J., Sonesson, G., Konderak, P. (eds.) Meaning, Mind and Communication: Explorations in Cognitive Semiotics, pp. 83–99. Peter Lang, Frankfurt am Main (2016)
4. Mendoza-Collazos, J.C.: On the importance of things: a relational approach to agency. Cogn. Semiot. **13**(2), 1–11 (2020)
5. Mendoza-Collazos, J.C., Sonesson, G.: Revisiting the life of things: a cognitive semiotic study of the agency of artefacts in Amazonia. Public J. Semiot. **9**(2), 30–52 (2021)
6. Mendoza-Collazos, J.C., Zlatev, J., Sonesson, G.: The origins and evolution of design: a stage-based model. In: Pagni, E., Theisen, R.S. (eds.) Biosemiotics. The Natural Foundations of Symbolism. Springer, Cham (2020)
7. Mendoza-Collazos, J.C.: La agencia de las cosas: Una semiosis de las redes de transporte en Bogotá. DeSignis (in press)
8. Gallagher, S.: Philosophical antecedents of situated cognition. In: Robbins, P., Aydede, M. (eds.) The Cambridge Handbook of Situated Cognition, pp. 35–51. Cambridge University Press, Cambridge (2008)
9. Johnson, D., Verdicchio, M.: AI, agency and responsibility: the VW fraud case and beyond. AI Soc. **34**(3), 639–647 (2019)
10. Niño, D.: Elementos de semiótica agentiva. Utadeo, Bogotá (2015)
11. James, W.: Pragmatism: A New Name for Some Old Ways of Thinking. Longmans, Green, and Co, New York (1907)
12. Gallagher, S.: How the Body Shapes the Mind. CUP, Cambridge (2005)
13. Gallagher, S.: The natural philosophy of agency. Philos. Compass **2**, 347–357 (2007)
14. Sheets-Johnstone, M.: The Roots of Morality. Penn State Press, Pennsylvania (2008)
15. Sheets-Johnstone, M.: Thinking in movement: further analyses and validations. In: Stewart, J., Gapenne, O., Di Paolo, E. (eds.) Enaction: Toward a New Paradigm for Cognitive Science, pp. 165–181. The MIT Press, Cambridge (2010)
16. Sheets-Johnstone, M.: Fundamental and inherently interrelated aspects of animation. In: Foolen, A., Lüdtke, U., Racine, T., Zlatev, J. (eds.) Moving Ourselves, Moving Others. John Benjamins, Amsterdam (2012)
17. Thompson, E.: Mind in Life: Biology, Phenomenology, and the Sciences of Mind. Harvard University Press, Cambridge (2007)
18. Hutchins, E.: Enaction, imagination, and insight. In: Stewart, J., Gapenne, O., Di Paolo, E. (eds.) Enaction: Toward a New Paradigm for Cognitive Science, pp. 425–450. The MIT Press, Cambridge (2010)
19. Goldstein, S., Naglieri, J. (eds.): Handbook of Executive Functioning. Springer, New York (2014)
20. Zlatev, J.: Meaning = life (+ culture). Evol. Commun. **4**(2), 253–296 (2002)
21. Parthemore, J., Whitby, B.: Moral agency, moral responsibility, and artefacts. In: Gunkel, D., Bryson, J., Torrance, S. (eds.) Proceedings of AISB/IACAP World Congress. University of Birmingham, Birmingham (2012)
22. Latour, B.: On interobjectivity. Mind Cult. Activity **3**(4), 228–245 (1996)
23. Appadurai, A. (ed.): The Social Life of Things: Commodities in Cultural Perspective. Cambridge University Press, Cambridge (1988)
24. Clark, A.: Being There: Putting Brain, Body, and World Together Again. MIT Press, Cambridge (1997)
25. Sutton, J.: Material Agency, skills and history: distributed cognition and the ar-chaeology of memory. In: Knappett, C., Malafouris, L. (eds.) Material Agency: Towards a Non-anthropocentric Approach, pp. 37–56. Springer, Boston (2008)

26. Watts, C.M.: On mediation and material agency in the Peircean semeiotic. In: Knappett, C., Malafouris, L. (eds.) Material Agency: Towards a Non-anthropocentric Approach, pp. 187–208. Springer, Boston (2008)
27. Malafouris, L.: How Things Shape the Mind: A Theory of Material Engagement. MIT Press, Cambridge (2013)
28. Latour, B.: Pandora's Hope: Essays on the Reality of Science Studies. Harvard University Press, Cambridge (1999)
29. Gibson, J.J.: The Ecological Approach to Visual Perception. Psychology Press, New York (1979)
30. De Sousa Santos, S.: Una epistemología del sur: La reinvención del conocimiento y la emancipación social. Siglo XXI editores, Barcelona (2015)
31. Hutchins, E.: The social organization of distributed cognition. In: Resnick, L., Levine, J., Teasley, S. (eds.) Perspectives on Socially Shared Cognition, pp. 283–307. American Psychological Association, Washington (1991)
32. Hutchins, E.: The role of cultural practices in the emergence of modern human intelligence. Philos. Trans. R. Soc. Lond. B **363**, 2011–2019 (2008)
33. Latour, B.: We Have Never Been Modern. Harvard University Press, Cambridge (1993)
34. Latour, B.: Reassembling the Social. An Introduction to Actor-Network Theory. Oxford University Press, Oxford (2005)
35. Clark, A., Chalmers, D.: The extended mind. Analysis **58**(1), 7–19 (1998)
36. Ward, L.: Dynamical Cognitive Science. The MIT Press, Cambridge (2002)
37. Cowley, S., Vallée-Tourangeau, F.: Cognition Beyond the Brain: Computation, Interactivity and Human Artifice. Springer, London (2013)
38. Hutto, D.D., Myin, E.: Radicalizing Enactivism. Basic Minds without Content. MIT Press, Cambridge (2013)
39. Hutto, D.D., Myin, E.: Evolving Enactivism: Basic Minds Meet Content. MIT press, Cambridge (2017)
40. Sonesson, G.: Postphotography and beyond. From mechanical reproduction to digital production. VISIO **4**(1), 11–36 (1999)
41. Mendoza-Collazos, J.C.: Design and manufacturing of an electric vehicle for car-sharing in Bogotá. In: Proceedings of MOVICI-MOYCOT 2018: Joint Conference for Urban Mobility in the Smart City, 1–6. IET Digital Library, Medellín (2019)

The Practice of Ergonomics in the Creation of Technical Specifications for Offshore Platform Projects

Marina P. Mercado$^{(\boxtimes)}$ (ID), Priscila B. C. Leite (ID), Camila P. Marins (ID), Fernanda Tinoco (ID), and Francisco J. C. M. Duarte (ID)

Department of Production Engineering, Federal University of Rio de Janeiro, Rio de Janeiro, RJ, Brazil

{marinapmercado,camila.marins,fernanda.tinoco, duarte}@pep.ufrj.br, priscila.blasquez@coppe.ufrj.br

Abstract. Ergonomics in design is intended to close the gap between what is designed and the real work. This study seeks to discuss the creation of technical ergonomics requirements for the basic design stage of workshops on offshore platforms. Thus, this paper also intends to show how the ergonomics discipline contributes to integrating knowledge on the real work of the maintenance crew with the design. This case study uses procedures, data collection, and analysis guided by the Ergonomics of the Activity's theoretical framework, focused on design projects [1]. The results of this research indicate the contribution of ergonomics to improve the work of maintenance crews, which occurred both through the construction of new layout and equipment list, and through the development of technical specifications. Hence, this work points to the need for new studies on platform maintenance work, in addition to studies that deepen the debate on consolidating ergonomics practice in design projects.

Keywords: Maintenance · Basic design · Offshore · Workshop · Oil and gas · Petroleum

1 Introduction

One of the difficulties identified in design projects is the gap between what is designed and the crews' real work [1]. This hiatus in which ergonomics can be inserted as a design discipline. However, ergonomics' participation in design is still seen with the expectation of delivering products similar to those of other disciplines.

The design process of oil platforms has a specific organization, often guided by technology-centered criteria [2]. This study is based on the ergonomics team's participation in the basic design of new offshore platforms. At this stage of the project, the creation of technical specifications for the hull and topside areas of the platform were directed to ergonomics. This paper will discuss the development process of these specifications by formulating documents for the workshops.

© The Author(s), under exclusive license to Springer Nature Switzerland AG 2021
N. L. Black et al. (Eds.): IEA 2021, LNNS 219, pp. 217–222, 2021.
https://doi.org/10.1007/978-3-030-74602-5_33

The purpose of this paper is to show the creation process of technical ergonomic requirements for workshops. In this context, this study also intends to show how the discipline of ergonomics integrated knowledge on the maintenance crew's real work into the technical documents.

2 Methodology

This research consists of a case study of qualitative and exploratory approach with procedures for data collection and analysis guided by the theoretical framework of the Ergonomics of the Activity, focused on design projects [1].

Work analysis in reference situations is used for this theoretical framework. The following stages were carried out to meet the proposition of the theoretical background: a) demand analysis; b) analysis of the organizational, technical, economic, and social environmental aspects; c) analysis of the work activities and situation in the reference situation; and d) validation of the study and recommendations to improve the work.

The survey was conducted in a Brazilian energy company from 2018 to 2020. Ethical procedures that guide ergonomics practice and follow the code of ethics established by the Brazilian Association of Ergonomics [3] were used, and the following precautions were taken:

- Research subjects were previously informed about the study and agreed to their participation,
- The company's management formally authorized the study, and
- Names and certain information were kept confidential and not reported.

The data was analyzed using primary and secondary sources of record. The primary source analysis consists of recording the project's technical discussions and meetings and the notes on the reference situations' analysis. The secondary source analysis refers to the Brazilian regulatory standards, the company's data regarding the reference situations and the project, and the ergonomic analysis reports of previous projects. These analyses allowed the participation in technical discussions with the project disciplines and the development of documents.

For the work activity analysis in the platform's different environments, 12 visits were made to the four platforms selected as reference situations, as shown in Table 1. The platforms were selected because they have characteristics similar to the future project. This paper will only cover data relating to the activities of maintenance crews.

Several meetings were held to develop the design and create the specifications, among which five were exclusively aimed to discuss workshop documents such as layout, equipment list, and technical specifications. These meetings were held with representatives of the architecture, operation, and maintenance teams, among others.

The maintenance crew's activities were also discussed in other situations, such as weekly meetings of the ergonomics team, Design Review (DR) sessions, etc.

In both meetings and DR sessions, intermediate objects such as 2D plans (printed and digital), workshop equipment lists, and the 3D model. The purpose of using these resources was to assist in the communication, anticipation of results, and recording the history of project decisions [4].

Table 1. Visits made in reference situations.

Reference situation	Visit period
Platform A	November 2 to 4, 2018
Platform B	May 17 to 20, 2019
Platform B	July 8 to 11, 2019
Platform A	July 19 to 21, 2019
Platform A	August 8 to 11, 2019
Platform A	September 3 to 6, 2019
Platform B	September 2 to 6, 2019
Platform B	November 11 to 14, 2019
Platform C	December 8 to 15, 2019
Platform C	January 12 to 16, 2020
Platform A	March 7 to 10, 2020
Platform D	March 14 to 17, 2020

Source: Prepared by the authors (2021)

3 Results

The results show that ergonomics contributed to improving the maintenance crew's work. This contribution occurred both by creating ergonomics technical specifications and the definition of new layouts and equipment list.

The chapter addressing technical specifications were previously structured by the project management team, so the specifications' presentation was divided according to the platforms' environments, including the workshop. The contributions related to the maintenance crew's work were inserted mainly in this chapter. However, that crew's work is not restricted to these areas, as maintenance work is done throughout the platform. Therefore, in addition to the workshops' specifications, we have also added contributions related to support points for the maintenance crew in the operational area to reduce the number of trips to the workshop and increase problem-solving efficiency.

In this process of building the specifications, exclusive meetings were held to discuss the workshops. The first one took place before the first visit to the reference situations and was attended by the ergonomics team (including the researchers and company ergonomists), the architecture team, and platform maintenance supervisors. The architecture team presented the workshop equipment list and updated layout (digital and printed) for the design discussion at that meeting. As a follow-up, a new version of the workshop equipment list and layout was issued.

As presented in the method, these documents were taken to the reference situations on several visits to be validated with workers from different units and maintenance crews. This allowed us to collect information through work observation, interviews, and confrontations with workers. This information returned for new exclusive meetings of the workshops, generating constant reformulation of documents.

Besides these meetings with specific themes, other moments of interaction with designers also contributed to exchanging knowledge and information on the maintenance crew's work, such as the DR event and other periodic meetings.

As a result of the discussions, 50 specifications were created in the technical specifications workshop chapter, distributed as follows: 6 on initial conditions; 17 on layout, furniture, and equipment of the set of workshops; 12 specific to the mechanical workshop; 7 specific to the instrumentation workshop, 4 specific to the electrical workshop; 3 for the boiler-room; and 1 for the PSV workshop.

For example, a technical specification was created recommending the installation of screens in the workshops with an equipment monitoring system, such as in the control room. Upon analyzing the maintenance crew's work, it was seen that it involves more than just maintenance itself. The crew's duties include the operation of equipment responsible for the hull's operation, such as air conditioning and ventilation systems, water and sewage systems, electrical installations, etc.

Another example of a specification created concerned the physical arrangement of workshop equipment. Work observation allowed us to identify that the saw and hydraulic press machines were fixed close to the bulkhead, making it impossible to use them for larger parts. Thus, it was specified that the equipment's positioning must consider the size of the parts that will be used on them, and therefore, these must be at a minimum distance of 1 m from the bulkheads.

In addition to the ergonomics technical specifications, some contributions had to be transferred to the technical specifications of other disciplines due to the bidding process and distribution of documents to the vendors. For example, the ergonomic specifications for battery rooms were inserted in the electric technical specification because the work by the company responsible for the construction and assembly project of the battery room is based on the electric technical specification.

Based on the work analysis, it was seen that the type of battery influences the frequency and maintenance required and, consequently, the access to the battery banks. Thus, the first premise of the design was to consider the type of battery that should be used and, based on this definition, provide sufficient space for its maintenance and operation, such as access for filling and density measurement of the batteries. There should also be space to allow for the movement of trolleys for battery removal and exchange, as well as load handling devices that consider the type of handle, weight, and dimensions of each unit to be exchanged.

4 Discussion

The participation of ergonomics provided reflections on the maintenance work and the contribution of ergonomics and design dynamics. This process sought to bridge the gap between real work and design, based on the reference situations analyses. To this end, there was the integration of users and designers by creating discussion forums that encompassed different rationales and stakeholders of the project.

The maintenance crews' work is not limited to the workshops' physical space; their work may occur in any of the platform's environment. It also includes administrative and equipment operation activities. The specifications created were only possible given the knowledge of the real work done.

In this project, the ergonomics team's initial demand was to deliver specifications for the offshore platform areas. However, the knowledge acquired on the work did not only translate into the creation of ergonomics technical specifications. Part of this knowledge was also used to create layouts and equipment lists and contribute to the technical specifications of other disciplines.

Thus, the analysis of the maintenance crew's work ratified that the knowledge generated goes beyond the technical documents created. It includes new ways of thinking about the project dynamics itself, with greater integration between the disciplines involved.

In the basic design phase, ergonomics' specifications depend on the possibility of anticipating design decisions. Depending on the level of anticipation, direct specifications can be created, as in the case of the workshop equipment arrangement. In other situations, the specifications depend on future design decisions and are placed as assumptions/constraints to assist designers in the next steps, such as the battery room example. Thus, ergonomics' participation does not exhaust the knowledge on the best work practices; instead, it provides elements that increase the margin of maneuver of both the designer of the next phases and the worker of the future units.

The limits imposed on this work, including the availability of places onboard for analysis in reference situations, should be considered. Also, the discussion was restricted to the maintenance crew of the units' operational department, without considering the work of the outsourced crews and other departments.

Thus, further analysis of offshore maintenance work is required to encompass other crews and see how the design of other areas of the platform impacts the maintenance crew's work.

5   Conclusions

This work presented the integration of ergonomics in an offshore platform project, its collaboration with the maintenance crew's work, and its constraints.

The recognition of the ergonomist as a project stakeholder has not yet been consolidated. The ergonomic discipline's demand is usually directed to contributions related to worker's health and safety, disregarding their skills to improve the execution of activities and productivity. This disparity was evidenced in the technical specifications construction, where recommendations were not restricted to the workshop environment, extrapolating to other areas of the platform where the maintenance crew also works.

Hence, this work points to the need for new studies on platform maintenance work and the consolidation of ergonomics practice in projects.

References

1. Daniellou, F.: A ergonomia na condução de projetos de concepção de sistemas de trabalho. In: Falzon, P. (ed.) Ergonomia, pp. 303–316. Blucher, São Paulo (2007)
2. Duarte, F.: Complementaridade entre ergonomia e engenharia em projetos industriais. In: Duarte, F. (ed.) Ergonomia e Projeto na Indústria de Processo Contínuo. Lucerna, Rio de Janeiro (2002)

3. ABERGO - Brazilian Association of Ergonomics. Norma ERG BR 1002 - Código de Deon-tologia do Ergonomista Certificado (2003). https://www.abergo.org.br/arquivos/normas_ergbr/norma_erg_br_1002_deontologia.pdf. Accessed 07 Feb 2021
4. Jeantet, A.: Les objets intermédiaires dans la conception. Éléments pour une sociologie des processus de conception, Sociologie du travail, no. 3/98, pp. 291–316 (1998)

Inclusion of Debates on Real Work Situations in Alarm Management at a Gas Logistics Terminal

Anderson Nogueira de Lima[1]([⊠]) [iD], Carolina Maria Do Carmo Alonso[2] [iD], and Francisco José de Castro Moura Duarte[1] [iD]

[1] COPPE, Federal University of Rio de Janeiro, Rio de Janeiro, Brazil
anderson.lima@coppe.ufrj.br
[2] Faculty of Medicine, Federal University of Rio de Janeiro, Rio de Janeiro, Brazil

Abstract. Alarm management is a set of processes and techniques aiming to enable alarm systems to support operators for safer and more efficient operations. The consideration of the operational knowledge in the procedures stands as an opportunity and a challenge since it requires specific conditions. This article presents and discusses how the inclusion of debates about real work situations can contribute to the improvement of the solutions proposed by alarm management committees. Qualitative content analysis on meeting minutes and participant observation of an Alarm Management Committee using a report on real work information showed it was used on more than 60% of solutions applied to a gas transfer terminal, indicating a broad application and adoption. Yet, our findings suggest that the debates addressed alarms regarding variability and emerging strategies, and may consider entire subsystems instead of single alarms.

Keywords: Alarm management · Oil industry · Human factors · Bad actors · Return of experience

1 Background

1.1 Using Experience to Prevent Disasters

Historically, several industrial disasters are related to the inadequate performance of alarm systems. In the oil and gas industry, Three Longford gas explosions, Milford Haven Refinery, and Buncefield Oil storage depot are the most expressive events. The deterioration of alarm performance is related to the announcement failures, alarms announced outside the ideal time range, an avalanche of alarms that lead the operator to not diagnose the situation, or avalanches that cause some alarms not to be announced [1–3].

To prevent these issues, several efforts were made to handle alarm systems, seeking to actually help the operators to understand what is happening in the plant and make the right decisions. Alarm management is a set of organized practices and processes that can be implemented in a system, aiming at both efficiency and security gains. They can range from the design and implementation of the system to its monitoring and improvement of the system during use [1, 2, 4–6].

From a wider perspective, the alarm rates and interface are one factor, from a context where diverse organizational and human factors play their role in industrial safety. The Return of Experience (RoX) is one of these factors involved in the alarm management process, as in any work system design and modification aiming for safety improvement [7].

Taking into consideration the Return of Experience is one of the challenges - what conditions allow the RoX into the alarm management process?

1.2 Alarm Management Process

Several publications address how to organize the alarm management process, being the macroprocess suggested by ANSI/ISA 18.2 one of the most cited among all major publications. It organizes the process in three big loops [1, 2, 5, 6].

The monitoring and management of change loop fits the alarm into the philosophy standards, and evaluate its relationship with the plant, suggesting its definitions: set points, prioritization scale, consequences and corrective actions [2].

It is assumed that over the life of the plant, it is necessary to readjust some alarms. The reasons are diverse: implementation of technological improvements, changes in production processes, continuous learning, all potentially foster changes in the alarm system. Then, the monitoring and maintenance loop considers the operation of the system, as its maintenance. Both processes are bound to the monitoring and assessment, which prioritize alarms to enter the monitoring and management of change loop [2].

The cornerstone of the process, the philosophy, is a document that describes all following work processes, based on basic definitions, with the audit process, include all processes into the audit and philosophy loop [2].

On the monitoring and assessment loop, the bad actor's treatment is a possible method to select alarms to treat. Bad actors are the alarms most announced in a unit. The literature suggests that the announcement of alarms follow the Pareto principle - 20% of the most frequent alarms represent 80% of the total announcements. In this way, it would be possible to make quick gains. With few treatments, it would be possible a sudden improvement in the alarm system [8].

1.3 Bad Actors' Treatment on Practice

Some difficulties were observed during the bad actors' analysis meetings where one of the researchers participated in a gas transport plant.

Prompts are virtual points of control, that linked to sensors on the plant, may trigger when a value/signal is reached. If the prompt is set as an alarm, it is announced to the operator when triggered.

The focus on handling signals and adjusting the absolute and variation limits are important, but are not sufficient to resolve issues of decision and interpretation of work situations. Furthermore, even the experience of the users involved, when detached from the real work situation, loses the sensitivity of addressing the variability and unpre-dictability, and relies on prescribed conditions, rarely matching situations where the alarms were announced.

With the impossibility of resorting to monthly Ergonomic Work Analysis [9] or another method for analyzing real work, a report was developed, in order to guide the debates of the meeting with elements of real work.

Our hypothesis is that this information helps the commission to make decisions suited to deal with work situations that deviate from the prescriptions of the procedures.

Thus, we divided this study into six parts. Below, we explain the objective of this study, following the method of Qualitative Content Analysis (QCA) [10] applied to the minutes of the meeting and participant information. In the results section, we describe how the commission was formed and the organizational context of this effort, as the QCA of the contents of the meeting minutes and participant observation. The penultimate section of the article discussion emphasizes some treatments that were possible from considerations about the real work. Based on the evidence, the study concludes that the information about the real work contained in the report lead to a better Return of Experience, with solutions considering real work strategies and constraints.

2   Objective/Question

To present an analysis on how promoting debates of real work situations on bad actors treatment, by using a report with operational information, could be used by an Alarm Management Committee to justify changes in the alarm system. The limits and potentials of the method are explored.

3   Methodology

Given the purpose of the study, was chosen to conduct an exploratory qualitative research through the development of a case study. The case addressed in this article occurs in a gas logistics plant. The most important processes are gas transfers, between the plant's tanks, between other plants via pipelines, or with ships. The Alarm Management Committee (AMC) in this plant is composed of four professionals - two maintenance representatives, an operational coordinator and a control room operator.

Nine AMC meetings were held from September 2019 to August 2020. The first four meetings lasted 4 h and the subsequent five had an average duration of 2 ½ hours. From a list of 20 most played alarms in the plant, the committee should assess whether the alarm announcements were relevant, and how to decrease the alarm rates. It is worth noting that not all 20 alarms are necessarily handled in all meetings.

The data collection strategies were participant observation of nine AMC meet-ings and the analysis of the minutes of those meetings. All data were analyzed using Qualitative Content Analysis procedures [10].

4   Results

The first section sets out the organizational context, how the meetings were conducted and how the report was constructed. The second section presents the results of the qualitative content analysis of the meeting minutes. The third section illustrates some notable scenarios, where the debate about real work had a significant impact on the conduct of the resolution with data from participant observation.

4.1   Context of the AMC Meetings

Since August 2019, AMCs were installed in several units of an oil and gas logistics company, by director's determination. The company's standard on alarm management is inspired by ANSI-ISA 18.2, using the same process structure along with adaptations and improvements.

At the considered gas plant, the AMC meetings were held monthly. It aimed to investigate the characteristics of bad actors' alarms and applied techniques to reduce unwanted announcements, or even their removal from the system.

In the first two meetings, the discussions were guided by operational procedures, alarm adjustment techniques recommended in the company's internal procedures and the list of the 20 most announced alarms in the month. The preparation of the reports arose from the perception that the information available for the meeting was not sufficient to support the resolution of many alarms.

Table 1.   Report elements per meeting

Additions/Meetings	M1	M2	M3	M4	M5	M6	M7	M8	M9
Operational information			✓	✓	✓	✓	✓	✓	✓
Validation with peers					✓	✓	✓	✓	✓
Equipment information								✓	✓
Briefing								✓	✓

Starting on the third meeting, a report was built using operational information – list of all operations occurred in the month, and a description of unexpected or unwanted conditions associated with systems where bad actors were found – based on change-of-shift reports and personal observations. The report was made by the control room operator, main author of this study. As the feedback was positive, report usage was established.

More elements were included, seeking to meet the needs that were revealed during the meetings. Validation with peers consisted of discussion with coworkers of at least two different teams about operational conditions or particular issues, in order to get multiple perceptions and an agreement about the state of affairs. Before meeting #6, only peers of the same team were consulted. Equipment information was an inquiry about maintenance notes, reports of odd behavior or mal-functioning of equipment involved in the investigated alarms. A quick briefing about the major findings was added to guide the discussion. The Table 1 illustrates the additions to the report during the nine analyzed meetings.

4.2 Qualitative Content Analysis

Nine minutes were analyzed, covering nine meetings and 11 months of operations (Sep/2019 to Aug/2020). The meeting minutes were organized as a table as numbered rows, with columns corresponding to deliberations, responsible person and deadline. The rows regarding bad actors' treatment have the following items:

Tag - the short name of the prompt; **Alarm description** – a description of the prompt, as shown for operators; **New description** – in case of description adjustment; **Justification** – the reasons to support the change; and **Recommended action** – the changes required to improve the alarm efficiency.

In Qualitative Content Analysis (QCA), building a coding frame allows to make a systematic description of the data [10]. In order to inquire how real work debates based on the reports influenced the bad actors treatment, we analyzed the cells corresponding each justification and recommended action, classifying it by the kind of evidence that supported the decision. With one dimension, "decision support", we identified four categories, as presented below.

The signal treatment consisted of adjustment of variable signals and tolerance values, mainly taking into consideration the sensor properties and the project limit requirements. The decisions supported by operational procedures are based on written standard procedures, which take into consideration system design requirements, risk assessment analysis, quality standards and other technical specifications. The decisions supported by experience use unwritten work procedures and logics as argument. Consists on the worker experience in dealing with the plant. The decisions supported by real work context uses the workers experience too, but applied in information about the real work context where the alarms were announced, provided by the report.

A short description of each category is shown in Table 2, with the total occurrences in number and percentage.

The results show that the treatment using signal treatment and operational procedures – prescribed methods – made 12% of the occurrences. The major part of the solutions relied on the operator's knowledge. Although the report was not available in all meetings, most bad actor resolutions were based on debates about real work - 63%.

In some instances, a change was noted in how the Committee treated the alarms when using real work situations. Here, we illustrate three scenarios as examples.

Scenario #1: Mass transfer with high rate of false alarms - a discussion on estimates and sensor reliability based on operational information
This scenario shows how an estimative of flow was not reliable using level indicators, and should be done using other variables.

In the operations of receiving gas from ships, many variables are monitored, as pressure, flow and temperature. A bad actor analyzed was a huge number of alarms announced for level rate, which in this case is a flow measurement – since it indicates a volume variation. As verified by the report, this operation did not have any odd episode, as

Table 2. Occurrences and percentage of categories

Codes	Short description	Occ.	%
Signal treatment	Treatment based on adjustments of process variables	3	3,3%
Supported by operational procedure	Treatment based on documented operational information	8	8,9%
Supported by experience	Treatment based on past experience but not necessarily related to the episode where the alarms were announced	22	24,4%
Supported in a real work context	Using work experience along information provided by the report	57	63,3%

leakages or overpressure. At this specific system, there was no flow meter - the level rate was supposed to estimate the transfer flow. The level sensor was a floating gauge device – calibrated for a still surface. It was argued that although flow monitoring is important, the transfer causes disturbance on the liquid's surface, enough for the gauge to oscillate generating false high and low flow indications - false alarms. It was concluded that this alarm should be removed, because it was not reliable. The variable can still be observed - for estimating the rate and comparing with the ship information, and monitoring should be based on multiple pressure sensors available. This way, it would be possible to estimate flow variations instantly by pressure oscillation.

Scenario #2: Restrictions change alarm usage and operational strategy
In this scenario, a situation where an unusual operating condition and their effect on alarm rates is portrayed, which highlighted an operational variable that is related to performance.

The terminal has two kinds of gas tanks, with completely different storage conditions: refrigerated storage (temperatures around -40 °C and maximum pressure 0.1 kgf/cm^2) and pressurized storage (Temperatures over 10 °C and pressure above 3 kgf/cm^2). The operation of transferring gas from the low temperature tanking for the high-pressure tanking is made using a heat exchanger to warm the gas using sea water.

The pipelines involved in the operation of pressurized gas are built to withstand a range from $+10$° to $+50$ °C. Usually, the temperature of the gas leaving the heat exchanger stays between 15° and 18 °C. As the plant is situated in a tropical area, there is no risk of lowering more the temperature down the pipeline. A low temperature alarm is set to 13 °C. In case the temperature reaches below 13 °C, the operator should increase the flow of sea water, or reduce the flow of gas. It is a stable process, and this alarm is rarely announced. Surprisingly, this alarm was featured as a bad actor in one of the meetings.

The debates used to build the report helped to understand the issue. In a certain transfer operation, from refrigerated storage from shore to a ship with pressurized storage, the vessel had problems dealing with high pressure. It caused the vessel to ask for lower transfer rates, and even to halt the operation. To make the transfer as efficiently as possible, the team decided to transfer the gas with the lowest possible value within safe limits, to minimize the pressure on the ship tanks. This alarm was announced several times in a transfer because the operation required multiple corrective interventions, as controlling the temperature was difficult since the backpressure of the ship made difficult to keep a steady flow. Despite appearing as a bad actor, an assessment of the situation allowed us to conclude that all were relevant. This strategy allowed the best transfer rate possible inside safety limits, contributing to a quicker operation.

Scenario #3: System working outside prescript conditions
This scenario describes a system working out of the normal operational conditions, and its effects on all alarms associated.

When transferring from pressurized storage to refrigerated storage, the gas must be cooled to temperatures of $-30°$ to -40 °C. The cooling operation is done using a compressor unit, which uses a cooling fluid in a closed gas circuit at low temperatures, with takes away the heat from the gas in two heat exchangers in series. This operation is particularly complicated, since the rate and temperature of the two gas streams must match in order to keep the exchanger liquid/vapor levels and pressure in control. High coolant levels on the exchangers could make liquid reach the compressors - a very dangerous situation. The system automatically shut the process in case the levels reach a threshold. An accident is avoided, but it causes a loss of cooling fluid and time. The use of a cooling fluid with characteristics different from those ideally designed, with a mechanical problem in the compressors that reduced the efficiency of the system, caused an abnormal fluctuation in the pressure and levels of the heat exchangers. In this way, the level and pressure alarms ended up appearing as bad actors. As these two conditions - different cooling fluid and performance issues on the compressors - could happen again, the Committee decided to propose a formal change in the procedure, recommending new level goals and alarm margins. An interface feature would be installed, allowing to change the margins more easily.

We purposely refrain from considering the evolution of alarm rates, since it cannot reflect the approach results due the variability in the number of operations and the operating conditions from month to month. We also avoid considering the evolution of the types of justification for alarms, considering that the series is too short.

5 Discussion

The code framing of the alarm justifications showed that 63% of the cases used the report as support for the proposed changes, which suggest a wide application of the method.

It was also possible to notice that some sources of variability influenced more than one process variable. Thus, the resolutions could treat subsystems, covering variables and alarms that did not appear as bad actors in that situation.

The inclusion of debates about the real work for the discussion allows a discussion beyond the technical knowledge formalized in the procedures and manuals - it recognizes process variations and emergent operational strategies associated with it. Hence, it guides the discussion and complements the understanding of the occurrences, respecting the strictly technical dimension of the systems. These results are consistent with the considerations of Gauthey [7], where the return of experience quality increases with methods that allow the analysis of real work situations.

Alarm management techniques can be used to solve problems based on techno-centric projects, as it adds knowledge produced by users back in the system. The excess and redundancies of sensors and alarms are described since 80s, due increasing digital automatization of the processes [11]. This issue, when approached by an alarm management Committee with real activity information, enough resources and organizational support, may provide the system a better delimitation of operational margins – the plasticity, as stated by Béguin [12].

As the system recommend changes results in lower alarm rates and better control of the plant, this initiative matches the model proposed by Daniellou [4], where human and organizational factors, when coordinated and considering the activity of work, increase safety and production levels.

As a limit of this approach - and any bad actors treatment method, we point that it is confined to experienced situations. Plant behavior under unprecedented abnormal situations cannot be accessed by this method.

6   Conclusions

This research demonstrated that the discussion of real work situations was used as support of the majority of recommended changes by the AMC. It also allowed the development of solutions to reduce bad actors that incorporated the plant's operational context in addition to the prescribed situations, contributing to safer and more efficient operations. Yet, allowed at some conditions, the treatment of a whole subsystem.

As a limit of this study, it is considered that oil and gas logistics operations, despite the proximity to the refining industry, are not continuous processes.

We plan to apply this method in other industrial units of the same company, to investigate the reproducibility of the results.

One of the possibilities that we expect for further inquiry is the elaboration of a list of requirements for the alarm data extraction tool, so it can better support the analysis of real work situations, e.g., showing multiple variables on a timeline.

The strategies for the use of alarms by operators deserve further investigation. We find evidence that operators can use alarms or alerts as a warning to maintain awareness of the behavior of a process variable, without necessarily having an associated action. These strategies have a direct consequence on the rate of alarms/alerts.

References

1. EEMUA - Engineering Equipment and Materials Users Association: Alarm Systems - A guide to design, management and procurement. Publication 191, London (2013)
2. International Society of Automation: ANSI/ISA-18.2-2016 - Management of Alarm Systems for the Process Industries. Research Triangle Park, NC, USA (2016)
3. Mehta, B.R., Reddy, Y.J.: Industrial Process Automation Systems. Elsevier (2015)
4. Daniellou, F., Boissières, I., Simard, M.: Human and organizational factors of safety: state of the art. FonCSI (2011)

5. NAMUR: NA 102 - Alarm Management (2008)
6. Norweigian Petroleum Directorate: YA-711 Principles for alarm system design, pp. 1–25 (2001)
7. Gauthey, O.: Le Retour D'expérience - Etat Des Pratiques Industrielles. Les Cahiers De La Sécurité Industrielle, p. 57 (2008)
8. Hollifield, B., Habibi, E.: The Alarm Management Handbook. PAS, Houston, TRexas (2010)
9. Wisner, A.: Understanding problem building: ergonomic work analysis. Ergonomics **38**, 595–605 (1995). https://doi.org/10.1080/00140139508925133
10. Schreier, M.: Qualitative Content Analysis in Practice. Sage Publications (2012)
11. Duarte, F.J.C.M., Santos, P.: A configuração das telas de sistemas digitais de controle de processo. In: de Castro Moura Duarte, F.J. (ed.) Ergonomia e Projeto na Indústria de Processo Contínuo, pp. 187–198. Lucerna, Rio de Janeiro (2002)
12. Béguin, P.: Taking activity into account during the design process. Activites **4** (2007). https://doi.org/10.4000/activites.1727

Ergonomic Simulation: The Work Dimension in the Integrated Operations Centres Design in the Oil Industry

Barbara Oggioni[1]([✉]) [iD], Francisco José de Castro Moura Duarte[1] [iD], and Pascal Béguin[2] [iD]

[1] Programa de Engenharia de Produção, COPPE, Universidade Federal do Rio de Janeiro, Rio de Janeiro, Brazil
barbarap@pep.ufrj.br
[2] Institut d'Études du Travail de Lyon, Université Lumière Lyon 2, UMR 5600-LABex IMU, Lyon, France

Abstract. This study aims to reflect on how the work dimension can be considered in Integrated Operations (IO) projects through a work simulation from a participatory ergonomic perspective. This research presents a case study of an Onshore Collaborative Centre (OCC) design, where an Ergonomic Work Analysis and three Ergonomics Simulations cycles were performed to support the discussions with workers and managers to create design solutions. The results show the organization of a participatory ergonomics approach in IO projects, which includes the structuring of the participatory dynamics in the design process from the Ergonomic Work Analysis and Simulations. The simulation is a method that can transform work into an important factor both in modifying the project and in technical choices. It also allows for the inclusion of different actors and their perspectives. However, for the simulation to be an effective means of participation, it is necessary to have an integration between the work analysis and the expectations of the project.

Keywords: Ergonomic simulation · Participation · Design process · Integrated operations

1 Introduction

1.1 The Work Dimension in Integrated Operations (IO) Projects

Integrated operations, as a new model of work, has emerged from the initiatives of several oil and gas companies to improving operational performance and reduce costs. According to Haavik [1], the petroleum industry domain, with harsh environment and remoteness of operations, induce requirements for low offshore staffing and high degree of sensor-based monitoring, combined with support and management from remote centers of coordination.

Projects of this nature have impacts on different operating units, such as the advent of operations support rooms, which has been transforming offshore and onshore work

N. L. Black et al. (Eds.): IEA 2021, LNNS 219, pp. 232–239, 2021.
https://doi.org/10.1007/978-3-030-74602-5_35

towards greater integration. To this end, several teams in Onshore Collaborative Centres (OCC) began to analyze data, recommend process optimization and predictively monitor possible equipment failures on board. To Moltu and Nærheim [2], this type of rooms makes operations and maintenance work more feasible between the onshore-based operation unit and the offshore operations.

Some studies indicate that such collaborative rooms encourage cooperation, integration of teams in real time, more intense flow of information and knowledge within the asset, leading to a new organizational culture [3, 4]. There is a prerogative that work processes become integrated and collaborative from the available technology and physical environment.

Although studies emphasize the importance of considering human factors and the end-users participate in IO projects and in the change process, this participation is focused on their experiences as input to the experts [5] and on the training and preparation through an intensive program of change management [6], mainly focused on the probable resistances coming with the project implementation [7].

From an ergonomic point of view, more than involving training, meetings and consultation, participation "is seen as providing the opportunity for real, early and full involvement of the people involved (operators, supervisors, etc.) in the making of decisions about their jobs, systems, workplace and organization" and "such involvement will include the ability to influence, or to control, such decisions or the relevant decision makers" [8].

This study aims to reflect on how the work dimension can be considered in Onshore Collaborative Centres design through a work simulation from a participatory ergonomic perspective. For such purpose, this paper presents a case study of an OCC design, where an ergonomic work analysis and three simulations cycles was performed to support the discussions with workers and managers from Brazilian oil and gas industry to create design solutions.

1.2 Participatory Ergonomics

A participatory ergonomics approach to workplace assessment and design will aim at modifying the representations of work that are involved in design and not simply bring new bricks of knowledge to the designers [9]. According to the authors, introducing a participatory approach in the design process requires a social construction, for a clear negotiation between the parties, and technique, which consists in the definition of methods that allow a confrontation between different types of knowledge.

Among these methods, work simulation appears as an ubiquitous method to participatory ergonomics approach in the design process, which involves dealing with un-predicted variability, mobilizing personal and collective resources, experiencing con-traditions and debates about values between human actors [10]. Simulating work situations is a work oriented method that puts workers and others stakeholders at the center of the design process [11–14], allowing work to be a decision-making criterion, similar to economic and technical criteria, which are often the only criteria taken into account [12].

However, the aim of the simulation is not to prescribe the right way of performing the tasks [14]. In this sense, it is impossible to fully anticipate and predict the future, because activity is constructed by a given operator as a response to a given context [10]. Nonetheless, the simulation brings the possibility of staging and manipulating certain elements that are considered significant to achieve a goal, and to drop other less interesting ones [15].

In this study, an ergonomic participatory approach based on methods such as analysis and simulation of work was used, from the perspective of activity ergonomics approach. The analysis of the activity makes it possible to understand the difficulties that workers encounter in their work and the adjustments that they implement to deal with the variability [16]. And the simulation, when considering the activity point of view, allows to stage some idea or design hypothesis through a model, a mock-up or a prototype, in order to experience and learn from them, to identify what is causing problems and troubles, and to suggest a possible resolution to depict [10].

2   Methods

This research presents a case study of an Onshore Collaborative Centre design, where an Ergonomic Work Analysis and three Ergonomics Simulations cycles were performed to support the discussions with workers and managers to create design solutions. The subsequent analysis of the ergonomic design process used in the case study aimed to understand how Work Analysis and Ergonomics Simulations can contribute as participatory methods in IO projects.

2.1   Case Study Context

This research was carried out in one of the oil production units of the studied petroleum industry, from February 2017 to April 2018, which operates in the exploration of the pre-salt area. To optimize operation in this environment, with platforms about 280 km offshore and in ultra-deep water at depths of 2,200 m, for example, the unit needs increasingly structured support onshore.

To this end, the production unit initiates several onshore support initiatives for offshore production and starting an OCC, following the trend of operational integration of the international oil and gas industry. With the expansion of the pre-salt operation and the arrival of new platforms by 2021, the production unit started the OCC restructuring project to expand its capacity to support maritime operations.

The design of the new OCC would move its place of operation, currently in separate rooms, to a large center that would be located in an old, unoccupied restaurant and kitchen in the same building. The aim was that the new OCC would be able to accommodate the increase in staff and to allow for reinforced interactions between teams, making the integrated support character effective.

2.2   Case Setting and Participants

The participants in the study are composed by the existing OCC teams, which are: 3 predictive monitoring cells of equipment and systems on board offshore platforms; 1 logistics support team; 1 operational support team, which controls the gas network and provides emergency support for offshore operations; 1 support team for gas flow planning and optimization; 1 infrastructure support team for the OCC itself and the IO management team, which were the project demanders.

The first stage of the study of work, the phase of prior analysis [17], sought to understand the work globally, its main tasks, as well as the main interactions between teams, inside and outside the OCC. The objective was the construction of integration hypothesis between the OCC teams, represented by a sociogram, which would guide the construction and the simulation of layout proposals. To this end, the existing process mapping documents made available by the company were analyzed, and open interviews and non-systematic observations were conducted with the OCC teams.

After the validation of the integration hypothesis with managers and workers, the ergonomics team returned to the field to further study the work. According to Maline [17] and Daniellou [14], the objective of deepening work analysis within the framework of a simulation approach is to identify typical work situations. It is a projective, scenario-making phase, and depends on prior analysis, as a scenario is no more than a case of assembling variables with certain criteria, identified during the previous phase and belonging to all areas of the situation to be conceived.

Maline [17] highlights that a scenario respects the systematics of a work situation. In the OCC project, the following variables were analyzed: (1) elements of the work activity; (2) elements of the task to be performed; (3) monitoring and platform support characteristics; (4) characteristics of the organization; (5) incident types and emergency situations; and (6) elements of the time course.

The simulation phase was organized in 3 stages. The first stage started discussions with teams and managers about two layout alternatives generated by the ergonomics team from the study of work. The main objective was to select one of the two proposals for discussion in the next simulation sections. The resources used were paper schematic floor plans and pens for interventions by workers and managers.

The second stage was held at the exact location that would be transformed to house the new CCO. The resource used was "game board", which is a rigid board, with the vinyl-printed schematic floor plan for writing and erasing, with pieces representing the workstations that could be moved. The board was used as a support for discussion about the organization of spaces.

As a result of the second stage of simulation meetings, an ergonomics team reproduced the layout associated with a three-dimensional (3D) package for use in the third stage of simulation meetings, that took place 20 days later. Like to the second stage, the meeting was held in the environment to be modified and the game board, the floor plans printed on paper including and the 3D model images, was used as support.

During the simulations, the ergonomists presented the project that was developed and made questions regarding the space and the work activity to be performed in it. The questions were based on typical work situations, structured in the study phase of the teams' in-depth work. The team of ergonomists had the main function of being mediators and the main objective was to lead the participants to reflect on their own work and present their space organization proposals.

The ergonomists' mediation had to adapt to the different situations during the simulations, with each new layout proposal made by the participants, information about the work situations was again put "in play" for discussion, as the propositions of reflection on the work without the influence of technical devices and the reflection on how emergency situations would be conducted, for example.

3   Results

The results of the work analysis and simulations are presented in this section, divided into two parts. First, we present the result of the work analysis that allowed the generation of the first layout alternatives and the mapping of the work situations used in the simulations. Then, the layout evolution in the different phases of the simulations, contextualized by the content analysis of the discussions held by the participants. Here, the example of monitoring teams is used to illustrate this development.

3.1   The Role of Work Analysis

First, with the Work Analysis, it is possible to characterize the existing integration between the OCC teams. The creation of a sociogram allowed visualizing the relational and communication intensity within the team, and among other teams. Recording the different frequencies of interactions between cells guided the grouping and the required proximity between teams in the space design. The nature of integrated work guided discussions with project managers to validate the sociogram. Based on the work analyzed and the integration groups identified, the ergonomics team started the first OCC layout studies.

Subsequently, on the understanding of team functioning, data analysis strategies and integration with other teams, the ergonomics team compiled the typical situations of the teams to construct scenarios in the final simulation meetings, contributing to the reflections about future work and the intended environment design with elements of real work.

3.2   The Role of Simulations

The three simulation cycles show how innovative proposals were created at each stage. The first simulations contributed to equalizing the knowledge of the project among the participants (operators and managers). For the second and third cycle of simulations, the use of a game board and a virtual model enabled a reflection on the layout of the workstations since it was possible to study new possibilities and modify the layout during the discussions about the operation space in different work situations.

Taking the case of the monitoring team as an example, the first and second simulation cycle has the influence of technical devices on most of the dynamics. The videowall guided the layout by both operators and management. The occupation is discussed more in function of a technical disposition than in function of the work, even with the work situations being put for the discussion. To encourage the change of logic, the ergonomists requested that only the work be considered, removing the concern of adjusting the layout according to a technical device.

Thus, monitoring operators reported how information exchanges were made to analyze a possible deviation, data searches in different systems, the possibility of grouping between two operators around a monitor for case discussion and training. These typical work situations were mostly held in informal corridor meetings between workstations.

In the third simulation cycle, operators proposed a new layout, which was discussed between the three monitoring teams earlier: *"(...) The videowall is impacting what the* [monitoring] *team is most important today, which is the interaction!"*.

The operators' proposal was to organize the workplaces in half circles so that operators could hold meetings at the center and still have some video viewing when they needed it. In this way, from the operators' point of view, they would be able to meet the needs of the team's integrated work and the requirements of the need to concentrate information on large screens placed by management and the IO team. Figure 1 shows the result of layout development in secondary and tertiary simulation.

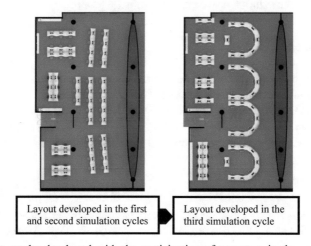

| Layout developed in the first and second simulation cycles | Layout developed in the third simulation cycle |

Fig. 1. Layout results developed with the participation of operators in the second and third simulation cycles.

4   Discussion

The results show that simulation is a method that can transform work into an important factor both in modifying the project and in technical choices. It also allows for the inclusion of different actors and their perspectives. However, for the simulation to be an effective means of participation, it is necessary to have an integration between the work analysis and the expectations of the project.

The analysis of the work and the simulation maintain dialectical ties during the conduction of the project. The work analysis allows producing knowledge of the work, which guides the choices that are made during the design. The detailed analysis of the activity allows the debates about the work in the simulations to concretely contribute to the transformation of the working conditions.

As an example of the monitoring team presents, operators organize small meetings to build a shared context about the state of the platform. Applying the "typical work situations" during the simulations made it possible to put the work on the scene, even when managers insisted on an integrated vision from large screens, such as video wall. Without a staging, based mainly on the elements of the activity, the discussion about the work would not take place and would have focused on technical devices.

The solution found by the monitoring operators, which aimed to meet both the technological demands of managers and the interaction through the meetings between workers, demonstrates how it is possible to deal with the differences between actors so different from the same project and create innovative solutions.

According to Béguin [18], the design is characterized by heterogeneous points of view; operators and designers can legitimately discourse-give. But these discrepancies are the driving force behind the modification of the characteristics of the object being designed, that is, the criteria are modified, the specifications adjusted, and the purposes redefined so that the solution is acceptable within the group.

5   Conclusions

New technologies do not bring and do not solve alone the collective dimension that is needed for implementing "Integrated operations". It is necessary to know and bring elements of work to the project. Ergonomic Work Analysis and Ergonomic Simulation as a participatory ergonomics approach allows reflection, new developments and, above all, brings the view of work as an important decision variable in the IO design process.

References

1. Haavik, T.: Remoteness and sensework in harsh environments. Saf. Sci. **95**, 150–158 (2017)
2. Moltu, B., Nærheim, J.: IO design gives high efficiency. SPE Econ. Manag. **2**(1), 774–784 (2010)
3. Edwards, A., Roberts, S.: iValue, an intelligent energy strategy for an integrated gas major. In: SPE Intelligent Energy Conference and Exhibition. Society of Petroleum Engineers, pp. 25–27 (2008)
4. Lima, C., Lima, G., Quelhas, O., Ferreira, R.: Integrated operations: value and approach in the oil industry. Braz. J. Oper. Prod. Manag. **12**, 74–87 (2015)
5. Moltu, B.: Good IO-design is more than IO-rooms. In: Rosendahl, T., Hepsø, V. (eds.) Integrated Operations in the Oil and Gas Industry: Sustainability and Capability Development, 1st edn. IGI Global, Hershey (2013)
6. Lima, C., Lima, G., Castro, J.: Improving value in oil business with integrated operations: a practical case of knowledge management. Int. J. Knowl. Manag. **11**(3), 55–72 (2015)
7. Siqueira, C., Cunha, V., Meneghelli, R., et al.: Challenges in managing people to implement an integrated operations systems: a Petrobras case study in an operational unit of exploration and production. In: SPE Intelligent Energy International, Utrecht, The Netherlands (2012)
8. Wilson, J.: Participation - a framework and a foundation for ergonomics? J. Occup. Psychol. **64**, 67–80 (1991)
9. Garrigou, A., Daniellou, F., Carballeda, G., Ruaud, S.: Activity analysis in participatory design and analysis of participatory design activity. Int. J. Ind. Ergon. **15**, 311–327 (1995)

10. Béguin, P., Duarte, F., Bittencourt, J., Pueyo, V.: Simulating work systems: anticipation or development of experiences? An activity approach. In: Proceedings of the 20th Congress of the International Ergonomics Association (IEA 2018), vol. IV, pp. 494–502. Springer, Cham (2018)
11. Andersen, S., Broberg, O.: A framework of knowledge creation processes in participatory simulation of hospital work systems. Ergonomics **60**(4), 487–503 (2017)
12. Béguin, P.: Learning during design through simulation. In: 11th International Symposium on Human Factors in Organisational Design and Management & 46th Annual Nordic Ergonomics Society Conference, pp. 867–872 (2014)
13. Broberg, O., Conceicao, C. A framework of participatory ergonomics simulation. In: Proceedings of the 20th Congress of the International Ergonomics Association (IEA 2018), vol. IV, pp. 391–395, Springer, Cham (2018)
14. Daniellou, F.: Simulating future work activity is not only a way of improving workstation design. Activites **4**(2), 84–90 (2007)
15. Béguin, P.: Une approche opérative de la simulation. In: Astier, P., Oudart, A.-C. (eds.) Analyses du travail et formation: contributions de la didactique professionnelle - Les Cahiers d'Etudes du CUEEP N° 56 (2005)
16. Daniellou, F.: The French-speaking ergonomists' approach to work activity: cross-influences of field intervention and conceptual models. Theor. Issues Ergon. Sci. **6**(5), 409–427 (2005)
17. Maline, J.: Simuler le travail: Une aide à la conduite de projet. ANACT, Montrouge (1994)
18. Béguin, P.: A concepção dos instrumentos como processo dialógico de aprendizagens mútuas. In: Falzon, P. (ed.) Ergonomia Construtiva, pp. 205–222. São Paulo, Blucher (2016)

Situated Relational Networks: Empowerment and Entrepreneurship in the Rocinha Slum

Isabella Nunes Pereira[1] ⓘ, Aline Brufato[1] ⓘ, Felipe Loureiro[1](✉) ⓘ,
and Roberto Bartholo[1,2] ⓘ

[1] Production Engineering Program, Federal University of Rio de Janeiro, Rio de Janeiro, Brazil
[2] Universität Erlangen-Nürnberg, Erlangen, Brazil

Abstract. The paper presents a qualitative study on entrepreneurship in the Rocinha slum, Rio de Janeiro, Brazil, from the perspective of the effectuation approach developed by Saras Sarasvathy. Effectuation is the key for interpreting four case studies focused on the social, economic, and cultural relationships between the slum and the north-eastern region of Brazil – the origin of many of Rocinha's residents. The interviews indicated the importance of relational links between Rocinha and Northeast of Brazil either in the slum's economic dynamism or its identity affirmation, an aspect revealed in one interview with an entrepreneur who sends the rent income to relatives in the Northeast, for example. As a possible unfolding of future research, the effectuation approach seems adequate for the study, not only for startups, but also for the operation of such initiatives in those contexts marked by radical uncertainties, as is the Rocinha slum in Rio de Janeiro.

Keywords: Situated entrepreneurship · Effectuation approach · Relational networks · Rocinha slum

1 Introduction

Rocinha is one of Rio de Janeiro's biggest slums, and its population growth rate is higher than the city's. According to the latest official data - available from the Demography Census 2000–2010, developed by the Brazilian Institute of Geography and Statistics (IBGE) -, Rocinha's population grew 23%, while the average growth in the city was 7.9%. The slum is located in one of Rio's most valued neighbourhoods, providing a significant part of the workforce – both formal and informal - for many middle and upper-class residences and businesses in the region. According to the Census 2010 – Table 1 - the average commute time to work place for Rocinha's residents expresses the importance of its location.

Rocinha's proximity to the wealthiest regions of a highly cosmopolitan city such as Rio de Janeiro and the access to networks (relational and technical) facilitates the characterization of Rocinha as an internationalized slum. Where relational patterns of the *glocal* are inherent of entrepreneurship dynamics in Rocinha (see Google My Maps shorturl.at/gFQ35). Following this characterization, the paper analyses entrepreneurship in Rocinha, through four cases in different sectors, building on effectuation approach and

Table 1. Δt average commute time to workplace for Rocinha's residents

% residents	Δt commute time
7%	5 min or less
34%	6 to 30 min
47%	Between 30 min and 1 h
11%	Between 1 and 2 h
1%	More than 2 h

Source: Demography Census 2010, Brazilian Institute of Geography and Statistics (IBGE).

focusing on the impact of territorial dynamics in entrepreneurial activities – especially on the relevance of personal trust as a vector for transformation (Sarasvathy 2001; Lomnitz and Sheinbaum 2004).

2   Effectual Entrepreneurship in Rocinha Slum

The effectuation approach builds on Herbert Simon's "bounded rationality" theory, which argues that it is necessary to consider radical uncertainties in the decision-making environments in which entrepreneurs operate (Simon 1969). The entrepreneur's attitude towards the future is at the core of the effectuation approach: "Under conditions of uncertainty, the actions and interactions that the entrepreneur has to undertake, including the decision to take action at all, increase in complexity and ambiguity. In other words, most entrepreneurial opportunities in the world have to be made through the actions and interactions of stakeholders in the enterprise, using materials and concepts found in the world. Opportunities are, in fact, artifacts" (Sarasvathy et al. 2020 p. 12).

The effectuation approach introduces a new lens on a well-known phenomenon, providing alternative rationality to the conventional models based on planning, market-analysis, and benchmarking (Sarasvathy 2004). It argues that entrepreneurial decisions are immersed in uncertainties and contingencies and can offer new relational opportunities for businesses since "effectual strategies are useful when the future is unpredictable, goals are unclear and the environment driven by human action" (Sarasvathy 2008 p. 73). The core of the effectuation approach lies in the following principles:

1. *Bird-in-hand* – The starting point comes from the available resources: the entrepreneur's identity (who I am); previous knowledge (what I know); and available network (whom I know). It is essential to acknowledge that the entrepreneur's identity depends on and is frequently affected by the available knowledge and the density of the networks.

2. *Affordable-loss* – What can the entrepreneur afford to lose to begin and sustain an entrepreneurial endeavor, based on the worst-case scenario? The aim is to help deal with uncertainty and encourage the development of creative solutions that can allow the entrepreneur to operate with controlled costs and risks.
3. *Crazy-quilt* – Emphasizes cooperative relational networks, partnerships, without following static selection criteria. The entrepreneur allows many stakeholders to participate in the activity.
4. *Lemonade* – Based on the entrepreneur's ability to explore the unpredictability of contingencies in Search of creative opportunities.
5. *Pilot-in-the-plane* – Discerning what is and what is not manageable among the contingencies, aiming at controlling what can be controlled by the entrepreneurial activity – or that can support it.

In this study, we will apply the five principles to four cases of entrepreneurship in the Rocinha slum to assess whether the effectuation approach can be an adequate interpretive key.

3   Four Cases of Situated Entrepreneurship in Rocinha

This paper is a development of the pioneering research developed by the primary author in her Ph.D. thesis on entrepreneurship in Rocinha (Pereira 2014). It was based on data collected through qualitative field research during the Covid-19 pandemic. The four cases that will be analyzed through the five principles of the effectuation approach (Table 2) belong to four different areas: (I) restaurant; (II) real estate business; (III) travel agency; and (IV) Afro-Brazilian martial arts (*capoeira*).

4   Findings

Table 2. Effectuation's five principals in four cases in Rocinha

1. BIRD-IN-HAND	
I	In 1985, the entrepreneur came from Bahia, in northeast Brazil, to work as a housekeeper in Rio de Janeiro, settling at Rocinha. After a few years, she became manager at a food franchise, where she remained for 10 years. In 2007, she opened her restaurant at Rocinha, focusing on Brazilian regional food. In 2020, during the Covid-19 pandemic, she moved her restaurant to a neighboring slum to cut costs. This move was only possible due to her experience in cooking and managing restaurants and keeping at least part of her network of suppliers

(*continued*)

Table 2. (*continued*)

II	The entrepreneur was born and raised in Rocinha and had a degree in design from one of the most prestigious universities in Rio de Janeiro. In 2015, he closed his own design business and began working with his mother as a real estate broker in her agency, established in Rocinha for over 40 years. This career-move was possible because of the relational networks built by his mother, and he brought to the business his knowledge on information technology and the intention to optimize the company's key processes,
III	The entrepreneur was born and raised in Rocinha, where his grandparents operated numerous businesses. Rooted in his community, his activity focuses on local endeavors with *Rocinha's samba school* and an informal transportation cooperative. In 2014, he opened the first community-based travel agency in Rocinha. The business became viable because of his deep relationship with the community and previous experiences with collective initiatives, even without having any prior experience in tourism
IV	In 1979, the entrepreneur came from Bahia to Rio de Janeiro while having no relatives or acquaintances. However, encounters with three people marked his trajectory: i. Grande Otelo, a world-famous Brazilian actor, contacted one of his sons, who practiced *capoeira* and allowed him to start teaching *capoeira* in Rio; ii. Moraes Moreira, a famous Brazilian musician, also from Bahia, who introduced him to his artists' Community; and iii. João do Pulo, *capoeira* master in Rocinha, invites him to replace one of his teachers. Since then, he established himself as a *capoeira* master in Rocinha, building on his ability as a *capoeira* master and on his capacity to develop and sustain relational networks
2. AFFORDABLE-LOSS	
I	The entrepreneur intended to keep her business in Rocinha, but she had to keep the restaurant closed for 4 months while still paying the full rent during the pandemic. She then reached her financial limit and decided to move to a neighboring slum to operate with lower costs. *"I thought I wouldn't keep investing money with no return, and went to Rio das Pedras. I am here, and the business is going, but my heart stayed in Rocinha"*
II	When the entrepreneur chose to succeed his mother in her real estate business, he gave up on his own design business, which opened in 2010 as his college degree's culmination. His mother's company provided a steady, regular income amid an uncertain context. *"We were overwhelmed with work that was one of the reasons for closing the business. I could not take it anymore, and it came to the point where I would rather not sign new clients. It was tough to work. I was thinking about what I should do with my life, and, without knowing what to do, I joined my mother. My mother retired, but she keeps working, and now I am working with her"*
III	During the pandemic, there was a substantial reduction of tourist flow in Rocinha, and the entrepreneur thought about closing the business. Analyzing the financial situation in broad terms, he chose to keep the agency even with much lower demand. *"I have my agency, I could have already rented the space, but the agency is a reference, the Money is coming in, and I am buying supplies, paying my debts, and living one day at a time."*

(*continued*)

Table 2. (*continued*)

IV	After his mother died in Bahia, the entrepreneur decided to go to Rio and start a new life. *"My life was just her and me, so I thought to myself, what am I going to do with my life now?"* In Rio, he lived in dire conditions for 25years while pursuing ways to sustain himself with *capoeira* as both a career and a way of life. He declined offers from experienced masters, focusing on his training and pursuing his way: his shirt and rope in Rocinha, where his *capoeira* group was rooted.*"[…] no man, I'll give you the rope, you have to stay with me, you are very good […] I thought: I build this group, so I said - now I am crazy, I won't be called to go anywhere, I am Building a capoeira group and have to be careful now because doors will be closed to me and everything will be back at square zero, I am going to all capoeira meetings to show my shirt, show my name, and since I had some students, I took the students, and we walked around Rio going to these meetings"*
3. LEMONADE	
I	Since it was financially impossible to remain in Rocinha, the entrepreneur decided to move to a neighboring slum. *"I never thought about leaving Rocinha. I scraped all my savings, my husband's and took a loan to pay for the costs and keep my things. I ended up losing half my things, and now I am here, in Rio das Pedras, and had to reinvent myself"*
II	The entrepreneur was able to apply his expertise as designer and business manager in the modernization of his mother's business, focusing on information technologies and operational management and the consolidation of his mother's tacit knowledge – especially during the unprecedented challenges posed by the pandemic
III	The entrepreneur opened his business in 2014, focusing on community-based tourism to respond to the predatory tourism that existed in Rocinha.*"In 2014, I opened the agency because the tourism we had here gave nothing back to the community, created no jobs and no income. We decided to dive into this segment so that the slum could be empowered and own this tourism. I don't want a boom without infrastructure, receiving 100 tourists every day is not that. I want half of that, but with quality, so that the person leaves here understanding who we are; understanding our reality"*
IV	When the entrepreneur chose to create his *capoeira* group in Rocinha, giving up on other opportunities, he began to strengthen his network in *capoeira* - which reaches far beyond Rocinha – in order to deal with the uncertainties of his business
4. CRAZY-QUILT	
I	Settling in a new community, the entrepreneur had to rebuild her network of clients and suppliers. All of her efforts were focused on this reshaping of long-established networks.*"It is complicated, but, at the same time, it is good for me because you leave your comfort zone. This renews you, renews people and subjects. Everything is different. The only thing I have to learn is how to deal with my feelings"*

(*continued*)

Table 2. (*continued*)

II	The business is based on the relational capital built by the entrepreneur's mother over the years. Acknowledging that, the successor focuses on the consolidation and actualization of this capital, supporting it with information technologies and communication. *"I have 'computerized' the whole process. She doesn't know how to work with WhatsApp, internet, these things, I am her right arm, but her contact is essential."*
III	The entrepreneur knew how to identify the opportunity for a niche based on the interface between local and global dynamics. Rocinha's location is privileged since the touristic dynamics in the city's wealthiest regions may include visits to the site. *"It is all about contact, right? [...] I proposed to create a business with no financial conditions, without knowing anything, not studying tourism, not speaking English, not speaking Spanish, if you consider all of that, you'll see that now I am a reference in the world"*
IV	For over two decades, the entrepreneur became known and came to know the dynamics of the *capoeira* market in Rio do Janeiro. His rootedness in Rocinha was strongly based on this relational capital accumulated over the years
5. PILOT-IN-THE-PLANE	
I	The entrepreneur used economic rationality to decide to move to a neighboring slum and establish a new business. *"It was an attitude more from the head than from the heart, and we ended up revising the costs, now everything is controlled. I am reshaping myself. I am shaping even my feelings. I still don't know how to behave"*
II	The entrepreneur/successor took control of the real estate business, aiming to modernize processes and develop contact with clients
III	Even in a context of radical uncertainty, the entrepreneur was able to save his energies, focusing on controlling what he was able to control. *"Now is the day to day, now is about working, making money, investing, keeping the pantry full, the expenses paid, and be happy."*
IV	The entrepreneur does not follow pre-established business plans, and his connections with the site are not only economic. *"I wished but never planned, and to this day, I still don't plan much. [...] In capoeira, there is a move called 'negative and dodge'. You must know the time to dodge and the time to back off. [...] you act as you'll move, but you don't, if you move at the wrong time you'll get hit, you'll end up in the floor"*

5   Conclusions

The four cases of entrepreneurship in the Rocinha slum allow us - with caution -, to present some convergences that may be pertinent to future research. In summary, we can argue that the qualitative research corroborates the proposition – considered common-sense among Brazilian researchers – which Rocinha's population is mainly from the north-eastern origin, a historical migratory flow from impoverished regions to the Southeast of Brazil. This flow was not limited to establishing the slum, unfolding into relational networks that stretch to this day. These relational networks are active not only in the creation of opportunities for formal and informal work – they also sustain and dynamize economic and meta economics links between residents of north-eastern origin and their hometowns.

Three of the four entrepreneurs (I, III e IV) are of north-eastern origin. In case I, the entrepreneur came from the Northeast, and the restaurant focused on north-eastern food. In case III, the entrepreneur's grandparents came from the Northeast, belonging to one of the first migratory flows that established the slum. The community-based tourism promoted by the agency focuses on the affirmation of this cultural identity. In case IV, the *capoeira* tradition from Bahia expresses the entanglement between African Brazilian traditions and Brazil's Northeast.

Even in case II, the only one in which the entrepreneur is not of north-eastern origin, this close relationship becomes evident: most of the agency's revenue comes from renting rooms, apartments, and shops whose income is sent to the owner's hometown in the Northeast. In many cases, clients came from the Northeast, worked in Rio for years until they were able to buy a property, and have then come back to their hometowns where they can live comfortably with the profits from the rent in Rocinha- where the cost of living is much higher. Thus, the four cases corroborate the proposition that there is a strong connection between Rocinha and the Northeast region of Brazil, not only in economic terms but also in cultural identity and belonging.

The four cases also point towards the importance of college education and extension projects in the qualification of the young workforce from Rocinha and/or in the repercussion over the territory's configuration. It becomes evident in the modernizing proposal by the entrepreneur in case II. Initiatives such as the community-based tourism agency of case III have constituted a new field for academic research – becoming the subject of dissertations and thesis in many Brazilian universities-and for extension projects and grant and research programs.

Lastly, the four cases suggest that the effectuation approach can be an adequate interpretative key for understanding the dynamics and rationalities of entrepreneurial activities in slums. Complex sites characterized by a radical uncertainty – than official programs promoted by Brazilian institutions such as the Support Service for Micro and Small Businesses (SEBRAE).

In all cases, the logic behind the actions of the entrepreneurs seems to be much more convergent with goals other than growth and scale. The focus of their entrepreneurial activities seems to prioritize a way of living. The adherence to the principles of the effectuation approach in entrepreneurial activities in the Rocinha slum reveals a dynamic shaped by complex reciprocity networks between individuals and groups that occupy different levels in different power structures (Lomnitz 1988; Lomnitz and Sheinbaum 2004).

Although the effectuation approach can be adequate not only for the study of startups but also for research into the operative sustainability of entrepreneurial activities in complex environments such as Rocinha, where social, economic, and political contexts may rapidly change, the research has apparent shortcomings, based on interviews with only four entrepreneurs, and it would not be wise to propose generalizations. However, it does point towards the relevance of relational networks for the development of entrepreneurial activities. As Lomnitz and Sheinbaum (2004) underlines, these networks can be classified into two types: horizontal (usually family and friends) and vertical (usually employers and landlords), and in many cases, these types are intertwined. This seems to be an exciting field for future research, particularly in studying the entanglement between the principles of effectuation, sites, and relational networks.

References

Google My Maps. Rocinha, Rio de Janeiro. https://www.shorturl.at/gFQ35. Accessed 4 Feb 2021

Instituto Brasileiro de Geografia e Estatística (IBGE), Censo Demográfico (2000). https://www. ibge.gov.br/censo/. Accessed 4 Feb 2021

Instituto Brasileiro de Geografia e Estatística (IBGE), Censo Demográfico (2010). https://censo2 010.ibge.gov.br/. Accessed 4 Feb 2021

Lomnitz, L.A.: Informal exchange networks in formal systems: a theoretical model. Am. Anthropol. **90**(1), 42–55 (1988). https://doi.org/10.1525/aa.1988.90.1.02a00030

Lomnitz, L.A., Sheinbaum, D.: Trust, social networks and the informal economy: a comparative analysis. Rev. Sociol. **10**, 5–26 (2004). https://doi.org/10.1556/revsoc.10.2004.1.1

Pereira, N.I.: Efeituação Situada: Redes e Empreendedorismo na Rocinha. Tese de doutorado no Programa de Engenharia de Produção - COPPE/UFRJ (2014). https://producao.ufrj.br/index. php/br/informacoess-academicas/teses-e-dissertacoes/doutorado/2014-1/61-54/file

Sarasvathy, S.D.: Causation and effectuation: toward a theoretical shift from economic inevitability to entrepreneurial contingency. Acad. Manag. Rev. **26**(2), 243–63 (2001). https://doi.org/10. 5465/AMR.2001.4378020

Sarasvathy, S.D.: Making it happen: beyond theories of the firm to theories of firm design. Entrep. Theory Pract. **28**(6), 519–531 (2004). https://doi.org/10.1111/j.1540-6520.2004.00062.x

Sarasvathy, S.D.: Effectuation: Elements of Entrepreneurial Expertise. Edward Elgar, New Horizons in Entrepreneurship Series (2008)

Sarasvathy, S.D., Dew, N., Venkataraman, S.: Shaping Entrepreneurship Research Made, as well as Found, 1st Editio. Routledge (2020)

Serviço de Apoio às Micro e Pequenas Empresas (SEBRAE). https://www.sebrae.com.br

Simon, H.A.: The Sciences of the Artificial. MIT Press, Cambridge (1969)

Foundations for a Prospective Approach to Work. Supporting Concrete Utopias

Pueyo Valérie[(⌧)]

University Lumière Lyon 2, Environnement Ville Société UMR 5600, Labex IMU, Lyon, France
valerie.pueyo@univ-lyon2.fr

Abstract. This article sets out the foundations of a prospective approach to work that aims right now to build a desirable world of tomorrow. The postulate is indeed that it is from work and activity that this is achievable. It presents how this proposition accompanies concrete utopias and constitutes a paradigm shift for ergonomics.

Keywords: Prospective approach to work · Concrete utopias · Work · Activity

1 Introduction

Thinking Ergonomics 4.0 forces us to think about the future of work. To do so, two perspectives can be adopted. The first is to identify and predict what the future evolution of work and productive environments will be. This leads to questioning emerging technologies, organizational, regulatory, economic and social transformations in all their diversity. The challenge is then to develop useful knowledge and methods to take care of work in the face of these new trends.

The second is to contribute now to making tomorrow's world desirable by considering that today's world is going through crises that are not unrelated to a crisis of Work. Work being understood as a socio-historical political regime [1] configuring the "to work" (which is called activity in ergonomics in the French-speaking tradition). But, far from considering these crises as inevitable, we can think, *a contrario*, that they are decisive moments during which one must exercise choices and act. They are therefore opportunities and open up alternatives. So, they are a turning point that opens up a new uncertainty. This is our position, and this is why we adopt Gaston Berger's formula: *"Tomorrow will not be like yesterday, it will be new and it will depend on us. Tomorrow is less to be discovered than to be invented"* [2].

It is with this conviction aimed at fighting against destiny that Gaston Berger founded prospective in the aftermath of the Second World War in France. He then noted a society with drastic time accelerations, a loss of sense, marked by human over-power. He withdrew the idea that Humanity must think about the consequences of its actions, consider different possible worlds and work for the one that suits us. Gaston Berger's observation could be taken up word for word today and his position is more relevant than ever. Therefore, it is in this same perspective that we propose to found a Prospective approach

N. L. Black et al. (Eds.): IEA 2021, LNNS 219, pp. 248–255, 2021.
https://doi.org/10.1007/978-3-030-74602-5_37

to Work. Its ambition: to contribute through and from work and activity to "inventing tomorrow's world", here and now, by integrating the challenges of the environment, access to health, education, etc.

This requires three explanations. The first concerns the backgrounds of Prospective approach to Work. The second relates to the nature of the movements that the Prospective approach to Work proposes to accompany or bring to light. The third looks at the challenges to be taken up and the approach to be conceived. In conclusion, this leads us to question ourselves. Does Prospective approach to Work constitute a change of "paradigm" for Ergonomics?

2 The Backgrounds of Prospective Approach to Work

The first background of Prospective approach to Work is a position relative to the place of work and activity. In order to make tomorrow's world desirable and more humane, work and activity are central. But in what way and for what reasons?

First of all, our postulate is that work is central because it *"lies at the crossroads of several convergences such as those of social life, economic life and politics (as living, acting and deciding together)"* [3]. It is also so because what we are talking about when we speak of work is neither a profession, nor a job, nor a social function, but the very production of the conditions of human existence. By production of the conditions of human existence we do not refer to work as a means of subsistence or a factor of production among others. What we mean, in accordance with the position defended by the ILO, is that work is a field of human creativity, of self-realization, participating in action on the world through technology and know-how [4]. Thus, work is an area of manifestation of freedom allowing expression, human elevation and emancipation.

From this perspective, work is a field through which and thanks to which humanity expresses and produces itself [5] - what makes the human - through the "shaping" of an open, non-reified world, which constitutes a living environment, an "ecumene". Thus work "frames" *"the capacity.../...to put one's environment in order.../...to take root (i.e.).../.../...to give meaning to one's environment, to unite material necessity and spiritual value, (to) participate in one's vital environment"*. In this perspective, one obeys the objective conditions of existence without submitting [6]. This is a far cry from the dominant representation of work: a domain of necessity and constraint.

However, looking at work in its current dominant regime, this is massively what it is all about. It must be noted that this regime is problematic: it is globally deleterious for Humans and the world and constitutes little and for little the domain of creativity and realization presented above. On the contrary, it is based on massive reification. So much so that one can consider with Simone Weil that in this regime, it is things that direct human activity and not the other way round [5].

But that's not all. For if work is a domain dated at the crossroads of the social, political and economic, which structures the indispensable factory of the Human being and his environment, it is through activity, that it is played out in essence. In fact, it is through activity that the Human being can pass *in concreto* day after day from the potential to the real. It is by activity, that the Human puts himself in action. An action in the world but also on and "with" the world. A "real" action by which "active" human have the world as their "material". For if one follows Weil's position, " *The world is then an environment endowed with meaning through activity as a manifestation of man's spirituality over matter.../... to work is the central activity through which man mediatizes his power.../... is a mediation in a double sense. First of all, it weaves a link between me and myself, which exists in time. And it links my spirituality .../... and the informed world over which I exercise my power"* [6]. The work that underlies it is then the condition by which the world itself becomes a medium for man. Thus, activity is a human experience - singular and unique for each and every one of us - which nevertheless has "an anthropological dimension characteristic of the modes of human interaction with his or her environment" [7], an activity that is finalized, yet open to possibilities and limitless possibilities that are currently assignable.

The second background to Prospective approach to Work is made up of principles proposed by Berger in 1964. Then, as now, it was a question of thinking of prospective as an anthropological ethic, a Humanism concerned with emancipation and the ends of human activity. One must therefore constantly ask oneself, with Paul Valéry, the question *"what do we want and what should we want?* "This essential question does not have a simple answer. And it obliges us to define, choose, exclude or at least subordinate between different values. But it is always the preoccupation of the Human being and of human facts in, on and with the world that ultimately constitutes a compass.

This being said, the principles on which this ethic is based are as follows. 1) If the concern of the Human being is essential, Human being is not the measure of all things. He thinks of himself in the world. But it is at his level that actions are carried out.; 2) Humanity must think of its acts responsibly, globally and in time; 3) It is necessary to focus on human problems in order to elaborate a "real praxis" that is a real alternative beyond the existing one. Berger thus links the ideal and concrete dimensions by holding Hegel's position that *"the ideal is more real than the real"* [8]. However, for it to be real, it must be given substance and done, 4) So, *"It is a question - to tackle - not (of) problem(s) to be solved if one can, but (of) project(s) to be realized if one wants"* [8]. 5) This implies seeing "far". It means forming a desirable future to fight against fate, not chance [9]. For seeing far ahead does not mean planning ahead as a precautionary measure, but rather asking oneself the question of the future that may be suitable for acting accordingly here and now, without fatality. It also implies seeing "broadly" in an integrative and systemic way. Finally, it implies seeing "in depth", beyond appearances and easy interpretations, which obliges us to take risks and act in freedom.6) It also means committing to the common good and not to particular interests. 7) And for this, we must bring together people from different backgrounds and professions - researchers, engineers, creative workers - committed to political action, crossing their gaze to transform the world. These men change things from where they are, each in his own place. Then, these *"men [...] will not only be able to bear a theoretical, external, abstract testimony, but (also) will be able [...] to give the fruit of deep experiential wisdom"* [10], 8) Finally, it is necessary to propose "a 'fable' of the World" [10]. A fable towards which one would like to go in hope and will. It is not an affabulation but a narrative of a "towards what" and a "for what".

As we have seen, the formation of the "towards what" and the "for what" cannot do without a statement of values and normative dimensions useful for action. Since the

Prospective approach to Work has as its project to contribute through and from work and activity to "inventing tomorrow's world", it is important to present the normative dimensions that allow us to think about what truly human work can be, *i.e.* a field of manifestation of freedom, expression and emancipation.

In the perspective of the French-speaking tradition of Ergonomics, a truly human work is above all a framework centered on the capacity to act in, on and for the world that is the activity. This is why the third background of Prospective approach to work is made up of normative assets to think of an "accomplished" activity, a source of health and added value, in a word desirable. The following are therefore some features of what is desirable for activity as a way of acting and being in the world: 1) It must be an authentic act that participates in transforming the world. This means that this act makes it possible to do things that are considered to be done, to carry out acts or works (building something permanent and visible for society) and to make them happen, *i.e.*, to have something to do with it, and finally to be a recognized and legitimate protagonist in this shaping of the world [11]; 2) It must be situated in the register of Action [12] which refers to several dimensions. Action (i) is "a being-with", a product of a plurality of singular points of view, in the public space, demanding meaning, values in dialogue around the same "object"; (ii) corresponds to the desire to *"make something new on our own initiative"*, (iii) is linked to human affairs and (iv) is therefore political; 3) It must make sense from the point of view of values and be of value to others, especially in terms of utility, accuracy and authenticity; 4) It must constitute an experience of the environment that contributes to establishing a relationship of order, *i.e.*, of intelligibility between things, coherence, adequacy, and which is a source of satisfaction because of the harmony that results from it [13]; 5) An experience that, moreover, allows us to significantly organize and divide up the world in order to get out of it [14]; 6) This experience must also be rooted *i.e.* i) be part of a heritage and a history, a historico-cultural environment *"keeping alive treasures of the past"*, which one can make his own and in his own hand, ii) but also be part of a present among others and iii) be tended towards *"presentiments of the future"* [15].

With the backgrounds of the Prospective approach to Work being laid out, for which interventions and for which projects have we thought of it?

3   Nature of Movements Concerned, Associated Challenges and Elements of the Approach

As stated in the introduction, the Prospective approach to work aims to contribute to desirable futures through work and activity. This is why it proposes to accompany, from this point of view, projects that are part of concrete utopias [16]. What are these projects in concrete utopias [13]? They are all brought together by a focal point: the aim is to bring about a world in which humans are in harmony with their environment and can live an authentic, non-alienated life, attentive to others and to the Planet. But more precisely, they are based on three specific ideas. The first is that they give rise to vital impulses for change questioning the established order that is considered unsatisfactory. The second is that they consider that this established order of things is neither definitive nor closed. This is not inevitable. Other ways have to be found and made to happen. Because the world, although overflowing with problems, is full of movements but also of possibilities and possibles. These projects are therefore both instructive and resolutely full of hope. The third is that they propose to discover and mobilize these possibilities and possibles in order to bring out a *perhaps* that *can be* and that, given the problems of the world, is *a duty to be*. Also, if they have a utopian dimension that calls into question what already exists and imagines other paths, they are very concrete. They start from real problems and the will to act in and on the world by going through experiments. The watchword is what must be done. They are therefore neither fictions nor unfeasible dreams. They are projects that aim to bring out a different, a perspective.

These projects represent challenges in more than one way. Indeed, if the starting point for these concrete utopias is a dream associated with a diagnosis of what is problematic and the conviction that there is a need to act, it is clear that they cannot be realized without the mobilization of multiple actors. These are epics based on the commitment of a plurality. So, how can a shared project emerge? How can we do it from singular contributions to be coordinated, in cooperation, based on diagnoses, wishes, explorations that make it possible to establish together, what is troubling and what perhaps needs to happen in the future? How, moreover, can we cut out something that can be done by several people? Something that is inscribed in an environment (often on the scale of a territory) while there is an abundance of possible paths, criteria (e.g. sustainability of resources, well-being, social integration, etc.), values, points of view? How can we move forward in these projects when we cannot, by the very fact of these ambitions, stick to techniques that mobilize what is feasible, known, foreseeable and certain, under penalty of reproducing the existing that is the problem? How can we accompany this adventurous risk-taking over time and over the long term? How to identify, explore and experiment with forms of possibilities and then crystallize what has been acquired and reorientated? Finally, how can we give time and space to these long-term explorations without them being confronted with institutional difficulties or the existing norms in breach of which they are placed? With, however, one necessity: that of ultimately enabling standardization processes that overhaul existing standards? And, above all, how can we ensure that work and activity at the heart of these projects as a way of manufacturing the conditions of existence and being in the world? In all these challenges that concern the emergence of a towards what, a for what and a how, there is a necessity: more than taking care of work and activity, it is a question of putting them back at the heart. As much in their emergence as in their conduct. This is the ambition of Prospective approach to Work.

Why is it so? Because, in addition to the centrality of work and activity for us, we can observe that some of these projects fail or lead to the exhaustion of those who commit themselves to them. What explains this? First of all, some of these projects, inscribed in the transition to sustainable development forget to think about work and activity [17]. Yet, they are struck by them and need to be reinvented and reconfigured. But this is neither simple nor quick, and it cannot be carried by individuals left alone to face this challenge. It requires profound developments [14]: professional transitions. If we are not careful, the result is disorder and disturbances that cannot be absorbed by the actors [18]. Secondly, these initiatives sometimes develop out of dreams disconnected from reality and practical dimensions, on the margins of institutions potentially providing frameworks for action. While others are driven by institutions that aim by rule and new "technical" criteria to govern living together. In both cases, then, the dialectic between the for what, the toward what and the how is non-existent. This leads either to ideal projects without materiality, or to technical devices without a soul. Intenable in one case, empty of meaning in the other.

As we have seen, the examination of utopian projects or projects with reformist ambitions indicates the difficulties to be overcome. But others prove beneficial from the point of view of health and work. From them, we draw elements structuring a normative path for prospective action through, on and from work and activity. This concerns as much the emergence of the for what, the towards what as the how. Three of these major elements can be cited. 1) The first element is the permanent concern to establish a table of correspondences between a perspective, "ideal and assignable" means, criteria, focal points, an approach, trends identified in society and desirability (*i.e.* the desires of individuals increased by others). The second element is the investigation of other projects constituted as references. References that will be examined in particular how doing it is a creative act that allows new directions and new means to be discovered. The third is the existence of industrious experiential devices [13]: supporting concrete utopias. They are at their service and allow us to organize the how in a very concrete and long-term way. From the Foucaldian concept of device, they inherit the functional properties of constituting a systemic form, in the background, orienting, structuring and selecting. They also inherit from it the abundance of what composes it. They are industrious because they consider the activity of daily life up to these political stakes. Finally, they are experiential because they offer opportunities to experiment and develop an experience that guides, organizes and gives meaning. We have referred to these devices as *basic contracts*. These contracts are made up of principles, precepts, criteria, approaches, steles, scraps and monuments elaborated by the protagonists. They constitute a framework for the activity of each party. They organize and compose the capacity to act, *i.e.* the activity. In a way, they are the foundation of a new work regime constantly preoccupied with activities tending towards one for what and one towards what, busy forming living conditions and a desirable future. They thus prove to be operators of order, coherence, satisfaction and integration that allow each person to be in their place, in their environment, among others.

This last element particularly marks the approach we are proposing with the Prospective approach to Work. Indeed, in this approach we accompany (i) the emergence of a concrete utopia, and (ii) the conception of a basic contract, *i.e.* a support for utopia which frames the capacity to act in polyphony, over the long term and along an uncertain path open to the unhoped-for. This path between the foundation of utopia and the conception of the associated basic contract is composed of three steps. The first one is to formulate an informed critique. This step requires an understanding of what is missing, which should be by considering the existing order space, the difficulties, the troubled experiences. This leads to the formulation of a practicable utopian wish for its concrete expression. This wish is examined in the light of the interests, needs, desires and desirables of the actors, society, beneficiaries, institutions and the environment. It also examines the obstacles, not to give up but to test the will of the protagonists who will have to find ways and positions to confront them in reason and conscience. The second one aims to examine the resources, that is, the possibilities and the possibles to be conceived. Possibilities refer to means and goods that are already there but not yet activated and that acquire meaning, legitimacy and value according to the stated wish. Possibles are both the knowledge available to achieve the wish, the determinants of the time to be able to do otherwise (technically, societally, etc.), the will of the people involved and finally the ability to implement a process over time. At the end of this step, the challenge is to form a coherent configuration - a table of correspondences (via a dialectic of ideal ends and means) that marks a for what and a towards what and already elements of the how. The third step is then devoted to the design of a basic contract designed to start from, by and for the activities implemented in their polyphony at the service of the perspective.

4 Conclusion

Does working in prospective on concrete utopias bring about a paradigm shift for Ergonomics? At the very least it constitutes a change of focus. Indeed, such projects go beyond the frameworks usually implemented in ergonomic interventions. At the level of the multiplicity of actors (citizens, structures, municipalities, institutions,…), the cooperation that binds them, the perimeters that go beyond the traditional legal boundaries of firms, the criteria and challenges encountered (environmental, territorial development, etc.), the cooperation that they require, or the temporalities caught in long histories and trajectories.

But it seems to us that beyond these changes of focus, Prospective approach to Work on Utopias leads to a change of paradigm. Until now, ergonomics has been part of existing frameworks in order to improve the conditions of exercise for employees, to promote the consideration of activity in productive environments, or to work for the participation of actors in the management of design projects. In any case, the aim of the intervention is to improve the existing system by taking into account the characteristics of human functioning, by producing knowledge about the activity, or by recognizing the expertise of employees in dialogues with designers. However, in all these projects, it can be said that the ergonomist and the employees concerned are taken within the existing frameworks. They are "external", *i.e.* extrinsic to the specific wills of the actors, their values, their wishes. So, the challenge is to make these projects as favorable as possible to humans. However, it is by no means expected that we will embark on a path of reform. It is not a question of profoundly modifying the framework of action and its perspectives. It can therefore be said that ergonomics has so far developed along an adaptative path. Continuing to work along this path is necessary and legitimate because there is still much to be done to give workers a place within a massively deleterious work regime. But is it enough?

Indeed, in view of the crises, it is no longer just a question of adapting work to human, but of participating in more reforming adventures. To put it another way, it is no longer a question of regulating and adjusting what is being done, but of contributing normatively to what could be done. In doing so, the object of interventions is no longer simply to produce knowledge about human functioning or activity, but to accompany projects that raise the question of what a human world is. In addition to the fact that this question is abyssal, it refers to forms of conduct of action that are completely new for the discipline: it is no longer a question of being part of a project with an existing framework, but of contributing through and from the activity to the emergence of a project and a framework at the crossroads of multiple possible points of view and orientations. We leave behind a universe in which the project of some would dominate or oppose the project wishes of others, as is traditionally the case. And that is quite another thing! Thus, Prospective approach to work implies assuming the political scope of work, from the point of view of living together, its governance and the normative dimensions that the discipline can identify from the point of view of work and activity. All of this requires exchanges and debates, all of which in any case responds to the expectations of audiences engaged in these paths exploring utopian forms.

References

1. Lavialle, C.: Le travail en question, XVIIIème-XXème siècle. PUF, Paris (2017)
2. Berger, G.: Phénoménologie du temps et prospective. PUF, Paris (1964)
3. Guérin, F., Pueyo, V., Béguin, P., Garrigou, A., Hubault, F., Maline, J., Morlet, T.: Concevoir le travail, le défi de l'ergonomie. Octarès, Toulouse (2021, in press)
4. Peccoud, D.: Le travail décent : Points de vue philosophiques et spirituels. OIT, Genève (2004)
5. Weil, S.: Réflexions sur les causes de la liberté et de l'oppression sociale. Gallimard, Paris (1955)
6. Taïbi, N.: L'expérience ouvrière de Simone Weil. Paris (2007)
7. Béguin, P., Robert, J., Ruiz, C.: Travail et Travailler. In: Brangier, E., Valey, G. (eds.) Dictionnaire encyclopédique de l'Ergonomie. 150 notions clés. Paris, Dunod (2021, in press)
8. Berger, G.: Methode et résultat. In: Berger, G., Bourbon-Busset, J., Masse, P. (eds.) De la prospective. Textes fondamentaux de la prospective française 1955–1966. Paris, L'harmattan (1958)
9. Lecourt, D.: Philosophie et prospective. Les Docs d'Aleph, 23 (2004)
10. Berger, G.: L'idée de l'avenir. Les Annales, Nouvelles séries, 118 (1960)
11. Sznelwar, L.I.: Quand travailler c'est être protagoniste et le «protagonisme» du travail. Thèse présentée à l'école polytechnique de l'université de Sao Paulo pour le titre de professor-livre-docente (2013)
12. Arendt, H.: La condition de l'homme moderne. Paris, Calman-Levy (1983/1961)
13. Pueyo, V.: Pour une prospective du travail. Les mutations et transitions du travail à hauteur d'Hommes (2020). https://hal.archives-ouvertes.fr/tel-02480599
14. Béguin, P.: Conduite de projet et fabrication collective du travail: une approche développementale. Document de synthèse en vue de l'habilitation à diriger des recherches. Université Victor Segalen, Bordeaux 2. 149 p. Soutenance le 19 Novembre 2010 (l'ED 303 ne délivre pas de mention) (2010)
15. Weil, S.: L'enracinement. Prélude à une déclaration des devoirs envers l'être humain. Paris, Gallimard (1990/1949)
16. Bloch, E.: Le principe espérance, tome I. Gallimard, Paris (1976)
17. Pueyo, V., Béguin, P.: Supporting professional transitions in innovative projects. In: Bagnara, S., Tartaglia, R., Albolino, S., Alexander, T., Fujita, Y. (eds.) Proceedings of the 20th Congress of the International Ergonomics Association (IEA 2018). Advances in Intelligent Systems and Computing, vol. 824. Springer, Cham (2019). https://doi.org/10.1007/978-3-319-96071-5_204
18. Pueyo, V.: Travailler dans une unité expérimentale à l'INRA. Quel modèle à l'interface science société? Rapport de recherche INRA-Alenya, 49 p (2018)

Helping a Robot to be "Autonomous": The Expertise of a (Human) Roboticist in a Manufacturing Plant

Natalia Radicchi[(⊠)], Luciana Detoie, Rodrigo Ribeiro, and Francisco Lima

UFMG – Universidade Federal de Minas Gerais, Belo Horizonte, MG, Brazil
{nradicchi,ldetoie,rodrigoribeiro,fpalima}@ufmg.br

Abstract. The creation of robotic systems demands the formalization of how-to-do rules. However, professional workers interact with the world in a way that goes beyond formal rules, such as when facing unforeseen and context-dependent events. The solution to replace human tasks by robotic systems consists in the creation of "micro-worlds", which presuppose controlled environments, with fixed rules, in which robots are able to operate successfully. Accordingly, such micro-worlds must be designed, built, supervised, maintained and optimization by (human) roboticists who make sense of what robots must and must not do. To address this interaction between them, this article discusses cases that show how experienced workers use their perceptual skills to anticipate and solve problems on the robots under their supervision. Through the analysis of the "course of action" (Theureau, 2004) of real events, its goal is to show how human activity is directed by getting a sense of the situation during the interaction with the machines and how the context influences such sense. As a result, it contributes with Industry 4.0 in its aim to increase automation to maximum power, enabling robots to perform increasingly complex functions. On the other hand, it argues against its assumption that human performance in automated environments is a residual problem to be solved – i.e., eliminated. The actual challenge is how to design micro-worlds that enable and enhance the human-robot integration in the shopfloor for guaranteeing quality, safety and efficiency.

Keywords: Robots · Industry 4.0 · Autonomous systems · Micro-world · Perception

1 Introduction

Industrial robots, by definition, are machines capable of operating and performing movements autonomously, without the need for direct or remote human guidance. Eventually, these autonomous movements accurately replace gestures previously performed by human operators, as in the case of welding robots, focus of this paper. However, even with these machines it has not yet been possible to completely reproduce the abilities of human beings [1]. Once acknowledged that these limitations exist, even with the advance of automation, the main point of this paper consists in discussing just how much autonomous can a robot be vis-à-vis the roboticist that supervises it. We argue that robots are functional within limits defined by their "micro-worlds", whose boundaries and conditions of possibility are actively guaranteed by the human operators around them in the shopfloor. Their "care" with the robots appeared in three types of activity during the research fieldwork in a manufacturing plant: supervision, maintenance and "optimation" of the robots, the latter understood as modifications made by the operators, who improve robots' performance beyond its nominal or current operation [2].

With the increase in IT capacity in Industry 4.0, and the promises of increasing performance of artificial intelligence (AI) incorporated to automatic systems in order to give them more autonomy, there is a reinforcement of the idea that human activity tends to disappear or take a merely residual place. This belief leads to configurations of design and of "labour division" that make it difficult to integrate the movements of automata with the activity of the roboticist[1]. As a result, the work needed to create, expand and maintain the micro-worlds in which robots operate is hindered or impeded, affecting both the performance of automata and human operators. We argue that the operators' support for robots calls for human embodied skills and cognition, such as perceptual skills and judgements, that are impossible to be objectified and, thus, delegated to automata. When observing the work of "supervision", the fieldwork challenge remains on how to access the consciousness in action and the human perception when they are taking care of the automata. For an in-depth and effective analysis of human action, it is necessary to divert the focus from the level of consciousness to identify the incorporated and situated knowledge that shows up in the course of action.

Based on a case study carried out on a line of welding robots in the automotive industry of heavy vehicles, this article is organized in five sections. First, the concept of micro-world is presented, showing how human work is a prerequisite for it to function properly. This is followed by discussions that reflect the attempts to integrate individuals and automata and how skills and knowledge built by experience is a mandatory passage for such integration (Sect. 2). In order to analyse embodied skills and cognition underlying action and its contribution to human-robot integration, it is argued how the Theory of the Course of Action allows for the empirical substantiation of this hypothesis (Sect. 3). Addressing the empirical evidence, we elucidate how the workers' interventions occur and how their abilities influence the work with automata (Sect. 4). In conclusion, a reflection is made emphasizing the need to design automata without neglecting the dimensions of the activity and how the human being still maintains a main role – and not a residual one – in human-machine interaction.

2   Human-Machine Integration

Artificial Intelligence (AI) still faces the challenge of guaranteeing, through algorithms or configurations emerging from neural networks, the correct functioning of machines. The creation of an artificial system demands the formalization of how-to-do rules, as an attempt to objectify the practical knowledge of human beings. Dreyfus [3] observes that "AI researchers have been trying to solve the problem of making computers, which

---

[1] Here, we call roboticists, specialist professionals who main contribute to taking care of the robots and to maintain the micro-world conditions.

are synthetic tools, sensitive only to the shape or outline of their inputs, behave like human beings, who are sensitive to semantics or meaning." The difficulty in inserting all the skills and knowledge of an "activity" in the machine lies in the impossibility of explaining all the background that transcends the sphere of information itself. It is a fact that individuals act differently from machines. To "follow a rule", in the Wittgensteinian sense, presents tacit, circumstantial and judgemental aspects that are essentially human [4]. Designers of automated, robotic systems are then faced with the "regress of rules" [5] and the impossibility of defining all the relevant aspects for the execution of any activity.[2]

The proposed solution for robots to perform human tasks is the creation of "micro-worlds", defined by Dreyfus [6] as a restricted model, which contains well-defined rules and variables that work well within a "closed system". In fact, it is already known that, for some well circumscribed situations, computers can easily outperform humans. That said, even the creation of a micro-world depends on anticipating the data and situations that the machine will work with. Real-world problems are subject to unpredictable events and those humans who are able to solve them do not follow pre-defined rules. Thus, going against the assumptions underlying the hard A.I., the validity of the micro-world concept for real situations is not achieved through the expansion of its limits or the aggregation of more than one micro-world. "A micro-world is limited by and closed within itself, and it is not possible, either by combination or by extrapolation, to make it to reflect real everyday situations" [6]. Therefore, if automated, robotic systems work only within the limits of their micro-worlds, human expertise is no longer a residual problem. It plays the role of giving meaning to what happens at the interfaces between their micro-worlds and the world that surrounds them.

In practice, it is difficult to be flexible in integrating humans and robots when the latter are designed as black boxes and when the practical knowledge of human beings is overlooked during the design phase. When designing micro-worlds, a legitimization and emphasis of theoretical knowledge is privileged, mainly the programming part, and little attention is given to the skills and knowledge of those who will "take care" of the robots. In this sense, the human experience in supervising and maintaining robots is seen as a "residual" knowledge, which would be replaced by scientifically based knowledge, that is, as something that would tend to disappear as technology advances. In contrast, we argue that the human experience should be seen as the element that guarantees the system reliability and improves its performance through "optimation" [2][3]. Thereby, it

---

[2] The "regress of rules" occurs due to the fact that rules do not contain the rules for their own application. As a result, when formalizing a rule for a robot, another rule should be written to explain how to apply the first rule. However, since the second rule is also subjected to the same problem, a third rule should be written to explain how to apply it, and so forth. As we can see, this logic continues for as many rules as an obstinate engineer wants to write, showing, therefore, that there is no philosophical or practical solution to the problem of the rules not containing rules for their own application, as any attempt to solve it would lead to the infinity regress of rules.

[3] Lima and Silva [2] explain that: "'optimation' is the positive counterpoint of the activity of "supervision", thus denying that, even in highly automated systems, humans are a mere receptor or passive link in the control cycle. 'Optimation' consists in assigning values and principles of evaluation or effectiveness to the functioning of the technical system: deciding whether the system is working properly and, above all, whether it could work better".

is essential to recognize the limitations and the limits of a micro-world in order to avoid an approach based on technocentric principles – i.e. that classifies human activity as something to be ruled out or reduced as most as possible.

Therefore, it is necessary to analyze how human beings interact with the world and how this experience is required to operate automated, robotic systems. A first approach to the question could be the confrontation between the experiments of the Chinese Room [7] and the Spy [8], which demonstrates the absence of meaning and the fallibility of any automaton, but still leaves the effective integration between perceiving and getting a sense of the world and automata micro-worlds. The classical experiment of the Chinese Room is ambiguous and inconclusive, since it claims that the performance of the illiterate operator in Chinese is equivalent to that of a Chinese speaker, which makes consciousness an epiphenomenon. Collins' spy "thought experiment" recognizes the equivalent performance, that could be intentionally reproduced through the training of a spy undercovered in another culture. However, he states that it would be impossible for the spy to deceive everyone in all kinds of situations. The spy is always going to be unmasked, just as an automatism is always going to fail at some point or situation[4] [9, 10].

3   The Course of Action as a Methodological Approach

Creative solutions to the problems that the real, practical world creates, which are unpredictable and not always limited to the boundary conditions previously inserted in artificial systems, has brought the need to deeply explore the human-machine relationship (H-M) with an anthropocentric perspective. By observing real situations and considering the Theory of the Course of Action [11], it was possible to uncover how roboticists' experience and sense of activity guided their action during the interaction with the machines. The results, far from covering all possible situations and aspects of H-M interaction, unravel particular details of it that arose from the fieldwork and to propose some recommendations for the design of robotic (micro-world) systems and for the later organization of work in the industrial plant.

The interaction between roboticists and robots described in this document were observed in routine situations within the working environment where they were both placed. After collecting information (speeches, images, videos) and conducting self-confrontation interviews in some cases, an analysis of roboticists' course of action when carrying out some activities took place to uncover the embodied skills and cognition behind their "*knowing how*". Theureau's Course of Action Theory (CAT) [11] invites an analysis of activity through the tetradic sign, inspired by Peirce, which integrates the analysis of one's action, perception, cognition, and experience within a given situation. This theory offers resources to access what Theureau calls "situational pre-reflective consciousness", which is where cognitive, non-representational phenomena, linked to perception and action, manifest themselves. The experience and knowledge acquired in

---

[4] Collins [2004, p. 136] changed his mind later on, saying that, if spies develop "interactional expertise" – the expertise of talking fluently about a domain without having practical experience – they will never be caught. Please see Ribeiro and Lima (2015) [10] for a critique of Collins argument that practice is not necessary for becoming fluent in a language.

previous situations and which are called upon by the situation are called the *Referential* and it links to the *Representamen* - whats is taken into account in the situation - to illustrates to the individual the many possibilities of action to be done in the scene (situation). Based on audiovisual records and traces of the activity, the self-confrontation interview enabled to replace the roboticists "in situation" (i.e. with regard to the action being analysed) and to make explicit the pre-reflexive consciousness present in their action at the moment they anticipated or actd to adjust any malfunction of the robots.

4   Human-Machine Interaction and the Micro-world

The research took place in a large machinery industry, which uses welding robots in part of its production line. The experience of the main roboticist we analysed included programming, maintenance (mechanical and electrical) and welding. From all of them, the one that the company highlighted as the most complex was programming. The idea widespread in the company was that the roboticist was someone who understood a lot about the machine and that his "know how" to refine the robot program distinguished him from the others roboticists. However, during fieldwork it was possible to witness different types of actions related to the supervision, maintenance (correction and anticipation) and optimization of the robots, which showed that these automata did not act alone. Operators with different types of skills and distinct levels of expertise substantiated a valuable material that uncovered the diverse ways of human-machine interaction. These cases were then compared with the original design of the robot and of its micro-world in order to highlight what could be improved.

4.1   Supervising the Robots

As interviewees said during fieldwork, the robots are designed to be "autonomous", to work with very little or no human help at all. Nonetheless, what has been seen, in practice, is that it is the attentive supervision of the operators that ensures the performance of the robotic system. The robotic welding line demands direct supervision from operators who are responsible for replacing the welded parts, turning on the robots and maintaining the expected working conditions (i.e. their micro-world). In addition, there is the maintenance team, responsible for exchanging and adjusting components, checking welding process consumables, calibrating, etc. Finally, there is the figure of the roboticist, who acts in the development of programs, analysis of welding specifications, failure diagnostics, operational improvement, among others.

In the analyzed cases, it was possible to find examples where the operators themselves made operational adjustments, reprogramming and even workarounds on the operation's routine, to guarantee the continuity of the plant production.

> *"sometimes, for not stopping the production, there is a trick that is not right... when you have a big collision the gear goes like this (...) so, its absolute zero is somewhere, but its reference has to change, because its gear was out." (Roboticist)*

Some components and artifacts, however, do not allow operators to adjust the robots during the operation nor even in during maintenance. In these cases, the solution was to call the manufacturer and request the adjustment of the design. This was observed in a situation in which the roboticist needed the manufacturer support to increase the range limit of the welding arm of one of the robots, thus improving the quality of its welding. According to the roboticist, for that type of adjustment, the structure of the machine was a *"black box"*, that is, it did not allow access to change the program parameters.

4.2 Maintaining Robots' Micro-world

Regarding the maintenance of the welding robots, operators and maintenance workers acted in three types of situations: (1) when they could anticipate a problem and a potential stop of the machine; (2) when, in the middle of an ongoing problem, they needed to make a diagnosis to restore the functioning of the system; and (3) in situations of scheduled maintenance. Regarding the former, sometimes the operators could "feel" that something was wrong with the machine even before the emergency sensors were triggered and the machine effectively stopped. This required learning to "listen" to what the weld "was saying", or "feeling" the machine "pop", when the sound of the weld was slightly different than usual[5]. The operator was, then, able to anticipate the problem and the alarm itself and, consequently, avoid stopping the machine (situation 1). As a result, they could avoid production loss and rework, and make preventive maintenance "on the spot". When the machine had already stopped due to an equipment problem, human experience also turned out to be of great value to accelerate the process of diagnosing the problem and re-establishing the working conditions (situation 2). In one of the analyzed cases, when the robot stood still and the roboticist was not in the facilities, the man responsible for robots maintenance was an electrician that knew the robots, but had no experience with welding. Of the several options he suggested (ground cable and terminals replacement, welding machine replacement, re-setting the parameters of the program, etc.), none of them solved the problem. Contacted by cellular phone messages, even from distance, the roboticist could then suggest some actions (coupling head and wire feeder checking) that were useful for solving the problem later on. Analyzing the situation and seeking to understand how the roboticist managed to suggest a more accurate solution than the electrician that was on site, he stated that it was his welding experience that allowed him to make such suppositions.

> *"Inside the robot it is really hard indeed. You have to change components for components until you find it* [i.e. the problem], *sometimes you open it and you don't... The check is not visual, you don't have an instrument to measure.(...)* [In this case] *I saw the weld... it is called 'cold weld'. The material didn't spread. (...) then you have to understand a little bit of welding, welding process* [for a correct diagnosis]. *Nothing to do with* [checking] *the robot* [insides]" (Roboticist)

Analyzing in detail the suggestions made by the electrician, it was possible to see how close they were to his experience in electrical maintenance. In contrast, it was quite interesting to verify the importance of experience in the welding process (i.e. the

---

[5] When a sound, which should be constant, was interchanged with clicks, metallic noises or in stronger intensity.

perceptual skill of seeing a "cold weld") in order to diagnose the causes of the failure and correct the problem. The machine operator, who works directly with it and has some experience in manual welding, even though not in charge of solving the maintenance problem that day, made suggestions very similar to those made by the roboticist. When interviewed, this worker mentioned, again, the relevance of (his) experience with welding as a means to justify (his) proposals to solve the welding robot problem.

> *"The welder, when he is welding, he feels, he goes 'smoothly', you see, the welding is totally melting. Now,* [when] *it starts to pop, to hit, there is something wrong (...) For the robot it is the same system, but it is automatic. It won't know that it's splashing. It won't stop. The welder, on the other hand, does the opposite, he notices it there, he stops."* (Operator)

Regarding the scheduled maintenance (situation 3), what was clear from the roboticist's speech it rarely took place as planned. Part of this was because the maintenance workers, knowing 'their' robots intimately and knowing which components were able to act for longer, did not replace the components on the stipulated dates.

4.3 "Optimation" Robots' Micro-world

In the optimation work, the relevance of practice could once again be highlighted. Refusing to passively accept the performance of a ready-made technical system, the main roboticist and some operators proposed new projects to improve the robots. In one day, the roboticist mentioned an operator's suggestion to "balance" production by changing the operation of "his" robot.

> *"...he gave me an idea: 'What do you think about 'taking this off' (...) 'oh, those 10 min are a gain for the company'. 10 minutes for each piece, we manufacture 1000 pieces a year, 10 minutes for each piece is a whole lot of money."* (Roboticist)

On another occasion, the roboticist reported the search for a new supplier to find a cable that would technically support the operation, but would also represent a good cost-benefit ratio for the company. According to him, there was a joint work with the supplier's technician to fix the component geometry, leaving the robot "ready for welding". In this case, the solution went beyond the pre-established conditions in the original design, respecting the particularities of the machine and the financial conditions of the company.

5   Analysis and Final Considerations

The success in the creation and development of robots and their micro-worlds depends on respecting the users' requirements and involving them, when possible, in the design process. Autonomy cannot be guaranteed in all situations, as robots cannot make sense even of the micro-world they are in not to mention of the world surrounding them. It is known that automation and robotic systems adds a logical layer to work operations and that many times human actions are facilitated or even made possible only through the use of such machines and systems. However, human experience cannot be neglected as a determining factor and facilitator for them to work properly the conception of these projects, nor can it be disregarded that the interaction with the machines continues to happen even with automated systems.

When it comes to the supervision and maintenance of robots, considering that it is not possible to foresee all the rules that allow their constant operation, it is expected that adjustments and adaptations are always necessary. The routine operation itself takes care of presenting new situations that, added to previous experiences, increase the skills and knowledge towards helping the robots to be "autonomous". It is this experiential baggage that must, therefore, support engineers and programmers during the design of the micro-world, allowing for a better H-M interaction in the shopfloor. Bohle [12] points out that the *subjective involvement* with the machine facilitates the integration between operators and their artifacts. Moreover, the author states that *"An individual's capability to acquire on-the-job skills and empirical knowledge, such as feeling for material or the correct understanding of certain machine sounds, is the result of a way of working in which sensorial perception and feeling play an important part in coping with the task in hand."*.

Designing and building robots and their micro-worlds is complex and require a great deal of knowledge and experience from engineers and programmers. By the same token, the knowledge and skills of many "roboticists", are necessary to anticipate and make sense of the signals issued by the automatisms in real situations (i.e. supervision), to fix problems (i.e. maintenance) and to make adjustments in the robot itself and its connection with the micro-world (i.e. optimation). The point is now how to better integrate such experiences in order to smooth and improve the system as a whole. As Bohle [12] points out and we have exemplified, it is the "subjective involvement" with the machine that facilitates the integration between operators and their artifacts. For making the best out of roboticists' experiences, however, the design of robots and their micro-worlds must foresee and support such integration, adopting an anthropocentric approach. This will not lead, however, to "autonomous systems": "automation, added to standards and operational procedures, tries to systematize aspects of human experience, but will always be dependent on it". Human expertise is the strongest link.

References

1. Goldberg, K.: Robots and the return to collaborative intelligence. Nat. Mach. Intell. **1**, 2–4 (2019)
2. Lima, F., Silva, C.: A objetivação do saber prático na concepção de sistemas especialistas: das regras formais às situações de ação. In: Duarte. Ergonomia e Projeto em indústrias de processos contínuos, pp. 84–121. Lucerna, Rio de Janeiro (2000)
3. Dreyfus, H.: A Internet: Uma Crítica filosófica à educação a distância e ao mundo virtual, Massachusetts, pp. 15–16 (2009)
4. Ribeiro, R.: Knowledge transfer. Unpublished doctoral dissertation, Cardiff University, School of Social Sciences, Cardiff, UK, pp. 24–25 (2007)
5. Wittgenstein, L.: Philosophical investigations. Blackwell, Oxford (1976 [1953])
6. Dreyfus, H., Stuart, D.: Why computers may never think like people. In: Computers in the Human Context: Information Technology, Productivity, and People, pp. 125–143 (1989)
7. Searle, J.: Can computers think? In: David, J.C. (ed.) Philosophy of Mind: Classical and Contemporary Readings. OUP USA (2002)

8. Collins, H.: Artificial Experts Social Knowledge and Intelligent Machines. MIT Press, Cambridge (1990)
9. Ribeiro, R., Lima, F.: Interactional expertise as a third kind of knowledge. Phenomenol. Cogn. Sci. **3**, 125–143 (2004)
10. Ribeiro, R., Lima, F.: The value of practice: a critique of interactional expertise. Soc. Stud. Sci. **46**, 1–30 (2015)
11. Theureau, J.: O Curso da ação. Método Elementar. Belo Horizonte: Fabrefactum Editora Ltda. (Brazilian translation of 'Le cours d'action: méthode elémentaire' (2nd edition, Octarés Éditions) (2014 [2004]))
12. Böhle, F., Milkau, B.: Computerised manufacturing and empirical knowledge. AI Soc. **2**, 235–243 (1988)

Reasoning Territorial Projects Through the Making of a Milieu

Jeanne-Martine Robert[1]([✉]) and Pascal Béguin[2]

[1] UMR 5600 EVS, Université Lumière Lyon 2, Lyon, France
jeanne.robert@univ-lyon2.fr
[2] Institut d'Etudes du Travail de Lyon, LL2, UMR 5600 EVS, Labex IMU, Lyon, France

Abstract. The purpose of this communication, based on a project which aims to the revival of an ancestral agricultural production in the South of France (the picking of linden flowers), is to discuss territorial project. Territory can be defined as governance concerns of a given space delimited by its borders. But it appears that this agricultural production can be understood as *"the making of a milieu"* through the work done with the lime. Our hypothesis is that we need to better articulate these two "spheres", the territory and the milieu, in order to manage projects at the scale of a geographical area.

Keywords: Territory · Milieu · Work · Project management

1 Problem Statement

The history of lime tree culture in the geographical area of the Baronnies in France dates from a century and a half. From the 19th century, this tree has been cultivated for its flowers picked by hand and dried, before to be sold to the traders. Lime tree production from the Baronnies has been 90% of the overall French production (with about 400 tons of dried lime tree flowers sold during the season of production). But during the 1980s, and despite projects for supporting the production, nobody has been able to prevent the *"death of the lime tree"*. However, it is currently experienced a revitalization of harvesting and marketing practices due to a project supported by a territorial entity: the «Natural Regional Park of Baronnies Provençales» (NRP). Thus, we can identify three phases of lime tree work by pickers and traders: the emergence of a unique environment, its crisis and its expected renewal through a territorial project.

The fluctuating value of the lime tree accordingly to these periods, appears as being linked to the *making of a milieu*: the possibility or the impossibility for the stakeholders to create an environment thanks to their work done with the lime trees. Based on the work of Georges Canguilhem [1], we apprehend the *"making of a milieu"* as a normativity which does not consist to dominate a space or to fight *"against an environment"*, but to develop a flexible relation of composition within the environment and to transform it, a manner to match [2], and to harmonize relationships with the multiple and heterogeneous [3] in order to establish a balance of life, including when the environment is changing (due, for example, to climate, economic, demographic or legislative reasons). From this point of view, making a milieu within an environment testifies the vital, but fragile creativity of humans to invent new ways of living and doing with what surrounds them.

The main challenge of a territorial project is then to question how one can allows and supports the inhabitants of a geographical area to make a milieu. As such, a territorial project questions the articulation between the administration of territorial resources on the one hand, and the manner of the inhabitants to develop ways of doing and living together in order to have a desirable and valuing life on the other hand.

After having quickly presented our method, this communication will illustrate what we name "*the making of a milieu*", and how the «*death of the lime tree*» can be understood as the collapse of that milieu. Then, we will question territorial project management.

2   Method

The analysis presented here is based on ethnography of the lime tree culture and on the implementation of a territorial project to enhance the value of the lime tree. These two actions were carried out for the NRP.

The ethnography was conducted over 8 months in 2017. 75 semi-directive interviews were carried out on the memory and current events in the harvesting and marketing of lime trees. They were conducted in such a way as to diversify the points of view of the inhabitants of the area and the actors in the sector: pickers, traders, pharmacists, but also elected officials and technicians from the area. These interviews were supplemented by participant observation of public events of valorization as well as of the harvest. A botanic study of linden cultivars was also conducted in collaboration with the botanist Luc Garraud of the CBNA of Gap-Charance. This study has allowed establishing hypotheses on the links between populations of wild and domestic lime trees.

Finally, we are conducting a project for the territorial valorization of the lime tree carried by the NRP. Public meetings, with the actors of the sector, have initiated this project in 2018. Since January 2020, within the framework of a European LEADER project, 8 experiments have been carried out in order to weave links between the actors of the sector and the territory in order to develop resources for the work of the lime tree in relation to a valuable and sustainable life in the Baronnies.

3   The Making of Lime Milieu

The work of the lime tree emerges at the end of the 19th century, at the meeting point of three spheres: that of the plantation of a plant resource, that of the trade of aromatic plants and that of peasant agriculture in the Baronnies. The lime trees were present before the development of trade in the form of wild forests in the mountains of the region. This is the species Tilia Platyphyllos. From the second half of the 19th century, plants from these forests were planted along the roads during road repair works. From the 1880s onwards, these trees were picked for the trade of dried lime blossoms as a part of the developing trade of aromatic plants in the South-East of France. At that time, the peasant agriculture of the region was undergoing a major transformation as sericulture, vines and madder disappeared. The lime tree became, along with lavender, one of the region's cash crops.

The weaving between these three spheres started with the development of road-side lime picking. The picking has been initially organized by herb traders, grocers or wholesalers who resold the lime tree on the national market, to herbalists, hospitals and pharmacies. The lime tree was sold in bulk, packaged in boxes of 5 to 10 kilos. It was then identified and qualified by its visual aspect: a lime tree whose flowers were in full maturity with large yellow bracts. This lime tree was first named "Tilleul de Carpentras", due to the main station where wholesalers shipped their products.

Starting in the 1910s, farmers planted lime trees from the wild forests on their land, along the edges of other productions: field edges, roadsides, farm yards. Scattered orchards of up to fifty trees strongly marked the landscape of the Baronnies. These plants were then grafted in order to match the characteristics of the lime tree, the criteria of the trade and the characteristics of the work of picking. The linden was picked by hand, directly from the tree by climbing up ladders 5 to 8 m high. Flowering lasts a few days. It is vulnerable to weather changes. The flowers can become grey or stained depending on their exposure to sunlight and humidity and break easily once dried. The grafting work allowed then to spread out the time of picking, to facilitate the picking gesture, to privilege flowers which lose less water when drying, which keep a yellow color... The most widespread cultivar was the named "Bénivay", commercial standard, adapted to packaging in cardboard boxes: flexible, yellow and with large bracts. The development of pruning from the 1960's allowed picking the flowers on branches on the ground. Thus, all members of the families of the pickers participated to the picking. Picking extended outside the agricultural sector and employees took their annual leave to do the picking. Thus, almost all the inhabitants of the Baronnies were pickers at the time of flowering. The lime tree became a complement in a system of generalized poly-activity.

Lime tree fairs multiplied until the 1980s. At these fairs, pickers sold dried lime blossoms to wholesale companies in the region. These were moments of great sociability. They were also moments of tension between pickers and traders over the purchase price, which was constantly rising and falling, particularly in relation to lime blossom imports from Eastern Europe and China. The development of cultivation and trade generated a process of valuation of the lime tree. The region became the only production area in France with 400 tons of lime trees produced in the 1950s, representing up to 90% of French consumption. Its commercial reputation grew internationally and the Buis-les-Baronnies fair became "the capital of the lime tree". Lime tree money took on a singular value: it was the first "fresh money" after the winter restrictions. It allowed to live and, with the development of loans, to make investments. Because of the little work (in the agricultural sense) that the picking required, apart from the pruning, the lime tree was lived like a "manna fallen from the sky", or "the gold of the Baronnies". But the valuation of the lime tree was not only economic. It was also linked to the social experience of fairs and the gathering that brings together all the inhabitants, all generations.

Throughout the 20th century, around the linden tree, a whole diversity of work practices corresponded and wove a milieu. The work done with the linden tree, by the merchants and by the pickers, allowed a multiplicity of heterogeneous phenomena and dimensions to be held together. These work practices gave rise to a weaving, a field of adjusted forces that made it possible to create a milieu that allowed life to take place.

4   The Unknot of the Milieu

From the 1980s onwards, what was matched will gradually come unknot. This was expressed by regular and increasingly important crises around the purchase prices of linden at fairs. But these crises were the expression of a deeper phenomenon. A series of changes in work practices and in the social environment led to unknotted the milieu and to what has been experienced as "the death of the lime tree".

The first dimension was changes in the commercial practices of mass distribution. First, it appeared a change in the conditioning of the lime tree flowers. At the beginning of the 1960s, the lime tree will be conditioned in little bags called "infusettes". It was then crushed and could no longer be qualified visually. Then, the Baronnies lime tree was mixed with imported lime tree and devalued. The second one was the diffusion of herbal teas with more pronounced artificial flavors that changed consumer's habits. On the farmers' side, the development of fruit crops (apricots and cherries) balanced the harvesting of the lime tree with the harvesting of fruits that ripened at the same time and brought in more money. Fluctuations in the supply of linden at fairs as a result of climatic events (such as frost) and the cost price of the fruit, accentuated the fluctuations in the purchase price of linden from one year to the next.

In terms of harvesting practices, rural desertification and difficulties in the transmission of farms made it increasingly difficult to carry out manual harvesting, which required a large amount of labor that was previously carried out by family or neighborhood members. The widening gap between purchase prices and the cost of wages made it all the more complicated to use paid labor. In addition, the change in legislation on work at heights on farms made it impossible to hire employees for harvesting.

With each crisis, the producers organized themselves around a Producers' Union, which experienced several revivals and carried out valorization actions. The lime tree was named "Tilleul des Baronnies" in order to recognize the work of production. Experiments were carried out to enhance the value of the lime tree other than in the form of herbal tea. Studies were conducted on the active ingredients to differentiate the Baronnies lime tree from other imported lime trees. A quality bonus system was granted for a few years. The Tourist Offices were trying to support this effort by carrying out promotional activities for the tourists. Several quality label projects have been initiated to protect the Baronnies lime tree from importations. None of these projects succeeded in bringing together pickers and traders. All of these actions did not enable them to weave links between them and to match their working practices with a changing environment.

The fairs closed one after the other between 1990 and 2003, when the most important fair closed. Newspapers printed about the death of the lime tree. Disillusionment and anger mark the speeches of the pickers of this period. It is the burial of the lime tree. It enters into a process of negative valuation. The complementary role of the picking is denigrated. The actions of tourist valorization are considered as meaningless folklore. The linden tree, "it's nothing anymore". What dies there are not the trees, nor the pickers, nor the merchants. What is dying is a certain way of living and working together. A death produced by the unknotted of all the elements previously held and matched together, in the way of disintegration. The breakdown of the relations between gatherers and merchants lead to a process where every one develops work practices without any adjustment to the others. The memory of events will be forsaken, without transmission.

The lime trees were abandoned, and no longer pruned. Some are uprooted or, for road-side trees, pruned according to road safety regulations. Small linden trees grow back in hedges. The landscape of the lime tree "becomes wild". It marks the abandonment of a culture and the de-weaving of an environment.

Today, this death is weighed against a fragile revival of picking and trade. In fact, from the 2000s, a trade of organic quality lime trees by wholesale companies newly arrived in the region has emerged. Over time, this trade leads to a slight increase in the purchase price. It contributes to the maintenance of the harvesting work by pickers, whether farmers or not, most of whom are aging. Picking is also taken over by PPAM pickers (Perfume, Aromatic and Medicinal Plants) who develop their own marketing channels in markets that are more remunerative than those of wholesalers. However, this revitalization remains uncertain because both pickers and traders are encountering difficulties. Organic quality trade standards impose certification constraints that are difficult to implement and control that disqualify much of the production. Abandoned trees have grown and make pruning difficult. Drying places have often disappeared or are no longer adapted to the standards of organic quality trade. Both pickers and traders are inventing new work practices, from the invention of new pruning techniques to the implementation of organic certification contracts. But their practices develop in isolation, without coordination, without reciprocal adjustment. This makes the emergence of a new environment precarious, even impossible.

5 Thinking Territorial Project as Supporting the Making of a Milieu

Interventions and research studies carried out in ergonomics are massively centered on firms (as productive organization). But this focus is deeply questioned in order to meet the challenge of the making of a milieu. There is a need to question action and change far from the boundary of each firms, in order to create a together crisscross from a diversity of actors (and economic entity), producers, botanists, traders, etc., whose the work is currently disconnected and untwined. Additionally, the project is supported by a administrative entity (the «Natural Regional Park of Baronnies Provençales»), but the geographical area of lime tree production is under the authority of a diversity of administrative divisions (departments, municipalities) and institutions at different scales (regions[1], but also the French State and European Community), whose actions and expectations are not *a priori* articulated, and which can even be discordant when viewed from the perspective of lime tree cultivation. Thus, elected officials can oppose each other on programs to support local agriculture, such as between complementary linden or apricot monoculture, according to their own economic and political reference models. In this context, four dimensions appear to be strategic in territorial project.

The first dimension questions the relevant scale of action. Making a milieu does not stop at the boundaries of an administrative area. In the case of linden, the production area extends beyond the Baronnies as far as another area (the Diois), where some of

---

[1] The territory of the Natural Regional Park of Baronnies Provençale extends over two distinct administrative regions.

the wholesale companies purchasing linden are currently located. Consequently, the territory must be understood as a physical space inhabited by human groups, who give themselves a particular representation of their history and their singularity, and within which an appropriation of their links is played out, in their economic, cultural and political dimensions. This is very different from a space delimited by an administrative or economic authority or jurisdiction. The notion of *"project territory"* seems relevant [4]. It designates the scale from which a cross-disciplinary dialogue between the stakeholders and the administrative and policy entities present on the "project territory" must be woven.

The second dimension relates to the interdependency between the stakeholders. The idea of making a milieu is consistent with that of a work system, in which the whole (actually the "milieu") is more than the sum of its parts. The ability of the stakeholders to make such a system lies in their cooperation. To cooperate consists in taking into account the constraints of others in the choices and arbitrations that each person makes in the context of their own activity [5]. Mendes & Coll. [6] analyzed in detail the dynamics of changes in a system of actors who cooperate. She studied the process of systemic change due to the introduction of humidification (projection of water during the extraction - cutting, smoothing and polishing- of marble plaques) in order to reduce pneumoconiose cause by dust inhalation in the Brazilian mining sector. The introduction of technical humidification (a quite simple artifact) led to unexpected difficulties (regarding the safety of electrical devices due to water, the quality, etc.). The research shown that a central issue is then the ability to adjust and reconstruct the whole work system by proximity and propagation between the workers. For example, taking into account the constraints and difficulties that are encountered by operators using the new technical devices for humidification appears as an uncertain problem to be solve by the electrician. But the solution provided by the electrician will question quality, etc. ... Renata Wey named that process of reconstructing the whole by proximal cooperation a *"systemic appropriation"*. That idea of a "systemic appropriation" is important for reasoning project management. It suggests that the system is discovered as we move forward, and that the difficulties of ones must be taken into account by others to find a possible outcome. This means that interdependency is not only something to do. It is a resource to lead the project by following the propagation of the constraints encountered within a revealed system, understood as a milieu that has to be weaved.

The third dimension relates to the constitution of the actors. The cooperation, under-stood as mentioned above, refers to a quality of exchanges and dialogues between the actors in interdependence. But it also assumes that the stakeholders need to maintain symmetrical relations. However, the relations between the actors can be asymmetrical. In that case, the questions and issues of the ones may become overwhelming, and being imposed to the others. In the Baronnies Provençales, the traders of lime tree flowers have procedural and organizational resources that are without comparison with those available to the pickers, who produce linden in self-subsistence and polyactivity, and who are not organized. The ability of the pickers to identify, to transmit and to make their understanding and problems heard is then very limited. This raises the question of the constitution of a "collective actors". Indeed, the lack of an organization that brings together pickers currently prevents them from playing a role in the dialogue with whole-sale companies, but also from having access to support from public institutions. The question is therefore to explore forms of organization that could meet their current needs and work constraints while giving them a place in the territory.

The fourth dimension refers to "boundary object". This question is by no means new in project management. In ergonomics, there are recurrent references to the use of scale models and graphics representations, prototypes, mock up, etc. as resources which help to support the participation of the end users to the design process (see for example [7]). However few discussions has been centered on the characteristics of these objects, and their use [8]. For a territorial project, cartography appears as being a useful resource. In the case of the lime tree, one of the boundary objects identified is a map that lists the trees for harvesting on the territory. This map plays a two-fold role in project management. On the one hand, it enables the "project territory" to be depicted. On the other hand, it helps to positioning in space the place of the different actors of the territory, so that it is a support for defining their cooperation. Therefore, its implementation allows pointing out a share space, and to establishing the conditions of a dialogue and a cooperation dynamics often impossible on other subjects. It allows to experiment the matching of their interests and to weave links between them.

6 Discussion

It is possible to define project management through three dimensions: it is a goal-oriented process, framed by its temporal dimension, and involving a collective of people from different professional orientations and expertise [9]. The collective dimension is probably not the sole question raise by territorial projects. But in focusing on "the making of a milieu", it appears has being a central focus: there is a need to create a together crisscross from a diversity of disconnected untwined actors (and economic entity). This weaving is a necessity for life. In consequence, we can note that normativity [10] joins the stakes of sustainability understood as *"creating an environment in which people can develop their full potential and lead productive, creative lives in accord with their needs and interests"* [11]. However, such an approach call for a better understanding of the dynamics of institutionalization that appears as different level (e.g. moving from territorial administrative entities to a territorial project, contributing to the emergence of collective actors).

Insofar as the mechanisms specific to the development of territories contribute intrin-sically to the development of work systems, it is not sufficient to apprehend the territorial dimension as a simple determinant. Territorial projects are matrices from which living human territories will be built. From that point of view, ergonomics would be led to contribute, from the perspective of work issues, to the contemporary development of a territorial science thought in terms of systems of activities, whose concepts, modes of operation and methods of analysis need to be better defined.

References

1. Canguilhem, G.: La connaissance de la vie. Vrin (1993)

2. Ingold, T.: Faire: anthropologie, archéologie, art et architecture. Editions Dehors, Bellevaux (2017)
3. Dewey, J.: L'art comme expérience. Gallimard, Paris (2010)
4. Di Meo, G.: Géographie sociale et territoires, coll. Fac-géographie (1998)
5. Béguin, P.: Design as a mutual learning process between users and designers. Interact. Comput. **15**(5), 709–730 (2003)
6. Mendes, R.W.B., Pueyo, V., Béguin, P., Duarte, F.J.C.: Innovation, systemic appropriation and prevention in the granite mining sector: the case of humidification. WORK: J. Prevention Assess. Rehabil. **57**(3), 351–361 (2017). https://doi.org/10.3233/WOR-172566
7. Broberg, O., Andersen, V., Seim, R.: Participatory ergonomics in design processes: the role of boundary objects. Appl. Ergon. **42**(3), 464–472 (2011)
8. Bittencourt, J.M., Duarte, F., Beguin, P.: Simulation with a Lego scale model and other intermediary objects. In: Proceedings of the XI International Symposium on Human Factors in Organizational Design and Management, Denmark, Copenhagen (2014)
9. Béguin, P.: Acting within the boundaries of work systems development. Hum. Factor Ergon. Manuf. Serv. Ind. **21**(6), 543–554 (2011)
10. Canguilhem, G.: Le normal et le pathologique. PUF, Paris (2013)
11. UNDP Homepage. https://www.undp.org/. Accessed 09 Jan 2021

Automation and the Future of Human Work: An Everlasting Debate Renewed by the Work Activity

Daniel Silva[1(✉)] ⓘ and Liliana Cunha[1,2] ⓘ

[1] Centre for Psychology at University of Porto (CPUP), Porto, Portugal
{danielsilva,lcunha}@fpce.up.pt
[2] Faculty of Psychology and Educational Sciences of the University of Porto, Porto, Portugal

Abstract. Driven by digitally enabled machines, robotics and artificial intelligence, the speed and pace at which tasks can be automated are unprecedented. The changes in the nature of the work activity caused by an "automation revolution" is the motto for the current debate on automation and the future of human work. This debate has crystalized, so far, into forecasts estimating the extent to which occupations are "automatable". But what are the real effects of automation in the content and pace of work? What is the place of the human activity within work environments increasingly automated? Through a research approach from the "point of view of activity", two studies were designed to investigate these questions. Study 1 was conducted in two cork processing companies, whereas study 2 followed an exploratory strategy with Portuguese experts involved in the design of future automated driving situations. The findings suggest the activity constitutes the critical "link" between the theoretical definition of work automated processes and the real work. But such link remains "hidden" compared with the complexity of the automation apparatus. Diverging from techno-deterministic interpretations, the perspective of our research is to contribute to monitoring the ongoing transformations of work evoked by automation considering the operational leeway for workers develop their experience, preserve their health, and revalue their work practices.

Keywords: Automation · Work activity · Technology · Automatable work

1 Introduction

In light of a digital era, it is common today the discourse about an "automation revolution" in work [1], brought about by the proliferation of advanced automated assembly lines, collaborative robots, working algorithms, and the first forms of automated vehicles. Such technological innovations have put again on the top of researchers and policymakers' agendas the debate on the future of human work, in the face of growing concerns about the obsolescence of human activity in production. Despite being an ongoing debate, it is far from new [2–5]. The analysis of the relations between work activity, technological progress, and society is held since the end of the 1950s, with the introduction of automation into more and more branches of industrial activity [6]. Since then, and in the course of successive waves of technological innovation (from automatization and robotization to microelectronics and computerization of work), the debate concerning the consequences for work activity and society at large is periodically renewed [7–10]. But why is the current technological wave different?

Dominated by the digitalization of the economy, the current automation wave is distinctive in its speed and wide-scale of diffusion, transforming the working methods in an ever-increasing number of activities, from manufacturing to the services sector [5]. The road transport industry constitutes the most recent example of a sector in which automation is transforming human work activity. A second contingent factor contributing to this distinctive feature concerns the theoretical and political discourses linking technology to the "modernization" of production to meet the challenges of this century. In this vein, a set of restructuring processes are now suggested under an emerging model called the "fourth industrial revolution" (also referred to as "Industry 4.0", "Industry of the Future", or "Work 4.0"). This "new" model holds the promise of a straightforward relationship between technological performance and productivity gains, improved quality, and competitiveness [e.g., 11].

2 Automation is not a Monologue: A New Appeal to Work Psychology and Activity Ergonomics

Whilst the transformation of work induced by this emerging model portends significant change in production by its "techno-centred" properties [10, 12], it is also true that other impacts are kept as "discrete" areas of interest, namely the modifications in the work activity and their consequences for workers. This tendency is rooted on an "un-dialectical technological determinism" [4], assuming technological performance implies progress, particularly for those workers who view their repetitive and routine tasks replaced by monitoring tasks. These new tasks are often seen as more complex and abstract. In this sense, the work activity is taken as an "immaterial" reality [13], or a "technical abstraction" [9], in a more and more automated world, and therefore without anchor points for analyzing the transformations evoked by automation.

In the past, Terssac and Coriat [7] shed light on how such interpretations could be doubly reductionist. First, it could lead to the "marginalization" of workers' know-how when they are compared to the properties of automatisms in machinery. Second, by comparing to the workers' role, automatic operations of technical devices are described as "invariant" functions. In turn, the activity tends to be described not by its content, but in terms of residual and predefined "substitutions", only mobilized in performing fragmented tasks that cannot be assigned to technology yet.

Nevertheless, what does research reveal by adopting the point of view of work activity? At this point, work psychology and activity ergonomics have important contributes by mobilizing activity-oriented categories of analysis [10, 12, 14]: (i) the pace of work and new physical and cognitive demands; (ii) the modes of appropriation and usage of technological artefacts; (iii) the resources to develop and preserve the work experience; (iv) the risks and their impacts on workers' health; or (v) the evolution of workers' criteria on what is a "job well done". Quite often such dimensions are seen as "residual and temporary forms" in the modernization of work [9]. Exempting them from the analysis is a further step towards deterministic visions, dictating automation as the only factor shaping the future of human work in a predefined way.

3 Research Issues

Grounded in this frame, our goal is to present two ongoing Portuguese studies dedicated to analyzing the consequences of automation. The work activities under analysis belong to different sectors (cork industry; and road transport), having in common the fact that automation technologies are inducing a set of reconfigurations that deserve to be scrutinized while debating the future of human work. Study 1 is based on fieldwork in two cork companies. Study 2 is part of a Portuguese research project, involving engineers, automation designers, human factors experts, and work psychologists, which aims at analysing the future situations of automated driving. Through these ongoing studies, we intend to explore the impacts of automation in the content and pace of work, and how workers develop and preserve their "reserves" of experience.

4 Method

4.1 Study 1: The Case of Cork Companies in an Industrial District

Our first study takes place in two small-sized cork companies, located in the "cork district of Santa Maria da Feira" (a small county in the north of Portugal), which constitutes the major cork industrial district in the world. Obeying to a continuous process of geographical agglomeration throughout the 20th century, this "industrial district" stands out by two factors: most of the clustered companies are dedicated to the manufacture of natural cork stoppers; and this territory forms at present a "pool of specialized workers" in cork.

Data for this study were collected through ergonomic analysis of work activity (EAWA). In each company, we carried out interviews with managerial staff (to explore the milestones of technological change), on-the-job observations (open observations, and then systematic observations of reference situations were performed), three individual sessions of guided analysis in the workplace, and two sessions of collective allo-confrontation [15].

4.2 Study 2: The Case of Automated Vehicles

Discourses on road transport advocate that driving is undergoing an "unparalleled revolution" towards the "mobility of the future". Promising advantages in terms of road safety, congestion, or accessibility, automated vehicles have garnered significant investments by the automotive industry and mobilized a broad research interest worldwide. In Portugal, a research project with conditional levels of automation is ongoing in a driving simulator [16]. Following an exploratory strategy, data for our second study was collected through semi-structured interviews with researchers participating in this Portuguese project. The professionals were selected based on their expertise in the design of driving scenarios used in simulation stages. Three interviews were conducted, each lasting circa 90 min, recorded and transcribed verbatim. Interview topics included the design of simulation scenarios, human-automation relationship, and the role of human activity in automated driving situations. After a reading dedicated to generating an initial narrative (in vivo codes) from each interview, second coding followed an inductive approach guided by emerging themes [17].

5   Results and Discussion

5.1   "Finding the Sound of My Machines"

The two analyzed cork companies underwent processes of technological evolution in the last two decades regarding the general increase in automation. According to the managerial staff of each company, these processes resulted mainly in the introduction of automated machines driven by the need to meet growing quality demands and increase the production speed. The managers emphasized that such performance allows competing with the rising market share of companies producing plastic stoppers, which in the early 2000s were "threatening" the sustainability of the cork district.

In the first company, the analysis focused on the activity performed in the rectifying section, where through different automated machines the cork stoppers are counted, polished (in the body of stoppers), rectified (in the ends of stoppers) and selected ("chosen") according to quality classes. In this rectifying section, only one operator works per shift, who is responsible for 5 automated machines (see Table 1).

In turn, in company 2, the analysis was focused on the work activity in the gluing section. In this section, each worker is responsible for two automatic gluing machines, which produce the "capped stoppers", i.e., cork stoppers where the end is placed in a cap (of wood, PVC, porcelain, glass, or metal) through heated glue (see Table 1).

The rectifying section (in company 1) was implemented in 2015, and since then it has undergone a significant process of technological change through automated machines (the digital-enabled pre-sorting machine was the last one to be adopted, in 2019). The automation of the process of stoppers rectifying has diminished manual operations, mainly in counting and visually selecting stoppers according to their quality. However, the juxtaposition of different automated machines has imposed changes in the pace of work and gives rise to new temporal demands. Factors associated to these demands are the need to prevent incidents in the machines' functioning and ensure the stoppers selection made by the selecting machines are in tandem with company's parameters of quality for each stoppers' classes. To better illustrate the variability of "operative commitments" [18] performed to meet these demands, we analyzed observation-based data collected during a systematic observation of a morning shift (see Fig. 1). Here, we present an excerpt from a chronicle of activity treated with ActoGraph® software [19].

The analysis of this chronicle showed how the operative sequences and pace of the work are largely determined by machines, inasmuch as interruptions for managing incidents are frequent. In this excerpt, 48.3% of the total time is devoted to managing, clearing jams, removing rejected stoppers, and restarting, mainly in the two selecting machines (1). In fact, these two machines are the most demanding for the workers (67.5% of the total time is dedicated to operations required by them), who have now to manage

Table 1. Characteristics of the work situations from the workers' perspective.

	Section	Machines	Core operations in activity	Uncertainty and complexity
Company 1	Rectifying	Pre-sorting machine Rectifying machine Polishing machine 2 selecting machines	- Feeding machines' pockets with stoppers - Programming machines for automatic selection according to different quality classes - Supervising the automatic selection of stoppers and identification of deviations or faults - Clearing jams	- Jammed stoppers in machines' pockets - Stoppers from lower-quality classes require additional efforts to anticipate incidents - Differences between the programmed selection and the actual selection made by selecting machines
Company 2	Gluing	6 automatic gluing machines (two per worker)	- Feeding machine's pockets with stoppers and caps - Anticipating jams - Adjusting and testing machines according to sizes of stoppers and caps - Selecting manually defective stoppers	- New caps requiring machines adjustment and testing - Smaller stoppers lead to more jamming (requiring a continuous vigilance) - Jammed stoppers in the machine's gluing mechanism (after clearing, this mechanism must be manually adjusted)

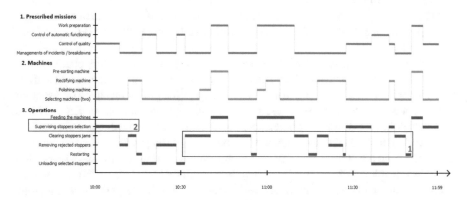

Fig. 1. Chronicle of the activity of a female worker in the cork stoppers rectifying section.

two main "temporal frameworks" [20], with different situational requirements. Besides the management of incidents related to jams, the human supervision over the automatic selection is crucial (2), since the worker compares the selection carried out by machines with the manual selection of stoppers (in which these workers have experience). In case of significant differences in terms of quality, the workers' criteria on what is a quality cork stopper prevail, and then the selecting machine is stopped in order to be programmed. The workers' criteria on quality are developed throughout years of experience, and they are based on knowledge of cork and its defects. This know-how was generated from (i) the handling and touching natural cork stoppers; (ii) the observation of defects, and the visual comparison of defects (comparing different quality classes); and (iii) in some cases, the smell of stoppers.

In company 2, the automatic gluing machines were introduced in 2012, leading to the substitution of the manual procedure (i.e., the workers no longer stick the caps on the end of the stoppers, one by one). Unlike what happened in the manual gluing method, operators now work the entire shift standing up, and moving between the two automatic gluing machines for which they are in charge. Here, the objective of the analysis was to explore how the workers mobilize their reserves of action in the face of growing human-machine configurations, identifying the operations that contribute to workers' expertise.

According to workers, two situations were highlighted. First, diagnosing and anticipating incidents to forestall machines from stopping; and second, the gestures in manual adjustment of the machines' gluing mechanism (see Table 1). The discussion of the operative modes mobilized in each of these situations was carried out through a crossed allo-confrontation session. The workers explained how they collect and filter signals about machines functioning and work setting to anticipate incidents or breakdowns. For example, the most prominent source for diagnosing is what workers have named as 'the sound of my machines': "*At the beginning, I had to learn to find the sound of my machines in amidst all the noise from the factory. Without looking at the screen* [positioned on the back of the machines], *you know the problems are coming* [...] *When you catch it* [the sound], *firstly, you will hear the caps in the machine's pocket, with a little slower pace, and shortly after it is the speed of the stoppers passing by in the gluing mechanism, look, it is different, isn't it? We need to act fast*", explains a worker with 6 years of experience in the gluing section.

Regarding the adjustment of the machines' gluing mechanism, this operation was identified as a core dimension of the workers' expertise, involving a sequence of actions: removing the jammed stoppers; manual calibration of the gluing mechanism; programming the machine; test, and then restart. In their interaction with automated machines, the workers have developed competences mobilized in this adjustment and recalibration. But this process takes time and work experience, through which workers represent and appropriate the automatic process of gluing and, accordingly with these representations, they develop gestures needed in handling auxiliary tools (e.g., a "hook-spanner") to proceed manually the adjustment. De Keyser and Van Daele [18] showed how the development of such mental representations about automatic movements of machines, if even partial, could support their control.

According to the workers' perspective, the know-how involved in this operation is decisive to confer a sense of autonomy and control in performing the activity, besides contributing to define what they consider an "expert worker" in the gluing section.

5.2 Mobility of the Future: New "Grey Areas" for the Human Activity?

In study 2, the interviewed researchers had a background in transportation systems engineering, and currently they participate in activities associated with the architecture of simulation scenarios to explore the moments when drivers regain manual control of vehicles. One of the respondents justified the interest for these control transitions (between the human and automation system) explaining that *"These moments are posing major concerns in terms of safety, and somewhat they have remained as "grey areas", and not only in legal terms"*. In fact, automation capabilities made possible today by technology progress enable advanced automated driving situations; however, humans are expected to supervise automation and they are requested to resume control in critical situations for which automation is not able to handle with yet [21, 22]. In this context, one of the interviewed researchers stated that the challenge is to inform car manufacturers on: *"The minimum takeover-request lead time needed for drivers resume manual control of their vehicles in an appropriate and safe manner [...] We are also interested in what happened after human takes control, the quality of maneuvers"*.

Regarding the role of drivers, the researchers stated that today's driving simulated-based experiments are dedicated to predicting the future driving performance, i.e., the probable human behavior when interacting with vehicle automation. In this way, through "prospective simulations" using prototypes [23], the aim is to have drivers play out their probable future role based on the driving scenarios suggested by the researchers. Depending on the automation level, the driver could perform non-driving tasks, and, in these circumstances, the driving will become a "hands and feet free" activity. However, it is far from being an "attention-free" activity, at least up to the state of "fully automated driving environments". In this sense, the respondents emphasized that simulator experiments analyze two probable roles for the human in vehicles of the future: *"With controls within the vehicle, firstly, the driver will be a supervisor, and then will act as an "emergency driver" to correct critical maneuvers. In the highest level of automation, the driver will be just a passenger [...] But till then, the "supervisor" and "emergency driver" roles will rely on the level of automation technology and its reliability"*.

Yet, the researchers also expressed that increased automation might not be synonymous of higher levels of safety, mainly when drivers are expected to act as supervisors. Their concerns reflect one of the best known "ironies of automation" [24]. The operation of these vehicles is built upon the assertion of a "human recovery ability" in the presence of abnormalities or unexpected events. One researcher expressed the underlying irony of an "apparent shared control" in automated vehicles: *"Who is effectively responsible for the vehicle? Automation is operating the vehicle, and the human driver is told that he/she may look outside or perform other tasks, but, at the same time, he/she should be aware to act after the sound* [an audible alarm from the system]. *In these circumstances, optimal periods of time for takeover requests need to be defined with large safety margins, leading to very cautious situations [...] The problem lies on the fact that these margins could dramatically narrow the situations where automated vehicles could really operate"*.

Such concerns and challenges lead the researchers to question whether the drivers should be placed in such "grey" situations, and they showed some reservations on the real deployment of conditionally automated vehicles (with takeover requests) on public roads.

6 Conclusions: New Ways of Mobilizing the Activity

The "modernization of work" brought about by automation technologies holds the promise to address multiple economic challenges, among which productivity, shortened delivery times, and increased efficiency are the most common. But, instead of globalizing the expected results and maintaining the characteristics of each work situation on the margins of technological change [8], work psychology and activity ergonomics research have reinforced the importance to scrutinize the transformations of work from the activity's perspective [12, 14]. Albeit with different levels of automation maturity, the first results of our studies indicate that automation brings profound changes in work content and requires the development of new human-machine relationships. On the other hand, our findings show that automation gives rise to new sources of complexity and variability, mobilizing the individual and collective activity to deal with the unpredictability and dynamism of the environment.

At a time when "dystopic" visions on a fully automated world of work are far from being a reality, the challenge is to analyze the ongoing transformations of working and employment conditions to question what the future human work will be like. Our research will be further developed in the contexts presented, contributing to argue against visions that depict technology merely as a tool at the service of tasks. On the contrary, automation technologies should not be detached from the appropriation and usage processes undertaken by workers while developing their work experience, finding new sources of autonomy, and (re)building the meaning of work.

Acknowledgments. This work is supported by the FCT − Portuguese Foundation for Science and Technology under Grant SFRH/BD/139135/2018; by the Fundação Calouste Gulbenkian ("CORK-In" project); and by the Centre for Psychology at University of Porto (FCT UIDB/00050/2020).

References

1. Skidelsky, R., Craig, N.: Work in the Future: The Automation Revolution. Palgrave Macmillan, London (2020)
2. Cavestro, W.: Automation, skills and the content of work. Int. J. Syst. Sci. **19**(8), 1407–1418 (1988)
3. Rolle, P.: Asir y utilizar la actividad humana. Cualidade del trabajo, cualificación y competencia. In: Lahire, B., Rolle, P., Saunier, P., Stroobants, M., Alaluf, M., Postone, M. (eds.) Lo que el trabajo esconde: materials para un replanteamiento del análisis sobre el trabajo, pp. 197–208. Bifurcaciones, Madrid (2005)
4. Howcroft, D., Taylor, P.: Plus ca change, plus la meme chose? – researching and theorising the 'new' new technologies. New Technol. Work Employ. **29**, 1–7 (2014)

5. Goos, M., Arntz, M., Zierahn, U., Gregory, T., Carretero Gómez, S., Gozález Vázquez, I., Jonkers, K.: The Impact of Technological Innovation on the Future of Work. European Commission, Seville (2019)

6. Friedmann, G.: O futuro do trabalho humano. Moraes Editores, Lisboa (1968)

7. Terssac, G., Coriat, B.: Micro-électronique et travail ouvrier dans les industries de process. Sociologie du Travail **4**, 384–397 (1984)

8. Lacomblez, M., Melo, A.: Informatisation des petites et moyennes entreprises et conditions du travail – analyse de cas au Portugal. Commission des Communautés Européennes, Porto (1989)

9. Clot, Y.: Le travail sans l'homme? Pour une psychologie des milieux de travail et de vie. La Découverte, Paris (1995)

10. Barcellini, F.: Quelles conceptions de la coopération humains-robots collaboratifs? Une expérience de participation au projet de conception d'un démonstrateur de robotique collaborative. Activités **17**, 1–29 (2020)

11. Davies, R.: Industry 4.0: Digitalisation for productivity and growth. European Parliamentary Research Service, Brussels (2015)

12. Bobillier Chaumon, M.-E.: Technologies émergentes et transformations digitales de l'activité: enjeux pour l'activité et la santé au travail. Psychologie du Travail et des Organisations **27**(1), 17–32 (2021)

13. Rot, G., Vatin, F.: Le travail et l'automation: réflexions sur l'activité productive. Progressistes 20 (2018)

14. Caroly, S., Hubaut, R., Guelle, K., Landry, A.: Le travail digital, un enjeu pour les psychologues du travail: L'exemple de l'industrie 4.0. Le Journal des Psychologues **367**, 27–32 (2019)

15. Mollo, V., Falzon, P.: Auto- and allo-confrontation as tools for reflective activities. Appl. Ergon. **35**(6), 531–540 (2004)

16. Lobo, A., Ferreira, S., Silva, D., Cunha, L., Simões, A., Couto, A.: On the road to automated vehicles: from perception to use. In: Lusikka, T. (ed.) Proceedings of the 8th Congress of the Transport Research Arena (TRA 2020). Traficom, Helsinki (2020)

17. Miles, M., Huberman, A., Saldana, J.: Qualitative Data Analysis: A Methods Sourcebook. Sage, California (2014)

18. De Keyser, V., Van Daele, A.: Fiabilité humaine, securité, automatisation: Le cas de conducteurs de tours a commande manuelle ou numérique. Le Travail Humain **49**, 117–135 (1986)

19. Boccara, V., Delgoulet, C., Zara-Meylan, V., Barthe, B., Gailard, I., Meylan, S.: The role and positioning of observation in ergonomics approaches: a research and design project. In: Bagnara, S., Tartaglia, R., Albolino, S., Alexander, T., Fujita, Y. (eds.) IEA 2018. AISC, vol. 824, pp. 1821–1828. Springer, Cham (2019)

20. Zara-Meylan, V.: Quelles conceptions temporelles pour analyser l'activité? Une proposition issue de recherches en ergonomie dans l'horticulture. Activités **13**, 1–28 (2016)

21. Silva, D., Cunha, L.: "Automated but not alone": how the possible forms of future human activity are analyzed in the advent of automated vehicles? In: Russo, D., Ahram, T., Karwowki, W., Di Bucchianico, G., Taiar, R. (eds.) IHSI 2021. AISC, vol. 1322, pp. 90–96. Springer, Cham (2021)

22. Haué, J.-B., Le Bellu, S., Barbier, C.: Le véhicule autonome: Se désengager et se réengager dans la conduite. Activités **17**, 1–26 (2020)

23. Bobillier Chaumon, M.-E., Rouat, S., Laneyrie, E., Cuvillier, B.: De l'activité de simulation à l'activité en simulation: Simuler par stimuler. Activités **15**, 1–25 (2018)

24. Bainbridge, L.: Ironies of automation. Automatica **19**(6), 775–779 (1983)

Reflections on the Activity Perspective in Hospital Work Permanence Actions During COVID-19

Talita Naiara Rossi da Silva[1]([✉]) [iD], Lívia Bustamante van Wijk[2] [iD],
Thainá de Oliveira Rocha[1] [iD], Nicole Beltrame Medeiros de Souza[1] [iD],
and Selma Lancman[1] [iD]

[1] Universidade de São Paulo Medical School, São Paulo, Brazil
talitarossi@usp.br
[2] Hospital of Universidade de São Paulo, São Paulo, Brazil

Abstract. The situation that emerged from recognizing the COVID-19 pandemic in 2020 required a university hospital's efforts to reorganize the work and care activities in this period. This study aims to present actions to support workers' permanence in the hospital context at work in pandemic times. The development of actions was based on the activity ergonomics and, therefore, recommended recognizing actions in real work situations involving workers directly. The interventions covered 14 sectors, involving 140 workers. During the actions, the team recorded the activities in a field diary to document the care provided and prepared reports with the identified demands, which were organized into five categories: i) information and communication management, ii) the establishment, improvement, or continuous monitoring of protocols, iii) hospital workers' health care, iv) establishment of collective spaces to refresh and align conducts; and v) adequacy of work conditions and processes. The interventions with hospital workers in the COVID-19 pandemic contributed to the exchange of experiences and knowledge between same-sector and inter-sector workers and sharing perspectives regarding work dynamics. The foundation of the actions in activity ergonomics has contributed to increasing the visibility of situations that pre-existed the pandemic and structured a new perspective on health and work in the hospital, recognizing the active participation of workers.

Keywords: Health workers · COVID-19 · Hospital · Ergonomics · Permanence at work

1 Introduction

COVID-19 is a global health, social, and economic emergency that has been imposing unprecedented challenges on health workers since early 2020. These professionals and those directly caring for COVID-19 patients or engaged in other activities are highly exposed to the risk of infection and death and deal daily with the suffering and mourning of the population. They are subjected to long working hours, fatigue, exhaustion, stigma, physical and psychological violence [1]. Health workers are still afraid to infect their families and communities and experience close people's distancing, which leads to weakened bonds and social support [2].

The hospital studied is one of the services underpinning the health care and teaching platform at University of São Paulo and is responsible for care, teaching, and research activities. It is a secondary-level hospital serving the university community and the population of a circumscribed region of São Paulo's municipality where the University Campus is located. The hospital was not a reference for the care of COVID-19 patients during the pandemic. Nonetheless, it was active in the Health Care Network of the region, following cases that arrived at the emergency room or started to show symptoms compatible with this disease during hospitalization. In these situations, the hospital carried out the necessary referrals to other referral services and ensured care continuity for cases that, perhaps, could not be transferred. This hospital context required efforts to reorganize work, care, and teaching activities. Procedures and flows have been modified in light of the new care required to minimize COVID-19 transmission risks.

The hospital also cooperated with the reorganization of a hospital complex that was a reference in the care of COVID-19 patients in the health care network. For example, between March and August 2020, the hospital received patients and teams from the gynecology/obstetrics, pediatrics, ophthalmology, and otorhinolaryngology clinics, which required restructuring the spaces and recomposing the teams linked to the hospital and the hospital complex to work under this new circumstance.

Thus, the hospital studied was reorganized to accommodate clinics, patients, students, and residents transferred from another service. It had to review its care and safety protocols for workers and patients to minimize the risks of COVID-19 transmission. It is also noteworthy that the hospital had been undergoing a significant budget crisis since 2014, including two Voluntary Dismissal Programs, non-replacement of employees, and job insecurity, which led to team disarticulation and a climate of uncertainty regarding the future of the hospital and its vocation as a teaching and research institution [3].

In late 2019, USP recruited emergency doctors, physiotherapists, speech therapists, occupational therapists, nurses, and nursing assistants, who started their activities in early 2000. Integrate, dovetail, train, and allow teams to being more than clusters were challenging tasks that involved all hospital workers. At this time, the hospital was surprised by the COVID-19 pandemic, which demanded new reorganizations of all health services underlying University's teaching care platform and the definition of new work processes.

In this context, the Laboratory for Research and Intervention in Health and Work (LIIST) linked to the Occupational Therapy Course at FMUSP, which develops workers' health actions within the mentioned services, also restructured its work. This study aims to present the actions to support workers' permanence at work in the hospital context during the pandemic.

2   Method

The actions to support work permanence presented in this study were based on activity ergonomics. Thus, they recommended carrying out actions in real work situations, directly involving workers [4, 5].

These actions aimed at i) promoting spaces for dialogue between workers in the sector to expand access to information on personal and group care strategies in the pandemic; ii) building spaces for reflection to facilitate the relationships between workers at the hospital and increasing personal and professional resources to face the challenges experienced in the work processes; iii) supporting the reorganization of the teams of the hospital and the integration of new professionals hired for a specified time; iv) identifying the needs for the transformation of specific work processes in each sector to reduce the risk of infection, promote workers' health, prevent dismissals and foster adherence to guidelines and regulations.

The development of the actions started with contacts with the heads to schedule meetings with workers' groups in each sector. On average, three meetings were held with each sector during working hours. The number of meetings was defined jointly with each group that assessed the need for further discussions on work in the sector.

The actions carried out were documented in a field diary, and the identified demands and information were systematized in reports. These reports were presented to the hospital's Superintendence to broaden discussions aimed at improving work conditions and organization.

3 Results

Permanence at work support actions reached 14 care, administrative, or support sectors and involved 140 workers. The identified demands were organized into five categories: information and communication management; establishment, improvement or continuous monitoring of care protocols; health care for hospital workers; creation of collective spaces for updates and alignment of conducts and adaptation of working conditions and processes.

Concerning information and communication management, workers described the lack of clarity and limited time for transmitting reports and guidelines related to the pandemic and work processes, gaps in conduct protocols between sectors and professionals without access to reports sent by e-mail. These issues were observed in workers' concerns, for example, on the use of personal protective equipment and application of protective measures fitting work's reality; the need for physical distance in small and poorly ventilated spaces.

The occupational therapy team's presence in work situations allowed identifying weaknesses in the work's organization and facilitated the access of all workers to information. It also favored the discussion on concerns with the Hospital Infection Control Commission, followed by feedback to workers; reduced access time to information and guidance and; identification of workers without access to institutional e-mail and forwarding this data to the internal communication sector.

The second category of demands, establishment, improvement, or continuous monitoring of protocols, includes the escalation of updating and training actions in line with each clinic's particularities and subsequent monitoring to verify the assimilation and application of knowledge and trained competencies. For example, a quick intubation course guided the teams on the proper steps and procedures. However, some sectors had greater difficulty in accessing the materials and medications to perform them. This category also included the need to reorganize work processes to reduce likely COVID-19 infection.

The reflections carried out with the workers' groups were established as spaces for exchanging experiences and knowledge about work and care protocols. This practice of reflecting on the activity allowed better adequacy of the new protocols to each sector's real work, characterized by changes in the work routine, overload, and the lack of spaces to align multidisciplinary teams.

The third category, health care for hospital workers, included demands associated with creating a flow of care for workers in the context of COVID-19 and the establishment of guidelines for the removal of workers with flu-like symptoms and COVID-19 signs. There were several concerns about the safety of professionals with symptoms and the risk of exposure to others. There was even a lack of uniformity and protocols related to the number of days that each worker should be removed without clarifying these differences to professionals and the sector. Also, several types of health control for hospital workers were disrupted with the advent of the pandemic and reorganizations in the hospital and the municipality's health care network.

Concerning the fourth category, creating collective spaces for updates and conduct alignment, workers claimed the opening of spaces for dialogue and participation in decision-making on work processes. They also stressed the need for hierarchical reorganization in sectors and between sectors to build more horizontal relationships, a greater appreciation of all professional categories, better division of work between different professions, and participatory elaboration of strategies and ways of working.

Finally, the fifth category, the adaptation of working conditions and processes, included the need for improving working conditions and processes in different hospital sectors. This issue was already recurring but was aggravated by the pandemic due to the need to minimize transmission and infection risks among workers.

Several streamlining actions were required to ensure the distance between workers without harming the communication between them. For example: streamlining the flow at the pharmacy counter for delivering the prescription and collecting medication; allowing the opening of secondary doors to increase air circulation; increasing natural ventilation areas in underground working environments; implementing electronic drug prescription to minimize contact between workers and decrease the physical circulation of documents; reviewing administrative flows that previously included the use of paper and face-to-face contact for exclusively remote actions, via telephone or e-mail.

4 Discussion

The actions carried out with hospital workers in the COVID-19 pandemic contributed to the exchange of experiences and knowledge between workers in the same sector and intersector, and the sharing of perspectives regarding work dynamics and readjustment needs to face the pandemic. This situation enabled the construction of alignments on the work processes and identifying aspects that must be jointly reassessed by the team, for example, a better consolidation of teamwork. The actions also enabled some adjustments in work environments and processes and greater engagement of workers and their know-how in the search for improvements in the quality of care and their health care.

The demands identified in each sector's actions were presented to the hospital's Superintendence so that they could be better studied in future actions. The opportunities for collective discussion about work represented a social construction instead of merely producing solutions to the problems identified initially [4]. In this sense, they contributed to structuring a new perspective on work, promoting greater recognition of difficulties and solutions based on the experience of workers and the exchanges between them.

The context of several modifications, many of them provisional and temporary, for example, emergency reorganizations necessary with the advent of the pandemic and recruitment of professionals for a specific time, work situations highly vulnerable to infections, have hindered the use of the preferred method for activity ergonomics, namely, the ergonomic analysis of work. The initial demand for occupational therapy actions in 2020 was the first characterization of work in different sectors. In this case, it is recommend using methods that allow the brief recognition of the most critical work situations that may be subjected to more in-depth and accurate analyses [5].

We decided to adopt reflective practices to preserve the approach to real work situations and workers' involvement in actions. These activities were established as discussion groups on work from a critical analysis of the activity with the workers. Thus, workers in each group discussed their activities and made their representations explicit. Reflective practices enable the construction of new knowledge and representations for action based on social experiences and interactions between workers. These practices produce workers' changes and can result in work changes [6].

Finally, it should be noted that hospital work is essentially collective. Different professionals carry out specific activities that complement each other and sometimes occur in the same workspaces. The course of individual workers' actions is intertwined in a cooperative relationship between service users and workers and between them and their peers [7]. The reflections on the work with the teams that were also reconfiguring became a facilitating space for the construction or strengthening of technical and social commitments that allow working together in the different work teams [8].

5   Final Considerations

The foundation of the actions in activity ergonomics and reflective practice with the workers contributed to increasing the visibility to pre-existing situations in the pandemic, such as work environments without ventilation and conflicting hierarchical relationships. However, these actions mainly allowed structuring a new perspective on workers' health in the hospital. In this sense, work is recognized as a determinant of health, and the active participation of workers is fundamental in reflecting on the activities carried out and building improvements.

References

1. World Health Organization. Coronavirus disease (COVID-19) outbreak: rights, roles and responsibilities of health workers, including key considerations for occupational safety and health. https://apps.who.int/iris/bitstream/handle/10665/331510/WHO-2019-nCov-HCWadv ice-2020.2-eng.pdf?sequence=1&isAllowed=y. Accessed 08 Feb 2021

2. World Health Organization. Mental health and psychosocial considerations during COVID-19 outbreak. https://www.who.int/docs/default-source/coronaviruse/mental-health-considera tions.pdf. Accessed 08 Feb 2021
3. Lancman, S., Sato, A.T., Hein, D.T., Barros, J.O.: Precarização do trabalho e sofrimento psíquico: ação em psicodinâmica do trabalho em um serviço de farmácia hospitalar universitário. Rev. Bras. Saúde Ocupacional **44**(e33), 1–9 (2019)
4. Guérin, A., Kerguelen, A., Laville A., Daniellou, F., Duraffourg, J.: Understanding and transforming work: the practice of ergonomics. In: ANACT Network Editions, Lyon (2007)
5. Daniellou, F., Béguin, P.: Metodologia da ação ergonômica: abordagens do trabalho real. In: Falzon, P.: Ergonomia, 1ed, Blucher, São Paulo, pp. 281–301 (2007)
6. Mollo, V., Nascimento, A.: Práticas reflexivas e desenvolvimento dos indivíduos, dos coletivos e das organizações. In: Falzon, P.: Ergonomia Construtiva, 1ed, Blucher, São Paulo, pp. 283–303 (2016)
7. Martin, C., Gadbois, C.: A ergonomia no hospital. In: Falzon, P.: Ergonomia, 1ed, Blucher, São Paulo, pp. 519–533 (2007)
8. Dejours, C.: Subjetividade, trabalho e ação: uma visão de conjunto. In: Dejours, C.: Trabalho e emancipação, pp. 23–44. 1ed, Paralelo 15, Brasília (2012)

Analyzing the Activity of Brazilian Airline Industry Professionals in Assisting Passengers with Disabilities

Flávia Helen Moreira da Silva[1], Marina Greghi Sticca[1(✉)],
Talita Naiara Rossi da Silva[1], Heloisa Giangrossi Machado Vidotti[2],
and Nilton Luiz Menegon[2]

[1] University of São Paulo, Ribeirão Preto, Brazil
marinagreghi@ffclrp.usp.br, talitarossi@usp.br
[2] Federal University of São Carlos, São Carlos, Brazil
menegon@dep.ufscar.br

Abstract. This study aims to analyze airline industry professionals' work activity in assisting passengers with disabilities in identifying possible service improvements. Semi-structured interviews and observations of airport, airline, and service provider workers' activity were carried out in 16 airports in the five Brazilian regions. The critical incident methodology was also adopted to map difficulties in providing services to passengers with disabilities and factors that facilitate service and operations. A descriptive, statistical analysis of the participants' characterization data and thematic analysis of the interviews were performed. The following challenges were identified during the travel cycle: i) situations of non-accountability by families, which requires the follow-up by airline professionals; ii) non-boarding due to medical documentation requirements; iii) lack of follow-up or passengers' embarrassment due to inadequate communication between professionals; iv) difficulties related to the lack of infrastructure or an insufficient number of employees; v) constraints and conflicts with passengers with disabilities who refuse to comply with security procedures; vi) accidents when boarding wheelchair users; viii) damage and loss of assistive equipment; viii) difficulties in handling situations involving people with mental disorders. Concerning service provision facilitators, people mentioned aspects related to i) airport infrastructure; ii) the training of employees to assist passengers; iii) availability of prior information before boarding. The analysis of airline transport professionals' activity allowed gathering information to support processes to improve management related to the accessibility, airport infrastructure, assistance equipment, and services provided to passengers with a disability or reduced mobility.

Keywords: Work analysis · Accessibility · Air transportation

1 Introduction

This work is nested in a Brazilian multicentric research project entitled "Improving the Civil Aviation Accessibility" developed by the Federal University of São Carlos

N. L. Black et al. (Eds.): IEA 2021, LNNS 219, pp. 288–295, 2021.
https://doi.org/10.1007/978-3-030-74602-5_42

(UFSCar), in collaboration with the University of São Paulo (USP), together with the National Civil Aviation Secretariat (SNAC). It aims to identify the main barriers to the participation of passengers with disabilities in Brazilian airports; develop a manual with criteria, guidelines, and best practices for accessibility in national and international civil aviation and develop material to support the training of airport operators and the assessment of accessibility at airports and flights to verify adherence and implantation of practices established in that manual.

The issue of air transport accessibility has been discussed internationally, and several studies have highlighted the difficulties of passengers with disabilities in all travel stages [1–7]. In Brazil, restrictions on the participation of passengers with disabilities in civil aviation are also being highlighted in research projects coordinated or developed by this study's authors.

The research arose from gaps identified over several studies conducted in civil aviation since 2012 by the group of the Laboratory of Ergonomics, Simulation, and Project of Productive Situations (SimuCAD/Grupo Ergo & Ação/PSPLAB), from the Production Engineering Department (DEP), Federal University of São Carlos (UFSCar), especially the development of guidelines and training that consider the experiences of passengers and workers to respond to accessibility problems in air transport.

This paper aimed to analyze airline professionals' work activity to assist passengers with disabilities in identifying possible service improvements.

1.1 Assistance for People with Disabilities in Air Transport

The profile of passengers in the airline industry has been changing in recent years. The number of people with special assistance needs (PNAEs) using air transport [3, 7, 8] is rising. PNAEs' classification covers older adults, pregnant women, nursing mothers, people accompanied by a lap child, people with reduced mobility, or anyone with limited autonomy as a passenger due to a specific condition, and people with disabilities, which are the focus of this study [9].

According to the World Health Organization [10], disability is part of the human condition. It is complex, dynamic, multidimensional, related to body structures and functions, and contextual, environmental, and social factors. Almost all people will experience temporary or permanent disability and decreased functionality associated with the aging process throughout life. This perspective is reaffirmed in the 2006 United Nations Convention on the Rights of Persons with Disabilities (CRPD), which established that disability results from interactions between people with disabilities and behavioral and environmental barriers. These interactions can prevent the full, effective, and equal participation of these people in society [11]. Thus, environmental factors, such as products, technology, built environment, support, relationships, attitudes, services, systems, and public policies can facilitate or hinder the participation of people with disabilities [10, 12].

The literature review shows that part of the difficulties of PNAEs is related to the services provided by airport or airline employees. These services are prescribed in Brazil in ANAC Resolution 280 [9], which provides for procedures related to passengers' accessibility with special air transport assistance. Article 14 of that Resolution lists 12 activities in which the airline must assist the PNAEs. Some of them are the responsibility of airmen, as they correspond to airport ground services. Worth mentioning are check-in and baggage drop-off, travel from the check-in counter to the aircraft, going through border and security controls, boarding and disembarking the aircraft, seat accommodation, departure from the disembarkation plane, and transfer or connection between flights.

Studies point to the need to improve the training of professionals in the airline industry to identify difficulties, communication, and interaction with these passengers [13–16] and change in the negative attitude of workers having direct contact with passengers with disabilities [17].

1.2 Activity Analysis

Activity analysis can be considered a methodology that aims to understand the behavior of users or operators and their operational strategies by analyzing processes and interactions in a given setting [18]. It increases knowledge about the repertoire of activities during the operator's interaction with the user.

Work activity derives from the integration between the work situation elements, which can be determined outside the worker and, simultaneously, transform him. Thus, the activity analysis aims to identify the activity determinants, the inconsistencies, and potential risks to occupational health and system dysfunctions [19].

2 Methods

2.1 Participants

One hundred fifteen workers linked to airports (n = 56), airlines (n = 47), and service providers (n = 12) participated in the survey in 16 national and international airports in the five Brazilian regions. Most participants were aged 30–39 years (f = 42.6%), 24.3% of airport participants had a graduate level, and complete higher education was observed among airline and service provider participants (f = 20.9% and 4.3%, respectively). Most of the participants held management, supervision, and coordination positions, but workers in services and direct assistance to passengers, projects, maintenance, and security also participated in the study.

2.2 Procedures

Semi-structured interviews and observations of these professionals' work were carried out in real situations of assistance to passengers with disabilities. In the interviews, they were asked to describe how they assist people with disabilities within their respective functions. The critical incident methodology was also adopted to map difficulties in providing services to passengers with disabilities and factors that facilitate service and operations.

2.3 Data Analysis

A descriptive statistical analysis of the participants' characterization data and thematic analysis of the interviews were performed using the MaxQDA 2020 software (trial version). The following thematic categories were created: i) typical service situations by travel stage; ii) critical incident episodes per travel stage; iii) facilities for assisting people with disabilities by travel stage.

3   Results

3.1   Typical Situations for Servicing Passengers with a Disability or Reduced Mobility

In the pre-boarding stage, the factor that appears most frequently (N = 31) in the respondents' report refers to monitoring passengers with disabilities while waiting, whether accompanied or not, to prepare to respond to requests for assistance. Situations in which the family does not accompany the passenger, requiring professionals from the airport or airline to follow-up and assist with all their needs, such as, for example, assistance in using the toilets, have been reported. It was also found that the lack of accessibility from airports, for example, can prevent passengers with disabilities from performing their activities, such as traveling to the boarding area independently.

Access to prior information about passengers with disabilities was also reported as an activity performed by airlines (N = 10). According to the respondents, passengers can identify their needs when purchasing air tickets, which facilitates accessibility resources to serve passengers.

For example, the aircraft can be allocated to the bridge-boarding (finger) if passengers have mobility difficulties. According to the respondents, this information must be provided in advance to facilitate the organization of services and equipment availability. The allocation of passengers in reserved areas at check-in was also mentioned as a service activity so that passengers with disabilities can wait for boarding (N = 9) to favor the follow-up and assistance process. The availability of equipment (wheelchairs) and the adaptation of the location to these passengers' needs were mentioned as necessary service factors.

Another item mentioned by airline employees was the verification of passengers' needs at check-in. According to the respondents (N = 7), identifying the needs facilitates the service, as it is possible to check the necessary equipment and identify demands in the next stages of the trip (Table 1).

Regarding the boarding and disembarking stages, the need to accompany passengers with disabilities during these air travel stages was mentioned more frequently (N = 36). The reports point out a concern of the attendants in carrying out a follow-up that meets passengers' needs, for example, concerning the equipment required for transportation.

Another factor reported by workers in typical service situations is making equipment available for the loading and unloading of wheelchair users. In this category, airline employees, the airport, and third-party companies reported having to adapt the service needs to the existing equipment (chairs that climb the stairs and ambulift) and airport structure (remote or bridge boarding/disembarkation).

Priority boarding and passenger accommodation in the aircraft's front rows were also described as typical service situations for passengers with disabilities in these stages of the trip.

Respondents also mentioned resource management as a typical activity related to the service of passengers with disabilities or reduced mobility. The main categories identified regarding resource management refer to: i) the need to ensure the functioning, availability, and maintenance of equipment, ii) issues related to airport infrastructure, and iii) team management to serve passengers with disabilities. Situations in which it

Table 1. Thematic categories and frequencies related to typical service situations (pre-boarding, boarding, and disembarking).

Thematic categories	(f)
Pre-boarding	
Waiting monitoring	31
Access to information in the system about passengers with disabilities	10
Differentiated safety inspection	9
Priority space allocation	9
Questioning service needs	7
Medical care	3
Passengers with disabilities service system	1
Boarding and disembarking	
Boarding and disembarking monitoring	36
Provision of equipment for boarding wheelchair users	31
Priority boarding	8
Front row accommodation	3

is necessary to request equipment or service (van, taxi) that can assist passengers with disabilities and guarantee equipment maintenance services, such as wheelchairs, have been reported. Airport employees also reported the need to adapt the terminal structure (elevators, stairs, and toilets) to these passengers' needs, inspecting, maintaining, and improving accessibility.

Also, airline employees reported the need to carry out team management to attend to these passengers' needs and train them. According to reports, airport and airline teams must be prepared to meet the needs of passengers with disabilities.

Regarding information flow management concerning passengers with disabilities, airport and airline respondents quoted the importance of receiving advance information to schedule flights and allocate equipment and resources necessary for service.

3.2   Critical Incidents

The following were quoted in the pre-boarding stage: i) situations related to relatives of passengers with disabilities, such as non-accompaniment, which requires professionals to perform activities that were not foreseen; ii) situations of denied boarding for passengers with disabilities due to unanticipated arrival for boarding, medical problems preventing the trip or failure to complete documents related to the health of passengers (MEDIF, for example), required for boarding, iii) structure that hinders mobility (lack of or inadequate elevators), use (non-adapted toilets), and special guidance (absence of tactile floor).

The following were mentioned in the boarding and disembarkation stage: i) difficulties for passengers with physical disability related to infrastructures, such as the lack of boarding bridges, which requires the use of chairs that climb stairs, for example; staff shortage, and the lack of training of employees, for example, in handling the wheelchair. Accidents have been reported in wheelchairs with falling passengers with reduced mobility for these reasons, ii) difficulties related to the passengers, either because they refuse to be served or because they feel insecure with the alternatives provided in the boarding process. One example mentioned was the passenger's refusal to use the chair that climbs the stairs because he felt insecure, and no other alternative was provided to him which culminated in an uncomfortable boarding situation for the passenger (Table 2).

Table 2. Thematic categories and frequencies related to atypical service situations (pre-boarding, boarding, and disembarking).

Thematic categories	(f)
Pre-boarding	
Situations of non-accountability by families, which requires the follow-up by airline professionals	5
Non-boarding due to medical documentation requirements	5
Lack of accessible structure	4
Boarding and disembarking	
Boarding of passengers with a physical disability (Difficulties related to the lack of infrastructure during embarkation and disembarkation or an insufficient number of employees)	25
Boarding of passengers with a physical disability (Associated with the passenger)	10
Difficulties in dealing with people with mental, cognitive, intellectual disabilities and autism spectrum disorder (ASD)	8
Damage/loss/delay in returning wheelchairs	6

3.3 Facilitators for Serving Passengers with Disabilities or Reduced Mobility

Concerning service provision facilitators, people mentioned aspects related to i) airport infrastructure and facilities, such as accessible signage, check-in space reserved for passengers with disabilities, adapted counters, boarding facilities, such as ambulift, boarding bridges, and ramps, wheelchairs, parking spaces reserved for people with disabilities; ii) the training of employees to assist; iii) availability of prior information before boarding; iv) communication between passengers and employees and among employees to inform about the needs of passengers and to advise on the particularities of personal assistance equipment.

4 Discussion

By analyzing the real work activities from the workers' perspective, we observed difficulties, operational strategies adopted in assisting passengers with disabilities, management, and infrastructure conditions that also interfere in the service and training needs.

As a suggestion for improving accessibility conditions, necessary betterments were highlighted in the infrastructure of Brazilian national and international airports, such as, for example, enhanced accessibility equipment and installation of tactile flooring. Management-related issues were also identified, such as increasing the number of employees to meet priorities, maintaining equipment, and eliminating remote boarding positions. As for training, we identified difficulties in performing work activities resulting from skills gaps and related to the lack of resources or other operational or infrastructure-related factors. These difficulties will provide for the development of training content based on typical worker's situations, considering the challenges and issues arising in the service process.

We also found that accidents involving boarding passengers with physical disabilities and reduced mobility are frequent, which may be related to low levels of practical training in wheelchair handling skills. Therefore, it is crucial to expand the provision of specific training geared to daily service situations and address more practical experiences to develop techniques and skills in driving passengers.

5 Conclusion

The analysis of the activity of Brazilian airline transport professionals allowed gathering information to support processes for the improvement of management related to the accessibility and infrastructure of airports, equipment for assistance and embarkation/disembarkation of people with disabilities, and services provided by airlines and airports to these users in the global airline transport industry. The data collected at this stage of the research will support: i) the elaboration of a manual with criteria, guidelines, and best practices for accessibility in the national and international civil aviation; ii) the development of training to train airport operators; iii) the assessment of accessibility at airports.

References

1. Darcy, S.: (Dis)Embodied air travel experiences: disability, discrimination and the effect of a discontinuous air travel chain. J. Hospitality Tourism Manag 19, 1–11 (2012)
2. Chang, F.C., Chen, C.F.: Identifying mobility service needs for disabled air passengers. Tourism Manag 32, 1214–1217 (2011)
3. Chang, F.C., Chen, C.F.: Meeting the needs of disabled air passengers: factors that facilitate help from airlines and airports. Tourism Manag. 33, 529–536 (2012)
4. Chang, Y.C.: Cabin safety intentions of passengers with reduced mobility. J. Air Transp. Manag 25, 64–66 (2012)
5. Poria, Y., Reichel, A., Brandt, Y.: The flight experiences of people with disabilities: an exploratory study. J Travel Res 49(2), 216–227 (2010)
6. Small, J., Darcy, S., Packer, T.: The embodied tourist experiences of people with vision impairment: management and implications beyond the visual gaze. Tourism Manag 33, 941–950 (2012)
7. Davies, A., Christie, N.: An exploratory study of the experiences of wheelchair users as aircraft passengers–implications for policy and practice. IATSS Res. 41(2), 89–93 (2017)

8. Da Silva, T.N.: Contradições e descontinuidades nos sistemas de atividade do transporte aéreo brasileiro: restrições às viagens e as estratégias de passageiros com deficiência, idosos e obesos. PhD Thesis. Federal University of São Carlos, p. 272 (2016)
9. Brasil. Agência Nacional de Aviação Civil. Resolução nº 280,p. 17 (2013)
10. Saúde da, O.M., Mundial, B.: Relatório Mundial sobre a Deficiência. Tradução Secretaria de Estado dos Direitos da Pessoa com Deficiência de São Paulo (2011)
11. Brasil. Convenção sobre os Direitos das Pessoas com Deficiência: Protocolo Facultativo à Convenção sobre os Direitos das Pessoas com Deficiência: Decreto Legislativo nº 186, de 09 de julho de 2008: Decreto nº 6.949, de 25 de agosto de 2009. 4ª Ed., rev. e atual. Brasília: Secretaria de Direitos Humanos, p. 100 362.4 C766 (2010)
12. Organização Mundial da Saúde. Classificação Internacional de Funcionalidade Incapacidade e Saúde (CIF). Genebra, Suíça (2004)
13. Major, W.L., Hubbard, S.M.: An examination of disability-related complaints in the United States commercial aviation sector. J. Air Transp Manag 78(C), 43–53 (2019)
14. Silva, da T.N.R., Guarda, de J.B.S., Silva, da L.L.G., Figueiredo, J.P., Menegon, N.L.: Passageiros com deficiência no transporte aéreo brasileiro: diferentes atores, perspectivas semelhantes. Gestão Produção, 24(1), 136–147 (2017)
15. da Silva, T.N.R., Silva, A.L.R., Caetano, V.O., Silvestrini, G.A., Menegon, N.L.: Passageiros com deficiência visual no transporte aéreo: avaliação da acessibilidade em aeroportos. Cadernos Brasileiros de Terapia Ocupacional 27(2), 372–383 (2019)
16. Poria, Y., Beal, J.: An exploratory study about obese people's flight experience. J. Travel Res. 56(3), 370–380 (2017)
17. Kim, S.E., Lehto, X.Y.: The voice of tourists with mobility disabilities: insights from online customer complaint websites. Int. J. Contemp. Hospitality Manag. 24(3), 451–476 (2012)
18. Garrigou, A., Daniellou, F., Carballeda, G., Ruaud, S.: Activity analysis in participatory design and analysis of participatory design activities. Int. J. Ind Ergon. 15(5), 311–327 (1995)
19. Guérin, F., Laville, A., Daniellou, F., Duraffourg, J., Kerguelen, A.: Compreender o trabalho para tranformá-lo: a prática da ergonomia. Tradução Guiliane M.J. Ingratta, Marcos Maffei, pp. 25–26. Edgard Blucher, São Paulo (2001)

Working in Times of COVID 19: Challenges for Mental Health

Claudio Marcelo Brunoro[1] and Laerte Idal Sznelwar[2]([✉])

[1] Instituto Trabalhar, São Paulo, Brazil
[2] Departamento de Engenharia de Produção da Escola Politécnica da,
Universidade de São Paulo, São Paulo, Brazil
laertesz@usp.br

Abstract. Some changes in the scenario radically transformed the course of work in the days of COVID 19. This paper is based on different testimonies made by different protagonists working at the university: teachers, administrative personal as well as students. These reports were analyzed, considering mainly the relationship between mental health and work, from the theoretical framework of activity ergonomics and psychodynamics at work. The results show different consequences; among then some will be addressed in this text, we highlight: Uncertainty - loss of certainty - if there was any; Dismantling of routines; Installation of doubt regarding many aspects of the work; Relationship with death; Many things taken for granted and immutable become fluid and questionable.

Keywords: Mental health · Challenges for the future · Pandemia · Transformation work · Mental suffering

1   Introduction

The Pandemic period that started in 2020 will certainly be marked by history. From one moment to the next, everyone is forced to protect himself from an invisible threat, practicing social isolation among other important measures to prevent the spread of the coronavirus.

In the world of work, many changes happen abruptly, causing consequences for those who work and for customers and users of products and services provided by different companies and institutions. If, on one hand, sanitary measures were necessary, like closing work places and continuing production virtually, on the other, many professional actions needed to continue happening on sites, like industries and some essential activities, like hospitals and other health services.

This scenario also impacted the university environment, causing consequences for the work of teachers, researchers, administrative teams, as well as the educational activities of the students themselves. For most Universities, the possibility of face-to-face work has become unviable, both in classrooms or other learning environments (laboratories, collaborative spaces, etc.) for the case of teachers and students, and in offices for administrative and teaching teams. It was necessary to make use of communication

N. L. Black et al. (Eds.): IEA 2021, LNNS 219, pp. 296–301, 2021.
https://doi.org/10.1007/978-3-030-74602-5_43

technologies, through the increased use of virtual rooms for synchronous (live) classes and meetings.

This abrupt change, in addition to the threat of the pandemic itself, had many consequences in terms of how to develop working activities and had to be rapidly incorporated by everyone who kept working. However, not everyone was prepared to continue their work routines in this new format, in addition to all the challenges of the most different orders: the need to work at home in contact with the family, specially with children that couldn't go to school, as well as others who had their own working tasks (Guérin et al. 2001); the need for equipment and guaranteed access to good internet and adequate working stations and places.

Without intending to be an exhaustive study, this article systematizes the results of testimonies from different actors in the university environment regarding the impacts caused by this new scenario, especially for people's work and studies. These results were analyzed, considering mainly the relationship between mental health and work, as well as the impact on the mental health of these people from the theoretical framework of activity ergonomics and psychodynamics at work. The results show different consequences in terms of quality of each one's performance and also related to anguishing situations, especially in regard to isolation (Dejours 2018) (Muller 2018).

2   Theoretical References

Discussing the effects of COVID 19 on work requires first highlight the understanding of work and its relationship to mental health.

This first statement regards the fact that, when dealing with work, we do not refer only to an employment relationship, and also we don't consider work as a mere occupation. Work, in the sense of action, refers to what is "alive", to what is added by people in a production system (of goods or services) in order to guarantee that the production actually happens. Work is giving from oneself so that the objectives of production are achieved; objectives related to each one and also in terms the collective and the organizational goals.

Living Work is eminently human action; it's not related to machines or mechanical and computerized systems functioning. It is about what is "alive" in the production, since those who work, in fact everyone, are protagonists of their life, of their work (Sznelwar 2015). For this reason, it is essential to highlight that the experience of working (live work) cannot be confused with a mere "execution" of what is foreseen and provided by the procedures (Hubault, Bourgeois 2016). Even, because production doesn't happens adequately in reality if people don't translate what is considered in the prescription (task) into working activities. When acting only according to the procedure, an action known as "standard operation" or "strike of the zeal", the production results are not obtained satisfactorily. In order to overcome these challenges, the subject needs to find his way of doing things, his ways of circumventing the difficulties and variability found in contact with materials, with machines, with tools, with processes, with customers, with time that is allocated to perform (Abrahão et al. 2009; Daniellou, Rabardel 2005).

Thus, working towards the development of mastery, skills and competence is linked to how subjects acquire a certain mastery over things. In other words, the possibility of personal development, included in some professional universe, is dynamic and needs to be taken care of and always replenished. In other words, from doing it's possible incorporate new knowledge and skills (Brunoro 2013) (Bolis et al. 2014).

Remember that the activity of one depends on the work of others; there is no isolated work. Nothing is done alone, all work is done with others and for others; all work is addressed to someone, to the other (Dejours 2012). This reinforces the importance of knowing that, even though it is experienced individually, lived and incorporated; work is an experience that constitutes the collective (Dejours et al. 2018). There is no human without the collective, without the relational. Unfortunately, the dissemination of desolate scenarios in organizations is a fact enhanced by the processes of individualization of work, the demobilization of collectives and the relentless pursuit of overcoming others and oneself since organizational models based on competition have become prevalent in many areas of our economy. The significant amount of sick-leaves to work-related mental disorders is one of its undeniable consequences, especially in terms of individual performance assessment. We reinforce the view that nothing is neutral in the world of production and work.

Work, which is central to everyone's life, provides conditions for the development of each one's subjectivity, for the consolidation of collectives, for the enrichment of subjectivity, in short, a process aimed at professional growth, health construction and the realization of oneself (Sznelwar, Hubault 2015).

Building paths towards the emancipation of subjects and collectives should be the objective of working and of production systems (Dejours 2012). Otherwise, if the human being is treated by other human beings who have the power of decision in companies and institutions as a "thing" (Honneth 2008), we are facing a favorable scenario for the emergence of pathogenic suffering and, consequently, to the appearance of high levels of absenteeism, turnover, disorders, diseases and accidents. In short, a desolate, mortified scenario, where survival depends on psychical defensive mechanisms to face this suffering (Dejours Dejours 1986; Molinier 2013).

3   Method

In order to carry out this study, some testimonies of different actors from the university environment were collected throughout the pandemic period in 2020, especially from the Engineering courses at the University of São Paulo. Contributed to this study: teachers, undergraduate and graduate students, administrative professionals.

The collection of these testimonies was carried out according to people's interest in contributing to the study from a semi-structured questionnaire. The guiding question of this script for the testimony was: **How is your experience as a professional/student related to this pandemic period? What are the main impacts for your work/learning activities?**

The collected testimonies were analyzed in the light of the ergonomics of the activity and the psychodynamics of work, with special attention to the relationships between work and mental health, as well as the impacts on the subjectivity of those who responded to the questionnaires and those who participated at different virtual meetings organized to present and discuss the results. The elements that emerged in the testimonies were categorized and grouped in different categories.

4   Results and Discussion

4.1   Time

The personal relation with time during the pandemic is different since it brought a perspective that we always try to postpone or anesthetize as much as possible, the proximity and fear of death. The relationship with time has changed, what was previously regulated in a certain way by the routines of our daily lives, collapsed. Even for those where the impact did not result in isolation or radical changes in their work, there was a disorder in the chain of their activities.

It is important to reflect on the subjectivity of time, since it is not exclusively about measured time, but about lived time. The impression that everything has become more intense, that the transit times between one activity and another have been reduced to something practically non-existent, or have been extended, as for many of those who depend on public transport to work, are significant issues. How many do not know exactly what day it is today, how many forget to do things because they are in a kind of "cloud", where apparently time is suspended. Will there be repercussions, both at individual and collective levels, regarding this drastic change in the relationship with time? Especially because they are multiple activities that touch, intertwine, with many interruptions and lack of control over different variables.

4.2   Space

Something significant has also changed with regard to space, especially those who stayed at home. What was previously related in a continuity, was broken. What is outside of my shelter has become a threat, it is not a focus on social violence, but on an invisible and very overwhelming threat, a virus. Being practically restricted to the domestic space, has and will have an impact on our subjectivity still little known. Living with people close to you, when you're not alone, has become something that, in space and time, has also been exacerbated. Those who live with many people in small spaces, in addition to the risks of transmitting the disease and, often, the precarious living conditions, have to live 24/7 with the same people, loved or less loved. This also has its risks, there are also signs of an increase in domestic violence, especially against women.

There is another issue related to the domestic space as a working space and it concerns the conditions for working. Thinking about adaptable jobs, including different aspects, including lighting is a big challenge. How to do this, who is responsible for working conditions, is the employer? People themselves?

We have been working at home for a long time, remembering the case of factions in the textile industry, work in agriculture where the border between domestic and work is not very evident, as well as other professions, where part of the work is done at home, like that of teachers. It should also be noted the existence, in many countries, of dangerous activities developed in the domestic space, including what is done at the bottom of the yard; an example is micro smelting.

The space is different, even if we manage to have windows to the world, when we use electronic media to contact loved ones, to work, to browse what is available to access.

4.3 What Changes

First, as a reflection - Work, considered as a regulated, constrained activity, requiring mastery and accumulated knowledge, ceases to be, at least in part, at that moment.

Second, when we talk about work, we always need to refer to what work. Even though there was more or less exacerbated disorder for all, inequalities in relation to work have not been reduced. It would not be a surprise if we note that they have intensified, deepened. This concerns not only the loss of work and entrepreneurial activities, but also issues that can be dealt with in the precarious universe. We cannot fail to see what is evident, which are the working conditions of couriers, which are currently in great demand. The signs of greater precariousness in his work are becoming increasingly evident, including a reduction in the value of the unit of his work.

5 Conclusion

The word uncertainty hangs in the air; we do not know what to do, how to do it, if we have changed something in hierarchical relationships, if we have appropriated the modes of production in another way, if there is a greater expropriation of the modes of production, if the experiences and knowledge are shared, or still other ways of working are emerging? Actually we don't know! What the results of this study shows are related to the difficulties to dealt of uncertainty, loosing certainty was one of the main consequences. Another aspect, related to the dismantling of routines and the difficulty in developing possible short-term scenarios, obliged the protagonists to review procedures constantly due not only to the changing scenarios, but also to deal with new protocols and procedures. This also means the issue of loss of mastery and the need to take ownership of new know-how without the time needed to obtain mastery. Living and working isolate and the fear related to the risk of death was also one of the main issues. Many things taken for granted and immutable become fluid and questionable.

If this is a situation affording suffering, *on the other hand, this is an opportunity!*

There is an evident risk of an increase in work-related mental health problems; otherwise there is an opportunity for deeper reflections on work and its importance for human development. What is the content and the possibilities afforded by work to develop and enrich subjectivities? Another perspective that we should find against is the possibility to go even deeper into defensive, alienating mechanisms for denying suffering.

References

Abrahão, J.I., Sznelwar, L.I., Silvino, A., Sarmet, M., Pinho, D.: Introdução à Ergonomia: Da prática à teoria. Blücher, São Paulo (2009)
Bolis, I., Brunoro, C.M., Sznelwar, L.I.: Mapping the relationships between work and sustainability and the opportunities for ergonomic action. Appl. Ergon. **45**, 1225–1239 (2014)
Brunoro, C.M.: Trabalho e Sustentabilidade: contribuições da ergonomia da atividade e da psicodinâmica do trabalho. In: 2013 Tese (Doutorado) – Universidade de São Paulo, São Paulo (2013)

Daniellou, F., Rabardel, P.: Activity-oriented approaches to ergonomics: some traditions and communities. Theor. Issues Ergon. Sci. **6**(5), 353–357 (2005)

Dejours, C.: Por um novo conceito de saúde. Revista Brasileira de Saúde Ocupacional **14**(54) (1986)

Dejours, C.: Avaliação do trabalho submetida à prova do real: crítica aos fundamentos da avaliação. Blücher, São Paulo (2008)

Dejours, C.: Trabalho vivo: trabalho e emancipação. tomo 2. Paralelo 15, Brasília (2012)

Dejours, C., Deranty, J.P., Renault, E., Smith, N.H.: The return of work in critical theory: self, society, politics. Columbia University Press (2018)

Guérin, F., Laville, A., Daniellou, F., Duraffourg, J., Kerguelen, A.: Compreender o trabalho para transformá-lo. A prática da ergonomia. Blücher, São Paulo (2001)

Honneth, A.: Observações sobre a reificação. Civitas-Revista de Ciências Sociais **8**(1) (2008)

Hubault, F., Bourgeois, F.: A atividade, recurso para o desenvolvimento da organização do trabalho. In : Ergonomia Construtiva. São Paulo, Editora Blücher, pp. 127–144 (2016)

Molinier, P.: O trabalho e a psique – uma introdução à psicodinâmica do trabalho. Paralelo 15, Brasília (2013)

Muller, J.Z.: The Tyranny of Metrics. Princeton University Press, Princeton (2018)

Sznelwar, L.I.: Quando trabalhar é ser protagonista e o protagonismo do trabalho. Blücher, São Paulo (2015)

Sznelwar, L.I., Hubault, F.: Subjectivity in ergonomics: a new start to the dialogue regarding the psychodynamics of work. Production **25**, 354–361 (2015)

Does the Sense of Work Make Sense? Some Issues Related to the Future of Work in the Light of Psychodynamics of Work

Laerte Idal Sznelwar[1]([⊠]) and Seiji Uchida[2]

[1] Departamento de Engenharia de Produção da Escola Politécnica da Universidade de São Paulo, São Paulo, Brazil
laertesz@usp.br
[2] Instituto Trabalhar, São Paulo, Brazil

Abstract. The main proposal of this paper is to discuss questions related to the work of nursing assistants in two different hospitals in Brazil using as a key reference the concepts and methods related to Psychodynamics of Work. Work in caring situations, a typical service relation is, in many situations, treated in a similar rationality as an industry, based on teleological purposes. In fact, this kind of work is not only related to the technical aspects of the professions involved, since it's meaning is related to compassion and it's quality depends of cooperation among different actors, including the patient and his family. The results published on this paper are related to what nursing assistants that participated on our study testimony in relation with their working experience.

Keywords: Psychic health · Sense · Future of work · Psychodynamics of work

1 Introduction

Imagine a scenario where what was planned went down the drain; imagine a scenario where a significant part of professional competences are questioned; imagine a scenario where it is necessary to change the way of doing in a radical way; imagine a scenario where contact with others becomes virtual; imagine a scenario where time and space dedicated to work became fluid. Imagine?

The situation, experienced by many workers, belonging to the most different professional categories is very delicate. In addition to the precarious processes of work relationships and the constant threats arising from the automation processes and data sciences where it is propagated that, in the future, work will be restricted to few and elite professional categories, there was the advent of the COVID-19 pandemic; these disturbing facts question, even more, the importance and centrality of work for the constitution of subjects, collectives, organizations and even society as well. In the field of psychic health and the approach related to psychodynamics of work, there are significant signs of the emergence of pathogenic suffering, which not only relate to individualized and individualizing ways of evaluating performance, but also with respect to fear about the future and continuity. Subject's existence as professionals, as someone contributing to the production of goods and services and to the development of society is questioned (Hubault, Bourgeois 2001) (Hubault 2011).

2 Research Objective/Question

One of the key issues that we propose to discuss is related to the subjects' life itinerary and what work provides as a potential for their development, as well as that of the professions themselves. Our position is that any work that does not allow professional development, constant learning and recognition of the usefulness and beauty of doing is opposed to human needs in the pursuit of health and self-realization; it is therefore an existential damage. Epistemophilia, considered by Freud as inherent to the human, due to its incompleteness, vulnerability and fragility, is one of our properties that needs to be treated with care, to be welcomed; so that everyone can develop their abilities as fully as possible, aiming at building a more just, inclusive and favorable society for the development of culture. Therefore, it is essential that tasks should be designed in a way that allows workers to build a successful path in a particular professional field. For these reasons, we defend the thesis that Taylorism and Fordism, even if considered as overcome by many, are still strongly present in our minds. Considering as trivial and natural the division of labor that leads to the fragmentation of production processes into small, meaningless tasks that do not allow a career development is one of the consequences of this process of naturalizing political choices made in history.

3 Methodology

The results presented on this paper are related to two different studies made with nursing teams, specifically with nursing assistants in public hospitals in São Paulo, Brazil. The method used is based on the psychodynamics of work's approach and different groups were organized in order to provide a space for the professionals to talk about their living experiences at work. The proposal for the participants was to freely talk about their work, about their professions and what they would like to testimony about their working experiences at the hospital. In one of the studies it was possible to organize five different meetings, the last one was organized to validate the rapport made by the researchers. The other study was conducted as a focus group because the participants didn't have more time in their agenda. A session to validate was conducted virtually.

4 Results

The results will be presented partially as a synthesis, because the rapports are very long. We've chosen to present them answering to the question: "What it means to be a nursing assistant":

..... is to like what you do, to take care of old people, adults, youths, child and babies. It means looking at work differently, knowing that having this job is good and rewarding. To know that this profession is a kind of priesthood that requires dedication and humanity.

..... is to suffer and endure the death of patients.

.... means taking care of a variety of patients with their respective problems. Knowing how to deal with the elderly with their attachments and dependence; with babies who do not speak where it is necessary to guess and feel for them, with children who demand time and attention and so on.

... is to deal with the patients' companions (husband, wife, relatives, friends, etc.) and play different the roles, like providing psychological, social and spiritual support.

... it means also recognizing personal limits, as when experiencing unbearable suffering in the care of certain patients in a certain type of hospital unit.

... is to have tacitly the desire that the care provided cures the patient. But in reality there is an intense awareness that care is not enough, that it does not prevent death, does not prevent chronic problems, does not prevent sudden falls in the curing process, etc.

... is to develop skills that often remain hidden from the eyes of others colleagues at the hospital. It is taking the risk of seeing these skills seen as personal characteristics and not as the know-how of this activity. It is even being questioned when exercising this knowledge and keeping silent when another professional disqualifies their knowledge.

... it is also having the possibility of being recognized by the family of the patients like when someone testimony that they took care of someone very well. This kind of recognition is very important.

... it's also dealing with the possibility of patients' death. What to do when you have a closed diagnosis that a patient will die? How to be prepared to receive news of death when it comes by surprise? It's complicated to deal with losses.

... is to put themselves in the patient's and companions' place and see how they would like to be treated and cared for. To have compassion on them, to suffer with them and better understand their feelings.

.... is to be a a reference for patients, to participate in their day to day, in their history and in their life. Being a reference means being the person that patients turn to because they need support. At the same time, being a nursing assistant is having to deal with the anguished, distressed and intense request to clarify the sick condition of the patient, often terminal. In fact they have restrictions, they cannot speak about many thinks related to the situation, as it is the competence of the doctor.

.... is learning to deal with the other's body in the most profound intimacy. It means overcoming, in addition to the modesty, shame and resistance of the patient to see his body being stripped, overcoming his difficulty in exposing the sick body (ugly, smelly, uncontrolled, full of marks and signs, etc.).

... is often experiencing the feeling that no matter how much you do, there is always something to do.

.... is seeking to ensure that what the patient asks for will be attended to. It's trying to meet and solve the demand immediately while in the patient room, because when he leaves, he "forgets" the patient in the previous room to dedicate himself entirely of the next patient.

.... is having to constantly experience the pressure of the responsibility of never making mistakes. Doing everything right all the time, it is never being able to disconnect, because they deal with many details.

... is working together with different colleagues, doing thinks to help others when they need and receiving their support in order to do a better work and effectively help patients.

... is also prepare to get sick. It means preparing to be cared for, being dependent on others. It means also to fear the risks of not being treated as well as they treat their patients. And to be painfully aware of everything that lies ahead when you get sick, because they already know how it all ends. Being patient is not easy.

5 Discussion

From the results obtained in those two studies based on an approach inspired psychodynamics of work, some questions emerge related to the work of care in a hospital. Dealing with professional experience it's far more complex (Morin 2007) than we could expect if we cope with a more instrumental approach.

The implementation of the ideas related to the New Public Management in hospitals is one of scenarios considered in our studies (Alonso et al. 2015). Suffering and the life of different protagonists (Sznelwar 2015) in production are still not enough known by managers in those institutions. One of the very strong indications is related to the fact that it is considered that the professional career must have a development that is reflected in a vertical rise, that is, in the fact of becoming a chief, a leader or even a manager. This is nonsense, since professional development is much more anchored in learning, in the development of skills and know-how that are constituted when work situations are favorable. Developing does not mean becoming a leader, but a better professional, more capable of acting. Another main question that is relate do the fact that in those groups is related to cooperation (Hubault 2017) with colleagues; if work organization is conceived without a team constitution it becomes even hard to work as nursing assistant. The constitution of a profession depends on the possibility of being part of a certain collective based on more or less stable rules. This contribution of each worker to the enrichment of the profession reinforces the identity of each one and is fundamental in the realization of oneself and in the search for health. According to Dejours, a path towards emancipation can be followed through the effective participation of subjects in organizations that encourage rather than discourage cooperation, enabling individuals to participate in deliberation processes related to how their work can be constantly transformed and organized (Dejours 2012).

People guide their actions through the formation of meaning and beliefs, and it's related to the enrichment of subjectivity (Böhle, Milkau 1998). This is in contradiction the typical instrumental rationality and corresponds to different rationalities, like the *pathic* point of view, based on psychoanalytic' concepts. In this perspective, according to Dejours it is not possible to measure work because work is related to the individual's subjective experience (Dejours 2011) For this author, given the impossibility of measuring the work, it is common to translate it into a measure of working time and understand - erroneously - that through this measurement the work will be evaluated (Dejours 2003).

It is important to emphasize that the measurement of time explains the duration of the activity and not its intensity, effort, quality and the real content of the work, in addition to not consider the immaterial values of caring services, such as trust, cooperation and pertinence is a great source of misunderstanding on organizations, specially in hospitals. In other words, the choices of management highlights the lack of recognition caring work of the nursing assistants, especially with regard to what is not described in the tasks of patient care, which leads to a conflict when the organization considers care as a mere execution, typical of a reification process.

6   Conclusions

The proposal of those studies, a kind of action research (Coughlan, Coghlan 2002) was to afford to the participants the possibility to appropriate the meaning of their work, an action that is based on a different kind of dialogue, were for each one it was possible to talk about their experience, to listen to others and to build something in common. It was a possibility to contribute by developing discussions related to something central in their liver, the meaning of their work. This is a proposal whit the principal aim to allows professionals to face challenges that stimulate our intelligence, ingenuity, sensitivity, ability, skill, knowledge, feelings, in a word an activity that mobilizes our being, specially compassion when thinking about nursing activities (Molinier 2000). According to the Psychodynamics of Work, professional actions in their real dimension is understandable only if we apprehend the effort invested by the subject when this one carries out this work in unforeseen, adverse conditions, full of obstacles and non-prescribed situations. And to the extent that the contribution of the nursing team can be recognized; in terms of how caring work is useful and aesthetically beautiful.

Thinking about the future of work and whether there will be work in the future has an important relationship with the meaning of work. Discussing the question of meaning requires, at least in part, a look at the past, at least what happened in the 20th century, where, as already said, the dominant ideology was based on a disaggregation of what would be working. From a vision focused on movement and energy expenditure, one of the foundations of taylorism, the question of intelligence at work was partially integrated, mainly in some types of activity considered to be less sensible to very restrictive procedures and, more recently, the issue of subjects' engagement. All of these processes, which we consider to be different waves of how to manage people at work, are based on reifying ideas, disaggregated from what people effectively would have a potential for being, specially regarding an emancipative perspective (Dejours 2012). From the point of view from which we are seeing the issue of work, in the fundamental case for the subjects in relation to their incompleteness and their desires, it helps us to better think about the meaning and the future of the human and his work.

References

Alonso, J.M., Clifton, J., Díaz-Fuentes, D.: The impact of New Public Management on efficiency: an analysis of Madrid's hospitals. Health Policy **119**(3), 333–340 (2015)

Böhle, F., Milkau, B.: De la manivelle à l'écran. L'évolution de l'expérience sensible dês ouvriers lors des changements technologiques, coleçäo DER d'EDF, Eyrolles, Paris (1998)

Coughlan, P., Coghlan, D.: Action research for operations management. Int. J Oper. Prod. Manag. **22**(2), 220–240 (2002)

Dejours, C.: L'évaluation du travail à l'épreuve du reel. INRA Editions, Paris (2003)

Dejours, C.: Para uma clínica da mediação entre psicanálise e política: A psicodinâmica do trabalho. In: Lancman, S., Sznelwar, L.I. (orgs.) Christophe Dejours: da psicopatologia à psicodinâmica do trabalho. 3.ed. Brasília: Paralelo 15; Rio de Janeiro (2011)

Dejours, C.: Trabalho e emancipação (Trabalho Vivo, tomo II). Paralelo 15, Brasília (2012)

Hubault, F.: Os desafios relacionados à mobilização da subjetividade na relação de serviço. In: Sznelwar, L.I. (org.) Saúde dos bancários. Publisher São Paulo (2011)

Hubault, F.: Corps, activité, espace – nouvelles interpellations de l'économie dématérialisée. In: Hubault F. (coord.). Les espaces du travail ; enjeux savoirs, pratiques – actes du séminaire Paris1. Editions Octarès Toulouse, pp. 3–12 (2017)

Hubault, F., Bourgeois, F.: La relation de service: une convocation nouvelle pour l'ergonomie? In: Hubault, F., La relation de service, opportunités et questions nouvelles pour l'ergonomie, pp. 5–32, Octares Editions, Pais (2001)

Molinier, P.: Travail et compassion dans le monde hospitalier. In: Relation de service: regards croisés. Cahiers du Genre (28), pp. 49–70, L'Hamattan, Paris (2000)

Morin, E.: Restricted complexity, general complexity. In: Gershenson, C., Aerts, D., Edmonds, B. (eds.) Worldviews, science and us: Philosophy and complexity, pp. 5–29. Singapore, World Scientific (2007)

Sznelwar, L.I.: Quando Trabalhar é ser Protagonista e o Protagonismo no Trabalho. Blucher, São Paulo (2015)

When Autonomy Fails: The Fallback Pilot Paradox and an Innovative Solution to Unlock Human Intervention into Autonomous Systems

Felipe M. S. Turetta[1,2(✉)], Francisco Lima[2], and Rodrigo Ribeiro[2]

[1] EMBRAER Center of Engineering and Technology, Belo Horizonte, MG, Brazil
felipe.turetta@embraer.com.br
[2] UFMG – Universidade Federal de Minas Gerais, Belo Horizonte, MG, Brazil

Abstract. Fully autonomous systems without any human interventions are not achievable in practice, but one day the levels of autonomy will probably high enough so the system will be considered autonomous for "practical reasons" and the pilots will only intervene very rarely. This will deepen a problem that is already present in current automatic systems, the "out of the loop pilot syndrome". This paper explores, the paradox of a "pilot for an autonomous system" and how he can build any situation awareness, showing that SA level 2 might be the key for unlocking interventions. It shows also the current conventional solutions for human machine interface design, and proposes a new type of HMI, called Parallel synthetic task.

Keywords: Autonomous systems · Situation awareness · Human-Machine-Interface

1 Introduction

The ideal of fully autonomous systems has been in the horizon for some decades but regardless of the efforts from the industry and academia some barriers proved too hard for computers to trespass. Recent advancements in software (e.g. deep learning and convolutional neural networks) and hardware (e.g. LIDAR), however, appears to be able to cope with some of those barriers and the hopes of full autonomy are renewed in the scientific community.

That said, given the experience from many decades, most technology roadmaps are more cautious than they were in the past and most of them foresee a period for "technological maturing" where the system, although capable of full autonomy, will still be monitored by a human, so confidence can be gained in the design. In the aviation and urban air mobility market, this human monitor is usually referred as a "fallback pilot".

This situation reminds us of an old problem between ergonomists stated back in 1983 by Bainbridge in her paper "Ironies of automation": "By removing the easier parts of one's task, automation can make the difficult parts even more difficult". Then one

N. L. Black et al. (Eds.): IEA 2021, LNNS 219, pp. 308–315, 2021.
https://doi.org/10.1007/978-3-030-74602-5_45

could argue by extrapolation that the fallback pilot task is "impossible", since all the tasks have been removed from him.

Endsley's theory of situation awareness [6] appears to support this extrapolation. She defines situation awareness as *'being aware of what is happening around you and understanding what that information means to you now and in the future'*. Thus, situation awareness is a critical resource to monitor the system, decide if its behavior is correct and intervene if necessary. She also states that in order to build adequate situation awareness the user needs to be in the loop, something that is quite difficult (if not impossible) to attain if the system operates autonomously within a black box. This brings us to what we call "the fallback pilot paradox": It is impossible for someone to monitor and intervene successfully in the operation of an autonomous system (at all times), simply because he is out of the loop in practice and in principle.

Still the industry is not aiming for perfection, but for an improvement over the current situation, and that may be achievable if we use the technologies and expertise built over the last decades adequately. Designers may resort to conventional solutions to the paradox, but new technologies may have enabled new and unconventional solutions. This paper aims to discuss the nature of the problem and outline some of the conventional approaches to deal with this paradox, but also to propose a new kind of solution that is entitled as Parallel Synthetic Task interface.

2   The Paradox of an Autonomous System Pilot

In this section, we will define an autonomous system, present an overview of situation awareness theory and then elaborate on why the fallback pilot task is so challenging (Table 1).

Table 1. Sheridan and Verplank's 10 levels of automation [10].

Level	Description of Interaction
1	Human does the whole job up to the point of turning it over to the computer to implement
2	Computer helps by determining the options
3	Computer helps determine the options and suggests one, which human does not need to follow
4	Computer selects action and human may or may not do it
5	Computer selects action and implements it if human approves
6	Computer selects action, informs human in plenty of time to stop it
7	Computer does whole job and necessarily tells human what it did
8	Computer does whole job and tells human what it did only if human explicitly asks
9	Computer does whole job and tells human what it did and it, the computer, decides what should be told
10	Computer does whole job if it decides it should be done, and if so tells human, if it decides it should be told

2.1 Autonomous Systems

The concept of autonomy is a tricky one, and the authors believe that it is actually not a good term to be used for artificial systems [4, 5]. Still it is the term that the industry is currently using. It is necessary to define that for the purpose of this paper (and spread out in the industry), the term automatic (or automated) refers to the capability of performing a predefined routine, while the term, autonomy refers to the added capability of sensing and measuring the environment, performing some kind of decision making and applying changes to that routine. Several scholars and entities have defined the concept of "levels of autonomy", showing the increasing participation of the machine not only in taking the actions (like in automatic systems), but also in decision-making. In the academy the most famous scale it is probably the 10 levels of autonomy first described by Sheridan and Verplank in 1978 as levels of automation (since this automation/autonomy division was not clear at the time), but today commonly associated with autonomy.

For the purpose of this analysis, the fallback pilot paradox effectively starts at Sheridan's level 6. This is the turning points from automation to autonomy (even though this is a complex gray area) and it is where the fallback pilot paradox starts to get worse than a traditional man-machine interface.

2.2 Situation Awareness and Decision Making

The term "Situation Awareness" (SA) is largely used in safety critical industries and it is recognized as a critical resource for the decision-making process. For Endsley et al. the formation of situation awareness occurs in three basic steps that she calls SA Levels. The first level is the perception of the elements in the environment, for a combat pilot this would be the perception of another aircraft obtained by direct visual contact, through a radar monitor etc. The second level is the comprehension of the situation, or the ability to merge the information obtained in level one SA into a meaningful context. In the combat situation level 2 SA would allow the pilot to know if the other aircraft is an enemy and potentially engaged in intercepting him. Level 3 SA is the ability to project future status of the situation. In order to attain that in addition to having a well-formed level 2 SA, the person needs to have a good knowledge of the system dynamics in order to be able to consider time into the evolution of the situation. In our combat pilot example, with level 3 SA he would be able to perceive if the enemy will be able to intercept him, and approximately how long it would take depending on his own courses of action.

The link between SA and decision-making can be illustrated by using a model created by military strategist John Boyd in 1975 [8] called the OODA loop. It consists in a feedback loop with the Observe-Orient-Decide-Act phases. Those phases can be nested with Endley's three levels of SA to form the model depicted in Fig. 1.

Notice that in addition to the nested model a yellow path has been included to illustrate an expert operator capability. According to the phenomenological stream ergonomists [11] and philosophers [5] humans have the capability of intuitive expertise, where they can trigger a response to an event directly after a stimulus and understanding, without conscious information processing. The flow in yellow cannot be mimicked by any computer system by principle due to its lack of understanding. This is why SA level 2 appears to be the point where the fallback pilot should focus his attention the most.

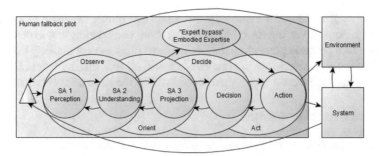

Fig. 1. Adapted Nested OODA-SA model with an expert bypass.

2.3 The Fallback Pilot Paradox

With this initial definition, it is possible to postulate the fallback pilot paradox:

1. An autonomous system cannot be relied to effectively alert a fallback pilot if the need for intervention arises;
2. A fallback pilot cannot effectively build the necessary situation awareness to decide when to intervene, and if he can, the system is not autonomous.

The first part of the paradox is an application of Gödel's incompleteness theorem [13] in this situation. Any system design is made with the goal of being complete (considering all foreseeable situations) and consistent (not contradicting itself). Unfortunately, Gödel's theorem states that an axiomatic or rule-based system (such as a software) cannot demonstrate its own consistency. In other words, monitoring cannot be done solely by alerts issued by the system itself, as they are bound to be incomplete. Of course, there will be failure scenarios where a suitable alerting can be designed, but not for all the possible, future scenarios. Those other scenarios need to be monitored or anticipated by an element outside the system (the fallback pilot). That is why current aircraft Autoland systems and cars auto steer systems, require pilots to maintain hands on the controls and alertness of the environment so that they can intervene quickly if required. This may work well on auto lands, since an aircraft landing is a rather short period, but is a considerable issue for long drives. This is when the second part of the paradox comes into place.

The second part is the consolidation of our current knowledge on situation awareness and complex systems. Adequate situation awareness cannot be built because in order to make future projections of the system behavior (level 3 SA) the fallback needs considerable knowledge of the system's dynamics and the current, ongoing context. In order to have that, he or she needs considerable training, operational experience and situated understanding. To obtain this situated understanding (level 2 SA) he needs to actively monitor the system and environment (level 1 SA). The problem is that with an autonomous system, fallback pilots are almost never performing the tasks thus, their expertise can be said to be always incomplete. Several theories of learning could be cited to support this statement; Engeström et al. [7] would say the "boundary crossing" would never be made, or Vygotsky [12] would state that the learned meaning would never become a lived meaning. In other words, the fallback pilot's expertise would always be one of school, never one of practice. In addition, considering that experience is a prerequisite for properly perceiving the environment [9], it is very unlikely that the fallback pilot would be able to attain even level 1 SA in an abnormal situation. Even if the knowledge and skill were present, there would still be the issue of dynamic coping.

3   Conventional Solutions

As discussed previously it is hard to draw a clear line in order to state if an autonomous vehicle with a fallback pilot is ontologically different from, for example, a modern aircraft with several automated features. If it is, probably the same design strategies will work well (maybe with a higher dose). If it is not, it is still worth analyzing the best practices currently available to deal with automated systems.

Endsley et al. [6] lists 50 principles for a user centered design, thoroughly addressing human factors issues in the design of complex systems. It is interesting to notice that most of them remain applicable to the autonomy scenario, only a few contradictions that arise mainly from the nature of this scenario. For example, one of the principles is "Automate only if necessary", but even though a human could perform some tasks better, full autonomy is the designers' goal and the "added value" for some systems (like autonomous cars). When (and if) technology eventually enables an equivalent level of safety there is no reason for not automating in those cases, something that might be different on other applications like nuclear power plants and maybe even airliners.

Since the issue at our hands is the one of recognizing the need for an intervention, and being able to intervene successfully into an autonomous system, we will review the principles that most affect it.

"Taking advantage of parallel processing capabilities" is an example as the design for both autonomy and automatic systems should leverage on the human capability use different senses jointly such as sight and hearing. "Make critical cues for schema activation salient" and "Use information filtering carefully" also have an increased importance in the autonomy scenario, since it leaves the pilot out of the loop.

The entire category of "Certainty principles" deals with sensor reliability, missing information and composite data. It is critical that the fallback pilot has a clear awareness of this kind of information, since due to the lack of understanding and meaning; machines are quite susceptible to bad decisions under unreliable data. The Air France 447 accident [2] is a good example of what an automated system can do when it receives unreliable data. In situations like this one it is the fallback pilot responsibility to identify the unreliable source and take appropriate action, as the system does not know "what makes sense or does not" [6, 13].

"Providing transparency and observability" and "Mapping system function to mental models of users" are essential to allow the fallback pilot to understand the modes and operate at a higher level of abstraction than the system itself, which is the only way he will be able to spot situations that the system is unable to handle. This higher level of abstraction is what Endsley calls "global SA". The fallback must not only understand the premises and limitations of the system, but also have the tools and indications to identify when one of those limitations is about to cause a failure. This also relates to the principle "Make modes and system states salient".

Alarm design is perhaps the most interesting category for our discussion. "Don't make people rely on alarms - provide projection support" is at the heart of the fallback paradox, since if a perfect alarm system could be designed (as explained in the second part of the paradox through Gödel's theorem), then the modes of failure it is foreseeing could be treated further to make the system resilient to it. This is not possible and there will always be "unknown unknowns", and thus the fallback pilot must be able to diagnose the system at a higher level (just as meta-mathematics is for mathematics) than just "relying" on the alarm. This resonates with principle "Support the assessment and diagnosis of multiple alarms", as a multiple failure event may easily indicate a design error, or a low probability event for which the system is not prepared. However, maybe the most interesting discussion is over principles "Reduce false alarms", "Set missed alarm and false alarm trade-offs appropriately" and "Minimize alarm disruptions to ongoing activities". On an automated system it is usually the norm to try to balance the rate of false to missed alarms (see Fig. 2), as false alarms cause system trust problems increasing the response time (as pilots starts seeking to confirm the alarm by many other means or even ignore it) and missed alarms are a hazard by itself.

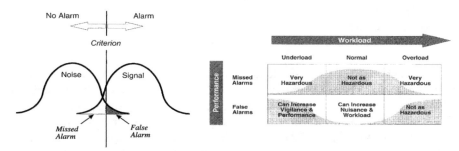

Fig. 2. Left: Missed x False Alarms tradeoff [6]: page 153]. Right: Missed x False Alarms effect on performance at different workload levels [6]: page 158]

On an automated system, adding workload to the equation complicates the issue further as can be seen in Fig. 2(right). This is because the workload level usually varies considerably during the operation (for example in a typical flight workload is higher during takeoff and landing than it is during cruise). Fortunately, adding workload appears to be less of a problem for the fallback pilot of an autonomous system, as the workload is expected to be low throughout the entire operation. This suggests that for this kind of operation it may be suitable to favor false alarms considerably in order to have near zero missed alarms, while still using the false alarms to increase vigilance and performance. However, maybe there is an even better way to use this effect, by combining it with the principle "Provide SA support rather than decisions".

4   An Innovative Solution: Parallel Synthetic Task

As discussed previously, false alarms can be used to increase vigilance and performance during low workload situation, but with the drawbacks of creating distrust in the system and increasing response time when a true alarm occurs. But what if it is possible to create a mechanism that could have those advantages without the drawbacks? If an interface could be created to engage the pilot in monitoring tasks without confusing the pilot in real alarm situations? This interface could not be labeled as an alarm, as per the definition of the word it is directly linked to a hazard. It is also not a monitor, since its use implies a somehow passive behavior. We need something that is active and can engage the fallback into the situation so that he is in the loop and able to intervene if required, thus it is a "Task". We also do not want that he directly executes the "real task", as this is up to the autonomous system, we want something that really "Provides SA support rather than decisions", and enables intervention if required. Thus, it occurs in "parallel" with real task and it is not itself; thus it is artificial or "synthetic". This new kind of HMI is called Parallel Synthetic Task (PST).

It should be designed to have the following characteristics:

1. Salient system and environment relationships in order to enable the fallback pilot to build the SA required for monitoring the system
2. Not increase workload to prohibitive levels or create an increase in response time to real task demands
3. Not create false perceptions
4. Not allow tunneling into the PST and leaving the real task unattended.

An example of a PST for an autonomous car would be confirming obstacles on the road, already tagged in augmented reality by the system. In some situations, the driver would tag the obstacle first, on others the computer. This would engage the fallback in active monitoring and the information could create new alarms. Of course, in this case, the PST would remove part of the "added value" of autonomous system, but this could be used during the test phase of the system. Another example could be asking the pilot of an airliner, the maximum difference between the airspeed in the three indicators. This appears to be more effective than just asking to "Check Airspeed", as the calculation will definitely engage the pilot's attention and salient any abnormal difference. Still those are only simple examples and actual implementations will need considerable case-by-case engineering.

In some operational scenarios at vehicles or automated industrial units, operators develop strategies denominated "functional games", that allows them to maintain an alertness level to intervene when required [3]. Studies with simulators reproducing vehicles with SAE autonomy level 4, shows that splitting the attention between the road and a different activity (multitasking), is what allows successful engagement during reversion to manual operation [14]. Those cases corroborate the pertinence of the notion of a parallel activity, although it still needs to be better specified.

5 Conclusion and Future Works

The paper has laid down the theoretical founding for a new type of Human-Machine interface, the Parallel Synthetic Task. Maybe some alerts had already explored this idea in the past, but apparently, the formal concept has never been formulated before. With this formalization, more ergonomists may look at it with different eyes and come up solutions for increasing fallback pilots' situated awareness in autonomous systems. As Bainbridge stated, "a man can take notes of parameters without knowing what they mean", but if a PST can be designed to connect parameters and meaning, better interventions into autonomous systems may be unlocked. In other words, while an emergency checklist tries to solve the problem directly, a PST tries to engage the pilot intelligence and understanding, so that he can solve the problem. A deep study of accidents like the Air France 447, in which the lack of understanding of the situation (level 2 SA) was a critical issue, may contain valuable guidance for the next phases of this research, as it appears that SA level 2 is the main weakness of computer systems.

References

1. Bainbridge, L.: Ironies of automation. Automatica **19**(6), 775–779 (1983)
2. BEA -Bureau d'Enquêtes et d'Analyses. Final Report On the accident on 1st June 2009 to the Airbus A330–203 registered F-GZCP operated by Air France flight AF 447 Rio de Janeiro - Paris 2012. Ministère de l'Écologie, du Développement durable, des Transports et du Logement (2012)
3. Clot, Y.: La fonction psychologique du travail. Presses Universitaires de France-PUF (1999)
4. Collins, H.M.: Artificial experts – social knowledge & intelligent systems. MIT Press (1990)
5. Dreyfus, H.L.: What Computers Still Can't Do: A Critique of Artificial Reason. MIT Press; Revised ed. (1992)
6. Endsley, M.R., Bolte, B., Jones, D.G.: Designing for situation awareness: an approach to user-centered design (2003). ISBN 0–7484–0966–1 (hbk.) - ISBN 0–7484–0967-X (pbk.)
7. Engeström, Y., Engeström, R., Kärkkäinen, M.: Polycontextuality and boundary crossing in expert cognition: learning and problem solving in complex work activities. Learn. Instr. **5**, 319–336 (1995)
8. Frans, O.: Science Strategy and War, The Strategic Theory of John Boyd. Routhledge, Abingdon, UK (2006)
9. Ribeiro, R.: The role of experience in perception. Human Studies **37**(4), 559–581 (2014). https://doi.org/10.1007/s10746-014-9318-0
10. Sheridan, T.B., Verplank, W.L.: Human and computer control of undersea operations. MAN-MACHINE SYSTEMS Laboratory, of. Mechanical engineering - Massachusetts Institute of Technology Report (1978)
11. Theureau, J.: O Curso da ação: método elementar. Fabrefactum, Belo Horizonte (2014)
12. Vygotsky, L.S.: A construção do pensamento e da linguagem. Translation: Paulo Bezerra. São Paulo: Martins Fontes Editora (2000)
13. Newman, J.R, Nagel, R.: Gödel's proof. New York University press (1958)
14. Haué, J-B., Le Bellu, S., Barbier, C.: Le véhicule autonome: se désengager et se réengager dans la conduit. Activités, 17-1 | 2020, mis en ligne le 15 avril 2020, consulté le 17 avril (2020). https://doi.org/10.4000/activites.4987

Academic Productivism Analyzed from the Perspective of the Ergonomics of Activity: Perception of the Post-graduated Teacher

Marina Helena Pereira Vieira[1](✉) ⓘ, Andréa Regina Martins Fontes[2] ⓘ, Sandra Francisca Bezerra Gemma[3] ⓘ, and Uiara Bandineli Montedo[1] ⓘ

[1] Department of Production Engineering, University of São Paulo, São Paulo, Brazil
[2] Department of Production Engineering, Federal University of São Carlos, Sorocaba, Brazil
[3] School of Applied Sciences at University of Campinas, Limeira, Brazil

Abstract. The teaching work is characterized by a new perspective in academic procedures, based on the intensification of activities and high charge for publication in recognized journals. This paper analyzes teachers' work in the context of postgraduation higher education in a public university, identifying the main constraints to which this professional category is subjected, especially the evaluation system for intellectual production. The methodology employed can be classified as an exploratory and descriptive case study using Activity-Centered Ergonomics concepts. Data collection includes perception questionnaire, work diary, observation participant and semi-structured interviews applied to all teachers who work in the Production Engineering department of a federal public university located in a medium-sized city in the state of São Paulo, Brazil. Results identified the studied teachers' main constraints such as excessive tasks; lack of recognition, collectivity and institutional support; and demand for productivity). In their perception, teachers that don't work in the postgraduate program are less stressed than those who do, although both groups have physical and mental overloads. Teachers who work in postgraduate school suffer and feel frustrated with the great weight given to publications in detriment of other activities as or more important for teaching work. It should also be noted that there is no enough financial or institutional support to achieve the goals. The evaluation of intellectual production must consider the different activities of the teaching workload to avoid suffering and contribute to increasing quality to the scientific knowledge production.

Keywords: Ergonomics work analysis · Teacher's work · Teacher evaluation · Centered-activity ergonomics · Academic productivism

1 Introduction

The teaching work is characterized by a new perspective in academic procedures, based on the intensification of activities and high charge for publication in recognized journals, contributing to developing physical and mental disorders in professors [1]. This

© The Author(s), under exclusive license to Springer Nature Switzerland AG 2021
N. L. Black et al. (Eds.): IEA 2021, LNNS 219, pp. 316–322, 2021.
https://doi.org/10.1007/978-3-030-74602-5_46

reproduction of features of the flexible capitalist economy on work in an academic environment results in the precariousness of teacher's work [2–4].

A consequence of neoliberal approaches to educational reforms has been the increased workload that includes considerably longer working hours than in the past, an ever-expanding teaching role, and most noticeably, a significant increase in nonteaching and largely administrative duties [5].

Other researchers [3, 4, 6] discuss the precariousness of teacher's work, highlighting the devaluation of the professor's image, lack of material and human resources of schools, increased work rhythm, and other conditions that contribute to the physical and mental overloads. These are impacting the perception of satisfaction, welfare, safety and health for this category negatively.

These difficulties are even more intensified in the Master's degree and Doctoral degree programs. The authorization and recognition are granted for a fixed term, depending on the CAPES' (Coordination for the Improvement of Higher Education Personnel) evaluation criteria, which is prioritized publications as the primary indicator of a teacher's productivity.

According to CAPES [7], the requirements for authorization, recognition and renewal of postgraduate courses depend on, among other factors: the existence of a previously consolidated research group in the area of knowledge; the control and completion of administrative reports and; a system evaluation for the professors involved, which translates into the internal policies of accreditation and disqualification of professors in the program, based essentially on the amount and classification of their published articles [1].

The program productivity is measured mainly by the number of publications and classification of the journals that publish them, characterized by the excessive valuation of academic production quantity and tendency to devaluate its quality [8]. These quantitative criteria, however, consolidate academic productivism empty of content and meaning. It is the production of knowledge reduced to a race for publishing [9].

The research is based on Activity-Centered Ergonomics approach that confronts the work designed by the organization and the conditions for its execution with the effective work developed by the professionals [10], that is, it places work activity at the centre of the analysis, seeking answers to the demands that arise from productive situations [11].

All work is expressed in the form of workload [12]; therefore, it is pertinent to ask how the conditions and organization of work, the content of the activity and interpersonal relationships contribute to the workers' welfare, especially considering how changes in the field of work are understood and experienced by the working class [13].

In this scenario, the article analyzes the work of teachers in the context of postgraduation higher education in a public University, based on the Activity-Centered Ergonomics, identifying the main constraints to which this professional category is submitted. It will be considered, mainly, the evaluation system for CAPES's intellectual production, which validates and classifies the quality of Brazilian graduation programs and is replicated in the universities' internal regulations. This replication has a direct impact on the workload of post-graduate teachers.

This paper is organized in five sections: the present one introduces the problem, objective and some reference authors about the main theme; the second section presents the methodology applied to develop the research; the third section presents the results, the fourth section, the discussion; and the last one, the conclusions.

2 Methodology

The methodology employed can be classified as an exploratory and descriptive case study using Activity-Centered Ergonomics concepts. Data collection includes: perception questionnaire, work diary, observation participant and semi-structured interviews applied to all teachers who work in the Production Engineering department of a federal public university located in a medium-sized city in the state of São Paulo, Brazil. The study considers the responses of all 21 professors, 15 of them work in the postgraduate program. The objectives of the used tools are presented below:

- perception questionnaire, operationalized from literature and based on instruments validated in other studies;
- work diary, created with the central idea of having a simple script to follow the teachers' daily work within a predetermined period;
- participant observation, for one year, participating in board meetings, administrative activities, following attendance and classes; and
- interviews with semi-structured scripts, carried out as a way to support the construction of the narrative about the reality of the teaching work in graduation program, confronting the main aspects indicated in the questionnaire's essay questions with the interviewees' verbalizations.

These multiple instruments have been combined to triangulate data and support the rigorous application of the case study.

3 Results

As previously mentioned, the obtained results came from data collection with teachers from the Department of Production Engineering of a Federal public University in Brazil.

The studied teacher's squad is composed of 53% of women and 47% of men. Approximately 50% had been working for 6 to 10 years, almost 20% had been working for 11 years, since the beginning of the course. Young researchers can characterize it: 58.8% aged between forty-one and forty-five years, 22% were below forty, and 17% were over forty-five.

The results were divided into two topics highlighted by the interviewers as a cause of discomfort and suffering: workload and quantitative evaluation of teaching work.

3.1 Teachers Workload

The teachers' workload involves teaching, research, extension, administrative tasks inside and outside the department, participation in internal committees, collegiate bodies, and other charges. The workload is related to physical, cognitive and organizational aspects; the interviewees pointed out complaints about body pain due to the adoption of static postures for long periods, mental exhaustion due to work overload, and insecurity due to lack of institutional support.

As for the teachers' perception of the physical wear and tear of their work, considering the multiple tasks performed by these workers, the ones demand the most significant physical workload were: preparing classes that required moving around in the campus to organize spaces and collect materials (88,2%); applying tests (70,60%) and; registering grades in the university system (47,1%).

Regarding mental requirements, undergraduate students' guidance was considered the most stressful task (94%), mainly due to the volume of completed work to read, correct and revise in the same period at the end of semesters. In the sequence, preparing tests, updating classes and guiding graduate students, are in second place in the list of activities that demand high cognitive charge, indicated by 88% of the interviewees.

As for organizational factors, there is a need to deal with a lack of resources and lack of support to answer questions and make decisions during administrative activities.

3.2 Evaluation of Teaching Work

The teaching work evaluation was a widespread complaint in the reports for demanding abusive goals for publications and internal evaluations about intellectual production. According to interviewees, the evaluations expose the teachers to their colleagues and do not represent the workload they perform throughout the year.

Teachers' perception from aggressive charging for results (such as publications in high-impact journals) was identified by about 65% as the main problem. The workplace conflicts were emphasized in reports about individualism and few or none interaction among the colleagues. Communication among teachers was considered unsatisfactory by 53% of interviewers. It's an essential issue because collective work could decrease individual pressure and reach department goals.

Graduate professors must maintain a high amount of publications, in well-evaluated journals, of course. Other professors who form the department are invited to join the graduate program only if they also have an excellent article publications flow. As the intellectual production and its respective publication in journals that feature high strata, it is one of CAPES's main requirements for a good evaluation of the programs.

However, these quantitative assessment parameters that place some colleagues in a prestigious position do not always encompass all teaching, research, extension and administrative tasks in the best possible way. In the response of one of the interviewees, it is possible to identify some notes that show constraints:

"Other variables that make the work environment tense are the demands for the professor to remain in the postgraduation program, in the sense of requiring publications in journals. Doing quality research takes a lot of time, and at the same time, the teacher must dedicate him or herself to administrative tasks, which takes a long time and is not recognized or valued. This situation creates a permanent state of tension" (Verbalization of the interviewed teacher).

The results also showed that there are no activities that encourage the community. The dissemination of research in articles that tend to be better when involving various professionals does not occur because a joint publication assigns fractions and therefore reduced grades for the professors involved.

To deal with these difficulties, the professors allege focusing on the job's advantages, such as time flexibility and on-site availability, which engender autonomy to perform the activities. By more than 70% of the teachers, this autonomy is a positive factor. Research satisfaction, good university infrastructure, freedom to self-manage time, job stability, among others, also contribute to job satisfaction and coping with work problems.

4 Discussion

The intellectual evaluation system proposed by CAPES is replicated in the accreditation and discreditation processes for teachers in postgraduation. These impacts raise feelings of oppression, emotional distress and propagate individualistic attitudes. Although some professors agree with the formal assessment procedures, it can see that the studied course is turning less multidisciplinary, since quantitative areas are reaching with more facility the imposed goals than qualitative areas [1].

From the interviews, it can infer that the refinement of the publication requirements and the excessive heft given to the production of articles, often end up distorting the teaching activity and putting relevant aspects, such as teaching itself, in a background-position. Teaching in a post-graduate program is placed between the dichotomy between the pleasure of knowledge producing and wearing the charge for intellectual production.

Despite the deleterious effects that academic productivism generates in the teaching community, it is recognized that research publications in relevant journals, which other researchers read, are fundamentally crucial to science's progress. The context of the university is based on the pillars of teaching, research and extension, but is highly evaluated by the research pillar, generating mental and psychological strain, forcing the teacher to treat publication as the primary goal be achieved, in detriment of other activities that are essential to the context of education.

In Brazil, there is no researching career and this activity is delegated to the professors with PhD degrees who aggregate postgraduate activities. Even with all the difficulties, the results show that teachers feel satisfied with being part of the graduate program, making it essential to discuss and improve this context. Work must be analyzed on interactions done in the collective, recognized by confidence among colleagues [14].

The proposal of work that ultimately leads to satisfaction, in a collective dimension, and health built through self-realization and professional development, is instilled in the concepts of Activity-Centered Ergonomics [15]. This approach allows real work centrality as a key element for the worker to be seen as a protagonist of action in the production system [16].

Work-related issues must be understood of human action, creating opportunities to discuss constraints and impasses (e.g. discuss increased workload, ask for tasks to be better distributed, have more freedom to refuse to attend meetings, be able to ask for help to colleagues).

More than merely highlighting individual reasons that might lead to ailments, the main issue is that this work organization generates an outcome of suffering either illness or pleasure. In other words, the problem lies on the opportunity provided by the factors of work organization for the mobilization of intelligence in a context based on trust and genuine cooperation, which enables health-building, professional development, and especially self-realization.

Moreover, it is proposed that, ultimately, living in a society can be built (or rebuilt) through coexistence in the workplace, through genuine respect in interpersonal relationships (solidarity, trust and cooperation), through the extraordinary force of work as a source of the civilizing process [17]. But to do so, it is necessary to assume that it is possible to transform work.

5 Conclusion

Based on the analysis presented in this article, the main constraints identified in teaching work were: excessive tasks; lack of recognition; lack of collectivity; lack of institutional support; and mainly, evaluation criteria and demand for productivity. Teachers' percept that the evaluation of intellectual production is an oppressive and short-sighted process, which does not reflect a good teacher's performance in the exercise of his teaching, research, and extension.

The main pleasure sources mentioned by these workers were: building knowledge to produce scientific and methodological solutions to contribute to the development of science; teaching and training students who will be the professionals responsible for the demands of the future in terms of technology, management, politics, among others, and; guiding and orientating research, which usually involves highly spirited students.

The rules of classification and evaluation of intellectual production should consider the various activities of the teaching workload. Only in this way will it avoid being a source of suffering for teachers and effectively contribute to achieving the quality of higher education and scientific production knowledge.

References

1. Vieira, M.H.P., Fontes, A.R.M., Gemma, S.F.B., Montedo, U.B.: Produtivismo na pós-graduação na perspectiva da ergonomia da atividade. Educação e Pesquisa 46, e220223 (2020). https://doi.org/10.1590/s1678-4634202046220223
2. Léda, D.B.: "Correndo atrás": as repercussões da economia capitalista flexível no cotidiano do trabalho docente. In: 6th Seminário da Regulação Educacional e Trabalho Docente (REDESTRADO), pp. 1–13. Anais da Redestrado, Rio de Janeiro (2006)
3. Mancebo, D.: Trabalho docente: subjetividade, sobreimplicação e prazer. Psicologia 20(1), 77–83 (2007)
4. Rodrigues, A.M.S., Souza, K.R.D., Teixeira, L.R., Larentis, A.L.: A temporalidade social do trabalho docente em universidade pública e saúde. Ciência Saúde Coletiva 2(25), 1829–1838 (2020)
5. Fitzgerald, S., McGrath-Champ, S., Stacey, M., Wilson, R., Gavin, M.: Intensification of teachers' work under devolution: a 'tsunami' of paperwork. J. Ind. Relations 61(5), 613–636 (2019)
6. Silva, T.A.A., Souza Júnior, G.R.: Análise da precarização e intensificação do trabalho docente no Instituto Federal de Pernambuco. Cadernos CiênciasSociais UFRPE 1(16), 126–145 (2020)

7. CAPES. Coordenação de Aperfeiçoamento de Pessoal de Nível Superior. Avaliação do Sistema Nacional de Pós-Graduação. Brasília, DF: Capes. (2014). https://capes.gov.br/avaliacao/sobre-a-avaliacao/. Accessed 20 Jun 2020
8. Patrus, R., Dantas, D.C., Shigaki, H.B.: O produtivismo acadêmico e seus impactos na pós-graduação stricto sensu: uma ameaça à solidariedade entre pares? CadernosEbape 13(1), 1–18 (2015)
9. Pimenta, A. G. (Des)caminhos da pós-graduação brasileira: o produtivismo acadêmico e seus efeitos nos professores pesquisadores. 324f. Tese (Doutorado em Educação – Centro de Educação, Universidade Federal da Paraíba (2014). https://repositorio.ufpb.br/jspui/handle/tede/4823. Accessed 10 Jun 2020
10. Guérin, F., Laville, A., Daniellou, F., Duraffourg, J., Kerguelen, A.: Compreender o Trabalho Para Transformá-lo: A Prática da Ergonomia. Edgard Blücher, Fundação Vanzolini, São Paulo (2001)
11. Ferreira, M.C., Freire, O.N.: Carga de trabalho e rotatividade na função de frentista. Rev. AdministraçãoContemporânea 5(2), 175–200 (2001)
12. Torres, C.C., Abrahão, J.I.: A atividade de teleatendimento: uma análise das fontes de prazer e sofrimento no trabalho. Rev. Bras. SaúdeOcupacional 31(114), 113–124 (2006)
13. Vilela, E.F., Garcia, F.C., Vieira, A.: Vivências de prazer-sofrimento no trabalho do professor universitário: estudo de caso em uma instituição pública. Rev. Eletrônica de Administração 19(2), 517–540 (2013)
14. Dejours, C.: Subjetividade, trabalho e ação. Rev. Produção 14(3), 27–34 (2004)
15. Brunoro, C.M., Bolis, I., Sigahi, T.F., Kawasaki, B.C., Sznelwar, L.I.: Defining the meaning of "sustainable work" from activity-centered ergonomics and psychodynamics of Work's perspectives. Appl. Ergon. 1(89), 103209 (2020)
16. Sznelwar, L.I.: Quando Trabalhar é ser Protagonista e o Protagonismo do Trabalho. Editora Blucher, São Paulo (2015)
17. Dejours, C.: Travail vivant: Tomo 2 - Travail et emancipation. Payot, Paris (2009)

Does the Work Managed by Numbers Have a Future? The Introduction of New Public Management in Public Services in Brazil: The Example of the Judiciary

Leonardo Wandelli[1] and Laerte Idal Sznelwar[2]([⊠])

[1] Labor Court 9th Region, Paraná, Brazil
[2] Escola Politécnica da Universidade de São Paulo, São Paulo, Brazil
laertesz@usp.br

Abstract. In this paper we propose to present the results and a discussion related to actions developed within the judiciary system in Brazil. Based on the approach of work psychodynamics and activity-centered ergonomics, a discussion is proposed relating the impacts of the neoliberal managerial system on the subjectivity and the health of magistrates. In addition a debate on the risks for democracy both at the level of collective work within the judiciary and at the level of the society and on the rule of citizenship is proposed.

For the Psychodynamics of Work, work is always a challenge for oneself; any kind of work also involves the interpretation of conflicting rules in face of singular situations where the reality always transcends what had already been planned. It also requires committing, assuming the strategic and ethical risks involved. In this sense, the work of magistrates is an exemplary case; even in a type of work with a stable relationship, good salaries and an important social role, the degradation of professional ethos, cooperation and deontic activity.

Keywords: New public management · Neoliberalism · Mental health · Psychodynamics of work · Activity-centered ergonomics · Macroergonomics

1 Introduction

Judicial work also involves empathy and even compassion in face of the drama of the subjects. To become a good judge, the subject has to improve his practices without losing the feeling of compassion. To work on oneself and to transform oneself into a better person is important to build better judgments. The problem is that the reality of work, the possibilities in order to "honor life" through work, are seriously affected. Disaffection, disengagement in the pursuit of justice, loss of solidarity and cooperation, defensive individualism, challenges the magistrates. The defensive cynicism and the psychic and somatic disorders are more prevalent. The emergence of individual and collective psychic defense strategies, which block the capacity for critical thinking, promotes adherence to managerial discourse acts as a rationalization of ethical suffering, a kind of naturalization. It is undeniable that living with the dilemma of choosing between submission to managerial logic and the traditional professional ethos is starting to have major impacts on magistrates. Resist is risky and costly, but adhering is also risky, since it implicates a loss of meaning. Also judges, when they are subject and/or submit to neoliberal management techniques, lose a large part of their freedom to think and act. One can even wonder with great concern whether judges, exposed to these management methods deny the suffering experienced in their work, would in turn be able to develop their professional actions with lucidity. In fact, one of the consequences of psychic defense mechanisms is the impoverishment of the ability to think and reflect. It is also a risk to the ability to analyze, engage and maintain impartiality with respect to the trials that are under their control.

Work remains the key issue in the social, ecological and legal crisis introduced by neoliberal governance. Work as a commodity is a paradigm established in capitalism even under the social state, empties the meaning of work as such, since only the exchange of working time for wages counts, leaving aside the issues of content of the work. With corporate governance by numbers, which extends the cybernetic imagination to all human activities, the worker is reified. To this is added management by fear, exercised both at the level of companies and at the level of public institutions, by the threat of destinies spread by neoliberalism, of social descent, precariousness and misery.

2   Method

Based on a request from the National Council of Justice (CNJ), the regulatory and control body of the Brazilian judiciary, a first research was carried out in order to study the work of judges, having as questions of based on the possible impacts of work organization methods on the mental health of judges (Sznelwar 2014). The main goal of this action-research was to facilitate the reflection of the participants, in order to identify work experiences and better understand their experiences as well as to promote a possibility of exchange on issues that are normally not addressed, such as those related to pathogenic suffering (Lancman, Heloani 2004). The methodology used was based on interviews, focus groups and documentary and bibliographical research (particularly with regard to the rules and history of the judiciary in Brazil). Focus groups were organized with judges working in different kinds of courts, with extensive validations being carried out in different courts, according to the precepts of psychodynamics at work.

This research was followed by a second, based on a request from the Regional Labor Court of Justice in Paraná, in southern Brazil. (Wandelli, Tavares 2015). The investigation was carried out by a group of researchers made up of judges and officials from the court itself, with the participation of a professor as supervisor and consultant, as well as another research professor. This research, based on concepts and precepts of PDT, was characterized by a participatory and action research method. The objective of the research was to study the question of the impact of the mechanisms of evaluation of the work of the social actors of the judiciary on the subjectivity, the mental health and the characteristics of the work of these professionals.

3   Results and Discussion

The judiciary in Brazil has undergone a series of normative changes and a profound transformation of the institutional culture in recent years, brought about by the National Council of Justice (CNJ) and other higher councils, instituted by a constitutional amendment. Based on the concern for rationalization and effectiveness/efficiency, a diversified set of measures has been implemented, largely inspired by the management models of private companies. Among them, the mechanisms for evaluating the work of judges, through criteria for approval during the probationary period and career promotion, all based on quantifiable results. Achieving, or even surpassing, the production objectives set by the higher authorities concerning the results of the work of judges, as well as the results obtained by each court, also define the criteria for the allocation of resources. Performance indicators allow governance based on comparative statistics of the quantities and speeds of procedural acts, which is one of the pillars of the established changes.

While it can be recognized that in part these changes have brought about gains in streamlining and modernization, on the other hand, there is widespread concern among professionals that they have also led to a detour in the meaning and content of the work of judges, on the organization of work and also on their status. The focus of the evaluation process on statistical control and the obtaining of results, in addition to breaking with the qualitative sense of effectively contributing to the achievement of justice, accentuate competition between magistrates and between courts. Several signs of deterioration in cooperation are identified. This further weakens informal peer-to-peer work evaluation mechanisms, the possibilities to show and discuss the strategies adopted to report difficulties with other magistrates of the same level of jurisdiction, as well as with colleagues of different degrees, affecting significantly the judgment of beauty (Dejours 2003), essential to the construction and reinforcement of identity. In addition, professional ethics, in its role as mediator of judicial performance and of relations with society, of deliberative practices between judges and their professional identity, is questioned. The pressure for quantifiable results and the introduction of electronic processes aimed at improving the work process, as well as at better control, pave the way for the emergence of actions, which are at the limit, or even exceed, what is considered as ethical and corresponding to the traditions of the profession. It is precisely in these situations that pathogenic suffering processes emerges; in this case, when the subjects do not find solutions to act in accordance with the rules and traditions of the profession of the judiciary; a kind of suffering settles, nominated as ethical suffering (Dejours 2009). This is the way opened for the exacerbation of defenses; initially individual, then collective, or even defensive ideologies that promote the degradation of living together and prevent more cooperative processes, based on solidarity among colleagues.

The main structuring element of the discourse of the interviewed magistrates is their relationship with the professional ethos. It is not enough to be nominated, "sit in the chair and become a judge". Learning the technical and ethical values and standards of the profession is only possible with effort, in concrete work experience and in relationship with colleagues. This process takes time and requires persistence in face of the resistance of the real, throughout day to day and throughout a professional lifetime. It is around a set of technical and ethical norms, in their porosity and openness, that the dimension of the profession is organized, as well as its meaning within social life. This meaning that will serve as mediation for the construction of identity and self-esteem. This normative settings are partly formal - including the Constitution, procedures, codes of ethics, normative acts; and are partly informal, even tacit and unconscious, which are collectively constituted in the relationship within each one experience of work, and the collective relationship whit peers.

Many judges, especially older ones, report that the motivation for choosing a profession was marked by the desire to contribute to the realization of justice, including the improvement of social relations. Contributing to reducing non-compliance with laws, modifying social reality to bring it as close as possible to the provisions of the Constitution and legal texts is essential to the sense of work and a source of satisfaction for the judge. But in face of the repetition of similar cases, the sensation of "wiping ice" appears (Sisyphus work).

There is an acceptance that there would be no other way to evaluate and that disconnection with the meaning of judicial work would be inevitable, in the dual dimension of singular justice and effectiveness. This denotes a justifying rationalization, since the development of other evaluation criteria is possible, but there is no investment in research and development to find other ways. The risk is that of magistrates' reification, since there is a felling that when evaluated by numbers, "we become a number too". The bond with the meaning of work is lost, with the community construction of the professional ethos and with the sublimation pathways that allow the appropriation of effort and suffering, disappearing the role of the subject, which is reduced to a number. Doing a good work is in contradiction with the need to achieve the required statistical results, the way to obtain the institutional recognition. Several strategies of adaptive behaviors arise, among them multiple references to ways of "playing with the rules of the game", and even to modify the conduction of the processes to achieve better statistical results, even though this is far from the best for the citizens. Pressure to adapt each one to the "rules" is great and presents itself as a dilemma.

4   Final Discussion

The link between the impacts of the neoliberal managerial affects on subjectivity and health of magistrates. It has consequences also for democracy both at the level of collective work within the judiciary and at the level of the Republic as well. A dialogue between Psychodynamics of Work (PDW), and a critique of governance by numbers based on the work of jurist Alain Supiot (2015, 2019) can help us to understand the issues related to what's happening with this kind of work, as well as the public management. Judicial work implies, at the same time, the exercise of independence, impartiality and, in a certain contradictory way, of sensitivity, empathy and even compassion in face of the drama of people. Compassion is the propensity to act to alleviate the suffering not deserved by others, a feeling that arises from the fear of suffering; he or his loved ones, in a similar way. It is already known how compassion can engender both the commitment to the other and their exclusion (Adorno; Horkheimer, 1985; Arendt, 2008). To become a good judge, according to research participants, one have to improve yourself as a person once it's necessary to develop the ability to appreciate situations in order to better decide. To work on one and to transform oneself into a better person is a mission in which, the work itself, in the triangular relation with the matter, with the others and with oneself is an essential resource. The work of the judges could have all the elements for that. The problem is that, as we have seen, the mechanisms of dialogue on the reality of work, of recognition and "honoring life" through work, through which judicial work could contribute to this personal improvement, are seriously affected. Disaffection, disengagement in the pursuit of justice, loss of solidarity and cooperation, defensive individualism, question the propensity for individual and collective development, especially if we take into account, intersubjective relationships and public actions.

Defensive cynicism; psychic and somatic disorders knock the door. The emergence of psychic defense strategies individual and collective, which block the capacity for critical thinking, promotes adherence to managerial discourse. This is a kind of rationalization of ethical suffering. In fact, many magistrates express certain naturalization, even their commitment to this new discursive strategy. It is undeniable that livings with the dilemma of choosing between submission to managerial logic and the traditional professional ethos have impacts on magistrates. Resist is risky and costly, but adhering to this breaking in professional traditions, in the meaning of work is also risky. Also judges, when subjected to neoliberal management techniques, lose a large part of their freedom to think and act. One can even wonder, with great concern, whether magistrates who are submissive and submit others to methods of managing based on management techniques such as those described here, would be able to well exercise their profession, with lucidity. One of the consequences of psychic defense mechanisms is the impoverishment of the capacity to think and reflect. It is also a risk to the ability to analyze, engage and maintain impartiality with regard to the processes that are under their guardianship. How they will be in good conditions to judge?

Supiot states that work remains the key issue in the social, ecological and legal crisis introduced by neoliberal governance. The work-commodity paradigm (Polanyi 2012), which is established in capitalism even under the welfare state, empties the meaning of work as such, since only the exchange of working time for wages counts, leaving aside from the stakes the content of the work (how to work, according to the rules of the profession) and why to work, as well as the results. With public management by numbers, which extends the cybernetic imagination to all human activities, worsens this situation because the worker is no longer conceived as a "mechanical machine", but under the model of "a computer program": the already written - program - and only modifiable in a top to bottom sense, submits the programmable worker, who is evaluated by performance indicators deviating from any concrete experience of the work. To this is added the management by fear, exerted at the level of companies as well as at the level of nations, by the threat of the destinies diffused by neoliberalism, of social descent, precariousness and misery.

On the other hand, Supiot argues that the digital revolution brings in a potential for positive transformation, more than in the sense of liberation from work, in the sense of liberation at work, of the exemption from repetitive and calculating activities in order to allow workers to devote to the most fruitful and creative elements of human work. Also in this regard, Dejours (2015) argues that it is possible to manage companies and organizations in quite different ways even under capitalism and pleads for a real labor policy, commensurate with the centrality of living work for human sociability. The action research experiences reported here confirm - that by promoting thought processes by workers, as in the case of judges and justice officials, about their own work, it not only opens a path to critical understanding, but also the construction of strategies of resistance and initiatives of transformation which can open spaces of emancipation related to the role of the law for the protection of people. The analysis, the reflection related to each ones work has an important impact on the way can transform the working person and help to change working situations.

References

Adorno, T.W., Horkheimer, M.: Dialética do Esclarecimento. Jorge Zahar, Fragmentos filosóficos. Trad. Guido Almeida. Rio de Janeiro (1985)

Arendt, H.: A condição humana. Forense Universitária, Trad. Roberto Raposo. Rio de janeiro (2008)

Dejours, C.: L'évaluation du Travail à l'épreuve du réel. INRA Editions, Paris (2003)

Dejours, C.: Travail Vivant. Payot, Paris (2009)

Dejours, C., Choix, L.: Souffrir au travail n'est pas une fatalité. Paris, Bayard (2015)

Lancman, S., Heloani, R.: Psicodinâmica do trabalho: o método clinico de intervenção e investigação no trabalho. Produção **14**(3), 77–86 (2004)

Polanyi, K.: A grande transformação: As origens de nossa época, 2nd edn. Elsevier/Campus, Rio de Janeiro (2012)

Supiot. A. Gouvernance par les nombres. Cours au Collège de France (2012–2014), Paris, Fayard (2015).

Supiot, A.: Le travail n'est pas une marchandise. Contenu et sens du travail au xxie siècle: Leçon de clôture prononcée le 22 mai 2019. Collège de France (2019). https://doi.org/10.4000/books.cdf.7026

Sznelwar, L.I.: (Coord.). Trabalhar na magistratura, construção da subjetividade, saúde e desenvolvimento profissional" In: Conselho Nacional de Justiça (CNJ). Relatório Metas Nacionais do Poder Judiciário – Brasília: Conselho Nacional de Justiça (2014)

Wandelli, L.V., Tavares, L.N.M.: (Coords.). Impactos dos mecanismos de gestão e avaliação do trabalho judicial na subjetividade e saúde psíquica de servidores e magistrados: uma abordagem a partir da interface da psicodinâmica do trabalho com a ergonomia da atividade e análise organizacional. Curitiba, Tribunal Regional do Trabalho da 9ª Região (2015)

Food Well-Being: Territory, Work and Cooperation

Amanda Fernandes Xavier[1](✉) ⓘ, Francisco José de Castro Moura Duarte[1] ⓘ,
Márcia Regina Fortes Fernandes Xavier[1] ⓘ, and Francisco de Paula Antunes Lima[2] ⓘ

[1] Production Engineering Program - COPPE, Federal University of Rio de Janeiro (UFRJ),
Av. Horácio Macedo, 2030, Rio de Janeiro, RJ 21941-598, Brazil
`{amandaxavier,duarte}@pep.ufrj.br`
[2] Production Engineering Department - DEP, Federal University of Minas Gerais (UFMG),
Av. Antônio Carlos, 6627, Belo Horizonte, MG 31270-901, Brazil
`fpalima@ufmg.br`

Abstract. The magnitude of the current health and economic crisis has high-lighted the criticality of the food sector for life and social stability. Production and consumption represent critical environmental impacts on soil degradation, water pollution, and biodiversity reduction. The generation of waste is also significant. In addition to these territorial impacts, food can create several fundamental functionalities such as work, health, services and social relationships. This article presents an analysis, based on the Functional and Cooperative Economy (FCE) approach, of two initiatives that cooperate for food well-being in Rio de Janeiro, the first related to food production and distribution, and the second to collection and treatment of organic waste. The objective is to characterize the challenges and limits of these initiatives' current economic model and build guidelines for transforming their economic models. Through collective dynamics and interactions with company managers, the importance of a higher articulation of these initiatives with beneficiaries and territorial actors, capable of increasing the relevance of the solutions offered about their expectations and needs, and an evolution of functionalities and performances of uses. This collective engagement will allow the sharing of material and immaterial resources, in a convergence of interests and actors that act in the service of a territorial project with economic, social, societal and environmental intentions.

Keywords: Functional and Cooperative Economy · Food well-being · Work · Territory

1 Problem Statement

The present consumption levels threaten society's well-being and the environment's state. Food is an important area of our daily lives but represents one of the consumption areas of great environmental concern [1]. According to the EAT-Lancet Commission, the global food system (which entails production, processing, distribution, preparation, and consumption of food) requires transformational change for humanity to feed the

N. L. Black et al. (Eds.): IEA 2021, LNNS 219, pp. 329–336, 2021.
https://doi.org/10.1007/978-3-030-74602-5_48

world's global population while staying within the biophysical limits of the planet [2]. Over-consumption leads to unhealthy diets in some parts of the world, while hunger and malnutrition are prevalent in others [3]. The generation of waste is also significant. According to research [4, 5], 56% of household waste in Brazil is food waste and garden pruning. These impacts on the territories and the extent of the current health and economic crisis highlighted the criticality of the food sector for life and social stability.

Reflecting a model of financial performance, centred on the mass production of material goods, and the growing global interdependence [6], this imbalance of local ecosystems reinforces the distance between territorial relations and local needs [7–10]. It is necessary to review economic models and find new forms of consumption and production, reflecting on the limits of the current economic dynamics, not only because of their inability to respond to economic challenges but also to consider social challenges [11, 12]. Accompanying those who eat from a food well-being perspective implies integrating solutions combining a set of goods and services, implemented by a diversity of actors gathered within a territorialized ecosystem [11].

In this study, we contributed to the perspective of the Functional and Cooperative Economy (FCE) in a territorial food context, understanding the issues of sustainability within an approach that leads to the renewal of the social bond, the requirement of social equity and, still, a renewal of governance models for companies and territories [11]. This FCE approach considers the issues of subjectivity and its relationship with work, questioning the Taylorist-Fordist assumptions of the hegemonic economic model, in an attempt to enrich the different social representations that exist about human work [13, 14].

The present study's objective is to characterize the challenges and limits of the current economic model of two initiatives that cooperate for food well-being in Rio de Janeiro and build guidelines for transforming its economic models, based on the FCE approach.

2 Background Theory

The Functional and Cooperative Economy approach was initially developed by the ATEMIS laboratory (Analysis of Work and Changes in Industries and Services) and by IEEFC (European Institute for the Economy of Functionality and Cooperation), both located in France. It stems from the adverse effects of the dominant industrial economic model, centred on the logic of mass production of material goods and financial performance [6], unable to put the economy at the service of the great functionalities of life, such as the health [15–17].

This new economic configuration aims to provide integrated solutions for services and goods that no longer rest on simple sales, but on service, relationships based on immaterial resources. These solutions should allow less consumption of natural resources, greater well-being for people and better economic development [18]. The FCE proposal recovers the work's centrality and competences due to their immaterial values. Cooperation is a fundamental element and develops in all its directions: horizontal, between peers; vertical, between hierarchical positions; and transversal, between providers and their customers, for example [6].

This interactionist approach allows the other's recognition and creates resilience for economic relations, so weakened in the current scenario. Sustainability is also recognized as the intertwining of social, environmental, and economic pillars anchored in a familiar territory [17, 19]. Thus, among the fundamental bases of FCE, the territory becomes the space for the materialization of transactions and the recognition of work through the service. A "service relationship" is created when the customer becomes a participant in the service together with other local actors, who combine goods and services to solve a problem. Therefore, the perception of the territory emerges, not as a geographical space, but as a political space for transformation and cooperation, the basis for a social resignification of work, for a new way of producing and commercializing [16, 19].

3   Methodology

This research constitutes an exploratory work, following three main stages: (i) construction of a conceptual-theoretical framework; (ii) research and study of public information of companies; (iii) monitoring of company directors, following an approach inspired by the work of the ATEMIS laboratory and the IEEFC. More than 300 companies have already followed this approach, applicable to any industrial or service company, whatever their field of activity and status.

The monitoring and intervention approach followed three dynamics:

1. Collective dynamics based on FCE principles, through space for reflection animated by researchers of the FCE approach. Six meetings were held, one per month, by nine company directors from different sectors. The basis of these meetings was a device in stages where we tried to identify and debate for each company: (i) the limits of the current economic model; (ii) the positive and negative externalities, as well as the actors involved; (iii) strategic immaterial resources; (iv) the performance of the use of material resources; (v) integrated solutions for goods and services (vi) the construction of cooperative ecosystems, (vii) the diversification of the flow of income and investment and (viii) governance, engagement and cooperation. This device is known as "FCE Radar" [11];
2. Individual interactions with each manager: interviews were conducted to learn about the economic model of each company, composed of: (i) exchange model (value proposition and main customers), (ii) production model (division and working conditions), strategic resources, management challenges and productivity levers), (iii) business model (profitability and revenue bases, value sharing) and (iv) governance model (strategic decision actors, the perimeter of responsibility and effects induced by the company's activity);
3. Interações em pares de dirigentes: reuniões 1 ou 2 vezes por mês, que permitiu a criação de vínculos e de relações de confiança base para as reflexões coletivas.

The results of this monitoring and intervention process of two companies, related to the production and distribution of food and the collection and treatment of organic waste, will be presented below.

4 Results and Cases Analysis

4.1 Case 1: Junta Local

Case 1 Results

Junta Local is an initiative that brings together local producers, from small agroecological farmers to collectives and cooperatives, through street markets in neighbourhoods in Rio de Janeiro and the sale of products through the "virtual bag" platform. The model is based on articulating producers' network, providing short chains, from the direct producer to the final consumer, favouring fair trade, and valorizing local production. For this, there is a curatorship and a search for alignment with the premises, vision and values of the Board, through an associative model that carries out various activities to support member producers. Producers actively engage in this process, participating in decision-making processes and contributing ideas and efforts.

The company collects a fixed monthly fee and a rate of 18.5% of the producers' sales, defined jointly in assembly. Producers are guiding decisions and, thus, converging demands and collecting solutions. Some key partners are: the Secretary of State for Culture and Creative Economy; the Municipal Secretariat for Development, Employment and Innovation; and other local ventures, such as bars, gastronomic collectives and culinary spaces of innovation.

With the pandemic crisis in 2020 and the cancellation of street markets, the Board's solution was to invest in the online sales platform, representing a significant sales increase. This allowed selling the products on a larger scale and even greater financial returns, with an average ticket increase of 70%. This increase in scale led to a rise in the logistics chain and the operational demands assumed by its internal team (composed of 9 people), which centralized all distribution. The lack of space for receiving products, storing and assembling orders (because they do not have a warehouse), and the absence of more cooperative partners in outsourced services, such as the cold chain, are emerging as the main challenges. Besides, with street markets cancelled since March 2020 and social isolation, the relationship between producers and consumers has been damaged. Likewise, the articulations between the producers themselves since the assemblies have been changed to a virtual approach. This highlighted the weaknesses of current governance, which cannot reconcile decision-making with horizontal and transversal reflection spaces. To respond to these challenges, Junta Local started this year (2021) its operations in a physical space, called Galpão K, to centralize the logistical processes and, above all, interaction with the community.

Case 1 Analysis

The company "Junta Local" has a strong socio-economic and territorial impact, due to the relevance of its value proposition, focused on fair trade and health through healthy foods. As an independent platform, its economic model is based on decision autonomy, with higher monetary returns to the market. Its production model has several challenges, with productivity levers that were, with the pandemic, centred on the technological progress of the virtual platform and economies of scale by online sales. Its integrated solutions must rest on employee relations, recovering the centrality of work

[11, 18]. In this context, the performance of work processes is vital. It needs to better mobilize its immaterial resources, through the understanding and engagement of the actors involved, in a co-production work based on the potential of the client's demand, the organization, the prescription, the business rules [20].

Thus, the company must develop its work organization and management model, understanding the real work of the associated producers, their resources (material and immaterial), spaces and productive process, needs and expectations, and networking methods. This understanding can enable better routes and mutualization of resources, reducing costs and promoting the democratization of products for new customer segments. This interactionist approach will recognize the work of associates and resilience for economic relations, reducing the dependence on scalability [17, 19], which is especially important in crisis times.

Furthermore, it is necessary to have a precise understanding of the ways of organizing work and the beneficiaries' ways of life and consumption, through collective listening and reflection to aggregate all this knowledge as the basis of a new cooperative and territorial governance. The perception of the territory emerges not as a geographical space, but as a space for the materialization of relational transactions and the recognition of work through the service [16, 19]. Cooperating with the beneficiaries will reflect a better use performance linked to the scope of "food well-being", resulting from an implication of those who are fed by the evolution of food uses: the diversity of products consumed, the ways of preparing food, the knowledge of the nutritional dimensions, the health of those who eat, among others [11].

The current physical space, "Galpão K", should reflect a more robust distribution centre structure, improving the dynamics of receiving, classifying/separating products and managing inventories. It can explore as an opportunity to share the use of material goods and the development of reverse logistics (of bags and other products). It is also crucial that Junta Local, as the operator of this dynamic space, promotes integration, training and social and professional insertion among several territorial actors, including the residents of the surroundings with their existing local dynamics, is not only physical but cultural and aggregating space. The perception of this space of proximity, reflection and cooperation highlight the value of (collective) work as a fundamental part of the recognition of people as a society [8, 16, 17].

4.2   Case 2: Dr. Catador

Case 2 Results

The Dr. Catador initiative proposes collecting and treating organic waste through composting, transforming the waste into fertilizer. The initiative is associated to the Environmental Education Center (CEA, in Portuguese), a project focused on developing green awareness and environmental training, especially for children, through partnerships with local schools, through the dynamics of composting, biogas production, community garden and courses. It is an individual enterprise, centred on alliances that are essential to the business, such as a Sports Social Club that provides the local and human resources, and a local University, which helps through internship agreements. The Dr. Catador initiative has loyal customers, concerned with sustainability and community engagement, reinforcing its immaterial resources.

The income is associated to the adhesion contracts in two types of contracting: (i) supportive plan, focused on the collection and treatment of organic waste; and (ii) sponsor, for clients associated with CEA. The CEA project aims to be a space for exchanging reflective experiences and practices. Before the pandemic, the centre received sporadic visits from Dr. Catador's customers. With social isolation, all activities were suspended. The ideal was for the sponsoring plan to finance the CEA activities. However, there are no deliveries of differentiated values that make the differences pertinent. The manager prioritizes the cheapest plan, striving to escalate a more significant number of clients.

For composting activities, the company has three employees provided by the Club, who demonstrate their perception of their importance. The work requires strength, logistical skills and the ability to solve operational problems. For the collection, the initiative has an outsourced employee, whose activities occur without articulation with the others. CEA project, in turn, has been underutilized, not only due to the pandemic but also due to the manager's low perception of the immaterial values of that space. There is no clear division for the manager between Dr. Catador and CEA project, which are still confused in the same entity and economic activity. CEA's work seeks to address the territory's issues, but intuitively and without a participatory work from clients and other local actors. Even with a value proposal of relevance and sustainable values, the territory is still exogenous to the business, with no proper occupation and appropriation of values and effective delivery of what is proposed.

Case 2 Analysis

The Dr. Catador initiative is an alternative relevant to the territory's needs and the only one that develops this activity in the region. The project faces several challenges, financial and operational, mainly related to the management and work organization model.

The work activity challenges come from the configuration of the relationships, resulting from the outsourcing of labour and the lack of knowledge about what the operators feel, think, do, and about their exciting understanding of the activity performed. There are also material difficulties, as some service tools are outdated, contributing to the overload of operators and waste of valuable time. It is crucial for the manager to know the activity and the heuristic dimension of his employees [21] and to work in a cooperation that is not only vertical but horizontal between operators, with the development of skills and informal collaboration, indispensable for the operation of the company [22].

The manager has been developing new membership and service packages that enable customer loyalty with medium and long-term contracts. The packages need to offer higher added value to the associated customers, expanding the offer with a plurality of goods and services, bringing the greater financial return and minimizing the dependence on the scalability of organic waste collection. To this end, cooperative governance is pertinent, which can be overcome through a territorial ecosystem that brings collective solutions, shared management and articulated with different local actors [11]. The new membership and service packages can help consolidate the identity of Dr. Catador and CEA project. This delimitation will contribute to the recognition of intangible and strategic values, which will boost the construction of the ecosystem related to the food well-being of the territory.

It is imperative to structure new governance mechanisms for cooperation with territorial collectives. A decisive step is to bring together interested actors who share a cooperative stance, based on a new vision of territorial development, which captures an economic, social and environmental value for a group of interested parties, in a sustainable idea of the company [8, 23]. The process of building this ecosystem is already underway; different local actors meet weekly to discuss, exchange experiences and reflect on a territorial project. It is vital to create a governance that favourably creates this cooperative ecosystem, avoiding silo actions, which tend not to bring benefits to the territory. The actors' pertinence and willingness to cooperate is another essential factor that contributes to the engagement between them [11].

5   Final Considerations

Despite their relevance for the value proposal and positive socio-economic and territorial impact, the cases studied powerfully illustrate the limits of the dominant economic model, which worsened in the pandemic, due to the centrality of the volume logic with productivity levers centred on technological progress and economies of scales. For a territorial well-being food project in Rio de Janeiro, due to the work of the initiatives discussed here, it is essential to have an economic configuration that provides integrated solutions based on service relations based on immaterial resources, through a process of greater collective engagement with beneficiaries and territorial actors. On the one hand, forming partnerships with complementary actors that demonstrate relevance in their local performance can strengthen the initiatives' value proposition, focusing on the plurality of services and minimizing the dependence on scalability. On the other hand, cooperative territorial governance may recover the centrality of work, reflecting on the methods of use, ways of life, and organizing work.

This approach to the Functional and Cooperative Economy highlights the value of collective work as a fundamental part of recognizing people as a society and the intertwining of the social, environmental and economic pillars of sustainability, anchored in common territory. To this end, the next steps are the continuation of collective dynamics and interactions with company managers, in a new cycle of monitoring and intervention to transform their economic trajectories based on the insights presented here.

References

1. Moll, S., Watson, D.: Environmental pressures from European consumption and production. In: A Study in Integrated Environmental and Economic Analysis; European Topic Centre on Sustainable Consumption and Production, Copenhagen, Denmark (2009)
2. Willett, W., Rockström, J., Loken, B., Springmann, M., Lang, T., Vermeulen, S., Garnett, T., Tilman, D., De Clerck, F., Wood, A.: Food in the anthropocene: the EAT-lancet commission on healthy diets from sustainable food systems. Lancet 393, 447–492 (2019)
3. O'Neill, B.C., Oppenheimer, M., Warren, R., Hallegatte, S., Kopp, R.E., Pörtner, H.O., Scholes, R., Birkmann, J., Foden, W., Licker, R.: IPCC reasons for concern regarding climate change risks. Nat. Clim. Chang. 7, 28–37 (2017)

4. Garcez, L., Garcez, C. Lixo. 1a edição, São Paulo. Cailis (2010). 28 p.
5. Campos, LS.: Inclusão de catadores como estratégia para a integração do sistema municipal de gestão de resíduos sólidos. Tese de Doutorado, DEP. Universidade Federal de Minas Gerais (2020)
6. Lima, F.D.P.A., Dias, A.V.C.: Financeirização, Trabalho e Saúde: a Economia como Doença Social. In Desenvolvimento Colaborativo para a Prevenção de Acidentes e Doenças Relacionadas ao Trabalho, 1st edn. ExLibris, São Paulo (2020)
7. Baldassarre, B., Keskin, D., Diehl, J.C., Bocken, N., Calabretta, G.: Implementing sustainable design theory in business practice: a call to action. J. Clean. Prod. **273**, 123113 (2020)
8. Maillefert, M., Robert, I.: Nouveaux modèles économiques et création de valeur territoriale autour de l'économie circulaire, de l'économie de la fonctionnalité et de l'écologie industrielle. Revue d'Économie Régionale & Urbaine, v. Décmbr, 5, 905 (2017)
9. Du Tertre, C., Vuidel, P.: Modèle économiques- quoi de neuf? Les Limites du Modèle Industriel. Mise en Débat des Modèles de L'Économie Circulaire et de L'Économie Collaborative. Club EF & DD (2014)
10. Vaileanu-Paun, I., Boutillier, S.: Économie de la fonctionnalité. Une nouvelle synergie entre le territoire, la firme et le consommateur? Innovations (1), 95–125 (2012)
11. Du Tertre, C., Vuidel, P., Pinet, C.: Développement durable des territoires: L'économie de la fonctionnalité et de la coopération. Horizontes Interdisciplinares da Gestão - HIG **2**(5), 1–25 (2019)
12. Bocken, N., Smeke Morales, L., Lehner, M.: Sufficiency business strategies in the food industry: the case of Oatly. Sustainability **12**(3), 824 (2020)
13. Dejours, C.: Trabalho vivo: trabalho e emancipação. Paralelo, Brasília, 15 (2012)
14. Sznelwar, L.I., Uchida, S., Lancman, S.: A subjetividade no trabalho em questão. Tempo Soc. **23**(1), 11–30 (2011)
15. Zwanka, R.J., Buff, C.: COVID-19 generation: a conceptual framework of the consumer behavioral shifts to be caused by the COVID-19 pandemic. J. Int. Consum. Market. 11 (2020)
16. Du Tertre, C.: Économie servicielle et travail: contribution théorique au développement "d'une économie de la coopération." Travailler **29**(1), 29–64 (2013)
17. Hubault, F.: Le bien être un enjeu sensible pour le management dans l'économie du service. In: Karsenty, L. (coord). Quel management pour concilier performances et bien-être au travail? Editions Octarès (2015)
18. Ademe, A., Vuidel, P., Paquelin, B.: Vers une Économie de la Fonctionnalité à Haute Valeur Environnementale et Sociale en 2050: Les Dynamiques Servicielle et Territoriale au Coeur du Nouveau Modèle. Synthèse. Agence de l'Environnement et de la Maîtrise de l'Energie (ADEME) (2017)
19. Roman, P., Muylaert, C., Ruwet,C., Thiry, G., Maréchal, K.: Intégrer la territorialité pour une économie de la fonctionnalité plus soutenable. Développement durable et territoires **11**(1) (2020)
20. De Gasparo, S., Debuc, T., Guyon, M.: Quand les ergonomes se mêlent de la performance. Actes du 51ème Congrès de la SELF, Marseille 21–23 (2016)
21. Du Tertre, C.: Economia de serviço e trabalho: contribuição teórica do desenvolvimento da cooperação"| Economie servicielle et travail: contribution théorique au développement" d'une économie de la coopération". Trabalho Educação **27**(3), 15–42 (2018)
22. Daniellou, F., Laville, A., Teiger, C.: Ficção e realidade do trabalho operário. Revista Brasileira de Saúde Ocupacional **17**(68), 7–13 (1989)
23. Du Tertre, C.: Functional and Cooperative Economy in territories. A support tool setting FCE on Euro-pean territory. CREPE EFC/ERASMUS+ (2016)

Part II: Systems HF/E (Edited by Paul M. Salmon)

EHF Audits: State of the Art and Lessons Learned

Colin G. Drury[1]([✉]) and Patrick G. Dempsey[2]

[1] Applied Ergonomics Group Inc., Boulder, CO 80304, USA
[2] National Institute for Occupational Safety & Health, Pittsburgh, PA, USA
pbd8@cdc.gov

Abstract. An ergonomics/human factors (EHF) audit is a methodology for regular review of the fit between people and their working systems. Its objective is to provide proactive guidance on problems or good practices, so that actions can be taken to improve the EHF of a work system, often with an emphasis on safety. An EHF audit can be an appropriate measure of the performance of the EHF function. The objective of this paper is to review the current state of EHF audits from a variety of EHF perspectives and domains, so as to address their value and shortfalls. Audits in the literature and in EHF practice were reviewed (Drury and Dempsey 2020) by considering the audit's objective structure and typical questions, as well as noting the balance between breadth, depth and application time. While much of that review concentrated on the data collection instrument, often a checklist or questionnaire, details of how the audit was to be used were noted. This included the sampling scheme and how results of the audit data collection were to be analyzed and presented to management and workforce. The current paper extends the review to lead to lessons learned that can be applied to future audit systems.

Keywords: Audit · Safety · Lessons learned

1 Why Audit EHF?

EHF audits stand beyond evaluations of individual workplaces or functions to provide input into the state of the level of EHF implementation within a larger system. As such, an EHF audit can provide reliable and valid input into the evaluation of both the organization's level of EHF effectiveness and of the specific functions within the organization charged with EHF design and implementation.

Outside the EHF community, an audit refers to a careful examination of records, such as financial accounts, to "…be certain that acceptable policies and practices have been consistently followed" (Carson and Carlso 1977, p. 2). As Koli (1994) noted, a financial audit comprises four steps:

1. Diagnostic investigation. Describe the business and highlight areas requiring increased care and high risk.
2. Test for transaction. Trace samples of transactions grouped by major area and evaluate.

© The Author(s), under exclusive license to Springer Nature Switzerland AG 2021
N. L. Black et al. (Eds.): IEA 2021, LNNS 219, pp. 339–345, 2021.
https://doi.org/10.1007/978-3-030-74602-5_49

3. Test of balances. Analyze content.
4. Formation of opinion. Communicate judgment in an audit report.

All four have relevance to EHF audits: different audits may be needed for different areas of concern, sampling of tasks is more usual than a complete audit of all tasks, each task must have an analysis, and the final results must be communicated to management for action.

2   Examples of Current Audit Systems

We shall follow our own precepts by referencing only a sample of all published EHF audits drawn from the comprehensive review of Drury and Dempsey (2020) which reviewed 30 current and historical EHF audit systems.. The description is meant to give a depiction of available audits, and also to convey the utility of this particular assessment approach that we believe can be used to develop useful and useable assessment tools.

The so-called International Ergonomics Association (IEA) Checklist was presented at the first Congress of the IEA (see Burger and De Jong 1962). The checklist was designed to cover a range of occupational contexts. This was done by using the concept of functional loads (1. physical, 2. perceptual, and 3. mental) as rows of a matrix and system components (A. worker; B. environment; and C. working method, tools, machine) as columns of a matrix to plan the analysis. The ergonomist determines which cells are relevant for the particular analysis being performed. A checklist was provided for each cell requiring analysis, creating an approach that was modular and efficient. This provides the historical context but also foreshadows the form of more current audits.

A more recent modular audit system was developed for assessing ergonomics of aircraft inspection and maintenance activities (Koli et al. 1998). These audits were computerized as the Ergonomics Assessment Program (ERNAP) as described by Meghashyam (1995). While more context-specific than the approach suggested by Burger and De Jong (1962), ERNAP was designed for inspection and maintenance activities that are nonrepetitive in nature. The approach follows specific tasks assigned to technicians by task cards at the start of each shift rather than assessing a workplace. Extensive task analyses of inspection and maintenance tasks were used to develop generalizable function descriptions of inspection and maintenance work (Drury et al. 1990).

The International Labour Office (ILO) in collaboration with the IEA developed "Ergonomic Checkpoints" (ILO 2010) which are easy-to-use checklists for assessing materials handling and storage, hand tools, machine safety, workstation design, lighting, premises, hazardous substances and agents, welfare facilities, and work organization. There are 132 checkpoints, each of which is a checklist item under one of the categories mentioned. Information on how to correct identified deficiencies are given for each checkpoint. The checkpoints are also freely available as a mobile application. The checkpoints are intended to cover a fairly broad range of work settings and were designed to be easy to understand and use.

More recently, Dempsey et al. (2017) developed an extensive set of audits for three types of mining operations (bagging operations, haul truck operations, maintenance and repair operations). The audits are available from the National Institute for Occupational

Safety and Health (NIOSH) in a paper form as well as a more convenient electronic version, ErgoMine (NIOSH 2016), that is available as a free Android application (https://www.cdc.gov/niosh/mining/works/coversheet1906.html). The three types of operation are all quite different. Bagging operations tend to be repetitive requiring materials handling tasks including palletizing and carrying, while maintenance and repair operations additionally involve non-repetitive tasks performed at various locations on a mine site. Haul truck operations involve equipment access during ingress and egress, driving, and tasks associated with refueling and minor maintenance. Like the Ergonomic Checkpoints, each audit item leads to one or more associated practical solutions. Current work is extending ErgoMine to include more specific checklists to address slips and falls as well as a managerial feature to track recommendations and whether they have been addressed.

3   Lessons Learned from EHF Audit Systems

In any organization, "Lessons Learned" can be important inputs into system improvement, although not without their potential difficulties, (Voit and 2006). In this section we address issues in practical audit system design that have arisen in the examples given above and in Drury and Dempsey (2020).

3.1   Use of Legal vs. EHF Good Practice Standards

There is a temptation to use regulatory considerations as the standards for EHF audits, but this will not often be wholly satisfactory. For example, Dempsey et al. (2017) used information from relevant regulations (Title 30 of the United States Code of Federal Regulations) when developing their audits, but they also used information from sources including injury surveillance analyses, task analysis and laboratory studies to develop audit items and associated remedial recommendations. One laboratory study was initiated due to a lack of specific guidance on the selection of grated walkway materials used at mine sites. Pollard et al. (2015) performed a study to evaluate slip potential of commonly observed walkway materials. Specific recommendations were added to the audit about selecting walkway materials that offered higher slip resistance to prevent slips and falls.

There is no reason that EHF audits should not use a mixture of legal requirements and current best practice as the basis for the standards against which to audit. A similar consideration is applicable to the actual audit measurements. If an audit question asks directly whether a measurement exceeds some standard, there can be a temptation for the auditor to mentally round up or down to give a desired outcome. This tendency can be reduced by having the auditor merely record the actual measurement, which is then compared to the standard at the later analysis stage.

3.2   Breadth, Depth and Application Time

As Drury and Dempsey (2020) noted: "Ideally, an audit system would be broad enough to cover any task in any industry, would provide highly detailed analysis and recommendations, and would be applied rapidly. Unfortunately, the three variables of breadth, depth, and application time are likely to trade off in a practical system." Breadth of an audit can mean either many different workplaces in one domain, or many similar workplaces across domains. Depth means the amount of detail included in the audit, not just "is automation involved?" but more probing items such as "can controls and/or displays change modes automatically?" Application time is clearly an increasing function of both breadth and depth; hence trade-offs are likely in these three aspects of the audit system.

3.3 Data Collection Instrument

Almost all EHF data collection methods have been used as audits: checklists, questionnaires, interviews, group techniques, and archival data. Most published audit systems use checklists or questionnaires, so that standard design considerations for these are directly applicable to help ensure that users of checklists make minimal errors. Recent examples can be found in using checklists for procedure design, e.g., Drury and Johnson (2013). Any data collection instrument needs to be usable by different levels of user familiarity, from repetitive daily use to occasional use. This means that some level of additional help may be needed for the occasional user, such as more detailed embedded instructions within a checklist. These are much easier to include when the data collection instrument is presented on an electronic system rather than as a paper form (see Drury, Patel and Prabhu 2000 for more detail). ErgoMine (NIOSH 2016) includes a number of graphics and parameter definitions such as an illustration pointing to the third metacarpophalangeal joint to assist users with measuring "knuckle height" for materials handling tasks.

This brings up the issue of developing more automated instruments than the traditional paper-and-clipboard. Electronic systems work well in areas such as procedure design (Pai 2003) and form the basis of a number of recent audits of mining tasks (Dempsey et al. 2017). Electronic systems can easily include branching logic if certain items are only completed based on the response to other items: This is much more convenient to the user and reduces the chances of error. The results can also be more easily stored and retrieved should the auditor wish to compare results across time.

3.4 Sampling Scheme

In any sampling, we must define the unit of sampling, the sampling frame and the sample choice technique. For an EHF audit, the unit of sampling is not as self-evident as it appears, but a good start is to use the natural unit of the job that is composed of a number of tasks. Note however that one person performing one simple set of tasks is no longer the norm in most developed economies. Teams often rotate between tasks or workplaces, and many jobs have rather ill-defined tasks as they move from direct action to system supervision.

Definition of the sampling frame is more obvious as it derives from the scope of the audit, whether a section, a department, a whole plant or perhaps a geographically extended area for on-site maintenance jobs. Organizations often have defined responsibilities by location or region for ergonomics and safety, and the sampling frame can be chosen to be consistent with these 'natural' organizational boundaries.

Choice of the sampling technique is also rather straightforward and well-covered in EHF texts. Typical concepts are Random, Stratified Random, and Cluster sampling, although in practice a "sample of convenience" is a tempting alternative. This latter strictly prevents statistical inference from the sample and should therefore be avoided. In particular, if the choice of which tasks to observe is left to the audit user on the ground, it may be easy to obtain biased (or at least non-random) results if the auditor has some idea of which jobs may give "better" or "worse" EHF outcomes. Again, the solution is randomness in sampling unless *every* task in the sampling frame is to be included.

3.5 Data Analysis and Presentation

A comment is warranted concerning how data are analyzed and interpreted. Following Koli (1994), Dempsey et al. (2017) designed their audits so that users measured rather than assessed aspects of tasks. Certain dimensions and weights are entered, and the application then interprets the data entered using coded logic to provide the interpretation of whether a remedial recommendation was warranted. This simplifies the auditing task and eliminates the potential reduction of reliability and validity that a judgement could introduce. This approach may increase the complexity of analyzing the results, but the logic can be coded once into a computerized format that will ultimately make it easier for future end users.

Whether a simple checklist or a more extensive modular audit system, there are two levels of analysis: immediate action to improve the specific task and analysis across the whole sample to assess EHF performance level. The first analysis of collected data should focus on presenting the user with a set of actionable and feasible solutions to address the ergonomics or safety deficiencies suggested by the audit. In other words, the audit system should be designed with the user in mind, just as with any system or tool. This allows the user to focus on implementing solutions rather than merely examining and collating the data. At the sample or system level the objective is to integrate and summarize the collected data across tasks or workplaces. Care is needed at this level to resist oversimplification, e.g., by managers demanding a single number for EHF effectiveness which may disguise uneven levels of EHF effectiveness across the sampling frame.

Two of the audit systems described earlier – ErgoMine and Ergonomics Checkpoints – provide users with recommendations for each item where a deficiency is noted. ErgoMine (NIOSH 2016) provides the user a list of recommendations specific to their responses. In order to increase feasibility, several alternatives are given when there are a range of solutions (e.g., automatic palletizer as ideal to eliminate palletizing, versus rotating lift tables to reduce biomechanical stresses while palletizing). The Ergonomic Checkpoints are not as context specific; therefore, the approach utilized was to provide several alternatives that have potential to cover a variety of workplaces. For example, the checkpoint on whether mechanical devices are used for lifting, lowering and moving heavy materials (Checkpoint 9 under Materials storage and handling) shows examples of a portable gantry, hydraulic floor crane, an overhead gantry, and manually powered lift device.

3.6   Audit System Reliability and Validity

For an audit methodology to be of value, it must have demonstrated levels of validity, reliability, sensitivity, and usability. We have covered usability above, but the other three parameters are all critical aspects of proving that an audit system can meet its goals. These measures are traditionally covered in methodology texts, e.g., Wilson and Corlett (1990). Validity is perhaps the most difficult to demonstrate for an audit system, although several studies in Sect. 2 have had their validity measured. Content and construct validity were carefully assessed for the ErgoMine (NIOSH 2016) system (see Dempsey et al. 2017). A retrospective predictive validity for an audit of aviation maintenance was established with some effort by Hsiao et al. (2013a, 2013b). Reliability shows how well a measurement device can repeat a measurement on the same sample unit, e.g., multiple auditors assessing the same workplace or task. As is well known, reliability sets an upper limit on validity and so is an important measure, as well as being relatively simple to assess. "Sensitivity defines how well a measurement device differentiates between entities" (Drury and Dempsey 2020). Sensitivity is not just the precision of the measurement (number of significant figures) but the ability to detect small actual changes in EJF conditions.

4   Conclusions and Recommendations

Auditing has a long history in ergonomics going back to the first IEA Congress (Burger and De Jong 1962), and there have been a number of successful implementations in sectors ranging from mining to transportation. While the research required to properly develop and evaluate audit systems can be significant, audits can be easily implemented using a variety of approaches from pen and paper to applications implemented on mobile devices. A recent survey of professional ergonomists (Lowe et al. 2019) indicated that a high percentage of ergonomists in a number of countries use observation-based assessment tools. Given the robustness of auditing, we believe there is potential for auditing to solve a number of needs for tools to assist ergonomists.

Like many ergonomics assessment tools, there are limited data on validation of longer-term use of audits and the effect on outcome measures such as productivity, errors or injury rates. Mobile applications can provide data on factors such as where mobile apps are used, how many times they are used, and how many items were completed, but these data do not provide information on the degree of implementation of findings or the downstream effects of implementing recommendations. Additional studies will be needed to better understand these outcomes.

Disclaimer: The findings and conclusions in this paper are those of the authors and do not necessarily represent the official position of the National Institute for Occupational Safety and Health, Centers for Disease Control and Prevention. Mention of any company or product does not constitute endorsement by NIOSH, CDC.

Patrick Dempsey, co-author of this Contribution, is an employee of the US Government.

References

Burger, G.C.E., de Jong, J.R.: Aspects of ergonomic job analysis. Ergonomics **5**, 185–201 (1962)

Carson, A.B., Carlson, A.E.: Secretarial Accounting, 10th edn. South-Western, Cincinnati (1977)

Dirken, J.M.: An Ergonomics Checklist Analysis of Printing Machines, vol. 2, pp. 903–913. ILO, Geneva (1969)

Dempsey, P.G., Pollard, J., Porter, W.L., Mayton, A., Heberger, J.R., Gallagher, S., Reardon, L., Drury, C.G.: Development of ergonomics audits for bagging, haul truck, and maintenance and repair operations in mining. Ergonomics **60**(12), 1739–1753 (2017)

Drury, C.G., Dempsey, P.G.: Human factors and ergonomics audits. In: Salvendy, G., Karwowski, W. (eds.) Handbook of Handbook of Human Factors and Ergonomics. Wiley, Hoboken (2020)

Drury, C.G., Johnson, W.B.: Writing aviation maintenance procedures that people can/will follow. Proc. Hum. Factors Ergon. Soc. Annual Meet. **57**, 997–1001 (2013)

Hsiao, Y.L., Drury, C., Wu, C., Paquet, V.: Predictive models of safety based on audit findings: part 1: model development and reliability. Appl. Ergon. **44**(2), 261–273 (2013)

Hsiao, Y.L., Drury, C., Wu, C., Paquet, V.: Predictive models of safety based on audit findings: part 2: measurement of model validity. Appl. Ergon. **44**(4), 659–666 (2013)

Koli, S.T.: Ergonomic Audit for Non-repetitive Task," unpublished M.S. thesis, State University of New York at Buffalo, Buffalo (1994)

Koli, S., Chervak, S., Drury, C.G.: Human factors audit programs for nonrepetitive tasks. Human Fact. Ergon. Manuf. **8**(3), 215–231 (1998)

Lowe, B.D, Dempsey, P.G., Jones, E.: Ergonomics assessment methods used by ergonomics professionals. Appl. Ergon. **81** (2019). https://doi.org/10.1016/j.apergo.2019.102882. Article 102882

Meghashyam, G.: Electronic ergonomic audit system for maintenance and inspection. In: Proceedings of the Human Factors and Ergonomics Society Annual Meeting, vol. 39, pp. 75–78. Human Factors and Ergonomics Society, Santa Monica (1995)

NIOSH: ErgoMine 1.0. By Dempsey, P.G., Pollard, J.P., Porter, W.L., Mayton, A.G., Heberger, J., Reardon, L., Fritz, J.E., and Young, M. Pittsburgh, PA: U.S. Department of Health and Human Services, Public Health Service, Centers for Disease Control and Prevention, National Institute for Occupational Safety and Health, Mobile App (2016)

Pai, S.: Effectiveness of Technological Aids in Checklist Use. unpublished Master's thesis, State University of New York at Buffalo, Buffalo, NY (2003)

Pollard, J.P., Heberger, J.R., Dempsey, P.G.: Slip potential for commonly used inclined grated metal walkways. IIE Trans. Occup. Ergon. Human Fact. **3**(2), 115–126 (2015)

Voit, J.R., Drury, C.G.: Supporting Vicarious Learning with Collaborative Lessons Learned Programs. IEEE-SMC Part 1. **36**(6), 1054–1062 (2006)

J. R. Wilson, J.R., Corlett, E.N. (eds.): Evaluation of Human Work. Taylor & Francis, London (1990)

Requirements for Measuring Inspection System Performance

Colin G. Drury[✉] and Catherine Drury Barnes

Applied Ergonomics Group Inc., Boulder, CO 80304, USA

Abstract. A recurrent in Ergonomics/Human Factors (EHF) studies of the performance of quality inspection systems is: How to obtain valid measures of system performance. Such measures are needed to determine whether the whole system meets the enterprise's needs, and also as a baseline for measuring the effectiveness of interventions, e.g., human/automation integration. The methodology used in the paper was to select, review and analyze the findings of over 50 years of inspection studies (e.g., Drury 2019) in a variety of domains starting in manufacturing (e.g., See 2012), but continuing into maintenance, security screening, and medical imaging. In all of these domains a similar need emerges to accurately measure inspection system performance This paper provides an analysis of the issues involved, alternatives for measurement and recommendations for a comprehensive approach. The major issues in performance measurement are presented. For most applications we recommend one type of study for human, automated and hybrid systems: the Test Sample method.

Keywords: Quality · Systems · Measurement · Methodology

1 Why Measure Inspection Performance?

This issue of how to measure inspection system performance continues to arise in most new studies requested by industry and other domains where inspection is an important part of the system. Examples beyond the obvious ones in manufacturing include aircraft structures (Drury and Spencer 1997), security screening (Koller et al. 2009), agricultural products (USDA 1994) and food products (Chapman and Sinclair 1975). The reasons that are given, or implied, for requiring inspection performance measurement are:

1. Obtain a single measure of inspection system performance, so as to characterize outgoing quality.
2. Obtain a single measure of inspection system performance, to modify quality control calculations (Bennett 1975).
3. Obtain a single measure of inspection system performance to characterize inspection reliability and therefore predict service failures, for example in aging aircraft (Drury and Spencer 1997).
4. To evaluate system improvements, ranging from improved training to increased inspection automation (Drury and Sinclair 1983).

© The Author(s), under exclusive license to Springer Nature Switzerland AG 2021
N. L. Black et al. (Eds.): IEA 2021, LNNS 219, pp. 346–353, 2021.
https://doi.org/10.1007/978-3-030-74602-5_50

In the over-60-year history of Ergonomics/Human Factors (EHF) in inspection and quality control (e.g., Belbin 1970) each study has faced this measurement problem, and early advice was given on the different alternatives to obtain valid and reliable measurements of the human/system performance. The book by Harris and Chaney (1969) devoted a chapter to the measurement issue, concentrating on two methods. Sinclair (1979) added a third method in his advice on the problem. These three methods still form the basis of deciding on measurement techniques, so that the current paper re-examines them in the light of modern development in quality control systems. This is not a comprehensive review, classifying studies, counting the number of each type of measurement type and bringing together data from different sources: That has been done many times, see Drury (2019) for review of these sources and See (2012) for more details. Rather, we shall use representative studies as examples to illustrate the techniques in a more modern context. As noted at the beginning of this paper, new studies have to address these issues, so that a treatment is a single paper will be useful to EHF professionals in the future.

2   Measurement of Inspection Performance and EHF

First it should be noted that there are two types of inspection, known as Attributes and Variables in the quality assurance field. Attributes inspection examines the product for specific discrete defects such as cracks in aircraft structures, scratches on automobile paintwork or blemishes on fruit. Variables inspection, in contrast, measures a key aspect of quality, e.g., size of a ball bearing or reflectivity of a surface, using interval or ratio levels of measurement. As argued elsewhere (Drury 2019), variables inspection can and should be more of an automated activity with little if any human intervention. Hence, we concentrate in this paper on attributes inspection.

In order to characterize inspection system performance for a particular defect or set of defects, three measures are needed:

1. The actual fraction defective arriving at the inspection system, denoted by p'
2. The probability that a defective item is rejected, or Hit, denoted by $p_2 = $ p(reject|rejectable)
3. The probability that a non-defective item is rejected, or False Alarm, denoted by p_1 = p(reject|acceptable)
4. The time (or use of other resources) required to perform the inspection task, denoted by t.

From these four measures, other indicators of interest to the enterprise can be deduced, e.g., the fraction defective after inspection, throughput of the inspection system. Drury and Addison (1973) provide explicit formulae for such calculations. Note also that the measures above do not include any for inspector well-being, such as those covered in the review by Drury (2019).

The four performance measures are not independent. For example, probability of a Hit and probability of a False Alarm are typically correlated, probability of both Hits and False Alarms increase with time per item inspected, and the probability of both Hits and False Alarms increase with increasing incoming fraction defective. The forms of these relationships are well-understood using appropriate models of human and system functioning, see for example Drury (2002).

Finally, many inspection jobs require the inspector to not only classify each item on an Accept/Reject basis but to provide a deeper level of classification. First, defects may need to have a judgement of severity beyond Accept/Reject as different levels of severity may lead to different actions. For example, a garment may have a defect whose severity is minimal so that mending is possible, or the whole item can be sold at a discount, or the whole garment must be scrapped. Chapman and Sinclair (1975) give a numerical example from their study of chicken carcass inspection. Alternatively, an item of product may contain multiple defects of the same or different types (e.g., cracks, mis-coloration and surface scratches on kitchen cabinet doors). The EHF professional needs to decide whether data recording and subsequent analysis should proceed at the defect level or at the whole item level. Finally, a whole batch of product may need to be characterized according to rule-based standards, such as a shipload of agricultural products (USDA 1994). In these cases measures such as p(Hit) and p(False Alarm) will not tell the whole story of quality to managers or customers, although individual defects or items may still be the basis for performance measurement at a detailed level. In still other cases, defects may be mis-classified resulting in detrimental effects on system performance and quality.

3   Requirements for Valid and Reliable Measurement of Inspection Performance?

The objective of measuring inspection system performance is to obtain reliable and valid numerical values of the four variables listed. Reliability is relatively simple to assure as the four measures have well-known properties and performance is often consistent within a single inspector (e.g., Drury et al. 2009). However, these same authors showed that there are often strong and consistent differences in performance *between* different inspectors, so that multiple representative inspectors need to be used in performance evaluations.

To ensure validity, the EHF professional needs to control those independent variables relevant to the specific needs of the performance evaluation. A useful classification of the variables that need to be controlled in given in See (2012). For example, in evaluating human and automation for the inspection of roller bearings, Drury and Sinclair (1983) needed to have a set of defect types fully representative of those encountered at the inspection station and in particular those relevant to the final customer of the bearings. Anything less than the full set would compromise validity. At the same time, the defects had to represent the desired range of defect severity. Ensuring that the desired set of defect types and their severities are presented to the inspection system requires that a listing of defect types and severities is known. In the paper cited, developing such a defect list required many hours of meetings between production personnel, quality assurance personnel, management and customer representatives. This is not at all unusual in inspection studies. In some industries such defect lists and limit standards are published by national or international bodies such as the United States Department of Agriculture's detailed Visual Reference Images (2016), covering many types of agricultural products such as wheat or soybeans.

Other independent variables that must be controlled, or at least measured, include those characterizing the inspectors (see Drury et al. *op cit*), the physical environment of inspection and the person-to-person interactions involving the inspectors that define their interpretation of instructions and management expectations.

4   The Three Methods for Measuring Inspection Performance?

Here we return to early studies and review papers, as the basis for the methods recommended has not changed materially. Harris and Chaney (1969) were early practitioners who classified two methods of measuring inspection performance: Job Sample and Repeated Inspection (Sect. 2). The Job Sample (which we refer to as Test Sample) is given the most attention, with detailed instructions on how to prepare the sample, instruct the inspectors, and record, analyze and present the data. Less attention, and a lower recommendation, is given to the Repeated Inspection method (which we refer to as Reinspection of Production).

Sinclair (1979) presents all three methods, which he labels Separate Test, Labeling Defects in Production and Reinspection (which we refer to as Test Sample, Labelled Items in Production and Reinspection of Production respectively.)

More recent papers tend not to discuss and justify an explicit choice of method, but rather present and detail the method used as if it were the logical (or even correct) choice.

4.1   Reinspection of Production

Reinspection of Production is where actual production is re-inspected after the main inspection, hopefully by a more reliable system (e.g., not under production time constraints). Both the accepted and rejected items need to be inspected so that the two primary measurements of Hits and False Alarms can be measured (e.g., Drury and Addison 1973). This method requires little preparation in that no test sample is needed, does not interrupt production inspection, and has good face validity for management and workforce. However, there is no control over the items reaching the inspector, so that some defect types and severities may not occur, the relative frequency of defects may be unrepresentative, and the reinspection itself is unlikely to be perfect. The lack of sample preparation required means that what is typically an important step in understanding inspection performance is missed: A detailed examination of what is and is not rejectable for each type of defect (e.g., the master defect list of Drury and Sinclair 1983).

As with all of the methods of measuring inspection performance, the ethics of the testing situation need to be carefully considered. Reinspection of Production may not may not be part of regular operations, with differing requirements for obtaining informed consent. In the Drury & Addison (1973) study, reinspection was part of normal production so what was analyzed was already-recorded ("archival") data, and the results of the measurements were discussed with the inspectors after the measurement periods rather than before. Note that there was no requirement at that time to obtain informed consent in an industrial (not research) setting. If there had been no reinspection in place already, then inspectors would need to be informed of the new measurements before they were put in place, so that they could give informed consent. It is recommended for the future that informed consent be required in all inspection studies.

4.2 Labelled Items in Production

The method known originally as Labelling Defects in Production uses known defects inserted into the production stream before inspection. Unobtrusive markings on these known items, e.g., numbers that fluoresce under ultraviolet light, allow these inserted items to be retrieved post-inspection from both the accepted and rejected product. In this paper we term the method Labelled Items in Production as for any sensible understanding of the inspection system performance the probability of False Alarm also needs to be known, so that known good items also need to be labelled and placed in the stream coming to the inspector. This method also has good face validity, and does not require that the status of all production items be known, just the labelled items. However, as Sinclair (1979) points out, the addition of defects not expected at that particular time may change inspectors' mental models of the process and hence their inspection performance.

In addition, the sample itself may deteriorate over time, whether stored or from repeated use. The author has seen the extremes of carefully-prepared samples covered in dust in laboratory drawers, and samples so badly scratched as to be of little use in future performance measurement. This "wear and tear" of samples also makes the individual items more easily recognizable to inspectors, so that repeated testing, especially with feedback of results to the inspectors, can lead to progressively better performance. It is a mistake to think that because test items are from hard substances, they will be immune to wear and tear. One inspection manager described hardened steel test samples as "like ripe peaches" after each additional handling during inspection tests.

When a set of labeled items are artificially introduced into a production system, inspectors need to be informed beforehand to ensure informed consent.

4.3 Test Sample

When a test of inspection performance is performed with just the test sample and not with items embedded within production, it becomes the Test Sample method. This method also requires a carefully-assembled sample of items with characteristics known as well as possible. Again, this sample must be comprised of known good items and the whole range of relevant defects, each at a variety of severity levels. The Test Sample is again a potentially-valuable enterprise resource for re-use on other inspectors or on hybrid or automated inspection systems. Again, sample deterioration and learning by the inspectors are potential problems.

The Test Sample method typically consists of having inspectors inspect only the test sample, while recording Hits and False Alarms based on the inspectors' decisions, e.g., Dalton and Drury (2004). The conditions of inspection can be much more closely controlled than the two previous methods, although at the cost of less direct realism, affecting face validity. For example, Dalton and Drury (2004) tested novel lighting for sheet steel inspection in an off-line lighting rig, rather than inspecting a continuous steel sheet moving past the inspector. The loss of realism was balanced against the ability to take more detailed measurements, e.g., of time taken to inspect each test item, and the opportunity to conduct structured interviews with the inspectors following the test. This extra data allowed detailed modelling of the inspection process. Typical examples of the use of Test Samples are for precision machined parts (See 2015), steel roller bearings (Drury and Sinclair 1983), automotive paint samples (Lloyd and He 1998) and airport security screening of baggage (Koller et al. 2009). More unusual examples are for characterizing Non-Destructive Inspection of aircraft structures (Rummel 2014) and even software inspection, e.g., De Lucia et al. (2007).

5 Inspection Performance Measurement Conclusions and Recommendations

Three methods for measuring inspection performance have been presented, and although measurement of inspector well-being has been undertaken, e.g., See (2015), this essential element of EHF evaluation is still relatively uncommon. The actual performance measurements have been presented, although reference to the original literature is advised. For example, if p(Hit), p(False Alarm) and time per item are all available (as in the Test Sample method) then more detailed analysis can reveal whether performance deficits have arisen from the search or the decision components of the inspection task (see Drury and Spencer 1997; Koller et al. 2009). For any inspection task, the actual task first needs to be understood in detail to be prepared for the complexity of measurement and control required. The author has never worked on an inspection task without at least a prior Task Analysis, and often a Hierarchical Task Analysis, e.g., Drury and Watson (2002). Such an analysis also helps in communicating with management, technical staff and the inspectors themselves to ensure that all agree to the same set of facts concerning the inspection system and its objectives.

In order to consolidate recommendations for inspection performance methodology, Table 1 presents a synopsis of the methods available based on the material presented here.

It should be clear from this summary that a Test Sample is the most comprehensive and practical means of testing the performance of an inspection system. As an example, Drury and Sinclair (1983) used a Test Sample to evaluate both inspectors and an automated system for precision aircraft parts, concluding that neither system was particularly accurate, and in follow-up studies made system changes to address the issues found in both systems. There will be some situations where higher face validity is required, so that Reinspection of Production and Labeled Defects in Production still have a place in EHF studies of inspection. Clearly there is a trade-off between characteristics of the three methods in terms of validity and depth., which should be appreciated before any study is started. Also, note that all three methods require an accurate defect list, with limit standards before the study can be started. In addition, it is recommended that (a) each study begin with an HTA of the inspection system, (b) informed consent is routinely required and (c) inspector well-being data is routinely collected to provide a balanced view of the performance results.

Table 1. Comparison of methods on performance issues.

Performance issue	Reinspection	Labelled items	Test sample
Defect list needed	Yes	Yes	Yes
Sample needed	No	Yes	Yes
Item labelling needed	No	Yes	Yes
Face validity	High	Moderate	Lower
Depth of measurement	Low	Higher	Highest
Depth of analysis	Low	Higher	Highest
Informed consent needed	Yes	Yes	Yes

Acknowledgements. The authors wish to acknowledge their obvious debt to their colleagues Douglas H. Harris and Murray A. Sinclair who first codified and expanded the classification of methodologies expounded in this paper.

References

Belbin, R.M.: Inspection and human efficiency. Appl. Ergon. **1**(5), 289–294 (1970)

Bennett, G.K.: Inspection error: its influence on quality control systems. In: Drury, C.G., Fox, J.G. (eds.) Human Reliability in Quality Control, pp. 1–10. Taylor and Francis, London (1975)

Chapman, D.E., Sinclair, M.A.: Ergonomics in inspection tasks in the food industry. In: Drury, C.G., Fox, J.G. (eds.) Human Reliability in Quality Control, pp. 231–251. Taylor and Francis, London (1975)

Dalton, J., Drury, C.G.: Inspectors' performance and understanding in sheet steel inspection. Occup. Ergon. **4**, 51–65 (2004)

De Lucia, A., Fasano F., Scanniello, G., Tortor, G.: Comparing inspection methods using controlled experiments. In: Electronic Workshops in Computing, The British Computer Society, pp. 1–10 (2007)

Drury, C.G.: A unified model of security inspection. In Proceedings of the Third International Aviation Security Technical Symposium, Atlantic City, NJ, Federal Aviation Administration, pp. 27–30 (2002)

Drury, C.G.: Belbin on inspection: a 50-year retrospective. In: Bagnara S., Tartaglia R., Albolino S., Alexander T., Fujita Y. (eds.) Proceedings of the 20th Congress of the International Ergonomics Association (IEA 2018). Advances in Intelligent Systems and Computing, vol 824. Springer, Champlain IL (2019)

Drury, C.G., Addison, J.L.: An industrial study of the effects of feedback and fault density on inspection performance. Ergonomics **16**, 159–169 (1973)

Drury, C.G., Holness, K., Ghylin, K.M., Green, B.D.: Using individual differences to build acommon core dataset for aviation security studies. Theor. Issues Ergon. Sci. **10**(5), 459–479 (2009)

Drury, C.G., Sinclair, M.A.: Human and machine performance in an inspection task. Hum. Factors **25**, 391–9 (1983)

Drury, C.G., Spencer, F.W.: Human factors and the reliability of airframe visual inspection. In: Proceedings of the 1997 SAE Airframe/Engine Maintenance & Repair Conference (AEMR'97), also SAE Technical Paper 972592, (1997)

Drury, C.G., Watson, J.: Good practices in visual inspection. Aircraft Maint. Technol. 74–76 (2002)

Harris, D.H., Chaney, F.B.: Human Factors in Quality Assurance. Wiley, New York (1969)

Koller, S.M., Drury, C.G., Schwaninger, A.: Change of search time and non-search time in X-ray baggage screening due to training. Ergonomics 52(6), 644–656 (2009)

Lloyd, C.J., He, Y.: An objective measure of severity for small topographical defects in automotive paint. SAE Technical Paper Series 982316 (1998)

Rummel, W.D.: Nondestructive evaluation – a critical part of structural integrity. Procedia Eng. 86, 375–383 (2014)

Sinclair, M.A.: The use of performance measures on individual examiners in inspection Schemes. Appl. Ergon. 10(1), 17–25 (1979)

See, J.E.: Visual inspection: A review of the literature (Report SAND2012–8590).: Sandia National Laboratories, Albuquerque, NM (2012)

See, J.E.: Visual inspection reliability for precision manufactured parts. Hum. Factors 57(8), 1427–144 (2015)

United States Department of Agriculture: Rice Inspection Handbook. USDA Washington, DC (1994)

United States Department of Agriculture: Visual Reference Images, USDA Washington, DC (2016)

Testing the Reliability and Validity of Net-HARMS: A New Systems-Based Risk Assessment Method in HFE

Adam Hulme[1]([⊠]), Neville A. Stanton[2], Guy H. Walker[3], Patrick Waterson[4], and Paul M. Salmon[1]

[1] Centre for Human Factors and Sociotechnical Systems, University of the Sunshine Coast, Sunshine Coast, Australia
ahulme@usc.edu.au
[2] Transportation Research Group, University of Southampton, Southampton, UK
[3] Centre for Sustainable Road Freight, Heriot-Watt University, Edinburgh, UK
[4] Human Factors and Complex Systems Group, Loughborough University, Loughborough, UK

Abstract. There is growing interest in the use of systems-based risk assessment (RA) methods in human factors and ergonomics (HFE). Despite this, there has been a lack of formal reliability and validity testing undertaken to determine whether systems-based RA methods have the capacity to reliably and accurately identify potential risks within complex systems. The purpose of this study was to test the intra-rater reliability (within subject stability) and criterion-related validity ('gold standard' performance) of the Networked Hazard Analysis and Risk Management System (Net-HARMS). Net-HARMS is a new and innovative systems-based RA method that supports analysts with the identification of emergent risks. Emergent risks represent new risks that are created when risks from across a complex system interact with one another. Reliability and validity measures for Net-HARMS were obtained using the Signal Detection Theory (SDT) paradigm. Matthews Correlation Coefficient (MCC) was used to analyze the complete SDT data to measure the strength of the correlation between risks. Findings indicate a weak to moderate level of reliability and validity for Net-HARMS based on the MCC score. The results suggest that there is merit to the continued use of Net-HARMS following a series of methodological recommendations that aim to enhance the reliability and validity of future applications.

Keywords: Risk assessment · Reliability and validity · Signal detection theory · Net-HARMS

1 Introduction

Risk assessment (RA) is a critical aspect of Human Factors and Ergonomics (HFE) research. Unlike accident analysis which takes a reactive approach, examining events after they have happened, RA aims to proactively identify hazardous system states that could conceivably contribute to an adverse incident [1].

N. L. Black et al. (Eds.): IEA 2021, LNNS 219, pp. 354–362, 2021.
https://doi.org/10.1007/978-3-030-74602-5_51

The use of systems-based RA methods to identify potential hazards and risks within complex safety-critical systems is increasing [1–6]. A systems-based RA approach acknowledges that risks within complex systems are created due to the complex inter-actions among a network of human and non-human factors. These factors operate at various scales and interact within and across multiple levels.

Despite growing interest around systems-based RA methods, there has been a lack of formal reliability and validity testing undertaken. Reliability and validity testing can indicate whether our safety methods 'work' as intended. This includes whether systems-based RA methods have the capacity to consistently and accurately identify risks within complex systems. There is a pressing need to test the reliability and validity of systems-based RA methods to advance knowledge in HFE and to ensure meaningful organizational changes are made to enhance safe working practices.

The Networked Hazard Analysis and Risk Management System (Net-HARMS) [5, 6] is a new, cutting edge systems-based RA method in HFE. Net-HARMS supports analysts with the identification of 'emergent risks' which are created when risks across all levels of a complex system interact with one another. Currently, Net-HARMS is the only RA method that includes this emergent risk feature whilst retaining a focus on a whole systems approach. An important next step is to subject Net-HARMS to reliability and validity testing to better understand how the method performs when used by experienced HFE and safety practitioners.

The purpose of this study is to test the intra-rater reliability and criterion-related validity of Net-HARMS in order to establish an evidence-base for its continued use into the future. Future directions and recommendations are proposed.

2 Methods

2.1 Net-HARMS

Net-HARMS [5] was developed based on the findings of a review which found that most RA methods do not support the identification of risks across work systems [1]. Net-HARMS provides two key advances over existing RA methods. First, it enables analysts to identify risks across the overall system, as opposed to 'sharp end' risks only. Second, Net-HARMS enables analysts to identify emergent risks that arise when different risks combine and interact with one another. The Net-HARMS risk modes taxonomy contains three categories and 10 risk modes:

Task

1. T1: Task mistimed
2. T2: Task omitted
3. T3: Task completed inadequately
4. T4: Inadequate task object
5. T5: Inappropriate task

Communication

6. C1: Information not communicated

7. C2: Wrong information communicated
8. C3: Inadequate information communicated
9. C4: Communication mistimed

Environmental

10. E1: Adverse environmental conditions

Applying Net-HARMS involves first developing a Hierarchical Task Analysis (HTA) [7, 8] of the target system. The HTA is converted into a task network which shows the core tasks and the relationships between those tasks. Task risks are identified by applying the Net-HARMS risk mode taxonomy (as above) to each task node within the task network. Following the task risk phase, the risk mode taxonomy is applied once more to identify emergent risks that arise when task risks interact with one another [6].

2.2 Study Design

A test-retest study design was used to evaluate the performance of Net-HARMS in terms of its capacity to identify potential risks impacting the design and safe operation of a metropolitan rail level crossing system (see Sect. 2.4). Nine participants used the method to perform a RA for the rail level crossing system during two workshops (led by AH and PS) separated by four weeks (Time one (T1) and Time two (T2)). The stability of the risks identified, and thus the reliability of the method, was determined by comparing participants' analyses between T1 and T2 (i.e., a within-subject analysis). Accuracy of the identified risks, and thus the validity of the method, was determined by comparing participants' analyses against an expert analysis, both at T1 and T2 (i.e., a criterion-related validity assessment). Reliability and validity measures are highest when the identified risks at T1 and T2/expert analysis are considered the same. Ethical approval was granted by the USC's Human Ethics Research Committee (A191245).

2.3 Participant Characteristics

To be eligible to take part in the study, participants were required to have direct experience with, and/or specialized knowledge about, HFE research and/or the science of accident analysis and RA. Participants were recruited through authors' research network. Sample demographics are presented in Table 1.

The occupation, qualification, work sector, context, and length of time employed in the current role of the participants can be viewed in Table 2.

Table1. Participant age and gender

Age range (years)	Frequency (%)
25–34	3 (33.3)
35–44	3 (33.3)
45–54	1 (11.1)
55–64	2 (22.2)
Gender	
Male	6 (66.7)
Female	3 (33.3)

Table 2. Participant employment characteristics

	Occupation	Qualification	Sector	Context	Employed (yrs.)
1	HFE consultant	Master's	Industry	Consultancy	1–2
2	HFE PhD student	Master's	University	Research	0–1
3	HFE consultant	PhD	Industry	Consultancy	10–20
4	HFE manager	Master's	Government	Transport	10–20
5	HFE specialist	PhD	Government	Rail	10–20
6	Ergonomist	Master's	Government	Work safety	10–20
7	HFE Fellow	PhD	University	Research	2–5
8	HFE PhD student	Master's	University	Research	2–5
9	HFE Fellow	PhD	University	Research	10–20

2.4 Materials

Electronic spreadsheets, analysis templates, and guidance documents to support the application of Net-HARMS were made available to participants on the morning of each workshop. The two-hour analyses were performed using a personal computer with spreadsheet processing software.

The participant group was provided with materials from a rail level crossing study that included the tasks and networks required to undertake the analyses [9]. Specifically, four out of a total 15 tasks from the 'rail level crossing system lifecycle task network' were chosen: (i) operate rail level crossing; (ii) performance monitoring; (iii) risk management; and, (iv) mange infrastructure [9].

2.5 Workshop Procedures

Participants were provided with a description of the Net-HARMS risk modes taxonomy, a flow diagram that outlined the steps required to complete a full analysis, and an electronic spreadsheet containing two tabs corresponding to the task risk and emergent risk phases. One hour was spent on the task risk and emergent risk phase, respectively.

2.6 Expert Analysis

One author (PS) with 21 years' experience of applied HFE and safety science research in areas such as road and rail safety, aviation, deference, healthcare, workplace safety, and cybersecurity completed the full Net-HARMS analysis. This analysis was subsequently inspected by two authors (AH and NS) who made suggestions to refine risk descriptions where necessary following open review and consensus.

2.7 Risk Comparison Procedure

One author (AH) closely inspected each risk reported at T1 and T2, or against the expert analysis, to perform a risk comparison analysis. A risk comparison was performed up to the furthest point that a participant reached at either T1 or T2 for reliability, or how far a participant reached at both T1 and T2 against the expert analysis for validity.

2.8 Signal Detection Theory (SDT)

The SDT paradigm [10] was used to evaluate reliability, as well as validity against the expert analyses. SDT uses a 'confusion matrix' which is a suitable approach when dealing with binary classification data (Fig. 1).

| | | Participant T2 (Reliability) Expert (Validity) | |
		Yes	No
Participant T1/T2	Yes	Hit (H)	False Alarm (FA)
	No	Miss (M)	Correct Rejection (CR)

Fig. 1. The SDT matrix and taxonomy

Based on the SDT matrix, four possible categorical outcomes following a comparison of risks at T1 and T2/expert analysis were made: (i) Hit; (ii) Miss; (iii) False Alarm; and, (iv) Correct Rejection. Thus, if the risks for a given participant were comparable at T1 and T2/expert analysis, a Hit was recorded using the SDT paradigm. If the risks were different, both a False Alarm and Miss were recorded. Correct Rejections were computed by subtracting each participant's False Alarm frequency from a pooled False Alarm value across the participant group.

2.9 Data Analysis

Matthews Correlation Coefficient (MCC) was used to analyze the complete SDT data (Eq. 1). The MCC measures the strength of a correlation between the predicted positive and negative values – in this case T1 risks – and the observed or 'true' positive and negative values – in this case T2 risks (i.e., reliability) or expert risks (i.e., validity).

$$MCC = \frac{H \times CR - FA \times M}{\sqrt{(H + FA)(H + M)(CR + FA)(CR + M)}} \tag{1}$$

The MCC is a reliable statistical approach that produces a relatively 'high' score, but only if the prediction obtains respectable scores in all four matrix categories (i.e., Hits, Misses, False Alarms, and Correct Rejections) [11]. Like other correlation coefficients, the MCC is normalized and operates on a scale from -1.0 to $+1.0$, where: $+1.0/-1.0$ is a perfect positive/ideal negative correlation; and, 0.0 means no relationship between a set of responses. The reliability and validity of Net-HARMS is higher as the MCC score approaches positive 1.0. The MCC scores were graphed using box plots to visualize the spread of data.

3 Results

The reliability of Net-HARMS was variable, indicated by a weak to moderate positive MCC score (M [SD] = .32 [.31]; Mdn [IQR] = .31 [.56]) (Fig. 2).

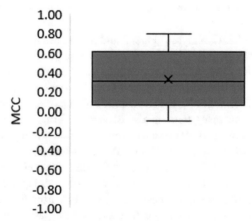

Fig. 2. Reliability MCC score for Net-HARMS. The mean and median MCC score is indicated by a cross and horizontal line, respectively.

The validity of Net-HARMS was variable, indicated by a weak to moderate positive MCC score at both T1 (M [SD] = .30 [.28]; Mdn [IQR] = .40 [.36]) and T2 (M [SD] = .40 [.33]; Mdn [IQR] = .50 [.33]) (Fig. 3).

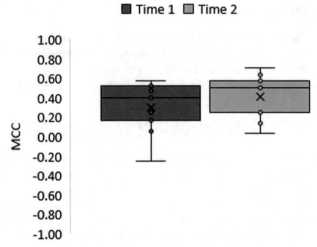

Fig. 3. Validity MCC scores for Net-HARMS at T1 and T2. The mean and median MCC score is indicated by a cross and horizontal line, respectively.

4 Discussion

The purpose of this study was to test the intra-rater reliability and criterion-related validity of Net-HARMS in order to establish an evidence-base for its continued use into the future. Indeed, ongoing methodological and analytical refinement may be necessary should results from rigorous quality control and methods testing studies indicate room for improvement.

According to the MCC analyses (Figs. 2 and 3), the reliability and validity of Net-HARMS was variable, indicated by a weak to moderate positive correlation coefficient between the predictive class, or T1 risks, and the observed class, or T2 risks (i.e., reliability), and between the predictive class, or T1 and T2 risks, and the observed class, or expert risk analyses (i.e., validity). Based on these findings, there is merit to the continued use of Net-HARMS; however, there is also a need for further research to explore why higher correlation coefficients and levels of reliability and validity were not obtained.

Four main reasons likely justify the results in this study, including: (i) the high-level nature of the tasks and controls described within the 'rail level crossing system lifecycle task network'; (ii) the need for further in-depth training and practice in the use of novel systems-based RA approaches; (iii) difficulties around applying the methods from a conceptual and procedural perspective; and, (iv) the particular characteristics and features of the chosen safety-critical system.

Regarding point one (i) above, the task network used in this study [9] was described at a 'high-level', which may have introduced greater variation in the risk descriptions provided, both between T1 and T2 (reliability) and between T1/T2 and the expert analysis (validity). Instead of a high-level network, a detailed task network would contain very specific system tasks thereby supporting analysts with equally refined risks. A more detailed task network could also result in many more tasks and relationships, increasing the time taken to undertake a Net-HARMS analysis.

In terms of point three (iii) above, this paper does not include the results from an individual phase analysis. For example, Net-HARMS includes two phases; a task risk identification phase and an emergent risk identification phase. The MCC score reflected a combined task and emergent risk phase resulting in an overall reliability and validity score for the method. The emergent risk phase is, however, arguably more difficult relative to the former, both conceptually and in practice, as analysts are required to identify new risks based on the interactions between existing system task risks. Thus, due to its conceptual and procedural complexity, the emergent risk phase might compromise the stability and accuracy of the identified risks. Future empirical testing is therefore required to confirm or deny this possibility.

Finally, this study has shown that some analysts performed better than others when identifying risks. Investigating the underlying reasons for individual differences during the delivery of RA methods training represents a fruitful avenue of future HFE research.

5 Conclusion

Net-HARMS appears to support analysts with the identification of stable and accurate system risks, albeit up to a certain point. Further training around the use of Net-HARMS is advocated along with a continuing need to test the reliability and validity of RA and HFE safety methods.

References

1. Dallat, C., Salmon, P.M., Goode, N.: Risky systems versus risky people: to what extent do risk assessment methods consider the systems approach to accident causation? A review of the literature. Saf Sci **119**, 266–279 (2017)
2. Leveson, N.: Engineering a Safer World: Systems Thinking Applied to Safety. MIT Press, Cambridge (2011)
3. Hollnagel, E.: FRAM, the Functional Resonance Analysis Method: Modelling Complex Socio-Technical Systems. Ashgate Publishing Ltd, Surrey (2012)
4. Stanton, N.A., Harvey, C.: Beyond human error taxonomies in assessment of risk in sociotechnical systems: a new paradigm with the EAST 'broken-links' approach. Ergonomics **60**(2), 221–233 (2017)
5. Dallat, C., Salmon, P.M., Goode, N.: Identifying risks and emergent risks across sociotechnical systems: The NETworked hazard analysis and risk management system (NET-HARMS). Theoret. Issues Ergon Sci **19**(4), 456–482 (2018)
6. Hulme, A., McLean, S., Dallat, C., Walker, G.H., Waterson, P., Stanton, N.A., Salmon, P.M. Systems thinking-based risk assessment methods applied to sports performance: A comparison of STPA, EAST-BL, and Net-HARMS in the context of elite women's road cycling. Applied Ergonomics 91 (2020, in press)
7. Kirwan, B., Ainsworth, L.K.: A Guide to Task Analysis: The Task Analysis Working Group. CRC Press , Boca Raton (1992)
8. Stanton, N.A.: Hierarchical task analysis: Developments, applications, and extensions. Appl. Ergon. **37**(1), 55–79 (2006)
9. Salmon, P.M., Read, G.J.M., Walker, G.H., Goode, N., Grant, E., Dallat, C., Carden, T., Naweed, A., Stanton, N.A.: STAMP goes EAST: integrating systems ergonomics methods for the analysis of railway level crossing safety management. Saf. Sci. **110**, 31–46 (2018)

10. Green, D.M., Swets, J.A.: Signal Detection Theory and Psychophysics. Wiley , Cambridge (1966)
11. Chicco, D., Jurman, G.: The advantages of the Matthews correlation coefficient (MCC) over F1 score and accuracy in binary classification evaluation. BMC Genom. **21**(1), 6 (2020)

Approach to Measure, Analyze and Develop the User-Centered-Complexity of Technical Products

Andreas Kaufmann[✉], Florian Reichelt, Marcel Racs, and Thomas Maier

Institute for Engineering Design and Industrial Design, Department of Industrial Design Engineering, University of Stuttgart, Pfaffenwaldring 9, 70569 Stuttgart, Germany
andreas.kaufmann@iktd.uni-stuttgart.de

Abstract. To measure the complexity of the technical product interface literature provides no methodology. This contribution starts with an overview of the state of the art and a categorized summary of the most relevant literature regarding product-related complexity. A methodical approach is presented for measuring human-machine-interface (short: HMI) - complexity including the product complexity and the degree of automation. For both HMI complexity and product complexity, a parameterization is used to obtain a measurable value. With the help of this parameterization a relationship between these three variables could be established. The degree of automation as a variable is used in the form of a balancing buffer to compensate border crossings depending the HMI complexity as well as the product complexity. These borders are individually marked of the respective product in combination with the user group. A brief evaluation of the methodology on the basis of different example products is carried out.

Keywords: Complexity · Measurement · User-centered-development · Human-machine-interface · Technical products

1 Objective and Literature Review

Literature provides many different definitions of complexity which differ depending on the discipline, the research issue, and the focus of observation [1]. Complexity is also perceived very differently in the various scientific fields, which is why there is no consistent definition so far [1, 2].

Complexity can be considered in different ways. One approach is to distinguish between subjective and objective complexity. Subjective complexity describes the activity or action of a subject within a system and describes behaviors in dealing with complex systems [2]. Thereby, the limited ability of a person to absorb and process information must be focused [3]. Changing the scale, the focus of observation, or the persons' level of knowledge can lead to a change in subjective complexity without an actual change in the system [4]. Objective complexity is commonly called structural complexity in literature and describes the structural dimension of the system. In this context, the elements of the system are connected to each other and therefore build the structure of the system [1].

© The Author(s), under exclusive license to Springer Nature Switzerland AG 2021
N. L. Black et al. (Eds.): IEA 2021, LNNS 219, pp. 363–370, 2021.
https://doi.org/10.1007/978-3-030-74602-5_52

In the field of technical product complexity, there are various approaches addressing complexity. A differentiation needs to be drawn between company-related and product-related complexity.

Product complexity can be described by a structural component, subdivided into the number of product components and its relations and functions [2, 5]. Another aspect of product complexity is described by the dynamics of the system and the interaction with other systems [1, 3]. In the user-centered consideration of HMI and usability, the human being and its understanding of the system must also be included. In this context, product complexity depends on the user and the user's prior knowledge and understanding of the system and can be described by uncertainties and lack of transparency [2].

To gain an overview of the relevant aspects of product complexity, extensive research was carried out and suitable parameters for describing product complexity were identified. These parameters can be seen in Table 1 on the left and were examined for the frequency of their references in literature.

Table 1. Literature review on various complexity aspects.

Characteristics of complexity			HMI development [6]	Human Supervisory Control [7]	Digital interfaces [8]	Product complexity [9]	Product portfolios [5]	Modular construction [10]	Complexity assessment [11]	Dimensions and indicators [12]	Measuring complexity [13]	Methodical development [14]	Designer-Artifact-User System [15]	Interpretative framework [16]	Organizations and complex systems [3]	Material flow systems [1]	Complexity management [17]	Complexity in construction projects [2]	The science of complexity [18]	Σ
HMI →						**Product complexity**			**Complexity assessment**			**Organizational complexity**					**Empirical investigations**			
Complexity Parameters	Variety and diversity	Variety of elements		x		x	x	x	x	x	x	x	x	x	x	x	x	x		14
		Type of the elements		x	x	x	x	x		x	x	x		x	x		x			12
		Number of elements	x	x	x	x	x	x	x	x	x	x	x	x		x	x	x	x	16
		Heterogeneity of element distribution	x			x				x		x		x	x	x			x	8
	Relations and connectivity	Correlations between elements	x	x	x	x	x	x	x	x	x	x		x	x	x	x	x	x	16
		Type of relations (relation content)		x		x	x	x	x	x	x	x		x	x	x			x	12
		Number of relations (link density)	x	x	x	x	x	x		x		x				x				9
		Uneven distribution of relations						x		x		x		x						4
	Product related parameters	Product architecture				x	x		x	x					x		x			6
		Functionality/functions	x	x		x	x		x	x					x		x			8
		Performance capability		x		x		x	x											4
		Life cycle / durability				x			x	x			x	x			x			6

The literature sources addressed above have been sorted and grouped according to their thematic focus. Based on the summarized amount of references, which can be seen on the right, the four most important parameters can be identified. Parameters with lower importance are shaded and therefore only partially relevant for this work. The shaded sections provide a better impression of the depth and breadth of the literature search conducted. In summary, the literature review showed that there are few studies addressing the complexity of user-centered product design. There is a clear research gap when considering product complexity in relation to the complexity of HMI and the associated usability of products. Additionally, an approach to adjust complexity for users by changing the degree of product automation or, vice versa, to measure product and HMI complexity by the degree of automation has not been researched yet.

2   Methodical Approach

As described in chapter one there is a need for a methodical approach that describes the interrelationships of three variables, which are the degree of automation (DoA), product complexity (PC), and the HMI complexity (HMIC).

Literature provides main parameters to describe complexity and make it measurable to a certain degree, as shown in chapter one. The methodology described in this paper is based on the composition of these parameters and transfers them to the specific product and HMI complexities.

2.1   Theoretical Principles

When it comes to technical interface design, the relationship between control element (CE) and the active part (AP) is very important. A major goal in the user centered HMI-development is to achieve a compatibility of the control element and the active part of the product. Thus, intuitive operating can be verified. [19] This link between AP and CE is a major factor for the methodical approach presented in this contribution.

2.2   Degree of Automation

Automation can be seen as the central link between the functions of a product and the control elements. The degree of automation (DoA) depends on the number of product functions and the number of control elements. Figure 1 shows the correlation and examples of how the degree of automation can be understood.

An electrical seat adjustment can serve as an example of a product for the lowest degree of automation (no automation). The operation of the seat's active parts is directly related to the according control elements. For each function of the product there is a corresponding actuator. The automation-ratio is 1:1.

In comparison, a high DoA can perform all functions of a product by means of a single control element. For example, a passenger of an autonomous vehicle can activate the vehicles' function with very few controls. A high automation ratio is 1: a high number.

Thus, the purpose of automation can be seen as the translation of user interaction into product functions. Whereas the DoA describes the complexity of the machine logic, which is only used as a black box in this contribution. Accordingly, the DoA is not determined and measured.

However, the degree of automation is a central relation between the HMI and the operating principle and thus between the HMI complexity and the product complexity.

Fig. 1. Illustration of the degree of automation using the example of an electrical seat adjustment (left) and an autonomous vehicle cockpit (right)

2.3 Product Complexity

To measure the product complexity (PC) a parameterization is necessary. For this reason, objective key parameters were identified, which could be derived and transferred from the state of the art. The parameters are the number of active parts (NAP), the number of functions per active parts (NFAP), the correlation between active parts (CAP), and the variety of active parts (VAP). The most important parameter is NAP. The other three parameters can be seen as similar important and are added in the calculation before they are multiplied by the factor 0.5, as shown in Table 2. The addition to the NAP results in the actual value of the product complexity, which is divided by the maximum value to get PC.

2.4 Complexity of the Human-Machine-Interface

Simultaneously to the parameterization of the product complexity, the HMI complexity is determined. The different parameters are the number of control elements (NCE), the number of functions per control element (NFCE), the correlation between control elements (CCE), and the characteristics of the control element (VCE).

Considering the HMI complexity, the user is essential. Depending on the user or intended user group, the permissible HMI complexity shifts. Professional users can handle much more complex HMIs than a nonspecialist. For this reason, it is necessary to include the characteristics of the user group in the evaluation of the HMI complexity. The assessment of the user group needs to be made by the user of the methodical approach, since this one has the expertise to make a valid assessment. The user group is categorized based on the parameters expertise HMI (EH) and expertise product (EP). The expertise regarding the HMI is very important to find out if there is experience in operating the relevant HMI. The experience can be measured by the frequency of usage, see Table 3. The expertise regarding the product indicates the experience the user has with similar products. The user is not aware of the specific HMI but has some experience with a product of a competitor, for example. To calculate the overall expertise EH is more important than EP. The expertise (E) is compared with the HMI complexity (IC) in order to be able to recognize a possible excessive demand on the user. Table 2 shows the calculation of the different complexity variables. The numerical example in Table 2 is the percussion drill, which serves as an evaluation example in chapter four.

Table 2. Calculation of the Complexity regarding the Product and the HMI (Example Percussion Drill).

	Product Complexity			Human-Machine-Interface Complexity					
	PC		0-4	E		0-4	IC		0-4
Parameter	Number of APs	NAP	1	Expertise HMI	EH	0	Number of CEs	NCE	2
	Number of functions per AP	NFAP	2				Number of functions per CE	NFCE	1
	Correlation between APs	CAP	2	Expertise Product	EP	2	Correlation between CEs	CCE	1
	Variety of APs	VAP	2				Variety of CEs	VCE	3
Calculation	$PC = \dfrac{NAP + (0,5*(NFAP + CAP + VAP))}{10}$			$E = \dfrac{(EH + 0,5\,EP)}{6}$			$IC = \dfrac{NCE + NFCE + (0,5*(CCE - VCE))}{10}$		
Results	PC	**0,40**		E	0,17		IC	0,2	HMIC = (1-E)+ IC	**HMIC 1,03**

		Ranges of Value (PC)			Ranges of Value (HMIC)	
Ranges of Value	PC Range 0 - 1	PC > 0,7	High PC	HMIC Range 0 - 2	HMIC > 1,5	HMIC is too high, Recommendations need to be considered
		PC 0,3 - 0,7	Moderate PC		HMIC 1-1,5	HMIC is high, Recommendations should be considered
		PC < 0,3	Low PC		HMIC 0,75-1	HMIC is moderate, Recommendations can be considered
					HMIC < 0,75	HMIC is manageable

Design Recommendations	PC > 0,7	Indicator HMIC can be to high; DoA is important and	Raising the DoA to lower NCE and/or NFCE
	PC = 0,3 - 0,7	Indicator that HMIC might be in moderate level	Lower NCE with the help of adaptive control elements
	PC < 0,3	Indicator that HMIC is in low level	Lower PC so the IC and HMIC is getting lower
			Reduce the CCE
			Increase EH and/or EP with the help of trainings
			Increase the VCE to increase intuitivity in operating

2.5 Ranges of Value

The range of values for the evaluation of the different parameters, shown in Table 3, is fixed on an established scale from 0 to 4. Where 0 is the lowest rating and 4 the highest [20].

Table 3. Ranges of Value for the 10 different parameters.

	EH / EP		NAP NCE		NFAP NFCE		CAP CCE		VAP VCE
0	No Experience	0	0 APs / CEs	0	Ø 1 Function per AP / CE	0	0 Corr. between APs / CEs	0	0 % diff. types of APs / CEs
1	Rare Use	1	1-7 APs / CEs	1	Ø 2 Functions per AP / CE	1	Ø 1 Corr. between APs / CEs	1	25 % diff. types of APs / CEs
2	Occasional Use	2	8-49 APs / CEs	2	Ø 3 Functions per AP / CE	2	Ø 2 Corr. between APs / CEs	2	50 % diff. types of APs / CEs
3	Frequent Use	3	50-100 APs / CEs	3	Ø 4 Functions per AP / CE	3	Ø 3 Corr. between APs / CEs	3	75 % diff. types of APs / CEs
4	Daily Use	4	> 100 APs / CEs	4	> Ø 4 Functions per AP / CE	4	Ø > 3 Corr. between APs / CEs	4	100 % diff. types of APs / CEs

The individual ranges of value for the different parameters are defined qualitatively with the focus to a holistic evaluation method for technical products. For the application of the method, it is necessary to adjust these ranges to the specific selection of products which should be investigated. The ranges of value were defined by the assumption that very different products are evaluated in this paper. Regarding the number of APs and CEs, it is assumed that a number of more than 100 is a very complex product. Above this number, the HMI is not easily operable, which means that as the number increases, adjustments must be made either way. Therefore, this classification was chosen for this application. The lowest range for these parameters (NAP/NCE) besides 0 is between 1 and 7. This number refers to the work of Miller who defined 7 ± 2 information units (chunks) as the limit of working memory with respect to a point in time. [21] The ranges of value in between are scaled appropriately, as are the value ranges of the other parameters. Table 3 is defined for the evaluation carried out in chapter four and has no general validity, especially regarding completely different compositions of products.

3 Application Area and Resulting Design Recommendations

The area of application of the method is diverse. One scope is the analysis of own or third-party products (benchmark) to check whether there are deficits in the implementation of the HMI with regard to complexity or whether the degree of automation must be increased.

In the case of a new development, it is important to pay attention to the resulting complexity in the HMI concept phase. If necessary, automation concepts must be adapted in order to regulate the HMI complexity to a level that is appropriate for the user groups. In case of a new development there is just the PC and no HMI complexity existent. In this case the complexity of the HMI is calculable with the PC. The PC then indicates possible problems which can occur with the HMIC.

The result of the methodical approach is a design recommendation for the characteristics and interaction of the three variables. The possibility of determining two of three variables allows a design recommendation for the degree of automation. In general the result of the methods are recommendations for all three variables and their parameters of how to manage the complexity.

The ranges of value of the calculation are described in Table 3. The design recommendations with the ranges of value resulting from the calculation are included.

4 Evaluation

For a brief evaluation the method was applied to three different example products. The ranges of value are adjusted to the specific evaluation, to confirm that different products with widely differing complexities can be examined. The evaluated products are a seat adjustment in a vehicle, a percussion drill, a control armrest of a tractor, and a autonomous vehicle. The results are shown in Fig. 2. The assumed expertise of the user in these examples is at $EH = 0$ and $EP = 2$. Figure 2 shows a qualitative distribution of the complexities and the degree of automation. The solid triangle is the actual distribution and the dashed triangle is the distribution after the design recommendation was applied or with the implemented degree of automation. The arrows indicate the change in the respective example.

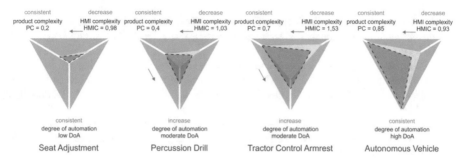

Fig. 2. Evaluation examples

5 Conclusion

The elementary result of this contribution is, besides the discovered research gap with the help of the literature review, the awareness that product development requires a functioning interrelation between product complexity, HMI complexity, and the degree of automation. Here, a complexity limit of the HMI must be complied. This limit is linked to the user or user group. If the HMI complexity overstrains the user, a regulation must be provided. This can be implemented by increasing the degree of automation, as described in this contribution. In this context, the product complexity can usually not be reduced. It is therefore necessary to increase automation in order to achieve reduction in HMI complexity while maintaining product complexity. Another way to reduce the HMI complexity is to increase the expertise of the user with trainings or tutorials. Thus the HMI complexity becomes operable.

6 Outlook

In order to expand this methodical approach, it is necessary to conduct further evaluations with different products. This provides an opportunity to refine the approach and address potential weaknesses. With the help of further evaluation examples the calculation can be specified. Further considerations are necessary to be able to integrate this methodical approach into the product development process.

References

1. Krenn, B.: Bewertung von Komplexität in Materialflusssystemen der Prozessindustrie am Beispiel der Stahl- und Feuerfestindustrie. Department of Industrial Logistics at the University of Leoben, Dissertation (2008)
2. Hoffmann, W.: Zum Umgang mit der Komplexität von Bauvorhaben – Indikatorbezogenes Modell zur Bewertung von Komplexität in Bauprojekten. Department of Constructional Engineering, Technical University Kaiserslautern, Dissertation (2017)
3. Bandte, H.: Komplexität in Organisationen. Dissertation, 1st edn. DUV, Wiesbaden (2007)
4. Pommeranz, I.: Komplexitätsbewältigung im Multiprojektmanagement. Department of Economics, University of Augsburg Dissertation (2011)

5. Jacobs, M., Swink, M.: Product portfolio architectural complexity and operational performance: incorporating the roles of learning and fixed assets. J. Oper. Manag. **29**(7–8), 677–691 (2011)
6. König, C.: Analyse und Anwendung eines menschzentrierten Gestaltungsprozesses zur Entwicklung von Human-Machine-Interfaces im Arbeitskontext am Beispiel Flugsicherung. Department of Mechanical Engineering, Technical University of Darmstadt, Dissertation (2012)
7. Li, K., Wieringa, P.: Understanding perceived complexity in human supervisory control. In: Carsten, O., Vanderhaegen, F. (eds.) Cognition, Technology & Work, vol. 2, no. 2, pp. 75–88. Springer, London (2000)
8. Wu, L., Zhu, Z., Cao, H., Li, B.: Influence of information overload on operator's user experience of human–machine interface in LED manufacturing systems. In: Carsten, O., Vanderhaegen, F. (eds.) Cognition, Technology & Work, vol. 18, no. 1, pp. 161–173. Springer, London (2016)
9. Schuh, G.: Produktkomplexität managen – Strategien – Methoden – Tools. 3rd.edn. Hanser, Munich (2017)
10. Blackenfelt, M.: Managing complexity by product modularisation – Balancing the aspect of technology and business during the design process. Department of Machine Design, Royal Institute of Technology, Stockholm, Dissertation (2001)
11. Budde, L.: Integriertes Komplexitätsmanagement in produzierenden Unternehmen – Ein Modell zur Bewertung von Komplexität. School of Management, Economics, Law, Social Sciences and International Affairs, University St. Gallen, Dissertation (2016)
12. Orfi, N., Terpenny, J., Sahin-Sariisik, A.: Harnessing Product Complexity: Step 1 – Establishing Product Complexity Dimensions and Indicators. In: The Engineering Economist, vol. 56, no. 1, pp. 59–79, Taylor & Francis (2011)
13. Vesterby, V.: Measuring Complexity: Things That Go Wrong and How to Get It Right. 1st edn. In: Emergence: Complexity and Organization, vol. 10, no. 2 (2008).
14. Lindemann, U.: Methodische Entwicklung technischer Produkte. Springer-Verlag, Heidelberg (2005)
15. Maier, J., Fadel, G.: On the complexity of the designer-artifact-user system. In: International Conference of Engineering Design ICED 03, vol. 14, Stockholm (2003)
16. Benedettini, O., Neely, A.: Complexity in services: an interpretative framework. In: Schoenherr, T., Seshadri, S. (eds.) 23rd Annual Conference on Production and Operations Management Society (POMS), Chicago, Illinois, U.S.A. (2012)
17. Götzfried, M.: Managing Complexity Induced by Product Variety in Manufacturing Companies – Complexity Evaluation and Integration in Decision-Making. School of Management, Economics, Law, Social Sciences and International Affairs, University of St. Gallen, Dissertation (2013)
18. Heylighen, F.: Building a science of complexity. In: Conference of the Cybernetics Society, London, (1988)
19. Schmid, M., Maier, T.: Technisches Interface Design. Bewertung und Gestaltung. Springer , Anforderungen (2017)
20. Verein deutscher Ingenieure e.V.: Konstruktionstechnik – Technisch-wirtschaftliches Konstruieren –Technisch-wirtschaftliche Bewertung – Blatt 3. Beuth Verlag, Berlin, Germany (1998)
21. Miller, G.A.: The magical number seven, plus or minus two: some limits on our capacity for processing information. Psychol. Rev. **63**, 81–97 (1965)

That Was Close! A Systems Analysis of Near Miss Incidents in Led Outdoor Activities

Scott McLean[1](✉), Lauren Coventon[1], Caroline F. Finch[2], and Paul M. Salmon[1]

[1] Centre for Human Factors and Sociotechnical Systems, University of the Sunshine Coast, Sippy Downs, Australia
smclean@usc.edu.au

[2] School of Medical and Health Sciences, Edith Cowan University, Joondalup, WA, Australia

Abstract. The analysis of near miss incidents is recognized as an important component of safety management. The aim of this study is to present a systems analysis of near miss incidents in the Australian Led Outdoor Activity (LOA) sector. This study utilized the LOA specific incident reporting and learning system, Understanding and Preventing Led Outdoor Activity Data System (UPLOADS), to analyze near miss incidents in LOAs in Australia. UPLOADS is based on Rasmussen's risk management framework and uses a modified AcciMap framework. Data for the current analysis was provided by 18 LOA providers across a 12-month period between September 2018 to September 2019. The LOA providers represented all Australian states and territories. The results demonstrate that a network of factors from across the system contribute to near miss incidents. These include, local government, parents, schools, LOA organizations, supervisors, participants, and the environment. The current findings will help LOA providers better understand near miss incidents and improve their safety efforts.

Keywords: Led Outdoor Activity · Safety · Incident reporting · AcciMap · Near miss

1 Introduction

To prevent future adverse incidents, it is critical to learn from past adverse events and near misses [1–3]. The use of a formal incident reporting system is now widely accepted as an effective means of understanding and preventing incidents and near misses in safety critical domains [1, 4, 5]. However, many incident reporting systems are criticized for failing to collect appropriate data that supports incident prevention [6]. In addition, whilst systems thinking models of accident causation are accepted as state-of-the-art [7], they are not typically used in the analysis of near miss incidents. Previous research has shown that near miss incidents display similar characteristics to adverse incidents [8]. As such, understanding the systemic factors contributing to near miss incidents is important to inform incident prevention strategies [8].

The Understanding and Preventing Led Outdoor Activity Data System (UPLOADS) is an incident reporting system developed to improve the safety of the Australian Led

N. L. Black et al. (Eds.): IEA 2021, LNNS 219, pp. 371–375, 2021.
https://doi.org/10.1007/978-3-030-74602-5_53

Outdoor Activity (LOA) sector. LOAs are defined as facilitated activities that occur in an outdoor or recreational setting and have specific learning objectives [9]. Activities undertaken by LOA participants include abseiling, high ropes courses, camping, canoeing, kayaking, and rafting, among others. UPLOADS is underpinned by Rasmussen's Risk Management Framework (RMF) [10], and the associated AcciMap technique [11]. The RMF suggests that all sociotechnical systems are comprised of a hierarchy, each of which contain different actors, organizations and technologies that share responsibility for production and safety [10]. The AcciMap method is used to identify and represent the network of contributory factors and where they reside across the systems hierarchy [12]. LOA providers use UPLOADS to submit their near miss and adverse incidents that occur during LOAs [4, 13]. Previous analyses of adverse incidents reported to UPLOADS have demonstrated that the decisions and actions of actors from across multiple levels of the system interact to enable adverse events [11, 14]. The purpose of this study was to present an analysis of the near miss incidents submitted to UPLOADS to determine the near miss incident characteristics and the interacting network of contributory factors.

2   Method

Data for the current analysis was provided by 18 LOA providers across a 12-month period between 2018 and 2019. The LOA providers represented all Australian states and territories. UPLOADS was developed to support Rasmussen's RMF [10] and associated AcciMap method to provide an understanding of systemic influences on incidents and near misses in LOA. The modified AcciMap utilized for UPLOADS is presented (Fig. 1). UPLOADS provides a standardized method for reporting and analyzing near miss incidents across five hierarchical levels representing the LOA system:

- Governance (local government, regulators);
- Clients (schools, parents);
- LOA planning and management (program design, program scheduling);
- People involved in incidents (participants, other people);
- Resources and activities (equipment, environment).

The near miss incidents reported to UPLOADS capture information regarding the activity type (e.g. bushwalking, kayaking, mountain biking), the circumstances at the time of the incident (e.g. incident type, time location, severity), participant information (e.g. name, age, gender, treatment received), a written incident description, the contributory factors involved in the incident, and the interactions between the contributory factors. The potential severity of near miss incidents were defined as; no impact, minor, moderate, serious, severe, and critical. Participation of all persons involved in programs was collected to calculate the relative frequency (per 1000 program participation days) of near miss incidents (near miss incidents per activity/Program Participation Days x 1000). Participation of all people is also recorded for each activity type to calculate the relative frequency of near miss incidents for activities (near miss incidents per activity/Activity Participation Days × 1000).

LOA providers submit their incident reports to the National Incident Dataset (NID) which then forms a national repository that is analysed by the research team. For the

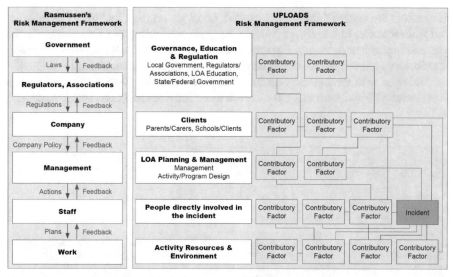

Fig. 1. Rasmussen's RMF (Green) alongside the adapted framework for the LOA Sector (Purple); and examples of how contributory factors from across the system can interact to contribute to incident causation. (McLean, Coventon, Finch, Salmon, 2021, Under Review).

data to be eligible for inclusion in the current analysis, the data must meet the following criteria:

- Data was complete and entered in accordance with the UPLOADS app training material;
- Participation data included the breakdown of activities and the number of participants involved in each activity per day;
- Incident reports included descriptions of each contributory factor and the relationships between contributory factors.

3   Results

In total, 143 near miss incidents from 357,691 Program Participation Days were submitted to the NID across the 12-month period. This equates to a near miss incident rate of 0.4 per 1000 program participation days.

The LOA activities with the most frequent occurrence of near miss incidents were Walking/running (n = 40), Harness outdoors (n = 35), Camping in tents (n = 19), and Freshwater activities (n = 16). Potential incident severity was reported as; no impact (n = 6), minor (n = 13), moderate (n = 35), serious (n = 52), severe (n = 26), and critical (n = 11).

The contributory factors and relationships between them were used to develop an Accimap of the near miss incidents. The most frequently reported contributory factors from across the system levels were included, Local government facilities, Communication from schools, Management policies, Program scheduling and resourcing, Participant and Supervisor decisions, Equipment and clothing (Fig. 2). Relationships between contributory factors were identified across all levels of the system hierarchy (Fig. 2).

Activities with the highest near miss incident rate (per 1000 activity participation days) included Walking/running (0.4), Fresh water activities (0.2), and Harness activities (0.2).

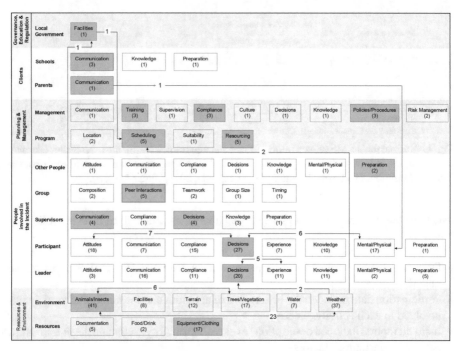

Fig. 2. Near miss incident contributory factors and relationships.

The absolute number of contributory factors are presented in parenthesis. Lines connecting the contributory factors represent the relationships. The value embedded within the relationship represents the number of times a relationship was reported. The shaded boxes represent the most frequently reported factors across the five levels. For figure clarity, only the most prominent relationships are presented.

4   Discussion

This study supports previous research suggesting that near miss incidents share similar characteristics to adverse incidents in that they are created by a network of contributory factors spanning the overall work system (in this case the LOA system) [8, 15]. The current analysis demonstrates that the decisions and actions of actors from across multiple levels of the LOA system interact to create near miss incidents. As such, an incident reporting tool that considers the network of contributory factors such as UPLOADS, is appropriate for understanding near miss incidents in LOAs. Despite the overall low rate of near miss incidents (0.4), there were 37 (26%) incidents classified with a potential severity of severe or critical. This result highlights that despite successful outcomes, there were multiple incidents nearing fatal outcomes. Further work should explore the protective factors which prevented the incidents analyzed from progressing to an adverse outcome.

Minimizing near miss incidents in LOAs may be achieved through a detailed understanding of the network of contributory factors demonstrated in the current analysis. This allows LOA providers to focus their safety efforts on removing the whole network of contributory factors causing near miss incidents.

References

1. Jacobsson, A., Ek, Å., Akselsson, R.: Method for evaluating learning from incidents using the idea of "level of learning." J. Loss Prev. Process Ind. **24**(4), 333–343 (2011)
2. Jacobsson, A., Ek, Å., Akselsson, R.: Learning from incidents–a method for assessing the effectiveness of the learning cycle. J. Loss Prev. Process Ind. **25**(3), 561–570 (2012)
3. Lindberg, A., Hansson, S.O., Rollenhagen, C.: Learning from accidents–what more do we need to know? Saf. Sci. **48**(6), 714–721 (2010)
4. Goode, N., et al.: Translating systems thinking into practice: a guide to developing incident reporting systems. CRC Press, Boca Raton (2018)
5. Nielsen, K.J., Carstensen, O., Rasmussen, K.: The prevention of occupational injuries in two industrial plants using an incident reporting scheme. J. Saf. Res. **37**(5), 479–486 (2006)
6. Dekker, S., Just culture: balancing safety and accountability. Ashgate Publishing, Ltd. (2007)
7. Salmon, P.M., et al.: The big picture on accident causation: a review, synthesis and meta-analysis of AcciMap studies **126**, 104650 (2020)
8. Thoroman, B., Salmon, P.: An integrated approach to near miss analysis combining AcciMap and Network Analysis. Saf. Sci. **130**, 104859 (2020)
9. Salmon, P.M., et al.: Injury causation in the great outdoors: a systems analysis of led outdoor activity injury incidents **63**, 111–120 (2014)
10. Rasmussen, J.: Risk management in a dynamic society: a modelling problem. Saf. Sci. **27**, 183–213 (1997)
11. McLean, S., et al.: Applying a systems thinking lens to injury causation in the outdoors: evidence collected during 3 years of the understanding and preventing led outdoor accidents data system. Injury Prev. **27**(1), 48–54 (2021)
12. Rasmussen, J., Suedung, I.: Proactive risk management in a dynamic society. Swedish Rescue Services Agency (2000)
13. Salmon, P.M., et al.: Rasmussen's legacy in the great outdoors: a new incident reporting and learning system for led outdoor activities. **59**, 637–648 (2017)
14. Mclean, S., et al.: Incidents in the Great Outdoors: A systems approach to understanding and preventing led outdoor accidents. In: 64th Human Factors and Ergonomics Society Annual Conference, Chicago, USA (2020)
15. Thoroman, B., Goode, N., Salmon, P.: System thinking applied to near misses: areview of industry-wide near miss reporting systems. Theoret. Issues Ergon. Sci. **19**(6), 712–737 (2018)

Validation of Ergonomic Criteria for the Evaluation of Simplex Systems

Viviane Perret[1]([⊠]), Neville A. Stanton[2], Cédric Bach[1], Guillaume Calvet[1], and Aline Chevalier[3]

[1] Human Design Group, Toulouse, France
{viviane.perret,cedric.bach,guillaume.calvet}@hdgroup.fr
[2] University of Southampton, Southampton, UK
n.stanton@soton.ac.uk
[3] Laboratoire Cognition, Langue, Langage, Ergonomie (CNRS UMR 5263), Université de Toulouse, Toulouse, France
aline.chevalier@univ-tlse2.fr

Abstract. The increasing complexity of interconnected systems, organizations and environmental instability open on one hand new functional features and unexpected levels of systemic efficiency, but on the other hand leads to great challenges to maintain a good level of usability. We assume that the complex systems should be adapted to human capacities and goals through a structural integration of such complexity by the interactive systems. These systems should be both: structurally complex from technological and organizational standpoint; and conceptually simple from operator's standpoint, in other words it should be *simplex*. In order to design an efficient balance between *complexity* and *simplexity* a new kind of user centered methods are necessary. But, current available methods in ergonomics to assess Human-Simplex System Interactions (HSSI) are limited in the field of Human Oriented Approach of Complexity, also called Human System Integration (HSI). In this paper, we present an experimental assessment of an evaluation method based on a set of Ergonomic Criteria able to support human factors specialists during an inspection task of complex systems. This experimental study aimed to assess if these Ergonomic Criteria are useful and efficient. Thirty-one HSI Designers performed an ergonomic inspection of two Simplex Systems in order to capture a maximum of usability/assistance flaws. The results show that the criteria are reliable and valid. The use of these Criteria allowed to identify more flaws and also more flaws shared between assessors. Nevertheless, the satisfaction results revealed the need to improve the level of maturity of these criteria.

Keywords: Human system integration · Evaluation methods · Heuristic evaluations · Complexity · Usability

1 Introduction

The technological (r)evolution has scaled up the implementation of multimodal and interconnected systems within a more and more wider complex network [1]. To face challenges posed by the complexity of reality on human agents, simplex [5, 7] systems should be both: (a) structurally complex from technological and organizational stand-point; and (b) conceptually simple from operator's standpoint. The challenge of a Human oriented design dealing with simplex interactions opens new investigations for Human Factors (HF) research. Designing the fair balance of resources the human agents mobilize would require a set of ergonomic rules defining features of simplex systems. In view of the ergonomic researches [6], we focused on an Ergonomic Criteria based method, supporting the HF specialist to perform a usability diagnosis task of structurally complex systems. The current limitations of ergonomic criteria (e.g., [2, 4]) are to not explicitly integrate ergonomic properties supporting the user dealing with complexity in situation, such as space-time relationships (4D). To overcome these limitations, we developed a first ergonomic criteria list based on the codification of 810 recommendations extracted from an analysis of 27 scientific and industrial documents published between 1978 and 2015. The updated version of these Ergonomic Criteria [11] following a first usability assessment is arranged in six main categories subdivided in 3 hierarchical sub-levels. This list is composed of 32 elementary criteria indicated with a star in the Table 1.

Table 1. List of ergonomic criteria for human simplex system interactions (HSSI)

1. Compatibility	**2. Guidance**
1.1 Users	2.1. Presentation of items
1.1.1. Basic Human Capabilities*	*2.1.1. Sensory Modalities**
1.1.2. Core Competencies*	*2.1.2. Legibility**
1.1.3. User's Tasks & Goal*	*2.1.3. Grouping / Distinction of Items**
1.2. Coordination	*2.1.4. Salience**
1.2.1. Physical Locations*	*2.1.5. Right Time, Location & Behavior**
1.2.2. Synchrony & Asynchrony*	2.2. Content of Items
1.2.3. Agents' Responsibilities*	*2.2.1. Significance**
1.2.4. Interoperability between systems*	*2.2.2. Accuracy**
	2.2.3. Relevance*
	2.3. Prompting
	2.3.1. Action Activation*
	2.3.2. Actions Plan*
	2.3.3. Status Information*
	2.4. Immediate Feedback*
3. Adaptability	**4. Actions and Information Costs**
3.1. Level of control	4.1. Substantial Actions*
3.1.1 Shared Control*	4.2. Repetitiveness & Frequency*
3.1.2. Control recovery*	4.3. Informational Load*
3.1.3. Vigilance Management*	**5. Homogeneity & Consistency***
3.1.4. Time-Lags Management*	**6. Threats & Error Management**
3.2. Flexibility	6.1. Error Protection*
3.2.1. Evolving User's Experience*	6.2. External Threats Protection*
3.2.2. Individual Needs & Preferences*	6.3. Error Correction*

The adoption of a method is facilitated if this method is both *reliable* and *valid* [14]. The *reliability* seeks to identify if the participants results are well grouped; while the *validity* seeks to define if their results are well aligned with the targeted goal [14]. Thus, we aimed to meet to two research questions: Do the proposed *criteria* help to: (1) improve exhaustivity and accuracy of identified problems? And (2) identify more similar problems within assessors? In this paper, we first present the method elaborated to assess *reliability* and *validity* of the *Ergonomic Criteria* we propose to support ergonomic inspection of *Human Simplex System Interactions* (HSSI). We then present our main results. Finally, we discuss and conclude on the contribution of our study and consider perspectives for further research about *Ergonomic Criteria for HSSI*.

2   Methodology

2.1   Stages of the Experiment

The participants had to perform an inspection task [2, 4]. They had to identify a maximum of problems related to bad usability or lack of assistance from the system (i.e., simplexity flaws). Two methods were used separately to evaluate two simplex systems. 16 participants took part individually in a Document based Inspection (DI). The document used to guide the inspection was the *Ergonomic Criteria for the HSSI* we sought to assess. 15 participants took part individually in an Expert Inspection (EI), in other words solely based on the participants' expertise. This group was the Control Group.

The systems to inspect had deliberately issues (i.e., willingly erroneous design hypothesis; presentation that did not match with the system capability). The systems were also contrasted enough to assess the stability of the *Ergonomic Criteria*. The first system was an aeronautical concept of operations related to the integration of RPAS (Remotely Piloted Aircraft Systems) into a controlled air traffic. This concept proposed the integration of an onboard transponder in a RPAS to enable it to fly in a civil controlled airspace and to follow the same procedures as those currently applied in the air-traffic management. The second system was a generic smartphone application. This app was a crowd sourced and community-based traffic/navigation application marketed for car drivers. In the context of our study, the participants had to inspect this navigation application by considering the pedestrian needs. The app was presented on the same smartphone for each participant.

Each session was video recorded, and mainly conducted in a meeting room, partially outdoor for the navigation app. We introduced the evaluated systems one by one. Their presentations were counterbalanced between participants. Each inspection was limited to 30 min. For the navigation app, we exposed the 2 steps required to perform the inspection: (1) 10 min was proposed to explore the system in outdoor pedestrian situation; (2) then, for 20 min, participants had to notify identified problems, and inspect the additional services allowing to plan a journey. Before performing the inspection, the DI group had unlimited time to read and to be familiarized with *Ergonomic criteria*. They were informed they had access to the document all along the session. At the end of the experiment, the DI group was asked to fil the SUS questionnaire (*System Usability Scale*) [3]. With this experimental design, we analyzed data from 30 h video recording and participants' notes.

2.2   Participants

31 volunteers had an advanced level of education in ergonomics or usability engineering. We integrated the engineer profiles in the study target population to take into account the *Ergonomic criteria* understanding by non-specialists in human factors involved in human oriented complex system design process. All the participants had previous experiences, at least once, with the design of systems involving one or several operators, dynamic processes, and high-tech systems (that are components of systemic complexity). They knew heuristic methods. 83.87% worked or studied in the research on transportation (e.g., aeronautic, automotive, railway, shipbuilding). The DI group were 22 to 56 years old ($A = 31$, $SD = 9.58$). The EI group were 20 to 56 years old ($A = 30.93$, $SD = 9.91$).

2.3   Material

The experimental apparatus used was the *Ergonomic Criteria for HSSI*, two simplex systems, and the SUS questionnaire [3].

   The *Ergonomic Criteria* were outlined on three supports: (a) a sheet introducing the criteria tree structure; (b) a leaflet presenting the criteria short definitions; (c) a document report showing each criterion one by one with detailed definitions, rationales, and, for elementary criteria, ergonomic recommendation examples, and when required, exclusionary rules. For each *simplex system*, we briefly exposed the context, goal, and available features to answer this goal. We identified, for the *Aeronautical Concept*, 24 key issues, from publications [8, 9, 13] and an interview with a RPAS designer. We illustrated communications between agents to put these issues forward. By inspection, we identified 13 key issues on *Navigation app* guidance for a pedestrian.

2.4   Data Collection and Analysis

The data collected was the participants' notes and verbalizations. We implemented qualitative and quantitative analyses. The calculation of *Reliability and Validity* metrics is based on a repository. The repository lists problems assessed as correct (*true positive*) [2]. First, we performed a thematic analysis to formalize problems expressed by participants. We followed SESAR's guidelines [12] to use a common framework and coherent format during the transcoding of the identified-flaws [2]. Then, we excluded from problems expressed by the participants, problems which were not present / identified as positive (*false positive*). To have a consent on the final repository used to compute the scores, two experts involved in the research were in charge of validating problems assessed as correct or to be rejected. The repository was composed of 42 correct problems for the aeronautical concept, and 28 for the navigation app.

   We evaluated the *reliability of the criteria* through: the *effectiveness* measured via the average percentage (a) of problems well-identified per participant, and (b) of participants having well-identified a problem [2]; the *convergence* referring to the extent to which two analysts identified the same problem [2]. We evaluated the *validity of the criteria* through: (1) the *completeness* measured via 3 indicators based on well-identified problems, i.e., the diversity based on the problem categorization into *Ergonomic Criteria for HSSI*; the distinctiveness based on the problem classes specifically revealed when using a method;

the preciseness based on the rate of problems only highlighted by DI against the set of identified problems; (2) the *Predictive value* of the diagnosis defined from Matthews' correlation coefficient (*Phi*) score. For each participant, we first categorized the identified problems in 4 categories (*Correct Identification, False Alarms, Miss, Correct Rejection*), and then, computed the *Phi* score; (3) the *stability* defining if the methodological tool support stays similar regardless the specific features of system which is measured by the comparison of previous results for each system. To determine the impact of usability modifications implemented on the *criteria* [11], and how to improve them (if required), we evaluated the *satisfaction of the criteria* through the SUS questionnaire results [3], and participants comments from the DI group. We compared these results to those from a previous study focused on *criteria* usability [11].

3   Results

3.1   Reliability of the Criteria

About the *effectiveness,* results highlighted that the group using the *criteria* (DI) has significantly identified more problems compared to the control group (EI) ($F(1.58) = 14.34$, p $= .0003$, η^2p $= .20$) (Fig. 1). Regarding *convergence*, the highest threshold of well-identified problem rate by a same number of participants is around 20%. For DI, this threshold always involved a convergence between participants. The comparison of the thresholds to the average percentage of participants having well-identified a common problem outlined that the convergence threshold matched for DI to problems identified for: (a) the aeronautical concept by 25% of participants (EI: specific to one participant); (b) the navigation app by half of the participants (EI: 33% of participants). These results highlighted that the proposed *ergonomic criteria* are reliable as methodological tool to access to ergonomic properties of HSSI.

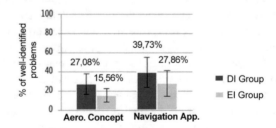

Fig. 1. Average percentage of well-identified problems per participant

3.2   Validity of the Criteria

First of all, we were able to categorize the set of well-identified problems by both groups with the *Ergonomic Criteria for HSSI*. We extracted 17 problem classes by categorizing the well-identified problems with the corresponding complexity dimensions [10]. In regard to *completeness,* when considering 100% rate as a diversity of problems allocated over the *criteria* set, the diversity for DI is around 6-point higher than for EI for both inspected systems (i.e., 72% against 66% for the aeronautical concept; and 66% against 59% for the navigation app). For distinctiveness, we observe that 11.76% of the problem classes is only identified by DI. With regard to preciseness, the rate of the problems only highlighted for DI against the set of problems identified on both systems is 31.43% (38.10% for the aeronautical concept, 21.43% for the navigation app) (Fig. 2).

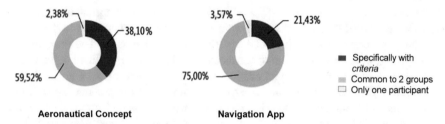

Fig. 2. Percentage of problems specifically identified with *criteria,* common to both groups, and by only one participant

Regarding *Predictive value,* there is no *Phi* score below 0 for DI contrary to the control group (Fig. 3). For both inspected systems the *Phi* score was significantly higher when the *criteria* was used ($F(1.58) = 16.12$, p < .0001, $\eta^2p = .22$). The problem categorization highlighted there is less *False Alarms* for DI (for DI, 2 FA for both systems, against for EI, 7 FA for the aeronautical concept and 5 FA for the navigation app).

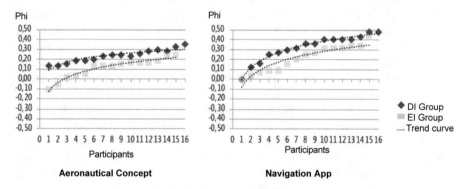

Fig. 3. Distribution of the Phi scores

Finally, the *criteria* assistance is similar regardless the specific features of system. Indeed, a significant effect is raised for DI whether it was for the *effectiveness* or the *predictive value.* In addition, regardless the inspected system, for DI: (a) more than 90% of well-identified problems are common to at least two participants of this group; (b) diversity of well-identified problems is 6-point higher; (c) at least one additional problem class is identified; (d) more *Ergonomic Criteria* are covered; (e) problems related to the *operators' knowledge, interactions guidance*, and s*pace-time relationships* are more identified and distinguished.

In conclusion, these results outline that the proposed *ergonomic criteria* are also valid as a method to access to ergonomic properties of HSSI.

3.3   Satisfaction of the Criteria

The average SUS score was 52.66 ($SD = 13.77$), considered as marginal low according to [3]. We extracted the *strengths* and *weaknesses* of the *criteria* thanks to the average score on every item seen in the light of the participants' verbatims. (a) The *strengths* (i.e., items $\geq 2,50$) were the integration & consistency of the *criteria*, outlined in the interest in the *criteria* scope, and their organization. (b) The *weaknesses* (i.e., items < 2) were the perceived difficulty to learn and use them. Compared to the previous version [11], participants well appreciated the criteria completeness and organization. To conclude, the results highlighted the modifications to be made to the *Ergonomic criteria* in order to improve their maturity as to reorder some of them, and to simplify and explicit the wordings (main point pointed out).

4   Discussion

This study showed that the *Ergonomic criteria* we propose as a methodological support for user centered inspection of HSSI can be considered as *reliable* and *valid*. Complementary studies should be performed to test if results stay: (a) homogenous over time by comparing exposed results with those of a similar study performed with the same participants (i.e., within-analysts test/retest [14]); (b) stable on a wider range of system complexity levels; (c) similar if all the participants are trained in human factors. The repository of correct problems could be developed thanks to integration of identified problems from user tests [2]. Considering the results, we can hypothesize the more complex a system, the more *criteria* usefulness (e.g., decrease false alarms; similar performance between most complex system DI, and simplest system EI).

The satisfaction results revealed the need to improve the *Ergonomic Criteria* maturity level. Indeed, one of the main challenge to propose usable criteria is to find the suitable level of abstraction so that the criteria can be both, cognitively accessible (i.e., easily remembered; easily construct mental model); and flexible to evolution, and the extent of the targeted object. The second challenge is to find the right wordings so that most part of the targeted population can understand them at a standard level.

Acknowledgments. This study took place under a research visit within the Transportation Research Group at the University of Southampton as a part of a research thesis supported by CNRS, Airbus, and Human Design Group. We would like to thank the many volunteers and contributors for their time and the quality of their suggestions and comments.

References

1. Bach, C., Perret, V., Calvet, G.: an integrated approach of human oriented interactions with complexity. In: Harris, D. (eds.) Proceedings of the 14th International Conference, EPCE 2017, Held as Part of HCI International 2017, Vancouver, BC, Canada, pp. 247–265. Springer (2017)
2. Bach, C., Scapin, D.L.: Comparing inspections and user testing for the evaluation of virtual environments. Int. J. Hum. Comput. Interact. **26**(8), 786–824 (2010)
3. Bangor, A., Kortum, P.T., Miller, J.T.: An empirical evaluation of the system usability scale. J. Hum. Comput. Interact. **24**(6), 574–594 (2008)
4. Bastien, J.M.C., Scapin, D.L.: A validation of ergonomic criteria for the evaluation of human-computer interfaces. Int. J. Hum. Comput. Interact. **4**(2), 183–196 (1992)
5. Berthoz, A.: La Simplexité. Odile Jacob, Paris (2009)
6. Chauvin, C., Hoc, J.M.: Intégration de l'ergonomie dans la conception des systèmes homme-machine. In: Millot, P. (ed.) Ergonomie des systèmes homme machine. Hermès, Paris (2013)
7. e Cunha, M.P., Rego, A.: Complexity, simplicity, simplexity. Eur. Manag. (28), 85–94 (2010)
8. Kochenderfer, M.J., Holland, J.E., Chryssanthacopoulos, J.P.: Next-generation airborne collision avoidance system. Lincoln Lab. J. **19**(1), 17–33 (2012)
9. Olson, W.A.: Airborne Collision Avoidance System X. Tech Notes - MIT Lincoln Laboratory (2015)
10. Perret, V., Bach, C., Calvet, G., Chevalier, A.: A user-centred approach of complexity: toward development of a method to support simplex systems design. In: Proceedings of HCI-Aero 2016, Paris, France (2016)
11. Perret, V., Calvet, G., Chevalier, A., Bach, C.: Critères ergonomiques pour les Interactions Homme- Système Simplexe : Support à la classification de problèmes ergonomiques ?. In B. Barthe, Gonon, O., Brun, C. (eds.), Actes du 52e congrès de la Société d'Ergonomie de Langue Française, Présent et futur de l'ergonomie, Toulouse, France, pp. 443–447 (2017)
12. SESAR: Human Performance Reference Material Guidance (2013)
13. SESAR: D02 - TEMPAERIS Final Report (2015)
14. Stanton, N.A., Young, M.S.: Giving ergonomics away? The application of ergonomics methods by novices. Appl. Ergon. **34**, 479–490 (2003)

Matching-Based Comprehension of Emergency Safety Symbols Among Filipinos: User-Centered Quality Measure

Maela Madel L. Cahigas and Yogi Tri Prasetyo[(✉)]

Mapúa University, 658 Muralla St., 1002 Intramuros, Manila, Philippines
ytprasetyo@mapua.edu.ph

Abstract. In the occurrence of natural calamities and accidents, emergency safety symbol is an implicit comparison to proper usage of equipment and appropriate action to follow. The study aims to investigate the relationships and significant differences among demographic factors, comprehension scores, type of identification responses, and cognitive design features that are all associated to emergency symbols. A total of 236 participants accomplished the entire questionnaire. Comprehensibility design of 15 emergency symbols were investigated through demographic factors (age, gender, and educational attainment), type of identification responses (correct, partially correct, incorrect, and opposite meaning), and cognitive design features (familiarity, simplicity, spatial recognition, and semantic closeness). The study incorporated descriptive statistics, Pearson correlation analysis, ANOVA, and Tukey Post-Hoc test. Symbols 3, 13, and 15 passed $\geq 85\%$ comprehensibility requirement of American National Standards Institute (ANSI). Symbols 2, 3, and 5–11 were classified as critically confusing with greater than 5% "opposite meaning" value. Symbol 3 (93.73%) was the most familiar signage while symbol 5 (62.71%) was the least familiar signage. The simplest sign was symbol 3 (95.51%) and symbol 9 (73.9%) was the most complex. Symbol 3 (93.22%) had the highest value of spatial recognition while symbol 9 (74.15%) had the lowest percentage. Highest semantic closeness was acquired by symbol 15 (92.46%) and the least percentage was obtained by symbol 14 (72.63%). Comprehension scores were significant and positively correlated to familiarity (0.62), semantic closeness (0.61), spatial recognition (0.60), and simplicity (0.52). Gender and educational attainment were significant to comprehension scores. Statistical analysis utilized in the study provided interrelationship between the identified factors relative to comprehensibility of emergency safety symbols.

Keywords: Emergency safety symbol · Comprehensibility · Cognitive design features · Statistical analysis

1 Introduction

Emergency safety symbol is a communication strategy that aims to provide instructions and information relative to unforeseen circumstances. Integrating human engineering principles to visual emergency signals helps people easily recognize the signs in precise manner [1]. Symbols are considered to be ergonomically acceptable if greater number of people are able to perceive the intended meaning of the symbol, hence directly related to excellent cognitive design features.

Cognitive features and effectiveness of symbols are measured through assessments. Variables that influence effectivity of symbols are human-related factors (age, familiarity, and gender) and graphic design features (color, layout, text style, shape, orientation, and placement) [2]. If a particular symbol is not properly developed, it can lead to accident, or worse, death. There are number of experimental studies that conduct comprehension-based assessments. Responses are categorized as correct [3, 4], partially correct [4], incorrect [3, 4], and opposite meaning [3, 4]. Cognitive design features are tested through familiarity [2, 4–6], spatial compatibility [4], standardization [4], simplicity [5, 6], meaningfulness [5], and semantic closeness [5, 6]. Moreover, color green is associated to emergency safety symbols; whereas, green is supplemented with concepts of "go" and "safety" in emergency context [7].

The study aims to investigate the relationships and significant differences among demographic factors, comprehension scores, type of identification responses, and cognitive design features that are all associated to emergency symbols. The demographic factors considered are gender, age, and educational attainment. Comprehension scores represent percentage of correct answers. Identification responses are divided to correct, partially correct, opposite meaning, and incorrect. Cognitive design features stipulate familiarity, simplicity, spatial recognition, and semantic closeness. Descriptive statistics, Pearson correlation [6], and Analysis of Variance (ANOVA) [6] are utilized to analyze comprehensibility of emergency safety symbols.

2 Methodology

2.1 Experimental Procedure

Google forms, an online survey tool, was utilized to collate responses of participants. The questionnaire consists of three sections: (1) demographic profile; (2) identification of emergency symbols; and (3) assessment of symbols' cognitive design features. The assessment accumulated 236 respondents, which comprised of 120 males and 116 females with varying age and educational attainment as shown in Table 1.

The second section of the questionnaire was structured with 15-item emergency safety symbols in a multiple-choice type of test. Participants were asked to select the most appropriate description among the four given choices, and responses may be deemed as correct, partially correct, incorrect, and opposite meaning (Table 2). The information of the selected symbols was extracted from the published document made by International Organization for Standardization (ISO), subsequent to document reference number of ISO:7010:2019(E). Moreover, American National Standards Institute (ANSI) generated ANSI Z535 [3–5] to measure effectiveness of symbol. This standard was utilized in this study, and symbols were considered as comprehensive if the percentage of correct responses had a value of $\geq 85\%$. Moreover, opposite meaning was considered as a negative type of response as it may lead to accident; a value greater than 5% indicates that the symbol was critically confusing [3].

Table 1. Demographic profile of respondents.

Characteristics	Category	N	Percentage (%)
Gender	Male	120	50.85
	Female	116	49.15
Age	≤17	2	0.85
	18–24	116	49.15
	25–34	52	22.03
	35–44	36	15.25
	45–54	21	8.90
	≥55	9	3.81
Educational attainment	High school student	4	1.69
	High school graduate	8	3.39
	College level w/o diploma	36	15.25
	Vocational degree graduate	4	1.69
	Bachelor's degree graduate	154	65.25
	Postgraduate student	10	4.24
	Master's degree graduate	18	7.63
	Doctoral degree graduate	2	0.85

Once identification test was accomplished, participants were asked to complete the last part of the questionnaire. Figure 1 shows the sample questionnaire to assess cognitive features related to the symbol. Four cognitive design features were evaluated, namely familiarity [2, 4–6], simplicity [5], spatial recognition [4], and semantic closeness [5]. Furthermore, the third section of the questionnaire utilized five-point Likert scale; this aims to measure the extent of four cognitive features relative to each symbol.

Statistical Analysis. Participants' responses were initially analyzed through descriptive statistics. Thus, the data collated from all three sections of the questionnaire was summarized. Descriptive statistics was useful in organizing the data accordingly.

Pearson correlation analysis and Analysis of Variance (ANOVA) are statistical methods that have been commonly and successfully used in most survey research in behavioral and social science studies [6]. Pearson correlation was used to identify significant relationships between comprehension scores and four cognitive design features. Furthermore, ANOVA was utilized to explore relationships and significant differences between: (1) comprehension scores and demographic characteristics; (2) cognitive design features and demographic characteristics; and (3) type of identification responses and cognitive design features. Afterwards, Tukey Post-Hoc test was used to identify the exact group under the variables with significant differences. For Pearson correlation and ANOVA, significant level was set to 0.05. If p-value $\leq$ 0.05, there is a significant difference between the compared variables. However, if p-value $>$ 0.05, then there is no significant difference between the compared variables. SPSS 26, a statistical software, was used to generate the significant results.

Table 2. Emergency safety symbol comprehension assessment.

Symbol	Emergency Safety Symbol	Type of Identification Response			
		Correct	Partially correct	Incorrect	Opposite meaning
S1		Emergency telephone	Telephone booth	Telephone conversation	Emergency smartphone
		84.75%	11.86%	2.54%	0.85%
S2		Emergency stretcher	Medical bed	Bedside care	Intensive care unit (ICU)
		67.80%	14.41%	3.39%	14.41%
S3		First aid	Pain reliever	Holy cross	Complex grab kit
		88.98%	0.00%	0.85%	10.17%
S4		Evacuation assembly point	Evacuation temporary refuge	Evacuation modular relief tent	Evacuation escape route
		83.05%	11.86%	2.54%	2.54%
S5		Oxygen resuscitator	Respiratory equipment	Medical oxygen generator	Breathing extinction device
		19.49%	38.98%	20.34%	21.19%
S6		Emergency exit (left hand)	Emergency exit stairs	Evacuation point	Emergency exit (right hand)
		32.20%	37.29%	11.02%	19.49%
S7		Emergency escape breathing device	Oxygen resuscitator	Emergency patient	Asphyxia valve
		61.02%	24.58%	0.85%	13.56%
S8		Eyewash station	Safety shower	Eye irrigation area	Wear eye protection
		65.25%	3.39%	22.03%	9.32%
S9		Child seat presence and orientation detection system	Open safety bar of chairlift	Evacuation chair	Emergency safety chair
		74.58%	10.17%	0.85%	14.41%
S10		Break to obtain access	Obtain safety equipment	Door opens by pulling	Deactivate access to equipment
		55.08%	7.63%	28.81%	8.47%
S11		Child's life jacket	Lifebuoy	Emergency patient	Anti-pressure device
		66.95%	23.73%	0.00%	9.32%
S12		Turn clockwise to open	Turn clockwise to activate emergency alarm button	Turn counterclockwise to activate emergency alarm button	Turn counterclockwise to open
		50.00%	44.92%	4.24%	0.85%
S13		Tsunami evacuation building	Evacuation assembly point	Running man	Modular relief tent
		89.83%	6.78%	2.54%	0.85%
S14		Emergency stop button	Emergency shower stop button	Activate emergency shower button	Activate emergency alarm button
		38.98%	4.24%	6.78%	50.00%
S15		Emergency window with escape ladder	Rescue window	Search and rescue transponder	Safe zone (fall prevention)
		88.14%	8.47%	1.69%	1.69%

3 Results and Discussion

Type of identification responses were compared through ranking method. Result shows that S13 received the highest percentage (89.83%) of correct answers and S5 had the lowest percentage (19.49%). It means that "tsunami evacuation building" symbol was the most comprehensive and "oxygen resuscitator" symbol was hardly recognized by the participants. Four types of identification responses were also analyzed in each symbol. Correct responses dominated S1–S4, S7–S13, and S15. For S5–S6, partially correct had the highest ranking. Out of the 15 identified emergency safety symbols, S14 was the most critically confusing because responses dominated the category of opposite meaning. S14 was designed to imply "emergency stop button" with 38.98% correct responses. Its opposite meaning was to "activate emergency alarm" that comprised 50% of the total responses. If an emergency occurred and a person has to activate the alarm, then it would definitely fail its purpose because the button was intended to stop emergency alarm. Consequently, a lot of people could have been unaware of the current emergency and that their lives could be at stake. Aside from S14, S2-S3 and S5-S11 each acquired value of $\geq 5\%$ in opposite meaning responses, and thus these symbols were deemed to be critically confusing as well [3].

Emergency Telephone	Cognitive Design Features	Description	5-Point Likert Scale				
			1 Strongly disagree	2 Disagree	3 Neutral	4 Agree	5 Strongly agree
	Familiarity	I am familiar with this symbol.	○	○	○	○	○
	Simplicity	The symbol is designed with simplicity.	○	○	○	○	○
	Spatial recognition	Position of image(s) within the symbol is arranged properly.	○	○	○	○	○
	Semantic closeness	Displayed symbol is closely related to its intended meaning.	○	○	○	○	○

Fig. 1. Assessment of cognitive features.

Comprehension scores presented in Table 3 refers to respondents' correct answers in identifying emergency symbols. Previous studies [3–5] used ANSI Z535 comprehensibility standard of 85%. Using the same standard, S3 (88.98%), S13 (89.83%), and S15 (88.14%) passed the criterion. This means that only 3 out of 15 (20%) emergency symbols can easily be identified. Although respondents had a hard time in identifying the remaining 7 symbols, their assessment in symbols' cognitive features were high in percentage (at least 62%) as shown in Table 3 as well. Respondents were most familiar with S3 and least familiar with S5. Simplicity of symbol was also assessed. S3 was described to be the simplest and has uncomplicated design while S9 was complex. For spatial recognition, appropriateness of images incorporated within the space were evaluated. S3 had the highest percentage and S9 had the lowest value. Suitability of symbol to its description pertains to semantic closeness. S15 was closely related to its description while S14 had the least semantic closeness relationship.

Two factors, comprehension and cognitive design features, were both subjected to Pearson correlation. All elements were significant ($p \leq 0.05$) and positively correlated with each other. Therefore, respondents' ability to comprehend the symbols was directly dependent to the four cognitive features; whereas, familiarity had the most impact (0.62), followed by semantic closeness (0.61), then spatial recognition (0.60), and least impact was simplicity (0.52). Contrary to the result of previous study with pharmaceutical pictograms [5], the highest rank was semantic closeness and the least rank was familiarity. For road signs [4], spatial recognition was identified to be insignificant. Although there

Table 3. Results of the assessment.

Symbol	Comprehension score (%)	Familiarity (%)	Simplicity (%)	Spatial recognition (%)	Semantic closeness (%)
S1	84.75	78.47	86.1	84.58	84.58
S2	67.8	74.92	85.34	84.07	83.56
S3	88.98	93.73	95.51	93.22	91.44
S4	83.05	76.69	80.76	83.81	81.78
S5	19.49	62.71	78.73	79.49	78.22
S6	32.2	76.95	84.07	80.76	80.51
S7	61.02	63.22	79.49	79.49	78.47
S8	65.25	74.15	80.25	81.02	80
S9	74.58	63.98	73.9	74.15	73.9
S10	55.08	67.03	78.98	78.98	75.42
S11	66.95	69.83	81.27	78.47	77.46
S12	50	71.69	83.56	82.03	82.54
S13	89.83	80.25	88.39	88.39	87.37
S14	38.98	68.05	77.2	77.2	72.63
S15	88.14	83.05	89.41	90.42	92.46
Highest	S13 (89.83%)	S3 (93.73%)	S3 (95.51%)	S3 (93.22%)	S15 (92.46%)
Lowest	S5 (19.49%)	S5 (62.71%)	S9 (73.9%)	S9 (74.15%)	S14 (72.63%)
Mean	64.41	73.65	82.86	82.41	81.36
SD	0.24	0.08	0.05	0.05	0.06
Variance	0.0447	0.0066	0.0028	0.0025	0.0032

were similarities in terms of cognitive features, results still vary because different type of symbols was observed in each study.

Among the three demographic characteristics, gender and educational attainment were significant (Table 4) to the comprehension score of participants. There is no proven significant relationship between respondents' age and their capability to answer the questions. Tukey Post-Hoc test can't be performed to gender because it only had 2 set of groups. Results in Table 4 also shows definite group within educational attainment relative to respondents' comprehension scores.

Respondent's gender had significant difference (Table 5) with semantic closeness of symbol 12 (SC12). S12 had 82.54% semantic closeness and was considered to be relatively high compared to other symbols. Thus, decisions of female and male sub groups were important in terms of semantic closeness. Also, age was significant to

Table 4. ANOVA (left) and Tukey Post-Hoc test (right) between demographics and comprehension.

Source	df	F	Sig.	Educational Attainment		Sig.
Gender	1	14.86	0	High school student	Vocational degree	0
Age	4	0.5	0.73		Bachelor's degree	0.04
Educational attainment	6	2.79	0.01		Postgraduate student	0.02
					Master's degree	0.01
				Vocational degree	High school student	0
				Bachelor's degree	High school student	0.04
				Postgraduate student	High school student	0.02
				Master's degree	High school student	0.01

familiarity of symbol 6 (F6), spatial recognition of symbol 15 (SR15), and semantic closeness of symbol 15 (SC15). In Table 3, symbol 6 had low comprehension score (32.2%) but with high familiarity score (76.95%). It was previously mentioned that S15 passed ANSI criteria and it had the highest semantic closeness percentage (Table 3). Furthermore, the simplicity of symbol 5 (SM5) was statistically different with S1 and S11. It was stated in Table 3 that S5 had the lowest comprehension score, and S1 and S11 has simplicity percentage of 86.1% and 81.27%, respectively. These simplicity values were absolutely higher compared to S5's simplicity score of 78.73%. Indeed, S5 had more complex structural design compared to S1 and S11.

Table 5. Significant differences between demographic characteristics and cognitive design features & cognitive design features and type of identification responses.

Source	Dependent variable	df	F	Sig.
Gender	SC12	1	3.93	0.05
Age	F6	4	3.91	0
	SR15	4	2.66	0.03
	SC15	4	2.47	0.05
SM5	S1	1	9.74	0
	S11	1	11.52	0

Comprehensibility test used in this study had limitations. Questionnaire may be designed the other way around; wherein emergency symbols could be deemed as the choices. Future researchers may opt to redesign symbols after the initial test. Subsequently, post-comprehensibility test and post-cognitive assessment may be incorporated to determine if there are significant differences in the applied changes.

4 Conclusion

Interpretation of emergency safety symbols must be logical, easy, and effective. The study utilized descriptive statistics, Pearson correlation analysis, and ANOVA with Tukey Post-Hoc test. Most participants were able to state the correct answer for S13 (89.83%) while S5 (19.49%) was the least comprehensive symbol. Furthermore, huge number of participants correctly identified the appropriate description for S1–S4, S7–S13, and S15. Out of 15 emergency symbols, 3 symbols passed ANSI Z535 principle, namely S13 (89.83%), S3 (88.98%), and S15 (88.14%), in descending order. S14 was the most critically confusing when compared to other symbols using the ranking method in each type of identification response. Moreover, opposite meaning percentage for S2, S3, and S5-S11 were greater than 5%. These symbols were highly recommended for design enhancement. Participants' responses relative to four cognitive design features were analyzed as well. Respondents were most familiar with S3 (93.73%) and least familiar with S5 (62.71%). S3 had the highest simplicity and spatial recognition percentage while S9 had the lowest percentage for the aforementioned cognitive features. S15 (92.46%) had the highest semantic closeness and S14 (72.63%) had the least percentage value.

Using Pearson correlation analysis, results revealed that comprehension scores and four cognitive design features were all significant and had positive correlation. Significant correlation for cognitive design features was arranged to familiarity (0.62), semantic closeness (0.61), spatial recognition (0.60), and simplicity (0.52), in highest to least impact respectively. ANOVA and Tukey Post-Hoc test was used in the latter part. Gender and educational attainment were significant to comprehension scores of participants. Additionally, respondent's gender was significant to SC12, age was significant to F6, SR15, and SC15, and SM5 was statistically different with S1 and S11. Intervention of ergonomics comprehensibility assessment is crucial in prescribing standard design of symbols, thus there is a need to create concrete guidelines to provide safety information for contingency plans and to eliminate risks of accidents.

References

1. Kroemera, K., Marras, W.: Ergonomics of visual emergency signals. Appl. Ergon. **11**, 137–144 (1980)
2. Rogers, W.A., Lamson, N., Rousseau, G.K.: Warning research: an integrative perspective. Hum. Fact. J. Hum. Fact. Ergon. Soc. **42**, 102–139 (2000)
3. Seo, D.C., Ladoni, M., Brunk, E., Becker, M.W., Bix, L.: Do healthcare professionals comprehend standardized symbols present on medical device packaging?: An important factor in the fight over label space. Packag. Technol. Sci. **30**, 61–73 (2016)
4. Bañares, J.R., Caballes, S.A., Serdan, M.J., Liggayu, A.T., Bongo, M.F.: A comprehension-based ergonomic redesign of Philippine road warning signs. Int. J. Ind. Ergon. **65**, 17–25 (2018)

5. Ahmadi, M., Mortezapour, A., Kalteh, H.O., Emadi, A., Charati, J.Y., Etemadinezhad, S.: Comprehensibility of pharmaceutical pictograms: effect of prospective-user factors and cognitive sign design features. Res. Soc. Admin. Pharm. **17**, 356–361 (2020)
6. Chi, C.-F., Dewi, R.S.: Matching performance of vehicle icons in graphical and textual formats. Appl. Ergon. **45**, 904–916 (2014)
7. Kinateder, M., Warren, W.H., Schloss, K.B.: What color are emergency exit signs? Egress behavior differs from verbal report. Appl. Ergon. **75**, 155–160 (2019)
8. Hiranchiracheep, S., Yamazaki, A.K., Foypikul, W.: A preliminary surveying of the meaning of colored pictogram instructions for emergency settings in manufacturing. Procedia Comput. Sci. **96**, 1528–1534 (2016)

Situation Awareness and Automated Shuttles: A Multi-road User Analysis

Gemma J. M. Read[1]([✉]) [ID], Alison O'Brien[1], Neville A. Stanton[1,2] [ID],
and Paul M. Salmon[1] [ID]

[1] Centre for Human Factors and Sociotechnical Systems, University of the Sunshine Coast,
Maroochydore, QLD, Australia
gread@usc.edu.au

[2] Transportation Research Group, University of Southampton, Southampton, UK

Abstract. Automated shuttles are currently being trialed as a new transport solution however to date there has been a lack of studies investigating how other road users interact with these new types of vehicles. The aim of this study was to understand the situation awareness (SA) of road users (driver, cyclist, motorcyclist, pedestrian) interacting with an automated shuttle on a public road. Naturalistic data were collected, and the Event Analysis of Systemic Teamwork was used to develop task, social and information networks for a scenario when all four road user types interacted with the automated shuttle at a T-intersection. The findings provide early insights into SA of different road users when interacting with automated shuttles at unsignalized intersections. Such insights could be used to improve the design of shuttles and road environments to support the SA and decision making of human road users.

Keywords: Automated shuttle · Situation awareness · Driver · Cyclist · Motorcyclist · Pedestrian

1 Introduction

Automated shuttles are currently being trialed worldwide as a novel public transport solution. However, there is little research into how human road users interact with them and what issues might arise as a result (Stanton et al. 2020). Non-optimal design of shuttles may lead to road user misunderstandings of shuttle intentions, which could in turn lead to safety or efficiency issues, negatively impacting public acceptance of these new technologies. In addition, it may be that the features of existing road environments or aspects of road user behaviour create issues between road users and automated shuttles. Naturalistic research into the interactions between road users and automated shuttles is therefore critical to support their safe implementation.

Situation awareness (SA) can be broadly defined as understanding 'what is going on' (Endsley 1995). Incompatibility in SA of different road user types at intersections has been identified as playing an important role in road crashes. For example, Salmon et al. (2013, 2014) found that driver SA did not incorporate some of the more flexible

© The Author(s), under exclusive license to Springer Nature Switzerland AG 2021
N. L. Black et al. (Eds.): IEA 2021, LNNS 219, pp. 393–400, 2021.
https://doi.org/10.1007/978-3-030-74602-5_56

behaviours that can be performed by cyclists and motorcyclists at intersections such as lane filtering or hook turns. This was due to flaws in the design of intersections and a lack of experience interacting with these users, leading to under-developed schema for these behaviours. Automated shuttles represent a novel road user type. Thus, current road users will not have had an opportunity to develop schemata for their behaviour. The aim of this study therefore was to understand the SA of road users (a driver, cyclist, motorcyclist and pedestrian) when interacting with an automated shuttle on a public road. By analyzing SA, insights can be gained regarding how the design of automated shuttles and the road environment could be optimized to support the decision making of the human road users with whom it will interact.

The Event Analysis of Systemic Teamwork (EAST) framework (Stanton et al. 2019) was adopted for the analysis. EAST has previously been used to investigate road user behaviour at intersections (Salmon et al. 2014) as well as other aspects of autonomous vehicles, such as understanding the changing role of drivers (Banks and Stanton 2019) and how Connected and Autonomous Vehicles will be integrated into the transport system (Banks et al. 2018). However, previous studies have not focused specifically on automated shuttles, nor used data from naturalistic trials to inform EAST models. Furthermore, to our knowledge, this is the first naturalistic study of road user SA when interacting with an automated shuttle.

EAST uses network-based representations of tasks, social interactions and information concepts to understand systems. Social networks are used to identify social actors (both human and non-human) who interact within the scenario under analysis, and the relationships between them. Task networks describe the activities that are performed and the relationships between activities, and information networks represent the information that is used and how different concepts are linked. Information networks are commonly used to represent and analyse SA (e.g. Salmon et al. 2013).

2   Method

2.1   Design

A small-scale naturalistic on-road study was undertaken involving the research team who interacted with an automated shuttle being trialed on a public road in Australia. Given the novelty of naturalistic studies around automated vehicles, this study represented a pilot study involving researchers only, in line with other recent studies (e.g. Endsley 2017). Four research team participants took the roles of driver, cyclist, motorcyclist and pedestrian. Each participant held extensive experience in the road user role they held, however, they did not have previous experience on the route used in the study, nor previous experience of interacting with automated shuttles on the road.

Data collected to inform the EAST networks included video recordings taken from the perspective of the road users, concurrent verbal protocols as they negotiated the study route and post-study retrospective written reflection on the task based on the critical decision method (CDM) technique. This is achieved by 'thinking aloud' while concurrently performing the task of interest, with the protocols later transcribed for analysis. The verbal protocol approach has been used in several previous studies focused on understanding road user behaviour and SA (e.g. Read et al. 2018; Salmon et al. 2014; Walker et al. 2011). The CDM, usually conducted as an interview, contains a series of probes designed to elicit retrospective data about decision making processes during a scenario (Crandall et al. 2016).

While the video recording and verbal protocol data were collected across a longer route, for the purposes of this paper a specific scenario was selected for analysis. This was an interaction between the shuttle all four road users at a T-intersection (see Fig. 1). As can be seen in Fig. 1, the T-intersection is unsignalized, has no line markings, approach signage or pedestrian footpaths.

Fig. 1. Overview of interaction. Automated shuttle shown in yellow. Map data ©2021 Google.

2.2 Materials

The automated shuttle involved in the study was an EasyMile EZ10 model (see Fig. 2). At the time of the study it was being trialed in a low-traffic environment in Queensland, Australia. The shuttle can carry 6 seated passengers and 6 standing passengers, in addition to a safety operator. The safety operator was present on-board the shuttle at all times, however there was no driver's seat, and the position of the safety operator on-board was not clearly visible or obvious to other road users. The shuttle operated at a maximum speed of 20 km/h within a 40 km/h road speed zone. The trial route for the shuttle was a 3.9 km return loop with several stops provided for passengers to embark/disembark. The shuttle was programmed to follow a pre-defined route. It used GPS, localisation signage and obstacle detection to achieve the driving task. The safety operator was able to intervene and take over manual control at any time and approved certain shuttle actions such as proceeding through intersections.

Audio recording equipment was used to record the continuous verbal protocols they provided while traversing the route. GoPro cameras were used to capture the forward and rear view of the car, and were mounted on the handlebars of the motorcycle and bicycle, and helmets of the motorcyclist and cyclist. The pedestrian wore a head-mounted GoPro, with rear view captured via a chest strap mounted GoPro. A 14-question CDM survey was developed based on Crandall and colleagues (2006).

Fig. 2. The EZ10 Shuttle

2.3 Procedure

Prior to attending the study location, research team participants practiced providing a continuous verbal protocol while driving with coaching provided by experienced team members. At the study location, research team participants familiarized themselves with the shuttle route by riding the automated shuttle. They then organized the attachment of the recording equipment and travelled, as their road user type, the same route as the shuttle in a loop for two trials of approximately 20 min each. The pedestrian walked a modified, shorter route encompassing two intersections, including the T-intersection selected for analysis. All research team participants provided continuous verbal protocols as they traversed the route.

Approximately one week after the on-road data collection participants completed the CDM survey. Participants were provided with, and requested to review, the forward-facing video taken from their perspective during the study and the transcript of their verbal protocol before completing the CDM questions, providing as much detail as they could remember about their experience negotiating the T-intersection.

2.4 Data Analysis

The audio and visual recordings were downloaded and verbal protocols were transcribed verbatim for each road user as they approached and traversed the intersection.

A workshop was held with three of the research team members to build the EAST networks from the data gathered. The data used to build the networks included the forward-facing video recordings, verbal protocol transcripts, and responses relating to four specific questions from the CDM survey: What did you see, hear or notice? What information did you have available to you at the time of the decision? Did you use all the available information? What was the most important piece of information you used in formulating your decision? The draft networks were then reviewed by all members of the research team and final versions created.

3   Results

3.1   Task Network

The task network (Fig. 3) shows the tasks that were undertaken by each road user and the shuttle during the scenario and their interrelations based on the sequencing of tasks and the influence of tasks on each other. A total of 11 tasks were identified. The most highly connected tasks were 'approach intersection', 'monitor and respond to obstacles', 'provide indication' and 'follow pre-programmed route'. Interestingly, while the first three tasks were conducted by all road users, 'follow pre-programmed route' was only conducted by the shuttle.

3.2   Social Network

The social network (Fig. 4) shows the actors involved in the T-intersection scenario and the interactions between them. These include both physical interactions (e.g. the cyclist operating the bicycle) and visual detection by one actor of another during the approach and traversal of the T intersection. A total of 11 social actors were identified. Visual inspection of the network shows that the shuttle itself is an influential node in this network with many connections with other actors. This is due to its sensors obtaining comprehensive information from the road environment.

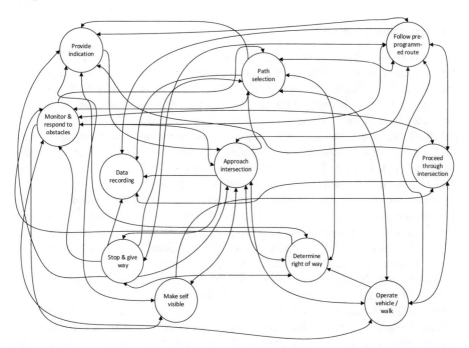

Fig. 3. Task network

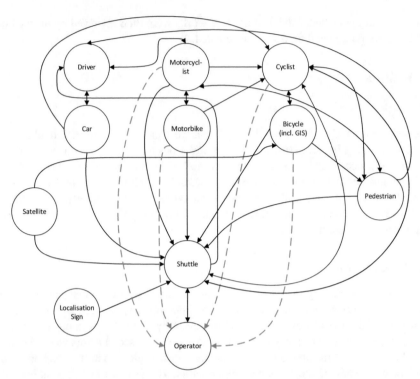

Fig. 4. Social network. Note, dotted lines indicate assumptions (data not available).

3.3   Information Network

The information network (Fig. 5) shows the concepts that formed road user SA during the scenario. A total of 27 information concepts were identified. Visual inspection of the network suggests that the concept of 'shuttle' is relatively more frequently connected to other nodes in the network. This may suggest that until automated shuttles become well embedded in road user schemata they will be somewhat of a novelty and could potentially misdirect attention and SA away from other road users or hazards in the road environment. Other nodes such as 'direction', 'pedestrian' and 'car' were also more highly connected. The focus on 'direction' may be due to the intersection scenario, with road users focused on determining the intended path of others.

It was also interesting to note that different road users used different combinations of SA concepts during the scenario. For example, the pedestrian had unique SA concepts associated with determining their 'crossing point', the relevant roads at an unsignalized intersection via looking at a 'street sign', the 'noise' generated by the motorcycle, and consideration of the road 'rules' relevant to the situation.

There were also different information requirements based on the task being performed. For example, the cyclist was continuing through the intersection while the shuttle, in the on-coming direction, pulled forward into the intersection to turn right. A task for the cyclist in this situation was to 'make self visible', yet they could not confirm that the shuttle had detected their presence and was intending to stop and give way. The information network showed that the cyclist was concerned with whether the shuttle giving way, and was also interpreting the shuttle's 'indications', however the cyclist remained uncertain about the shuttle's intention throughout the interaction.

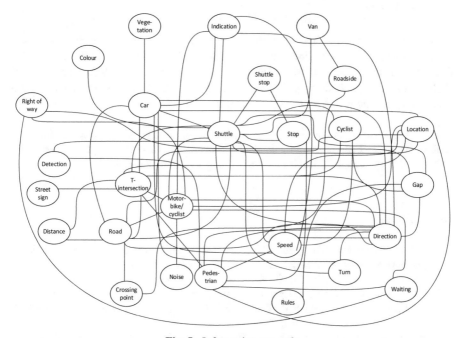

Fig. 5. Information network.

4   Discussion

The insights gained from the application of EAST in this study can be used to inform the design of automated shuttles and the road environment in which they will operate. In relation to the design process, it is recommended that SA requirements be formally specified for each road user type, including sub-types where appropriate (e.g. adult pedestrians, children, pedestrians with disabilities). Requirements should also consider the tasks that users undertake in a structured and systematic manner, using a framework such as EAST.

In terms of SA requirements generally, a key insight was that with no driver on-board, there is no opportunity for road users (e.g. cyclists) to make eye contact to confirm that they have been detected (as would be the case with a human driver). An externalised information display could provide this information. However, road users must still gain experience and build schema to respond appropriately to such displays.

Although small in scale, this study represents the first naturalistic investigation of multiple road users interacting with an automated shuttle. As it was limited to a single case study interaction at an unsignalized intersection, future research should recruit a larger sample and study interactions within various road environments including roundabouts, signalized intersections, zebra crossings, and straight roadways.

5   Conclusions

This study provides early insights into the SA of different road users when interacting with automated shuttles. In line with previous research it indicated that SA differed for different road user types, and for different tasks (Salmon et al. 2013; Salmon et al. 2014; Walker et al. 2011). Such insights could inform ways in which automated shuttles are designed to communicate with other road users.

Acknowledgements. This research was conducted in partnership with the Royal Automobile Club of Queensland (RACQ) and Redland City Council. The views expressed are those of the authors and do not necessarily reflect the views of the partner organisations.

References

Banks, V.A., Stanton, N.A.: Analysis of driver roles: Modelling the changing role of the driver in automated driving systems using EAST. TIES, **20**(3), 284–300 (2019)

Banks, V.A., Stanton, N.A., Burnett, G., Hermawati, S.: Distributed cognition on the road: Using EAST to explore future road transportation systems. Appl. Ergon. **68**, 258–266 (2018)

Crandall, B., Klein, G., Hoffman, R.R.: Working Minds: A Practitioner's Guide to Cognitive Task Analysis. MIT Press, Cambridge (2016)

Endsley. Autonomous driving systems: A preliminary naturalistic study of the Tesla Model S. J. Cogn. Eng. Decis. Making, **11**(3), 225–238 (2017)

Endsley. Toward a theory of situation awareness in dynamic systems. Hum. Factors **37**(1), 32–64 (1995)

Read, G.J.M., Stevens, E.L., Lenné, M.G., Stanton, N.A., Walker, G.H., Salmon, P.M.: Walking the talk: comparing pedestrian 'activity as imagined' with 'activity as done'. Accid. Anal. Prev. 113, 74–84 (2018).

Salmon, P.M., Lenne, M.G., Young, K.L., Walker, G.H.: An on-road network analysis-based approach to studying driver situation awareness at rail level crossings. Accid. Anal. Prev. **58**, 195–205 (2013)

Salmon, P.M., Lenne, M.G., Walker, G.H., Stanton, N.A., Filtness, A.: Exploring schema-driven differences in situation awareness between road users: an on-road study of driver, cyclist and motorcyclist situation awareness. Ergonomics **57**, 191–209 (2014)

Stanton, N.A., Eriksson, A., Banks, V.A., Hancock, P.A.: Turing in the driver's seat: can people distinguish between automated and manually driven vehicles? Hum. Factors Ergon. Manuf., 30, 418–425 (2020).

Stanton, N.A., Salmon, P.D., Walker, G.H.D.: Systems Thinking in Practice: Applications of the Event Analysis of Systemic Teamwork Method. CRC Press, Boca Raton (2019).

Walker, G.H., Stanton, N.A., Salmon, P.M.: Cognitive compatibility of motorcyclists and car drivers. Accid. Anal. Prev. 43, 878–888 (2011)

A Human Factors and Ergonomics Systems Approach to Exploring Sensory Design for Inclusive Public Space

Nicholas Stevens[1]([✉]), Tobias Volbert[2], Linda Cupitt[2], Erin Stevens[1], and Paul M. Salmon[1]

[1] Centre for Human Factors and Sociotechnical Systems, USC, Maroochydore, QLD, Australia
nstevens@usc.edu.au
[2] 7 Senses Foundation, Brisbane, QLD, Australia

Abstract. People experience the world around them in vastly different ways through a diverse range of sensory inputs and outputs. The purpose of this research was to explore a sociotechnical systems approach to support sensory urban design and establish an archetype model for public space design and evaluation. The research involved the construction of a Work Domain Analysis, the first phase of the systems analysis approach, Cognitive Work Analysis. The resultant model incorporates key sensory design principles to build an in-depth and integrated understanding of accessible, engaging and inclusive public space. The model was then applied to two existing public spaces to assess the impact of a holistic sensory design approach. Key findings illustrate the importance of integrating sensory design elements into public spaces to achieve increased levels of sensory affordance for all users, regardless of ability.

Keywords: Sensory urban design · Systems HFE · Work domain analysis · Public spaces · Sociotechnical systems

1 Introduction

Current practice in public space design is underpinned by inclusive accessibility principles [1–3]. More specifically, principles of universal design aim to 'design environments to be usable for all people, to the greatest extent possible' and guide the development of accessible urban spaces [4]. In Australia, like elsewhere, there exists a range of building and engineering standards that provide guidance for the design and construction of public space. However, key criteria within these standards largely focus on physical accessibility needs (i.e. ramps and rails), while largely overlooking inclusive design for people with intellectual disability.

To support the design of more inclusive public spaces, the 7 Senses Foundation [5] has established a set of guidelines promoting accessible and sensory engaging design for multiple abilities. Whilst these guidelines provide important considerations for public space, the development of methodologies for realizing inclusive designs are limited [6].

N. L. Black et al. (Eds.): IEA 2021, LNNS 219, pp. 401–408, 2021.
https://doi.org/10.1007/978-3-030-74602-5_57

A critical next step is the provision of appropriate frameworks and empirical assessments of the potential utility and impact of such guidelines. The aim of this paper is to present an exploratory study which was undertaken in response to these gaps.

1.1 Sensory Urban Design

Sensory urban design is an approach which seeks to include all public space users, regardless of ability. It aims to move beyond purely visual aesthetics in urban design to create spaces that actively engage all the senses [7]. The 7 Senses Foundation is a community organisation established in 2013 that integrates seven senses into community development and urban initiatives. Their core mission is to 'create healthier and happier neighborhoods and communities that include people of all abilities and wellness and cultivate activity and play' [5]. Sensory focused design enables conscious adaptation of the built and natural environment to improve each person's sensory and motor development opportunities. The seven senses include a range of abilities including: hearing, taste, smell, touch, vision, awareness of our body's position (proprioception), and movement through space and balance (vestibular) [1, 5, 8].

1.2 The Public Space Domain

The term public space may be defined as 'space within the urban environment which is readily available to the community regardless of its size, design or physical features and which is intended for, primarily, amenity or physical recreation, whether active or passive' [9].

A public space may range from a suburban recreational park, to a formal town square and will therefore vary in size and location depending on the intended use. Regardless, its design needs to consider the inclusion of all possible users. The Australian Institute of Health and Welfare [10] details 3 cohorts for inclusion:

1. Multi-generational such as elderly people, young children, teenagers;
2. Mainstream populations such as individuals, families, couples; and
3. People with disabilities including acquired brain injury; physical; neurological; speech; intellectual; psychiatric; vision; hearing; autism; and deaf-blind.

Public space will occur within rural, regional and metropolitan areas. Accordingly, the form and quality of surrounding infrastructure which supports its use, i.e. public amenities, transport, and community facilities will vary. As such any model development, as proposed here, must be generic in nature and therein widely applicable.

2 Methods

2.1 Cognitive Work Analysis (CWA), and Work Domain Analysis (WDA)

Central to this research is the use of a Human Factors and Ergonomics systems analysis and design framework, Cognitive Work Analysis (CWA) [11]. The study involved applying the first phase of CWA, Work Domain Analysis (WDA), to create a systems model of an 'ideal' public space that seeks to achieve the 'inclusive public space for all' concept. The aim was twofold: first, to showcase the utility of using systems analysis methods such as WDA in urban design applications; and second, to provide a design model that incorporates safety, engineering, and sensory design considerations. The second part of the study involved assessing two public spaces, in South-east Queensland, Australia, to analyze the extent to which they meet the archetype inclusive public space model.

The WDA allows for the identification of all system components and their inter-dependencies within a domain via the use an Abstraction Hierarchy (AH). The AH describes the system in question across five levels: 1) Functional purpose – describes the overall purpose(s) of the system; 2) Values and priority measures – the criteria that the system uses for measuring progress towards its functional purpose; 3) Purpose-related functions – the functions (and activities) of the system that are necessary for achieving the functional purposes; 4) Object-related processes – the functional capabilities and limitations of the physical objects in the system that enable the purpose-related func-tions; and 5) Physical objects – the artefacts within the system that afford the physical functions [12]. By building an AH of a domain, such as a public space, it is possible to detail each component, its relationships and map the causal linkages.

2.2 Building the WDA

The WDA was developed and refined by experts from the disciplinary fields of landscape architecture, urban design, public health, community development and human factors. Two of the analysts have previously applied CWA in urban design contexts, whilst another has extensive experience of applying CWA across a range of domains including defence, road and rail transport [6].

A draft AH was constructed by the urban design and public health practitioners. This analysis considered and included the 7 Senses approach and also the range of national and international policy and literature as it relates to public space and sensory design. This AH was subsequently reviewed by all experts at an analyst workshop. Any disagreements about the inclusions or the linkages between levels of AH were resolved through discussion until consensus was met.

3 Results

A summary of the AH is presented in Fig. 1. The top two levels are complete; however due to size restrictions the lower three levels show only a summary of the nodes. The following results do not endeavor to outline all the relationships; rather provide an overview of the levels and some interactions of the AH to demonstrate the applicability and usefulness of this HFE approach.

3.1 Functional Purpose

From the literature, policy and practice it was concluded that three functional purposes are extant when generating and supporting sensory based inclusive public spaces. These include: 'a healthy and happy community'; 'an inclusive and connected community'; and 'a healthy and active individual'. These functional purposes focus primarily on how users operate within the domain and their interactions with each other and their community. It is only when considering the levels below within the AH can the significant relationships and interdependencies be fully analyzed and understood.

3.2   Values and Priority Measures

Values and priority measures are presented on the second level and seek to outline the criteria against which to evaluate the system's functional purposes [12] - twelve values and priority measures were established. These range from objective measures such as 'conform to built environment standards and rules' and 'maximize actual safety'; through to values concerned with social equity and urban design; 'enable individuality' and 'maximize engaging design elements' (Fig. 1).

With such a diverse range of values and priority measures two notable issues are revealed. The first is that some values and priority measures may conflict with one another. For example, maximizing engaging elements whilst adhering to design standards and optimising safety may be challenging in practice. The second issue is the difficulty for stakeholders to understand whether the diverse range of values and priorities are being met. It is questionable whether current approaches exist to assess whether design elements are engaging or if individuality is being enabled.

An example of these interrelationships can be found when considering the value and priority measure of 'maximize community connectedness'. This priority measure is connected 'up' to each of the functional purposes of the system and is therefore central to the overall success. Further, the AH highlights that it must be supported by a range of purpose related functions, on the level below. The purpose related functions which support 'maximize community connectedness' and *how* it is achieved include each of the seven senses, in addition to purpose related functions concerning: local character; local ownership and agency; diversity; quality of design; places to meet and wait; active and passive engagement; walkability and way-finding.

3.3   Purpose-Related Functions

This level aims to identify the functions, or activities, of the system that are necessary to achieve the functional purposes [12]. It provides a crucial link and can be used to break down the AH into means-ends relationships; or a 'why', 'what' and 'how' delineation. For example, if the purpose related function of 'provide visual sensory experience' represents the '*what*'; then the values and priority measure on the level above ('maximize engaging design elements', 'enabling individuality' and 'maximize comfort') are '*why*', while the object related processes (on the level below) such as 'landmark', 'provides greenery and vegetation', 'provides shade and shadow', and 'provides water display' represent the '*how*' in terms of achieving the purpose-related functions. These means-ends relationships work across all levels of the AH and are central to operationalizing design outcomes.

For efficiency, in Fig. 1, the purpose related functions of the WDA have been grouped to represent: 'sensory-related functions' (e.g., provides tactile experiences, provide

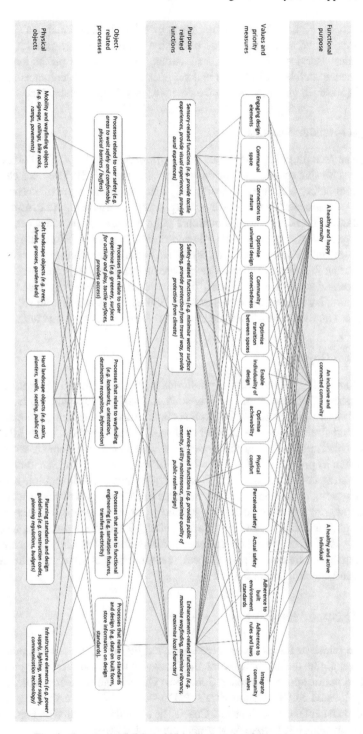

Fig. 1. Summarised WDA AH for inclusive public space design

visual experiences, provide aural experiences); 'safety-related functions' (e.g., minimize motorized traffic speeds, provide protection from travel way, provide protection from climate); 'service-related related functions' (e.g., provides public amenity, utility maintenance, delivery of utilities and services to need); and 'enhancement-related functions' (optimise vibrancy, maximize diversity, enable local character).

3.4 Object-Related Processes

The object-related purposes level refers to the *affordances* of the physical objects found within a system that enable the purpose-related functions [12]. They are categorized here into user safety (e.g. areas to wait safely and comfortably, provides shelter), user experience (e.g. greenery, surfaces for activity, access), way finding (e.g. route decision making, destination recognition), functional engineering (e.g. provides sanitation fixtures, transfers electricity) and standards and design (e.g. store information on design standards, store information on road rules). When linking the objects to their affordances, it is evident that the object-related processes are often afforded by multiple objects. For example, 'provides surface for objects' is an affordance of parking space, pavement surface, fences, lawn, tables, and chairs/seats. While objects which offer the affordance of a 'greenery and vegetation' include lawn, trees, shrubs, grasses, and annual plants.

3.5 Physical Objects

At the bottom of the AH, the range of public space physical objects are identified. These include aspects of infrastructure design, such as tactile surface indicators, pavement surface and stormwater grates, as well as associated amenities including toilets, drinking fountains, and street signage. A number of these objects can offer similar affordances, despite how dissimilar they may be. For example, while lawn and ramps are very different in form, both may provide a 'safe surface for mobility', in addition to providing a 'surface for activity and play'. Similarly, one physical object may provide multiple affordances within the system, e.g. fences can deter vehicles from using pedestrian space; provides shade/shadow; provide a tactile surface to touch; provide a physical barrier; provide a surface for play and activity; and provide a psychological buffer between pedestrian and the roadway. It is important to note that some objects may not actually be located within the public space but are critical to its success, including budgets, road rules, maintenance standards, and construction codes.

4 Public Space Evaluation

The second phase of this study involved applying the model to existing public space contexts to examine the extent to which they achieved the 'ideal' inclusive public space design. Two public spaces located in South-east Queensland were considered. The first case study, located on Upper Main Street, Palmwoods, represents a small square within a regional town center on the Sunshine Coast. The second was located on Fairfield Road, Fairfield, represents a suburban recreational park in Brisbane.

Each area was visited by two researchers and notes were made regarding the presence or absence of elements from the object-related processes and physical objects levels of the AH. A ranking was assigned to each object related process to reflect the extent to which it was supported by objects in the space. This was determined based on the number of physical objects found that linked up to each object related process. These rankings were decided through consultation between an urban planning expert and a public health professional. Guidelines were agreed upon to determine 'none, low, medium, high or exceeding' ranking.

4.1 Summary Analysis of Case Studies

Each of the two chosen case studies represents a very different public space context. However, there were many similarities identified in relation to each location's limitations and strengths for inclusive sensory design. Physical objects found missing within both contexts include bike racks, public transit stop, drinking fountains, water feature, large rocks, animal habitat boxes, grasses, tactile surface indicators and maps. The AH identifies that these objects play a significant role within the system in terms of reducing optimal user comfort, way finding, functional engineering and planning standards, and design affordances (Fig. 1). As a result, there is impact up the model to the purpose-related functions, values and priorities and the overall functional purpose of the public space system. In both contexts a large proportion of sensory affordance did not differ as a result of available physical objects, they were largely low to medium rankings indicating that more could be done in the design of these public spaces.

5 Discussion

The aim of this study was to explore sensory design for optimising the inclusiveness of public space, incorporating the 7 Senses approach. Moreover, WDA was proposed as a useful tool to both the design and evaluation of public space designs. The findings indicate that this sensory approach is useful in moving the design of public space towards better inclusion of a broader community. Significantly, the study has established new knowledge for a sensory design approach allowing for its further development, future research and application in best practice urban planning and design. WDA does indeed provide a useful framework with which to design and/or evaluate public space designs.

The implications of this study into future development of human factors and urban design research and practice are extensive. There is potential to extend existing research, exploring sensory design of public spaces, beyond the first phase of CWA into the other four remaining phases of CWA [12]. One important line of inquiry involves using these phases to go beyond specification of public space designs to develop permanent sensory public spaces. The formative nature of CWA is useful for this, as it enables design concepts to be evaluated and reiterated at the paper design concept level. In addition, the strategies analysis phase will enable designers to anticipate how different users will use the public space (e.g. people with disabilities, elderly).

6 Conclusion

This paper demonstrates how the socio-technical approach of CWA can significantly contribute to better understanding of the impacts and influences of inclusive public spaces design. By constructing a Work Domain Analysis of the 'ideal' public space system, the authors have developed a comprehensive model of public space in community contexts. In addition, this paper has incorporated sensory design principles from the 7 senses approach.

It presents an inclusive design focus which moves beyond just physical accessibility or 'sensory zones', to make sensory design elements integrated into the entire system. This study provides a clear framework based on best practice literature and design guidelines, nationally and internationally, in addition to incorporating professional opinion and expertise across a range of influential sectors.

References

1. Australian State Government of Victoria. Urban Design Charter for Victoria (2009). https://www.dtpli.vic.gov.au/planning/
2. Centre for Universal Design. 7 Principles of Universal Design (1997). https://www.universaldesign.ie/exploreampdiscover/the7principles
3. UNICEF. Australian Child Friendly Cities Model (2013–2015) (2013). https://www.unicef.org.au/Discover/Australia-s-children/Child-Friendly-Cities/
4. Gray, J.A., Zimmerman, J.L., Rimmer, J.H.: Built environment instruments for walkability, bikeability, and recreation. Disab. Health J. 5(2), 87–101 (2012)
5. The 7 Senses Foundation (2014). https://www.7senses.org.au/
6. Stevens, N., Salmon, P.: Safe places for pedestrians. Accid. Anal. Prev. 72, 257–266 (2015)
7. Abedi, M., Mofidi, M., Behzadfar, M.: Investigation role of sensory stimulus in perception of urban spaces. Int. J. Acad. Res. 3(2), 201–205 (2011)
8. Sensory Processing Disorder (SPD) Australia. Sensory Processing Disorder Australia (2014). https://www.spdaustralia.com.au/
9. Kellet, J., Rofe, M.: Creating active communities: UniSA, Institute for Sustainable Systems and Tech (2009). https://www.heartfoundation.org.au/
10. Australian Institute of Health and Welfare (AIHW). Australia's health 2012 (2012). https://www.aihw.gov.au/
11. Vicente, K.J.: Cognitive Work Analysis: Toward Safe, Productive, and Healthy Computer-Based Work. CRC Press, Boca Raton (1999)
12. Jenkins, D.P., Stanton, N.A., Salmon, P.M., Walker, G.H.: Using work domain analysis to evaluate the impact of technological change on the performance of complex socio-technical systems. Ties 12(1), 1–14 (2011)

When Instrumentation and Human Performance Contribute Jointly to the Outcome of a Human-System-Integration (HSI) Mission: Brief Review

Ephraim Suhir[1,2,3,4]([✉])

[1] James Cook University, Townswille, QLD, Australia
[2] Portland State University, Portland, OR, USA
[3] Technical University, Vienna, Austria
[4] ERS Co., Los Altos, CA, USA

Abstract. The objective of this brief review is to demonstrate how analytical ("mathematical") probabilistic predictive modeling (PPM) can be effectively employed to predict the outcome of a Human-System-Integration (HSI) mission or an extraordinary situation, when the reliability of an instrumentation (both its hard- and software) and human-in-the-loop (HITL) performance contribute jointly to the outcome of the mission or the situation. The general concepts are illustrated by numerical examples. It is concluded that analytical modeling should always be considered, in addition to computer simulations, in any HSI undertaking of importance: these two modeling techniques are based, as a rule, on different assumptions and employ different calculation procedures, and if the calculated data obtained using these two approaches are in agreement, then there is a good reason to believe that the obtained results are accurate and trustworthy.

Keywords: Probabilistic predictive modeling (PPM) ·
Human-System-Integration (HSI) · Human-in-the-loop (HITL)

Acronyms

ASD	Available Sight Distance
HCF	Human Capacity Factor
HF	Human Factor
HITL	Human in the Loopuman in the Loop
HSI	Human-System Integration
MWLMWL	Mental Workloadental Workload
PDF	Probabilistic Predictive Modeling

1 Incentive

By employing quantifiable and measurable ways to assess the role of various intervening uncertainties associated with the MWL and HCF [1, 2] and treating the HITL [3, 4] as a

N. L. Black et al. (Eds.): IEA 2021, LNNS 219, pp. 409–413, 2021.
https://doi.org/10.1007/978-3-030-74602-5_58

part, often the most critical one, of the complex man-instrumentation-equipment-vehicle (or another object of control, including, say, another human)-environment system [5–7], one can improve dramatically the human's performance, the HSI and predict, minimize and, when possible and appropriate, even specify the probability of the occurrence of a HSI related casualty. The never-zero probability of such casualty has to be established beforehand and made adequate for a particular application of importance. No improvements in the HSI are possible, if this interaction is not quantified. In the review that follows the use of the PPM [8–12] is addressed. This technique enables quantifying, on the probabilistic basis, the role of the HF and improve his/hers HCF, so that the HITL would be able to successfully cope, when necessary, with an elevated MWL. The emphasis is on situations, when reliability of the instrumentation and human performance contribute jointly to the outcome of an HSI related mission or an off-normal situation.

2 Brief Review

The convolution technique developed in connection with the helicopter landing ship situation [13] and extended in application to the famous "Miracle-on-the-Hudson" event [14] is chosen to illustrate the possible application of the MWL-HCF bias in the HITL related missions and situations. It is shown how applied probability based (see, e.g. [15]) concepts could and should be used, in addition to traditional psychological activities and efforts, when there is a need to evaluate, quantify, optimize and, when possible and appropriate, even specify the human ability to cope with an elevated MWL. When adequate human performance in a particular critical HITL situation is imperative, ability to quantify the HF is highly desirable. Such quantification could be done by comparing the actual or anticipated MWL with the likely ("available") and established in advance HCF. The MWL vs. HCF models and their modifications can be helpful particularly, after appropriate algorithms are developed and sensitivity analyses are conducted, to evaluate the role that the human plays, in terms of his/hers ability (capacity) to cope with a MWL in various situations, when HF, instrumentation performance and uncertain and often harsh environments contribute jointly to the success and safety of a mission; to assess the risk of a mission outcome, with consideration of the HITL performance; to develop guidelines for personnel selection and training; to choose the appropriate simulation conditions; and/or to decide if the existing levels of automation and the reliability of the employed equipment (instrumentation) are adequate. Other possible HSI models are also indicated [4, 16].

Let us address, as a suitable example, the situation when a steadfast obstacle is suddenly detected in front of the moving train. Consider first a situation when the ASD $\hat{S}$ assessed by the system's radar and/or LIDAR is much more accurate than the estimates that of the machinist, when he/she takes over, so that this distance could be treated as a non-random variable. It is also natural to assume that the random pre-deceleration ("constant speed") distance S_0 and the deceleration ("constant deceleration") distance S_1 are distributed in accordance with the Rayleigh law. Indeed, the most likely values of these distances cannot be zero, but cannot be very long (large) either. In addition, in the emergency situations of the type in question, short distances are much more likely than large distances, and, because of that, the maxima (modes) of their PDFs should be heavily skewed towards the short distances. The Rayleigh distribution is the simplest one that possesses these features. Weibull distribution could be another option.

The probability P_S that the random distance $S = S_0 + S_1$, which is the sum of two Rayleigh-distributed random distances, S_0 and S_1, exceeds a certain level $\hat{S}$ can be found as a convolution of the two Rayleigh distributions as S

$$P_S = 1 - \int_0^{\hat{S}} \frac{s_0}{\sigma_0^2} \exp\left(-\frac{s_0^2}{2\sigma_0^2}\right)\left[1 - \exp\left(-\frac{(\hat{S} - s_0)^2}{2\sigma_1^2}\right)\right] ds_0 = e^{-(1+\eta^2)s^2}$$

$$+ e^{-s^2}\left(\frac{1}{1 + 1/\eta^2}(e^{-s^2/\eta^2} - e^{-\eta^2 s^2}) + \sqrt{\pi}\frac{s}{\eta + 1/\eta}[\Phi(\eta s) + \Phi(s/\eta)]\right).$$

Here $f(s_{0,1}) = \frac{s_{0,1}}{\sigma_{0,1}^2} \exp\left(-\frac{s_{0,1}^2}{2\sigma_{0,1}^2}\right)$ are the probability density distribution functions of the random variables S_0 and S_1, $\sigma_{0,1}$ are the modes (most likely values) of these variables, $s_{0,1} = \sqrt{\frac{\pi}{2}}\sigma_{0,1}$ and $\sqrt{D_{0,1}} = \sqrt{\frac{4-\pi}{2}}\sigma_{01}$ are their means and standard deviations, respectively, and $s = \frac{\hat{S}}{\sqrt{2(\sigma_0^2+\sigma_1^2)}}$ and $\eta = \frac{\sigma_1}{\sigma_0}$ are the dimensionless parameters of the convolution and $\Phi(\alpha) = \frac{2}{\sqrt{\pi}}\int_0^\alpha e^{-t^2} dt$ is the Laplace function (probability integral). The calculated probabilities P_S are shown in Table 1. As evident from the table data, the available sight distance (ASD) parameter s plays the major role, while the ratio η of the deceleration and the pre-deceleration distances is less important. Intuitively, it is felt that it should be this way.

The role of the ASD variability could be accounted for based on the following simple reasoning. It is natural to assume that the ASD is a normally distributed random

Table 1. Calculated probabilities P_S of obstruction assuming non-random ASD

s/η	0	1.0	2.0	5.0	10.0	20.0
0	1.0000	1.0000	1.0000	1.0000	1.0000	1.0000
0.25	0.9394	0.9975	0.9962	0.9870	0.9719	0.9579
0.5	0.7788	0.9656	0.9515	0.8890	0.8413	0.8071
0.75	0.5698	0.8629	0.8232	0.7059	0.6424	0.6058
1.00	0.3679	0.6848	0.6259	0.5817	0.4324	0.3997
1.50	0.1054	0.2818	0.2399	0.2181	0.1344	0.1197
2.0	0.0183	0.0645	0.0534	0.0328	0.0253	0.0216
3.0	1.234E−4	6.562E−4	5.395E−4	2.852E−4	1.980E−4	1.577E−4
4.0	1.254E−7	1.064E−6	6.384E−7	2.673E−7	2.078E−7	1.125E−7
5.0	1.389E−11	1.231E−10	9.847E−11	4.853E−11	2.924E−11	2.085E−11

variable. This is because the probabilities that the actual ASD values could be greater or smaller than the radar or Lidar read are equally likely, and therefore the corresponding probability density distribution function should be symmetric with respect to its mean (the most likely, median) value. Then the probability P_A that this variable is below a certain value s is $P_A = \frac{1}{2}[1 - \Phi(s)]$. Obstruction will be avoided, when the random sum $S = S_0 + S_1$ of the two random distances, S_0 and S_1, is below a certain level $\hat{S}$ (the probability of this situation is $1 - P_s$) and, in addition, the actual ASD distance is above this level (this probability is $1 - P_A$). Then the probability that the obstruction is avoided is $(1 - P_s)(1 - P_A)$, and the probability of the obstruction, which is an opposite event, is

$$P_{SA} = 1 - (1 - P_s)(1 - P_A) = P_A + P_s - P_A P_s = \frac{1}{2}[1 - \Phi(s) + P_s(1 + \Phi(s))]$$

The calculated probabilities P_{SA} (Table 2) reflecting the role of the ASD variability indicate that consideration of this variability results in a rather insignificant increase in the predicted probabilities of obstruction, and that the difference rapidly decreases with the decrease in these probabilities. For very low probabilities of obstruction (two last lines in Table 2), the ASD variability does not make any difference at all.

Table 2. Calculated probabilities P_{SA} of obstruction considering random ASD

s/η	0	1.0	2.0	5.0	10.0	20.0
0	0.5000	0.5000	0.5000	0.5000	0.5000	0.5000
0.25	0.9613	0.9984	0.9976	0.9917	0.9821	0.9731
0.5	0.8318	0.9738	0.9631	0.9156	0.8793	0.8368
0.75	0.6319	0.8827	0.8487	0.7484	0.7281	0.6627
1.00	0.4176	0.7096	0.6553	0.6146	0.4770	0.4469
1.50	0.1206	0.2940	0.2528	0.2314	0.1491	0.1346
2.0	0.0201	0.0662	0.0551	0.0346	0.0271	0.0234
3.0	1.334E−4	6.662E−4	5.495E−4	2.952E−4	2.038E−4	1.677E−4
4.0	1.254E−7	1.064E−6	6.384E−7	2.673E−7	2.078E−7	1.125E−7
5.0	1.389E−11	1.231E−10	9.847E−11	4.853E−11	2.924E−11	2.085E−11

3   Conclusion

Analytical MWL/HCF models and their possible modifications and generalizations can be helpful when developing guidelines for the evaluation of the probability of failure of a mission or of an off-normal situation and for personnel selection and training; and/or when there is a need to decide, if the existing methods of reliability and ergonomics engineering are adequate in particular situations, and if not, whether additional and/or more advanced and, perhaps, more expensive equipment or instrumentation should be developed, tested and installed to meet the safety requirements. The emphasis was on missions and situations, when the equipment/instrumentation (system's) and HITL performance contributed jointly to the outcome of the mission or an off-normal situation of importance. Although the obtained numbers make physical sense, it is the approach, and not the numbers per se, that is, in the author's opinion, the main merit of the carried out analyses.

References

1. Suhir, E.: Mental Workload (MWL) vs. Human Capacity Factor (HCF): A Way to Quantify Human Performance. In: Gregory and Bedny, I. (eds.) Applied and Systemic-Structural Activity Theory. CRC Press, Boca Raton (2019)
2. Suhir, E.: Adequate trust, human-capacity-factor, probability-distribution-function of human non-failure and its entropy. Int. J. Hum. Factor Model. Simul. 7(1) (2019)
3. Suhir, E.: Human-in-the-loop: Probabilistic Predictive Modeling, Its Role, Attributes, Challenges and Applications, Theoretical Issues in Ergonomics Science, July 2014
4. Suhir, E.: Human-in-the-loop: application of the double exponential probability distribution function enables one to quantify the role of the human factor. Int. J. Hum. Factor Model. Simul. 5(4) (2017)
5. Suhir, E.: Reliability and Accelerated Life Testing, Semiconductor International, 1 February 2005
6. Suhir, E.: Probabilistic Design for Reliability, Chip Scale Reviews. vol.14, no. 6 (2010)
7. Suhir, E.: When Reliability is Imperative, Ability to Quantify It is a Must, IMAPS Advanced Microelectronics, August 2012
8. Reason, J.T.: Human Error. Cambridge University Press, Cambridge (1990)
9. Hollnagel, E.: Human Reliability Analysis: Context and Control. Academic Press, London (1993)
10. Kern, A.T.: Controlling Pilot Error: Culture, Environment, and CRM (Crew Resource Management). McGraw-Hill , London (2001)
11. O'Neil, W.A.: The human element in shipping, keynote address. In: Bi-annual Symposium of the Seafarers International Research Center, Cardiff, Wales, 29 June 2001
12. Harris, D.: Human Performance on the Flight Deck. Bookpoint Ltd., Ashgate Publishing, Oxon (2011)
13. Suhir, E.: Probabilistic modeling of the role of the human factor in the helicopter-landing-ship (HLS) situation. Int. J. Hum. Factor Model. Simul. (IJHFMS) 1(3) (2010)
14. Suhir, E.: Miracle-on-the-hudson: quantified aftermath. Int. J. Hum. Factor Model. Simul. 4(1) (2012)
15. Suhir, E.: Applied Probability for Engineers and Scientists. McGraw-Hill, New-York (1997)
16. Suhir, E.: Likelihood of Vehicular Mission-Success-and-Safety. J. Aircraft 49(1) (2012)

Part III: Ergonomic Work Analysis and Training (EWAT) (Edited by Catherine Delgoulet and Marta Santos)

Steering Group: An Action-Training Tool in the Ergonomic Work Analysis

Vicente Nepomuceno[1](✉) ⓘ, Denise Alvarez[2] ⓘ, Fernanda Araújo[3] ⓘ, and Marcelo Figueiredo[2] ⓘ

[1] Federal University of the State of Rio de Janeiro, Rio de Janeiro, Brazil
[2] Fluminense Federal University, Niterói, Rio de Janeiro, Brazil
[3] Federal University of Rio de Janeiro, Rio de Janeiro, Brazil

Abstract. The text analyses steering groups (SGs) in ergonomic actions. The SGs are considered as training and strategy tools by ergonomists. They are also seen in their function of co-training and co-analysis of work and of construction of a common language in interventions, which are part of the training paradigm of actors in and for the analysis of work, for and by action. Its background is the complexity of Ergonomics and Training interventions, the sustainability of the ergonomic action and the reciprocal learning. This is the register of the experience of an ergonomic action accomplished in a coal mining cooperative to discuss its wrongs and rights. The focus is on the relevance of the discussion, as there is little dissemination of structured methodology on SG organization. The main issue is on how to structure SGs in ergonomic work analyses (EWAs) that conciliate transformation of labor situations and training of workers. An ergonomic action with work analysis, SG structuring and Meetings on the Work (MWs) was carried out. The results point out indications to what one has to consider when structuring technical, political and operational steering groups.

Keywords: Tools of ergonomic action · Ergonomics and training · Steering group · Clinical and strategical knowledge · Participatory ergonomics

1 Introduction

The article presents an ergonomic action accomplished in a coal mining cooperative, where ergonomists used the construction of steering groups (SGs) as a training and strategic tool. Registering this experience to discuss its wrongs and rights is relevant as there is little dissemination of structured methodology on organizing SGs in interventions that articulate Ergonomics and Training [1].

We intend to analyse the performance of these co-analysis tools of work, or reflection and action-training practices [2, 3] and also of the building of a common ground [4, 5], comparing them to other experiences. The issue here is: how to structure SGs in ergonomic work analyses (EWAs) that conciliate transformation of work situations and training of workers?

This type of ergonomic action has been studied since the end of the XX century [6] and has, at least, as a perspective, two types of knowledges: clinical, observer of

N. L. Black et al. (Eds.): IEA 2021, LNNS 219, pp. 417–424, 2021.
https://doi.org/10.1007/978-3-030-74602-5_59

words and the emergence of different knowledges; and strategic, that creates favorable conditions in the organization to transform situations [7]. The suggestion of creating groups responsible for the carrying out of the process was already seen in Guérin *et al.* [8], who thought them inserted in a pre-existing structure in the enterprise or in an *ad hoc* structure.

Vidal sees the importance of creating different groups for the social construction: Interest Group (IG), Focus Groups (FGs), Monitoring Group (MG) and Support Group (SGr) [9, p. 69]. According to him, the IG together with ergonomist-researchers configures the Ergonomic Action Group (EAG), which should learn the EWA, oriented by the ergonomists. The SGr must be integrated by people with decision-making power, to whom the EAG will report during the intervention. The MG is similar to the SGr, being composed by people who hold technical authority to make decisions in the ambit of the intervention, but who cannot participate in it as a whole. The FGs are created in accordance to work situations under focus. The EAG and the FGs are focused on the operational articulation, while the MG and the SGr are of strategic articulation. The dynamic of these groups must allow the construction of consensuses during the EWA steps.

In the literature directly linked to Ergonomics and Training we find references to the so called ERGO groups or Ergogroup. Within them two groups are created: the steering committee and the Ergogroup. Chicoine, Tellier & St-Vincent [10] highlight the composition of these groups who conduct the intervention: the committee, composed by the industrial plant director or personnel manager, one representative of the work union and the ergonomist; the Ergogroup, created at the beginning of the intervention, directed by the ergonomist and of permanent action. The latter has as characteristic: (1) to analyse more than one labor situation; (2) have its members trained by the ergonomist; (3) to fix ergonomic expertise in the enterprise; (4) incorporate occasional collaborators along the intervention; (5) be composed by two experienced operators, one supervisor, one technical specialist and the ergonomist.

Daniellou & Béguin [11] emphasize that the implementation of groups must be thought with the task of political and technical steering of the intervention, however, they do not define *a priori* configuration for them. The political steering refers to the definition of objectives, the implementation of means, the necessary arbitration in the different steps; on the other hand, the technical steering deals with the construction of solutions and the coordination between specialties.

The creation of support structures is a fundamental step for the social construction of the intervention, but, besides this, the ergonomist must be observant to his/her positioning within the enterprise. According to the authors, positioning is a dynamic and evolutional management where the ergonomist identifies the actors with whom he/she will construct the intervention and verifies if they are in positions that make actions possible. At the same time, he/she must be attentive not to consider a person solely for their function in the hierarchy. He/she must also plan the contacts to be made in each step of the EWA and the level of relation sought with the different actors. It is important to consider also the constraints that weigh on the actors in relation to their respective positions. This exploitation will allow the ergonomist to identify who must be associated to the intervention's steering and who must be kept informed of the progress of the project.

These contributions inspired us to construct the dynamic of the ergonomic action put in practice in the cooperative, presented below.

2 Methodology

Influenced by these authors, we opted to create three action and training spaces: the steering group (SG) to technically conduct the intervention; the management group in which, at each visit, ergonomists and top management would meet to talk about the progress of the project and its referrals, which we consider our political steering; the Meetings on the Work (MWs), with mini-tractor operators (MT) to analyse the coal cleaning and displacement operation activity, a critical situation chosen for analysis. At each visit we worked for 4 days, together with the technical SG, and registered data and analyses in reports handed to top management. In addition, we produced internal research reports with impressions on the context and social construction. Both were analysed at the end of the ergonomic action.

We acted this way during the 4 steps of the ergonomic analyses during 13 months in the research "Miners for the study of self-management work – META(*)"[1]:

(1) identification and demand analysis: "contribute to coal productivity of around 4,500 tons/day", as average production oscillated under this level;

(2) creation of the technical SG, co-analysis of the global cooperative functioning and definition of the production bottleneck, that was the coal cleaning operation;

(3) analysis of the MT operator activity in performing the coal cleaning and sending it to the surface, training of SG in analysis of the activity;

(4) discussion of the pre-diagnosis in MWs [12] and construction of recommendations, training of MT operators and confection and co-analysis of recommendations.

The definition of the demand was drawn up from interviews of ergonomists with key-sectors of the cooperative. The results of interviews were presented to production workers, who complemented the information. In presentations, workers were invited to participate in a group that would conduct an improvement project, viewing to tion.

The structure of the SG was thought for the intervention's technical conduction, to identifying and analysing demand. It was necessary to gather the knowledges to identify the causes of irregularity in daily production. The group was formed by 7 voluntary workers: 1 cooperative vice-president (ex-tractor operator), 2 engineers, 1 supervisor, and 3 caretakers. A co-analysis of the global functioning of the cooperative, training in ergonomic analysis (work analysis and activity analysis) was carried out together with the SG, and the production bottleneck was defined: the coal cleaning activity, done by the mini-tractor operators (MT).

---

[1] (*)META – In Portuguese, META means "objective", "goal", which linked the name of the study group to the objective of the task itself, in a word play impossible to be translated (translator's note):(*)META – In Portuguese, META means "objective", "goal", which linked the name of the study group to the objective of the task itself, in a word play impossible to be translated (translator's note).

To continue the training in EWA, we had to understand the work activity of the MT operation. Before initiating interviews and observations to understand the work activity, we carried out a "mini course" with the members of the SG, whose contents were the foundations of the EWA and its steps and the concepts of task, activity, variability, and control.

The analysis of the mini-tractor operator's (MT) activity in performing the coal cleaning and sending it to the surface and training of the SG in analysis of the activity was carried out after the "mini-course" with the SG. Interview and observation scripts for MT operators were elaborated together with the SG. There was concern in adapting the language of questions to make it closer to the reality of interviewees.

The division of the SG and of researchers to carry out the interviews was also discussed. Some expressed discomfort in interviewing a colleague ("but we already know what happens in this work. We don't need to do these interviews"). This feeling of workers can also be observed in Gaudart *et al.* [13], training with trade unionists who perceived in workers the same discomfort in interviewing colleagues. Our intention was to instigate the learning of the look, the attention, the interest.

After carrying out interviews, results found were shared and we made the observations of the activity. Following the observations, the material was evaluated. This step was intended to bring us closer to the activity of the MT operation and conclude a pre-diagnosis of the causes of production irregularity.

The discussion of the pre-diagnosis was carried out in MWs [12], where there was also the construction and co-analysis of recommendations and training of MT operators. The MWs intend to be collective chats where the activity is the theme in focus and work is debated. We carried out 6 meetings with 6 tractor operators and some SG members. The meetings began with the presentation of a key concept, then a series of utterances collected in the previous step were chosen individually and commented by operators. From these utterances, difficulties were discussed and work was reflected upon. In the sixth meeting we presented a synthesis with a diagnosis and concluded a series of recommendations. At the end, we delivered a list of recommendations to be implemented by the SG, with the authorization of the top management to modify the tractor cleaning operation and contribute in the production regularization.

3   Results and Discussion

The ergonomic action resulted in 17 actions of recommendation constructed by MT operators, SG workers and researchers. Three support structures were created:

1) Management Group, operationalized in meetings with the top-management;
2) Steering Group, technical group, personnel in key-functions in the organogram;
3) Operational Group, with operators of the production bottleneck, participants of the MWs.

In the META research we opted to create, in each visit, meetings of researchers with management without the personnel of the technical SG. It was a way of authorizing the path planned by the SG and of verifying eventual deviations, besides requesting liberation of personnel, rooms and information. Nevertheless, meetings with management did not occur as planned, as their participation was passive. In each visit it became more difficult to find management personnel and there was a progressive distancing, even with us insisting on making ourselves available to the cooperative.

The technical SG involved supervisors and engineers in a training space for researchers and workers and the taking of decision on research actions. It triggered internal changes related to understandings of the work process and framing of functions. The SG presented substantive changes in the ways of action within the cooperative and in the understanding of the work process. Its members incorporated in their language terms and concepts of the activity ergonomics. Along the ergonomic action, we perceived that SG meetings allowed the change in work representations of its members allowing a training which habilitated them to act beyond limits set by their functions. One of the positive results of this change of representation in technical SG members was expressed by a production supervisor. On the day we carried out the observations of the activity, he told us that our work was very important, since we were "teaching the cooperative to listen to the other". He said something as: "Now I can be me, I don't have to be harsh with somebody who has produced little, I can speak with kindness". Despite these changes, however, the group was not able to follow up the actions of recommendation, since only actions focused on changes in machinery were implemented.

The positioning during intervention seems to us to be little studied in EWA manuals. To some extent, we incurred in a contextual evaluation error when considering that the position in the organogram for training of SG would allow the implementation of recommendations. The presence of the vice-director had seemed to us sufficient as a representative of the institutional power of the cooperative's management, however, it was not.

This mistake had been signaled by Daniellou & Béguin [11], when stressing to the necessity of constructing support structures with the presence of key actors. We opted to prioritize voluntary participation, both in the SG and the MWs, a choice that, despite its advantages, showed limits. The production caretakers and supervisors, strategic members of the cooperative and fundamental professional in the construction of changes in production, declined participating. Without their participation, it was not possible to change their representation in the situation of work and, neither, change elements present in the organization of work. Therefore, their participation was essential, even if compulsory.

To bring to the SG a member of the MW, be it a MT operator or a production caretaker, in conformity with MATRIOSCA [14], would have been a more interesting choice than create MWs and subsequently analyse this work only with members of the technical SG, as we did.

Another dissociation that showed itself mistaken was between the technical SG and the meeting with management. We should have constructed more spaces between management and this SG and not allow the space of management only with researchers. The SG should have been our social and political construction not only our technical construction.

It seems to us that in projects focused on a demand of productivity, the management of the ergonomists position should be even more careful. Expectations of those involved lie in short term results; a "production driven" discourse, more patronal, is anticipated. It is necessary to develop spaces of joint construction and mediation with management, stemming from real proposals, *i.e.*, after the diagnosis, which must be foreseen in the initial plan. The existence of a technical SG was authorized, although the implementation of changes had not been negotiated, even if it did not involve resources. Following up these modifications would have brought new and important issues to the SG. As warned by Daniellou & Béguin [11], the dimensioning of the ergonomists action must be done according to conditions that had been able to be constructed against the context. However, it may be restricted to a job while its determinants are located elsewhere. If one acts this way, they will be ineffective. We tried not to be restricted to the MT operator job, suggesting changes in the work organization. Nevertheless, these strategic changes were suggested without having gained a position of trust with management and supervision. This led us to not reach the transformation of these situations.

4   Conclusions

Our main objective was to answer the question: how to structure SGs in ergonomic work analyses (EWAs) that conciliate transformation of work situations and training of workers?

Initially we presented some approaches to structuring EWA support groups and methodologies from the Ergonomics and Training fields. Benchmarks that reinforced the importance of these support structures in the technical construction and political process of the intervention. Following that, we explained the methodology developed, an action-research that conciliates the EWA with training devices, carried out during 13 months in a coal cooperative. From this experience we point out challenges and learnings on the structuring of these SGs. The intervention showed that:

1. The process of participation and training of SG allowed a change in representation on work that led workers to reconstruct their way of acting at the workplace. It allowed them to appropriate the concept of activity, incorporating it in everyday life.
2. The construction of separate support groups – technical group and political group with the management seems to be a good strategy to take advantage of the availability of members of top management. However, it proved ineffective, as it did not allow top management to engage in the project.
3. The building of groups from functions present in the organogram presents limits. There are conflicts in organizations and it is necessary to be more attentive to the positioning of ergonomists than to these functions.
4. In projects focused in the increase of productivity it is necessary a closer positioning with key actors, having in mind that demands as these make it more difficult and subtle the epistemological convergence [15] among ergonomists and key actors.
5. The strategy of construction of recommendations to be implemented by SG without the presence of ergonomists was a mistake. It would be necessary to organize the project in a way that ergonomists could follow up the implementation of recommendations (as the Ergogroups do) [16].

6. The political steering must be thought from the beginning of the project guaranteeing conditions of implementation of actions for the SG. In the ergonomic action addressed we managed very limited conditions, restricted to machinery, the same difficulty reported by Bellemare *et al.* [16].

References

1. Neves, M.Y., Alvarez, D., Silva-Roosli, A.C.B., Masson, L.P., Oliveira, V.A.N.: Ação-formação: uma leitura das contribuições da Ergonomia da Atividade. Fractal: Revista de Psicologia **30**(2), 112–120 (2018)
2. Arnoud, J., Falzon, P.: A coanálise construtiva das práticas. In: Falzon, P. (ed.) Ergonomia Construtiva, pp. 305–321. Blucher, São Paulo (2016)
3. Mollo, V., Nascimento, A.: Práticas reflexivas e desenvolvimento dos indivíduos, dos coletivos e das organizações. In: Falzon, P. (ed.) Ergonomia construtiva, pp. 283–303. Blucher, São Paulo (2016)
4. Teiger, C., Lacomblez, M. (coords.): (Se) Former pour transformer le travail. Dynamique de constructions d'une analyse critique du travail. Presses de l'Université Laval/ETUI, Québec/Bruxelles (2013)
5. Santos, M., Alvarez, D.: Language issues in the activity of interaction with the company players: building tools to guarantee a 'Common Ground'. In: Proceedings of the 20th Congress of the International Ergonomics Association (IEA), volume IV, Florence, pp. 366–373 (2018)
6. Teiger, C., Laville, A.: La cooperation syndicats-recherche aux sources de la dynamique "recherche-formation-action" – L'expérience du laboratoire d'ergonomie du CNAM (1965–1990). In: Teiger, C., Lacomblez, M. (coords.). (Se) Former pour transformer le travail. Dynamique de constructions d'une analyse critique du travail, pp. 59–83. Presses de l'Université Laval/ETUI, Québec/Bruxelles (2013)
7. Lacomblez, M., Teiger, C., Vasconcelos, R.: A Ergonomia e o "paradigma da formação dos atores": uma parceria formadora com os protagonistas do trabalho. In: Bendassolli, P. F., Soboll, L. A. P. (orgs.). Métodos de pesquisa e intervenção em psicologia do trabalho: clínicas do trabalho, pp. 159–183. Editora Atlas, São Paulo (2014)
8. Guérin, F., Laville, A., Daniellou, F., Duraffourg, J., Kerguelen, A.: Compreender o trabalho para transformá-lo: A prática da Ergonomia. Blucher, São Paulo (2001)
9. Vidal, M.C.R.: Guia para Análise Ergonômica do Trabalho (AET) na Empresa. Editora Virtual Científica, Rio de Janeiro (2003)
10. Chicoine, D., Tellier, C., St-Vincent, M.: Work Involving Varied Tasks: An Ergonomic Analysis Process for MSD Prevention. IRRST, Québec (2007)
11. Daniellou, F., Béguin, P.: Metodologia da ação ergonômica: abordagens do trabalho real. In: Falzon, P. (ed.) Ergonomia, pp. 281–301. Blucher, São Paulo (2007)
12. Schwartz, Y., Durrive, L. (ed.): Trabalho e ergologia: conversas sobre a atividade humana. EdUFF, Niterói (2010)
13. Gaudart, C., Petit, J., Dugué, B., Daniellou, F., Davezies, P., Thery, L.: Impacting working conditions through trade union training. Work **41**(2), 165–175 (2012)
14. Duarte, S., Vasconcelos, R.: Análise da atividade, participação e sustentabilidade da ação transformadora: reflexões a partir do Projeto Matriosca. Laboreal **10**(1), 32–46 (2014)
15. Vasconcelos, R.: O papel do psicólogo do trabalho e a tripolaridade dinâmica dos processos de transformação: contributo para a promoção da segurança e saúde no trabalho. Doctoral thesis presented at the Faculty of Psychology and Education Sciences of the University of Porto. Porto (2008)

16. Bellemare, M., Marier, M., Prévost, J., Montreuil, S., Perron, N.: From diagnosis to transformation: how projects are implemented in a participatory framework. In: Proceedings of the XIVth Congress of the International Ergonomics Association (IEA), San Diego, pp. 724–727 (2000)

Analysis of Clinical Reasoning Processes During Scanning Chest X-Rays Based on Visual Perception Patterns

Hirotaka Aoki[1]([⊠]) [iD], Koji Morishita[2], Marie Takahashi[2], Rea Machida[1], Atsushi Kudoh[2], Mitsuhiro Kishino[2], and Tsuyoshi Shirai[2]

[1] Tokyo Institute of Technology, Tokyo 152-8550, Japan
aoki.h.ad@m.titech.ac.jp
[2] Tokyo Medical and Dental University, Tokyo 113-8510, Japan

Abstract. One of the most critical differentiator of skills in chest x-rays diagnosis is an effective information acquisition strategy coupled with thorough medical knowledge. However, well-experienced doctors frequently find it difficult to explicitly explain their skills because such skills are implicit and automated. To uncover characteristics of skills in chest x-rays diagnosis, we monitored eye movements as well as their debriefing utilizing the eye movement data, seventeen medical doctors including experts, intermediates, and residents during diagnosing twenty chest x-rays. Based on debriefing and eye movement data, we discuss possible application of eye movement data for effective education system.

Keywords: Gaze pattern · Expertise analysis · Clinical reasoning process · Debriefing · Chest X-rays

1 Introduction

Eye movement data analysis has been recognized as not only a powerful means to reveal expertise in medical image interpretation (e.g., [1]), but also a novel and effective educational tool to show expert's sophisticated performance (e.g., [2–4].) In the present paper, we report on a concept and its preliminary implementation of eye movement data-based expertise analysis for educational purpose in chest x-rays diagnosis. We performed a series of experiments in which seventeen medical doctors ranged from expert to residents conducted chest x-rays diagnosis. From the debriefing utilizing eye movement data, we elicited hidden scanning strategies during diagnosis evaluation of a pedagogically informed intervention based on eye-movements of programmers. Based on the preliminary results, we discuss the potentials of eye movement data for effective education system.

© The Author(s), under exclusive license to Springer Nature Switzerland AG 2021
N. L. Black et al. (Eds.): IEA 2021, LNNS 219, pp. 425–431, 2021.
https://doi.org/10.1007/978-3-030-74602-5_60

2 Experiment

2.1 Participant

Thirteen medical doctors and six residents were recruited. The individual attributes are summarized in Table 1. Ethics approval was granted by the Tokyo Institute of Technology Review Board (2020038) and the Tokyo Medical and Dental University Review Board (M2020-103). All participants provided written informed consent prior to the experiment.

Table 1. Participants' individual attributes

Group	Clinical department	No. participant	Experience (year)
Group 1	Radiology	4	7–22
Group 2	Respiratory medicine	4	12–25
Group 3	Emergency and critical care	5	5–13
Group 4	Resident	6	0.6–1.6

2.2 Chest X-Ray Image Test Set

A test set of twenty x-ray images of twenty patients' chest radiographs were selected. In selection processes, each radiograph was carefully examined by two radiologists, one professor who is an expert having extensive experience (>45 years) and skill in interpreting chest x-ray images and another one who is the third author of the present paper, to identify all of possible symptoms. In addition, the expert gave his rating to each image representing how difficult possible lesions/signs could be found and how difficult the case could be diagnosed (i.e., identifying the root cause of the lesions/signs) in five point scale (1: very easy ~5: very difficult). In the data analysis, five out of the twenty images were used. The details of the five images are summarized in Table 2.

2.3 Task

The experimental task was to perform x-ray chest image interpretation. Each participant was asked to report lesions found and his/her diagnostic decision for each image. Additionally, a participant was asked to give his/her ratings about how difficult possible lesions/signs could be found and how difficult the case could be diagnosed in five point scale (1: very easy ~5: very difficult).

Table 2. X-ray images

X-ray image	Patient (age, gender)	Finding	Diagnosis	Rating score	
				Identification of lesions	Diagnosing
1	59, man	Tumor shadow	Obstructive pneumonia	1	5
2	58, man	Nodule shadow	Lung cancer	2	1
3	69, woman	Ground-glass attenuation	Lung cancer	1	1
4	78, man	Consolidation	Lung cancer	1	1
5	83, man	Nodule Granular shadow Nodule shadow/Reticular shadow	Lung cancer	2	2

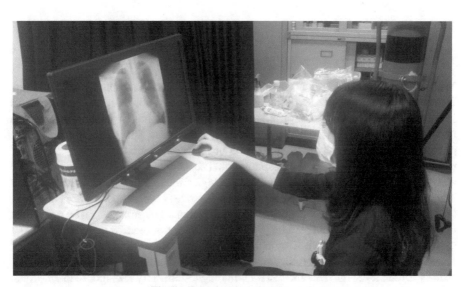

Fig. 1. Experimental environment.

2.4 Procedure

Upon arrival at our experimental site, each participant was briefed on the overall objective of the experiment, the tasks to be conducted, debriefing procedures, calibration processes of our eye tracker (Tobii X-3 120, Sweden), and questionnaire. Before starting, a participant completed one practice circuit using two images. After carrying out calibration for the eye tracking system, experimental tasks composed of 20 image interpretations were started. After interpreting an image, a participant verbally report his/her findings and diagnostic decision based on the findings. Then he/she was asked to give rating scores of difficulty perceived. Eye movement data during interpretation task were recorded. The experimental environment during interpretation task is shown in Fig. 1.

After the image interpretation task, a debriefing session with eye movement data began. In the session, eye movement data recorded while seeing images 1–5 (see Table 2) were shown to each participant. By examining the participant's own eye movement data, he/she was asked to explain the reasons why specific areas were gazed at as much as possible. In the end of experiment, a participant provided responses to the questionnaire about his/her expertise and experience, and his/her recognition of effectiveness of eye movement data as an education tool.

2.5 Data Analysis

In the present paper, we focus on elicitation of visual scanning strategy of individuals. To do so, we first examine the verbal protocols obtained from the debriefing session. Then we visualize the eye movement data to vividly represent the coincidence of the strategy elicited.

3 Result

3.1 Visual Scanning Strategies Inferred by Debriefing with Eye Movement Data

Table 3 shows the key statements included in verbal protocols for each participant group. Based on the protocols, we could classify them inductively. For example, the statements included in class 1 seem to show a strategy of postponement of lung field interpretation in order not to overlook critical but small/less-visible lesions. Statements in class 2 seem to be similar with class 1, but they seem to be show another strategy of avoidance of preconception by applying redundant/additional scanning rule. Statements in classes 3 and 4, on the other hand, seem to indicate strategies relating to application of routines in interpretation. Class 3's statements refer to the strategy where specific area that, they think, are important are revisited not to overlook lesions. The strategy can be something like a "critical area revisited" strategy. Class 4's statements seem to be relating to more strict routine strategy, that is a "Complying with one's mental checklist at any moment." From relatively low skilled participants (e.g., resident), we could obtain verbal protocols such as "First I try to find lesions. Just after finding lesions, I try to diagnose them." Such statement included in class 5 seems to indicate a less-sophisticated strategy of single lesion focusing that may be a cause of overlooking. The classifications of strategies inferred from verbal protocols are also shown in Table 3.

Table 3. Verbal protocols obtained.

Class	Statement	Strategy inferred
1	"I know that the lesions, especially lesions found first, attract too much attention, causing medical oversight. So I always try not to see the lesions" "I always examine the lung field at the end of image interpretation. Because the lesions in the lung field seems to be too salient, blinding other lesions" etc.	Postponement of lung field interpretation
2	"After I find some lesion, I try to find another one even though it is very much unlikely to exist" etc.	Avoidance of preconception by applying redundant/additional scanning rule
3	"First I examine the peripheral of lung, because I believe that it is a critical area causing medical oversight" "I try to pay attention to bones" etc.	Critical area revisited
4	"At any moment, I always examine by the following sequence: Quality of image -> apex right lung and pleura -> costo-phrenic angle -> diaphragm -> right mediastinum -> left mediastinum -> apex left lung and pleura -> costo-phrenic angle -> diapharagm -> behind the trachea -> behind the heart -> lung field (up to down) -> ribs, etc.	Complying with one's mental checklist at any moment
5	"First I try to find lesions. Just after finding lesions, I try to diagnose them." etc.	Single lesion focusing

3.2 Visualization of the Corresponding Eye Movement Data

For the purpose of education/training, the understanding of effective strategy for visual scanning while image interpretations are the key success factor. To enhance the understanding in training, we think that the appropriate visualizations of eye movement data, which is directly connected with each effective strategy, are necessary. Figure 2 shows an example watching sequences visualized based on a participant taking strategy of "Complying with one's mental checklist at any moment." In this figure, a single fixation is represented by a circle, and the order of fixations are shown by numbers. In addition, the noises such as very short fixations are eliminated so that the visual scanning pattern can be clearly understood.

3.3 Expectation of Eye Tracking as a Teaching Tool

As shown in Fig. 2, the visualized eye movement data focusing on visual scanning pattern seem to represent a participant's strategy vividly. By combining textual instructions

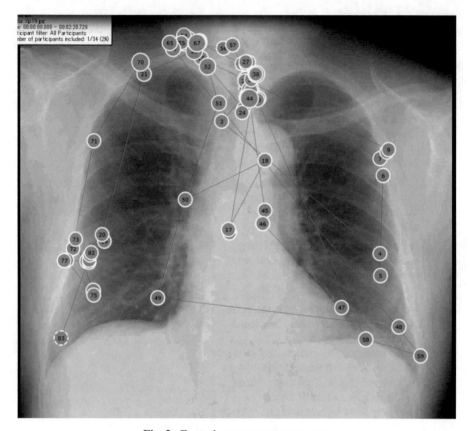

Fig. 2. Example eye movement pattern.

regarding image interpretation strategy with the visualized eye movement, we can expect
to develop very effective education system, especially for residents. In our experiment, all
of the participants showed positive attitudes toward such education system (mean score:
4.4, Do you expect the eye movement data-based education system to be successful? 1:
Definitely no ~5: Definitely yes.)

4 Discussion and Conclusion

This paper shows an idea for the application of eye movement data for the analysis
of expertise/skill in x-ray image interpretation and development effective education
system. We carried out a series of experiments in which experts to novice medical
doctors performed image interpretations and diagnosis for twenty cases. A procedure to
implicit hidden mental strategies and to visualize eye movement data was demonstrated.
In our plan, we will continue analyzing all data obtained in the experiment. We will
characterize eye movement patterns in individual levels, and identify the relations of
the patterns and expertise levels. In addition, we plan to find key factors relating to

overlooking. These analyses will be great helps to understand detailed skills in image interpretations as well as to elicit useful implications for effective training.

Acknowledgments. This research was partly supported by Grant-in-Aid for Scientific Research (C), No. 18K04599m the Japan Society for the Promotion of Science. We would like to acknowledge Prof. Yukihisa Saida and Prof. Keiichi Akahoshi, Tokyo Medical and Dental University, for their great supports for our study.

References

1. van der Gijp, A., Ravesloot, C. J., Jarodzka, H., van der Shaaf, M.F., vandr Schaaf, I.C., van Schaik, J.P.J. and ten Cate, T.J.: How visual search relates to visual diagnostic performance: a narrative systematic review of eye-tracking research in radiology. Adv. Health Sci. Educ. **22**, 765–787 (2017)
2. Jarodzka, H., Balslev, T., Holmqvist, K., Nyström, M., Scheiter, K., Gerjets, P., Eika, B.: Conveying clinical reasoning based on visual observation via eye-movement modelling examples. Instruct. Sci. **40**, 813–827 (2012)
3. Litchfield, D., Ball, L.J., Donovan, T., Manning, D.J., Crawford, T.: Viewing another person's eye movements improves identification of pulmonary nodules in chest x-ray inspection. J. Exp. Psychol. Appl. **16**, 251–262 (2010)
4. Seppänen, M., Gegenfurtner, A.: Seeing through a teacher's eyes improves students' imaging interpretation. Med. Educ. **46**, 1113–1114 (2012)

A Comparison of the Knowledge, Awareness and Practice of Ergonomics Between Lecturers in the Faculty of Engineering and College of Medicine in a Nigerian University

Blessing Chiagozikam Atueyi[1]([✉]), Stephen C. Nwanya[2],
Echezona Nelson Dominic Ekechukwu[3,4,5] [iD], Obiageli Theresa Madu[6],
Emmanuel N. Aguwa[4,7], and Onyemaechi Valentine Ekechukwu[2]

[1] Fifth Year Undergraduate, Department of Medical Rehabilitation, College of Medicine,
University of Nigeria, Nsukka, Nigeria
Blessing.atueyi.200625@unn.edu.ng
[2] Department of Mechanical Engineering, Faculty of Engineering, University of Nigeria,
Nsukka, Nigeria
[3] Department of Medical Rehabilitation, FHST, University of Nigeria, Nsukka, Nigeria
nelson.ekechukwu@unn.edu.ng
[4] Environmental and Occupational Health Unit, Institute of Public Health, College of Medicine,
University of Nigeria, Nsukka, Nigeria
[5] LANCET Physiotherapy Wellness and Research Center, Ibadan, Nigeria
[6] Department of Nursing Sciences, Faculty of Health Sciences and Technology,
College of Medicine, University of Nigeria, Nsukka, Nigeria
[7] Department of Community Medicine, Faculty of Medical Sciences, College of Medicine,
University of Nigeria, Nsukka, Nigeria

Abstract. Lecturers are bearers of knowledge and are expected to dispense them. However, professional exposures influence the degree of Knowledge Awareness and Practice (KAP) of a given phenomenon like ergonomics that is multidisciplinary. The level of the KAP of Ergonomics among lecturers appears unknown. This study assessed and compared the level of KAP of Ergonomics between Lecturers in Engineering Faculty and College of Medicine, University of Nigeria.

This cross-sectional survey sampled the KAP of lecturers in the College of Medicine (CoML) and the Faculty of Engineering (FEngL). Their sociodemographics and KAP of Ergonomics were assessed using a self structured questionnaire. Data obtained were analyzed using frequency, percentage, mean, standard deviation and independent t-test. The level of significance was set at 0.05.

A total of 75 lecturers (33 CoML and 42 FEngL), majority of whom were males (65.3%) and at the level of the rank of Lecturer II or I (48.0%). More FEngL (73.8%) than CoML (69.7%) wrongly reported that ergonomics fits workers to their work, while more CoML (78.8%) than FEngL (71.4%) wrongly reported that document in a computer workstation should be placed flat on the table. Overall, there was no significant difference ($p > 0.05$) in the mean ergonomics knowledge ($58.01 \pm 27.65\%$ vs 61.22 ± 28.80), awareness ($68.18 \pm 30.79\%$ vs $64.88 \pm 29.89\%$) and practice ($46.21 \pm 30.79\%$ vs $45.53 \pm 22.23\%$) of the participants (CoML vs FEngL respectively).

© The Author(s), under exclusive license to Springer Nature Switzerland AG 2021
N. L. Black et al. (Eds.): IEA 2021, LNNS 219, pp. 432–437, 2021.
https://doi.org/10.1007/978-3-030-74602-5_61

COML and FEngL have a fair knowledge/Awareness of Ergonomics but their practical application is poor. There is need for lecturers to advance their knowledge, awareness and practice of Ergonomics through training and retraining.

Keywords: Ergonomics · Lecturers · Awareness · Knowledge · Practice · College of medcine · Faculty of engineering

1 Introduction

Professionals in the fields of engineering and health appear to be indispensible in the practice of ergonomics. While the engineers typically design tools and other devices to suit the human user, their counterparts in health manage the sequelae from a possible miss-match and/or poor application of ergonomics by the end user. It is therefore expected that professionals in the fields of engineering and health should have not only have a sound knowledge and awareness of the science of ergonomics; but also demonstrate good practice of ergonomics both in their work setting and otherwise. Academics are custodians of knowledge and researchers who transmit knowledge to budding professionals. By virtue of the job descriptions of academics in engineering and health science, one should expect them to have a sound knowledge, awareness and practice of ergonomics. When a job is considered as having a high risk, some of the intervention needed is to reduce the risk for the worker who must perform that job. Ergonomics is a discipline that applies information about human behaviour, abilities, limitations and other characteristics to the design of tools, machines, tasks, jobs and environments for productive, safe, comfortable and effective human use [1].

Ergonomics is known to be well established in many countries. However, in Industrially Developing Countries (IDCs) like Nigeria, it is less well known and less practiced. Fortunately, there is a growing awareness of the crucial role that ergonomics can play in these IDCs. Lecturers are bearers of knowledge and are expected to dispense them. However, professional exposures influence the degree of Knowledge Awareness and Practice (KAP) of a given phenomenon like ergonomics that is multidisciplinary. Not only that the level of KAP among academics in Engineering and Health Sciences is unknown, comparison of these factors between these two cohorts is yet to be established. This study assessed and compared the level of KAP of Ergonomics between Lecturers in Engineering Faculty and College of Medicine, University of Nigeria.

2 Method

2.1 Participants

This cross-sectional survey involved 75 participants (49 males and 26 females) who were recruited from the College of Medicine (CoML) and the Faculty of Engineering (FEngL) at the University of Nigeria Enugu. The inclusion criteria were as follows; being registered as a lecturer in University of Nigeria Enugu, between the age ranges of 18 to 60 years, absence of any disorder that would distort the ability to correctly answer the questionnaire such as physical disability, psychiatric and psychological disorder. Thirty-three (33) lecturers from the CoM and forty-two (42) lecturers from the FEng participated in the study. All participants gave a verbal consent and met inclusion criteria.

2.2 Materials

The material used for this study is a self structured but validated questionnaire. The online version of the questionnaire was created with googleforms and was also used for participants that couldn't be reached physically. The questionnaire was divided into two sections; the first section of the questionnaire assessed the participants' socio-demographics which consisted of sex, educational level, department, rank and post qualification experience. The second section assessed the participants Knowledge, Awareness and Practice of Ergonomics; this consisted of 7 close-ended questions on knowledge of ergonomics and 8 close-ended questions each for the awareness and practice of ergonomics.

2.3 Data Analysis

Data obtained were analyzed using frequency, percentage, mean, standard deviation and independent t-test. This was done using statistical package for social sciences (SPSS) version 23. The level of significance was set at 0.05.

3 Results

3.1 Demographic Characteristics of the Participants

A total of 75 lecturers (33 CoML and 42 FEngL) participated in this study and majority of them were males (65.3%), although there were more female participants in the CoM (45.5%) than those in FEng (26.2%). Most of the participants attained post graduate educational level (73.6%) and were at the rank of leturer I/II (51.4%). The Post Qualification Experience (PQE) for most of the participants was less than 11 years (55.9%) but more participants in the CoM (51.6%) had PQE of 11–20 years.

3.2 Summary of the Knowledge of Ergonomics among lecturers in FEng and CoM

Most of the participants reported to have heard of ergonomics before the survey (82.7%), yet very few participants correctly reported that ergonomics fits workers to their work (13.3%). More participants in the FEng than CoM (FEng vs CoM) correctly reported that Ergonomics prevents injuries to workers (76.2% vs 72.7%), improves job satisfaction (78.6% vs 66.7%), does not decreases overall performance (71.4% vs 57.6%), and does not increases mechanization and cost (45.2% vs 27.3%). On the other hand, more participants in the CoM than FEng (CoM vs FEng) correctly reported that Ergonomics does not fit workers to their work (18.2% vs 9.5%) but cuts across all disciplines (81.8% vs 69.0%). Overall, majority of the participants from FEng had a good knowledge of Ergonomics (31.0%), while most of their counterparts in CoM had a poor knowledge of Ergonomics (33.3%). However, there was no significant difference (t = 0.489, p = 0.627) between the mean knowledge scores of participants in FEng (61.22 ± 28.79) and their counterparts in CoM (58.00 ± 27.65).

3.3   Summary of the Awareness of Ergonomics among lecturers in FEng and CoM

Majority of the participants in this study correctly reported that prevention of awkward postures was a way of subverting WRMSDs (82.7%). However more of the participants in CoM than FEng (CoM vs FEng) correctly reported that preventing repetitive movements (48.5% vs 33.3%), avoiding constrained positions (84.8% vs 61.9%), switching between sit and stand work posture (72.7% vs 64.3%) without avoiding work for days (63.6% vs 61.9%) as some methods of preventing WRMSDs. Meanwhile more participants in FEng than CoM (FEng vs CoM) correctly reported that preventing awkward posture (83.3% vs 81.8%), observing work breaks (76.2% vs 69.7%), performing stretches during work (64.3% vs 60.6%) but not necessarily buying expensive furniture (76.2% vs 66.7%),as some ways of preventing WRMSDs. In general, the participants in CoM were more aware of Ergonomics (78.8%) than their colleagues in FEng (73.6%). On the contrary, there was no significant difference ($t = 0.468$, $p = 0.641$) between the mean Ergonomics awareness scores of participants in CoM (68.18 ± 30.79) and their counterparts in FEng (64.88 ± 29.89).

3.4   Summary of the Practice of Ergonomics among lecturers in FEng and CoM

In response to the question on how best to lift a heavy object from the floor, more participants in CoM than FEng (CoM vs FEng) correctly reported that not bending the back over the object while standing (60.6% vs 40.5%), nor moving the object away from the body (39.4% vs 38.1%) nor raising the objects using the back muscles (51.5% vs 38.1%) were the proper techniques for carrying out the task. On the other hand, more participants in FEng (83.3%) than CoM (66.7%) correctly reported that firmly holding onto the object was an important lifting technique. In response to the principles to be observed while working with the computer, more participants in FEng than CoM (FEng vs CoM) correctly reported that screen should not be above eye level (57.1% vs 48.5%), keyboards should not be on the same level with the screen (61.9% vs 48.5%) and documents should not be placed flat on the table (14.3 vs 9.1%). On the other hand, more participants in CoM than FEng (CoM vs FEng) correctly reported that work stations should be positioned perpendicular to the window in an office (51.5% vs 42.9%). In general majority of both the participants in FEng (61.9%) and CoM (70.8%) poorly observed the practice of Ergonomics. Also, there was no significant difference ($t = 0.122$, $p = 0.903$) in the practice of Ergonomics between the participants in FEng (45.53 ± 22.23) and their counterparts in CoM (46.21 ± 25.86).

4   Discussion

Most of the participants reported to have heard of ergonomics before this study; however, only few of the participants correctly reported that ergonomics fits workers to their work. One out of ten lecturers in FEng and one out of five lecturers in CoM knew that ergonomics fits work to the worker. Designing a work to fit the worker inorder to improve their efficiency and optimize safety is considered as the key emphasis of ergonomics [2]. Failure to correctly respond to this question may be a strong indicator of poor knowledge of ergonomics among these cohorts. Correspondingly, this appears to be worse for the participants in FEng although the difference in their general knowledge of ergonomics was not significant. The knowledge of ergonomics is an underlining step that aids its right application. Ignorance of ergonomics in the field of engineering and health poses a great risk for the safety of humans. A study that assessed the knowledge of ergonomics among medical laboratory scientists in Nigeria also reported a poor knowledge of ergonomics among these cohorts [3]. Also in accordance to the findings in this research, a study done in Malaysia assessed the knowledge of ergonomics among civil and structural engineers. It was reported that there was a poor knowledge of ergonomics among these cohorts particularly on the Prevention through Design (PtD) principles which needed to be improved [4]. Lecturers in the field of Engineering and Medicine needs to be thoroughly informed about the ergonomics and its right application as this would help in the equipping of professional practitioners working in these field with the required ergonomic skills needed for practice.

Participants in FEngL and CoML were reported to poorly observe the practice of Ergonomics with no significant difference between the two cohorts. This is similar to the low practice levels reported by Fauziyah & Handayani (2017) [5] and Siddiqui, et al. (2016) [6] among Indonesian industrial workers and Pakistani dental practitioners respectively. A common denominator among these studies is that there were done in low and middle income countries (LMICs). A sound ergonomic practice is an effective way to reduce exposure to the risk factors of WMSDs [7, 8]. The lack of this may be responsible for the increasing WMSD prevalence in this population that has been termed "an impending epidemic" [9]. Physiotherapists, Nurses, Dentists and other healthcare workers are involved in a wide range of physically demanding manual jobs which could pose a great risk of WMSDs [10]. This is due to long hours involving repetitive movements, less time to rest, static and awkward postures and challenges with work environments [11]. When the health workers are affected with WMSDs, this would reduce the workforce and pose a threat to the health of individuals and the nation at large. Safety professionals in engineering apply ergonomics in designing products for human users. Research has proven that sound ergonomic design is one of the most effective ways to reduce exposure to risk factors that are known to causes WMSDs [7, 8].

Finally, it is pertinent that lecturers (especially FEngL and CoML) who are the bearers of knowledge be richly informed about the subject matter 'Ergonomics' in order to impart this knowledge on budding professionals.

5 Conclusion

Lecturers in the College of Medicine and Faculty of Engineering have a fair knowledge/Awareness of Ergonomics but their practical application among these cohorts is poor. There is a great need for an increased knowledge and awareness of ergonomics among lecturers who are the dispensers of knowledge. When lecturers are properly informed about the subject matter Ergonomics, this will positively affect students under their tutelage, hence a great way of reaching out to the society and nation at large.

6 Recommendation

There is need for lecturers to advance their knowledge, awareness and practice of Ergonomics through training and retraining. It is recommended that researchers in the field of ergonomics should carry out relevant studies as well as media publicity on reasons why ergonomics should be part of our daily activities.

References

1. Sanders, M., McCornick, E.: Human Factors in Engineering and Design. McGrraw Hill, New York (1993)
2. Damaj, O., et al.: Implementing ergonomics in construction to improve work performance. In: Proceedings of 24th Conference of the International Group for Lean Construction, Boston, MA, USA, pp. 53–62 (2016)
3. Oladeinde, B., et al.: Awareness and knowledge of ergonomics among medical laboratory scientists in Nigeria. Ann. Med. Health Sci. Res. **5**, 423–427 (2015)
4. Ibrahim, C.K., Belayutham, S.: A knwoledge, attitude and practices (KAP) study on prevention through design: a dynamic insight into civil and structural engineers in Malaysia. Architect. Eng. Des. Manag. **16**, 131–149 (2020)
5. Fauziyah, H., Handayani, T.: Knowledge and practices of ergonomic working positions among Industrial workers. UI Proc. Health Med. **3**, 92–95 (2017)
6. Siddiqui, T., et al.: Assessment of knowledge, practice and work environment related to ergonomics among dental students and dental practioners. Int. J. Contemp. Dent. Med. Rev. (2016)
7. Quellet, S., Vezina, N.: Work training and MSDs prevention: contribution of ergonomics. Int. J. Ind. Ergon. **44**, 24–31 (2014)
8. Middlesworth, M.: MSD Prevention: How to prevent Sprains and Strains in the Workplace (2015)
9. Epstein, S., et al.: Prevalence of work-related musculoskeletal disorders among surgeons and interventionalists: a systematic review and meta-analysis. JAMA Surg. **153** (2018)
10. Waters, R.T.: Introduction to Ergonomics for Healthcare Workers. Rehab. Nurs. **35**, 185–191 (2010)
11. Gadjradj, P., et al.: Ergonomics and related physical symptoms among neurosurgeons. World Neurosurg. **134**, e432–e441 (2020)

Building Spaces for Discussion: Getting the Diversity of Practices Speak

Camille Bachellerie[1]([⊠]), Danie Jon[2,3], Alexis Chambel[2,3,4], and Camille Toulisse[5]

[1] Conservatoire national des arts et metiers, CREAPT, Paris, France
camille.bachellerie@lecnam.net
[2] AECTT-EVS UMR 5600, Université Lumière Lyon 2, Lyon, France
danie.jon@univ-lyon2.fr
[3] Kardham, Marseille, France
[4] Parcours Doctoral National en Santé Travail, Paris, France
[5] Head of the Internal Occupational Health Service of Département de l'Ain, Paris, France
camille.toulisse@ain.fr

Abstract. This article aims at explaining the setting up and the progress of the Junior Practice in Reflection Committee of the SELF's "day of exchange on practices". Here we describe how the day took place in February 2020 in Paris. We are going to explain how the engineering of the discussion is organized and what effects are expected when we are talking about the practice of ergonomics. Beyond this description, our approach is to document about the engineering discussion around the implementation of a reflexivity on the practice among novice ergonomists.

Keywords: Discussion engineering · Reflective practice · Practice diversity · Professional enrichment

1 Introduction

The Junior Practices in reflection Committee (JPR) was born out of a two-fold observation; the existence of problems specific to young practitioners and the lack of space to instruct those. From that basis, it was proposed to the SELF (French Speaking Ergonomics Society) to create a committee dedicated to exchanges on the practice of ergonomics for and by junior practitioners. This committee has a twofold objective of creating an ephemeral framework for exchanges between junior practitioners while at the same time articulating these exchanges with the various instances that make up the profession and manufacture the discipline. Since its creation in 2014 and at a rate of about three days per year, it has brought together nearly 200 participants from all over France but also from various fields of ergonomics practice (occupational health service, consultant, internal, doctoral student, etc.). Finally, these spaces of exchange have crossed borders, with a first office in Quebec from 2014 to 2017 and an office in Peru since 2018. The interest of this symposium is to present what has been developed by the committee in terms of exchanges on practice while opening this presentation to other forms of practice. These axes will take the form of four communications. The first communication will return to the theoretical foundations of the JPR Committee. The second paper will present the story of a young practitioner. Without wanting to be representative, it will serve as an example to show what is discussed in the JPR meeting days. The third communication will present the implementation of the exchange on practice and we will be able to illustrate here the methodology we use and the intermediate objects that it mobilizes. The fourth communication will come back to the specificities of the deployment of the office in Peru and issues that this may raise.

This article represents the third part of a symposium; it is dedicated to the description of the discussion engineering method deployed by the JPRs during the days organised by the Committee. First of all, we will show how the French ergonomics context calls for the creation of different spaces for discussion on practice. Next, we will describe the different forms of discussion and why the JPR Commission has chosen the engineering of discussions on practice. Finally, we will concretely illustrate our point with an example of a day organised by the JPR in February 2020 in Paris.

2   The Challenge of Spaces for Debate in a Context of Diversity of Practices

The observation on the diversity of professional practices in ergonomics has been shared for many years in France (Daniellou 2003; Daniellou 2008; Falzon 2019) and these different forms of practices and areas of specialisation are recognised. The JPR are part of this tradition of taking a close interest in all forms of practices.

The practices conditions of ergonomist are various. Each one acts within its own regulatory and organizational frameworks, which will determine the room for maneuver allocated to them. These diverse practices conditions stem from the fact that ergonomists work in a variety of environments (institutional structures, occupational health service, job retention, engineering firms, research, etc.) but also have different areas of intervention: designing an aeronautical workshop in a factory, organising the progress of a building site, keeping a person with disabilities in employment, preventing musculoskeletal disorders, designing a digital interface, etc. Sometimes, the diversity of these objects calls for the development of specific methods according to the sectors in which ergonomists work. Thus, some of them form associations to talk about a specific object: *"It is therefore normal that there should be profession confrontations limited to the same type of object"* (Daniellou 2008, p. 13).

In this sense, ergonomists are grouped into different associations and the discussion held there can be of several kinds: conditions of practice, statutes, professions or even the objects of intervention. If we take up Yves Clot's expression (1999), these spaces consist of *"making the profession speak"* in order to draw up the rules of the profession among peers. Ergonomists can then talk about their successes and difficulties in establishing these crafts rules. Obviously, the aim of these groups is not to produce "generic lessons" but rather to showcase professional experiences, each time singular, but which may resonance with the experiences of peers.

The diversity of practices constitutes a richness for French ergonomics because it avoids the modelling of a universal form of intervention which should be applied everywhere and to everyone; on the contrary, it makes it possible to build a practice which is adaptable and can respond to the various situations encountered by ergonomists. However, this should not prevent ergonomists from thinking collectively about this practice. As Daniellou reminds us in 2008 in an introduction to the *Journées de Bordeaux pour la Pratique*: *"The fact that everyone manages and that there is no reflexive capitalisation anywhere, the idea that an intervention is different every time and that everything has to be rebuilt is the opposite of the idea of a profession. My position is that we need models which capitalise on what experience is likely to work in a given context and framework of constraints. From experience, i.e. from the decantation of the lived experience of ergonomists who have been at the front in various situations"* (Daniellou 2008, p. 20).

However, the diversity of ergonomists' status, working conditions and areas of intervention may constitute a risk of isolation, particularly when it is a first experience. In this case, the first resource that appears to novice ergonomists is reference to academic models and methods. However, this resource remains limited, as these models and methods, which are rich in generic lessons, are constantly evolving according to the situation faced with. In this respect, opening spaces for reflexivity makes it possible to discuss these practices without falling into the pitfall of standardization. These spaces of reflexivity make it possible, through discussion, to develop what Yves Clot (1999) calls *"gender"* and *"style"*: even if the overall model of an intervention remains the same, it must be constantly adapted to the situation, so everyone will develop a style according to *"gender"*.

According to Daniellou (2008), the profession of ergonomist is the result of a construction of crafts rules that are themselves fueled by the practice: "The trade is therefore a collective work around "how we do in such and such a situation", around our activity in terms of difficulties in managing certain forms of situations" (p. 14–15). Thus, if we take up Daniellou's expression, these places of meeting and discussion can constitute "work of the craft".

According to Falzon (2019), the ergonomist's activity is arbitration: "How are decisions of opportunity made? What arbitration do I have to make at any given time?" (p. 120). This arbitration skill is developed through experience, which enables us to make relevant compromises in the situation: *"Arbitration skill is one of the skills to be developed. There is what we wish to do, what we can really do in a situation and which we can judge ourselves acceptable, what colleagues may find acceptable, and then also what seems unacceptable. Arbitration decisions are decisions of the profession, of profession collectives."* (Falzon 2019, p. 121).

By making the diversity of practices speak, one is led to review one's own practice, to examine it differently in the light of what others are doing and thus to widen the scope of possibilities. However, the diversity of practices cannot be decreed; it is a process that is the result of the development of professional practices (Van Belleghem 2008). The challenge here is therefore not only recognising this diversity but also to collectively share these practices in order to contribute to their development: *"We are relying on Yves Clot's proposal, which consist of recreating, in a way, diversity of doing things, so that can find their way around and share them"* (Van Belleghem 2008, p. 113). It means recognising these practices as professional know-how, highlighting them, without considering them as deviations from what would be a 'norm'. This is what Yves Clot calls *"the sense of doing well"* (p. 117, 2019), where the development of work *"well done"*, in the sense of the organisation and the worker, lies in the existence of controversies over what makes these criteria. Here, as Christophe Dejours and Isabelle Gernet (2012) point out, these "*spaces of deliberation*" (p. 84) allow for debate and negotiation of rules, the creation of new knowledge and cooperation. The challenge here is therefore to integrate diversity in order to contribute to the process of diversification and development of practices.

3 Building a Space for Discussion

As we have just seen, the practice of ergonomics in France therefore exists in various forms and in various contexts of intervention. In order to discuss the diversity of ergonomics practice and to enable young practitioners to express the issues and questions that are specific to them (Cromer et al. 2016), the JPR commission proposes a "day of exchange on practice" up to three times a year. These days provide a framework for bringing together novice ergonomists to discuss and debate a theme, different for each day.

The purpose of these moments is not only discussion or expression. The challenge is to arrive at a reflexivity on practice (Schön 1983), both individual and collective. To do this, it is first necessary to be able to offer the conditions "*for the emergence and effective realisation of the exchange of practices*" (Cromer et al. 2016). Talking about one's practice also requires taking the "risk" of sharing one's experience, one's satisfaction or dissatisfaction with the intervention with others. Talking about one's practice would therefore also require talking about oneself and revealing oneself. Thus, the space for exchange on practice is not only a place to gather, but also a framework that exists thanks to the engineering of discussion (Ibid.), which guarantees a safe and constructive environment. This participates in the establishment of operating rules "*in order to create a climate of listening, trust and benevolence, allowing everyone to express themselves freely*" (Ibid.).

This discussion engineering is worked on in three stages: before, during and after the day (Ibid), and considers several structuring elements: the framework, the facilitation, the participants, and the interaction between these three elements.

The first stage is the preparation of the framework of the discussion space and the structuring of the roles (animator, participant, reciter). The commission is composed up to 5 members, and for each day two of them take the role of animator and a third person takes care of the logistics.

Throughout the day, the animators guide the participants towards reflexive work. They begin by setting a safe framework stating certain rules such as benevolence towards other participants. They then make sure that the time allocated to the different stages is respected and encourage everyone to speak.

Very often, the two remaining members participate in the day as participants in the sub-groups to regulate the exchanges and to help the other participants in the reflexivity. Indeed, this preparation time also allows the constitution of sub-groups from the list of participants. We pay particular attention to the fact that these sub-groups are made up of different areas of activity (consultants, in-home practitioners, etc.), always with the aim of promoting discussion between different forms of practices. This distribution also makes it easier for everyone to gain height. Each sub-group is structured around a reciter, whose storytelling is also worked on upstream in cooperation. The challenge is to structure the narrative into reflexive professional storytelling. Without this, they cannot play their role as boundary objects and allow a reflexive exchange on practice. This point is more detailed in the first two papers of this symposium.

Then, the theme to be discussed during the day is chosen either based on a survey addressed to young practitioners at the beginning of the year or according to the demands and needs emerging after previous days. The theme is divided into sub-questions to provide a reference point for the discussions during the day. These themes consider the diversity of ergonomic practices and are chosen so that they can be discussed for all forms of practices and intervention situations.

The second stage is the day's session. It is the time and space of exchange on practice and reflexive work that constitutes the main issue of the exchange day. After a brief presentation of the committee and the rules of operation, the day is divided into four steps:

- 1st step: Storytelling and questioning the participants' understanding.
- 2nd step: Sharing with the other participants about situations which the storytelling echoes in their own practice, followed by work on the theme addressed. Intermediate objects can be used to give substance to the discussion and as a support for the debates. Animators move between each sub-group to guide the discussion.
- 3rd step: Sharing of each person's work and taking height, assisted by the animators.
- 4th step: assessment of the day going around the table, where all participants are asked what they thought of the day (feedback, satisfaction, dissatisfaction) but above all what they retained (a key concept, an idea, etc.).

Finally, the third stage, the after-day stage, also contributes to the construction of the discussion space. It is a moment of assessment which, based on the course of the day, the feelings of the animators and participants members of the committee, the after-day discussions between the members but also on the feedback from the participants, allows the days to evolve in a perspective of improvement. By preserving and solidifying what works and by modifying the elements that may have caused problems or hindered the reflexive work, this is how each of the days evolves; not only the engineering of the discussion but also the themes and the emergence of new ones for the coming days. A report on the day is then communicated by the committee, which allows each participant to have a trace of the exchanges and allows the committee to have material for events and articles that are shared within the community.

4   Description of the JPR Discussion Engineering Methodology Based on an Example

This section aims to illustrate how a day for exchange on practice unfolds. As an example, we describe here how it took place in February 2020 in Paris.

The theme chosen was "multidisciplinary in intervention". We then divided this theme in three sub-questions to help the participants to explore it. This enables us to clarify the content of this exchange in giving an outline:

- Creating the conditions for the intervention: how does the ergonomist take position according to his/her possibilities to act and those of the other actors in the intervention?
- Can the ergonomist do everything? How do the boundaries of our practice move according to our intervention and the actors involved in?
- What methodologies and tools should be used to support this multi-professional collaboration?

To encourage discussion on these themes, we ask the participants to create a visual representation of their intervention along the day. We called these representations: "intervention maps" to represent the phenomena linked to the intervention in a spatial configuration, that would give meaning to the way in which the ergonomist acts. Participants are divided into three sub-groups, rather than a full group, to encourage reflection and discussion. We then divide the day into four main stages: First, each sub-group, based on a practitioner's experience, the other participants draw up an "intervention map" from the reciter's storytelling. Second, from the intervention maps that each participant individually developed, we ask the participants to create an intervention map together (Fig. 1). Third, still in sub-group, we asked the participants to create a new map (Fig. 2). This represents the ideal of the spaces, movements and actions that the ergonomist could have made during the intervention. Finally, we meet all together for a plenary session. This debriefing takes place in three times: one rapporteur per group presents the last two maps to all the participants (Fig. 3).

Fig. 1. Each group works on a "intervention map" based on the narrative.

This is followed by a collective discussion about similarities and differences between all these maps. This allows us to take an overview of the particularities of each intervention that have been presented. Then, the animators take few minutes to underline the strong ideas that come out of the debate.

Finally, at the end of the day, we lead a round-table discussion to gather the opinions of each participant on the day's progress and content. Here is an example of verbatim: *"Exchanges are free, allow us to realise that we are not alone and that we are facing the same difficulties. Discovering the interventions of others is really enriching. The format is great, thank you very much!"*.

Fig. 2. Examples of maps developed collectively in sub-groups

Fig. 3. Whole group presentation of each group's intervention maps

5 Conclusion

Throughout the day, we ask the participants to write down their expectations regarding the proposed theme. This collecting step is crucial because it allows us to appreciate what the participants retain from the day and the elements that they will use for their own future interventions. Thus, different levels of feedback are identified: a very broad level of expectation that concerns ergonomics in general and its practice with great appeal for discussion among peers. We also reach a shared consensus on the need to consider the multidisciplinary in the interventions.

Thanks to this feedback, we can observe viewpoints changes on different aspects of practice. However, we do not know to what extent these changes in points of view give rise to real changes in practice. To really measure whether these effects are taking place, the Commission would need to adopt a diachronic approach to participants' practice, between a "before" and an "after" participation in a one-day event. While such knowledge would be very interesting for the development of the discussion engineering set up by the Commission, but an approach of this type would require a non-negligible amount of time and investment and would take us away from the Committee's aims: to create a reflexive space for young practitioners and to diffuse this approach throughout our scientific and professional community.

Today, because of the health crisis, we are keen to develop our methodology so that it can be adapted to virtual meetings. If these remotely events cannot replace face-to-face discussions, it invites us to question ourselves on a new form of discussion engineering that we are going to set up during the 2020–2021's winter in order to keep the reflexivity of young practices alive.

Finally, more than ever in this context, we are committed to continuing to promote the diversity of practices and their encounters, beyond our geographical borders. This is why a new office of the Commission has been set up in Peru; the challenge here is to take up elements that have already been developed by the Commission in order to adapt them to the local context of the practice of Peruvian ergonomics. This will be the content of the fourth and final paper of this symposium.

References

Daniellou, F.: Dix ans de pratiques de l'ergonomie: Avons-nous beaucoup changé? Actes des Journées de Bordeaux pour la Pratique, Bordeaux, Mars **2003**, 13–23 (2003)

Daniellou, F.: Diversité des domaines d'intervention, nouvelles pratiques de l'ergonomie, qu'avons-nous encore en commun? Actes des Journées de Bordeaux pour la Pratique, Bordeaux, Mars **2008**, 11–22 (2008)

Clot, Y.: La fonction psychologique du travail. Presses universitaires de France, Paris (1999)

Clot, Y.: Les conflits de la responsabilité. In: Bourdu, E., Lallement, M., Veltz, P., Weil, T. (eds.) Le travail en mouvement. Presses des Mines, pp. 112–121 (2019)

Cromer, D., Elwert, L., Hubert, K., Francou, F., Couillaud, S.: De l'échange sur la pratique à son enrichissement. In: 51ème Congrès de la SELF, Marseille, France (2016)

Dejours, C., Gernet, I.: Travail, subjectivité et confiance. Nouvelles Revue de Psychosociologie **13**, 75–91 (2012)

Falzon, P.: Fil rouge JDB 219. Evolution des contextes et des pratiques d'intervention : vers différents métiers d'ergonomes?. Actes des Journées de Bordeaux pour la Pratique, Mars 2019, Bordeaux, pp. 111–125 (2019)

Schön, D.A.: The Reflective Practitioner: How Professionals Think in Action. Ashgate, New York (1983)

Van Belleghem, L.: Diversité des domaines d'intervention, nouvelles pratiques de l'ergonomie: Qu'avons-nous encore en commun ? Fil rouge. Actes des Journées de Bordeaux pour la Pratique, Mars **2008**, 109–125 (2008)

What is a Good Scenario in Vocational Training Design? Considerations Based on a Literature Review

Vincent Boccara[1]([⊠]) [iD] and Maria Sol Perez Toralla[2]

[1] CNRS, Laboratoire Interdisciplinaire des Sciences du Numérique, Université Paris Saclay, Orsay, France
vincent.boccara@universite-paris-saclay.fr
[2] Atitlan, Orsay, France
mariasol.perez@atitlan.fr

Abstract. The notion of scenario runs through many more or less formalised currents in the domain of vocational training design. However, the notion of scenario and scriptwriting (i.e., scenario design) does not seem to have stabilised well in ergonomics and in the field of vocational training. With this in mind, we conducted a systematic review of the scientific literature in the field of vocational training in order to better understand how authors define these notions of scenario and scriptwriting and how they report on them in their publications. Using the systematic literature review methodology PRISMA, we identified a corpus of 91 scientific articles over the period 2000–2019 from an initial corpus of 1051 articles. We present here the first results of this work by highlighting the main aspects of the definitions attributed to the concept of scenario. We then focus on 17 characteristics which govern what the authors consider to be a "good scenario". Finally, we focus on the most quoted characteristics of a good scenario: realism.

Keywords: Scenario · Scriptwriting · Vocational training · Ergonomics

1 Introduction

Vocational training is a major challenge for employability throughout a person's career and for the performance of companies in a context of rapidly changing markets and means of production. Learning opportunities in training courses are strongly impacted by the design, facilitation, and evaluation of training course. However, the design and evaluation phases are often underestimated and under-equipped compared to the facilitation phase, when they are particularly important in the design of vocational learning systems.

From our experience, we have been involved in the last years in several research project mobilizing the topic of the scenario of human activity in complex systems [1–3]. In these projects, one of the issues at stake was to elaborate and script scenarios to train the trainees to complex work situations. These training systems could used physical mock-ups as well as digital simulation, 3D, virtual reality, augmented reality, or mixed reality technologies, video game or gaming techniques to increase the realism of training situations in order to

© The Author(s), under exclusive license to Springer Nature Switzerland AG 2021
N. L. Black et al. (Eds.): IEA 2021, LNNS 219, pp. 446–453, 2021.
https://doi.org/10.1007/978-3-030-74602-5_63

promote learning. In all of these systems, one of the major challenges in the project was the scenario design for the learning situations, i.e., the temporal organization of events and the different possible learning paths for learners.

To our knowledge, there are several "currents" in design training (e.g. scenario-based training [4–6], but few formalized methods and tools available to design a rich and complex scenario that is consistent with the real work activities for which we want to train. Moreover, in the scientific literature in ergonomics or in the field of vocational training, the notion of scenario seems to be poorly defined and polysemic. At least four ways of defining a scenario can be identified. In the field of training, the scenario is designed by instructors to meet pedagogical objectives [7]. It represents a procedure, a guide to be followed to complete a task, or a situation that learners are trained to perform [4–6]. The scenario can refer to a simple, usual, normal situation as well as an emergency, complex, rare situation. In the field of ergonomic design, the scenario is a tool that enables the representation of (existing or future) uses or situations, to support the design of an artefact, a work situation, or even a work organisation [8–10]. Scenario design is generally based on the contribution of designers and users with different profiles. In the field of decision-making, a scenario refers to a dynamic interactive model, composed of variables that must be manipulated to identify the different possible solutions to respond to a complex situation [11]. In the field of safety, the scenario refers rather to a model, built from real and past data, which represents an accident, an incident or typical situation in which these occur [12, 13].

Although there are many ways of building scenarios the scripting of vocational training environment is often based on the extraction of information contained in prescriptive documents supplemented by the so-called "expert opinion" method. The resulting scenarios are then structured as follows: to a procedure X to be taught, an X' scenario (which reproduces the procedure as faithfully as possible) is matched by an X" script. We can add to these scripts "game modes": uncovered level versus expert level, with or without assistance, in limited or no time, etc. These game modes are not, however, variations of the implementation of the procedure with regard to the characteristics of the situation. The staging remains structured by a prescribed procedure to be followed; deviations from this procedure are traced. From this perspective, the script architecture is structured based on a library of prescribed procedures rather than situations.

Within this context, we decided to conducted a review of the scientific literature on both "scenario" and "scenario design" in the field of vocation training to explore these notions from a triple point of view: conceptual, methodological and pragmatic.

2 Method

To investigate this question, we conducted a systematic review of the scientific literature according to the PRISMA method (Preferred Reporting Items for Systematic reviews and Meta-Analyses) [14]. The method is structured in four parts: 1) delimitation of the perimeter, which consists in defining the databases of scientific literature to be consulted, the key words related to the research questions and the reference period; 2) identification, which consists in consulting the databases selected on the basis of the keywords chosen to constitute the first corpus of articles, 3) selection, which aims at restricting the first corpus to a list of sources to be read in details based on inclusion and exclusion criteria and, 4) eligibility, which corresponds to the study of the selected sources to obtain the list of sources that respond directly to our research questions.

In the present systematic review, we consulted the Sciences Direct database and two French reviews (Activités and Travail Humain) between 2000–2019 with the keywords: "training AND scenario AND simulation". The first corpus was a set of 1051 articles. The second phase of selection was based on the reading of the titles and summaries of the articles to identify the extent to which they were part of the corpus of articles to be read in detail. These phases lead us to a corpus of 97 scientific articles. In the third phase we read in detail these 97 articles. We retained 91 articles and rejected six based on our inclusion and exclusion criteria.

For each of the 91 articles, we conducted then a systematic analyses according to 11 variables: 1) the year of publication of the article, 2) the country of origin of the authors, 3) authors' discipline, 4) the type of publication, 5) the definition of a scenario, 6) the process of designing a scenario, 7) the composition and structure of a scenario, 8) the animation of a scenario, 9) the technological environment of a scenario game, 10) the scope of a scenario, 11) the theoretical framework mobilized by the authors concerning scriptwriting.

We focus here on two of these variables: the 5th variable that defines a scenario, and the 6th variable that presents the quality criteria of a scenario in vocational training from the point of view of the authors.

3   Results

3.1   How to Define a Scenario in Vocational Training?

This first part of the results aims to give an account of how scenarios are defined and presented in the scientific literature on vocational training and simulation.

To do so, we have relied on two complementary perspectives of description. The first refers to the identification in each article of the definitions explicitly given by the authors to the notion of scenario. The second refers to the selection and then the analysis of all the passages in the articles which shows the way in which the authors use the notion of scenario without explicitly defining it.

With regard to explicit definitions, only five articles out of 91 (i.e., 4.5%) contain an explicit definition of the notion of scenario of the type "A scenario is…", "we define a scenario as…". Thus, more than 95% of the articles mobilize the notion of scenario without explicitly defining it. 17 articles (including the five preceding ones) present extracts that can provide information on the definition of the notion of scenario (i.e., 19% of the 91 articles in the corpus).

Based on the 17 articles that give a definition or elements for defining a scenario, we identify tree perspectives for defining a scenario in the field of vocational training: 1) pedagogical and/or evaluative, 2) anticipation and decision-making, 3) reproduction of the characteristics of an event in the field of security.

From a pedagogical and/or evaluative perspective, the training scenario is designed by researchers or trade experts, who may also be instructors, to meet pedagogical objectives

[7, 15, 17, 18]. It provides a learning context [16, 18] and aims to implement learning situations [7, 15]. It represents a procedure [19], a guide to be followed to carry out a task [20] or to use a tool [21]. They can also represent a situation in which learners are trained and in which they must decide and/or act [15, 16]. Training scenarios are based on training objectives [7], training standards [20], or occupational standards [19]. As a result, scenarios can define expected actions [19], pre-defined options [18]. However, the implementation of such scenarios is most often said to be flexible, i.e. the learner's action has an effect on how the scenario unfolds. This is translated in different ways. For example, the reference solution is not the only possible solution in the development of the scenario [15], the pre-defined structure of the scenario is used as a guide and not as a strict procedure to be followed [19], or the content of the scenario is adapted dynamically during its implementation according to what the learner achieves [17].

From an anticipation and decision-making perspective, the scenario can take the form of a dynamic interactive model. This model is made up of variables that need to be manipulated to identify different possible solutions [11, 21] The design of a probabilistic scenario means defining a set of events, the probability of occurrence or non-occurrence of which is varied to explore the different alternatives to respond to a complex and urgent situation [11]. This type of scenario is designed by a group of experts with different visions.

In the field of security, the scenario rather refers to a standard model, built from real and past data. The design of an accident scenario consists, at the minimum, in identifying the common characteristics of a set of accidents [13] and may also be based on the identification of discriminating characteristics to define a typology [12]. This type of scenario constitutes a descriptive model. For example, it represents a type of occupational accident, which can be used in the field of occupational safety and health [12]. It describes the nature of a risk, the recommended actions, and the possible consequences if these actions are not implemented [22]. It can also provide a prototypical road accident situation, used as a prevention tool [13].

These tree approaches are intended to provide a reading grid for understanding, more generally, how the authors define the notion of scenario. However, they do not make it possible to cover all the meanings mobilized by the authors in their articles in relation to the ways of describing the design or use of a scenario.

These three perspectives for defining a scenario are based on a limited number of articles (17 articles out of 91) since most authors do not define this notion. A complementary approach to understanding how scenarios are defined in the literature is to look at the elements that compose them or the characteristics that are sought by the designers of these scenarios during their building.

3.2   17 Categories of Criterion for Evaluate a Good Scenario

Among the 91 articles of the corpus, 32 articles (35%) did not mention any quality criteria for simulation scenarios. From the 59 other articles of the corpus, we identified 139 criteria of quality. Each article mentions an average of 2.5 criteria (Med = 1; SD = 3.1; min = 0: max = 12). More specifically, 34/59 articles mention between 1 and 3 criteria, 17/59 articles mention between 4 and 7 criteria and 8/59 articles mention between 8 and 12 criteria.

The 139 quality criteria are organized according to three sets of criteria relating to the scenario (13 categories, 95 criteria), the facilitation (3 categories, 26 criteria) and the design (2 categories, 18 criteria). For each set of criteria and each category, the number of criteria reflects their diversity.

The criteria relating to the scenario are both the most varied (95/139 criteria, i.e. 68%) and the most mentioned (168/226 occurrences, i.e. 74%) in the corpus. They are divided into thirteen categories as follows:

1. 31 criteria relate to the *"realism"* (67 occurrences), i.e. the extent to which a scenario reproduces reality in a faithful manner,
2. 23 criteria relate to *"what the scenario allows to include or represent"* (28 occurrences),
3. 11 criteria refer to the *"coherence"* (21 occurrences), i.e. the extent to which the scenario reproduces reality in a faithful manner,
4. 9 criteria relate to the *"competencies"* that the scenario allows to be practiced or developed (13 occurrences),
5. 7 criteria relate to the *"usefulness"* of the scenario with respect to the intended use objectives (13 occurrences),
6. 5 criteria relate to the *"adaptation"* of the scenario to be adapted to the participants (10 occurrences),
7. 3 criteria relate to the *"representative"* of the scenario (three occurrences), i.e. the scenario is representative of the participants, i.e. the scenario is not representative of the participants' needs, but rather of their needs, i.e. to the fact that it is typical,
8. one criterion refers to its *"precision"* (six occurrences), i.e. the richness of the details it presents,
9. a criterion refers to the *"complexity"* (three occurrences), i.e. the diversity of the data it contains and its level of difficulty,
10. a criterion refers to the *"economic character"* (one occurrence),
11. a criterion relates to *"completeness"* (one occurrence),
12. a criterion relates to the *"significance"* (one occurrence), i.e. the extent to which it is meaningful,
13. a criterion relates to the *"validity"* (one occurrence), i.e. the fact that it allows measurement of what it is supposed to measure.

Among these thirteen categories, six categories refer not only to a single criterion, and this criterion is made up of a single level of the taxonomy (that of the category), i.e. significance, representativeness, precision, economic character, complexity, and completeness of the scenario. For the other seven categories, the criteria are made up of one to four levels of taxonomy. Within the same category, there may therefore be a criterion consisting of a single level of taxonomy (e.g. "realism"), others resulting from the combination of two levels (e.g. "environmental realism"), three levels (e.g. "realism of the physical environment"), or four (e.g. "realism of the physical environment in situ").

There are 26 design criteria which represent 32 occurrences. They are divided into two categories: 1) 18 criteria (22 occurrences) refer to the design approach, i.e. the principles and strategies that guide and direct the design of a scenario; 2) eight criteria (ten occurrences) refer to the design methods, i.e. the techniques and tools used to design a scenario. The design criteria result from the combination of two to four levels of taxonomy.

The criteria relating to animation are both the least varied (18/139 criteria, i.e. 13%) and the least mentioned (26/226 occurrences, i.e. 12%) in the literature. These criteria are divided into three categories as follows: 1) ten criteria (fifteen occurrences) refer to actors, i.e. the people involved in the implementation of the scenario as facilitator or player; 2) seven criteria (seven occurrences) refer to guidance, i.e. the means used to support the participant's activity during a scenario; 3) one criterion (four occurrences) refers to pedagogy, i.e. the teaching methods used to animate a scenario. The criteria relating to animation result from the combination of one to four levels of the taxonomy.

4   Discussion: The Importance of Realistic Scenarios

In discussion, we would like to come back to the criterion most frequently cited by the authors: the "scenario realism" (67 occurrences). Realism can be defined by the authors as *"a scenario that mimics reality"* [23]. The realism of the scenario can be linked to a choice of facilitation when the number of actors aims to be consistent with the number of people needed to carry out the simulated situation [24], to the consideration of the specificities of its field of application [16], to the context that it allows to reproduce [25], or to the realism of the story that it aims to bring into play [22].

In addition, the dimensions contributing to the realism of the scenario are also related to the forms of learning sought. For example, active learning pedagogy requires the construction of realistic scenarios that allow learners to intellectually, emotionally and physically confront unexpected situations in order to prepare for future vocational situations [26].

Furthermore, the dimension of realism is also found in the criteria relating to the design and facilitation of scenarios. For some authors [7] the design of the story by an instructor allows for the construction of a realistic scenario. From a facilitation perspective, authors [27] explain the need for extras to understand the roles to promote the realism of the script. Thus, considering all the quality criteria of a script, its conception and animation, this quality criterion is the most sought-after by authors.

Finally, these results are consistent with the findings we have made in the research projects we have been involved in. In these projects a major issue was also the realism of the script. However, the reference taken to instruct this realism remains vague: is it the task, the work situations, the psychological processes, the physical environment, the social environment, etc.? A striking point of these first results is also the very large number of articles that use the term scenario without giving a definition of this term. It seems therefore an interesting perspective to better stabilize a definition and to adopt a more structured method to guide the processes of scenario-based training design.

References

1. Boccara, V., Delgoulet, C.: Works analysis in training design. How ergonomics helps to orientate upstream design of virtual training environments. Activités **12**(2), 137–158 (2015). https://www.activites.org/v12n2/V12n2.pdf

2. Couix, C., Boccara, V., Fucks, I.: Training design for a proposed job of operating the remote monitoring system for risk prevention (RMSRP) in French nuclear power plants. In: Proceedings 19th Triennial Congress of the IEA, Melbourne, 9–14 August 2015
3. Boccara, V., Delmas, R., Darses, F.: L'ergo-scénarisation : un enjeu majeur des environnements virtuels de formation. Revue du Service de santé des armées **45**(5), 603–611 (2017)
4. Stacy, W., Freeman, J.: Training objective packages: enhancing the effectiveness of experiential training. Theor. Issues Ergon. Sci. **17**(2), 149–168 (2016)
5. Cannon-Bowers, J.A., Burns, J.J., Salas, E., Pruitt, J.S.: Advanced technology in scenario-based training. In: Cannon-Bowers, J.A., Salas, E. (eds.) Making Decisions Under Stress: Implications for Individual and Team Training, pp. 365–374. American Psychological Association (1998). https://doi.org/10.1037/10278-014
6. DoE: Training Program Handbook: A Systematic Approach to Training. DoE, Washington (1994)
7. Peeters, M., van den Bosch, K., Meyer, J.J.C., Neerincx, M.A.: The design and effect of automated directions during scenario-based training. Comput. Educ. **70**, 173–183 (2014)
8. Daniellou, F.: L'ergonomie dans la conduite de projets de conception de systèmes de travail. Ergonomie, 359–373 (2004)
9. Vincent, C.J., Blandford, A.: Usability standards meet scenario-based design: challenges and opportunities. J. Biomed. Inform. **53**, 243–250 (2015)
10. Nelson, J., Buisine, S., Aoussat, A., Gazo, C.: Generating prospective scenarios of use in innovation projects. Le travail humain **77**(1), 21–38 (2014)
11. Turoff, M., Bañuls, V.A., Plotnick, L., Hiltz, S.R., de la Huerga, M.R.: A collaborative dynamic scenario model for the interaction of critical infrastructures. Futures **84**, 23–42 (2016)
12. Duguay, P., Cloutier, E., Levy, M., Massicotte, P.: Profil statistique des affections vertébrales avec indemnités dans l'industrie de la construction au Québec. Le travail humain **64**(4), 321–342 (2001)
13. Distefano, N., Leonardi, S.: A list of accident scenarios for three legs skewed intersections. IATSS Res. **42**(3), 97–104 (2018)
14. Moher, D., Liberati, A., Tetzlaff, J., Altman, D.G.: Prisma group: preferred reporting items for systematic reviews and meta-analyses: the PRISMA statement. PLoS Med. **6**(7), e1000097 (2009)
15. Liao, S.H., Ho, Y.P.: A knowledge-based architecture for implementing collaborative problem-solving methods in military e-training. Expert Syst. Appl. **35**(3), 976–990 (2008)
16. Borders, J., Polander, N., Klein, G., Wright, C.: ShadowBox^{TM}: flexible training to impart the expert mindset. Procedia Manuf. **3**, 1574–1579 (2015)
17. Wray, R.E., Folsom-Kovarik, J.T., Woods, A., Jones, R.M.: Motivating narrative representation for training cross-cultural interaction. Procedia Manuf. **3**, 4121–4128 (2015)
18. Chan, P.G., Schaheen, L.W., Chan, E.G., Cook, C.C., Luketich, J.D., D'Cunha, J.: Technology-enhanced simulation improves trainee readiness transitioning to cardiothoracic training. J. Surg. Educ. **75**(5), 1395–1402 (2018)
19. Saint-Dizier de Almeida, V.: Comment améliorer la compréhension de l'entretien d'annonce de diagnostics médicaux sérieux. Activités **10**(10–2) (2013)
20. Macris, A.M.: Enhancing enterprise resource planning users' understanding through ontology-based training. Int. J. Knowl. Learn. **5**(5–6), 404–422 (2009)
21. Bañuls, V.A., Turoff, M., Hiltz, S.R.: Collaborative scenario modeling in emergency management through cross-impact. Technol. Forecast. Soc. Chang. **80**(9), 1756–1774 (2013)
22. Lesch, M.F.: A comparison of two training methods for improving warning symbol comprehension. Appl. Ergon. **39**(2), 135–143 (2008)

23. Haugland, V.L., Reime, M.H.: Scenario-based simulation training as a method to increase nursing students' competence in demanding situations in dementia care. A mixed method study. Nurse Educ. Pract. **33**, 164–171 (2018)
24. McKittrick, J.T., Kinney, S., Lima, S., Allen, M.: The first 3 minutes: optimising a short realistic paediatric team resuscitation training session. Nurse Educ. Pract. **28**, 115–120 (2018)
25. Jones, B., Potter, C.: Applying best practice in simulation: critical care response team training. Clin. Simul. Nurs. **13**(9), 442–445 (2017)
26. Lindgren, C.: Do you know your outcome of realistic scenario training? Procedia-Soc. Behav. Sci. **46**, 863–869 (2012)
27. Bierer, J., Memu, E., Leeper, W.R., Fortin, D., Fréchette, E., Inculet, R., Malthaner, R.: Development of an in situ thoracic surgery crisis simulation focused on nontechnical skill training. Ann. Thorac. Surg. **106**(1), 287–292 (2018)

Creation of the Junior Practices in Reflection Committee of the French Speaking Ergonomics Society: Historical Genesis and Theoretical Foundation of the Exchange on Practice

Alexis Chambel[1,2(✉)], Danie Jon[1,2,3], Camille Bachellerie[4], and Camille Toulisse[5]

[1] AECTT-EVS UMR 5600, Université Lumière Lyon 2, Lyon, France
danie.jon@univ-lyon2.fr
[2] Parcours Doctoral National en Santé Travail, Paris, France
[3] Kardham, Paris, France
[4] Conservatoire national des arts et metiers, CREAPT, Paris, France
camille.bachellerie@lecnam.net
[5] Head of the Internal Occupational Health Service of Département de l'Ain, Paris, France
camille.toulisse@ain.fr

Abstract. This article is part of a wider symposium which aims to present what has been developed by the Junior Practices in Reflection Committee of the French Speaking Ergonomics Society (SELF) in terms of exchange on practice. It is the first communication of a symposium and focuses more specifically on the genesis of the Committee. We will first develop the needs that led to its emergence, then the conceptual anchoring, particularly the use of the storytelling that is mobilised. Finally, the various actions that have been implemented since its creation will be developed.

Keywords: Reflective practice · Ergonomics of the activity · Discussion engineering · Junior practice

1 Introduction

This article is the first in a series of four constituting a symposium. It presents the Junior Practices in Reflection Committee (JPR) of the French Speaking Ergonomics Society (SELF) and the reflective spaces, the "days for exchange on the practice", that has been set up since its creation. This symposium first communication looks more specifically at the genesis of the Commission.

Before going into more detail on the genesis, it seems important to come back to the object of these exchanges: the practice. Commonly used term, it carries by essence a certain polysemy. First, it can be mobilised from the perspective of opposition to knowledge, in reference to the traditional concept of *logos* and *praxis*. It is then often reduced to the simple application of knowledge. The expression can also be used to characterise the repetition of the action from the perspective of mastery of a skill. While

© The Author(s), under exclusive license to Springer Nature Switzerland AG 2021
N. L. Black et al. (Eds.): IEA 2021, LNNS 219, pp. 454–461, 2021.
https://doi.org/10.1007/978-3-030-74602-5_64

these two approaches give us some clues to what the practice is, it is important to better delineate its contours.

The practice of a profession can be defined as *"a situated professional activity, oriented by purposes, goals and standards of an occupational group. It results in the application of knowledge, processes and skills in action of a person in a professional situation."* [2]. Contrary to the usual representation of simple application, it implies a reflection of its own, which is performed before, during and after the action [17]. Moreover, this definition has two important characteristics:

- First, it offers the possibility to think about the articulation between the individual and the collective, which refers to the concept of "community of practice" [13, 23] and can be synthetically defined as a group of individuals united around three structuring dimensions: mutual commitment, sense of joint enterprise and shared repertoire of resources. We will return more particularly to this notion in the course of the text.
- Then, it makes practice part of its relationship to action. It is a setting in motion of knowledge and methods in articulation with the complexity of situations, with the contingencies of reality that the ergonomist has to deal with. It can thus be differentiated by its situated character from other similar concepts such as technique, which refers rather to a know-how, to a precise method that may be disconnected from the situation.

Therefore, talking about one's practice refers to a personal way of doing things, marked by both singularity and repetition, in accordance with a form of collective action, and shared within a community structured around common norms and goals.

It is fundamentally this need for a space for discussion on practice that led to the first members of the Committee in 2014: Sarah Couillaud, Damien Cromer, Laurène Elwert, Fabien Francou et Karen Hubert and the SELF then chaired by François Hubault, to set up a specific Committee on this subject. However, the object of our Committee is more restricted, it concerns the Junior Practices, understood as up to 6 years of practice of the profession of ergonomist. This positioning is based on a two-fold observation: the existence of problems specific to novice ergonomists and the lack of space to instruct them. We will develop these different points in a first part, before getting to the heart of our methodology in a second part: the mobilisation of the reflexive professional storytelling, finally concluding on the declinations and the contribution of this engineering to the various forms of discussion we are developing.

2 Genesis of the Committee

Although the Committee is not intended to represent novice practitioners, it is nevertheless possible for us, based on our own experience and the literature, to put forward hypotheses. These relate first to the specific difficulties encountered by novice practitioners who participated in the creation of the Committee. They also relate to what prevents their instruction in existing spaces within the community.

2.1 Reflection on the Difficulties Encountered by Novice Practitioners

The profession of ergonomist has been the subject of numerous studies in the field of ergonomics of the activity, particularly from a formative perspective [3, 10, 21]. It can be characterised from three perspectives [12]. The first views ergonomics as a diagnostic activity, the second as a design activity and the third as a collaborative problem-solving activity, thus placing it in the service domain. These three perspectives provide food for thought, both in terms of the relationship with experience and the difficulties encountered by the ergonomist [4].

The first two points of view lead us to consider the repertoire of situations available to the ergonomist. In the first case, it is a question of carrying out a process of categorisation of the situation encountered regarding the known categories. In the second, the situation reference frame feeds "an iterative, non-linear resolution process based on the experience of past solutions" [4]. One of the difficulties for ergonomists is the "limit of their reference system" [21]. Indeed, the practice of ergonomics is characterised by an extreme diversity of classes of situations that may be encountered by the practitioner. In their encounter with reality, the practitionner draws on the library of situations they has experienced in order to enter into dialogue with the singular case they finds themself confronted with. The existence in their experience of similar, or at least approximate, cases then enables them to provide a more satisfactory response, both from the point of view of their own values and objectives, but also regarding the relevance of their action.

Although this difficulty is not exclusive to young practitioners, it is nevertheless more marked during the beginning of the professional career, when this library of situations can only marginally be enriched by the practice of the ergonomist themself. This leads some authors [3, 10, 12] to underline the importance of developing this library of situations during the training of ergonomists. The sharing of experience then becomes one of the methods envisaged.

The works on training, more specifically in the field of professional didactics, also shed some light on the difficulties that young practitioners may encounter. By focusing on conceptualisation for action, these works have made it possible to identify "pragmatic concepts" [16], concepts which can be defined as *"schematic and operative representations, elaborated by and for action, which are the product of a historical and collective process, and which are transmitted essentially through experience and companionship"* [16]. We will simply retain here the anchoring of these concepts with action and practice. Rather, it is their relationship with other concepts and fields of knowledge [22] that is important for our purposes.

The first link that deserves to be developed is the relationship to the theoretical concepts acquired during the formation. Based on work on the operation of nuclear power plants, Pastré [15] shows that the knowledge acquired during training cannot be used directly but is subject to "pragmatisation". This process can be defined in a synthetic way as the creation of an operational model that makes it possible to move from an understanding of the operation to the actual operation. In the context of ergonomics, a parallel can be drawn with the intervention. It is one thing to know the theoretical sequence, its different stages and its composition. It is another to combine this knowledge with the complexity of reality to carry out an intervention.

The second link concerns the relationship to daily concept and is specific to service activities. In this type of activity, a process of professionalisation of daily concepts takes place [14]. For our action in everyday life and throughout life we mobilise a whole set of concepts organising our activity which differs from the pragmatic concept because it is not associated with a professional activity. For example [14], "Doing the housework" for a home helper will require adjustments because it is not the same to do the housework for one or another person's home. This will require some respect for the place where the person lives and adaptations to the person's quality criteria. In the same case, another daily concept of "helping the other" may also require adjustments, sometimes helping means letting go to develop autonomy. As these concepts are already mobilised in action in everyday life, it is not pragmatisation that is at stake *"since it is already mobilised in everyday situations"* but a process of professionalisation [14]. If the author takes the concept of help as an example, it seems more relevant for our purpose to evoke the concept of observation, at the heart of the practice of our profession. Observing the other as an ergonomist is not just looking at the progress of an action or an object as would be the case on a daily basis, but it is mobilising know-how and methods to understand the activity. It means doing it in a way that is always singular according to the particularities of the situation and the operators with whom they are conducted. Observation will thus require adjustments in its practice, adjustments made according to the singularity of the situation, based on a set of clues taken all along from the work environment, the worker or oneself… It is this work of putting together a set of elements to create an operative and professional model of observation which will be necessary for the beginner ergonomist.

We therefore hypothesize a double process of pragmatization and professionalization of the concepts which takes place in the early stages of the professional practice of the ergonomist. This process is difficult, it is not without certain clashes and questions, which require space for discussion. However, while the existence of problems specific to young practitioners, or at least more marked ones, explains the need for exchange, it does not necessarily explain the difficulty of instructing them in existing spaces and with the community as a whole.

2.2 The Lack of Reflective Space for Practice

The ergonomics community offers many opportunities for exchange. They take extremely diverse forms, ranging from the most formal and wide-ranging events repre-sented by the various congresses to the simplest meetings, such as the convivial moments offered locally by the various ergonomics associations. However, each of these spaces, although they participate in the life and construction of our community, are the result of specific objectives that do not really fall within the scope of the debate on profes-sional practice. The closest events, the congresses, seem to us rather to pursue a logic of construction of a professional identity. They enable the development of the profes-sional "gender" [7], which can be succinctly defined as collective practice, the rules of the profession, but they do not aim to debate individual "styles" [7] understood as an individual declination of the "gender", which differs for each ergonomist.

Moreover, talking about ones practice is not easy. It is necessary to talk about oneself and sometimes about one's difficulties and failures. It may be a matter of assuming certain wanderings, other times of sharing a concession that is difficult to make to one's

458   A. Chambel et al.

professional ethics to allow the intervention to be carried out. This requires a "protective framework" [1] to be able to do so. If we take the example of the Congress, the public character can thus limit this possibility of free speech. In any case, this difficulty in speaking out is even more marked for the young practitioner, whose confidence in they own practice still benefits only marginally from the benefits of experience.

But it is perhaps another object which complicates the speaking out of young practitioners and which relates to social relationships. While studies on the impact of speaking in groups focus mainly on other social relationships [5, 6], we hypothesize that certain factors such as experience, prestige and, more generally, status within a community can have an impact on speaking. Far be it from us to attempt to erase other, much more documented social relationships, but rather to underline the idea that, despite all the goodwill we can show, we remain part of a multitude of social relationships that no amount of discussion engineering can perfectly erase. In practice, it may thus be difficult for the young practitioner to speak to more experienced people. It will be even more complex for they to move from a listening and learning posture to enter an egalitarian position and debate they practice.

Here again, this is only an attempt on our part to explain the Committee's challenge by the need felt by some young practitioners to gather and talk about their difficulties, a need that is now reflected in the objectives that the Committee has set itself: the creation of spaces for exchanges on practice, the development of the professional network and encouraging the setting in motion of these exchanges within the profession.

3 The Heart of Our Engineering: The Reflexive Professional Storytelling

To meet this need of young practitioners, the Committee organises exchange days on practice. However, for a discussion on practice to take place, it is not enough to simply decree it. A real engineering must be thought out for the exchange to be operational [11, 20]. The core of the one we have chosen is based on the mobilisation of professional storytelling from the young practitioners themselves and is inspired by the work of Beaujouan [3]. However, unlike this work, this is not a "professional storytelling with didactic aims" [3], but a reflexive professional storytelling.

An example of a professional storytelling will be provided in the second paper[1] of this symposium, so we will not detail the characteristics of the storytelling itself here. However, it seems important to situate it in relation to certain uses of storytelling that have inspired it or are relatively close to it.

The fundamental difference between professional storytelling with a didactic aim [3] and reflexive professional storytelling lies in its purpose. In the original works, the professional storytelling is mobilised to enable the transmission of teaching within the framework of the training of ergonomists. This difference is not anecdotal since it will induce adjustments in the construction of the professional storytelling, the objective not

---

[1] Eisenbeis A., Bachellerie C. (2021), Contributions and construction of the professional storytelling within the framework of a Junior Practices in Reflection day: the example of a design project in a munici-pality, IEA 21st Triennial Congress.

being centered on the message and its intelligibility, but on its capacity to become a tool for convening and mobilising the individual experience of each participant. It must therefore have sufficient elements and depth to allow for debate and not be a teaching tool, but rather a questioning one.

Storytelling is also a classic tool within a community of practice [13]. It enables the transmission of experience within the community and the collective construction of a common history. Here too, although the creation of links is the object of the stories we mobilise, it differs from this conventional use by their inclusion in the temporality of the event that the day represents. They are not intended to circulate outside these spaces. However, *"the shared practice within a CoP [Community of Practice] acts as a cement between the members or as a source of coherence that collectively allows them to search for meaning in the way they consider and apply their profession"* [9] and it is this linking function that is sought in the mobilisation of the storytelling during the JPR days of exchange on practices.

Thus, it is more of a "boundary object" [18, 19] within a community of practice, *"these objects are often the provisional result of the process of reification of practice by the members"* [9]. This process of reification, the ability to make practice tangible and debatable, is the central purpose of the reflexive professional storytelling. Qualifying the reflexive professional storytelling as a boundary object highlights all its other characteristics, such as the interpretative flexibility that will open the debate between practitioners. It is thus both concrete and abstract, specific and general, conventional and customisable [19]. Concrete as it deals with a real experience. Abstract as this experience is reconstructed, narrated. Specific, because each intervention is a specific case, with elements related to the practice of ergonomics of the activity. General, because of its capacity to allow the expression of the different forms of activity ergonomics such as in-house practice, consultancy, in an occupational health service or as a researcher, but also all the different professional types of participants. Conventional as it is always an intervention, with certain specific codes. Customizable, because at any time it can be completed and enriched by the participant.

It finally allows the production of knowledge by the participants. This knowledge is first of all of a conceptual and collective nature. It is however, also and above all an individual and reflexive nature for each practitioner.

4 Conclusion: Storytelling, A Tool with Multiple Variations

Since the creation of the Commission, the foundations of this engineering have been developed in several formats. The first takes the form of a full day, around a specific theme. This will be more detailed in symposium's third article[2]. To date, 13 events have been held on this model, which remains the core of the commission's activities.

On the SELF 54th congress in 2019, a new format was tested in a shorter time frame [8]. It was open to all practitioners regardless of their experience. Taking the form of 3 workshops, they showed the interest of this type of approach for the whole community. However, they also confirmed the need to maintain time for exchange between novice

---

[2] Bachellerie C. et al. (2021), Building spaces for discussion: getting the diversity of practices speak, in: IEA 21st Triennial Congress.

practitioners to allow free expression. In particular by the observation of the expert posture from which it was difficult to emerge. Therefore, to this day, we favor the development of the interface with the community and the organisation of mixed events in parallel and in addition to the events aimed for novice practitioners.

In order to create a link during the confinement period from March to May 2020 in France, another format has been tested. Throughout this period, weekly and distance meetings were offered to young practitioners. They enabled them to discuss topics related to the impact of the health crisis on the current and future practice of ergonomists. These sessions were rich in exchanges and gave rise to a summary article. On the form, they were an opportunity to start a reflection on a new distanced engineering which construction continues today. Without being able to replace the face-to-face, it is a necessary adaptation in response to the crisis we are going through.

This engineering has also given rise to international developments, which will be the subject of the fourth paper of this symposium[3]. Participation in this congress is also part of this dynamic of dialogue with the international community.

As a result of these diverse experiences, the SELF's JPR Committee has evolved both in the actions it undertakes within the community and in the forms of discussion on its practice. The experience acquired over the years also shows the effectiveness of the methodological protocol that has been developed and the conviction of the interest of these discussion forums for novice ergonomists.

References

1. Albert, V.: 5. Vers une démarche d'intervision. Supervisions éco-systémiques en travail social, Relation, pp. 81–94. ERES, Toulouse (2007)
2. Altet, M.: Une démarche de recherche sur la pratique enseignante: L'analyse plurielle. Revue française de pédagogie 138(1), 85–93 (2002)
3. Beaujouan, J.: Contributions des récits professionnels à l'apprentissage d'un métier: Le cas d'une formation d'ergonomes. (Thesis). Bordeaux 2 (21 novembre 2011)
4. Beaujouan, J., Daniellou, F.: Les récits professionnels dans une formation d'ergonomes. Le travail humain 75(4), 353–376 (2012)
5. Blanchard-Laville, C. (Éd.): Variations sur une leçon de mathématiques: Analyse d'une séquence, "l'écriture des grands nombres. L'Harmattan, Paris (1997)
6. Chevet, M.: L'impact du genre dans la relation entre enseignant-e-s et apprenant-e-s. Ela. Etudes de linguistique appliquée 142(2), 163–174 (2006)
7. Clot, Y.: La fonction psychologique du travail. Presses universitaires de France, Paris (1999)
8. Cromer, D., Cléret, M., Marié, J., Toulisse, C., Chambel, A., Bachellerie, C.: Quand les expériences se rencontrent: Une opportunité de développement des pratiques de chacun. 55ème Congrès de la SELF, Comment contribuer à un autre monde? Tours, France (2019)
9. Daele, A.: Les communautés de pratique. Encyclopédie de la formation, 721–730. PUF Paris (2009)
10. Daniellou, F.: Entre expérimentation réglée et expérience vécue. Les dimensions subjectives de l'activité de l'ergonome en intervention. Activités, 03(3–1). ARPACT - Association Recherches et Pratiques sur les Activités (2006)

---

[3] Mestanza M., et al. (2021), The exchange on practice: an issue for the development of novice ergonomists in Peru in a context where practices of ergonomic are heterogeneous, in: IEA 21st Triennial Congress.

11. Detchessahar, M.: Quand discuter, c'est produire... Pour une théorie de l'espace de discussion en situation de gestion. Revue française de gestion, (132), 32–43 (2001)
12. Falzon, P.: 1. Nature, objectifs et connaissances de l'ergonomie. Éléments d'une analyse cognitive de la pratique. Ergonomie, Hors collection, pp. 15–35. Presses Universitaires de France, Paris cedex 14 (2004)
13. Lave, J., Wenger, E.: Situated Learning: Legitimate Peripheral Participation, p. 138. Cambridge University Press, New York (1991)
14. Mayen, P.: Quelques repères pour analyser les situations dans lesquelles le travail consiste à agir pour et avec un autre. Recherches en éducation **4**, 51–64 (2007)
15. Pastré, P.: La conceptualisation dans l'action : Bilan et nouvelles perspectives. Éducation permanente (n° 139), 13–35 (1999)
16. Samurçay, R., Pastré, P.: La conceptualisation des situations de travail dans la formation des compétences. Education permanente (123), 13–32. Université de Paris-Dauphine (1995)
17. Schön, D.A.: The Reflective Practitioner: How Professionals Think in Action. Ashgate, New York (1983)
18. Star, S.L.: Ceci n'est pas un objet-frontière! Revue d'anthropologie des connaissances **4**(1), 18–35 (2010)
19. Star, S.L., Griesemer, J.R.: Institutional ecology, 'translations' and boundary objects: amateurs and professionals in Berkeley's museum of vertebrate zoology, 1907–39. Soc. Stud. Sci. **19**(3), 387–420 (1989)
20. Van Belleghem, L., Forcioli Conti, E.: Une ingénierie de la discussion? Chiche! Actes du 50ème Congrès de la SELF. Présenté à Articulation performance et santé dans l'évolution des systèmes de production, Paris (2015)
21. Viau-Guay, A.: Analyse de l'activité déployée par un ergonome lors de difficultés profession-nelles: Contribution à la formation initiale (2009)
22. Vidal-Gomel, C., Rogalski, J.: La conceptualisation et la place des concepts pragmatiques dans l'activité professionnelle et le développement des compétences. Activités, 04(4–1). ARPACT - Association Recherches et Pratiques sur les ACTivités (2007)
23. Wenger, E.: Communities of Practice: Learning, Meaning, and Identity, p. xv, 318. Cambridge University Press, New York (1998)

Identification of Sensitive Driving Situations to Guide the Design of a Learning Tool for Automated Vehicle Drivers

Hugo Cusanno[1,2]([✉]), Christine Vidal-Gomel[1], and Sophie Le Bellu[2,3]

[1] Université de Nantes, CREN E2661, Nantes, France
`Hugo.cusanno@univ-nantes.fr`
[2] Renault SAS, Boulogne-Billancourt, France
[3] Université de Bordeaux, ENSC, IMS Cognitique UMR5218, Bordeaux, France

Abstract. This paper presents a research process aiming at studying the activity of drivers in automated vehicles (AV). To do this, we carried out *in situ* observations and conducted interviews with two different populations: professional and novice drivers in automated driving (AD). The results obtained by triangulation highlight a series of "sensitive" situations specific to automated driving. The clinical analysis of these situations shows changes in the relations and mediations involved. Some of them have common characteristics, making it possible to classify the sensitive situations identified. These changes require a potential adaptation of "traditional" driving schemes, necessary for the appropriation of the AV by the drivers. These results allow us to provide recommendations for improving AV prototypes, and to consider the design of a learning tool to support the appropriation of these systems. This device should, at a minimum, make it possible to familiarize vehicle drivers with sensitive driving situations, in order to initiate the transformation of their schemes upstream, and to cognitively relieve them in real driving situations.

Keywords: Automated driving · Sensitive driving situations · Instrumental genesis · Learning tool design

1 Introduction

Technological innovation progress in the automotive industry is leading manufacturers to offer more and more features in vehicles. It also brings new driving modes intended to either help, assist and even partially or completely replace the driver. These new driving modes have been categorized by the SAE into five levels (Society of Automotive Engineers 2018). In this paper we will only focus on SAE Levels 3 and 4. These levels offer a driving mode in which the role change between the driver and the system disrupts the driving activity from manual to highly automated, and vice versa (Kyriakidis et al. 2019). This change is not trivial and requires knowing it better in order to guide and support future automated vehicles (AV) drivers. Therefore, we set up a research process that allows us to engage a reflection on how to guide appropriation (instrumental genesis in the sense of Rabardel 1995; Verillon and Rabardel 1995), first of the AV itself, but also

N. L. Black et al. (Eds.): IEA 2021, LNNS 219, pp. 462–470, 2021.
https://doi.org/10.1007/978-3-030-74602-5_65

of the learning tools we contribute to develop. We consider automated driving, just like "traditional" driving, to be an instrumented collective activity (Mundutéguy and Darses 2007; Vidal-Gomel et coll. 2014). It is from this angle, and with a situational approach, that we deployed a process to analyze professional (people working for the company whose job is to drive vehicles and prototypes under various conditions in order to test the maximum functionalities and limitations) and novice AV drivers' activity (Cusanno et al. 2019, 2020). We first conducted a study with professional drivers and then completed and compared it with a second study aimed at analyzing the activity of novice AV drivers. We seek to understand the transformations produced in the drivers' activity and possible difficulties during the instrumental genesis (op. cit.). This, in order to guide the design of future AVs and the design of learning tools to support their appropriation by drivers new to these systems.

2 Methodology

2.1 Two Populations Studied; Two Methodologies Deployed

A Collection of Professional AV Drivers' Experience and Knowledge. The first study allowed to follow nine professional AV drivers experts (in the sense of Lefèbvre 2001), in a four-step research process: (1) exploratory semi-structured interviews, (2) instrumented observations on open roads in AV prototype, (3) individual auto-confrontation interviews, and (4) a collective allo-confrontation interview (Mollo and Falzon 2004). Details in Cusanno, Vidal-Gomel et Le Bellu (2020).

A Study to Understand AV Novice Drivers' Difficulties. The second study is based on an experiment carried out as part of a European project aims to carry out experiments with automated levels 3 and 4 SAE vehicles. It takes place on various experimental sites or open roads in Europe, in order to assess the impact of automated vehicle deployment, on its acceptability, mobility, traffic, road safety, etc. We study more specifically the driving activity of twenty AV novice drivers. We follow their progress during three consecutive driving sessions of around 1 h 30 each (t0, t0 + 1 month, t0 + 4 months) with an AV prototype on the highway. Two persons are systematically present in the vehicle. A safety driver (who followed specific training created by a driving school trainer to handle the dual command), seated in the right front passenger seat, is responsible for ensuring the safety of the experiments by taking back control of the vehicle in potentially risky driving situations. And a supervisor, seated in the right rear seat, oversees by checking that the system is operating correctly. An ergonomist is also present in the vehicle during driving sessions 1 and 3. He oversees the participants' pre-driving briefing, including a short indoor training session (30 min) and a test on track (45 min) to get started with the prototype. During the drive, participants are asked to verbalize their feelings aloud; the ergonomist is responsible for taking notes and verbal reminders. He then conducts auto-confrontation interviews with each participant, based on an interview guide created upstream.

2.2 Equipment Used for Open Road Experiments

AV Prototype. For both studies we used the same prototype which is an AV level 3–4 SAE draft. In addition to "traditional" manual driving, it offers an automated driving mode available on highway with at least two lanes. When AD is available, the driver must meet certain restrictive conditions inherent in the prototype to activate it. Once AD is activated, the vehicle manages all aspects of driving and the driver can theoretically have other occupations. The driver can take back control whenever he wants. The vehicle can also ask the driver to take over driving, in 60 s, if it arrives on a section of highway that is no longer suitable for AD. To achieve this, the driver has the choice between pressing the accelerator or brake pedal, or moving the steering wheel, or pressing a button on the steering wheel.

Instrumented Data Collection. In both experiments, the vehicle was equipped with audio-video data collection systems. We used two cameras, one facing the driving scene, close to the driver's point of view, and the other facing the driver himself. We recorded the driver's verbalizations while driving with a dictaphone and took notes. Audio-video recordings were also made during in-room interview sessions.

2.3 Data Processing

Our goal is to identify characteristics of driving situations that are potentially difficult, risky, or requiring increased attention for AV novice drivers. We call them "sensitive situations". The qualitative data from the two studies were treated in the same way. All interviews audio recordings were transcribed, and the videos were analyzed chronologically, situation after situation. We then proceeded to thematic analyzes of the interviews, which we put in front of the corresponding video sequences and simultaneous verbalizations. The most recurring situations were analyzed in more detail from a clinical point of view (Clot and Leplat 2005) using the CIAS (Collective Instrumented Activity Situation) model of Rabardel (1995; Verillon and Rabardel 1995). This model makes it possible to identify the relations and mediations at stake in a situation between the subject (S; the driver), the instrument (I; the AV), the object of the activity (O; the driving), and other people (P; other drivers, passengers, etc.). Thus, we can approach the scheme transformations potentially required for a more effective management of these situations, from the point of view of professional and novice AV driver. Thanks to the triangulation (Apostolidis 2003; Olsen 2004) of data from the two studies, we sought to characterize what could be the instrumental genesis of future AV drivers.

3 Results

3.1 A List of 32 «Sensitive» Driving Situations Specific to AD

The study of AV professional drivers identified 27 sensitive situations. This list was confirmed and completed thanks to our second study in which we collected 25 sensitive situations, including 20 similar to the first study. This brings us to a total of 32 sensitive situations. The clinical analysis of each of these situations allowed us to categorize them from the point of view of system operation and the experience of the participants:

- Cat. 1: Sensitive situations related to AD activation (N = 6). E.g. If the driver activates AD while being too close to the preceding vehicle, the system will brake to recover the safety distance, creating surprise and discomfort for the driver.
- Cat. 2: Sensitive situations related to nominal AD operation (N = 7). E.g. When the AV passes by an insertion lane, it does not anticipate the insertion of other vehicles as a human driver would.
- Cat. 3: Sensitive situations related to nominal AD operation but critical from the driver's point of view (N = 6). E.g. When the AV passes a large truck, it does not shift in its lane like a human driver might do to keep a lateral safety distance.
- Cat. 4: Sensitive situations related to AD limits known by the system, leading to a quick take over request, only in AD Level 3 SAE (N = 5). E.g. If the system detects a work area on the road, it will then ask the driver to take over the driving, giving him 10 s to act.
- Cat. 5: Sensitive situations related to AC limits not recognized by the system and critical from the driver's point of view (N = 3). These situations require voluntary action by the driver, without assistance from the system; The driver must know how to recognize and anticipate these situations to take over the driving. E.g. If an emergency vehicle wants to pass, the AV is not able to locate it precisely and let it pass, so the driver must make the decision to act quickly.
- Cat. 6: Sensitive situations related to the deactivation of AD (take over the driving) (N = 5). E.g. If the driver deactivates in a curve, he must keep the correct angle with the steering wheel to avoid swerving in the lane.

3.2 Three Classes of Sensitive Situations: Mobilized Relations and Mediations

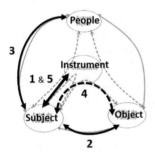

Fig. 1. CIAS model: situation of deactivation in a curve (cat. 6)

Analysis of sensitive situations based on the CIAS model (op. cit.) allows us to identify common characteristics between some of our situation categories. We classify them this way: (A) activation and deactivation situations (cat. 1, 4 and 6), (B) driving situations managed by AD (cat. 2 and 3), and (C) the ambiguous situations of AD (cat. 5). In this section we use the graphical representation of the CIAS model emphasizing the relations (solid lines) and mediations (dotted lines) between entities. As a reminder: the subject (S; the driver), the instrument (I; the AV), the object of the activity (O; the driving), and other people (P; other drivers, passengers, etc.). We present below (cf. Fig. 1) an example of a class (A) CIAS model of a situation of deactivation in a curve (cat. 6):

To deactivate AD and take over the drive (subject's goal), the subject must: (a) analyze and understand the messages coming from his vehicle (dashboard interface, sounds, etc.) indicating that he must take control (1: **S-I relation**); (b) understand the driving activity (speed, lane, angle of turn, etc.) of his vehicle (2: **S-O relation**); (c) become aware of the state of surrounding traffic and other vehicles behaviors (3: **S-P relation**); and (d) associate the possible actions according to the situational context, and be able to anticipate and decide on the action to deactivate (4: **S-I-O mediation**). Once AD is deactivated, the driver can check the intended result by looking the same interfaces (5: **S-I relation**).

In this class of situations, the main differences with "traditional" driving are understanding the new AV interfaces (1: **S-I relation**), and knowledge of activation and deactivation procedures depending on the context (4: **S-I-O mediation**).

For class (B), the main differences with "traditional" driving lie in the understanding of the AV driving behavior depending on the situations (**I-O relation**), and in the driver's ability to potentially inhibit some of his "traditional" driving automatisms in these situations (**S-I-S reflective mediation**). Class (C) combines both the differences with "traditional" driving identified in class (A), and those identified in class (B). However, **S-I-S mediation** is not present since the AV does not indicate anything specific to the driver. This is due to the contrast between the AV behavior (**I-O relation**) and the context perceived by the subject (**S-O and S-P relations**).

3.3 Two Different Populations, Two Ways to Apprehend AD

Our observations show that the management of the AV driving activity differs from one population to another. Professional drivers are more conscientious because they play the role of driver, safety driver and supervisor of the second study at the same time. They are therefore extremely focused on driving tasks, on traffic monitoring, but also and above all on monitoring the AV behavior. Also, traces of their professional activity remain visible, especially when they report that they usually take over the driving at the last moment in order to let the AV try to manage the situations and record as much data as possible that will be used to improve the prototype. Some of them told us they felt exhausted after just two hours of driving due to cognitive load this activity represents:

«After two hours we are exhausted. You are not driving but it's even worse, you have to expect the worst at any time, so you have your hands an inch from the wheel, your eyes are on the road really everywhere at the same time, and you can take over the drive at any time». Study 1, subject 1.

Conversely, more than 60% of novice drivers delegate this responsibility to the safety driver, and are more trustful because he can manage problematic situations:

«We have a human safety driver; we tend to trust him. [...] This is a bias: we trust him, so we are not in supervision mode». Study 2, subject 8.

Professional drivers are aware of and express changes in their management of certain situations, reflecting an adaptation of "traditional" driving schemes. This allowed us to gather advices and recommendations to better appropriate the AV (Cusanno et al. 2020):

«The thing that I did unconsciously because I am used to doing it, is to take enough distance from the van in front of us before activating, otherwise you start your regulation by braking and it is not very pleasant». Study 1, subject 2.

This "Results" section aims at highlighting the differences with "traditional" driving through AD experienced situations. The results represent the current state of the art on the developments of AV prototype tested, so they will probably evolve. Indeed, the classification of situations that we propose constitutes an entry for: (1) taking them into account by the designers to improve systems, and (2) their integration into learning tools for future AV drivers in order to facilitate appropriation of these new systems. Our research mainly focuses on this second point.

4   Discussion

4.1   Traces (Among Professionals) and Clues (Among Novices) of a Potential Instrumental Genesis of the AV

These results show that the introduction of an AD mode leads to a modification of the relations and mediations at stake in driving situations that already exist in "traditional" driving. The driver will have to adapt by learning to manage them differently (classes B and C). In addition, completely new driving situations, including their own relations and mediations, are emerging. The driver will have to learn to manage them (class A). The observation of drivers' adaptations in these new situations can translate potential schemes transformations. Thus, when a driver favors the use of the accelerator pedal each time he deactivates and says during auto-confrontation interview: *«Often it is the accelerator because I used... there is also the habit that I have with the cruise control.»* (study 2, subject 4); we can think that he assimilated this scheme of use from the cruise control for the deactivation of AD. On the other hand, regarding the activation of AD, we observe failures at the start of the first driving session in more than 60% of novice drivers. However they manage to adapt before the end of this session: *«The first time, indeed, I didn't even succeed on the first try [...] It was not so easy for me at first to know when it was the right time or not. At the end I was a little more comfortable»* (study 2, subject 10). In this specific case, we believe that error plays a fundamental role in learning (Dehaene 2018) and allows these drivers to accommodate some of their action schemes in order to achieve their goal (in this case, the goal is to activate AD). Finally, we observe gestures and verbalizations that may suggest an active inhibition (Pascual-Leone 1987; Houdé 2000) of certain automatisms (or schemes) of "traditional" driving. For example, the inhibition of the reflex to press on the brake pedal when there is a cut-in, or the inhibition of the action on the steering wheel to shift into the lane when overtaking a truck (Cusanno et al. 2020). These scheme transformations (or their absence in certain subjects) are observable in both populations studied. We hypothesize that they are the markers of the subjects' instrumentation processes (Rabardel 1995).

We also observe changes in the nature of certain mediations, moving from pragmatic (preparing an action on driving) to epistemic (knowledge of driving management by the AV), reflecting the attribution of new functions to artefacts. This allocation of new functions concerns the use of the AV interfaces, no longer to manage class B situations (driving situations managed by AD) but to control their smooth running and the AV actions. Other mediations keep the same nature but are given new functions, such as the use of controls (steering wheel and pedals) to deactivate AD. We believe that these modifications, observed in both populations, are markers of an AV instrumentalization process (Rabardel 1995).

Thus, we were able to recompose, on one hand a subject (driver) instrumentation process, and on the other hand an artefact (AV) instrumentalization process which are, according to Rabardel, the instrumental genesis constituents.

Finally, the object of professional drivers' activity differs from novice drivers. Their in-depth knowledge of the capabilities and limitations of AD, acquired through their empirical experience, enabled them to develop a representation of the system that provides an appropriate trust in AV (Lee and See 2004). They can recognize sensitive situations and anticipate the AV behavior. This ability allows them to establish a reliable and quick diagnosis, and take appropriate decisions in dynamic situations (according to the model of Hoc and Amalberti 1994; Hoc and Amalberti 2007). Raising the awareness of future AV drivers to these situations via an appropriate educational content could be a lead to follow to help them (Le Bellu, in prep.). This educational content could be supplemented with advices and recommendations issued by professional AV drivers. Their "professional" point of view (Goodwin 1994) allows them to analyze their own activity and be aware of their schemes' adaptations, by externalizing this meta-knowledge, which could be the subject of advices.

4.2 Limits

The methodological limitations of the first study with professional drivers are discussed in detail in Cusanno, Vidal-Gomel and Le Bellu (2020). Regarding the second study, note two main limitations: 1) the vehicle used is an unfinished AV prototype (for example, failure during activation can be partly explained by a complex activation procedure inherent in the prototype), 2) the safe presence of the safety driver in the vehicle during the driving session (more than half of the participants report having explored the use of the AV more than if they had been alone).

5 Conclusion

The results of these two studies allow us to attempt to reconstruct the instrumental genesis of a driver during the appropriation of an AV, thanks to the analysis of the new relations and mediations at stake in sensitive driving situations specific to AD. The first study allowed us to approach different integration levels of the new schemes developed by professional drivers and to collect advices and recommendations for getting started with the AV. The results of the second study are consistent with those of the first study concerning the sensitive situations identified and the potential schemes transformations associated with these situations. They also make it possible to consider the importance of trust for the appropriation of the AV by drivers new to this technology. Session 3 results analysis will confirm and complete these results after three sessions in AV. Note that these two studies report the current state of the art in SAE level 3–4 AV prototype design, and the results presented in this paper will be taken into account to improve future AD systems.

Moreover, we can now think about the design of a learning tool for AV appropriation by considering these results which guide the choice of educational content to be integrated. This content should be scalable to adapt to changes in future AD systems. For example, it would be interesting to try to facilitate the drivers' schemes transformations by presenting the sensitive AD situations upstream. Mayen and Gagneur (2017) talk about pedagogy of situations. This could potentially relieve the driver cognitively in real driving situations, in particular by preparing the inhibition of certain existing schemes (Houdé 2000). More broadly, the idea of orchestrating a system of instruments, integrating devices offered beyond onboard artefacts, for learning (Trouche 2003) could make it possible to play on the redundancy and complementarity of shared knowledge. The advices and recommendations gathered in the first study could be included alongside more general information about AV and AD. Thus, the onboard learning tool that we have to design should be thought as part of the way in which the orchestration is designed.

References

Apostolidis, T.: Représentations sociales et triangulation : enjeux théoricométhodologiques. Méthodes d'étude des représentations sociales, 13–35 (2003)

Clot, Y., Leplat, J.: La méthode clinique en ergonomie et en psychologie du travail. Le travail humain **68**(4), 289–316 (2005)

Cusanno, H., Vidal-Gomel, C. Le Bellu, S.: Comment guider les genèses instrumentales pour la prise en main du véhicule autonome? In: Actes du 5ème Colloque International de Didactiques Professionnelle, Former & développer l'intelligence professionnelle, Montréal, 23, 24 et 25 oct 2019, pp. 145–158 (2019)

Cusanno, H., Vidal-Gomel, C., Le Bellu, S.: Comment guider les genèses instrumentales pour la prise en main d'un véhicule automatisé ? In: Actes du 55ème Congrès de la SELF, L'activité et ses frontières. Penser et agir sur les transformations de nos sociétés, Paris, 11, 12 et 13 jan 2021, pp. 336–341 (2020)

Dehaene, S.: Apprendre!: les talents du cerveau, le défi des machines (Learning!: The talents of the brain, the challenge of machines). Odile Jacob, pp. 293–321 (2018)

Goodwin, C.: Professional vision. Am. Anthropol. **96**, 606–633 (1994). https://doi.org/10.1525/aa.1994.96.3.02a00100

Hoc, J.M., Amalberti, R.: Diagnostic et prise de décision dans les situations dynamiques. Psychologie française **39**(2), 177–192 (1994)

Hoc, J.M., Amalberti, R.: Cognitive control dynamics for reaching a satisficing performance in complex dynamic situations. J. Cogn. Eng. Decis. Mak. **1**(1), 22–55 (2007). https://doi.org/10.1177/155534340700100102

Houdé, O.: Inhibition and cognitive development: object, number, categorization, and reasoning. Cogn. Dev. **15**(1), 63–73 (2000)

Kyriakidis, M., de Winter, J.C., Stanton, N., Bellet, T., van Arem, B., Brookhuis, K., Martens, M.H., Bengler, K., Andersson, J., Merat, N., Reed, N., Flament, M., Hagenzieker, M., Happee, R.: A human factors perspective on automated driving. Theor. Issues Ergon. Sci. **20**(3), 223–249 (2019)

Le Bellu, S.: Are we ready for driving an automated vehicle? Need to support the familiarization of future users (in prep.)

Lee, J.D., See, K.A.: Trust in automation: designing for appropriate reliance. Hum. Factors **46**(1), 50–80 (2004)

Lefebvre, C.: Vers une formation à la conduite automobile intégrant des connaissances conceptuelles et des métaconnaissances. Recherche-transports-sécurité **70**, 16–40 (2001). https://doi.org/10.1016/S0761-8980(01)90225-0

Mayen, P., Gagneur, C.A.: Le potentiel d'apprentissage des situations : une perspective pour la conception de formations en situations de travail. Recherches en éducation **28**, 70–83 (2017)

Mollo, V., Falzon, P.: Auto-and allo-confrontation as tools for reflective activities. Appl. Ergon. **35**(6), 531–540 (2004)

Mundutéguy, C., Darses, F.: Perception and anticipation of others' behavior in a simulated car driving situation. Le travail humain **70**(1), 1–32 (2007)

Olsen, W.: Triangulation in social research: qualitative and quantitative methods can really be mixed. Dev. Sociol. **20**, 103–118 (2004)

Pascual-Leone, J.: Organismic processes for neo-Piagetian theories: a dialectical causal account of cognitive development. Int. J. Psychol. **22**(5–6), 531–570 (1987)

Rabardel, P.: Les hommes et les technologies; approche cognitive des instruments contemporains. Armand Colin (1995)

Society of Automotive Engineers: Taxonomy and definitions for terms related to driving automation systems for on-road motor vehicles (2018). www.sae.org/standards/content/j3016_201806

Trouche, L.: Construction et conduite des instruments dans les apprentissages mathématiques: nécessité des orchestrations. hal-00190091 (2003)

Verillon, P., Rabardel, P.: Cognition and artifacts: a contribution to the study of though in relation to instrumented activity. European journal of psychology of education, 77–101 (1995)

Vidal-Gomel, C., Delgoulet, C., Geoffroy, C.: Compétences collectives et formation à la conduite d'engins de secours dans un contexte de spécialisation des sapeurs-pompiers en France. Perspectives Interdisciplinaires sur le Travail et la Santé (16–4) (2014)

Contributions and Construction of the Professional Storytelling Within the Framework of a Junior Practices in Reflection Day: The Example of a Design Project in a Municipality

Antoine Eisenbeis[1][(✉)] and Camille Bachellerie[2]

[1] Mairie de Meudon, Meudon, France
[2] Conservatoire national des arts et metiers, CREAPT, Paris, France
`camille.bachellerie@lecnam.net`

Abstract. This article is the second of a four-step symposium presenting the activity of the Junior Practices in Reflection Committee (JPR). It presents a bibliographical review and an example of a storytelling by a young practitioner that take place within the framework of the JPRs. A design project is presented for a school registration reception in a municipality. It will present the methodology implemented with the project's actors, the tools used and its role in the project. All to consider the constraints of the agents and the public received and to ensure a quality of service. A professional storytelling, like the one presented, is used as a fulcrum for the discussion between junior practitioners.

Keywords: Professional storytelling · Design project · Junior practitioner · Reflective practice · Public administration

1 Introduction

The Junior Practices in reflection Committee (JPR) was born out of a two-fold observation; the existence of problems specific to young practitioners and the lack of space to instruct those. From that basis, it was proposed to the SELF (French Speaking Ergonomics Society) to create a committee dedicated to exchanges on the practice of ergonomics for and by junior practitioners. This committee has a twofold objective of creating an ephemeral framework for exchanges between junior practitioners while at the same time articulating these exchanges with the various instances that make up the profession and manufacture the discipline. Since its creation in 2014 and at a rate of about three days per year, it has brought together nearly 200 participants from all over France but also from various fields of ergonomics practice (occupational health service, consultant, internal, doctoral student, etc.). Finally, these spaces of exchange have crossed borders, with a first office in Quebec from 2014 to 2017 and an office in Peru since 2018. The interest of this symposium is to present what has been developed by the committee

N. L. Black et al. (Eds.): IEA 2021, LNNS 219, pp. 471–477, 2021.
https://doi.org/10.1007/978-3-030-74602-5_66

in terms of exchanges on practice while opening this presentation to other forms of practice. These axes will take the form of four communications. The first communication will return to the theoretical foundations of the JPR Committee. The second paper will present the storytelling of a young practitioner. Without wanting to be representative, it will serve as an example to show what is discussed in the JPR meeting days. The third communication will present the implementation of the exchange on practice and we will be able to illustrate here the methodology we use and the intermediate objects that it mobilizes. The fourth communication will come back to the specificities of the deployment of the office in Peru and issues that this may raise.

This article presents the second paper of the symposium. It will first explain what a professional storytelling from a theoretical point of view is, followed by an example presented during a day of exchange and then discussed. This concerns the design of a reception for a school service in a town hall and the contribution of the ergonomist in this multidisciplinary project.

2   The Contribution of Professional Storytelling to JPRs

This section intends to provide a theoretical review on the use of storytelling in professional development, without claiming to be exhaustive.

2.1   The Practice of Ergonomics: A Specific, Situate and Unique Activity

The ergonomist's profession is complex, due to the singularity of the work situations studied (Beaujouan and Daniellou 2012). The approach taught does not provide ready-made solutions, which makes learning complex (Lancry et al. 2006; cited by Beaujouan 2013). Following his training, the ergonomist builds himself throughout his professional career and specially in his first experiences. Thus, the JPR Committee is part of the continuity of professionalisation.

As indicated in the first article of the symposium[1] and following Falzon (2004), Beaujouan (2013) proposes the contributions of a professional storytelling as part of a training course, the cognitive activity of the ergonomist profession is described, as characterized by three points of view:

- As an activity of diagnosis and intervention on a process, this activity being based on rules. […]
- As a design activity and associates it with a poorly defined problem-solving process […]
- As an activity which considers ergonomic practice as an activity of collaborative problem-solving and refers "*to a situated construction, particular to the case encountered, linked to the particular circumstances which, here and now, present themselves to the ergonomist or are constructed by him*" (Falzon 2004, p. 32 cited by Beaujouan 2013, p. 355 and 356).

---

[1] Chambel A. et al. (2021) Creation of the Junior Practices in Reflection committee of the French Speaking Ergonomics Society: historical genesis and theoretical foundation of the exchange practice, IEA 21st Triennial Congress.

These cognitive activities specific to the ergonomist require specific and adapted training devices, particularly through the implementation of scenarios to integrate in this construction.

In addition, skills must be developed as an ergonomist (Beaujouan 2013; p. 52–54):

- A capacity to reflect on professional practice;
- A capacity for subjective deliberations of the practice;
- A capacity for "dialogue with situations";
- Strategic and relational capacities;
- Diagnostic and prognostic capacities;
- Ability to build bridges between the particular and the general.

The JPR days of exchange on practice are a continuation of these arrangements that have been put in place. Members are graduates but have not fully acquired all of the skills and competencies of the ergonomics profession that are acquired throughout the professional career.

To understand this complexity of the profession, the days of exchange on the practice, have professional storytelling as their starting point as they allow projection into situations.

2.2 Professional Storytelling and Storytelling Function

Beaujouan (2013, p. 27) proposes six properties to define professional educational storytelling: the succession of intentional actions, the constancy of the agent, the transformation of predicates, the structured process, the proposed plot, and the final evaluation.

These stories described by Beaujouan in 2012 have several functions and contributions (p. 109).

Concerning the framework of the JPR days, some stories allow the use of the following functions of the storytelling:

- The "didactic function" which makes it possible to enrich the library of cases of its recipients to help them build and solve complex problems.
- The "configurational function" of the storytelling concerns its ability to account for independent events (consecution) in a whole making sense (consequence) in order:

  - to feed the pragmatic concept development process
  - to be at the origin of inferential processes under certain conditions, in particular that of being able to raise the level of analysis of the storytelling in order to draw more general lessons (Soulier 2006)
  - to be a driving force in the way in which the understanding of the action will strive to make up for its success or failure by giving the subject the opportunity to reconstruct causality where he lived from contingency (Pastré 1999)

- The "reflective function" allows awareness by distancing from past experiences invites us to read our past, present, and future by dialoguing with ourselves and giving the opportunity to better understand ourselves

- And "projective function" as an opportunity to experience action scenes by proxy by acting cognitively and immersing oneself in the skills to be mastered. (Beaujouan 2013, p. 109–110)

Some of these functions are less marked, in particular the didactic function, which is more of an incidental effect and is not the main objective of the Committee.

However, "not everything is a professional storytelling" (Beaujouan 2013, p. 186): it must be prepared.

As part of the days of exchange organisation (the presentation of the day's progress is presented in the third paper of this symposium), several people with different roles are involved:

- The novice practitioner expressing the professional storytelling as the reciter
- The organizers of the days as animators
- Novice practitioners participating in the day.

A discussion time takes place upstream between an organizing member of the day and a novice practitioner in order to prepare him to present his story. The objective is to help the reciter construct this professional storytelling to be as relevant as possible and to serve as a support to fuel the discussion for the novice practitioners participating in the day.

Construction landmark for the use of professional stakeholders (Beaujouan 2011 p. 186) can be used by organizers to ask good questions.

In the second part, the example of a professional storytelling will be presented.

3   Role and Contribution of a Young Ergonomist: The Example of a Design Project for a School Enrolment Reception

The presented project emerged following the need to refresh the premises and the evolution of the service with the dematerialization of registrations. The request comes from the education department and technical services to initiate a reflection and take into account the functional needs of the reception area.

3.1   Context

This intervention takes place in a city near Paris. The local authority employs 700 agents for 45,000 inhabitants. The city's missions are for example the management of schools, town planning, culture, and even green spaces.

The intervention takes place more precisely at the reception of the education directorate which manages registration for the canteen, leisure centers or nurseries. 4000 parents must register with the city annually. It should be noted that the intervention takes place in a context of dematerialization, with less and less reception from the public, as well as during the period of the health crisis of COVID-19.

The ergonomist is part of the human resources department in the occupational health service. With 2 years of experience, his profession is new for the city. His objective is to integrate users and their needs into the architectural projects. His main role is to make the link between the operational services and the technical services.

3.2 Actions

It seems essential to talk about the strategy implemented by the ergonomist to integrate architectural design projects. At the beginning there were no ergonomist and the human resources department was not working on architectural projects. He first met the Director of Buildings to explain what he could do in this area. Concrete demonstration of the methodology positioning work was carried out in order to participate in design projects, with the aim of integrating the constraints of workers and users.

During the renovation, the ergonomist brought together around the table various actors in the design but also in the service for which it is intended, which was not always the case before. The following actors were associated according to their roles and skills:

- The Director of Buildings, who manages all the buildings owned by the city;
- A plan designer, who masters 3D modelling;
- The person in charge of the technical center, who realizes custom-made offices;
- The director responsible for the operationality of the service;
- The service manager responsible for the quality of service;
- The administrative officers of the education service, who receives the citizens everyday.

The ergonomist also provided a project methodology. To this end, it carried out interviews and observations to collect the needs of actors in the field. These needs were transmitted to the technical services for the realization of plans and simulations via modelling software.

Following the design on the software, the agents were able to bring up the elements to be improved according to their work constraints.

3.3 Final Results at Different Levels

First, the user agents were integrated into the design project and for the renovation of their workplace, taking their constraints into account.

Second, a modelling of the reception area was carried out using modelling software to simulate the work activity and project oneself into the future space.

At the time of writing this paper, the goal is to work in the coming months with technical services and agents to discuss and to improve each scenario.

Following the simulations, the idea is to adjust the macroscopic and microscopic elements of the scenarios by taking into account the feedback from the agents. The most suitable scenario, depending on the technical, functional, and financial constraints will be chosen.

The ergonomist set up the structuring of the project, which is based on multidisciplinary in the intervention. In the short term, this approach made it possible to create a tool for carrying out the redesign project and the ergonomist supported the actors in taking it up. In a longer-term vision, we believe that such an approach could be reused by the design actors in a subsequent project.

During this project two main difficulties were encountered. The first is the reluctance of technical service agents regarding the usefulness of ergonomic intervention, hence the need to create an approach that is understandable and reproducible by these same actors. The second was dependent on the context of the health crisis in which this intervention was carried out, a source of obstacles for multidisciplinary work.

This story underlines the importance of the ergonomist's strategic stance and knowledge of the positioning of the actors is essential on this type of project, in order to obtain degree of latitude for the intervention. This experience makes it possible to open a new reflection on the escalation of needs by the manager, without the ergonomist having to intervene. For example, it involves a guide to the points of attention to be taken into account in order to take into consideration all the constraints during design.

4   Discussion and Conclusion

Professional storytelling serves as the foundation for discussion engineering as well as projection into action. It allows the practice to be placed in a concrete context and is used from "action" to arrive at general questions. Participants can then more easily establish links with their own practices.

The presentation of a project allows first of all, to relate to theoretical elements learned during the student training. In this example, we can cite the strategic analysis of actors or characteristic action situations.

A story is also used to enrich the situation library. In this project, participants who have never performed an intervention on a reception desk have the elements to tackle this situation in their professional environment. The challenges of dematerialization can also be discussed.

The other novice ergonomists participants can also offer their contributions to the novice practitioner expressing the story which can be used to question himself again about the project.

In addition, other participants can get a first glimpse of how another organization works. In this intervention, the one-day participants do not necessarily come from the same type of structure (consultants, interns in a private company, doctoral student, etc.). In this story, they may have elements on the organization of a territorial public service, and the actors specific to this structure. They can then discover the positioning of the ergonomist in a design project.

A formalization of the preparation of a professional story, within the framework of the JPR, could be the subject of another communication.

A professional story serves as a starting point for discussions that take place during the JPR days. In the third article of the symposium[2], it is explained how, from a professional storytelling, the organizers use discussion engineering to enable the exchange on practice.

[2] Bachellerie C. et al. (2021). Building spaces for discussion: getting the diversity of practices speak, IEA 21st Triennial Congress.

References

Beaujouan, J.: Contributions des récits professionnels à l'apprentissage d'un métier. Le cas d'une formation d'ergonomes (2011)

Beaujouan, J., Coutarel, F., Daniellou, F.: Quelle place tient l'expérience des autres dans la formation d'un professionnel? Apport et limite du récit professionnel (2013)

Beaujouan, J., Daniellou, F.: Les récits professionnels dans une formation d'ergonomes (2012)

Falzon, P.: Nature, objectifs et connaissances de l'ergonomie. Éléments d'une analyse cognitive de la pratique. Ergonomie, Hors collection, pp. 15–35. Paris cedex 14: Presses Universitaires de France(2004)

Lancry, A., Leduc, S., Valléry, G.: Le lien générationnel dans la formation et la pratique des ergonomes. In: Valléry, D.G., Amalberti, R. (eds.) L'nalyse du travail en perspectives. Influences et évolutions, pp. 229–237. Toulouse: Octarès Edition (2006)

Pastré, P.: La conceptualisation dans l'action : Bilan et nouvelles perspectives. Éducation permanente, (n° 139), 13–35 (1999)

Soulier, E.: Le storytelling dans les organisations et le rôle des systèmes et technologies de l'information et de la communication. Dans E. Soulier, Le Storytelling, concepts, outils et applications. Paris: Lavoisier (2006)

Delphi and Bayesian Networks in the Analysis of Fatigue in Air Traffic Events in Practical ATC Instruction

Larissa Maria Gomes de Carvalho⬦, Talitha Cruz de Oliveira⬦, and Moacyr Machado Cardoso Junior$^{(\boxtimes)}$ ⬦

Aeronautics Institute of Technology, SJC 12228-900, Brazil
{larissalmgc,Moacyr}@ita.br

Abstract. Risk management is an ongoing process that involves the planning of an organization's resources, whether human or material, aiming to reduce and/or eliminate the occurrence of certain risks, in addition to mitigating the effects of those that may happen. The objective of this work was to propose the use of the Delphi method and the Bayesian Networks in the evaluation of the influence of fatigue on occurrences of air traffic involving the process of practical instruction. To achieve this objective, a preliminary report corresponding to the exercise from February 2019 to February 2020 was considered. The report pointed out that of the 15 existing sectors that cover the airspace region within the scope of the São Paulo Operations Center/In Brazil, sectors T7, T8, and T5 (grouped with T3 and/or T4) had more occurrences. Three (03) controllers who act as instructors, assigned probability values considering (a) the influence of fatigue during practical instruction (b) the sectors involved, (c) the complexity of the tasks to be performed, and (d) the existence or not of adverse weather conditions. The results points out that the complexity of the task is the most prominent factor for fatigue and the consequent occurrence of incidents, followed by the existence of meteorological conditions and the operation in sector T5 (grouped to T3 and/or T4). The developed research reached, in general, its objectives, being able to contribute as a tool for risk management and decision making during the practical instruction process.

Keywords: Fatigue · Air traffic control · Practical instruction · Delphi method · Bayesian networks

1 Introduction

1.1 Problem Statement

Risk is defined as the possibility of the occurrence of an event capable of causing damage, thus being a threat to activity in systems considered to be sociotechnical complex. (Amundrud, Aven and Flage, 2016) [1]. Air traffic control is characterized as a complex and dynamic system that requires strategies for developing professional skills and maintaining proficiency in training controllers.

In the São Paulo region, this control is exercised by the Regional Flight Protection Service (SRPV-SP) and covers the so-called São Paulo and Rio de Janeiro Terminals, as well as the "Tubulão" (which connects the two Terminals). Currently, it refers to 0.4% of the national airspace, but it has the legitimacy of control and responsibility for approximately 37% of the national air movement. Statistics confirmed 946 thousand air movements distributed in the seven main Brazilian airports (Guarulhos, Congonhas, Viracopos, Galeão, Santos Dumont, Campo de Marte and Jacarepaguá) in the year of 2019.

The training of a controller requires a set of skills and abilities, psychomotor, cognitive, and emotional skills, as well as sequential, gradual, and appropriate training to the complexity of the task (Cassiano, SK., 2017) [2]. The military organization, responsible for air traffic control in São Paulo, has a specific training sector, where the process of constant training and capacity building is structured and is governed by regulations and standards from the Department of Airspace Control (DECEA).

ICA 100-18 deals with the technical qualification of air traffic controller (DECEA, DECEA Ordinance No. 237/DGCEA, OF DECEMBER 4, 2018) [3–6, 10]. According to this regulation, it is the role of the instruction control body to provide theoretical/practical instruction in the courses and operational stages of the ATC Body in which they are qualified and to apply the foreseen assessments. In addition, they must maintain close supervision on the training of interns in the operational position, to guarantee the safety in the provision of ATC. In the case of instruction to the trainee in an ATC Organ operational position, the responsibility for conducting the operation will lie with the ATC Organ Instructor who is supervising it. The technical criteria for the performance of the instructor function are listed in the same standard and are: a. have a valid Technical Qualification from the body corresponding to the category for which one will be instructing; b. having exercised the duties corresponding to this Technical Qualification for at least 24 (twenty four) months, consecutive or not, in the respective body; c. have at least Operational Concept B (good); d. is appointed by the Head of the Organ; e. have completed the training course for ATC Organ Instructor recognized by DECEA; f. having completed the ATC Organ Instructor Preparation Internship, with a minimum workload of 10 h, of the body for which the instruction will be given; and, g. is considered fit by the organ's Operational Council.

In accordance with international standards related to aviation, the International Civil Aviation Organization (ICAO), which governs and supervises the activities and provision of air services, to which Brazil is a signatory, formally recognized through the State Letter (State Letter) SP 59/5.1–14/91, of December 15, 2014 the need to consider fatigue as an important criterion that impacts air activities and the maintenance of operational safety, and, therefore, proposed regulatory frameworks. Fatigue is conceptualized as a physiological state of reduced capacity for mental or physical performance resulting from sleep loss, prolonged wakefulness, circadian phase and/or workload that can impair a person's alertness and ability to perform tasks properly in accordance to the safety-related operational requirements (Fatigue Management Guide for Air Traffic Service Providers, ICAO, 2018, 2016) [7–9].

Bayesian networks graphically represent the Bayesian inference of probabilities, being, therefore, a model of conditional dependencies between the elements of the system.

It is based on the classical probability theory, in which it is defined that mutually exclusive events have an independent probability of occurrence and that there are interconnected events, that is, in which the probability of occurrence of one influences the probability of occurrence of the others, thus defining the called Bayes Rule or conditional probability [10, 11].

This rule allows the construction of the probability conjunction tables for random variables, represented by the chain rule, according to (Eq. 1).

$$P\left(\bigcap_{k=1}^{n} A_k\right) = \prod_{k=1}^{n} P\left(A_k \middle| \bigcap_{j=1}^{k-1} A_j\right)$$

(1)

From the application of this property to the variables of interest, it is possible to build a network relating the factors of cause and effect graphically, thus facilitating the understanding of the interested parties.

According to a preliminary report, the statistics showed that in the period from February 2019 to February 2020, 27 occurrences of air traffic involving the investigation process were found.

1.2   Objective/Question

To understand the influence of fatigue during the operational stage, three sectors were investigated using the data collected from the occurrences through elicitation and aggregation carried out by interviews with 03 controllers who exercise instruction, followed by the probability analysis through the Bayesian Networks.

1.3   Methodology

Considering the Delphi Method to be an effective approach to elicit and aggregate data from the preliminary analysis, an interview was initially carried out with 03 controlling specialists who work on the instruction. They were informed about the objective of the work, and answered questions that addressed the complexity scenarios, the shift of work, the task complexity and the subjective fatigue load in each scenario, considering the presence or absence of adverse weather conditions.

The application of the Delphi Method took place by making two tables available for each stakeholder to complete, as will be shown on next Section.

With the results obtained, an average was made for each specification based on the 03 specialists. Then, the tables were validated with each one. The results found were then aggregated and the probabilities were calculated using Bayesian Networks, using the variables Sector, Meteorological Condition, and Task Complexity as the primary nodes of the model (causes), while Fatigue is the secondary node and there is the tertiary node, Incident. In this case, both the secondary and the tertiary node represent the effects or consequences of the process. The scheme will be shown on the next Section as well.

2 Results

2.1 Identified Methods

In this section, after using the Delphi method according to the results of the requests made with each controller that assumes the role of instructor, it was possible to perform the aggregation of the results and use the Bayesian networks, through the Netica software. Tables 1 presents the aggregated values grouped by sector, while Table 2 shows the aggregated probability of occurrence of incidents according to the fatigue level.

Table 1. Aggregated values for sector T7, T8 and T5 + T4/T3.

Sector	Meteorological condition	Task complexity	Fatigue		
			High	Medium	Low
T7	Existent	High	66.7	23.3	10
T7	Existent	Low	40	36.7	23.3
T7	Non existent	High	50	43.3	6.7
T7	Non existent	Low	23.3	26.7	50
T8	Existent	High	63.3	26.7	10
T8	Existent	Low	46.7	33.3	20
T8	Non existent	High	36.7	46.7	16.6
T8	Non existent	Low	20	23.3	56.7
T5 + (T4/T3)	Existent	High	80	13.3	6.7
T5 + (T4/T3)	Existent	Low	46.7	36.7	16.6
T5 + (T4/T3)	Non existent	High	70	23.3	6.7
T5 + (T4/T3)	Non existent	Low	33.3	30	36.7

Table 2. Aggregated values for sector probability of occurrence of incident according to the fatigue levels

Fatigue	Incident	
	Happens	Does not happen
High	63.3	36.7
Medium	40	60
Low	23.3	76.7

A preliminary analysis shows that for the condition in which all input variables are equally distributed, the high fatigue level is already with a probability of 48.1% and that the occurrence or not of incidents has close probabilities (occurrence is likely to 47.6% and no occurrence of 52.4%), (see Fig. 1).

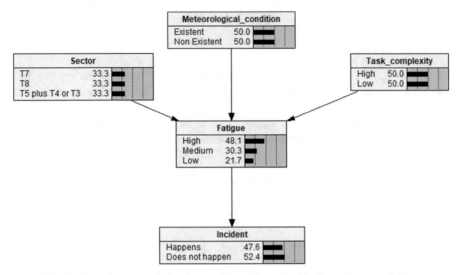

Fig. 1. Bayesian network for the condition of equally distributed input variables.

a) When the existence of a meteorological condition reaches 85.5% probability, the probability of high fatigue reaches 54.6% and the occurrence of incidents has an equal probability of occurrence or non-occurrence, that is, both are 50%. The same situation occurs when the high complexity of the task reaches a probability of 73.5%, therefore the complexity of the task is a more relevant factor for high fatigue and the occurrence of accidents than the existence of meteorological conditions.

b) The analysis of the sectors shows that the T8 sector is the least influential in the generation of fatigue, because when its probability reaches 0%, it leads to a 51.3% probability of high fatigue and 48.7% of occurrence of fatigue incidents; and when it reaches a probability of 100%, it leads to a 41.7% probability of high fatigue and 45.4% of incidents.

c) Analyzing T7, it is possible to report that, for a 0% probability of occurrence, the probability of high fatigue reaches 49.6% and that of incidents occurring reaches 48%. When it has a 100% probability of occurrence, that is, all operations are performed in this sector, the probability of high fatigue reaches 45% and the occurrence of incidents is at 46.7%.

d) It is noted that the T5 + T4/T3 sector is the most influential in the generation of fatigue and the probability of the occurrence of incidents, as it presents the following results: 0% probability for T5 + T4/T3 leads to the probability of 43, 3% high fatigue and 46.1% of incidents; 100% probability for T5 + T4/T3 leads to 57.5% probability of high fatigue and 50.6% of incidents.

2.2 Discussion

Therefore, according to the results, it is possible to infer that highly complex tasks are the most relevant factors in the generation of fatigue and consequently heavily contribute to the occurrence of air traffic incidents. Another scenario that causes insecurity concerns the existence of weather conditions in the T5 sector, grouped with T3 and/or T4.

It is important to consider that during the elicitation, the experts raised some interesting questions about the use of these methods. According to them, the Delphi Method and the Bayesian Networks fail to apprehend the complexity of the system, because, for that, many other variables ended up not being considered. The concept of fatigue itself, here, is limited to the workload at the time the control is performed. Nevertheless, when assessing the influence of fatigue, one should consider the circadian rhythm, the sleep-wake cycle, the self-inflicted overload, the lifestyle, the way in which the scale of work is organized, respect for personal physical limitations and psychological, internal managerial regulation, organizational and work organization issues, as well as shared accountability. As reported by one of the controllers, the occurrence sometimes happens after the operator has worked very well in an extremely complex scenario. The moment one "lets their guard down" because they believe that the complexity has decreased. Alternatively, it happens in a moment of monotony when complexity is low.

3   Conclusions

The results indicate that the complexity of the task is the most prominent factor for the occurrence of incidents, followed by the existence of meteorological conditions and the operation in sector T5 (grouped to T3 and/or T4).

Therefore, the research developed achieved, in general, its objectives, and can contribute as a tool for risk management during the process of practical instruction. However, despite generating considerable indicators, other methods of risk management and analysis, such as resilience engineering, can be used to apprehend the complexity of the complex socio-technical system that is air traffic control and the influence of fatigue on practical instruction.

References

1. Amundrud, O., Aven, T., Flage, R.: How the definition of security risk can be made compatible with safety definitions. J. Risk Reliab. **231**, 286–294 (2016)
2. Cassiano, SK.: Learning to fly: the role of learning in operational safety. Conexão Sipaer Mag. **8**(3), 2–18 (2017)
3. DECEA: Department of airspace control. Ordinance Nº 227/DGCEA. ICA 100-12: Air Rules. Rio de Janeiro (2016)
4. DECEA: Airspace control department. Ordinance No. 11/DGCEA. ICA 100-18: Technical Qualification for Air Traffic Controller. Rio de Janeiro (2018)
5. DECEA: Airspace control department. Ordinance No. 186/DGCEA. ICA: 100-37: Air Traffic Service. Rio de Janeiro (2017)
6. DECEA: Airspace control department. Operational Personnel Management System. Rio de Janeiro (2019)
7. CANSO; ICAO; IFATCA: Fatigue management guide for air traffic service providers civil air navigation services organisation. [s.l: s.n.] (2016)
8. OACI: International civil aviation organization. Manual for the Oversight of Fatigue Management Approaches (2016)

9. OACI: International civil aviation organization. Fatigue Management Guide for Air Traffic Services Providers (2018, 2016)
10. SRPV-SP: Regional flight protection service of the state of São Paulo. Operational Model of the São Paulo Approach Control. São Paulo (2018)
11. Towards Data Science: Introduction to Bayesian networks. https://towardsdatascience.com/introduction-to-bayesian-networks-81031eeed94e. Accessed 2 July 2020

Ergonomic Analysis of the Material and Sterilization Center in a Private Brazilian Hospital

Angelica Garcia Juns[✉] and Julieth Paola Salamanca Gomez

Sirio-Libanes Hospital - Institute of Education and Research (IEP), Sao Paulo, Brazil
angelica.gjuns@hsl.org.br

Abstract. The Center for Material and Sterilization of the Surgical Center of the Sírio Libanês Hospital, the focus of this study, presents data showing a high incidence of absenteeism related to musculoskeletal illness. The present work is a primary study with a qualitative research-action design, with a methodological approach in Ergonomic Workplace Analysis (EWA), aiming to raise an overview of the working conditions that supports improvements for the sector. Of the 44 workers participants 61.36% consider the conditions of comfort of the environment and workstations in the sector to be good or excellent. In the focal groups throughout the workers there was an unanimity regarding their professional fulfillment in the MSC, they referred that they would not trade their jobs for any other. However, ten physical and organizational aspects were identified by workers as workstations with ergonomic problems that need to be improved in order to be more suitable and comfortable, with their respective recommendations. As well, it is relevant too for workers to approach the psychosocial aspects of their labor: highlighting their professional identity and recognition within the Material and Sterilization Center, the Hospital and Nursing.

Keywords: Patient safety · Ergonomic analysis · Sterilization Center

1 Introduction

1.1 The Context of the Material and Sterilization Center of the Sirio Libanes Hospital's Surgical Center

The Sirio Libanes Hospital (HSL) was one of the first in Brazil to implement the World Health Organization concept of "Safe Surgery", keeping its infection rates related to surgical procedures below international rates. It has a large and modern structure with the capacity to sterilize surgical equipment through automated procedures.

As established in the Brazilian National Health Surveillance Agency Resolution n°15 [1], the objectives/main goals of the Material and Sterilization Center (MSC) are:

• To receive, check, process and sterilize health products for the entire hospital complex.

N. L. Black et al. (Eds.): IEA 2021, LNNS 219, pp. 485–491, 2021.
https://doi.org/10.1007/978-3-030-74602-5_68

- Ensure the sterilization process aiming at the quality of the service provided, through chemical, physical and biological monitoring.
- Provide health products that meet the demand and complexity of the procedures carried out at the hospital complex.

In 2016, due to a partnership with a company world leader in solutions for sterilization, the LEAN Process was implemented for the modernization and innovation of the physical area and procedures of the MSC in HSL. It started operating with a physical area of $12916,7\ ft^2$ and with new automated procedures (state-of-the-art equipment, the first in Latin America): tunnel washers, reducing the cleaning time to 15 min, new high-temperature autoclaves, new double-console ultrasonic washers that make it possible to wash, dry and lubricate instruments in the same cycle, a car washer for containers and hospital utilities with a total capacity of 48 cars in 8 h, turning the MSC and the HSL a reference in Latin America for their new process flows.

Even though it is modern and highly technological, the MSC draws the attention of the Occupational Medicine sector for presenting data with a high incidence of absenteeism related to musculoskeletal illness.

1.2   Brazilian Laws and Subsidies for Carrying Out an Ergonomic Workplace Analysis

The Brazilian Ministry of Labor developed the Regulatory Norms (NR) to ensure compliance with the Chapter V - Occupational Safety and Medicine, Title II - General Labor Protection Standards for the Consolidation of Labor Laws. There are 37 Norms that detail the obligations, rights and duties proposed in the decree, to be fulfilled by employers and employees. NR 17 is one of them and addresses specifically Ergonomics: it aims to establish parameters that adapt working conditions to the psychophysiological characteristics of workers, making the employer responsible for the development of an Ergonomic Workplace Analysis - EWA [1–5].

The NR17 Application Manual [6] defines the Ergonomic Workplace Analysis as "a constructive and participatory process to solve a complex problem which requires knowledge of the tasks, the activity developed to perform them, and the difficulties faced to achieve the required performance and productivity". This methodology aims to apply the knowledge of ergonomics and through broader job descriptions transform work situations, being the protagonist the worker.

Since 2018, the institution's ergonomist carried out ergonomics analysis in the sector. A resident nurse of the Nursing Residency Program, motivated by working in the sector and listening to workers complaints of overload due to efforts at work, joined the ergonomist for the development of her Conclusion Work of the Residency, which generated the research presented here.

2   Methods Adopted to Understand the Work Using EWA

The residency conclusion work elaborated between March 2020 and January 2021, as the basis of the scientific study, adopted a qualitative research-action design, with a methodological approach in Ergonomic Workplace Analysis (EWA) based on the NR17 Application Manual and the Ergonomic Activity Analysis [6–8].

This type of analysis method is a constructive and participatory process. The main objective/goal of applying the EWA is to modify these work situations by improving conditions. This methodology was applied through the following steps.

A global analysis which aimed to understand the institution in its administrative structure, the product, the technical dimension of production, the organization of production and work and the legislative dimension and development regulations.

An analysis of the worker population based on the responses to the questionnaire applied on-line to 44 MSC workers. It was used to collect and analyze the occupation, gender, age, weight, height, BMI, shoulder and elbow height to the floor, time in this institution/sector, level of education, employment, and shift job.

An analysis of the initial demand and context based on the illness profile of workers in the sector, through the analysis of data related to absenteeism, provided by Occupational Medicine. It was used the short-term leave (up to 15 consecutive days) due to musculoskeletal diseases in 2019.

An analysis of the prescribed tasks and context of the MSC carried out through the sector's regulatory legislation, design of its demand and flow, the manual of standard operating procedures and the documents of risk analysis.

The researchers observed the workers in their work routines to collect data of the real situations: operating methods, variabilities, layout of the environments, elements of the work organization, requirements of the tasks, equipment, etc. Activity recording methods were implemented (including photographic/filming records under the approval of all those involved in the research, without identifying the subjects). Physical traction and compression measures were applied to some activities of pulling and pushing objects with the help of a Portable Digital Dynamometer. Measures were also performed using a measuring tape: manual reach heights, distance from the operator to the task, visual range etc.

Focus groups were carried out with the workers to obtain their opinions and build together the analysis of the work. A total of 22 nursing technicians participated. The analysis of the results of the groups was carried out through content analysis [9], a tool used in the healthcare field for qualitative data. The objective of this method is to find the meaning or meanings of the workers' statements and responses through the application of the three phases of the method: pre-exploration phase of the material or of fluctuating readings; the selection of units of analysis (or units of meaning); the categorization and subcategorization process: the grouping was performed through frequency, quasi-quantitative and implicit relevance.

The data collected in the previous stages, and previously analyzed, were presented to the workers, aiming to detect errors of interpretation and the need to include points that had not yet been clarified, thus ensuring the smoothness of the procedures and the relevance of the results.

3   Results

3.1   The Main Issues Related to Physical Overload at Work

Of the 44 on-line survey participants, 34.10% considered the work conditions of comfort of the MSC environment to be regular, while 61.36% considered them to be good or excellent. However, 4.54% consider them to be bad or very poor.

When questioning whether if the workers consider that work overloads their bodies and causes illness, 79.55% responded affirmative. Through the explanation box included in the survey in this question, the workers explained their response by associating this event with the lifting of heavy materials, performing repetitive movements, the posture maintained during the workday, long periods of standing up, the height of the benches and sinks, the lack of professionals, the improper functioning of the conveyor system and stress.

The study identified ten workplaces, activities or equipment with physical ergonomic problems: transportation (dirty and clean materials) of materials with a trolley, the purge's sinks, the purge's conveyor system (at the entry of the Tunnel Washers), discharge of materials at the exit of the washers, inspection and preparation of materials on bench, receipt and devolution of consigned materials, management of private materials, trachea dryer, autoclave and arsenal.

The main workstation with ergonomic problems that workers perceive as a need to be improved is the assembly and disassembly of the racks on the Washer machines. The automated Tunnel Washers (thermal disinfectors) constantly present technical failures such as: unevenness of the modules, non-identification of the rack by the sensors and irregular conditions of the rollers. The workers then need to perform a manual physical force to push or pull the rack when it is halt, either due to the rollers not functioning or because it is horizontally misaligned between the modules. The weight of the racks is variable and, when using consigned materials, they have a greater load and can reach over 23 kg, without any measure for control of this load distributed in the racks. Under the measured conditions, the maximum force required to pull the rack reached 122 N.

3.2   The Main Content of Group Interviews: Organizational and Psychosocial Aspects

The focus groups were directed to the relevant points identified with the help of the online questionnaire previously applied anonymously. As an initial questioning for the groups, there were two main triggering questions: "What is it like to work at the HSL MSC?"; and "What does it mean to be a nursing technician at the HSL CME?".

Thus, organizational problems related to frequent solutions given to violations of the SMC rules by customers and suppliers (doctors, instrumentalists and material companies) were identified. The pressures for the surgery schedule to be respected are constant. However, any planning error or unforeseen in the process prior to the sterilization of the material ends up affecting the MSC, which is pressured not to generate delays in surgery, errors or shortages of material. As examples: some doctors believe that they need much more material to operate than the standard items; the delivery of material from suppliers takes place outside the period so that there is time for pre-surgery preparation; the surgery scheduling sector works based on the material limit, making it necessary to prioritize the same material for more than one surgery on the day. As consequence, the worker feels obliged to rush, overloading himself physically and psychologically.

The work scales between the different tasks are not rotated by all workers because they depend on experience and preserved functional capacity, and the team has many new members not yet trained and others with physical limitations due to health problems. Those who work on scales repeatedly that are consider heavier feel more overloaded and stressed.

Working at the MSC is a unique and differentiated service, consisting of a set of specific knowledge, which requires a specialized workforce, a proactive and united team, with the same mission and vision: to provide a quality service to the hospital and guarantee patient safety. Although the activities in the sector do not require formal training, they are of high technical complexity. However, the MSC professionals see other health professionals treating them as "bedpan washers". Workers do not feel that they receive the deserved recognition. They work at their best and believe that they create an overload for themselves when trying to do the job well, despite the adversities, to ultimately be neglected by other areas. This lack of recognition is even the reason that so many organizational problems exist: the other areas do not see how their actions generate an overload on the SME nor demonstrate to understand the importance of the MSC's procedures. This context is seen by them as one of the reasons for illness in the sector.

Among themselves and within their sector they recognize the value of their work, the meaning and the objective: they see that they perform an essential activity. All participants stated fulfillment, gratitude and desire to remain in the sector.

3.3 Recommendations and Improvements for the Working Conditions

All the activities analyzed were followed by recommendations for improvements for the group of managers related to these work processes. Some solutions had already been foreseen in the area's budget by managers, since 2019, when they were monitored by the institution's ergonomist.

This is a place where management is very close to the reality of production work, works side by side and knows the needs of workers. In addition, they recognize the necessary improvements and value the opportunities to ensure greater safety and health.

However, with the global pandemic of COVID-19, the hospital experienced low occupancy and expenditure retention throughout almost the entire year of 2020, eliminating equipment purchases and some solutions already foreseen. With this analysis reviewing all conditions to be improved, new action plans are underway to ensure a future schedule of improvements in working conditions.

4   Discussion

The HSL MSC, within the Brazilian reality, stands out for its excellent working conditions. Most workers consider the working conditions to be good or excellent and this is reflected in the quality of service, highly participative management and a long collective construction, especially of the nurses who manage it. It is a place of technology, with the latest generation procedures, focused on Innovation and Sustainability. However, there will always be processes to be improved to ensure greater safety and health for workers.

The technological solutions showed malfunctions mainly after a few years of use and started to depend on the adaptations of the human and unforeseen efforts in the design of the projects. The interface with the automated washing conveyor system, for example, while bringing the benefits of Lean Process in the item management, produces biomechanical overload by generating the need to manually maneuver the racks on the conveyor every time the system halts.

When, in order to make the automated machine work properly, manual labor is necessary, which generates an overload on the operator, we are faced with a paradox of this technology: the conveyors that should direct themselves, without any effort or need for the worker's attention, demand the reallocation of the racks to correct paths and physical efforts to beat the rollers, made for a load that should move by itself. The lack of integration between engineering and operation and maintenance functions is a problem not yet solved by organizations, even when it regarding the internal activities. With the subcontracting of the project, the problem becomes more complex [10].

The work product delivered by the MSC directly contributes to quality, safety and efficiency in patient care. However, the team does not feel recognized and believes that this is a factor that contributes to illnesses, as it affects the way they work. Also, the professional identity, so strengthened internally in the team through mutual recognition of the value of work, the complexity of tasks, the specificity necessary to perform the function, is threatened by the external view that disqualifies and does not see these nursing technicians as part of the patient care.

Professional identity in Nursing is a continuous, multidimensional and collective process that is based on practices historically built to define itself. For the nursing technicians of the MSC, the construction of this identity, and consequent image and self-esteem, is still a greater struggle, since even within the area of hospital nursing, they have difficulty in asserting themselves and defining their institutional role. The conception of identity involves meanings or attributes, the roles that individuals play in a given institution, and the image built around this, concerns external perception (positive or negative) [11].

Therefore, acting on action plans aimed at the organization of work that include other sectors, clients and suppliers, in the adjustments, with respect to the work flows at the MSC, showing the MSC Production standards and the complexity of the operations, can be a recognition strategy. In addition to its usefulness, the external judgment of recognizing this complexity, the time and technical care required in production, may be essential to grant a more professionalized status, reflecting "beauty", the art of work, recognized by workers and managers of the MSC.

To Dejours [12], "recognition is an element of structuring or destructuring power of work in relation to its psychic economy". For this reason, the valorization of the theme by the workers during the data collection and the correlation made by themselves between this factor and their illness are such a valued point in this research. It is understood here a correlation that deserves to be analyzed by the institution in greater depth and understood as essential to the construction of Health at work.

5   Conclusion

This analysis can take into account a large number of approaches for understanding the work, it allowed to expand the relationship between ergonomics and the sector, from just one way of identifying biomechanical overload to a channel for discussing all aspects of the work: organizational, technological and psychosocial.

The production of spaces for exchange between workers, the reflections mediated by the EWA method and their participation brought reflections from the nursing technicians that allowed to demonstrate how the involvement of workers is highly relevant to ensure health development in the sector.

Acknowledgements. We would like to express our deepest appreciation to the Center for Material and Sterilization of the Surgical Center of the Sírio Libanês Hospital's team for their trust, generosity and commitment to make this study happen.

References

1. Brazil. Resolution - RDC n° 15, of March 13, 2012. Provides for requirements of good practices for the processing of health products and other measures. https://bvsms.saude.gov.br/bvs/saudelegis/anvisa/2012/rdc0015_15_03_2012.html. Accessed 13 Apr 2021
2. Brazil. Decree-Law n° 5,452, of May 1, 1943. Approves the Consolidation of Labor Laws. Rio de Janeiro (1943). https://www.planalto.gov.br/ccivil_03/decreto-lei/Del5452.htm. Accessed 06 Sep 2020
3. Brazil. Constitution (1988) Constitution of the Federative Republic of Brazil. Brasília, DF: Federal Senate (1988). https://www.planalto.gov.br/ccivil_03/Constituicao/Constituicao.htm. Accessed 06 Sep 2020
4. Brazil. MTB Ordinance n° 3,214, of June 8, 1978. Approves the regulatory norms - NR - of Chapter V, Title II, of the consolidation of labor laws, related to occupational safety and medicine. Federal Official Gazette of 06 July 1978 - Supplement. https://sit.trabalho.gov.br/portal/images/SST/SST_legislacao/SST_portarias_1978/Portaria_3.214_aprova_as_NRs.pdf. Accessed 13 Apr 2021
5. Brazil. MTb Ordinance n° 876, of November 24, 2018. Amends item 17.5.3.3 and repeals items 17.5.3.4 and 17.5.3.5 of Regulatory Standard No. 17 - Ergonomics. Official Gazette of the Union of 25 October 2018 – Section 1. https://sit.trabalho.gov.br/portal/images/SST/SST_normas_regulamentadoras/NR-17.pdf. Accessed 13 Apr 2021
6. Brazil. Ministry of Labor and Employment. Regulatory Standard No. 17. Application Manual, 2 (2002)
7. Wisner, A.: Inside work: ergonomics, method and technique. FTD/Oboré (1987)
8. Guérin, F., et al.: Understand the work to transform it: the practice of ergonomics. Edgard Blucher (2001)
9. Campos, C.J.G.: Content analysis method: tool for the analysis of qualitative data in the health field. Rev. bras. enferm. [Internet] (2004)
10. Salerno, M.S., Aulicino, M.C.: Engineering, maintenance and operation in continuous processes: elements for the design of mobile and interpenetrating organizational boundaries.) Gestão & Produção, **15**(2), 337–349 (2008)
11. Castells M. The information age: economy, society and culture. The power of identity. Paz e Terra, vol. 2, p. 24 (2002)
12. Dejours, C.: The madness of work. 5th edn. Cortez – Oboré, São Paulo, p. 158 (1992)

The Exchange on Practice: An Issue for the Development of Novice Ergonomists in Peru in a Context Where Practices of Ergonomic are Heterogeneous

Mirtha Mestanza[1]([✉]), Camille Toulisse[2], Camille Bachellerie[3], Danie Jon[4,5], and Alexis Chambel[4,5,6]

[1] Aquaergo, Lima, Perú
Mirtha.mestanza@aquaergo.com
[2] Head of the Internal Occupational Health Service of Département de l'Ain, Paris, France
camille.toulisse@ain.fr
[3] Conservatoire national des arts et métiers, CREAPT, Paris, France
camille.bachellerie@lecnam.net
[4] AECTT-EVS UMR 5600, Université Lumière Lyon 2, Lyon, France
danie.jon@univ-lyon2.fr
[5] Kardham, Marseille, France
[6] Parcours Doctoral National en Santé Travail, Paris, France

Abstract. Ergonomics in Peru is influenced by a very heterogeneous practice: the ergonomics of activity and human factors . In this context, the JPR days in Peru allow novice practitioners to share their practices and make them evolve.

Keywords: Exchange of practice · Ergonomics of the activity · Human factors · Peru

1 Introduction

The Junior Practices in reflection Committee (JPR) was born out of a two-fold observation; the existence of problems specific to young practitioners and the lack of space to instruct those. From that basis, it was proposed to the SELF (French Speaking Ergonomics Society) to create a committee dedicated to exchanges on the practice of ergonomics for and by junior practitioners. This committee has a twofold objective of creating an ephemeral framework for exchanges between junior practitioners while at the same time articulating these exchanges with the various instances that make up the profession and manufacture the discipline. Since its creation in 2014 and at a rate of about three days per year, it has brought together nearly 200 participants from all over France but also from various fields of ergonomics practice (occupational health service, consultant, internal, doctoral student, etc.). Finally, these spaces of exchange have crossed borders, with a first office in Quebec from 2014 to 2017 and an office in Peru since 2018. The interest of this symposium is to present what has been developed by the

N. L. Black et al. (Eds.): IEA 2021, LNNS 219, pp. 492–499, 2021.
https://doi.org/10.1007/978-3-030-74602-5_69

committee in terms of exchanges on practice while opening this presentation to other forms of practice. These axes will take the form of four communications. The first communication will return to the theoretical foundations of the JPR Committee. The second paper will present the story of a young practitioner. Without wanting to be representative, it will serve as an example to show what is discussed in the JPR meeting days. The third communication will present the implementation of the exchange on practice and we will be able to illustrate here the methodology we use and the intermediate objects that it mobilizes. The fourth communication will come back to the specificities of the deployment of the office in Peru and issues that this may raise.

In this fourth communication, we will speak exclusively about the development of the SELF JPR Commission office in Peru and the implementation of the days of reflection on the practice. Indeed, this document does not aim to measure the impact of the exchange days on the practice of young Peruvian ergonomists because until now two days of exchanges have taken place since the creation of the commission. Due to the global situation, the 2020 events could not take place and will be postponed to the year 2021. Thus, this document based on the 2 days realized aims to show: the development of the JPR days in Peru, how they allow novice practitioners to share their practices and to make them evolve, the differences with France as well as the difficulties encountered, and all this in a context where the practice of ergonomic are heterogeneous.

2 Context

The observation on the diversity of professional practices in ergonomics has been shared for many years in France (Daniellou 2003; Daniellou 2008; Falzon 2019) and these different forms of practices and areas of specialisation are recognised. The JPR are part of this tradition of taking a close interest in all forms of practices.

Peru, like other countries in America, is influenced by the two currents of ergonomics: activity ergonomics and human factors ergonomics. In this country, we find novice ergonomists trained in one of the two currents, or novice ergonomists with mixed training (Cromer and Mestanza 2019). Novice practitioners trained in human factors ergonomics focus their practice on a normative approach. This practice focuses on man as a machine, and the adaptation of the machine to man is their main concern (Darses and Montmollin 2006). On the other hand, those trained in activity ergonomics aim to transform work, supported by an analysis centred on the activity of the workers. Moreover, this practice focuses on the human being as an actor in the work system (Darses and Montmollin 2006).

15 new ergonomists are trained each year in Peru, and this for all training (courses, University Diploma and Master). Moreover, with various training and practical these novice Peruvian ergonomists find themselves alone in the field and without accompaniment. That is to say that they do not have opportune spaces to express their difficulties, mistakes and also successes during their first years of practice. Ergonomists experience professional difficulties that have an impact both on them and on their interventions (Viau-Guay 2009). There are conferences or courses that they attend and where they can express themselves in Peru, but with a learning rather than an exchange objective. Thus, in a context where ergonomics is new and practices are diverse, it is important

to generate discussion spaces that allow novice Peruvian ergonomists to have reflexive exchanges about their practice (Schön 1983). These spaces for exchange could enable them acquire strategies, compare their analyses, see the advantages and disadvantages of each practice, and enrich their own.

3 Peruvian Office of the Junior Practices in Reflection Commitee

The idea of implementing exchange days on the practice in Peru emerges thanks to two favorable factors. The first factor is the presence in Peru of three ergonomists trained in France. They know, from their training, the importance of adopting a reflective posture, regularly and intentional, in order to become aware of one's way of acting, or reacting, in the practice of ergonomics (Schön 1983). The second factor is the knowledge of the success of the SELF's JPR Committee in France and Quebec, during the SELF congress symposium in 2016: *"De l'échange sur la pratique à son enrichissement"* (From the exchange on the practice to its enrichment).

Aware of the difference in the reality of training and practice of ergonomics between France and Peru, we knew that reproducing the exchange days on the practice in Peru would be a great challenge. For this reason, it was essential to participate virtually (one of the three ergonomists) in a few days of exchange of the JPR Committee in France. This way, a link has always been kept with France with the members of the French JPRs office. During these days, it was possible to sort out the elements replicable or not in Peru on the structuring as well as the engineering of the discussion set up in France (Cromer and Mestanza 2019). These will be developed in the construction and development part of the Peruvian JPRs.

Thus, an office of The Junior Practices in reflection in Peru was created in 2018 with the support of the SELF. The SELF has validated this as a Committee that fosters the exchange on practice and emerging communities of novice practitioners in ergonomics of activity. The Peruvian office is run by three ergonomists trained in France. It has been agreed so far to organize 2 days per year. The main objectives of these exchanges are kept intact and are:

- To provide a space for exchanges and discussions
- Fostering debate between practitioners (ergonomics of the activity and human factors)
- Participate in building new practices
- Enabling participants to develop their networks.

4 Construction and Development of the Junior Practices Days in Peruvian Ergonomics

The Day Before: Exchange days requires prior preparation. Here, we will present the organization of the days, highlighting the elements that can be replicated or not from France to Peru.[1]

---

[1] Bachellerie C. et al. (2021). Building spaces for discussion: getting the diversity of practices speak, IEA 21st Triennial Congress.

Just like in France, the members of the office create the necessary conditions for the realization of the day and also everything concerning logistics. The place and the schedule are strategically chosen because in Peru there are many ergonomics professionals; who work alternately between the city and the mining industry and therefore it is necessary to adapt to the schedules. The network of novice ergonomists is small, which facilitates the organization of the days. The organizers propose, by email, between 3 or 4 possible dates. Once the date and the place are chosen, a communication is made on social networks (Facebook, Instagram, LinkedIn) as well as on the SELF website in order to reach other possible participants. Registration is free as in France and is done by email (Fig. 1).

Fig. 1. Information poster for the Peruvian *practical reflection days in 2019*

Unlike in France, not all participants are ergonomists, so it is necessary to broaden the field of influence to occupational physicians and other health, hygiene, and safety professionals. Moreover, some of them are not available for a whole day because of their work. The agreed schedules for the two days carried out were in the afternoon (14:00 to 18:00). Registrations are limited to 12 people for organizational reasons and to guarantee a quality of exchange, as the organizers can moderate small groups of 4 people especially as the participants are not familiar with this type of days. Indeed, they are used to attending conferences where participants listen and ask a few questions at the end of the presentation. Moreover, some participants are reluctant to show their work for fear of being judged, confidentiality of information, etc., which requires the facilitator to provide a caring setting. Finally, the facilitator asks the participants to bring items related to their current interventions (plans, presentations, photos, videos, etc.) to facilitate the exchanges.

The Day: As in France, the organizer opens the day and the participants are welcomed in a selected room to encourage exchanges. Each participant introduces themself and expresses they expectations (Cromer and Mestanza 2019).

Unlike in France, where the committee is beginning to be known, the participants do not know the Committee, its objectives and the methodology of the day's proceedings.

It is therefore necessary to have a very detailed explanation of the operating rules. In the two days carried out in Lima and Arequipa, there were 6 participants per day. For this reason, it was not necessary to divide the participants into small groups. The exchanges were therefore carried out with the whole room. Each participant had between 30 and 50 min to share their intervention while exchanging with their peers. There was no specific preparation time before the day, but participants were asked to bring their work (slides, plans, models, etc.). There were no specific themes developed, as it was first necessary to familiarize participants with this new exchange methodology.

The first day session of the Peruvian office took place on May 3, 2019 in Lima from 14:00 to 18:00, in the premises of the Universidad Nacional de Ingenieria. The novice practitioners presented their current interventions and the topics discussed were varied. We show below a summary illustrating the topics discussed and the picture of the participants of the day (Fig. 2).

Participant Day 1: This was an intervention in a company in charge of toll collection in Lima. The novice ergono-mist presented a very thorough diagnosis of the health and safety issues with uncertain recommendations. It also evoked and explained a problem of positioning around the company's occupational physician. Thus, all the participants discussed the importance of including the analysis of work in the diagnosis. They noted that it was important to make the link between the determinants of work, the activity and the effects on the company in the diagnosis (attention time to users and the quality of atten-tion to toll users). This is in order to generate a more complete diagnosis and more meaningful to the other interlocutors (quality, production and management). This way, the novice ergonomist could improve his or her positioning in order to achieve work transformation.

Fig. 2. Summary illustrating the topics covered and participants picture from Day 1, 2019.

The second day took place on June 8, 2019 in Arequipa from 14:00 to 18:00. The novice ergonomists presented their interventions and the topics discussed were var-ied. We show below a summary illustrating the topics discussed and the picture of the participants of the day (Fig. 3).

The After-Day: Just like in France, after the day we produce a report with the objectives of the day, the names of the participants, the topics discussed and a picture with all the participants that have authorized it. The idea is not to produce an analytical and exhaustive document, but to transcribe the issues raised, the brakes and levers identified, highlighting the links that could be made. This work allows us to reach a higher level of "sedimentation" of the exchanges (Cromer and Mestanza 2019). Likewise, participants

Participant Day 2: This was an intervention in a control room design project at the time of implementation. It showed us the problems of the work spaces at the time of the installation of the work team. The novice ergonomist made a very sustained diagnosis of the health problems of the users in order to find a new arrangement of the work spaces after the construction. It is very likely that the new layout did not come to fruition because the control room had been inaugurated and the management would not want to reinvest. The team discussed the importance of involving the ergonomist in the upstream stages of the project, i.e. at the "programming" or "design" level.

Fig. 3. Summary illustrating the topics covered and participants picture from Day 2, 2019.

receive a certificate of participation that novice Peruvian ergonomists request much more often than in France.

5 Results

During the two days, the novice ergonomists were able to present their current interventions and the topics discussed were varied. From these days and the exchanges that took place, the following elements and observations emerged:

- **The profession of ergonomist in Peru.** The influence of the two currents of ergonomics: human factor and the ergonomics of the activity, implies a certain difficulty in the practice of the novice practitioners because the idea of the profession of ergonomist is not the same for the various professionals (applicants and responders). Sometimes the applicants have human factor training and their expectations are different from those of the ergonomists answering the requests.
- **The positioning of the ergonomist is very weak around the company's occupational physician.** The main applicants in Peru are occupational physicians and health and safety team. They are very open to the transformation of work, but they generally have little decision-making power in organizations. Some novice ergonomists do not have strategies to improve their positioning to reach decision-makers and transform work.
- **The difference between implementing health and safety improvements and transforming work through ergonomic intervention.** The improvements implemented in Peruvian companies are generally centered on the control of professional risks. However, these proposals of improvements can be incoherent with the real work and the functioning of the man at work which is not taken into account.
- **Diagnosis is very intensively focused on the health problems of uses and very little on performance or quality.** The lack of analysis of work in the training of ergonomists means that diagnoses are very focused on occupational health, which

may be lacking in the diagnoses, as this does not always speak to decision-makers and therefore does not allow the transformation of work to be achieved.

- **The importance of including ergonomics in the design of workspaces at the «programming» or «design» level.** The participation of ergonomists in the management of projects is little known in Peru and they are generally called upon at the handover stage of a project when there are problems between users and workspaces.

This set of themes developed during the days shows the need for novice ergonomists to have spaces conducive to exchanges in order to build new practices in the convergence of the two currents of ergonomics.

Following the days, the participants were able to give us their feedback and one of the returns illustrates all the opinions of the participants:

"The reason I participated in the JPR day is because I looked for real solutions that other participants have integrated into their projects. This day was different from others (conferences, congresses, etc.) because I had the opportunity to show my mistakes, successes, and the progress of my work. In addition, I benefited from the experience of the other participants. It remains in my mind the importance of the ergonomist's positioning to achieve the transformation of the work. Since that day, I approach problems in work with a systemic approach, I do not look for an immediate solution, and otherwise I take a step back to find the root cause of the problem. During the next sessions, I expect to find experiences in other sectors, in other forms, to solve problems and in this way open my mentality to new ideas". (Cromer and Mestanza 2019).

The JPR days are very innovative sessions that allow novice ergonomists to identify their blockage problem in their interventions and find possible solutions. The participants are looking forward to future days because they find their problems in other novice ergonomists and they participate in the construction of new practices. In the same way, the recognition of the practice, influenced by the two currents of ergonomics, allows them to find new intervention strategies, compare their analyses, see the advantages and disadvantages of each practice, and enrich their own. These days also allow participants to build their network with fellow ergonomists and other professionals.

6   Conclusion

Thereafter it will be necessary to make the days evolve. First of all by increasing the number of participants by improving the communication of the days through audiovisual support, ergonomics training, networking, etc.

Also, it will be important to select specific themes to be developed for the next days. Indeed, the large number of topics covered in the time allotted does not allow for in-depth and reflective exchanges. The topics are certainly infinite, but it is important to prioritize them in relation to the expectations of the participants. Indeed, if a precise theme is not developed, then the subjects risk being overlooked and multiplied, especially since the participants' functions can be very heterogeneous (occupational physicians, health and safety engineers, ergonomists, etc.). From these two days we have learned that it is necessary to focus the participants on a particular subject in order to gain more height on it and to meet the main objectives of the Junior Practices in reflection Committee.

By comparing the topics discussed during the JPR days in France with those of the days held in Peru, we find common issues such as the positioning of the ergonomist, working with stakeholders, demand analysis, etc.. Thus, whether we are in Peru, France, Quebec or elsewhere, some of the concerns of novice ergonomics practitioners are similar and have no borders.

References

Schön, D.A.: The Reflective Practitioner: How Professionals Think in Action. Ashgate, New York (1983)

Van Belleghem, L.: Diversité des domaines d'intervention, nouvelles pratiques de l'ergonomie: qu'avons-nous encore en commun? Fil rouge. Actes des Journées de Bordeaux pour la Pratique, Mars 2008, 109–125 (2008)

Schön, D.: The Reflexive Practitioner: How Professionals Think in Action. Basic Books, USA (1983)

Schön, D.: Educating the Reflective Practitioner. Jossey-Bass, San Francisco (1987)

Cromer, D., Mestanza, M.: Debate de la práctica, un instrumento para la construcción de la carrera del ergónomo que traspasa las fronteras, Laboreal [En línea] **15**(N°2) (2019)

Cromer, D., Elwert, L., Hubert, K., Francou, F., Couillaud, S.: La comission SELF Jeunes Pratiques en Réflexion: de l'échange sur la pratique a son enrichissement. In: Symposium. Actes du 51ème Congrès de la SELF, Marseille (2016)

Clandestine Activity Among Care Assistants in France: Questions for Training?

Grégory Munoz[1]([⊠]), Pierre Parage[2], and Pascal Simonet[3]

[1] Centre de Recherche en Education de Nantes (CREN-EA 2661), Université de Nantes,
Chemin de la Censive du Tertre, BP 81227, 44 312 Cedex 3 Nantes, France
gregory.munoz@univ-nantes.fr
[2] Université de Nantes et Conservatoire National des Arts et Métiers de Nantes, Nantes, France
[3] Centre de Recherche en Education de Nantes, Nantes, France
http://www.cren.univ-nantes.fr/

Abstract. Our approach focuses on the analysis of the activity of care assistants (CAs) working in residential care facilities for elderly dependents (EHPAD in France). We wonder about the link between activity analysis and training: how could this analysis question training?

Keywords: Analysis of activity · Suffering · Clandestine activity · Training · Professional didactics

1 Introduction

In previous work (Parage and Munoz 2013), we had identified a form of clandestine activity (Dejours 2003) among CAs, faced with the exacerbated productivity carried out in organizations that are therefore "paradoxical" (De Gaulejac 2011), in that they require, for example, both to be in a care relationship with patient and to treat as many patients as possible in a constrained time. This clandestine activity allows them to be less subject to situations of ethical conflict (Gollac and Bodier 2011; Bodier and Wolff 2018), by taking control of their work, sometimes even against the collective. Stimulated by a dialogue between the approaches of professional didactics or vocational didactics (Pastré 2011; Mayen 2015) ergonomics (Wisner 1997; Falzon 2014) and the clinical psychology of activity (Clot 2009, 2010), which seek to understand work with a view to professional development, we have been interested in the question of the resumption of this activity characteristic of CAs by trainers.

2 Theoretical Framework

2.1 Ethical Conflict

Dejours invites us to think not only that reality makes itself known to the subject in the mode of suffering, but that it is this suffering that allows him to overcome the resistance of reality, on the one hand, and to transform the world, on the other hand (Dejours 1998).

© The Author(s), under exclusive license to Springer Nature Switzerland AG 2021
N. L. Black et al. (Eds.): IEA 2021, LNNS 219, pp. 500–507, 2021.
https://doi.org/10.1007/978-3-030-74602-5_70

In work, ethical suffering is a consequence of ethical conflict. This appears in situations when operators respond to a prescription by explicitly carrying out immoral tasks whose consequences are clearly harmful to others (Dejours 1998). Ethical conflict can thus engender ethical suffering, resulting not only in physical (e.g. MSDs) and psychological (e.g. burn out) disorders, but also in forms of ethical resignation such as submission or resignation; or even in forms of ethical resistance leading to the resumption of one's own activity, or the emergence of clandestine activity (Parage and Munoz 2017a).

Ethical conflict crystallizes when the rules prescribed by the institution come into opposition, on a deontological or moral level, to individual rules and/or rules constructed by the work collective. Ethical conflict can therefore be considered as a conflict of values.

2.2   Cognitive Conflict

Cognitive conflict arises when reality is different from the representation we make of it. Thus, from a constructivist perspective, it is an essential resource for learning and skills development. Faced with this conflict, the subject often has two options:

- Either he gets bogged down in the conflict, unable to solve the problem at hand or to take a stand in a clear dilemma. In this case, his adaptation to the situation remains subject to his past reference points;
- Either he comes out of the conflict by a qualitative leap that enables him to transform the situation. We can then speak of conceptual genesis (Rabardel and Pastré 2005).

In work situations, cognitive conflict is mobilized by the incompressible gap between prescribed work and real work, in which the professional constructs acceptable compromises according to the specificity of the situations. The evolution of the prescription reexamines the goals and forms of provisional construction of the subject's operative model (Pastré 2005). Cognitive conflict can then be considered as a conflict of goals.

2.3   Ethical and Cognitive Conflict

Our position as didacticians leads us to see professional intelligence as a response to both types of conflict and particularly to the way in which value conflicts and goal conflicts are actualized in individuals. In a previous paper, we started from the hypothesis that ethical conflict influences cognitive conflict by potentially modifying the subject's operative model (Parage and Munoz 2017a), but is it not appropriate to explore reverse causality? Can cognitive conflict not be at the origin of a displacement of the ethical conflict? The audience of trainers allows us to consider the question at two levels: 1/ from the point of view of the profession of care provider and 2/ from the point of view of the function of trainer.

3 Methodology

Through the use of instruction interview to the double (Oddone et al. 1981; Clot et al. 2002), we gain access to some of the actors' activity. On the one hand, CAs are questioned in order to understand their ethical suffering and the intelligence of the situations they deploy to deal with it. On the other hand, by modifying the technique of instruction interview to the double, we offer the trainers participating in our survey fictitious CA testimonies, elaborated from our analysis results, which present the exacerbated pressures of the work. We seek to see how they position themselves with respect to the expression of these pressures at work.

3.1 CA-Side Data Collection Method

Our collection method, relating to the analysis of the work, is based on the comments made during look-alike instruction interviews conducted with 4 operators in residential care facilities for elderly dependents (EHPAD in France): 3 CA and 1 hospital agent. The look-alike instruction method involves the researcher questioning the operator by asking him to instruct him on what he needs to know in the event of replacing him in his work.

3.2 CA-Side Data Analysis Method

Our analysis proceeds on two levels. The first level attempts to locate the suffering identified in the actors, in order to determine their level of responsibility according to Jaeger (2009). In this presentation, we limit ourselves to the most salient points.

The second level explores the signs of intelligence at work through conceptualization in actors' actions (Vergnaud 2007), in order to help the professionals on suffering.

3.3 Data Collection on the CA Trainer Side

Concerning the trainers, we have modified the protocol of the instruction to the look-alike insofar as the reference situations were not the subject of a negotiation between subject and analyst. On the other hand, we have chosen to produce two guidelines developed by CAs in the framework of our previous study (Parage and Munoz 2017a), in order to orient the subjects towards the question of the pressures exerted on the work of CAs.

As an example, we propose the first testimony on which the dear one asks to be instructed:

"For newcomers to the service, what is difficult is to take the pace of the work... For example, at the moment, even though she's been here for three weeks, we have a colleague who is systematically late on the cart and I regularly have to do one or two rooms on her side to keep up the pace... However, she has at least two years of experience in this job... In fact, she listens to the patients too much, so she wastes her time...".

3.4 Data Analysis on the CA Trainer Side

The angle of ethical conflict is considered on the basis of: 1/ the three forms of moral and ethical responsibility (Jaeger 2009); and 2/ the positions of each trainer with regard to ethical suffering (Dejours 2003; Molinier 2008). Concerning cognitive conflict, we rely on one or two organizers of the activity (Pastré 2011), whose links with ethical conflict will be explored. In conclusion, we question the relationship of trainers to clandestine activity.

4   Results

Our first results position the CAs surveyed in an ethical suffering (Dejours 1998; Molinier 2008), between resignation, sometimes akin to a withdrawal, and resistance, presenting a collective or individual commitment (Munoz and Parage 2019). By resorting to a conscious and assumed clandestine activity, examples of which we will present, some have built, essentially through their experience, fragile and tenuous forms of resistance to the injunctions of productive activity. Based on our first results, we hypothesize (Parage and Munoz 2017) that conflicts of purpose among CAs change regimes. They move from a logic of "and" (care and cure) to a logic of "or", painfully forcing professionals to decide. From this point of view: "development in working adults is inseparable from the construction of their experience, powerful and fragile at the same time" (Pastré 2011, p. 6).

The managerial discourse, taken up in part by trainers, shifts the suffering from an ethic of institutional responsibility to an ethic of professional responsibility (Jaeger, 2009), which can hinder the actors' power to act (Rabardel 2005; Clot 2009, 2010).

4.1   Positioning of CAs in the Face of Suffering

For P and O, suffering is turned towards oneself. O indicates for example: "I was going to have a depression in there...". For M and S, it is referred to the collective. S says about his relationships with his colleagues and his hierarchy: "I still need it, but I no longer feel in osmosis with it all (...), I need to have colleagues with whom I have fun, with whom I get along, who bring me things, etc.". But sometimes with the hierarchy you find leaders who are not up to the task. But maybe it's me who's not up to the job.

With regard to ethical suffering, two main trends seem to emerge:

– Either it is related to the responsibility of the institution, and seems to be dissolved in forms of ethical resignation provisionally justified by conformation to the work collective (for P & O);
– or it is related to professional and/or personal responsibility, which leads to a certain detachment from the collective and an individual remobilization through forms of clandestine activity, testifying to a certain ethical resistance (for M & S).

The main trends of our study in understanding are summarized in Table 1 below.

Table 1. Positioning of professionals in the face of suffering

	Conflict	Suffering	Responses	Perspectives
O	Relating to institutional responsibility	Explicit Lack of acknowledgement	Ethical resignation Conformation to the collective	Depression Work stoppage
P	Relating to institutional responsibility	Contained suffering Lack of training	Ethical resignation Conformation to the collective	Step point Building experience
M	Related to personal responsibility	Explicit Lack of collective	Ethical resistance Clandestine activity	Being a sophro-logue and intervening in institution
S	Related to professional responsibility	Measured Lack of cooperation	Ethical resistance Clandestine activity	Choosing your establishments

4.2 Care Assistants and Ethical Conflict from the Trainer's Perspective

Concerning the relationship to the profession of care worker, we find the representations that we have already highlighted (Parage and Munoz 2017a):

– The constraints weighing on the very object of the work, particularly the pressure of time, which reduces the profession to nursing, even though the relationship with the resident is recognized as an inherent part of care (FO3: "We run after time, a stopwatch in the belly"; FO1: "Discussing with patients is also care");
– The relationship with the institution, which is experienced as a lack of human resources, thus updating the dilemma between quantity and quality (FO2: "Ten to fifteen minutes per resident is not enough"; FO3: "Ten to fifteen drops per CA is impossible").

While CAs had diversified ethical positions, the trainers seem to relate globally the drifts of the activity to an ethic of institutional responsibility, invoking the incompressible character of temporal constraints. Moreover, the responses to be given to the register of constraints differ significantly from what CAs have to say:

– The need to approach problems from the point of view of communication, organization and teamwork;
– The need to get back in control (FO1: "It's up to them to make things happen"; FO3: "They seem to refrain from thinking");
– The need to mobilize colleagues to take action.

Thus, the managerial discourse that tends to be relayed by the trainers shifts the suffering from an ethic of institutional responsibility to an ethic of professional responsibility. At FO1, the principles introduced by the institution around the concept of humanitude open up sufficient space to mobilize CA. Thus, we do not detect any obvious signs of ethical under-friendliness among the trainers.

For FO2, ethical suffering seems to dissolve into a form of ethical resignation justified by the heaviness of the system. The formation of CA then appears essentially as a great role-playing game in which no one is fooled. For FO3, the position of trainer is an opportunity to reaffirm and disseminate an ethic of professional responsibility. Ethical suffering then feeds forms of ethical resistance that are assumed but which remain incantatory (FO3: "You have to stand firm on your values").

The main trends in the analysis of the trainers are summarized in Table 2 below.

Table 2. Synthesis of the positioning of the trainers

	Ethical conflict/caring profession	Ethical conflict/training profession	Consequences/training	Responses/training
FO1	Relating to institutional responsibility	Related to professional responsibility	Absence of tangible signs of ethical suffering	Humanitude as a unique frame of reference for management and training
FO2	Relating to institutional responsibility	Relating to institutional responsibility	Ethical resignation Training as a consensus around immobility	To limit oneself to the treatment of the problems raised from a communication point of view
FO3	Relating to institutional responsibility	Relating to institutional responsibility	Ethical resistance Remobilization on values (care, tutoring, relationship with the resident)	Acting locally to remobilize the work collective

5   Discussion

Three orders of discussion deserve to be posed: theoretical, methodological, and didactic. According to the theoretical order, how are cognitive conflict and ethical conflict articulated? For example, how do trainers, often coming from the field, deal with the dilemmas present in the testimonies and the sometimes stated clandestine CA activity? Can we infer forms of clandestine activity specific to their position as trainers (Parage and Munoz 2019)? About the dilemma between care and cure, updated in the question of the place of personal hygiene (the toilet) in relation to the relationship with the resident? How are each of the actors positioned? What is its position within the initial training referential? According to the methodological order, what is the limit or the power of the recourse to instruction to the double to grasp the activity?

6 Conclusion

According to the didactic order, if an important preoccupation of the actor with a professional didactics or vocational didactics (Mayen 2015) point of view is to improve the training devices, how can he conceive with the actors' new devices making it possible to cultivate the intelligence of the situations without falling into the denial of the activity?

References

Bodier, M., Wolff, L.: Les facteurs psychosociaux de risque au travail. Octarès, Toulouse (2018)

Clot, Y., Fernandez, G., Carles, L.: Crossed self-confrontation in the "Clinic of Activity". In: Bagnara, S., Pozzi, S., Rizzo, A., Wright, P. (eds.) Proceedings of the 11th European Conference on Cognitive Ergonomics, ECCE 11, pp. 13–18. Istituto di Science e Technologie Della Cognizione, Rome (2002)

Clot, Y.: Clinic of activity: the dialogue as instrument. In: Sannino, A., Daniels, H., Gutiérrez, K. (eds.) Learning and Expanding with Activity Theory, pp. 286–302. Cambridge University Press, Cambridge (2009)

Clot, Y.: Le Travail à coeur, pour en finir avec les risques psychosociaux. La Découverte, Paris (2010)

Dejours, C.: Souffrance en France – La banalisation de l'injustice sociale. Seuil, Paris (1998)

Dejours, C.: L'évaluation du travail à l'épreuve du réel. INRA, Paris (2003)

De Gaulejac, V.: Travail, les raisons de la colère. Le Seuil, Paris (2011)

Falzon, P. (ed.): Constructive Ergonomics. CRC Press, Boca Raton (2014)

Gollac, M., Bodier, M. (eds.): Mesurer les facteurs psychosociaux de risque au travail pour les maîtriser. Rapport du Collège d'Expertise, remis au ministre du travail. DARES, Ministère du travail et de l'emploi, Paris (2011). https://travail-emploi.gouv.fr/IMG/pdf/rapport_SRPST_d efinitif_rectifie_11_05_10.pdf

Jaeger, M.: Du principe de responsabilité au processus de responsabilisation. Vie Sociale 3, 73–81 (2009)

Mayen, P.: Vocational didactics: work, learning, and conceptualization. In: Filliettaz, L., Billett, S. (eds.) Francophone Perspectives of Learning Throught Work, pp. 201–219. Springer, Cham (2015)

Molinier, P.: Les enjeux psychiques du travail : Introduction à la psychodynamique du travail. Payot, Paris (2008)

Munoz, G., Parage, P.: L'activité clandestine des aides-soignant(e)s comme intelligence des situations. Colloque International de Didactique Professionnelle 2019, organisé par l'Association RPDP en partenariat avec l'Université de Sherbrooke, 23–25 octobre 2019, Longueuil, Québec (communication#40, pp. 186–193) (2019). https://ki-learning.fr/RPDP2019/Actesduco lloqueV1.pdf#page=186

Oddone, I., Re, A., Briante, G.: Redécouvrir l'expérience ouvrière. Vers une autre psychologie du travail?. Editions sociales, Paris (1981)

Parage, P., Munoz, G.: De l'analyse du travail en vue du développement: une valeur pour le travailleur ou pour l'économie de la connaissance. Questions pour les formateurs, in Actes du colloque international. *Les questions vives en éducation et formation: Regards croisés France – Canada*, pp. 65–80 (2013). https://cren.univ-nantes.fr/wp-content/uploads/2017/06/lesactes7.pdf

Parage, P., Munoz, G.: L'activité clandestine chez les aides-soignants en EPHAD: un enjeu pour les formateurs. Actes du 4e colloque international de didactique professionnelle. *Entre pressions institutionnelles et autonomie du sujet: quelles analyses de l'activité en situation de travail en didactique professionnelle*, Thème 3: Analyse de l'activité en situation de travail pour la formation et l'apprentissage : entre contraintes institutionnelles et potentiels pour les apprentissages professionnels (communication n° 3118) (2017). https://rpdp2017.sciencesconf.org/data/3118_PARAGEPierreMUNOZGregory.pdf

Parage, P., Munoz, G.: Les formateurs(trices) face à l'activité clandestine des aides-soignant(e)s. Colloque International de Didactique Professionnelle 2019, organisé par l'Association RPDP en partenariat avec l'Université de Sherbrooke, 23–25 octobre 2019, Longueuil, Québec, (communication#41, pp. 194–201) (2019). https://ki-learning.fr/RPDP2019/ActesducolloqueV1.pdf#page=194

Pastré, P.: La didactique professionnelle. Approche anthropologique du développement chez les adultes. PUF, Paris (2011)

Rabardel, P.: Instrument subjectif et développement du pouvoir d'agir. In: Rabardel, P., Pastré, P. (Dir.) Modèles *du sujet pour la conception : dialectiques activités développement*, pp. 11–29. Octarès, Toulouse (2005)

Wisner, A.: Aspects psychologiques de l'anthropotechnologie. Le Travail Humain **60**(3), 229–254 (1997)

Dialogues with Health Workers in a Hospital to Combat the Covid-19 Pandemic

Simone Santos Oliveira[1]([⊠]) [iD] and Lucia Rotenberg[2] [iD]

[1] National School of Public Health, Oswaldo Cruz Foundation (Fiocruz), Rio de Janeiro, Brazil
simone@ensp.fiocruz.br
[2] Oswaldo Cruz Institute, Fiocruz, Rio de Janeiro, Brazil

Abstract. We describe the analysis of the work-health relationship in coping with the Covid-19 pandemic in a public hospital from data derived from a questionnaire and the accomplishment of Groups of Meetings on Work based on the three-pole dynamic device. Health workers have faced exhausting routines, making complex use of themselves to care for patients. They experienced overload and exhaustion, besides feeling of powerlessness in the face of the number of deaths and uncertainties. The constant changes in the protocols generate insecurity in the action. The importance of the meetings is evident in order to strengthen the teams' trust and cooperation in facing the work's variability.

Keywords: Health work · Covid-19 · Hospital · Cooperation · Work meetings

1 Introduction

The Covid-19 outbreak that has haunted the world, classified as a pandemic by the World Health Organization (WHO) on March 11, 2020 has brought numerous challenges to countries.

The high rate of the disease in Brazil required a restructuring of the Public Health System in order to meet the new demand and not to collapse services at the three levels of care (primary, secondary and tertiary). Thus, Campaign Hospitals and expansion of beds were built up throughout the country. In Rio de Janeiro, in addition to these modalities, the new Covid-19 Pandemic Hospital Center was built, linked to the National Institute of Infectious Diseases of the Oswaldo Cruz Foundation (INI/Fiocruz).

Due to its permanent character, the Hospital Center (HC) has specific characteristics that differ from the campaign units built for temporary operation. Intended for critically ill patients diagnosed with the disease, HC was built in less than two months at Fiocruz's headquarters, providing 195 beds for the treatment of the disease. Occupying a total area of 11,720 square yards, composed of a workforce of more than 1,000 professionals, including doctors, nurses, nursing technicians, physiotherapists, pharmacists, psychologists, social workers and other support categories, its inauguration took place on 05/19/2020.

In the context of the HC, one of the biggest concerns is the high contamination rate of health professionals, which leads to absenteeism and death. However, not only contamination is a concern for these workers. Stress, anguish, depression, fatigue, long hours, can also compromise the well-being of those who are essential in the fight against the pandemic [1, 2].

In this sense, the research question seeks to contribute to the understanding of the work and health relationship with a view to supporting HC workers, especially with regard to psychosocial aspects with the theoretical-methodological framework of Activity Ergonomics and the Ergology perspective.

2 Theoretical-Methodological Perspective

Activity Ergonomics establishes the important distinction between prescribed work and real work [3]. The ergological perspective expands the concept of prescribed work, suggesting the notion of predecessor norms [4]. These approaches converge with the perspective of Occupational Health Surveillance (OHS), which is based on the ideas and principles arising from the Italian Workers' Movement (IWM) to fight for health, represented by the principle of worker participation in studies [5]. In this framework, Ergology developed the three-pole dynamic device (3PDD), a knowledge production model that proposes a meeting between materials generated by different scientific disciplines, knowledge and values generated by workers' experiences [6]. The 3PDD is expressed in the Meetings on Work (MoW) that seek to highlight the debate of norms and values present in the activity.

Recognizing the complexity of work and the practice experience of workers is essential for preventing illnesses and promoting health. It is noteworthy, therefore, that working is an act of managing lags, the activity being guided by a prescription, but never being restricted to it, and it is always modified by the subject in the course of action.

2.1 Research-Intervention Procedures

Questionnaire applied in three moments with an interval of 20 days between them: Moment 1 - expectations of performance in the emergency context; the impacts of Covid-19 on the health of workers, friends and family; depression, anxiety and stress - through the Depression Anxiety and Stress Scale - DASS-21 [7]; Moment 2 - Inventory on Work and Risk of Illness - WRI [8] which proposes to evaluate the psychosocial context of work and its relationship with illness, composed of four interdependent scales; Moment 3 - Maslach Burnout Inventory - MBI [9], an instrument with 22 items that assesses Burnout rates.

For the purposes of this presentation, we will only use the partial results of the first and second moments. It is noteworthy that the DASS-21 scale considers sensations and feelings experienced by people in the seven days prior to its completion, and cannot be considered a diagnostic instrument for mental disorder. The WRI scale has been psychometrically analyzed, thus making it possible to assist in the diagnosis of critical indicators at work, assessing the psychosocial context of work and its relationship with illness. It is composed of interdependent scales: Work context assessment scale (WCAS) - composed of three factors: work organization, working conditions and socio-professional relationships; Human cost at work scale (HCWS) consists of three other factors: physical cost, cognitive cost and emotional cost; Scale of indicators of pleasure and suffering at work (SIPSW) composed of four factors: two of them evaluate pleasure and two evaluate suffering at work.

After analyzing each factor and the set, the interpretation can be measured as satisfactory (meaning positive result and producing pleasure at work); critical ("extreme situation", potential negative cost and suffering at work) and severe (situation that produces human cost and suffering at work). The last two situations require attention and procedures, in order to mitigate or eliminate the causes.

Meeting on Work Groups (MoW) – an ethical-epistemological attitude adopted, placing in debate the different knowledges – that of workers' practice experience and technical-scientific knowledge for producing new knowledges, anchored on the 3PDD. Five meetings were carried out: two with nursing teams, two with nursing technicians and one with registered nurses. Meetings were at the Hospital Center, during the shift, with an average of one hour long each, with the participation of 5 to 8 workers indicated/invited by immediate management.

Manager Training Workshop – to develop from concrete cases the managers' capacity of analyzing work situations based on the theoretical-methodological elements developed by the Ergonomics of Activity and Ergology, constructing a specific regard and listening.

Intervention proposals – based on the diagnosis developed by Training management groups contribute to the improvement of conditions and well-being of workers.

3   Results and Discussion

In the first moment of the questionary, 219 workers from all professional categories participated, with a larger number of nursing technicians (28%), followed by nurses (18.7%), physiotherapists (15.5%) and doctors (10.9%). The mean age was 36 ± 8 years, with physiotherapists and nursing technicians slightly younger.

Feeling apprehensive about working in the pandemic was common in all categories, especially among doctors, since more than half of them reported this condition (54.2%). It is interesting to highlight that almost all doctors reported that they felt more stressed than before the pandemic; for other categories the proportions were around 50%.

High frequencies of stress, anxiety and moderate and severe depression were observed, especially for physicians (54.2%, 37.5% and 25%, respectively), followed by the physiotherapists in the sample (26.5%, 35.3% and 14.7%, respectively).

From the stratification of the DASS-21 scale results, 20 workers were identified to having reached critical levels of symptoms of stress, depression or anxiety. These workers belonged to the following categories: doctors (7), physiotherapists (5), nurses, (2) pharmacists (2), nutritionist (1), nursing technician (1), radiology technician (1) and administrative assistant (1). They were contacted and offered support at the institution's Occupational Health Center. Of these, four workers expressed a desire for support, the others already had some type of mental health monitoring.

The second stage of the questionnaire was attended by 133 workers for the diagnosis of critical indicators at work using the IWRI scale. Figure 1 shows the percentage of workers who evaluated each of these factors (Work Organization, Working Conditions and Social and Professional Relationships) as *critical* or *severe*, that is, indicating a limit situation and a source of suffering at work.

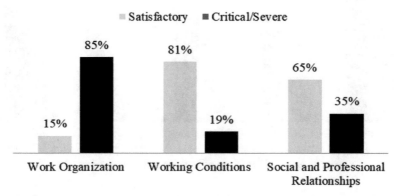

Fig. 1. Work context assessment scale WCAS organization and working conditions and socio-professional relations

In Fig. 2, the percentage that indicated the physical, cognitive and affective costs at work as *critical* or *severe*, therefore potentializes and producers of suffering.

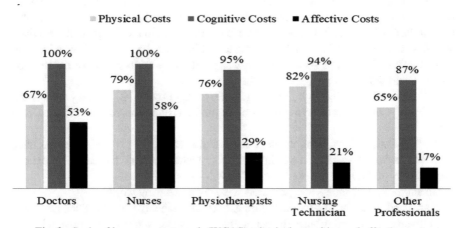

Fig. 2. Scale of human cost at work (WCAS), physical, cognitive and affective costs

In this Fig. 3 we present the percentage of workers who evaluated experiencing *critical* or *severe* professional fulfillment and freedom of expression. That is, for these percentages of workers these factors are experienced in a more negative way, increasing their suffering at work.

The dialogues established at the meetings gave visibility to the great challenge experienced by workers during this time of pandemic. A diverse challenge of many facets and, in this case, of the HC, inaugurated in the eye of the pandemic hurricane, the challenge of constituting teams and receiving patients simultaneously, very well expressed by one of the nurses:

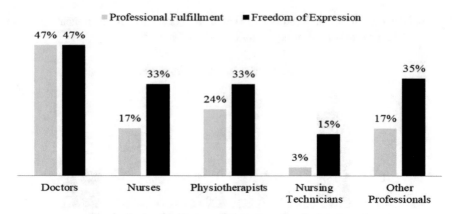

Fig. 3. Scale of indicators of pleasure and suffering at work

"Imagine that you decide to build a house, but at the same time you want to live inside it (…) we are raising the walls and already living inside, wanting to use the toilet and putting up a slab and the house is ready" (MoW 1 – worker 3).

These teams were formed by professionals, from different backgrounds and experiences, sometimes none in emergency, intensive care or even in-hospital.

"The hospital opened and continues (…) we didn't know each other, there were three shifts (…) and we didn't know the nurses, the technicians, because we had never seen them in our lives, we didn't know if they were able or not to receive patients and that's how it was. You have this or that experience, and in come the patients, it was like that, nerve-racking. The desire we had was to war paint our faces, because we didn't know how it would work" (MoW2 – worker 4).

For those who participated in the beginning of this process, it was very exhausting, requiring a permanent correction of problems and constant improvement indicated by them.

"When I came down here, when patients started to arrive, I stayed at the entrance, because I'm from screening, it was hell with four technicians and two nurses, we didn't know where we literally put our heads" (MoW 5 - worker 3).

In addition, procedures and protocols were created during work:

"As I said, it has been very challenging, because each day is new and we have been participating in everything since the beginning of the process, making the hospital flows, routines (…) we are always there trying to improve the processes" (MoW 1 - worker 4).

An issue identified as very mobilizing, considered stressful, was related to difficulties with a completely computerized environment, differentiated digital systems and communication via tablet, since the use of paper is not allowed in the hospital:

"The issue of computerization, working with a tablet, I come from five years at a hospital (…) where there wasn't any of this, so, for me when there was a demand, I had to adapt and it is being a challenge, because we are in an era, we are living at a time with people saying: *'let's do a live', 'let's talk to the family'*, until I adapted to these little things it was a challenge" (MoW 1 - worker 2).

Due to the nature of the pandemic, contamination generates fear and insecurity, which is mainly expressed in the handling of Personal Protective Equipment (PPE). The act of dressing up and undressing is an important challenge because in addition to the risk of contamination, it creates embarrassment for using the bathroom and taking breaks.

"The biggest challenge is to get used to this outfit, I think we are not used to it up to now. For example, there is no chair or table for us to sit on, there is no time for us to sit, relax and there are extremely heavy shifts, because you have a patient who is there and suddenly he's a *gonner*, and so on and you don't rest. Being dressed up and sometimes you want to go to the bathroom to pee and you're not be able to" (MoW 5 - worker1).

"In order to go to the bathroom, we need to enter an environment, remove all the dressing (…) and then put on a whole new dressing, so, for example, sometimes we end up holding back longer because of all this work or we also hold back because this shift is more difficult and so you don't waste that time" (MoW 5 – worker 2).

The quality, adequacy and quantity of PPE contributes to the balance of mental health, in addition to ensuring working conditions and regular breaks.

Good work environment with its organizational culture, make up one of the ingredients of competence (Schwartz, 1998) and opens space for the constitution of cohesive and cooperative collectives.

"The group is very cohesive, we managed it in a short time, I even play with them that in a short time we managed to produce a lot and have a lot of affinity (…) they represent the construction of this here. Everything we have achieved to date has been built up by everyone who is here, we arrived with a blank piece of paper and put each piece together, everything was thought by us" (MoW 1 – worker 8).

However, interpersonal relationships and communication between teams present the usual conflicts between categories of hospital environments.

"The issue of doctors fitting in and not standing on the pretext of ego. We try to balance the multi teams, both nursing, and physiotherapists, anyway… And soon, because, every hour they ask for something and sometimes the institution does not have it registered and they do not want to understand, so for me it is a daily struggle in relation to that" MoW 1 – worker 6).

Although the amount of compensation being seen as positive and motivating, it does not prevent many professionals from needing other links to supplement their income, generating an overload of work:

"The salary floor here is a little better than the others, but I still think it can improve, so that we don't have to have another job and can support myself with this one only" (MoW 5– worker 4).

"The issue is controversial: I think the vast majority here work in two places, so there is this overload" (MoW 5– worker 1).

"I know people who work in three" (MoW 5– worker 3).

"I know someone who works in four and I don't know how he does it" (MoW 5 – worker 2).

Due to the diversity of origins, of previous works, adapting to the HC environment was also challenging, especially for professionals coming from the private sector: "we suffered so much harassment out there that it became normal for us" (MoW 1 - worker 6).

Issues that should not be overlooked by management, as the greatest challenge is, having the courage to come back for another day of work.

Recognition is essential for the balance of the psychological health of workers, capable of transforming suffering into pleasure [10] when saving lives:

"The most rewarding thing was last week, when we had a patient in her 90s (...) when she was discharged, we took her out of bed, sat her on a chair, and when we were taking her out, she said: 'wait', and she prayed Lord's Prayer, asking for a blessing to all employees, it was gratifying" (MoW 3 - worker 4).

"It is very gratifying to hear the patient thanking you for the care you are taking. One of the patients, I played with her, I said: 'very soon you will be out of here, you're going home', and she said: 'I want to, but sometimes I don't want to, because I will miss you all', hearing this is very gratifying; that feeling of accomplishment, that you are doing a good job" (MoW 3 - worker 1).

We highlight the necessary care for health workers, strengthening the dynamics of recognition that can be given by users, by society, co-workers and fundamentally by the hierarchy. There is a consensus on the high social value of hospital work, however, on the other hand, it can lead to actions of neglect of protection measures due to the urgency of solving the patient's problem [11].

4 Conclusions

Despite the speed imposed by the urgency of responding to the pandemic not allowing the workforce's hiring processes to have an ideal acuity with regard to professional experience in hospitals and in emergencies, there was a cooperation of teams in facing the variability of work. Workers have faced exhausting routines, making complex use of themselves to care for patients. They experienced overload, exhaustion, and the feeling of powerlessness in the face of the number of deaths and uncertainties. The constant changes of protocols generate insecurity in action. It highlights the importance of dialogue spaces for the strengthening of trust and collectives.

It is noteworthy that incorporating health care for workers "in times of rapid and complex change, such as the case of the Covid-19 pandemic, requires changes in practices that are historically rooted both in the managers involved and, in the Health and Safety at Work teams, that, as a general rule, are excluded from strategic management and accommodated with the naturalization of excluding practices" [12].

That is why we proposed Training Workshops with managers, which are in the process of starting, to raise awareness and create means for a greater understanding of the complexity of work and its transformation.

References

1. Lai, J., et al.: Factors associated with mental health outcomes among health care workers exposed to coronavirus disease 2019. J. Am. Med. Assoc. 3(3), 1–12 (2020)
2. Walton, M., Murray, E., Christian, M.D.: Mental health care for medical staff and affiliated healthcare workers during the COVID-19 pandemic. Eur. Heart J. Acute Cardiovasc. Care 9(3), 241–247 (2020)

3. Daniellou, F., Laville, A., Teiger, C.: Ficção e realidade do trabalho operário. Rev. bras. saúde ocup. **68**(17), 7–13 (1999)
4. Schwartz, Y.: A abordagem do trabalho reconfigura nossa relação com os saberes acadêmicos: as antecipações do trabalho. In: Souza-e-Silva, M.C., Faïta, D. (eds.) Linguagem e Trabalho: construção de objetos de análise no Brasil e na França, pp. 109–126. Cortez, São Paulo (2002)
5. Oddone, I., et al.: Ambiente de trabalho: a luta dos trabalhadores pela saúde. Editora Hucitec, São Paulo (1986)
6. Schwartz, Y., Durrive, L.: Trabalho e Ergologia: Conversas sobre a atividade humana, 2nd edn. EdUFF, Niterói (2010)
7. Vignola, R.C.B., Tucci, A.: Adaptation and validation of the depression, anxiety and stress scale (DASS) to Brazilian Portuguese. J. Affect. Disord. **155**, 104–109 (2014)
8. Mendes, A.M., Ferreira, M.C.: Inventário sobre trabalho e risco de adoecimento – ITRA: instrumento auxiliar de diagnóstico de indicadores críticos no trabalho. In: Mendes, A.M.C. (ed.) Psicodinâmica do Trabalho: teoria, método e pesquisas, pp. 111–126 Casa do Psicólogo, São Paulo (2007)
9. Maslach, C.: Comprendiendo el burnout. Cienc Trab. **11**(32), 37–43 (2009)
10. Dejours, C.: Da psicopatologia à psicodinâmica do trabalho. In: Lancman, S., Sznelwar, L. (eds.) Christophe Dejours:da psicopatologia à psicodinâmica do trabalho. Paralelo 15. Fiocruz, Rio de Janeiro (2004)
11. Silva, C.O.: Vida e Trabalho no Hospital [tese de Doutorado]. Escola Nacional de Saúde Pública-Fiocruz, Rio de Janeiro (2002)
12. Almeida, I.M.: Proteção da saúde dos trabalhadores da saúde em tempos de COVID-19 e respostas à pandemia. Rev. bras. saúde ocup. **45** (2020)

Impact of High Production Demands in Knowledge Transmission and Learning: Contributions of Work Activity Analysis

Cláudia Pereira[1]([✉]) [iD], Catherine Delgoulet[2] [iD], and Marta Santos[1] [iD]

[1] Center for Psychology at University of Porto; Faculty of Psychology and Educational Sciences, University of Porto, Porto, Portugal
{cpereira,marta}@fpce.up.pt
[2] Conservatoire National des Arts et Métiers, CRTD, Paris, France
catherine.delgoulet@lecnam.net

Abstract. Production demands are one of the constraints that challenges work activity, knowledge transmission and learning in workplace.

In order to understand, through the analysis of real work activity, how working conditions within a context based on a pull flow model interferes with knowledge transmission and learning, a case study was conducted within a specific and crucial function in a Lithograph production line in a Portuguese metalomechanic company. Data was collected through the analysis of the real work activity of Printing Lithographers (PL) and Auxiliary Printing Lithographers (APL).

Data show that PL is a function with high variability and fluctuating demands, in a pull flow logic, that affects knowledge transmission and learning opportunities: these occurs through brief/momentary explanations and demonstrations during production, depending on current problems and on PL' availability.

The results underpin the pertinence and originality of the study in terms of understanding the impact that certain working conditions have on knowledge transmission and learning in pull flow organizations, particularly in the Portuguese context, and contributes also to scientific enrichment about the importance of using work analysis in real work contexts.

Keywords: Work analysis · Work conditions · Knowledge transmission · Learning

1 Introduction: Working Conditions and Its Relations with Knowledge Transmission and Learning

In light of the contributions of Work Psychology and Ergonomics of the Activity, studies on knowledge transmission between workers and learning in workplace should consider the understanding and analysis of work activity and its conditions, since these have an impact on the way that knowledge transmission and learning can occur in professional contexts (e.g., [1, 2]).

N. L. Black et al. (Eds.): IEA 2021, LNNS 219, pp. 516–523, 2021.
https://doi.org/10.1007/978-3-030-74602-5_72

In different activity sectors (e.g., health, manufacturing, transportation, aviation, construction), several studies on working conditions, and their impact on dimensions such as health, safety, the activity itself, refer to constraints like physical demands, related to heavy load lifting; painful postures; repetitive efforts; cognitive demands, such as extensive planning, work coordination; temporal and task demands, related to production pressures, meeting deadlines, workload, that affects performance and occurrence of errors at work (e.g., [3–7]).

In the particular case of operational activities in industry, the sector in which our case study fits, the issues of physical (physical load of materials/equipment; postures) and cognitive demands (complex tasks; having to learn new things; having to solve unforeseen problems) that affect performance at work; low autonomy in the way the work is carried out; and work intensity, namely working at high speed, working to tight deadlines, and with pace determinants (speed of machines; direct demands from others, direct control) are particularly relevant [8, 9].

These conditions reflect, in part, the presence of lean production practices, which are demanding (due to frenetic working rhythms) and common in several industries, since they imply a focus on reducing wasteful activities while expecting the optimization of productivity and quality, considering customers' demands, and with cost effective [10, 11]. We refer, in specific, to pull flow practices, which aim to facilitate production so that companies produce the necessary quantities on time (pull) and which imply the definition of product families (e.g., by sizes, type of material to be produced, size of orders) sustained and accompanied by layout arrangements (flow) [12].

This form of organization then reveals the presence of the productive component of the activity (action object-oriented and motivated by the performance of tasks). But, work activity also has a subject-oriented component, that is, a constructive activity, directed to the development of knowledge, skills, conceptualizations developed from the productive activity, to this one and that transforms back the workers' knowledge [13]. Constructive activity has positive effects on learning and knowledge transmission, since it is also through contact with concrete work situations that learning occurs, experience is developed and transmission is sustained (e.g., [14–16]). However, it is known that these processes are conditioned by issues such as work intensification (which encompasses the working conditions described above), precarious employment or flexible management practices [1]. So, we wonder: in workplaces with these kind of constraints (some more presents than others depending on the context), in what form it is present knowledge transmission and learning opportunities?

The contributions illustrated support our understanding of production demands as being a constraint that continues to challenge the workers' activity, specially within contexts based on a pull flow organizational model which limits the possibilities of anticipating future work and reinforces flexibility and reactivity. However, studies on the impact that high production demands have on knowledge transmission and learning in industry (namely in some types of industry and in the Portuguese context) has not been found. To address this gap, our aim was to investigate, through the analysis of real work activity, how working conditions within a context based on a pull flow model interferes with knowledge transmission and learning within a specific and crucial function for the business in a lithography production line from a industrial metalomechanic company.

2   Methodology

2.1   Research Questions

To conduct the research on the issue and goal exposed, a case study with a practical purpose [2] is been conducted. The following research questions were defined: i) What are the most critical working conditions in the lithography activity? ii) How does the transmission of knowledge in daily life occur and what learning opportunities are there for workers? iii) What impact do critical working conditions have on the carrying out of knowledge transmission initiatives and on workers' learning?

It is not the object of this text, but it is important to mention that one of the objectives of the project in which this case study is integrated will be to define, in light of the data obtained, actions that enhance the transmission of knowledge and learning in the context.

2.2   Context and Participants

The case study is being carried out in a Portuguese metalomechanic company. Part of this company's core business is the production of metal packaging (from sheet metal cutting, to printing the engravings, and packaging assembly).

After an initial analysis of the different areas of activity (analysis of micro-demographics data, understandings on HR positioning in relation to the areas and impact on the business), it was decided that the research would be on one of the two production lines in the area of lithography (roughly 20 workers on both production lines). The factors underlying this decision are the fact that it is one of the most critical areas for the company, because of the type of work it entails, the demographic characterization of the teams (it will be the second most aged of the company in the next 5 years), and the importance for the business.

The participants are three Printing Lithographers (PL), that assume the responsibility for the quality' control of engraving and colors on tinplate and the formal role of seniors and experts, responsible for transmitting their knowledge to APL, aged between 37 and 46 years; and three Auxiliary Printing Lithographers (APL), aged between 23 and 37 years, of one of the production lines. The seniority of these workers varies between 3 and 26 years. Workers are organized in teams of one PL and one APL in each shift (with the presence of a third/four worker responsible for placing the tinplates at the beginning of the production line). The teams work in three weekly rotating shifts between morning, afternoon and night (work 3 × 8).

2.3   Data Collected and Procedure

Based on an activity-oriented approach [17], the focus of the data collection was the work activity of PL and APL.

Data was collected through the analysis of the real work activity: through systematic observations and in-hand records of workers' verbalizations to characterize working conditions. This collection was intended to answer the research questions, but also to develop materials that were discussed with workers, Human Resources (HR) and Department leader. These materials were: 1) a scheme of the productive process, consisted of the main operations, resources used, and workers involved [18]; 2) activity chronicles using Actograph® [19] on the most critical activity of PL (quality' control of engraving and colors on tinplate), by systematically recording this critical task in 15 different orders (big and small orders; orders from the same product and from different products); and, 3) scheme with 22 tasks to be learned by the APL, according to their degree of difficulty of learning, developed from the workers' perceptions about the difficulty of the tasks (the identification of the tasks was made from the combination of observations and analysis of internal documents). The data collected and organized in these materials were analyzed in an integrated way.

3 Results

3.1 High Production Demands Revealed Through Work Analysis

The work analysis conducted (and materialized in the scheme of the productive process and activity chronicles of quality' control of engraving and colors on tinplate) allowed to constitute the production dynamics in the line, showing that PL is a work with high variability and fluctuating demands, in a pull flow logic. In every shift workers receive the orders' sheet (organized with the clients' orders and according with the size of tinplates, the size of the orders, or the type of product to print), and have to carry out as many orders as possible (if they do not complete all orders, these are continued by colleagues of the next shift). These orders can be delivered once per shift, or, in case production is responding quickly to orders, more than once per shift. The orders' sheet workers receive differs mostly according to the number of orders from customers and the number of orders they can respond to in a shift varies: there are days where they have multiple small orders (e.g., orders up to two thousand tinplates) and different products (e.g., industrial paint cans; oil cans; specific oil cans for cars); in others fewer orders, but larger (e.g., six thousand tinplates) and with similar products (e.g., dry shampoos for different types of hair and deodorants).

In addition, the control of the quality of engraving and colors of the tinplate it's a task that requires a high attention and thoroughness in order to reduce printing errors and avoid waste of material for the company. This task is accompanied by an intense noise emitted by the printing machines. And, although they have to produce as many orders as possible, this is conditioned by the voluntary interruptions they sometimes have to make in the production flow, to correct imperfections, or by the unpredictable and frequent shutdowns that occur in almost every orders' production in the machines due to failures (e.g., jammed sheets; lack of tinplates in the machines).

The results show also the impossibility, for workers, to anticipate how many orders will be completed and the performance criteria to carry out as many orders as possible in a shift, assuring quality product and avoiding errors and waste of material, revealing, thereby, the existence of high production demands of clients, and as a consequence, high work rhythm. Although not yet sufficiently explored, this complexity of work that combines multiple demands (e.g., quality, optimization of productivity, efficiency, responsibility, flexibility, reactivity) and its conditions of realization (work 3×8) are seen as enablers of negative impact on health, with emphasis on generalized fatigue.

3.2   Impacts on Knowledge Transmission and Learning

The working conditions exposed illustrate the absence of specific moments for transmission or learning, being the focus the production of orders. The workers state that these conditions make it hard to plan or anticipate moments for the transmission in the workplace. We have found that, besides an initial and short (roughly 16 h) training of framing in the function, there are only occasional short trainings, given by external professional technicians and on specific technical issues (e.g., cleaning of some equipment's in machines), leaving the transmission in the day-to-day conditioned by the high production demands. The knowledge transmission occurs through brief/momentary explanations and demonstrations during production, depending on current problems and on PL' availability.

Regarding APL learning, the results, in particular from the scheme with tasks to be learned by the APL, according to their degree of difficulty of learning, reveal that most of the tasks are perceived with an intermediate level of difficulty (e.g., changing equipment on the machines; preparing the next order), also mentioning that the most difficult to learn (e.g., learning how to insert the right amounts of water and ink into the machines; making adjustments to the colors in the patterns) are also those that imply a greater permanence in the function, to face new orders and new problems, in order to gain experience. However, we found that it is only in PL breaks that APL stays in charge (the rest of the time they support PL work), which is understood by them as something that slows down the learning process and the construction of experience, trust and autonomy at work.

It was also realized that the company doesn't provide conditions for knowledge transmission, but expects it to happen in day-to-day work. Thus, the discussion with HR and Department leader around the materials produced were understood as a first step towards understanding the need to think of ways of knowledge transmission (e.g., through training actions) for learning the PL function.

4   Discussion

4.1   A Hybrid Work Activity, but Production Above All?

Work analysis on PL function reveals the existence of a hybrid work activity [20], where high production demands are a central element in the way the activity is carried out daily and managed by workers, privileging performance criteria like production and quality, thus, compromising the constructive activity and the knowledge transmission and learning of this function.

It became clear that the work activity occurs in a pull flow model, under certain norms and procedures. Although these lean practices consider that workers have the right-duty to interrupt production flow when anomalies or defects are identified and they must be encouraged to participate in decisions about production, thus favoring learning and responsibility [10], we realized that is only the possibility for workers to intervene/interrupt production in the face of defects that appears to happens in this company.

The results on the working conditions and the workers' perception on knowledge transmission and learning, sustain the need and importance of defining moments for transmission to promote learning [21]. In particular, we believe that the fact that the APL only have the chance to assume the function in the PL breaks, limiting, for example, the possibility of encountering unforeseen challenges and having to solve them, and the impossibility they have to reach certain degrees of difficulty of learning tasks, can be critical issues for them (for their learning and the prosecution of the work) since these are known as elements that influence workplace learning [9, 16].

The data allow us to anticipate that it is also a critical issue to the health of PL, because the way they face knowledge transmission relies on an expectation to preserve their own health (e.g. reducing fatigue, if there's a APL with sufficient knowledge and ability to cover their breaks, which is not always the case). Yet it is necessary to collect more data in the field to sustain this reflection.

The discussion with HR and Department leader points towards the importance that a possible investment in the development of their workers and improvement of work situations can preserve their health while maintaining performance criteria.

4.2 Contributions of Work Analysis

In the scope of this study, work analysis assumed an important role in four aspects: to guide the researcher in the form of data collection; in the explanation of the object of study through an activity-oriented approach; in the recognition, by workers, of the constraints associated with their work; and, to enhance the analysis and discussion of the results.

It was this approach that made possible the clear comprehension of the PL work activity, its conditions and constraints, and the understanding of the situations of knowledge transmission and learning present in the production line. Assuming the practical purpose of this case study and that the work analysis, beyond the study and understanding of the work, contributes to clarify or raise questions with companies' key players and, consequently, improve the contexts and situations of work at its end [2, 22], it was also important to support the development of tools for reflection and discussion with the company, with potential use in the design of actions to transmit knowledge and content that enhance learning.

Despite its valuable contributions, it is also worth mentioning some constraints associated with the researcher's activity in the analysis of the actual work activity, already evidence in the literature [2], namely, the difficulty of asking questions due to some physical constraints, such as the need to maintain some physical distance in order not to hinder the required movements of the activity and the intense noise of the production machines.

5 Conclusion

Research has already shown how work intensification has effects on economic performance in manufacturing (e.g., [23]) and on workers' health (e.g., [24]). This study aimed at understand how working conditions within a context based on a pull flow model interferes with knowledge transmission and learning within a specific and crucial function for the business of an industrial company.

Results showed that high production demands (followed by high work rhythm) condition moments of knowledge transmission and learning opportunities and that work analysis had an important contribution to demonstrate the real activity and to put these issues in discussion with company decision power' interlocutors.

We believe that these first results underpin the pertinence and originality of the study in terms of understanding the impact that certain working conditions have on knowledge transmission and learning in pull flow organizations, particularly in the Portuguese context where scientific evidence is lacking in this regard, thus promoting its discussion. The study also contributes to scientific enrichment about the importance of using work analysis in real work contexts.

The next steps in the study are to pursue the work with workers, HR and leaders, in order to deepen the analysis and identify ways to adjust some of the current circumstances in order to enhance transmission and learning in the workplace.

Acknowledgments. This work was supported by the FCT under Grant PD/BD/143112/2018.

References

1. Cloutier, E., Ledoux, E., Fournier, P.-S.: Knowledge transmission in light of recent transformations in the workplace. Relations industrielles/Ind. Relat. **67**(2), 304–324 (2012)
2. Leplat, J.: Repères pour l'analyse de l'activité en ergonomie. Presses Universitaires de France, Paris (2008)
3. DiDomenico, A., Nussbaum, M.: Interactive effects of physical and mental workload on subjective workload assessment. Int. J. Ind. Ergon. **38**, 977–983 (2008)
4. Hancock, P.A., Williams, G., Miyake, S.: Influence of task demand characteristics on workload and performance. Int. J. Aviat. Psychol. **5**(1), 63–86 (1995)
5. Hwang, S.L., Yau, Y.J., Lin, Y.T., Chen, J.H., Huang, T.H., Yenn, T.C., Hsu, C.C.: Predicting work performance in nuclear power plants. Saf. Sci. **46**(7), 1115–1124 (2009)
6. Memarian, B., Mitropoulos, P.: Production practices affecting worker task demands in concrete operations: a case study. Work **53**, 535–550 (2016)
7. Sluiter, K.: High-demand jobs: age-related diversity in work ability. Appl. Ergon. **37**, 429–440 (2006)
8. Eurofound: Metal industry: working conditions and job quality. Working Conditions Survey (2014)
9. Eurofound and International Labour Organization: Working conditions in a global perspective. Publications Office of the European Union, Luxembourg, and International Labour Organization, Geneva (2019)
10. Forza, C.: Work organization in lean production and traditional plants: what are the differences? Int. J. Oper. Prod. Manag. **16**(2), 42–62 (1996)

11. Soliman, M., Saurin, T., Anzanello, M.: The impacts of lean production on the complexity of socio-technical systems. Int. J. Prod. Econ. **197**, 342–357 (2018)
12. Doolen, T., Hacker, M.: A review of lean assessment in organizations: an exploratory study of lean practices by electronics manufacturers. J. Manuf. Syst. **24**(1), 55–67 (2005)
13. Rabardel, P., Samurçay, R.: From artifact to instrument-mediated learning. In: International Symposium Organized by the Center for Activity Theory and Developmental Work Research. University of Helsinki, Finland, pp. 1–23 (2001)
14. Delgoulet, C., Gaudart, C., Chassaing, K.: Entering the workforce and on-the-job skills acquisition in the construction sector. Work **41**(2), 155–164 (2012)
15. Thébault, J., Delgoulet, C., Fournier, P.S., Gaudart, C., Jolivet, A.: La transmission à l'épreuve des réalités du travail. Educ. Permanente **198**, 85–99 (2014)
16. Tourmen, C., Leroux, A., Beney, S.: What is learned during the first moments of work? Work **41**, 5231–5234 (2012)
17. Daniellou, F., Rabardel, P.: Activity-oriented approaches to ergonomics: some traditions and communities. Theor. Issues Ergon. Sci. **6**(5), 353–357 (2005)
18. Pereira, C., Santos, M., Delgoulet, C.: HR challenges for knowledge transmission in a Portuguese industrial lithography company. Actes du 55ème Congrès de la SELF, L'activité et ses frontières. Penser et agir sur les transformations de nos sociétés. Paris, 11, 12 et 13 janvier 2021, pp. 178–183 (2020)
19. SymAlgo Techonologies: Actograph® (2018)
20. Rémery, V., Markaki, V.: Travailler et former: l'activité hybride des tuteurs. Educ. Permanente **206**, 47–60 (2016)
21. Maubant, P.: Penser l'apprentissage pour penser la transmission à autrui. In: Wittorski, R. (ed.) Comprendre la transmission du travail, pp. 123–142. Champ Social, Nîmes (2015)
22. Teiger, C., Montreuil, S.: The foundations and contributions of ergonomics work analysis in training programmes. Saf. Sci. **23**(2/3), 81–95 (1996)
23. Valeyre, A.: Forms of work intensification and economic performance in French manufacturing. East. Econ. J. **30**(4), 643–658 (2004)
24. Volkoff, S., Buisset, C., Mardon, C.: Does intense time pressure at work make older employees more vulnerable? A statistical analysis based on a French survey "SVP50." Appl. Ergon. **41**(6), 754–762 (2010)

Co-design of a Learning Analytics Tool by Computer Scientists and Teachers: The Difficult Emergence of a Common World

Joël Person(✉) , Christine Vidal-Gomel, Philippe Cottier, and Coline Lecomte

CREN (Centre de Recherche en Education de Nantes), Université de Nantes, Nantes, France
joel.person@univ-nantes.fr

Abstract. We present here the first part of an ongoing study conducted at a French high school, about the co-design of tools exploiting Learning Analytics by teachers and Computer Sciences researchers. The device implemented by the IT specialists hardly meets the conditions that would allow for an effective participation of stakeholders in the design process. The object planned to be designed turns out to be disconnected from the real activity of teachers.

Keywords: Co-design · Learning Analytics · Learning dashboards · Participatory design · Teaching learning activity

1 Introduction

The computer data massively generated within an educational framework is an important thing to consider for educational institutions, which see it as a lever "at the service of pedagogical efficiency" [1]. The emerging technology of Learning Analytics (LA) would make it possible to model learners' behaviours and learning paths, and facilitate the diagnosis, prediction, remediation and personalization of those learning processes for teachers and learners [2]. Once collected and processed through algorithms, the data is made available to stakeholders of the education sector via visualization tools such as Dashboards. Even though most of those tools are implemented in ready-to-use software solutions, those often fall short of meeting the needs of downstream users [3, 4]. Another issue is the lack of data literacy[1] of recipients, who thus cannot properly interpret the information they get [5]. Making teachers participate in designing those tools could contribute to making them more relevant and acceptable to a professional community who, as far as France is concerned, feels "little experienced and little trained in digital technologies" [6]. In this case, the design process gathers together stakeholders from different worlds [7, 8] – teachers in different fields and computer scientists – around a complex object: LA. How can the co-design process work between teachers and computer scientists? What type of devices should be used?

---

[1] "The ability to read, understand, create, and communicate data as information. https://en.wikipedia.org/wiki/Data_literacy, last accessed 2021/01/21.

N. L. Black et al. (Eds.): IEA 2021, LNNS 219, pp. 524–533, 2021.
https://doi.org/10.1007/978-3-030-74602-5_73

The participation of downstream users to the design process is a concern in the field of EIAH[2] [9, 10], as well as Design Ergonomics [11, 12]. The object planned to be designed is complex and requires the mobilization of a design collective [13]. The participatory approach is recognized as a more efficient means of design [14], supported by the use of various tools that help with expression and creation [15]. However, this way of working depends on a specific participatory framework that aims at identifying the roles and areas of expertise of the various participants, as well as the institutional conditions that will ensure their cooperation throughout the design project [11, 12, 16]. In the case of activities relying on the use of digital artefacts and tools, this participatory aspect is particularly important in a context of technological determinism [17].

Moreover, studies conducted in the field of Ergonomics have clearly highlighted that, in order to make the designed object more relevant and efficient, it is useful to inform this kind of participatory process by determining what the typical situations of action and probable future activity of downstream users could be [12, 13, 16, 18]. Without being identical to future situations of use, typical situations of action intend to retain some "psychological fidelity" [19]: it is about understanding in what respects the situation duplicates psychological features of real operations, including task complexity, perceptual skills, decision-making, stress, organisational constraints, difficulties of use, etc.in order to inform the designing process. This reflection is based on the stakeholders' activity and requires the elaboration of intermediary objects [20] that serve as resources for the design process. The simulated situations proposed by Barcellini et al. (op. cit.) fulfil those functions by mobilizing the experience of participants. What happens in the design process when it is based on other types of devices such as, for instance, the games developed in the field of Computer Sciences to design LA-inspired tools [21]? We will address those questions by focusing on the Leap'Num research action project.

2 Field and Methodology

The Leap'Num research action project aims at studying the design and implementation of LA tools in a French high school[3], within the framework of their global digital project. It is in line with the dynamics of innovation supported by the project incubation mission of the Délégation au Numérique Educatif (Delegation for Educational Digital Technologies, DNE)[4]. Within this framework, we will analyze here the design process for a Dashboard informed by LA. Two Computer Sciences researchers, as partners of the project, offered to conduct a "participatory design" workshop built around a game played by five teachers and future potential users. This recreational device aimed at helping them express their needs in terms of learning data and get more familiar with the potentialities of LA [21].

---

[2] French-speaking community of TEL (Technology Enhanced Learning).

[3] The high school was inaugurated at the beginning of the school year 2017. Staff members are selected according to the adequacy between their profile and this project.

[4] The DNE project incubators aim at encouraging the emergence of new digital projects in order to potentially generalize their results.

2.1 Participants

Five teachers volunteered to participate in the project: Mathias and Thierry, physics and chemistry teachers, Daniel and Myriam, foreign languages teachers, and Cécile, a school librarian. They are aged between 36 and 50. They have been working in education for 18 years on average. 3 months prior, they attended a meeting presenting the research project and the group was formed via an enrolling process conducted within the team involved in the high school's digital project. The two computer scientists (Stéphane and Hervé) are teachers-researchers in computer sciences and have been working on the topic of Learning Analytics since 2015. They thus have an "expert" level of knowledge on this technology and its implications for teaching and training systems.

2.2 Situation Observed

The participants gathered in one of the meeting rooms of the establishment in the late afternoon for a duration of 1 h 45 min. The workshop was comprised of 4 successive phases orchestrated by one of the computer scientists (Stéphane) around a design aid tool [21]. The elements of the game (boards with sections, cards) served to trigger and guide a brainstorming session aimed at bringing out the presumed needs of teachers related to LA, and materializing them into a wireframe on paper. The production of this layout at the end of the workshop was meant to provide guidance for the creation of the Dashboard prototype that would later be implemented in a real work situation, with an iterative approach (Fig. 1).

Fig. 1. The wireframe produced at the end of the workshop

2.3 Data Collection

6 exploratory interviews were conducted before the workshop was organised, with the same 5 teachers and the high school headmistress. The topics addressed during these first encounters were related to the stakeholders' professional skills, their relationship

with digital technologies and their knowledge of the ongoing research project. Several visits allowed us to become more familiar with the high school, the staff and some of the available tools such as the ENT (Digital Work Environment).

For the duration of the workshop, two observers[5] took notes on the process, focusing on the participants' progress in the game, their understanding of the instructions, their questions to the facilitator, their manipulation of the cards and post-it notes.

We filmed the workshop session with the consent of the participants. Since self-confrontation sessions could not be conducted immediately afterwards due to the stakeholders' work schedule constraints, we completed our approach with 4 short interviews (SI) conducted with 4 of the teachers (Daniel, Cécile, Thierry and Mathias) and self-confrontation interviews (SCI) [22] conducted with the 7 participants (teachers and computer scientists) between March and July of the same year. During the SCI, the stakeholders were invited to verbalize their feelings regarding their involvement in the session, based on 8 to 10 key sequences from the video that we had selected for them to watch. They were significant moments where points of view that could influence the design process were expressed. Those interviews were also filmed.

2.4 Data Processing

All of the interviews and films were transcribed in writing. It was necessary to watch them multiple times to complete the verbatim account with valuable body language indications that enriched the analysis (turns to speak: whom does the speaker address?; manipulation of the elements of the game). The video was then transcribed and coded using the activity analysis software Actograph® [23], in order to quantify the speaking turns of each participant and identify the topics addressed.

This first phase was refined by means of a predicate-argument framework (PAF) adapted from the COMET method [24]. Developed as a tool for analyzing verbal interactions during collective design processes, COMET is based on the breaking down of a corpus into coded units according to a predicate-argument system. Our PAF, as briefly presented in the table below, was applied to 1319 speaking turns, i.e. 100% of our corpus (Tables 1 and 2).

Table 1. List of predicates and examples of arguments

Predicates	Propose (suggestion, new idea or need related to the Dashboard)	Validate (marks of agreement or confirmation, phatic expressions)	Point of view (opinions, personal or shared representations)	Evoke (personal information input)	Inform (arguments mainly centred on the game)	Question (various interrogations addressed to the computer scientists)
Arguments (Examples)	Functionalities Data Visual	Proposal Question Point of view	Assessment (positive, negative, mixed)	Experience Humour	Game Data Law	Game Visual aspect Access to the data

Through this coding system, we are trying to highlight the sequences that appear to us to be characteristic of the participants' involvement and respective logic during the

---

[5] A postgraduate student and a student in her second year of M.A in Education and Training Sciences.

Table 2. Extract from the coded verbatim account

129	15'00	MG:/So we also need to track what's happening on their smartphones, which means, uh…towards the public, towards their personal phones	Proposes	Tracking *(personal phones)*
130		DT:/Well there, in that case, it's in real time	Informs	Tracking

workshop. We will then proceed to a triangulation by confronting these phases to the various data collected within the framework of a clinical approach of the field and its stakeholders.

3 Results

We present here three types of results: 1) a lack of preparation; 2) a simplistic device; 3) A gap between two professional worlds.

3.1 A Lack of Preparation

Mathias was significantly more involved in the process than his colleagues (24, 94% of the total number of speaking turns). He arrived at the workshop with a very strong interest in the research project, which echoes his own pedagogical practices, notably those relating to the flipped classroom strategy. Conversely, the other participants were diversely involved due to their lack of knowledge of the project and/or the format of the workshop: *"I think we didn't know on what basis we should ask questions"* (Cécile – SI). Thierry questions his position: *"I don't know whether one of these two postures is useful at work: the first one where I'm lost and I don't know what is expected of me, I'm just watching, I'm trying to find my place. And the second one, I've found it but I'm no longer in a creation, research mode, I'm just making information available."* (Thierry – SCI).

The computer scientists' biased choice to orient the design process towards the creation of a Dashboard is retrospectively questioned: *"… but I found it surprising that we were starting with the idea of an interface, because for me, the interface is sort of the outcome of all the process of reflection before on what we want to do, where we want to go, what goals we want to achieve, etc."* (Daniel – SI).

Those remarks bring to light the need for a preliminary time of preparation between teachers and computer scientists. An initial phase of clarification [25] would perhaps have allowed for sharing out the steps of the thinking process between the partners [26], keeping in mind the goals and modalities of the collective design activity. However, it still does not tell us anything about the usefulness of this type of design tool for the teachers' work.

3.2 A Simplistic Device

From the Predicate-Argument coding system, we retain two main elements: on the one hand, the high number of validation marks (27, 98%), indicating a majority of consensual exchanges, and on the other hand, a low number of proposals (9, 25%), which, in what is supposed to be a participatory design workshop, raises questions. We notice that the "Inform" and "Evoke" predicates, which are often used (19, 18% and 16, 08%), are not translated into specific needs. The following extract from the verbatim account, which takes place at the beginning of the workshop, seems to us to be emblematic of proposals that were seemingly unanimously adopted, sometimes in a tacit way (validation through phatic expressions or silence and nodding), without there being a clear positioning or argumentation on the part of the stakeholders. We only find very localized moments of argumentation and counter-argumentation that are typically identified in design-related activities [26]. 6 moments qualify as contradictory exchanges: an attempt at collective synchronization at the beginning of the workshop; the possibility to share the Dashboard with the administrative staff; the competition with non-institutional resources (Youtube); the ethical issue surrounding the tracking of students' equipment; the goals of the profession; the possibility of a heuristic Dashboard (this last exchange occurred between the 2 computer scientists and the two physics and chemistry teachers) (Table 3).

Table 3. Extract from the coded verbatim account

n°	Time	Verbatim accounts	Predicates	Arguments
65	10'41	Mathias: Well to react we need to be able to observe/so we need explicit tracking, we start with this first major idea, I totally agree…in short, we don't really know what they are doing with it, in fact	Proposes Questions	Tracking Students' uses
66		Cécile:/Yes, that's right	Validates	Proposal
67		Magalie: uh-uh	Validates	Proposal

The participants experience a dual approach: they must take ownership of an original design mode that they discover "on the job" under the monitoring of researchers, and get familiar with LA through designing a teaching and learning Dashboard. The proposed design mode implies a simplification that leaves the stakeholders estranged from their professional activity. Of course it comes up in the verbal exchanges through the cases or anecdotes evoked, but it cannot be grasped in all its complexity [27]. For instance, the two physics and chemistry teachers have two different working methods, whether it is for the use of digital tools or the assessment of students. On a different note, during the phase of visualization of the Dashboard, a friendly disagreement arose between Humanities teachers and Sciences Teachers regarding their respective taste for charts. These exchanges bear witness to the existence of certain aspects of the profession that could not be debated in the workshop, in spite of their potential importance for designing new tools.

Thus, as a whole, the teachers seemed to be answering questions only to "play along" without appearing to express real needs in terms of Dashboards or any other LA tool to track students. E.g.: *"we add the geolocation option, since we can ask for whatever we want anyway..."* (Daniel – SC01). However, we do not know what student geolocation will be used for, why teachers are interested in it, or how it relates to the understanding of learning processes, i.e., the stated goal of LA. At the end of the workshop, the indicators suggested by the teachers concerned the consultation of educational resources prescribed on the ENT in order to understand whether and how students used them. The characteristics of the situations in which the Dashboard would be used were not defined. Let's note that this information is already available on the high school's ENT[6].

The format chosen to facilitate the collection of the teachers' needs relies on the game designed by the computer scientists and the representations inscribed therein [10]. This method provides a framework for action but does not really succeed in calling forth the emergence of a common world [8].

3.3 A Gap Between Two Professional Worlds

On the contrary, the computer scientists considered the session to be fruitful in the sense that the teachers' proposals provided enough "material" to develop a Dashboard, in spite of some acknowledged limitations of the device: *"So here, for me, everything is going pretty well, the board's content is extensive, I don't know if I'll be able to meet all the requirements, that's what I'm thinking, but anyway, we have plenty of material to work with."* (Stéphane – SCI).

Furthermore, within the configuration of the workshop, the teachers were seated around a table while one of the two computer scientists, standing up, acted as a facilitator, main interlocutor and decision-maker. Stéphane thus "untangled" a controversial situation: the issue surrounding the tracking of students' personal equipment. Although this request had initially been made by all the teachers, Thierry, who is particularly aware of the questions related to personal data protection due to his position as a RUPN[7], expressed his opposition to it. Technical information on how difficult it is to access students' data were too concise and muddled, the computer scientists did not share much of their knowledge with the teachers regarding the practical modalities of access to these digital traces. Even though they evoked a previous research project and the conditions in which they had been able to carry out the collection of students' personal data, no real answer was given to this question, other than the decision to narrow down the scope of the data collection: *"Ok, so here we lock up the collection...by doing this locally."* (Stéphane, SC01). The design process was thus oriented towards a new direction, announced by the facilitator of the game. No one picked up on the contradiction with the initial decision to follow the activity of students in autonomy, in class, online and outside of the school premises.

Ultimately, this lack of symmetry (in posture, level of expertise, goals) contradicts the notion of "participatory design" by creating a gap between the two worlds.

---

[6] The Digital Work Environment (ENT) E-Lyco is equipped with an integrated module (360°) enabling staff to track students' activities via their digital traces.

[7] RUPN: Referent for educational digital resources and uses. Website Eduscol. https://cache.media.eduscol.education.fr/file/Numerique_educatif/36/2/Missions_du_RUPN_499362.pdf.

4 Discussion: Conditions for Participatory Design

We tried to understand how the co-design of an artefact by teachers and computer scientists could work. The workshop was imposed upon teachers according to the computer scientists' representations, without prior consultation with the teachers and without taking into account their typical situations of action at work [18]. It thus fell short of reflecting the diversity of established uses within a heterogeneous social and technological environment, and did not enable teachers to project themselves in their future activity. LA and the Dashboard only fitted into the world [8] of computer scientists and the game did not fulfil its function as a bridge between their world and the teachers' world; it was too far removed from their professional activity.

The intermediary object [10] implemented is above all a tool for collecting specifications. The stakeholders' differences, be them interpersonal or linked to the specificities of the knowledge they have to transmit, were glossed over in favour of generic choices that do not correspond to any specific learning situation. Moreover, the whole process appears to be detached from the global research project, without any temporal landmarks that would make the various phases – coordination, design and validation – more visible to the stakeholders.

Lastly, it took place in a professional context that is saturated with solicitations [28], against which the temporal resources allocated to teachers turn out to be insufficient, notably to get used to the pervasive technologies that transform their work and that of their students.

The shortcomings we noticed in the device as well as some difficulties to access data that were reported later on, led us to start reengineering it with two volunteer teachers. This co-design work is centred on the analysis of a teaching situation mobilizing digital resources, which they elaborated according to their own experiences and pedagogical goals, and which appears to them as relevant for the mobilization of LA. Therefore, what is at stakes here for us is to "better take into account the diversity and variability of situations and operators" [13] and contribute to establishing the conditions of a real participatory design process.

References

1. MEN Dossier de presse rentrée 2018: L'école de la confiance. https://www.education.gouv.fr/le-numerique-au-service-de-l-ecole-de-la-confiance-3212. Accessed 21 Jan 2021
2. Siemens, G.: Learning analytics: the emergence of a discipline. Am. Behav. Sci. **57**(10), 1380–1400 (2013). https://doi.org/10.1177/0002764213498851
3. Bodily, R., Verbert, K.: Review of research on student-facing learning analytics dashboards and educational recommender systems. IEEE Trans. Learn. Technol. **10**(4), 405–418 (2017). https://doi.org/10.1109/TLT.2017.2740172
4. Matcha, W., Gasevic, D., Pardo, A.: A systematic review of empirical studies on learning analytics dashboards: a self-regulated learning perspective. IEEE Trans. Learn. Tech. **3**(2), 226–245 (2020). https://doi.org/10.1109/TLT.2019.2916802
5. Echeverria, V., Martinez-Maldonado, R., Shum, S.B., Chiluiza, K., Granda, R., Conati, C.: Exploratory versus explanatory visual learning analytics: driving teachers' attention through educational data storytelling. J. Learn. Anal. **5**(3), 72–97 (2018). https://doi.org/10.18608/jla.2018.53.6

6. Cnesco: Numérique et apprentissages scolaires. Cnesco (2020). https://www.cnesco.fr/fr/num erique-enseignements-et-apprentissages/. Accessed 21 Jan 2021
7. Bucciarelli, L.L.: An ethnographic perspective on engineering design. Des. Stud. **9**(3), 159–168 (1988). https://doi.org/10.1016/0142-694X(88)90045-2
8. Béguin, P.: Innovation et cadre sociocognitif des interactions concepteurs-opérateurs: une approche développementale. Le travail humain **70**(4), 369–390 (2007)
9. Linard, M.: Concevoir des environnements pour apprendre: l'activité humaine, cadre organisateur de l'interactivité technique. Sciences et Technologies de l'Information et de la Communication pour l'Éducation et la Formation **8**(3), 211–238 (2001)
10. Cottier, P., Choquet, C., Tchounikine, P.: Repenser l'ingénierie des EIAH pour des enseignants concepteurs. In: Dinet, J. (dir.) Usages, usagers et compétences informationnelles au XXIème siècle, pp. 159–193. Hermes Lavoisier, Paris (2008). ISBN 978-2-7462-2193-2
11. Darses, F., Reuzeau, F.: 24. Participation des utilisateurs à la conception des systèmes et dispositifs de travail. In: Falzon, P. (ed.) Ergonomie, pp. 405–420. PUF, Paris (2004). https://doi.org/10.3917/puf.falzo.2004.01.0405
12. Folcher, V.: Conception pour et dans l'usage: La maîtrise d'usage en conduite de projet. J. Hum. Mediat. Interact./Revue des Interactions Humaines Médiatisées **16**(1), 39–60 (2015)
13. Béguin, P., Cerf, M.: Formes et enjeux de l'analyse de l'activité pour la conception des systèmes de travail. Activités, **1**(1) (2004). https://doi.org/10.4000/activites.1156
14. Carroll, J.M.: Encountering others: reciprocal openings in participatory design and user-centered design. Hum.–Comput. Interact. **11**(3), 285–290 (1996)
15. Sanders, E.B.N., Stappers, P.J.: Co-creation and the new landscapes of design. Co-design **4**(1), 5–18 (2008). https://doi.org/10.1080/15710880701875068
16. Barcellini, F., Van Belleghem, L., Daniellou, F.: Design projects as opportunities for the development of activities. In: Falzon, P. (ed.) Constructive Ergonomics, pp. 150–163. CRC Press, Roca Baton (2014)
17. Fluckiger, C.: Innovations numériques et innovations pédagogiques à l'école. Recherches **66**, 119–134 (2017)
18. Daniellou, F.: L'ergonomie dans la conduite de projets de conception de systèmes de travail. In: Falzon, P. (ed.) Ergonomie, pp. 359–373. PUF, Paris (2004). https://doi.org/10.3917/puf.falzo.2004.01.0359
19. Baker, S., Marshall, E.: Simulators for training and the evaluation of operator performance. In: Bainbridge, L., Ruiz Quintanilla, S.A. (eds.) Developing Skills with Information Technology, pp. 293–312. Wiley, Chichester (1989)
20. Vinck, D.: De l'objet intermédiaire à l'objet-frontière. Revue d'anthropologie des connaissances **3**(1), 51–72 (2009)
21. Gilliot, J.M., Iksal, S., Medou, D., Dabbebi, I.: Conception participative de tableaux de bord d'apprentissage. In: Proceedings of IHM'18: 30e Conférence Francophone sur l'Interaction Homme-Machine, pp. 119–127, Brest, France (2018)
22. Mollo, V., Falzon, P.: Auto-and allo-confrontation as tools for reflective activities. Appl. Ergon. **35**(6), 531–540 (2004)
23. Boccara, V., Delgoulet, C., Zara-Meylan, V., Barthe, B., Gaillard, I., Meylan, S.: The role and positioning of observation in ergonomics approaches: a research and design project. In: les auteurs Congress of the International Ergonomics Association, pp. 1821–1828. Springer, Cham (August 2018)
24. Darses, F., Détienne, F., Falzon, P., Visser, W.: COMET. A method for analysing collective design processes. Research report RR-4258, INRIA (2001).
25. Daniellou, F.: Des fonctions de la simulation des situations de travail en ergonomie. Activités **4**(2) (2007). https://doi.org/10.4000/activites.1696

26. Darses, F., Falzon, P.: La conception collective: une approche de l'ergonomie cognitive. In: de Terssac, G., Friedberg, E. (eds.) Coopération et conception, pp. 123–135. Octarès, Toulouse (France) (1996)
27. Goigoux, R.: Les schèmes de régulation de l'activité des enseignants. Recherche en éducation **33**, 42–50 (2018). https://doi.org/10.4000/ree.2067
28. Lantheaume, F.: Tensions, ajustements, crise dans le travail enseignant: un métier en redéfinition. Pensée plurielle **2**, 49–56 (2008). https://doi.org/10.3917/pp.018.0049

How to Train for Everyday Work - A Comparative Study of Non-technical Skill Training

Gesa Praetorius[1,2](✉) [iD], Steven C. Mallam[1] [iD], and Salman Nazir[1] [iD]

[1] Faculty of Technology, Natural Sciences and Maritime Sciences, University of South-Eastern Norway, Borre, Norway
gesa.praetorius@usn.no
[2] Linnaeus University, 39281 Kalmar, Sweden

Abstract. This paper presents a comparative study of training of non-technical skills in the maritime and lignite power domains. Non-technical skills (NTS) are the cognitive, social and personal resource skills that complement technical skills in operations within high-risk domains. Training NTS is essential to maintain safety in operational contexts, such as onboard a merchant vessel or in the operation of a lignite power plant. Contextual interviews and observations have been conducted across 8 operator training courses, three maritime and five lignite power. The results indicate that the training approaches and their execution differs greatly despite having a common theoretical basis. While training in the observed maritime courses often combined longer theoretical lectures with group exercises and high-fidelity simulations, the focus of the training remained on the use of specific NTS techniques or tools to prevent accidents and incidents. In contrast to this approach, the training in the lignite power domain primarily focused on how to integrate selected NTS into daily operations. While the lignite training also utilized incident examples and shorter lectures, the focus remained on simulating everyday work tasks and to apply newly learned practices as part of routine operations and standard operational procedures. Further, trainees in the lignite training courses were empowered to take charge of their learning processes, as parts of the training let them recreate situations from their work within the simulator. This article highlights lessons learned from each domain with the goal of improving training practices for NTS in high-risk operations.

Keywords: Maritime Resource Management · Crew Resource Management · CRM · Non-technical skills · Safety training · Training simulators

1 Introduction

Maritime vessels and lignite power plants can be considered as complex socio-technical systems operating in high-risk domains. While each industry provides an essential service to society, their operations are inherently dangerous and adverse events, such as accidents, may have severe consequences for the general public and the environment.

© The Author(s), under exclusive license to Springer Nature Switzerland AG 2021
N. L. Black et al. (Eds.): IEA 2021, LNNS 219, pp. 534–542, 2021.
https://doi.org/10.1007/978-3-030-74602-5_74

Thus, training operators in how to adapt to changes in operational contexts, deal with the complexity arising from the many variables that may affect each system and beyond the operators' control, as well as to learn how to act flexibly in the event of disturbances, are essential for safe and efficient operations [1].

While operator training until the late 1970s often focused on technical skills, such as being an expert navigator or hold fundamental knowledge of chemical processes, non-technical skills training has since gained increasing popularity. Non-technical skills (NTS) can be defined as "*the cognitive, social and personal resources skills that complement technical skills, and contribute to safe and efficient task performance*" [2, p.1]. These skills are often divided into seven areas: situation awareness, decision making, communication, teamwork, leadership, as well as the ability to manage stress and cope with fatigue [3].

NTS training stems from the aviation domain where several accidents by the late 1970s had been attributed to human error. Investigations identified deficiencies in coordination of work, communication and decision making as root causes. One of the prominent accidents often associated with the development of NTS training, which is often referred to as Crew Resource Management (CRM), is the collision of two aircraft on Tenerife in 1977. Decision making, fatigue and leadership were identified as causes for the accident that resulted in 583 fatalities [1]. Because of this and other adverse events, the aviation industry started to investigate pilot error and to develop courses focused on how to prevent these unwanted outcomes. The first CRM course was developed by NASA and launched in the late 1970s [4]. While CRM initially was intended to only include staff in the cockpit, it has gradually been developed and adapted for a multitude of programs including air traffic controllers, and maintenance staff [3].

CRM for NTS training has since been adopted by several of high-risk industries, such as in the healthcare, maritime, and nuclear power domains [5]. The courses typically encompass a mixture of classroom-based lectures, computer-based training modules, and group discussions often complemented by simulator training. Further, courses also often make use of exercises, including discussions of incidents and accidents [6].

2   Aim and Research Questions

This paper presents findings from an exploratory study within the maritime and lignite power domains with a focus on how NTS are trained within each domain. The aim is to identify potential improvements and lessons to learn for NTS training approaches in complex settings.

The following questions have guided the data collection and analysis:

- How are NTS trained within each of the two domains?
- What are the commonalities and differences in the training approaches among two domains?
- What lessons can be learned to inspire NTS training approaches in high-risk environments?

3   Methodology

The methodological approach in this study has been explorative, using observations and contextual interviews. Three maritime and five lignite power plan training courses focused on NTS training were observed. The observations were combined with contextual interviews [7] with instructors and trainers to increase the understanding for the learning objectives and design of each training course.

3.1   Maritime Training

Three maritime non-technical skills courses were observed during 2018 for this study. The courses were provided as Maritime Resource Management (MRM) providing NTS training for operators serving in different departments onboard. An overview of the courses is presented in Table 1.

Table 1. Maritime Non-Technical Skills (NTS) Training Courses

Course	Organizer	Format	Participants	Participants' background
Course 1	Oil & gas company	Simulations, lectures, group discussions	14	Bridge officers, engineers, deck personnel
Course 2	Swedish Naval College	Lectures, group exercises and group discussions	20	Navy officers and reserve officers
Course 3	Swedish maritime academy	Lectures, group discussions, seminars, simulations	31	Maritime students

The first course was provided for operators working onboard special purpose vessels within the oil and gas domain. The participants of the course came from different departments within the same company and some of them serving together on the same vessel. The second course observed was provided by the Swedish Naval College. The participants were active navy officers, as well as people serving in the military reserve force of the Swedish Armed Forces. The third course visited was held at a Swedish maritime academy with maritime trainees in the last year of the BSc education in marine engineering (n = 10) and nautical science (n = 21)

3.2   Lignite Power Plant Training

The Lignite Power Plant (LPP) training courses were part of operator training provided on behalf of a large power company. All courses were provided by same independent training provider.

Five training courses for operators of LPPs in Germany were observed during the Spring and Fall 2019. The courses were short training solutions (4–5 days in duration). The training program is organized into a stepwise system, where five main courses running from basic technical skills (Courses 1 and 2) to more specific operations and tasks (Courses 3–5) for operators at differing points in their career. These multi-day courses contain a mixture of lectures, simulation scenarios and discussions, and are required for continued certification, as well as promotion to more senior positions (e.g. shift supervisor).

As all courses contain both technical and non-technical skill training elements, the courses which explicitly focus on NTS training and skills were visited across four separate weeks (Courses 3 and 4), with four separate pools of trainees. In total, approximately 50 h of training were observed during these visits with 18 differing control room operators. In the advanced courses, trainee numbers are kept low, with 3–4 operators typically trained together in a group across an entire week.

4 Results

4.1 Maritime NTS Training

The maritime NTS courses observed combined a mixture of teaching methods, including group discussions, lectures focused on theoretical concepts underlying NTS, and simulator exercises in full mission bridge and engine-room simulators. The lectures focused on generic knowledge of NTS, while group discussions and simulator exercises were often based on previous accidents and incidents, sometimes using incident reports as basis for discussions and for simulation exercise design. The training courses were provided by experienced instructors who formerly served within either the Navy or Merchant fleet, complemented by expert lecturers on certain topics. In one of the courses, the theoretical lectures on situation awareness, teamwork, decision-making and leadership were provided by a former airline pilot.

The lectures differed in depth and lengths between the courses, but generally covered situation awareness, decision-making, the effects of fatigue and stress management, communication, teamwork and leadership. Several of the involved lecturers chose to present theoretical concepts, such as Endsley's model of situation awareness [8], while others relied on examples from the aviation domain, or previous experiences from working onboard to explain NTS. Furthermore, all three courses used examples from accidents within the lectures to exemplify the loss of certain NTS. In addition to theory, techniques and tools, such as closed-loop communication, challenge-response, short-term strategy or FORDEC (facts, options, risks/benefits, decision, execution check) [9], were taught in the classroom-based lectures.

Two of the three courses used extensive time for exercises in high-fidelity simulators to facilitate the application of learned techniques and knowledge within settings resembling close to real life operations. During the simulations, different approaches for role distribution and responsibilities in the team were used. In the course for the oil and gas company, the participants were encouraged to exchange roles and positions to increase the mutual understanding for each other's work. In the the course provided to the, the roles were rotated so that each participant was in command of the team at least once. However, no exchange of positions and roles between engine-room and bridge team were conducted. This can be explained as the course being directed towards students in maritime degree programs with a limited experience of working onboard. As a consequence, participating in these simulations does not only serve to train NTS, but also roles and responsibilities, as well as familiarization with the different technologies on the bridge and engine-room.

In both courses the simulator scenarios were designed to challenge the participants. This included, amongst other things, heavy weather conditions, fire in the engine-room, equipment not functioning properly, or the need to make modifications to a planned operation or voyage based on a sudden change in the operational context. One of the instructors explained that simulators are the basis of a learning arena in which participants can practice operations in a safe space, where MRM or NTS are integrated with technical skills. Further, all three courses used accidents and incidents as examples to emphasize the importance of NTS for operations in high-risk systems. In one course, simulation exercises were built on incidents that had occurred in the company, while another course used accident reports as basis for group discussions, in which the trainees were asked to identify important NTS, or the lack thereof, based on official investigation reports.

None of the three courses used questionnaires, behavioral markers or other forms of formative or summative assessment to evaluate the training in relation to the desired learning objectives and goals. While the course participants were asked to provide a course evaluation, these evaluations did not relate to NTS or NTS learning goals. This is interesting to note as the courses provide what is needed to gain, or maintain, certification of human element and bridge, or engine-room, resource management as required to be able to serve in a commanding position onboard a vessel.

4.2 Lignite Power Plant NTS Training

The LPP courses primarily focused on operator training through high-fidelity simulator training combined with short lectures and exercises on decision making, communication and leadership. In particularly, Course 3 contains two days where lectures and exercises on NTS were mixed with simulation scenarios and discussions. Further, accident examples from the process and aviation domains were used as examples of NTS in operations which were used as cases to discuss amongst trainees. In comparison to the maritime domain, the main course instructor did not have operational experience within an LPP. Instead, he had an engineering background complemented by pedagogics and didactic training.

Within the observed courses, short lectures and exercises were carried out not in a separated classroom or lecture space, but rather within the simulator environment itself. According to one of the instructors, the goal of the course's NTS training is to improve the overall teamwork among plant operators, including the shift supervisors, and to increase the operators' awareness of the importance of clear communication and joint decision making amongst shift teams. However, most parts of the observed training courses were focused on technical skill training through simulations rather than NTS training. As the plant operation is very complex in itself, the instructor explained that learning is increased if the trainees are not exposed to extraordinary circumstances, but rather practice how to regain control and return to normal operations after a low frequency event, such as a start-up of operations after a power outage. Normal operations, according to the instructor, are already complex enough to pose regular challenges to the trainees, which makes it unnecessary to pre-plan incidents or build exercises upon earlier accidents.

Within the courses observed, leadership was generally trained by operators being able to take the role of shift supervisor during parts of the simulated operations. Communication was trained first as a single exercise without simulation (see [10] for a detailed description) and later integrated into a specific operational simulation, especially through trigger questions during the debriefing after an exercise. During the exercises the operators mostly remained in the same role that they would normally have within the shift team at their specific LPP. Only in one case, as none of the participants were currently working as shift supervisor, the most experienced operator was asked to step into this role.

Further, in two of the observations it was noted that parts of the training simulation were based on the trainees' experience. Each day of the course ended with an hour of simulation during which the trainees had the opportunity to recreate a situation that had surprised them during operations, i.e. the operators' experiences and curiosity to explore and test potential solutions to an encountered situation in real-life operations. Thus, the course intertwined formal learning of NTS with actual operations and surprise grounded in the operators' experience from everyday work.

5 Discussion

Despite a common theoretical basis the two domains approach the training of NTS quite differently.

5.1 Comparison Between Courses

The MRM courses generally used a traditional approach to NTS training. Lectures are provided in classroom-based settings mixed with group discussions and short exercises. To compliment the theoretical approach, the lectures and exercises were mixed with high-fidelity simulations in most of the observed courses. The simulations were often based on either very complex operational settings or previous incidents to trigger the use of specific techniques, such as closed-loop communication, taught during the lectures. The focus of the simulations and exercises was mostly on how to avoid incidents and accidents through the use of NTS in operations. However, no specific freeze technique or any other means to facilitate the use of specific skills or tools were applied during the simulations. Further, the use of high-fidelity simulation may also have had certain drawbacks. Especially in the course directed towards cadets, the simulation often trained both technical and NTS simultaneously which may have blurred the distinction in between the different set of skills, as well as it may have triggered the students to focus more on the technical than non-technical skills.

The LPP training was more focused on anchoring knowledge on NTS in everyday operations at a plant with a focus on three of the NTS: communication, leadership and decision making. Less focus was placed on specific techniques and the only explicit tool taught to the operators was the use of the FORDEC approach to joint decision making in challenging situations.

Further, the audience and aim of the courses differ vastly. Within the LPP training, all trainees were professional operators working within the same company, but potentially in differing plants and shifts. The instructor emphasized that this mixture of attendees triggers and increases the sharing of experiences, and thus learning of strategies and reasoning across shift teams. In the maritime courses, the participants were quite diverse. The maritime students represented a set of novices with limited operational experience, which might explain why more focus was paid to technical rather than non-technical skills during the simulations. The navy personnel had a varying degree of expertise reaching from novices with limited time served onboard to professional sailors with many years of experience in the engine and deck departments. The participants in the third course were all experts within their own department onboard but represented other departments beyond deck and engine-room. It is therefore particularly interesting that all of trainees across the differing courses received the same generic NTS knowledge despite the large differences in proficiency and operational contexts.

Further, the ratio between the number of trainees and instructors varied across courses and between the domains. While the maritime courses had at least 14 participants in each, the trainer-to-trainee ratio in the LPP courses was very low (e.g., typically 1:2–1:5) and the courses depended on a high level of trainee interaction and peer discussion. The trainees themselves were all current professional LPP control operators, and thus specialists in their field. The trainer-trainee dynamic organizes the trainers in the position of facilitator, with a focus on probing trainees with questions for introspective and peer analysis, rather than as an authoritarian figure who "provides" information and definitive answers to problems.

It is also noteworthy that not all instructors in the LPP domain had an operational background, while all maritime instructors had previously served onboard for many years. This introduces different dynamics, in maritime the expert instructor designs and provides the training, in which the design is often anchored in very demanding and often extraordinary operational circumstances. The trainees participate in the simulation but have little ownership of the exercise. It can thus be said that the MRM courses emphasize NTS for accident avoidance, while the LPP training courses emphasize the complexity of everyday work rather than extraordinary operational circumstances.

As everyday work constitutes the majority of operational conditions, it can be argued that training NTS to promote normal operations should be emphasized to a larger extent within maritime operator training. As in the LPP courses, it should be possible to design exercises that are less based on accidents and high stress events, and more anchored in what represents everyday work. Further, the ability of trainees to provide input to the simulation design creates more engagement and ownership, as well as it might provide greater value for actual operations. Trainees are encouraged to engage in peer-to-peer discussion throughout the simulation scenarios and evaluate each other's actions and decisions in debriefing. Thus, there is potentially a higher degree of transfer between what is trained in courses and the actual work settings.

Earlier research on MRM has shown that the degree of transferal between training and real-life settings might be low and that there is a general lack of studies evaluating the long-term effect of NTS training [11]. It has recently also been discussed that the focus on individual NTS may hinder effective team training. Thus, an approach rooted in resilience engineering with focus on adaptability and flexibility on a team level might serve as a potential improvement to the current training regime [12].

Further, both courses showed only a limited range of formal assessment methodologies with regards to trainee performance. There is research suggesting that behavioral markers and knowledge-based questionnaires pre- and post-training may help to identify concrete learning outcomes and training results, such as changed attitudes or changes in task performance [e.g. 13], but these might not be enough to understand to what extent acquired knowledge is actually applied in operations. Further, traditional assessment methods focus on individual performance, but often fail to reflect team performance. Thus, potential methods for summative and formative performance assessment of teams can potentially contribute to both an increased understanding of NTS and their application in both LPP and maritime operations and beyond.

6 Concluding Remarks

Maritime NTS training focuses on the connection between theoretical knowledge and demanding operations that are typically less common for operators to encounter in their work, while addressing the complexity of everyday work in relation to NTS is limited. This potentially hampers the transferability of training content and may also affect the participants' perception of the validity and relevance of training if only extraordinary or relatively uncommon scenarios are used. A more participatory approach to training design with less emphasis on mishaps and incidents should be explored. The lignite power domain may serve as inspiration for this. Further, methods to assess and understand team performance especially with regards to NTS should be developed. These can potentially both increase trainee understanding, as well as more effectively transfer NTS knowledge from training to operations in high-risk domains.

Acknowledgements. This research has received funding from the European Union's Horizon 2020 research and innovation programme under the Marie Skłodowska-Curie grant agreement No. 823904. The authors would further like to acknowledge the financial support of the Swedish Mercantile Marine Foundation as well as thank all the interview participants and administrative support staff from the industrial facilities.

References

1. Flin, R., O'Connor, P., Mearns, K.: Crew resource management: improving team work in high reliability industries. Team Perform. Manage. 8(3/4), 68–78 (2002). https://doi.org/10.1108/13527590210433366
2. Flin, R., O'Connor, P., Crichton, M.: Safety at the Sharp End: A Guide to Non-technical Skills: Ashgate (2008)
3. Thomas, M.J.W.: Training and Assessing Non-Technical Skills: A Practical Guide. CRC Press, Boca Raton (2018)

4. Helmreich, R.L., Foushee, H.C.: Chapter 1 - why CRM? empirical and theoretical bases of human factors training. In: Kanki, B.G., Anca, J., Chidester, T.R. (eds.) Crew Resource Management (Third Edition), pp. 3–52. Academic Press (2019)
5. Hayward, B.J.H., Lowe, A.R., Thomas, M.J.W.: Chapter 15 - the migration of crew resource management training. In: Kanki, B.G., Anca, J., Chidester, T.R. (eds.) Crew Resource Management (Third Edition), pp. 421–447. Academic Press (2019)
6. Salas, E., Wilson, K.A., Burke, C.S., Wightman, D.C.: Does crew resource management training work? an update, an extension, and some critical needs. Hum. Factors **48**, 392–412 (2006)
7. Kawulich, B.B.: Participant observation as a data collection method. Forum Qual. Soc. Res. **6**(2) (2005). https://doi.org/10.17169/FQS-6.2.466
8. Endsley, M.R.: Toward a theory of situation awareness in dynamic systems. Hum. Factors **37**(1), 32–64 (1995)
9. Hörmann, H.J.: FOR-DEC. A prescriptive model for aeronautical decision-making. In: Fuller, R., Johnston, N., McDonald, N. (eds.) Human Factors in Aviation Operations. Proceedings of the 21st Conference of the European Association for Aviation Psychology (EAAP), pp. 17–23. Aldershot, UK: Avebury Aviation (1995)
10. Tusher, H.M., Mallam, S., Praetorius, G., Yang, Z., Nazir, S., Stock, W.: Operator training for non-technical skills in process industry. Comput. Aided Chem. Eng. **48**, 1993–1998 (2020)
11. Havinga, J., de Boer, R.J., Rae, A., Dekker, W.S.: How did crew resource management take-off outside of the cockpit? a systematic review of how crew resource management training is conceptualised and evaluated for non-pilots. Safety, **3**(4) (2017). https://doi.org/10.3390/safety3040026
12. Praetorius, G., Hult, C., Österman, C.: Maritime resource management: current training approaches and potential improvements. TransNav, Int. J. Marine Navigation and Safety of Sea Transport. **14**(3), 573–584 (2020). https://doi.org/10.12716/1001.14.03.08
13. Röttger, S., Vetter, S., Kowalski, J.T.: Effects of a classroom-based bridge resource management training on knowledge, attitudes, behaviour and performance of junior naval officers. WMU J. Maritime Affairs **15**(1), 143–162 (2016). https://doi.org/10.1007/s13437-014-0073-x

Computational Platform for Training Hydroelectric Power Plant Operators in Resilience Skills

Angela Weber Righi[1]($\boxtimes$) (ID), Priscila Wachs[2] (ID), Tarcisio Abreu Saurin[3] (ID),
André Manzolli[4] (ID), Felipe T. R. Tovar[4] (ID), Fábio Y. Nara[4] (ID), Eduardo M. Yamão[4] (ID),
Luis Gustavo T. Ribas[4], Harlen F. Bório[4] (ID), and Gelson L. Carneiro[4] (ID)

[1] Federal University of Santa Maria (UFSM), Avenida Roraima, 1000, Santa Maria 97105-900, RS, Brazil
angela.w.righi@ufsm.br

[2] Federal Institute of Education, Science and Technology of Rio Grande do Sul – Canoas Campus (IFRS – Canoas), Rua Maria Zélia Carneiro de Figueiredo, 870, Canoas, RS 92412-240, Brazil

[3] Federal University of Rio Grande do Sul (UFGRS), Rua Osvaldo Aranha, 99, 5°Andar, Porto Alegre, RS 90035-190, Brazil

[4] Lactec Institutes - Mechanical Systems Division, Av. Pref. Lothário Meissner, no. 1, Curitiba, PR 80210-170, Brazil

Abstract. Resilience is an important characteristic of a hydroelectric power plant operation. Training in resilience skills (RS) can improve the resilience of systems. The aim of this study is to develop a computational platform to train hydroelectric power plants operators, using the Resilience Engineering perspective. A plant was recreated in a virtual environment, in which the trainees and the instructors see real images of the installations and equipment, moving inside the plant, based on the simulation of four basic scenarios that contemplate the exercise of eleven RS categories. A module for assessing trainee performance is the basis for a debriefing session with instructors at the end of the simulation. Tests of the platform were carried out with plant operators and adjustments were made aiming at the use of it in the formal training program of the company involved.

Keywords: Computational platform · Resilience · Complex systems · Training · Hydroelectric power plant

1 Introduction

The sociotechnical systems (STS) are characterized by their complexity, due to factors such as the growing scale of operations, intensive use of information technology and a changing external environment [1]. Resilience is essential to cope with such characteristics. According to Hollnagel [2], resilience "is the intrinsic ability of a system to

A. Manzolli, F. T. R. Tovar, L. G. T. Ribas and H. F. Borio—Institution of the authors during the project implementation period.

adjust its operation before, during, or after changes and disturbances, so it can sustain the necessary operations". A hydroelectric power plant is a complex STS and its operation requires individuals, teams and organizations to be able to cope with challenge situations and have a resilient performance.

The scientific discipline dealing with such practices is called Resilience Engineering (RE), which is a safety management paradigm in STS [2]. This chapter is focused on resilience skills (RS) training development, one of the practices that enhance the resilience performance at the individual, team and organizational levels. RSs are "skills of any kind (social, cognitive, motor, etc.) necessary to adjust performance in order to maintain safe and efficient operations during expected and unexpected situations" [3].

Therefore, the aim of this study is to develop a computational platform to train hydroelectric power plants operators. It is worth noting that this chapter presents the main results of a "Research & Development Project" (R&DP) called "Platform for training hydroelectric power plants operators in non-technical skills with the Resilience Engineering perspective". A comparison between this project and another related to power grid electricians training was published by Wachs et al. [4].

2 Method

2.1 The Research and Development Project

The R&DP was registered (number 461900035) at ANEEL (Brazilian electric energy national agency). The project was conducted through the participation of researchers from two main institutions, the Federal University of Rio Grande do Sul (institution A, the first three authors were at that institution during the time of the project) and the LACTEC Institutes (institution B). AES Tietê was the company in the electric sector that participated and financed the three-year project.

2.2 Research Design

The Cognitive Task Analysis (CTA) [5] was adopted, and the CTA data collection techniques were used, namely: interviews, real work observations and analysis of documents. A total of eight interviews with expert hydroelectric power plant operators were made, using the Critical Decision Method [5]. Approximately 40 h of real work observation were carried out in two different hydroelectric power plants, in different shifts of work and with different operators. Some of the documents analyzed were standard operational procedures, safety goals, service orders, operational performance reports. The analysis of the database generated by CTA allowed the identification of RS, work constraints, systems redesign opportunities and training scenarios.

To develop the computational platform (virtual environment), a mathematical model of the power plant was built based on photographs, videos and sounds, as well as an application to reproduce such a model in order to offer an immersive interface. To recreate the virtual environment of the plant, it was necessary to record and process more than 16,000 videos and images, as well as modeling plant's logic consisting of 795 operating commands. The LabVIEW, Java and PostgreSQL software environments and languages were used to develop and implement the computation platform (virtual environment).

A reference power plant was chosen by the company representatives, in which the data for the logical and mathematical modeling were collected aiming at the virtual recreation of its operation. The chosen plant has a capacity of 132 MV generation, characterized as medium-sized, since it has similarity between the other power plants of the company.

2.3 Research Steps

A total of six steps were taken to develop the training platform, based on Saurin et al. [4]: (i) resilience skills (RS) and work constraints identification; (ii) definition of training scenarios; (iii) simulation protocol development; (iv) trainees assessment report definition; and (v) computerized platform development; (vi) training program evaluation.

Prior to the mentioned steps, an intensive literature review was conducted and recurrent meetings among the different institutions were held along the R&DP. Some steps were taken in parallel, as (iii) and (v).

RS and Work Constraints Identification. In order to select raw segment in the database (described on 2.2), it should be related to: (i) RS, which could be identified from the informal work practices report, as well as from decisions and actions associated with typical RS categories presented in literature [5], such as decision making, teamwork, hazard identification, among others; (ii) constraints that create the need to use RS, such constraints would later be useful for the design of the training scenarios; (iii) possible redesign of the system to facilitate or reduce the need to use RS. The third result is not used to the training development itself but give insights to the system redesign and the system's resilience.

After individual extraction of the raw sections by the different researchers, a comparison was made between the selected sections and a single listing was obtained, through a consensus, of the results associated with items (i), (ii) and (iii). This listing still received adjustments after being submitted to the validation of an expert designated by the company.

Definition of Training Scenarios. This step includes the definition of training goals, quantity of training scenarios, basic scenario characteristics, challenge characteristics (constraints) to be added to increase the complexity of the scenario and expected performance.

Two premises were adopted to design the basic scenarios: to cover the main technical activities of the operators, such as starting and stopping a generating unit; and possibility of generalizing the scenarios for several hydroelectric power plants.

Simulation Protocol Development. The simulation protocol consists in procedures on how to conduct the training session. The protocol provides the following steps: (i) to fill in a simulation data registration document, such as real and virtual start times, instructor and trainees names; (ii) choose the scenario and adjust computerized platform for it; (iii) briefing session, explaining the training goals and presenting how the computerized platform works; (iv) perform scenario (trainees and instructor); (v) trainees self-assessment (using a checklist); (vi) instructor assessment (also using a checklist); (vii) debriefing session, discussion about performance in the scenario and learning opportunities.

Trainees Assessment Report Definition. Areport is generated by the computerized platform and includes information about the actions performed during the simulation, pertinent to each trainee, in the actual sequence of occurrence, and the results of the trainees' self-assessment and the instructor assessment. This report guides de discussion during the debriefing session.

Computerized Platform Development. To be as similar as possible to the real environment, the trainees should be able to move virtually through the plant, to visualize its state and to control it by the interaction with their indicators and controls. The computational tool was designed as follows: (i) Model Server: calculates a set of variables using logical-mathematical models; (ii) Database Server: it stores information about the simulation and interfaces between the other modules that exchange information; (iii) Instructor Terminal: allows the instructor to control the simulation; (iv) Trainee Terminals: contains the immersive interface where operators will be trained or tested; (v) Training Terminal: runs an application in which the instructor defines the parameters of the simulation and carries out the assessment.

Training Program Evaluation. Although a hydroelectric power plant representative participated in every step of the R&DP, a final evaluation of the training program was carried out. Besides the already mentioned company representative, 2 operators participated in the training session, going through all the steps required at training protocol.

3   Results and Discussion

Four training scenarios were developed (Table 1), each of them contemplated: (i) a problem, which triggered the need of some RS; (ii) the expected solution; (iii) expected RS; (iv) the constraints that create the need to use RS. Such scenarios are called "basic" scenarios, as they can give rise to a number of specific training scenarios. An intentional or random incorporation of new constraints, as well as the intensity of each constraint and the timing of insertion in the simulation cad be added to the basic scenario. Two trainees are expected to each scenario, one called "machine room operator" and the other "control room operator".

Table 1. Training scenarios summary. *PG = power generator; COGE = energy generation control room

Scenario	Task	Summary of Initial Condition	Simulated Actors	Expected action
1	Start	PG1 is stopped for generation control. Auxiliary service via PG 2; heavy weather; time: 7:00 pm PG2 and PG3 with 40 MW each	COGE	Starting the machine in a maximum time of 30 min (pass PG2 for synchronization manually; identify failure on PG3)
2	Stop by urgency or emergency	Auxiliary service in PG3; machines in the system: PG1, PG2, PG3; time: 3:00 pm; good weather; PG3: temperature = 70 °C	COGE, supervisor maintenance	stop the PG urgently (not in emergency)
3	Stop for generation control	PG2 + PG3 on bar I with 20 MW each; PG1 on bar II with 40 MW; dry season; time: 10 pm	COGE	Find information, connect circuit breaker to manual
4	PG 2 bar transfer	3 PGs in bar I, auxiliary service PG1; PG1-40 MW; PGs 2 and 3-30 MW; requests COGE (for shortcoming in area D), transfer from a PG to bar II; good weather, hot summer; time: 7:30 pm	COGE	PG II bar transfer (sequence 8)

Table 2 shows the RS required and the work constraints presented in each basic scenario. As can be seen RS 1, 2, 7, 8 and 9 are required in all scenarios. Similarly, work constraint 1 is present in all scenarios, while constraints 2 and 5 are present in three scenarios. The diversity of RS requested, and work constraints presented in the scenarios are aligned to the variability inherent to complex systems, requiring resilience.

Table 2. Required RS and presence of work constraints by scenarios.

	RS	1	2	3	4
1	To interpret information from supervisory controllers, equipment or the environment	X	X	X	X
2	To draw up action strategy to reestablish plant operations	X	X	X	X
3	To determine priority actions		X	X	
4	To identify sources of stress and fatigue	X			
5	To coordinate activities with maintenance staff		X		
6	To coordinate activities with other actors		X		X
7	To coordinate activities with the COGE	X	X	X	X
8	To coordinate activities with the other shift worker	X	X	X	X
9	To understand the role of each piece of equipment in the plant's operations	X	X	X	X
10	To recognize the power plant as an interconnected generation system				X
11	To recognize the implications of stopping generation unit		X		
Constraints					
1	Increased operational workload	X	X	X	X
2	Equipment failure or damage	X	X	X	
3	Failure of the supervisory control system			X	
4	Problems outside the power plant	X			X
5	Time pressure		X	X	X
6	Increased bureaucratic workload		X	X	

A hydroelectric power plant was recreated in a virtual environment, in which the instructors and trainees see real images of the installations and equipment, moving inside the plant, based on the simulation of four basic scenarios that contemplate the exercise of eleven RS categories (Fig. 1, 2 and 3). A module for assessing trainee performance is the basis for a debriefing session with instructors at the end of the simulation.

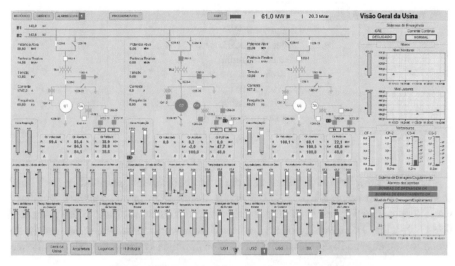

Fig. 1. Main screen of the supervisory system [4].

Fig. 2. Solution to display videos in virtual panels.

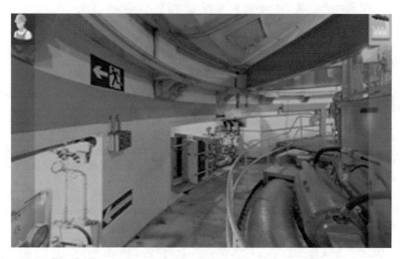

Fig. 3. Power plant navigation: access point to heat exchangers.

Evaluations of the platform were carried out with plant operators and adjustments were made aiming at the use of the same in the formal training program of the company involved. In general, the analysis of the platform among the operators verified that the computational platform and the proposed training meet the initial goals of the project. They identified the need of RS during the execution of the scenarios, being able to perceive their greater or lesser use in each training session performed. The reliability of the proposed scenarios, as well as the developed environment, was highlighted. The R&DP deliverable was compatible with the reality experienced in a hydroelectric power plant.

4 Conclusions

The computational platform developed in the mentioned project and presented in this chapter allows the training of hydroelectric power plants operators in RS, using a virtual environment training platform with 4 different scenarios. The platform and training protocol were elaborated and validated through participation of the operators during the development process.

Concerning the theoretical contribution of the study, it can be evidenced the inclusion of the Resilience Engineering perspective in the development of regular training for operators, beyond the technical training. This approach integrates technical and resilience development. The use of a computational platform to simulate a real environment is an alternative for complex systems that operate uninterrupted.

Acknowledgments. We thank the other project partners: Marco Aurélio Deboni and Wagner de Freitas Ciarelli, from AES Tietê; Flávio Carra, reference hydroelectric power plant coordinator; Fábio Lofrano Dotto, from Farol Consultoria; AES Tietê employees, especially the power plant operators; and Brazilian electric energy national agency (ANEEL).

References

1. Carayon, P.: Human factors of complex sociotechnical systems. Appl. Ergon. **37**(4), 525–535 (2006)
2. Hollnagel, E., Woods, D., Levenson, N.: Resilience Engineering. Ashgate, Concepts and precepts. Aldershot (2006)
3. Saurin, T., Wachs, P., Righi, A.W., Henriqson, E.: The design of scenario-based training from the resilience engineering perspective: a study with grid electricians. Accid. Anal. Prev. **68**, 30–41 (2014)
4. Wachs, P., Righi, A.W., Saurin, T., Henriqson, E., Manzolli, A., Tovar, F.T., Nara, F.Y., Yamão, E.M., Ribas, L.G., Borio, H.F.: Resilience skills training: simulations using physical and virtual scenarios. In: Proceedings of the 6th Resilience Engineering International Symposium, pp. 1–14, Lisboa (2015)
5. Crandall, B., Klein, G., Hoffman, R.: Working Minds: a Practitioner's Guide to Cognitive Task Analysis. The MIT Press, Cambridge (2006)

Part IV: HF/E Education and Professional Certification Development (Edited by Chien-Chi (Max) Chang and Maggie Graf)

Little Less Conversation, Little More Action Please: The Pecha Kucha Student Thesis Competition

Dora Hsiao[1], Larissa Fedorowich[2], Shofwan Hermanta[3], Rohmat Khaironi[3], Daniel P. Armstrong[4] (iD), Christopher A. B. Moore[4] (iD), Maksym Khmara[5], and Sadeem M. Qureshi[5,6(✉)] (iD)

[1] Galvion, Inc., Montreal, Canada
[2] Ergonomist, Montreal, Canada
[3] Trunojoyo Madura University, Madura, Indonesia
[4] University of Waterloo, Waterloo, Canada
[5] Applied Aerospace Manufacturing (AMF) Program, Fanshawe College, London, Canada
slqureshi@ryerson.ca
[6] Ryerson University, Toronto, Canada

Abstract. Are you tired of listening to presentations that go on and on that put you to sleep? Do you think you can do better? As part of the Student/ECR committee, the IEA2021 is hosting a 'Pecha Kucha' (PK) competition for students. This will give students a chance to showcase their overall thesis topics. PK is derived from a Japanese word for 'chit-chat' and signifying a concise, fast-paced method of delivering a presentation. PK is a creative and imaginative way to explain complex research, within a short time period. The competition will be following the traditional Pecha Kucha format, where participants will be restricted to showing 20 slides, for 20 s each, with a total of six minutes and 40 s to speak on their thesis topic, in the realm of Ergonomics.

Keywords: Pecha kucha · Student competition · Innovative presentation method · Student thesis

1 Introduction

The world is evolving. People are getting busy, long meetings with too many slides, rambling and a lack of direction make the average person less productive. One of the reasons why there is a disconnect between research done in academic institutes and the industry, is because research is complex. Students unknowingly, used to explain these ideas in a complex way. There is a need for a tool that can effectively communicate complex topics quickly and in an effective way. Pecha Kucha may help!

1.1 What Is Pecha Kucha?

The Pecha Kucha is a new and innovative way of executing presentations, where the speaker gets 20 slides that change automatically after every 20 s. The speaker must

N. L. Black et al. (Eds.): IEA 2021, LNNS 219, pp. 553–559, 2021.
https://doi.org/10.1007/978-3-030-74602-5_76

synchronize their speech with slide change. The idea of PK was conceived back in the mid-2000s. Originally, it was designed by/for architects but it got adopted by other domains as well, given its creative style. PK is similar to an extended elevator pitch with powerpoint slides, that relies on brevity and concision. The speaker has limited slides and lacks the option to go back or skip ahead. Therefore, the speaker is forced to streamline their content. In addition, PK has a very visually appealing presentation style. Utilizing singular impactful images, enhances the presentation and can captivate the attendees.

1.2 Our Motivation

The inspiration for this special session was to provide participants an opportunity to present their thesis topic in a novel and engaging way. Buckley and Hirsch [1] reported that conferences become much more attractive if there are student competitions. The PK format was selected to encourage students to use their creativity to captivate their audience, and present their research through storytelling and accompanying visuals.

2 Methods

2.1 Pre-conference Competition

Students were asked to submit a mini-PK, in the form of a 1–2 min video 6-months prior to the congress. The submissions included a high-level overview of the research, including a brief background and methods, main results/findings and the impact of the research. A panel of judges reviewed all submissions, and ultimately invited six students to present at the congress.

2.2 Main Competition

The competition follows the traditional PK format, where the six finalists were restricted to showing 20 slides, for 20 s each (20 × 20), with a total of six minutes and 40 s to speak on their thesis topic, in the realm of Ergonomics. The session was 60-mins long and winners were announced on the final day of the congress. Following each presentation, a small Question and Answer round was conducted. The final competition was graded on the quality of presentation (including synchronization), visual appeal and creativity, preparation and presentation, and research impact.

A panel of three judges with various backgrounds were invited, including representatives from the workforce (practitioners) and academia (professors/researchers).

3 Finalists

The competition received a wide range of submissions across several domains, such as aviation, healthcare, neural networks, biomechanics, workload assessment tools, manual order picking, design of smart washer tools and telemetry devices etc. The following are the finalists invited to present at the IEA2021 as part of the main competition. A brief description for each is provided below.

3.1 Mental Workload Assessment and Job Mapping Using NASA TLX

Unbalanced workload jobs due to unsystematic job mapping could affect mental workload especially for managerial jobs. High mental workload has been predicted as the reason for high labour turn-over at a manufacturing company, where employees experience high workloads in their day-to-day job. This condition could lead to hidden costs such as high labour turn-over and delayed job costs. This study assessed mental workload and re-mapped the workload using NASA-TLX in order to balance between the load and the amount of personnel in the jobs. Based on six indicators called mental demand, physical demand, temporal demand, performance, frustration levels, and efforts, mental workloads of 16 managerial jobs were assessed for the company. Job mapping was also conducted after the assessment by corresponding the results to government regulation about physical workload and calculating over the mental workload. The result shows that there are 6 jobs (delivery, drafter, cashier, purchasing admin, marketing admin and casting admin) which need 1 personnel addition, 1 job (PPIC) needs 3 personnel additions, and 1 job (HRD) needs 1 personnel reduction. This topic was submitted by Shofwan Hermanta Putera.

3.2 Human Factors of Reduced Flight Crew Operations: Concept, Development and Evaluation

The present work has demonstrated how Human Factors and Ergonomics methods enable the conceptualization, development, and evaluation of the complex sociotechnical system of Reduced Flight Crew Operations (RCO) of an airliner. RCO refers to its evolutionary cockpit crew development in the future. The copilot is dis-placed from the cockpit by adding additional automation, and a remote copilot as ground-based, redundant human support for the single-pilot. Both agents conduct the copilot's previous functions and can assist or resume command and control in case of an emergency. The workload-centered concept of RCO includes mandatory flight planning and navigation support by the remote-copilot to one single-piloted aircraft at a time during departure and arrival. In contrast, cruise is supported in case of need. This is the reason why it is called the dedicated support concept of RCO. Cognitive Work Analysis combined with social network analysis as well as STAMP and STPA allocated functions, specified user requirements, and gave design advice. A human-in-the-loop flight simulation showed a higher workload on the copilot caused by (single-)pilot incapacitation and during arrival independently from the crewing configuration. All copilots landed the aircraft safely. RCO represents a viable and promising concept for future aviation at early human-centered design stages. This topic was submitted by Daniela Schmid.

3.3 Vital Interactive Device

Air ambulances drastically change all the time. Upon doing some initial research, we concluded that there is a significant lack of understanding the importance of air ambulance communication systems. Due to our research, we discovered there is a lack of communication between the air paramedic near the patient and the receiving doctor. The aim of this study is to develop tools that enable timely transmission of correct information from paramedics to doctors - a critical element in the health and safety of patients. In this industrial partnered project, customer requirements were developed after detailed discussion. These requirements included: ecological friendly materials, simple installation, and clear medical software. The device must have an ability to restore or duplicate data and must be equipped with a save button which will benefit the doctor. Our device should not interfere with the aircraft avionics frequencies for pilot gain. Our concept is made of durable composites which makes it lightweight and shock resistant and more practical for air paramedics. The monitor works on SATCOM so that there is no interference with the aircraft's system and guarantees the smooth data transfer to the doctors. Generally speaking, the device is developed for nurses, paramedics, doctor's usage and technicians, engineers who will maintain this product as well. Moreover, further testing is required before gaining approval from Transport Canada or the Federal Aviation Administration (FAA). This topic was submitted by Maksym Khmara.

3.4   Neural Networks to Predict Cervical Spine Compression and Shear

Military helicopter pilots around the globe are at high risk of neck pain related to their use of helmet-mounted night vision goggles. Unfortunately, it is difficult to design alternative helmet configurations that reduce the biomechanical exposures of the cervical spine during flight because the time and resource costs associated with assessing these exposures are prohibitive. Participants (n = 26) performed flight-relevant visual scanning tasks under 4 helmet conditions while EMG and motion capture data were recorded. These data were used to drive an EMG-driven musculoskeletal model of the neck. The outputs of this model were cervical compression and anteroposterior shear. These outputs were leveraged to develop neural networks to predict cervical spine compression and shear given head-trunk kinematics and intervertebral moments, data can be rapidly generated through virtual simulation. These neural networks are capable of differentiating between different helmet conditions in terms of associated cervical spine compression and anteroposterior shear exposures during flight-relevant head movement. The neural networks developed in this study may be useful in helping to prevent neck pain related to military helicopter flight by providing a virtual approach to rapidly assess the biomechanical implications of various helmet designs. This topic was submitted by Christopher Moore.

3.5   Understanding Personal Determinants of Movement Strategy to Improve Lift Training

This research aims to evaluate whether modifiable personal factors explain why some lifters define a movement objective that attempts to minimize resultant loading on their spine. A series of studies will be conducted to evaluate whether any of; ability to perceive relevant sensory feedback, experience, knowledge on lifting mechanics, strength capacity or body mass, are associated with defining a movement objective that aims to minimize spine loading when completing lifting demands. Using results from these studies a probabilistic model will be developed to predict the range of likely lifting strategies and corresponding spine loads given modifiable personal factors as inputs (as illustrated in Fig. 1). Using the generated model, the combination of modifiable personal factors that result in the lowest predicted magnitudes of spine loads will be identified.

This identified combination of modifiable personal factors can then be used to inform the development of lift training programs. Such lift training programs would aim to improve the modifiable factors that result in reduced spine loads. It is expected that strategically improving modifiable personal factors that result in predicted reductions in spine loads will be an effective training approach, where to date lift training has been shown to be a generally ineffective injury reduction strategy. This topic was submitted by Daniel P. Armstrong.

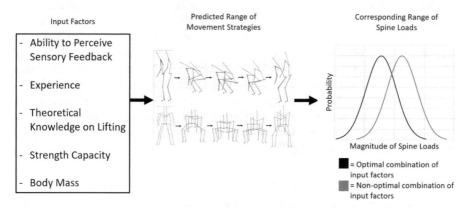

Fig. 1. An overview of the proposed probabilistic model where given a combination of input factors a range of predicted movement strategies and corresponding spine loads will be predicted. Through model iterations an optimal combination of input factors that result in lowest magnitude of predicted spine loads will be identified.

3.6 Design of Smart Washer Tools Using an Anthropometry Approach

Washing hands in general, namely the hands of a baker, are used to turn on the water tap which results in the water tap becoming dirty. After, clean hands are used again to turn off the water tap, so that the hands are again exposed to bacteria. The aim of this research is to design a safe "smart washer" automatic hand washing device according to anthropometry. The methods used in this research is research and development to design automatic hand washing tools. As well as the anthropometric method to determine the size in tool design. The percentile used is 50% and the anthropometry used is Indonesian people aged 17–23 years. The result of this research is an automatic hand washing device with the help of an ultrasonic sensor to detect distances. Washing hands with the help of this tool only requires placing the hands at one point. When the sensor detects that the hand is 16–20 cm away from the sensor, it will emit soap, a distance of 11–15 cm will release water, and a distance of 5–10 cm will emit hot steam as a dryer. The impact of this research is expected to reduce the use of tissue, thus reducing tree cutting. It may also reduce the spread of the COVID-19 virus by washing hands safely and comfortably. This topic was submitted by Rohmat Khaironi.

4 Discussion

Pecha Kucha has seen an exponential growth in popularity [2]. Including this type of session in the congress proceedings puts IEA2021 in a position that harnesses creativity and newer tools i.e. makes way for newer and exciting things. As highlighted in the report on 'Supporting Early Career Professionals and Students within the IEA and its Federated Societies' by Buckley and Hirch [1], the conference becomes much more attractive if there are student competitions - this session addresses that need.

Our student competitors presented their thesis topics from a diverse range of research fields. These topics included: Job mapping using the NASA TLX helps predict and inform mental workload; Strategically improving modifiable personal factors that result in predicted reductions in spine loads may be an effective training approach; A Vital Interactive Device may be critical to timely transmission of information from air ambulances to doctors; Neural networks may be useful in helping to prevent neck pain due to helmets in military helicopter flight; Reduced Flight Crew Operations represents a viable and promising concept for future aviation at early human-centered design stages; An anthropometrically informed design of an automatic hand washing device including environmental and health implications.

4.1 3-Minute Thesis (3MT) Vs. PK

In the past, 3MT has always been the 'go to' competition for most organizers. One limitation of the 3MT competition is that the 3-min restriction does not provide adequate time to explain ones' research. Above all, 3MT has only one slide; most students overload this one slide and try to by-pass the system. Thus, defeating the overall purpose. The PK format for this student competition helped guide presenters in delivering creative and engaging presentations, in a novel way. Where, they had limited yet adequate time and slides that forced them to avoid rambling and streamline their discussion. The 'no text' policy in the slides provokes the student to think out of the box and forces them to explain their complex research topics in an easier way.

4.2 Limitations

Perhaps, the biggest inhibitor of this competition was the uncertainty around the possibility of in-person conference due to COVID-19 pandemic restrictions. This likely impacted the number of submissions and could impact the congress attendance as well. At the time of this writing, we are still unsure if the congress will be hybrid or in-person. In addition, we must recognize, the Pecha Kucha format is still relatively new, and it may be unfamiliar to many, which may have led to reduced interest. Organizing these types of competitions in annual Human Factors/Ergonomics conferences may increase awareness and will inspire practitioners and researchers to incorporate this in their work-life.

5 Conclusion

The popularity for Pecha Kucha has been growing exponentially. Including this type of competition in the congress proceedings puts IEA2021 in a position that harnesses creativity and newer tools i.e. makes way for newer and exciting things.

References

1. Buckley, K., Hirsch, L.: Supporting Early Career Professionals and Students within the IEA and its Federated Societies (2019)
2. CNBC Homepage. https://www.cnbc.com/2019/04/29/pechakucha-japanese-inspired-technique-will-radically-improve-your-powerpoint-presentations.html. Accessed 01 June 2020

Human Factors and Ergonomics by Distance Learning: Successes, Challenges and Opportunities

Glyn Lawson[✉] and Sue V. G. Cobb

Human Factors Research Group, University of Nottingham, Nottingham NG7 2RD, UK
{glyn.lawson,sue.cobb}@nottingham.ac.uk

Abstract. While interest in online and blended learning has surged during the COVID-19 pandemic, distance learning courses have been available for several decades. This paper provides a reflective review of the Ergonomics and Human Factors distance learning courses offered by the University of Nottingham. Some of the successes of these courses include the adoption of new collaboration technologies and the high quality practical work conducted in the students' own workplaces. Challenges remain around maintaining student engagement, managing the impact of students' other responsibilities on their learning, and parity of the student experience. Opportunities exist for blended learning and adopting additional technologies such as immersive virtual learning environments.

Keywords: Online · Education · Digital · Human factors · Ergonomics

1 Introduction and Overview of the Human Factors and Ergonomics Distance Learning Courses at the University of Nottingham

The University of Nottingham (UoN) has offered Distance Learning (DL) courses in Human Factors and Ergonomics (HF&E) since 2001. These courses, offered as a Postgraduate Certificate (PGCert) and then a Masters of Science (MSc) from 2006, are aimed primarily at practitioners. They offer a flexible route to gaining formal qualifications, both of which are recognized by the Chartered Institute of Ergonomics & Human Factors, the main body representing the profession in the UK. While the courses have been offered for several decades, there has been renewed interest during the COVID-19 pandemic, in part due to uncertainty around the travel restrictions which may be in place when the next cohort starts. Indeed, online delivery has become normalized during the pandemic and, alongside blended learning, is likely to continue post-COVID-19 [1, 2]. Interestingly, the delivery of the UoN DL courses was largely unaffected by the pandemic, as the course is offered 100% online – there is no requirement for students to attend UoN in person. Rather, some of the learning from the delivery of the courses informed the transition of UoN face-to-face courses to a blended learning model. While online learning in ergonomics is not new [3], this paper presents an outline of the DL

© The Author(s), under exclusive license to Springer Nature Switzerland AG 2021
N. L. Black et al. (Eds.): IEA 2021, LNNS 219, pp. 560–566, 2021.
https://doi.org/10.1007/978-3-030-74602-5_77

courses in HF&E at UoN and their key characteristics, before presenting successes, challenges and opportunities. Some of the material will be relevant to those considering DL courses in HF&E; other parts will be more widely applicable to any blended mode of education in HF&E, or other cognate disciplines. A recurring theme throughout the paper is the importance of focusing on the end-user needs; in-line with an HF&E approach, learning design, technology and processes which do not meet the specific needs of DL students are unlikely to be successful.

The UoN programs aim to produce graduates who understand the complex inter-relationships between people, technology, management and systems, and prepare these students for careers in industry or research. They provide students with a fundamental understanding of HF&E, and teach them how to apply this knowledge to analyze products and work situations. The programs also develop transferable skills, such as critique, communication, and information acquisition.

An overview of the courses is shown in Table 1. This shows the preferred running order of modules (top to bottom), although this is subject to flexibility, for example if students transfer from another UoN PGCert course in Usability and Human Computer interaction. Students may study more than one module at a time to accelerate their learning, or interrupt their studies. There is also an option to move between the courses, subject to certain requirements. Each module represents approximately 300 h of student work. While MSc students are required to complete all six modules, PGCert students complete the first module then choose one of the three options. The PGCert is usually complete in 1–2 years; the MSc in 2–4 years.

Table 1. Program overview

Module	Start month	MSc	PGCert
Ergonomics application in the workplace	September	Core	Core
Ergonomics methods	March	Core	Option
Human factors in interactive systems	September	Core	
Ergonomics in work organizations	March	Core	Option
Human factors in context	September	Core	
Practical ergonomics investigation	March	Core	Option

Entry requirements usually include a first degree from a diverse range of backgrounds, such as engineering, psychology, design, or health sciences. This diversity enhances the cross-disciplinary nature of the course. Importantly, and unlike the face-to-face MSc, the majority of the students join the DL courses several years after completing their undergraduate education. Many are looking to develop skills for their current role; others are looking to transition into an HF&E position. Several of the students are international and complete the course from their own countries.

As mentioned above, the teaching is 100% online. Most of the content is hosted on Moodle, which comprises a variety of learning resources, including electronic reading lists, activities, diagrams, case studies, and reflection exercises. However, the collaboration and interactivity usually occurs through Microsoft Teams. For example, tutorials are run through Teams, and students will often contact their tutors through Teams with questions. There is also some peer-to-peer interaction. Communication still occurs through email, particularly more formal/official announcements. Assessment is also conducted online, and is not usually timed, in part due to the challenge of working across multiple time-zones and remote proctoring.

Students are assigned a personal tutor, and in recent years this has been the same person as the course director, given the overlap in responsibilities. However, for each module there is also a module convener, who takes responsibility for the teaching content within that module.

2   Successes

In broad terms, successes of the program is evidenced by the steady stream of students recruited to the course, and the graduates produced over the last two decades. Students on the courses are generally happy, and make few complaints or criticisms.

One of the key strengths of an applied course, such as HF&E, is that many students undertake the course in order to develop their professional qualifications and expertise. As such, many of the students are able to apply their learning directly to their work and several comment on how practical and useful the course material is. Another measure of success is the quality of individual projects undertaken as the final module of the course. Students can choose their own project topic and many choose to conduct a research study to investigate a problem, or to apply HF&E methods or design principles to effect some change in their work(place). As these are 'live' projects, student motivation and enthusiasm is very high. Where projects are supported by employers or clients, students have a unique opportunity to examine real issues and propose realistic solutions. Not only does this contribute to actual change in the workplace, but also consistently high grades for the individual projects of DL students, with some published in scientific journals [4, 5].

Looking at specific successes, the adoption of Microsoft Teams has had a big impact on the student experience, as found by others who have adopted this technology during the pandemic [6, 7]. Prior to Teams, most collaboration was conducted through emails, announcements and discussion forums in Moodle, and Adobe Connect conference calls. Whilst these techniques can facilitate distanced communication between students and tutors, the pattern was often high student engagement at module start, followed by gradual disengagement over the following months, often resulting in only one or two students responding to tutor announcements and leaving unanswered comments for other students. In part, this is a consequence of the nature of professional distance learning students; they do not work through the course material at the same pace and therefore arrive at suggested 'discussion points' at different times. Often, when students posted a comment to the discussion forum, other students were not at the same point and therefore did not reply – when they did reply, other students had already moved on beyond this point. Delays in response to asynchronous discussion may have exacerbated students' feelings of isolation. Tutors monitoring the discussion forums provide feedback on student comments, but this is not the same as peer exchange of ideas and thoughts about the topics that they are learning. This is particularly valuable for an applied course, such as HF&E, as the diversity of contexts within which the student cohort are working, offers great opportunity for sharing of experiences and insight regarding the practical application of HF&E methods in the workplace and other environments. Lack of interaction and social presence with learning peers has a negative influence on student perception of their learning experience [8, 9] and collaboration has long been recognized as important to the success of distance learning [10]. Whilst the previous technologies provide the opportunity for collaboration, Teams puts collaboration at the forefront, with improved usability and access to messaging, meetings, and video/voice calls. For UoN DL students, this has made a huge impact; increasing contact with academic staff and, most notably, peer-to-peer interaction. The ease by which students can add comments, messages, "like", and call tutors has transformed the level of interactivity on the course, and subsequently enhanced the student experience. This is reflected in positive student feedback, even though several of these students had their first encounter with Teams on the DL course. However, the feedback is integral with the human use of this technology; it is not just the platform they like, but that their tutors respond in a supportive and timely manner. This resonates with prior research which recognizes the importance of the instructor in online education, and in particular their ability to demonstrate empathy when interacting with students, a positive attitude towards online learning, and technical competence [11].

The importance of the humans in the system extends beyond timely messages to Teams. Improved accessibility to shared communication channels, and the use of 'social media' communication tools such as 'thumbs up' and 'smiley faces', used both by students and tutors, also helps to break the student-tutor barrier that some mature students may be familiar with. Recognizing that it is OK to 'chat' with tutors and that tutors are willing to invest time in student-led interactions, has increased student-tutor engagement. Indeed, responding to probing questions from diligent students who notice that 'work as imagined' in text-books does not always match 'work as done' in practice, leads to lively and interesting discussions from which the tutors also learn new insights. Teaching professional students is entirely different for tutors than standard HEI teaching and there is much to be gained from sharing of expertise from both sides.

3 Challenges

Despite the aforementioned successes, there are a number of challenges associated with DL HF&E courses. Perhaps foremost is the fact that the students often have significant responsibilities outside of their learning (e.g. family, jobs/careers) which can impact on their ability to study. This necessitates flexibility in the program of study, which often manifests as extensions for assignments, or interruptions to study; these are encountered more often than for face-to-face students.

Related to the demographics of the student population, several have been out of academia for a number of years. These students sometimes need a bit of extra support in areas such as academic writing, and in particular technical skills such as structuring reports and academic referencing. This is relatively easy to accomplish, but it is important to offer this support, particularly during the early stages of their learning as they (re)familiarize themselves with academic work.

Despite the success of new collaboration technologies, student engagement and isolation remains a concern. This is confounded by factors such as having a cohort that is working across multiple time zones, so real-time collaboration with the whole class is difficult. To improve access to tutorials, they are often run twice: once in the morning and once early evening. However, the students demonstrate different approaches to their learning. Perhaps linked to their other responsibilities, some students prefer to be "left alone" to work through the learning content and assignments; others prefer far more interaction with the tutors. But there remain challenges in developing peer-to-peer interaction, beyond pleasantries, which has the potential to enhance learning and benefit from the wealth of professional experience in a variety of different sectors held by the students.

Related to their professional roles, there are fantastic opportunities available to students, and assignments have been conducted in areas such as surgery, aerospace, emergency medicine, rail and others. However, this can result in a disparity in student experience; the students who do not have access to these exciting workplaces may have to use alternatives such as home office, garage etc. Relatedly, any practical work for the course must consider what equipment/workplace/participants the students can access. These problems are not insurmountable, but require consideration when setting assignments. Other problems can arise from tension between university work and that of the employer. For example, university processes may require the student to gain ethics and health and safety approval to conduct coursework in a workplace they might actually access on a regular basis.

Finally, the distance learning students necessarily follow a different academic calendar to face-to-face students. This raises administrative challenges, as many of the tasks which are usually automated require greater human intervention, for example, module registrations.

4 Opportunities

Even before the COVID-19 pandemic there were indications that blended learning held opportunities for DL students. Specifically, some students have visited the campus, in order to meet their tutor, and also to have an in-person lecture/classroom experience. Relatedly, some in-person students have made use of DL resources, and have expressed a desire for greater flexibility for remote participation in the course. Much of this has been achieved during the pandemic, as face-to-face students have had a mix of in-person and online resources, in part facilitated through digital technologies. There is clearly opportunity to continue with some form of blended offering in the future.

While the current courses offer a degree of specialization (e.g. through selection of topics for assignments), there may well be the opportunity for even more customization. For example, we currently offer only PGCert and MSc courses; students may wish to embark on even smaller courses as part of their Continued Professional Development or skill development. They could perhaps weave a selection of these smaller course to obtain a formal qualification , and perhaps with a specialism (e.g. Design Ergonomics;

Healthcare Human Factors; Ergonomics in Health and Safety). This customization may also help address the diverse needs of the cohort, particularly in recognition of prior research which shows demographic differences can affect outcomes in online learning [12].

Digital technologies also offer further opportunities, particularly for distance learning. For example, Professor Gary Burnett at UoN developed the "Nottopia" virtual learning environment [13] during the COVID pandemic, for which students create avatars and engage in virtual classrooms. This received overwhelmingly positive feedback, particularly for offering a pseudo-in-person experience for students who were not able to access campus in person. While further research work is needed to understand the effectiveness of immersive learning technologies [14], these, and other technologies, offer opportunities to enhance the student experience for distance learners. However, returning to the main theme of this papers: it is essential that the users are considered first and foremost. Technology, which neither suits the needs of distance learning students, nor offers perceived benefits, is likely to fail.

5 Conclusions

The University of Nottingham has offered distance learning in Human Factors and Ergonomics for several decades. The courses are generally successful, largely due to the time investment of academic staff and commitment to the course and its students. However, digital technologies have also been used to enhance collaboration, thereby improving engagement of the students. These experiences may be useful for any provider considering online courses. However, all universities are likely to change following the COVID-19 pandemic. These experiences may be useful across a range of programs at both Undergraduate and Postgraduate levels. Key to the success of any course however is a focus on the people: understanding their needs, motivations, and backgrounds, and designing a learning experience which meets these requirements.

References

1. Radha, R., Mahalakshmi, K., Kumar, V.S., Saravanakumar, A.R.: E-learning during lockdown of covid-19 pandemic: a global perspective. Int. J. Control Automation **13**(4), 1088–1099 (2020)
2. Cahapay, M.B.: Rethinking education in the new normal post-COVID-19 era: A curriculum studies perspective. Aquademia, **4**(2), ep20018 (2020)
3. Weiss, P.L.T., Schreuer, N., Jermias-Cohen, T., Josman, N.: An online learning course in ergonomics. Work **23**(2), 95–104 (2004)
4. Bowie, P., Ferguson, J., MacLeod, M., Kennedy, S., de Wet, C., McNab, D., Kelly, M., McKay, J., Atkinson, S.: Participatory design of a preliminary safety checklist for general practice. British J. General Practice **65**(634), e330–e343 (2015)
5. Trudel, C., Cobb, S., Momtahan, K., Brintnell, J., Mitchell, A.: Human factors considerations in designing for infection prevention and control in neonatal care–findings from a pre-design inquiry. Ergonomics **61**(1), 169–184 (2018)

6. Henderson, D., Woodcock, H., Mehta, J., Khan, N., Shivji, V., Richardson, C., Aya, H., Ziser, S., Pollara, G., Burns, A.: Keep calm and carry on learning: using Microsoft teams to deliver a medical education programme during the COVID-19 pandemic. Fut. Healthcare J. **7**(3), e67–e70 (2020)

7. Favale, T., Soro, F., Trevisan, M., Drago, I., Mellia, M.: Campus traffic and e-Learning during COVID-19 pandemic. Comput. Netw. **176**, (2020)

8. Caspi, A., Blau, I.: Social presence in online discussion groups: testing three conceptions and their relations to perceived learning. Soc. Psychol. Educ. **11**, 323–346 (2008)

9. Kurucay, M., Inan, F.A.: Examining the effects of learner-learner interactions on satisfaction and learning in an online undergraduate course. Comput. Educ. **115**, 20–37 (2017)

10. Beldarrain, Y.: Distance education trends: Integrating new technologies to foster student interaction and collaboration. Distance Educ. **27**(2), 139–153 (2006)

11. Volery, T., Lord, D.: Critical success factors in online education. Int. J. Educ. Manage. **14**(5), 216–223 (2000)

12. Rizvi, S., Rienties, B., Khoja, S.A.: The role of demographics in online learning; A decision tree based approach. Comput. Educ. **137**, 32–47 (2019)

13. University of Nottingham Press Release Wednesday 16 December 2020. https://www.nottingham.ac.uk/news/next-frontier-in-engineering-learning-uks-first-university-module-taught-wholly-in-vr. Accessed 07 Feb 2021

14. Beck, D.: Augmented and virtual reality in education: immersive learning research. J. Educ. Comput. Res. **57**(7), 1619–1625 (2019)

How Ergonomics and Related Courses Are Distributed in Engineering Programs? an Analysis of Courses from Brazilian Universities

Esdras Paravizo[1]([⊠]) [iD], Maria L. F. Fonseca[2] [iD], Flávia T. de Lima[3] [iD],
Sandra F. B. Gemma[4] [iD], Raoni Rocha[5] [iD], and Daniel Braatz[1] [iD]

[1] Department of Production Engineering, Federal University of São Carlos, São Carlos,
SP, Brazil
esdras@estudante.ufscar.br

[2] Ergonomics and Simulation Laboratory, Federal University of Itajubá, Itajubá, MG, Brazil

[3] School of Education, University of Campinas, Campinas, SP, Brazil

[4] Ergonomics and Occupational Health Laboratory, School of Applied Sciences,
University of Campinas, Campinas, SP, Brazil

[5] Department of Production Engineering, Administration and Economics,
Federal University of Ouro Preto, Ouro Preto, MG, Brazil

Abstract. Courses on ergonomics, occupational health, safety, and work design are usually present in engineering programs, providing an opportunity for raising students' awareness of the importance of work sciences. However, the distribution of these courses across different engineering specializations is unclear. This paper analyses 71 engineering programs from five specializations (chemical, civil, electrical, industrial, mechanical), from 10 Brazilian universities to identify courses related to the Work Engineering (WE) field, which articulates ergonomics, work design, and occupational health topics. In total, 89 unique courses were found, occurring 113 times across the programs analyzed. The Industrial Engineering programs were the ones with the most relevant courses (62,5% of the programs had 3 or more WE-related courses). The analysis of the titles of the courses highlighted that "work", "safety" and "ergonomics" were the most recurrent themes addressed in the courses. On the other hand, the topic "health" is practically ignored in Brazilian engineers' training. In general, the results emphasize the relatively small number and uneven distribution of WE courses in engineering programs, further supporting the need to build an interdisciplinary field of knowledge applied to engineering and in close collaboration with Ergonomics.

Keywords: Work engineering · Ergonomics education · Engineering programs · Work design education · Work sciences

1 Introduction

Current engineering problems have become much more complicated due to population growth and the demands arising from it, making engineering education a vital issue for

N. L. Black et al. (Eds.): IEA 2021, LNNS 219, pp. 567–574, 2021.
https://doi.org/10.1007/978-3-030-74602-5_78

any nation. In the Engineering undergraduate programs in Brazil, Ergonomics, Occupational Health, Safety, and Work Design are core disciplines to understanding human work. In this paper, we argue that this set of ergonomics and related courses that can be articulated and integrated into engineering programs, compose the field of Work Engineering (WE). The WE field can be understood as an interdisciplinary field of knowledge that articulates theories, methodologies, practices and knowledge of the work sciences, particularly those related to health, safety, ergonomics and design (Braatz et al. in press).

People's work can be seen as a complex phenomenon, with varied characteristics and multiple meanings, demanding analysis from different perspectives (Neves et al. 2018). Therefore, as interdisciplinary disciplines, the work-related sciences (such as ergonomics, work design, occupational health, and safety) offer contributions related to economic, social, cultural, psychological and technological aspects, promoting reflection on human work, improving decision-making and increasing responsibilities towards interventions.

The relevance of research on Ergonomics education is evident through the efforts that have been conducted in the last decades. For instance Landau (2000) discusses ergonomics education in Germany at the end of the 20th century, while Bridger (2012) highlights the International Ergonomics Association's role in the globalization and standardization of ergonomics and human factors.

More recently, in the IEA 2018 Conference, there were several presentations and papers reporting ergonomics education initiatives across the globe. To highlight a few, Cuenca and Aslanides (2019) report the experiences and expectations of professional Ergonomics Education in Argentina. Similarly, Black and Village (2019) report on the Human Factors/Ergonomics (HFE) education and certification in Canada, while Legg and Stedmon (2019) highlight the fragility of HFE programs, from a New Zealander program. Furthermore, the discussions on the topic in the IEA 2018 conference culminated in a paper by Oakman et al. (2020) deepening the reflection on tertiary education challenges and the path forward.

Nonetheless, the discussion of ergonomics education focuses primarily on programs at a tertiary level, both academic (masters and doctorates) and professional. According to Järvelin-Pasanen; Räsänen (2019) the University of Eastern Finland has become the only university where Ergonomics is studied as a significant subject in undergraduate, masters and doctoral degrees (Järvelin-Pasanen and Räsänen 2019), although it is usual to find HFE-related courses in a variety of undergraduate programs, especially in the field of engineering.

The importance of integrating courses related to HFE, specifically occupational health and safety, in engineering programs has recently been recognized by the Brazilian Ministry Education which required engineering schools to offer such courses in their programs. Nonetheless, little to no data exists on the availability of courses on ergonomics and related themes in Brazilian engineering programs. Thus, the purpose of this article is to provide an initial understanding of how courses related to the topics covered by WE (particularly those related to health, safety, ergonomics, and work design) are distributed across undergraduate engineering programs in Brazil and across the different areas of engineering expertise (industrial, mechanical, civil, chemical and electrical). Furthermore, we aim to get a sense of the most recurrent topics and areas related to WE are currently being taught in Brazil's engineering programs. In the next section, we detail the method employed to carry out this study.

2 Methods

The study followed a mixed-methods approach, in which secondary data on Brazilian engineering programs was collected and analyzed both quantitatively and qualitatively. Five engineering programs (criteria: most enrollments in 2019, according to the Ministry of Education) were selected for the analysis; thus, we analyzed Civil, Mechanical, Electrical, Chemical, and Industrial (Production) Engineering programs.

To select the universities offering these courses, we focused on Brazil's top 10 public institutions in 2020 (USP, UNICAMP, UFRJ, UFMG, UNESP, UFSCar, UFSC, UnB, UFRGS, UNIFESP), according to an international university ranking. Thus, 71 engineering programs of this university pool were analyzed.

Each program curriculum was screened for the courses they offered on WE. This screening process followed a 4-step process. Firstly, in a collective discussion, we defined 5 general keywords (i.e., "ergonomics", "work", "health", "safety", "design") that should be looked for at the career curriculum, focusing on keywords appearing in courses' title, objectives and description. Secondly, a set of inclusion/exclusion criteria was defined to analyze further the courses found and keep only those related to WE. The third step comprised the removal of duplicated courses. In the final step, there was a collective discussion to review the included courses, based mainly on the authors' experience, resulting in removing courses that were not related to ergonomics and related topics. In this process, the authors collectively read the course title, objectives and topics (when available) of all the courses marked as "possibly relevant" to the study. Then, there was a discussion on whether each of these courses was related to the work engineering field, based on the information available and the authors' previous experiences and expertise (3 authors are senior researchers and university professors).

This process's outcome was a pool of courses offered in engineering programs that deal with WE, which was then quantitatively analyzed to provide an overall understanding of the offering of such courses in top engineering programs from Brazilian universities.

3 Results

The initial screening (step 1) found 1246 courses containing the keywords in their title and course objectives/description. These courses' objectives and description were qualitatively analyzed (step 2), narrowing down the number of relevant courses to a total of 164 courses. Further analysis removing duplicated courses and a final contextual evaluation of their title (steps 3 & 4), objectives, and course topics lead us to a total of 89 unique courses (and 113 occurrences, since some courses were shared across multiple programs) on WE in the programs analyzed. Additionally, it was possible to identify the courses' status (mandatory or elective); out of the 113 courses offered 66,37% (n = 75) were mandatory and 33,63% (n = 38) were elective.

In terms of the number of engineering specializations analyzed, there was not a considerable variation: Electrical Engineering programs were the most recurrent ones, amounting to 23,94% (n = 17) of the programs analyzed, followed by Industrial Engineering 22,54% (n = 16), and Mechanical Engineering 19,72% (n = 14). Chemical and Civil Engineering programs appeared 12 times each on the sample, making up 16,90% of the sample. Table 1 summarizes this information.

Table 1. The number of programs of each engineering specialization analyzed and the number of programs offering 0, 1 or 2, or 3 or more courses on WE.

Engineering Specialization	# of Programs Analyzed (%)	# of Programs with n courses on WE (%)		
		n = 0	n = 1 or n = 2	n ≥ 3
Industrial	16 (22,53%)	0 (0%)	6 (37,5%)	10 (62,5%)
Electrical	17 (23,94%)	12 (70,59%)	4 (23,53%)	1 (5,88%)
Mechanical	14 (19,71%)	5 (35,71%)	7 (50%)	2 (14,29%)
Chemical	12 (16,9%)	2 (16,67%)	10 (83,33%)	0 (0%)
Civil	12 (16,9%)	6 (50%)	6 (50%)	0 (0%)
Total	**71 (100%)**	**25 (35,21%)**	**33 (46,48%)**	**13 (18,31%)**

Of the 71 engineering programs analyzed, 35,21% (n = 25) did not have any courses on WE, 46,48% (n = 33) offered between one and two courses only and 18,31% (n = 13) offer 3 or more courses (to a maximum of 8). Further analysis identified how this distribution of the courses offered varied across the different engineering specializations. The overview of these results is shown in Table 1.

It was also possible to identify how the 113 courses occurrences are distributed across the different engineering specializations: 54,87% (n = 62) are on Industrial Engineering programs, 15,04% (n = 17) on Mechanical Engineering programs, 13,27% (n = 15) on Chemical Engineering programs, 8,85% (n = 10) on Electrical Engineering and 7,96% (n = 9) on Civil Engineering programs. Figure 1 shows the number of engineering programs analyzed for each specialization and how many courses on WE were found through this analysis.

Furthermore, to compare the different engineering specializations concerning the number of WE courses offered, it is possible to create a "courses per specialization" indicator (CPSI). This indicator can be calculated by dividing the number of WE courses offered in a specialization by the number of programs in that specialization. For instance, the CPSI for Industrial Engineering is calculated by dividing 62 (number of WE courses offered in Industrial Engineering programs) by 16 (number of Industrial engineering programs analyzed). Thus, the CPSI for Industrial Engineering is 3,88. Similarly, the CPSI for Electrical Engineering is 0,59 (calculated by dividing the 10 WE courses offered by the 17 programs analyzed). The CPSI for each program is also shown in Fig. 1.

An additional analysis tried to identify the most recurring topics of the courses identified. By searching the titles of the 89 courses with a set of keywords (i.e., work, safety, ergonomics, organization, engineering, hygiene, design, health, psychology, sociology),

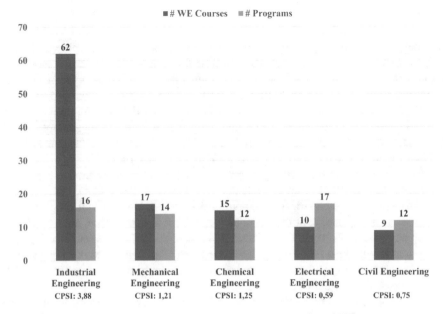

Fig. 1. The number of engineering programs analyzed and the number of WE courses occurrences.

it was possible to get an overall understanding of the courses' focus. There was a total of 146 occurrences of these keywords in courses' titles, with "work" (also equivalent to "occupational") being the most recurring one with 39 hits. The "health", "psychology" and "sociology" keywords were the least occurring ones with 2, 6, and 4 appearances each. Figure 2 summarizes the number of occurrences of each keyword in courses' titles.

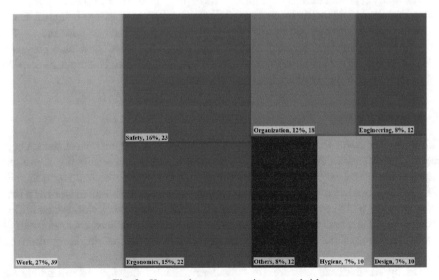

Fig. 2. Keywords occurrence in courses' titles

4 Discussion

The courses' analysis supports the perception that ergonomics, health, safety, and work design courses are not sufficiently present in Brazilian engineering programs. However, whenever courses on WE are offered, they are more likely to be mandatory than elective.

Furthermore, it is possible to identify Industrial Engineering as the one with the closest proximity to WE; more than 60% of the Industrial Engineering programs had 3 or more courses on the target topics (and no program with a complete absence of the subjects surveyed). On the other hand, Electrical Engineering was the one with the highest proportion (70,59%) of programs without any course on WE.

Thus, the Industrial Engineering overall experience can be considered as a positive reference for other engineering specializations. It is incontestable that engineers from specializations such as electrical, civil and mechanical engineering will act directly in the planning, design and control of productive systems and, therefore, are responsible for impacting people's work. Thus, offering WE courses in the other engineering specializations should be a first-order priority for those who tend not to have any course discussing such topics. And even those programs that already offer some courses on WE could improve the number of courses offered.

While ergonomics education is traditionally focused on the tertiary level for the preparation of professionals that will work specifically in HFE, there are opportunities to improve the availability of WE courses in bachelor programs, mainly those related to engineering. The motivation for that is clear: raising students' awareness of the importance of work, health, safety and HFE aspects and their intertwined nature with design, could lead to the formation of professionals who can address those issues in their future practice. This demand for WE competencies comes directly from society and, in the Brazilian case, is further supported and required by the new Curricular Guidelines for engineering courses established by the Education Ministry.

The study reported here is exploratory. Its explicit goal was to provide researchers and educators in HFE with an overview of how the WE courses are being addressed in engineering programs. As a secondary goal, this paper aimed to raise the issue of an improved articulation between engineering and HFE in undergraduate programs, possibly triggering a discussion on how to better contextualize and incorporate core WE topics into the different engineering specializations.

5 Conclusion

This paper highlights the issue of the lack of importance that human work has on engineering formation, which directly impacts the health, safety, and well-being of workers. Changes in engineering programs (more courses, more professors and researchers on WE teaching), and an overall focus on an integrative approach to human work as a focal point could be a start to address the issues raised, thus improving working conditions decrease accidents and work-related diseases. Curricular guidelines changes (with the explicit inclusion of the WE topics as an integral part of the engineering curriculum) can also be an opportunity for triggering these changes, as seen in Brazil.

The approach discussed here, for considering the ergonomics and related courses as part of an interdisciplinary field of knowledge called Work Engineering can be a useful strategy to highlight the relevance of these topics' presence within the different engineering specializations' programs.

This study is an initial approach to understand how these topics are addressed in engineering programs. The keyword-oriented search based on information available on institutions' websites is sufficient for this exploratory study; however, they might have missed courses related to WE but did not mention the keywords in their title, objectives, and topics' summary. Furthermore, the data collection was carried out in 2020 on the institutions' sites' information. Outdated information and other inaccuracies on the information available at the sites might have impacted the data collected.

Additionally, this study is focused on Brazilian public universities that rank among the best of the country (and in some instances Latin America). This sample of universities and courses is not necessarily representative of the overall population of institutions in Brazil or the world. Further studies could extend this approach to analyze engineering programs across the world and perform a more in-depth analysis of the syllabi of the WE-related courses found. This could provide more insight into what is being taught, the primary references employed, and educators' pedagogical and evaluation strategies in these courses. Including qualitative analysis, approaches could also lead to a better understanding of professors' perceptions.

Finally, it should be noted that the objective is not to make engineering programs "less technical or technological", but to highlight the importance of people (especially the workers) and human work within socio-technical systems.

References

Black, N., Village, J.: Human factors/ergonomics education and certification: the Canadian experience. In: Bagnara, S., Tartaglia, R., Albolino, S., Alexander, T., Fujita, Y. (eds.) Proceedings of the 20th Congress of the International Ergonomics Association (IEA 2018). IEA 2018. Advances in Intelligent Systems and Computing, vol. 826, pp. 818–825. Springer, Cham (2019). https://doi.org/10.1007/978-3-319-96065-4_85

Braatz, D., Rocha, R., Gemma, S.F.B.: Engenharia do Trabalho: saúde, segurança, ergonomia e projeto. 1st edn. Ex-Libris, São Paulo (in press)

Bridger, R.S.: An international perspective on ergonomics education. Ergon. Des. **20**(4), 12–17 (2012). https://doi.org/10.1177/1064804612455637

Cuenca, G., Aslanides, M.: Use of reflexive practice in students of industrial engineering for the construction of knowledge in ergonomics. In: Bagnara, S., Tartaglia, R., Albolino, S., Alexander, T., Fujita, Y. (eds.) Proceedings of the 20th Congress of the International Ergonomics Association (IEA 2018). IEA 2018. Advances in Intelligent Systems and Computing, vol 825, pp. 1007–1008. Springer, Cham (2019). https://doi.org/10.1007/978-3-319-96068-5_111

Järvelin-Pasanen, S., Räsänen, K.: Ergonomics integrated into degree program in health promotion in the university of Eastern Finland. In: Bagnara, S., Tartaglia, R., Albolino, S., Alexander, T., Fujita, Y. (eds.) Proceedings of the 20th Congress of the International Ergonomics Association (IEA 2018). IEA 2018. Advances in Intelligent Systems and Computing, vol. 821, pp. 304–309. Springer, Cham (2019). https://doi.org/10.1007/978-3-319-96080-7_35

Landau, K.: Ergonomics in Germany. Proc. Human Factors Ergon. Soc. Ann. Meeting **44**(38), 890–892 (2000). https://doi.org/10.1177/154193120004403858

Legg, S.J., Stedmon, A.W.: Fragility of tertiary ergonomics/human factors programmes. In: Bagnara, S., Tartaglia, R., Albolino, S., Alexander, T., Fujita, Y. (eds.) Proceedings of the 20th Congress of the International Ergonomics Association (IEA 2018). IEA 2018. Advances in Intelligent Systems and Computing, vol. 821, pp. 186–191. Springer, Cham (2019). https://doi.org/10.1007/978-3-319-96080-7_22

Neves, D.R, Nascimento, R.P, Felix, M.S.J, Silva, F.A, Andrade, R.O.B.: Sentido e significado do trabalho: uma análise dos artigos publicados em periódicos associados à Scientific Periodicals Electronic Library. Cad. EBAPE.BR **16**(2), 318–330 (2018). https://doi.org/10.1590/1679-395 159388

Oakman, J., Hignett, S., Davis, M., Read, G., Aslanides, M., Mebarki, B., Legg, S.: Tertiary education in ergonomics and human factors: quo vadis? Ergonomics **63**(3), 243–252 (2020)

Toward Contextual Education and Research in Ergonomics: A Latin American Vision

Juan Carlos Velásquez Valencia[1] ⓘ, Karen Lange-Morales[2](✉) ⓘ,
Gabriel García-Acosta[2] ⓘ, Lessby Gómez Salazar[1] ⓘ, Jairo Ernesto Luna García[2] ⓘ,
Aida Josefina Rojas Fajardo[1] ⓘ, José Javier Aguilar Zambrano[2] ⓘ,
Andrés Fandiño-Losada[2] ⓘ, and Jose Orlando Gomes[3] ⓘ

[1] Universidad del Valle, Cali, Colombia
[2] Universidad Nacional de Colombia, Bogotá, Colombia
klangem@unal.edu.co
[3] Universidade Federal do Rio de Janeiro, Rio de Janeiro, Brazil

Abstract. This work presents elements for an epistemological approach to the research lines of the proposed Doctorate in Ergonomics in Colombia and how they aim to respond to the context and needs of the region. Considering the characteristics of the context, the development of ergonomics in the region and the history and strengths of the research groups involved, three research lines are proposed: Ergonomics, work and health; Ergonomics, innovation, design and organizations and Ergonomics, social impact and sustainability.

Keywords: Ergonomics · Research · Doctorate · Latin America · Good living

1 Context

Ergonomics has taken multiple paths with different dimensions, as can be seen in both the definition by the International Ergonomics Association (IEA) and in the topics of their technical committees. At the worldwide level, the importance of studies on the informatic revolution (ICTs) and the Internet of Things (IoT); macroergonomics, which has now gone beyond the field of productive organizations and is applied to any type of organization; or the perspectives in ergoecology, whose approach contemplates the relationships between the diverse human activities and the conditions of the ecosystems, to maintain a dynamic equilibrium and resilience with the biodiversity. This implies huge challenges and responsibilities for Latin America (LA), so rich in cultural and environmental biodiversity, as well as natural resources. To understand all of this only under the modern vision implies seeing that richness as mere resources, whose exploitation is in many cases aligned with the questionable paradigm of progress, growth and development, disconnected from the nature that provides them. Therefore, the challenge would include a vision of ergonomics beyond the postmodern, one that is emergent and emancipated from LA.

N. L. Black et al. (Eds.): IEA 2021, LNNS 219, pp. 575–581, 2021.
https://doi.org/10.1007/978-3-030-74602-5_79

In Latin America, the development of ergonomics began at the industrial engineering and industrial design faculties, subsequently spreading to the health disciplines (occupational and physical therapy). While there are postgraduate programs in LA offering specializations and Master's Degrees in ergonomics, there are no programs for specific doctoral training in Human Factors and Ergonomics (HFE). An exploratory review of recent academic publications in the official languages of LA (2016–2020), found 168 products published in Spanish and 440 in Portuguese, including articles, books and theses. The most commonly addressed topics were associated with occupational health (32.7%), health (15.5% and ergonomics (14.3%). The countries with the largest number of such publications were Brazil, Peru, Ecuador, Colombia and Mexico.

In Colombia, ergonomics began in the late 1960 s, with industrial hygienists trained abroad and when, in the framework of the Iberian American Congress in 1969, the topic was addressed with cases and methods associated with ergonomics. In 1996, the Sociedad Colombiana de Ergonomía (SCE) (Colombian Ergonomics Society) was created, which existed briefly until the 1980 s. Since then, programs for specializations in ergonomics have been created along with laboratories and training as part of curricular programs for industrial design, physiotherapy, occupational therapy and industrial engineering, among others. In 1997, the program for Specialization in Ergonomics at the Escuela Colombiana de Rehabilitación (Colombian School for Rehabilitation) was created. It was focused on the ergonomics of activity. There are currently seven active programs for specializations in ergonomics in the country. However, given its importance, there is a need to go beyond the productive sectors to reach those in which public policies are established, seeking to advance in building an sustainable environmental, economic and political system; now more than ever, if we consider the limiting situation that the Covid-19 pandemic has imposed on humanity, and particularly on societies that lack strong health and working systems such as ours.

In this context, what characteristics should a doctorate in ergonomics have that systematically addresses the problems of the Latin American context?

2   Definition of a Doctoral Program in Latin America

2.1   Methodology

The fundamental pillars of a doctorate are its epistemological approach, along with its research lines. This work presents an introduction to those lines. For the definition, the following procedure was applied: location of research groups at the participating universities, analysis of the history of those groups (academic products and strengths), selection of the IEA technical committees relevant to that history and interests, and culminating in the creation of a matrix comparing the domains of ergonomics and the strengths of the groups and the technical committees of the IEA. These inputs were analyzed in the light of epistemological and paradigmatic reflections, to conclude with the proposed research lines.

2.2 Needs of a Doctoral Program in Latin America

Ergonomics requires comprehensive, multi- and transdisciplinary research, which contemplates the improvement of physical, sociocultural, economic and educational conditions. The basis of the systematic thinking of our multi- and transdisciplinary field, gives us a considerable advantage when understanding and structuring complex problems (wicked problems), and allows us to offer synergic and holistic solutions. It is essential to reflect, improve and research contexts in which technology transferences have been made (anthropotechnology) to what are considered "developing" countries, whose implementation frequently causes difficulties due to inadequate adaptations stemming from physical, cognitive, social and cultural incompatibilities, i.e. ignoring idiosyncrasy, attitudes and customs. As it advances, anthropotechnology should be rearranged, with future studies, so that ergonomics would incorporate technical tools and aids for work, processes and organization in the dynamics of product innovation teams, among other aspects.

2.3 Some Epistemological Aspects

The aim is to open up scientific research to new possibilities and perspectives; such is the case with the so-called «epistemologies of the South». When based on the epistemology of the North, development and well-being are impossible goals for the countries of the South to fulfill. Under its logic of linear time, history has a single and known meaning, which in recent centuries has been called conquest, colony, progress, revolution, growth, development or globalization. All of these concepts are associated with economic growth and thus the notion of well-being is also associated with that logic. The parallel, asymmetrical history disconnected from this linear vision of progress is bizarre or does not exist. This logic, as proposed by Boaventura de Sousa, «produces lack of existence while declaring as backward everything that, according to the rule of time, is asymmetrical in relation to what is advanced» [1]. Lack of existence is associated with 'absent agents' and assumes a residual form, in other words, preventive, wild, obsolete, and underdeveloped.

According to this theory and practice, «lack of existence is produced in the form of an unsurmountable, while natural, inferiority. People are inferior because they are insurmountably inferior and, therefore, they cannot constitute a credible alternative compared to what is superior» [2]. The epistemological debate about ergonomics is thus about proposing parallel and asynchronous lines in building ergonomic knowledge and practice, which acknowledges the needs of the populations, distant from or absent from the concept of development.

Based on the epistemologies of the South, epistemological reflection also takes place around concepts such as that of Sumak Kawsay (Quichua) or Suma Qamaña (Aymara), which very roughly translates as 'good living'. Good living makes it possible to counteract the modern and hegemonic categories that propose a dualism between developed and underdeveloped countries (based on the economics of development and financial economics), and which do not take ancestral knowledge into consideration; the latter involves greater harmony between human life and nature, and possible release from the slavery of subsistence within capitalism, which has become the only meaning of life for most Latin Americans. In this framework, the reductionist vision of well-being, fixated on Gross Domestic Product (GDP) and focused on the financial, will be debated and the possibility will be explored for a sustainable life, in which human progress and well-being do not signify economic growth but rather resonance with existence.

2.4 Research Lines

The need thus arises to strengthen research in the field of ergonomics, based on a perspective that takes up the thinking of the Global South, guided by the epistemologies of the South. A doctorate is designed located in the cities of Bogotá and Cali, Colombia, with three research lines: 1) Ergonomics, work and health; 2) Ergonomics, innovation, design and organizations, and 3) Ergonomics, social impact and sustainability.

Ergonomics, Work and Health. An ergonomic vision focuses on the productive processes, which is where it establishes its efforts as a discipline and a profession. However, there is another trend that focuses its actions on the workers, not only as a workforce, in other words, linked to the production of goods and services, but is also concerned with understanding the effects of the processes of consumption in scenarios outside of the job, where the worker as an individual and as part of the collective undertakes other kinds of activities, such as rest, recreation and education, among others.

Ergonomics thus recognizes in these environments of work and consumption, not only the identification and control over conditions that could deteriorate health but also, and especially, the determinants and determination of processes of health and illness and how they affect social performance. Under this dynamic, ergonomics enlarges its frame of action and gathers and nurtures its action, permeated by the culture, politics, norms and laws as well as other phenomena that determine human activity and its effects on productive processes and processes for consumption, in other words, in social processes, understanding that the worker is the central nucleus of this relationship.

Therefore, ergonomics focused on workers' health, not only increases its frame of action to cover protection in labor scenarios but is also interested in comprehensive protection for workers and design of the environments where they live and work; from this perspective, social relationships and everything that affects them become the target of study for ergonomics, thus aiming at the well-being of the worker and good living in the environment.

In relation to the above, it may be concluded that some of the topics of interest of the research line in ergonomics, work and health are: analysis of labor accidents, from a perspective of complexity; study of labor situations and the prevention of musculoskeletal disorders; mental integrity, ergology and the prevention of psychosocial risks; working conditions in the informal economy; safety of the patient and the caregiver; and the management and organization of health services.

Ergonomics, Innovation, Design and Organizations. In this research line, the interests of ergonomics and innovation complement each other, with the former providing approaches and tools to achieve the objective of the latter, i.e. changes in products, processes and organizations to improve both the productivity of systems and people's well-being. In this relationship, design serves as the coordinating backbone between ergonomics and innovation, as a creative act able to generate ruptures and proposals that modify lifestyles, with products, processes ore organizational structures in an incremental or radical manner.

In the relationship between ergonomics and innovation, two possibilities may be sketched out. On the one hand, there is the relationship between the ergonomics of conception and product innovation, supported in participative processes. On the other hand, there is a relationship between macroergonomics and anthropotechnology with the innovation of processes and organizational innovation, supported by the comprehension of sociotechnical systems as well as in participative processes.

With ergonomics for design (ergonomía de concepción in Spanish), the design encounters principles and methods that enable it to deal with and resolve labor matters and consumer aspects associated with well-being, health, safety, usability, emotionality, inclusion, participation and validation, among others. In this sense, seven trends are identified based on ergonomics and the human factors that support the design and development of products and services [3]: Collaborative design, user-centered design, customer-centered design, usability, universal design, experience-based design and transcultural design.

In terms of the relationship between ergonomics, design and organizations, macroergonomics opens up the spectrum for application of ergonomics in the organizational realm, based on scaling the sociotechnical approach using the "simplest" interactions such as the use of a manual tool by a person, and including more complex scenarios such as the analysis and design of organizations using such variables as complexity, formalization and centralization.

Considering the above context, the research line in ergonomics, innovation, design and organizations aims to contribute in the wide-ranging and varied realms of innovation, design and organizations, the development and application of methods for approach and validation that show the contribution by the systemic approach, analysis of the activity and the productive processes in relation to the joint design of situated solutions.

Ergonomics, Social Impact and Sustainability. A systematic review of publications about the relationship between ergonomics and sustainable development between 1992 and 2011 [4], shows two approaches. The first is aimed at the inclusion of ergonomics for the preservation of natural capital, through the design and development of products and constructions, including ICTs and smart systems. The goal has been to reduce and conserve consumables and resources (energy, raw materials and consumables). The second approach is aimed at social and human capital, particularly as embodied in corporate social responsibility. Based on health and safety, it contributes towards social sustainability, understanding that human capital must be maintained over time. The contribution of ergonomics to the ability to work and to have and maintain jobs, is an essential condition in corporate social responsibility.

From a theoretical perspective, Thatcher, Zink and Fischer [5] recognize four approaches based on the HFE and aimed at sustainable development and sustainability. The first are the human factors and sustainable development. This involves achieving a balance between the different types of capital (economic, social and natural), to ensure sustainable labor in all geographic regions and over time, having a dialogue with the concepts of corporate social responsibility. The second approach is Green Ergonomics, which is aimed at interventions based on HFE with a pro-nature approach, proposing four principles for application to design. The third approach is that of Ergoecology, conceptualized as the product of the interaction between the ergonomic system and the factors of the surroundings of the system. Finally, the authors recognize work on concepts of sustainable labor systems.

This line seeks to enlarge the sphere of action of ergonomics, stressing the importance of a symmetrical approach between the social and the environmental, as key factors for reaching sustainability in any anthropic system, along with expansion of the concept of social responsibility beyond the corporate approach. The specific topics of the line to be worked on include ergoecology, green ergonomics and a systemic approach to sustainable labor systems, along with social impact and social and environmental responsibility [6].

3 Discussion

Ergonomics must face multiple challenges in Colombia and LA; these include the future of work and the work of the future, informal work, the forces of the popular economy, and the collective and cooperative construction of work, the onset of aging and its relationship to vulnerable populations and the contribution towards poverty reduction, underappreciated vernacular technologies, new technologies transferred without adaptation or option for assimilation, and technical-scientific developments that not only impact employment but also all of the dimensions of human occupation or activity. These challenges may be addressed under the concept of systemic-complex thinking and using the ecology of knowledge, now that, in its development, ergonomics has transcended labor environments and become extended to all scenarios of human activity and interaction.

4 Conclusions

The epistemogical debate and challenge of ergonomics in the countries of the Global South is about proposing parallel and asynchronous lines in the construction of knowledge and ergonomic practice, which would address the needs and aspirations of the populations, remote or absent from the concept of development or headed in the direction of unsatisfactory development and living, to concentrate part of the efforts on epistemological reflection about good living and biocentric shifts.

Neither does this involve abandoning once and for all the understanding of well-being and quality of life; it is rather to understand them in a situated space-time context, visualizing their limitations, to open up to an epistemology that perceives the gaps that persist in the modern vision. It should aim for a vision that includes emerging local paradigms of pluri- and inter-identities and which would fundamentally be transformations both in the context of work as well as in the diverse activities of life and human existence.

Latin America can propose and teach new ways of understanding work and human activities, analyze and promote them as other aesthetic, ethical and ecological forms, disconnected from modernity and postmodernity. The doctoral program in ergonomics for Latin America aims to be part of the ontological and epistemological emancipation from modernity, in which the challenge is no longer to understand and repeat models and methods that are born and operate in contexts rooted in the modern vision of work.

References

1. de Souza-Santos, B.: Descolonizar el saber, reinventar el poder. Montevideo: Trilce, pp. 24–25 (2010)
2. de Sousa-Santos, B.: Epistemologías del sur. Utopía y praxis Latinoamericana. Revista Internacional de Filosofía Iberoamericana y Teoría Social. **16**(54), 17–39 (2011)
3. Puentes Lagos, D.E., García-Acosta, G., Lange-Morales, K.: Tendencias en diseño y desarrollo de productos desde el factor humano: una aproximación a la responsabilidad social. Iconofacto **9**(12), 71–97 (2013)
4. Radjiyev, A., Qiu, H., Xiong, S., Nam, K.: Ergonomics and sustainable development in the past two decades (1992–2011): Research trends and how ergonomics can contribute to sustainable development, Appl. Ergon. (46) 67–75 (2015)
5. Thatcher, A., Zink, K.J., Fischer, K.: How has HFE responded to the global challenges of sustainability? In: Thatcher, A., Zink, K.J., Fischer, K. (eds.) Human Factors for Sustainability. Theoretical Perspectives and Global Applications. CRC Press, Taylor & Francis (2020)
6. Moray, N.: Ergonomics and the global problems in the 21st century. Ergonomics **38**(8), 1691–1707 (1995)

Placing Students in an Operational Learning Situation as "Human Factors and Ergonomics Engineering" in a Vehicle Design Project

Mohsen Zare[1]([✉]) [iD], Hugues Baume[1], Jean-Bernard Bluntzer[1] [iD], Regis Barret[1], and Felicie Walgenwitz[2]

[1] ERCOS Group (Pôle), Laboratory of ELLIAD-EA4661, UTBM-University of Bourgogne Franche-Comté, 90010 Belfort, France
mohsen.zare@utbm.fr
[2] Training and Education Management Department, UTBM-University of Bourgogne Franche-Comté, 90010 Belfort, France

Abstract. This study aimed to place the students in an operational situation as Human Factor and Ergonomics (HFE) engineers within a vehicle architecture project and propose them as learning objectives using the different ergonomics tools to evaluate the occupant packaging of a vehicle. A Computer-Aided Design (CAD) application has been proposed, enabling the users to generate a 3D digital model, called digital mockup, of a car without in-depth knowledge in the use of CAD software. The students' groups used the CAD application and reproduced a digital mockup after measuring the different dimensions in a real car. This quickly generated car model allows them to evaluate occupant packaging elements, such as posture, reach-capability, and visibility by ergonomics tools. Most users of the CAD application were satisfied and believed that it saved their time significantly. However, the CAD application needs to improve in several aspects to better responds to the vehicle interior design needs.

Keywords: Learning practice · Ergonomics · Automotive design · Occupant packaging

1 Introduction

The automobile industry is currently facing a milestone in its development. What will the automobile look like in ten years? Will it be ultra-compact, low-tech, and sustainable, or ultra-high-tech? Today, cars are undergoing significant changes: firstly because of developing Connected and Autonomous Vehicles (CAV), secondly, because of the immediate need to switch back to reasonably-sized vehicles to continue the drastic reduction in energy consumption. Such developments will put ergonomics at the core of the architecture of these future vehicles: The new electric and hybrid propulsion systems create new architectural potential with a positive impact on the passenger cabin. Flat floors and elimination of the engine compartment might require rearranging onboard functions. Autonomous driving will offer new onboard activities, mainly for the "driver," who must sometimes take over control of the car rapidly. The "driving position" and seating functions will change radically. Furthermore, energy-efficient vehicles will be more compact and lighter but will still have to accommodate their passengers comfortably and efficiently. Consequently, ergonomics and vehicle architecture will be the core of new vehicle development to find the best compromise to achieve user comfort and performance.

To consider human factors and ergonomics on board in upcoming cars' new situations, future HFE engineers must learn the ergonomics methodologies for occupant packaging of vehicle interior design. Such training prepares engineering students for careers in automotive design and provides them with skills applicable to other product design areas.

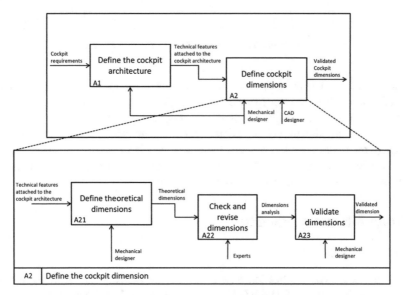

Fig. 1. Generic step of cockpit dimension definition extracted from car engineering process.

Generating an initial digital model of a simple car for ergonomics evaluations of occupant packaging is time-consuming and sometimes complicated for many HFE students. They lack sufficient knowledge of mechanics and use of digital mockup built with Computer-Aided Design (CAD) software based on expert rules (mechanical, ergonomics, or styling principles) [1, 2]. Thus, we need a digital mockup that configures quickly different vehicle types without in-depth knowledge of CAD software. This digital mockup generated into the CAD software must simulate a simplified model of a car composed of the various surfaces defining the interior space, particularly the cockpit [3, 4]. Moreover, the digital mockup needs to be in adequation with the industrial design process [5] that each student will face in his future industrial career.

Figure 1 shows a generic conceptual model extracted from a car engineering process defining the cockpit dimension based on an industrial process [5, 6]. In the first step (A1), the digital mockup allows the student to choose the cockpit architecture based on the automobile silhouettes. Figure 2 shows the simplified silhouette used to develop a car: Sedan, Estate, SUV, Hatchback, and Cabrio. The second step (A2) allows the student to define the cockpit dimensions with the revision of the theoretical dimension based on simulation of the digital mockup.

| Sedan | Estate | SUV | Coupé | Cabrio |

Fig. 2. A simplified silhouette is used to develop a vehicle [7].

Based on this conceptual model, this study aims to propose a learning situation for human factors engineering students close to the reality of the professional environment of automobile design. A CAD application is presented that quickly generates the simplified 3D geometrical architecture of the vehicle, enabling the students to analyze occupant packaging for interior vehicle designs using ergonomic tools. The following sections present the development of the CAD application, feedbacks from students about learning situations, and the conclusion/limitations of this study.

2 Materials and Methods

2.1 Digital Mockup

We developed a CAD application based on a digital mockup driven by expert rules. This CAD application is built with CAD software (CATIA from Dassault Systèmes) and Microsoft Visual Basic Application. This CAD application is based on the parametric features of the software, allowing the user to, after configuring the vehicle silhouette, export the preliminary model and then resume it in the CAD software combined with the Digital Human Modeling (DHM). This model can be used to evaluate human-vehicle interactions in the next stage of the engineering process.

The digital mockup needs to integrate the early phases of the engineering process of a vehicle. Figure 3 describes the proposed approach to define the digital mockup. Based on our approach, we need to determine scalable dimensions in our digital mockup. Therefore, an explicit set of expert rules relative to the cockpit architecture were defined.

On the one hand, the expert rules from the technical environment need to be defined. These rules, named "*Design requirements*," are mainly coming from the styling and engineering area. For example, the styling team can represent different features, such as the user interfaces, which can be placed in various locations on the dashboard. The engineering team can also determine some specific features and their localization, such as the air ducts, which need to be rightly positioned to heat the whole cockpit correctly.

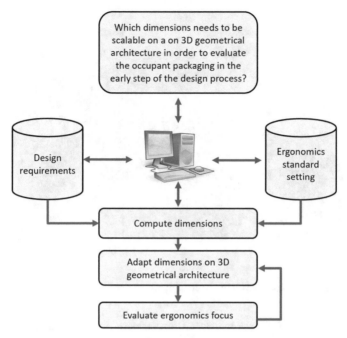

Fig. 3. The proposed approach to establish a digital mockup of a vehicle for ergonomics evaluation.

On the other hand, the rules come from the ergonomics environment named "Ergonomics standard-setting." For example, we can expose the ingress/egress process, driving the sitting positions and dimensions.

After the computation of these different expert rules, which can evolve at each new engineering process, the digital mockup allows the student to adapt the dimensions using its inexplicit knowledge. With the use of a digital manikin implemented into the digital mockup, the student is finally able to evaluate interactions of occupant-vehicle and study how the modifications of the vehicle parameters affect occupants.

Figure 4 shows the result of the digital mockup into the CAD system. The cockpit is displayed with the digital manikin integration and the simplified features of the vehicle: i.e., roof, windshield, dashboard, steering wheel, front and rear seats, floor, and four wheels. As described earlier, the digital mockup is built using the parametric technology of the CAD software. It is developed regarding the engineering process's two steps: *"Define cockpit architecture"* and *"Define cockpit dimensions."*

To choose the cockpit architecture, the user needs to select a set of features corresponding to the vehicle silhouette presented in Fig. 2. An algorithm activates or deactivates the proposed features. For example, Eq. (1) shows the algorithms of the activating/inactivating of the roof through a user parameter, which is an available command

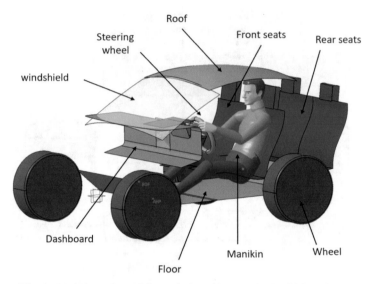

Fig. 4. Digital mockup of the cockpit architecture in the CAD software.

for the student in the software interface. Furthermore, the user can directly edit each construction parameters based on the expert rules to define the cockpit dimension.

$$If('Roof\_activity' == true)$$

$$\{'Roof\backslash Component\_Activity' = True\}$$

$$Else$$

$$\{'Roof\backslash Component\_Activity' = False\}$$

(1)

2.2 Study Population

The second phase of this study was to evaluate the effectiveness of this new educational practice on a group of students. 34 HFE engineering students participated in the study. We created 15 groups, including two or three students, and each group must work on a particular car, for example, Peugeot 2008, Fiat 500, etc. They went to the car dealers to measure the different dimensions of their specific vehicle, allow them to reproduce the architecture cockpit of the car with the CAD application explained above. Each group worked on a car to evaluate human-vehicle interactions with DHM tools. Five manikins with different anthropometric features (5th, 50th, 95th, 75th foot/25th trunk, and 75th trunk/25th foot) were implemented in the digital mockup allowing the student to understand the effects of modifications of the vehicle design parameters on occupants' packaging.

Each student group was followed during the project, and they answered a questionnaire about the efficiency of the CAD application. A pedagogical specialist interviewed ten groups regarding the effectiveness of digital mockups and learning situations. We assessed the level of satisfaction following user feedback.

3   Results

The CAD application proposed for the learning to design occupant packaging of different vehicles meets HFE engineers' needs to work on the car interior designs project. This CAD application is intended to facilitate the geometrical configuration of a car and enable students to carry out ergonomics evaluation of the interior space with DHM tools.

The first step of the work consists of a series of measurements on the real car. The requested dimensions are measured, then entered into the CAD application. The digital model is updated and represents the outline of the desired vehicle. Finally, the students could test some parametric design methods of vehicle interior based on the Society of Automotive Engineers (SAE) standards. They can also use several DHM tools to analyze the human task and adapt occupant packaging for different minikins in terms of posture, accessibility, and visibility.

3.1   User Experience Feedback

The participants reported a high level of satisfaction about the handling and the understanding of the CAD application (Table 1). However, the opinions were inconsistent for the measurement phase in the reference (real) vehicles. Many dimensions of a real car were difficult to measure. Furthermore, the participants were semi-satisfied regarding the digital mockup graphic representation compared to the real vehicle (Table 1).

Table 1. Student feedback concerning the proposed CAD application for generating a simplified vehicle digital mockup (N = 34).

CAD Application features		Satisfied % (n)	Neither satisfied nor dissatisfied % (n)	Dissatisfied % (n)
Learning		61.7 (21)	12 (4)	26.3 (9)
User interface		41.2 (14)	26.5 (9)	32.3 (11)
Graphic representation of the digital model	Driver position	47.2 (16)	17.6 (6)	35.2 (12)
	Seat	85.3 (29)	0	14.7 (5)
	Floor/pedal	76.5 (26)	0	23.5 (8)
	Roof/windshield	85.2 (29)	8.9 (3)	5.9 (2)

3.2   Interview About Pedagogical Objectives

A specialist of pedagogical engineering interviewed ten groups of students using the CAD application. This interview showed that the measurement phase on the real car is time-consuming and error-prone. Some students also have problems working with CAD software (Catia V.5). It was estimated that using the CAD application saved between 6-10 h time. Furthermore, the students believe that the CAD application guided them and reproduced the most useful surfaces automatically. However, it is noted that the digital mockup generated through the CAD application needs to be adjusted.

The students' groups proposed to provide more help in the CAD application and enhance the guiding features of the tool to facilitate the generating a digital mockup. They also ask to integrate into the CAD application a library of other vehicles.

4   Conclusion

The CAD application generates the digital mockup of the vehicle interior designs provided a real learning situation for HFE engineering students. This learning situation was close to the professional reality that enables the students to analyze occupant packaging based on a simplified 3D geometric architecture of a vehicle. However, this CAD application needs to be improved to provide a more realistic model, especially on the dashboard and the instrument panel, to meet the stylistic specificities of each vehicle studied [8, 9].

References

1. Bluntzer, J.B., Sagot, J.C.: M. Mahdjoub. In: Bernard, A. (ed.) Global Product Development, pp. 545–551. Springer, Heidelberg (2011)
2. Prasad, B.: Concurrent Engineering Fundamentals, vol. II: Integrated Product Development (1996)
3. Ulrich, K.: Res. Policy **24**, 419 (1995)
4. Chometon, A.: Architecture Automobile Tendances Evolutions Sécurite Design Ergonomie Confort Perfor. Hybrid. Niv, C (Ellipses, Paris (2011)
5. Pahl, G., Beitz, W., Feldhusen, J., Grote, K.-H.: Engineering Design: A Systematic Approach, 3rd edn. Springer, London (2007)
6. Robertson, D., Ulrich, K.: Sloan Management Review 19 (1998)
7. Designed by pch.vector/Freepik. https://www.freepik.com/free-vector/automobiles-models-icon-collection_8270941.htm
8. Bluntzer, J.-B., Ostrosi, E., Sagot, J.-C.: Proceedings of the institution of mechanical engineers. Part D: J. Automob. Eng. **229**, 38 (2015)
9. Ostrosi, E., Bluntzer, J.-B., Zhang, Z., Stjepandić, J.: J. Comput. Des. Eng. **6**, 719 (2019)

The Gap Between Human Factors Engineering Education and Industry Needs

Bella (Yigong) Zhang[✉] and Mark Chignell

University of Toronto, Toronto, Canada
`yigong.zhang@mail.utoronto.ca, chignell@mie.utoronto.ca`

Abstract. Traditional Human Factors Engineering (HFE) education focuses on bridging the gap between human and system design. Given the rapid, and accelerating technological advancement, particularly in areas such as machine learning and data science, how should HFE education adapt to better equip students for working in industry? This project sought to identify and understand the gap between HFE education and industry needs by surveying human factors engineering students and practitioners concerning their impressions of the gap and how it can be addressed.

Keywords: Human factors engineering · Education · User experience · Practitioner survey · Industry needs

1 Introduction

In recent years the field of human factors and ergonomics has expanded and changed to meet the challenges of new internet and communication, and healthcare, technologies. In today's digital economy, big data is everywhere – our society is being transformed by the ubiquity of data. With the assistance of ever more pervasive software and hardware technologies, an increasing amount of data is created, stored, and distributed on a daily basis. The surfeit of ("big") data affects the practice of human factors engineering (HFE) by providing vast amounts of data about human behaviour that can guide design. In the meantime, it is also an opportunity for the HFE discipline to assist in human-centerd system design with automated data analysis and machine learning systems [1]. In areas such as cybersecurity, there is often a great deal of tacit knowledge that is available to domain experts but not to machine learning systems, for instance in the case of data exfiltration [2]. In such cases, collaborations between human experts and machine learning algorithms may provide better results than either party alone, using an interactive machine learning approach. From an HFE perspective, emerging topics such as interactive machine learning and explainable AI represent a new example of human-machine collaboration, which is core to the discipline of human factors and ergonomics.

Human factors engineers play an important role in designing effective and safe automation solutions and avoiding catastrophe or undesired outcomes. In the face of accelerating change, HFE needs to adapt further in order to meet the challenges and opportunities created by the recent explosion in areas such as data science and machine

© The Author(s), under exclusive license to Springer Nature Switzerland AG 2021
N. L. Black et al. (Eds.): IEA 2021, LNNS 219, pp. 589–594, 2021.
https://doi.org/10.1007/978-3-030-74602-5_81

learning. To better integrate human factors into intelligent systems and organizations, there is an increasing number of emerging research areas, such as explainable artificial intelligence, human-centered data science, human-centered design of artificial intelligence, interactive machine learning, and human-automation interaction. However, research results need to be translated into industry practice, and thus it is important that HFE education keeps up to date with the latest results, and industry needs, so that future generations of human factors engineers will be prepared to contribute and benefit emerging fields.

There has been relatively little research on how human factors engineers can better work with data scientists, nor has there been much research on how we can impart data science skills in HFE education programs, though there has been recent discussion among HFE educators [3, 4]. Thus the following questions need to be addressed if we are to have the information needed to design up to date HFE curricula.

- How do we provide future human factors engineers with the skills to play their role in the emerging era of automation and data?
- How can human factors engineers better serve the systems and organizations that are increasingly dependent on data analytics and artificial intelligence?

The research reported in this paper is intended to provide an important first step towards answering these questions.

2 Objective

In this research, we aim to understand the unmet training needs for future human factors engineers by surveying HFE students and practitioners and interpreting their responses. The results of this research identify the perceived gap between that education and industry needs. The research should provide insights that will inform the design of future HFE education curricula.

3 Methodology

We conducted two surveys, one with HFE students and the other with HFE practitioners. The surveys comprised 11–12 questions in a combination of multiple-choice, Likert scale, and open-ended questions. All responses to the survey were anonymous and voluntary. We promoted the surveys on the Human Factors and Ergonomics Society member forum, LinkedIn HFE/UX Technical groups, and through researchers' alumni network. If interested audience self-identified as HFE/UX practitioners/students, they could participate in the survey research voluntarily after agreeing to the consent at the beginning of the survey.

The student survey sought to understand the perceived needs of undergraduate and graduate students who specialize in HFE at major universities. This survey had two sections: 1) education experience; 2) evaluation of the respondent's education experience. The HFE practitioner survey focused on identifying skillsets that were desired, but currently missing, based on the work experience of the respondents and on the recommendations of the respondents for changes in the HFE curriculum. The survey questions covered the practitioners' education and work experience, as well as their reflections on their work demands relative to the education they received.

4 Results

In the HFE student survey, 58 students from 26 universities participated. Over half of the respondents were pursuing their graduate degrees (Fig. 1). Figure 2 shows the students' rating on the HFE education they received from their home university. There are three main takeaways from the student survey results (Fig. 2). First, over half of the students did not feel confident in working with data scientists on data-driven products (Statement 1–4, in Fig. 2); secondly, the students were generally satisfied with the HFE education they have received (Statement 5 & 7 in Fig. 2); lastly, the students thought that HFE education should incorporate more data science skills in the curriculum (Statement 6 in Fig. 2).

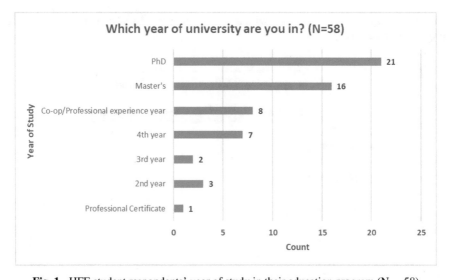

Fig. 1. HFE student respondents' year of study in their education program (N = 58)

We received 99 responses for the HFE practitioner survey. Most of the respondents had worked in industry for over 5 years (Fig. 3). Over 60% of the respondents had graduate degrees in HFE, and a further 37% had bachelor's degrees. The top three gaps areas in their education that were identified by the practitioners were 1) Understanding basic principles of artificial intelligence, advanced data analytics, big data, data visualization, 2) Real-life projects with clients and internship opportunities, 3) Practical User Experience (UX) research and design skills. The top three areas of change practitioners would like to see in the future human factor engineering education were 1) incorporate more materials in HCI, UX, UI, and visual design, 2) teach advanced data analytics tools and

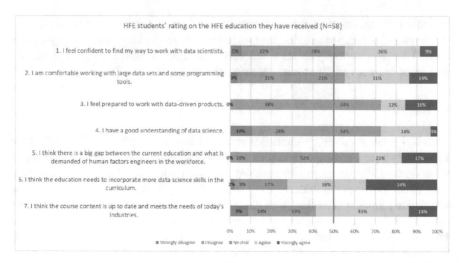

Fig. 2. HFE students' rating on the HFE education they have received (N = 58)

statistics to equip students to work with big data sets, and 3) apply theories in hands-on projects or case studies.

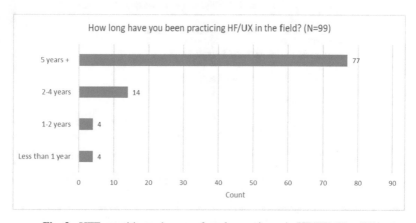

Fig. 3. HFE practitioners' years of work experience in HF/UX (N = 99)

5   Discussion

Based on the survey results, we learned that there is an urgent need to integrate a data science perspective into the existing HFE curriculum. As most HFE educators are not sufficiently trained in data science and automation, the implementation of the revised curriculum will require educators to proactively get training in data science and seek more interdisciplinary teaching collaboration between faculties. Due to the practical nature of the HFE discipline, educators should promote more hands-on learning in both undergraduate and graduate HFE education. This echoes earlier calls for more problem-based learning in engineering education (e.g., [5]). Problem-driven learning from examples should also assist in learning how to collaborate in teams and learning from reflection on experience, which is increasingly recognized as important components of engineering education (e.g., [6]).

Besides the obvious need to create more internship opportunities, we recommend collaborating with HFE practitioners in the field and establishing a database of up-to-date case studies in the HF/UX field to make it easier for educators to integrate relevant, practical, and trending materials into the HFE courses. Lastly, it will be useful to create more collaborative opportunities for HFE educators around the world to learn best practices from one another and establish an up-to-date, recognized, standardized but customizable HFE curriculum.

There are three major limitations of the surveys. First, due to overlaps between HF and UX, we did not make a differentiation between respondents who are more specialized in HF or UX. Second, the respondents self-identified themselves as students or practitioners in HF/UX and participated in the research without the researchers scrutinizing whether they qualified for participation. Lastly, more respondents to the student survey would help improve the accuracy and validity of the results. We will continue to promote the survey to gather more responses.

6 Conclusions

HFE has been traditionally more academic and has focused on safety-critical industries. With the increasing prevalence of emerging mobile technologies and big data, the HFE profession is faced with opportunities and challenges to expand and adapt to the changing work context. To better serve quickly evolving systems and organizations, it is important that we, educators and practitioners, welcome the opportunity to collaborate with new industries, expand the practical knowledge of students and emerging practitioners, and keep the HFE curriculum relevant to industry needs.

Acknowledgments. We want to thank the Human Factors and Ergonomics Society for promoting our surveys and our colleagues who have supported us by participating in the surveys.

References

1. Drury, C.G.: Human factors/ergonomics implications of big data analytics: chartered Institute of Ergonomics and Human Factors annual lecture. Ergonomics **58**(5), 659–673 (2015)
2. Chung, M.H., Chignell, M., Wang, L., Jovicic, A., Raman, A.: Interactive machine learning for data exfiltration detection: active learning with human expertise. In: IEEE Transactions on Systems, Man, and Cybernetics: Systems, 2020, vol. 2020, pp. 280–287 (2020)
3. Hannon, D., et al.: A human factors engineering education perspective on data science, machine learning and automation. Proc. Hum. Factors Ergon. Soc. Annu. Meet. **63**(1), 488–492 (2019)
4. Hannon, D., et al.: The Education of the Human Factors Engineer in the Age of Data Science (2020)

5. Brodeur, D.R., Young, P.W., Blair, K.B.: Problem-based learning in aerospace engineering education. In: ASEE Annual Conference Proceedings (2002)
6. Turns, J.A., Sattler, B., Yasuhara, K., Borgford-Parnell, J.L., Atman, C. J.: Integrating reflection into engineering education. In: ASEE Annual Conference and Exposition, Conference Proceedings (2014)

Part 5: Organisation Design and Management (ODAM) (Edited by Laerte Idal Sznelwar)

A Prospective Ergonomics Approach for the Design of a Planning Support System in the Road Freight Transport (RFT)

Eugénie Avril[1]([⊠]), Virginie Govaere[2], Liên Wioland[2], Jordan Navarro[3,4], and Julien Cegarra[1]

[1] Laboratoire Science de La Cognition, Technologie et Ergonomie (EA7420), Université de Toulouse, INU Champollion, Albi, France
`{eugenie.avril,julien.cegarra}@univ-jfc.fr`
[2] Département de l'Homme au Travail, INRS, Paris, France
`{Virginie.govaere,Lien.wioland}@inrs.fr`
[3] Laboratoire d'Etude des Mécanismes Cognitifs (EA3082), Université Lumière Lyon 2, Bron, France
`Jordan.navarro@univ-lyon2.fr`
[4] Institut Universitaire de France, Paris, France

Abstract. The Road Freight Transport (RFT) sector is continuously evolving, being confronted with intense competition and growing pressure from customers and suppliers, tight delivery times, and many regulations. All these factors lead the RFT sector to face multiple economic, environmental, and safety challenges. In these companies, the planner has a central position. The tasks of planner include supervising the transport round, keeping contact with the drivers during delivery, providing new instructions when needed, ensuring order follow-up with customers, etc. Such tasks require a high cognitive load which implies difficulties for planners in assessing the consequences of their decisions in terms of economic, environmental, and safety dimensions. In this study, principles of prospective ergonomics have been tested to support the transition from a human-based decision making to a computer-supported decision-making to anticipate the future computer-supported decision-making. We focused on the effect of system transparency and reliability. We confronted six planners with planning problems. We modified information available on planning to provide high and low levels of transparency. Starting from real issues, we also generated reliable and unreliable solutions (for these latter by adding invalid data). For each problem, planners were asked to assess the quality of the proposed solutions and indicators. The results showed than planners give a higher score to reliable scenarios displaying reliable information than to a less reliable scenario in which information is modified. This assessment of scenario is more adequate and easier with high transparency than with low transparency of information.

Keywords: Transparency · Automation · Road freight transport · Reliability · Planning support system

N. L. Black et al. (Eds.): IEA 2021, LNNS 219, pp. 597–603, 2021.
https://doi.org/10.1007/978-3-030-74602-5_82

1   Introduction

The Road Freight Transport (RFT) is a sector in constant evolution that is confronted to strong competition and growing pressure from customers and suppliers, tight delivery times and many regulations to follow [1]. In addition, there is an increase in competitiveness and flexibility factors, linked in particular to the rapid growth of e-commerce (675% increase in internet sales in 10 years) and the development of new modes of delivery (Uber collaborative platform). All these factors lead the RFT sector to face multiple economic, environmental and safety challenges. These challenges also stress the need for efficient planning support systems. The planner has a strategic central position in a company: he/she is at the core of communications between management, drivers and customers [2]. In particular, the planner is in charge of planning and monitoring transport rounds. Planner tasks includes supervising the transport round, keeping contact with the drivers, providing new instructions when needed, ensuring order follow-up with customers and so on. All of those occurs while participating in the management of unforeseen events such as breakdowns, traffic jams due to traffic accidents, customer delays, and so on. Such tasks are considered cognitively demanding. Therefore, planners have difficulties in assessing the consequences of their decisions in terms of economic, environmental and safety dimensions. In this study, a prospective ergonomics approach was favored to assess the influence a new support system allowing integration and better visibility for planners of these dimensions. It is clear that the future decision-support tools are likely to evolve rapidly. Currently, various approaches are investigated to integrate new tools in the logistic sector. These approaches could influenced the design of aids systems (artificial intelligence with automatic learning, etc.). Also, it is important to understand the behavior of human operator with regard to these new tools which can be more or less transparent [3].

More precisely, in a multidisciplinary consortium (also including experts planner) we designed a new planning support system proposing (1) the generation of different planning on the basis of a database and user–entered data (delivery times, drivers and trucks available…) (2) visual indicators evaluating the quality of each planning (and each change in those planning) in the three dimensions aforementioned. To anticipate the future computer-supported decision-making, we focused on the effect of system transparency and reliability. More precisely, transparency correspond to the ease of understanding the system. This level of transparency is important, especially because planners have to make decision based on both the system proposals and their own understanding of the situation [4]. But in this planning system, more transparent solutions also have a negative aspect of requiring simpler way of planning and designing indicators.

2   Research Methodology

2.1   Participants

Six male expert planners aged from 40 to 45 years old participated in this study. Three participants were planners in the same road freight transport company in the North of France, and three others were planners in the same road freight transport company in Paris region. Planners have been with the companies for a long time. Five out of the six planners also had experience as drivers, which allowed them to know the constraints of the drivers.

2.2 Apparatus

We used information with a high level (condition 1) or a low level of transparency (condition 2). In the high level of information, raw information of the planning were available. However, for the low level of transparency, information of the planning were aggregated through used of indicators (condition 2). For each condition, we constructed scenarios where we manipulated the reliability of the information presented (reliable or less reliable). These two conditions were applied in both companies within their specific context.

First Condition with High Transparency. The reliable scenario consists in a delivery route usually carried out in the participating company. It is performed without planning support system aid, and the route is regularly practiced through its execution. We considered it reliable because it corresponds to the practice that planners usually implement. Reliable information was provided and validated by experts that not participated in the experiment. In the first condition, raw data were displayed to the participant: as shown in Fig. 1, the driver's arrival at the *warehouse* is 4.30 am; after loading the truck, the driver is leaving the warehouse at 5.25 to the *site 1* located 22 km away and 35 min of *drive*; the time spent at *site 1* corresponds to 20 min of unloading; the driver then moves to *site 2* (40 min and 17 km); the time spent at *site 2* corresponds to 20 min of unloading; finally, the driver returns to the *warehouse* (30 min and 18 km). The total duration of the delivery route (three hours and 20 min) and the total kilometers (57 km) are also given.

		Customer : NAME					
	Warehouse	Move	Site 1	Move	Site 2	Move	Warehouse
	4.30 am	5.25 - 6 am	6 - 6.20 am	6.20 - 7 am	7 - 7.20 am	7.20 - 7.50 am	7.50 am
Duration	00:55	00:35	00:20	00:40	00:20	00:30	
Kilometers		22		17		18	

Total duration	03:20:00
Total kilometers	57

Fig. 1. An example on reliable scenario in the first condition

Based on these reliable scenarios, the raw information was modified to change its reliability. For example, we display the same information in Fig. 2. However, the number of kilometers is modified to deviate from the reliable scenario.

Second Condition with Low Transparency. In the second condition, scenarios corresponded to the previous reliable delivery route from the first condition. We added three indicators (I) that qualified the planning regarding economic, environmental, or health

Customer : NAME						
Warehouse	Move	Site 1	Move	Site 2	Move	Warehouse

	4.30 am	5.25 - 6 am	6 - 6.20 am	6.20 - 7 am	7 - 7.20 am	7.20 - 7.50 am	7.50 am
Duration	00:55	00:35	00:20	00:40	00:20	00:30	
Kilometers		13		10		30	

Total duration	03:20:00
Total kilometers	53

Fig. 2. An example of less reliable scenario with raw data modified in the first condition.

and safety costs (Fig. 3). These costs were calculated from various sources and data gathered from the participating companies. Thus, these indicators corresponded to aggregate information. Each indicator was presented through a number that corresponded to the cost of the delivery route for each of the dimensions (safety/health, environmental, and economic). The higher the number, the higher the cost of the delivery route.

Customer : NAME						
Warehouse	Move	Site 1	Move	Site 2	Move	Warehouse

	4.30 am	5.25 - 6 am	6 - 6.20 am	6.20 - 7 am	7 - 7.20 am	7.20 - 7.50 am	7.50 am
Duration	00:55	00:35	00:20	00:40	00:20	00:30	
Kilometers		22		17		18	

Total duration	03:20:00
Total kilometers	57

Safety 456	Physical: 111 Mental: 166 Emotional: 179	Economic 57	Environmental 15

Fig. 3. An example of reliable scenario with aggregated information in the second condition.

For the less reliable scenarios, indicators was modified (Fig. 4.)

Customer : NAME						
Warehouse	Move	Site 1	Move	Site 2	Move	Warehouse

	4.30 am	5.25 - 6 am	6 - 6.20 am	6.20 - 7 am	7 - 7.20 am	7.20 - 7.50 am	7.50 am
Duration	00:55	00:35	00:20	00:40	00:20	00:30	
Kilometers		22		17		18	

Total duration	03:20:00
Total kilometers	57

Safety 365	Physical: 89 Mental: 133 Emotional: 143	Economic 46	Environmental 12

Fig. 4. An example of less reliable scenario with aggregated information in the second condition.

The reliable and less reliable scenarios were, in each phase, presented on paper to the participants as if a decision support system had created them.

2.3 Procedure

A planner was confronted with five comparisons. A comparison was composed of a reliable scenario presented systematically with the same scenario in which information was modified, i.e., less reliable scenario.

The experts had to rate each scenario a scale from "1" (low-quality proposition of the decision support system) to 5 (very good quality proposition of the decision support system) and explain their choice for each scenario in each comparison. The explanations were recorded with a voice recorder during the experiment.

3 Results

3.1 First Condition with High Transparency

In the first company, the reliable scenarios were assessed at a mean of 3.47 ($SD = 0.64$) and the less reliable scenarios at 2.67 ($SD = 0.62$). In the second company, the reliable scenarios had a mean of 3.73 ($SD = 0.88$) and the less reliable scenarios of 2.2 ($SD = 1.01$).

Despite their uses and operational efficiencies, the planners affirmed that a route is determined based on a compromise between different constraints (economic constraints specific to the company and constraints in terms of the quality of service provided to the customer). Finally, a delivery route is not considered a "really good" quality but is somewhat acceptable in a given context.

The differences in the means of the scenarios between these two companies cannot be interpreted strictly because the scenarios were based on company data, which were not the same (different customers, different departure times, and the like). Explanations of the planners during the experiment are not presented in this short paper but it allowed to conclude that that (1) the planners' evaluations were the result of a compromise, (2) one of the planners used only a part of the indicators to construct evaluation, and (3) reliable information (i.e., reference) was not always considered as reliable.

3.2 Second Condition with Low Transparency

In the first company, the reliable scenarios were assessed at a mean of 3.13 ($SD = 0.91$) and the less reliable scenarios at 2.93 ($SD = 1.03$). In the second company, the reliable scenarios had a mean of 3.26 ($SD = 0.88$) and the less reliable scenarios of 3.4 ($SD = 0.73$). Finally, it should be noted that as in condition 1, (1) the indicators were considered reliable as long as they resembled the planners' representation of the perceived difficulty of the delivery route and (2) this representation influenced the score given, regardless of underestimation or overestimation.

4 Discussion

Our objective was to examine the transparency and the reliability of a decision support system in the road freight transport sector. Expert planners were confronted with multiple solutions proposed by the decision support system containing high transparency in condition 1, and low transparency in condition 2. In each phase, we showed two propositions of the decision support system to the participants. One scenario displayed less reliable information compared to the other scenario.

Our hypothesis were (1) that a reliable information, whether high or low transparency (raw or aggregated information), should be better perceived and assessed compared to information with a lower level of reliability; that (2) information with a high level of transparency should be evaluated better than information with a low level of transparency.

Our first hypothesis was confirmed. In both companies, the planners gave a higher score to the reference scenario than the modified scenario. In the first phase, the planners in both companies gave a higher score to a less reliable scenario. This result implied that planners are sensitive to the reliability of the decision support system, which is in line with studies on reliability in the human-machine interaction domain [5, 6]. For next researches, it would be interesting to study the real use of scenarios longitudinally when implementing such planning system. Indeed, such studies would allow to assess differences in the use of such programs (depending on the reliability of the system) based on the expertise of the operators. Moreover, it had been highlighted that the perceived usefulness of the system influences the use of a decision support system [4]. For this reason, comparing the results of the evaluations of the scenarios and their real use will be interesting, especially when using unreliable scenarios. However, it should be noted that whether utilizing a reliable or unreliable scenario, both must also integrate the context of the situation. As explained in the introduction, planning involves many factors [2]. For instance, planners can use an incorrect scenario because they recognize a "margin of time" on this specific day. Our second hypothesis was also confirmed. We found that information with a high level of transparency is better evaluated than information with low transparency (indicators). However, we can also notice that with high transparency, more scenarios were considered equal with the same score to low transparency. These results showed that the score is more discriminating with the high transparency: planners give a higher score to the modified scenario more often with the low transparency. We can suppose that the aggregation of the information in the low transparency condition leads the operators to score based on their representation. The compromises planners made in this representation led to frequently assigning a higher score to a less reliable scenario. In condition 1, with reference indicators, the planners did not give a higher score systematically to the reference indicators calculated based on various elements. This suggests that for a decision support system in the RFT sector, displayed information aggregated leads to more difficulty to recognize unreliable information.

Research has shown that increasing the transparency of automation might help participants assess the reliability of automation. For example, providing operators with explicit reliability information leads to faster and more accurate trust calibration [7, 8]. In our study, we can suppose that indicators' lack of transparency induced operators to evaluate the reliability of the indicators based on their perceptions. Even if the planners had participated in the calculation of these indicators, in practice, the indicators need to be displayed with a scale which would serve as a reference. That is to say, the position of the indicator on a scale should include a minimum and maximum based on the calculation of all others indicators of the others planning proposed by the decision support system. This is an essential point because multiple studies have stated the positive effect of transparency on trust and operators' perceived reliability of an automated system [9].

Such results have several consequences for the design of planning support system. This showed the importance of study the planning activity.

References

1. Govaere, V., Wioland, L., Cegarra, J., Gourc, D., Clément, A.: Smart planning-approaching the characteristics of a valid, balanced transport round. In: Congress of the International Ergonomics Association, pp. 387–396. Springer (2018)
2. Khademi, K. : Les processus cognitifs dans les activités d'ordonnancement en environnement incertain. (Doctoral dissertation, Toulouse Jean Jaures II University) (2016)
3. Bhaskara, A., Duong, L., Brooks, J., Li, R., McInerney, R., Skinner, M., Loft, S.: Effect of automation transparency in the management of multiple unmanned vehicles. Appl. Ergon. **90**, (2021)
4. Cegarra, J., van Wezel, W.: Revisiting decision support systems for cognitive readiness: a contribution to unstructured and complex scheduling situations. J. Cogn. Eng. Decision Mak. **6**(3), 299–324 (2012)
5. Bagheri, N., Jamieson, G.A.: The impact of context-related reliability on automation failure detection and scanning behaviour. IEEE Int. Conf. Syst. Man Cybern. **1**, 212–217 (2004)
6. Parasuraman, R., Manzey, D.H.: Complacency and bias in human use of automation : an attentional integration. Hum. Factors **52**(3), 381–410 (2010)
7. Lee, J.D., Moray, N.: Trust, self-confidence, and operators' adaptation to automation. Int. J. Human-Comput. Stud. **40**(1), 153–184 (1994)
8. Wang, L., Jamieson, G.A., Hollands, J.G.: Trust and reliance on an automated combat identification system. Hum. Factors **51**(3), 281–291 (2009)
9. Hussein, A., Elsawah, S., Abbass, H.A.: The reliability and transparency bases of trust in human-swarm interaction: principles and implications. Ergonomics, 1–19 (2020)

Beyond Human Factors and Ergonomics: An Inter-professional Model of Practice to Optimize Function, Workplace Design and Conditions

Marie-Christine Beshay[1](✉) and Jeanne Guérin[2]

[1] M|CARE Occupational Therapy and Rehabilitation, Ottawa, ON K1Z 7M4, Canada
mbeshay@mcaretherapy.com
[2] Ergonovix Inc., Laval, Québec J7C 6B3, Canada
ergo@jeanneguerin-ccpe.com

Abstract. Using an integrated, collaborative and holistic approach in the understanding and solution implementation to Human Factors and Ergonomics is essential as employees face increasing demands, experience complex conditions and are required to perform at higher levels of function. This paper highlights the positive impacts of instilling a model of practice that promotes successful collaboration between employees, employers and Subject Matter Experts (SME) with the aim of improving employees and industry's health while contributing to the enhancement of the science of Human Factors Ergonomics, Occupational Therapy, Traditional and Alternative Medicines. Inspired by the Industrial Athlete model first introduced at the Boeing company in 2005 to support their factory workers, the authors have developed a more comprehensive and holistic model based on lessons learned where SMEs and experts from various disciplines collaborate from the onset by using their unique professional lens to address workers and workplace related injuries and solve Human Factors and Ergonomics issues to ensure optimal and sustainable results [1, 2]. Utilizing an interdisciplinary model of practice promotes the offering of services that are built on trust, knowledge transfer and expertise which benefit the employees' health and well-being and allows for successful implementation of strategies, directives and changes, while ensuring that both employees and employers access professional support from industry experts and assuring that their respective needs are identified at program inception. This collaborative approach allows for a seamless integration of disciplines that aim to benefit workers in their ability to excel in their role while receiving the care they need efficiently.

Keywords: Human factors · Ergonomics · Collaboration · Occupational therapy · Traditional medicine · Alternative medicines · Subject matter experts · Industrial athlete · Return to work · Workplace injuries · Workplace health and safety

1 Introduction

Human Factors and Ergonomics aim to enhance human safety and comfort to promote overall performance and well-being, often evaluating individuals and/or groups, immediate work environments and possible solutions within the realm of employment conditions. This can lead to an oversight of significant personal factors to each individual, therefore rendering interventions short-sighted and ill-fitted to the people and companies' long-term needs. In-depth knowledge of occupations, functionality, design and of the complexity of human factors are fundamental and essential to be able to provide succinct, precise and optimal solutions which will benefit both clients and employers, save costs, prevent injuries and promote long-term productivity.

In the Human Factors and Ergonomics industry, there are many disciplines that promote functional solutions to enable workers to seamlessly integrate to their respective workplace. Much of the focus however is based on a review of their daily physical tasks, their environmental setup and a brief intake of the history of their injuries. Several disciplines also offer support in the realm of workplace injury prevention, in which case, the focus is primarily on preventing frequently occurring physical injuries stemming from repetitive tasks within their role and those categorised as higher risks. Client and employer files requiring intervention and support from a human factor and ergonomics expert often lie in the hands of a single sourced provider who will use their unique set of skills to identify and address relevant issues. Using a unique lens of Human Factors and Ergonomics embodies potential discrepancies in the analysis and understanding of job functions, of cognitive, psychological, emotional, psychosocial and physical conditions.

A model of practice is proposed whereby a spirit of collaboration between experts in the field is instilled honing in on individual strengths and areas of expertise stemming from each discipline to provide a comprehensive review and analysis of all influencing factors on employees' wellness in the workplace. By endorsing concerted efforts from the onset rather than working in silos and competing for roles within the workplace wellness industry, SMEs are encouraged to work together to complement each other's strengths to offer quality, professional and comprehensive care that ensure long-term, exhaustive and effective program planning, solution implementation to better the human factor and ergonomics industry.

2 Collaboration Rather Than Competition

In foreplaning for industry leading environments, seeking support from experts in the field of Human Factors and Ergonomics, an inter-professional collaboration is proposed. The system targets excellence, applicability and comprehensiveness to ensure industries could rely on services that encompass depth and inclusiveness in its ability to assess, analyze and provide solutions. The results target the uniqueness and complexity of each individual within each department and role to promote wellness, productivity and enhanced workplace performance.

Inspired by the Industrial Athlete program and in reflecting on current industry needs as well the prevalence of physical injuries where "1 in every 10 Canadian adult [suffers from] a repetitive strain injury (RSI) serious enough to limit normal activities" and of increased mental health illnesses in the workplace, the authors identified that the current model of practice in the Human Factor and Ergonomic industry of working with a sole service provider renders a disservice to employees and employers by risking overlooking significant factors essential to their productivity [3]. These workplace related illness, injuries and disease have been exacerbated in recent months, partly due to stressors and the lack of synergy with remote work due to the COVID-19 pandemic [4].

The notion of the Industrial Athlete is based on considering workers' need to utilise their mental and physical talents to perform their daily tasks while accessing their individual and unique set of skills, strengths, flexibility, coordination and endurance as would an athlete. The similarities drawn between an athlete and an industry worker is based on the risk of injuries of athletes arising from the repetitive use of skills, postures, and tasks [5]. The distinction that highlights the uniqueness of an athlete is their extensive and comprehensive access to a team of rehabilitation specialists involved throughout their journey with a focus on both injury prevention and rehabilitation should an injury occur, with the sole focus of a prompt return to previous activities.

"The Boeing Industrial Athlete Program combines services such as industrial massage, conditioning exercises, stretching, and physical and occupational therapy. This program is designed to improve the physical and mental resilience of employees" [6]. Similarly, innovative Industrial Athlete Programs have incorporated models of practice from the sports medicine discipline which have further rendered success to the implementation of this program within the workplace. This includes the implementation of: 1) a prevention focus, which assures employees and workers have access to preventive and protective equipment to ensure that from the onset, workers are setup to succeed within their work environment; 2) a conditioning approach which allows for appropriate training targeting potential areas of weakness and enhancing overall performance, and therefore allowing for an improved adaptation and adoption to work demands, as well as enhanced endurance, which has a direct positive impact on health and well-being; 3) an early intervention process to streamline screening and identification of issues as quickly as possible, followed by established measures to initiate the decrease of the severity of the identified issue and allowing for expedited support from the appropriate care provider and team of experts; 4) a standardized approach to instate rehabilitation and progressive treatment to address both physical and mental health injuries, focusing on improving function to promote prompt return to work related activities and demands [6].

A review of the literature has allowed the present authors to consider and analyse successes and shortcomings from previously introduced models of practice, to produce a revised approach that is applicable and adapted to the reality facing employees and workers.

The proposed model aims to optimize the support offered by subject matter experts (SME) to individuals and groups by providing comprehensive sustainable and efficient solutions to address their issues using a multifaceted approach based on the principles of collaboration, interdisciplinary practices and early intervention fundamentals, with the ultimate goal of aiding employees and employers optimize their functional status, their performance and productivity, whilst striving for the same level of excellence, efficiency and stamina used by competitive athletes.

3 Program Inception Through an Inter-professional Lens

Occupational therapists are health professionals with in-depth knowledge and expertise about human function, anatomy and physiology, with a thorough understanding of disease and injuries and their impact on an individual's physical, cognitive, emotional, and psychosocial function and the limitations that will translate into their ability to interact within their environment to perform their daily tasks, activities and occupations [7]. Occupational therapists consider a holistic approach to optimize the function of individuals by adapting their environment to meet their needs, by performing comprehensive evaluations of the person's environment and completing in-depth activity and task analysis. Their ability to understand the job demands of workers, and the impact of their injuries as well as prevailing risks in their environment whilst considering all factors that may be influencing their productivity and performance including issues stemming from mental health and physical health renders their position unique in their ability to collaborate and contribute to problem solving long-term solutions that aim to support workers to remain active contributors within their employment settings.

The Association of Canadian Ergonomists define ergonomics and human factors as the "discipline concerned with the interactions between humans and other elements of a system (environment, people and objects) with the goal of optimizing human well-being and overall system performance" [8]. The role of the ergonomists and human factors expert is to evaluate the person, their tasks, their environment and their workload to identify misaligned factors that will inform the development of functional and practical solutions that will allow clients to perform their roles.

Psychologists specializing in return to work recognize essential factors that present as quality markers for successful work reintegration including interpersonal functioning skills, job satisfaction, cognitive functioning, level of motivation, job-specific requirements and workplace setup. Their unique lens used in vocational rehabilitation and integration allows clients to receive support and interventions by specialists who understand the often-invisible factors that influence physical performance, endurance and productivity [9].

Kinesiologists are experts in understanding and designing targeted systemic and musculoskeletal conditioning program to aid individuals retrain their muscles, endurance, tolerance and overall performance as part of a rehabilitation team to optimize a workers' physical stamina and ability to assume the physical load and tolerances required to be successful in their duties [10].

4 Systematic Factors

The environmental reality for many employers is tainted by the high prevalence of workplace related injuries and illness which are associated with increasing rates of absenteeism year and after year [11]. In 2020, the national rate of absenteeism throughout all industries was an average of 11.6 days, where nearly 6% of employees nation-wide were absent due to an illness or disability [12]. Systematic costs to insurers and employers were calculated to be an estimated $16.6 billion in 2012 [13].

When taking into account the increasing rates of individuals with chronic conditions, including mood disorders and back problems, individuals with complex physical and mental health needs as well as the increasing systematic cost of absenteeism and rate of re-injury for those who have either returned to work without appropriate support, or returned to work without a personalized progressive return to work plan, it is essential for functional supports and models of practice to be developed and integrated to allow for successful workplace integration and promote supportive workplaces centered on wellness.

5   Model Implementation

In light of the rapidly evolving systematic needs on workplaces, pressures instilled on employees to pursue their work regardless of environmental conditions, a phenomenon particularly concerning with employees having to shift to remote and adapted work as a result of the COVID-19 pandemic, it is evident that a revised and widespread approach to support workers and employers be successful in maintaining their productivity is necessary.

The proposed model (Fig. 1) focuses on an integrated and collaborative approach to provide a comprehensive solution to employers and to industry leaders to offer high-level expertise and supports using an inter-professional lens.

Fig. 1. Inter-professional Model of Practice

A subject matter expert (SME) in this model would act as a case manager and would be identified as the main contact point with employers, stakeholders and support personnel. The SME has in-depth knowledge of physical and mental health conditions, as well as a thorough understanding of environmental barriers, conditions and facilitators. The SME would take on the responsibility of screening all requests from employers and workplaces including work related prevention initiatives, wellness promotion programs, workplace modifications and adaptations and return to work files. The screening process would allow the SME to gain an overview of each request and to complete an overall need-based assessment to allow for the efficient and prompt assignment and assembly of industry experts who represent complementary disciplines who will work collaboratively to effectively aid employees reach their optimal level of wellness, workplace integration and productivity.

6 Discussion

The implementation of a comprehensive executive team of industry experts, inspired by models of professionals who work with athletes, aims to enhance efficiency in aiding employees return to work safely and rapidly following an injury, in assuring accessible and functional workplaces and in reducing the risk oversight in the promotion of workplace wellness. The applicability of this model in a workplace setting would involve an umbrella vision focused on program development in collaboration with employers and will incorporate essential elements based on education, knowledge transfer and targeted interventions. This approach will yield long-term cost-savings, reduce losses associated with absenteeism and reduced productivity, and will ultimately promote efficient inter-professional collaboration.

7 Conclusion

Optimizing and streamlining efforts between industry leaders will not only create bridges between disciplines who have worked for years in silos, and often in the shadows of one another, but will also allow for the opportunity to create allies, and most importantly will bring to the forefront the importance of workplace wellness, accessibility and inclusivity centered on Human Factors and Ergonomics.

References

1. Betsy Case, Boeing Frontiers, June 2005. https://www.boeing.com/news/frontiers/archive/2005/june/i_ssg.html. Accessed 15 Feb 2021
2. Basu, S., Wechsler, L.S., Smith, D.R., Towler, C.D., Curley, C.M., Rogers, K., Hermans, T.L.: Boeing Technical journal, Industrial Athlete: Implementation and Effectiveness of a multifaceted Program for the Prevention of Occupational Injury (2016). https://www.boeing.com/resources/boeingdotcom/specialty/innovation-quarterly/December-2016/BTJ_Industrial_Athlete_full.pdf. Accessed 15 Feb 2021
3. Public Services Health & Safety Association. https://www.pshsa.ca/safe-environments/topics/musculoskeletal-disorders-msd-ergonomics#home-pshsa-logo. Accessed 15 Feb 2021
4. Statcan, Mental health among health care workers in Canada during the COVID-19. https://www150.statcan.gc.ca/n1/en/daily-quotidien/210202/dq210202a-eng.pdf?st=nau0Yjmf. Accessed 15 Feb 2021

5. Personal training on the net. https://www.ptonthenet.com/articles/The-Industrial-Athlete---Part-1-2101. Accessed 15 Feb 2021

6. Gagne, R.: The Industrial Athlete: Preparing the employee for the physical demands of the job. Fit2WRK, vol. 1.09 (2015)

7. American Occupational Therapy Association. https://www.aota.org/About-Occupational-Therapy/Professionals/WI/Ergonomics.aspx. Accessed 15 Feb 2021

8. Association of Canadian Ergonomists. https://ergonomicscanada.ca/en/our-profession/about-ergonomics. Accessed 15 Feb 2021

9. Mental Health Promotion. http://www.mentalhealthpromotion.net/resources/assessing-fitness-for-duty-and-rtw-readiness-for-people-with-mental-health-problems.pdf. Accessed 15 Feb 2021

10. Ontario Kinesiology Association. https://oka.on.ca/document/243/OKA%20Position%20Statement%20-%20Wellness%20and%20EHBS%20Whitepaper%20-%20April%2016%202019.pdf. Accessed 15 Feb 2021

11. Zhang, W., McLeod, C., Koehoorn, M.: The relationship between chronic conditions and absenteeism and associated costs in Canada. Scandinavian J. Work, Environ. Health **42**(5), 413–422 (2016)

12. Statistics Canada. https://www150.statcan.gc.ca/t1/tbl1/en/tv.action?pid=1410028501&pickMembers%5B0%5D=4.1&pickMembers%5B1%5D=2.2&cubeTimeFrame.startYear=2016&cubeTimeFrame.endYear=2020&referencePeriods=20160101%2C20200101. Accessed 15 Feb 2021

13. Stewart, N.: Missing in Action: Absenteeism Trends in Canadian Organizations, The Conference Board of Canada (2013)

A Reflexive Method to Evaluate a New Safety Management Program

Vincent Boccara[1]([✉]) [ID], Catherine Delgoulet[2] [ID], Stella Duvenci-Langa[3], Fabien Letourneaux[4], and Audrey Marquet[2]

[1] Laboratoire Interdisciplinaire des Sciences du Numérique, Université Paris Saclay, CNRS, Orsay 91400, France
vincent.boccara@universite-paris-saclay.fr
[2] Conservatoire National des Arts et Métiers, CRTD, Paris 75005, France
catherine.delgoulet@lecnam.net
[3] SNCF, Network Technical Direction, St-Denis, France
[4] SNCF, Research and Innovation Department, St-Denis, France

Abstract. This communication aimed to present a reflexive method to evaluate how a new safety management program is being implemented in the daily practices of managers. This method was built during an experimentation in a partnership research (E-safety project), in order to be then deployed by the managers and safety actors of the railways company. We conducted a study according to five steps: 1) preparation phase with the sponsor of the evaluation, 2) kick-off meeting with the director of one of the company's infrastructure maintenance facilities, 3) data collection by semi-structured interviews, 4) analysis of the data collected and 5) co-construction of a diagnosis on the implementation of the safety program in the daily practices. Here, we focus on the step three. Participants were twelve managers representing the four levels of the management line of this site and two support services. More the results concerning the assessment of the safety program, we aimed to present the method, its principles, the type of quantitative and qualitative analysis conducted and figures. These results then lead to discuss the interest of moving towards a constructive approach of safety.

Keywords: Safety program · Reflexive method · Assessment

1 Introduction

This work reports on exploratory research aimed at developing a process for evaluating a safety management program to be deployed in 2015 in a major French railway company in order to stem railway accidents.

1.1 A Safety Program as a Tool of Safety Culture Change

This safety program is a set of principles (risk prevention approach, general rules), actions (prevention actions, risk management, training sessions, etc.) and resources for managers

N. L. Black et al. (Eds.): IEA 2021, LNNS 219, pp. 611–617, 2021.
https://doi.org/10.1007/978-3-030-74602-5_84

(video, documents, tools, for information, monitoring and experience feedback, etc.) in order to manage safety in their daily practices. It was deployed with the manager line as a special target to strengthen their role in the safety management system.

For the company, this program is a strategic and multidimensional tool to support a desired change in safety culture [1]: from rules-based safety to a more integrated safety culture [2]. In this company, the notion of "integrated safety" combines two meanings. The first one refers to the articulation between the different forms of safety (passengers, workers and infrastructure or equipment) that were previously considered separately and the articulation between the forms of safety form the socio-technical system as a whole. The second one is related to the renewed approaches to safety that emphasize the capacity of all the workers to take initiatives to be able to cope with variability and unforeseen events of the real work [2, 3]. It refers to the articulation of the work of designing the rules that are required of workers (rule-based security) and how workers manage safety in real work situations (managed safety).

1.2   How Evaluate a Safety Program?

Research in the field of evaluation of programs for the prevention of health and safety risks to workers or systems is relatively numerous and diverse. They are distinguished in particular by the scope of the evaluation task (a training program vs. a set of actions and tools) and the approach implemented [4–7]. Three initial observations are listed below.

A frequently used methodology is that of pre- and post-test. It is used to measure quantitatively or qualitatively changes in risk perceptions and their acceptability, preventive actions implemented, etc. before and after the deployment of a program. The work mainly involves questionnaire-based surveys, sometimes combined with interviews or observations in real work or training situations. The evaluation focuses on representations and opinions relating to the actions implemented or the perceived degree of deployment of a program. In most cases, the evaluation is normative; it identifies deviations from what was expected. This methodology seems interesting for the evaluation of actions that are limited in form (e.g. training) and time (e.g. a few months of deployment), but becomes difficult to conduct: a) when the evaluation concerns a multidimensional program involving various actions and tools, which may be deployed over several years before bearing fruit; b) if the program evaluation is commissioned after the first deployments, which is common in companies.

The population surveyed is often homogeneous (very often operational staff or managers who learn, and more rarely trainers or experts), which leads to a monocular evaluation, through the prism of the perceptions and actions of the specific population. The prior knowledge, skills and practice of these people in terms of safety work is not known, nor are the various prevention campaigns in which they have already had the opportunity to participate. The counters are reset to zero, without knowing where the survey population "starts" from.

Another trend noted is the segmentation of safety issues in relation to other dimensions of work (work organization, productivity, quality, staffing). For example, the studies focus on the "safety actions" implemented (in number and sometimes in kind), without considering the actual conditions of work, whether in terms of organization, material and human resources, etc. The work is therefore not concerned with the actual conditions of work. However, in their daily work, managers and operational staff do not manage production on the one hand and safety on the other, they work by trying to hold the two dimensions together. Moreover, accidents and incidents are multi-causal, so actions that impact safety are not always focused on this dimension, and the cumulative or rebound effects of HRM or organizational actions can just as easily support or make it difficult to work safely.

Given the project's start date (after an initial phase of deployment of the security program in the company) and the company's decision to move from regulated security to managed security, the objective of the exploratory study was a) to build an evaluation approach that allows to take pictures at defined intervals (regular or in connection with specific events) to provide elements for piloting the deployment of such a program over the years within the framework of an evaluative-formative approach; b) to broaden the spectrum of the population under consideration by working with the entire managerial line and support activities in charge of the deployment of such a program, and to consider the prior experience of these workers in promoting safety at work; c) to avoid a compartmentalized approach to safety by relying on a systemic approach that seeks to understand how this program fits into the missions of managers and their practices.

The evaluation process is here considered as an individual, collective and organizational tool for continuous improvement in order to manage together production and safety and then, to develop the safety at work. In this perspective, the evaluation process differs from more "classical approaches" (Kirkpatrick 1994). It had three main characteristics: 1) reflexive, 2) collective, 3) based on real work analysis.

2   Method

This study was conducted in order to evaluate a safety program organized according to six axes for transforming safety management: 1) proactive safety behavior and learning from errors and problem, 2) risk management, anticipate, identify and priorities actions, 3) mastering the interfaces with contractors, 4) simplifying procedures based on real work, 5) building the conditions for everyone's involvement, 6) acquiring innovative equipment. Based on these six axes, the company developed a set of 38 resources according to several forms: documents (e.g. Fair Culture Kit), videos (e.g. train of safety), software (e.g. monitoring platform for actions carried out), network (e.g. OHF referents), training (e.g. OHF training), processes (e.g. experience feedback) which were disseminated within the company.

We conducted a study according to five steps. The first step was a preparation phase with the sponsor of the evaluation in order to explain the general framework of the method regarding the comprehensive and reflexive approach. The second step was a kick-off meeting with the director of one of the company's infrastructure maintenance facilities to position this framework and explain the objectives of the research. The third step was a data collection by semi-structured interviews. Participants were twelve managers representing the four levels of the management line of this site and two support services: from the top management to the first level of supervision through Human Resources, production programming or Health-Safety-Environment department. The semi-structured interviews were structured according four phases: 1) the vocational career and its turning points, 2) the daily work as manager and how safety issues are played out, 3) the known and used resources of the new safety program (and others) to manage safety and production in practice discussed from a sorting cards method and the story of an experienced safety event and, 4) the professionalization process to safety issues as they experience and mobilize it for others. The fourth step consisted of processing and analysis of the data collected. The fifth step was the co-construction of a diagnosis on the current state of safety in practices, with a view to identifying areas for improvement and concrete actions to be implemented within a defined timeframe.

3   Results

In this communication, we focus the presentation of the results on the step three, which allowed the development of original analysis and productions. The third step was a data collection by semi-structured interviews.

3.1   The Vocational Career and its Turning Points

The 12 managers have between 11 and 40 years of seniority in the company ($M = 28,18$; $SD = 11,16$). They have held management positions for at least 1 year and some for more than 30 years ($M = 13,9$; $SD = 9,15$). They have been in their position for 1 year up to 7 years ($M = 3,09$; $SD = 2,43$). These managers, as we hypothesized, therefore have significant experience of issues related to safety at work and have for the most part been involved in other occupational and industrial risk prevention campaigns prior to the deployment in 2015 of the safety management program concerned here.

Given these conditions, most managers consider in first analysis that this program does not change much to the main principles of safety in the field. However, the most senior managers (those who knew the company before the 1990s) have seen significant changes over the past 20 years or so in terms of: a) the place given to safety and b) the material means allocated: *"I would say, basically, that things are much better than they were during a period, which I experienced* [in the 1990s], *when safety was of the third order"*. *"Before, we didn't have the right tools, now we have them, but they still have to be reliable"*. In addition, some note that if the program does not disrupt practices, it has *"formalized something. Therefore, we have given more of a name, a legitimacy to the different innovations, to the different things that exist in the field"*. This safety management program is therefore not perceived as disruptive, but managers are identifying guidelines that formalize practices that have remained tacit until now.

3.2   The Daily Work as Manager and How Security Issues are Played Out

Three main missions are distinguished: production, safety and HR management. They are associated with four transversal missions: communication, reporting, relational and professionalization. All participants consider that one of the challenges of their daily work is to articulate the missions of Production, HRM and Safety in order to succeed in "working safely" (and avoid their juxtaposition or even contradiction in action). These missions were organized in radar graphic. We worked then on the basis of "typical cases" built from interviews with participants. Each "typical case" is the synthesis of specific cases, with reference to similar themes, told by several participants. It refers to two or more missions of the managers, thus shaping particular configurations. The radar graphic was based on three construction principles in order to describe the articulation of missions in the daily work of managers: 1) the arrangement of missions creates particular configurations, 2) each configuration is made up of one or more typical cases, 3) each typical case may have a favorable or unfavorable safety outcome from the point of view of the actors interviewed. Presented in the form of "radars graphic" of favorable and unfavorable configurations, they make it possible to work on the basis of factual elements related to the deployment of the safety program. From the twelve interviews, we identified a total of 66 specific cases (26 favorable and 40 unfavorable) which were organized into 23 typical cases (10 favorable and 13 unfavorable) illustrating 13 configurations.

For example, we present below a typical case of positive valence articulating the missions of production, safety, human resources and reporting: *"The software applications facilitate teamwork by making it possible to take over someone else's work. They facilitate the tracing of operations or human resource processes (salary) and their follow-up. They allow you to keep a memory of the state of the situation. They also make it possible to delegate part of the work, for example monitoring, before validating as a manager"*. The outcome of this typical case, whose main theme is digitalization, is judged to be both favorable and unfavorable to safe working. On the one hand, digitization facilitates reporting, the monitoring of safety clearances and the coordination of the company's players. It also allows a "memory" of the situation and its evolution to be kept. On the other hand, digitalization is not yet fully completed and the company is still in transition. In some cases, this incomplete digitalization leads to the need for double reporting in national software and in the company's local software, which generates an excess of reporting work. This reporting work is considered too important by the managers, for whom it does not directly ensure a safety function, but rather allows feedbacks in real time for a set of actors in the management and support functions. This reporting work in competition with field work with their teams contributes to a loss of meaning in their work among managers. The incomplete digitalization can also make it difficult to coordinate between actors who still work on paper and others who have moved to digital management.

3.3   The Known and Used Resources of the New Safety Program

Based on the card sorting, we analyzed the extent to which the safety program was a resource system for the participants. From a "quantitative" point of view, the resource system can be understood on the basis of two indicators: 1) the average number of people at the level of each resource category, 2) the number of people at the level of each resource. This makes it possible to distinguish resources "known" by employees from resources "used" in their work and to put into perspective, on the one hand, a level of knowledge of resources within the sample studied and, on the other hand, a declared level of use of resources in work. In this way, we can identify deviations/conformities with prescriptions or deviations/conformities with expectations by distinguishing between knowledge and use of resources. This allows to put the best known and most used resources into perspective, which provides information on the core of the resource system shared by the participants. On the other hand, identifying resources that are little or unknown and used by the managerial line allows to identify elements of the program that are not resources for the participants. In our case, we identified two resources. However, these resources had not yet been disseminated to all levels of the company at the time of the study. For example, 8/38 resources emerged as well-known resources by all the interviewed managers. These resources are in relation to four of the six axes of the safety program: the third and the sixth axes were not represented.

From a "qualitative" point of view, these treatments make it possible to show which categories and resources of the safety program are most or least known or used. We can also identify that a set of resources are declared to be known or used by the interviewees even though they have not yet been deployed at the time of the study. This type of result is not to be banished from interpretation; on the contrary, it is very interesting. They may mean that respondents attribute resources (tools, procedures, etc.) to the safety program that are not part of it. This provides information on the one hand on the quality of the dissemination of the program, the way in which the actors of the company have appropriated (or not) the resources and also more generally the way in which the actors apprehend the safety program. On this last point, one interpretation may be that the actors appropriate the guiding principles of the program more than they retain all the resources as presented in the program's prescriptive documents.

Finally, the added resources are indicators of the existence of local resources that the participants consider to be related to the management of safety in their work. In this example, nine additional resources were thus identified by the twelve participants interviewed. These resources showed the links with existing resources in work situations and the integration of the program with existing safety management practices.

3.4 The Professionalization Process to Safety Issues

The word of "professionalization" did not resonate with the participants during the interviews. The elements gathered often remained very general, or even left the participants questioning during the interviews. The word "professionalization" is not mentioned spontaneously or evocatively; it is replaced by other terms used on a day-to-day basis in the company such as: "training", "skills assessment", "qualifications", "the transmission of knowledge between old and new" or "the construction of safe work experience".

4 Discussion

The first results show how an evaluation approach based on a collective approach across the entire management line of a railway establishment, anchored in the analysis of the realities of the work of these managers and their subordinates, is a source of lessons learned in the deployment of the safety program at the various hierarchical levels. The inventory of the knowledge and use (shared or not) makes it possible to assess the level of deployment of the various resources of the safety program within the company, as well as the level of control. The identification of favorable or fearful management mission configurations also allows the multidimensional and systemic nature of occupational safety management to be considered. Finally, considering the prior experience of these managers leads to an understanding of how they position themselves in relation to the program analyzed and the effects they perceive.

With this method, the challenge is not to provide only an expert point of view, but rather to support the construction of a reflection based on the analysis of actual work to support the changes deemed collectively necessary for working safely. This method has to be seen as a tool for the direction committee in order to guide continuous safety improvement.

Finally, beyond an integrated approach to safety in the workplace, these results underline the constructed nature of safety. They invite to draw a parallel with other studies, that propose to develop an analytical framework for a constructed safety approach [8–11].

References

1. IAEA: Safety culture. Safety series No. 75-INSAG-4. IAEA, Vienna (1991)
2. Johansen, J.P., Almklov, P.G., Mohammad, A.B.: What can possibly go wrong? Anticipatory work in space operations. Cognt. Technol. Work **18**(2), 333–350 (2016)
3. Hollnagel, E.: Epilogue: RAG – The resilience Analysis Grid. In: Hollnagel, E., Pariès, J., Woods, D., Wreathall, J. (eds.) Resilience Engineering in Practice: A Guidebook, pp. 275–296. Aldershot, UK Ashgate, Studies in Resilience Engineering (2010)
4. Baril-Gingras, G., Bellemare, M., Brun, J.P.: The contribution of qualitative analyses of occupational health and safety interventions: an example through a study of ex- ternal advisory interventions. Saf. Sci. **44**, 851–874 (2006)
5. Stave, C., Marianne Törner, M., Eklö, M.: An intervention method for occupational safety in farming — evaluation of the effect and process. Appl. Ergon. **38**, 357–368 (2007). https://doi.org/10.1016/j.apergo.2006.04.025
6. Berthelette, D., Leduc, N., Bilodeau, H., Durand, M.-J., Faye, C.: Evaluation of the implementation fidelity of an ergonomic training program designed to prevent back pain. Appl. Ergon. **43**, 239–245 (2012). https://doi.org/10.1016/j.apergo.2011.05.008
7. Van Eerd, D., Mae Ferron, E., D'Elia, T., Morgan, D., Ziesmann, F., Amick, B.C., III.: Process evaluation of a participatory organizational change program to reduce musculoskeletal and slip, trip and fall injuries. Appl. Ergon. **68**, 42–53 (2018). https://doi.org/10.1016/j.apergo.2017.10.015
8. Nascimento, A, Cuvelier, L. Mollo, V., Dicciocio, A. Falzon, P.: Constructing safety: from the normative to the adaptive view. In: Falzon, P. (ed.), Constructive Ergonomics, Chapter 8, pp. 111–125. CRC Press, Taylor & Francis Group, Boca Raton (2015)
9. Rocha, R., Mollo, V., Daniellou, F.: Work debate spaces: a tool for developing a participatory safety management. Appl. Ergon. **46**, 107–114 (2015). https://doi.org/10.1016/j.apergo.2014.07.012
10. Rocha, R., Mollo, V., Daniellou, F.: Contributions and conditions of structured debates on work on safety construction. Saf. Sci. **113**, 192–199 (2019). https://doi.org/10.1016/j.ssci.2018.11.030
11. Galey, L., Nascimento, A., Cuvelier, L., Judon, N., Delgoulet, C., Boccara, V., Marquet, A. Audignon, S., Gaillard, I., Garrigou, A.: From regulated and managed to constructive safety in the industry. In: 21th World Congress Ergonomics, 13–18 June. Vancouver: Canada (2021)

Training of Occupational Health and Safety Professionals in Design Thinking

Ole Broberg$^{(\boxtimes)}$ 🆔 and Sisse Grøn

DTU Management, Engineering Systems Design, Technical University of Denmark,
2800 Lyngby, Denmark
obro@dtu.dk

Abstract. Within realistic time constraints we successfully trained six occupational health and safety professionals in applying a Design Thinking (DT) approach to solve complex musculoskeletal and psychosocial problems at work. DT may be defined by the double diamond model pointing to a non-linear and user-centred problem-solving process iterating through divergent and convergent phases A key characteristic of DT is the ability to frame a problematic situation in new and interesting ways. The training was done in a full-day workshop followed by a learning-by-doing phase in which they planned and completed design sprint workshops in companies. The professionals went from novices into advanced beginners according to the Dreyfus model of skill acquisition. In the overall question of the usefulness of DT in OHS management, the average rating went from 6 before the training course to 9.5 after. In an evaluation of the DT approach on a 1–5 scale they rated design sprints at 3.8 to be more appropriate to manage complex problems than the methods they normally used. However, more experience seems necessary to adopt the DT mind set of an iterative process, in which they need to decide which tools to use in an emergent, nonlinear and iterative fashion.

Keywords: Design Thinking · Occupational health and safety professionals · Training program · Complex problems

1 Introduction

Many companies are looking for more agile and flexible approaches to solve complex safety and health challenges such as musculoskeletal and psychosocial problems. This is an opportunity for occupational health and safety (OHS) professionals to introduce new methods for problem solving. We propose the design thinking (DT) approach as a candidate for this endeavour. A key characteristic of DT is the ability to frame a problematic situation in new and interesting ways. It was our assumption that the 'designerly' way of problem framing and solving were well suited for complex workplace problems and for promoting a participatory approach.

The motivation for the project is based in the context for Danish OHS professionals. They are characterized as "an occupational group of professionals characterized by heterogeneity and multidisciplinary in approaches and methods" [1]. Hence, when

© The Author(s), under exclusive license to Springer Nature Switzerland AG 2021
N. L. Black et al. (Eds.): IEA 2021, LNNS 219, pp. 618–623, 2021.
https://doi.org/10.1007/978-3-030-74602-5_85

Danish OHS professionals take part in managing complex OHS problems they do that in a myriad of different approaches. We suggest that Design Thinking has the ability to provide an overall problem-solving process, which may guide OHS professionals.

DT may be defined by the double diamond model pointing to a non-linear and user-centred problem-solving process iterating through divergent and convergent phases (Fig. 1). The first diamond focusses on exploring and defining the problem, while the second diamond focusses on developing and testing solutions. The iterative process through the two diamonds may be done in an intensive *design sprint* by a small group of participants [2].

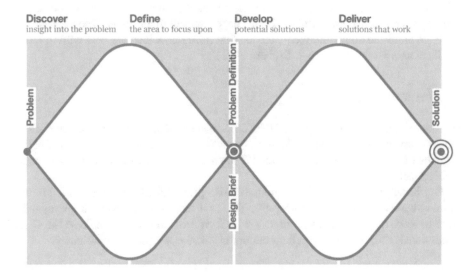

Fig. 1. The double diamond model (Design Council 2007).

Saidi et al. studied how DT can complement a human factor engineering approach [3]. They point to a number of features in DT that are not present in human factor engineering: 1) DT is driven by feedback from users, 2) the multidisciplinary teams in DT provide input from diverse expertise, generating a wider variety of possible solutions, 3) the testing and iteration of low fidelity prototypes is a useful entry point for preliminary assessment of solutions, 4) the principle of fail fast and often, can be helpful in the management of risks before implementing a solution, and 5) the emphasis on empathy creates opportunities for stakeholders to identify expressed and underlying needs. We assume these points also to be valid when it comes to how DTI can contribute to OHS management.

As DT is spreading to new areas there has been some studies on how to teach and train DT for non-designers. Seidel & Fixson points to the dilemma that non-designers face difficulties in learning the tools and mind-set of DT as they do not have a training as designers [4]. They set out to investigate how relative novices can learn effective DT methods given realistic time constraints for training. They identify three group of tools that they see as the core of DT in training non-designers: need-finding tools, brainstorming tools, and prototyping tools. In addition to learning the tools, Seidel & Fixson also point to the need for adopting a designer's mindset [4]. This includes encouraging a climate of debate, developing a sense of empathy, and promoting respect of different viewpoints.

Finally, Seidel & Fixson point to a challenge that non-designers will meet in learning the DT approach [4]: the use of DT tools is dynamic and requires adaption over time. It is not a linear problem-solving process. DT learners have to adapt to a process in which they need to decide which tools to use in an emergent, nonlinear and iterative fashion.

In adapting DT to the area of OHS management two questions may be raised: 1) Why is DT worth introducing to OHS professionals? 2) How can OHS professionals as non-designers learn to practice DT? In this paper we will focus on the second question. We have indicated some arguments for the first question, which we deal with in more details in another paper (Grøn & Broberg 2021).

2   Methodology

In order to explore the potentials of DT in OHS management we designed an interactive research project [6] aiming at elucidating (i) how OHS professionals can be trained in the DT approach and tools, and (ii) how the DT approach contributes to OHS management. In this paper we focus on (i).

Our basic philosophy for the training of OHS professionals was to ground it in the learning-by-doing theory by Dewey [7]. This is a hands-on approach to learning. In order to learn the students must interact with their environment. In this case the OHS professionals must interact with their current professional practice environment.

Table 1. Training program activities and data collection methods.

Activity	Data collection
Baseline OHS professionals	Interviews
Training workshop	Questionnaire
Design sprint 1	Observation and questionnaire
Reflection workshop	Questionnaire
Design sprint 2	Observation and questionnaire
Design sprint 3	Observation and questionnaire
Evaluation workshop	Interviews and questionnaire

The training program included three main activities (Table 1): 1) a full-day training workshop and a handbook introducing the DT approach and tools, 2) the OHS professionals applying the approach and tools in a case in their own organisation or with a client, and 3) a reflection workshop in between in which the professionals shared and evaluated experiences. In the training workshop, the researchers introduced the design sprint as a key feature of DT and a way to involve relevant stakeholders in the problem solving [2]. A design sprint was defined as a very compact version of going through the phases in the double diamond model. The main task for the participant hereafter was to plan and facilitate two or three design sprints of 3–4 h in their own or client company in order to solve a real-world psychosocial or musculoskeletal problem.

Six experienced OHS professionals were recruited for the training program. Four were internal professionals in companies and two were professionals in an occupational health service consultancy. The case companies included a pharmaceutical manufacturer, a mail distribution centre, and two municipality services. The two first cases focussed on musculoskeletal problems, and the two last-mentioned on psychosocial problems.

Quantitative and qualitative data were used in evaluating the learning outcome. The participants filled in a questionnaire at five different points along the training program. For each DT element the respondent was asked to rate his/her 'knowledge of', 'preparedness to apply' and actual 'applying in my work'. In this way it was possible to follow the OHS professionals' self-reported progress in learning DT models and tools. After design sprint 2 or 3 the OHS professionals rated their overall experience with the DT approach and the outcome.

The quantitative data were supplemented by observation of OHS professionals facilitating design sprints in companies, and semi-structured interviews with the six participants after they had completed the sprints.

3 Results

The results indicated a steep learning curve after the training workshop assessed on a 1–10 rating scale. This included basic DT elements such as the DT concept, the Double Diamond model, and the design sprint approach (Fig. 2).

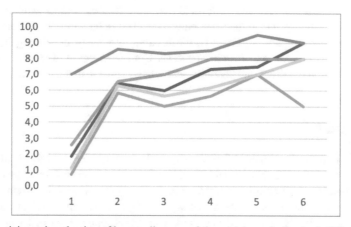

Fig. 2. Participants' evaluation of how well prepared they are to apply five basic DT elements in their practice. In the x-axis number 1 refers to before the training workshop and number 6 to after the completion of the third design sprint workshop in a company. (n = 6)

In the overall question of the usefulness of DT in OHS management, the average rating went from 6 before the training course to 9.5 after design sprint 3 (Fig. 3). In an evaluation of the DT approach on a 1–5 scale they rated design sprints at 3.8 to be more appropriate to manage complex problems than the methods they normally used. The degree to which the design sprint contributed to a better understanding and definition of the problem was also rated at 3.8. Expecting that elements from DT will be part of their future work practice were rated at 3.6.

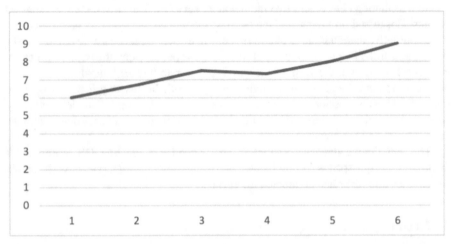

Fig. 3. Participants' evaluation of how useful Design Thinking is in OHS management. In the x-axis number 1 refers to before the training workshop and number 6 to after the completion of the third design sprint workshop in a company. (n = 6)

Observations and interviews confirmed that the OHS consultants were able to plan and facilitate design sprints in their company. However, in handling the double diamond process they were sometime surprised by the iterative nature, e.g., in defining the problem by a continuous naming and framing process. Confusion could also arise on how to articulate the problem focus and keeping clear when you were in the problem or solution diamond.

4 Discussion

The results indicate that basic DT skills may be learned quickly by OHS professionals in a compact training program based on learning-by-doing. The professionals went from novices into advanced beginners according to the Dreyfus model of skill acquisition [8]. However, more experience seems necessary to adopt the DT mind set of an iterative process. The study also indicated that the DT approach opens up a new role for OHS professionals as a planner and facilitator of design sprints for company stakeholders to solve complex problems. However, this study has been a 'DT push' project for a limited number of participants and more studies are needed to document the benefits of DT skills among OHS professionals and to optimise a training program and handbook.

5   Conclusion

OHS professionals may learn DT and a new role through a compact training program based on learning by doing. Adopting the iterative design process seems to a major challenge for OHS professionals. Applying DT in companies may open up new approaches for handling complex OHS problems in a participatory way.

References

1. Madsen, C.U., Hasle, P., Limborg, H.J.: Professionals without a profession: occupational safety and health professionals in Denmark. Saf. Sci. **113**, 356–361 (2019)
2. Knapp, J., Zeratsky, J., Kowitz, B.: Sprint: How to Solve Big Problems and Test New Ideas in Just Five Days. Bantam Press, London (2016)
3. Saidi, T., Mutswangwa, C.T., Douglas, T.S.: Design Thinking as a complement to human factors engineering for enhancing medical device usability. Eng. Stud. **11**(1), 34–50 (2019)
4. Seidel, V.P., Fixson, S.K.: Adopting Design Thinking in novice multidisciplinary teams: the application and limits of design methods and reflexive practices. J. Prod. Innov. Manage. **30**(S1), 19–33 (2013)
5. Grøn, S., Broberg, O.: Design thinking: a new approach for OHS professionals to address complex problems. In: Proceedings on 21st International Ergonomics Association Triennial Congress. Springer (2021, forthcoming)
6. Eklund, J., Pettersen, J., Elg, M., Bolling, A.: Interactive research for production and work environment. In: Proceedings on Nordic Ergonomics Society Annual Conference. NES (2008)
7. Dewey, J.: Democracy and Education: An Introduction to the Philosophy Of Education. WLC Books, New York (2009). (Original work published 1916)
8. Dreyfus, S.E., Dreyfus, H.L.: A Five-Stage Model of the Mental Activities Involved in Directed Skill Acquistion. Storming Media, Washington D.C. (1980)

Need-Seeking: Creating, Discovering or Recovering Needs?

Stéphanie Buisine[1](✉), Amandine Taton[1,2], and Andréa Boisadan[1]

[1] CESI LINEACT, 92000 Nanterre, France
sbuisine@cesi.fr
[2] Châlons-Agglo, 51000 Châlons en Champagne, France

Abstract. Need-seeker approach, which orients new product development towards the satisfaction of future needs, has been recognized as one of the most efficient innovation strategies to date. But finding future needs to address remains a challenge for companies, entrepreneurs and practitioners, as they lack a methodological framework to structure their approach. In this chapter, we first elaborate on three paradigms for need-seeking: discovery of future needs, creation of new needs, and recovery of fundamental needs. We then provide examples of methods supporting each paradigm, and tentatively position them in terms of reliability and affordability, so that innovation teams can make informed choices in their application. Thereby, we expect to contribute to the field of prospective ergonomics and its concrete implementation, as well as to the promotion of radical innovation based on needs and uses rather than based solely on technology.

Keywords: Prospective ergonomics · Radical innovation · Future needs · Future uses

1 Innovation

From a macroeconomic viewpoint, innovation is acknowledged as a major factor of productivity, economic growth and population wellbeing [1]. It is considered as key to nurture western industry [2] and to reach a balance between social and economic approaches of growth [3].

Radical innovation shapes world's long-term transformations as it produces a significant impact on existing markets or creates new markets [4]. Radical innovation is implemented through products recognized as new (as opposed to incremental innovation, which relies on improvement of existing products) and this novelty can be testified by the introduction of a new technological feature and/or by new uses of existing technological solutions. While technological innovation is lengthy to develop and limited by the advance of science and research, innovating by making new uses of existing technologies is potentially unlimited and can be fruitful in a short term, provided that it is supported by a relevant and structured methodological approach.

1.1 Need-Seeker Innovation Strategy

Innovation observatories around the world highlight three main strategies developed within the companies that invest highest on research and development worldwide [5], namely: Technology-driver strategy (whose priority is to develop products of superior technological value, which may result in radical innovation based on new technology), Market-reader strategy (which focuses on creating value through incremental innovation and customization of products) and Need-seeker strategy (which aims to find unstated customer needs of the future, be the first to address them, and result in radical innovation through new uses). Although the three strategies all possess their own success stories, a long-term analysis [5] clearly shows that Need-seeker outperforms the two other strategies in terms of leading position on the market and financial return on investment. Hence innovation analysts recommend developing Need-seeker strategy in order to stimulate progress and growth. However, need-seeking is not straightforward as traditional ergonomic methods for needs analysis rather turn into a Market-reader approach. Need-seeking as in prospective ergonomics remains to be structured methodologically to be more widely adopted by practitioners, entrepreneurs and companies.

1.2 Discovery and Creation Paradigms

Need-seeking is mostly defined as *anticipating* future needs [5], but the very notion of anticipation is subject to debate, as one may consider the future as more or less deterministic, more or less chaotic, and therefore more or less likely to be anticipated. In this respect, entrepreneurship approaches notably contrast the discovery and creation paradigms, which can be illustrated through the metaphor of *mountain-climbing* vs. *mountain-building* [6]. On the one hand, the discovery paradigm (*mountain-climbing*) assumes that future needs can be approached (i.e., anticipated) through the careful study of current uses and unsatisfied needs. In other terms, the mountain exists and the challenge is to be the first one to reach the top: this paradigm fosters competition between companies on existing markets (which can also be called Red-ocean strategy – [7]). On the other hand, the creation paradigm (*mountain-building*) considers that the future cannot be predicted (or anticipated) and is to be invented. The mountain does not exist, the demand has to be created (Blue-ocean strategy – [7]). The latter view entails much more uncertainty but empowers creative people and inventors, as innovation opportunities appear here as endogenous to any company or entrepreneur. Conversely, if future needs are to be discovered, or anticipated, innovation opportunities are exogenous per se and entrepreneurs have to surround themselves with people exhibiting sharp analysis skills and experience.

To these worldviews, we add a third paradigm, relying on re-discovering, or recovering, fundamental needs. This is a pragmatic approach which does not attempt to anticipate but does not rely on pure creation either.

1.3 Recovery Paradigm

Before elaborating on this paradigm, it seems useful to clarify what we mean by "needs" in the need-seeker strategy. We do not aim to search for some new psychological needs, as these are defined as innate and universal – hence it seems pointless to create, discover or recover new needs. For example, in Self-determination theory [8], human motivation process relies on three psychological meta-needs (need for autonomy, for competence, and for relatedness). Need-seeker innovation strategy rather focuses on functional needs, which determine product use. For example, World Health Organization [9] lists bodily, individual and societal functions, and we believe that innovation may impact these functional needs, either by meeting them (i.e., providing functional solutions), or by stressing them (e.g., when a product appears poorly usable).

Accordingly, we posit that many technological and/or use innovations can be interpreted, not as the discovery or creation of new functional needs, but as the recovery of fundamental functional needs. For example, augmented, tactile, tangible or spoken interaction solutions allow direct manipulation of data, which is not a recently appeared functional need, but represents a fundamental need we have unlearnt with previous interaction solutions (e.g., soft keys, mouse and keyboard). When one develops expertise with a technological solution, be it an imperfect one, s/he may feel satisfied and no longer experience the fundamental need behind. The recovery paradigm consists in seeking this fundamental need to inspire new functional solutions and generate use-based innovation.

2   Need-Seeking Methods

In the present section, we describe and illustrate examples of need-seeking methods implementing the creation, discovery and recovery paradigms. Fig. 1 below emphasizes that these three paradigms can be organized along a double continuum: methods for discovering (anticipating) future needs may be the most reliable ones (with a high likelihood of generating successful innovations as outcomes) but the most difficult ones to put into practice (because they require time and specific resources). On the other end of the continua, methods for creating needs are affordable to any organization but appear as highly uncertain: an infinite number of ideas can be generated, among which the probability to pick up the next successful innovation may be quite low.

Methods attempting to recover fundamental needs lie in between the two ends of the continua: they require more resources than creation methods but remain less costly to implement than discovery methods. Similarly, they may offer an interesting tradeoff in terms of reliability and likelihood of success.

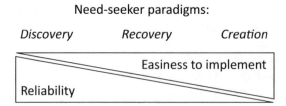

Fig. 1. Need-seeker paradigms (discovery, recovery and creation) organized along a double continuum: Reliability of the approach (likelihood of success in terms of innovation outcomes) and easiness to implement (in terms of time, investment or specific resources).

2.1 Discovering Future Needs with Lead Users

Needs analysis as traditionally performed in User-centered design process is highly relevant for improving existing products (i.e., incremental innovation) but may not be fruitful for discovering future needs. On the contrary, it may generate the so-called Innovator's dilemma [4] and thereby inhibit radical innovation: companies willing to develop solutions as close to market demands as possible are likely to miss radical innovation opportunities, because a majority of users prefer sticking to current dominant designs and tend to spontaneously reject a radical change in their habits.

Therefore, collecting ideas of radically different solutions or evaluating them should be performed with a specific kind of users, who are positioned ahead of Rogers' [10] curve of innovation adoption. Lead users are such minority users with whom companies are likely to discover future needs or future uses. By definition, lead users are precursors and are at the leading edge of important trends in the market. The Lead user method [11] consists in involving in the innovation process such users with a specific profile, exhibiting both strong critical-thinking skills with regard to existing products and strong creative-thinking skills to imagine alternative uses. Case studies (e.g., in the domain of sport or open-source software – [11]) have shown that involving lead users in an innovation project may grant access to needs that will later be experienced by many users and therefore may open successful innovation opportunities. The method was also formally tested with 3M company [12] in the sector of medical supplies and gave rise to the biggest innovation wave in 50 years in this division [13].

Although very effective, this method remains costly to implement, as finding Lead users requires time and formalizing their needs and ideas requires a skilled team.

2.2 Creating New Needs with Personas

Less costly methods might be found in the Lean startup framework [14] in which designers and entrepreneurs often rely on Personas to imagine user-centered, undreamed-of concepts that they subsequently test and improve through short iterations and continuous customer involvement. The Persona is a concept formalized by Cooper [15], Pruitt and Grudin [16] and Pruitt and Adlin [17]. It is a fictitious character representing a segment of population. According to Blomquist and Arvola [18], "a Persona is an archetype of a user that is given a name and a face, and it is carefully described in terms of needs, goals and tasks". Representing a group through an archetype fosters empathy to designers and supports feeling and interpreting action, thoughts and emotions of the target segment [19, 20]. Personas can be used all along the design process, in the design, implementation, or test and measure phases [17, 19]. They can be materialized as posters or storyboards including a name, a face, a general biographical note (e.g., age, occupation, hobbies), and specific information related to the project (e.g., attitudes, expectations, and concerns regarding the target sector or activity), as well as virtual characters or avatars [20].

On a theoretical viewpoint, Persona efficiency may be related to priming process, which refers to "the incidental activation of knowledge structures, such as trait, concepts and stereotypes, by the current situational context" [21]. The mere activation of a concept or a stereotype (here: the Persona profile) activates some associated semantic information networks likely to shape ideation accordingly: in an automatic and unconscious way, one's thoughts, ideas, and behaviors are influenced by the concepts activated [21, 22]. This phenomenon may explain why Personas help designers imagine concepts that are adapted to users. However, this often results in an overwhelming number of ideas among which designers struggle to identify which one may result in actual need creation and successful innovation. Hence the uncertainty of the method.

2.3   Recovering Fundamental Needs with Extraordinary Users

As previously stated, this approach consists in uncovering fundamental needs hidden by long-term use of products and technologies, in order to find new solutions – radically-new solutions to old needs. Typical or representative users may not be able to access their fundamental needs, which are deemed to be satisfied for a long time by contemporary products. To elicit hidden fundamental needs, it is more fruitful to refer to non-typical, or extraordinary users [23] whose functional needs are not satisfied by contemporary products designed for typical users. Those can be found among off-standard or off-target users. Off-standard users are those experiencing a limitation in their capabilities while using products (e.g., children, seniors, users with a disability), and off-target users are those who do not belong to the marketing segment of the product and have never had the opportunity to develop expertise its use (e.g., children, non-users).

Because children's capacities are under development, they may experience, depending on their age, several limitations, be they physical (e.g., height, grip), motor (e.g., strength, dexterity) or cognitive (e.g., literacy, understanding). These characteristics are likely to highlight functional needs in terms of easiness, simplicity, accessibility, and so on. For example, it is reported that the first graphical user interface was invented because the challenge was to design a computer that would be so simple that a child would be able to use it [24]. This special need of children later proved to be generalizable to the whole population. Children are also capable of expressing spontaneously "impossible" demands that adults would self-censor. For example, in reaction to his 3-year-old daughter insisting to see instantly the photos he took of her, Edwin Land ended up inventing the Polaroid in 1943 [25].

The integration of the special needs of users with disabilities into mainstream product design is called Universal design [26, 27]. Its primary purpose is product accessibility, whereas our aim is to foster radical innovation through the generalization of special needs. For example, addressing special needs of people with severe motor impairment (wheelchair users) gave rise to radical innovation in the sector of fitness equipment for the general population [23]. Stretching their (lower limbs') muscles is a fundamental need of wheelchair users (to avoid muscle retraction, recover after surgery, maintain joints, manage pain, etc.) that they can hardly meet autonomously. The design of a fitness device to practice stretching revealed that it is actually a fundamental need for everyone: it happened to become a radical innovation and a best-seller in fitness industry, which was previously focused on weightlifting and cardio training only.

Finally, people with no prior experience of a given product may be more likely to express unmet functional needs than expert users. The expert may indeed have developed routines and strategies to increase efficiency and overcome limitations of the product so that s/he may no longer see them. For example, in a pedagogical experiment [28], needs of users and non-users of nail polish were analyzed through a simple user test.

Target users (women) did not comment much on nail polish devices, just mentioned that the brush used for the test was not flexible enough and too small. On the contrary, off-target users (men) commented a lot on the devices (bottle, cap, brush), which appeared highly unusable with fingernails freshly painted; they also emphasized the difficulty to paint nails of the dominant hand (with their non-dominant hand) and so on – obvious fundamental needs that target users did not mention. These may nonetheless be actual needs for all, as target users interviewed in this study were still 60% dissatisfied and 80% to find nail polish application difficult (this reached 100% of off-target users).

All in all, because it requires field studies, the Extraordinary user method appears as more costly to implement than the Persona method, but more affordable than the Lead user method, because lead users hold a much more specific profile and are more difficult to spot out of the general population. In terms of reliability, the Extraordinary user method may be less effective than the Lead user method, but more reliable than methods for creating new needs, which are subject to the highest uncertainty.

3 Conclusion

To face innovation challenges of the twenty-first century, companies should learn from proven successful strategies and strive to implement them in their own framework, adapt them for their own market and customers, in compliance with their own constraints and organizational culture. We focused here on Need-seeker innovation, a strategy acknowledged as efficient to generate new products, services or business processes based on "future needs". To help practitioners, entrepreneurs and companies knowingly structure their own Need-seeker approach, we first described three paradigms supporting respectively the discovery of future needs, the creation of new needs, and the recovery of fundamental needs. We provided examples of methods in each paradigm illustrated by a few application cases and discussed their reliability and affordability. We thereby expect to contribute to the promotion of need-seeking, prospective ergonomics, and radical innovation based on the value added to customer uses and need satisfaction.

References

1. OECD: Oslo Manual: Guidelines for collecting, reporting and using data on innovation. 4th edn. OECD, Paris (2018)
2. Midler, C., Beaume, R., Maniak, R.: Réenchanter l'industrie par l'innovation. Dunod, Paris (2012)
3. Le Masson, P., Weil, B., Hatchuel, A.: Les processus d'innovation: Conception innovante et croissance des entreprises. Hermès Science, Paris (2006)
4. Christensen, C.: The Innovator's Dilemma. Harvard Business Review Press, Boston (2016)
5. Jaruzelski, B., Staack, V., Goehle, B.: Proven paths to innovation success. Strategy Bus. 77, 2–16 (2014)
6. Alvarez, S.A., Barney, J.B.: Discovery and creation: Alternative theories of entrepreneurial action. Strategic Entrepreneurship J. 1, 11–26 (2007)
7. Kim, W.C., Mauborgne, R.: Blue Ocean Strategy: How to Create Uncontested Market Space and Make the Competition Irrelevant. Harvard Business School Press, Boston (2005)

8. Deci, E.L., Ryan, R.M.: The "what" and "why" of goal pursuits: human needs and the self-determination of behavior. Psychol. Inq. **11**, 227–268 (2000)
9. World Health Organization: International classification of functioning. In: Disability and health: ICF (2001)
10. Rogers, E.M.: Diffusion of Innovations, 5th edn. Free Press, New York (2003)
11. Von Hippel, E.: Democratizing Innovation. MIT Press, Cambridge (2005)
12. Von Hippel, E., Thomke, S., Sonnack, M.: Creating breakthroughs at 3M. Harvard Bus. Rev. **77**, 47–57 (1999)
13. Lilien, G.L., Morrison, P.D., Searls, K., Sonnack, M., von Hippel, E.: Performance assessment of the lead user idea-generation process for new product development. Manage. Sci. **48**, 1042–1059 (2002)
14. Ries, E.: The Lean Startup: How Today's Entrepreneurs Use Continuous Innovation to Create Radically Successful Businesses. Crown Business, New York (2011)
15. Cooper, A.: The Inmates are Running the Asylum. Macmillan, New York (1999)
16. Pruitt, J., Grudin, J.: Personas: practice and theory. In: Proceedings of the Conference on Designing for User Experiences, pp. 1–15. San Francisco (2003)
17. Pruitt, J., Adlin, T.: The Persona Lifecycle: Keeping People in Mind Throughout Product Design. Morgan Kaufmann Publishers, San Francisco (2010)
18. Blomquist, A., Arvola, M.: Personas in action: ethnography in an interaction design team. In: Proceedings of the Second Nordic Conference on Human–Computer Interaction, pp. 197–200. ACM Press (2002)
19. Bornet, C., Brangier, E.: méthode des Personas: Principes, intérêts et limites. Bulletin de Psychologie **524**(2), 115–134 (2013)
20. Buisine, S., Guegan, J., Barré, J., Segonds, F., Aoussat, A.: Using avatars to tailor ideation process to innovation strategy. Cognit. Technol. Work **18**, 583–594 (2016)
21. Bargh, J.A., Chen, M., Burrows, L.: Automaticity of social behavior: direct effects of trait construct and stereotype activation on action. J. Person. Soc. Psychol. **71**(2), 230–244 (1996)
22. Dijksterhuis, A., Van Knippenberg, A.: The relation between perception and behavior, or how to win a game of trivial pursuit. J. Person. Soc. Psychol. **74**(4), 865–877 (1998)
23. Buisine, S., Boisadan, A., Richir, S.: L'innovation radicale par la méthode de l'utilisateur extraordinaire. Psychologie du Travail et des Organisations **24**, 374–386 (2018)
24. Isaacson, W.: Steve Jobs. JC Lattès, Paris (2011)
25. Nonaka, I., Zhu, Z.: Pragmatic Strategy. Cambridge University Press, Cambridge (2012)
26. Vanderheiden, G.C.: Design for people with functional limitations resulting from disability, aging and circumstance. In: Salvendy, G. (ed.) Handbook of Human Factors and Ergonomics, pp. 2010–2052. Wiley, New York (1997)
27. Vanderheiden, G.C., Tobias, J.: Universal design of consumer products: current industry practice and perceptions. In Proceedings of the XIVth Triennal Congress of the International Ergonomics Association and 44th Annual Meeting of the Human Factors and Ergonomics Association, pp. 19–22 (2000)
28. Buisine, S., Bourgeois-Bougrine, S.: The creative process in engineering - Teaching innovation to engineering students. In: Lubart, T. (ed.) The creative process - Perspectives from Multiple Domains, Chapter 7, pp. 181–207. Palgrave Macmillan, London (2018)

Sharing an Autonomous Taxi Without a Driver Through Guided Imaginary Projection to Identify Sources of (Dis)comfort

Beatrice Cahour[1]([✉]), Marie Hoarau[1], and Anna Rossi[2]

[1] CNRS i3 Telecom, Paris, France
beatrice.cahour@telecom-paristech.fr
[2] Faurecia, Nanterre, France

Abstract. Future shared robot taxis should reduce traffic congestion in cities, and in order to design services adapted to the needs of users, the sources of comfort and discomfort must be specified. In order to project people into the use of this future mobility, the technique of Guided Imaginary Projection was used with 40 men and women between 22 and 66 years of age. It made it possible to specify the effect produced by the absence of a driver, a driver who usually takes on the role of mediator who reassures, organizes and manages the unexpected events. Recommendations for the design of such services were drafted.

Keywords: Autonomous taxi · Comfort and discomfort · Guided imaginary projection · Interactions · Security · Feeling of control

1 Problem Statement

This study is looking at future autonomous shared cars (full autonomy of level 5), also known as shared autonomous taxis or robotic taxis. These vehicles would be capable of travelling on different types of road, in built-up areas as well as on expressways, without a driver or attendant.

These shared autonomous taxis offer great promise. As electric vehicles, they should be more environmentally friendly, relieve road congestion and limit road accidents (ERTRAC Working Group 2017b, 2017a). But for significant effects to be observed, it is important that these robotic taxis be shared. Indeed, the electrification of autonomous vehicles alone will not prevent the harmful effects of the private car on the environment. Sharing vehicles should be more beneficial: it should limit the number of vehicles produced and make the trips produced by each vehicle profitable (Pélata et al., 2019; Saujot et al., 2018). Although several models of vehicle sharing exist, the idea here is to share the same vehicle with strangers during a journey, such as short distance carpooling, as opposed to car-sharing which consists of making a vehicle available to various users, without them having to live together for the duration of a journey. The shared robotic taxi therefore represents a paradigm shift from the personal owner-vehicle to a shared autonomous vehicle service, involving cohabitation in the passenger compartment with strangers and without a driver.

N. L. Black et al. (Eds.): IEA 2021, LNNS 219, pp. 631–638, 2021.
https://doi.org/10.1007/978-3-030-74602-5_87

For the user, the shared robotic taxi seems to be closer to two types of services that currently exist: car-pooling and Chauffeur-Driven-Car (CDC) in pool mode, thus shared with strangers. Studies concerning these modes of transport show the predominant role of the driver both in car-pooling (Adelé and Dionisio 2020; Cahour et al. 2018; Créno 2016) and for CDCs in solo mode (Kim et al. 2019) or in pool mode (Morris et al. 2020; Pratt et al. 2019). In carpooling or in CDC, drivers have both an organisational role, for example for helping the identification of the vehicle and choosing routes, and a role as facilitator of on-board interactions. Its absence in the context of shared robotic taxis therefore raises the issue: does the absence of the driver in a shared robotic taxi have an effect on tyhe appropriation of the service and in which way?

Although many prospective studies exist on level 5 autonomous vehicles and partly on shared robotic taxis (Becker and Axhausen 2017; Narayanan et al. 2020), they most often take place in the form of a priori acceptability questionnaires, i.e. without taking into account the participants' travel activity or, under the paradigm of declared choice, which does not question the motives of the choices made by the participants.

There are also experiments which are more ecological, but generally with routes with predefined stops (such as a bus) and not door-to-door, or with support persons in a level 2 or 3 shuttle to ensure that everything runs as smoothly as possible. Of particular interest is the study by Kim et al (2019) using the Wizard of Oz paradigm. This paradigm makes it possible, by hiding the driver behind an occulting system, to make participants believe that the vehicle is autonomous. This study specifically documents the interactions between the driver and the users of an autonomous CDC service in order to design a prototype that compensates for the absence of a driver. However, in this study, the vehicles are not shared and the routes are imposed, which does not quite answer our question.

2   Methodology

We wanted the participants to mobilize the robot taxi in a usual mobility activity. The futuristic service that was imagined with a working group including car manufacturers[1] is similar to a shared CDC service (such as Uber pool), but with an autonomous car without driver. The paradigm of the Wizard of Oz and the other classic projective methods, by imposing a scenario and a route, were not adequate for this objective. We then chose a mode of imaginary projection in a trip with the shared robotic taxi service that we presented to the participants.

2.1   Population

The 40 participants in the study (20 men and 20 women, aged 22 to 66, m. = 43.4, standard deviation = 15.12) were recruited by mailing list and word of mouth. Four age

[1] We thank the P.F.A (Plateforme de la Filière Automobile) for the financing of this study, and the PFA Working Group including Samuel Baudu (Faurecia), Luciano Ojeda (PSA), Jean-François Forzy (Renault) and Stéphanie Coeugnet (Institut Vedecom) ; this group helped us to imagine an adequate service, and gave feedbacks on the methodology and recommendations for future services.

groups were balanced: 10 participants aged 22 to 30, 10 aged 30 to 45, 10 aged 45 to 60, 10 over 60. Their professions are varied, some are also students or retired.

So that participants could easily project themselves in the use of this type of service, the criteria for inclusion in the study were to have already used either a CDC in pool mode, or a CDC in solo mode and carpooling. The important point was that participants could easily imagine sharing a vehicle with strangers from a smartphone application that geolocates them[2].

2.2 Protocol[3]

The aim was to project the participants into a simulation of the use of the shared robotic taxi so that the participants could understand it "as if" they were using it; it allows them to describe sources of comfort/discomfort after having almost tested the service and not just on the basis of an abstract and global representation. This projection into future and non-existent use can be done through films (Cahour and Forzy 2009), but then it is not the participant who acts, or through virtual reality, but it is very complex to simulate a taxi robot with several people entering, exiting and interacting. The method of Guided Imaginary Projection, developed by Allinc et al. (2018) for the use of still inexistent modes of transport, seemed very appropriate. It proceeds with the following steps.

Phase 1: Presentation of the Service. Le service de robot-taxi a été expliqué aux participants à l'aide de plusieurs images représentant l'application sur smartphone et l'intérieur du véhicule. L'ensemble des étapes de l'usage du service étaient détaillées: comment réserver, identifier le véhicule, rentrer dans le véhicule, l'organisation du trajet, les informations, l'espace, moyen de contact avec un superviseur lointain, les bagages, les arrêts du véhicule, l'arrivée à destination, la notation après-coup, etc. (Fig. 1).

Phase 2: The Guided Imaginary Projection (GIP). Participants are invited to close their eyes and imagine a journey they could make on board such an autonomous shared taxi. They are guided by the interviewer so that the imaginary journey is as detailed as possible. As the choice of route is completely free, the participants can project themselves into the use they imagine they could make of this service without any limits whatsoever. They are regularly asked to verbalize what happens to them in their imaginary journey, what they do, perceive, think or feel during this journey. The objective is to help them have an embodied position of talk, not an abstract one, and to immerse them in this imaginary journey.

Phase 3: Sources of Comfort and Discomfort. Participants are then invited to answer questions about potential sources of comfort and discomfort they have encountered

---

[2] Nevertheless, we note that 8 participants did not meet these criteria: 7 participants over the age of 60 (it turned out that older persons make very little use of shared services) and 1 pre-test participant that we included in the study because he did not show any difficulties during the GIP phase.

[3] We first intended to have face to face interviews but it was difficult with the Covid situation; we then tested the videoconference interviews and it appeared to be very satisfying. All the interviews were therefore conducted by videoconference.

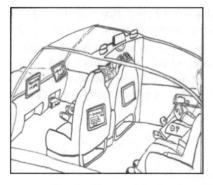 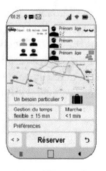 

Fig. 1. Figures of the interior of the car and of the smartphone application

(some of which they verbalized during GIP) or might encounter while using this service in various situations.

Phase 4: General Questions. Finally, participants answer demographic questions (age, etc.) and questions about their car-sharing service usage habits.

2.3 Analysis of the Verbal Data

The parts of the protocol containing the Guided Imaginary Projection (phase 2) and the questions on the sources of comfort and discomfort (phase 3) were transcribed and then categorized according to 8 categories, already identified in the literature on car sharing (Allinc 2018, Allinc et al. 2015, Créno, 2018), and adapted to the shared taxi robot:

- interactions (with passengers and with the service),
- feeking of security (aggression or accident),
- feeling of control (time, route and automaton),
- availability of information,
- interior design,
- values,
- multi-activity,
- others.

Finally, a count was made of the sources of comfort/discomfort mentioned by the participants. Where relevant, i.e. where there appeared to be a difference between participants according to their gender or age, a Fisher's test was carried out to identify differences between populations on small numbers.

3   Results

We will develop here results concerning the three first sources of comfort/discomfort: interactions, security and control. Then we will focus on the effects of the driver's absence.

3.1   Main Sources of Comfort and Discomfort

We report here the most interesting elements, some categories, although mentioned by the participants, are not developed.

Interactions: They represent a source of comfort or discomfort for all participants, with great differences between and within individuals: 40% of participants find it comfortable to talk with other passengers, 37.5% prefer to respect the standards of politeness and then to make the journey in a calm manner. 60% of participants imagine that some passengers might behave badly, which could be a source of discomfort for them: these participants thus mention noisy or rude passengers.

Security: 30% fear sharing the vehicle with an alcoholic passenger and 20% mention fearing the presence of an aggressive passenger.

Concerning accidents, 55% of the participants consider that they would feel safe in the robot taxi. Paradoxically, among these participants, 6 consider that they would still be afraid of the driving of the robot-taxi and 5 participants stipulate that they would monitor the driving of the vehicle during the PrIG. These participants consider this fear to be irrational or novelty related: they imagine that driving the robot taxi will be safer, but that they will need some time to feel reassured on board. In contrast to these participants, other participants (25%) consider that they will definitely have fears about the taxi robot's ability to drive safely, and in particular to adapt to unexpected situations such as a child crossing out of a pedestrian crossing.

Control of the Trip: This category is the one that most often questions the use of the service. 67.5% of participants would find it uncomfortable to lose time or make extra detours because of other passengers. If, at the time of booking, vehicles take too long to arrive, 40% of participants would look for another means of transport; this time varies greatly from one participant to another: between 10 and 30 min. 5 participants consider that it will be more comfortable for them to use the vehicle when there are no time constraints. One participant specifies that she would not use the vehicle to go to work.

Technical Bugs: Although the service presented to the participants is defined as reliable at all levels, some participants fear the occurrence of uncontrollable bugs of the automaton: when opening the vehicle door (30%), problem with seat allocation (30%), loading of the application too long when making a reservation (30%). It should be noted that this last technical problem would lead to the search for another mode of transport.

3.2   Effect of the Driver's Absence

As one of the participants pointed out, all the problematic situations mentioned are all the more so because there is no driver.

Interactions: For the management of interactions, the absence of a driver is perceived as uncomfortable by 6 participants because they consider that there is a risk of having no one to talk to. For 3 participants, the driver is a moderator who acts as a link between the participants, manages small incidents, or reassures about deadlines. For 2 participants, the absence of a driver is uncomfortable because he is the one who gives advice on tourism. For 2 participants, his absence makes the experience less convivial.

On the other hand, for other participants, the absence of a driver is a source of comfort: no imposed discussions (3 participants), no price changes (2 participants), no scams or mistakes (2 participants).

Aggression Risk: With regard to the risk of aggression, the absence of a driver is also a source of discomfort for 6 participants who consider that the call button or emergency stop does not replace the driver who can intervene immediately. However, one participant considers that the driver can be the one who aggresses.

Accident Risk: If, as we saw above, the autonomous vehicle can be perceived as safer in terms of accidents (55% of participants), this is directly attributed by 20% of participants to the absence of a driver who may be drunk, tired or driving badly. For 2 participants, the absence of a driver makes it possible to talk without distracting the driver.

On the other hand, accident management seems more complicated for 3 participants, especially for administrative questions of insurance.

Control of the Trip: The absence of a driver is a major source of discomfort for the control of the trip. Regarding technical breakdowns, 7 participants imagine that they are all the more uncomfortable as there is nobody to manage them. Regarding the journey, 10 participants find it uncomfortable not being able to negotiate detours, stops or shortcuts with a contact person as they can with the driver.

Information Availability: With regard to the availability of information, especially when identifying the vehicle, while 10 participants (i.e. 25%) consider that the autonomous vehicle should be easily identifiable, partly due to the absence of a driver, 9 participants (i.e. 22%) would like a distinctive sign or a light signal to ensure that the vehicle is theirs in a place heavily frequented by robot taxis. 4 participants specify that this is due to the absence of the driver: usually, the driver calls or signals to his passengers.

Car Design: Concerning the design of the interior, 10 participants feel a feeling of "strangeness" or "vertigo" due to the absence of the driver in the vehicle.

Values: Finally, in terms of values, 6 participants are concerned about the loss of jobs caused by the absence of a driver, and 3 feel that there is a form of dehumanization linked to the absence of a driver.

4   Discussion

This study allowed us to identify a large number of sources of comfort and discomfort when imagining the use of a shared robot-taxi. The Guided Imaginary Projection methodology, which aims to have future users "live" an experience of the service in an imaginary way, therefore seems to be effective for projecting in future uses that cannot yet be tested in the real world.

These elements will enable us to issue recommendations in order to limit the sources of discomfort of such a service. Some of these recommendations will relate to the design of the interactions with the vehicle and the service, which will aim to compensate for the absence of a driver: this may involve a charter for the use of the service for passengers, a protocol automatically triggered in the event of an accident or incident in conjunction with the remote operator, and the personalization of the interactions with the vehicle. However, certain sources of discomfort seem difficult to circumvent, such as user values, for example.

Our participants are users who already have experience of vehicle sharing so that they can more easily project themselves into the service, which is a sort of Uber-pool without a driver. It might be interesting to interview other populations, perhaps less familiar with shared systems or with special needs (disabled people, parents with young children, single teenagers), in order to identify whether they raise other sources of discomfort.

References

Adelé, S., Dionisio, C.: Learning from the real practices of users of a smart carpooling app. Eur. Transp. Res. Rev., **12**(1), 39 (2020). https://doi.org/10.1186/s12544-020-00429-3

Allinc, A.: Sources de confort et d'inconfort psychologiques dans les transports et conditions pour l'usage de modes plus respectueux de l'environnement [Ph.D. thesis]. Télécom ParisTech. (2018)

Allinc, A., Cahour, B., Burkhardt, J.-M.: The guided imaginary projection, a new methodology for prospective ergonomics. In: Congress of the International Ergonomics Association, pp. 1340–1347 (2018)

Allinc, A., Cahour, B., Burkhardt, J.M.: Sources of psychological comfort and discomfort in transport modes. Proceedings of the Conference on Cognitive Ergonomics ECCE 2015, 1–3 juillet, Varsovie, Pologne (2015)

Becker, F., Axhausen, K.W.: Literature review on surveys investigating the acceptance of automated vehicles. Transportation, **44**(6), 1293–1306 (2017). https://doi.org/10.1007/s11116-017-9808-9

Cahour, B., Forzy, J.F.: Does projection into use improve trust and exploration? the case of a cruise control system. Saf. Sci. **47**(9), 1260–1272 (2009)

Cahour, B., Licoppe, C., Créno, L.: Articulation fine des données vidéo et des entretiens d'auto-confrontation explicitante : Étude de cas d'interactions en covoiturage. Le travail humain **81**(4), 269–305 (2018)

Créno, L.: Covoiturer entre inconnus : Des risques perçus à la construction de la confiance, panorama des expériences vécues des usagers. [Ph.D. thesis]. Télécom ParisTech. (2016)

ERTRAC Working Group.: Automated Driving Roadmap (2017a)

ERTRAC Working Group.: Integrated Urban Mobility Roadmap (2017b)

Kim, S., Chang, J.J. E., Park, H.H., Song, S.U., Cha, C.B., Kim, J.W., Kang, N.: Autonomous taxi service design and user experience. Int. J. Hum. Comput. Inter. 1–20 (2019)

Morris, E.A., Zhou, Y., Brown, A., Khan, S., Derochers, J.L., Campbell, H., Pratt, A.N., Chowdhury, M.: Are drivers cool with pool? Driver attitudes towards the shared TNC services UberPool and Lyft Shared. Transp. Policy (2020). https://doi.org/10.1016/j.tranpol.2020.04.019

Narayanan, S., Chaniotakis, E., Antoniou, C.: Shared autonomous vehicle services : a comprehensive review. Transp. Res. Part C: Emer. Technol. 111, 255–293(2020). https://doi.org/10.1016/j.trc.2019.12.008

Pélata, P., Dumont, M., Bruel, F.: Quel futur de la mobilité dans les grandes villes? Le journal de l'ecole de Paris du management **3**, 30–37 (2019)

Pratt, A.N., Morris, E.A., Zhou, Y., Khan, S., Chowdhury, M.: What do riders tweet about the people that they meet? Analyzing online commentary about UberPool and Lyft Shared/Lyft Line. Transp. Res. Part F: Traff. Psychol. Behav. **62**, 459–472 (2019)

Saujot, M., Brimont, L., Sartor, O.: Mettons la mobilité autonome sur la voie du développement durable. Studies **02/18**, 48 (2018)

Work of Articulation Around Interdependencies in the Project Management: Maintenance and Modernization Projects in High-Risk Industry

Christelle Casse[1]([✉]) and Nathalie de Beler[2]

[1] Université Louis Lumière Lyon2, Lyon 69, France
`c.casse@univ-lyon2.fr`
[2] Electricité De France (EDF), R&D, Clamart 92, France

Abstract. This paper focuses on project management activities in the field of maintenance of high-risk industries. It studies the resources and constraints of project managers, at individual and collective levels, to anticipate and manage the multiple coordination and interdependencies in the projects and to do the « articulation work».

Keywords: Project management · High-risk industry · Maintenance · Articulation work

1 Introduction

This paper focuses on complex projects subject to very strong temporal constraints, in which each hazard may have significant repercussions. The complexity of the project generally stems from the combination of the complexity of the technical system and the division of project tasks, generally introduced by the diversity of expertise mobilized in the design and functioning (Adler 1995). For Charles Perrow (1984; 2011), the behavior of a strongly coupled complex system becomes uncertain whenever there are hazards.

For project managers, dealing with uncertainty requires a high degree of adaptability to cope with unexpected events (Bechky and Okhuysen 2011). The project management activity consists mainly in coordinating a number of mutually dependent tasks, both because they mobilize the same resources, (at the human, material, logistical and spatial levels…), potentially interfere with each other or because they are temporally linked. Project managers partly anticipate the interdependencies in the project planning and partly manage them in real time because of the planning uncertainties or unexpected events. Thus, project managers manage dynamic environment (Amalberti 1996; Amalberti and Hoc, 1998; Van daele and Carpinelli 2001).

"The objective of planning in dynamic environments is the control of processes, i.e. keeping its (partly autonomous) evolution within acceptable limits" (Van Daele and Carpinelli 2001 p. 2). Upstream and real time planning is made particularly complex in maintenance projects because of the dispersion of spaces, people, tasks and therefore sequential (vertical) and horizontal potential interactions. The management of interdependencies depends on the formal and informal work of cooperation and negotiation among project members (Kellogg et al. 2006), which evolve as one moves closer to the actual implementation of operations. Anselm Strauss (1988) characterized this activity by the notion of "articulation work".

This approach highlights the existence of professional groups that distribute competences, provide cognitive frameworks and material devices, and define a legitimate distribution of roles and responsibilities. However, it also insists on the fact that this articulation of tasks is not static. Contingent situations constantly renew the work of articulation, and the interactions and negotiations needed between project managers and technicians. According to Strauss, articulation work makes it possible to develop trajectories, which group sequences of tasks around a singular situation. However, the dynamic nature of the activity, the emergence of hazards and the existence of strong resource constraints call into question these trajectories. Both notions of trajectory and articulation allow the analysis of complex projects, in which a large number of sub-projects and professional interact and which are characterised by the propagation of hazards linked to resource constraints. They complement the planning approach to analyse the recompositions and adjustments that take place in real time during the implementation phases.

This research aims at identifying the competencies, resources and difficulties of the project members to identify and manage the interdependences, such as sequential links between operations, availability of multiple skills required to complete an operation, skills or equipment sharing or co-activity in the same space. We focus on the articulation work performed, the distribution of responsibilities and tasks to complete maintenance operations while managing the relations between them,

2 Context: An Outage of Production for Maintenance

Our paper is based on a research-action concerning the optimization of managing tasks in the maintenance and modernization projects of a high-risk industry in France. In order to study the activity of piloting complex projects, we have analyzed annual maintenance outage in two energy production plants. The outage for maintenance is a complex domain submitted to numerous stakes and constraints: productivity, safety, security and environmental protection. Its main purposes consist of the replacement of parts of the resource of production, as well as periodic test, regulatory controls and maintenance activities on the equipment. The company –composed of 19 production units- adopted since the middle of the nineties an organizational structure called "outage project", cross-functional to the various departments of each unit. The project's organization main features rely on a national high-level requirement report, which describes the process of preparation, realization and collection of experience feedback of the outage project. The organization is supported by a dedicated structure which mobilizes from about fifty to one hundred people. The project management team (a dozen of persons) is almost 100% dedicated on the outage project from the preparation phase until the learning from experience phase.

The team plans and coordinates all the operations and has to manage a set of events of various natures: technical, organizational or human hazards and changes in regulation. Obviously, the Socio-Organizational and Human dimensions are essential to overtake these difficulties, to reach and maintain the performance of the outage projects at an acceptable cost (human, social, financial).

For several years, the outage projects did not reach the expected performance. The various analyses realized by the operator revealed recurring difficulties, such as Non-quality of maintenance, time wasting and deficiency in the resolution of technical hazards. Concluding that the organization would have reached its limits, the operator launched a 3 years R&D project in 2015, aiming at enlightening the mechanisms and the socio-technical and human factors that contribute to reach and maintain the targeted performance. The next chapter describes our method of investigation.

3 Methodology

Maintenance outages usually involve several thousand people for a short period of 30 to 95 days (planned). Our study is particularly interested in the management of hazards during the course of the project, their cause, and their possible consequences, the way in which they are identified, evaluated and managed collectively (Dille and Söderlund 2013). Our approach is qualitative, based on bibliographic study, observations of the daily operation of projects (10 days), semi-guided individual interviews (21 people) and learning from experience meetings (Table 1).

Table 1. Methodology

Method	Unit 1	Unit 2
Daily operation observation	7 days	3 days
Individual interviews	9 people	12 people
Collective feedback meetings	2 restitutions	1 restitution

The studies carried out on each unit were the subject of feedback meetings (restitutions) on unit and with the national management. The restitutions made it possible to validate and adjust the analyses and conclusions in order to refine the final diagnosis.

4 Results: Distribution and Mechanism of Articulation Work

The analysis of the daily operation and several incidents that occurred during maintenance, allows us to highlight how articulation work is distributed between project managers; its weaknesses, for instance in terms of anticipation; its main resources (in particular experience) and the effects of relations between professional groups on the improvement of its performance.

4.1 The Articulation Work Distributed Between All the Stakeholders

We noted a lack of involvement and training of maintenance technicians in the identification of interdependencies during preparation phase, due to the organization and their focalization on the core of their technical task. The project team's activity mainly consists of identifying the many potential interdependencies between tasks, assessing the degree of flexibility in the arrangement and implementation of tasks, and imagining recombinations. The people in charge of piloting the project must therefore be able to interact with technicians in charge of sub-parts of the project on more specific tasks, without having the same level of expertise. The preparation phase of maintenance projects is a highly structured, procedural key phase. Project teams must anticipate the sequential interdependencies between tasks and define the "critical path" of the maintenance outage which consists in defining a trajectory of the critical tasks in terms of performance and safety to optimize the organization.

To do this, the project management team uses standard schedules or those of previous outage to build the project planning. An imbalance appears between the anticipation of sequential interdependencies and transversal interdependencies, like co-activities, which are more difficult to grasp from the start. Interdependencies linked to co-activities or interactions between tasks are less predictable by definition because they result from the synchronicity of tasks that belong to independent tasks sequences. Indeed, they are more difficult to identify and support during preparation phase. This relies on the ability of maintenance teams to identify dependencies between their tasks and those of other technical teams, based on their experience. On the technical side, however, the maintenance teams have not developed the knowledge needed to identify these dependencies. The maintenance technicians are generally overwhelmed by the quantity of tasks to be programmed in a very constrained time frame, for which administrative and technical files must be drawn up, and human, logistical and material resources must be defined and organized. The structuring by task as well as the lack of cross-disciplinary meetings during the preparation phase make it difficult for them to get involved in these tasks in the upstream phase. Furthermore, as maintenance technicians are involved in both the outage preparation and ongoing maintenance work, their availability is very limited at this stage. The outage project managers have difficulties to reserve time with the technical specialists to anticipate the constraints of the project, the sequences of tasks and, even more so, the interdependencies with other technical teams. The outage project team, together with the support services, organizes cross-functional meetings to anticipate potential hazards and also to simulate outage project scenario. However, only a few technical managers are present at these collective meetings.

The conditions of negotiation between project teams and technical managers also have an impact on the ability to anticipate interdependencies in preparation phase. At this stage, it is not easy to put one task ahead of another, especially if it is not on the critical path. It is often easiest for the professional to wait for the implementation of the task to negotiate adjustments and to decide on priorities and potential disagreements between stakes.

The diversity of professional involved in the outage projects amplify the difficulty of anticipating interactions. Indeed, a national team is in charge of the modification of the installations. This team works alternately on all the company's units and has its own operating rules. Even if meetings are set up with the project team during the preparatory phase, its external position often leads to dysfunctions in the transmission of information between both teams, or even in the sharing of rules. For example, during our observations on one of the units, this team was working with outdated procedures in which new safety requirements were missing. It led to failures during the work. Furthermore, from a logistical point of view, its demands with regard to local needs were sometimes unsuitable or incomplete. In a large project requiring the erection of very high scaffolding to reach the ceiling of a building, the logisticians discovered after the erection that the scaffolding was 50 cm off the unit of the intervention. We also observed that the project managers did not anticipate the interdependencies between the operations carried out by this team and those managed internally, with consequences not only in terms of last-minute adaptations, but also in terms of delays and security loopholes.

4.2 Impact of Skills Profiles on the Work of Articulation

The structure of roles and competencies in the company gives more legitimacy to maintenance managers than to project managers, who are the ones who manage interdependencies and do the articulation work. Historically, the skills of maintenance professionals have grown on the basis of clearly identified and specialized technical teams and knowledge. The maintenance technicians, therefore, have structural and historical legitimacy in the company. The project managers have cross-functional positions that are not anchored in the traditional trades' structures. Even if the majority of the project leaders and managers comes from the technical professions, their role within projects, essentially centered on operations planning and "interface" management, gives them a more limited legitimacy in the operational structures. Furthermore, the increase in the number of interface positions between the project team and the technical services, notably to improve the circulation of information, has led the company to recruit more and more project managers from outside the company, sometimes after graduating from engineering schools. This dynamic has generated difficulties in integrating them into the operational teams. As they have neither the same language nor the experience of the technicians in contact with the operations and the field, these project managers suffer from a lack of recognition within the structure. Moreover, the standards describing these new roles are much less formalized than those for technician positions. The identity and tools of these managers, particularly the internal networks between them, are still under development within the company. Because their previous jobs structured their project management skills, they find it difficult to value them as specific skills that legitimize their role and action.

4.3 Experience and Cooperation as Resources for Articulation Work

Networking and managing the experiences and expertise of project members appear as the main resource for collectively anticipating and face hazards and their vertical and horizontal propagation risk into the project. In the context of the complexity and interdependence of the tasks, the experience appears to be the major resource of the project managers. Anticipation and adaptation practices are essentially based on skills derived from experience. Most of the time, the project members' career paths enable them to build up a vast experience of outages, which can be used to identify the interfaces between tasks and the management of hazards and new situations. This resource is all the more important as it compensates for a deficiency in the databases available to support project stakeholders in the search for solutions and adaptations. The existing databases are linked to learning from experience process (REX). They are dispersed and designed with specific architectures and consultation methods that do not facilitate the search of lessons learned from past. Everyone therefore mobilizes the bases they already know, and/or relies on their memory, personal notes or the knowledge of other professionals, particularly pillars of experience. The trajectories of the project members have led them to cross several collectives and networks of experts whom they call upon when necessary. The project managers' strategies in taking information, making decisions or taking action are strongly conditioned by their background and the networks in which they have been involved in the past. For example, a project manager who has had national responsibilities has a greater capacity to influence and question directives than his or her counterparts. It opens up strategic perspectives, not because he or she is at an advantage in terms of structure but because he or she has greater knowledge of the key actors and of the cross-cutting processes for organizing units and maintenance campaigns. The project managers' trajectories have shaped their identity, their ways of interacting with other professionals and their sensitivity to interdependencies. They have left their professional communities but are transferring their knowledge and networks to their new role in the service of maintenance projects and the management of interdependencies.

4.4 New Demands that Amplify the Work of Articulation

Difficulties in anticipating the consequences related to the introduction of new require-ments are increasingly frequent in the regulatory and normative arena, leading to degraded situations that spread throughout the project. The projects operate on rou-tines that allow both the organization and progress of the worksites optimizations. Each outage project introduces few new activities. However, certain activities or areas are subject to new regulations that introduce new constraints in the organization difficult to anticipate. These constraints lead to rigidity, particularly in the management of hazards. Environmental regulation, for instance, is becoming increasingly strict and changing practically at each outage project. We have thus observed the consequences of changes in national and local regulations concerning the discharge of polluted effluents related to unit's activity. The increase in requirements and limitations regarding discharges into rivers has had significant consequences for project stakeholders during our observations. Effluent discharge has become a very sensitive area requiring both regulatory and tech-nical expertise. Until now, this subject has not been an object of attention for outage project managers because it did not pose any particular constraint other than predicting treatment processes according to the tanks and planning automatic discharges. More-over, the operation team performed this task. Today, the limitations in terms of pollution and discharge rates are linked to the quantity and composition of the effluents produced by the unit, which is diverse during outage periods and comes from a variety of sources. The management of discharges requires upstream reflection on the discharges generated by the various maintenance operations and anticipation of chemical incompatibilities or transverse constraints that could block or slow down the progress of the outage project. Dedicated chemists must analyze each effluent reservoir to determine its detailed composition and to adapt the treatment and discharge methods. Moreover, analyses require time (several hours). It also depends on the flow of rivers and the weather, two external factors that are difficult to predict upstream. Effluent management therefore becomes a function to be managed in anticipation in a transversal way, requiring articulation between stakes. Hazards in terms of quantity, deadlines or type of composition can have significant repercussions on the saturation of reservoirs that were not designed to play the role of intermediate storage. Then, more than the occurrence of a new requirement, it is the many disturbances that its application to existing constraints causes that pose a problem.

5 Discussion

The interactionist approach makes it possible to explain why articulation work during the project remains predominant despite the focus on the preparation phase and the experience accumulated by the project stakeholders. Uncertainties, project organization and the modes of interaction between the technical lines and the project team favour adaptive management rather than anticipative. Indeed, the technicians are not very active in the anticipation of interdependencies linked to co-activity, which are more difficult to identify and anticipate. Thus, the project team relies on the experience of its members to manage interdependencies in a reactive manner. The experience and composition of the project team therefore appear to be essential resources for managing uncertainties in projects (Weick and Sutcliffe 2011).

However, our study shows the difficult position of the project team in relation to maintenance teams, which benefit from a legitimacy that is more firmly rooted in the organisation. The legitimacy of project managers cannot be taken for granted and they sometimes struggle to assert their authority. This calls into question the way in which project managers and leaders build their authority in relation to technical managers, especially when they come from the same backgrounds (Hodgson 2005).

It also raises questions about the project management methods used. Further reflection on the concurrent approaches to project management and development approaches could facilitate greater project plasticity for better integration of the technicians from the preparation phase (Beguin 2010). Our empirical results may help us to discuss the notion of resilience of project, considering that resilience is based on the ability to manage successfully the propagation of unexpected events into the project (Weick and Sutcliffe 2011; de Beler et al. 2018), which requires a management of interdependencies by the project managers from the beginning of the project preparation.

6 Conclusion

Improving the management of interdependencies in the outage projects requires different kinds of changes that constitute areas of development for the company, including:

- Organizational adjustments such as the availability of technical and project skills in the preparation phase, the streamlining and relief of management processes and tasks to refocus the professional on their core activity (in particular having the time to integrate new regulations);
- Support tools design for the early detection of interdependencies (eg planning simulations, simulation of co-activity in areas of space congestion) thus facilitating decision-making.
- "Cultural" changes, in particular by: emphasizing "preparing the organization for the unprepared", developing cross-teams simulation and learning from experience meetings to improve mutual knowledge and cooperation, promoting management methods based on trust and accountability, the principle of subsidiarity.
- Greater attention to the development and preparation of efficient project teams, of "collective intelligence", with an emphasis on team development, a clear definition of roles and responsibilities.

Acknowledgment. This research was conducted with Thomas Reverdy.

References

Adler, P.S.: Interdepartmental interdependence and coordination: the case of the design/manufacturing interfaces **6**(2), 147–167 (1995)

Amalberti, R.: La conduite des systèmes à risques. PUF, coll. Le travail humain, Paris (1996)

Amalberti, R., Hoc, J.M.: Cognitive activity analysis in dynamic situation: why and how? Travail Humain **61**(3), 209–234 (1998)

Atkinson, R., Crawford, L., Ward, S.: Fundamental uncertainties in projects and the scope of project management. Int. J. Project Manage. **24**(8), 687–698 (2006)

Bechky, B.A., Okhuysen, G.A.: Expecting the unexpected? How SWAT officers and film crews handle surprises. Acad. Manage. J. **54**(2), 239–261 (2011)

Beguin, P.: Conduite de projet et fabrication collective du travail: une approche développementale (Doctoral dissertation, Université de Bordeaux Ségalen, Bordeaux 2) (2010)

Corbin, J.M., Strauss, A.L.: The articulation of work through interaction. Sociol. Quart. **34**(1), 71–83 (1993)

Danilovic, M., Sandkull, B.: The use of dependence structure matrix and domain mapping matrix in managing uncertainty in multiple project situations. Int. J. Project Manage. **23**(3), 193–203 (2005)

Dille, T., Söderlund, J.: Managing temporal misfits in institutional environments: a study of critical incidents in a complex public project. Int. J. Managing Projects Bus. **6**(3), 552–575 (2013)

Floricel, S., Michela, J.L., Piperca, S.: Complexity, uncertainty-reduction strategies, and project performance. Int. J. Project Manage. **34**(7), 1360–1383 (2016)

Hodgson, D.: "Putting on a professional performance": performativity, subversion and project management. Organization **12**(1), 51–68 (2005)

Perrow, C.: Normal Accidents: Living with High-Risk Technologies. Basic Books, New York (1984)

Perrow, C. Complex organizations : a critical essay (Vol. 3rd). Random House, New York (1986).

Pich, M.T., Loch, C.H., Meyer, A.D.: On uncertainty, ambiguity, and complexity in project management. Manage. Sci. **48**(8), 1008–1023 (2002)

Sosa, M.E., Eppinger, S.D., Rowles, C.M.: The misalignment of product architecture and organizational structure in complex product development. Manage. Sci. **50**(12), 1674–1689 (2004)

Strauss, A.: Work and the division of labor. Sociol. Quar. **26**(1) (1985)

Strauss, A.: The articulation of project work: an organizational process. Sociol. Quart. **29**(2) (1988)

Weick, K.E., Sutcliffe, K.M.: Managing the Unexpected: Resilient Performance in an Age of Uncertainty, vol. 8. Wiley, New-York (2011)

Van Daele, A., Carpinelli, F.: Planification dans la gestion des environnements dynamiques: quelques apports récents de la psychologie ergonomique. Psychologie française **46**(2), 143–152 (2001)

Occupational Health and Safety Doctrine and Service Activity; Conceptualization, Methodology and First Result

Alexis Chambel[1,2,4](✉) and Valérie Pueyo[1,2,3]

[1] UMR 5600, AECTT-EVS, Lyon, France
[2] Université Lumière Lyon 2, Lyon, France
valerie.pueyo@univ-lyon2.fr
[3] IETL, Lyon, France
[4] Parcours Doctoral National en Santé Travail, Lyon, France

Abstract. This paper presents a thesis in progress. This research work focuses on the frameworks of thought and action that structure prevention in France, described as the health and safety doctrine, and their relationship with service activities. It involves both a work of conceptualization of this doctrine, operated from the notion of social apparatus in Foucault's philosophy, and the construction of an original methodology to question it from the work activity. This text also develops some preliminary results to illustrate the contribution of the methodological choices made.

Keywords: Occupational Health and safety · Service activity · Foucault · Social apparatus · Doctrine

This paper presents the thesis being carried out in France within the UMR 5600 (Environnement Ville Société) under the supervision of Valérie Pueyo. Begun on October 1st, 2019, this thesis is financed by the «Parcours Doctoral National en Santé Travail» coordinated by EHESP within the framework of the Plan Santé Travail 3. It is based on previous research work that has highlighted the existence of a "occupational health and safety doctrine" (Pueyo et al. 2019). We will come back to this term in more details, its characterization being one of the objects of the research work, but it can be succinctly defined as a framework of thought and action that structures the prevention of occupational risks. The hypothesis put forward is also the birth of these predicates in the industrial world and their inadequacy with the new forms of work represented by service activities (ibid.). The central objective of the thesis is to deepen this hypothesis and to identify more precisely the points of dissonance between the occupational health and safety doctrine of prevention and service activities.

It is important to specify right away that this is the Francophone occupational health and safety doctrine. Therefore, we do not presume any value of universality. For this reason, we will not revisit its content, which has also been the subject of previous communications (Chambel et al. 2021; Chambel et al. 2020), but rather its treatment as a research subject, which may prove relevant to the international community. For

N. L. Black et al. (Eds.): IEA 2021, LNNS 219, pp. 648–654, 2021.
https://doi.org/10.1007/978-3-030-74602-5_89

it is not a question here of reflecting on the «*frame*» (Pueyo 2020) represented by the occupational health and safety doctrine in disconnection from «*the substance*» (ibid.), which animates action, and more generally from activity. The originality of this work lies both in the way the prevention system is understood as a doctrine and the related conceptualization, but also in the link made with the work activity. The articulation between a conceptual object composed of elements of different scales (macro, meso, micro), the relatively vast perimeter of service activities and the reality of the situations experienced by the workers implies the development of an original methodology able of bringing these different dimensions into dialogue.

An initial conceptualization of the doctrine of prevention has been carried out; it can be assimilated to «*un dispositif*» (Foucault 1977), a social apparatus. We will begin by developing in greater details this central notion in this research work. This will allow us to present the methodology deployed before concluding with some preliminary results, as the fieldwork and data analysis is ongoing.

1 The Health and Safety Doctrine: A Social Apparatus

In Foucault's philosophy, the concept of social apparatus is characterized both by what it is and by its function. It can be succinctly defined as a set of elements that make up a system and guide action.

1.1 The Ontology of the Social Apparatus

The first characteristic of the elements of a social apparatus is their very great diversity. It can thus include «*discourses, institutions, architectural arrangements, regulatory decisions, laws, administrative measures, scientific statements, philosophical, moral and philanthropic proposals, in short: what is said, as well as what is not said*» (Foucault 1977). Thus, «*it can include virtually everything*» (Agamben 2006). Elements as diverse as the concept of risk, personal protective equipment or the action plan represented by information and awareness can thus find their place in the system represented by the occupational health and safety doctrine.

The systemic, more structuring characteristic refers to a set of «*plays*», «*changes in position, modifications of functions, which can also be very different*» (Foucault 1977). The social apparatus is then not the elements themselves, but the combinations of relations between them (Lafleur 2015). These relations are marked by a certain form of instability, of movement, for example, «*a given discourse may appear sometimes as a program of an institution, sometimes on the contrary as an element that makes it possible to justify and mask a practice that remains silent, or to function as a second reinterpretation of that practice*» (Foucault 1977). We will not go into more details here about these plays, which are extremely numerous within the doctrine, but perhaps the name "Health and Safety" already gives a clue to two conceptual fields that constitute, interfere with and influence each other.

1.2   The Function of the Social Apparatus

The social apparatus is a «*formation, which, at a given historical moment, had the major function of responding to an emergency*» (Foucault 1977). This functionalist dimension, this logic of orientation, inscribes the device in mechanisms of knowledge and power.

From the perspective of knowledge, it relies on certain types of knowledge and allows the production of certain others, in a form of self-feeding. For Vuillemin (2012), it is an «*operating table*», a form of reading grid. It gives a coherent orientation and cuts out a field, leaving by extension some elements in the shadow. Like the action of a prism on light, it decomposes reality into more or less elementary and interpretable units. But in doing so it gives a distorted, oriented and partial vision.

The link with power is reflected in its ability to guide action. Agamben (2006) speaks of «*docile enslavement*» and «*control without violence*». For Lafleur (2015), the social apparatus is used to evaluate, measure and isolate in a logic of domination. More generally, it is part of disciplinary mechanisms (Foucault 1975). This tendency to evaluation by measurement, to identify thresholds, to break down by risk or work unit in the doctrine of prevention echoes this logic of separation into elementary units, which can be dealt with by the fields of knowledge mobilized by the system.

«*That's the social apparatus: strategies of power relations supporting types of knowledge, and supported by them*» (Foucault 1977).

The occupational health and safety doctrine of prevention emerged in the middle of the 19th century in response to the deteriorating health of the working populations. The system it represents was thus historically constructed and developed in response to a model of work organization and industrial production. By using this model as a social apparatus, it is possible to better characterize the elements that come into tension with the activity in the classes of service situations.

2   Re-examining the Doctrine Based on Activity

In order to be in line with this logic of articulation of different dimensions and scale, of debating the doctrine with the reality of the activity, the production of knowledge about it is implemented by mobilizing approaches of analysis of real work. They are coupled with the concept of "classes of situations" from professional didactics in order to allow a categorization of situations based on the organization of the action and not on the productive system.

Professional didactics is particularly interested in the relationship between knowledge and action. In this paradigm, the worker carries out a work of conceptualization in action. This conceptualization mobilizes so-called pragmatic concepts (Samurçay and Pastré 1995) in that they differ from other types of concepts by their finalized properties (Vidal-Gomel and Rogalski 2007). This mechanism is carried out by and for action based on indicators linked to the situation, information that the worker takes from his/her situation. These indicators can be of an extremely diverse nature. They may be related to the physical environment, interaction with a user or other workers, work organisation, etc. Based on this conceptualization, the worker will deploy «*schemes*», a relatively stabilized organization of action while benefiting from a certain flexibility to adjust to the variability of reality. The major interest of this theory for our object and the link with the situation classes, since, as Pastré (2011), points out, the same scheme corresponds to one and only one situation class. By thus identifying the conceptual structure of the situation (made up of pragmatic concepts and indicators) and the different schemes deployed, it is possible to categorize situations and identify the related prevention needs. It also makes it possible to identify points of similarity or difference between service activities that at first glance.

For this research is also based on a comparative methodology, particularly adapted to apprehend global phenomena from singular situations (Plutniak and Kikuchi 2017). This comparison is carried out using several materials. The preferred means, when possible, is the inclusion of prevention actors in the conduct of *«prevention projects»* (Judon 2017) within structures. These prevention projects are characterised by the mobilisation of "intermediate prevention objects" (ibid.). We prefer the term prevention «boundary objects» (Star 2010; Star and Griesemer 1989) to this term because of their major characteristic: interpretative flexibility. Indeed, they must allow all the actors involved, workers and prevention workers alike, to express their points of view and representations of the situation, even though all these actors belong to different "professional worlds" (Béguin 2004).

The second method used, when it is not possible to directly integrate prevention workers into projects, is to carry out maintenance with prevention actors from these same projects. The aim here is to gather their points of view *a posteriori*.

3   First Prevention Project: Prevention Health and Safety Doctrine and Work Space

A first prevention project is being carried out with social mediators. Social mediation can be defined as an activity of intermediary between users and public and private services with a view to repairing the social link. The activity is marked by a great variability, particularly because of the extremely vast perimeter covered by the work of mediation.

The organization of the association is divided into two relatively hermetic types of activities. One is oriented towards the reception of the public with a distribution by site. The other represents what the association calls the field activity and which consists in going to meet the users, on mission of the public or private services. This meeting can be carried out in a physical way, or by telephone. The call of the users by the mediators of the field team is called phoning and represents for them a full-fledged activity, about one day per week.

The project of prevention covers several axes and all the activities, we will present here only one of the elements of the project, the action on the spaces for the activity of phoning. Indeed, the structure is currently undergoing a project to move one of the sites, this move project inducing to rethink the phoning space. 10h30 of observations have been carried out specifically on this activity, in a position of co-production with the mediators of a knowledge on their activity. One of the major elements identified during the observations is in the collective dimensions. Contrary to the common representation, the activity of the other mediators also in phoning activity is not only a hindrance linked to the co-activity, quite the contrary. During phoning, the mediators listen to what the other mediators are doing during waiting or reporting times on the software. This listening allows the development of skills, but also to break the boredom that the phoning activity can generate from time to time. Exchanges are also regularly set up, to share information on certain cases or, there again, simply to limit boredom. Collaborative situations can even be set up when a user does not speak French and a mediator helps his colleague to continue the mediation in English. Far from being anecdotal, all of these collective dimensions are essential to the health of mediators, whether they are skills development, collective development or strategies for managing boredom.

This knowledge produced then allowed the realization of a working group with 4 mediators, the technical referent, the team leader, the occupational health nurse and the occupational health physician in charge of the structure. A volumetric model was chosen as a prevention boundary object (Fig. 1). Particular attention was paid to certain characteristics: it was to enable the perspective of those involved in prevention to be expressed (identification of the position of the windows and the orientation of the buildings, position of the electrical sockets, etc.).

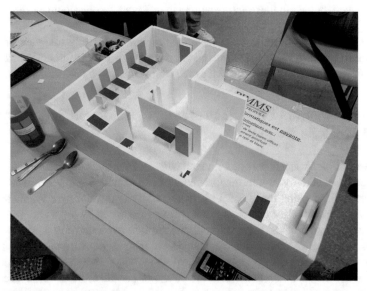

Fig. 1. Prevention boundary object representing the final solution chosen by all participants

The analysis of the data is still in progress at the time of writing, but it is already possible to indicate that prevention actors are mainly focusing their discourse on certain specific points. All of these elements are part of an environmental modeling of risk. In the foreground is the question of ambiences, both visual and auditory, from the angle of the discomfort that can be caused by bad lighting or general noise. The ground-level fall was also a point of vigilance, reflected in concrete terms by a reflection on circulatory flows with regard to the positions of substations and electrical wires. The chemical risk was also evoked through the printer and the potential toxic emissions linked to its use. The collective dimensions were more generally understood by the prevention specialists from the perspective of co-activity and per workstation. The surface area per workstation was also a point of vigilance, potentially echoing the minimum space standards per tertiary workstation.

These different dimensions were partly in tension with the needs expressed by the mediators. The mediators, while not neglecting the negative impact of co-activity, wanted to preserve the collective dimensions. Placing the offices facing the walls was thus quickly discarded. The partition envisaged to separate the position of the technical referent from that of the mediators never found its place, as the exchanges between these positions are essential to the activity. Elements related to the purpose of the action were also debated, such as the necessary proximity of a shelf or the printer.

The confrontation of these different positions via the mobilization of a boundary object nevertheless makes it possible to arrive at a satisfactory solution (Fig. 1), both from the perspective of the occupational health nurse and the occupational physician, but also from that of all the workers in the structure.

References

Agamben, G.: Théorie des dispositifs. (M. Rueff, Tran.) Po&sie **115**(1), 25 (2006)

Béguin, P.: Monde, version des mondes et monde commun. Bulletin de psychologie **57**(1), 45–48 (2004)

Chambel, A., Béguin, P., Pueyo, V.: Mutation du travail et doctrine de prévention. Actes du 55ème Congrès de la Société d'Ergonomie de Langue Française, pp. 298–303. Presented at the « L'activité et ses frontières » Penser et agir sur les transformations de nos sociétés, Paris (2021). https://ergonomie-self.org/wp-content/uploads/2021/01/SELF-2020-actes.pdf

Chambel, A., Pueyo, V., Béguin, P.: Mutation du travail et doctrine de prévention. Archives des Maladies Professionnelles et de l'Environnement, SI: 36e Congrès National de Médecine et Santé au Travail, **81**(5), 741 (2020)

Foucault, M.: Surveiller et punir: Naissance de la prison. Collection TEL. Gallimard, Paris (1975)

Foucault, M.: Le jeu de Michel Foucault. Dits et écrits Gallimard., vol. 3, pp. 298–329 (1977)

Judon, N.: Rendre possible un espace intermédiaire de dialogue pour coconstruire de nouvelles solutions de prévention dans un contexte d'incertitude: Cas des travaux de revêtements routiers (thesis). Bordeaux, 19 October 2017. https://www.theses.fr/2017BORD0705

Lafleur, S.: Foucault, la communication et les dispositifs. Communication. Information médias théories pratiques, vol. 33/2 (2015). https://journals.openedition.org/communication/5727

Pastré, P.: La didactique professionnelle: Approche anthropologique du développement chez les adultes. Formation et pratiques professionnelles. Presses universitaires de France, Paris (2011)

Plutniak, S., Kikuchi, C.: Comparer, comparaison, comparatisme»: Séminaire de lecture en sciences sociales de l'École française de Rome 2017–2018 (2017)

Pueyo, V.: Pour une Prospective du Travail. Les mutations et transitions du travail à hauteur d'Hommes (HDR). Université Lumière Lyon 2, 24 January 2020. https://hal.archives-ouvertes.fr/tel-02480599

Pueyo, V., Ruiz, C., Haettel, B., Béguin, P.: Connaissance des situations réelles de travail des aides à domicile et doctrine de prévention (Recherche réalisée pour la Direction Générale du travail dans le cadre du troisième Plan Santé au Travail (PST3)). Lyon (2019)

Samurçay, R., Pastré, P.: La conceptualisation des situations de travail dans la formation des compétences. Education permanente, (123), 13–32 (1995). Université de Paris-Dauphine

Star, S.L.: Ceci n'est pas un objet-frontière ! Revue d'anthropologie des connaissances, 4(1(1)), 18–35

Star, S.L., Griesemer, J.R.: Institutional ecology, 'translations' and boundary objects: amateurs and professionals in berkeley's museum of vertebrate zoology, 1907–39. Soc. Stud. Sci. **19**(3), 387–420 (1989)

Vidal-Gomel, C., Rogalski, J.: La conceptualisation et la place des concepts pragmatiques dans l'activité professionnelle et le développement des compétences. Activités, 04(4–1). ARPACT - Association Recherches et Pratiques sur les ACTivités (2007). https://journals.openedition. org/activites/1401

Vuillemin, J.-C.: Réflexions sur l'épistémè foucaldienne. Cahiers philosophiques **130**(3), 39–50 (2012)

Safety Leadership in Two Types of Safety-Critical Systems

Åsa Ek$^{(\boxtimes)}$ ⓘ and Mattias Seth

Ergonomics and Aerosol Technology, Department of Design Sciences,
Faculty of Engineering LTH, Lund University, Lund, Sweden
`asa.ek@design.lth.se`

Abstract. In safety-critical systems, such as aviation systems, nuclear power plants and hospitals, system failures can cause loss of life, environmental and property damage. Safety-critical systems consists of loose or tight interactions, they are more or less complex, and these characteristics affect the system's ability to prevent and overcome emerging system failures. The demand for good safety cultures, and safe and efficient work within these types of systems highlight the crucial role of safety leadership. This paper reports on findings from a small pilot study with the aim of exploring whether safety leadership in practice differs according to the built in properties of complexity and coupling in safety-critical organizations. Based on a literature review on safety leadership, interviews were conducted with one leader at a nuclear power plant, and one at a university hospital. The two systems can be viewed to have separate characters and differences in the way work is performed. Contrasts existed between safety leadership within the nuclear power plant and the hospital setting concerning flexibility in the organizations. The hospital setting were more suitable for adaptability and flexibility in relation to dynamical decision hierarchies. The nuclear power plant setting was viewed as more rigid with tightly coupled interactions, and the leadership and safety culture might be extra crucial within this system. Nevertheless, both interviewees promoted a transformational and inspirational leadership style. However, transactional leadership was preferable in critical situations.

Keywords: Socio-technical system · Safety · Resilience · Safety leadership

1 Introduction

1.1 Background

Complexity and ambiguity of socio-technical systems are continuously increasing. This is due to, for example technological advancements in combination with globalization and outsourcing. Many socio-technical systems such as nuclear power plants, hospitals, and aviation systems, can also be referred to as complex safety-critical systems, i.e., were system failures can cause significant loss of life and property damage (Reiman and Oedewald 2009). Complex organizations with safety-critical activities need to have abilities to adapt continuously to changing and unexpected circumstances (Weick and

© The Author(s), under exclusive license to Springer Nature Switzerland AG 2021
N. L. Black et al. (Eds.): IEA 2021, LNNS 219, pp. 655–663, 2021.
https://doi.org/10.1007/978-3-030-74602-5_90

Sutcliffe 2007), and to have resilient capabilities to detect and act in a flexible and safety conscious manner. Hollnagel et al. (2011), views safety as a dynamic property of a complex socio-technical system, produced during the daily functioning of the system and emerging from the activities and interactions of various elements of the system. The interactions of the elements can be categorized according to complexity and what type of coupling that is prevalent within the system. Couplings can be tight or loose, and they affect an organization's ability to prevent and overcome emerging system failures (Perrow 1984). In tightly coupled systems, sub-elements are interdependent, and the leadership is characterized as centralized and rigid. In loosely coupled systems, the sub-elements are independent, and leadership decentralized. Organizations with both complex and tightly coupled interactions are said to be extra susceptible to accidents (Perrow 1984; Rosness et al. 2004).

The increased demand for efficient and safe work within safety-critical systems highlight the role of adequate leadership. The research literature in safety science often emphasize the crucial and fundamental role of safety leadership and management in creating successful safety work and a good safety culture in a workplace or organization. Top management, but also middle management, supervisors, and safety representatives, are emphasized as creators and maintainers of organizational culture and that they affect safety and health in a workplace (Collins and Gadd 2002). The definition of safety leadership may vary, but one way is to say it is about: "the demonstration of safety values through the creation of a vision and the promotion of well-being through the art of engagement, honesty, and discipline" (Luke 2018). Safety leadership can be described with focus on behavioral characteristics and leadership strategies.

1.2 Aim of Paper

In a small pilot study, presented in the current paper, the aim was to explore whether safety leadership in practice differs according to the built in properties of complexity and coupling in specific safety-critical organizations. Are safety leadership practiced differently according to the type of organization in order to achieve safe performance? Based on safety leadership aspects found in a literature review, the aim was to get more knowledge about their application in practice in two types of safety-critical organizations; one nuclear power plant, and one university hospital. The two systems can be viewed to have separate characters and differences in the way work is performed.

A nuclear power plant is a very instruction-driven and tightly coupled operating system having several important system safety characteristics, e.g., the application of standardized operating procedures. In a university hospital, the system safety approach is not that prominent and healthcare professionals usually do not see themselves working according to standardized routines and methods, but on the basis of their competence. The hospital organization can be said to be loosely coupled and, compared to a nuclear power plant, allowing more flexibility in the execution of work. Thus, the approach to yielding high safety may probably be different in the two systems, especially concerning leaders' strategies and practical methods for achieving safety.

The aim of this paper is to 1) present findings from the literature review on safety leadership, and 2) to present findings gained from interviews conducted with one leader at a nuclear power plant, and one at a university hospital.

2   Methods

The study was a small pilot study. A literature review was conducted with focus on identifying concepts and aspects relating to safety leadership in safety-critical systems and organizations. Semi-structured and explorative interviews were thereafter conducted with two leaders, one leader at a nuclear power plant, and one leader (also physician) at a university hospital. An interview guide containing aspects on safety leadership found in the literature review was used in the interviews. Interviews were conducted via Skype and Zoom. Interviews were recorded, transcribed, and analyzed using content analysis.

3   Safety Leadership

This section contains a summary of the literature review on safety leadership which was performed in the pilot study. Due to space constraints, the summary focuses on behavioural characteristics and leadership strategies allowing organizations to be reliable and resilient.

Shared Mental Models of Safety. Shared mental models are essential for effective safety coordination and teamwork and includes shared understandings of common goals and each organizational or team member's role. A leader's responsibility includes the creation, maintenance, and accuracy of shared mental models in an organization (Johnston and Briggs 1968; Salas et al. 2005). Shared mental models include shared cognitive representations of an environment and how to tackle problems that may occur. Inconsistencies in mental models within and between e.g., teams in safety-critical systems, can lead to confusion and devastating consequences as a result from poor coordination (Fernandez et al. 2017). Shared mental models can be enhanced through various training methods such as simulation exercises, where e.g., leaders and team members practice each other's roles, which in turn increases the team's coordination and backup behaviors (Fernandez et al. 2017).

Safety Communication. Communication has been described as the most critical and essential leadership component in safety-critical systems (Fernandez et al. 2017). A leader's safety communication includes giving accurate pictures of the environment and of objectives to organisational members and teams, allowing them to develop shared mental models through updates and feedback communication (Vecchio-Sadus 2006). Communication allows the leader to coordinate teams' actions, establishing team members' roles, and their responsibilities (Murase et al. 2014; Vecchio-Sadus 2006). The use of closed-loop communication further ensures that everyone has received and interpreted the message as intended. Communication frequency between leaders and teams, as well as performance feedback, have been shown to relate to increased performance in safety-critical systems (Vecchio-Sadus 2006; Fernandez et al. 2017). Safety communication and feedback should include information on near-misses and incidents. A leader who encourage free communication of opinions and near-misses contribute to the establishment of a good safety culture (Cole 2000; Vecchio-Sadus 2006). A safety culture is underpinned if safety information is not received properly, which also negatively affects the organization's ability to be resilient (Wilcutt and Whitmeyer 2013). Feedback from leaders on organizational members' safety behaviors should be constructive, and risky behaviors should be immediately followed up, and specific instructions should be provided on how behavior can be improved (Fernandez et al. 2017; Salas et al. 2005).

Shared Leadership. In organizations who rely on vertical leadership, there is a clear decision hierarchy, where several members and teams solely rely on one hierarchical leader (Yukl 2008). These organizations rely on downward influence, where the focus is to enhance work performance by influencing organizational members' behaviors (Bienefeld and Grote 2014; Murase et al. 2014; Shuffler and Carter 2018). However, the prevalent complexity and ambiguity of safety-critical systems can make it impossible for one leader to manage all necessary tasks efficiently, safely, and in a timely manner (Fernandez et al. 2017). Instead, leadership in safety-critical systems should be shared between several persons, so called shared leadership, where employees, in critical situations, are allowed to follow the colleague that possess the best knowledge given the prevailed situation. This is much in accordance with the principles of high reliability organizations. Shared leadership further suggests that power and influence should be shared among several individuals (Bienefeld and Grote 2014; Fernandez et al. 2017; Murase et al. 2014).

Leadership Behavior and Strategies. Leaders have both direct and indirect effects on employees. The indirect effects constitute the establishment of rules, norms, procedures, and practices. The direct effects relate to the monitoring and control of employees' behaviors, carried out through direct interactions (e.g., safety observations, training sessions, and meetings) (Luke 2018).

According to Yukl (2008), a factor of leadership effectiveness is the followers' attitudes and perceptions of the leader. These attitudes are further dependent on the employees' respect, admiration, and trust in the leader (Cooper 2015). Cooper (2015) uses the term effective safety leadership, which is a leader within a safety-critical system that establishes a balance between caring and control. Important factors are thus the involvement of everyone in safety, showing appreciation, trusting the subordinates, listening to people, and acting on relevant safety information (Cooper 2015; Rasmussen 1997). Furthermore, by constantly challenging the status quo and questioning working patterns and safety work, a leader can drive corrective actions that are necessary in order to balance the work inside the safety margins (Ramthun and Matkin 2012).

Cooper (2015) forwards three leadership styles: transformational, transactional, and servant. They all constitute different leadership behaviors and strategies that leaders use and that shape an organization's safety culture (Cooper 2015; Flin and Yule 2004; Yukl 2008). Transformational leaders are charismatic, inspiring, stimulating, and considerate (Yukl 2008). They motivate organizational members by using a positive language, they are observant, and treat each member as an individual. Transformational leaders can question traditional assumptions, and encourage broad perspectives and diversity (Cooper 2015).

Transactional leaders focus on performance monitoring and promotes consequence management. They emphasize organizational members' responsibility for their own work, and sets up clear goals concerning desired outputs and needed performance requirements. This form of leadership style is important when wanting to ensure compliance with safety rules and regulations, and include leadership behaviors such as: safety observations, the provision of safety feedback to personnel, and taking actions against arising safety issues (Sadeghi et al. 2012). Transactional leadership is criticized of having a short-term focus because of the use of reward-punishment systems. Transactional leadership can be advantageous during crisis and emergencies, but are not preferable in the long run, since it lacks focus on employee well-being (Cooper 2015; Sadeghi et al. 2012).

The servant leadership style focus on building personal relationships by advocating open communication and a supportive environment, which increases safety performance and engagement (Cooper 2015). This leadership style engages in safety behaviors such as: active participation in safety meetings and safety committees, listening to employees' ideas and actions concerning how safety could be improved, and following up on any safety corrections to ensure their completion (Cooper 2015).

Which of these leadership styles that are the most effective depends on the prevalent situation, and leaders can use a combination of all three. However, servant leadership has shown to have a stronger influence on safety culture, such as employees' safety engagement, their safety behavior, and the reduction of incident rates. However, for a leader to engage in all these behaviors, the organization must provide a supportive environment and sufficient resources to leaders (Zenger et al. 2009).

Another division of safety leadership is inspirational and positional leadership. Inspirational leaders help to develop employees' knowledge, skills, and abilities, enabling them to participate more wholeheartedly in safety efforts. They are devoted to safety and have the ability to motivate employees to why it is important to follow set guidelines. Employees follow inspirational leaders because they want to, and because they are allowed to discover what feels right for themselves (Cooper 2015). In contrast, positional leaders operate more clearly under the virtue of power, since they tend to tell people what they want them to do, and people follow them not necessary because they want to, but rather because they have to (O'Reilly and Roberts 1976; Shuffler and Carter 2018).

Safety Culture and Safety Participation. A safety culture reflects the values, believes, and perceptions that members of an organization share in relation to safety. A positive safety culture is believed to have a positive impact on safety communication and learning (Reason 1997). The leadership (on all organizational levels) is often highlighted as having a main effect on an organization's safety culture, as well as employee safety participation, and reduced injury rate (Kim and Gausdal 2017). Safety participation has to do with the activities that employees engage in, and that contributes to the overall organizational safety, rather than safety of the self (Salas et al. 2005; Shuffler and Carter 2018). Safety participation is enabled through each organizational member's safety-related knowledge and motivation.

4 Results and Analysis

This section presents results from two interviews conducted in two safety-critical systems: one leader at a nuclear power plant, and one operations manager (physician) at a university hospital.

4.1 Leadership and Safety at a Nuclear Power Plant

The safety work within a nuclear power plant was by the interviewee characterized by carefulness and systematics. The workflow regarding critical tasks and interventions, follow carefully evaluated instructions, where several independent actors, internal and external, systematically establishes and reviews various safety documentation before any intervention can be initiated. The last actor is the Swedish Radiation Safety Authority who approves or rejects the intended working plans after reviewing the established documentation by the different actors. The documentation constitutes a tool for coordination and communication, which will ensure that the planned work tasks are conducted and achieved safely, and that everyone involved in performing the tasks are aware of the prevailing conditions and circumstances.

The interviewee forwarded that the organization had a high focus on engineering approaches regarding the calculation and evaluation of risks. Safety-critical work tasks were conducted according to the peer review principle, where two colleagues work side by side enabling them to check up on each other's work. Complex tasks were often divided into several sub-tasks, where highly specialized expert teams provided support. Thus, complex work tasks are performed by several specialized teams together, and safety is constantly overviewed by an appointed safety officer. As teams and divisions are to cooperate, before, during, and after a safety-critical operation, it is essential that the communication is well functioning (e.g., through physical meetings and closed-loop communication).

However, the interviewee forwarded that the greatest safety challenge within the organization was related to communication. The challenge is to ensure that everyone has understood the prevailing conditions related to the task to be performed, and how to avoid misunderstandings (i.e., in what order the work should be performed, what safety measures that needs to be considered, how to prepare, and how to conduct the work).

The interviewee's leadership could be categorized as inspirational leadership, even though the organization was managed through vertical, hierarchical leadership. According to the interviewee, one of the most important qualities of a leader is to "lead others, by first leading oneself". This connects to characteristics of inspirational and transformational leadership, that is, to reflect, to serve as a living safety example, to listen, and to inspire others. As a nuclear power plant organization is immense and include over a thousand employees, employee safety participation is vital. Safety training, and continuous learning for safety are vital components to maintain safety.

4.2 Leadership and Safety at a University Hospital

Interview results showed that during the last 15–20 years, the views and perspectives on leadership in the university hospital had changed. The prior working environment at the hospital was characterized by hierarchical and transactional leadership structures, but today, the focus had shifted towards shared leadership and transformational behaviors, a shift that the interviewee encouraged. The paradigm shift was derived from the increased organizational complexity, with increasingly larger personnel groups, and technological equipment becoming more and more integrated within the working environment. To cope with the inherent organizational complexity and ambiguity, and at the same time being able to carry out lifesaving interventions and operations in an environment comprised of time pressure and financial constraints, the leadership, as well as teamwork, have to function properly. Important components for preparing leaders and employees to handle such situations, was management courses for leaders, as well as simulation exercises for employees. These types of training interventions were well-established forms, and was widely used.

The interviewee highlighted the importance of the organization's ability to tackle critical situations as a high reliability and resilient organization. Having characters such as flexibility, redundancy, and dynamical decision hierarchies became especially evident during the outbreak of the Covid-19 pandemic. Acute and critical situations, like the pandemic, often require a transactional leadership, which also under normal circumstances are often used by leaders closer to the employees actually performing the activities (sharp end). In turn, transformational leadership behaviors were often used by administrative leaders, which operate further away from employees (blunt end). However, the seriousness of a situation decides whether a transformational or transactional leadership behavior is used, and whether a vertical or shared leadership is utilized. The interviewee forwarded that the abilities to quickly redirect resources, and to shift focus, were essential to the successful handling of critical situations. The hospital's personnel was continually trained, e.g., through simulation exercises, in order for the organization to maintain such abilities.

One of the most critical safety aspects according to the interviewee was communication, where a lack of communication, often due to time pressure, caused the majority of the reported incidents within the organization. The prevailing safety culture provided an environment where personnel felt free to communicate and report incidents, although differences was seen in different parts of the hospital organization. The interviewee found the organization being good at following up on incidents, with much focus on investigating why things went wrong. Interests was also expressed to investigate why things went right (safety-II-perspective). However, during safety feedback sessions, both perspectives were often discussed concerning occurred incidents.

5 Discussion and Conclusions

This paper reported on results from a small pilot study with the aim of exploring whether safety leadership in practice differs according to the built in properties of complexity and coupling in specific safety-critical organizations. An evident contrast existed between leadership within a hospital environment and a nuclear power plant with regards to flexibility and resilience in organizations. It seems that hospital settings are more suitable for the adaptability and flexibility behaviors concerning dynamical decision hierarchies. The hospital setting seemed better suited for testing different leadership strategies, since the work, compared to a nuclear power plant, were more adaptable and flexible, and not as tightly coupled. A nuclear power plant obeys rules, laws, and regulations that authorities have established for them, and much of the work has to be carefully evaluated and analyzed. Since this setting are more rigid and tightly coupled compared to a hospital, the leadership and safety culture might be extra crucial within a nuclear power plant, due to the absence of the ability to test different strategies and use shared leadership. Nevertheless, the views of the two interviewees agreed on which behavioral characteristics a leader should possess. Both interviewees promoted a transformational and inspirational leadership style. However, transactional leadership was preferable in critical situations.

Acknowledgements. This pilot study was supported by grants from the Swedish Radiation Safety Authority.

References

Bienefeld, N., Grote, G.: Shared leadership in multiteam systems: how cockpit and cabin crews lead each other to safety. Hum. Fact. **56**(2), 270–286 (2014)

Cole, K.: Crystal Clear Communication: Skills for Understanding and Being Understood, 2nd edn. Prentice Hall (2000)

Collins, A.M., Gadd, S.: Safety culture: a review of the literature. Health and Safety, Human Factors Group, Sheffield (2002)

Cooper, D.: Effective safety leadership - Understanding types & styles that improve safety performance. Professional Safety February, pp. 49–53 (2015)

Fernandez, R., Shachita, S., Rosenman, E.D., Kozlowski, S.W.J., Parker, S.H., Grand, J.A.: Developing team cognition: a role for simulation. Simul. Healthcare **12**(2), 96–103 (2017)

Flin, R., Yule, S.: Leadership for safety: industrial experience. BMJ Quality and Safety in Health Care **13**(2), ii45–ii51 (2004)

Hollnagel, E., Pariès, J., Woods, D. D., Wreathall, J.: Resilience Engineering in Practice: A Guidebook. Ashgate, Farnham, England (2011)

Johnston, A., Briggs, G.E.: Team performance as a function of team arrangement and work load. J. Appl. Psychol. **52**(2), 89–94 (1968)

Kim, T., Gausdal, A.H.: Leading for safety: A weighted safety leadership model in shipping. Reliabil. Eng. Syst. Saf. **165**, 458–466 (2017)

Luke, D.: Practical Guide to Safety Leadership - An Evidence-Based Approach. Routledge, New York (2018)

Murase, T., Carter, D., DeChurch, L., Marks, M.: Mind the gap: the role of leadership in multiteam system collective cognition. Leadership Quart. **25**(5), 972–986 (2014)

O'Reilly, C.A., Roberts, K.H.: Relationships among components of credibility and communication behaviors in work units. J. Appl. Psychol. **61**(1), 99–102 (1976)

Perrow, C.: Normal Accidents: Living with High-Risk Technologies. Basic Books (1984)

Rasmussen, J.: Risk management in a dynamic society: a modelling problem. Saf. Sci. **27**(2–3), 183–213 (1997)

Ramthun, A.J., Matkin, G.S.: Multicultural shared leadership: a conceptual model of shared leadership in culturally diverse teams. J. Leadersh. Organ. Stud. **19**(3), 303–314 (2012)

Reason, J.: Managing the Risks of Organizational Accidents. Ashgate, Aldershot (1997)

Reiman, T., Oedewald, P.: Evaluating safety-critical organizations - Emphasis on the nuclear industry. Report 2009:12, Swedish Radiation Safety Authority, Sweden

Rosness, R., Guttormsen, G., Steiro, T., Tinmannsvik, K. R., Herrera, A. I.: Organisational accidents and resilient organisations: Five Perspectives. Revision 1. Sintef, Norway (2004)

Sadeghi, A., Lope Pihie, Z.A.: Transformational leadership and its predictive effects on effectiveness. Int. J. Bus. Soc. Sci. **3**(7), 186–197 (2012)

Salas, E., Sims, E.D., Burke, C.S.: Is there a "big five" in teamwork? Small Group Res. **36**(5), 559–562 (2005)

Shuffler, M.L., Carter, D.R.: Teamwork situated in multiteam systems: key lessons learned and future opportunities. Am. Psychol. **73**(4), 390–406 (2018)

Vecchio-Sadus, A.M.: Enhancing safety culture through effective communication. Saf. Sci. Mon. **11**(3) (2006). Article 2

Weick, E., Sutcliffe, K.M.: Managing the Unexpected: Resilient Performance in an Age of Uncertainty. Jossye-Bass, San Francisco (2007)

Wilcutt, T., Whitmeyer, T.: The case for safety: The North Sea Piper Alpha disaster. NASA Saf. Center Syst. Fail. Case Stud. **7**(4), 1–4 (2013)

Yukl, G.: Leadership in Organizations, 7th edn. Pearson Education (2008)

Zenger, H.J., Folkman, R.J., Edinger, S.: The Inspiring Leader: Unlocking the Secrets of How Extraordinary Leaders Motivate. McGraw-Hill Education (2009)

From Regulated and Managed to Constructive Safety in the Industry

Louis Galey[1,2]([✉]), Adelaide Nascimento[2], Lucie Cuvelier[3], Nathalie Judon[4], Catherine Delgoulet[2], Vincent Boccara[5], Audrey Marquet[2], Sabyne Audignon[6], Irène Gaillard[7], and Alain Garrigou[6]

[1] University Paris Nanterre, Department of Psychology, LAPPS (EA 4386), Team TE2O, 200 avenue de la République, 92001 Nanterre Cedex, France
louis.galey@parisnanterre.fr

[2] Ergonomics Team, CNAM, CRTD, 41 rue Gay Lussac, 75005 Paris, France

[3] University Paris 8, UFR de psychologie, laboratoire Paragraphe, Team C3U, 2 rue de la Liberté, 93 526, Saint-Denis, France

[4] Institut National de Recherche et de Sécurité (INRS), Rue du Morvan, CS 60027, 54500 Vandoeuvre Les Nancy, France

[5] Université Paris Saclay, CNRS, LISN, Rue Von Neumann, Bat 508, 91403 Orsay Cedex, France

[6] University of Bordeaux, Inserm, Bordeaux Population Health Research Center, Team EPICENE, UMR 1219, 146 rue Léo Saignat, 33000 Bordeaux, France

[7] Centre d'Étude et de Recherche Travail Organisation Pouvoir (CERTOP) UMR 5044, University Toulouse Jean Jaurès, Maison de La Recherche, 5 allée Antonio Machado, 31058 Toulouse cedex 9, France

Abstract. Safety development is of high stakes in work environment, as recent accidents remind us. Despite several paradigms have proposed approaches to characterize and develop safety practices, it appears that more complementarity is still possible based on the consideration of real work. From a case study in the aeronautics industry (metal additive manufacturing), the objective of this article is to present an operationalization of the concept of constructed safety practices.

First, an analysis of regulated safety has been done from the actual safety practices prescribed (risk assessment, protection equipment, etc.). Then, a characterization of managed safety practices has been achieved regarding the current work activities and exposure situations to micro and nanoparticles. Finally, one confrontation interview with a worker was a mean to identify constructed safety practices development.

Constructive safety appears both in the individual or collective strategy built by the worker, and by the development of safety prescriptions based on a knowledge of managed safety practices. This exploratory work gives prospects to build another theoretical and practical prospect to act on the safety development.

Keywords: Participatory ergonomics · Industry of the future · Exposure situation · Measurement · Metal additive manufacturing

N. L. Black et al. (Eds.): IEA 2021, LNNS 219, pp. 664–671, 2021.
https://doi.org/10.1007/978-3-030-74602-5_91

1 Introduction

Changes in the work environment generate safety issues that are always high in technological innovations. Many sectors are concerned, from hospitals to industries with accidental risks or that may generate exposure to chemicals. Nanoparticles exposure appears in this context as a major occupational health issue. Many measures are in place to reduce and control this risk through prevention and protection recommendations. However, the prevention measures in the workplace promoted by public policies are still based on a dominant functionalist model (Reason 1990). A recent review (Galey et al. 2020a) indicates that nanotechnologies prevention strategies reproduce traditional model (Eastlake et al. 2016; Stone et al. 2017).

Alternative approaches have since been proposed, revealing characteristics of human activities and organizations (Morel et al. 2008) that make it possible to foster resilient firms (Cuvelier et al. 2019) in the face of risk (Hollnagel et al. 2007). Based on this work, "*managed safety*" (actual safety practices) as a complement to "*regulated safety*" (formal safety practices) has become a research subject in its own right incorporating the dichotomy between "work as imagined" and "work as done" as a resource for the understanding and transformation of work in the field of safety research. This dichotomy, refers to "*integrated safety*" (Johansen et al. 2016), is not limited to the regulatory and procedural dimensions. It considers jointly the necessary adjustments in real work situations. Other work has focused on "*safety in action*" to understand how workers perform safe work by adjusting safety requirements to suit work situations (De Terssac et al. 2009). This qualitative approach to safety development based on the analysis of actual work (Delgoulet et al. 2012; Dul et al. 2012) in relation to safety requirements has been constituted as an integrative and constructed approach to safety (Nascimento et al. 2014).

Although the latter concept makes a considerable contribution to understanding the dynamics of safety in organizations (Rocha et al. 2015, 2019), the definition of these components of safety remains unclear, as do the methodological perspectives and the nature of the data produced for research and interventions in the workplace.

From these approaches, we retain the importance of the analysis of the work activity. Moreover, there is no publication on the mobilization of this approach in settings where occupational exposures to toxic substances may occur. In activity centered ergonomics, work activity analysis is a starting point, analysing exposure situations in situ (Garrigou et al. 2011), to understand risk situations. It is an essential distinction from industrial hygiene (Zartarian et al. 2004), which focuses on the development of regulated safety practices from characterization of pollutant, mainly in the form of expert top-down prevention approaches.

This paper aims to contribute to the debates on the construction of safety by combining qualitative and quantitative analyses of work in settings where occupational exposures to toxic substances may occur. It presents the results of a study aimed at characterizing safety practices (regulated, managed and constructed) in order to develop them in one industry 4.0 from the aeronautics sector where exposures to nanoparticles may occur.

2 Method

Regulated safety practices are defined by the actions implemented by the company to protect operators from the risks associated with the handling of chemicals. These practices take the form of rules, prescriptions and safety devices based on what is foreseeable (normal operation and malfunction) (Daniellou et al. 2011). Regulated safety practices were analyzed based on safety prescriptions (risk assessment document, procedures, training, individual and collective protection equipment, organization of prevention in place in the company) and their consideration of work.

Managed safety practices are the work activities carried out by operators, actual exposures, representations, know-how, operating strategies and informal regulations in the performance of their work. The managed safety practices were analyzed on the basis of actual work situations and exposures experienced during the course of the work activity. Video observations as well as exposure and heart rate measurements were carried out. Concerning the measurement of exposure to micro and nanoparticles, the measurements carried out are based on international recommendations (OECD 2015; CEN 2018).

Finally, the constructed safety practices can be observed in the possibilities to act on the development of new safety practices from the analysed managed safety practices. These emerging practices should contribute to the evolution of regulated safety practices based on existing actual exposures and activities. The constructed safety practices were analysed based on the potential safety developments resulting from the implementation of the approach (construction of individual or collective practices, mobilization of strategic stakeholders, safety construction spaces, constructed prevention actions).

The dynamics around the constructed practices were observed in particular during confrontation interviews (Mollo and Falzon 2004) using video associated with real-time measurements of exposures (Galey et al. 2020b).

Table 1 summarizes the characteristics of the safety practices selected for analysis.

Table 1. Synthesis of the analysis of observed safety practices and their characteristics.

Safety practices	Description	Analysis criteria
Regulated	- Protective equipment - Prevention policies, procedures, safety documents - Organisation, distribution of roles, regulation space - Integration of NPs - Regulatory application	Updating, co-construction, work as imagined/work as done gap, operating phases, activity stages, vocabulary, accessibility/suitability, acute/chronic risks, articulation of risks, search for common/systemic causes

(continued)

Table 1. (*continued*)

Safety practices	Description	Analysis criteria
Managed	- Work activity - Physical strain - Exposure (aerosol)	- Event, degraded mode, objective deviation, prudence/risk taking/protective activity, room for maneuver, possibilities for action, collective strategy, seniority in the position, knowledge of exposure situations, fears and symptoms, denial/distancing/inoperative representation, contact/exposure/visible traces - Cardiac cost - Number concentration (nanoparticles), mass concentration (microparticles), granulometric distribution of chemical elements, transmission electron microcopy
Constructed	- Construction of individual or collective practices integrating managed and regulated practices	Presentation of the results of measurement and analysis of the activity to the operators, mobilization of strategic actors, mobilization of the safety construction area, actions planned and implemented integrating the activity

Starting from a mobilization of the companies' stakeholders (social construction), the methodology is based on a qualitative and quantitative analysis of the regulated, managed and constructed safety practices.

The aeronautic company, gathering 2800 employees, is specialized in the building of helicopters engines. The field targeted for the implementation of the method is made up of four operators working on two additive manufacturing machines. Data were collected during one intervention of a single operator on additive manufacturing equipment (2h34) and a confrontation interview (48 min).

3   Results

The safety levels appear to vary according to work situations. We note regulated safety practices developed in aeronautics, although managed safety practices lead to strong occasional exposures.

Regulated safety practices are high due to specific additive manufacturing developments that go beyond regulations. The company has a structured prevention organisation with players in the field with specific roles, procedures and protective equipment appropriate for this type of risk. We note the existence of a specific procedure for organising prevention on this additive manufacturing workstation. In particular, the procedure specifies the individual protective equipment to be used, the area where this equipment is to be installed, the maximum wearing time of this protective equipment of 2.5 h, the cleaning procedures for the parts produced to be carried out during human intervention, the work areas according to the planned tasks.

Managed safety practices show that the opportunities for protection during work activity are moderate due to the design of additive manufacturing and safety equipment. Although the operator makes use of the protections and applies careful maintenance know-how to the machine, the powder reloading device at the top of the printer has led to the development of exposing strategies during this operation. The physical intensity calculated from the heart rate indicates a light level. The aerosol measurement results show a low concentration of micrometric and nanometric particles, except for certain actions (when the operator retrieves the powders to sift them or transfers them from a shovel or bucket to reload the machine). Physico-chemical analyses confirm these exposure data by highlighting the presence of nickel, chromium and cobalt on a micro and nanometric scale that can be explained by the powders handled during the exposing actions identified.

Certain exchanges allow us to understand the development of practices, comparable to a constructed safety, in relation to the refilling of the additive manufacturing machine designed to be refilled from 10 kg bottles. Exchanges with the manufacturer of the machine have enabled discussions to be held about the know-how implemented by the operator to save time during this operation, described as follows during a self-confrontation interview based on measurements and video of work:

"Because I only put 10 kg in the bottle in relation to the weight to be lifted, I can only put 10 kg, there's 90 kg in the main tank [...] [main tank of powders to be refilled]. Instead of doing the manipulation 9 times, I do it in one go. And instead of spending an hour to fill the main tank, it takes me 10 min. [...] If you drop it, a little cloud will be created. After that, it's an operation that you have to do at some point, so... It's always the same, you mustn't go too fast to make it fall... Now I put it everywhere evenly, I hit it a little bit to pack it down, then I stay up, I don't move, otherwise I just go up, down, up, down. [...] I stand at the top, I'm next to it and I make small shovels so as not to load them too much, not to put them everywhere..."

The measurement results show that this strategy leads to invisible exposures, both for operators and management. The design of the machine and the time saved in this way of recharging is a way of keeping to work instructions. Indeed, it is forbidden for operators to wear their personal protection for more than 2.5 h because of the inconvenience caused. Moreover, the powder transfer gesture described by the operator without *"going too fast"* shows the construction of safety practices in the action exceeding the prescriptions, taking into account the knowledge of the dangers of the powders used.

Constructed safety practices are reflected in the opening up of spaces for discussion on exposure situations. The operators are involved collectively in these exchanges.

However, the presence of these spaces over time remains a question at the end of the intervention research. Determinants at the level of machine design are discussed and requirements for prevention are identified. A design project of a factory of the future makes it possible to envisage deep transformations of work situations at the organisational, technical and human level.

The methodology helps to mobilize company stakeholders to collectively develop new safety practices built from existing or new resources, with particular responsiveness in this aeronautics cases.

4 Discussion

This methodological development allows a global and in-depth characterization of safety practices, and the possibility to act on the development of safe work situations. However, implementation requires significant resources for measuring and analyzing safety practices. After an average data collection period of one week per company, one week was also required to process the data. Furthermore, the analyses of safety practices carried out are focused on a work situation, limiting the variability and possibilities for continuous adjustment of the system over time. Additional studies are necessary to test the method in other professional environments and ensure its transfer. It seems central in this approach to analyze the actual work activities to re-examine the safety requirements and development prospects.

In this way, the exposure and the work become a frontier object (Vinck 2009) to animate discussions and exchanges, between professions and disciplines in the field of occupational health. The work carried out and the exposures become objects of discussion for the actors of the company. The challenge of this work is to integrate work activity analysis in safety development of industry 4.0.

Our approach to constructed safety questions traditional approaches to regulated and managed, or even integrated safety, described as the articulation or integration of managed and regulated safety practices. Indeed, it appears that constructed safety practices can both result from the development of safety prescriptions based on a knowledge of managed safety practices (and vice versa), but also be constructed at the level of the subject in the performance of his or her work, mobilising knowledge derived from regulated safety according to the work situations and variabilities encountered, in order to develop individual or collective constructed safety practices. In this sense, the perspective we adopt on constructed safety tends towards the description of safety in action. (De Terssac et al. 2009). The notion of temporality and culture is essential in this meaning of constructive safety, referring to the origins of the theories of activity.

5 Conclusion

This work contributes to operationalizing and specifying the concept of constructive safety built from analysis of work activities and exposure measurements. Situations of exposure to chemical substances are made visible in an aeronautics company. In this case, it becomes possible to take into account the exposing work activities in the understanding of managed safety practices. Developments of constructed safety practices are still necessary and made possible from the knowledge produced on work activities and exposures.

References

Cuvelier, L., Woods, D.: Sécurité réglée et/ou sécurité gérée : Quand l'ingénierie de la résilience réinterroge l'ergonomie de l'activité. Le travail humain, **82**(1), 41–66 (2019)

CEN. Pr EN 17058—Workplace exposure—Assessment of inhalation exposure to nano-objects and their agglomerates and aggregates. CEN (2018)

De Terssac, G., Boissières, I., Gaillard, I.: La sécurité en action. In: Conception de systèmes socio techniques robustes, Octarès, pp. 128–134 (2009)

Daniellou, F., Simard, M., Boissières, I.: Human and organizational factors of safety: State of the art (Foundation for an Industrial Safety Culture). FonCSI (2011)

Delgoulet, C., Cau-Bareille, D., Chatigny, E., Gaudart, C., Santos, M., Vidal-Gomel, C.: Ergonomic analysis on work activity and training. Work (Reading, Mass.) **41**(2), 111–114 (2012). https://doi.org/10.3233/WOR-2012-1286

Dul, J., Bruder, R., Buckle, P., Carayon, P., Falzon, P., Marras, W.S., Wilson, J.R., van der Doelen, B.: A strategy for human factors/ergonomics: Developing the discipline and profession. Ergonomics **55**(4), 377–395 (2012). https://doi.org/10.1080/00140139.2012.661087

Eastlake, A., Zumwalde, R., Geraci, C.: Can Control banding be useful for the safe handling of nanomaterials? A systematic review. J. Nanoparticle Res. **18** (2016). https://doi.org/10.1007/s11051-016-3476-0

Galey, L., Audignon-Durand, S., Brochard, P., Debia, M., Lacourt, A., Lambert, P., Bihan, O., Martinon, L., Pasquereau, P., Witschger, O., Garrigou, A.: Towards an operational exposure assessment strategy to airborne nanoparticles by integrating work activity analysis and exposure measurement. Archives des Maladies Professionnelles et de l'Environnement **81**(3) (2020a). https://doi.org/10.1016/j.admp.2020.03.831

Galey, L., Audignon, S., Witschger, O., Bau, S., Judon, N., Lacourt, A., Garrigou, A.: What does ergonomics have to do with nanotechnologies? A case study. Appl. Ergon. **87**(103116) (2020b). https://doi.org/10.1016/j.apergo.2020.103116

Garrigou, A., Baldi, I., Le Frious, P., Anselm, R., Vallier, M.: Ergonomics contribution to chemical risks prevention: an ergotoxicological investigation of the effectiveness of coverall against plant pest risk in viticulture. Appl. Ergon. **42**(2), 321–330 (2011). https://doi.org/10.1016/j.apergo.2010.08.001

Hollnagel, E., Woods, D.D., Leveson, N.: Resilience Engineering: Concepts and Precepts. Ashgate Publishing, Ltd. (2007)

Johansen, J.P., Almklov, P.G., Mohammad, A.B.: What can possibly go wrong? Anticipatory work in space operations. Cogn. Technol. Work **18**(2), 333–350 (2016)

Mollo, V., Falzon, P.: Auto- and allo-confrontation as tools for reflective activities. Appl. Ergon. **35**(6), 531–540 (2004). https://doi.org/10.1016/j.apergo.2004.06.003

Morel, G., Amalberti, R., Chauvin, C.: Articulating the Differences Between Safety and Resilience: The Decision-Making Process of Professional Sea-Fishing Skippers. Hum. Factors J. Hum. Factors Ergon. Soc. **50**(1), 1–16 (2008). https://doi.org/10.1518/001872008X250683

Nascimento, A., Cuvelier, L., Mollo, V., Dicioccio, A., Falzon, P.: Constructing safety. In: Constructive Ergonomics, p. 95. CRC Press (2014)

OECD: Harmonized tiered approach to measure ad assess the potential exposure to airborne emissions of engineered nano-objects and their agglomerates and aggregates at workplaces. ENV/JM/MONO(2015)19, (55) (2015). https://citeseerx.ist.psu.edu/viewdoc/download?doi=10.1.1.696.3255&rep=rep1&type=pdf

Reason, J.: Human Error. Cambridge University Press, Cambridge (1990)

Rocha, R., Mollo, V., Daniellou, F.: Work debate spaces: a tool for developing a participatory safety management. Appl. Ergon. **46**, 107–114 (2015). https://doi.org/10.1016/j.apergo.2014.07.012

Rocha, R., Mollo, V., Daniellou, F.: Contributions and conditions of structured debates on work on safety construction. Saf. Sci. **113**, 192–199 (2019). https://doi.org/10.1016/j.ssci.2018.11.030

Stone, V., Führ, M., Feindt, P.H., Bouwmeester, H., Linkov, I., Sabella, S., Murphy, F., Bizer, K., Tran, L., Ågerstrand, M., Fito, C., Andersen, T., Anderson, D., Bergamaschi, E., Cherrie, J.W., Cowan, S., Dalemcourt, J.-F., Faure, M., Gabbert, S., Poortvliet, P.M.: The Essential Elements of a Risk Governance Framework for Current and Future Nanotechnologies. Risk Analysis: An Official Publication of the Society for Risk Analysis (2017). https://doi.org/10.1111/risa.12954

Vinck, D.: From intermediary object towards boundary-object. Revue d'anthropologie des connaissances **3**(1), 51–72 (2009)

Zartarian, V., Bahadori, T., McKone, T.: Adoption of an official ISEA glossary. J. Exposure Sci. Environ. Epidemiol. (2004). https://doi.org/10.1038/sj.jea.7500411

COVID-19 and Teleworking from Home: Understanding New Issues from a Macroergonomic Perspective

Lígia de Godoy[1]([envelope]), Marcelo Gitirana Gomes Ferreira[1],
and Michelle M. Robertson[2,3,4]

[1] Universidade do Estado de Santa Catarina – UDESC, Florianópolis, Brazil
[2] Northeastern University, Boston, USA
m.robertson@northeastern.edu
[3] D'Amore-McKim Business School, Boston, USA
[4] Office Ergonomics Research Committee, Boston, USA
director@oerc.org

Abstract. During the COVID-19 pandemic, remote work has been adopted by many organizations as a way to reduce the risk of contagion and preserve jobs and companies. This emergency situation led to a sudden and compulsory shift from the office to home, forcing the adoption of teleworking from home by people and organizations who had little or no experience with this type of workstyle modality. Also, important phases such as planning and resourcing workers and managers may have been passed over with minimal or no attention. This paper aims to raise and discuss experiences on the adoption of remote work during COVID-19 and issues that should be addressed to avoid possible negative outcomes. Experiences in the adoption of telework during the pandemic show consequences already discussed by the literature, like work-family conflict, but under specific circumstances, such as the closure of schools and daycare centers. Excess workload and technology invasion are also reported as difficulties of remote work in this scenario. Using a macroergonomic model, we address issues that should be verified to overcome these challenges, at different levels, considering factors related to the organizational, personnel, and technological subsystems, and the external environment. The use of a macroergonomic model intends to consider aspects from diverse areas that could influence individual, group, or organizational desired outcomes. The consequences of sudden and enforced remote work during COVID-19 reinforce the importance of planning and accompanying telework comprehensively.

Keywords: Remote work · Telework · Working at home · COVID-19 · Macroergonomics

1 Introduction

Remote work is a reality and much has been said about its advantages and implications for workers, managers, and society. During the COVID-19 pandemic, remote and telework,

N. L. Black et al. (Eds.): IEA 2021, LNNS 219, pp. 672–679, 2021.
https://doi.org/10.1007/978-3-030-74602-5_92

especially at home, were widely implemented in several countries to reduce the risk of contagion and, at the same time, preserve jobs [1]. As a result, remote work was adopted by people and organizations with little experience in this workstyle modality or that previously preferred not to adopt it [2]. Also, the implementation of remote work in a sudden way, especially during the first wave of contagion, which started in mid-March 2020, resulted in passing over some phases considered important before the implementation of this working style. Besides the urgency of moving the work to home, it was also a compulsory change for many workers and resulted in more employees of the same organization working remotely or from home. In addition, consequences of the pandemic, like worries about family member's health, lack of social contact and physical activities, and sharing the workspace with family can all be related to remote and telework during COVID-19 [3].

Considering these new scenarios, this paper aims to raise and discuss issues that must be verified and ways to overcome possible challenges and consequences of the adoption of telework under different situations, based on a macroergonomic model [4].

2   Remote Work, Telework and Working at Home

Considering the divergence between terms and definitions about remote work and telework in different countries, ILO's Technical Note [5] provides recommendations for the use of four different concepts, which are: "remote work", "telework", "work at home" and "home-based work". The terms are related, and even overlap at some point, and derive from the concept of default place of work. The default place of work is the location where the work would be expected to be performed. That could be the premises, facilities or site of the economic unit for which the work is carried out - which could be their own home, in case of independent workers who work mainly from home -, client's premises, facilities or site, or public spaces.

Remote work can be defined as "situations where the work is fully or partly carried out on an alternative worksite other than the default place of work" [5, p. 5]. This definition, as seen, presupposes the existence of a default place of work, excluding, for example, independent workers who do not have any fixed premises (not even their own home) to perform work. In addition, telework is considered a subcategory of remote work, comprising workers who work remotely with the support of Information and Communications Technology (ICT) or landline telephones. The definition of work at home is related to the workplace, being independent of the concept of default place of work. Therefore, work at home is the modality in which work is performed fully or partially in the worker's residence. Home-based workers, on the other hand, are "those who usually carry out their work at home, regardless of whether the own home could be considered as the default place of work" [5, p. 7].

The four mentioned concepts overlap at some point and can be combined to generate additional concepts, as follows: remote work from home, telework from home, and home-based telework. Figure 1 shows how the concepts interrelate.

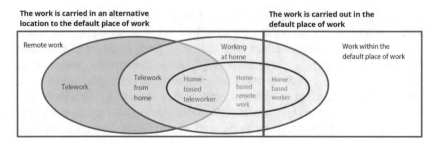

Fig. 1. Interrelation of the concepts of remote work, telework, working at home, and home-based work [5, p. 7]

3 Method

This article is based on data from the literature, mainly official international organization research, scientific articles, and working papers or preprints, due to being recent research and still under discussion. We report experiences in the adoption of remote work because of COVID-19 and, with the support of a macroergonomic model, presented next, we discuss strategies and issues to be verified from the implementation of this working pattern as seen during the pandemic.

3.1 Macroergonomics Work Systems Design Model

Robertson and Maynard [4] present a macroergonomics work systems design model that combines aspects at the organizational, group, and individual level, in a range from macro to microergonomics, indicating issues to be considered in telework implementation. These issues are related to the technological, personnel, and organizational subsystems, together with influences from the external environment. At each level of the model possible outcomes to measure the effectiveness of the telework program are given. We use this model to frame the micro, meso, and macroergonomics issues surrounding remote work and teleworking from home.

4 Results

4.1 Remote Work During COVID-19 Pandemic

Data from Brynjolfsson et al. [6] show a significant fraction of workers who began teleworking from home in March and April of 2020 in the United States (35.2%), which, added to those who were already working at home before the COVID-19 pandemic, represent almost half of the sample. In Brazil, 13.3% (8.7 million) of the workers who were employed and not away from work were performing their activities remotely in May 2020. This percentage decreased to 9.1% in November (7.33 million), following an increase in the number of employed people not away from work because of the pandemic [7].

In a Brazilian research about remote work during COVID-19, Bridi, Bohler, and Zanoni [8] report an increase in hours worked per day and days worked per week, as a consequence related by the participants. Also, the main difficulties pointed by the workers are the lack of contact with coworkers, more interruptions, and work-family conflict. In terms of advantages, the participants mentioned flexibility, no need to commuting and fewer worries about physical appearance.

Molino et al. [9] investigated technostress, which is the stress derived from the use of ICTs, among Italian teleworkers during the COVID-19 pandemic. They found a positive relationship between telework and workload and two technostress creators: techno-overload, related to the tendency of ICTs to make users work faster and longer, and techno-invasion, referring to the invasion of personal life by ICTs. That means that telework was related to working more and to the intrusion into worker's personal life because of the use of technologies. In contrast, telework by itself showed a negative relationship with work-family conflict and behavioral stress, showing positive and significant effects, though, indirectly through workload and technostress creators.

Del Boca, Oggero, Profeta, and Rossi [10] investigated the effect of COVID-19 on Italian working women and their male partners, regarding work, housework, and childcare arrangement, considering that one of the issues regarding remote work during COVID-19 was the closure of schools and daycare centers. The study shows an increase in housework and childcare done by working women and their partners, but more intensively by women working at home than men, especially regarding housework. Even though the male partners tend to spend more time with children during the COVID-19 crisis, this increase in hours spent is still greater for women, for whom the work-life balance is harder to achieve when their partners continue to work outside. Similarly, Lyttelton, Zang, and Musick [11], based on national data collected in the US before and during the COVID-19 pandemic, report that telework from home, called telecommuting in their study, increases time spent on childcare for fathers and mothers, but mothers still tend to do more housework. Also, during the beginning of the COVID-19 pandemic, mothers teleworking from home reported more frequent feelings of anxiety, loneliness, and depression than fathers in the same working condition.

In the study of Ipsen and Kirchner [12], about people teleworking from home in Europe at the beginning of the COVID-19 pandemic, early finds suggest that the managers surveyed, especially danish, found the situation more challenging than the employees. Waizenegger, Mckenna, Cai, and Bendz [3] interviewed knowledge workers from different countries who were forced to telework due to the pandemic. The participants related a substitution of spontaneous meetings by more planned and focused on, virtually, which has the advantage of enhancing its efficiency. It seems to have a downside for new employees, though, because they can be afraid to be bothering the colleagues or supervisors by asking questions. The wide use of remote work by an organization and the virtual meetings can have a positive effect on the integration of hybrid teams, that before the pandemic had only a few remote workers. However, it is worth pointing out that virtual meetings can be considered intrusive, depending on the duration or frequency, or even lead to "virtual meeting fatigue".

5   Discussion

Remote and telework have been widely discussed as a long-standing working pattern, especially after the beginning of the COVID-19 crisis, either because of the uncertainty about the end of the pandemic or the fear of new waves of contagion [13]. In addition, after what Papanikolaou and Schmidt [14, p. 4] calls "the largest global experiment in telecommuting in human history", discussions are emerging about the potential for remote and teleworking across countries and occupations [15]. The wide use of remote work in an emergency scenario resulted in its adoption by people and organizations that until then had little or no experience with it. Therefore, the implementation of the modality under these circumstances goes beyond previous concepts related to suitability to remote work, whether in terms of occupation or employee profile, which requires attention to its implementation, considering different characteristics and situations.

Although remote work is normally related to autonomy and flexibility of working schedule and place, the sudden and compulsory working at home because of COVID-19 can cause some challenges for workers, especially due to the domestic environment, which can lead to issues of mental health, productivity and work-life balance [3]. Some of the consequences of working at home during COVID-19 are already discussed by telework literature, like excess workload, work-family conflict, and social isolation [16], but the circumstances under these consequences can be different and must be considered, e.g. the closure of schools and daycare centers. The impact on families to teach their children remotely as well as working is a mental strain and contributes to the struggle of managing a work-life balance. The social isolation derived from the pandemic, needed to avoid contagion, is added to the social isolation that is known for being a possible consequence of remote work. This should be addressed by managers with the support of virtual tools (meetings, check-ups), considering different profiles of employees and family arrangements, e.g. people who live on their own [3]. Virtual tools also can be useful to provide online evaluation and training to help workers to set up their workstations, considering safety and ergonomic recommendations, and to identify risk factors and work-related health concerns. It is important to respect worker's confidentiality and privacy in these practices, considering the home environment and possible fear of reprisal [17].

According to Robertson and Maynard [4], one of the factors that lead to the success of a telework program is a carefully performed planning phase, prior to its implementation, considering different aspects of the sociotechnical subsystems. The authors also recommend that the planning phase encompasses a telework pilot study to evaluate the effectiveness of the implementation of the modality. Considering the urgency of the adoption of remote and telework because of the COVID-19 pandemic, these recommendations may not have been addressed properly, especially in the first wave of contagion. The importance of planning telework implementation from a macroergonomic perspective was also demonstrated during the COVID-19 crisis. Despite the emergency circumstance of its adoption, the experience showed some factors that should be considered to minimize possible consequences. Figure 2 shows an example of the use of the macroergonomic model in planning telework considering the pandemic experiences.

During COVID-19 lockdowns and restrictions, organizations had to structure themselves to deal with a larger portion of employees, or even entire teams, working remotely, which may become the "new normal" in the future. Organizations are considering flexible work style arrangements and how best to accommodate the safety and well-being of their employees in these new working conditions. Telework implementation in these

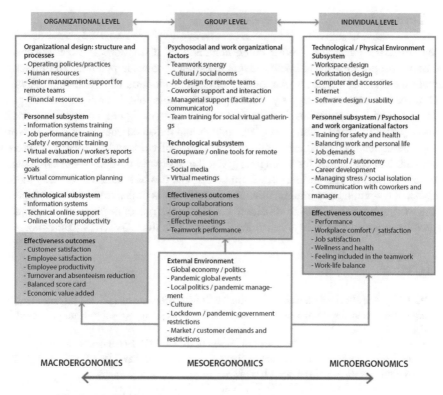

Fig. 2. Modified work system model for teleworking from home [4, 17]

circumstances reflects on the group and individual levels, especially the psychosocial factors and the technological subsystem, which requires heightened attention mostly because of the sudden need to adapting the residential environment to a work setting [3]. The individual level also comprises issues related to the pandemic, like stress and social isolation, emphasizing the need to balance work and personal life, which can be more problematic during the COVID-19 crisis [10, 11]. Therefore, the human resource department is of particular importance in these organizations and must be prepared to deal with remote workers, especially considering the psychosocial risks and the aggravating factors brought by the COVID-19 pandemic. Training and support for organizing work at home, to ensure a work-life balance, along with guidance for managing stress are important organizational actions. Also, home work conditions and performance goals must be clearly defined and periodically managed and discussed with supervisors, considering the risk of excess working hours [17]. Specific factors from the external environment are also important, such as global events related to the pandemic, governmental actions and restrictions, and market demands and restrictions. The expected outcomes are similar to those from the original model, such as productivity, at the organizational level, and job satisfaction and wellness, at the individual level.

6 Conclusions

The COVID-19 pandemic, among other technological disruptions and consequences, led many people to work at home, raising questions about the potential and effect of remote work across countries. Although the massive adoption of remote and telework took place in a state of emergency, it is important to point out that the COVID-19 pandemic resulted in experiences that can also contribute to designing knowledge work in relatively "new normal" situations. The sudden and enforced change to remote work led to consequences related especially to the balance of work and personal life, excess workload, and challenges for managers, given that a greater portion of the same organization adopted remote or telework from home. The use of a macroergonomic model assists in the planning and implementation of telework, encompassing a series of aspects of the work system that must be considered to reduce the risk of negative consequences, especially those arising from teleworking from home in the COVID-19 pandemic.

References

1. ILO: Keys for effective teleworking during the COVID-19 pandemic (2020). https://www.ilo.org/global/about-the-ilo/newsroom/news/WCMS_739879/lang--en/index.htm. Accessed 08 Feb 2021
2. Kramer, A., Kramer, K.Z.: The potential impact of the COVID-19 pandemic on occupational status, work from home, and occupational mobility. J. Vocat. Behav. **119**(103442), 1–4 (2020). https://doi.org/10.1016/j.jvb.2020.103442
3. Waizenegger, L., Mckenna, B., Cai, W., Bendz, T.: An affordance perspective of team collaboration and enforced working from home during COVID-19. Eur. J. Inf. Syst. **29**(4), 429–442 (2020). https://doi.org/10.1080/0960085X.2020.1800417
4. Robertson, M.M., Maynard, W.S.: Managing the safety and performance of home-based teleworkers: a macroergonomics perspective. In: Hedge, A. (ed.) Ergonomics Design for Healthy and Productive Workplaces, pp. 299–320. CRC Press, Boca Raton (2016)
5. ILO: COVID-19: Guidance for labour statistics data collection. Defining and measuring remote work, telework, work at home and home-based work (2020). https://www.ilo.org/wcmsp5/groups/public/---dgreports/---stat/documents/publication/wcms_747075.pdf. Accessed 08 Feb 2021
6. Brynjolfsson, E., Horton, J.J., Ozimek, A., Rock, D., Sharma, G., TuYe, H.-Y.: COVID-19 and remote work: an early look at US data. NBER Working Paper No. 27344 (2020)
7. Góes, G.S., Martins, F. dos S., Nascimento, J.A.S.: O trabalho remoto e a pandemia: o que a PNAD COVID-19 nos mostrou (2021). https://www.ipea.gov.br/portal/images/stories/PDFs/conjuntura/210201_nota_teletrabalho_ii.pdf. Accessed 08 Feb 2021
8. Bridi, M.A., Bohler, F.R., Zanoni, A.P.: O trabalho remoto/home-office no contexto da pandemia COVID-19, Curitiba: Universidade Federal do Paraná (2020). https://doi.org/10.13140/RG.2.2.14052.19842
9. Molino, M., Ingusci, E., Signore, F., Manuti, A., Giancaspro, M.L., Russo, V., Zito, M., Cortese, C.G.: Wellbeing costs of technology use during COVID-19 remote working: an investigation using the Italian translation of the technostress creator's scale. Sustainability **12**(5911), 1–20 (2020)
10. Del Boca, D., Oggero, N., Profeta, P., Rossi, M.C.: Women's work, housework and childcare, before and during COVID-19. IZA Discuss. Pap. No. 13409 (2020)

11. Lyttelton, T., Zang, E., Musick, K.: Gender differences in telecommuting and implications for inequality at home and work, 8 July 8 2020. https://doi.org/10.2139/ssrn.3645561

12. Ipsen, C., Kirchner, K.: Experiences of working from home in times of COVID-19: International survey conducted the first months of the national lockdowns (2020). https://doi.org/10.11581/dtu

13. Bonacini, L., Gallo, G., Scicchitano, S.: Working from home and income inequality: risks of a "new normal" with COVID-19. J. Popul. Econ. **34**(1), 303–360 (2020). https://doi.org/10.1007/s00148-020-00800-7

14. Papanikolaou, D., Schmidt, L.D.W.: Working remotely and the supply-side impact of COVID-19. NBER Working Paper 27330 (2020)

15. Dingel, J.I., Neiman, B.: How many jobs can be done at home? J. Public Econ. 189(104235) (2020). https://doi.org/10.1016/j.jpubeco.2020.104235

16. Gajendran, R.S., Harrison, D.A.: The good, the bad, and the unknown about telecommuting: meta-analysis of psychological mediators and individual consequences. J. Appl. Psychol. **92**(6), 1524–1541 (2007). https://doi.org/10.1037/0021-9010.92.6.1524

17. Robertson, M.M., Mosier, K.: Work from home: Human factors/ergonomics considerations for teleworking (2020). https://www.ilo.org/global/topics/safety-and-health-at-work/events-training/events-meetings/world-day-safety-health-at-work/WCMS_742061/lang--en/index.htm. Accessed 08 Feb 2021

Promoting Women Among Prison Officers: An Organizational Analysis

Stéphanie Hannart[1] ⓘ, Rafaël Weissbrodt[1][(✉)] ⓘ, and David Giauque[2] ⓘ

[1] School of Health Sciences, HES-SO Valais-Wallis, Agasse 5, Sion, Switzerland
{stephanie.hannart-oppliger,rafael.weissbrodt}@hevs.ch
[2] Swiss Graduate School of Public Administration, University of Lausanne, Lausanne,
Switzerland
David.Giauque@unil.ch

Abstract. This chapter summarizes the objectives, the approach undertaken, and the results related to action research carried out in correctional institutions in a Swiss canton. The aim was to identify organizational, managerial, and individual measures to feminize the profession of prison officer. After conducting about 50 semi-directed interviews with senior and middle management, as well as with male and female prison officers, several obstacles to this feminization were identified. Subsequently, a questionnaire was sent to all employees of these institutions to better identify the obstacles and the levers to the feminization of this profession. Recommendations were then proposed at the structural, organizational, and individual levels. This study emphasizes the importance of structural measures, such as changes in working hours or childcare support, as well as cultural measures, such as a change in the role of the profession and a change in mentality.

Keywords: Prison officer · Woman · Discrimination · Work organization · Management

1 Introduction

Prison officer is a traditionally male occupation. Yet, as part of the reintegration process, it is important for prisoners to keep in touch with the reality of society. This entails being confronted with women, including women in positions of authority. Furthermore, given the difficulty of recruiting qualified staff in sufficient numbers—for reasons such as the social stigma of working in prisons [1]—it is necessary to be able to employ both women and men and to retain them over the long term. As a matter of fact, since the 1970s, the profession of detention officer has slowly opened up to women, under the effect of various factors and constraints (politics, anti-discrimination laws, labor shortages, legal action taken by women, etc.) [2–5].

Depending on the culture of the institution, its mission, and its staff, female prison guards are confronted with discrimination, mockery, and abuse by male colleagues and supervisors, with detrimental impacts on their health and job satisfaction [4, 6, 7]. Stepping into an environment that has historically valued a virile and paramilitary culture, they face the challenge of demonstrating their abilities in the profession—whose criteria are essentially based on traditional male traits of physical strength, robustness, and hardness—while maintaining a certain degree of femininity. If they are perceived as too feminine, their skills are not recognized; if they adopt masculine behaviors, they risk rejection because they do not display the expected gender-stereotypical behaviors (such as empathy, communication, negotiation, and listening) [8]. In addition, an informal division of labor is common within teams and facilities. Women are generally assigned the tasks least likely to pose a security risk, such as support, administrative, or reintegration-related tasks. They also do more work with the least at-risk, juvenile, and female inmates [4, 7]. Finally, the glass ceiling effect found in traditionally male occupations explains the low presence of women in prison management positions [7]. However, women's ability and capacity for transformational leadership is widely recognized [9]. Female prison officers also seem to contribute to moderating the prison climate, decreasing violence and preventing conflicts [7].

In this context, a Swiss cantonal correctional service decided to carry out an organizational analysis in its various facilities and units, focusing on the work situation of uniformed female staff. The study aimed to identify the barriers encountered by women in their daily work and professional careers, as well as the resources and strategies they rely on to cope with these difficulties. Possible improvements were to be proposed, discussed, and prioritized. The rationale behind this project was that the proportion of female detention officers remained low, notwithstanding significant differences depending on the facility or unit. In addition, there were various indications that female officers faced professional difficulties linked to their status as women in this male-dominated profession.

2 Methods

The study was conducted by a research team comprising an ergonomist, an organizational sociologist, and a psychologist. After a preliminary visit to three correctional facilities, the study began with a review of international scientific publications on the subject. The following databases were searched for scientific publications on female custody officers: PsychInfo (database of scientific articles in psychology), Web of Science (interdisciplinary database), Science Direct (social sciences, health, etc.), Taylor and Francis Online (interdisciplinary database), and Google Scholar (search engine for scientific articles). The key search words used were related to the following four themes:

– Women: women working, female correctional officers, gender, human females, women, female.
– Prisons: correctional staff, jail employees, prison staff, prison personnel, prisons, correctional institutions, corrections officers, jail, personnel, officer.
– Inequalities: promotion, advancement, discrimination, sexism, inequality, male chauvinism, perceptions, bias, management, leader, leadership.
– Professional culture: culture, identity, work.

These keywords were combined in search equations. The articles selected for the literature review were selected based on the titles and abstracts of the references identified from these equations. These articles were read, summarized, and synthesized. This review provided a synthesis of the challenges faced by women. The literature review identified several recurring themes concerning the professional situation of female custodial and executive officers, as well as the difficulties they encounter in the promotion process. These themes were integrated into a conceptual model created by the research team. On this basis, semi-directive interviews were conducted, with the following objectives:

– To understand the main factors influencing the situation of uniformed staff, mainly women.
– To understand the reasons for the under-representation of women in the uniformed staff.
– To identify avenues to promote the entry of women into this profession and their professional development.

A total of 53 people (24 women and 29 men) took part in the interviews, which were all recorded in the form of minutes. The research team then proceeded to analyze these minutes thematically. This allowed us to identify the perceptions of the interviewees regarding the obstacles, but also the advantages, of the feminization of the profession of detention agent. This first thematic analysis of the interviews helped us to identify the main variables that could have an impact on this process of feminization. These variables were then integrated into a questionnaire that was sent to all employees of the different penitentiary institutions in the canton. In order to collect information from all the staff, but also to ensure that the results of the interviews (perceptions and experiences) were shared by a majority of the staff, a questionnaire was created by the research team. For certain dimensions of the questionnaire, scales that had already been scientifically validated were used; for others, questions were created based on the results of the literature review and interviews. Most of the items were closed-ended questions with four response modalities ranging from "disagree" (1) to "agree" (4), from "dissatisfied" (1) to "satisfied" (4), or from "never" (1) to "all the time" (4). The following dimensions were investigated, for a total of 114 questions:

– Motivations for entering this profession (16 questions)
– Medium-term wishes (11 questions)
– Motivations to change jobs (17 questions)
– Motivation and commitment to work (12 questions)
– Occupational health (5 questions)
– Job satisfaction (21 questions)
– Relationships between men and women (12 questions)
– Perception of displaced behaviors in the penitentiary institutions (7 questions)
– Individual data (13 sociodemographic questions).

A paper test was conducted with two female and two male detention officers. The anonymity of the responses was guaranteed, and the data were securely stored by the research team. To complete the questionnaire, the General Direction of the Prison Office communicated via the intranet and e-mail to all staff. A secure URL link was transmitted by the research team to all staff (prison agents and managers), according to the work email addresses provided by the General Direction. The link led to an introductory page outlining the context of the questionnaire, the confidentiality of the data, and the guarantee of anonymity; then a consent question had to be filled in before accessing the questionnaire. The URL link remained active for two weeks, with two reminders one week and four days before the closing date. Out of a total of 660 employees, 161 responded to our questionnaire, including 31 women and 130 men. The response rate was 24.4%. The sample is very representative of the population in terms of seniority, distribution by entity, function, age, and gender. The 40–49 age group is over-represented; conversely, the 20–29 age group is less present in the sample. Women are proportionately slightly overrepresented in the sample (19%) than in the overall staff (14%).

Results were discussed within the project's steering committee, comprising the head of office, representatives of the general management board, the head guard, and human resource specialists. A list of 28 avenues for action was developed in close collaboration between the research team and the steering committee. They were then presented, discussed, and prioritized during a meeting of the broader executive management team, including all prison directors.

3   Results

Both qualitative and quantitative samples were representative of the office's staff in terms of seniority, distribution by facility or unit, function, age, and gender. In the questionnaire survey, most of the differences in responses between women and men were not statistically significant due to the small size of the female sample. Nevertheless, trends could be identified.

3.1   Reasons for Entering the Occupation

Both women and men applied because of favorable wages and fringe benefits (mentioned by 94% of women and men participating in the online survey) and job security (women, 94%; men, 96%). Additional, more aspirational reasons were particularly noted by women: an interest in the security mission (women, 97%; men, 85%), a desire to be useful to society (women, 97%; men, 89%), a sense of public service (women, 94%; men, 87%), the appeal of the "esprit de corps" (women, 91%; men, 84%), and a desire to help (women, 74%; men, 62%). More men mentioned entering the profession because of the work schedules (women, 61%; men, 78%), on the recommendation of family and friends (women, 16%; men, 42%), or by chance (women, 13%; men, 29%). However, only the variable "recommendations from family and friends" showed a statistically significant difference between women and men.

During the interviews, many respondents stressed that their profession is not vocational. They entered it primarily for extrinsic conditions (salary, retirement, sometimes work schedules). Before working in prison, many of them had a variety of jobs, but did not find fulfillment or job stability there.

3.2 Desires for Development

Most survey participants, especially men, indicated that they wanted to stay in their position (women, 58%; men, 74%) or move up in their institution (women, 74%; men, 82%). Nearly half of both women (45%) and men (44%) said they would like to move up to another facility or service. Women were more likely to report a desire for career mobility and change within the same organizational entity (45%; men, 35%). Finally, the idea of changing jobs was more pronounced among men (women, 10%; men, 18%). More women than men wanted to change for a better work-life balance (women, 70%; men, 42%; p < .05), or out of disappointment with the current assignment (women, 34%; men, 21%). As for the men, they were more likely to want to take on other tasks (women, 74%; men, 88%; p < .05), take on responsibilities (women, 71%; men, 84%), or manage a team (women, 62%; men, 82%; p < .05).

The interviews showed that the prospects for vocational reconversion are very limited. Due to the specificity of their profession and the good wages and fringe benefits, prison officers can find themselves trapped in the profession. Internal mobility is therefore the only way to vary their activity. However, there are few opportunities to change in-house, especially for women. For example, female officers are denied access to workshops and high-security units; given their limited number in the facilities, their presence in the female detention units is mostly compulsory. Yet, gaining experience in the different functions of a prison increases the chances of promotion.

In addition, female agents mentioned encountering difficulties in balancing their private and professional lives. Atypical working hours were said to create difficulties in reconciling work and family life. In this context, hierarchical promotion was described as a way to access working schedules that were more compatible with family life. However, women considered that they have fewer career opportunities, and maternity was described as a hindrance to a career.

3.3 Sources of Work Motivation

Both female and male officers showed a high level of commitment and satisfaction in their work and mentioned a strong professional attachment to their entity. More than 80% of the survey participants indicated a good fit between their function and their needs. More men indicated being motivated by security tasks (86%) than by human contact with prisoners (74%). Women were even more likely than men to be motivated by security (90%), but they were equally motivated by human contact with inmates (87%). Men were also more likely to report feeling good about their prison service's culture (women, 72%; men, 87%).

The aspects of the work that the survey participants found most satisfactory related to the framework conditions (wages, occupation rate, and fringe benefits) and support among colleagues. Reasons for dissatisfaction were mainly related to management support, childcare facilities, replacement of sick colleagues, training and personal development opportunities, and the freedom to make suggestions. Women were more satisfied than men with the responsibilities entrusted to them (women, 87%; men, 73%) and, to some extent, with the support and competence of the hierarchy (women, 54%; men, 40%). On the other hand, they were less satisfied with the work-life balance (77%; men,

82%). The only statistically significant difference between women and men was in the support provided by male colleagues, which was less often considered satisfactory by female officers than by men (69%; men, 85%).

Despite the high overall level of satisfaction, 36% of women and 26% of men would not recommend their job, and 22% of men found it difficult to engage fully in the work. These differences between women and men were not statistically significant. However, other statistical analyses—not detailed here—showed that, overall, men were less satisfied and engaged than women.

3.4 Occupational Health

Most of the survey participants reported that they were globally in good physical and mental health (women, 100%; men, 93%). Nevertheless, more than a third of men and women stated that they were emotionally drained and stressed, and about a quarter said they were physically exhausted from their work. The differences between women and men were statistically non-significant. Regression analyses suggested that health status was poorer among those who experienced inappropriate behaviors and those with more dependent children; however, these relationships were found only among women.

3.5 Gender Relations

This theme was perceived very differently by women and men. Women more frequently felt that they were as capable of managing as men (women, 97%; men, 83%). They were less likely to feel that their management applied non-discriminatory practices (women, 68%; men, 79%) and less likely to feel that career opportunities were equal (women, 65%; men, 82%; $p < .05$). They were significantly more likely to say they had to do twice as much as men to be recognized in the same position (women, 58%; men, 16%; $p < .05$). Furthermore, only 41% of women considered that there was a steady increase in the number of women reaching hierarchical positions, compared to 68% of men ($p < .05$). However, about 50% of both men and women agreed that female officers were urged to take on support tasks rather than safety, technical, or managerial tasks. Finally, female officers were two to three times more likely than males to report inappropriate behavior: offensive or insulting gender-related language (women, 49%; men, 24%; $p < .05$), sexist jokes (women, 42%; men, 19%; $p < .05$), inappropriate relationships (women, 42%; men, 24%; $p < .05$), inappropriate gestures (women, 23%; men, 8%; $p < .05$).

The interviews confirmed the predominance of a clearly masculine work culture, valorizing physical strength and virility. Many female officers indicated that their job had made them harder and had led them to adopt typically male behaviors. Stereotypically, male officers tended to consider their female colleagues as physically and emotionally weaker. They also mentioned a concern that women may be more likely to be manipulated by inmates, or even to develop too intimate relationships with them, resulting in a security risk. However, some expressed stereotypes were also positive, with women being described as more able to anticipate and manage conflicts through dialogue. As managers, women tended to be seen as bringing new perspectives to the way teams are led, with a more participative leadership style.

Overall, a reserved attitude toward increased feminization was observed even among some women. According to a widely held view, a maximum quota of women must be maintained to ensure the security and proper functioning of the facility. The most frequently mentioned obstacle was the prohibition on women conducting strip searches. Men tended to indicate that this proscription caused additional "dirty work" for them. However, female officers noted that they performed other tasks in return. In addition, they contended that they received less support when working with female inmates than their male colleagues working with male inmates. Finally, the unsuitability of the premises for the presence of female staff was also mentioned in the interviews as complicating several aspects of the work, as was the unsuitability of some personal protective equipment to the female morphology.

4   Discussion

This organizational analysis adds to the limited ergonomics and human sciences literature on prison workers. Despite the impossibility of proceeding with activity observations in the field, due to security reasons, the study delivered rich and varied results, which confirm and complement findings from previous studies [3–9]. If the current organization of prisons were to stay the same, with a strong focus on the security paradigm, it would remain difficult for women to enter the correctional environment and be recognized for their skills. However, and this is an innovative contribution of this study, several factors have been identified that could change the situation.

Indeed, based on discussions within the project's steering committee, nearly 30 courses of action were formulated. They were grouped into four categories addressing the sociotechnical system as a whole: work organization (redesign of working schedules, promotion of more women to upper management positions, increased consideration for the reintegration of inmates, etc.), communication (promotion of the profession, development of a culture of dialogue, etc.), human resource management (more women targeted for recruitment, childcare support, strengthening of management skills, etc.), and technical and material aspects (video surveillance, adaptation of personal equipment, etc.). These avenues for action were discussed and prioritized with the management board of the detention service. An action program will be implemented over the coming months and years.

The example of Quebec's detention facilities [2] illustrates that these recommendations can greatly increase gender diversity in the workplace and reduce inequalities, provided there is long-term managerial and political support. Over the past two decades, Quebec institutions have developed a set of organizational measures that are close to the conclusions of this study. These changes have contributed to an evolution of organizational mentalities and practices, including a decrease in paternalistic attitudes and an appreciation of the importance of teamwork. Women currently represent more than 40% of the workforce in Quebec detention facilities; the increase in their presence has been accompanied by an increase in their numbers in decision-making positions. At the same time, changes in the way of working have gradually led to a significant decrease in the use of violence and a strengthening of dialogue with inmates; these changes benefit all uniformed staff as well as the prison population.

It thus appears that, in addition to improving the situation of female officers, the strengthening of gender diversity in the workplace is a response to the fundamental issues at stake in the evolution of the prison system.

References

1. Lemmergaard, J., Muhr, S.L.: Golfing with a murderer: professional indifference and identity work in a Danish prison. Scandinavian J. Manage. **28**(2), 185–195 (2012)
2. Brière, S., Pellerin, A., Laflamme, A.-M., Laflamme, J.-M.: Progression des femmes et mixité dans les services correctionnels au Québec: Des transformations possibles ? Relations industrielles **75**(1), 29–51 (2020)
3. Camp, S.D., Langan, N.P.: Perceptions about minority and female opportunities for job advancement: are beliefs about equal opportunities fixed? Prison J. **85**(4), 399–419 (2005)
4. Bruhn, A.: Gender relations and division of labour among prison officers in Swedish male prisons. J. Scandinavian Stud. Criminol. Crime Preven. **14**(2), 115–132 (2013)
5. Collica-Cox, K., Schulz, D.M.: Of all the joints, she walks into this one: career motivations of women corrections executives. Prison J. **98**(5), 604–629 (2018)
6. Dobrin, A., Smith, J.J., Peck, J.H., Mascara, K.: Perceptions of gender bias in the promotional process of a detention staff. J. Crim. Just. **41**(3), 522–538 (2016)
7. Batton, C., Wright, E.M.: Patriarchy and the structure of employment in criminal justice: Differences in the experiences of men and women working in the legal profession, corrections, and law enforcement. Feminist Criminol. **14**, 287–206 (2018)
8. Le Gendre, A.-C.: Female prison guards in prisons for men: between dissolution of sex differentiation and stereotypes reiterations. [Surveillantes dans les prisons pour hommes : entre indifférenciation des sexes et réitérations des stéréotypes sexués]. Nouvelle Revue de Psychosociologie **17**(1), 45–58 (2014)
9. Crockett, D.L.: An examination of factors contributing to the effectiveness of female administrators in corrections. Walden University, Public Policy and Administration, US (2018)

Effect of Debriefing Session on Emergency Training

Masaru Hikono$^{(\boxtimes)}$ ⓘ and Yuko Matsui

Institute of Nuclear Safety System, Inc, 64-Sata, Mihama, Fukui 919-1205, Japan
hikono.masaru@inss.co.jp

Abstract. Based on the lessons learned from the Great East Japan Earthquake related to nuclear power plant operation, a training curriculum (with the English name ECO-TEC training) was developed for improving the non-technical skills (NTSs) of emergency response teams at these plants. In this training, plant managers conducted an exercise involving initial response to a severe accident, followed by a debriefing session held to discuss good practices observed in the exercise and points requiring improvement. The debriefing session was set longer than the exercise and was considered to be as important as the exercise itself, that allows participants to recognize their own good practices and those of other members. In previously training situations, participants confirmed the lessons they learned at the post-exercise debriefing session, but whether that changed their performance was not confirmed. In this study, participants who underwent the training multiple times were used as subjects and the results of their post-exercise self-evaluation of NTSs, along with the results of third-party observations, were compared between the first and the second time they took the training. There were 20 multiple-time training participants. They were asked to evaluate their performance against certain targets, and four researchers watched videos of the exercise and evaluated the improvements in the participants' NTSs.

The self-evaluation results for NTSs showed that participants gave higher marks to their behavior for "reciting," "setting priorities," "concise reporting," and "having alternatives" after the second time. Improvement in NTSs was seen in various scenes through behavior observations. This indicated that the subjects drew on the lessons learned from the first time to attain higher NTSs the second time while making the NTSs their own. However, a direct causal relationship between the debriefing session and improvement in skill levels was not established, and therefore it is necessary to continue to collect data.

Keywords: Non-technical skills · Emergency training · Resilience engineering

1 Introduction

Enhancing the safety of socio-technological systems, which are constantly growing in size and complexity, is a challenge in many areas. To achieve this goal, merely improving the safety of engineered facilities is not sufficient. In the area of nuclear power generation, the focus of efforts shifted to ergonomics, human performance, and safety culture

N. L. Black et al. (Eds.): IEA 2021, LNNS 219, pp. 688–694, 2021.
https://doi.org/10.1007/978-3-030-74602-5_94

over time [1], drawing on the lessons of the Three Mile Island and Chernobyl accidents. As well, after the severe accident at TEPCO's Fukushima Daiichi Nuclear Power Station (hereafter "the Fukushima accident") following the Great East Japan Earthquake, proposals on the accident response capabilities of managers who take command in plant emergency response centers have also been included in various reports (from the government [2], an electric power company [3], an academic society [4], and the Institute of Nuclear Power Operations [5]). The importance of leadership training for managers has also been pointed out [6].

Hikono et al. [7] attempted to extract lessons mainly on the human aspects required of site managers from interviews with the plant manager at the time of the Fukushima accident. The skills related to human aspects are referred to as soft skills, CRM (crew resource management) skills, or non-technical skills (NTSs), and are attracting attention. According to Flin [8], NTSs are defined as skills such as the ability to quickly grasp circumstances, communicate effectively, and display leadership, as opposed to technical skills (expertise and skills directly related to a specific job), and which should be possessed by site staff to avoid human error and ensure safety. Improving NTSs and thereby responding swiftly and accurately to major disasters rarely experienced in daily tasks cannot be achieved merely by preparing manuals and desk-based work; it is effective to develop disaster response capabilities by regularly repeating practical exercises such as war game exercises through improvised role-playing, to strengthen the response capabilities that workers have acquired [9]. One of the characteristics of NTS training is its focus on debriefing sessions following exercises. Thomas [10] considered debriefing sessions as one of the important review processes for realizing the learning effects of NTS training. Furthermore, from the perspective of theoretical consistency between the skills to "respond" and "monitor" in resilience engineering and NTSs, some consider that it is more important for a first response team to develop the ability to grasp the available resources and diversity of interactions and to apply this knowledge to different circumstances, rather than to pursue the conventional training method of following a prescribed action program (such as an accident response manual) for accidents and incidents. Accordingly, it is important to develop a training program in which participants who work together are gathered to learn different perspectives from each other and jointly identify the necessary conditions for responding even to severe circumstances [11].

Hikono et al. [12] developed an NTS improvement exercise curriculum for emergency teams that stay at the site round the clock in shifts (Japanese name: "*taikan* exercise," English name: ECO-TEC, Experience / Core / Oversight – Training for Emergency Commanders) and they have been conducting the ECO-TEC training for manager-level employees [12]. In this training, as described in detail later, sufficient importance is placed on the debriefing as a process for learning something that is difficult to notice on one's own.

In ECO-TEC training, behavior markers were developed to evaluate the NTS of exercise participants [13] so that observers could evaluate NTS-related activities during exercises. Facilitators had been assigned in debriefing sessions to help participants remember the lessons they had learned, but the effect of the exercise for improving NTSs had not been verified. Thus, this study attempted to verify the effect of ECO-TEC by using multiple-time training participants as subjects and comparing the results of their self-evaluation of their NTSs (10 basic items), along with the results of third-party observations, between the first and the second time they took the training.

2 Outline of ECO-TEC Training

The participants were plant managers on holiday shifts who were requested to conduct an initial response to an incident that occurred late at night on a holiday. The participants were divided into groups of four or six members, and each member was assigned the role of general commander (overall supervision and command), unit commander (commander of each reactor unit; one or two persons), contact person (for each reactor unit the person in charge of making contact with parties in and outside the plant; one or two persons), or on-site coordinator (in command of the front-line team that responds to an emergency). After being briefed on the rules of the exercise and the background to the initial incident to which they had to respond, the participants moved to an emergency response center (or meeting room) where they responded to the initial incident in real time for approximately 40 min. The focus of ECO-TEC is to improve eight categories of NTSs including communication capability (communication, decision-making under stress, human characteristics under stress, delegation of authority, grasping of circumstances, assessment of circumstances, organizational management, and advance preparation for emergency situations) obtained from the 99 lessons derived from interviews with the plant manager at the time of the Fukushima accident [7]. In addition to the initial response to the incident, for which they gathered at the emergency response center, the participants also had to handle a quick succession of interruptions (e.g., threats by a stranger on site, people being injured or going missing, breakdown of communication lines, intimidating inquiries from the outside, subordinates disobeying orders, etc.). New interruptions were presented to them by controllers calling in by telephone from a separate room. The only resources available to the participants were the four or six members themselves and audio telephones, and the participants had to gather information, analyze, and grasp the conditions of the plant using these limited resources, and make decisions and issue orders as the shift members in charge while handling a succession of interruptions in addition to the initial incident. Through this setting, the participants were required to grasp the available resources and their various interactions and apply this knowledge to different situations that arose. The exercise was fully recorded by audio and video. A roughly 60-min debriefing session was held after each exercise. The training session took approximately 2 h in total. Also, about 1 week before the day of the exercise, a manual describing a minimum set of 10 basic actions expected to be taken in the exercise (hereafter, "the 10 basic actions") was distributed to the participants, who were also asked to set their targets for the exercise. These actions are summarized in Table 1. After the exercise, the participants filled out a questionnaire with a self-evaluation on their understanding of the situation and implementation of NTSs, and engaged in a debriefing session with all staff involved, sharing the good behaviors and points requiring improvement and drawing in-depth lessons. The debriefing session was treated as an important procedure alongside the exercise and was allocated more time than the exercise itself as a valuable learning opportunity for the participants to recognize the NTSs exhibited by themselves and other team members. Figure 1 shows the flow of ECO-TEC training.

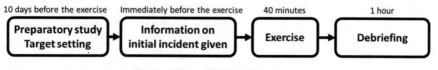

Fig. 1. Flow of ECO-TEC training.

The action:

- is related to NTSs (meeting the purpose of the exercise);
- is in line with workplace rules and operational circumstances (high frequency);
- has low scenario dependence (can be observed under different scenarios); and
- is readily observable from outside (can be used by many observers).

3   Analysis Framework

Multiple-time participants in the ECO-TEC training held from FY2016 to FY2018 were selected as analysis subjects. The changes in their self-evaluation for the 10 basic items and their basic actions during the exercise were observed by third-parties. The self-evaluation was conducted on a scale of 5 (5: did well, …, 1: did not do well). Video recordings of the exercise were viewed by four researchers (some with experience working at a nuclear power plant), who each wrote down what they noted (good practices and points requiring improvement). As the lessons identified in debriefing sessions, the comments written in the questionnaire were categorized based on the basic actions and used.

4   Results

4.1   Multiple-Time Training Participants

Twenty multiple-time participants to the training were analyzed. They were all male and were managers who are required to work holiday shifts at a power plant. All participants had either a one-year (17 persons) or two-year (3 persons) interval between the first and the second training.

4.2   Basic Actions

Figure 2 shows the results of self-evaluation on the 10 basic actions. The higher the rating, the higher the self-evaluation (the respondent felt he did well). Among the 10 actions, a higher number of subjects tended to feel that they did better the second time than the first time for "reciting," "setting priorities," and "having alternatives."

Table 1. 10 Basic actions.[a]

Basic action	Good practice observed in the exercise
1. Building a team	In a team with a less experienced commander, experienced members were seated close to the commander
2. Clarifying goals	Commanders clearly stated their decisions, allowing members to share goals and act quickly
3. Briefing	The commander announced, "Briefing starts now" to get everyone's attention and ended the briefing with a clear "That's all"
4. Reciting	Important information such as number of people was recited in telephone conversations. Commanders also repeated the information when receiving a report
5. Setting priorities	The commander ordered a certain task to be put off due to low priority, so that the time could be spent on another task
6. Drawing attention	Important matters were reported after drawing the members' attention by clearly saying, "This is important"
7. Asking if unclear	The circumstances of the other party were confirmed by asking, "Is your situation such and such?"
8. Grasping other members' circumstances	The commander encouraged less experienced members to "Ask if anything is unclear"
9. Voluntarily collecting information	When grasping the situations of members, various locations were contacted to find out how many workers of what job types were in each place
10. Having alternatives	In response to a phone call about a missing tool, the decision was made to take an action other than that regularly taken

[a] The basic actions attached importance to the process from the introduction of interruptions to decision-making, and consisted of actions to increase resources (human resources, time margin, and information) or to create rules, norms, workspaces, or atmosphere, and were selected based on the following perspectives [13].

4.3 New Lessons Learned in the First Training

Out of the 10 basic actions, more than half of the analysis subjects wrote that they learned new lessons regarding "briefing (11 persons)," "concise reporting (12 persons)," and "voluntarily collecting information (10 persons)" from the training.

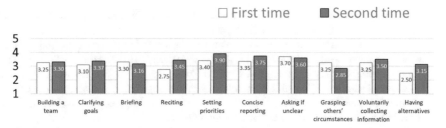

Fig. 2. Results of self-evaluation by multiple-time participants (for the 10 basic actions).

4.4 Third-Party Observations

Three examples of improvement in NTSs observed by observers are given below.

(1) Team building: For the first time training, the reporting of statuses when the members gathered was done without any particular structure, and the commander did not speak. However, the second time, the commander told everyone their roles and what they were expected to do.

(2) Briefing: The first time, the briefing session faded out because the commander himself responded to an interruption by telephone. The second time, the commander clearly announced the start of the briefing and instructed the members not to take phone calls during the briefing.

(3) Reciting: The first time, members loudly uttered unimportant remarks, such as "yes, yes," obstructing other members' conversations. The second time, members recited what the other party said and immediately reported the key points concisely to the commander.

5 Discussion and Conclusion

It was observed that multiple-time participants had acquired a higher skill level by drawing on the insights and lessons learned in the first training and setting targets in line with their roles for the second training. This indicates that debriefing sessions, which encourage members to learn more lessons, should be enriched. However, a direct causal relationship between debriefing sessions and improvement of skills was not established, and therefore it is necessary to continue to collect data. Improvement in NTSs may not necessarily be attributed only to ECO-TEC training but also to other types of training and personal learning by each member. In the future, it is necessary to consider the relationship between the lessons learned by individuals and their actions in more depth.

References

1. Frischknecht, A.: A changing world: challenges to nuclear operators and regulators. In: Itoigawa, N., Wilpert, B., Fahlbruch, B. (eds.) Emerging demands for the safety of nuclear power operations -challenge and response, pp. 5–15. CRC Press, Boca Raton (2005)

2. Investigation Committee on the Accident at the Fukushima Nuclear Power Stations, Final Report, Media Land, Tokyo (2012). (in Japanese)
3. TEPCO: Fukushima Nuclear Accident Summary & Nuclear Safety Reform Plan. (in Japanese) https://www.tepco.co.jp/cc/press/betu13_j/images/130329j0401.pdf. Accessed 20 Jan 2021
4. Atomic Energy Society of Japan, Investigation Committee on the Nuclear Accident at the Fukushima Dai-ichi NPP Final Report, Maruzen Publishing, Tokyo (2014). (in Japanese)
5. Institute of Nuclear Power Operations, INPO 11–005 Special Report on the Nuclear Accident at the Fukushima Daiichi Nuclear Power Station (2011)
6. Kugo, A.: The need for leadership in nuclear power plants. Thermal Nuclear Power **66**(8), 451–460 (2015). (in Japanese)
7. Hikono, M., et al.: Learning non-technical skill lessons from testimony given in the investigation of the nuclear accident at the Fukushima nuclear power stations. J. Inst. Nuclear Saf. Syst. **23**, 153–159 (2016). (in Japanese)
8. Flin, R.: Sitting in the Hot Seat: Leaders and Teams for Critical Incident Management. Wiley, Chichester (1996)
9. Flin, R., O'Connor, P., Crichton, M.: Safety at the Sharp End: A Guide to Non-technical Skills. Ashgate Publishing, Burlington (2008)
10. Thomas, M.J.: Training and Assessing Non-Technical Skills: A Practical Guide. CRC Press, UK (2018)
11. Bergström, J., Henriqson, E., Dahlström, N.: Some Thoughts on how to align the theoretical understanding of team performance with resilience engineering theory. In: Nemeth, C.P., Hollnagel, E. (eds.) Resilience Engineering in Practice. Becoming Resilient, vol. 2, pp. 127–137. Ashgate Publishing, Burlington (2014)
12. Hikono, M., Matsui, Y., Kanayama, M.: Development of emergency response training program for on-site commanders (1). In: 2017 International Congress on Advances in Nuclear Power Plants (Kyoto, Japan), 17382 (2017)
13. Hikono, M., Matsui, Y., Iwasaki, M., Morita, M.: Development of behavior markers for emergency response training. In: Bagnara, S., Tartaglia, R., Albolino, S., Alexander, T., Fujita, Y. (eds.) Proceedings of the 20th Congress of the International Ergonomics Association (IEA 2018). IEA 2018. Advances in Intelligent Systems and Computing, vol. 821. Springer, Cham. (2019). https://doi.org/10.1007/978-3-319-96080-7_6

Assessment of Psychosocial Risk Factors at Work: A Literature Review on the COPSOQ Evolution

Flavio Koiti Kanazawa[1](✉) and Teresa Patrone Cotrim[1,2] (iD)

[1] Faculdade de Motricidade Humana (FMH), Universidade de Lisboa (ULisboa), 1499-002
Cruz Quebrada, Portugal
kanazawaflavio@uol.com.br, tcotrim@fmh.ulisboa.pt

[2] Centro de Investigação em Arquitetura, Urbanismo e Design (CIAUD), Faculdade de
Arquitetura (FA), Universidade de Lisboa (ULisboa), 1349-063 Lisboa, Portugal

Abstract. The third version of the Copenhagen Psychosocial Questionnaire
(COPSOQ-III) was developed in response to new trends: professional life, theoretical concepts and international experiences. The use of validated questionnaires
in the assessment of psychosocial risk factors at work is of great relevance because
it contributes to international comparability of data, and consistently and robustly
data collection. The present study aims to review the literature about the evolution of validation studies of COPSOQ towards the 3rd version. The literature
review was based on scientific articles about the validation of COPSOQ-III. The
COPSOQ-III has already been validated in several countries (Germany, Canada,
Spain, France, Sweden and Turkey). The psychometric properties assessed more
frequently are reliability, ceiling and floor effects, and distinctiveness. In general,
the middle version of COPSOQ III showed adequate internal consistency. Regarding construct validity, it is worth to say that COPSOQ does not have a global score
based on the item responses to represent a latent construct.

Keywords: COPSOQ-III · Psychosocial risk factors · Validation · Literature
review

1 Introduction

The third version of the Copenhagen Psychosocial Questionnaire (COPSOQ-III) was
developed in response to new trends: professional life (changes in working conditions
due to globalization and computerization, intensified by the 2008 economic crisis); theoretical concepts (applied to health, productivity and worker turnover, which can facilitate
integration from the perspective of occupational health and human resources management); international experiences (increasing use in new countries, requiring adaptation
to different national contexts) (Burr et al. 2019).

The use of validated questionnaires in the assessment of psychosocial risk factors at work is of great relevance because it contributes to international comparability of data, and consistently and robustly data collection. The present study aims to review the literature about the evolution of validation studies of COPSOQ towards the 3rd version.

2 Methodology

The article is structured in three parts: the first one gives a perspective of the relevance of the psychosocial factors; the second presents the evolution of the COPSOQ from the first version until the third one; and the third part concerns the literature review regarding the validation of the third version.

Literature review of scientific articles developed for validation of COPSOQ-III and published on the international website of COPSOQ until December 2020 (https://www.copsoq-network.org/validation-studies/). The search on the site resulted in 26 articles, classified by countries (International-1; Australia-1; Canada-1; Chile-2; China-1; Denmark-1; France-2; Germany-2; Iran-2; Malaysia-1; Poland-1; Portugal-2; Spain-3; Sweden-6; Turkey-1). Of these 27 articles, 21 articles referring to the validation of COPSOQ-I and II were excluded, resulting in 6 articles about the validation of COPSOQ-III (International-1; Canada-1; Spain-1; Sweden-2; Turkey-1).

3 Results

3.1 Psychosocial Risk Factors at Work

In 1984, the International Labor Organization (ILO) and the World Health Organization (WHO) defined psychosocial risk factors as resulting from interactions between the work environment, job content and organizational work conditions, with workers' capabilities, and their culture, needs and personal extra-job considerations that may, through perceptions and experiences, influence health, work performance and job satisfaction (ILO 1986). This definition highlights the dynamic interaction between the work environment and human factors. Negative interaction may generate emotional disturbances, behavioural problems and biochemical modifications, determining an increased risk of mental and physical illnesses. On the other hand, when the interaction is in balance, it may generate a sense of control and self-confidence, improving motivation, work capacity and satisfaction, and contributing to better health (ILO 1986).

The First European Survey of Enterprises on New and Emerging Risks gave special attention to psychosocial risk factors, and showed that 40% of organizations found more difficult to deal with psychosocial risk factors than with traditional health and safety risks (EU-OSHA 2010). Even though is clear the importance of assessing and monitoring psychosocial risk factors in the business environment, there are still doubts about management methodologies, and many companies find difficult their implementation in dynamic scenarios and economic recession (Camerino et al. 2014, in Cotrim et al. 2017).

3.2 Evolution of the Copenhagen Psychosocial Questionnaires (COPSOQ-I, II and III)

The Copenhagen Psychosocial Questionnaire (COPSOQ) is an instrument for assessment psychosocial risk factors and for organizational development in the work environment for all types of work, in any sector of activity, for workplaces of different dimensions, or even, for private or public companies; available in 25 languages, making it possible to compare results between countries (Cotrim et al. 2017; Kristensen et al. 2005; Llorens et al., 2019; Silva et al. 2011). The COPSOQ was developed by a team of researchers from the Psychosocial Department led by Tage S. Kristensen and Vilhelm Borg at the Danish National Research Centre for the Working Environment (1995–2007) (Llorens et al. 2019). From 2007 the International COPSOQ Network (https://www.cop soq-network.org) leads the research towards its development (Llorens et al. 2019). It is widely cited by the International Labour Organization (ILO), World Health Organization (WHO), European Agency for Safety and Health at Work (EU-OSHA), and in hundreds of international scientific journals (Llorens et al. 2019).

The COPSOQ is an instrument that doesn't have tolerance levels regarding the exposure of workers to psychosocial risk factors, so it is pertinent to compare the results found with the reference values of the general population (serving as a short-term exposure target), providing a classification of the exposures of the workers under study; and the continuous application of the research allows to monitor the performance of prevention actions (Llorens et al. 2019). It covers a wide range of domains, including: demands at work, work organization and job contents, interpersonal relations and leadership, work-individual interface, social capital, conflicts and offensive behaviours, health and well-being, and personality (Burr et al. 2019; Cotrim et al. 2017; Llorens et al. 2019; Silva et al. 2011).

After investigating several Danish and international questionnaires, and without finding a possible standard questionnaire, the team of researchers decided to develop COPSOQ-I (Kristensen et al. 2005) based on the following instruments: Setterlind Stress Profile, Whitehall II, Short Form-36, QEAW-Questionnaire on the Experience and Assessment of Work (Germany), QPS Nordic-General Nordic Questionnaire, QSQ-Occupational Stress Questionnaire (Finland), JCQ-Job Content Questionnaire, and Questionnaires from Denmark (Kristensen 2002; Kristensen et al. 2005).

The second version of the Copenhagen Psychosocial Questionnaire (COPSOQ-II) was developed based on the theoretical considerations and practical results found in the application of COPSOQ-I. It was based on the following principles: (i) change the instrument at most every 5 years; (ii) make changes to the scales and items only when they show problems in the psychometric tests or in practical use (e.g. Quantitative demands); (iii) perform the elimination of scales only when they are not used for research or in a practical way (e.g. Sensory demands and Freedoms at work); (iv) carry out the inclusion of new scales only when there are new theories or new perspectives (e.g. Recognition, Trust, Justice, Work-family conflict and Depressive symptoms) (Cotrim et al. 2017; Pejtersen et al. 2010).

The COPSOQ-II presented three versions as COPSOQ-I: the "Short" version was intended for use in workplaces with less than 30 workers or for self-assessment; the "Middle" version to be used by occupational health professionals for the assessment and prevention of occupational risks; and the "Long" version in a research environment. However, later it was found that, also, in the research environment there was a need for shorter versions and that the "Middle" version had enough reliability (Cotrim et al. 2017; Pejtersen et al. 2010; Silva et al. 2011). In the "Short" version, the number of items in the scale scales was kept between 1 to 2 items/scale, while in the "Long" and "Middle" versions, they were kept between 3 to 4 items/scale, which was a balance between precision and load in the respondents; and yet, the items with a nominal "yes" and "no" response were changed to five-points Likert scales (Cotrim et al. 2017; Pejtersen et al. 2010). The development of COPSOQ-II incorporated scales from COPSOQ-I (Cognitive stress symptoms, Meaning of work, Predictability, Role conflicts and Social community at work); some scales from COPSOQ-I were excluded (Behavioural stress, Coping, Degree of freedom, Feedback at work, Mental health, Sense of coherence, Sensory demands, Social relations and Vitality); and new scales were added (Bullying, Burnout, Depressive symptoms, Family-work conflict, Justice, Mutual trust between employees, Recognition, Self-efficacy, Sleeping troubles, Social inclusiveness, Stress, Trust regarding management, Variation, Work-family conflict and Work pace). Taking into consideration trends in research news domains were added to COPSOQ-II: Offensive behaviours and Values at workplace (Pejtersen et al. 2010).

The COPSOQ-III structure contains items and factors with the designation: "Core" - 21 scales and 32 items, "Middle" - 18 scales and 28 items, and "Long" - 38 scales and 92 items, which correspond to the versions "Short", "Middle" and "Long" (Llorens et al. 2019). New items and scales were introduced in COPSOQ-III, existing items and scales changed in their description, and existing items were reallocated to new scales (Cotrim et al. 2017). The development of COPSOQ-III excluded one scale from COPSOQ-II: Social inclusiveness; reintroduced a scale from COPSOQ-I with new nomenclature: Control over working time (from Degrees of freedom); and new scales were added to COPSOQ-III: Illegitimate tasks, Insecurity over working conditions, Quality of work and Work engagement. Some scales were renamed: to Horizontal trust (from Mutual trust between employees), to Vertical trust (from Trust regarding management), to Organiza-tional justice (from Justice), to Recognition (from Rewards), to Sense of community at work (from Social community at work) and to Work life conflict (from Work-family con-flict). Regarding the domains in COPSOQ-III, one has been renamed to Social Capital (from Values at the workplace level) (Burr et al. 2019; Llorens et al. 2019).

3.3 International Studies of Third Version of the Copenhagen Psychosocial Questionnaire (COPSOQ-III)

The main information presented by the six studies regarding the validation of the third version of COPSOQ-III is summarized in Table 1 and Table 2.

Table 1. Summary of information from the 6 articles under study

Authors, Year; Country; Activity; Sample	Questionnaire (base)	Statistical Analysis
1. Berthelsen et al. 2020; Sweden; random samples and convenience sample of non-managerial employees; n = 2.847	COPSOQ III (middle version); 32 core items + 15 items middle items + 29 long items	**1. Correlation Analysis** • Bivariate correlation: Psychosocial Factors **2. Reliability** • Internal Consistency (Cronbach Alpha [α] and Spearman-Brown Coefficient)
2. Berthelsen et al. 2019; Sweden; private and public companies-human service; n = 1.316	COPSOQ III (middle version)	**1. Rasch Model** • Reliability (PSI-Person Separation Index); Chi-Squale Test; Residual values
3. Burr et al. 2019; Canada, Spain and France (random samples); Germany (industries); Sweden (private and public companies-human service); Turkey (service sector and manufacturing); n = 23.361	COPSOQ III (middle version); Added 2 factors COPSOQ III (long version)	**1. Correlation Analysis** • Bivariate correlation: Psychosocial Factors **2. Reliability** • Internal Consistency (Cronbach Alpha [α])
4. Ramkissoon et al. 2019; Canada; industries; n = 4.113	COPSOQ II (short version); COPSOQ III (beta version - core); Added 1 factor "Global Rating of Workplace Psychological Health and Safety"	**1. Factor Analysis** • Confirmatory Factor Analysis (CFA) **2. Correlation Analysis** • Bivariate correlation: Psychosocial Factors • Convergent validity: Psychosocial Factors X Global Rating of Workplace Psychological Health and Safety **3. Linear Regression** • Correlation Psychosocial Factors X Global Rating of Workplace Psychological Health and Safety
5. Useche et al. 2019; Spain; professional drivers; n = 726	COPSOQ III (Enterprise version-2018); GHQ-12 (Goldberg-General Health Questionnaire)	**1. Factor Analysis** • Exploratory Factor Analysis (EFA) • Confirmatory Factor Analysis (CFA) **2. Correlation Analysis** • Bivariate correlation: Psychosocial Factors • Convergent validity: Psychosocial Factors X Indicator of psychological distress **3. Reliability** • Internal Consistency (Cronbach Alpha [α] and Composite Reliability Index [CRI])

(*continued*)

Table 1. (*continued*)

Authors, Year; Country; Activity; Sample	Questionnaire (base)	Statistical Analysis
6. Şahan et al. 2018; Turkey; call center, hospital, plastic manufacturing, and metal industry; n = 1.076	COPSOQ III (middle version); Added 29 items COPSOQ III (long version)	**1. Factor Analysis** • Exploratory Factor Analysis (EFA) • Confirmatory Factor Analysis (CFA) **2. Correlation Analysis** • Convergent validity: Psychosocial Factors X Job Satisfaction and Burnout **3. Reliability** • Internal Consistency (Cronbach Alpha [α])

The COPSOQ-III has already been validated in several countries (Germany, Canada, Spain, France, Sweden and Turkey), in several business sectors (call center; hospital; plastic, metal and general industries; professional drivers; human services; diverse areas; and still, in public and private organizations) (Berthelsen et al. 2019; Burr et al. 2019; Ramkissoon et al. 2019; Şahan et al. 2018; Useche et al. 2019).

The psychometric properties assessed more frequently were reliability (Cronbach Alpha), ceiling and floor effects (fractions with extreme answers), and distinctiveness (correlations with other dimensions) (Burr et al. 2019; Şahan et al. 2018; Useche et al. 2019). Some studies also analyzed the factorial structure of the instrument (Ramkissoon et al., 2019; Şahan et al. 2018; Useche et al. 2019).

In general, the middle version of COPSOQ III showed adequate internal consistency (Burr et al. 2019; Şahan et al. 2018; Useche et al. 2019).

Regarding construct validity, it is worth to say that COPSOQ does not have a global score based on the item responses to represent a latent construct (Berthelsen et al. 2019). Nevertheless, scales are grouped in domains that are theoretically justified: work demands, interpersonal relations and leadership, influence and development, health outcomes, others (Burr et al. 2019; Şahan et al. 2018; Useche et al. 2019).

Table 2. Reliability analysis results from the 6 articles under study.

Authors, Year	Reliability Analysis (Cronbach Alpha Coefficient [α]; Spearman-Brown Coefficient; Composite Reliability Indices [CRI]; Person Separation Index [PSI])
1. Berthelsen et al. 2020	**1. Scale:** • **α > 0,7** = >17 scales (total of 17 scales with 3 or more items); • **Spearman-Brown Coefficient > 0,7** = > 6 scale (total of 7 scales with 2 items) • **Spearman-Brown Coefficient < 0,7** = > 1 scale: "Quality in Work" (0,69)
2. Berthelsen et al. 2019	**1. Scale:** • **PSI > 0,7** = > 1 scale (total of 1 scale with 6 items): "Social Capital" (0,83) • **PSI > 0,7** = > 1 scale (total of 1 scale with 2 groups [3 items + 3 items]): "Social Capital" (0,78)
3. Burr et al. 2019	**1. Scale:** • **α > 0,7** = > 20 scales (total of 23 scales with 2 or more items); • **α < 0,7** = > 3 scales: "Commitment to the Workplace" (0,64); "Control over Working Time" (0,69) e "Demands for Hiding Emotions" (0,66) **2. Scale - Specific Population:** • **α < 0,7** = > 3 scales: "Job Insecurity"-2 items (France-0,66 and Germany-0,67); Meaning of Work-2 items (France-0,62); "Predictability"-2 items (France-0,62 e Turkey-0,66); "Work Pace"-2 items (Spain-0,69) **3. Item-Total:** • **α > 0,4** = > 59 items (total of 60 items); • **α < 0,4** = > 1 item: Demands for Hiding Emotions: "Having to be kind and open to everyone" (0,30) **4. Item-Total - Specific Population:** • **α < 0,4** = > 3 items: Demands for Hiding Emotions: "Requirements not stating opinion" (Spain-0,34); Control over Working Time: "Holidays" (Turkey-0,38) and "Leave work for private business" (Turkey-0,28)
4. Ramkissoon et al. 2019	Reliability analysis was not performed. Have been performed: Factor Analysis, Correlation Analysis and Linear Regression

(continued)

Table 2. (*continued*)

Authors, Year	Reliability Analysis (Cronbach Alpha Coefficient [α]; Spearman-Brown Coefficient; Composite Reliability Indices [CRI]; Person Separation Index [PSI])
5. Useche et al. 2019	**1. Domain:** • **α > 0,7** = > 5 domains (total of 5 domains): "Demands" (0,919); "Influence and Development" (0,854); "Interpersonal Relationships and Leadership" (0,911); "Job Insecurity" (0.852); e "Strain" (0,901); • **CRI > 0,7** = > 5 domains (total of 5 domains): "Demands" (0,983); "Influence and Development" (0,970); "Interpersonal Relationships and Leadership" (0,984); "Job Insecurity" (0,981); e "Strain" (0,989)
6. Şahan et al. 2018	**1. Scale:** • **α > 0,7** = > 22 scales (total of 25 scales); • **α < 0,7** = > 2 scales: "Control over Working Time" (0,543); "Demands for hiding emotions" (0,696); "Predictability" (0,660)
Indices acceptable: • α ≥ 0,7 (For Scale)	• α ≥ 0,4 (For Item-Total) • Spearman-Brown Coefficient ≥ 0,7 • PSI ≥ 0,7 • CRI ≥ 0,7

4 Conclusion

The first international study was carried out in six countries (Canada, Spain, France, Germany, Sweden, and Turkey) using different social and cultural contexts (Burr et al. 2019), what strengths the results. It is necessary to develop further studies to validate the third version of COPSOQ worldwide. Recently, the global scenario imposed by Covid-19 is affecting workers differently from the studies analyzed. Further studies are needed as working contexts are changing quickly.

References

Berthelsen, H., Westerlund, H., Bergström, G., Burr, H.: Validation of the Copenhagen psychosocial questionnaire version III and establishment of benchmarks for psychosocial risk management in Swede. Int. J. Environ. Res. Public Health **17**, 3179 (2020)

Berthelsen, H., Westerlund, H., Pejtersen, J.H., Hadzibajramovic, E.: Construct validity of a global scale for workplace social capital based on COPSOQ III. PLoS ONE **14**(8), e0221893 (2019)

Burr, H., Berthelsen, H., Moncada, S., Nübling, M., Dupret, E., Demiral, Y., et al.: The third version of the Copenhagen psychosocial questionnaire. Saf. Health Work **10**, 482–503 (2019)

Cotrim, T., Bem-haja, P., Amaral, V., Pereira, A., Silva, C.F.: Evolução do Questionário Psicossocial de Copenhaga: Do COPSOQ II para o COPSOQ III. Int. J. Work. Condit. **14**, 105–115 (2017)

European Agency for Safety and Health at Work: European Survey of Enterprises on New and Emerging Risks - Managing safety and health at work. Bilbao: EU-OSHA (2010)

International Labour Organisation: Psychosocial factors at work: recognition and control. In: Report of the Joint ILO/WHO Committee on Occupational Health, Ninth Session, Geneva, 18–24 September 1984, Occupational Safety and Health Series No. 56. Geneva: ILO (1986)

Kristensen, T.S., Hannerz, H., Høgh, A., Borg, V.: The Copenhagen psychosocial questionnaire-a tool for the assessment and improvement of the psychosocial work environment. Scand. J. Work. Environ. Health **31**(6), 438–449 (2005)

Kristensen, T.S.: A new tool for assessing psychosocial factors at work: the Copenhagen Psychosocial Questionnaire. TUTB Newslett. **19–20**, 45–47 (2002)

Llorens, C., Pérez-Franco, J., Oudyk, J., Berthelsen, H., Dupret, E., Nübling, M., Burr, H, Moncada, S.: COPSOQ III. Guidelines and questionnaire (2019)

Pejtersen, J.H., Kristensen, T.S., Borg, V., Bjorner, J.B.: The second version of the Copenhagen psychosocial questionnaire. Scand. J. Public Health **38**, 8–24 (2010)

Ramkissoon, A., Smith, P., Oudyk, J.: Dissecting the effect of workplace exposures on workers' rating of psychological health and safety. Am. J. Ind. Med. **62**, 412–421 (2019)

Silva, C., Amaral, V., Pereira, A. C., Bem-haja, P., Pereira, A., Rodrigues, V., Cotrim, T., Silveiro, J., Nossa, P.: Copenhagen Psychosocial Questionnaire - COPSOQ - Portugal e países africanos de língua oficial portuguesa. Aveiro: Departamento de Educação, Universidade de Aveiro (2011)

Şahan, C., Baydur, H., Demiral, Y.: A novel version of Copenhagen Psychosocial Questionnaire-3: Turkish validation study. Arch. Environ. Occupational Health **74**(6), 297–309 (2018)

Useche, S.A., Montoro, L., Alonso, F., Pastor, J.C.: Psychosocial work factors, job stress and strain at the wheel: validation of the Copenhagen psychosocial questionnaire (COPSOQ) in professional drivers. Front. Psychol **10**, 1531 (2019)

Activity – The Core
of Human-Technology-Organization

Johan Karltun[1], Anette Karltun[1(✉)], and Martina Berglund[2(✉)]

[1] Department of Supply Chain and Operations Management, School of Engineering, Jönköping University, Jönköping, Sweden
{johan.karltun,anette.karltun}@ju.se
[2] HELIX Competence Centre and Logistics and Quality Development, Linköping University, 581 83 Linköping, Sweden
martina.berglund@liu.se

Abstract. Human work activities are at the core of value adding processes creating system performance. The concept of human, technology and organization (HTO) is used in different cases as it offers a framework for understanding and developing work. The aim of this paper is to elucidate the character of work activities and their significance in using the HTO concept. The aspects elaborated on are: the relation between the objectives of the organization and the activity, the organizational context of the activity, the variability of the individual and the work process, the influence of history, the relation between the individual and the activity and finally how activity can be studied. Looking at three short examples from different industries, it can be concluded that the HTO concept is beneficial to use in order to better understand the studied activities in the examples. However, there must be clearly identifiable tasks to really benefit from the HTO concept.

Keywords: HTO · Work system · Interaction · Performance · Work-As-Done

1 Introduction and Background

Rapid technical developments and digitally mediated work provide future working life challenges. Organizational structures, work processes and procedures must be prepared to support and assist employees to manage and interact with technology as well as the increasing organizational complexity in such work. Regardless of technology development and increasing complexity, most operations remain dependent on human work activities within the foreseeable future. As a consequence, the need for understanding the conditions for involved humans in such work activities increases as the demands change. The development of work requires incorporating the entire system, including the technical system and the social system as in sociotechnical systems theory. However, the importance of the work activity and its mutual dependence with the human performing it in interaction with the system needs to be better considered when designing for individuals and activities involved in performing work. We suggest that by using the human-technology-organization (HTO) concept [1], these requirements for understanding and developing work are easier to meet.

© The Author(s), under exclusive license to Springer Nature Switzerland AG 2021
N. L. Black et al. (Eds.): IEA 2021, LNNS 219, pp. 704–711, 2021.
https://doi.org/10.1007/978-3-030-74602-5_96

The HTO concept offers a holistic view on operations to deal with increasing complexity in work systems by focusing how interactions between humans, technology and organization are integrated in work activities (Fig. 1). Human aspects that are regarded involve e.g., physical, cognitive, and social aspects, while technology encompasses tangible and intangible tools and environmental characteristics. Organization, finally, includes both formal aspects, such as goals and written instructions, and informal aspects in terms of organizational culture and informal work practice [2].

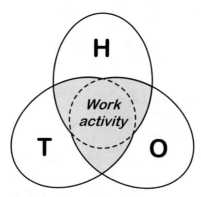

Fig. 1. Humans, Technology and Organization with shaded fields representing the interaction during different activities. Parts of the H, T and O are involved in different ways and to varying extents in different activities.

In HTO we consider how the activity takes place in the interplay between the humans, the technical system and how the work is organized around the activity. By emphasizing that humans are those who set the work in motion, it is acknowledged that most operations will remain dependent on human work activities. To get a grip on the activity as the core in the HTO concept it needs to be further explained. There are some characteristics that different theories on activities agree on [3]:

- Individuals perform activities to achieve one or several goals related to the role of the individual and the task as well as to the overall goals of the organization.
- The conditions for performing the activity are mediated by the technology and the organization as well as by the characteristics of the individual.
- Activities are unique due to individual diversity and variability as well as due to the variability of the context.
- Activities have roots in the past as they are designed and performed using the experiences and skills of the individual and the history of the context.
- To study the activity requires cooperation between the analyst and the individual and the analysis is mostly a joint production.
- Understanding activities generates knowledge about:

  - the physiological and psychological work conditions
  - how the individual is used and the costs that may bring
  - the tacit competences activated and
  - forms of collective interaction.

It is thus in the activity that the interaction between human, technology and organization takes place. Only there, the individual and the context are integrated into an execution. To understand and be able to develop work in more complex systems that are not easily reduced to a few reasonably independent and clearly delimited tasks, we can use the HTO concept to grasp the system character. This is done by analyzing what concrete technological enablers are available for humans and what organizational support that is at hand and compare with what is needed.

The aim of this conceptual paper is to elucidate the character of work activities and their significance in using the HTO concept. In the following sections of this paper, we highlight different aspects of activity linking these to other theories and earlier research. Three empirical cases are later presented and discussed to illustrate the perspectives taken on activities in relation to HTO.

2   Different Aspects of Activity

2.1   Objectives in Relation to Activity

Activities involve human performance, are related to the task and work performed and as such also related to the overall organizational goals and the strategies applied to reach them. An organization's operational strategy is always linked to what work is performed and the way it is performed. As the strategy scholars put it: "In reality, the strategic management of any operation cannot be separated from how resources and processes are managed at a detailed day-to-day level" [4]. The link between the daily operations and the overall goals has also been focused by researchers in business administration. One of the most well-known ideas is the balanced scorecard [5] which broadened the focus on strategic level to also include different aspects more directly related to operational work and how it is organized. Other examples of theories linking strategies to operational level are strategic consensus [6, 7], Hoshin Kanri [8] and knowledge management [9]. There are thus a number of efforts and tools to align goals at the operational level with the goals of the organization.

Goal conflicts at the manufacturing shop floor exist with main tensions between economic, technological and individual objectives related to optimization, constraints and subjective problems respectively [10]. The goals related to these problems regard for example speed or takt time, quality, safety, ergonomics and effectiveness. Many lean-inspired production systems do support a priority of these aspects that should be followed when the goals are conflicting [11].

However, the individual objectives are dependent on the individual performer and cannot always be known or foreseen. A conclusion is that the context in which the activity is performed must be defined to understand and describe the activity [12].

2.2   Understanding the Organizational Context for the Activity

A way to describe the specific conditions under which the work is performed and how the individual is affected is offered by Porras and Robertson [13] in their change-based framework. The framework describes the work setting as a socio-technical system built by four sets of factors: organizing arrangements, social factors, physical setting and technology. The individual worker in the setting interprets the whole system and adjusts his/her behavior to what he/she considers appropriate for the situation at hand and the experienced requests signaled by the system. It is claimed that in order to change the behavior of the worker, there must be changes made in the work setting that make the workers interpret the system differently and accordingly change their on-the-job behavior. The outcome of such a change is both development of organizational performance and the individual. This view of change and the individual as more affected by the context than the opposite, is also supported in a change process theory called task alignment. It emphasizes the importance of starting the change process where work is done and using the prescribed tasks as the outset [14].

The physical context influences how activities are performed. The behavior setting theory highlights how the physical environment (the milieu) is originally designed for certain social and cultural behaviors [15]. The milieu includes a combination of time, place and artefacts that will generate certain patterns of behavior. The development of the physical context and the individual's unique background are thus intertwined in the performing of work activities.

The industry as such, the characteristic of similar businesses, also provides an outset for understanding the context for activities. The specific characteristics of the industry regarding competitive environment, customer requirements, and societal expectations are identified as influencing the contextual conditions within an organization [16].

2.3 Variability with Respect to the Individual and the Work Process

There is variability in the work activity which stems from variability with respect to the humans and the overall work process. Except for diversity among the employees in terms of gender, experience [12], ethnic background, etc., there is also intra-variability over time regarding abilities and performance for a specific individual. This variability is commonly acknowledged, and it is the starting point for designing workplaces to be able to adapt them to as many employees as possible. In design of artefacts, there are different methods to design for human variability with respect to anthropometric data [17] and a need to understand variability in human movements [18].

There is also system variability, both normal and incidental variability [12]. Normal variability can be due to e.g., recurrent variation in material, process outcome, or number of incoming orders to process, while incidental variability can be due to errors leading to insufficient quality. Variability in human safety behavior depends on how a certain behavior is maintained by its consequences, habituation to an eliciting stimulus, risk discounting, consequence dimensions and verbal behavior at the workplace [19]. In complex and uncertain high-risk systems there is also a need for the individual to continuously adapt their activities to system variability, disturbances, and different types of constraints to keep the system safe [20].

2.4 Influence of the History on the Individual and the Context

Earlier history also influences the individual's behavior and the work context. In activity theory [21], the importance of explicitly including the history is emphasized, in particular the history of collective activity systems to understand real-life activities. Each individual has a unique history [22] and his/her experiences has contributed to a unique personality. This also includes the individual's knowledge and competence, ranging from being a novice to an expert [23]. As a novice, rules can be applied to characteristics identified in the context to help the individual perform his/her work. This is in contrast to the expert, whose skills are internalized in the individual who performs the work activity without consciously thinking of it. As a result, each individual has a subjective way of performing work activities.

2.5 Activity and the Individual

Activities are thus dependent on the person who performs them as they are adapted by the performer to his/her personality, skill, experience, knowledge as well as to his/her physical and physiological ability. Human performance varies since it is locally optimized as the individuals tend to apply shortcuts, heuristics, and expectation-driven actions in daily work activities [24].

While prescribed work consists of what the employer demands the operator to do according to predetermined conditions and expectations, work as done consists of real conditions and actual results i.e., work activities. Work activity could then be viewed as a strategy for adaptation to the real work situation and its actual conditions. This is what generates the actual outcome.

2.6 Studying the Activity

To understand the dynamic contextual factors and develop actionable knowledge in practice, it is necessary to understand the differences between work as prescribed and work as done. This is thus about real activities performed in daily work which is a core issue in activity analysis [12]. In activity analysis it is further essential to understand the functioning of the company from an activity perspective, i.e., how the activity is supported by the current conditions as it affects the production outcome. It is vital that the researcher has a multifaceted understanding of the performed activity to spot the fundamental difficulties [12], which must be done in collaboration with the workers.

An interactive research design offers a suitable approach to study work activities in a close collaboration between the researcher and the individual employees to understand and develop activities and their relation to dynamic contextual factors [25, 26]. Interactive research stresses the development of actionable knowledge where theory development in academia and practices evolve iteratively through a common platform for researcher – practitioner collaboration [27].

3 Discussion

The advantage of using the HTO concept and defining the studied and improved activities is that it drives a holistic view of the activities, thereby not delimiting but opening up the understanding of the work as done. This is also a main reason behind the adoption of an HTO view in many safety critical systems assessments. The following examples illustrate how the HTO concept was used in three different cases.

For deboning work several different technological and organizational solutions exist, with more or less advanced technical support. In this example, these solutions had a large impact on the activity performed and the outcome. This applied both to the outcome (volume and quality) and how the deboners were affected physically and psychologically by work [28]. The interdependencies between H, T and O were keys to understanding and improving the work.

In this example, it was clear that the technical solution of the workflow regulated to a large extent the organizational conditions and hence also the ergonomic conditions for the work. All the studied solutions offered both advantages and disadvantages regarding ergonomics, basically offering a balance between physical strain and psychological stress. The influence of specifics in the histories of the studied solutions on the conditions for work was very apparent in this hard job with very long traditions.

Health care systems are complex and demand multilevel as well as horizontal interactions to support clinical performance, and hospital managers' skills in creating supportive conditions for quality improvement (QI) activities aligned with profession-based reality is crucial for high quality outcome. In this example, hospital managers were able to translate and decompose national policy guidelines and regulations into specific objectives to support clinical work activities (H) by providing an Information and Communication Technology (ICT) based management system (T). Further, care developers were assigned by hospital managers to support clinical work and facilitating QI. They acted like glue in the organization (O) as they facilitated QI-processes and mediated valuable learning between hospital departments [9, 29].

In this second example the use of a technical ICT-system made it possible for hospital managers to enhance and support development of quality at the operational level and to work across several hierarchical levels. This was further supported by the organizational mean of using care developers. Together these efforts did have a direct developmental effect on the care giving activities in the different wards. The HTO concept in this case thus constituted a useful tool for understanding how value-creating frontline activities were affected by H, T, and O factors and interactions in various sections of a complex system.

New product introductions are challenging. When it includes collaboration between companies and production plants in other countries, different national cultures influence individual behavior and challenge mutual understanding. In this example, cross-cultural communication included human aspects but also ICT. Further, project management included adaptation of organizational and technical arrangements to employees working in different countries and time zones and with different backgrounds.

In this example, it became obvious that the way tasks are described and designed differed a lot between the national cultures involved. Moreover, the accepted relation concerning task (work-as-described) and activity (work-as-done) between the national cultures differed significantly. This had large consequences on the collaboration and the challenges met during the process [30]. Applying an HTO-perspective for analyzing the challenges showed that all three parts, H, T, and O, on their own and in integration with each other, were challenged in terms of encountered problems and need for further development.

In all the examples, the different aspects of activity could be understood and improved by analyzing and viewing the activity using the HTO concept and thereby being able to distinguish important features of the work situation. However, for the HTO concept to be useful, significant and typical activities of tasks must be identified. This can also be seen as a limitation. If this cannot be done, the HTO concept is difficult to apply in the analysis as the interactions integrated in the activity are challenging to identify.

4 Conclusion

It can be concluded that it is of high importance to consider the activity in depth when using the HTO concept to analyze a workplace or work setting. The activity directly connects the work done with the performer and the contextual conditions for doing the work. It integrates the variability of the process and the individual with the goals of the activity, the work, mediating technology, and the overarching organizational goals. The activity thus bears traces of both the individual and the overall business and the joint effort of system efficiency and well-being.

References

1. Karltun, A., et al.: HTO – a complementary ergonomics approach. Appl. Ergon. **59**, 182–190 (2017)
2. Berglund, M., et al.: HTO – A Concept of Humans, Technology and Organisation in Interaction. Linköping University Electronic Press, Linköping (2020)
3. Daniellou, F., Rabardel, P.: Activity-oriented approaches to ergonomics: some traditions and communities. Theoret. Issues Ergon. Sci. **6**(5), 353–357 (2005)
4. Slack, N., Lewis, M.: Operations Strategy, 5th edn. Harlow, Pearson (2017)
5. Kaplan, R.S., Norton, D.P.: The Balanced Scorecard: Translating Strategy Into Action. Harvard Business School Press, Boston (1996)
6. Mirzaei, N.E., Fredriksson, A., Winroth, M.: Strategic consensus on manufacturing strategy content: including the operators' perceptions. Int. J. Oper. Prod. Manage. (2016)
7. Veloso Saes, E., et al.: Manufacturing strategy in small firms: unveiling the drivers of strategic consensus. Prod. Plan. Control 1–19 (2020)
8. Jolayemi, J.K.: Hoshin kanri and hoshin process: a review and literature survey. Total Qual. Manage. Bus. Excel. **19**(3), 295–320 (2008)
9. Karltun, A., et al.: Knowledge management infrastructure to support quality improvement: a qualitative study of maternity services in four European hospitals. Health Pol. **124**(2), 205–215 (2020)
10. Scherer, E.: The Reality of Shop Floor Control - Approaches to Systems Innovation. In: Scherer, E. (eds.) Shop Floor Control - A Systems Perspective. Springer. Berlin (1998)
11. Scania, Scania Production System. 2007, Scania CV AB
12. Guérin, F., et al.: Understanding and transforming work. The practice of ergonomics. Lyon: Anact Network Edition (2007)
13. Porras, J.I., Robertson, P.J.: Organizational development: theory, practice, and research. In: Dunette, M.D., Hough, L.M. (eds.) Handbook of Industrial and Organizational Psychology, pp. 719–822. Consulting Psychologists Press, Palo Alto (1992)

14. Beer, M., Eisenstadt, R.A., Spector, D.B.: Why change programs don't produce change. Harward Bus. Rev. 158–166 (1990)
15. Westlander, G.: Ekologisk psykologi och behavior settingteorin. Studentlitteratur (1999)
16. Gordon, G.G.: Industry determinants of organizational culture. Acad. Manage. Rev. **16**(2), 396–415 (1991)
17. Garneau, C.J., Parkinson, M.B.: A comparison of methodologies for designing for human variability. J. Eng. Des. **22**(7), 505–521 (2011)
18. Burgess-Limerick, R., Green, B.: Using multiple case studies in ergonomics: an example of pointing device use. Int. J. Ind. Ergon. **26**(3), 381–388 (2000)
19. Lebbon, A.R., Sigurdsson, S.O.: Behavioral perspectives on variability in human behavior as part of process safety. J. Organ. Behav. Manage. **37**(3–4), 261–282 (2017)
20. Rankin, A., et al.: Resilience in everyday operations: a framework for analyzing adaptations in high-risk work. J. Cognit. Eng. Dec. Mak. **8**(1), 78–97 (2014)
21. Engeström, Y.: Activity theory and individual and social transformation. In: Engeström, Y., Miettinen, R., Punamäki, R.-L. (eds.) Perspectives on Activity Theory, pp. 19–38. Cambridge University Press, Cambridge (1999)
22. Daniellou, F.: Epistemological issues about ergonomics and human factors. In: Karwowski, W. (ed.) International Encyclopedia of Ergonomics and Human Factors, Part 1, pp. 43–46. Taylor & Francis, London (2001)
23. Dreyfus, H.L., Dreyfus, S.E.: Mind Over Machine: the Power of Human Intuition and Expertise in the Era of the Computer, vol. 231. Free Press, New York (1986)
24. Hollnagel, E.: Understanding accidents-from root causes to performance variability. In: Proceedings of the IEEE 7th Conference on Human Factors and Power Plants (2002)
25. Aagaard Nielsen, K., Svensson, L.: Action and Interactive Research: Beyond Practice and Theory. Shaker Publishing, Maastricht (2006)
26. Svensson, L., Ellström, P.-E., Brulin, G.: Introduction–on interactive research. Int. J. Action. Res. **3**(3), 233–249 (2007)
27. Karltun, J., et al.: Studying resilient action strategies of first line managers. Soc. Sci. Protoc. **4**, 1–15 (2021)
28. Karltun, J.: Technical and organizational system solutions for deboning and their ergonomics implications. In: NES 2010, Stavanger (2010)
29. Karltun, A.: A novel approach to understand nested layers in quality improvement. In: Human Factors in Organizational Design and Management – XI. Copenhagen (2014)
30. Berglund, M., Harlin. U.: Boundary Crossing in Product Introductions considering Humans, Technology and Organization. In: Human Factors in Organizational Design and Management – XI. Copenhagen (2014)

Trends in Emergency Preparedness Activities Taken by Participatory Workplace Improvement Programs

Kazutaka Kogi[1(✉)], Yuriko Takeuchi[1], Yumi Sano[1], Etsuko Yoshikawa[2], and Totu Yoshikawa[3]

[1] Ohara Memorial Institute for Science of Labour, Tokyo, Japan
k.kogi@isl.or.jp
[2] Japanese Red-Cross College of Nursing, Tokyo, Japan
[3] National Institute of Occupational Safety and Health, Kawasaki, Japan

Abstract. Emergency preparedness actions conducted through participatory programs for improving working environment of local government workers in a district of a prefecture were analyzed. Modified versions of the mental health action checklist listing locally feasible types of improvements were used for proposing potential improvements. Common types of achieved improvements and their relation to emergency preparedness were analyzed. The majority of 348 improvements reported in five years from 2014 to 2018 concerned work methods and physical environment factors. Nearly 30% of these improvements addressed communication measures for sharing information or mutually supporting co-workers. Emergency preparedness actions accounted for about 5%. In each year, participating workplaces often implemented two or more improvements, and emergency preparedness actions tended to be taken in combination with improved communication measures. These results confirmed that adequate emergency responses could be facilitated through group discussions utilizing locally adjusted action checklists covering communication-related improvements. It was suggested important for enhancing emergency preparedness to organize dialog-based participatory steps assisted by action checklists indicating locally appropriate responses extending to workplace-level communication measures.

Keywords: Emergency responses · Workplace environment improvement · Participatory program · Stress control · Communication measures · Action checklist

1 Introduction

The prominent roles of participatory workplace environment improvement programs are widely recognized as means of enhancing safety and health at work [1, 2]. Experiences in these participatory programs in varied sectors clearly indicate that these multi-area improvements often include enhanced emergency preparedness [3, 4]. This is noteworthy as workplace-level emergency preparedness plans aligned with local work teams are gaining importance [5, 6]. This is also emphasized in view of recent experiences in disaster preparedness plans, major-accident prevention programs, and stress control schemes [7]. Well-prepared emergency plans at the workplace are particularly important in view of recent experiences in natural disasters, new types of infectious diseases or stressful working conditions.

The progress in promoting participatory workplace environment improvement programs in various sectors has shown good evidence that emergency preparedness plans are included among multifaceted improvements done by the workers in these different sectors [5, 6]. This proves that commonly effective preparedness responses can be attained by building on practices adjusted to local situations [8, 9]. This is because these plans are better arranged through participatory steps organized by close management-workers collaboration. Multifaceted workplace improvements can relatively easily result from participatory steps focusing on feasible improvement actions as local priority measures. Emergency preparedness actions are frequently among these local priorities and thus relatively straightforwardly included among priority measures agreed on by the participants of these programs.

Recent developments in preventing COVID-19 infection at the workplace are highly relevant to these emergency preparedness actions discussed in this paper. Attention should be drawn to team-work elements of preventive actions that can certainly be facilitated by participatory steps taken at each workplace. Sustaining initiative of workplace people is the equally essential aspect of preventive actions taken in each local situation.

Usually, locally feasible improvement options are proposed by participating workers and managers of the participatory programs by utilizing locally adjusted action checklists listing feasible options in multiple technical areas [3, 4]. Through these recent experiences commonly utilizing action checklists, it has been proven that emergency preparedness plans are certainly among local priorities in discussing workplace improvements such as better work methods, physical environment needs, and work-support measures. It has become a usual process to take into account emergency responses as an important area of improvement priorities. In this way, emergency preparedness actions are often among the priorities opted through participatory workplace improvement programs. Therefore, it is beneficial to examine the types of emergency preparedness actions frequently proposed by such participatory programs.

The outcomes of recent participatory workplace environment improvement programs thus indicate common types of emergency preparedness actions as workplace-level priorities [4, 7]. It is useful to learn from these recent outcomes of participatory programs generally applicable emergency response measures that can be reasonably proposed by workplace-level discussions. Such measures are certainly among priority improvements in each local situation. It is practical to analyze the results of participatory action-oriented processes to know effective types of preparedness actions that can be collaboratively taken at the workplace. These useful actions could be incorporated as commonly valid preparedness responses in workplace-level planning processes.

2   Methods

Emergency preparedness actions implemented through participatory programs for improving working conditions and environment in prefectural government workplaces of a district in H Prefecture were analyzed. The workers in each of these workplaces held a short joint meeting and proposed locally feasible workplace environment improvements. Joint actions for implementing priority improvements were undertaken and reported. Common types of these actions and their relation to emergency preparedness were studied.

The results of 348 workplace-level improvements undertaken during 2014–2018 in about 50 workplaces in the district were compared. These improvements were undertaken by workers in respective workplaces through group discussions utilizing a locally adjusted version of the mental health action checklist for proposing immediate improvements [4]. Each action checklist listed locally feasible improvement actions in six technical areas: A-sharing information, B-working time arrangements, C-work methods, D-physical environment, E-social support, and F-emergency preparedness. Each action checklist was used as a means for facilitating proposals of immediate actions. How emergency preparedness actions in dealing with potential disasters, fires, or stressful situations were implemented in association with other improvements was studied. How these actions changed from year to year and how they were combined with other types of workplace improvements were examined. The results were discussed to know practical sets of workplace-level emergency plans..

3   Results

3.1   Improvement Actions by Participatory Programs

Workplace improvement actions taken by workers of prefectural government workplaces of the studied district were similar in different years. This was obviously because these actions focused on immediately feasible improvements in each workplace. Usually, these improvements were undertaken in multiple technical areas including work methods, mutual communication, physical environment, and emergency preparedness plans. The trend of these improvement actions in the five-year period studied is shown in Table 1.

While the majority of these workplace-level actions were conducted for improving work methods or physical improvement, a notable number of improvements were also undertaken for improving information sharing, social support measures, and emergency preparedness. It is noted that many such improvements concerned improved means of communication among workers. While these communication-related actions contributed to better work-related relationships among workers, they would also improve emergency response activities.

The use of modified versions of the mental health action checklist listing locally feasible improvements in the six technical areas presented in this table obviously Encouraged participating workers to undertake these multifaceted improvements. While the workers proposed and implemented many improvements in their daily work methods and physical environment factors, they also paid due attention to communication means and emergency plans. This is confirmed by the similar distribution patterns of improvement actions in these years. Communication-related improvements accounted for more than 20% of all the improvement actions, and emergency preparedness actions for about 5%. Improvements related to social support for workers also accounted for about 5%.

Table 1. Workplace environment improvements by workers in local government workplaces.

Year	2014	2015	2016	2017	2018	Total
Number of reporting workplaces (% of 53 workplaces)	40 (75%)	40 (75%)	32 (60%)	42 (79%)	45 (85%)	199 places
A. Sharing information	19	14	16	20	13	82
B. Working time arrangements	4	7	4	3	2	20
C. Work methods	26	26	19	23	32	126
D. Physical environment	26	14	9	15	20	84
E. Social support	5	4	2	4	4	19
F. Emergency preparedness	1	3	5	3	5	17
Total number of improvements	81	68	55	68	76	348

Frequent types of improvements that were more or less relevant to emergency preparedness are presented in Table 2. Many improvements concerned sharing activity schedules among all workers of each workplace or holding additional meetings regularly. Concerning social support measures, strengthening mutual support measures was also frequently mentioned. About emergency preparedness actions, joint planning of emergency preparedness measures was frequently mentioned while training sessions on emergency steps were undertaken in a few cases.

Table 2. Types of improvements conducted in five years about better communication and emergency responses.

Technical area	Types of improvements frequently undertaken	Number of action
A. Sharing information	-Sharing activity schedules among co-workers	53
	-Holding staff meetings regularly	23
E. Social support	-Specific measures to mutually support at work	16
F. Emergency preparedness	-Agreeing on emergency preparedness plans	13
	-Training sessions on emergency steps	3

We should note that planning of emergency preparedness measures was taken into account as part of workplace improvements. We should also note that improvements concerning communication means within each workplace also contributed to upgrading such measures. Participatory action-oriented programs could thus draw attention of workers to upgrading emergency preparedness measures.

3.2   Relation of Emergency Preparedness with Other Actions

The tendency to implement emergency preparedness actions together with other workplace improvements seems important in promoting preparedness activities. There were many workplaces in which improvements in two or more technical areas were conducted within the same year. Table 3 shows how many workplaces conducted workplace improvements in different technical areas in the same year. In particular, improvements about work methods as well as other types of improvements were often combined with improvements in sharing information. These results may indicate that workplace-level improvements tended to be implemented in a combined manner.

Table 3. Numbers of workplaces that took actions in the paired areas in the same year during 2014–2018.

Technical areas	Also in A	Also in B	Also in C	Also in D	Also in E
B. Working time arrangements	3				
C. Work methods	26	5			
D. Physical environment	14	5	23		
E. Social support	3	6	2	4	
F. Emergency preparedness	4	1	4	4	3

(A. Sharing information)

In the case of improvements in emergency preparedness actions (technical area F in the table), a majority of these improvements were done in association with those in other technical areas. Nearly one half of them were done together with improvements in sharing information or in social support actions. Improvements in work methods were often related to managing work-related information materials.

Examples of improvements implemented in the same workplace that undertook emergency preparedness actions are shown in Table 4. Apparently, workers of those workplaces in which emergency preparedness actions were agreed on tended to also pay keen attention to improving internal communication measures. Examples of these communication-related improvements were sharing information on work-schedules, holding extra meetings of team members, improving mutual support measures or enhancing co-working relationships through informal gatherings. Thus, most of those improvements in the area of emergency preparedness were frequently combined with improvements in internal communication within the work teams.

These data confirm that workplace environment improvements conducted through co-workers' discussion as in the participatory programs reviewed tended to focus on

Table 4. Examples of workplace improvements implemented together with emergency preparedness actions.

Technical areas	Examples of actions taken with emergency preparedness
A. Sharing information	-Posting activity schedules on the wall -Holding brief meetings regularly
B. Working time arrangements	-Observing no-overtime days as planned jointly -Prior consultation about paid leave days
C. Work methods	-Improving filing and storage systems -Joint measures for preventing mistakes at work
D. Physical environment	-Improved air conditioning -Improved lighting systems
E. Social support	-Drafting new manuals for tasks done by those absent -Holing informal gatherings more frequently

team-based communication measures and in this context pay due attention to emergency preparedness actions suited to each local situation.

As locally effective emergency preparedness actions, we should include not only establishing emergency response plans but also team activities such as emergency action training or improved communication among team members. The sequential participatory steps were assisted effectively by the use of locally adjusted action checklists listing broad-ranging improvement actions focusing on team-based communication, mutual support, and avoiding acutely stressful work situations. Therefore, the use of locally designed action checklists covering these broad ranges of collaborative actions within each workplace can assist workplace people in agreeing also on implementing emergency preparedness actions.

The overview of these local priority measures including emergency preparedness actions, as achieved by participatory programs involving dialog-based action planning, clearly indicated the merits of participatory steps involving work-team members. In particular, the action-oriented nature of debate tools such as a list of locally feasible, broad-ranging actions is important in facilitating such planning processes. The multi-action-oriented composition of the action checklists used in the reviewed programs is exemplary in this context.

4 Discussion

We can confirm that participatory steps for improving workplace environment through multifaceted action planning can pay due attention to emergency preparedness actions adapted to each workplace. When participating workers are guided to propose locally feasible improvements in multiple technical areas, they certainly pay due attention to emergency preparedness actions. While the majority of proposed improvements may center aroundwork methods and physical environment, they tend to equally propose essentially important means of communication and emergency preparedness plans. It is important that action-oriented proposals concerning emergency preparedness are often put forward in close connection with other types of communication-related improvements. The multifaceted nature of proposed improvements and their mutual close association are both important in promoting workplace-level improvements. The merit of participatory workplace environment improvement programs actually consists in such mutually linked and action-oriented nature of improvements taken at the initiative of local workers.

About workplace-level emergency preparedness actions, we may note not only emergency preparedness plans but also emergency response training in collaborative activities linked with various kinds of emergency situations. Further, the participating workers are well aware of the other linked needs for securing day-to-day communication measures among team members. The importance of sharing information about daily activities and mutually supporting routine activities is clearly noted by the participating workers. This close association among communication-related improvements seems essential for improving emergency preparedness activities as joint team actions within each workplace.

These participatory steps for taking emergency preparedness actions in a composite manner could be facilitated by utilizing group-work tools listing locally achievable practices. The relatively short list of these mutually interrelated workplace-level improvement actions seems to significantly facilitate group dialog and proposals of readily feasible improvements in multiple technical areas. This characteristic use of action checklists actually led to proposals of meaningful improvement actions involving emergency preparedness actions. Since these actions are also readily achievable in nature, the participatory steps taken can lead to meaningful actions also in relation to emergency preparedness. We should thus promote, through participatory programs, the usage of locally adjusted action checklists that include feasible emergency preparedness actions. In organizing participatory workplace environment improvement programs, we should carefully design an action checklist of immediate improvements so as to include emergency preparedness aspects within the workplace environment.

Recent experiences in establishing daily work routines effective for preventing COVID-19 infection and other work-related infection cases seem very relevant to multifaceted preventive activities discussed in this paper. Preventive activities with regard to such new types of infections are very relevant to emergency preparedness actions examined in this paper. In particular, the use of locally adjusted action checklists that list multifaceted workplace improvement measures including emergency preparedness actions should be recommended. It is suggested to review these recent experiences and associated routines as directly related to a variety of actions for enhancing emergency preparedness at the workplace.

In particular, the close relationships between improvements about internal communication at the workplace and emergency preparedness actions attract our attention. At the workplace level, workers consider improved communication in daily team work as essential, and this attention to smooth and sustained communication measures may certainly lead to joint attention to improved emergency preparedness plans. It is suggested to organize participatory programs at the initiative of local workers aiming at multifaceted workplace improvements for safe and healthy working conditions so as to improve workplace-level actions related to emergency preparedness in each local situation.

References

1. Kogi, K.: Participatory methods effective for ergonomic workplace improvement. Appl. Ergon. **37**(4), 547–554 (2006)
2. Tsutsumi, A., Nagami, M., Yoshikawa, T., Kogi, K., Kawakami, N.: Participatory intervention for workplace improvements on mental health and job performance among blue-collar workers: a cluster randomized controlled trial. Occup. Environ. Med. **51**(5), 554–563 (2009)
3. Kogi, K.: Practical ways to facilitate ergonomics improvements in occupational health practice. Human Factors **54**(6), 890–900 (2012)
4. Kogi, K., Yoshikawa, T., Kawakami, T., Lee, M.S., Yoshikawa, E.: Low-cost improvements for reducing multifaceted work-related risks and preventing stress at work. J. Ergon. **6**(1), 1–7 (2016)
5. Yazdani, A., Newmannm, W.O.: How compatible are participatory ergonomics programs with occupational health and safety management systems? Scandinavian J. Work Environ. Health **41**(2), 111–123 (2015)
6. International Labour Office: Ergonomic Checkpoints, 2nd edn. International Labour Office, Geneva (2010)
7. International Labour Office: Stress at Work Prevention Checkpoints. International Labour Office, Geneva (2012)
8. Yoshikawa, E., Kogi, K.: Outcomes for facilitators of workplace environment improvement applying participatory approach. J. Occup. Health **61**(5), 415–425 (2019)
9. Dul, J., Bruder, R., Buckle, P., Falzon, P., Marras, W.S., Wilson, J.R., van de Doelen, G.: A strategy for human factors/ergonomics: developing the discipline and profession. Ergonomics **55**(4), 377–395 (2012)

Ergonomics for Real Change: An Initial Look at System Facts and Concerns

Karen Lange-Morales[1]([⊠]) [iD] and Andrew S. Imada[2] [iD]

[1] Universidad Nacional de Colombia, Bogotá, Colombia
klangem@unal.edu.co
[2] A. S. Imada & Associates, Carmichael, USA

Abstract. For ergonomics to create real change, it needs to address the immediate technical problem to be solved as well as the human, organizational, and societal context of the change. This contribution presents a qualitative-interpretative analysis that reflects on vignettes from real life experiences. These cases will create sketches that will be familiar to ergonomists and change agents in organizations. Using this storytelling format, we will convert the focus of analysis from traditional change strategies to this broader conceptualization of systems. This will include questions about the journey (history) to the scenario, the actors' motivations, agendas, agency and the organizational causes. Defining matters of fact (MoF) and matters of concern (MoC) is similar to accident investigation analysis as they define proximal and distal causation to the event. The paper suggests a way to conceptualize these contextual variables into the ergonomics change process.

Keywords: Ergonomics · Matters of fact · Matters of concern · Real change

1 Introduction

Ergonomics has proved to be useful at different scales and scenarios. In the 1980s, the realization that interventions at a microlevel were insufficient to have the desired impact was the origin of macroergonomics. This shift allowed ergonomics to enhance its field of action, thereby improving interactions between humans and other elements of the system. Macroergonomics was a major step in addressing what French philosopher Bruno Latour defines as matters of fact (MoF), setting aside what he calls matters of concern (MoC) [1]. Traditional microlevel ergonomics focuses on matters of fact (MoF). For example, analyzing the causes of disorders like carpal tunnel syndrome and proposing physical and design changes to mitigate this malady. However, even if this approach is capable of alleviating human suffering, it is incapable of capturing interactions beyond the defined cause-effect relationship. Our experience as ergonomists has shown that there are other aspects that play a greater role in creating real change. Therefore, the objective of this paper is to illustrate the importance of looking beyond MoF in the development of interactions, in order to introduce key aspects of MoC for ergonomics.

While other writers have proposed taking a broader systems view [2], systems ergonomics and mesoergonomics [3], this paper contributes to systems thinking by

N. L. Black et al. (Eds.): IEA 2021, LNNS 219, pp. 720–725, 2021.
https://doi.org/10.1007/978-3-030-74602-5_98

pointing out a major difference – intent. Systems have been classified as natural and human designed [4]. The major difference is that natural systems do not have a known purpose. For example, while we recognize the relationships among system elements in a natural system (e.g., water, clouds, rivers, trees, and animals), there is no known purpose for this cycle. Human designed systems are created to 'serve a purpose' or achieve an outcome (e.g., to get across a river). Checkland further classifies human made systems into "hard" and "soft" systems. Hard systems are ones where most of the people can agree on the objective of the system (e.g., to cross the river). Soft systems have multiple objectives from the many actors' point of view and cannot be taken as a given. It is reasonable to expect that different actors (owners, employees, unions, customers, shareholders, and vendors) have different perspectives of what the system is supposed to accomplish. To date, we have assumed that systems have a singular purpose, or at least an agreed upon purpose, as in a hard system. Latour's concepts of MoF and MoC beg us to take multiple perspectives on what the parties' interests are and why they may behave the way they do within the same system. Many actors have different points of view of what the system's purpose is for them.

This paper is organized in three parts. The first one presents four vignettes taken from the experiences of the authors. The second part reflects on these narratives, identifying MoF and MoC related to these stories and organized in categories typically used in HF/E domain. Finally, the closing section discusses and summarizes the learnings. Regarding methodology, the vignettes were chosen because they raised questions that could not be answered just by looking into the ergonomic system [5]: To understand causes, the consultants had to look beyond the traditional elements considered and their classical way of approaching how the problem was triggered.

2 Looking into Real Life

From an extensive range of vignettes accumulated during more than twenty years of consultancies, we selected four to illustrate the differences between MoF and MoC.

2.1 The Injured Flower Cutter

After working as a contract employee for a flower exporter, a woman is hired based on her hard work and productivity. Two months after she is hired, she claims a disability due to repetitive strain injury. The Occupational Health Manager was upset, considering that it was a problem that this woman "got through" into the company.

What is particularly relevant in this case is the hiring practice to onboard motivated applicants. All those who are hired must first work as independent contractors for 11 months, after which time, the best workers will be contracted again but by another outsourcing company for subsequent 11 months. This practice is done to evaluate people's productivity without hiring them. After supervisors are sure that the person has a work behavior that meets their expectations, they hire the workers as a permanent employee. Becoming a permanent employee is very desirable and people are highly motivated to perform at high levels to gain entry. This requires 22 months of peak performance to gain entry into the organization. Was the injury caused by the selection process, the employee's motivation/agenda/needs, or the matters of fact?

2.2 Experienced Planter Reluctant to Seed with a New Tool

A new tool for making holes in the ground was tested and presented to a group of planters. Technical trials considering posture, times, quality of sowing plants showed great results. However, not all the workers were convinced. Planters recently hired are quite happy with the new tool, but the most experienced and recognized as 'the best sower' of the group reject it absolutely.

The company manager said: "They are stubborn. They have to obey and accept the change". The consultant was not satisfied with this conclusion. Although change implies conflict, she thought that there could be other reasons for his attitude. Inquiring a bit more in the situation, she discovered that the experienced planter rejected the new technology because he was afraid of losing his status as the best at his job. He was afraid that with the proposed technology everyone would be able to seed the same way, and his social world was threatened. In other words, losing his finger nails or hurting his knees was unimportant, compared with losing a social status and his self-esteem.

2.3 Driver with Injured Right Hand

The company was evaluating automatic transmissions on their truck fleet to make a system-wide change to reduce costs, injuries and improve performance. It came to a supervisor's attention that one of his drivers, who operated an automatic transition, was complaining about pain in her right wrist. He wondered: how could this be with no forward shifting? He suspected that the pain was related to off the job video game playing and this was an excuse.

After several rides with the consultant, the conversation moved to off hour activities and the driver admitted that she did spend a lot of time playing video games. Aware of the supervisor's suspicions, she said that the videogaming was not the cause of the problem, neither was the shifting. She confessed that when she was young, her father would hit her. She would raise her right arm to protect herself. Repeated trauma probably induced forearm injuries, likely caused ulnar and possible wrist pain. However, it was too embarrassing to talk about this personal experience at work and risk potential ridicule. It was easier to attribute the cause to something work related.

2.4 Food Stand Worker

After the redesign of a retail food stand, there was unusual resistance from some of the workers. The source of the resistance could be traced to a strong informal leader. Despite the analyses and demonstrations about why the work was now easier to perform, she continued to insist that the new design was inferior.

Instead of arguing with the worker, the consultant decided to spend time with her and get to know her better. He finds out about some of her personal interests to start the discussion and get to understand her better. After several visits, the food stand worker finally confides the real reason she does not like the workstation. The counter had been lowered about 21 cm, adhering to simple material handling principles. In doing so, the customers could see more of her when she turned around. "They can see my big behind" she admitted as the reason. It was a compelling moment, where one human tells another about a fear or shame that she was experiencing at work.

3   Discovering MoF and MoC

From these vignettes we can identify proximal and distal causes to organizational events. This requires zooming in and out to get a multiple perspectives of the problem to understand the events, in order to suggest interventions that can address the real causes.

Translating Latour's abstract concepts into our realm of systems thinking, we might start by saying that Matters of Fact (MoF) assume that the purposes, goals and/or objectives of the systems are as designed. To date, we have accepted the designer's or organizational intentions as given. That is, we treat it as a "hard system", one that most people can agree on the objective – system as designed. These are generally regarded as indisputable, stubborn, and simply there [6].

Matters of concern (MoC) emerge when you immerse the system and MoF into a social context. This context draws upon the emotions, opinions, attitudes and interests of the actors. Unlike MoF, MoC are not governed by the given objectives of hard systems. Instead, motivations, emotions and self-interests redefine purposes priorities, and hence actions. MoC are disputable, and their obstinance is different; they cannot be argued to be irrelevant, even if they are to the system as designed because they provide meaning to the interactions.

The kinds of human activities and interactions we study is what happens to MoF once it is placed in the social milieu and multiple MoC. Our methodology of talking to many of the stakeholders – besides the systems designers – allows us to zoom in and out from the traditional systems view. This visualization maps the multiple stakeholders' perspectives together to understand the complex sociotechnical system. This includes financial, physical conditions, infrastructure, recent events, politics, and temperament to name a few. It is messy, but so are the causes for the interactions that occur within social systems. Hard systems are perfectly suited to be designed and solved using linear methods like systems engineering; human activity systems are not.

Table 1 presents some of the MoF and the MoC that we identified in the selected vignettes. Because of our role as external technical experts with extensive experience with the companies, we are able to see these needs and concerns from multiple levels, which allows multiple causation models.

4   Discussion

Discerning these proximal and distal causes requires a unique set of skills to see the problem and solution at multiple levels from the actors' perspective. Accessing this also requires unique skills involving emotional intelligence. For actors to reveal their needs, which may be unknown even to them, requires organizational acumen, keen observational skills, trust, empathy and openness. These are qualities some ergonomists already possess because of their practice, but we need to go beyond the traditional academic understanding of MoF.

By definition, HFE has a systems approach. This means addressing different scales, as proximal and distal causes, is not new. However, the difference relies on which causes are considered as part of the system and which are not. The first aspect to understand a (work) situation as a system is defining its purpose. All elements are organized around this

K. Lange-Morales and A. S. Imada

Table 1. Matters of facts and matters of concern identified in the vignettes.

Vignette	Matters of Fact	Matters of Concern
Flower cutter	• Newly hired worker files an injury complaint • Repetitive motion, cycles per minute, temperature, duration affect injury risk • Tools, seating, cushioning, support, posture affect risk • Organization: Productivity, cost avoidance, quality • Occupational health staff: Prescribe solutions based on MoF to avoid injuries, losses, claims	• Flower cutter's life motivation: Income, job security, physical and mental well-being
Seed planter	• Improved tool is introduced to improve planters' output • Manager: 'Stubborn' workers resist accepting change • Organization: Productivity, costs, injuries	• Newer workers: Faster, safer, easier work • Experienced worker: Fear of losing status, respect if everyone is able to produce equally
Driver	• Automatic truck transmissions reduce right hand exertion • Driver who operates an automatic transmission complains of right arm pain • Driver does spend time playing videogames • Organization: Design choice to reduce injuries, costs and performance	• Supervisor: Fear of being taken advantage of by a video gamer • Driver: Fear of exposing personal information and ridicule. Pressures to conform to safety performance
Food stand worker	• Proper design improves productivity, comfort and speed of service • Experienced worker voices complaint about the improved design • Organization – Improved design increased speed of service and revenue	• Food Stand worker: How people see me is important. Embarrassment because the new counter height reveals her rear end

purpose, highlighting those aspects that have to do directly with the established purpose, and ignoring other elements that are apparently not. Real life is complex and reduction is necessary to deal with its complexity. Nevertheless, in the process of simplification, MoC can be left out because they are not part of the designed system. However, as our vignettes illustrate, they can have profound effects on how people act and how we interpret situations. In real life, systems have not one, but many purposes to many people.

5   Conclusions and Future Work

Interaction between humans and other elements of a system is not just a matter of facts but also (and especially) a matter of concern. It is important that ergonomics discipline and practitioners realize this and act accordingly. We propose this conceptualization as a means to addressing these matters. Without it, we will continue to solve immediate problems without making real change.

References

1. Latour, B.: What is the style of matters of concern? Spinoza Lecture I at the University of Amsterdam, Van Gorcum (2008)
2. Wilson, J.R.: Fundamentals of systems ergonomics/human factors. Applied Ergon. **45**(1), 5–13 (2014)
3. Karsh, T.T., Waterson, P., Holden, R.J.: Crossing levels in systems ergonomics: a framework to support 'mesoergonomic' inquiry. Appl. Ergon. **45**(1), 45–54 (2014)
4. Checkland, P.: Systems Thinking, Systems Practice. Wiley, New York (1999)
5. García Acosta, G.: La ergonomía desde la visión sistémica. Bogotá, Unibiblos (2002)
6. Stephan, P.F.: Designing 'matters of concern' (Latour): a future design challenge? In: Jonas, W., Zerwas, S., von Anshelm K. (eds.) Transformation design. Birkhäuser Basel, pp. 202–226 (2015)

Improve Creativity in Future-Oriented Design with the Prospective Persona

Antoine Martin[✉], Marie-France Agnoletti, and Éric Brangier

Université de Lorraine, PErSEUs, 57000 Metz, France
antoine.martin@univ-lorraine.fr

Abstract. As ergonomics is confronted with future-oriented design projects, ergonomists must investigate how design could create novel and adapted ideas. In often ill-defined contexts, prospective ergonomics proposes to rely on methods and knowledge related to creativity, to foster the design process. In this paper, we introduce the *prospective persona* method, which is the implementation of the persona method applied to individuals who experience uses or artefacts that are identified as being precursory. The objective of this persona is to improve constraints management by adding the description of needs little known to designers. The study presented in this paper aims to compare the quality of ideation during a creativity task using ordinary persona, *prospective persona* or no persona. Our results show an effect of *prospective persona* on creativity. *Prospective persona* allows for a higher number of new ideas than ordinary persona and is the source of more feasible ideas the non-use of persona. We therefore recommend the use of *prospective persona* in future-oriented creativity design phase.

Keywords: Prospective persona · Prospective ergonomics · Creativity

1 Creativity in Future-Oriented Design

The design of future and innovative artefacts is now a central issue in ergonomics. In this context, prospective ergonomics aims to define future artefacts, by following a multi-step approach. After identifying and generating future needs, ergonomists or designers must define preliminary ideas of artefacts (product, service, technology or system) (Brangier and Robert 2014; Robert and Brangier 2012) which are new and adapted to their future users and contexts (Bonnardel and Didier 2020). The design of future artefacts can be considered as an ill-defined and open-ended problem (Bonnardel 2000; Bonnardel 2009; Bonnardel 2012 Bonnardel 2012; Bourgeois-Bougrine et al. 2018; Eastman 1969), which implies that not all the information necessary for their resolution is stated and they do not admit a single solution. The representation of designers about the problem (*space problem*) and the artefact to be designed (*search space*) is therefore incomplete and imprecise (Bonnardel 2009, 2012). For these reasons, prospective ergonomics proposes to rely on methods and knowledge related to creativity, to foster the design process by helping designers to enhance their representations of the problem and the artefact to design (Brangier and Robert 2014); Robert and Brangier 2012). Indeed, design is

N. L. Black et al. (Eds.): IEA 2021, LNNS 219, pp. 726–736, 2021.
https://doi.org/10.1007/978-3-030-74602-5_99

considered as a creative activity which is mainly supported by two cognitive processes (Bonnardel 2009):

- **Constraints management**: the constraints make it possible to redefine the search problem and space search thus allowing the designer to better understand the context in which the designed system will evolve and to which it must fit. Prescribed, constructed and inferred constraints act as guides that allow the production and selection of ideas (Bonnardel 2012);
- **Analogical thinking**: analogical thinking makes it possible to extend the search space to fields or ideas which are not necessarily linked to the design problem, but which can inspire the generation of new ideas. This analogical transfer promotes and amplifies the generation of ideas from one context to another.

If many methods and tools exist to stimulate creativity (brainstorm, C–K method, TRIZ etc.) we have chosen to focus on the use of persona which makes it possible to integrate data from users' future needs and research into the creative step of prospective ergonomics approach.

2 Towards the Representation of Future Needs and Users: The Prospective Persona

Personas are fictitious and archetypal representations of users. They are concretely represented by textual and visual descriptions (Pruitt and Grudin 2003). Personas are used to enrich designers' mental representations of users (Bonnardel and Pichot 2020) and can be applied whether in the creative or evaluative phase of design process (Pruitt and Adlin 2006). When used for the creativity phase, personas are considered as creativity supportive cognitive tools, because they allow for constraint management and perspective taking (Bornet and Brangier 2013). Constraint management help narrow the search space, while perspective taking facilitate understanding users (Brangier et al. 2012). Several studies have shown a positive effect of personas on creativity. Brangier et al. (Brangier et al. 2012) have shown that experts produce more ideas, more original ideas, and ideas from more different fields when they were presented with personas and functions, than when they were not presented with specific material. In another study (Bornet and Brangier 2016) did not find significant results regarding the number of ideas generated, the originality of the ideas and the number of topics they addressed. However, they observed that the ideas selected by the client come mostly from the group with persona. (So and Joo 2017) tested the effectiveness of persona as a primer for a creative task. Their results show that participants who were primed with persona produced more original ideas than participants in the control condition. Finally, (Bonnardel and Pichot 2020) compared the difference to a creative task performed in the experimental condition for participants using a classic (or static) persona versus participants using a dynamic persona. Their results indicate a higher creativity score for the dynamic persona than for the classic persona. The latter study suggests that there are some persona methods that are more effective than others.

In the case of prospective ergonomics, personas aim to allow designers to apprehend users who do not exist, and to speculate on the future needs of future users (Bornet and Brangier 2013, 2016). But the literature reports the use of ordinary personas to speculate on future users' needs in order to generate new ideas for artefacts (Barré et al. 2018; Bonnardel and Pichot 2020; Bornet and Brangier 2013, 2016; Brangier et al. 2012, 2019).

Here we propose to use *prospective persona* that presents potential future users' needs, in order to generate new and adapted ideas of artefacts. It is built on the basis of data collected from precursory users − individuals who experience activities or artefacts that are identified as being precursory or prospective (Martin et al. 2021) − on their present and future needs. This methodological variation of the persona is a switch from a paradigm where we propose to designers to speculate on users' future needs, to a paradigm in which we depict users' future needs to designers. The *prospective persona* is in line with the work of (Fergnani 2019) but unlike Fergnani's future personas, which correspond rather to proto-personas (persona not based on data from user research) aiming to make a prospective scenario more concrete, our proposal of *prospective persona* corresponds to the use of persona to describe future needs anticipated during future oriented user searches. The prospective persona method can be considered as a part of the extraordinary users' method (Buisine et al. 2018) which consists in integrating users with particular abilities (children, non-users, precursory users etc.) into the design process to promote creativity. Buisine et al. (Buisine et al. 2018) also suggested that this method could be facilitated using persona who represents these specific users. It also allows rare users to be included in the design process.

3 Research Question and Hypothesis

This study aims to measure the effect of the *prospective persona* method on future artefacts definition. Our assumption is that the prospective persona, by describing future needs that are less common and accessible to designers than present needs, is at the origin of an enrichment of the designers' representation of the users, by constraint management. The prospective persona might also allow for perspective taking, which allows knowledge about future users to be incorporated into the definition of artifact ideas. This led us to the following hypothesis:

– **Hypothesis**: Ideas of future artifacts developed with the *prospective persona* might be newer and more adapted than those developed with ordinary persona or without persona.

4 Method

4.1 Participants

36 participants took part in the study, 5 were excluded because they did not complete the full protocol. Participants were engineering and master students specializing in energy, they were 8 women and 26 men aged between 20 and 29 ($M = 22.56$, $SD = 2.02$). Participants were randomly assigned to the conditions: Control (no use of persona; $n =$

10 after exclusion), ordinary persona (use of ordinary persona; $n = 11$ after exclusion) and *prospective persona* (use of *prospective persona*; $n = 10$ after exclusion). Participants were not paid and gave their informed consent before participating in the study.

4.2 Material

2 personas were used in the creativity sessions: an ordinary persona and a *prospective persona*. These personas were derived from real data collected through needs anticipation interviews on energy for housing conducted in a previous study (Martin et al. 2021). The ordinary persona is based on data collected from ordinary users, while the *prospective persona* is based on data collected from precursory users on their presents and future needs. It should be noted that what characterizes a prospective persona, is the specific pattern of needs and activities, i.e. the combination of its position on these variables.

Personas were built to vary only the data specifically related to precursory and ordinary users. Thus, prospective and ordinary personas have the same number of words, the same identity and the same context of use, so that their only differences lie in the patterns of activities and needs that correspond either to a precursory user profile or to an ordinary user profile (see Table 1). Personas were pre-tested to verify their understanding, exclusivity and credibility.

Table 1. Differences and similitudes between ordinary and prospective persona.

		Ordinary persona	Prospective persona
Form	*Layout*	Identical	
	Number of words	Identical	
	Identity (name, age, picture and job)	Identical	
	Use context (household composition, home and mode of ownership)	Identical	
Content	*Needs (energy self-sufficiency, control/independence, involvement, comfort, respect for environment, profitability, enthusiasm for technology and cost)*	Profile dependent	
	Activities (sharing, installation/maintenance, supply, self-consumption, system management, storage, distribution, and consumption management)	Profile dependent	
	Knowledge related to energy in the habitat	Profile dependent	

4.3   Procedure

4 separates 1 hour creativity sessions took place. They were administered in person and were scripted to guarantee similar conditions for each session. Participants had to individually perform a common divergent thinking task, which took place in the following manner:

1. **Brief**: participants were orally given a brief about the course of the session and the subject.
2. **Ideation 1**: participants had 20 min to generate as many ideas as possible about solutions that can transform energy in the home in the context of energy transition.
3. **Persona acquaintance**: given to conditions, participants were then presented with an ordinary persona, a *prospective persona* or had to leave the room. Participants with persona had 5 min to read and understand their persona.
4. **Ideation 2**: participants had 15 min to generate as many ideas as possible about solutions that can transform energy in the home in the context of energy transition, participants in persona conditions had to use their given persona.
5. **Personas evaluation**: to rate personas' quality participants in the Ordinary persona and *prospective persona* condition had to assess persona perceived constraints management and perspective taking, using 3 Likert scales of 1 (strongly agree) to 7 (strongly disagree) for each dimension (inspired from Bornet 2014). Perceived constraints management persona focused on perceived enrichment of knowledge about users, perceived ability of the persona to inspire ideas and perceived ability of the persona to orient ideas. While perceived perspective taking focused on the perceived ability to put itself in their place, for perceived understanding of persona's thinking and for perceived ability to predict persona's reaction.
6. **Questionnaire**: The session ended with socio-demographic questions.

4.4   Data Analysis

Artifact ideas were independently categorized by two judges to identify original ideas. All disagreements were resolved after discussion. The creative quality of ideas has been assessed using the dimensions inspired by (Bonnardel and Pichot 2020):

- Fluidity (total number of ideas produced);
- Originality (statistical scarcity of ideas);
- Novelty (surprising and reforming character of ideas);
- Feasibility (acceptability and implementability of ideas);
- Relevance (applicability and effectiveness of ideas).

The fluidity and originality of ideas were calculated, and the novelty, feasibility and relevance of ideas were assessed independently and without regard to conditions by the researcher and an independent judge (sustainable development consultant). Judges were asked to rate on a Likert scale ranging from 1 (strongly agree) to 7 (strongly disagree) the surprising, reforming, acceptable, implementable, applicable and effective nature of each idea. Judges' disagreements were resolved through discussion. Inter-judge reliability was calculated using the Krippendorff Alpha test and was found to be good (α = 0.82). For each participant and dimension, mean scores and number of ideas positively rated were calculated. The mean score provides information on the general quality level of ideas, while the number of ideas provides information on the number of ideas of a certain quality level, it is a fluidity score by quality. Statistical analyses were performed using Jamovi 1.2.16 and JASP 0.12.1.

5 Results

5.1 Artefacts Ideas

To compare the difference in ideas scores between groups in Ideation 2, we performed ANCOVA using data from Ideation 1 as a covariate. For the few variables that do not meet the assumption of normality, we used the nonparametric Kruskal-Wallis test in Ideation 1 (to control the differences between groups) and Ideation 2 (to perform comparisons of scores between groups). No differences were found in Ideation 1.

221 ideas of artefacts were generated for a total of 106 unique ideas. Our analyses did not show any significant differences between conditions for idea fluency (F (2,1) = 2.21, $p = 0.129$, $\omega^2 = 0.059$), number of original ideas (F (2,1) = 0.734, $p = 0.489$, ω^2 = -0.017), number of feasible ideas (F (2,1) = 1.99, $p = 0.157$, $\omega^2 = 0.050$), number of relevant ideas (F (2,1) = 1.42, $p = 0.258$, $\omega^2 = 0.025$), ideas originality (H (2) = 4.65, $p = 0.098$, $\varepsilon^2 = 0.131$) and ideas relevance (H (2) = 4.76, $p = 0.092$, $\varepsilon^2 = 0.183$).

Nonetheless, there was a significant difference in number of novel ideas (H (2) = 7.36, $p = 0.025$, $\varepsilon^2 = 0.245$). A Dunn's post-hoc pairwise comparisons test displayed a significantly higher number of novel ideas for *prospective persona (M = 1.40, SD =* 1.07) than for ordinary persona *(M = 0.455, SD = 0.522)*, and for no persona *(M =* 1.60, SD = 1.35) than for ordinary persona.

We also observe a significant difference in ideas novelty (F (2,1) = 10.05, $p < 0.001$, $\omega2 = 0.397$). A Tukey post-hoc comparisons test displayed a significantly better ideas creativity score for the without persona condition *(M = 3.13, SD = 0.6)* than for ordinary persona *(M = 4.63, SD = 1.02)*, and *prospective persona (M = 4.24, SD = 0.57)*.

Finally, we note a significant difference in ideas feasibility (F (2,1) = 9.272, p = 0.001, $\omega2 = 0.389$). A Tukey post-hoc comparisons test displayed a significantly better ideas feasibility score for ordinary persona *(M = 2.77, SD = 0.6)* and *prospective persona (M = 2.80, SD = 0.728)* than for the without persona condition *(M = 4.27, SD = 0.91)*.

5.2 Personas' Perceived Quality

Comparisons between personas' quality were done using ANOVA or nonparametric Kruskal-Wallis test when data do not meet the assumption of normality. Analyses of the personas' quality show no differences between conditions for perceived enrichment of knowledge about users (F (2, 19) = 0.248, $p = 0.624$, $\omega^2 = -0.037$), perceived ability of the persona to inspire ideas (F (2, 19) = 1.79, $p = 0.238$, $\omega^2 = 0.023$), perceived ability of the persona to orient ideas (F (2,19) = 0.10, $p = 0.724$, $\omega^2 = -$ 0.045), perceived understanding of persona's thinking (H (1) = 0.00561, $p = 0.940$, ε^2

$= 2.80^{-4}$), perceived ability to predict persona's reaction (F (2, 19) $= 1.52$, $p = 0.233$, $\omega^2 = 0.024$) and perceived ability to put itself in their place (F (2, 19) $= 0.228$, $p = 0.39$, $\omega^2 = -0.038$).

6 Complementary Study

A complementary study was conducted to specifically explore the quality of the *prospective persona* compared to the ordinary persona, in terms of perceived constraint management and perceived perspective taking. 32 university students master specializing in energy took part in the study. The same 2 personas as in study 1 were used.

Participants had to perform a short online creativity task for *prospective persona* and ordinary persona. Then, they had to assess personas perceived constraint management and perceived perspective taking qualities.

To compare the difference in between personas' quality, and because all the variables do not meet the assumption of normality, we performed the nonparamatric Friedman test for repeated measures. Analyses of the personas' quality show no differences between *prospective persona* and ordinary persona for perceived perspective taking for both perceived understanding of persona's thinking (F (1) $= 2.25$, $p = 0.134$) and perceived ability to predict persona's behaviors (F (1) $= 1.19$, $p = 0.275$).

A significant difference in personas perceived constraint management was observed for both perceived enrichment of knowledge about users (F (1) $= 8.91$, $p = 0.003$) and perceived ability of the persona to orient ideas (F (1) $= 7.35$, $p = 0.007$). Prospective persona ($M = 3.22$, $SD = 1.7$) is perceived as better enriching knowledge about users than ordinary persona ($M = 4.38$, $SD = 1.81$), and prospective persona ($M = 3.34$, $SD = 1.31$) is perceived as orienting the ideation more than the ordinary persona ($M = 4.22$, $SD = 1.79$).

7 Discussion

The objective of this study was to measure the effect *prospective persona*, ordinary persona, or no persona, on the generation of future artifact ideas.

Our results show that using *prospective persona* or not using persona leads to more new ideas than using ordinary persona. Furthermore, the ideas generated in the non-persona condition are on average newer than those generated with a prospective or ordinary persona. This difference in results may seem counter-intuitive, but it can be explained by the indicators used. In fact, it indicates that the non-use of the persona and the use of the *prospective persona* are both at the origin of a greater number of ideas judged as new, compared to the use of an ordinary persona. However, the non-use of persona allows the overall generation of ideas that are newer than those of the prospective persona, even when they are not considered new. Finally, the use of ordinary or prospective persona gives rise to more feasible ideas.

There is therefore a difference in terms of creativity between the use of prospective persona, ordinary persona and no persona. Ordinary persona promote feasible but less new ideas, no persona promotes less feasible but new ideas, and *prospective persona* promote new and feasible ideas.

These results are consistent with those of (Bornet and Brangier 2016) who show that personas lead to the generation of more feasible ideas and they are consistent with (Lilien et al. 2002) who observe that methods based on the representation of ordinary users have a compliance effect that does not generate new ideas. They are also consistent with Mulet et al. (2017) and Pichot et al. (2020), who indicate that the productions judged to be the most novel are judged to be the least feasible. We find this relationship in our study. However the use of *prospective persona* seems to be the source of more balanced ideas that are both more feasible than those in none persona condition, and that are newer than those obtained with the use of the ordinary persona.

Thus, the ordinary persona through the representation of present needs seems to activate knowledge that relates to current ways of responding to these needs and which are therefore not new but are feasible. The *prospective persona*, through the representation of future needs, would allow the introduction of new knowledge that would be the source of new ideas since it responds to new needs that are not necessarily satisfied by current artefacts. This new knowledge would also be the source of feasible ideas because it responds to explicit and contextualized needs. The non-use of persona favors the generation of ideas that are new as these ideas attempt to respond to a new future context that therefore requires new solutions. However, this future context is equivocal and therefore does not support the generation of feasible ideas.

Concerning the perceived quality of personas, in the main study our results show no difference between the perceived capacity of prospective and ordinary personas to promote perspective taking and constraint management. However, the results of the complementary study indicate that the use of *prospective persona* is at the origin of a more important perceived constraint management than the use of ordinary persona. As in the main study, no difference was found in the perceived ability of prospective and ordinary persona to promote perspective taking. Thus, ordinary and *prospective persona* would allow the same level of perspective taking, but prospective persona would induce a better constraint management. The *prospective persona* therefore allows the designer to view the world from the user's point of view. This result is not surprising, as the *prospective persona* preserves the figurative characteristics of the persona, allowing it to promote the mental simulation of the user's behaviours and thoughts.

We explain this improvement in constraint management by adding prescribed design constraints. In the case of the ordinary persona, present needs are described, and it is up to the designer to infer or speculate on constraints related to future needs, whereas in the case of the *prospective persona*, these future needs are constraints that are explicitly prescribed. Future needs are constraints transmitted through the persona, they are non-trivial, less accessible and therefore new data, allowing the designer to redefine his problem space and research space. Thus, the designer, by enriching these representations thanks to these new and explicit future constraints, is able to produce ideas that are newer by enriching the research space with non-banal data, and ideas that are adapted by enriching the problem space with a future context. These results also support the idea that the management of constraints allows both the problem space and the research space to be defined.

The *prospective persona* would therefore allow the designer (1) to integrate users upstream of the design process and thus avoid only techno-centric ideas, (2) to avoid the design fixation effect that occurs when only present needs are taken into account, and (3) to generate ideas for artefacts that correspond to the future needs of users because they are not based on a hypothetical representation of user needs.

The *prospective persona* is not a structurally different method from the persona method, it is rather a variation of the persona method. This study thus allowed us to replicate the results concerning the persona method, which is sometimes considered too few (Bonnardel et al. 2016; Bornet and Brangier 2016).

8   Conclusion

The *prospective persona* method appears to be more beneficial than the ordinary persona for the definition of future artifacts, as it improves creativity by bringing in new future constraints that allow for more feasible ideas, as well as generating more new ideas than with the ordinary persona. These results also suggest that it is more beneficial to describe future needs, rather than leaving designers to speculate on future needs based on present needs. In addition to allowing the designer to enrich his representations to have new and adapted ideas, the *prospective persona* seems to foster perspective taking for designers, in order to make them easier to understand and take into users in the design process.

This study is a first step in the evaluation of the *prospective persona*. It has limitations that should be addressed by further studies. It could be replicated by varying the creativity task used and by mobilizing a more experienced population with a larger sample. This study could also be replicated by using a substantial number of prospective and ordinary personas to control aspects of the content that we might not have been able to control by seeking to include the same number of descriptions of needs and activities with the same number of words.

Acknowledgments. We would like to thank all those who took part in this study. We also warmly thank Perrine ROY for her participation. This work was supported partly by the French PIA project «Lorraine Université d'Excellence», reference ANR-15-IDEX-04-LUE.

References

Barré, J., Buisine, S., Aoussat, A.: Persona logical thinking: Improving requirements elicitation for multidisciplinary teams. CoDesign **14**(3), 218–237 (2018). https://doi.org/10.1080/15710882.2017.1301959

Bonnardel, N.: Towards understanding and supporting creativity in design: analogies in a constrained cognitive environment. Knowl. Based Syst. **13**(7–8), 505–513 (2000). https://doi.org/10.1016/S0950-7051(00)00067-8

Bonnardel, N.: Designing future products: what difficulties do designers encounter and how can their creative process be supported? Work **41**, 5296–5303 (2012). https://doi.org/10.3233/WOR-2012-0020-5296

Bonnardel, N., Didier, J.: Brainstorming variants to favor creative design. Appl. Ergon. **83**, 102987 (2020). https://doi.org/10.1016/j.apergo.2019.102987

Bonnardel, N., Forens, M., Lefevre, M.: Enhancing collective creative design: an exploratory study on the influence of static and dynamic personas in a virtual environment. Des. J. **19**(2), 221–235 (2016). https://doi.org/10.1080/14606925.2016.1129145

Bonnardel, N., Pichot, N.: Enhancing collaborative creativity with virtual dynamic personas. Appl. Ergon. **82**, 102949 (2020). https://doi.org/10.1016/j.apergo.2019.102949

Bonnardel, N.: Activités de conception et créativité: De l'analyse des facteurs cognitifs à l'assistance aux activités de conception créatives. Le travail humain **72**(1), 5 (2009). https://doi.org/10.3917/th.721.0005

Bornet, C.: Evaluation de la méthode des personas en intervention corrective, préventive et prospective. Université de Lorraine (2014)

Bornet, C., Brangier, É.: La méthode des personas: principes, intérêts et limites. Bulletin de psychologie, Numéro **524**(2), 115–134 (2013)

Bornet, C., Brangier, É.: The effects of personas on creative codesign of work equipment: aan exploratory study in a real setting. CoDesign **12**(4), 243–256 (2016). https://doi.org/10.1080/15710882.2015.1112814

Bourgeois-, S., Latorre, S., Mourey, F.: Promoting creative imagination of non-expressed needs: exploring a combined approach to enhance design thinking. Creat. Stud. **11**(2), 377–394 (2018). https://doi.org/10.3846/cs.2018.7184

Brangier, É., Bornet, C., Bastien, J.M.C., Michel, G., Vivian, R.: Effets des personas et contraintes fonctionnelles sur l'idéation dans la conception d'une bibliothèque numérique. Le travail humain **75**(2), 121–145 (2012). https://doi.org/10.3917/th.752.0121

Brangier, É., Robert, J.-M.: L'ergonomie prospective: fondements et enjeux. Le travail humain **77**(1), 1 (2014). https://doi.org/10.3917/th.771.0001

Brangier, É., Vivian, R., Bornet, C.: Méthodes d'ergonomie prospective appliquées à l'identification de besoins pour des systèmes d'énergie à base d'hydrogène: Étude exploratoire. Psychologie Française **64**(2), 197–222 (2019). https://doi.org/10.1016/j.psfr.2019.02.002

Buisine, S., Boisadan, A., Richir, S.: L'innovation radicale par la méthode de l'utilisateur extraordinaire. Psychologie du Travail et des Organisations **24**(4), 374–386 (2018). https://doi.org/10.1016/j.pto.2017.11.001

Eastman, C.M.: Cognitive processes and ill-defined problems: a case study from design. In: Proceedings of the 1st International Joint Conference on Artificial Intelligence, pp. 669–690 (1969)

Fergnani, A.: The future persona: a futures method to let your scenarios come to life. Foresight **21**(4), 445–466 (2019). https://doi.org/10.1108/FS-10-2018-0086

Hassenzahl, M.: The thing and i: understanding the relationship between user and product. In: Blythe, M., Monk, A. (eds.) Funology, vol. 2, pp. 301–313. Springer (2018). https://doi.org/10.1007/978-3-319-68213-6_19

Lilien, G.L., Morrison, P.D., Searls, K., Sonnack, M., von Hippel, E.: Performance assessment of the lead user idea-generation process for new product development. Manage. Sci. **48**(8), 1042–1059 (2002). https://doi.org/10.1287/mnsc.48.8.1042.171

Marshall, R., Cook, S., Mitchell, V., Summerskill, S., Haines, V., Maguire, M., Sims, R., Gyi, D., Case, K.: Design and evaluation: end users, user datasets and personas. Appl. Ergon. **46**, 311–317 (2015). https://doi.org/10.1016/j.apergo.2013.03.008

Martin, A., Agnoletti, M.-F., Brangier, É.: Ordinary users, precursory users and experts in the anticipation of future needs: evaluation of their contribution in the elaboration of new needs in energy for housing. Appl. Ergon. **94**, 103394 (2021). https://doi.org/10.1016/j.apergo.2021.103394

Mulet, E., Royo, M., Chulvi, V., Galán, J.: Relationship between the degree of creativity and the quality of design outcomes. DYNA **84**(200), 38–45 (2017). https://doi.org/10.15446/dyna.v84n200.53582

Norman, D.A.: The Psychology of Everyday Things. Basic Books, NewYork (1988)

Pichot, N., Bonnardel, N., Pavani, J.B.: Towards a general factor of Disruptivity: the most novel creative objects tend to be the least valuable and feasible ones (2020, Submitted article)

736   A. Martin et al.

Pruitt, J., Adlin, T.: The Persona Lifecycle: Keeping People in Mind Throughout Product Design. Morgan Kaufmann Publishers, an imprint of Elsevier, Elsevier (2006)

Pruitt, J., Grudin, J.: Personas: practice and theory. In: Proceedings of the 2003 Conference on Designing for User Experiences - DUX 2003, vol. 1 (2003). https://doi.org/10.1145/997078.997089

Robert, J.-M., Brangier, É.: Prospective ergonomics: origin, goal, and prospects. Work **41**, 5235–5242 (2012). https://doi.org/10.3233/WOR-2012-0012-5235

So, C., Joo, J.: Does a Persona improve creativity? Des. J. **20**(4), 459–475 (2017). https://doi.org/10.1080/14606925.2017.1319672

Using Mixed Methods to Strengthen Connections Between Human Factors and Complex Socio-technical Systems

Christian Mauri and Ari Antonovsky[✉]

University of Western Australia, Crawley, WA 6009, Australia
ari.antonovsky@uwa.edu.au

Abstract. This paper begins by identifying two habits that hinder the ability of human factors to assist organisations in looking beyond their tech-problems, to better understand their socio-technical problems, and develop solutions. First, the tendency toward prima facie acceptance of widely accepted, often vague claims (e.g. that "communication affects productivity"), which can result in the under examination of concepts and the appropriateness of their application to real world contexts. Second, the tendency for experimental psychology to investigate such claims by testing specific constructs using environments and subjects that at best can only simulate, and can never adequately capture, the complex real-world contexts in which they are to be applied. The authors argue that these shortcomings can be addressed through analysis consisting of a mix of technical and organisational issues using both qualitative and quantitative methods. This is then illustrated through a case study of the authors' recent project on navy vessel maintenance.

Keywords: Social and occupational ergonomics · Maintenance · Mixed methods · Systems thinking · Naval ships

1 Introduction

In the research and application of organisational ergonomics, there are two tendencies that can hinder the analysis of human factors (HF) in complex sociotechnical systems. First, there is a tendency toward the prima facie acceptance of assumptions that are often difficult to substantiate. Examples include the idea that ostensibly objective workloads, determined by performance and physiological measures, converge with the subjective perceptions of workloads as experienced by workers, ultimately resulting in a unitary workload construct that can be measured with the right methods Matthews et al. (2019). While the philosophical hazards of such reification have not been without scrutiny (Åsberg et al. 2011; Dekker and Nyce 2015), it is understandable, given that ergonomics is emerging from the intersection of psychology and design into a world that is increasingly concerned with generating and using quantitative data to inform outcomes. In response to this challenge facing the substantiation and measurability of HF concepts, (Matthews et al. 2019, p. 377) recommend moving toward operationalization, whereby,

N. L. Black et al. (Eds.): IEA 2021, LNNS 219, pp. 737–746, 2021.
https://doi.org/10.1007/978-3-030-74602-5_100

rather than assuming that a measurement is adequately capturing some real phenomenon described by a coherently formulated concept, priority is placed on demonstrating that numerically meaningful measurements can, more-or-less, predict real world outcomes. While this shift from a theoretically grounded discipline to a research-informed service may prove useful for addressing small design problems and strategies, it undermines the ability of human factors to inform understandings of complex socio-technical systems. Hence, particularly where organisational ergonomics is concerned, under-examination of concepts and the appropriateness of their application to real-world contexts must be addressed with understanding, rather than application, in mind. As this issue concerns the ontological value of theoretical propositions, we shall refer to it as the *conceptual validity critique*.

Second, there is a tendency for experimental psychology to investigate claims by testing isolated constructs using environments and subjects that at best can only simulate the complexities of the real-world contexts in which they are to be applied. While such demonstrations may provide numerical data that can then be used to predict outcomes and inform design – and are thus agreeable with operationalization – issues can occur when the tire of research-based design hits the road of the workplace. This is because, while they may be imagined as closed systems for analytical purposes, large and complex work environments will inevitably be more open and subject to contingencies than the controlled environments where studies are typically conducted. As Wilkin (2010, p. 236) observes, one way around this is to include the clause of *all things being equal* (*ceteris parabis*) when imagining the applicability of such research. The issue here, of course, is that real environments and simulated environments are not truly equal, with *ceteris parabis* thereby being yet another tendency that carries unnecessary risks for those seeking to make use of applied organisational ergonomics. As this issue revolves around questions of external verification of laboratory experiments vis-à-vis real work environments, we can call it the *ecological validity critique*.

To those familiar with the debates over the value of laboratory experiments in social psychology that pervaded the literature through the second-half of the twentieth-century, the ecological validity critique will sound familiar and perhaps even outdated. Responding to the critique, Berkowitz and Donnerstein (1982, p. 246) observe that the criticisms of laboratory experiments stem from assumptions about human behaviour and preconceptions of the purpose of laboratory experiments. In terms of the former, they rightly observe that, while the influence of the environment on human behaviour certainly should not be underestimated, this alone does not justify a blanket dismissal of claims based on experiments that do not simulate such external environments. While the details of a work environment may influence performance, attitudes and proclivities can also be carried across multiple environments, such as the tendency to "tune out" of meetings or professional development sessions that are deemed unimportant, repetitive, or boring. Laboratory experiments serve to test and substantiate such theoretical propositions to demonstrate that they *can* happen, with such claims not requiring the claim that they *will* in fact happen. In other words, as laboratory experiments are helpful in determining *possibilities*, critiques that focus on *probabilities*, such as whether personnel are more likely to "tune out" of a team meeting held on land or at sea, are not suited to purpose. Hence, the critique being presented here is not a blanket dismissal of findings developed off-site; but is rather levelled at the tendency to depend on one approach rather than using both in concert.

We contend that one way for the practitioner to address these issues is by using a clear framework and mixed method to address both quantitative and qualitative data. This is part of a larger organisational ergonomics project on how mixed methods can improve analysis of human factors in the context of complex socio-technical systems. The aim of the current paper is to illustrate how over committing to the quantitative/qualitative dichotomy undermines the ability of applied ergonomics to generate rich research on complex systems, resulting in research that is increasingly narrow, siloed, and of limited use to real world application. Once a case has been made for the use of mixed methods, a case study of research carried out by the authors on maintenance personnel working on an Australian navy vessel is presented.

2   Human Factors and Complex Socio-technical Systems

Many ergonomics practitioners have embraced sociotechnical systems theory as a means for investigating design and performance, as well as the value of drawing on worker experiences to help identify and describe relationships between ostensibly single issues (Carayon 2006; Carayon and Karsh 2000; Walker et al. 2008; Waterson et al. 2015). When studying systems, conceptual distinctions are made between technological, bio-logical, cognitive, and social *subsystems*, with attempts to pragmatically address one of these subsystems usually meaning the temporary bracketing-out of other subsystems. For example, manuals on engine maintenance do not tend to mention the effects of fumes on the lungs or the atmosphere, and maintenance instructors can deliver content without addressing the mental states or group dynamics of the people being instructed. S*ociotechnical systems theory* thus reflects the simultaneously modest and demanding attempt to address the relationships between social and technological subsystems, with the former involving factors like the interactions between and coordination of personnel, and thus workplace culture and the quality of communication and instruction, and the latter involving tools, equipment, software, and operational structures (Mumford 2006).

For the organisational ergonomic practitioner, systems theory requires the analysis of the complex interactions of components and human factors within and across subsys-tems, rather than limiting analysis to complicated processes (Carayon 2006; Walker et al. 2008). While the maintenance of a technological system is complicated, each procedure can in principle be understood and performed with sufficient individual knowledge and skill. Complexity enters the picture when one also attempts to account for the biolog-ical and cognitive factors of maintenance crew, the social factors of their training and workplace, and all the other elements referred to collectively as human factors (Dekker et al. 2011). Thinking in terms of complex systems thus requires one to think in terms of interactions and unintended consequences, rather than in terms of single constructs and unidimensional interventions.

3   Mixed Methods in Organisational Ergonomics

Åsberg et al. (2011, p. 409) draw attention to the meaning of *method, qualitative,* and *quantitative*. The term *method* – as derived from the Greek *me'thodos* (*meta*: *after* and *ho'dos*: *path*), which can be loosely translated as *along a path* – refers to the steps or approach taken in going about something. In this sense, *method* in the sciences refers to the approach and the steps taken when collecting data. Interviews, surveys, and observations are thus all *research methods*, in so far that they enable us to approach phenomena in particular ways to generate data that can inform our scientific understanding. Put differently, a *method* is a manner of collecting data, most often in the form of words and numbers, which are then used to describe and relate phenomena in terms of observable qualities and quantities. A so-called "qualitative method", such as interviewing workers on site, can generate qualitative data describing experiences of an issue, as well quantitative data on the prevalence and priority of said issue. This means that it is not the method that is quantitative or qualitative, but the data that it generates. Accordingly, committing to a method as "quantitative" or "qualitative" is at best a statement of intent, for it describes the type of data and manner of description one intends on generating ahead of time. The reality is that, so far that a method can produce mixed data, most methods are "mixed-methods". For these reasons, Åsberg et al. (2011) argue that there is in fact no such thing as *qualitative* methods or *quantitative* methods per se, and that these terms should be reserved for describing types of data. With this methodological point in mind, we shall continue to refer to "mixed methods" for the time being, as it is hopefully clear that we are using the phrase to refer to using a number of research techniques to generate both qualitative and quantitative data, and we are averse to prematurely presenting a neologism as an alternative.

We argue that much can be gained from approaches that generate and relate multiple types of data, for it is through such multiple descriptions that the dynamic relations and interactions of a complex sociotechnical system can be revealed and tested. *Revealed*, in so far that, along with drawing on information from the relevant literature, the practitioner can draw connections between ostensibly distinct organisational factors and components via an analysis of the narratives and perceptions – that is, the qualitative data – of personnel (Antonovsky et al. 2016). Such data can then be coded into themes and investigated as quantitative data in terms of frequency, significance, and relations to other themes. There are several benefits to such approaches for informing analysis and interventions: interviews can generate context-specific themes that a literature-based survey may have missed; surveys can then give a sense of how significant these themes are to personnel; testing the priority of these themes can reveal that personnel (or perhaps the practitioner) deem something to be more important than the quantitative data would indicate. Such analysis can reveal the complexities that exist in the relations in between personnel, social and technical subsystems, and the environment. This provides a multidimensional system analysis that accounts for complexity and supports interventions that are more relevant to the intended audience or workplace.

4   Case-Study: Using Mixed Methods to Examine Issues Identified by Naval Maintenance Personnel

Human factors constructs were used as the framework for examining the issues that hinder and assist the effective maintenance of naval vessels, based on the perceptions of the maintenance workforce. Preliminary data on failures and their causes was sourced from historical maintenance records. Ideally, these records would provide data on the occurrence of specific human factors in failures, however, the available data was sparse. Therefore, the information needed to be obtained directly from the workforce. The following project was conducted with the maintenance crew of an Australian navy vessel, which is not a warship.

The methodology used for this project was essentially a mixed method approach to workplace studies, utilising research methods to produce both quantitative and qualitative data. This method was developed through previous research conducted with off-shore petroleum production crews (Antonovsky et al. 2016). Quantitative data has the advantage of capturing insights into perceptions across entire workgroups and provides an indication of *what* is happening in the workplace. This data is only as good as the survey questions, which are based on their level of understanding of the issues faced by the workforce, and of the applicability of the chosen scale. Qualitative data provides more detailed insights into the knowledge and understanding of the people within the workplace and provides an indication of *why* issues arise. However, as this information is collected at the individual level it may only represent one person's perception. Applying a mixed methods approach can compensate for the deficiencies of both approaches.

4.1 Actions

For this project, the following data was collected; each type of data used as the basis for the next stage of data collection to gain a deeper understanding of maintenance on the vessel and the complex relations involved:

- Failure data from the vessel's database (Quantitative)
- Interviews with maintenance personnel from different departments and different ranks (Qualitative)
- A multiple-choice questionnaire distributed to the entire maintenance workforce (Quantitative)
- Analysis of the open-ended question included in the questionnaire (Qualitative).

Nominally one-hour interviews were conducted with a cross-section of the workforce (8 junior staff, 4 senior staff, and 2 officers) to examine any systemic conditions in the maintenance workplace that may have contributed to failures. The interview transcripts were thematically analysed, with statements coded according to sub-themes that recured throughout the interviews. In this part of the thematic analysis, the aim was to aggregate comments that reflected similar ideas, attitudes, or concerns. The sub-theme data was then analysed within a framework of human factors constructs, generating the following themes:

-Training	-Equipment & Spares	-Information
-Feedback from Systems	-Personnel & Workloads	-Maintenance Planning
-Administrative Processes	-Decision-making	-Ship-specific Issues

The number of times a sub-theme was mentioned was recorded, to determine which themes were more prominent across the workforce and worth including in the survey.

The frequency of factors and themes from this analysis was then used as the basis for constructing a questionnaire which was administered to the entire maintenance cohort.

This questionnaire contained both multiple choice questions (MCQs) and open-ended questions (OEQs), requiring statistical and thematic analyses, respectively. The purpose of the multiple-choice questions (n = 85) in the survey was to gauge the level of agreement with specific comments and concerns (Agree, Strongly Agree, Disagree, Strongly Disagree) and the frequency of issues (Always, Often, Sometimes, Rarely, Never). Analysis of the responses to the multiple-choice questions involved calculating, a) the mean (average) of responses to measure how important the issue was to crew, and b) the standard deviation to measure the diversity of opinions. Further analysis included calculating the differences between responses from marine technicians (MT) and electrical technicians (ET), and between different ranks.

In addition to the multiple-choice questions described above, eleven open-ended questions were asked that required the respondent to write any further comments that they had relating to the previous multiple-choice question. These questions requested additional detail and clarification of the important issues, or suggestions for improvement. The interpretation of these responses required a thematic analysis similar to that used for the interviews. Each comment was assessed for its main sub-themes and the sub-themes were aggregated into broader themes representing the commonalities in ideas relating to the question. The number of times a theme was mentioned in written responses could then be used as an indication of the relevance of issues across the maintenance workforce.

4.2 Results of Interviews

Based on the most-frequently mentioned sub-themes from the interviews (Fig. 1), Table 1 lists the human factors that in turn provided the thematic framework for individual questions (n = 96) in the questionnaire.

Figure 2 provides an example of one of the open-ended questions in the survey. Thematic analysis of the written responses to this question are shown. These provided quantitative data concerning the number of respondents who had similar ideas on the topic.

The results of the survey provided several forms of data that would be difficult to obtain using an approach limited to a single construct or methodology. For example, a quantitative indication of the level of agreement with statements that were frequently made during individual interviews was obtained. Mean scores provided an indication of how widespread the opinions of interviewees were across the entire cohort. The mean scores that were obtained ranged from 1.8 out of 5 (*"The replacement of obsolete parts is well-managed"*), which indicates lack of agreement with the premise of the question, to 4.7 out of 5 (*"It takes too long to order and receive parts or software up-dates"*), which indicates a high level of agreement. The survey data also indicated the diversity of opinions concerning interview statements. The standard deviation for statements ranged from 0.52 (*"You enjoy the challenges of your job"*), indicating a narrow diversity of opinions to 1.55 (*"Training ETs & MTs to cover each other's tasks would help balance the workload"*), indicating a wide diversity of opinions.

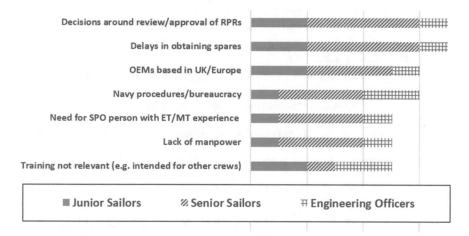

Fig. 1. The seven sub-themes most frequently mentioned in interviews, analysed through thematic coding, and arranged according to rank.

Table 1. HF themes derived from the interviews and examples of sub-themes used to construct the questionnaire.

HF themes	Number of questions	Example of "do you agree?" style questions used (sub-themes)
Spares & Equipment	14	The replacement of obsolete parts is well-managed?
Information	15	Maintainers are informed when a procedure change has been implemented?
Planning	11	The work of my team is well-coordinated with other departments?
Training	12	You receive regular training to remain up-to-date with new systems?
Workload	14	Your job requires you to perform too many different tasks to be effective?
Administration Tasks	11	Lessons learned from failed or inefficient maintenance actions are well-documented?
Communication	14	Your team members share a lot of information about the task?
Decision-making	5	The decisions made on actioning Requests for Problem Resolution make sense?

In addition, the OEQs generated concepts that were not considered in the design of the questionnaire. For example, a question concerning the efficacy of training methods (Fig. 2) generated responses related to cost, ease of organisation and fatigue. In addition,

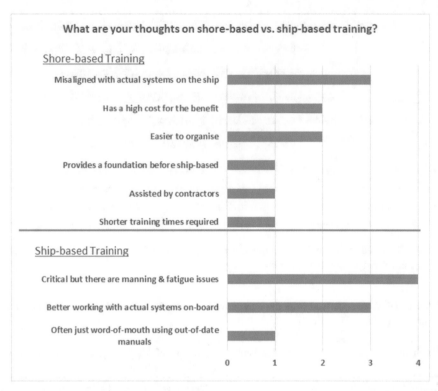

Fig. 2. Example of an OEQ, and the thematic analysis of responses which provided quantitative data concerning the frequency of shared ideas.

other OEQs generated responses that demonstrated that participants had a different interpretation of some of the questions from that of the researcher.

5   Discussion

As discussed earlier, the influence of any single factor is difficult to assess in a complex system, and the influence of a factor studied in another context or domain may not be relevant. While theoretical concepts can provide guidance as to the influence that distinct human factors may have, context-related ecological factors will ultimately determine the relevance of a specific construct. These methodology and outcomes demonstrate the first stage in a HF-based workplace analysis and intervention, namely, the collection of essential organisational data. This data informs the practitioner of the human factors that are most relevant to the organisation under study, and the influence these factors have on organisational effectiveness. By employing a mixed methodology to collect qualitative and quantitative data, the effects of interacting factors in a complex system can be investigated, thereby allowing for the identification and assessment of a broad range of interacting factors in terms of relevance, as well as the revealing of emergent issues. In the case study described above, the following were found to be advantages of the methodology for collecting data and efficiently identifying areas that will be prioritized for remedial interventions:

1. The utilisation of available organisational data provides a means of initiating discussions with the workforce about highly relevant workplace issues. Any quality of data may be used, as the intent is to generate discussion in a manner that surveyed personnel will likely find relevant, rather than to assess the validity of the output measures themselves.

2. As issues in a complex system are emergent, perception-based, highly context-dependent, or time-variant, it is important that the researcher has a basis early in the research for understanding the relevance of specific issues and sub-issues. The use of constructs and ideas generated from the interviews ensures the relevance and comprehensibility of the survey questions. To use a standardised scale for this type of research invites potential misunderstandings on the part of the participant, and misinterpretation and bias on the part of the researcher.

3. The intent of open-ended questions is to provide participants with the opportunity to express their ideas about the issues examined in the survey. This in turn provides the researcher with more detailed responses to the questions asked and insight to participants' interpretations of the meaning of questions. The OEQs thereby test the understanding of questions by the participant and interpretation of responses by the researcher. This reflects a double hermeneutic, whereby the participants interpret conditions in their workplace, while the researcher interprets the meaning given by the participants. The issues raised can then be related to a theoretical understanding of the way that specific human factors tend to operate in complex systems.

4. In addition, participants were found to offer supplementary information relating to the MCQs, as well as suggestions for improving human factors in their workplace, which the researcher can include in their recommendations for interventions and in the formulation of future research projects.

5. The current approach provides the basis for the longitudinal study of the effect of identified factors on output or performance measures, which are typically required to determine the value of interventions. In contrast, measurement of the influence of ostensibly isolated factors in a complex system is a more tenuous basis for recommending interventions.

Data collection and analysis are only the early stages of organisational and ergonomic investigations. Later stages typically address recommendations for interventions, based on the level of agreement, depth, and relevance of each issue raised, organisational priorities, and an awareness of the complexity involved in implementing changes – it is this latter condition that we will explore in future work.

6 Conclusion

In allowing the literature to inform the design of research projects and the identification of relevant themes, and then testing and revising these themes in response to the descriptions obtained from personnel working in real work environments, we reduce the risk of measuring less-relevant phenomena, described above as the *conceptual validity critique*. Likewise, as the descriptions provided by personnel in real work environments indicate that a particular phenomenon *can* happen but leave it up to the practitioner to determine probability, the challenge of substantiating such descriptions is comparable to those levelled at the laboratory experiments, which we described above as the *ecological validity critique*. Rather than fully embracing a completely empirical approach, we propose frameworks and methods geared toward not just generating, but substantiating, multiple data sources for understanding complex phenomena.

References

Antonovsky, A., Pollock, C., Straker, L.: System reliability as perceived by maintenance personnel on petroleum production facilities. Reliab. Eng. Syst. Safety **152**, 58–65 (2016)

Åsberg, R., Hummerdal, D., Dekker, S.: There are no qualitative methods–nor quantitative for that matter: The misleading rhetoric of the qualitative–quantitative argument. Theoret. Issues Ergon. Sci. **12**(5), 408–415 (2011)

Berkowitz, L., Donnerstein, E.: External validity is more than skin deep: some answers to criticisms of laboratory experiments. Am. Psychol. **37**(3), 245 (1982)

Carayon, P.: Human factors of complex sociotechnical systems. Appl. Ergon. **37**(4), 525–535 (2006)

Carayon, P., Hancock, P., Leveson, N., Noy, I., Sznelwar, L., Hootegem, V., Geert: Advancing a sociotechnical systems approach to workplace safety–developing the conceptual framework. Ergonomics **58**(4), 548–564 (2015)

Carayon, P., Karsh, B.-T.: Sociotechnical issues in the implementation of imaging technology. Behav. Inf. Technol. **19**(4), 247–262 (2000)

Dekker, S., Cilliers, P., Hofmeyr, J.-H.: The complexity of failure: implications of complexity theory for safety investigations. Safety Sci. **49**(6), 939–945 (2011)

Dekker, S., Nyce, J.: From figments to figures: ontological alchemy in human factors research. Cogn. Technol. Work **17**(2), 185–187 (2015)

Matthews, G., De Winter, J., Hancock, P.A.: What do subjective workload scales really measure? Operational and representational solutions to divergence of workload measures. Theoret. Issues Ergon. Sci. 1–28 (2019)

Mumford, E.: The story of socio-technical design: reflections on its successes, failures and potential. Inf. Syst. J. **16**(4), 317–342 (2006)

Walker, G., Stanton, N., Salmon, P., Jenkins, D.: A review of sociotechnical systems theory: a classic concept for new command and control paradigms. Theoret. Issues Ergon. Sci. **9**(6), 479–499 (2008)

Walker, G., Stanton, N., Salmon, P., Jenkins, D., Rafferty, L.: Translating concepts of complexity to the field of ergonomics. Ergonomics **53**(10), 1175–1186 (2010)

Waterson, P., Robertson, M., Cooke, N., Militello, L., Roth, E., Stanton, N.: Defining the methodological challenges and opportunities for an effective science of sociotechnical systems and safety. Ergonomics **58**(4), 565–599 (2015)

Wilkin, P.: The ideology of ergonomics. Theoret. Issues Ergon. Sci. **11**(3), 230–244 (2010)

Well-Being and Efficiency in Financial Sector Analyzed with Multiclass Classification Machine Learning

Gregor Molan[1]([✉]) [iD] and Marija Molan[2] [iD]

[1] Comtrade, Letališka cesta 29b, Ljubljana, Slovenia
gregor.molan@comtrade.com
[2] Institute of Occupational, Traffic and Sports Medicine, University Medical Centre Ljubljana,
Poljanski nasip 58, Ljubljana, Slovenia
marija.molan@kclj.si

Abstract. The main research goal is the identification of the most important well-being parameters determining worker's efficiency in the financial sector from 2005 until 2020 in the time of great changes in the socio-economic situation in Slovenia. Data were collected in 2005, 2010, 2015, and 2020 - key periods of important milestones in economic growths and declines in Slovenia for 2723 financial workers. All data are analyzed using the ML classification method to identify the most important attributes (well-being parameters) determining worker's efficiency. To prevent possible overfitting and/or underfitting there is a prescribed adequate tree depth for each decision tree as an additional domain knowledge added to the presented ML solution. We chose a binary decision tree learning, that is simple to understand and interpret with an ability to handle both numerical and categorical data.

Decision trees generated with the ML classification show, that workers with low efficiency (estimated as "poor" or "inadequate") were mostly out of work. In 2005 the most important influential factor was psychological fatigue. From 2010 to 2020, physical fatigue was the most important influential factor.

External socio-economic factors determine the level of well-being and efficiency. Adequate level of well-being is the basis of workers' efficiency and their health. The conclusions are based on the data from 2005 to 2020. Presented approach based on implementation of ML is a tool for identification of gripping points for intervention at work to maintain adequate level of workers well-being in a new working reality.

Keywords: Lack of well-being · Machine learning multiclass classification · Worker efficiency · Financial services · Economic conditions

1 Introduction

Subjective well-being describes the quality of individuals' live emotional reactions and cognitive judgements. In the work-place it also reflects workers' work satisfaction [1].

N. L. Black et al. (Eds.): IEA 2021, LNNS 219, pp. 747–754, 2021.
https://doi.org/10.1007/978-3-030-74602-5_101

Well-being as a reflection of personality, social influence, family impact and health, determines human behavior at the work-place.

There are different approaches to measure subjective well-being. For this purpose, OECD published guidelines for guidelines for measurement of subjective well-being [2]. Performance in real working situations depends on subjective perception of workers' well-being. Well-being is linked with health and productivity and workers who are in good psychical and physical condition achieve better performance [3]. The nature of work and workplace demands are changing and this may have considerable effect on worker well-being [4].

Huge amount of subjectively collected data demands adequate approaches to analyses these data. For this purpose, implementation of some multiclass classification algorithms offers more explainable connections between work and worker and between subjective well-being and performance [5]. Determination of connection between perception of well-being and performance, offers possibility to identify the most important influences of work on perception of well-being. Subjective perception of well-being components, like perception of stress, psychical fatigue, mode, and exhaustion shapes work's performance. Decrease of performance means expenses. Expenses are also investments in work-load components to adopt working environment to worker. Comparison of both expenses, decrease of performance and investments in work-load decrease, are basis for humanisation interventions. To identify all these relations, machine learning tools should be implemented.

2   Related Work

Formalization of relation between worker and work is presented in AH-model. The center of AH-Model is subjective evaluation of worker's well-being. It is defined as actual availability. Subjective evaluation of actual availability is reflection of perceived well-being and it is shaped with individual self-evaluations of his/her abilities, health, competencies, attitudes, experiences, motivation, and psychophysical conditions. The AH-model is formalized for machine learning [6]. It is upgraded with implementation of ML methods.

3   Original Contributions

The most important new approach is implementation of ML tools in analysis of connections between well-being and efficiency to identify less obvious relations between them. This approach offers the possibility to identify impacts of well-being as a basis for interventions in organization and external environment that determines work-load. Implementation of ML tool in analysis of well-being data is a step forward form purely statistical analysis.

4   Research Goal

The main research goal is the identification of the most important well-being parameters determining worker's efficiency in the financial sector from 2005 until 2020. This was a time of significance changes in the socio-economic situation in Slovenia but the basic content of the work of bank employees remained the same in the same environments. Identification of a lack of well-being enables efficient ergonomic measures to improve quality of worker's health and at the same time improve worker's efficiency.

5   Objective

The objective of this article is summarized in following items related to well-being and efficiency for workers in financial sector:

(a) Define time period for input data
(b) Define method for data analysis
(c) Define content of data
(d) Define prediction objects.

The final goal is to a identify key gripping points for ergonomic measures to improve quality of worker's health and to increase worker's efficiency.

6   Research Method

Data were collected in 2005, 2010, 2015, and 2020 - key periods of important milestones in economic growths and declines in Slovenia [7]. Our machine learning (ML) classification method analyzed well-being of 2723 financial workers. The most important influences of well-being on worker's efficiency should be identified [6] with implemented multiclass binary decision tree classification method [5]. Identified lacks of well-being are basis for implemented ergonomic measures as a participatory ergonomics [8].

6.1   Data Collection

Data on worker's well-being were collected with the questionnaire of availability from the AH-model with the efficiency data in the same period.

For each worker there is an efficiency, presented as a categorical value with 5 efficiency classes: E1 (excellent), E2 (good), E3 (average), E4 (low), E5 (bad).

Worker's well-being are 7 numerical independent attributes (physical and psychological fatigue, exhaustion, motivation, vigilance, mood, and stress) [6].

6.2   Decision Tree

The aim is to predict the efficiency class of the worker. All data are analyzed using the ML classification method to identify the most important attributes (well-being parameters) determining worker's efficiency. Results of the ML algorithm are decision trees. To prevent possible overfitting and/or underfitting there is a prescribed adequate tree depth for each decision tree as an additional domain knowledge added to the presented ML solution [9]. We chose a binary decision tree learning, that is simple to understand and interpret with an ability to handle both numerical and categorical data [10]. Such a decision tree classification method allows to use raw original data [11].

6.3 Graph Theory

To avoid ambiguity, here are some formal mathematical definitions and description of generated decision trees.

Definition. An **undirected graph** G is a pair G = (N, E), where N is a set of **nodes**, and E is a set of **edges**, i.e. two-sets (set with two distinct elements) of nodes.

Formally, a tree in graph theory is an undirected graph that has any two vertices connected by exactly one path [12]. In this article, results are presented with decision trees; they are binary trees, where each node has at most two children: left child and right child.

Decision trees generated with ML algorithm are presented on Figs. 1, 2, 3 and 4. The root nodes in these decision trees have the number $\boxed{1}$ in the box on the top of the node. Numbers in boxes on the top nodes are later $\boxed{2}$ for its left child and $\boxed{3}$ for its right child and so on. As it is presented on Fig. 3, there are node numbers $\boxed{4}$, $\boxed{10}$, $\boxed{11}$, and $\boxed{3}$ on the lowest level (tree leaf nodes), and it means that there are presented only relevant tree nodes - most of nodes are not presented.

Efficiency classes for workers' efficiency are presented as labels E1 and E2. In the second line in nodes are numbers of workers for each efficiency class. On Fig. 2 there are 4 efficiency classes "E1 E2 E3 E4", where for example on the node $\boxed{19}$, it is the 4th tree leaf, numbers "0 8 1 0" present that there are 8 workers with efficiency class E2, 1 worker with efficiency class 1, and no workers with efficiency classes E1 and E4. Consequently, the node $\boxed{19}$ is categorized as E2 as there are the most workers with efficiency E2.

The percentage number on the bottom of nodes is percentage of workers in a node. Leaf nodes on Fig. 3 have percentages that together represents all workers (23% + 9% + 26% + 42% = 100%).

7   Results

All analyzed workers had a good efficiency at the time of data collection. Decision trees generated with the ML classification show that workers with low efficiency (estimated as "poor" or "inadequate") were mostly out of work. The modal efficiency was E2 (good).

In 2005 (see Fig. 1) the most important influential factor was psychological fatigue. The marginal value for psychological fatigue was 2 and it is an adequate one. This explains about half of the whole 2005 sample. Workers with the perception of higher psychological fatigue also reported exhaustion. It was the time of high optimism in Slovenia and extensive economic growth. Workers in the financial sectors worked a lot, but they were also well paid. In those time, job in the financial sector was the excellent opportunity.

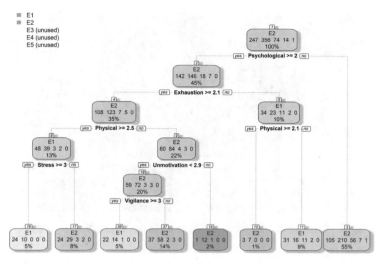

Fig. 1. Decision tree for worker's efficiency in the financial sector in 2005.

In 2010 (see Fig. 2) the most influential factor was perception of physical fatigue. Workers with a lower level of physical fatigue were more effective, and there were more than half of workers with such an efficiency. Workers with a higher level of physical fatigue, reported a decrease of vigilance and they were exhausted. They worked hard for excellent efficiency (E1). It was the time of the deepest economic crises in Slovenia with the decline of socio-economic conditions.

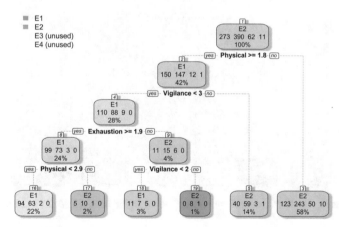

Fig. 2. Decision tree for worker's efficiency in the financial sector in 2010.

In 2015 (see Fig. 3) the most important influential factor was again physical fatigue. Workers with a higher level of physical fatigue were more effective. Their efficiency was excellent (E1). It was the time of better possibilities for everybody and a strong competition among financial workers and institutions.

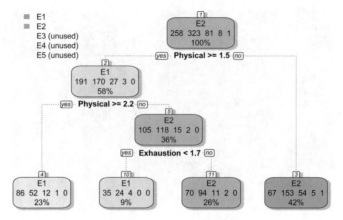

Fig. 3. Decision tree for worker's efficiency in the financial sector in 2015.

In 2020 (see Fig. 4) the most important influential factor was physical fatigue. The majority of workers had good efficiency (E2), and the minority were very effective (E1), all of them reported more physical fatigue. It was the time of change in ownership of financial institutions and coming of extensive digitalization of processes in financial institutions as well as generation changes. Older experienced financial workers retired and younger more competitive newcomers took their place.

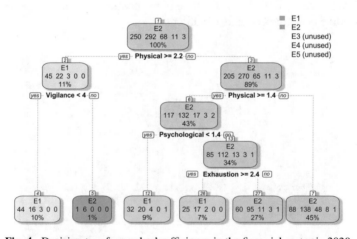

Fig. 4. Decision tree for worker's efficiency in the financial sector in 2020.

Identification of relations between perception of well-being and efficiency offers possibility to discover possible less visible impacts and influences. The domination of psychological fatigue reflects influences of workloads with limited influences of workers. In this situation work-loads demands work perceived with stress with limited duration. Good efficiency was enough for good salary.

In the last decade from 2010 to 2020, in the financial sector due to higher competition and new financial players financial workers had to work harder to achieve adequate or desired efficiency. The work, was due to static postures and longer work hours, physically more demanding.

The upgrade of AH-model with implementation of ML algorithm offers possibility to also discover the less visible relations and impacts on workers' well-being.

8 Conclusions

External socio-economic factors determine the level of well-being and efficiency. Adequate level of well-being is the basis of workers' efficiency and their health. The conclusions are for the era until the 2020, until the Covid-19, until the beginning of totally new working conditions and before the start of new era of the deepest economic crisis in the last century. The new reality in 2020 is extensive digitalization and remote work with less social support.

The new reality will be reflected also in changes of perceived well-being at work. New reality of remote work and work from home in less ergonomically adopted environment should be manifested in changes of well-being perceptions as it was before.

Presented approach based on implementation of ML is a tool for identification of gripping points for intervention at work to maintain adequate level of workers well-being also in new working reality.

8.1 Future Work

Test suites could be extended with development status weights to cover development of f-influences. Developed OIP-Model could be included in some of project management.

Declarations
Ethics Approval. Data were collected on the basis of individual approval of workers and the contract that governess data analysis and research between University medical centre Ljubljana and financial institutions.

References

1. Emmons, RA., Diener, E.: Personality correlates of subjective well-being. Pers. Soc. Psychol. Bull. **11**(1), 89–97 (1985). https://doi.org/10.1177/0146167285111008
2. OECD: OECD Guidelines on Measuring Subjective Well-being (Organisation for Ecnomic Co-operation and Development, Paris, France, 2013) (2013). https://doi.org/10.1787/978926 4191655-en. https://www.oecd-ilibrary.org/content/publication/9789264191655-en
3. JHSPH: From Evidence to Practice: Workplace Wellness that Works. Institute for Health and Productivity Studies (Johns Hopkins Bloomberg School of Public Health (JHSPH), Johns Hopkins Baltimore, MD, Baltimore, Maryland, USA). Johns Hopkins University (2015)
4. Adams, J.M.: The value of worker well-being. Public Health Reports **134**(6), 583–586 (2020). https://doi.org/10.1177/0033354919878434. PMID 31600480
5. Chaitra, P., Kumar, D.R.S.: A review of multi-class classification algorithms. Int. J. Pure Appl. Math. **118**(14), 17–26 (2018)

6. Molan, G., Molan, M.: Formalization of expert AH model for machine learning. Frant. Artf. Intell. Appl. **82** (2002)
7. The European Commission: Real GDP growth rate - volume (The European Commission, 2021). https://ec.europa.eu/eurostat/databrowser/view/tec00115/default/table?lang=en
8. Burgess-Limerick, R.: Participatory ergonomics: evidence and implementation lessons. Appl. Ergon. **68**, 289–293 (2018)
9. Ohn-Bar, E., Trivedi, M.M.: To boost or not to boost? On the limits of boosted trees for object detection. In: 2016 23rd International Conference on Pattern Recognition (ICPR), pp. 3350–3355. IEEE (2016)
10. Biswas, S., Blanton, R.D.: Statistical test compaction using binary decision trees. IEEE Des. Test Comput. **23**(6), 452–462 (2006)
11. Li, X., Ye, N.: Decision tree classifiers for computer intrusion detection. J. Parallel Distrib. Comput. Pract. **4**(2), 179–190 (2001)
12. Bender, EA., Williamson, S.G.: Lists, decisions and graphs (2010)

Towards Improving Esports' Working Conditions: Insights on Role of a Professional Players' Association

Esdras Paravizo[1]([⊠]) [iD] and Renato Luvizoto Rodrigues de Souza[2] [iD]

[1] Department of Industrial Engineering, Federal University of São Carlos, São Carlos, SP, Brazil
esdras@estudante.ufscar.br
[2] Department of Industrial Engineering, Federal University of Triângulo Mineiro, Uberaba, MG, Brazil

Abstract. The esports' scene is a multibillion-dollar industry with large global audiences. There is an increasing scholarly interest on the esports phenomenon, looking at it from a variety of disciplines. At the center of the esports ecosystem are the athletes who are members of teams that compete in leagues and tournaments, working in a still poorly regulated industry. Not surprisingly, the esports scene is usually characterized by poor working conditions, busy schedules and burnout. As a direct consequence, players' push for better working conditions is frequent and a possible avenue for pursuing such efforts is the establishing of players' association. In this context, this exploratory study aims to analyze the activities and initiatives carried out by the Counter Strike Professional Players' Association, to promote better working conditions for professional esports' players. The study qualitative analyses documents from the association, coding the initiatives and topics addressed by them. Results indicate that the association tries to address work conditions, regulations, player compensation and health issues by discussing guidelines and minimum standards of work with event organizers and teams organizations. We propose a model to understand the role of players' associations in dealing with these parties as well as with game developers, and the possible outcomes from these negotiations. The incorporation of Human Factor and Ergonomics specialists to players' associations can be a way to assist on driving for improvements on the esports scene.

Keywords: Esports · Work conditions · Players' association · Unions · Ergonomics and human factors

1 Introduction

The field of human factors and ergonomics (HFE) is known for its privileged position in terms of the industries and areas of interest. HFE methods and interventions are relevant in the context of traditional manufacturing settings to virtual environments design, always guided by the three fundamental characteristics of high-quality HFE as devised by [1]: a design-driven, systems approach, focusing on a double outcome: performance and well-being.

N. L. Black et al. (Eds.): IEA 2021, LNNS 219, pp. 755–761, 2021.
https://doi.org/10.1007/978-3-030-74602-5_102

An active line of research within the HFE community lies on the intersection of sports and HFE. A recent book edited by Paul Salmon and collaborators provide and overview of the most recent discussions and facets of HFE take on sports [2], putting forward the idea that sport can be seen as a complex socio-technical system and devising pathways to improving the interface between HFE methods in sports.

In parallel to traditional sports, professional competitive game playing - esports - have been increasingly gaining attention, both as an important entertainment market and business (with revenue estimates surpassing the billion-dollar threshold) and as a fruitful topic for scientific inquiry (with tens of thousands of studies and papers published in the last few years [3]).

This interest is also seen from the HFE perspective, as there are several opportunities for analyzing the esports' employing traditional HFE methods and approaches. For instance, [4] applied a questionnaire with esports athletes from Denmark uncovering that musculoskeletal pain is frequent in esports, mainly on athletes' back, neck and shoulders, possibly impacting their participation on esports activities. From the standpoint of the computer supported cooperative work community, researchers [5, 6] discuss organizational aspects and the collective nature of esports play, player communication and competition. Furthermore, hazard guides to esports have been created, highlighting the main risks esports athletes are exposed to, how to promote health in this scenario and how to improve performance as discussed by [7].

The discussion of the differences on esports and traditional, "real life" sports – and even if esports can be regarded as sports – is frequently debated. A sufficient starting point for the understanding of this discussion comes from [8] who conclude that esports match many of the sports' requirements for moving from merely a game to a sport in its own accord, except for the physicality and institutionalization. The authors contend that the fine motor skills required for esports play are not on par with the gross motor skills and physical prowess inherent to sports. With regards to the institutionalization of esports, the demonstration of esports as a stablished form of competition demands time, a broad body of rules, regulations and standards, a professionalization of the stakeholders of the ecosystem and the emergence of governing bodies, which the authors highlight that are not proven.

Specially with regards to the institutionalization aspect of esports, one of the relevant organizations that could assist on the professionalization and are a natural evolution for the field are players' unions. Unions and players' associations are frequent in traditional sports, raising interest from scholars as early as 1996 [9]. Dabschek [9] highlights that sports is a precarious occupation, with players facing injury risk, short careers and difficulties in transitioning to other employment afterwards, in addition to power imbalances between players and organizations which drive the idea of unionization. Similarly, in the esports ecosystem, discussions about the possible benefits and challenges for unionization are starting to emerge.

Among the many particularities unique to esports that may shape how the unionization process could unfold in this scene, [10] highlights the heterogeneity of the esports ecosystem, with numerous games and platforms, the organizations which usually field teams in different esports, the "nearly limitless power" of game developers over the teams and players and the intrinsic globalized nature of competition (not necessarily attached to a geographic location). The author highlights dissatisfaction over players' compensation, poor working conditions (e.g., long hours of practice), musculoskeletal disorders (e.g., Carpal tunnel syndrome), mental and physical issues (e.g. specially due to the heightened pressure from fans on social media) and the limited length of careers and transition opportunities as driving issues to the formation of unions. Another analysis on esports and unionization also highlights that players could be eligible from a legal standpoint to form unions and collectively bargain for better working conditions and other benefits.

Given this panorama, in 2018 a professional players association emerged in the Counter Strike: Global Offensive (a game developed by Valve) esports scene. The Counter Strike Professional Players' Association (CSPPA) intends to be a collective bargaining association aiming to "safeguard, protect and promote professional Counter-Strike players' interests"[1] (CSPPA, 2020), with a special focus on working conditions for players in the CS:GO industry.

The push from unions to improve working conditions may be an opportunity for an increase in the awareness of stakeholders and organizations of the importance of HFE aspects of work. In the case o esports unionization initiatives it is expected that players association could work to ensure a minimum standard of working conditions for the athletes. Thus, the aim of this study is to analyze the activities and initiatives carried out by the CSPPA to promote better working conditions for professional esports' players.

2 Methods

This study is exploratory, undertaking a qualitative approach based on documental analyses to identify and categorize the initiatives, programs and activities carried out by the CSPPA in 2020. The study focuses only on the CS:GO esports' scene for it is the one with the most consolidated player association so far. A pool of 9 documents available on the CSPPA website on their activities and 11 news articles reporting on the CSPPA were qualitatively analyzed, following the general inductive approach for qualitative data analysis presented in [11].

The analyzes focused on the identification of what were the aspects related to players' working conditions, regulation agreements, among other topics, discussed by the association, as well as their main partners in these discussions (e.g. teams' organizations, event organizers etc.). Both authors read the documents and codified their content. Eventual disagreements were discussed until a consensus was found. The overview of the topics and initiatives from the CSPPA that were found are presented in the next section.

3 Results

The analysis of the document pool selected shows that most recurrent aspects related to players' working conditions discussed by the association are related to tournament

---

[1] CSPPA – About us. Available on: https://www.csppa.gg/copy-of-csppa-aoa. Last accessed 09/02/2021.

schedule (e.g., matches starting time, days off between group-stage and play-off matches, facilities available for players, equipment for training and competition, etc.), regulations (tournament rules, players' code of conduct, players' compensation, players' break), health programs (specially mental health, burnout and stress mitigating initiatives), among other topics such as (travel to take part in tournaments, education programs, accommodation, amenities and security when traveling and the recognition of the players' union). Among the parties the association more closely interacts with are the players themselves, event organizers, teams' organizations and the game developer. Figure 1 shows an overview of the results from the analysis of the documents from CSPPA.

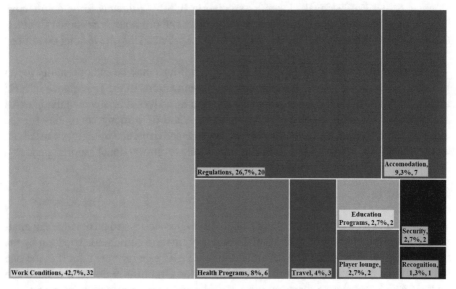

Fig. 1. Overview of the themes identified from the analysis of the CSPPA initiatives

4   Discussion

The results highlight the potential that collective bargaining bodies might have on the esports' scene to try and promote better working conditions for the players. For instance, one particular guideline elaborated by the CSPPA was the "Event Minimum Standards" which stipulates the responsibilities of event organizations when setting up an event in terms of the accommodation of players, the facilities for training and competition, amenities and the equipment (tables, chairs, hardware, etc.). When the CSPPA celebrates agreements with event organizers, they agree to ensure these basic conditions are met, which directly translates in a push towards the standardization and improved conditions for players.

Another example is the relatively small but impactful change articulated between the association and event organizers which pushed for the adjustment of matches' start time to avoid them going over midnight and the stipulation of a three-day rest period for players' going to the play-off stage of tournaments.

Another relevant initiative led by the association, related to mental health issues in the scene, was the partnering with two UK universities to undertake a mental health survey with players, coaches and other staff and a pilot program for promoting mental health education and clinical treatments for teams and players.

Nonetheless, many opportunities and some mishaps also impacted the association impact in the scene: the overall community (viewers & consumers of esports' content) tend to not understand the reality of professional players' work, nor the role and importance of a collective association that promote players' interests. Furthermore, when trying to act as an agent (assisting players in the negotiation of better contracts with teams) the association ended up having conflicts of interests which might have impacted the outcome of the negotiation (which led to the association not offering such services anymore).

Based on the current efforts identified from the CSPPA and the overview of the possible benefits originated from players' associations in esports, a model of the core interactions and outcomes of unions in esports is proposed in Fig. 2. This model considers players and coaches as the core participants of players' unions. Three core interactions of the unions in esports are identified: with the game developer, with the teams' organizations and with the event organizers. With each of those stakeholders, different demands and needs can be discussed.

For instance, with game developers the players' union may discuss and participate on the development process of the game, providing insight on gameplay issues derived from poor game design or interactions that should be addressed in future updates of the game. This proximity would tend to not "blindside" players and organizations in terms of changes in the game that may affect current strategies and on how the game is effectively played.

In terms of the team's organizations, players' unions are able to collectively bargain for fair contracts that consider players' health, IP, salaries and working hours and breaks. Especially considering that the teams' organizations are responsible for setting up players' main workplace, the union could be determinant to represent players interests and curtail predatory practices from teams' organizations, both in terms of the physical facilities and equipment made available and the work environment.

Finally, with regards to event organizers, the role of the players' union is to ensure that players have minimum working conditions at this secondary work location (in events' venues and practice facilities) as well as that they are not subject to extraneous schedules that do not allow for rest periods between matches and so on.

While it is understandable that mental workload and the drive for optimal and maximum performance is a crucial issue in the elite sports in general (as well as in esports), the focus of this study was on a more basic aspect: the minimum work conditions that athletes should have to enable them to pursue top-tier performance. These working conditions issues (e.g. frequent long travels, busy schedules, substandard facilities) hinder both player performance and health, and thus, must be addressed.

Raising awareness of players' unions with regards of HFE aspects and possible benefits towards the working conditions and overall improvement of the esports' scene

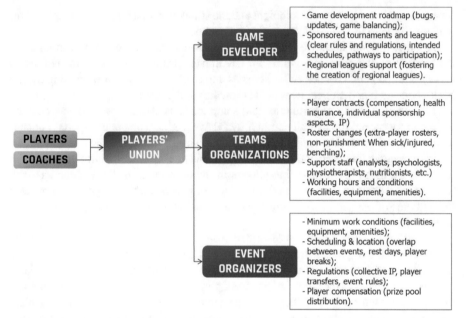

Fig. 2. Overview of the core interactions and possible outcomes of an esports' player union

can be a first point of contribution from HFE to esports. Incorporation of trained HFE specialists in teams' organizations could also lead to better working conditions and player performance.

5 Conclusion

Overall, this exploratory study identified the current initiatives carried out by a professional esports' players association and its focus on improving athletes' working conditions and related aspects. The model proposed for framing union interactions and possible outcomes can assist in framing future research questions on the topic, as well as assisting practitioners aiming to act in this field.

The institutionalization of sports, albeit still in course, can be further supported by the emergence of these players' associations and similar bodies that aim to collective bargain to balance out the significant differences in power among the stakeholders of the esports' scene.

The theme of esports' working conditions and mental health issues must be systematically addressed by the parties involved in the field. Players' associations might be an important driver in promoting a healthy scene, pushing event organizers and teams' organizations to consider players' needs and well-being in the definition of schedules, tournament formats and so on. In the future, the incorporation of ergonomics and human factors specialists in players' unions and teams' organizations could further bolster the opportunity to improve the work aspects of the esports' scene.

Further studies systematically looking at the esports' field from the lens of ergonomics and human factors are warranted, especially taking into account the possibilities brought by players' associations as drivers of improvements in players' working conditions. Future studies can provide an in-depth comparison of HFE long experience with traditional sports and how it can translate to the esports scene. Physical HFE approaches can focus on the musculoskeletal disorders athletes face, how the workspace design affects their health and performance. A cognitive HFE focus could gain insight on the mental workload aspects of players' work, the pressures associated with performance and an increased scrutiny from fans over social media, as well as the impact of the virtual environment and game style itself on players. Approaches looking at the organizational level, can focus on understanding the challenges in team coordination, communication, taking a systems ergonomics approach to this emerging field of scholarly interest.

References

1. Dul, J., Bruder, R., Buckle, P., et al.: A strategy for human factors/ergonomics: developing the discipline and profession. Ergonomics **55**, 377–395 (2012). https://doi.org/10.1080/001 40139.2012.661087
2. Salmon, P.M., McLean, S., Dallat, C., et al.: Human Factors and Ergonomics in Sport: Applications and Future Directions, 1st edn. CRC Press, Boca Raton (2021)
3. Reitman, J.G., Anderson-Coto, M.J., Wu, M., et al.: Esports research: a literature review. Games Cult **15**, 32–50 (2020). https://doi.org/10.1177/1555412019840892
4. Lindberg, L., Nielsen, S.B., Damgaard, M., et al.: Musculoskeletal pain is common in competitive gaming: a cross-sectional study among Danish esports athletes. BMJ Open Sport Exerc Med **6**, 000799 (2020). https://doi.org/10.1136/bmjsem-2020-000799
5. Freeman, G., Wohn, D.Y.: Understanding eSports team formation and coordination. Computer Supported Cooperative Work (CSCW) (2018)
6. Lipovaya, V., Lima, Y., Grillo, P., et al.: Coordination, communication, and competition in eSports: a comparative analysis of teams in two action games. In: ECSCW 2018 – Proceedings of 16th European Conference on Computer Support and Cooperative Work (2018). https://doi.org/10.18420/ecscw2018
7. Emara, A.K., Ng, M.K., Cruickshank, J.A., et al.: Gamer's health guide: optimizing performance, recognizing hazards, and promoting wellness in Esports. Curr Sports Med Rep **19**, 537–545 (2020). https://doi.org/10.1249/JSR.0000000000000787
8. Jenny, S.E., Manning, R.D., Keiper, M.C., Olrich, T.W.: Virtual(ly) athletes: where eSports fit within the definition of "sport." Quest **69**, 1–18 (2017). https://doi.org/10.1080/00336297. 2016.1144517
9. Dabscheck, B.: Playing the team game: unions in Australian professional team sports. J Ind Relations **38**, 600–628 (1996). https://doi.org/10.1177/002218569603800405
10. Ridenhour, K.F.: Traditional sports and esports: the path to collective bargaining. Iowa Law Rev **105**, 1857–1897 (2020)
11. Thomas, D.R.: A general inductive approach for analyzing qualitative evaluation data. Am J Eval **27**, 237–246 (2006). https://doi.org/10.1177/1098214005283748

Macroergonomic Assessment of a Colombian Floriculture Company

Elizabeth Pérez[1](✉) ⓘ, Yordán Rodríguez[2] ⓘ, and Claudia Patricia Giraldo[3] ⓘ

[1] School of Industrial Engineering, Universidad Pontificia Bolivariana, Medellín, Colombia
elizabeth.perezme@upb.edu.co
[2] National School of Public Health, Universidad de Antioquia, Medellín, Colombia
yordan.rodriguez@udea.edu.co
[3] Consultoría en Gestión del Riesgo Suramericana, Medellín, Colombia
cgiraldop@sura.com.co

Abstract. It is unusual to find ergonomic evaluations or interventions approached from a macroergonomic perspective in the Latin American context. The purpose of this study was to evaluate the ergonomic maturity level of a Colombian company in the floriculture sector using the Ergonomic Maturity Model (EMM), a macroergonomic tool. The evaluation was conducted in three stages: (1) preparation, (2) evaluation, and (3) improvement plan. An ergonomist conducted this process with the participation of five managers and 61 operational workers of the company. Several EMM tools were used to assist the evaluation process: evaluation matrix, weighting questionnaire, and a detailed questionnaire. As a result, the company was classified at the lowest maturity level (Level 1: Ignorance). Further, the maturity assessment results showed how managers and workers have different opinions and expectations about the development and application of ergonomics. We hope that the organization's discussions generated during the evaluation process will allow ergonomics to be gradually integrated into its processes.

Keywords: Ergonomic assessment · Ergonomic maturity model · Organizational ergonomics · Systems ergonomics

1 Introduction

For several decades, it has been proposed that to increase the impact of ergonomics in organizations, actions should be taken from a systemic perspective [1, 2]. Although this message has been gaining ground in academia and among ergonomics professionals, its actual application in the business sector is currently limited. In this sense, we believe that an important step to change this situation is to carry out macroergonomic assessments. This step will allow us to identify which aspects of the organization should be intervened, to integrate ergonomics into the production and service processes.

The integration of macroergonomic principles in the design and redesign of work systems has been gradually proliferating [3]. In our opinion, one factor that has driven this proliferation is the need for organizations to add value to their processes through

N. L. Black et al. (Eds.): IEA 2021, LNNS 219, pp. 762–766, 2021.
https://doi.org/10.1007/978-3-030-74602-5_103

ergonomics, which has been limited when only the traditional ergonomic approach, focused on the physical factors of the workplace, is used.

The company under study, which belongs to Colombia's floriculture sector, health, safety, and productivity problems have arisen. However, these problems have not been addressed from a macroergonomics perspective. Therefore, a macroergonomic study would allow the company to identify some improvement actions that could be taken to solve its organizational problems.

The purpose of this study is to evaluate the ergonomic maturity level of a Colombian company in the floriculture sector using the Ergonomic Maturity Model (EMM) [4, 5].

2   Methods

2.1   Ergonomic Maturity Model EMM

The EMM is a macroergonomic tool that allows companies to evaluate their capacity to introduce, apply, and develop ergonomics [4, 5]. Companies are classified into five gradual levels of maturity: (1) Ignorance, (2) Understanding, (3) Experimentation, (4) Regular use, and (5) Innovation.

For assessing the company maturity level, four macro factors operationalized in 12 factors are evaluated: (1) culture (acceptance and teamwork), (2) integration (strategic alignment, management, commitment, and resources), (3) performers (knowledge and skills, person in charge, compensation) and (4) surveillance (indicators, information systems, risk assessment) [4]. The maturity level of the company is the lowest level of maturity obtained among all the factors.

To assess the company's maturity, the EMM has tools that can be used at different moments during the assessment. The evaluation matrix [4] is the principal tool and represents the EMM. Through a description of each EMM factor's behavior, the matrix allows the company's level of maturity to be identified. It also allows the company to identify what actions to take to reach a higher ergonomics maturity level. The weighting questionnaire is another EMM tool that is recommended to identify the importance that the company attributes to the model's factors. Using a scale of 0–100%, respondents attribute a percentage of importance to each factor. The information collected can identify those factors within the company that could contribute to ergonomics development. Optionally, a detailed questionnaire can be designed to obtain more precise information on the company's maturity. It is recommended that the detailed questionnaire be designed by ergonomics experts in collaboration with the company's work team. It is recommended that the questions be short and respond to the behavior described for each factor in the EMM evaluation matrix.

2.2   Assessment Process with EMM

Sixty-one workers participated voluntarily in the maturity assessment, which was carried out in three stages.

Stage 1: Preparation. The evaluation process was explained to the company, highlighting the benefits that would be obtained. Meetings and training were held with managers, supervisors, and workers.

Stage 2: Evaluation. Maturity assessment was performed using three EMM support tools [4]: evaluation matrix, model factor weighting questionnaire, and detailed assessment questionnaire. In the first instance, the answers were collected individually. Later, the answers were discussed and consensual.

Stage 3: Improvement plan. A plan was developed focusing on the improvement of critical factors (lower level of maturity). The company's strengths and barriers concerning ergonomics were identified.

3   Results

The company was classified in maturity level 1 (Ignorance). This maturity level is due to the general lack of knowledge in the company about ergonomics and its application. For this reason, ergonomics is not considered a solution to the health, safety, and productivity problems existing in the company.

Figure 1 shows the maturity assessment results obtained with the EMM assessment matrix and the detailed questionnaire designed.

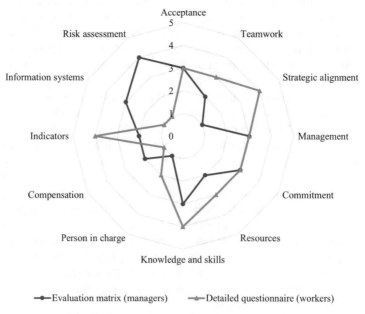

Fig. 1. Ergonomics maturity assessment results.

The evaluation matrix and the weighting questionnaire were applied to five company's top management. According to the evaluation matrix, the managers considered company level 1 of maturity (Ignorance). According to the weighting questionnaire, the most important factors were risk assessment and acceptance, while the strategic alignment and person in charge factors were the least important. The weighting questionnaire results are consistent with the maturity levels given to these factors by the company's managers using the evaluation matrix. When analyzing by factors, we can see that strategic alignment and person in charge were the factors to which management attributed the lowest maturity levels (see Fig. 1).

For a more detailed evaluation, a 52-question questionnaire was developed and applied to 61 workers. According to these workers' opinion, the level of maturity in ergonomics for the company was also 1 (Ignorance). According to the workers, the most critical factors to raise the company's maturity level were compensation, information systems, and risk assessment (see Fig. 1).

These results show how organizational stakeholders have different evaluations and perceptions about the degree of introduction and application of ergonomics. In this sense, the authors suggest that the evaluation groups be composed of representatives of workers at all organizational levels.

4   Discussion

In the company studied, the managers are not clear about the role of the ergonomist, they dedicate few resources to ergonomics projects, and they do not know how ergonomics can help fulfill the organization's strategic objectives. For this reason, the improvement plan was oriented towards the creation of an ergonomic culture. Workshops and training were proposed, focused on showing how ergonomics can generate value in organizational terms. The introduction of participatory techniques where workers are involved will be another crucial success factor in developing practical solutions.

In this case study, differences in opinions on ergonomics maturity between managers and workers were visible. The factors *risk assessment*, *information systems*, *indicators*, and *strategic alignment*, caused most opinion differences. Conducting pre-assessment training and including workers from all organizational levels in the assessment team and among the respondents can help in the consensus of the maturity assessment results.

Finally, it is worth mentioning that similar results to those obtained in this research have been reported in other sectors in the Colombian context [5].

5   Conclusions

The ergonomic maturity assessment provided a global vision of the company's current situation in terms of ergonomics. During the assessment process, the discussions generated new ideas to improve working conditions, initiating a transformation process within the organization. This research's systemic approach to address ergonomics can serve as a reference to extend the ergonomics profession's current scope in the Colombian context.

References

1. Hendrick, H.W., Kleiner, B.: Macroergonomics: Theory, Methods, and Applications, 1st edn. CRC Press, Boca Raton (2002)
2. Hendrick, H.W.: Macroergonomics: A Better Approach to Work System Design (2002)
3. Holden, R.J., Or, C.K.L., Alper, S.J., Joy Rivera, A., Karsh, B.-T.: A change management framework for macroergonomic field research. Appl. Ergon. **39**, 459–474 (2008)

4. Rodríguez, Y., Pérez, E.: Ergonomic maturity model: a practical macroergonomic tool. In: Bagnara, S., Tartaglia, R., Albolino, S., Alexander, T., Fujita, Y. (eds.) Proceedings of the 20th Congress of the International Ergonomics Association (IEA 2018), pp. 173–185. Springer, Cham (2019)
5. Rodríguez, Y., Pérez, E.: Diagnóstico macroergonómico de organizaciones colombianas con el Modelo de madurez de Ergonomía. Ciencias de la Salud **14**, 11–25 (2016)

Exploring the Impact of COVID-19 on Nurse Workload and Quality of Care via Computerized Simulation

Sadeem M. Qureshi[1]([✉]) [ID], Sue Bookey-Bassett[2] [ID], Nancy Purdy[2] [ID],
Michael A. Greig[1] [ID], Helen Kelly[3] [ID], Anne Vandeursen[3],
and W. Patrick Neumann[1] [ID]

[1] Human Factors Engineering Lab, Ryerson University, Toronto, ON M5B 2K3, Canada
s1qureshi@Ryerson.ca
[2] Daphne Cockwell School of Nursing, Ryerson University, Toronto, ON M5B 2K3, Canada
[3] University Health Network, Toronto, ON M5G 2C4, Canada

Abstract. COVID-19 is taking a significant toll on front-line healthcare professionals - especially nurses who provide care for patients 24/7. Given the trend for higher acuity levels among the COVID-19 patients and increased infection prevention and control (IPAC) precautions, such as donning and doffing personal protective equipment (PPE), the demands on front-line healthcare professionals have changed. To understand the changes, discrete event simulation (DES) was used to quantify the effects of varying COVID-19 policies on nurse workload and quality of care. We are testing a standard nurse-patient ratio of 1:5 where we vary the number of COVID-19 positive patients in that mix from 1 to 5. Preliminary modeling results show as nurses were assigned to more COVID-19 positive patients, the workload of nurses increased, and quality of care deteriorated. In comparison to the baseline (pre-pandemic) case, distance walked by simulant-nurse, mental workload, direct care time, missed care, missed care delivery time and care task waiting time, increased by up to 40%, 279%, -27%, 132%, 311% and 44%, respectively. The developed approach has implications for design of the healthcare system as a whole, including pandemic planning scenarios.

Keywords: Discrete event simulation · Healthcare ergonomics · Organizational design · Pandemic management

1 Introduction

1.1 Problem Statement

Healthcare professionals (HCP) are under tremendous stress and threat from COVID-19 [1]. This pandemic creates an enormous workload for an already overworked HCP population [2]. There is an increase in the volume of patients with severe illness, staff and equipment shortages and additional infection control practices resulting in long working hours [3]. There are currently no approaches to understand and quantify the

N. L. Black et al. (Eds.): IEA 2021, LNNS 219, pp. 767–772, 2021.
https://doi.org/10.1007/978-3-030-74602-5_104

workload of HCPs under pandemic outbreak scenarios such as COVID-19. Therefore, a tool is needed to test combinations of organizational design and staffing policies, such as attending to COVID-19 patients and COVID-19 care delivery routines, to determine the impact of these decisions on nurse workload and quality of care – Discrete Event Simulation (DES) is a potential solution.

1.2 Process Simulation in Healthcare

DES is an operations research tool that can be used to simulate the process of care delivery for nurses on a task-by-task basis [4]. It is used to assess and predict the efficiency of a proposed or an existing system [5]. DES has been effectively used for the analysis of system design alternatives and business modeling. It is a widely used tool in manufacturing and service industries to examine emergent behaviors [6–8]. Current approaches such as real-life trial and error, force workers to be exposed to untested work environments that can be hazardous to worker health and expensive to implement. DES is a tool that can virtually assess the effects of technical design and policy changes on the performance and outcomes of the system in question.

In healthcare, DES has been widely used to model patient flow for improving scheduling of patient admissions to improve patient throughput and minimize patient wait time, modelling operations in the perianesthesia units, emergency department, pharmacies, operating room scheduling, [9–12]. However, these studies have generally been limited to modelling from the perspective of a patient. Where, a patient is modelled in a fashion similar to modelling product flows in production systems. There is a scarcity of research focusing on nurse workload and care quality, despite the fact that nurses deliver 75% of the care in hospital settings [13] with the exception of Qureshi et al. [14]. They reported the creation and demonstration of a nurse-focused simulation approach by exploring the effect of nurse-patient ratios and patient acuity, on indicators of nurse workload and care quality. Qureshi [15] validated this approach by adapting this approach to a medical-surgical unit. The modeling results compared favorable to real-world outcomes. This research builds on this approach by making use of a validated modeling approach to examine the pandemic scenario workloads.

1.3 Research Question

The primary aim of this study is to develop a tool that can proactively test and quantify the implications for nurse workload and care quality parameters under varying pandemic scenarios in an acute care hospital unit. To address this aim, we ask the research question: How can acute care nurses operating under COVID-19 pandemic scenarios be modelled using Discrete Event Simulation (DES) to quantify the possible impacts on nurse workload and quality of care?

2 Methods

The demonstrator model was created using Rockwell Arena, a DES environment software. The demonstrator model simulates the working environment of nurses and the patient care delivery activities and quantifies the effects of changing technical design factors on nurse workload and care quality.

2.1 Model Inputs

Inputs to the model include: historical patient care data, nurse walking patterns, operational logic, unit layout and COVID-19 specific tasks. These are further explained below.

i) Historical patient care data was obtained as part of workload management report from an acute care hospital unit; *ii) Nurse walking patterns* and *iii) Operational logic,* both were created via multiple focus group sessions with experienced nurses (n = 29); *iv) Unit layout,* obtained by physically measuring the entire unit using Bosch (GLM 100); and *v) COVID-19 specific tasks* such as donning and doffing PPE.

2.2 Model Outputs

The model provided quantifiable outcomes of nurse workload and quality of care. Indicators of nurse workload for a simulated work shift included: *i) mental workload,* the stack of care tasks that need to be performed by the nurse; *ii) distance walked by nurse; and iii) direct care time.* Quality of care was quantified in terms of *i) missed care,* the number of care tasks not finished before the end of the shift; ii*) missed care delivery time* entails the time required to deliver the missed care. This is done by either the present nurse who has to work overtime or this burden falls on the next nurse. *iii) Care task waiting time,* the average waiting time before a care task is performed.

2.3 Experimental Design

The DES model tests the impact of the following conditions on nurse workload and quality of care*: COVID-19 patient assignment* entails the number of COVID19 positive, and COVID-19 negative patients assigned to one nurse. As illustrated in Table 1, we are testing a standard nurse-patient ratio of 1:5 where we vary the number of COVID-positive patients in that mix from 1 to 5. Where, the baseline condition is the pre-pandemic condition with zero COID-19 positive patients.

Table 1. The Experimental Design. Where, one nurse was assigned to a specific set of COVID-19 negative and COVID-19 positive patients.

Trial	COVID-19 negative patients	COVID-19 positive patients
Baseline (Pre-pandemic condition)	5	0
1	4	1
2	3	2
3	2	3
4	1	4
5	0	5

3   Results

A nurse focused DES modelling approach has been developed that demonstrates the ability to assess the impact of changing nurse-patient ratio and patient acuity on nurse workload and care quality. Preliminary results show an *increase* in nurse workload and a decrease in quality of care when nurses were providing care for COVID-19 positive patients. Where, the simulant-nurse walked a range of 7.9 to 11 km while carrying a mental workload of 15 to 57 tasks waiting to be performed. As a result, care tasks had an average wait time of 1 to 1.4 h. Due to this increased workload, 26 to 60 care tasks could not be completed before the end of the shift. Due to this excessive demand, a missed care delivery time of 2.3 to 8 h were recorded. In comparison to pre-pandemic (baseline) condition, +40% increase in distance walked by the simulant-nurse, +279% increase in mental workload, -27% decrease in direct care time, +132% increase in missed care, +311% in missed care delivery time and +44% increase in care task waiting time, were observed.

4   Discussion

Organizational design and healthcare policies dictate the workload of the human in the system, in this case, nurses, which impacts the quality of care. The developed simulation model integrated COVID-19 organizational policies and design in a 'virtual' environment to provide quantifiable impact on nurse workload and quality of care. The simulation model illustrated that attending to COVID-19 positive patients resulted in additional workload. The more COVID-19 positive patients assigned to the nurse, the greater the workload. A "tipping" point was observed for all indicators of workload and quality of care when the simulant-nurse was assigned to 4 or more COVID-19 positive patients. The model successfully provided evidence that nurses cannot manage the workload arising from the current organizational demands. Due to increased walking, direct care time decreased down by −27%. This increase missed care by up to +132% and the time required to deliver that care ranged from 2.3 to 8 h. Being unable to deliver timely care not only deteriorates quality of care but also employee morale [16, 17]. The consciousness of losing lives impacts the mental capability of nurses [18]. The model provides quantifiable evidence that the root-cause for this may be increased work demands.

These simulation models can be used as potential 'engines' in decision-making [19], that can help *administrators* understand and predict the impact of design decisions in terms of nurse workload and thereby the quality of care. *Policy makers* to test consequences of policy tradeoffs and technical design. Without specific quantitative models of the extra demands of pandemic care routines, healthcare system managers are essentially "flying blind". The developed modelling approach will help managers understand the implications of different scenarios on their staff – and hence on the system as a whole – in a range of possible pandemic scenarios. This research has implications for the design of the healthcare system as a whole, including pandemic planning scenarios. Furthermore, this research illuminates and quantifies the workload issues experienced by nurses on the COVID-19 front lines. While preliminary results are promising, a field validation study is currently underway to affirm the accuracy of this modelling approach.

5   Conclusion

Preliminary results suggest an increase in nurse workload and decreased quality of care, as nurses' patient assignments include an increasing number of COVID-positive patients. Further model development and validation are currently in-progress.

References

1. Canadian Federation of Nurses Unions: Nurses launch investigation into Canada's failure to protect health care workers from COVID-19 (2020)
2. Haas, S., Ann Swan, B., Jessie, T.A.: The impact of the coronavirus pandemic on the global nursing workforce. Nurs. Econ. **38**, 231–237 (2020)
3. Beckman, B.P.: COVID-19: never seen anything like this ever! J. Nurs. Adm. **50**, 3–7 (2020)
4. Qureshi, S.M., Purdy, N., Mohani, A., Neumann, W.P.: Predicting the effect of nurse–patient ratio on nurse workload and care quality using discrete event simulation. J. Nurs. Manag. **27**, 971–980 (2019)
5. Jun, J.B., Jacobson, S.H., Swisher, J.R.: Application of discrete-event simulation in health care clinics: a survey. J. Oper. Res. Soc. **50**, 109–123 (1999)
6. Dode, P.(Pete), Greig, M., Zolfaghari, S., Neumann, W.P.: Integrating human factors into discrete event simulation: a proactive approach to simultaneously design for system performance and employees' well being. Int. J. Prod. Res. **54**, 3105 (2016)
7. Greasley, A., Owen, C.: Modelling people's behaviour using discrete-event simulation: a review. Int. J. Oper. Prod. Manag. (2018). https://doi.org/10.1108/IJOPM-10-2016-0604
8. Perez, J., de Looze, M.P., Bosch, T., Neumann, W.P.: Discrete event simulation as an ergonomic tool to predict workload exposures during systems design. Int. J. Ind. Ergon. **44**, 298–306 (2014)
9. Lambton, J., Roeder, T., Saltzman, R., Param, L., Fernandes, R.: Using simulation to model improvements in pediatric bed placement in an acute care hospital. J. Nurs. Adm. **47**, 88–93 (2017)
10. Siddiqui, S., Morse, E., Levin, S.: Evaluating nurse staffing levels in perianesthesia care units using discrete event simulation. IISE Trans. Healthc. Syst. Eng. **7**, 215–223 (2017)
11. Swisher, J.R., Jacobson, S.H.: Evaluating the design of a family practice healthcare clinic using discrete-event simulation. Health Care Manag. Sci. **5**, 75–88 (2002)
12. Kovalchuk, S.V., Funkner, A.A., Metsker, O.G., Yakovlev, A.N.: Simulation of patient flow in multiple healthcare units using process and data mining techniques for model identification. J. Biomed. Inform. **82**, 128–142 (2018)
13. Nursing Task Force: GoodNursing, GoodHealth : An Investment for the 21st Century. Minist. Heal. Long-TermCare, Ontario, Canada (1999)
14. Qureshi, S.M., Purdy, N., Neumann, W.P.: Development of a methodology for healthcare system simulations to quantify nurse workload and quality of care. IISE Trans. Occup. Ergon. Hum. Factors **8**, 27–41 (2020)
15. Qureshi, S.M.: Developing an approach to quantify nurse workload and quality of care using discrete event simulation. Ryerson University, Canada (2020)
16. Konrad, R., et al.: Modeling the impact of changing patient flow processes in an emergency department: Insights from a computer simulation study. Oper. Res. Heal. Care **2**, 66–74 (2013)
17. Davey, M.M., Cummings, G., Newburn-Cook, C.V., Lo, E.A.: Predictors of nurse absenteeism in hospitals: a systematic review. J. Nurs. Manag. **17**, 312–330 (2009)

18. Yin, Q., et al.: Posttraumatic stress symptoms of health care workers during the corona virus disease 2019. Clin. Psychol. Psychother. **27**, 384–395 (2020)
19. Qureshi, SM., Purdy, N., Neumann, W.P.: A computerized model quantifying the impact of geographical patient- bed assignment on nurse workload and quality care. Nurs. Econ. **39**(1), 23–35 (2021)

When Design is Inspired by Theatre: Acting Techniques as Prospective Design Methods

Jacynthe Roberge[1](✉), Isabelle Sperano[2], Leigh Rivenbark[2], and Daniel Caja Rubio[1]

[1] Université Laval, Québec, Canada
`jacynthe.roberge@design.ulaval.ca`
[2] MacEwan University, Edmonton, Canada

Abstract. In acting training, psychophysical exercises are used to strengthen the relationship between mind and body, thus fostering a deeper understanding of the character [1]. Intrigued and inspired by the potential value of these techniques in design contexts, we explored their application for interaction designers as research methods in a pedagogical setting. To do so, we first created a single-session workshop that introduced design students to basic actor movement techniques in the winter of 2019. The goal of the workshop was to help students empathize with their users and discover solutions when designing digital products. Later, in the fall of 2020, we used reflections from the first activity to develop two longer workshops; both consisted of three sessions and were carried out consecutively in two different universities. In this article, we present a case study of those three workshops. After discussing considerations for the evolution of the workshops, we describe how each was conducted. Finally, we share our findings and insights that arose throughout the process.

Keywords: Interaction design · Acting techniques · Prospective ergonomics · Design methods

1 Introduction

Over the last decade, interaction designers have been creating an increasing number of new digital products that people can interact with at all times and in all places [1]. Creating useful innovative digital products for such varied contexts requires a deep understanding of human characteristics relevant to design, such as users' anthropometrics, behavioural aspects, cognition and social factors [2]. To do so, interaction designers have at their disposal a multitude of user research methods [3–5]. Most of these methods originate from the social sciences, more specifically from disciplines such as cognitive psychology, sociology and anthropology [6, 7]. Due to their disciplinary and academic origins, several of these methods lead the designer to base their understanding of the user on an intellectual construct. Although essential, this cerebral approach only allows limited access to the knowledge derived from the human body, and leads to creating a valuable but incomplete depiction of the user.

In acting training, psychophysical exercises are used precisely to strengthen the relationship between mind and body, thus fostering a deeper understanding of the character

N. L. Black et al. (Eds.): IEA 2021, LNNS 219, pp. 773–780, 2021.
https://doi.org/10.1007/978-3-030-74602-5_105

[1]. Engaging the body helps actors gain insights about a given character; insights they may not have gotten from a purely intellectual analysis. Intrigued and inspired by the potential value of these techniques for prospective design contexts, we explored their application for designers in interaction design courses.

This case study is based on workshops conducted in academic settings. A first version of this workshop was conducted in winter 2019, while the second and third versions were conducted consecutively in fall 2020. We adopted an iterative process so the results from the winter 2019 workshop informed how the fall 2020 workshops were conducted.

2   Research Goals and Questions

By adapting and using these acting techniques for a design context, we wished to examine first the **acceptability** of these acting techniques to designers. Were designers ready to step out of their comfort zone and fully engage in playing a role? Would they easily integrate these techniques into their current design project? Then, we were interested in investigating the **feasibility** of this approach. Were designers able to get intuitive insights about a user by applying acting techniques? Would the exercises used by actors to empathize with their characters also help designers do the same? Finally, we were interested in reflecting on the **relevance** of these activities in the design process. Would they reveal useful information to designers? Would it allow designers to enrich their understanding of the user and their context? Would it help them develop empathy for the user?

3   Workshop Version 1

3.1   Context

The first version of the workshop (Winter 2019) was conducted in an interaction design class with undergraduate design students (n = 12). The two-hour session was led by one interaction design and one acting professor, and took place in a theatre studio. Prior to the workshop, the students had designed a product in the form of a rudimentary physical prototype as part of the "develop" phase of the design process (see Fig. 1). The workshop was divided into three parts: Observe & Analyze, Embody, and Improvise. During each segment, students explored various acting exercises to help them engage with their products as if they were potential users.

3.2   Debrief and Reflection

The feedback we received from the student indicated that most of them could see where these techniques could prove useful when developing digital products and suggested potential future applications for design practitioners. While the workshop had positive outcomes, we identified various areas for improvement. First, we realized that a single two-hour session was too long and in-depth for design students; it did not feel well integrated in their design process. We discovered that the two stages (Observe & Analyze and Embody) should be expanded to provide more time for deeper learning, but that the third one (Improvise) should be removed as the necessary skills to improvise at a high enough level were too advanced for most of the design students. Also, it did not seem clear to some students how to concretely use the acting techniques in their project, possibly because some of the insights gained were unrelated to their projects at hand, and the analysis questions were not targeted enough. It is also possible that the workshop was presented too late in the project, so students were not able to fully incorporate the method in their design process.

4   Workshop Versions 2 and 3

4.1   Context

The second version of the workshop was held in fall 2020, and conducted in two interaction design classes at two Canadian universities. Participants of the second version of the workshop were graduate students (n = 22) while participants of the third version of the workshop were fourth-year undergraduate students (n = 11). Students in both classes had started their projects but were at a very early stage of the design process, namely the "discover" phase (Fig. 1). At this point, students received the design brief and started conducting user research.

The design problem was still ill-defined and they had no clear idea about the product or service they were going to build. By introducing acting techniques in the first design phase, we wanted to empower the students to benefit from these tools early in the process and apply them independently in subsequent phases (e.g., designing a persona or prototyping an experiment).

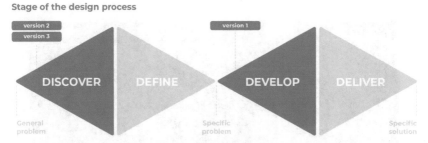

Fig. 1. Double diamond model (adapted from the UK Design Council) (Design Council. (2015). *The Design Process: What is the Double Diamond?* Design Council. https://www.designcouncil. org.uk/news-opinion/design-process-what-double-diamond.)

The second and third versions of the workshop were divided into three sessions that took place over three consecutive weeks. Acting assignments were given between the sessions in order to reduce the effects of the time gap between sessions and to encourage students to integrate these acting techniques into their design research process. All three sessions were led by an acting professor in collaboration with a design professor. After each session, each professor involved in the exercise completed an observation sheet in which they noted their thoughts and comments about the activities that were carried out. In the second version of the workshop, a second design professor took part in the sessions as a participant and filled a self-assessment questionnaire. Due to the particular context of the COVID-19 pandemic, all workshop sessions were held online.

Session 1: Observe and Analyze. The goals of the first session were to introduce design students to character movement, one of the main areas of acting training [8], and to provide them with tools to help develop the observation skills necessary to grasp the intricacies of someone's posture and movement. This introductory session lasted 75 min and consisted of lectures interspersed by practical exercises. During the session, the students explored three key concepts: psychophysical connection, observation, and movement analysis.

Psychophysical Connection. Character movement is a core component of acting training. In this area of study, students learn how to create the physicality of a character using various techniques. Character Movement is based on a concept called psychophysical connection [1], which proposes an interrelationship between mind (psycho) and body (physical). A person's psychology affects their physicality, and their physicality affects their psychology. In other words, what's inside affects the outside and vice versa. There are thus two main ways of approaching acting work: from the head and from the body.

After we introduced this fundamental concept, the students put it into practice by performing two psychophysical exercises. To help the students experience how emotions manifest themselves in the body, we asked them to work from the inside out, and create the physicality of someone who is depressed (Fig. 2a), shy (Fig. 2b), confident (Fig. 2c), etc. Next, we asked the students to take an outside-in approach, and stand in a physical pose associated with a specific emotion (e.g., high-power pose and low-power pose) and describe how it made them feel.

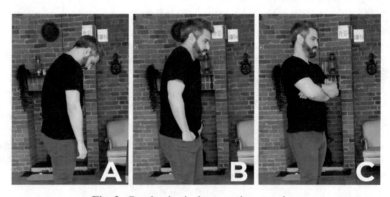

Fig. 2. Psychophysical connection exercises

Observation. An important step in acting training is the honing of observation skills [9]. To create an authentic character, the actor must first be able to accurately see the minutiae of human behaviour. Since observation is an essential skill that is developed through practice, acting students perform various exercises to become better "investigators of the ordinary" [10]. After a brief discussion about the importance of observation in acting training, students engaged in a series of warm-up games intended to sharpen their skills in this area.

Movement Analysis. Actor movement training involves a detailed study of posture and movement habits. This training helps the actor analyze and imitate the physicality of another person [11]. After an introductory lecture on movement analysis, the students examined their personal posture and movement habits. Using this analytical framework, they investigated the relationship between their physicality (posture and movement) and their psychology (emotions and thoughts). The students then shared their insights with a partner and participated in a debriefing about the exercise with the group.

To conclude this first session, we gave the students a homework assignment to analyze a user's posture and movement habits. They were also asked to include it in their design project as an additional user research method.

Session 2: Embody. The second session focused on a single central theme: character embodiment. The goal of this 75-min workshop was to introduce designers to the theory, and to practise character embodiment.

Actors often use embodying techniques to create believable characters. These techniques include imitating strangers, photographs, paintings, and even animals [12, 13]. Recent neuroscience research suggests that this kind of gestural mimicry, even at a subtle level, "has an impact on brain areas involved in self-processing [which] supports the contention of acting theorists that gestural and psychological approaches might be related paths towards achieving the same goal, namely the embodied portrayal of a character. It also lends support to theories of embodied cognition, which argue that a change in gestural expression can influence the way that people think and the emotions that they feel" [14]. Following this thought, we hypothesized that designers could also benefit from using gestural techniques to both develop empathy for a user and improve their acting skills in roleplaying and bodystorming work.

To help establish a footing for more complex embodying techniques, an acting professor led students through a series of basic warm-up exercises (Fig. 3). Students were then asked to apply their completed user movement analysis homework by embodying their user's personal movement habits. After moving like their user, the students answered a short series of questions in character to gain insights into their user's physical and psychological characteristics.

Fig. 3. "The Mirror Game" used as warm-up exercises

This second session's homework assignment was adapted from an exercise called "Emulating a Walk" from *Movement Training for Actors* by Jackie Snow [8]. As the name suggests, students had to watch their user at a safe and respectful distance, analyze their movement habits, and then move like this person for 15 min. Additionally, they were to reflect on insights they gained about their user by moving like them, and explore how they might apply these discoveries in the design process.

Session 3: Workshop Debriefing. During Session 3, we conducted a group debriefing in which design students exchanged views about their workshop experience of the last three weeks. This third session lasted about 30 min. No additional content (theoretical or practical) was presented during this meeting. The two main goals of this last session were to first find out if students had managed to integrate this method into their current design project and, if so, find out which facets of the method had been the most useful in their design process—we also discussed the types of insights gained with these techniques—and second, gauge the students' appreciation for and interest in using embodied acting techniques to collect data in design research. To do so, we asked specific questions regarding feasibility, acceptability (by designers), and relevance.

4.2   Reflection and Discussion

Observe and Analyze. During the exercises performed, the majority of students experienced the concept of psychophysical connection and thus understood that a person's body is a source of information about their state of mind and vice versa[1]. For them, this opened a door to a different way of accessing user knowledge[2].

Embody. While most students found the embodying exercises more challenging than their usual design activities, many commented on their usefulness and relevance, and on their potential outcome for their project[2]. By imitating (physically acting out) their users, most students discovered intuitive information about their psychological states[1]. Most students also considered using these techniques as an additional tool to get inside their users' heads, and foster a more holistic understanding of them. It is interesting to note that these techniques resulted in the most substantial insights when the users' characteristics (e.g., age, physical and mental abilities) were very different from those of the designers (See footnote 1).

Integration in the Design Process. The activities carried out during the workshop didn't have the same impact on both groups (second and third versions) regarding how students integrated the workshop outcome in their design process. Although both workshop versions were conducted at the same stage of the design process, there were two main differences. In the second version of the workshop, students had as yet no clear idea of their targeted users, but in the third version of the workshop, students knew precisely who they were designing for. Also, the homework assignments were optional in the second version of the workshop, but mandatory in its third version. These differences had a major impact on how the techniques were used by the students in their projects. Indeed, in the second version, students experienced the workshop as a novel learning experience, which was abstract and more detached from their project (See footnote 3).

---

[1] In accordance with our research goals and questions regarding **feasibility**.

[2] In accordance with our research goals and questions regarding **relevance**.

As for the third version of the workshop, these sessions acted like "seeds" planted at the beginning of a project that allowed the designers to gradually perceive the user in a richer way as the project progressed. Most of the students who participated in the third version reused the knowledge acquired during the workshop in the subsequent stages of their design project (e.g., while designing personas and carrying out user testing, creating videos of themselves, acting as their users, to use the product they designed)[3].

Overall, design students appreciated the creative and practical nature of the proposed method. It gave them a certain amount of freedom that they do not usually find in conventional research methods (See footnote 2).

Online Delivery: Benefits and Challenges. Online delivery made some of the techniques more difficult to teach, especially the embodying techniques. However, students encountered some benefits with online delivery that we did not foresee. During the online sessions (workshop versions 2 and 3), some felt more comfortable than during the face-to-face sessions (workshop version 1). They enjoyed being alone behind their screens, with the possibility of turning off their camera to do the exercises free from self-consciousness. While actors need to play their characters in front of an audience, designers don't need to develop this skill; for the latter, the endgame is knowledge, rather than performance. It is important to take this distinction into account between designers and actors in this type of workshop (See footnote 1 and 2).

In a future version of this workshop, we envision designers observing and embodying more than one user (as they would usually do with other methods). Also, these acting techniques should be used in conjunction with other design research methods to allow triangulation with other data in order to provide a more complete understanding of the user.

5 Conclusion

While these workshops were conducted in only a few classes, we think these embodied acting techniques could benefit ergonomics and design education. This may be especially true for prospective ergonomics, which looks for new methods of anticipating future needs and triggering responses to them. We believe teaching students fresh ways to observe, analyze and imitate their users compliments traditional head-centred design research methods by offering valuable body-based insights, thus providing a more holistic view of the user.

Acknowledgment. This conference proceeding would not have been possible without the collaboration of the students who took part in the different versions of our workshop. We thank the students from the Design Bachelor's degree at MacEwan University who took the workshop in winter 2019 as well as those who took it in fall 2020 (version 3). We also thank the students from the *maîtrise en design d'interaction* at Laval University School of Design who took the workshop in fall 2020.

---

[3] In accordance with our research goals and questions regarding **acceptability.**

References

1. Chekhov, M.: To the Actor: On the Technique of Acting. Martino Fine Books, Eastford (2014)
2. Ritter, F.E., Baxter, G.D., Churchill, E.F.: Foundations for Designing User-Centered Systems. Springer, London (2014)
3. Kumar, V.: 101 Design Methods: A Structured Approach for Driving Innovation in Your Organization. Wiley, Hoboken (2013)
4. Curedale, R.: Design research methods: 150 ways to inform design. Design Community College, Topanga (2013)
5. Martin, B., Hanington, B.: Universal Methods of Design. Rockport, Beverly (2012)
6. Randall, D., Harper, R., Rouncefield, M.: Fieldwork for Design. Springer, Cambridge (2007)
7. Clarke, A.J.: Design Anthropology: Object Culture in the 21st Century. Springer, Vienna (2011)
8. Snow, J.: Movement Training for Actors. Bloomsbury, London (2013)
9. Hagen, U.: Respect for Acting, 2nd edn. Wiley, Hoboken (2008)
10. Horowitz, A.: On Looking: A Walker's Guide to the Art of Observation. Scribner, New York (2014)
11. Adrian, B., Chelsea, C.: Actor Training the Laban Way: An Integrated Approach to Voice, Speech, and Movement, 1st edn. Allworth, New York (2008)
12. Clark, H.: The Silence of the Lambs great scene—Clarice & Hannibal's last meeting [Video] (2016). https://www.youtube.com/watch?v=2LrFsXAvzqc
13. SheenMachine. Inside The Actors Studio with Jim Carrey [Video]. Dailymotion (2015). https://www.dailymotion.com/video/x3d2umt
14. Brown, S., Cockett, P., Yuan, Y.: The neuroscience of Romeo and Juliet: an fMRI study of acting. Royal Society Open Sci. **6**(3), 1–20 (2019)

Capturing Future Trends in Customer Needs for the Design of Next-Generation Gas Station Services

Joao Gabriel Alves Ribeiro Rosa[✉], Fabiano Armellini, and Jean-Marc Robert

Polytechnique Montréal, Montréal QC, Canada
{joao-gabriel.alves-ribeiro-rosa,fabiano.armellini,
jean-marc.robert}@polymtl.ca

Abstract. This paper presents the data collection approach that was followed in the initial phase of a Prospective Ergonomics project on the design of future service stations in North America. The data collection involved different stakeholders and consisted of a review of technical documents, field observations, task analyses, and PESTEL analyses. Results show some statistics on the evolution of energy sources for vehicles and on the diversity of services offered at gas stations in Canada. They also highlight some political, social, and technological trends to consider when developing design scenarios for future service stations.

Keywords: Prospective ergonomics · New product development · Methods · Future gas station

1 Introduction

Design disciplines interested in the future seek to anticipate upcoming changes which are likely to be at the origin of future user needs and expectations, and determine the success of future products, services and processes. Prospecting and foresight have been repeatedly employed in New Product Development (NPD) to capture forthcoming trends for customer needs, technology capabilities, and society's evolution. Their results often lead to the construction of scenarios which have proven to be essential to support decision-making. These scenarios mobilize the imagination about the future through the identification and integration of variables and the construction of hypotheses that have a high probability of impact, be it positive or negative [1]. Nevertheless, forecasting and scenario building are a challenging task since they require a constant search for rich, reliable, and recent information from different sources. In addition, taking into account the ecosystem of the artefact to come is complex because it is broad, multifaceted, and with ill-defined boundaries [2].

The new branch of Prospective Ergonomics (PE), which is about the design of future things, promises to be useful in our project about the future. It concerns the detection and definition of current and future needs in order to design future products, services, processes or systems that will fulfill these needs [3]. It focuses on all aspects

N. L. Black et al. (Eds.): IEA 2021, LNNS 219, pp. 781–787, 2021.
https://doi.org/10.1007/978-3-030-74602-5_106

of ergonomics/human factors (e.g., performance, security, accessibility, emotions, satisfaction, user experience, aesthetics), follows a user-centered design approach, and puts emphasis on the development of prototypes for simulation and tests with different stakeholders [4]. Because PE is recent, case studies are still needed to show the approaches and methods in use, and the results obtained in real contexts.

This paper presents the data collection approach that was followed in the initial phase of a PE project on the design of future gas stations in North America. It is part of an ongoing research project whose objectives are twofold: provide empirical evidence on a PE field project with its approach, methods, and results, and help designers in their decisions for the design of future service stations. These stations are likely to undergo major changes in the coming years due to the environmental movement, the changes of energy sources in transportation, and the consumption trends of young generations. Furthermore, this multimillion-dollar business which is looking to have long-lasting facilities (40, 50, 75 yrs), and is facing high costs of construction and operations and tough competition in the market, seems aware of the importance of doing good design for the future. For this project, we are discussing with experts of different disciplines (engineering, design, human factors/ergonomics, computer science, management) and working in collaboration with a company in the oil industry which operates a network of service stations across Canada. Together, we aim at defining the foundations of service stations for the next 30 yrs.

2 Methodology

The methodology used for this project comes from two main disciplines: NPD and PE. It consisted of the following activities:

1) *Review of technical documents.* We reviewed various documents from government authorities (e.g., Ministry of Transport, control agencies) to know the safety rules governing the operation of service stations in a country. Gasoline and diesel are hazardous products from which the public, employees, suppliers of goods and services, and the environment must be protected.

2) *Field observation.* In 2019, the first author of this paper worked part-time as a cashier during two months in a gas station in Canada. This allowed him to observe what was going in a gas station on a daily basis, and learn about the procedures, culture, and the interactions between different stakeholders: owner, customers, employees, suppliers of goods and services, control agencies. So we had a better understanding of the practices, needs and expectations of each stakeholder, and could take them into account in our discussions on future gas stations.

3) *Task analyses.* We analyzed the activities performed by employees, customers, and suppliers of goods and services in gas stations. This allowed us to identify key elements that were likely to be affected by the changes to come (e.g., accessibility, security, hygiene, payment mode). These elements have been classified in three categories: decrease, be stable, increase. This helped us to make projections for the future of these activities.

4) *PESTEL analyses.* This acronym stands for Political, Economic, Societal, Technological, Environmental and Legal. We examined trends and data from different domains at the macro level to have an overview of what is happening in the world. We explored more carefully the information that seemed relevant for future gas stations. To this end, we carried out a PESTEL analysis, a long-established method in the fields of NPD and innovation. It offers a structure for the search of elements that affects our world. We examined data provided by statistical agencies, government departments and international organizations, and trend reports issued by different research companies. We reviewed patents and applications in the database of intellectual property offices, and other documents from regulatory agencies, multinational coalitions, newspapers and publications.

5) *Meet the experts.* We met with experts of diverse disciplines to discuss the impacts of different elements on future gas stations and to define the contents of prospective scenarios.

3 Results

Safety Requirements. Several safety requirements and restrictions imposed the government and city authorities apply to service stations for obvious reasons: vehicle fuel is a highly flammable product that is dangerous for people and damaging the environment, and several people (including smokers) and vehicles are on the move near the fuel pumps. Since it can be expected that service stations will continue to sell gasoline for another 10, 15, 20 yrs, these safety requirements will persist. Scenarios about future service stations must take them into account.

Diversity of Service Stations. Major differences exist between stations in terms of location (in the country, in a small vs. large city, along a highway), size, and diversity of products and services offered. They commonly offer three basic types of products and services: (1) products for vehicles (gas/diesel, oil, windshield washer fluid), (2) foods and drinks, and (3) tire inflation machine. In addition, they might also provide a large number of goods and services such as a car wash, lottery tickets, ice, firewood, catering services, rest areas, parking lots, etc. This explains why gas stations tend to be renamed service station. Depending on their characteristics, they may represent a break time or milestone point for travelers and drivers. It is logical to think that this will continue in the future.

Different Stakeholders. Depending on who participate in discussions on future service stations (owner, franchisee, employees, customers, supplies of goods and services, experts from various fields) different points of view and priorities emerge, and different scenario components are highlighted. This confirms the relevance of involving various actors and stakeholders in the design to cover as many issues as possible. Scenarios will seek to integrate these different perspectives. Note that they are not an end, they are a support to discussions between different actors and stakeholders.

PESTEL Analysis. Political Trends. The main political trends to take into account are the decisions made by different countries following the Paris Pact (2015) and the European Green Deal (2019). Several countries committed to a plan that will strongly modulate the world. In Canada, policies such as "Carbon Pricing" have been expanded over the past five years. Alberta, British-Colombia and Quebec stand out as the three provinces that meet the federal benchmark and will continue to implement their existing carbon pricing initiatives [5]. In 2019, there were "57 carbon pricing initiatives around the world implemented or scheduled to implementation" [5]. Other policies for a more environmentally friendly society are already being implemented as many countries (including Canada) have recently decided to ban the sale of new gasoline-powered vehicles in 2030, as we move to net-zero emissions by 2050. Canada's Energy Regulator projected in the publication "Canada's energy future 2018: Energy Supply and Demand Projections to 2040" that the percentage of sales of electric vehicles would account for 16% of the total, following a "reference case", and 64% in the "technology case" [6]. The "technology case" makes the assumption that a global shift towards low carbon energy technologies would take place [6]. Now (2021), less than three years after that projection, the growing policies (of which the ban on new gasoline-powered vehicles stands out) reach higher expectations than those represented in 64% of the number of electric cars for 2040.

PESTEL Analysis - Social Trends. The agenda and measures for a sustainable society are shaping the consumption habits of the population. Communities will value more respect for ecosystem, recycling, local purchasing, and quality food. We can see a change in consumption patterns in the registration of motor vehicles by fuel type in Canada (Table 1). Over the past five years, we have seen a staggering 290% growth in electric and hybrid-electric car registrations in Canada [7]. The province of Québec stands out since in the first and second quarters of 2020, new vehicles with zero emissions represented 6.8% of total new vehicle registrations in the province [8]. In Canada, this figure reached 3,5% [8].

Table 1. Evolution of the number of cars sold and propelled by different types of energy in Canada from 2015 to 2019

Type of energy	2015	2016	2017	2018	2019
Gasoline	1 776 345	+2,21%	+6,02%	−4,49%	−3,36%
Diesel	85 635	−16,83%	−8,15%	+8,33%	−16,60%
Battery electric	4 151	+20%	+78,77%	+152,70%	+57,57%
Hybrid electric	17 309	+25%	+5,11%	+54,84%	+8,58%
Plugin hybrid electric	2 737	+156,44%	+62,48%	+85,10%	−2,22%

Today in Canada, there are 12 369 service stations that sell petroleum products with an average revenue of 1.6 million Canadian dollars. The number of gas stations has been slightly decreasing over the years while the annual sales volume has been slightly increasing. Ontario, Quebec and Alberta are the three provinces with the highest concentration of gasoline stations. We can see as an example the evolution of the number of establishments and the sales volume in Québec in Table 2. Experts working in the field reported the objective of having more efficient and strategically superior gas stations in relation to location, business model and services offered. Ranging from 0,7 to 1,5 million Canadian dollars to build a station and over 100,000 Canadian dollars to invest in a franchise, service stations represent a changing billionaire market. The business model has been reassessed and adjusted over the years. In less than two decades, the logic surrounding the work of gas station attendant has changed to "do it yourself", due to technological advances and the search for cost savings.

Table 2. Evolution of the number of establishments and sales volume in Québec (1997−2019).

Years	Gas stations		Annual sales volume (millions of liters)	
	Number	Variation (%)	Total	Variation (%)
1997	5059		7565	
2010	2985	−41,00	8585	13,49
2013	2895	−3,02	8549	−0,42
2016	2876	−0,66	8797	2,89
2019	2821	−1,91	9103	3,49

Characteristics of Gas Stations. For the years 2016 and 2019, Fig. 1 shows the characteristics of gas stations in Quebec, and important changes in the business model [9, 10]. Next to the high percentages of convenience stores and self-services that stand out, we see the emergence of electric vehicles (EV) charging points and autonomous stations that in the last analysis (2013–2016) had no significant presence and were placed in the same group as gas bar.

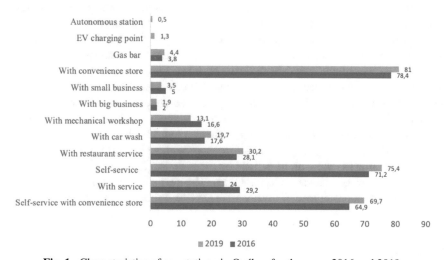

Fig. 1. Characteristics of gas stations in Québec for the years 2016 and 2019.

Impacts of the COVID-19. Following the COVID-19 pandemic, two main trends are expected to stay: 1) the concern for hygiene will remain a priority for a while and reinforce the model of human interactions without direct face-to-face presence; 2) the cashless mode of payment will be adopted more and more, to the point of becoming practically the only method of payment in use.

Technology. Preliminary results indicate that the Internet of Things (IoT) and the connection of people and objects will play an important role in future service stations. Scenarios have been designed in which the current logic of service stations is completely remodeled. As an example, the change of energy consumption of electric vehicles is only the tip of the iceberg when R&D centers are intensifying their works on battery capacity for more vehicle autonomy. Other trends, such as autonomous vehicles, and more recently flying cars, are the greatest threats to disturb the current situation. Their venue could lead to erasing current station services or, more likely, to redesign areas for self-programmed vehicles (potentially during the night) for a series of services such as preventive or corrective maintenance, tire inflation, and recharging. Such changes would lead to a major disruption with respect to the current situation.

Other scenarios where Artificial Intelligence plays a different role than the one described above were also developed. Intelligent virtual assistants could guide us before and during the recharge of the vehicle. Associated with augmented reality (another trend), they can provide an interactive experience when the client's presence is necessary or casual (e.g., Travel). Companies could work on this opportunity through endless new actions such as gamification, reinforcing their advertising, consolidating customer loyalty, etc.

4   Conclusion

Data collection is an ongoing activity throughout a complex project such as the design of future and long-lasting service stations. In this paper we presented the data collection that was followed in the initial phase of the PE design project; different stakeholders were involved with their practices, needs and expectations, and statistical findings and social trends were highlighted in order to be taken into account in the construction of diverse scenarios. These scenarios (about problems, human activities, use of new technologies, human-system interactions) are not an end, they rather provide support for discussion between stakeholders and are thus another source of data collection. Information selection for forward design strategies remains challenging because of the difficulty to find reliable prospective data, to work with variables (e.g., social, political, energy, economic trends) with ill-defined boundaries, and to have a clear portray of the future capabilities of innovative technologies. The next step of the project will consist in building virtual prototypes of forthcoming service stations and testing with different stakeholders.

References

1. Godet, M.: Prospective et planification stratégique. Economica, Paris (1985)
2. Adner, R.: Match your innovation strategy to your innovation ecosystem. Harvard Bus. Rev. **84**(4), 98 (2006)
3. Brangier, E., Robert, J.M.: Prospective ergonomics: foundations and issues. Le Travail Humain **77**(1), 1–20 (2014)

4. Robert, J.M., Brangier, E.: What is prospective ergonomics? a reflection and a position on the future of ergonomics. In: International Conference on Ergonomics and Health Aspects of Work with Computers, pp. 161–169. Springer, Berlin, Heidelberg (2009)
5. World Bank Group: State and Trends of Carbon Pricing 2019. Washington, DC: World Bank (2019). https://openknowledge.worldbank.org/handle/10986/31755. Accessed 08 Feb 2021
6. National Energy Board: Canada's Energy Future 2018: Energy Supply and Demand Projections to 2040. Canada Energy Regulator (2018)
7. Statistics Canada: Table 20–10–0021–01 New motor vehicle registrations, 2019. Statistics Canada (2019)
8. Statistics Canada: New Motor Vehicle Registration Survey, preliminary data for the first half of 2020. Statistics Canada (2020)
9. Régie de l'énergie Québec: Portrait du marché québécois de la vente au détail d'essence et de diesel: Recensement des essenceries en opération au Québec au 31 décembre 2019. Quebec Energy Regulator (2020)
10. Régie de l'énergie Québec: Portrait du marché québécois de la vente au détail d'essence et de diesel: Recensement des essenceries en opération au Québec au 31 décembre 2016. Quebec Energy Regulator (2017)

A Changing World: Challenges Related to Flexible or Precarious Work

Seiji Uchida[1] and Laerte Idal Sznelwar[2]([envelope])

[1] Instituto Trabalhar, São Paulo, Brazil
[2] Departamento de Engenharia de Produção da Escola Politécnica da,
Universidade de São Paulo, São Paulo, Brazil
laertesz@usp.br

Abstract. One of the first challenges we face in this article is to define "precarious". There is a lot of talk about job insecurity, as if it were a recent process, and therefore it is something relatively new in labor relations and production strategies in the capitalist world. We do not agree with this, even if it is not the intention of the authors, to place this process in contemporary times; it is something very old and, perhaps, something that has always existed when people had to work dominated by others. On the other hand, the advent of neoliberalism exacerbated these processes; even more when financial issues more and more govern production systems. So there is a lot to worry about when dealing with the issue of precariousness, since, as they become more accelerated and intense, these processes have an immense repercussion on the health of workers and also on social relations, also constituting a risk greater breakdown among the society.

Keywords: Health · Flexible work · Precarious work · Work organization

1 Precarious Work

This paper is inspired on the results of different interventions developed on different organizations - banks, public health services, the judiciary and universities. Based on the psychodynamic of work approach we will discuss recent changes that have taken place at work, especially as the methods of evaluation of workers' performance corroborated to introduce the issue of precariousness in different professional fields.

The precarious term has several connotations, its origins, distant in the history of mankind, have a strong meaning linked to what is exercised by permission; which is sustained because the landlord allows and tolerates, something that is in possession for a short period. It is still possible to refer to poor living conditions and the possibility that a change of place, regime, or ways of obtaining resources necessaries to survive. The risk of death is historically linked to the precarious, either because a certain population would be attacked, or because the risk of catastrophe would be imminent.

We are interested in thinking about precariousness in a particular sense. The one linked to the world of work. In this sense, we will reflect about this question within the context of the capitalist mode of production. When we reflect historically how the

N. L. Black et al. (Eds.): IEA 2021, LNNS 219, pp. 788–791, 2021.
https://doi.org/10.1007/978-3-030-74602-5_107

capitalist system developed, we observe that in relation to the world of work, there was always a struggle on the part of workers to guarantee conditions that would protect them from precarious situations. In this sense, Friedrich Engels' 1845 book on "The Situation of the Working Class in England" (2008) is classic. This author teaches us how important it is to understand this question within the particular historical determinations of each era. Harvey (Harvey 1992), following the School of Regulation, allows us to understand how each historical moment is determined by the capital accumulation regime. This system, according to this School (Lipietz 1991), the capitalist mode of production depends for continuing from crises and overcoming them. Overcoming occurs when a new accumulation regime is imposed in a hegemonic way. We had the crises of 1929, 1973 and the most recent one was on 2008 and further.

What would have changed in the last years to deal with a theme that has an opposite direction - that of flexibility, or better, that of precarious work?

1.1 Neoliberalism and the Situation in Brazil

Firstly, it's important to consider the political scenario in Brazil, with the entry of new labor legislation, it's still difficult to predict, since we do not know what, in fact, will change in labor relations. Otherwise our objective is to reflect and propose actions aimed at the future of work.

The advent of neoliberalism has exacerbated the precarious work processes, now under the hegemony of financial capital that has come to increasingly determine production systems. Therefore, there is much to worry about when dealing with the issue of precariousness, since, as they become more accelerated and intense, these processes have an immense impact on workers' health and also on social relations, also constituting a greater risk, a breakdown among the society.

According to Harvey (1992), the mode of production that follows Fordism, whose characteristic is the rigidity and control of all steps of production, comes under the sign of flexibility. Flexible capital accumulation becomes hegemonic. For a particular regime to exist, it is necessary that its reproduction scheme is coherent. In other words, the great challenge; "is to make the behaviors of all types of individuals assume some form of configuration that keeps the accumulation regime working" (Harvey 1992). In this sense, the materialization of this regime must "take the form of norms, habits, laws, regulatory networks, etc.; which guarantee the unity of the process, that is, the appropriate consistency between individual behaviors and the reproduction scheme" (Harvey 1992).

The process of flexible production led to flexible consumption. If, in the times of Fordism, production was standardized and on a scale, consumption was consistently mass and society at that time was mass society. Production was "pushed" according to production experts. Habits, behaviors and aesthetics preferences were determined by standardization. In Brazil many people bought and consumed the famous Volkswagen' Beetle. In the USA at the time of Ford, the Ford-T was bought en masse. In times of flexibility, demand now "pulls" production. It is what determines what will be produced. The consumer now wants variety and diversity. Customization is now sought and the society that now emerges is that of the individualism. Balman (2001) would say that a volatile and liquid reality emerges. Nothing remains; everything quickly becomes obsolete. Lipovetsky (1989) will consider as the ephemeral empire.

1.2 Precariousness, Subjectivity and Mental Health

This whole context encourages us to reflect on the impacts on the subjectivity of those who work, especially with regard to their health and mental illness at work.

Antunes (2020), in his book "The Privilege of Servitude", develops in a precise way the relationship between work and psychic illness in the context of flexible accumulation. His thesis is that "new diseases have been incorporated into the daily work world, typical of recent forms of work and production organization" (Antunes 2020). With the new international division of labor, according to this author, "a new map of accidents and occupational diseases" was established.

In order to understand this new reality of the emergence of new psychic disorders, it is important to bear in mind the process of flexibility that has been established in the current world, as previously mentioned. For Antunes (2020), "flexibility or flexibility today constitutes a sort of ordering synthesis of the multiple factors that underlie changes in the sociability of contemporary capitalism". Form the point of view of its impact on labor relations, "flexibility in work relations" is expressed in the drastic reduction of the boundaries between work and the space of private life, in the dismantling of labor legislation, in the different forms of hiring the workforce and in its denied expression, structural unemployment" (Antunes 2020).

Each country has dealt with its own implementation of the flexible capital accumulation regime. Laws, norms, rules, behaviors, etc., were created to reproduce this new accumulation regime. In the case of Brazil, it is important to consider the political scenario and with the entry of the new labor legislation. It is too early to predict what will happen, how the impact and the outcome of this reform will be. We do not know what will actually change in labor relations. Our role is to reflect and propose actions aimed at the future of work. With the flexibility of work and its relations, plus labor reform, the entire process brought with it a great precariousness of working conditions.

In our research, we observed how those processes produced job insecurity. With the growing process of individualization of work, together with individualized assessment and increased competition, solidarity relations have been broken. It is emphasized that the individual is now responsible for his career, he must create a competitive differential, he must think of work as a business and as owner, he must think "outside the box" and so on. How to think about the relations with others when the hegemonic rationality is now based on living at the risk of one own obsolescence? One must continually update, one must continually study so as not to be overtaken by the new generation. Concepts such as resilience, flexibility reveal what individual' characteristics must be developed in order to face an increasingly faster system, which changes continuously. This occurs through the impacts of ICTs (Information and Communication Technology) on work systems. These technologies intensify all these processes that were created by the flexible accumulation of capital. As Harvey says, there will be intensified spatio-temporal compression by these technologies.

Dejours (1988, 1999, 2010, 2012) throughout his career has reflected and contributed to the understanding of the impacts of work systems on subjectivity. His concern is to think about the possibility of the emancipation of the subject-worker. But, on those times it's necessary also to think about pathogenic suffering and the psychopathology of work, like depression and other diseases. Difficult and challenging times maintain and develop psychic sanity. Dejours argues that work is central to people's lives and alerts us to the deleterious effects of new work systems. When work allows the subject to find meaning and self-realization, the destination is positive, but the loss of meaning related to what people do and the impediment of self-realization, can lead the subject to unavoidable suffering and the consequences can be revealed as the emergence of severe illness and even suicides.

2 Final Discussion

Although this is not something new, since precarious employment relationships are already part of many people's lives, the fact that there are a number of aspects in the new legislation that increase the chances of hiring people in a flexible or precarious mode, it is necessary to question what the scenarios will be on the next years.

Probably, many colleagues and other professionals already live in a precarious situation, without any guarantee that they will have work in the near future, or even conditions to develop in the profession and, even without constituting a sufficiently profitable trajectory to guarantee a retirement in good conditions. So what changes, in addition to making situations legal today not provided for by law?

There are great challenges related not only for the professional role of ergonomists, psychodinamists, economists, engineers, managers, effectively concerned with work but for everyone at our contemporary societies. Work can be considered as a privileged social locus for the development of subjects, professions, collectives and culture? Or it'll remain and became more a more as a source for pathogenic suffering and alienation?

References

Antunes, R.: O Privilégio da Servidão – o Novo Proletariado de Serviços na era Digital. 2ª ed. Boitempo, São Paulo (2020)
Bauman, Z.: Modernidade Líquida. Zahar, Rio de Janeiro (2001)
Dejours, C.: A loucura do trabalho. estudo de psicopatologia do trabalho. 3ª ed., Cortez – Oboré, São Paulo (1988)
Dejours, C.: A banalização da injustiça social. Ed. Fundação Getúlio Vargas, Rio de Janeiro (1999)
Dejours, C.: Suicidio e trabalho. Paralelo 15, Brasilia (2010)
Dejours, C.: Trabalho Vivo. Paralelo 15, Brasilia (2012)
Harvey, D.: Condição Pós Moderna. Edições Loyola, São Paulo (1992)
Lipietz, A. Audácia. Uma Alternativa para o Século 21, Nobel São Paulo (1991)
Lipovetsky, G., do Efêmero, O.I.: A moda e seu destino nas sociedades modernas. Companhia das Letras, São Paulo (1989)

Restricted and General Complexity in Ergonomics

Tiago F. A. C. Sigahi[✉] and Laerte Idal Sznelwar

Polytechnic School, University of São Paulo, São Paulo, SP, Brazil
{tiagosigahi,laertesz}@usp.br

Abstract. Complexity theory has been used in ergonomics in response to reductionist views of work and organizations. However, there is still a lot of ambiguity and confusion in the use of concepts and theories of complexity. Defining the type of complexity approach used is essential to advance knowledge, as there are fundamental epistemological, ontological and methodological differences between them that influence the models of the human, of health and of work we produce.

Keyword: Complexity · Complex systems · Epistemology

1 Introduction

What assumptions underlie the way in which we know, think and act in the world? Which worldview guides the way we build problems? Although these are questions of philosophy, it is important that researchers in ergonomics and related fields ask them, as it affects the models of the human, of health and of work we produce (Wisner 1995; Daniellou 2006; Sznelwar 2020; Zilbovicius, Piqueira, and Sznelwar 2020).

Mainstream ergonomics espouses a basic philosophical stance, whether explicitly acknowledged or not, which is positivist, empiricist, and reductionist (Dekker, Cilliers, and Hofmeyr 2011). This way of thinking is built upon a Cartesian perspective, which is based on a separatist, isolating thought: It separates the subject from the object, science from philosophy, objective and reflective research, the disciplines from each other (Morin 2010, p. 26–28). This can be highly problematic as ergonomics has to deal with problems of complexity, emergence and sustainability which cannot be easily reconciled within this intellectual lineage (Dekker, Hancock, and Wilkin 2013).

As an alternative, complexity theory has been used in ergonomics in response to Cartesian-reductionist views of work and organizations, resulting in an increasing number of publications. In a paper published in the Ergonomics journal, Walker et al. (2010) pointed out that more than 80 journal papers from the mainstream ergonomics literature have used either the words "complex" or "complexity" in their titles. Today, considering the same parameters used by these authors – i.e., only the journals Ergonomics, Theoretical Issues in Ergonomics Science, Applied Ergonomics, and International Journal of Cognitive Ergonomics and Human Factors – this number increased to more than 150. If we add other relevant journals, such as International Journal of Industrial Ergonomics

N. L. Black et al. (Eds.): IEA 2021, LNNS 219, pp. 792–798, 2021.
https://doi.org/10.1007/978-3-030-74602-5_108

and Human Factors and Ergonomics in Manufacturing & Service Industries, the search results in approximately 300 articles.

Complexity has appeared in the ergonomics literature in both theoretical and practice-oriented discussions. For instance, Carayon (2006) discussed the dimensions of complexity of work systems, while Walker et al. (2010) aimed at translating concepts of complexity to the field of ergonomics, and Wilson (2014) proposed a framework delineating complexity features of systems ergonomics. Regarding complexity applications, there are examples in healthcare (Jun et al. 2010; Righi and Saurin 2015), aviation (Harris and Stanton 2010), investigation of accidents (Dekker et al. 2011), military (Rafferty et al. 2010), in the design and use of innovative technologies (Dekker 2012; Walker et al. 2009), road and rail (Stanton and Salmon 2011), sports (Salmon et al. 2010), etc.

Despite the great progress and growing interest of academia and industry in complexity theory (Frei and Serugendo 2011, 2012a, 2012b), when it comes to the meaning of complexity and related concepts there is still a lot of ambiguity and confusion. More than that, the question of what is "complexity" not only remains open, but also has very different, sometimes antagonistic, answers. In order to advance knowledge on complexity in ergonomics, it is important to distinguish complexity approaches. More specifically, there is a need to differentiate approaches regarding epistemological, ontological and methodological characteristics, and to understand the implications for research and practice.

It is not our intention to provide definitive answers to these questions, nor to carry out an extensive review of the literature on complexity in ergonomics, but rather to differentiate complexity approaches and illustrate with examples, stimulating reflections for those interested in conducting complexity-based ergonomics research and action.

This paper consists of a theoretical work based on the analysis of literature. Papers published in top journals in the field of ergonomics that used complexity theory were selected in order to illustrate the differences regarding complexity schools of thought.

2   Complexity in Ergonomics: Differentiating Schools of Thought

The definition of complexity refers to the idea of tissue, the fabric that joins the whole; it is related to the notion that reality is made up of ties and interactions (Morin 2007; Yolles 2019a). Complexity literature distinguishes between two schools of thought: Restricted complexity and general complexity (Morin 2007; Malaina 2015; Wells 2012; Byrne and Callaghan 2014). As stated by Morin (2016 p. 87–88), they have "the same data, the same principles of explanation, but differ by the arrangement of what is satellite and what is central". These differences reflect in the epistemological and ontological conception of complexity, in the objectives and methods used to achieve them, in the theoretical assumptions and bases, and in the phenomena of interest.

2.1   Restricted Complexity

Restricted complexity has its roots in nonlinear dynamics, evolutionary biology and artificial intelligence and is best represented by the Santa Fe Institute, considered one of the most important research centers on complex systems (Alhadeff-Jones 2008; Mitchell 2009; Yolles 2019a, 2019b).

In this view, complexity is an ontological dimension of the object of study – *the system is complex* –, a characteristic that can be completely described, predicted, explained and calculated (Allen, Maguire, and McKelvey 2011). Thus, complex problems are understood as complicated problems (Woermann, Human, and Preiser 2018).

This approach allowed important advances in formalization and modeling, but still remains under the positivist and reductionist paradigm (Cilliers and Preiser 2010; Mazzochi 2016). This view reinforced an upward logic in the scientific field that understanding complexity requires researchers to identify and organize the "laws of complexity" (Yolles 2019a). The central idea is that the complexity of the real world can be completely understood based on the understanding of simple rules that generate it. In essence, restricted complexity approaches reduce, simplify – "analyze" in its most original meaning, "divide to understand" – and may lose precisely the comprehension of the complexity of the system to be projected (Zilbovicius et al. 2020).

2.2 General Complexity

General complexity consists of an epistemological, cognitive, paradigmatic approach and is best represented by the works of French philosopher Edgar Morin (Alhadeff-Jones 2008; Well 2012; Malaina 2015).

In this view, complexity cannot be described in formal language; we can only have an approximate understanding of complexity using a plurality of descriptions (Cilliers and Preiser 2010) and this knowledge is provisional and contingent (Allen et al. 2011). The interested is in the limits of knowledge, in its incompleteness (Morin and Le Moigne 2000; Alhadeff-Jones 2008).

General complexity does not argue against reductionism *per se*; it states that it is necessary to reduce complexity to a point where research becomes possible (Human and Cilliers 2013, p. 31–32), where the world is intelligible to us (Human 2016, p. 425). The fundamental questions – to which there are no unique or definitive answers – refer to what are the assumptions that underlie the way in which we know, think and act in the world? Which worldview guides the way we build problems?

Thus, complexity is no longer reduced only to a characteristic of the system that can be completely explained by simple rules, but a question of interpretation, representation (Malaina 2015; Woermann et al. 2018; Yolles 2019a), i.e., how we see and conceive the world (Morin 2010) – *the way of looking at any system is complex.*

3 Illustrating Complexity Approaches in Ergonomics Literature

There are cases that is possible to easily identify the school of thought on which it is based. In general, restricted approaches are more straightforward to identify. For instance, Li et al. (2019) investigated user experience regarding smartphone texting methods and defined complexity as an indication of the number and type of characters used in a phrase. Lee et al. (2019) investigated the effects of in-vehicle information display on drivers, where visual complexity is a characteristic of the display defined by simple elements.

In other cases, restricted and general approaches can be confused, although it is possible to identify traits of one or the other. For instance, Liu and Li's (2012) discussion on the concept of task complexity illustrates different approaches to complexity. Task complexity has been recognized as an important task characteristic that influences and predicts human performance and behaviors. As explained by the authors, there are two perspectives of complexity with different theoretical foundations. The "objective perspective" is based on the assumption of the existence of an objective task external to and independent on task performers and the existence of a detached observer. In this approach, objective task complexity is the complexity of the prescribed task seen by the person prescribing the task. The "subjective perspective", on the other hand, advocates that task complexity is the complexity of the actual task for the person executing it. While in the objective perspective the *task is complex*, in the subjective perspective *the way to see the task is complex*.

Finally, general approaches to complexity in ergonomics are more related to the way of viewing production as a system of systems and work as a central element in the lives of people and society. The work sciences, in particular Activity-centered Ergonomics (Guérin et al. 2001) and Psychodynamics of Work (Dejours 2012), although they have different theoretical and methodological approaches, reveal the prevalence of the design-execution relationship paradigm as separate aspects and the impossibility of working and producing strictly following the predefined rules, especially those prescribed by certain production actors, such as engineers and managers (Brunoro et al. 2020). In this perspective, if everything were solved by the prescriptions, it would not be necessary *to work* – it would be sufficient *to operate*, in the sense proposed by the most classic and reductionist views of organizational schools based on the Taylorist-Fordist premises (Sznelwar, Uchida, and Lancman 2011). A general complexity approach leads us to question the utilitarian principle of economy-effectiveness (Morin, 2010 p. 160), which demands endless growth, imposes increasingly absurd goals and defends the ideology that men are beings with infinite overcoming capacity (Sznelwar et al. 2011, p. 27).

.

4 Concluding Remarks

Understanding the complexity approach being used is fundamental since some complexity-based models still remain in the epistemology of classical science (Woermann et al. 2018). This type of approach is represented by restricted complexity, which allowed important advances in the possibilities of modeling, favoring interdisciplinarity, opening the understanding to relational thinking, but it cannot get rid of the reductionist and positivist apparatus that must qualify it as "science" (Morin 2007; Yolles 2019a). It is important to distinguish this view from general complexity, which is essentially an epistemological approach and understands complexity fundamentally as a paradigmatic problem (Morin 2010, 2016).

On the one hand, there is a need to distinguish between restricted and general complexity, aiming at conceptual disambiguation, and theoretical, methodological and argumentation consistency. On the other hand, there is a need to connect and integrate them, because, first, although they are antagonistic in some aspects, they are also complementary, and second, a certain degree of restricted complexity is needed to produce and develop general complexity (Morin 2007). Understanding the type of complexity approach is important for future research in ergonomics since its underlying assumptions affect the way we build problems (Wisner 1995) and consequently the transformation of the work we want to see accomplished (Brunoro et al. 2020; Zilbovicius et al. 2020).

Ergonomics community may benefit from knowledge regarding how complexity has been used in the field. Different types of complexity approach represent different worldviews, thus influencing the variables taken into account in projecting and managing sociotechnical systems. There is a dialogical relationship between restricted and general complexity, and both theoretical and empirical work has to be done to support future research and actions based on complexity.

References

Alhadeff-Jones, M.: Three generations of complexity theories: nuances and ambiguities. Educ. Philos. Theory **40**(1), 66–82 (2008). https://doi.org/10.1111/j.1469-5812.2007.00411.x

Allen, P., Maguire, S., McKelvey, B.: The SAGE Handbook of Complexity and Management. SAGE Publications, London (2011)

Brunoro, C.M., Bolis, I., Sigahi, T.F.A.C., Kawasaki, B.C., Sznelwar, L.I.: Defining the meaning of "sustainable work" from activity-centered ergonomics and psychodynamics of Work's perspectives. Appl. Ergon. **89**, 103209 (2020). https://doi.org/10.1016/j.apergo.2020.103209

Byrne, D., Callaghan, G.: Complexity theory and the Social Sciences: The state of the art. Routledge, New York (2014)

Carayon, P.: Human factors of complex sociotechnical systems. Appl. Ergon. **37**(4), 525–535 (2006). https://doi.org/10.1016/j.apergo.2006.04.011

Cilliers, P., Preiser, R.: Complexity, difference and identity. Springer, Dordrecht (2010)

Daniellou, F.: Epistemological Issues about Ergonomics and Human Factors. In: Karwowski, W. (ed.) International Encyclopedia of Ergonomics and Human Factors, pp. 43–48. CRC Press, Boca Raton (2006)

Dejours, C.: Trabalho vivo: trabalho e emancipação - Tomo II. Brasília: Paralelo 15 (2012)

Dekker, S., Cilliers, P., Hofmeyr, J.H.: The complexity of failure: implications of complexity theory for safety investigations. Safety Sci. **49**(6), 939–945 (2011). https://doi.org/10.1016/j.ssci.2011.01.008

Dekker, S.W., Hancock, P.A., Wilkin, P.: Ergonomics and sustainability: towards an embrace of complexity and emergence. Ergonomics **56**(3), 357–364 (2013). https://doi.org/10.1080/00140139.2012.718799

Frei, R., Serugendo, G.D.M.: Advances in complexity engineering. Int. J. Bio-Inspired Comput. **3**(4), 199–212 (2011). https://doi.org/10.1504/IJBIC.2011.041144

Frei, R., Serugendo, G.D.M.: Concepts in complexity engineering. Int. J. Bio-Inspired Comput. **3**(2), 123–139 (2011). https://doi.org/10.1504/IJBIC.2011.039911

Frei, R., Serugendo, G.D.M.: The future of complexity engineering. Central Eur. J. Eng. **2**(2), 164–188 (2012). https://doi.org/10.2478/s13531-011-0071-0

Guérin, F., Kerguelen, A., Laville, A., Daniellou, F., Duraffourg, J.: Compreender o trabalho para transformá-lo: A prática da ergonomia. Editora Blücher, São Paulo (2001)

Harris, D., Stanton, N.: Aviation as a system of systems: Preface to the special issue of human factors in aviation. Ergonomics **53**(2), 145–148 (2010). https://doi.org/10.1080/00140130903521587

Human, O.: Complexity: E-special introduction. Theory, Culture Soc. **33**(7–8), 421–440 (2016). https://doi.org/10.1177/0263276415600105

Human, O., Cilliers, P.: Towards an economy of complexity: derrida, morin and bataille. Theory, Cult. Soc. **30**(5), 24–44 (2013). https://doi.org/10.1177/0263276413484070

Jun, G., James Ward, P., Clarkson, J.: Systems modelling approaches to the design of safe health-care delivery: ease of use and usefulness perceived by healthcare workers. Ergonomics **53**(7), 829–847 (2010). https://doi.org/10.1080/00140139.2010.489653

Lee, S.C., Kim, Y.W., Ji, Y.G.: Effects of visual complexity of in-vehicle information display: age-related differences in visual search task in the driving context. Appl. Ergon. **81**, 102888 (2019). https://doi.org/10.1016/j.apergo.2019.102888

Li, Y., You, F., You, X., Ji, M.: Smartphone text input: effects of experience and phrase complexity on user performance, physiological reaction, and perceived usability. Appl. Ergon. **80**, 200–208 (2019). https://doi.org/10.1016/j.apergo.2019.05.019

Liu, P., Li, Z.: Task complexity: a review and conceptualization framework. Int. J. Ind. Ergon. **42**(6), 553–568 (2012). https://doi.org/10.1016/j.ergon.2012.09.001

Malaina, A.: Two complexities: The need to link complex thinking and complex adaptive systems science. Emergence: Complex. Organ. **17**(1), 1–9 (2015). https://doi.org/10.emerg/10.17357.3f8320a4b0c3add74ffda2959beec5b2

Mazzocchi, F.: Complexity, network theory, and the epistemological issue. Kybernetes **46**(7), 1158–1170 (2016). https://doi.org/10.1108/K-05-2015-0125

Mitchell, M.: Complexity: A Guided Tour. Oxford University Press, Oxford (2009)

Morin, E.: Restricted complexity, general complexity. In: Gershenson, C., Aerts, D., Edmonds, B. (eds.) Worldviews, science and us: Philosophy and complexity, pp. 5–29. World Scientific, Singapore (2007)

Morin, E.: Science avec conscience. 14ª ed. Rio de Janeiro: Bertrand (2010)

Morin, E.: La méthode 1: La nature de la nature. Sulina, Porto Alegre (2016)

Morin, E., Le Moigne, J.L.: L'intelligence de la complexité. Fundação Peirópolis, Rio de Janeiro (2000)

Rafferty, L., Stanton, N., Walker, G.: The famous five factors in teamwork: a case study of fratricide. Ergonomics **53**(10), 1187–1204 (2010). https://doi.org/10.1080/00140139.2010.513450

Righi, A.W., Saurin, T.A.: Complex socio-technical systems: characterization and management guidelines. Appl. Ergon. **50**, 19–30 (2015). https://doi.org/10.1016/j.apergo.2015.02.003

Salmon, P., Williamson, A., Lenné, M., Mitsopoulos-Rubens, E., Rudin-Brown, C.M.: Systems-based accident analysis in the led outdoor activity domain: application and evaluation of a risk management framework. Ergonomics **53**(8), 927–939 (2010). https://doi.org/10.1080/00140139.2010.489966

Stanton, N., Salmon, P.: Planes, trains and automobiles: contemporary ergonomics research in transportation safety. Applied Ergonomics **42**(4), 529–532 (2011). https://doi.org/10.1016/j.apergo.2010.11.003

Sznelwar, L.I.: Quelle psychodynamique, pour quel travail, pour qui? Changements au travail- Nouveaux défis pour la psychodynamique du travail. Travailler **2**(44), 9–29 (2020). https://doi.org/10.3917/trav.044.0009

Sznelwar, L.I., Uchida, S., Lancman, S.: Subjectivity at work in question. Tempo Soc. **23**(1), 11–30 (2011). https://doi.org/10.1590/S0103-20702011000100002

Walker, G.H., Stanton, N.A., Salmon, P.M., Jenkins, D.P., Rafferty, L.: Translating concepts of complexity to the field of ergonomics. Ergonomics **53**(10), 1175–1186 (2010). https://doi.org/10.1080/00140139.2010.513453

Wells, J.: Complexity and Sustainability. Routledge, London (2012)

Wilson, J.R.: Fundamentals of systems ergonomics/human factors. Appl. Ergon. **45**(1), 5–13 (2014). https://doi.org/10.1016/j.apergo.2013.03.021

Wisner, A.: Understanding problem building: ergonomic work analysis. Ergonomics **38**(3), 595–605 (1995). https://doi.org/10.1080/00140139508925133

Woermann, M., Human, O., Preiser, R.: General complexity: a philosophical and critical perspective. Emergence: Complexity Organ. **20**(2), 1–18 (2018). https://doi.org/10.emerg/10.17357.c9734094d98458109d25b79d546318af

Yolles: The complexity continuum, Part 1: hard and soft theories. Kybernetes **48**(6), 1330–1354 (2019). https://doi.org/10.1108/K-06-2018-0337

Yolles, M.: The complexity continuum, Part 2: modelling harmony. Kybernetes **48**(8), 1626–1652 (2019). https://doi.org/10.1108/K-06-2018-0338

Zilbovicius, M., Piqueira, J.R.C., Sznelvar, L.: Complexity engineering: new ideas for engineering design and engineering education. Ann. Braz. Acad. Sci. **92**(3), e20191489 (2020). https://doi.org/10.1590/0001-3765202020181489

Transforming Organization of Work in Order to Promote Meaning and Mental Health: A Sustainable Perspective

Laerte Idal Sznelwar[✉]

Departamento de Engenharia de Produção da Escola Politécnica da Universidade de São Paulo,
São Paulo, Brazil
laertesz@usp.br

Abstract. In this paper we propose a conceptual discussion based on a dialogue between ergonomics and psychodynamics of work (PDW) in order to transform working situations to provide meaning for all protagonists; in regard to the concept that work is central to the lives of the subjects, it is an important path to search for self accomplishment and for the development of different professions, organizations and society. It is a complicated, difficult discussion, since many questions arise; questions that are dangerous, destabilizing, above all incomplete; therefore stimulating. It's also important to discuss about bleak scenarios workers are experiencing at this moment of our history, in many working situations. What is proposed in this paper is related to a specific issue based on questions related to life at work based on concepts of psychodynamics of work (PDW) and findings that come from actions developed in this field.

Keywords: Macroergonomics · Work organization · Sustainability · Mental health · Psychosocial issues · Psychodynamics of work

1 General Statements

Human being, inspired by a psychoanalytical perspective, concerns someone that desires, that is incomplete, that is contradictory and that is in search of something that he does not know well is, who has doubts about what he wants; well everyone lives his life in search of meaning. It is, therefore, a vision of perspective, of life project, of path that should allow the subjects to create a narrative and reinforce their identification processes. This search for is also something that does not have an end, as long as there is life, there is always something possible to aim for. Work would be a strong promoter, or even, a fundamental mean for everyone to build and continue on this path.

For Psychodynamics of Work, work is central to the lives of the subjects, it is a second chance, in addition to love and the centrality of sexuality so that we can constitute a life trajectory compatible with our desires; wishes in the sense used by Freud of WUNTCH, of desired (something distant and idealized).

Since this discussion is based on psychodynamics of work, it's important remain consistent with this discipline that includes many concepts and proposals (Dejours 1999, 2009) (Molinier 2006). A first inspiration came from Alain Wisner (Wisner 1994), one of the main authors of Ergonomics, with regard to intelligence. For him, and not only, every human being would be born with the potential to develop his intelligence; differences would be due to several factors, especially his life experience that, together with his inherited characteristics, would provide conditions for each and every everyone to seek and become more skilled, competent, wise.

In the perspective adopted in this article, and using an analogy with Wisner's thinking about the spread and the perspective of intelligence; desire (greatly simplifying the question) is a universal property of human beings. The search for something that makes sense, for a path that promotes realization, identification, is inherent to human kind and related to our incompleteness. Considering the incompleteness of human beings, the relationship between suffering and pleasure, as well as the perspective of life and death should be considered when we talk about work. When work does not provide conditions for this search, the search for meaning, it becomes an impediment, a propitious scenario for the emergence of pathogenic suffering.

Adopting the point of view, propagated by the psychodynamics of work and not only, but also by currents of philosophy and sociology of work; that work can and should make sense, we are inverting historical trends, or rather, predominant and hegemonic thoughts in history, which have propagated that work would be a background activity, a punishment, something to be done under the aegis of suffering, of pity and, for many, meaningless. It's the contrary; working has a profound potential for achievement, transforming, emancipating. This can be considered as a kind of utopia that could be formulated as follows: "Everyone has the right to an interesting, challenging job, which allows the construction of paths that favor the processes of self-realization, that allow the search for freedom and emancipation; that reinforces the collective life, the organization and the society as well".

The main reason to address those questions is related to the fact that work-related psychic disorders emerge in an intense, continuous and growing way in our societies. Another reason is related to the fact that it's important to reflect about the concepts of work in life time as well as to envisage actions that could help to transform the views on working in a radical way. We're talking about the importance of work in our life and societies and the risks for our health related to organizational choices related to working situations.

This means that work would perhaps be the main human environment in the search for meaning and that any type of activity that does not provide such conditions could be considered as an existential damage, since the role of organizations would be to guarantee for each human scenarios where it's possible to find a place and a role in society, express and develop their potentials.

The division of labor, which has existed for a long time in history, but has been deeply radicalized since Taylor and Ford, has become an almost insurmountable obstacle; it has shaped our minds for almost a century. The naturalization of the fact that it would be possible for human beings to repeat gestures and movements for hours, days, weeks, months, years is one of the worst legacy of the so-called Scientific Labor Organization.

This paved the way for reifying processes, legitimizing non-sense at work, alienation and all the consequences, social, political and cultural, as well as for the workers' health.

Sustaining this point of view, related to a fragmentation in working process as if it were inexorable and as the only way for the development of the production of good and services into the society would be considered as an impoverishment of the possibilities to reflect and adopt a critical positioning. Understanding that this is a historical issue and imagining other perspectives for the future is our purpose. But to do so, it is important to deconstruct this idea and build the world of work from an opposite perspective, which would be to provide conditions for everyone to have access to jobs that allow development, which are ways for their self-realization.

A small parenthesis, Adam Smith, one of the first thinkers of liberalism, noted that there would be an increase in efficiency in commercial production if production processes were divided into discrete tasks. On the other hand, he reinforced the importance of moral feeling and the role of the worker, showing concern about the risk of having his life consumed in monotonous, repetitive work, in short, meaningless. The same author, when dealing with the issue of moral sense, reinforces the importance of sympathy and cooperation.

Another parenthesis, when Charles Chaplin creates his film Modern Times (1936); he shows that modernity did not bring a perspective of emancipation. On the contrary, it brought the domain of machines, dominated by other humans, an instrument of domination and not of liberation. His brilliant allegory is a satirical perspective regarding the fact that when working does not provide conditions for the development of each one towards emancipation, when it does not provide the building of cooperative collectives, when it is not safe and is anchored in the repetition of something that does not make sense; working live become a desolation, the organization becomes a scenario in which the most different types of disorders will emerge, including psychic ones. Any similarity with what we are experiencing in contemporary times, where a true epidemic of psychic disorders linked to work emerges, is a simple coincidence. It is important to analyze and debate the organizational choices that, among others, harm, deprives the work of its meaning.

It's also possible to talk about the Sisyphus Myth - doing useless and meaningless work for all eternity - moving the stone to the top of the mountain until it rolls down, climbing again. Not only in this myth but also in other situations where work is used as a punishment are part of human kind (Arendt 2008); in this perspective the example of slavery, the movie Bent and the euphemism at the entrance to Auschwitz - Arbeit Macht Frei are relevant. Is submission to others something inexorable? (La Boétie 2002).

We must also clarify that when we speak of the working subject we do not position ourselves in an individualistic perspective! There is no human without the collective, without the relational. The individualistic lie propagated by neoliberalism has brought a series of losses to humanity. The spread of bleak scenarios in organizations is a fact and the expressive amount of sick-leave from work due to work-related mental disorders is one of its undeniable consequences.

The perspective of professions and professionalization enters in this debate because we realize that there was and is, increasingly, an attempt to untie the work of the professions. The use of the word occupation is notorious. It is not related to work, but mainly a reference to a generic human being, capable of doing anything, an without a professional perspective has long been sought, favoring alienating processes.

It is interesting to note that in certain sectors of the economy, if not the majority, the aim is to designate workers no longer by profession, but by some type of generic occupation. Let's look at the examples of bank employees, and others. It is not about someone who works in a certain sector of the economy and who, from his experience, the professional courses he will take, and how he becomes more and more knowledgeable about this type of economic activity becomes a, de facto, professional. It is quite the same for managers; they can be managers of anything; his qualification is "to be a manager", even if he understands nothing about the type of activity developed in a certain company, in a certain public or private institution. The idea of being a manager, as "something" generic means what? Would they be someone who has the skills to handle what? Would they be to be able to make people work under generic management guidelines? Or they would be much more than that, considering that, in fact, to lead teams, they need to become legitimate for the subordinates.

Worse still when the term collaborator is used in companies to designate workers in general. It is not true, it's used as a management technique, yet another hollowing out of what could make sense at work, what is actually being a professional in a certain company, in a particular sector of the economy.

Work is often confused with employment, with survival, with the possibility of acquiring what someone needs and desires in terms of goods and services. Although they are important, they are not enough and, depending on a series of historical-cultural issues, they can become a trap, like consuming to exist! The issue of unemployment, precarious employment, the lack of balance between work and other aspects of life, exhaustion, disrespect are quite significant and have been addressed. Other issues related to inadequate working conditions and their risks to health and physical integrity, injustice in relation to payment, issues of individualized performance appraisal have also been addressed. However, the question of self-realization is practically left out. It is a question strongly related to the perspective of finding meaning in work, when it comes to the search for the fulfillment of desires and the development of human capacities.

One of the main injustices in the world is in the social division of work; how many have access to interesting and challenging work, which allows for the development of skills and competences, which allows to live together with others; that is considered as useful and well done?

How can we imagine that we should work for long periods, not only with regard to working hours, but also throughout the working lives... until retirement, if this actually happens; considering the precarious nature of social relations including social security? What are the consequences of doing meaningless, repetitive things that do not allow the development of skills and competences? It's possible to develop subjectivity having boring jobs! What are the fears, concerns, and doubts; anxieties that arise from those living situations?

Adopting certain assumptions like those that advocate that people need to solve the most basic things before wishing is not true. It's like trying to invent a human that does not exist; it is not possible to separate the desire to do something useful and beautiful from what would be said basic needs, like feeding and reproducing. This can be considered as a kind of reification (Honneth 2007).

These questions reinforce the idea that the possibility of realization is much more radical, moving away from generic views that do not provoke a deeper reflection on the meaning of what we do, often restricted to fragmented tasks that cover very little if we consider the process production in a broader way.

Production, the social role of companies and work cannot be considered in a static way, as if it were something where each one and the collectives exercise and engage their intelligence, their body and their subjectivity to account for goals defined by others. The radical nature of the change in positioning lies mainly in the perspective of development, in the possibility of building a trajectory, a career, a life narrative that points to the ideas already developed here, such as emancipation, self-realization, for the construction of collectives and the professions; in short, as proclaimed by PDW concepts, for the development of culture and society (Sznelwar 2015) (Sznelwar and Hubault 2015).

New technologies have great potential to assist in the development of professional skills and abilities. However, this is not certain, or something inexorable; as it's known, depending on how the work is divided, companies will continue to provide repetitive and meaningless work. Technology has never been neutral in relation to work, and even its development can provide better or worse conditions for the development of people.

It should also be emphasized that having the conditions to develop professionally means experiencing situations that allow the construction of an increasingly comprehensive knowledge regarding a certain type of production, in a certain sector of the economy, and using different kinds of technologies. It is a perspective of continuous learning that is not restricted to allowing workers to learn and receive instructions. As is already known from what we have learned in the field of Ergonomics and Psychodynamics of Work, people are never restricted to what is prescribed by their tasks, since prescriptions can consider everything that happens. Actually everyone that works face the real, and it is always necessary to act taking into account what was not foreseen, since there are many emergent phenomena in production systems. If this is evident in the industrial world, let us imagine it in service situations.

2 Conclusion

It's important to state the need to change working perspective in order to provide interesting, challenging jobs, which allows the construction of paths that favor the processes of self-realization, that allow the search for freedom and emancipation in working systems; including a perspective of actually contributing to the development of organizations and society. This means that work would perhaps be the main human environment in which is possible to search for meaning and that any type of activity that does not provide such conditions could be considered as an existential damage, since the role of organizations should be to guarantee for each human being scenarios where each one can find a place and a role in society, express and develop potentials.

Some questions are finally addressed: Does it make sense to talk in the sense of work? Does it make sense to spread the idea that the meaning of work is for everyone? Based on those questions and the concepts presented in this paper, what is the meaning of work in a sustainable way?

804   L. I. Sznelwar

References

Arendt, H.: A Condição Humana. Forense Universitária, Trad. Roberto Raposo. Rio de janeiro (2008)

Dejours, C.: A Banalização da Injustiça Social. Ed. Fundação Getúlio Vargas, Rio de Janeiro (1999)

Dejours, C.: Travail Vivant. Payot, Paris (2009)

Honneth, A.: La réification: Petit traité de théorie critique. Gallimard Paris (2007)

La Boetie, É.: Discours de la servitude volontaire. Payot, Paris (2002)

Molinier, P.: Les Enjeux psychiques du travail. Payot & Rivages Paris (2006)

Sznelwar, L.I.: Alain wisner: o desenvolvimento da ergonomia e do pensamento sobre o « trabalhar. Martin Média, Travailler, (15), p. 55–70 (2006)

Sznelwar, L.I.: Quando trabalhar é ser protagonista e o protagonismo do trabalho. Blücher, São Paulo (2015)

Sznelwar, L.I., Hubault, F.: Subjectivity in ergonomics: a new start to the dialogue regarding the psychodynamics of work. Production 25, 354–361 (2015)

Wisner, A.: La cognition et l'action situées: conséquences pour l'analyse ergonomique du travail et l'anthropotechnologie. Proceedings of the 12th Triennial Congress of the IEA, Toronto, pp. 1–12 (1994)

Exploiting Forward-Looking Data in Prospective Ergonomics: The Case of Aviation

Karine Ung[(✉)], Philippe Doyon-Poulin, and Jean-Marc Robert

Polytechnique Montréal, Montréal, Québec, Canada
{karine.ung,philipe.doyon-poulin,jean-marc.robert}@polymtl.ca

Abstract. In this study, we investigated different sources of forward-looking data in the domain of aviation and pilot training that are of interest to human factors researchers and practitioners involved in the creation of future artefacts. We show how trends that are emerging for the future as well as unforeseen short-term events, such as the COVID-19 pandemic, impact decisions made on the design of future artefacts in aviation. In this respect, the case of anticipating pilot shortage is examined in relation with the design of a new form of training program: evidence-based training (EBT).

Keywords: Prospective ergonomics · Data source · Aviation · Evidence-based training · Pilot training · Pilot shortage

1 Introduction

1.1 Prospective Ergonomics

Ergonomic interventions have been mainly focused on correction and design (of already identified artefacts), and only recently on prospective and innovation [1]. Prospective Ergonomics (PE) deals with the design of future things. It consists in searching for current and upcoming needs in order to design future products, services, processes, or systems that will fulfill these needs [2]. This mode of intervention differs from traditional ones in several aspects: there is no initial demand from a client and therefore no mandate to the ergonomist; the need to fulfill is to be discovered; the artefact to create for this need is to be identified; and the future users of this artefact and their future activities have to be defined. The ergonomist who plans to launch a PE project must have initiative, be creative and a leader, and coordinate numerous activities that are normally associated to the development of new products or services: elaborate a project, analyse competitive artefacts, get financial support, build a team, manage the development process, etc. The activities involved in a prospective approach aim at gathering the relevant prospective information to orient towards the future and lead to creative and innovative ideas. PE can bring commercial advantages by developing new artefacts that can change human habits and be better adapted, more secure, less expensive, and/or more efficient.

N. L. Black et al. (Eds.): IEA 2021, LNNS 219, pp. 805–812, 2021.
https://doi.org/10.1007/978-3-030-74602-5_110

As a new approach, PE still has limited documented real-life cases and applications. There is therefore a need for guidance material and supporting tools in this domain [3]. This article identifies different sources of information that can support engineers, ergonomists, or designers in prospective activities in aviation. First, we provide an introduction of the concepts involved in the development of Evidence-Based Training (EBT) to address the forecasted pilot shortage. Second, we analysed prospective data in the large-scale domain of aviation and identify forward-looking data sources which can be used for future artefacts. Third, we discuss the results obtained and the limitations of this study. Finally, in the conclusion, we proposed new orientations and perspectives for future research in PE.

1.2 Safety Concerns of Airline Pilot Shortage

Aviation has seen continuous economic growth throughout the past decade. In 2019, the International Civil Aviation Organisation (ICAO) observed 1,303 scheduled airlines operated over 31,717 aircrafts, throughout 3,759 airports with the support of 170 air navigation services providers [4]. In 2017, the International Air Transport Association (IATA) predicted that air passenger numbers would increase to 7.8 billion by 2036, which is almost double of the 4 billion passengers at that time [5].

In light of the anticipated increase in the number of air travelers and high numbers of baby boomers retiring, pilot shortage was becoming a major issue. In 2019, Boeing's CEO had announced that pilot shortage was to be "one of the biggest challenges" facing the industry. Boeing also projected that 804,000 new civil aviation pilots worldwide were needed to maintain the global fleet in the next 20 years throughout commercial, business and helicopter industries [6].

These forward-looking data pointed towards an exponential growth in all sectors of aviation. Aviation industries believed in the benefits of the long-lasting and vital importance of air transport development as it became an indispensable means of transportation. To keep up with times, industries around the world have financed research programs to understand emerging trends in aviation and create artefacts services to get ahead of the industry. Multiple aviation organisations and associations have investigated the challenges concerning pilot shortage, and one of the most promising outputs is the development of new programs to accelerate pilot training.

In such circumstances, improved training methods are necessary to maintain safety standards while mitigating against pilot shortage by reducing training duration and costs. More specifically, training organisations have developed more efficient training programs with the goals of increasing pilot competencies and reaching higher safety levels. Traditional training uses repetitive testing in the execution of maneuvers (the "tick box" approach) to train pilots at managing situations that they have already practiced or encountered before. This method of training is no longer appropriate in this developing and dynamic industry and does not meet the needs of airline operations anymore.

1.3   The Need for a New Type of Training: Evidence-Based Training (EBT)

Evidence-Based Training, sometimes referred to as Competency-Based Training (CBT), arose from the concern that pilots needed to be trained to face novel and unexpected threats that do not deal with standard operating procedures. EBT aims at identifying, developing and evaluating pilot competencies in order to increase safety by managing threats and errors based on operations and training data. It has been supported by ICAO and IATA and quickly adopted by many airlines. EBT is a training and assessment method based on data and focuses on developing and assessing the overall capability of trainees across a range of pilot competencies rather than measuring their performance in events or maneuvers.

EBT differs from traditional training by including the aspects of pilot core competencies and evidence. Competencies are observable and measurable and are about activities that pilots need to operate safely. Evidence is the result of global safety and training data analysis. Both these elements in EBT aim at fostering pilot resilience, which is the ability of the crew to deal calmly and efficiently with unexpected situations. EBT is based on large sets of data (i.e., safety reports, pilot surveys, flight data records and analysis, etc.) such as those recorded during flights and training sessions. These data are used to identify threats, errors, undesirable aircraft states as well as typical failures observed in operation depending on routes and types of aircraft to be included in future training programs.

In light of forward-looking information in aviation and the forecast of the pilot shortage, aviation industries were looking for a way to train pilots faster and better. As a result, EBT was identified as a solution that can mitigate for pilot shortage by accelerating training while maintaining safety standards. Earlier in this paper, we had identified the lack of guidance and supporting tools in PE. We therefore use this case of pilot shortage to identify the sources of prospective data in aviation that can be exploited for future projects in this domain.

2   Problem

The major challenge in PE is the lack of examples of documented PE real-life cases that can provide lessons learned and best practices. The next section of this article identifies the forward-looking data sources that can be used in PE to identify future trends in aviation. They can be used as lessons learned and help with the design of products and services that do not yet exist in aviation.

3 Methodology

We reviewed commercial and scientific literature on air traffic and pilot demand. We identified data sources that provided statistics and forecasts concerning future traffic growth and pilot shortage. At the time of this study, the aviation industry was experiencing an industry downturn driven by COVID-19. We were therefore restricted to prospective data in aviation that were published prior to the COVID-19 pandemic because there are currently limited post-COVID-19 forecast data. We classified these sources as coming from universities, training organisations, aircraft manufacturers, international organisations and government organisations.

4 Results

The results of this study are identified sources of forward-looking data that can be used for PE studies in aviation. Even if these data are to be reviewed following the COVID-19 pandemic, they allow us to make several observations on findings that will still stand true post-COVID-19: several companies, organizations and specialists in the field of aviation publish prospective data on the field; forecasts stretch from periods ranging from 5 to 30 years; the sources of forward-looking information are numerous, diverse and well recognized by the community; and the information from these sources of information is recent, of different nature since it includes both quantitative data (statistical data, survey results) and qualitative information (expert judgments, trend analysis), and is considered reliable and rigorous.

We identified three international organisations, one flight training organisation, two aircraft manufacturers, two government organisations and one university that provide forecasts in aviation (see Table 1).

Multiple sources forecasted a need for additional pilots to meet the air traffic growth expected in the next 10 to 20 years. Concerning pilot demand, in 2020 CAE predicted that the civil aviation industry will need over 260,000 new pilots over the next decade. Also in 2020, Boeing anticipated the need for 763,000 new civil aviation pilots to fly and maintain the global fleet over the next 20 years. Concerning traffic growth, in 2019, IATA forecasted a growth of 3.7% in the number of air passengers annually over the next 20 years. In 2015, ICAO predicted an average global passenger traffic growth of 4.3% annually until 2035. On the aircraft manufacturing side, Airbus forecasted in 2019 a need for 39,000 new aircrafts in the next 20 years to meet passenger and traffic demands. Finally, in 2019, Embry-Riddle Aeronautical University provided scenarios with estimations on how various shortages of pilots in the USA will lead to increasing numbers of grounded aircrafts.

The IATA Monthly Traffic Statistics and the UK CAA do not provide prospective data, but they do provide the latest statistics showing the current trends in the domain. Even though they do not present forward-looking data, they can be used to anticipate trends in the near future and confirm past forecasts that were made on passenger and air traffic growth. Furthermore, most of the sources provide the information as charts and figures as part of a publication with very limited manipulation of data possible. The exceptions are Airbus, the FAA, the UK CAA and ACI which provide their statistics in a downloadable data spreadsheet on passenger, air traffic and airport traffic.

Table 1. Sources of prospective data in aviation concerning pilot demand.

	Type of organization	Title	Timeframe
CAE	Training organization	Pilot Demand Outlook	2020-2029
	At a glance: Provides a forecast of the pilot population over the next 10 years for airplanes and business jets. Also provides an estimate of the number of pilots needed to sustain operations in the next 10 years throughout different regions of the world [7]		
Boeing	Aircraft Manufacturer	Pilot & Technician Outlook	2020-2039
	At a glance: Boeing provides a 20-year fleet forecast for commercial aircrafts, business jets and civil helicopters. Based on the forecast, Boeing estimates the number of pilots, technicians and cabin crew members needed worldwide [8]		
Airbus	Aircraft Manufacturer	Global market forecast	2019–2038
	At a glance: Provides the demands of air travel and passenger aircrafts, network and traffic forecasts, freighter and services forecast for 2019–2038 [9]		
IATA	International Organisation	Monthly Traffic Statistics	Every month
	At a glance: Provides an overview of trends on the air passenger market for a single month collected from airlines. Describes variations in passenger revenue kilometers (PRKs) as compared to previous months throughout different regions [10]		
IATA	International Organisation	20-Year Passenger Forecast	2019-2039
	At a glance: Forecasts the evolution of the number of air travelers the next 20 years. Defines the drivers behind traffic demand and identifies traffic trends. Provides different possible scenarios to support industries' long-term strategic decision-making [11]		
ICAO	International organisation	Long-term Traffic Forecasts	2015-2045
	At a glance: Provides a global air transport outlook to 2030 and trends to 2040. Describes traffic forecast by regions of the world for international, domestic and freight traffic [12].		
ICAO	International organisation	Global and Regional 20-year Forecasts (DOC 9956)	2011-2031
	At a glance: Provides forecasts for pilots, maintenance personnel and air traffic controllers for the next 20 years [13].		
Airport Council International (ACI)	International organisation	World Airport Traffic Forecasts	2019-2040
	At a glance: Offers insights into the future evolution of air transport demand across the world between 2019-2040. The forecast breaks down into total passengers (broken down into international and domestic traffic), total air cargo and total aircraft movements [14].		

(continued)

810   K. Ung et al.

Table 1. (*continued*)

	Type of organization	Title	Timeframe
Embry-Riddle Aeronautical University	University	Effects of the Pilot Shortage on the Regional Airline Industry: A 2023 Forecast	2019-2023
	At a glance: Predicts how many aircrafts would have to be grounded by 2023 due to pilot shortage and impacts to passenger traffic. For US traffic only [15].		
Federal Aviation Administration (FAA)	Type of organization	Title	Timeframe
	Government organisation	Aerospace Forecast	2020-2040
	At a glance: Provides forecasts on emerging trends of the different segments of the aviation industry. For US traffic only [16].		
Civil Aviation Authority (CAA)	Type of organization	Title	Timeframe
	Government organisation	Aviation Market	Every year
	Provides airport traffic statistics, domestic and international airline traffic carried by UK registered airlines, and results from surveys of departing passengers. For UK traffic only [17].		

The statistics of this study point to the need for an accelerated pilot training as a solution to bring additional pilots into operations more quickly and efficiently in order to maintain current and future air traffic. In their paper, Embry-Riddle highlighted the need for new pilot pathway programs as an important topic for further research to mitigate pilot shortage. ICAO endorsed the implementation of EBT, which encouraged airlines to adopt this new training program. In their publications, CAE and Boeing emphasized the need to develop future aviation training standards. As of 2019, IATA offered EBT consulting services which helped airlines transition from traditional training to EBT. Airbus integrated EBT into their programs, influencing the training of the next generation of pilots.

5   Discussion

At the time of this study, this paper identified the latest forward-looking data in aviation and showed how these trends were exploited to create a training for a future need. Sources of aviation forecasts predicted a shortage in pilots that led to the development of innovative methods of pilot training. EBT was adopted by airlines, aircraft manufacturers and flight schools globally.

There were two main concerns regarding this study: the impacts of the COVID-19 pandemic and the efficacy of EBT. This analysis did not consider factors that could significantly impact the study, such as economic downturns, industry regulatory changes and disruptive events. In this case, the COVID-19 pandemic upended the forecasts and pilot shortage is not currently a challenge, with pilots grounded and uncertain about how to retain their license. This study therefore highlights a limitation of prospective: it lacks mitigation strategies when unexpected factors disrupt the predictions and change the needs. We have seen that prospective methods are grounded on analysing trends to anticipate future needs, but learning from this case study, PE should also try to anticipate disruptive factors and prepare for how they impact decisions made on the design of future products and services.

The second limitation involved the efficacy of EBT as a new training program with very limited data in operations. EBT has been adopted by training organisations and airlines for only a few years and there has been no published study or data on its level of efficiency. Initiatives should be made in the industry to encourage the organisations who implemented EBT to monitor and share their data on pilot training output. By sharing real operational data on an implemented and working EBT program, the whole industry could benefit from lessons learned and define ways to improve the program.

In all areas of interest, it is clear that any PE project (or more broadly speaking, any future artifact design project) should be based on good quality and diverse information to enable designers to be in the best possible position to make good decisions and achieve good results. However, having good baseline information does not guarantee that the design team will make good decisions and achieve good results.

6 Conclusion

We identified sources of forward-looking data in aviation and identified lessons learned for a pilot training. Up to now, research in aviation has been focused on designing for commercial purposes, customer needs, prevention or to increase safety. There have been limited studies in aviation that gathers sources of prospective data for the design of future artefacts. The downturn seen in aviation due to COVID-19 caused a major disruption, but as the industry recovers, we expect new forecasts post-COVID-19 to consider for prospective studies. In the near future, we hope to see more studies using a prospective approach with the potential to disrupt and innovate the industry of aviation.

Acknowledgements. This research was carried out as part of the activities of the IVADO Institute, thanks, in part, to financial support from the Canada First Research Excellence Fund.

References

1. Brangier, E., Robert, J.-M.: L'ergonomie prospective: fondements et enjeux. Le travail humain, vol. 77. Presses Universitaires de France, Paris (2014)
2. Robert, J-M., Brangier, E.: What is prospective ergonomics? A reflection and position on the future of ergonomic. In: Karsh, B.-T. (ed.): Ergonomics and Health Aspects, LNCS, vol. 5624, pp. 162–169 (2009)
3. Robert, J-M., Maldar, M., Taraghi, M., Seffah, A.: User Innovation, Lead Users and Crowd-sourcing for the Design of New Products and Services: Why, What and How?, pp. 730–743. Springer Nature Switzerland AG (2019)
4. Aviation Industry High Level Group, Aviation Benefits Report (2019).
5. IATA, 2036 Forecast Reveals Air Passengers Will Nearly Double to 7.8 Billion. Press Release No: 55 (2017)
6. Boeing Pilot & Technician Outlook, Flight Safety Foundation (2019).

7. CAE: 2020–2029 Pilot Demand Outlook. https://www.cae.com/cae-pilot-demand-outlook-2020/. Accessed 04 Feb 2021

8. Boeing: Pilot and Technician Outlook 2020–2039. https://www.boeing.com/commercial/market/pilot-technician-outlook/. Accessed 04 Feb 2021

9. Airbus Global Market Forecast: Cities, Airports and Aircraft 2019–2038. https://www.airbus.com/aircraft/market/global-market-forecast.html.Accessed 04 Feb 2021

10. IATA Monthly Traffic Statistics. https://www.iata.org/en/publications/store/monthly-traffic-statistics/. Accessed 04 Feb 2021

11. IATA 20-Year Passenger Forecast Global Report (2019)

12. ICAO Long-Term Traffic Forecasts, Passenger and Cargo (2018)

13. ICAO Global and Regional 20 Year Forecasts: Pilots, Maintenance Personnel, Air Traffic Controllers (Doc 9956).

14. Airport Council International, World Airport Traffic Forecasts 2019–2040 (2018)

15. Embry-Riddle Aeronautical University, effects of the pilot shortage on the regional airline industry: a 2023 forecast. In. J. Aviat. Aeronaut. Aerosp. **6**(3) (2019)

16. Federal Aviation Administration, FAA Aerospace Forecasts. https://www.faa.gov/data_research/aviation/aerospace_forecasts/. Accessed 04 Feb 2021

17. Civil Aviation Authority (CAA), UK Aviation Market. https://www.caa.co.uk/Data-and-analysis/UK-aviation-market/. Accessed 04 Feb 2021

Methodology Proposal to Access Cross-Functional Collective Activities of External Radiotherapy

Alexandra Wartel[1]([✉]), Céline Poret[1], Johann Petit[2], and Sylvie Thellier[1]

[1] Institut de Radioprotection et de Sûreté Nucléaire, 31 avenue de la Division Leclerc, 92262 Fontenay-aux-Roses, France
{alexandra.wartel,celine.poret,sylvie.thellier}@irsn.fr
[2] CNRS, IMS, Equipe d'ergonomie des systèmes complexes, 351 cours de la Liberation, 33405 Talence, France
johann.petit@bordeaux.fr

Abstract. In this paper we aim to present the methodology used in an Ergonomics research work to define the preparation for treatment in external radiotherapy. This research work concerns the analysis of the preparation for treatment in external radiotherapy activity and the difficulties workers are experiencing. Lack of fluidity during this step and between the different actors was noted by the IRSN (Institute for Radioprotection and Nuclear Safety) experts and the ASN (Nuclear Safety Authority). IRSN assumes that those lacks of fluidity may have an impact on workers activity and patients' safety. IRSN formulated a thesis subject on the basis of this hypothesis called "Human activity and transverse performance, the case of preparation for treatment in external radiotherapy".

Keywords: Radiotherapy · Process modelling · Team work

1 Fluidity and Collective Activity in External Radiotherapy

The first step of this research work was carried out in an external radiotherapy center to better understand what the preparation for treatment in external radiotherapy is, what fluidity is and the link between lacks of fluidity and patients' exposure to risk. According to the IRSN, the preparation of radiotherapy treatment presents lacks of fluidity qualified as a hazard. Let us consider that fluidity corresponds to an uninterrupted progression. The initial study has shown that preparation falls within the patient's global care, it is divided in interdependent steps, involving many trades at different times and places which contribute to its complexity (Thellier and Le Tallec 2019). In any case, the collaboration between the different professionals and the steps in the process allows the treatment administration, this led us to qualify it as a cross-functional collective activity (Motté and Haradji 2010; Poret et al. 2016). The field data collection performed for this study shows that there is no precise description of the preparation step and highlights the difficulties for the care team to adjudicate on a common definition.

2 Methodology

We started this work with observations, interviews and documents analysis. Initially, open observations[1] were used to discover the environment, the process and the professionals (informal interviews). They represent 60 h in the field and 2 h 30 min in meetings. Formal interviews represent 5 h 20 min. Consulting the radiotherapy center documents represents 7 h and 30 min. These documents concerned for example processing procedures, human and material resources, feedback committees. Other documents were used: radiation therapy courses of the chief physicist for example. The care center database includes an "operational process cartography" (Fig. 1) made by the care team. It details all the steps of the external radiotherapy process followed by this center. The first step "reception desk/secretariat" includes the creation of the patient file and the reception of the patient when he or she first presents himself or herself. The second step "Medical consultation" is the first appointment with the oncologist, who will explain to the patient and his family if they are present the course of treatment. This is also a time when the doctor asks the patient for certain information in order to establish the prescription. The third step "Appointment planning" is to plan the patient's various appointments in the radiotherapy department for the coming days and for the treatment sessions, according to the medical prescription. The fourth step "Paramedical consultation" allows the therapy technologists to explain to the patient in detail various tips and recommendations. The fifth step "Scanner" is to take a very precise image of the patient's body. The sixth step "Technical file's preparation" consists in gathering technical and specific information for the preparation of the treatment (scanner, radiation dose calculation, etc.). The seventh step "Setting up/treatment" verifies all the information necessary for the treatment and makes a first test and then delivers the treatment. The last step "End of treatment/ follow up" verifies that the treatment has gone well and monitors possible side effects.

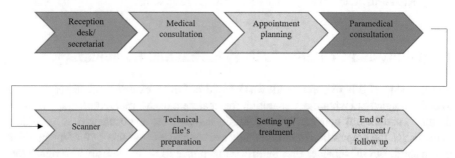

Fig. 1. "Operational process cartography" of the treatment carried out by radiotherapy department.

Exchanges with care team about the process revealed that preparation is unthought: there is no mention of it in the database and first interviews with the staff did not help to define it precisely. We elaborated a new process modelling (Fig. 2)[2] enriched with

---

[1] These are global observations that take place initially with a broad focus.

[2] Figure 2 is an illustration, it is not a question of understanding the details, but rather of showing what jumps out in relation to Fig. 1.

open observations and discussions with professionals (informal interviews) following the patient's file process. This helped complete the cartography (additional steps) and identify elements (or sources) of variability (doctor's adjustments, various patients' admissions ways, treatments' combination etc.). Elements that may have an impact on fluidity were drawn as well (orange circles).

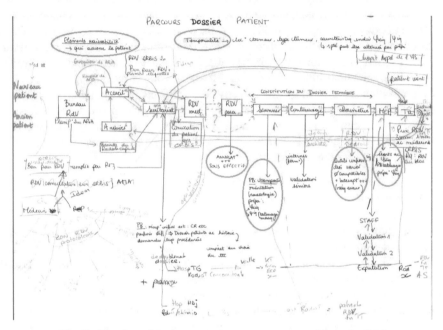

Fig. 2. Mapping of the treatment process reconstructed from the field

Because of the deadlines and objectives set beforehand, the second part of this methodology is less consequential: 3 h of interviews and 4 h of systematic observations. The aim of the systematic observations was to be present at a specific time and place to show and characterize the different types of interactions between professionals, which, based on open observations, would enable them to coordinate and make decisions (transmission of information via the file, by computer, by moving, over the phone, etc.), This has led us to the creation of observation grids used at a specific stage of the preparation: the scanner, and to choose two types of location (the most frequent) breast cancer and prostate cancer. Specifically, scanner steps, time, patient's file information, information given to the patient, and hazards/delays were recorded. We added three clarifications in the information entered in the patient's file: the information that the therapy technologist retrieves, the information that he gives to his colleagues and the stage of the care process concerned by this information.

For the following collective or individual interviews, we decided to discuss this new modelling highlighting the instrumentation of analyses. Given time and organizational pressure we did collective interviews only between people practicing the same trade. Different types of interactions were noticed during the discussions about the process modelling in collective or individual interviews. The trades that participated in these interviews were therapy technologists, administrative medical assistants, one radiation oncology physicist and one caregiver. Some of them used the process modelling to debate between them first and then with the ergonomist, it became an intermediate object (Vinck 2009) in the analysis work. Another professional (administrative medical assistant) added variability elements (above mentioned) by taking the sheet on which the process was modeled and writing on it. Then he explained it to the ergonomist. The co-construction of this new way of looking at the process therefore took place in the field with the professionals. In the absence of consensus on the definition of preparation it was decided to conduct additional, exploratory interviews with the various trades involved in several different establishment. According to the professionals met during the internship, the organization and type of institution (private/ public) could play an important role in the preparation (different deadlines between private and public) and in the fluidity of the process (difficulty to recover data, more or less flexible procedures). This can cause rushed work phases that can generate errors or delays in the start of treatment, eventually impacting the chances of remissions.

3   Results

The modelling highlights that preparation activity is a cross-functional collective activity difficult to delimit because professionals do not give the same contour and content of it. However this modelling allows to identify multiple types of preparation we can divide in two parts: preparation's object and types of treatment. The type of treatment chosen by the oncologist will have an impact on the object of preparation. The treatment chosen can be a classical treatment (carried out within the recommended timeframe depending on the location and stage of the tumor), an emergency treatment (carried out within 24 h to relieve the patient's pain), a re-irradiation (the patient has already received external radiotherapy in the past but the tumor has returned for example) etc. The objects of the preparation that will be impacted by these types of treatment are for example: patient's preparation, machines' preparation, medical files' preparation. For example, the preparation of the patient consists in making him or her an actor in his or her own care. To do this professionals "educate" the patients: be punctual at the sessions, do not move on the scanner table and later treatment, for some treatments come with a full bladder, do not eat certain foods. According to interviewed professionals, lacks of fluidity are hazards happening during preparation: the breakdown of a machine, a patient who does not come to a session etc. And these hazards can then cause an acceleration of the process or a slowing down or even a stoppage. This methodology was the occasion to put into debate what preparation is and transform professional's point of view about the process and the preparation during collective interviews by accepting colleagues' arguments and point of view for instance. It has also shown the difficulties that can be encountered in describing a process and that defining or characterizing a theoretical process leads to simplifying a real process, and making its diversity and variability "invisible".

4 Discussion

The originality of this work is double: to focus on the preparation of the treatment and fluidity associated (Munoz 2016; Nascimento 2009; Pernet 2013; Thellier 2017); and to include professionals in the process modelling. They therefore participate in part of the analysis of the activity, which is different from certain approaches where the ergonomist provides a diagnosis that will serve as a starting point for discussions and then co-construct solutions (Casse and Caroly 2017). This methodology is designed to meet a need to better understand the complexity of the real care process in its entirety (Motté and Poret 2018) because it concerns several professionals in many times and places with multiple care protocols, method etc. According to Van Belleghem (Van Belleghem 2014) this freedom to create an original methodology is possible because this work is part of a research having "low constraint to the exercise" supporting a high "practices' diversification potential".

5 Conclusion

This methodology integrating early in the work analysis the participation of professionals in external radiotherapy was developed to face the difficulties to define the preparation on the field and in institutional and professional documents. It helped collecting lots of information useful to the ergonomist comprehension and for radiotherapy professionals and to put in debate what preparation is. It has to do not only with methodology but also with results showing a new perspective on care process.

References

Casse, C., Caroly, S.: Les espaces de débat comme méthodologie d'intervention capacitante pour enrichir le retour d'expérience. Activites **14**(2) (2017). https://doi.org/10.4000/activites.3008

Motté, F., Haradji, Y.: 1. Construire la relation de service en considérant l'activité humaine dans ses dimensions individuelles et collectives. In: Ergonomie, conception de produits et services médiatisés, pp. 11–35. Presses Universitaires de France, Cairn.info (2010). https://doi.org/10.3917/puf.lepo.2010.01.0011

Motté, F., Poret, C.: La Simulation Réflexive Transverse: Une méthode pour ancrer l'activité humaine au cœur de la performance de l'entreprise. Activites **15**(1) (2018). https://doi.org/10.4000/activites.3123

Munoz, M.I.: «Prendre soin» du travail: Dispositifs de gestion du flux et régulations émergentes en radiothérapie (2016). https://www.theses.fr/2016CNAM1049/document

Nascimento, A.: Produire la santé, produire la sécurité: Développer une culture collective de sécurité en radiothérapie (2009)

Pernet, A.: Coproduire un soin sûr et efficace: Le développement des capabilités des patients en radiothérapie (2013). https://www.theses.fr/2013CNAM0906/document

Poret, C., Folcher, V., Motté, F., Haradji, Y.: Designing for the power to act together in organisations: the case of a business process. Activités **13**(13–2) (2016). https://doi.org/10.4000/activites.2917. Article 2

Thellier, S., Le Tallec, P.: L'analyse des risques d'un système sociotechnique complexe: Le cas de la radiothérapie. Cancer/Radiothérapie **23**(6–7), 510–516 (2019). https://doi.org/10.1016/j.canrad.2019.07.136

Thellier, S.: Approche ergonomique de l'analyse des risques en radiothérapie: De l'analyse des modes de défaillances à la mise en discussion des modes de réussite (2017). https://www.the ses.fr/2017CNAM1159/document

Van Belleghem, L.: Perspectives pour une stratégie de diversification des pratiques en ergonomie (2014)

Vinck, D.: De l'objet intermédiaire à l'objet-frontière. Vers la prise en compte du travail d'équipement. Revue d'anthropologie des connaissances **3**(1), 51–72 (2009). https://doi.org/10.3917/rac.006.0051

Work–Life Balance of Secondary Schools Teachers in Hong Kong

Kapo Wong[1](✉) , Alfred Tsz Shing Lai[1], Xiangcheng Meng[1] ,
Fion Choi Hung Lee[2] , and Alan Hoi Shou Chan[1]

[1] Department of Systems Engineering and Engineering Management,
City University of Hong Kong, Kowloon, Hong Kong, China
kpwong42-c@my.cityu.edu.hk, alan.chan@cityu.edu.hk
[2] Faculty of Business, UOW College Hong Kong, Kowloon, Hong Kong, China
fhung@uow.edu.au

Abstract. Work–life imbalance is a severe problem amongst most secondary school teachers in Hong Kong due to heavy workloads and long working hours. This paper examines the factors affecting the work–life balance of secondary school teachers in Hong Kong. An online questionnaire survey was conducted and 150 valid responses were received. In factor analysis, the correlations between work–life balance and five determinants, namely, time off for personal life, support from supervisor, support from co-workers, workload and work–family conflict, were assessed. High support from co-workers, low workload and low level of work–family conflict were positively correlated with high levels of work–life balance. The findings of this study could serve as a reference for the Education Bureau and principals to formulate policies to help the teachers cope with their workload problems. The implications for practitioners are provided to enhance work–life balance and wellness amongst teachers.

Keywords: Work–life balance · Teachers · Workload · Work–family conflict · Hong Kong

1 Introduction

Hong Kong is notorious for its tiresome working hours and punishing schedules [1]. In the education sector, teachers are facing these problems and enduring heavy workloads. These workloads might be generated from difficult demands of parents, the mandate of principals, uncooperativeness amongst co-workers and disobedience of students. Worldwide concern and attention on work–life imbalance amongst teachers has been increasing in the past years. Quality of education not only fundamentally depends on the proficient knowledge of the teachers but also on their health and wellbeing [2]. In 2019, the Education Bureau of Hong Kong implemented the 'One Executive Officer for Each School' Policy to increase administrative manpower and reduce the workload of administrative work amongst teachers and principals.

The purpose of this study was to understand the antecedents affecting the secondary school teachers' work–life balance. Upon reviewing past literature [e.g. 3–5], five factors

© The Author(s), under exclusive license to Springer Nature Switzerland AG 2021
N. L. Black et al. (Eds.): IEA 2021, LNNS 219, pp. 819–826, 2021.
https://doi.org/10.1007/978-3-030-74602-5_112

were identified and examined, namely, time off for personal life, support from supervisor, support from co-workers, workload and work–family conflict. This study also aims to raise awareness of the importance of work–life balance as well as improve the overall quality of education. Therefore, suggestions are provided to schools and the Education Bureau to address the problems of work–life imbalance confronted by teachers.

2 Literature Review

2.1 Work–Life Balance

In work–life balance, workers should have the liberty to completely enjoy both work and personal life [6]. In other words, workers are able to decide how to arrange their work and personal life roles to maintain healthy wellbeing. The advantages of achieving a balance between work and non-work roles benefit not only the wellness of workers but also the overall development of organisations, for example, by increasing productivity, lowering the rate of turnover and reducing absenteeism [7]. A sense of respect is contributed to the workers through the process of assisting in maintaining a healthy work–life balance. However, to attain a balanced work and life amongst teachers is an enormous challenge because most teachers are facing long working hours due to countless job duties and responsibilities [8–10].

2.2 Hypotheses

A number of factors were identified as indicators of work–life balance of teachers. Sufficient time off for personal life may improve the work–life balance [11]. It is believed that support from supervisors and co-workers may assist in maintaining a healthy work–life balance [12, 13]. Furthermore, low workload is inclined to enhance the work–life balance of teachers [3]. A low level of work–family conflict may improve work–life balance [14]. Therefore, five possible hypotheses were developed to evaluate the relationships of these five factors with work–life balance. The five hypotheses are shown in Table 1.

Table 1. Hypotheses between the five factors and work–life balance

Items	Descriptions
H1	Time off for personal life is positively correlated with work–life balance
H2	Support from supervisors is positively correlated with work–life balance
H3	Support from co-workers is positively correlated with work–life balance
H4	Workload is negatively correlated with work–life balance
H5	Work–family conflict is negatively correlated with work–life balance

3 Methodology

3.1 Sample and Procedure

In this study, an online questionnaire survey was conducted to collect data. The target participants of the survey were teachers in secondary schools in Hong Kong. The participants came from four secondary schools. A total of 150 completed questionnaires were received. The demographic profile of the respondents is shown in Table 2.

Table 2. Demographic information of the 150 respondents

Characteristics	Frequency	Percentage
Gender		
Female	88	58.7%
Male	62	41.3%
Age		
18–29	61	40.7%
30–49	72	48.0%
50–64	17	11.3%
Marital status		
Married	45	30.0%
Single	105	70.0%
Have child/Children		
Yes	21	14.0%
No	129	86.0%
Working years		
Less than 6 years	49	32.7%
6–10 years	54	36.0%
11 years or above	47	31.3%

3.2 Measure

The questionnaire contained 21 items, and the responses of the participants were measured on seven-point Likert scales, from 1 to 7 indicating "completely disagree" to "completely agree." All items were stated positively. The questionnaire had six sections, namely, time off for personal life, support from supervisors, support from co-workers, workload, work–family conflict and work–life balance.

Measurements of time off for personal life with five items and support from supervisors with three items were adapted from the study of Wong and Ko [15]. Measurements of support from co-workers with three items, workload with four items and work–family conflict with five items were adapted from the study of Torp et al. [16]. Work–life balance was measured by adopting one item adapted from the study of Brough et al. [17].

3.3 Data Analysis

The correlations between the five factors and work–life balance were evaluated by multiple regression. The reliability of each statement was evaluated by the value of factor loading and Cronbach's alpha. If the Cronbach's alpha is greater than 0.7, then it indicates an acceptable internal consistency [18]. If the factor loading is greater than 0.5, the reliability is satisfied. The composite reliability and factor loading were used for convergent validity. If the square root of the average variance of a factor was greater than the largest inter-construct correlations, then it indicated a satisfied discriminant validity [19].

4 Results

The results of factor analysis for composite reliability, factor loading, average variance extracted and Cronbach's alpha are reported in Table 3. The factor loadings of each item were greater than 0.7, satisfying the criteria. The composite reliability was greater than 0.6, and the average variance extracted was greater than 0.5. The value of Cronbach's alpha was greater than 0.7. The square root of the average variance of the factors was greater than the largest inter-construct correlations (see Table 4). Thus, the reliability and validity of the overall model were acceptable.

Multiple regression was used to analyse the relationships between work–life balance and the five factors, of which work–life balance was the dependent variable and five factors were independent variables (Table 5). The factors of time off for personal life and support from supervisors were unaccepted in the model ($p > 0.05$). The other three factors, namely, support from co-workers, workload and work–family conflict significantly affected the dependent variable. Work–life balance was positively correlated with support from co-workers (beta = 0.239; $p < 0.001$). Work–life balance was negatively correlated with workload (beta = 0.743; $p < 0.001$) and work–family conflict (beta = 0.148; $p < 0.005$).

5 Discussion

This study examined how the work–life balance of secondary school teachers in Hong Kong was affected by five factors. The results revealed that support from co-workers, low workload and low level of work–family conflict were critically related to work–life balance. Drawing on resource-based theory [20], gaining resources (e.g. support) is likely to maintain the satisfaction of balance. Therefore, if the teachers receive either tangible and intangible assists or support from co-workers, then their satisfaction of balance may be enhanced [21]. Furthermore, teachers work not only in school but also after leaving

Table 3. Results of reliability verification

Items	Mean	S.D	Factor loading	Composite reliability	Average variance extracted	Cronbach's alpha
TOPL1	3.16	1.746	0.779			0.795
TOPL2	3.347	1.461	0.771			0.791
TOPL3	3.353	1.795	0.812	0.888	0.614	0.791
TOPL4	3.427	1.462	0.745			0.793
TOPL5	3.460	1.933	0.810			0.795
SFS1	4.453	1.834	0.683			0.797
SFS2	4.140	1.375	0.655	0.754	0.507	0.797
SFS3	4.240	1.364	0.791			0.796
SFC1	3.840	1.754	0.859			0.805
SFC2	4.013	1.609	0.795	0.876	0.703	0.799
SFC3	4.174	1.735	0.859			0.801
LW1	4.020	1.981	0.857			0.789
LW2	3.773	1.493	0.843	0.907	0.710	0.789
LW3	3.687	1.800	0.843			0.786
LW4	3.653	1.776	0.828			0.784
LWFC1	3.653	1.584	0.759			0.786
LWFC2	3.700	1.478	0.769			0.786
LWFC3	3.507	1.350	0.737	0.879	0.591	0.790
LWFC4	3.627	1.717	0.775			0.785
LWFC5	3.580	1.664	0.805			0.783
WLB1	3.360	1.387	0.788	0.621	0.621	0.779

Note: S.D.: standard deviation

work, in acts such as the preparation of teaching, marking and calling parents [22]; therefore, the working hours of most teachers are extremely long and the workload is terrifically huge [23]. The long-term side effects of long working hours may jeopardise the health of teachers [24]. These effects may increase the rate of absence and lower the quality of teaching. The suffering of teachers is doubly damaging to schools. In addition, the conflict between work and family meant that the time, strain and behaviours of work (family) role interfere with family (work) role [25], possibly leading to difficulties in balancing work and personal life. The results of this study are consistent with the findings of Soomro et al. [14] who found a negative correlation between work–family conflict and work–life balance.

Further studies should be conducted to explore the reasons why work–life balance did not correlate with another two factors, namely, time-off for personal life and support from

Table 4. Correlation of the variables

Variables	1	2	3	4	5	6
1. Time off for personal life	0.784					
2. Support from supervisors	0.0114	0.712				
3. Support from co-workers	− 0.0162*	0.175*	0.838			
4. Low workload	0.034	0.053	0.057	0.769		
5. Low level of work–family conflict	0.016	0.023	0.049	0.182**	0.769	
6. Work–life balance	0.024	0.103	0.067*	0.074***	0.101***	0.788

Note: The values of square root of AVE are listed in diagonal
*$p < 0.01$, **$p < 0.005$ level, ***$p < 0.001$.

Table 5. Multiple regression of the five independent variables with work–life balance

Independent variables	Beta	Significance
Time off for personal life	0.010	0.825
Support from supervisors	− 0.044	0.351
Support from co-workers	0.239	0.000***
Low workload	0.743	0.000***
Low level of work–family conflict	0.148	0.002**

Note: **$p < 0.005$ level, ***$p < 0.001$

supervisors. Supports from supervisors may improve the balance of secondary school teachers as the employees can discuss with supervisors to mitigate their workloads. Several studies have found a positive correlation between work–life balance and support from supervisors [12]. Surprisingly, a non-significant result was found in this study.

This study provides important information for Educational Bureau to enhance teachers' wellbeing by establishing policies emphasising more on reducing the long working hours and heavy workloads. Principals should fully assist in maintaining the work–life balance of teachers by reducing unnecessary work, normalising flexible work arrangements and building a positive culture in school.

This study had several limitations. First, the sample size can be expanded and thus the reliability could be improved. Second, the survey was conducted during the occurrence of the pandemic and online learning became prevalent in the education sector. This change can be a critical challenge for most teachers. Therefore, the working conditions might be slightly different from those in "normal" situations [26].

6 Conclusion

The present study evaluates the determinants that affect the work–life balance of secondary school teachers in Hong Kong. The results showed that support from co-workers, low workload and low level of work–family conflict were uniquely related to work–life balance. These findings provide valuable implications for the Education Bureau and principals to develop appropriate strategies to reduce workload and minimise conflict. Further investigation is needed to be conducted to assess the relationship between work–life balance and support from supervisors.

References

1. Ninaus, K., Diehl, S., Terlutter, R., Chan, K., Huang, A.: Benefits and stressors–perceived effects of ICT use on employee health and work stress: an exploratory study from Austria and Hong Kong Int. J. Qual. Stud. Health Well-Being **10**(1), 28838 (2015)
2. Huyghebaert, T., Gillet, N., Beltou, N., Tellier, F., Fouquereau, E.: Effects of workload on teachers' functioning: a moderated mediation model including sleeping problems and overcommitment. Stress and Health **34**(5), 601–611 (2018)
3. Torres, A.C.: Is this work sustainable? Teacher turnover and perceptions of workload in charter management organizations. Urban Educ. **51**(8), 891–914 (2016)
4. Li, Y., Castaño, G., Li, Y.: Perceived supervisor support as a mediator between Chinese University teachers' organizational justice and affective commitment. Soc. Behav. Pers. Int. J. **46**(8), 1385–1396 (2018)
5. Virat, M.: Teachers' compassionate love for students: a possible determinant of teacher-student relationships with adolescents and a mediator between teachers' perceived support from coworkers and teacher-student relationships. Educ. Stud. 1–19 (2020)
6. Moore, F.: Work-life balance: contrasting managers and workers in an MNC. Empl. Relat. **29**, 385–399 (2007)
7. Byrne, U.: Work-life balance: why are we talking about it at all. Bus. Inf. Rev. **22**, 53–59 (2005)
8. Chen, J.: Understanding teacher emotions: the development of a teacher emotion inventory. Teach. Teach. Educ. **55**, 68–77 (2016)
9. Ho, S. K.: The relationship between teacher stress and burnout in Hong Kong: positive humour and gender as moderators. Educ. Psychol. **37**(3), 272–286 (2015)
10. Hue, M., Lau, N.: Promoting well-being and preventing burnout in teacher education: a pilot study of a mindfulness-based programme for pre-service teachers in Hong Kong. Teach. Dev. **19**(3), 381–401 (2015)
11. Gluschkoff, K., Elovainio, M., Kinnunen, U., Mullola, S., Hintsanen, M., Keltikangas-Järvinen, L., Hintsa, T.: Work stress, poor recovery and burnout in teachers. Occup. Med. **66**(7), 564–570 (2016)
12. Talukder, A.K.M.M.H.: Supervisor support and organizational commitment: the role of work–family conflict, job satisfaction, and work–life balance. J. Employ. Couns. **56**(3), 98–116 (2019)
13. Sloan, M. M.: Unfair treatment in the workplace and worker well-being. Work Occup. **39**(1), 3–34 (2011)
14. Soomro, A. A., Breitenecker, R. J., Shah, S. A. M.: Relation of work-life balance, work-family conflict, and family-work conflict with the employee performance-moderating role of job satisfaction. South Asian J. Bus. Stud. **7**(1), 129–146 (2018)
15. Wong, S.C., Ko, A.: Exploratory study of understanding hotel employees' perception on work–life balance issues. Int. J. Hosp. Manage. **28**(2), 195–203 (2009)
16. Torp, S., Lysfjord, L., Midje, H.H.: Workaholism and work–family conflict among university academics. High. Educ. **76**, 1071–1090 (2018)

17. Brough, P., Timms, C., O'Driscoll, M. P., Kalliath, T., Siu, O.-L., Sit, C., Lo, D.: Work–life balance: a longitudinal evaluation of a new measure across Australia and New Zealand workers. Int. J. Hum. Resour. Manage. 25(19), 2724–2744 (2014)
18. Taber, K. S.: The use of Cronbach's alpha when developing and reporting research instruments in science education. Res. Sci. Educ. 48, 1273–1296 (2017). https://doi.org/10.1007/s11165-016-9602-2
19. Dong, X. S., Wang, X., Daw, C., Ringen, K.: Chronic diseases and functional limitations among older construction workers in the United States: a 10-year follow-up study. J. Occup. Environ. Med. 53, 372–380 (2011)
20. Hobfoll, S. E.: Conservation of resources: A new attempt at conceptualizing stress. Am. Psychol. 44, 513–524 (1989)
21. Yang, Y., Islam, D.M.T.: Work-life balance and organizational commitment: a study of field level administration in Bangladesh. Int. J. Public Adm. 1–11 (2020)
22. Johari, J., Yean Tan, F., Tjik Zulkarnain, Z.I.: Autonomy, workload, work-life balance and job performance among teachers. Int. J. Educ. Manage. 32(1), 107–120 (2018)
23. Toropova, A., Myrberg, E., Johansson, S.: Teacher job satisfaction: the importance of school working conditions and teacher characteristics. Educ. Rev. 73, 71–97 (2020)
24. Wong, K., Chan, A.H.S., Ngan, S.C.: The effect of long working hours and overtime on occupational health: a meta-analysis of evidence from 1998 to 2018. Int. J. Environ. Res. Public Health 16(12), 2102 (2019)
25. Greenhaus, J. H., Powell, G. N.: When work and family are allies: a theory of work-family enrichment. Acad. Manage. Rev. 25, 178–199 (2006)
26. La Velle, L., Newman, S., Montgomery, C., Hyatt, D.: Initial teacher education in England and the Covid-19 pandemic: challenges and opportunities. J. Educ. Teach. 46, 596–608 (2020)

Author Index

Printed in the United States
by Baker & Taylor Publisher Services